THE CRB COMMODITY YEARBOOK 2002

Commodity Research Bureau

John Wiley & Sons, Inc.

Published by John Wiley & Sons, Inc., New York.
Published simultaneously in Canada.

Commodity Research Bureau
330 South Wells Street, Suite 1112
Chicago IL 60606-7104
312-554-8456
800-621-5271
http://www.CRBtrader.com
Email: info@CRBtrader.com

ISBN 0-471-21471-X

Printed in the United States of America

10 9 8 7 6 5 4 3 2 1

TABLE OF CONTENTS

Quality Service Since 1934

330 South Wells, Suite 1112
Chicago, IL 60606
Telephone: (800) 621-5271
Fax: (312) 939-4135
Email: info@crbtrader.com
Internet: http://www.CRBtrader.com

Dear CRB customers and futures traders:

On September 7th, 2001, the CRB division of Bridge was acquired by Logical Systems, Inc. of Chicago - parent and holding company of the largest network of futures and commodities Internet sites and data products. Since 1981, our technology has produced financial content, both printed and electronic, for many leading financial publications and institutions. Our products serve the casual investor as well as the professional trader. With the acquisition of CRB, we are now the only futures/commodities data supplier that has a total data solution in every format - from a digital data feed, to Internet delivery, to printed information. Offline and online, we continue to advance as the market and technology changes.

Our commitment to our customers has always been to provide the highest-quality, most accurate and timely data possible. We welcome CRB into our fold, and will continue to supply its customers with *Futures Perspective, CRB Commodity Yearbook, Futures Market Service, CRBtrader, CRB DataCenter,* historical charts, wall charts, and all of the other products you have come to trust CRB to provide. We have always believed that our customers provide our best source for new ideas and suggestions. We will continue to update and add to CRB's product line.

Please note that our address and phone numbers have changed. Additionally, you can now reach us on the Internet at **http://www.CRBtrader.com**, or email us at info@crbtrader.com.

Sincerely,

Davidson C. Lowdon

Davidson C. Lowdon
President & Publisher

ACKNOWLEDGEMENTS

The editors wish to thank the following for source material:

Agricultural Marketing Service (AMS)
Agricultural Research Service (ARS)
American Bureau of Metal Statistics, Inc. (ABMS)
American Forest & Paper Association (AF & PA)
The American Gas Association (AGA)
American Iron and Steel Institute (AISI)
American Metal Market (AMM)
Bureau of the Census
Bureau of Economic Analysis (BEA)
Bureau of Labor Statistics (BLS)
Chicago Board of Trade (CBT)
Chicago Mercantile Exchange (CME / IMM / IOM)
Coffee, Sugar & Cocoa Exchange (CSCE)
Commodity Credit Corporation (CCC)
Commodity Futures Trading Commision (CFTC)
The Conference Board
Economic Research Service (ERS)
Edison Electric Institute (EEI)
E D & F Man Cocoa Ltd
Farm Service Agency (FSA)
Federal Reserve Bank of St. Louis
Fiber Economics Bureau, Inc.
Florida Department of Citrus
Food and Agriculture Organization of the United Nations (FAO)
Foreign Agricultural Service (FAS)
Futures Industry Association (FIA)
International Cotton Advisory Committee (ICAC)
International Rubber Study Group (IRSG)
Johnson Matthey
Kansas City Board of Trade (KCBT)
Leather Industries of America
MidAmerica Commodity Exchange (MidAm)
Minneapolis Grain Exchange (MGE)
National Agricultural Statistics Service (NASS)
National Coffee Association of U.S.A., Inc. (NCA)
New York Cotton Exchange (NYCE / NYFE / FINEX)
New York Mercantile Exchange (NYMEX)
Commodity Exchange, Inc. (COMEX)
Oil World
The Organisation for Economic Co-Operation and Development (OECD)
Random Lengths
The Silver Institute
The Society of the Plastics Industry, Inc. (SPI)
United Nations (UN)
United States Department of Agriculture (USDA)
United States Geological Survey (USGS)
Wall Street Journal (WSJ)
Winnipeg Commodity Exchange (WCE)

THE COMMODITY PRICE TREND

In 2001, the Bridge Commodity Research Bureau's Futures Price Index closing value of 190.61 was 16.34 percent lower than the 2000 close of 227.83. It was the first decline in the index after two consecutive yearly increases. In 2000 the index rose 11.06 percent.

Overall, for the year most of the component commodities ended lower. After the huge 319.71 percent price increase in 2000, natural gas prices moved lower and declined 73.71 percent. All six of the Bridge/CRB Futures Price Subindices posted declines. These ranged from less than 1 percent to over 42 percent. The Energy Sub-index fell 42.42 percent to lead the decline.

Energy

The energy Sub-index fell 42.42 percent in 2001. In effect energy products reversed the strong performance of 2000 which saw natural gas lead the way higher with a gain of 319,71 percent. That impressive rally came to an end as natural gas prices fell sharply in 2001. Natural gas prices actually posted record highs in late December 2000. Prices then reversed form and fell as 2001 got underway. For all of 2001, natural gas prices declined 73.71 percent. The fundamental reason for the decline was that the high prices in 2000 led to more conservation. The high prices also encourage more exploration. The U.S. economy slowed which reduced the need for natural gas.

Heating oil prices also declined in 2001 though not near as much as natural gas. For the year heating oil declined 37.89 percent. In 2000 heating oil prices had increased by 31.33 percent. The high prices led to increased production of distillate and that along with a slowing economy drove price lower.

In 2001, crude oil prices fell 25.97 percent. In early 2001 the Organization of Petroleum exporting Countries (OPEC) reduced production but this was offset by increased production by non-OPEC countries. That along with slowing global demand allowed the supply of crude oil to increase putting pressure on prices. After the September 11 incident, prices moved higher only to decline again.

Grains

The Grains Sub-index showed a decline of 9.09 percent in 2001. This followed the 2000 gain of 11.36 percent. Among the components of the sub-index, corn declined 11.12 percent while soybeans declined 15.72 percent. In 2000 corn was up 13.33 percent while soybeans were up 8.18 percent. Wheat prices edged higher in 2001 after increasing in 2000.

Corn prices move lower in 2001 as there was increased foreign corn production. With this foreign supply increase and economic slowing, corn prices came under pressure. Soybean prices worked lower as there was increased global production of various oilseeds. While some foreign oilseed production has declined, soybean production has been increasing. Wheat price benefited from a decline in wheat production in the major exporting countries.

Industrials

The Industrial Sub-index declined 32.77 percent in 2001 after increasing in 2000. Cotton prices posted a sharp 42.85 percent decline in 2001. Cotton prices were pressured by high U.S. production and low consumption. The slowing economy reduced cotton use. Foreign production of cotton is also at high levels.

Copper prices in 2001 declined 21.83 percent. Copper prices came under pressure from high production and steadily increasing warehouse stocks. A slowing economy worked against higher prices. The major copper producer in 2001 agreed to reduce production and that should bring supply more in line with demand.

Livestock

The Livestock Sub-index declined 2.43 percent in 2001. The previous two years the index had recorded gains.

Live cattle prices fell 9.27 percent in 2001. The slowing U.S. economy reduced domestic demand for beef. Foreign demand for U.S. beef also slowed. After the September 11 incident, there was less dining out which cut into demand. Lean hog prices increased marginally by .40 percent. The U.S. inventory of hogs and pigs in 2001 was almost the same as in 2000.

Precious Metals

The Precious Metals Sub-index declined 7.12 percent in 2001. In 2000 the index increased. The decline was due mostly to platinum which declined 19.13 percent. Gold prices were up 1.97 percent while silver prices were down 1.01 percent.

The slowing global economy appeared to take a toll on platinum and palladium which find use in the automotive and electronics industries. Growing inventories of the metals pressured prices. After moving lower, gold prices rallied in the wake of September 11 before pulling back.

Imported

The Imported Sub-index fell a marginal .64 percent in 2001. The components of the sub-index were mixed. Coffee prices in 2001 declined 29.52 percent while cocoa prices moved sharply higher by 72.82 percent. Sugar prices trended lower for the year while orange juice was higher.

Cocoa has been one of the strongest commodities in terms of actual price increase. World production of cocoa has been less than consumption and that has led to a decline in cocoa stocks which has lifted prices. Coffee prices were burdened by world production exceeding consumption and prospects for a large Brazilian crop.

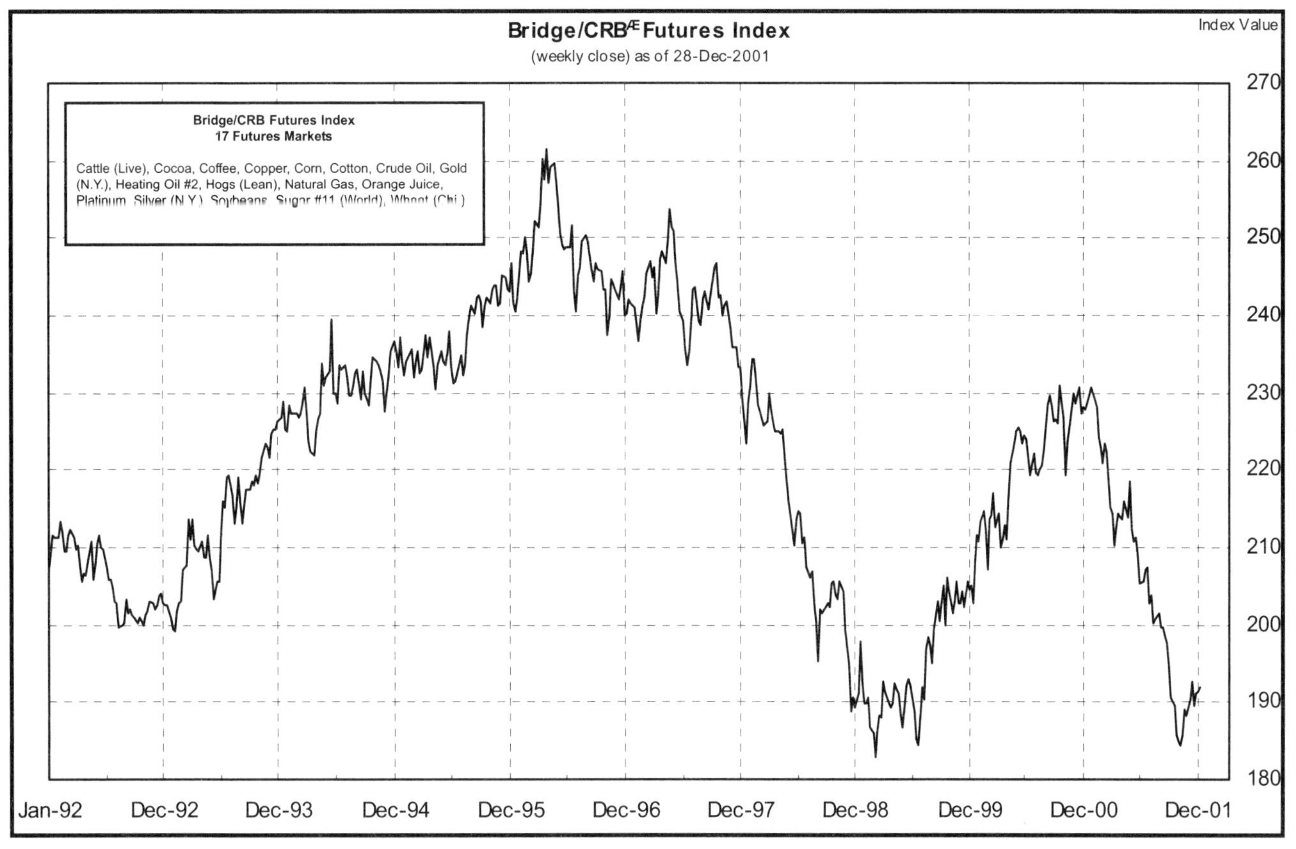

Monthly Bridge/CRB Futures Index High, Low and Close (1967=100)

Year		Jan.	Feb.	Mar.	Apr.	May	June	July	Aug.	Sept.	Oct.	Nov.	Dec.	Range
1992	High	212.20	215.30	212.90	210.30	211.70	212.90	209.10	204.90	203.50	202.90	203.60	204.30	215.30
	Low	206.90	207.20	208.60	204.50	204.90	208.00	203.00	198.20	199.30	199.10	199.20	201.20	198.20
	Close	211.20	209.60	209.80	204.80	208.00	209.30	203.10	201.00	200.40	199.90	203.10	202.80	----
1993	High	203.20	204.90	214.30	213.90	211.80	210.00	219.70	223.50	217.80	220.60	223.80	226.80	226.80
	Low	199.30	198.40	203.40	207.80	207.40	202.60	207.20	212.10	211.90	216.60	217.40	218.40	198.40
	Close	199.50	202.90	212.50	210.90	208.70	207.10	219.30	217.20	216.10	218.40	218.00	226.30	----
1994	High	229.80	229.20	231.00	227.80	239.20	239.70	234.70	235.40	234.40	235.20	234.70	237.18	239.70
	Low	226.20	225.70	227.40	227.80	225.20	235.90	230.40	228.00	228.60	227.00	228.80	226.97	225.20
	Close	225.60	227.60	227.70	225.00	235.50	230.40	233.70	231.90	229.90	233.30	229.20	236.64	----
1995	High	237.96	236.16	236.89	237.70	237.12	238.00	235.90	240.27	245.81	242.67	244.49	246.47	246.47
	Low	232.58	230.97	231.07	233.16	229.55	232.18	229.31	231.71	239.38	238.32	240.85	240.93	229.31
	Close	232.78	234.25	232.94	235.30	232.72	233.38	233.23	239.97	241.73	242.22	241.84	243.18	----
1996	High	247.56	251.21	253.50	263.79	261.24	252.92	251.90	252.04	250.35	249.59	247.08	246.85	263.79
	Low	238.63	245.62	242.72	250.19	251.79	246.64	240.09	242.83	243.10	237.78	235.99	238.12	235.99
	Close	247.53	248.77	251.40	256.09	254.07	248.67	241.99	249.46	245.63	237.83	243.36	239.61	----
1997	High	244.30	243.91	248.01	249.00	254.79	249.98	243.38	245.30	244.50	247.62	243.52	238.39	254.79
	Low	238.93	236.14	241.64	237.64	245.54	238.52	232.01	236.69	240.03	238.34	235.27	228.84	228.84
	Close	238.99	242.41	245.17	248.29	250.96	239.42	242.75	241.98	243.06	240.04	235.92	229.14	----
1998	High	235.36	236.08	231.74	229.09	226.67	216.75	216.75	207.48	205.03	206.57	206.73	197.29	236.08
	Low	221.56	223.97	223.04	223.42	214.03	208.42	205.99	195.18	196.31	201.34	195.18	187.89	187.89
	Close	234.28	227.65	228.88	223.99	215.90	214.63	206.00	195.68	203.30	203.28	195.42	191.22	----
1999	High	198.96	191.45	193.28	192.89	193.99	193.43	192.91	199.59	209.41	209.91	207.54	206.20	209.91
	Low	187.18	182.76	183.38	187.14	185.05	185.07	182.67	190.14	199.03	199.66	202.23	200.74	182.67
	Close	189.74	182.95	191.83	192.39	186.72	191.54	190.36	199.35	205.19	201.52	204.07	205.14	----
2000	High	213.70	215.29	217.88	214.15	226.12	227.29	225.69	228.02	232.20	234.38	231.46	233.37	234.38
	Low	201.43	206.74	209.61	207.61	211.86	222.23	217.42	217.76	224.74	218.38	220.93	225.46	201.43
	Close	210.46	208.78	214.37	211.03	222.27	223.93	218.61	227.41	226.57	219.28	229.79	227.83	----
2001	High	232.58	228.34	225.75	216.39	219.29	212.39	209.27	202.90	202.34	191.09	192.74	193.94	232.58
	Low	223.02	219.68	210.24	208.87	208.43	203.86	201.84	197.02	188.24	182.83	181.83	187.73	181.83
	Close	224.12	221.78	210.26	214.50	209.00	205.56	202.70	199.63	190.49	185.66	192.66	190.61	----

Source: Commodity Research Bureau (CRB)

CRB Indices

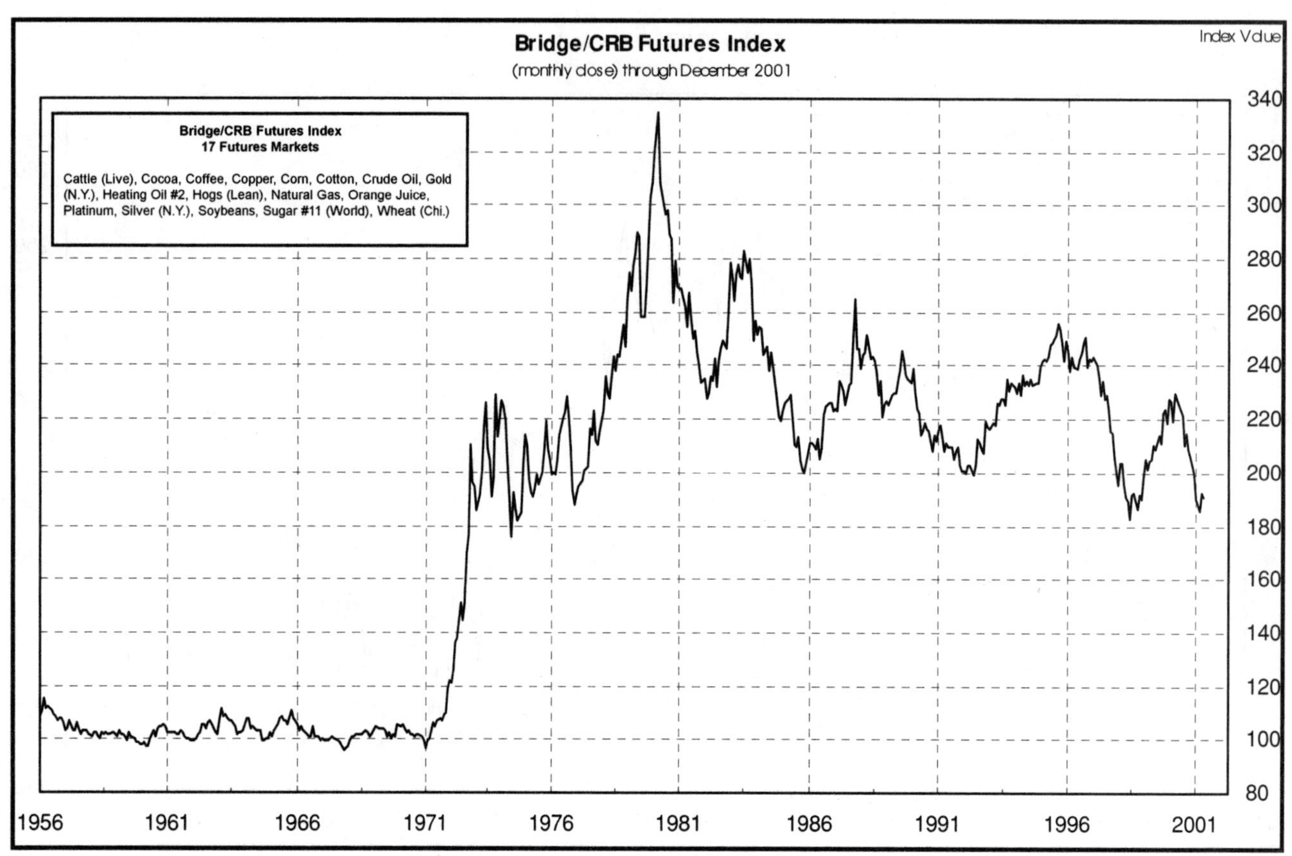

Bridge/CRB Futures Index
(monthly close) through December 2001
Index Value
Bridge/CRB Futures Index
17 Futures Markets
Cattle (Live), Cocoa, Coffee, Copper, Corn, Cotton, Crude Oil, Gold (N.Y.), Heating Oil #2, Hogs (Lean), Natural Gas, Orange Juice, Platinum, Silver (N.Y.), Soybeans, Sugar #11 (World), Wheat (Chi.)
340
320
300
280
260
240
220
200
180
160
140
120
100
80
1956
1961
1966
1971
1976
1981
1986
1991
1996
2001

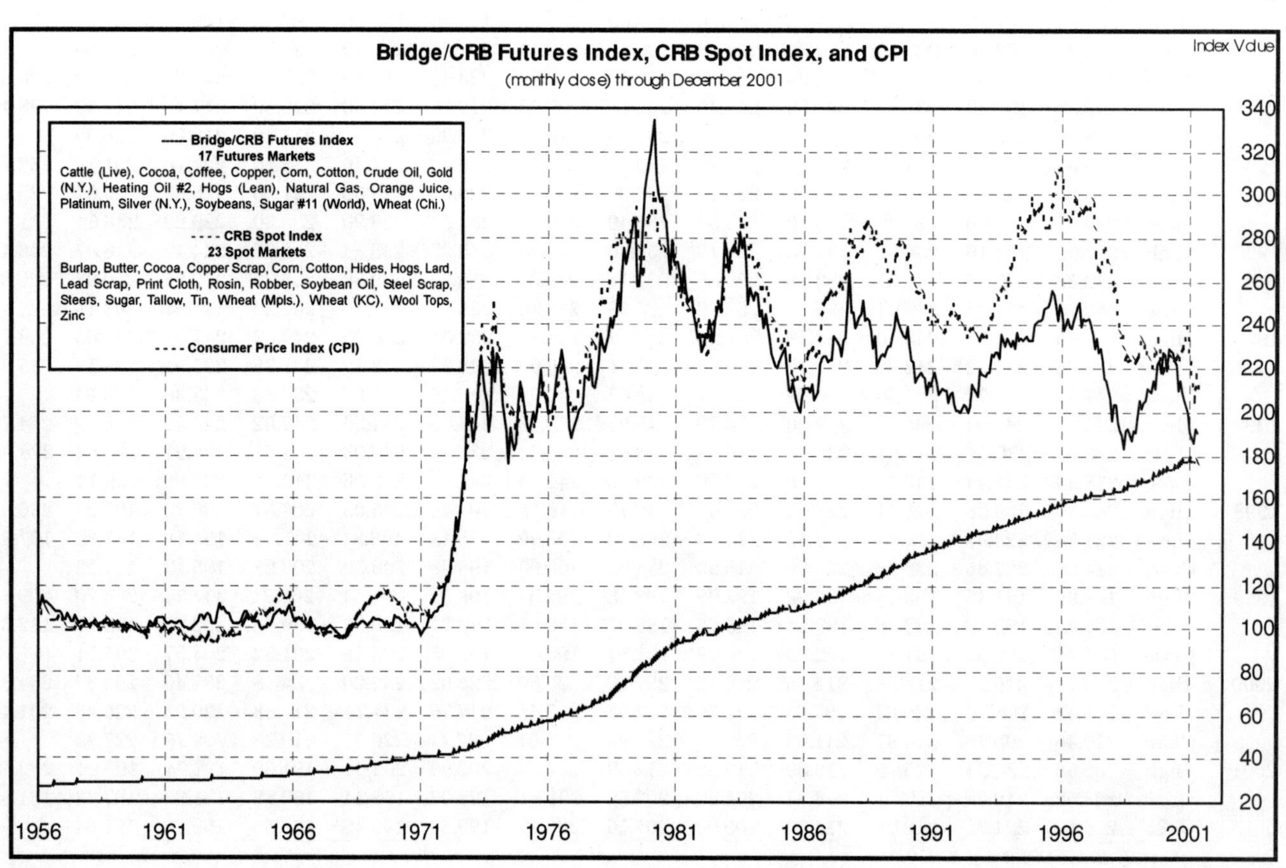

Bridge/CRB Futures Index, CRB Spot Index, and CPI
(monthly close) through December 2001
Index Value
Bridge/CRB Futures Index
17 Futures Markets
Cattle (Live), Cocoa, Coffee, Copper, Corn, Cotton, Crude Oil, Gold (N.Y.), Heating Oil #2, Hogs (Lean), Natural Gas, Orange Juice, Platinum, Silver (N.Y.), Soybeans, Sugar #11 (World), Wheat (Chi.)
CRB Spot Index
23 Spot Markets
Burlap, Butter, Cocoa, Copper Scrap, Corn, Cotton, Hides, Hogs, Lard, Lead Scrap, Print Cloth, Rosin, Robber, Soybean Oil, Steel Scrap, Steers, Sugar, Tallow, Tin, Wheat (Mpls.), Wheat (KC), Wool Tops, Zinc
Consumer Price Index (CPI)
340
320
300
280
260
240
220
200
180
160
140
120
100
80
60
40
20
1956
1961
1966
1971
1976
1981
1986
1991
1996
2001

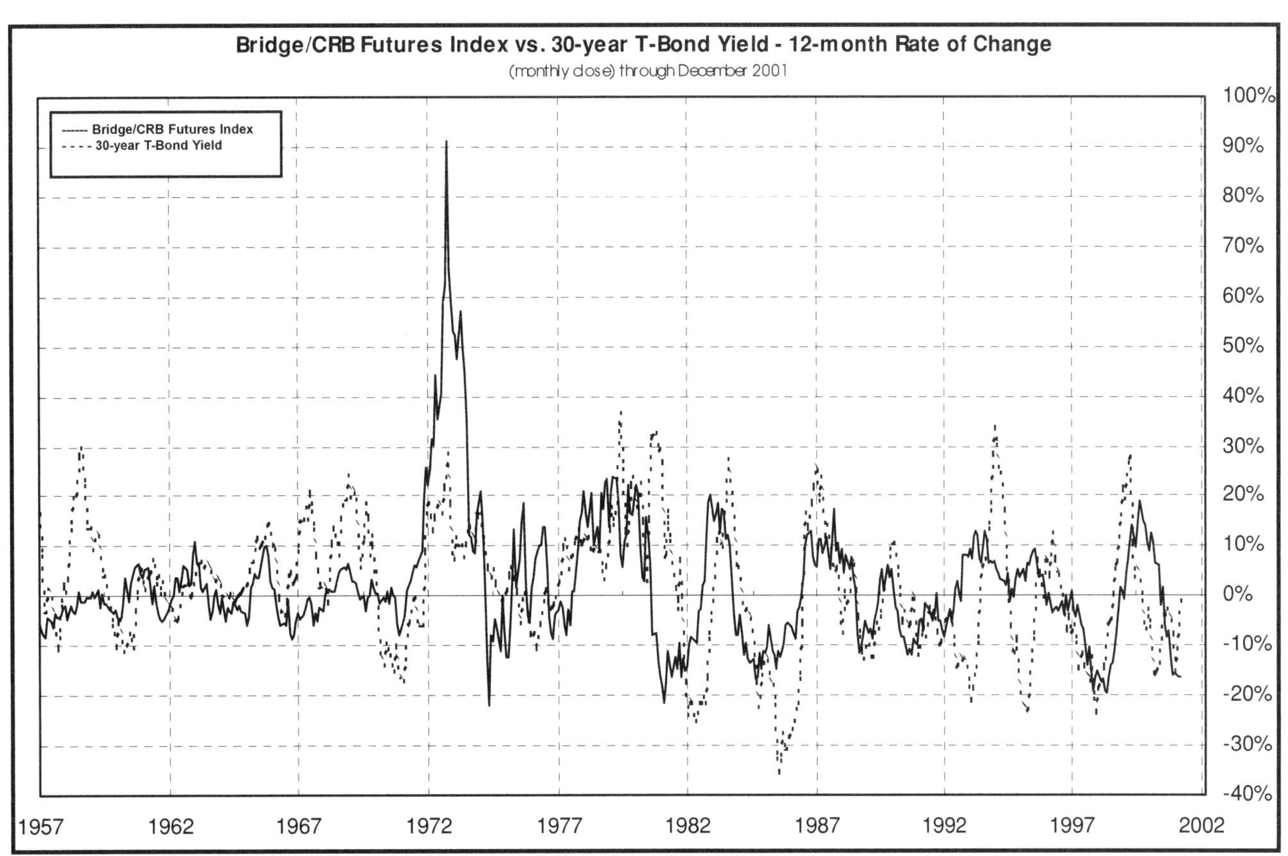
Bridge/CRB Futures Index vs. 30-year T-Bond Yield - 12-month Rate of Change
(monthly close) through December 2001
Bridge/CRB Futures Index
30-year T-Bond Yield
100%
90%
80%
70%
60%
50%
40%
30%
20%
10%
0%
-10%
-20%
-30%
-40%
1957
1962
1967
1972
1977
1982
1987
1992
1997
2002

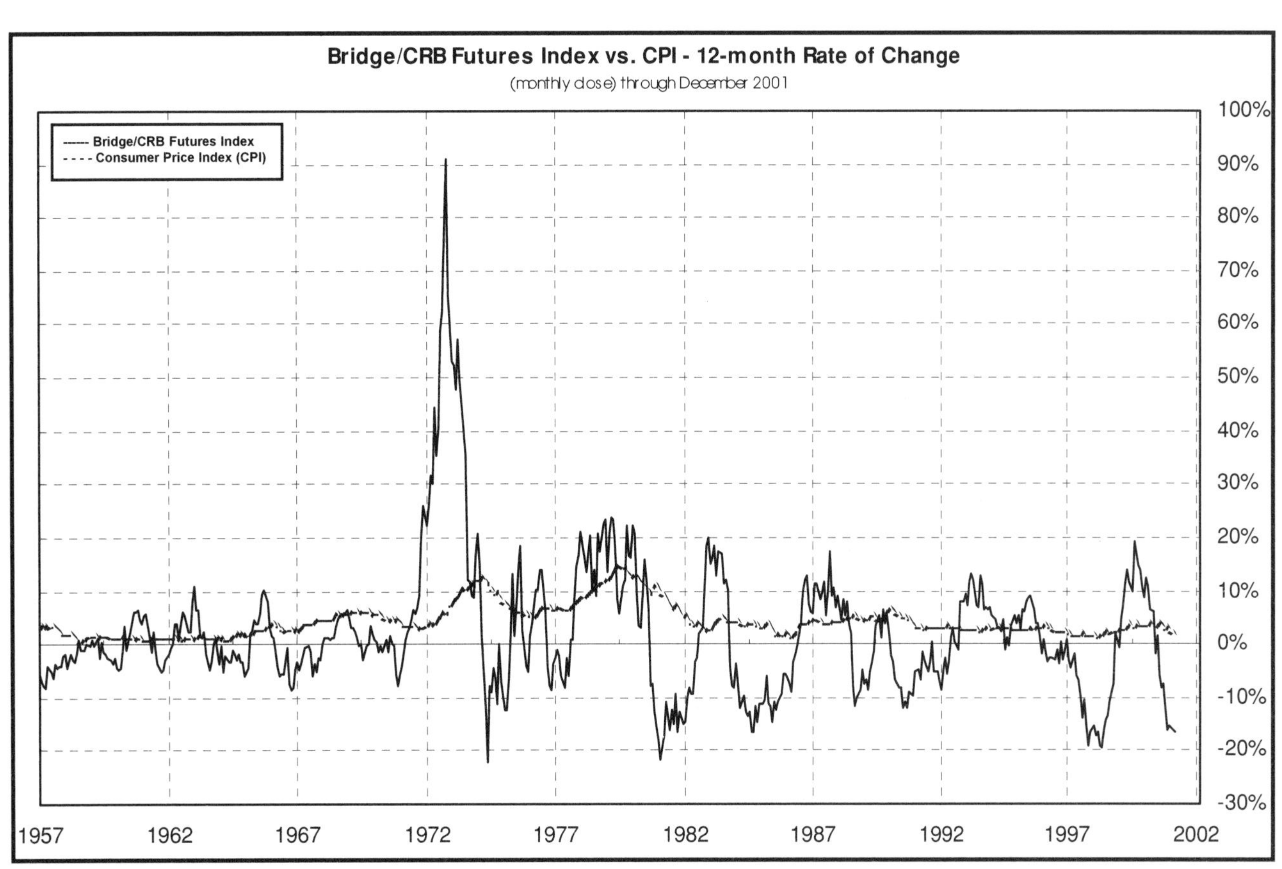
Bridge/CRB Futures Index vs. CPI - 12-month Rate of Change
(monthly close) through December 2001
Bridge/CRB Futures Index
Consumer Price Index (CPI)
100%
90%
80%
70%
60%
50%
40%
30%
20%
10%
0%
-10%
-20%
-30%
1957
1962
1967
1972
1977
1982
1987
1992
1997
2002

CRB Indices

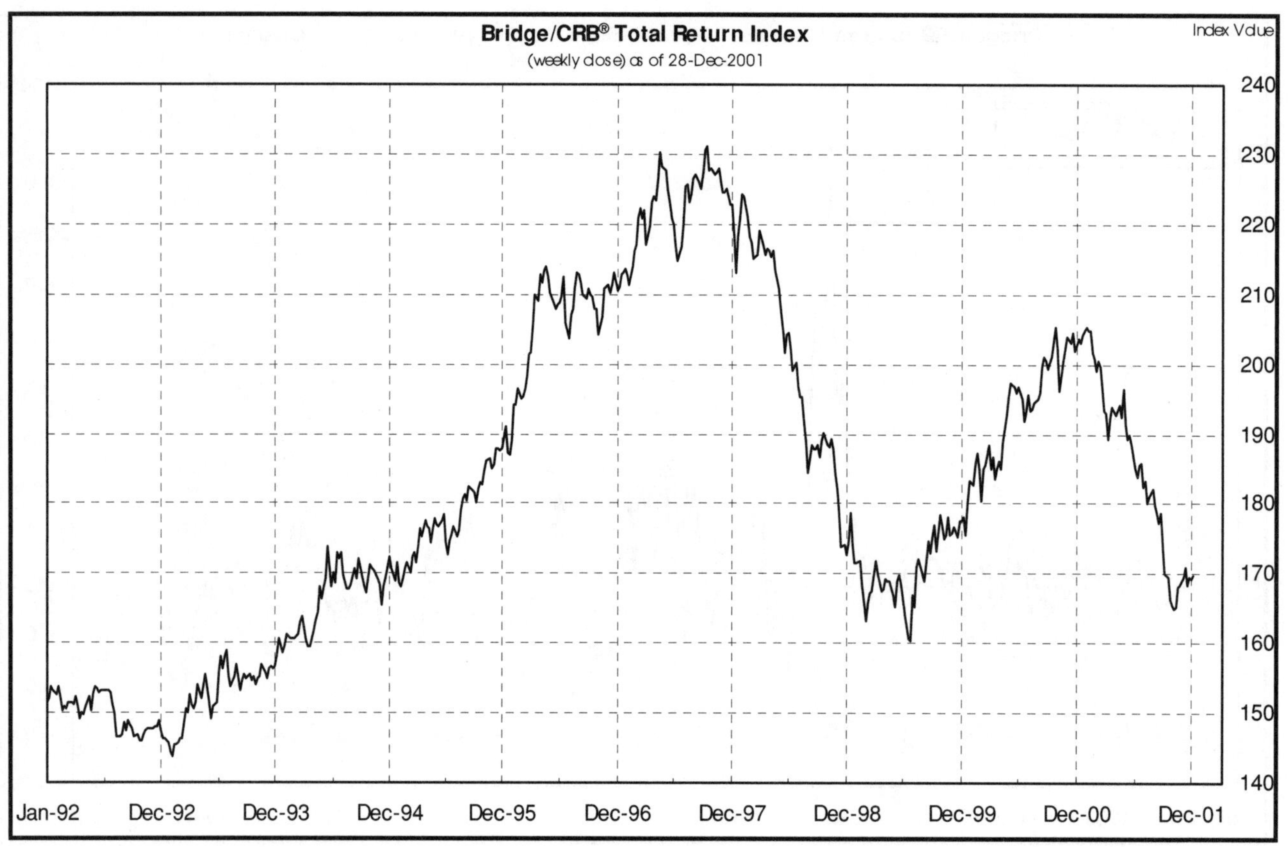
Bridge/CRB® Total Return Index
(weekly close) as of 28-Dec-2001
Index Value
240
230
220
210
200
190
180
170
160
150
140
Jan-92
Dec-92
Dec-93
Dec-94
Dec-95
Dec-96
Dec-97
Dec-98
Dec-99
Dec-00
Dec-01

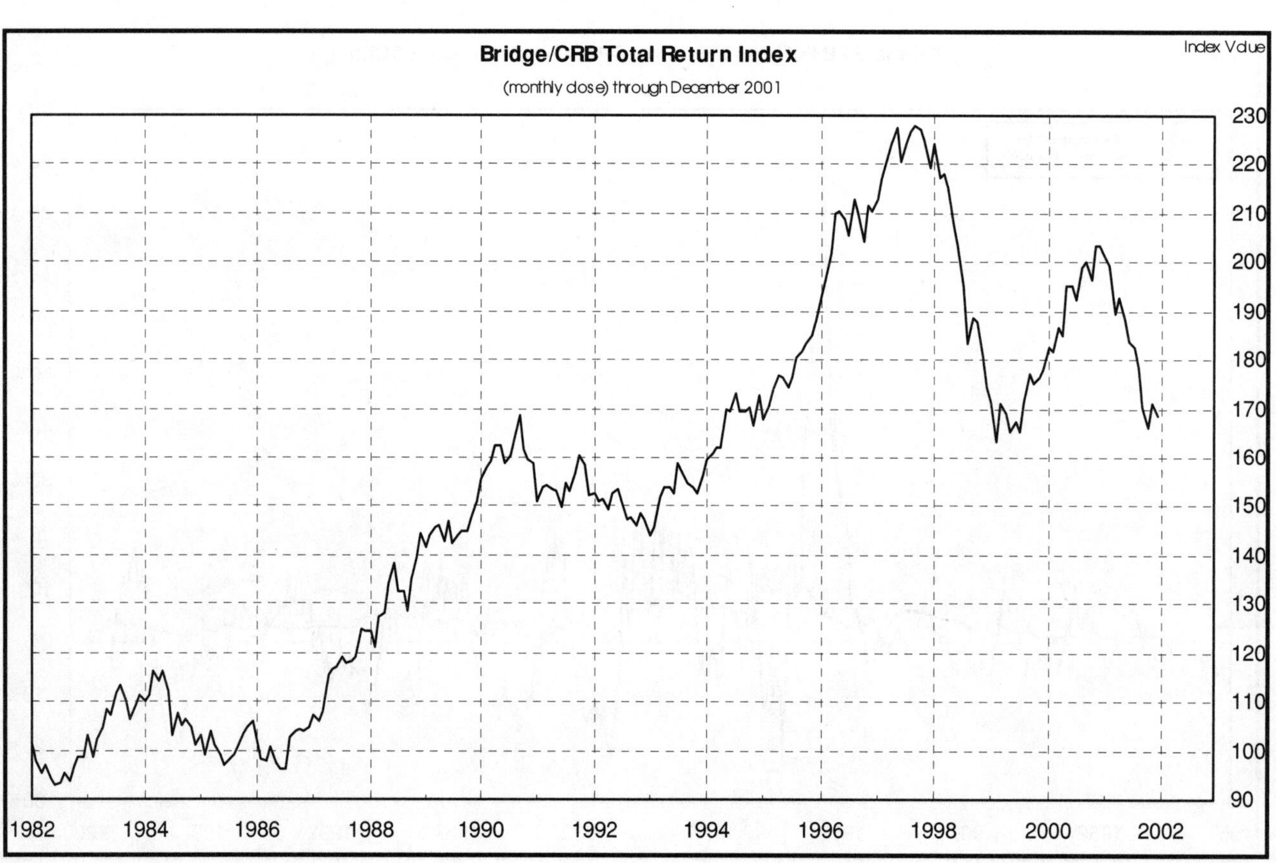
Bridge/CRB Total Return Index
(monthly close) through December 2001
Index Value
230
220
210
200
190
180
170
160
150
140
130
120
110
100
90
1982
1984
1986
1988
1990
1992
1994
1996
1998
2000
2002

CRB Livestock Sub-Index (1967=100)
(weekly close) as of 28-Dec-2001
Index Value
CRB Livestock Sub-Index
2 Futures Markets
Cattle (Live), Hogs (Lean)
290
280
270
260
250
240
230
220
210
200
190
180
170
160
Jan-92
Dec-92
Dec-93
Dec-94
Dec-95
Dec-96
Dec-97
Dec-98
Dec-99
Dec-00
Dec-01

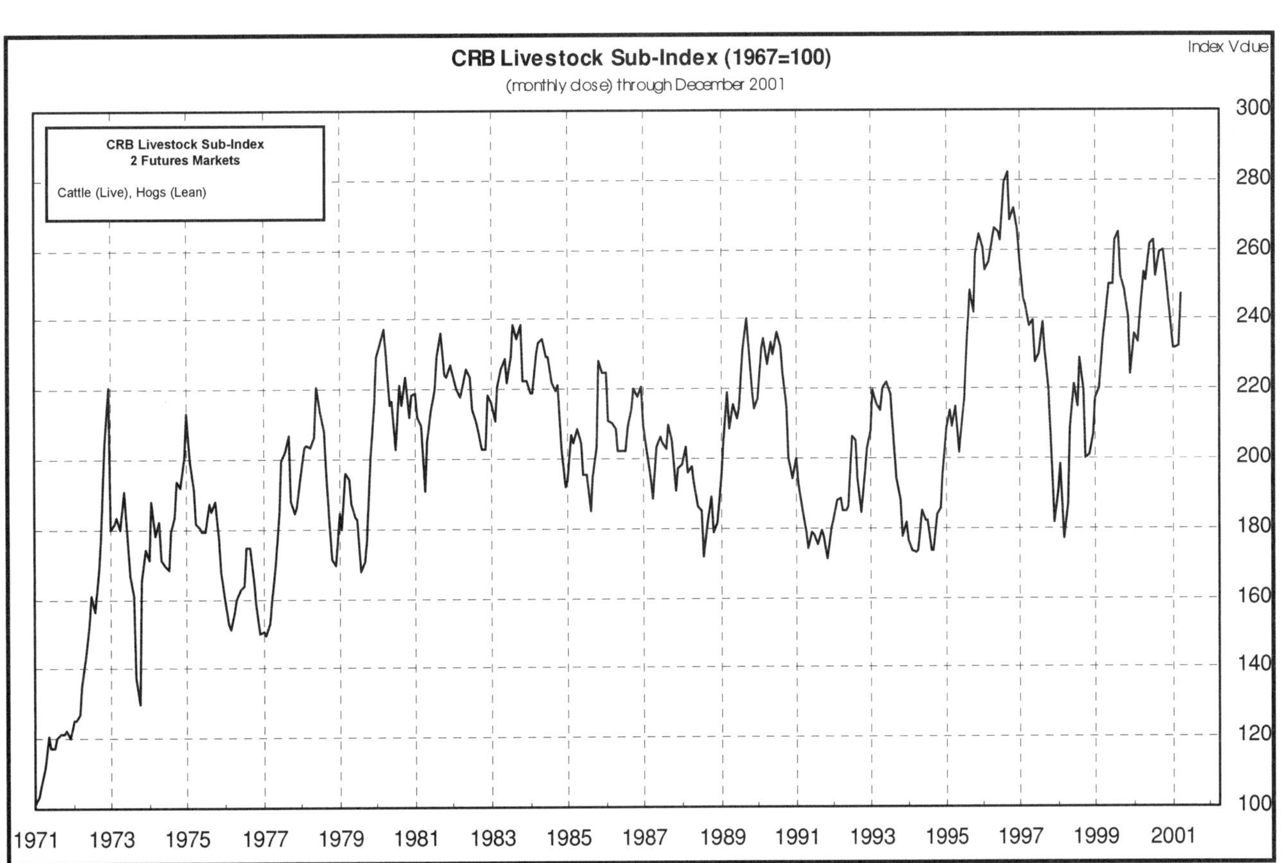
CRB Livestock Sub-Index (1967=100)
(monthly close) through December 2001
Index Value
CRB Livestock Sub-Index
2 Futures Markets
Cattle (Live), Hogs (Lean)
300
280
260
240
220
200
180
160
140
120
100
1971
1973
1975
1977
1979
1981
1983
1985
1987
1989
1991
1993
1995
1997
1999
2001

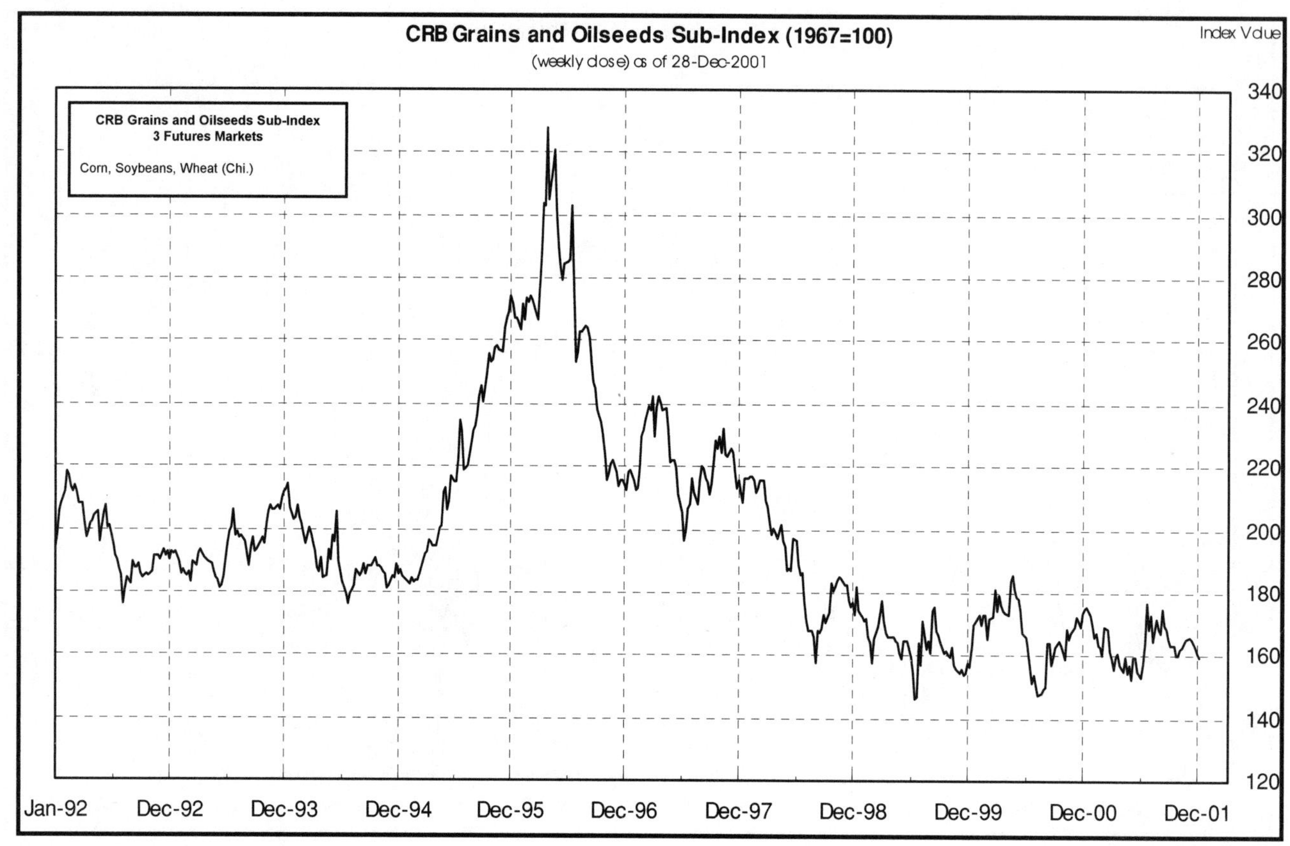
CRB Grains and Oilseeds Sub-Index (1967=100)
(weekly close) as of 28-Dec-2001
Index Value
CRB Grains and Oilseeds Sub-Index
3 Futures Markets
Corn, Soybeans, Wheat (Chi.)
340
320
300
280
260
240
220
200
180
160
140
120
Jan-92
Dec-92
Dec-93
Dec-94
Dec-95
Dec-96
Dec-97
Dec-98
Dec-99
Dec-00
Dec-01

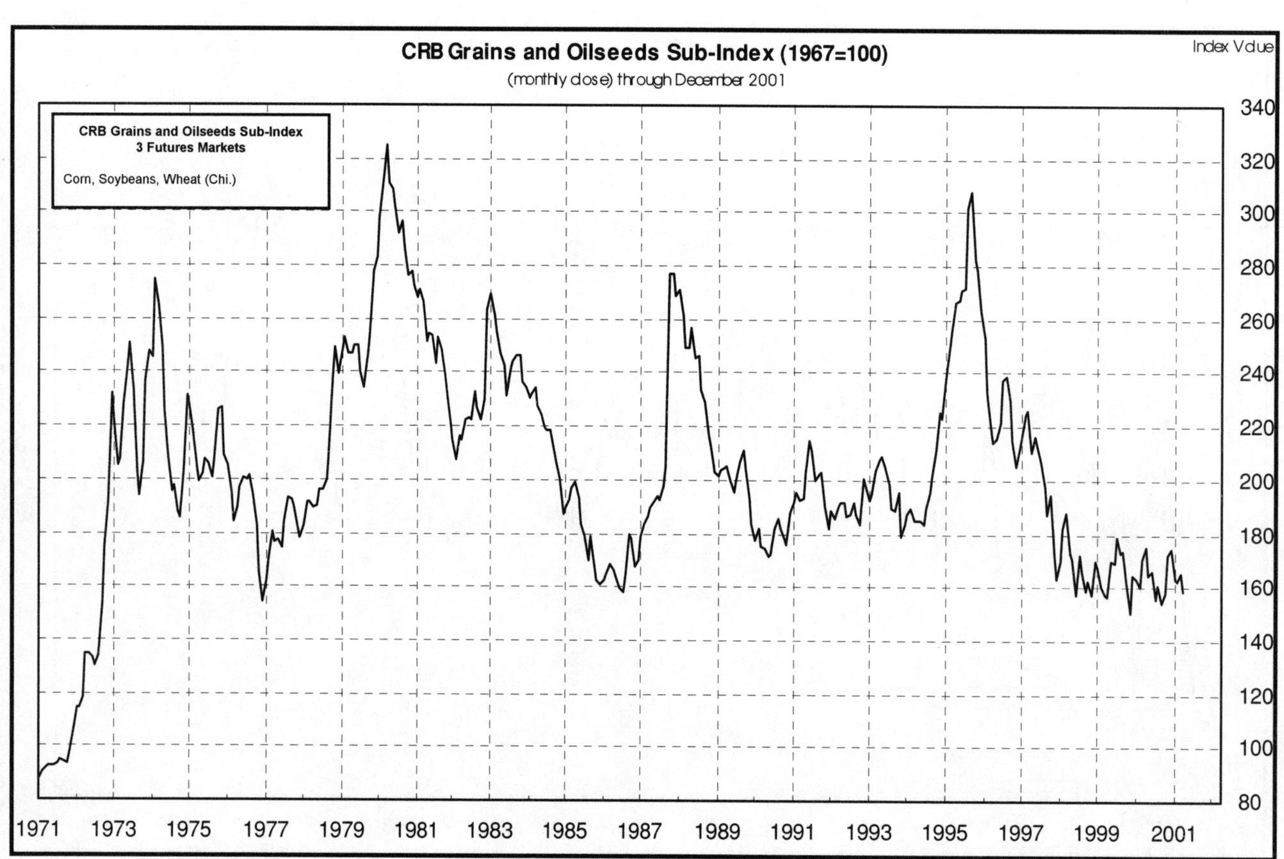
CRB Grains and Oilseeds Sub-Index (1967=100)
(monthly close) through December 2001
Index Value
CRB Grains and Oilseeds Sub-Index
3 Futures Markets
Corn, Soybeans, Wheat (Chi.)
340
320
300
280
260
240
220
200
180
160
140
120
100
80
1971
1973
1975
1977
1979
1981
1983
1985
1987
1989
1991
1993
1995
1997
1999
2001

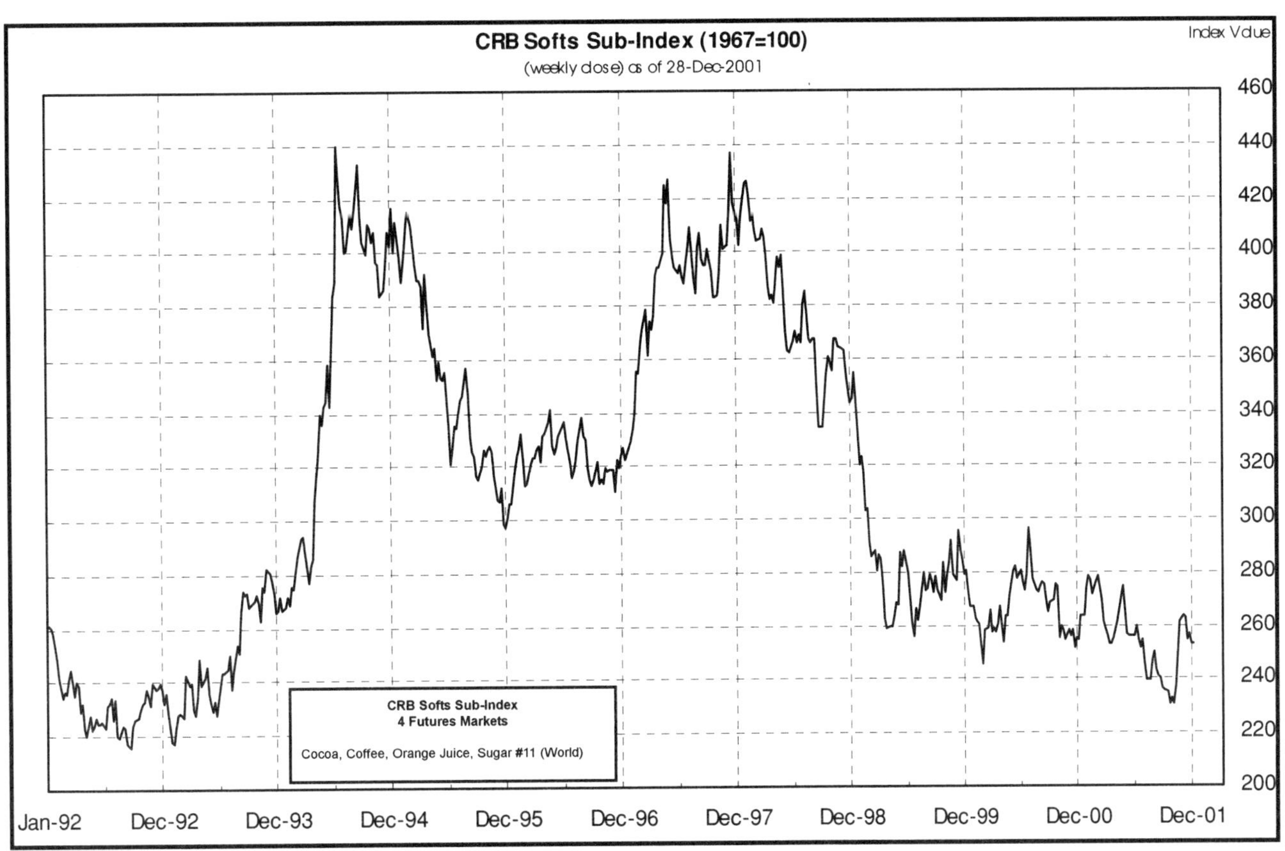
CRB Softs Sub-Index (1967=100)
(weekly close) as of 28-Dec-2001
Index Value
460
440
420
400
380
360
340
320
300
280
260
240
220
200
CRB Softs Sub-Index
4 Futures Markets
Cocoa, Coffee, Orange Juice, Sugar #11 (World)
Jan-92
Dec-92
Dec-93
Dec-94
Dec-95
Dec-96
Dec-97
Dec-98
Dec-99
Dec-00
Dec-01

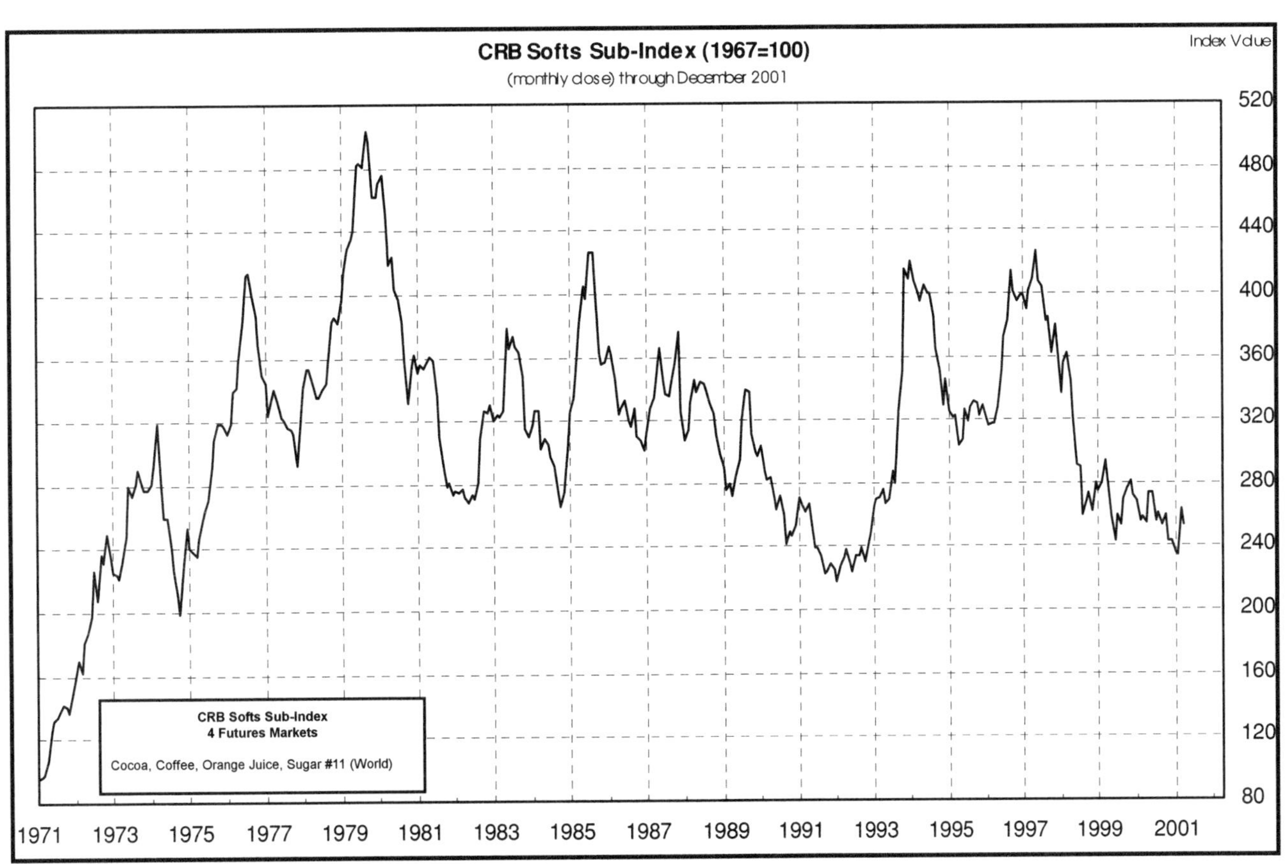
CRB Softs Sub-Index (1967=100)
(monthly close) through December 2001
Index Value
520
480
440
400
360
320
280
240
200
160
120
80
CRB Softs Sub-Index
4 Futures Markets
Cocoa, Coffee, Orange Juice, Sugar #11 (World)
1971
1973
1975
1977
1979
1981
1983
1985
1987
1989
1991
1993
1995
1997
1999
2001

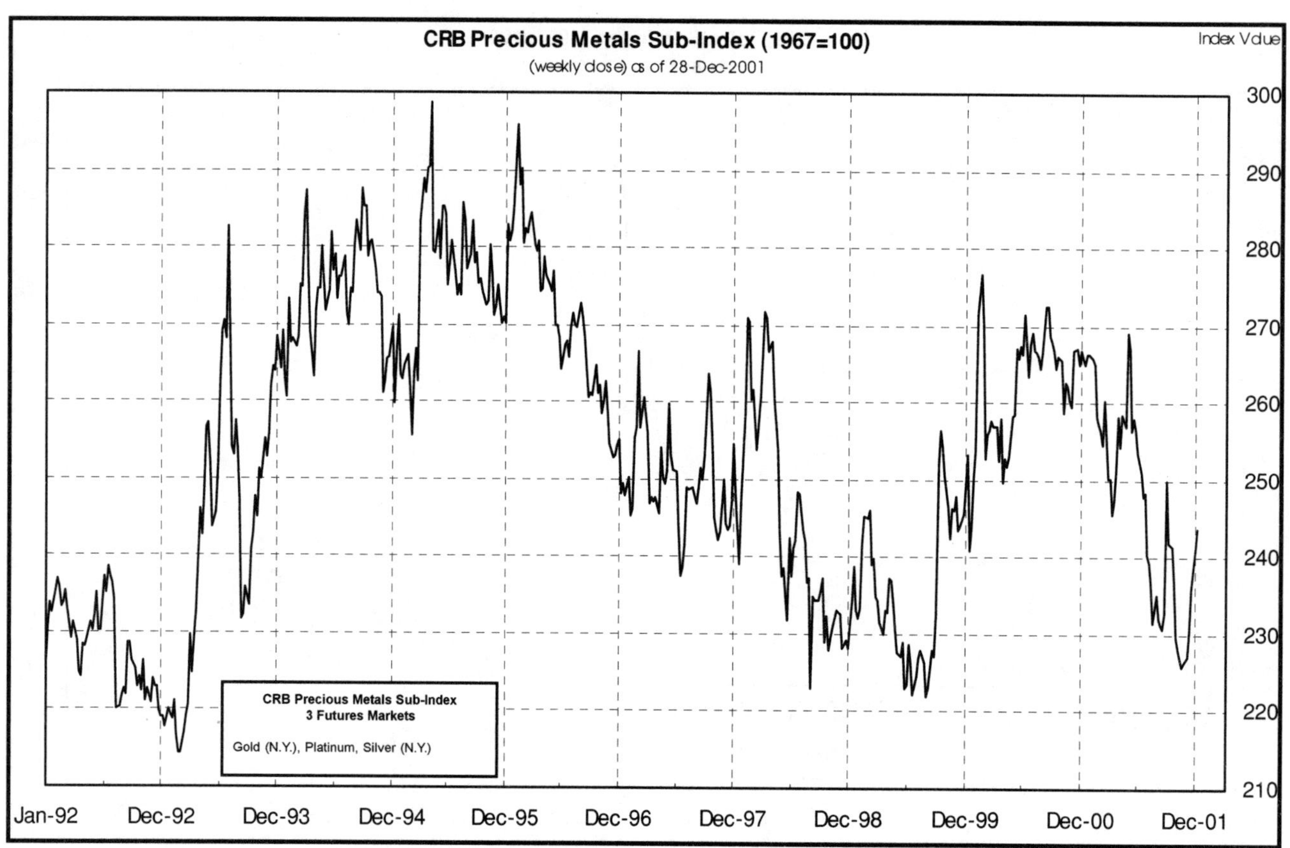
CRB Precious Metals Sub-Index (1967=100)
(weekly close) as of 28-Dec-2001
Index Value
CRB Precious Metals Sub-Index
3 Futures Markets
Gold (N.Y.), Platinum, Silver (N.Y.)
300
290
280
270
260
250
240
230
220
210
Jan-92 Dec-92 Dec-93 Dec-94 Dec-95 Dec-96 Dec-97 Dec-98 Dec-99 Dec-00 Dec-01

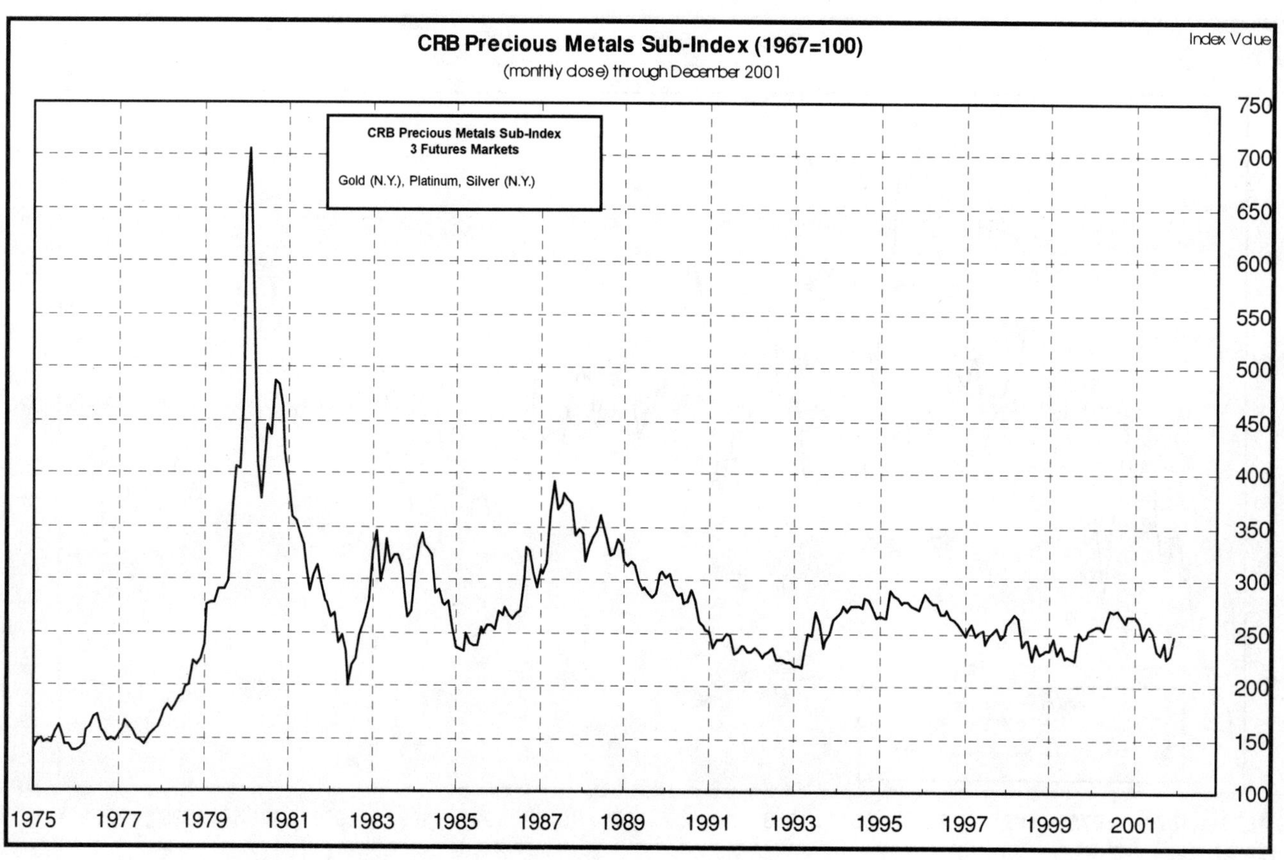
CRB Precious Metals Sub-Index (1967=100)
(monthly close) through December 2001
Index Value
CRB Precious Metals Sub-Index
3 Futures Markets
Gold (N.Y.), Platinum, Silver (N.Y.)
750
700
650
600
550
500
450
400
350
300
250
200
150
100
1975 1977 1979 1981 1983 1985 1987 1989 1991 1993 1995 1997 1999 2001

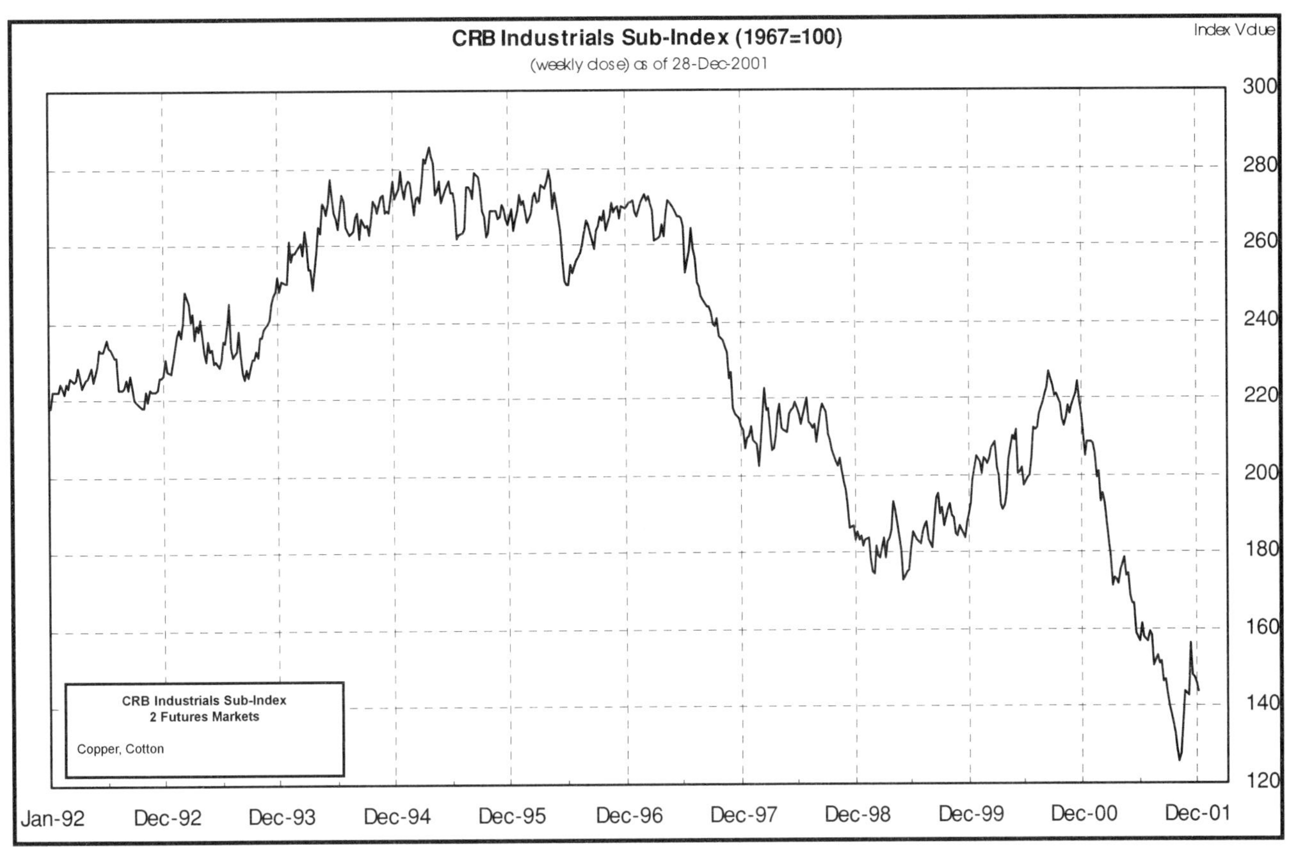
CRB Industrials Sub-Index (1967=100)
(weekly close) as of 28-Dec-2001
Index Value
300
280
260
240
220
200
180
160
140
120
CRB Industrials Sub-Index
2 Futures Markets
Copper, Cotton
Jan-92
Dec-92
Dec-93
Dec-94
Dec-95
Dec-96
Dec-97
Dec-98
Dec-99
Dec-00
Dec-01

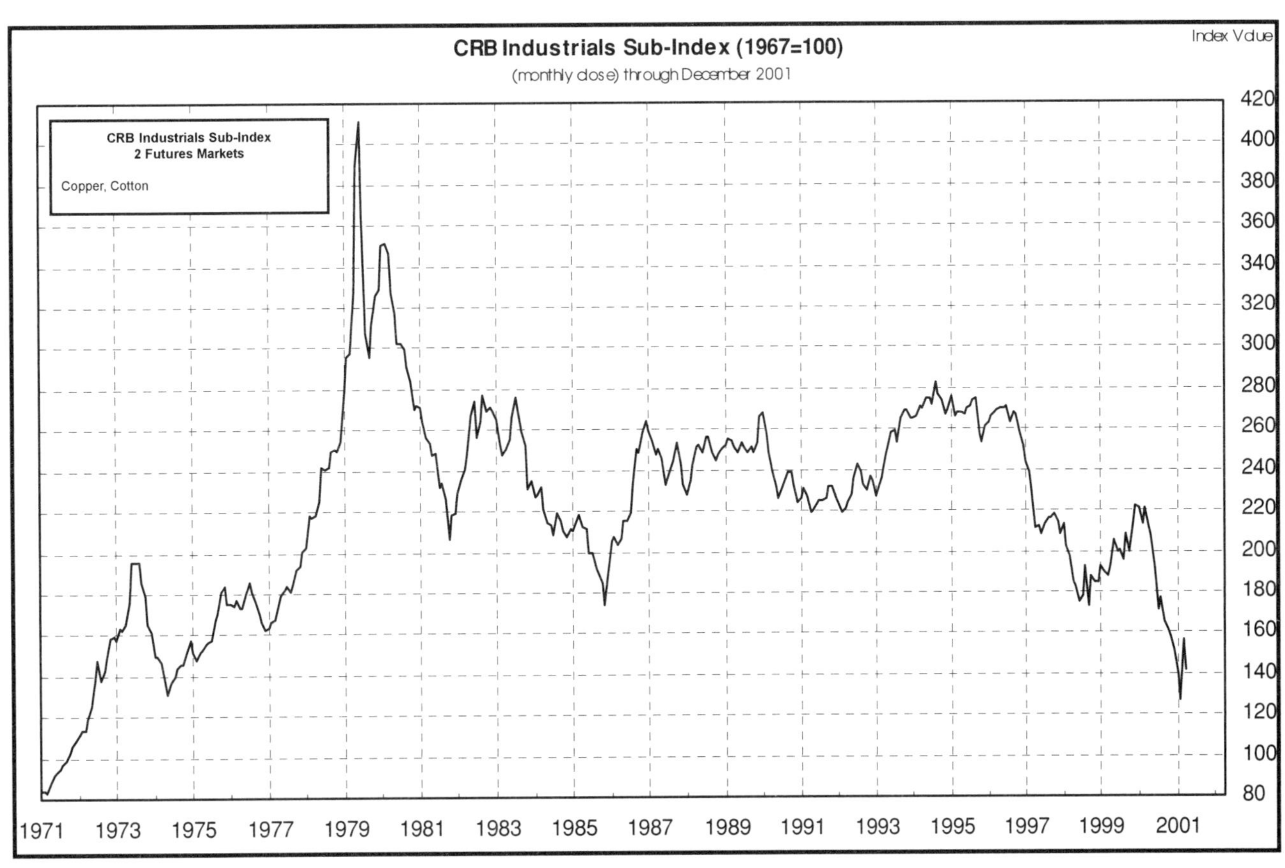
CRB Industrials Sub-Index (1967=100)
(monthly close) through December 2001
Index Value
420
400
380
360
340
320
300
280
260
240
220
200
180
160
140
120
100
80
CRB Industrials Sub-Index
2 Futures Markets
Copper, Cotton
1971
1973
1975
1977
1979
1981
1983
1985
1987
1989
1991
1993
1995
1997
1999
2001

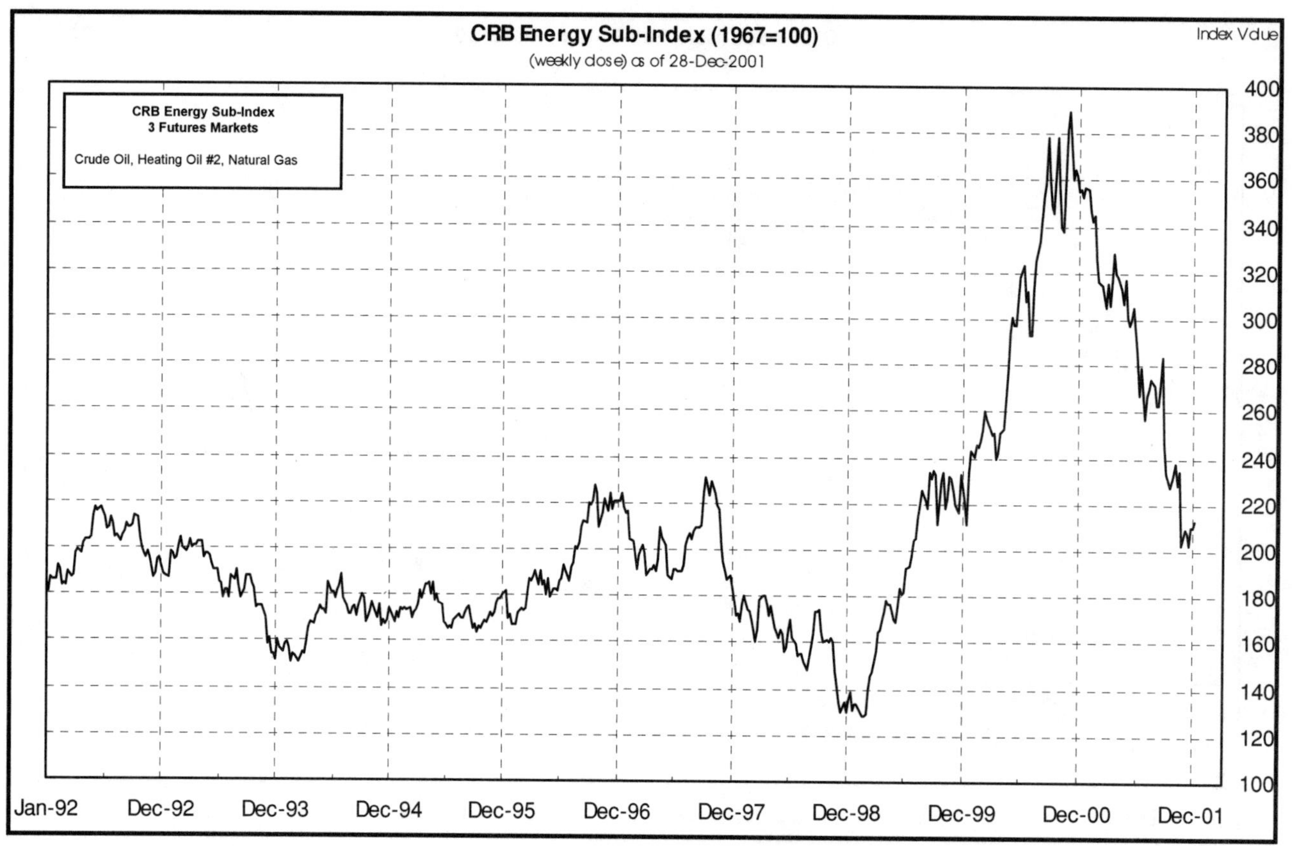
CRB Energy Sub-Index (1967=100)
(weekly close) as of 28-Dec-2001
Index Value
CRB Energy Sub-Index
3 Futures Markets
Crude Oil, Heating Oil #2, Natural Gas
400
380
360
340
320
300
280
260
240
220
200
180
160
140
120
100
Jan-92
Dec-92
Dec-93
Dec-94
Dec-95
Dec-96
Dec-97
Dec-98
Dec-99
Dec-00
Dec-01

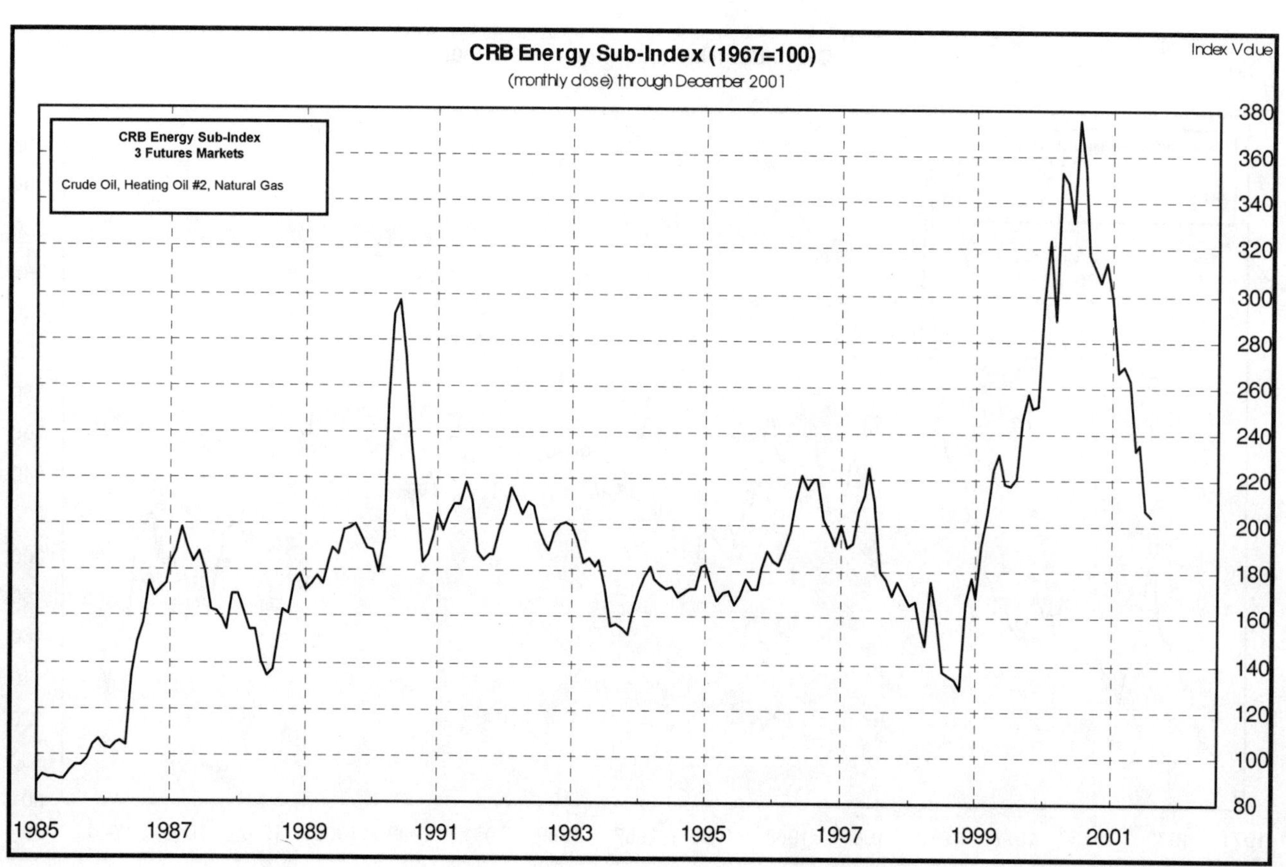
CRB Energy Sub-Index (1967=100)
(monthly close) through December 2001
Index Value
CRB Energy Sub-Index
3 Futures Markets
Crude Oil, Heating Oil #2, Natural Gas
380
360
340
320
300
280
260
240
220
200
180
160
140
120
100
80
1985
1987
1989
1991
1993
1995
1997
1999
2001

CRB Interest Rates Index (1977=100)
(weekly close) as of 28-Dec-2001
Index Value
CRB Interest Rates Index (1977)
3 Futures Markets
3-month T-Bills, 10-year T-Notes, 30-year T-Bonds
126
124
122
120
118
116
114
112
110
108
106
104
102
100
98
96
Jan-92
Dec-92
Dec-93
Dec-94
Dec-95
Dec-96
Dec-97
Dec-98
Dec-99
Dec-00
Dec-01

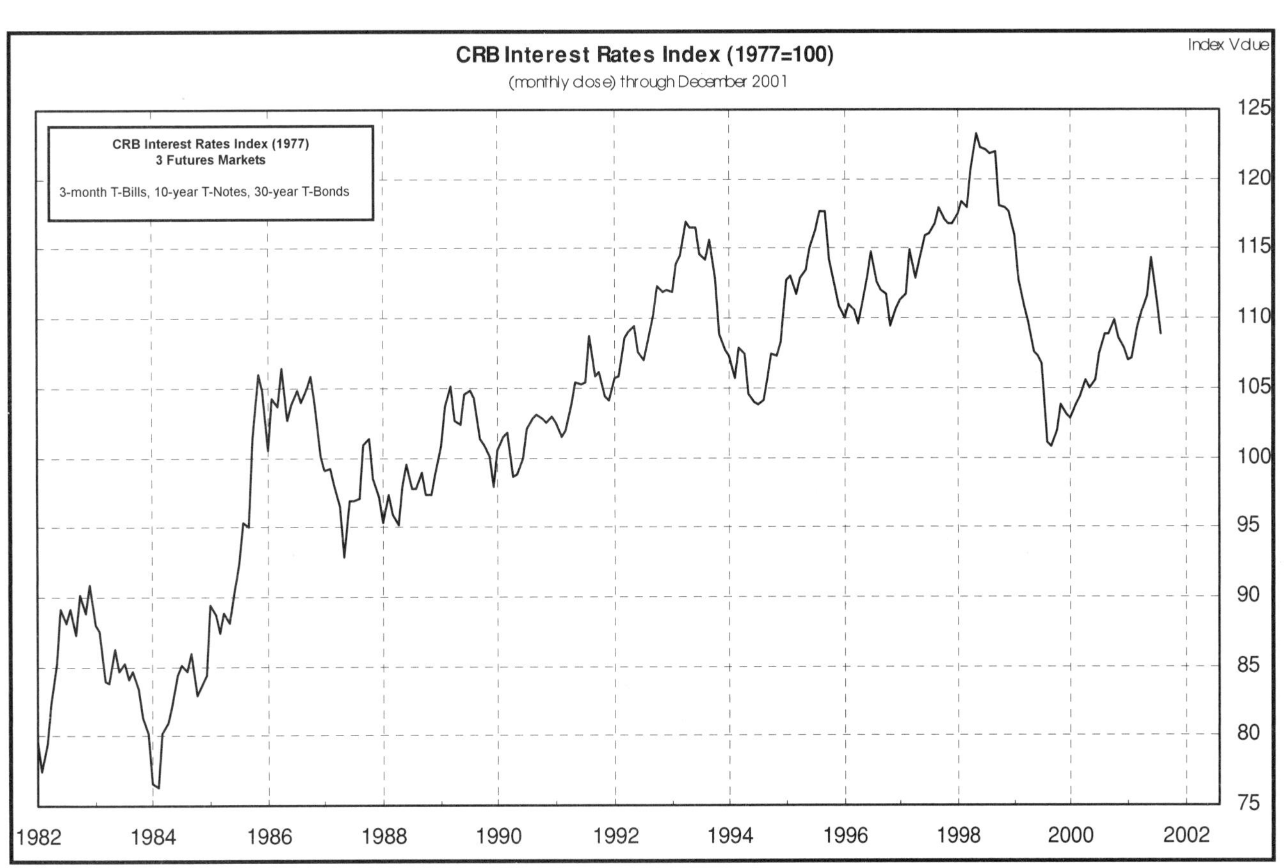

CRB Interest Rates Index (1977=100)
(monthly close) through December 2001
Index Value
CRB Interest Rates Index (1977)
3 Futures Markets
3-month T-Bills, 10-year T-Notes, 30-year T-Bonds
125
120
115
110
105
100
95
90
85
80
75
1982
1984
1986
1988
1990
1992
1994
1996
1998
2000
2002

CRB Metals Sub-Index (1967=100)
(weekly close) as of 28-Dec-2001
Index Value
CRB Spot Index
5 Spot Markets
Copper Scrap, Lead Scrap, Steel Scrap, Tin, Zinc
340
320
300
280
260
240
220
200
180
160
Jan-92
Dec-92
Dec-93
Dec-94
Dec-95
Dec-96
Dec-97
Dec-98
Dec-99
Dec-00
Dec-01

CRB Metals Sub-Index (1967=100)
(monthly close) through December 2001
Index Value
CRB Spot Index
5 Spot Markets
Copper Scrap, Lead Scrap, Steel Scrap, Tin, Zinc
380
360
340
320
300
280
260
240
220
200
180
160
140
120
100
80
60
1947
1952
1957
1962
1967
1972
1977
1982
1987
1992
1997
2002

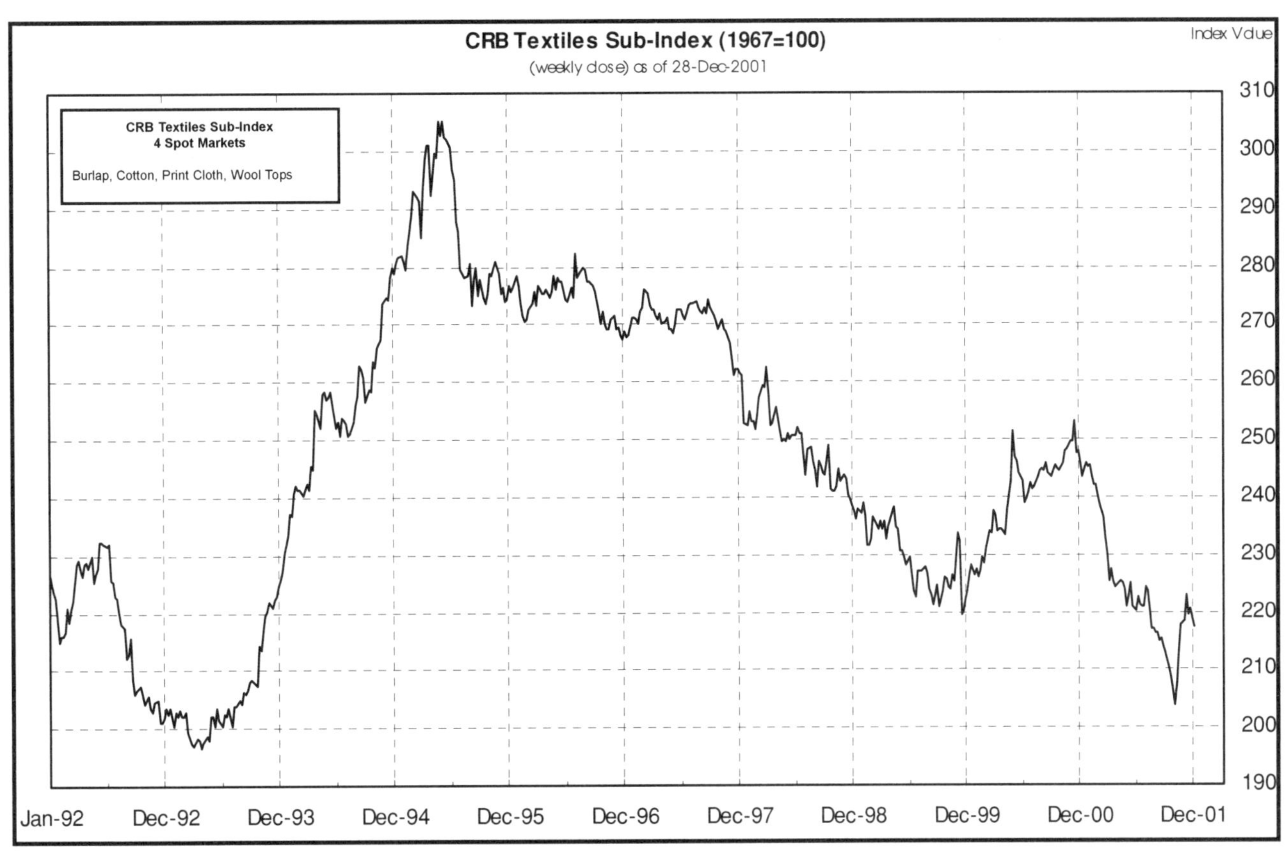
CRB Textiles Sub-Index (1967=100)
(weekly close) as of 28-Dec-2001
Index Value
CRB Textiles Sub-Index
4 Spot Markets
Burlap, Cotton, Print Cloth, Wool Tops
310
300
290
280
270
260
250
240
230
220
210
200
190
Jan-92
Dec-92
Dec-93
Dec-94
Dec-95
Dec-96
Dec-97
Dec-98
Dec-99
Dec-00
Dec-01

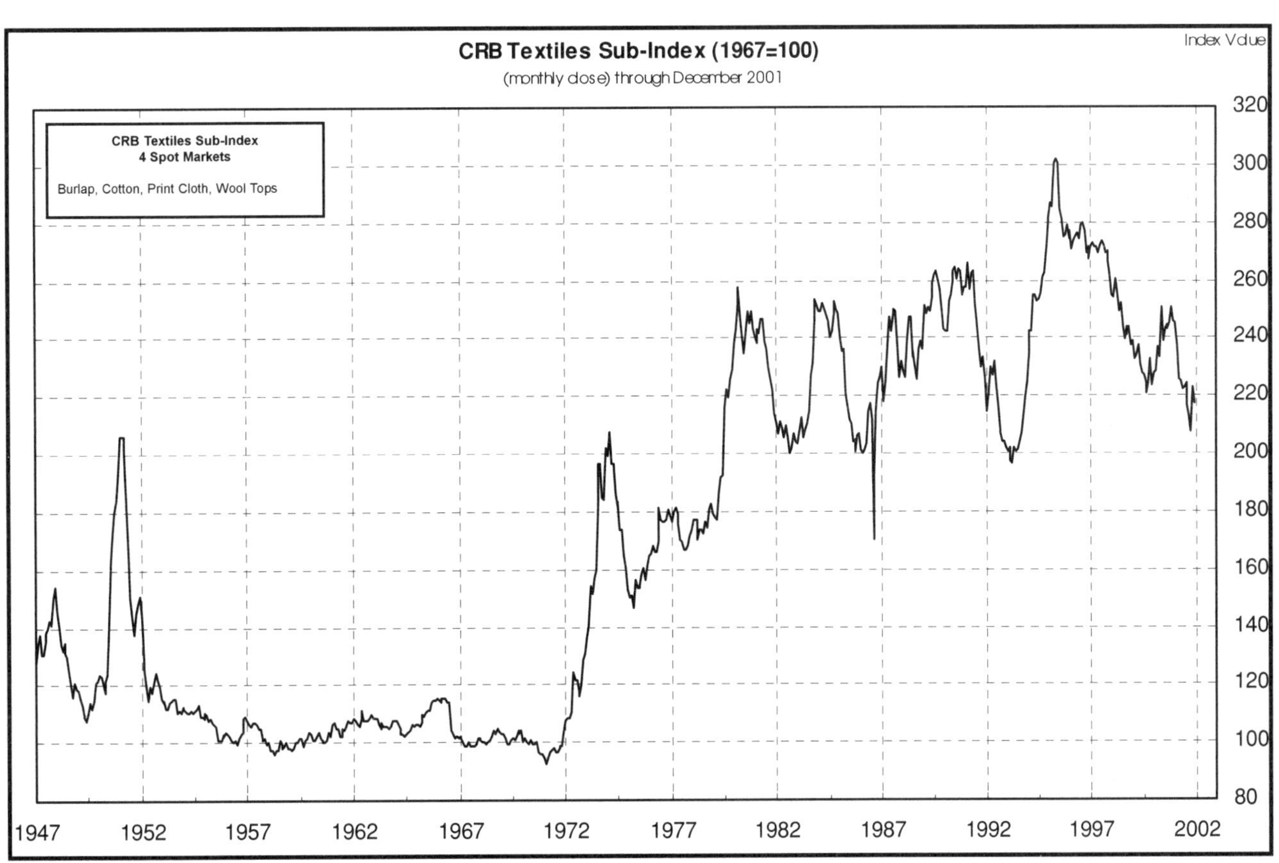
CRB Textiles Sub-Index (1967=100)
(monthly close) through December 2001
Index Value
CRB Textiles Sub-Index
4 Spot Markets
Burlap, Cotton, Print Cloth, Wool Tops
320
300
280
260
240
220
200
180
160
140
120
100
80
1947
1952
1957
1962
1967
1972
1977
1982
1987
1992
1997
2002

CRB Raw Industrials Sub-Index (1967=100)
(weekly close) as of 28-Dec-2001
Index Value
CRB Raw Industrials Sub-Index
13 Spot Markets
Burlap, Copper Scrap, Cotton, Hides, Lead Scrap, Print Cloth, Rosin, Rubber, Steel Scrap, Tallow, Tin, Wool Tops, Zinc
360
350
340
330
320
310
300
290
280
270
260
250
240
230
220
210
200
Jan-92
Dec-92
Dec-93
Dec-94
Dec-95
Dec-96
Dec-97
Dec-98
Dec-99
Dec-00
Dec-01

CRB Raw Industrials Sub-Index (1967=100)
(monthly close) through December 2001
Index Value
CRB Raw Industrials Sub-Index
13 Spot Markets
Burlap, Copper Scrap, Cotton, Hides, Lead Scrap, Print Cloth, Rosin, Rubber, Steel Scrap, Tallow, Tin, Wool Tops, Zinc
360
340
320
300
280
260
240
220
200
180
160
140
120
100
80
1947
1952
1957
1962
1967
1972
1977
1982
1987
1992
1997
2002

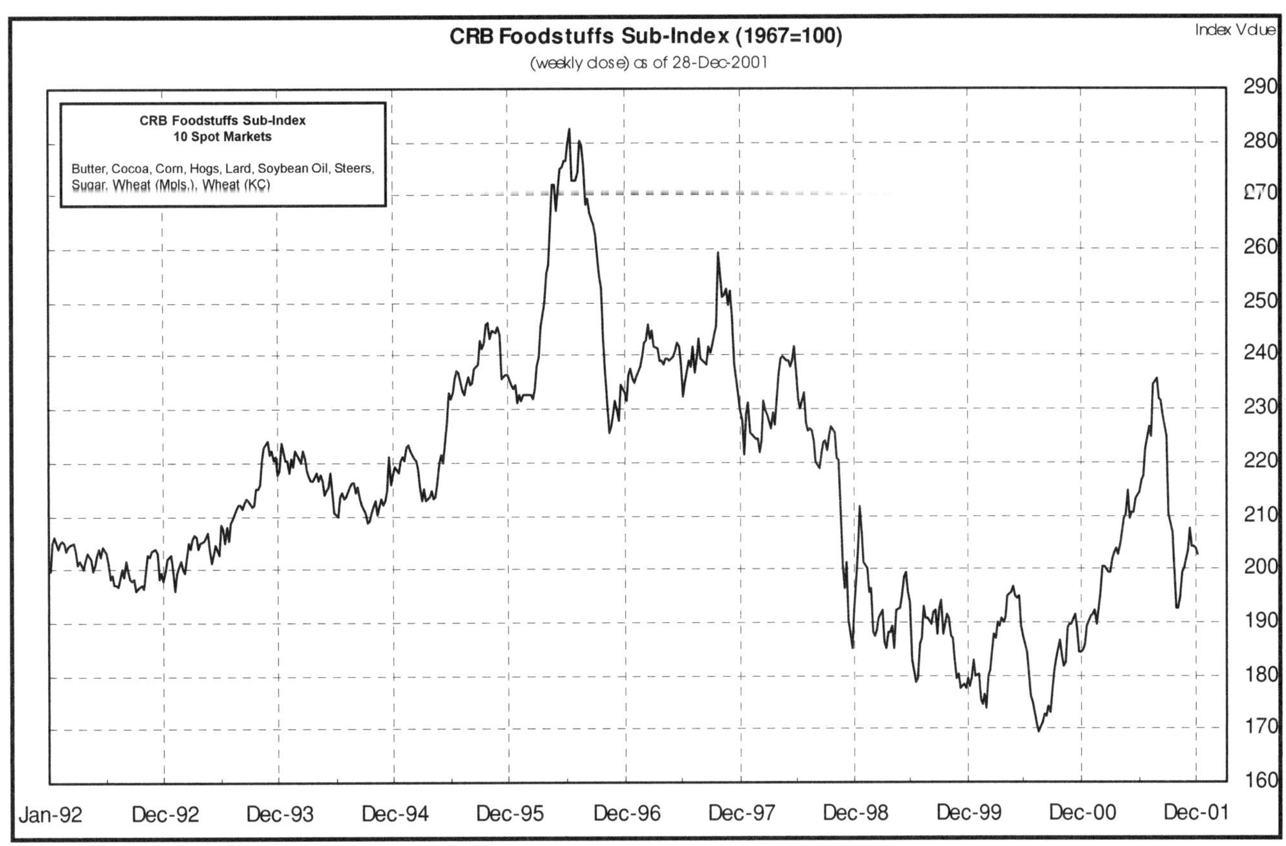
CRB Foodstuffs Sub-Index (1967=100)
(weekly close) as of 28-Dec-2001
Index Value
CRB Foodstuffs Sub-Index
10 Spot Markets
Butter, Cocoa, Corn, Hogs, Lard, Soybean Oil, Steers, Sugar, Wheat (Mpls.), Wheat (KC)
290
280
270
260
250
240
230
220
210
200
190
180
170
160
Jan-92
Dec-92
Dec-93
Dec-94
Dec-95
Dec-96
Dec-97
Dec-98
Dec-99
Dec-00
Dec-01

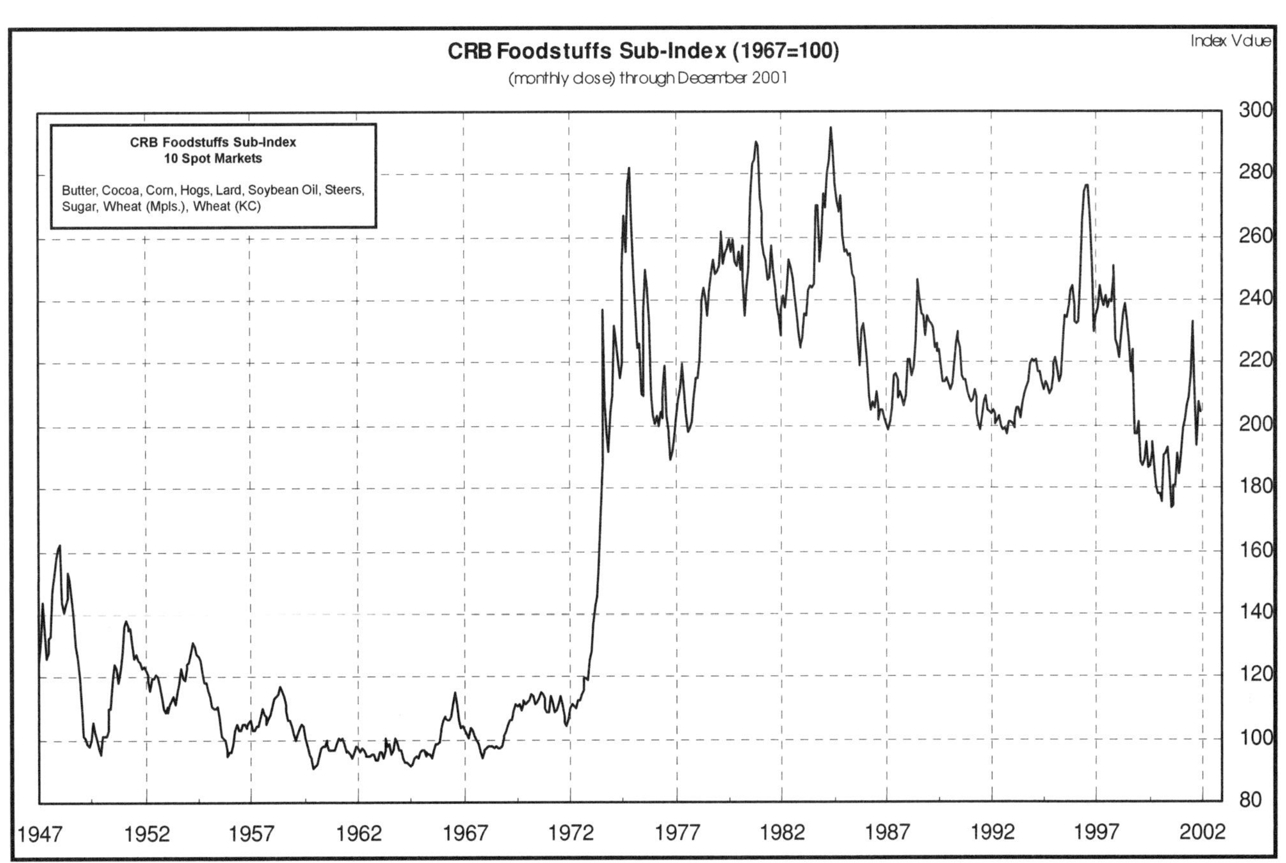
CRB Foodstuffs Sub-Index (1967=100)
(monthly close) through December 2001
Index Value
CRB Foodstuffs Sub-Index
10 Spot Markets
Butter, Cocoa, Corn, Hogs, Lard, Soybean Oil, Steers, Sugar, Wheat (Mpls.), Wheat (KC)
300
280
260
240
220
200
180
160
140
120
100
80
1947
1952
1957
1962
1967
1972
1977
1982
1987
1992
1997
2002

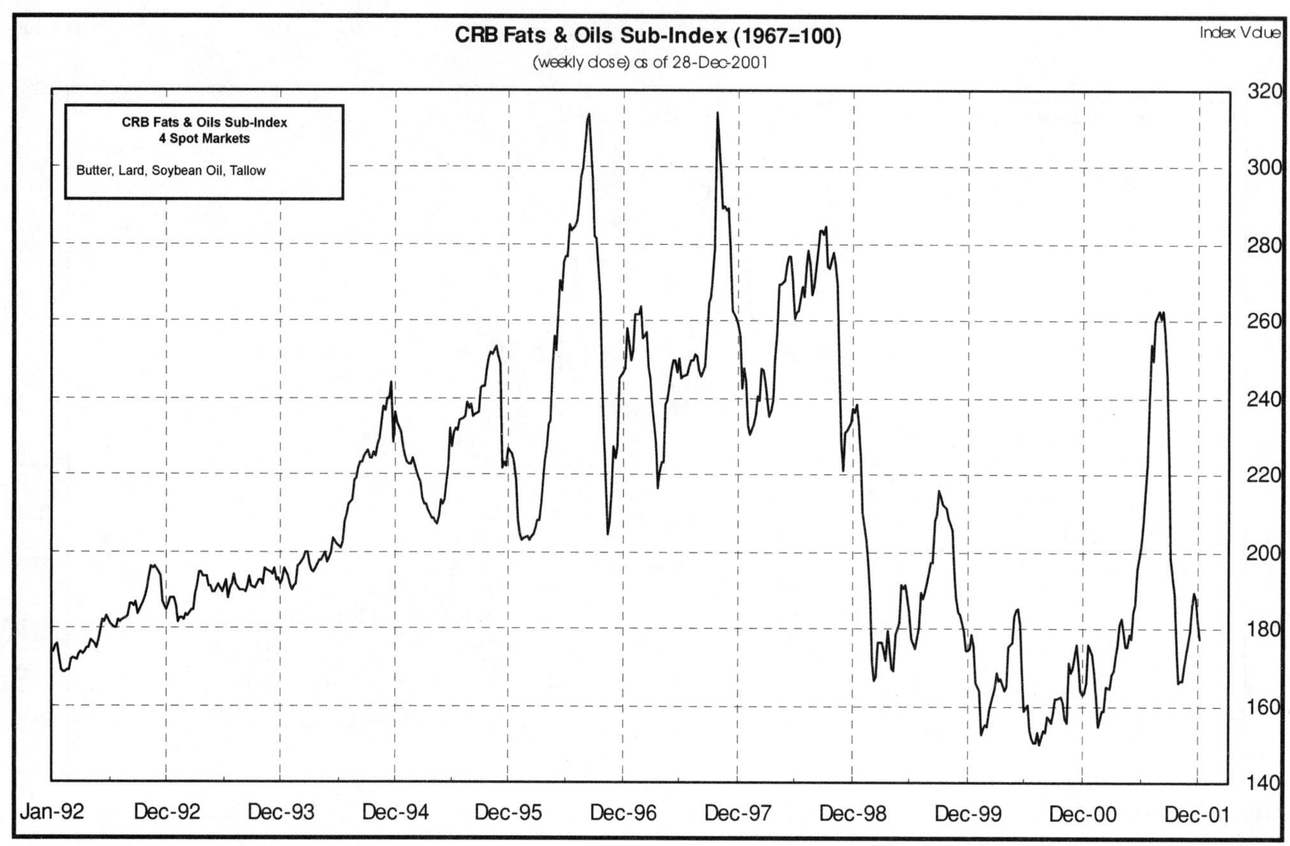

CRB Fats & Oils Sub-Index (1967=100)
(weekly close) as of 28-Dec-2001
Index Value
CRB Fats & Oils Sub-Index
4 Spot Markets
Butter, Lard, Soybean Oil, Tallow
320
300
280
260
240
220
200
180
160
140
Jan-92
Dec-92
Dec-93
Dec-94
Dec-95
Dec-96
Dec-97
Dec-98
Dec-99
Dec-00
Dec-01

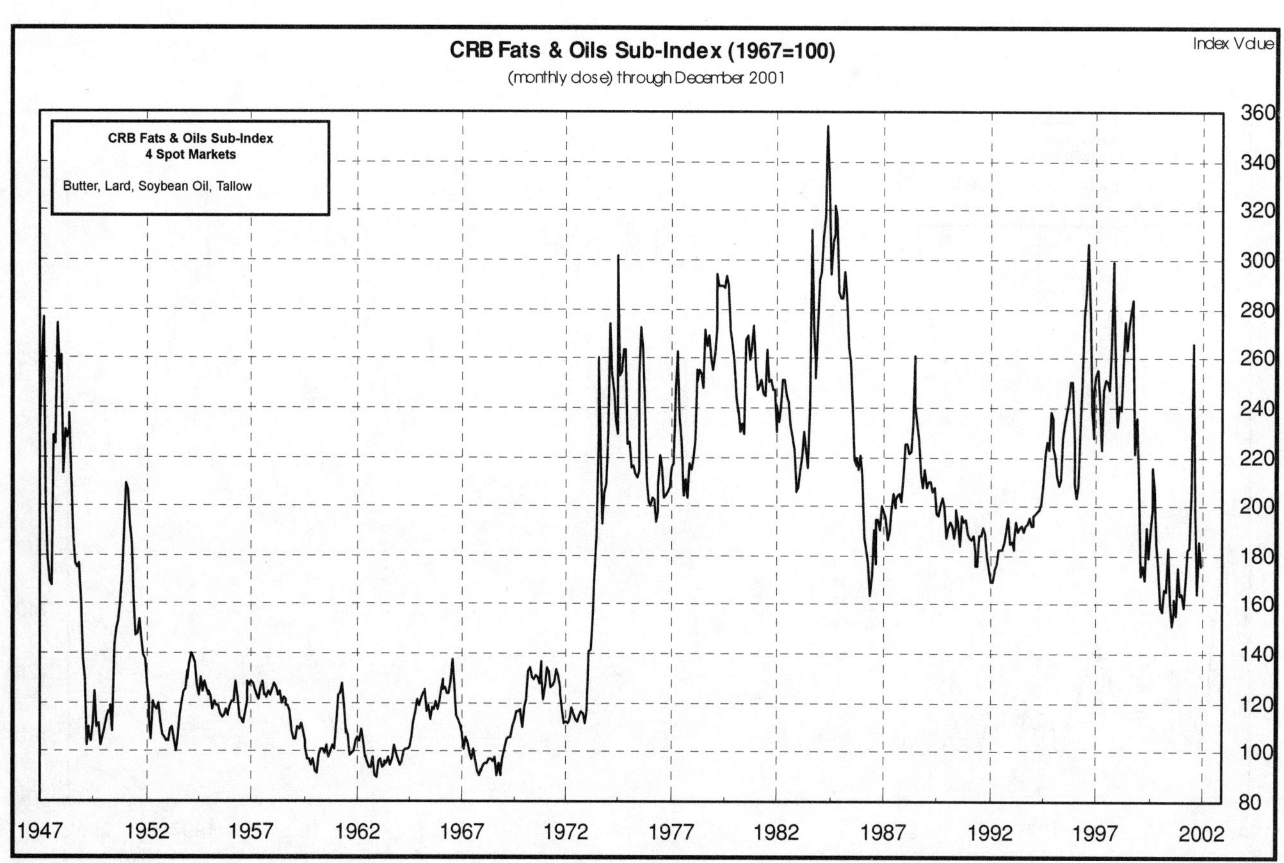

CRB Fats & Oils Sub-Index (1967=100)
(monthly close) through December 2001
Index Value
CRB Fats & Oils Sub-Index
4 Spot Markets
Butter, Lard, Soybean Oil, Tallow
360
340
320
300
280
260
240
220
200
180
160
140
120
100
80
1947
1952
1957
1962
1967
1972
1977
1982
1987
1992
1997
2002

CRB Livestock Sub-Index (1967=100)
(weekly close) as of 28-Dec-2001
Index Value
CRB Livestock Sub-Index
5 Spot Markets
Hides, Hogs, Lard, Steers, Tallow
400
380
360
340
320
300
280
260
240
220
200
Jan-92
Dec-92
Dec-93
Dec-94
Dec-95
Dec-96
Dec-97
Dec-98
Dec-99
Dec-00
Dec-01

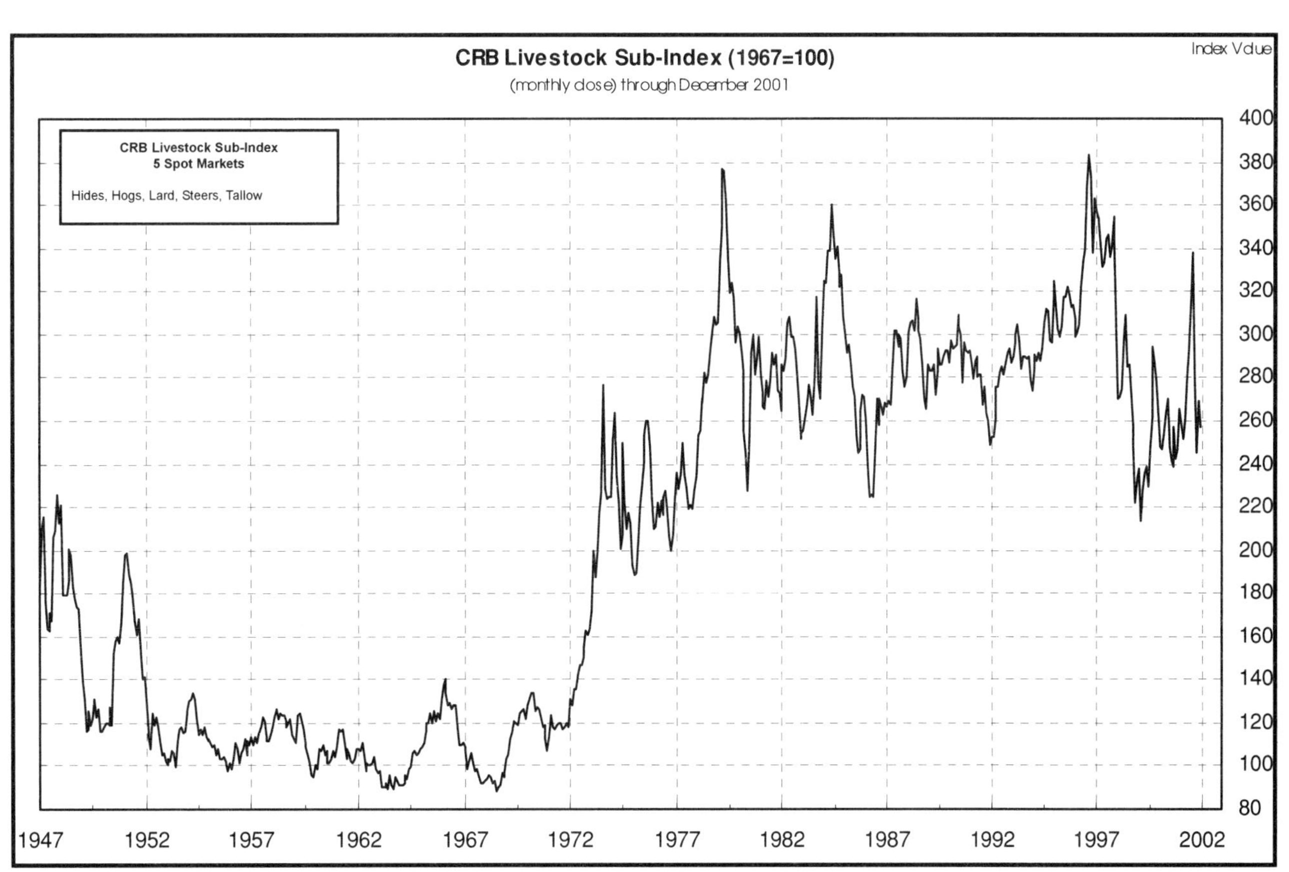
CRB Livestock Sub-Index (1967=100)
(monthly close) through December 2001
Index Value
CRB Livestock Sub-Index
5 Spot Markets
Hides, Hogs, Lard, Steers, Tallow
400
380
360
340
320
300
280
260
240
220
200
180
160
140
120
100
80
1947
1952
1957
1962
1967
1972
1977
1982
1987
1992
1997
2002

CRB Indices

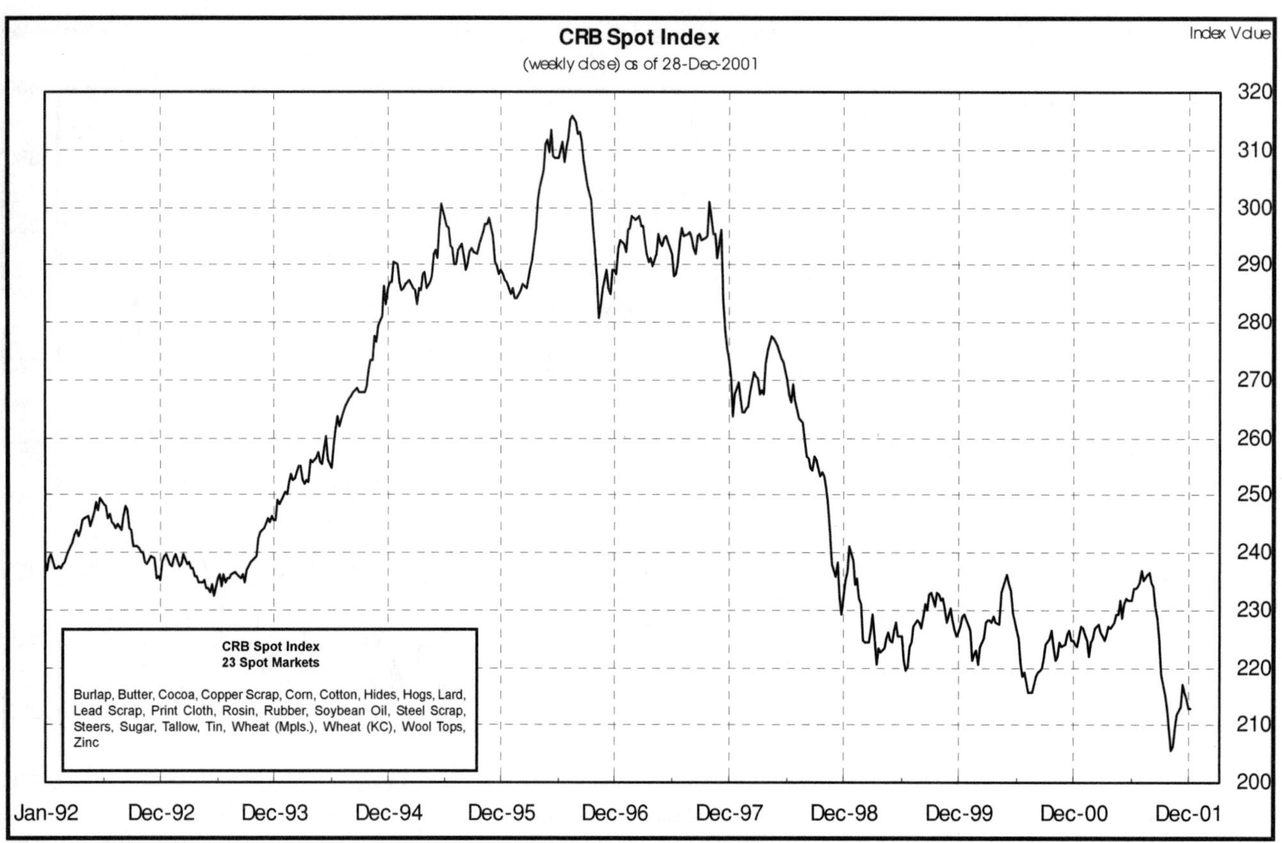

CRB Spot Index
(weekly close) as of 28-Dec-2001
Index Value
CRB Spot Index
23 Spot Markets
Burlap, Butter, Cocoa, Copper Scrap, Corn, Cotton, Hides, Hogs, Lard, Lead Scrap, Print Cloth, Rosin, Rubber, Soybean Oil, Steel Scrap, Steers, Sugar, Tallow, Tin, Wheat (Mpls.), Wheat (KC), Wool Tops, Zinc
320
310
300
290
280
270
260
250
240
230
220
210
200
Jan-92
Dec-92
Dec-93
Dec-94
Dec-95
Dec-96
Dec-97
Dec-98
Dec-99
Dec-00
Dec-01

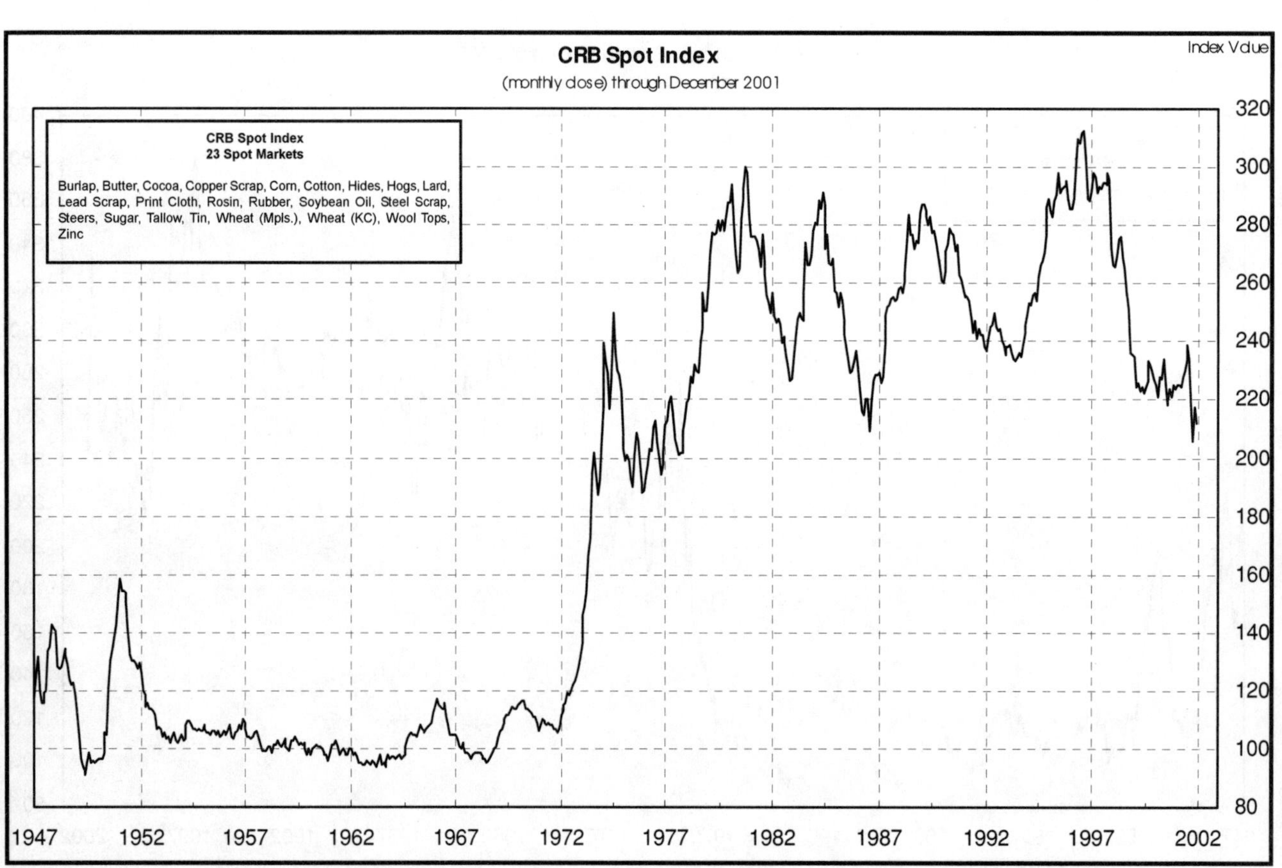

CRB Spot Index
(monthly close) through December 2001
Index Value
CRB Spot Index
23 Spot Markets
Burlap, Butter, Cocoa, Copper Scrap, Corn, Cotton, Hides, Hogs, Lard, Lead Scrap, Print Cloth, Rosin, Rubber, Soybean Oil, Steel Scrap, Steers, Sugar, Tallow, Tin, Wheat (Mpls.), Wheat (KC), Wool Tops, Zinc
320
300
280
260
240
220
200
180
160
140
120
100
80
1947
1952
1957
1962
1967
1972
1977
1982
1987
1992
1997
2002

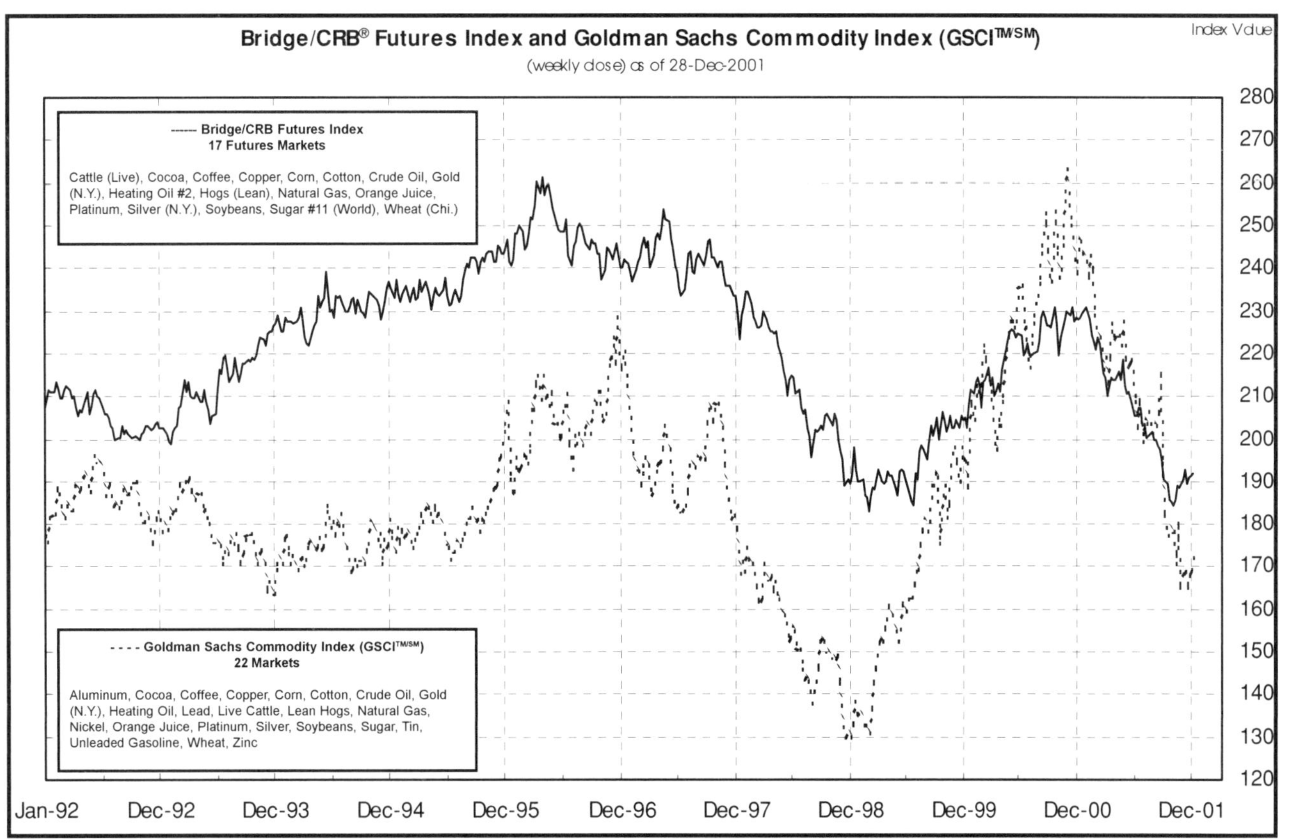
Bridge/CRB® Futures Index and Goldman Sachs Commodity Index (GSCI™/SM)
(weekly close) as of 28-Dec-2001
Index Value
------ Bridge/CRB Futures Index
17 Futures Markets
Cattle (Live), Cocoa, Coffee, Copper, Corn, Cotton, Crude Oil, Gold (N.Y.), Heating Oil #2, Hogs (Lean), Natural Gas, Orange Juice, Platinum, Silver (N.Y.), Soybeans, Sugar #11 (World), Wheat (Chi.)
- - - - Goldman Sachs Commodity Index (GSCI™/SM)
22 Markets
Aluminum, Cocoa, Coffee, Copper, Corn, Cotton, Crude Oil, Gold (N.Y.), Heating Oil, Lead, Live Cattle, Lean Hogs, Natural Gas, Nickel, Orange Juice, Platinum, Silver, Soybeans, Sugar, Tin, Unleaded Gasoline, Wheat, Zinc
280
270
260
250
240
230
220
210
200
190
180
170
160
150
140
130
120
Jan-92
Dec-92
Dec-93
Dec-94
Dec-95
Dec-96
Dec-97
Dec-98
Dec-99
Dec-00
Dec-01

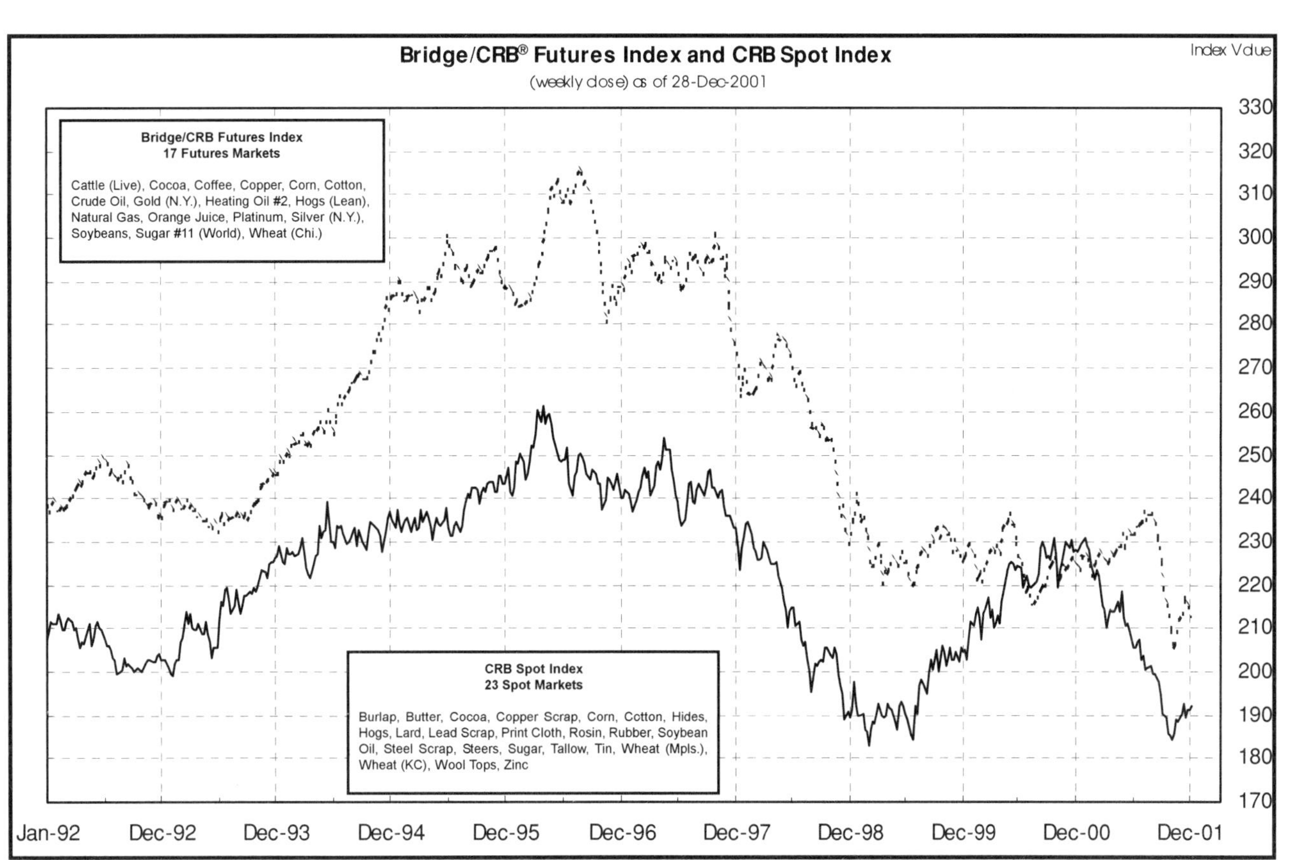
Bridge/CRB® Futures Index and CRB Spot Index
(weekly close) as of 28-Dec-2001
Index Value
Bridge/CRB Futures Index
17 Futures Markets
Cattle (Live), Cocoa, Coffee, Copper, Corn, Cotton, Crude Oil, Gold (N.Y.), Heating Oil #2, Hogs (Lean), Natural Gas, Orange Juice, Platinum, Silver (N.Y.), Soybeans, Sugar #11 (World), Wheat (Chi.)
CRB Spot Index
23 Spot Markets
Burlap, Butter, Cocoa, Copper Scrap, Corn, Cotton, Hides, Hogs, Lard, Lead Scrap, Print Cloth, Rosin, Rubber, Soybean Oil, Steel Scrap, Steers, Sugar, Tallow, Tin, Wheat (Mpls.), Wheat (KC), Wool Tops, Zinc
330
320
310
300
290
280
270
260
250
240
230
220
210
200
190
180
170
Jan-92
Dec-92
Dec-93
Dec-94
Dec-95
Dec-96
Dec-97
Dec-98
Dec-99
Dec-00
Dec-01

UNDERSTANDING AND ANALYZING THE COFFEE MARKET

by Walter Spilka

Introduction

Coffee is an invigorating beverage made from the roasted seeds of the coffee plant. Coffee's unique taste and aroma make it perhaps the most widely consumed beverage in the world. Coffee has a long history extending back over a thousand years. It is believed that the first coffee beans were consumed in the African country of Ethiopia where coffee was a wild plant. While there are many stories on how coffee spread throughout the world, it is believed that coffee plants from Ethiopia were taken to southern Arabia and cultivated in what is now Yemen. Coffee eventually made its way to Europe where the first coffee house was established in London in 1652. Soon after that coffee made its way to the United States where coffeehouses were established. From Yemen, coffee spread to what is now the Indonesian island of Java and Sri Lanka. There is a popular story that a French naval officer took a coffee plant from France back to Martinique in the Caribbean. Propagating the plant there, it spread through the Caribbean into Central and South America.

Coffee is a tree of the genus Coffea of the family Rubiaceae. There are some 25 species of coffee, most of which grow wild. There are two dominant commercially grown species, Coffea arabica and Coffea robusta. Coffea arabica or arabica coffee makes up about two thirds of world production with the remainder Coffea robusta or robusta coffee. Coffee made from arabica beans are milder tasting than robustas making them more popular in some countries while robusta coffees are more popular in other countries. Major arabica producing countries include Brazil, Colombia, Mexico, the Central American countries and some African countries like Ethiopia. Robusta producers include Brazil, Vietnam, Indonesia, India and a number of African countries. Some countries like Brazil and India produce both arabica and robusta coffee while most other countries produce only one or the other.

The coffee tree in the wild may attain a height of 30 feet or more and can live some 50 years. In commercial production, a coffee tree starts to yield coffee beans in 3-5 years after planting. Robusta trees tend to produce beans earlier. Yields increase and generally peak production is reached in about 15 years. Trees can continue to produce beans for many years but often with declining yields. Trees are therefore often replaced after 15 years. Since coffee is picked by hand, commercial coffee producers, top off the tree to keep it at a manageable height of 10-15 feet so the beans can be reached. The coffee tree produces a white flower which in turn gives way to the coffee seed or bean. There are a number of climatic factors that need to be monitored as they will act to determine the size and quality of the crop. Heavy rains during flowering can knock the flowers off the trees leading to a smaller crop. Very dry or drought conditions during flowering can lead to fewer flowers and a smaller crop. Under these conditions the trees can flower a number of times and timely rains can lead to additional flowering. Coffee trees grown in higher, cooler and drier conditions may flower once per year. In lower, warmer and wetter climates, multiple flowerings can occur. As a result, in some countries harvesting can take place more or less year round while in other countries the harvest occurs within a relatively short period. Coffee trees grow within a range of climates but virtually all production occurs within a range of 25 degrees north and south of the equator. Average temperatures of 70 degrees are most suitable though they can vary around that level. Coffee trees are very susceptible to freezing temperatures which can kill limbs and even the trees. A more important consideration may be the elevation the trees are grown at. Much robusta coffee is grown in lower elevations on rolling hills or tropical lowlands with the trees preferring warm, moist conditions. Robusta trees tend to be more hardy and less susceptible to disease. Coffee trees do better when not overexposed to direct sunlight. In some regions shade trees are planted to reduce sunlight. In many regions arabica coffee trees are planted on mountainsides where the terrain limits the amount of direct sunlight. Some of the finest arabica coffees are grown at elevations up to about 6,000 feet where the trees thrive in cooler conditions. The higher the elevation the greater the potential for frost. In general, the higher the altitude, the milder the coffee that is produced but higher altitude also incurs a higher cost of production.

The white flowers give way to the coffee cherry. The length of time from flowering to mature cherry depends partly on climatic conditions. In general, maturity takes about six months. From an initial color of green, the cherry ripens eventually becoming red. Inside the cherry are two coffee beans or berries which are rounded on one side and flat on the other facing together. Each bean is covered by a skin termed a parchment. When the coffee beans reach maturity as determined by their red color, they are harvested by hand.

There are two methods of harvesting and processing the harvested coffee beans. How the coffee is harvested depends on the method of processing. Processing of coffee can be either by the dry method or the wet method, the aim of both being to remove the various skins or coverings enveloping the two green coffee beans. Most coffee is processed by the dry method. With the dry method, all of the cherries on the coffee tree are picked and sun dried. The cherries are washed and then spread out to dry. They undergo fermentation and when dry, machines remove the outer coverings leaving the green beans. With the wet method, only the ripe cherries are picked and washed. This can require picking the same tree a number of times as the cherries reach maturity. Machines remove the pulp surrounding the parchment. The cherries are then placed in tanks to ferment and then washed again and dried in the sun or by machine. Hulling machines remove the parchment leaving the green coffee beans. There is a higher cost with the wet method and the resulting beans are considered to have better flavor and command a higher price. In the wet method there is more control over fermentation resulting in a better flavored bean. Both methods result in green coffee beans which are sorted, graded and put in 60 kilogram or 132 pound bags for export.

To obtain the unique aroma and flavor associated with coffee, the green coffee bean must be roasted. By itself the green bean has none of these characteristics. Roasting the coffee beans is as much art as science. It is the roasting process which initiates various chemical reactions in the beans that in turn bring out coffee's taste. In the process of heating the coffee beans in a roaster, the color changes from green to brown. The darkest roasts are termed Italian roasts. In effect the roasting process determines how the coffee will taste, the darker the roast the more intense the coffee taste. Some countries prefer dark roasted coffees, others lighter roasts. How coffee is priced is determined by the underlying characteristics and quality of the coffee. Mild washed arabicas, such as those from Colombia are priced at a premium to arabicas processed by the dry method, such as Brazilians. Robustas are priced less that arabicas.

Coffee Production

Over the last two years, coffee prices have trended lower. The major reason for this is that world production of coffee has exceeded consumption leading to a excessive buildup in coffee stocks which in turn has put downward pressure on prices. Coffee is produced in varying amounts in about 58 countries. Some 14 of these countries can be considered large producers and exporters of arabica and robusta coffee. The largest coffee producer and exporter of all is Brazil. Brazil produces about 30 percent of the world's coffee and of that total, about 24 percent is exported. The United States Department of Agriculture estimated that Brazilian coffee production in the 2001/02 season was 33.7 million bags, down 1 percent from the 2000/01 crop of 34.1 million bags. The Brazilian trees flower in October and November and the harvest begins in May extending for three months or more.

Factors that can affect the final size of the crop and world prices are dryness during the flowering period which can result in a poor flowering and smaller crop. Dryness in Brazil in late 1999 led to a decline in the crop of about 13% from the previous year. At the same time, heavy rains during flowering can knock the flowers off the trees resulting in a smaller crop. Of much more significance in the analysis of Brazilian production is the onset of winter in late June in the Southern Hemisphere. This is perhaps the most important time in the year in world coffee production because portions of the Brazilian coffee belt are susceptible to frosts or freezes which can damage the coffee tree reducing subsequent crops. Salomon Smith Barney Futures Research indicates that in the twentieth century there were 17 major freezes in Brazil or about one every five years. Of the 17 freezes, four occurred in June, nine in July and four were in August. The period of susceptibility is between June and late August. Looking at the pattern of these events, the chances of a freeze in the first half of June is small while it increases substantially in the last half of June and the first half of July. Statistically, the most likely time for a frost is between July 9-10. Freezes in Brazil are not common but they do occur with the chances in a given season about 1 in 4 or 1 in 3. When they occur or threaten to occur, coffee prices respond by staging explosive rallies in short order. Often the rallies are so strong they overdiscount the damage done and when an assessment of the damage is made, prices tend to move lower in a less rapid fashion. A number of meteorological factors have to occur simultaneously for a freeze to occur but these individual factors must be monitored on a daily basis to determine if a significant event is going to happen. Prices will anticipate an event. Another important factor to note about Brazil is that because of the sheer number of trees in production, there is an inherent ability to produce a very large crop with favorable weather. Brazil follows a two year production cycle with a large crop followed by a smaller crop. The 2001/02 crop was the small side of the pattern so the 2002/03 crop has the potential to be very large on a cyclical basis. This fact also has to be considered in analyzing production and subsequent price movements. A final factor to consider is the value of the domestic currency, the real, against the dollar. In 2001 the real declined in value versus the dollar which provided some protection against lower prices

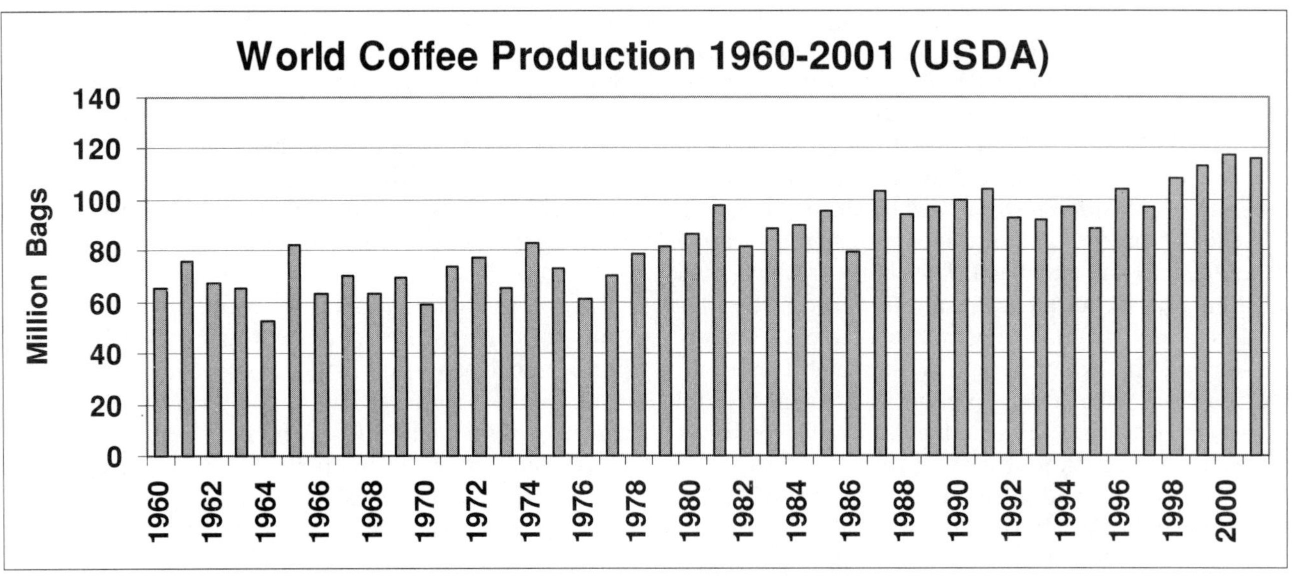

and an incentive for exporters to ship even more coffee. Further declines in 2002 and 2003 would likely result in larger exports from a larger crop.

Colombia is the third largest producer of coffee, growing mild washed arabicas that command a premium in the market. The U.S.D.A. estimated the 2001/02 crop at 11 million bags, up 5 percent from the previous year. About 90 percent of the crop is exported. Because of the climate, the harvest extends over much of the season with the main part in the October-December period. Weather is a factor as heavy rains have in recent seasons knocked flowers off the trees reducing the crop. The Colombian coffee industry has worked hard to protect the reputation of its higher regarded coffee.

A key production area for mild washed arabica coffees extends from southern Mexico through Central America. High mountains, adequate rainfall and mild temperatures make this region ideal for high quality coffee production. At the same time, costs of production tend to be higher and low prices over the last two years are now taking a toll on production. Low prices have caused a reduction in required maintenance and in the hiring of labor to pick the crops. Mexico's 2001/02 crop is estimated by the U.S.D.A. to be 5.5 million bags, up 4 percent from the year before but 11 percent less than two years ago. In Central America, the five producers; Guatemala, El Salvador, Honduras, Costa Rica and Nicaragua, are estimated to have a crop of 12.4 million bags, down 3 percent from 2001/02 and 13 percent less than two years ago. The significance of this is that the decline is expected to lower the overall quality of world production leading to a potential decline in consumption.

The two major Asian robusta coffee producers are Vietnam and Indonesia. Perhaps the most important development in the coffee market in the last decade has been the rise of Vietnamese coffee production. As recently as the 1997/98 season, production was estimated at 7 million bags. In 2000/01 production was estimate by U.S.D.A. at 15 million bags. With over 90 percent of the crop exported, this increase added a huge amount of coffee to the marketplace. The 2001/02 crop is estimated at 13.3 million bags and Vietnam has given strong indications that they intend to reduce the amount of coffee they produce. It remains to be seen whether this actually occurs. Indonesia's 2001/02 crop was estimated at 6.3 million bags, down 3 percent from the previous year.

Africa produces both robusta and arabica coffees. Well regarded arabica coffees are produced in Kenya and Ethiopia. The U.S.D.A estimates Kenya's 2001/02 coffee crop at 969,000 tonnes, down 5 percent from the previous year. Production has declined due to the effects of low prices and drought. Ethiopia's crop was seen at 3.8 million tonnes, up 3 percent from the previous season. Ethiopia is making an effort to produce more organically grown coffee which should command a premium in the market. The Ivory Coast is Africa's largest robusta producer. Low prices and dry conditions should mean that the 2001/02 crop will be 4.17 million bags, 4 percent less than in 2000/01. Uganda's robusta crop is estimated at 3.2 million bags, the same as in 2001/02.

Overall, world coffee production in 2001/02 is estimated by the U.S.D.A. at 115.8 million bags, down 1 percent from the previous year. Four years ago world production was 97.4 million bags. The increase in production of 18.4 million bags is some 19 percent. Of that total, 90 percent of the increase can be attributed to Brazil and Vietnam. It would appear that if pro-

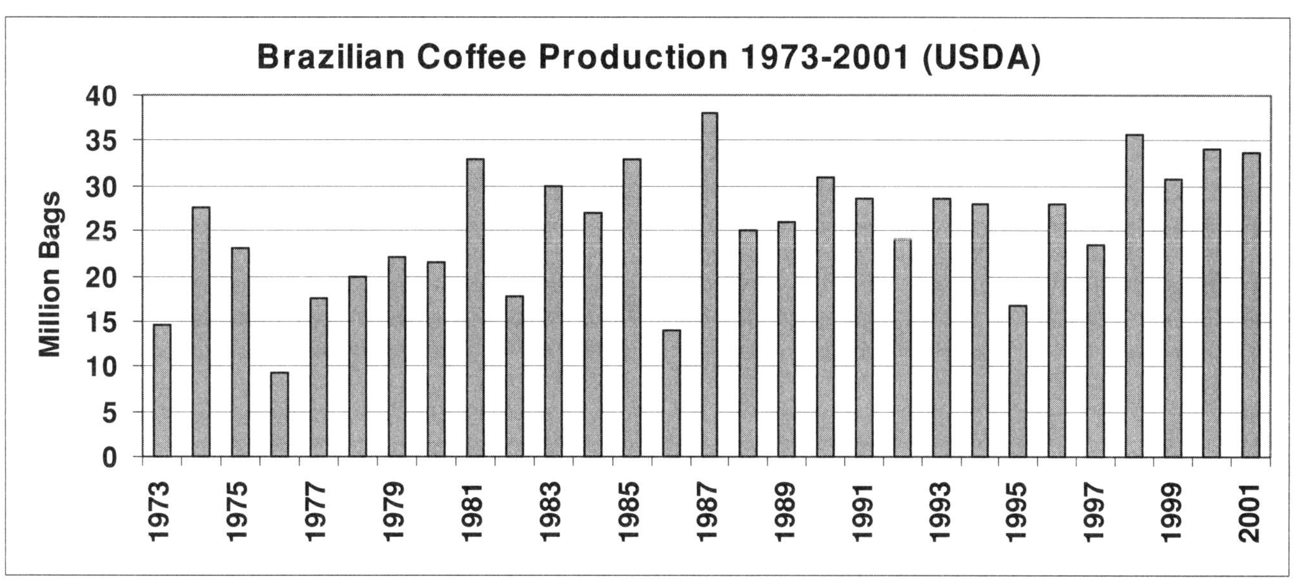

duction is going to decline, it will take a production decline in those two countries at the minimum.

Coffee Consumption

Global coffee consumption over time has trended higher with rising population, higher incomes and increased levels of economic activity and prosperity. When coffee consumption has fallen, it is usually the result of a sharp increase in retail prices or a contraction in economic activity. Coffee consumption is affected by a number of factors. The first factor is the retail price of coffee and its relation to the retail prices for other beverages like tea. Sharp increases in retail prices following a price spike have in the past led consumers to switch to other beverages and they do not always readily return to coffee when prices decline. Two frosts in Brazil in 1994 led to steep retail prices increases that caused consumers to hoard coffee and switch to other beverages. At the same time, retail prices do not decline as fast as they go up. Levels of disposable income and the general economic climate in a country can affect consumption. Studies have indicated that in higher income countries an increase in coffee prices of 1 percent leads to a decline in use of .2 percent to .3 percent. In lower income countries it can be assumed that this elasticity is higher. Declines in the value of the local currency can cause a decline in consumption. Climate also appears to play a part in coffee consumption. The International Coffee Organization has reported that the highest per capita levels of coffee use are in the colder climate countries of Finland, Norway, Denmark, Sweden and Austria. Part of the reason for high per capita use in these countries is that coffee is consumed socially and within families. At the same time, there is evidence that per capita use of coffee is declining in some developed countries in part because of competing beverages. U.S. per capita use of coffee is about a third that of Finland. The National Coffee Association reported that in 2000, U.S. per capita consumption was 1.31 cups per day compared to 2.1 cups in 1960.

There are some very positive developments in terms of consumption which should work to offset some of the per capita declines being seen. One is that coffee is being introduced and consumed in countries that have had very low per capita rates of use. In Asia, where tea is king, coffee is finding more acceptance. Large producers like Vietnam have the potential to see domestic use increase substantially. China, with a huge population of tea drinkers, is seeing coffee move out of the cities into the countryside. Russia is seeing more coffee consumed as quality improves. The other positive development is the increased popularity of specialty coffees and coffee shops. Coffee produced under strict conditions like organic coffee and coffee that meets high standards of taste can command large premiums which in turn leads to increased production and use. Coffee shops can introduce younger consumers to the beverage.

Consumption is estimated using net exports of production countries adjusted for changes in importing country stocks plus the consumption in producing countries. In recent seasons, global consumption has been increasing about 1.2 percent per year. The U.S.D.A. estimated world coffee consumption in 2000/01 at 111.1 million, less than one percent more than the previous year.

Coffee Stocks

Coffee prices have been moving lower since late 1999 when dry weather in Brazil drove prices higher. The primary reason for the decline has been produc-

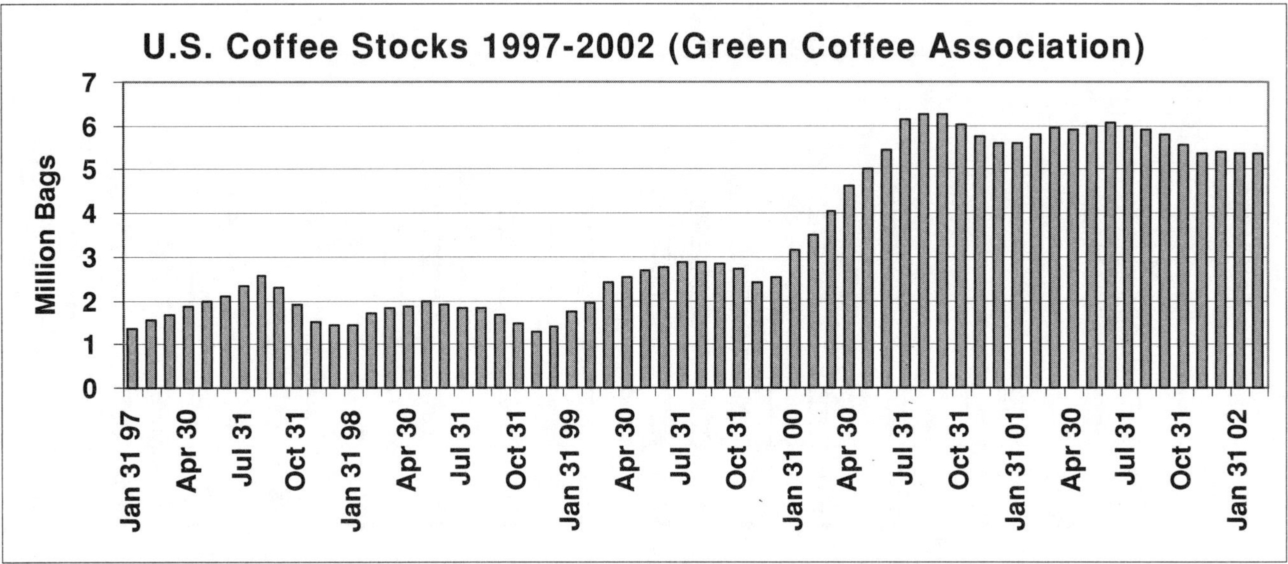

tion in excess of consumption leading to a steady buildup in coffee stocks. Coffee stocks in producing countries have been fairly steady. Brazil has managed to reduce its large stocks down to about six million bags. In turn, the stocks in the importing nations have increased substantially. Based on U.S.D.A. estimates, U.S. coffee stocks in September 2001 were 5.8 million bags, down 8% from the previous year but well above 1998 stocks of 1.7 million bags. European stocks in 2001 were 13.3 million bags, up 36% from the previous year. Japanese stocks were 1.7 million bags in 2001, up 9% from the previous year. In total, consuming country stocks totaled about 21 million bags. One illustration as to how much coffee stocks have increased is seen at the Coffee Sugar and Cocoa Exchange in New York. Certified warehouse stocks for delivery on January 4, 1999 were 84,665 bags. By March 17, 2001 they had reached 3.85 million bags. Since that peak, stocks have been slowly declining on a steady basis but as of March 18, 2002 they were still 2.5 million bags. Coffee producing country stocks in September 2001 were estimated at 24.4 million bags, up 15 percent from the previous year. World stocks of coffee increased in the 1998/99 season, the 1999/00 season and in the 2000/01 season. Based on estimated consumption in 2000/01 of 111.3 million bags, the current global stocks of coffee represent almost a five months supply. The ending stocks-to-use ratio is estimated to be .39 compared to .34 the previous season and .33 two seasons ago. As a general rule, a ratio of less than .30 represents a somewhat tight situation and would argue for higher prices to ration available supplies. A major question in the coffee market is when this buildup in coffee stocks will start to correct itself leading eventually to higher prices.

The Outlook for the Coffee Market

With prices for both robusta and arabica coffee trading at multi-year lows, the big question in the coffee market is when this trend will change. One direct effect of low prices is to reduce production. One worrisome effect of the low prices which have persisted for some time is that they are causing a decline in higher quality arabica coffees and that this will affect the overall quality of coffee worldwide leading consumption to stagnate or even decline. The situation in Central America is very troublesome now. It is possible that consumption could be adversely affected in the face of low prices, a time when consumption would be expected to increase. At the same time, production of lower quality coffees could well expand as producers have little in the way of alternative crops to grow. Declining currencies could well act to shield producers and exporters from the effect of low prices causing an increase in production. One effect that has been seen is that robusta coffee production as a percentage of world production has been increasing.

Adding to the difficulties facing the coffee market is the prospect that the 2002/03 Brazilian coffee crop will approach 40 million bags. The Brazilian Ministry of Agriculture has estimated the new crop at between 37.6 and 39.6 million bags. The 2003/04 crop is expected to show a cyclical decline. The prospect of a large crop has kept coffee prices under pressure and could push them still lower as harvesting gets underway. To offset this, Brazil will provide funding to remove 7-8 million bags of coffee from the market to be warehoused and sold in 2003 when prices should be higher. This would act to keep prices from moving much lower. Additionally, statements from Vietnam indicate that country will try to reduce production. Together these efforts could mean that coffee prices will not move much lower. In Brazil the fall will give

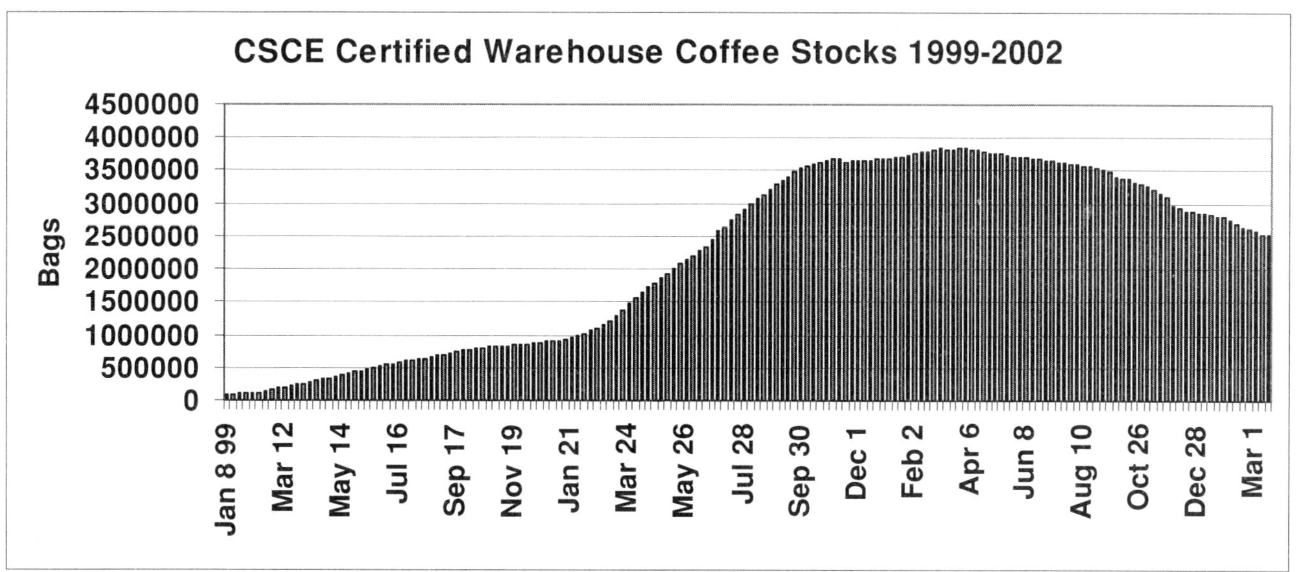

way to winter and the potential of a cold weather event that in itself would act to reduce coffee production. While not a likely possibility, there is the chance this could occur. Until coffee production is brought more in line with consumption, it is difficult to see how coffee prices will be able to move substantially higher.

Coffee Futures Markets

In Brazil, coffee futures and options are traded on the Commodity and Futures Exchange in Sao Paulo (BM&F). The Coffee, Sugar and Cocoa Exchange, Inc. a division of the New York Board of Trade trades coffee futures and options in New York City. The "C" contract calls for the delivery of washed arabica coffee that is produced in Mexico, several Central American and South American countries and in some Asian and Africa countries. The unit of trading is 37,500 pounds. Delivery months are March, May, July, September and December. Prices are quoted in cents per pound with the minimum price fluctuation being 5/100 cents per pound or the equivalent of $18.75 per contract. Exchange licensed warehouses are at the Port of New York, the Port on New Orleans and the Port of Miami. In December 2002 the Ports of Bremen/Hamburg and Antwerp will be included. The Exchange uses certain coffees to establish a "basis" with coffees judged better priced at a premium and the those judged inferior priced at a discount. Coffee considered at basis originate in Mexico, El Salvador, Guatemala, Costa Rica, Nicaragua, Kenya, New Guinea, Panama, Tanzania and Uganda. Coffee originating in Colombia has a 200 point premium. Coffee originating in Honduras, Venezuela and Peru has a discount of 100 points with coffee from Burundi, India and Rwanda at a 300 point discount while coffee from Ecuador and the Dominican Republic is priced at a 400 point discount. The Exchange notes that contract specifications are subject to change. In March 2002, the CSCE added a new coffee contract. The so called "mini" contract is very similar to the "C" contract. The differences are that the contract size is 12,500 pounds and the minimum price fluctuation is 5/100 cents per pound or $6.25 per contract. The contract months are February, April, June, August and November. While the "C" contract is finally settled by physical delivery the mini "C" contract is settled on a cash basis.

Coffee futures and options on robusta coffee are traded in London on the London International Financial Futures and Options Exchange. The contract calls for the delivery of robusta coffee from a number of countries including Brazil, India, Indonesia, the Ivory Coast, Uganda and Vietnam. The unit of trading is 5 metric tonnes with the minimum price movement $1.00 per tonne or $5.00 per contract. The contract months are January, March, May, July, September, November such that seven delivery months are available for trading. Exchange nominated warehouse locations are in London and the U.K. Home Counties. Other nominated warehouses are in Antwerp, Amsterdam, Barcelona, Bremen, Felixstowe, Hamburg, Le Havre, Marseilles-Fos, New Orleans, New York, Rotterdam and Trieste.

*　　*　　*

Walter Spilka is a coffee analyst at Salomon Smith Barney in New York. He was formerly an agricultural economist with the U.S.D.A. and has been a coffee trader. He received a doctorate in agricultural economics from the Virginia Polytechnic Institute.

Small Markets in a Big World: Commodity Market Volatility in the Information Age

by The Hightower Group

The return of volatility to the commodity markets will present tremendous opportunities for hedgers and speculators. By using combinations of futures, options and, in the case of hedgers, cash positions, traders can make the most of volatile markets. They can turn volatility into something to be desired, not feared. By approaching the market with "volatility plays," such as being long one futures contract and long three puts, timing becomes less essential for trading success.

Anyone who is a buyer or seller of physical commodities should accept the fact that today they can face extreme risk, the kind that can devastate their company's bottom line. In today's world information travels very far very quickly and market participants can react almost instantaneously. International events, which in previous decades would have taken weeks or even months to work their way though a market, can now do so in a matter of hours. Almost anything can happen, and in most cases these events are impossible to accurately predict.

Hedgers and Speculators alike (who recognize these factors and have a thorough understanding of option mechanics) can look to capitalize on changes in volatility in order to obtain an advantage over competition (in the case of the hedger) or for personal gain (in the case of the speculator).

In the 1990's holding inventories was considered taboo. "Just in time" inventory management was the mantra. It worked for retailers like The Gap and Wal-Mart, who were able to hold down costs managing their product inventories, so why not for buyers of physical commodities? After all, strong production kept supplies ample and held prices low and steady.

Unfortunately, those years of cheap prices and low volatility may have lulled buyers into a state of complacency. In the Appendix we have elaborated on an example of a corporate giant which may have underestimated its exposure to market volatility.

Entering a New Era of Volatility: The End of Deflation, the Return of Inflation

The odds have greatly increased for major volatility events to occur in several markets this year. With the US Federal Reserve declaring the recession over, the world economic cycle could kick into high gear, leading to a surprisingly strong demand for commodities. The US economy is showing strong signs of growth, and after eleven cuts in key interest rates during 2001/02, the Fed has made it clear they are in no hurry to choke off a recovery.

As the biggest economy in the world, a US-based world recovery is very real. Commodity prices as measured by the CRB Index is beginning to show signs of life after bottoming in November, 2001 and nearly retesting lows made in 1999. However, the CRB Index is still relatively cheap on an historical basis, leaving plenty of upside potential for prices to be impacted by a host of supply/demand problems, a lack of deflationary pressures and even some inflationary stimuli that appear to be developing. In fact, markets such as soybeans, precious metals and energies appear to have already made major bottoms.

While world soybean production has risen to record levels, it is barely keeping pace with burgeoning world demand, resulting in tight stock to usage ratios. Therefore, even a minor supply disruption could cause a price shock.

Energy prices could shoot even higher as tightening supplies collide with percolating US demand, while tensions continue to flare in the Middle East.

Following the events of September 11, 2001 the terrorism element will continue to keep markets on edge. This uneasiness appears to have boosted the desirability of precious metals, as no country is safe from an attack.

Increased volatility from weather could be a key factor this year, as there are indications of another El Nino weather anomaly developing. Will commodity markets be able to escape another El Nino event? While a severe El Nino event occurred during 1997/98, it had a very minor impact on commodity markets, as weather disruptions missed key growing areas. However, there is no guarantee of another total miss!

Structural Market Changes

Given the improving economic environment, there are several structural factors that could exacerbate a demand or supply driven move in prices. Physical commodity buyers have been lulled into hand-to-mouth purchasing practices that began when the economy was experiencing a deflation spiral.

Users did not want to stockpile commodities that were in plentiful supply and easily accessible since they ran the risk of tying up capital in a commodity that continued to lose its value.

In the current environment however, growing worldwide demand for basic commodities raises the risk of a supply squeeze when only minor disruptions develop. Controlling risk has been given up to boost return on shareholder equity. Adding to the volatility mix is an increase in small trader participation which could add to the "herd mentality" when a market shock occurs. Falling participation in some markets have made them more susceptible to volatility as fund traders represent a larger portion of total trade volume.

The enclosed charts give us a better view of sharp changes in prices which in the past may have taken a long time to develop but in the current world environment, the market is getter better at immediately re-establishing a market fair value when supply/demand fundamentals shift.

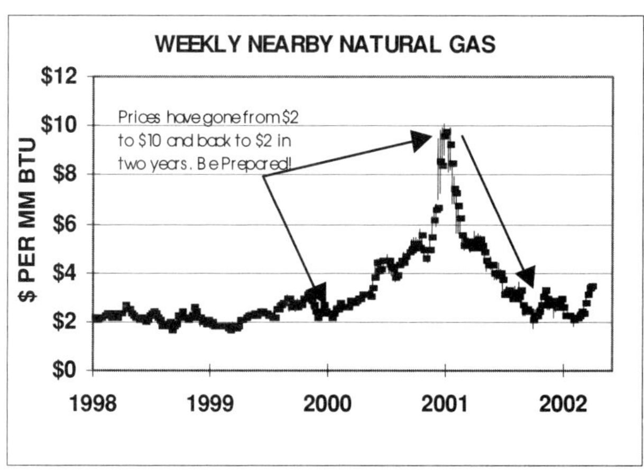

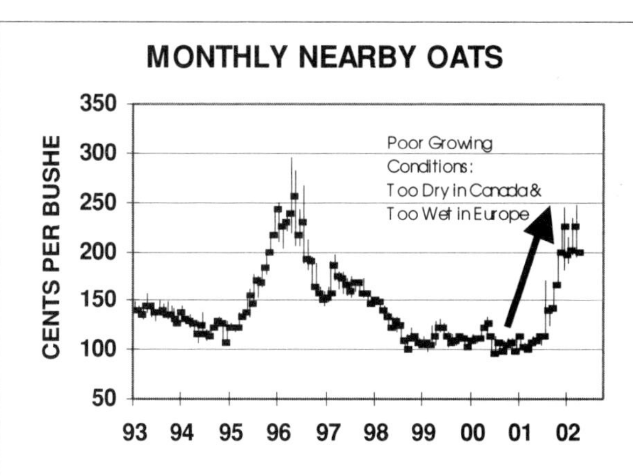

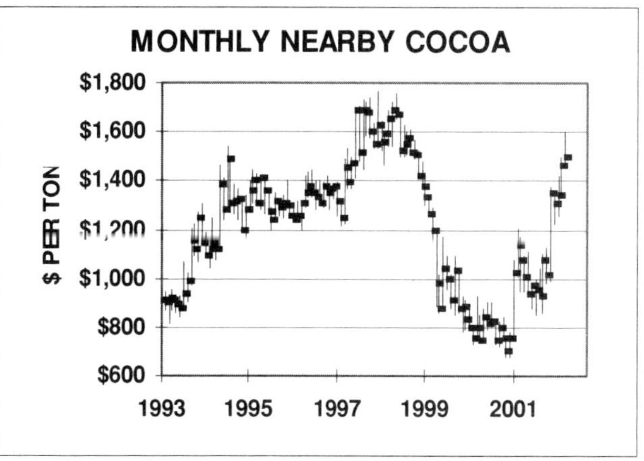

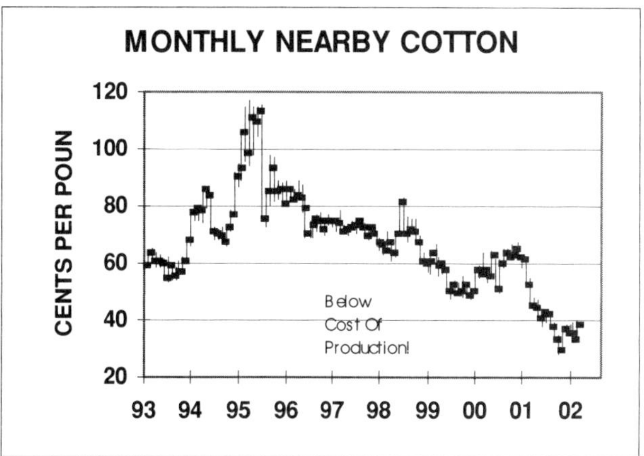

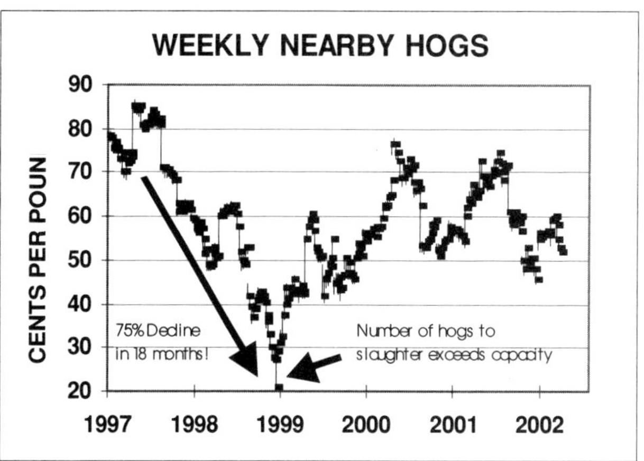

Don't assume relative value based on historical prices.

Consider what happened to hogs in 1998. Taiwan, a traditional supplier to Japan ran into problems with their hog production (foot & mouth disease). Japan looked to US for supplies and the US export market took off, driving up domestic pork and hog prices into the spring of 1997. This created tremendous opportunity for the US pork sector and hog producers responded by expanding production. Unfortunately, hog slaughter capacity didn't expand as quickly. (It's much easier, and cheaper, for a hog farmer to raise a few more hogs than it is for a meat packer to build a new plant.) So when the producers brought their hogs to market, the packers couldn't keep up. The result was a glut of market-ready live hogs with no place to go. Prices collapsed. Prior to that, prices were considered "cheap" when lean values were under $45.00/cwt. In 1998 the lean hog price fell to a new low of $20.70 for the nearby contract about 50% below the value which was previously thought to be cheep. Clearly, in this case the historical pricing structure proved a poor guide for value.

How Should Commercial and Individual Players Handle Such Explosive Volatility?

Back in the early 1980's, the CFTC authorized the trading of options on futures. This in effect allowed commodity producers and consumers to define their risk even more precisely. However, it seems that many corporate users continue to "call the market" with their hedge positions and imperil their organizations in the process.

In the current era of "Flash Volatility" no one can effectively define what is "fair value' and what is expensive. We suspect that over the course of the next several years, at least one commodity per year will make either a new all-time low or a new all-time high. Commodity market participants, producers or consumers, can ill afford make a value judgment toward prices that puts their entity at risk. However, one could employ what we call the "The Inside Out Method!"

The Inside-Out Method

In the "Inside-Out Method" commodity purchasers attempt to capitalize on unforeseen volatility explosions by contracting annual supply up front and then establishing a budget for option positions that will capitalize on price declines in case the current, fixed price level proves to be expensive. In other words, consumers should buy all their needs and "budget" for a put position that will blindly lower the initial price if a big event serves to knock down the price of the contracted commodity. The company has defined risk, will have a competitive advantage if prices explode and will in effect see their initial cost factor lowered if prices fall sharply. Through this method, risks are always under control and extreme volatility serves up a significant windfall to the hedger. By doing this, the hedger makes a friend of volatility and risk is, in effect, turned inside out!

On the other hand, commodity producers could sell their annual production and quantify how much call premium should be budgeted for them to participate in significant upside action. If prices stabilize and the calls never appreciate, then the producer probably would not have seen a better opportunity to sell his inventory. If prices were to freefall, the product is already sold. If the prices gain substantially, the producer still has the opportunity to gain from the move.

In both the long and short hedging stances, it is important to note that once the first step of fixing the cash price is made, the only pricing decision for the hedger after that is when to cut the windfall. By doing so, the hedger can go a long way towards removing emotion from the decision-making process. After having dealt with hedgers for over twenty years, it is clear to us that anxiety is usually the factor which fosters bad decisions. In the Inside-Out Method, extreme volatility is always a benefit! In a new era of wild, unannounced volatility, it would seem to make sense to lay a trap that benefits those with commodity risk instead of pushing them into an Enron-type disaster.

How Should Individual Speculators Handle an Era of Expanded Volatility?

Surprisingly enough, we think that the coming era is one where small investors should be participating in commodities, but this participation needs to be in a manner that capitalizes on volatility. Like corporate hedgers, individual speculators should get away from "calling the market" and instead look to invest in commodities with strong fundamental prospects and a potential to see excessive volatility. However, we strongly advise that speculators migrate toward options and futures combinations that truly define risk. Examples of these types of strategy are: 1) long futures and long a put or 2) short futures and long a call. Other examples would be to be 3) short a futures contract and long multiple calls or 4) long a futures contract and long multiple puts.

In our opinion, utilizing futures with multiple offsetting option plays is a way to play a long-term position in futures and benefit from excessive volatility. Traders will still have to have a right opinion in the market for the most part and will, most importantly, have to find a market that has the potential to become volatile. Traders can certainly invoke outright long option plays, but without an offsetting futures position, timing will be a critical element of success.

At the time of this writing (early April, 2002) we thought it would be interesting to throw out a specific example of a long-term investment position and let the reader measure the outcome at some later date:

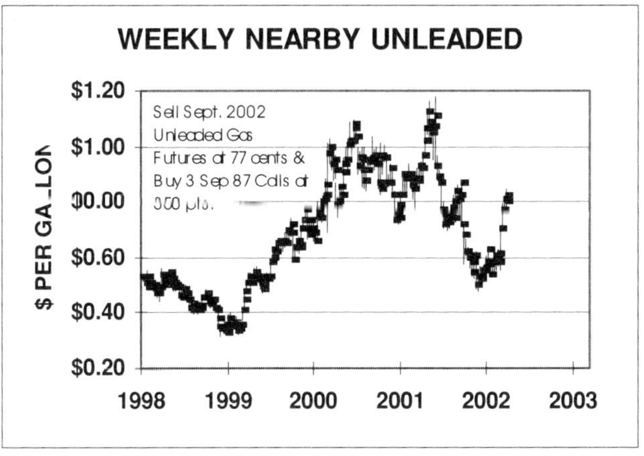

Unleaded Gasoline Example

As of this writing unleaded gas appears to be set for a possible significant upside rise and has already rallied from below 60 cents up to 80 cents. Long term position players could have sold September 2002 unleaded around 75 cents and bought three of the September 87 calls. This position can represent significant risk at expiration and only knowledgeable, experienced traders should implement such a position. The strategy has a bullish tilt but will, in effect, refund some of the call expense if the bull market turns into a bear market.

In most cases, a "keep it simplc" principle will apply in the coming era of wild trading, with long calls and puts potentially becoming more effective than they were in the listless recession era of the 90's. Hedgers and speculators alike can capitalize on this "new era" of volatility by anticipating the best and preparing for the worst in option trade selection.

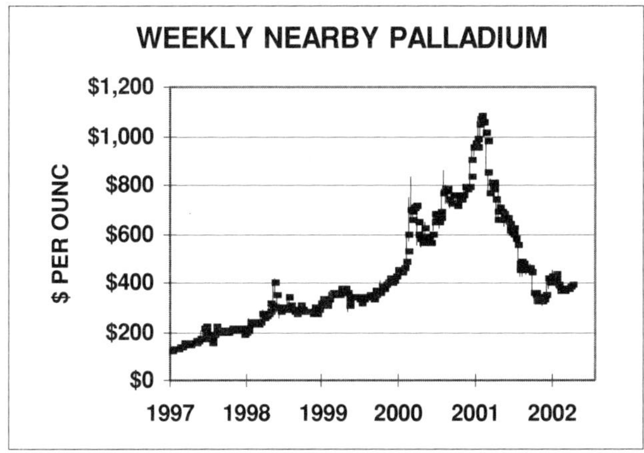

APPENDIX

An Example of Underestimating Volatility Can They Learn from Their Mistakes?

One of the most remarkable stories to emerge out of the 2001/02 commodity year was the Ford Motor Company's misread of the palladium market. Palladium has been a key element in air pollution control devices, specifically in catalytic converters. It used to trade around $100/oz and was a cheaper alternative to platinum, another metal that had similar uses. Ford led the way in developing palladium for this use in the late 1980s. Other car makers soon followed, and auto industry demand for the metal was estimated to have increased five-fold from 1992 to 1996. Most of the palladium was purchased from Russia, which had built up a substantial stockpile and was eager to sell.

In 1997 Russia began holding back palladium supplies and the price rallied to $350 an ounce. In the meantime auto sales were rolling and emission standards were climbing. The auto companies needed palladium and their main supplier was balking. Other manufacturers began looking at ways to reduce their need for palladium, but Ford apparently had no plan and was either hoping prices would eventually settle down or was assuming their competition was under the same pressures.

Ford was the number-one auto maker at the time and the number-one consumer of palladium. Prices didn't settle down; they kept climbing. Russia grew more unstable and Boris Yeltson resigned in December 1999. By February of 2000 palladium was trading at $835 per ounce!

Researchers at Ford began looking into ways to reduce their dependence on palladium, but in the meantime they began stockpiling the metal. The purchasing department, normally charged with purchasing relatively stable (at least less precious) commodities like steel and copper, was given the responsibility of securing the palladium. Their one concern was to make sure Ford had enough to keep production going. Apparently no effort was put into protecting the value of their considerable monetary investment in the precious metal.

By early 2001, prices climbed to $1,094 per ounce. Considering that if it takes an ounce of palladium for one catalytic converter, then in only a few years the commodity price fluctuation alone had increased the cost of each vehicle by $900!

In the meantime, Ford had a breakthrough. Their scientists developed a method to cut their dependence on the metal by 50%. Other automakers had done so as well. What would Ford do with all of the palladium they had been stocking up? Overall industrial demand was about to drop due to technological changes. A recession was kicking in. Supplies were becoming more plentiful because the higher prices had spurred mines to reopen in South Africa.

After peaking above $1,000 per ounce, prices fell to $350 during mid 2001. By the end of the year, Ford took a $1 billion write-off and was looking at ways to hedge commodity purchases in the future.

Ford Motors was caught up by historical events, but they also failed to heed a critical hedging tenet of measuring the best and worst case possible outcome of their actions. The big lesson for Ford and all users of commodities is that a failure to control or at least assess price risk can cause unforeseen exposure and blindside a company's balance sheet. Even when they were stocking up on all of that high-priced palladium, Ford could have protected the value of their inventory by buying puts. That way when prices eventually fell they could have at least recouped some of their costs.

---

* * *

Volume U.S.

U.S. Futures Volume Highlights

2001 in Comparison with 2000

2001 Rank	Top 50 Contracts Traded in 2001	2001 Contracts	%	2000 Contracts	%	2000 Rank
1	Eurodollar, CME	184,015,496	29.43%	108,114,998	17.29%	1
2	T-Bonds, CBT	58,579,290	9.37%	62,750,843	10.04%	2
3	T-Notes (10 Year), CBT	57,585,828	9.21%	46,700,538	7.47%	3
4	E Mini S&P 500 Index, CME	39,434,843	6.31%	19,211,355	3.07%	7
5	Crude Oil, NYMEX	37,530,568	6.00%	36,882,692	5.90%	4
6	E-Mini NASDAQ 100, CME	32,550,233	5.21%	10,817,277	1.73%	11
7	T-Notes (5 Year), CBT	31,122,401	4.98%	23,331,981	3.73%	5
8	S&P 500 Index, CME	22,478,152	3.60%	22,467,859	3.59%	6
9	Corn, CBT	16,728,748	2.68%	17,185,442	2.75%	9
10	Natural Gas, NYMEX	16,468,355	2.63%	17,875,013	2.86%	8
11	Soybeans, CBT	12,150,369	1.94%	12,627,950	2.02%	10
12	#2 Heating Oil, NYMEX	9,264,472	1.48%	9,631,376	1.54%	12
13	Unleaded Regular Gas, NYMEX	9,223,510	1.48%	8,645,182	1.38%	13
14	Wheat, CBT	6,801,541	1.09%	6,407,531	1.02%	15
15	Gold (100 oz.), COMEX Div. of NYMEX	6,785,340	1.09%	6,643,464	1.06%	14
16	Soybean Meal, CBT	6,743,772	1.08%	6,317,988	1.01%	16
17	Soybean Oil, CBT	6,034,325	0.97%	5,369,903	0.86%	18
18	Euro FX	5,898,429	0.94%	4,267,408	0.68%	20
19	NASDAQ 100, CME	5,586,750	0.89%	5,094,042	0.81%	19
20	Sugar #11, NYBOT	5,150,329	0.82%	5,933,850	0.95%	17
21	Dow Jones Industrial Index, CBOT	4,901,949	0.78%	3,572,428	0.57%	23
22	30 Day Federal Funds, CBT	4,686,695	0.75%	1,443,665	0.23%	35
23	Japanese Yen, CME	4,552,599	0.73%	3,965,377	0.63%	21
24	Live Cattle, CME	4,279,273	0.68%	3,681,512	0.59%	22
25	Canadian Dollar, CME	2,961,680	0.47%	2,460,134	0.39%	28
26	Swiss Franc, CME	2,901,939	0.46%	3,241,207	0.52%	24
27	High Grade Copper, COMEX Div. of NYMEX	2,856,641	0.46%	2,778,124	0.44%	26
28	Silver (5,000 oz), COMEX Div. of NYMEX	2,569,198	0.41%	3,117,017	0.50%	25
29	T-Notes (2 Year), CBT	2,389,165	0.38%	1,477,253	0.24%	34
30	Wheat, KCBT	2,357,004	0.38%	2,427,950	0.39%	29
31	Cotton, NYBOT	2,259,665	0.36%	2,597,757	0.42%	27
32	Coffee C, NYBOT	2,199,371	0.35%	2,134,961	0.34%	30
33	British Pound, CME	2,078,834	0.33%	2,029,542	0.32%	33
34	Lean Hogs, CME	2,018,339	0.32%	2,111,807	0.34%	31
35	Cocoa, NYBOT	2,005,817	0.32%	2,110,048	0.34%	32
36	One Month LIBOR, CME	1,315,593	0.21%	896,269	0.14%	41
37	Agency Debt (10 Year), CBT	1,189,389	0.19%	1,334,340	0.21%	36
38	Mexican Peso, CME	1,069,327	0.17%	1,117,304	0.18%	37
39	Wheat, MGE	967,666	0.15%	955,659	0.15%	40
40	Australian Dollar, CME	832,707	0.13%	749,555	0.12%	42
41	Russell 2000, CME	714,259	0.11%	508,726	0.08%	48
42	Feeder Cattle, CME	616,988	0.10%	582,279	0.09%	44
43	Orange Juice (Frozen Conc.), NYCE	577,496	0.09%	712,204	0.11%	43
44	Euroyen, CME	494,519	0.08%	1,079,074	0.17%	38
45	Nikkei 225, CME	476,274	0.08%	455,298	0.07%	49
46	Oats, CBT	440,854	0.07%	402,190	0.06%	50
47	S&P MidCap 400 Index	378,526	0.06%			
48	Municipal Bond Index, CBT	348,319	0.06%	551,634	0.09%	46
49	U.S. Dollar Index	342,948	0.05%			
50	Russell 1000 Index	313,318	0.05%			
	Top 50 Contracts	625,229,103*		484,770,006		
	Contracts Below the Top 50	3,894,340	0.62%	6,681,067	1.36%	
	Total	**629,123,443**	**100.00%**	**491,451,073**	**100.00%**	

* For 2000 Top 50 contracts totaled 486,896,065 including 3 contracts that are not among 2001's Top 50.

U.S. Futures Volume Highlights

2001 in Comparison with 2000

2001 RANK	EXCHANGE	2001 CONTRACTS	%	2000 CONTRACTS	%	2000 RANK
1	Chicago Mercantile Exchange (CME)	315,971,885	50.22%	195,106,383	39.70%	1
2	Chicago Board of Trade (CBT)	209,988,002	33.38%	189,662,407	38.59%	2
3	New York Mercantile Exchange (NYMEX)**	85,039,984	13.52%	86,087,640	17.52%	3
4	New York Board of Trade (NYBOT)*	14,034,168	2.23%	15,214,528	3.10%	4
5	Kansas City Board of Trade (KCBT)	2,375,133	0.38%	2,446,607	0.50%	5
6	Minneapolis Grain Exchange (MGE)	968,699	0.15%	958,420	0.20%	7
7	MidAmerica Commodity Exchange	582,872	0.09%	1,649,549	0.34%	6
8	Cantor Exchange (CE)	162,700	0.03%	325,539	0.07%	8
	Total	**491,451,073**	**100.00%**	**477,919,308**	**100.00%**	

** Includes Comex Division.

* Includes the New York Futures Exchange, New York Cotton Exchange and Coffee, Sugar and Cocoa Exchange.

U.S. Futures Volume 1997-2001

Cantor Exchange (CE)

FUTURE	CONTRACT UNIT	2001	2000	1999	1998	1997
WHEN issued 5 Year Notes	100,000 USD	26				
WHEN issued 10 Year Notes	100,000 USD	130				
6% U.S. Treasury Bonds (30-year)	100,000 USD	62,550	24,577	5,135		
6% U.S. Treasury Notes (5-year)	100,000 USD	42,024	75,662	85		
6% U.S. Treasury Notes (10-year)	100,000 USD	57,970	223,610	1,805		
Total		162,700	325,539	438,068		

Chicago Board of Trade (CBT)

FUTURE	CONTRACT UNIT	2001	2000	1999	1998	1997
Wheat	5,000 bu	6,801,541	6,407,531	6,570,025	5,681,569	5,058,645
Corn	5,000 bu	16,728,748	17,185,442	15,724,845	15,795,493	16,984,951
Oats	5,000 bu	440,854	402,190	371,406	442,874	397,332
Soybeans	5,000 bu	12,150,369	12,627,950	12,481,947	12,431,156	14,539,766
Soybean Oil	60,000 lbs	6,034,325	5,369,903	5,663,895	6,498,263	5,284,994
Soybean Meal	100 tons	6,743,772	6,317,988	6,326,897	6,553,846	6,424,945
Rice	200,000 lbs	121,661	169,133	139,592	157,764	171,973
Silver	1,000 oz	8,634	12,272	20,560	35,505	30,771
Mini Silver	1,000 oz	1,087				
Silver	5,000 oz	161	66	125	7	61
Gold	Kilo	4,867	7,173	10,247	13,363	13,620
Mini Gold	33.2 troy oz	717				
T-Bonds (30-year)	100,000 USD	58,579,290	62,750,843	90,042,282	112,224,081	99,827,659
Mini T-Bonds (30-year)	50,000 USD	4,383				
T-Notes (10-year)	100,000 USD	57,585,828	46,700,538	34,045,758	32,482,576	23,961,819
Mini T-Notes (10-year)	50,000 USD	213				
T-Notes (5-year)	100,000 USD	31,122,401	23,331,981	16,983,812	18,060,048	13,488,725
T-Notes (2-year)	200,000 USD	2,389,165	1,477,253	1,047,348	1,347,575	1,018,545
Agency Debt (10-year)	100,000 USD	1,189,389	1,334,340			
Agency Debt (5-year)	100,000 USD	1,919				
Mini Eurodollars	500,000 USD	483				
Mortgage	1,000 USD x Index	57,324				
Interest Rate Swap (10-year)	100,000 USD	58,884				
Municipal Bond Index	1,000 USD x Index	348,319	551,634	798,597	1,002,075	983,877
30-Day Federal Funds	5,000,000 USD	4,686,695	1,443,665	1,023,716	844,408	910,474
Dow Jones Industrial Index	10 USD x Index	4,901,949	3,572,428	3,896,086	3,567,512	755,476
Mini Dow Jones Industrial Index	2 USD x Index	20,728				
Dow Jones Transportation Index	20 USD x Index	2	4			
Dow Jones Utility Index	200 USD x Index	2	22			
Dow Jones AIGCI Index	100 x Index	4,292				
Total		**209,988,002**	**189,662,407**	**195,147,279**	**217,138,928**	**190,056,287**

Volume U.S.

Chicago Mercantile Exchange (CME)

Future	Contract Unit	2001	2000	1999	1998	1997
Lean Hogs	40,000 lbs	2,018,339	2,111,807	2,358,096	2,136,282	2,100,909
E-mini Lean Hogs	10,000 lbs	3,978	14,445			
Pork Bellies, Frozen	40,000 lbs	196,359	309,576	368,309	481,252	595,319
Butter	40,000 lbs	1,374	5,366	3,354	667	2,805
Fluid MIlk	50,000 lbs	88,016	45,527	45,753	30,734	4,188
Nonfat Dry Milk	44,000 lbs	48				
Class IV Milk	200,000 lbs	6,513	4,868			
Live Cattle	40,000 lbs	4,279,273	3,681,512	3,839,548	4,216,506	3,919,642
Feeder Cattle	44,000 lbs	616,988	582,279	650,071	738,567	837,165
E-mini Feeder Cattle	10,000 lbs	69	627			
Orient Strand Board Lumber	100,000 bd ft	10,264	532	535	505	1,115
Random Lumber	80,000 bd ft	206,840	221,168	287,856	249,847	260,318
T-Bills (90-day)	1,000,000 USD	31,113	16,763	41,260	104,180	199,084
Eurodollar (3-month)	1,000,000 USD	184,015,496	108,114,998	93,418,498	109,472,507	99,770,237
Euroyen	1,000,000,000 JPY	494,519	1,079,074	945,419	962,574	1,119,827
One Month LIBOR	3,000,000 USD	1,315,593	896,269	843,054	1,108,454	1,504,230
British Pound	62,500	2,078,834	2,029,542	2,738,600	2,645,017	2,664,401
Brazilian Real	100,000	3,937	2,067	59,104	79,509	49,092
Canadian Dollar	100,000	2,961,680	2,460,134	2,573,762	2,396,300	2,542,102
Deutschemark	125,000	3,232	21,076	1,497,389	6,884,026	7,044,783
Euro FX	125,000	5,898,429	4,267,408	3,002,453	17	
E-Mini Euro FX	62,500	13,244	29,942	1,775		
Japanese Yen	12,500,000	4,552,599	3,965,377	5,935,843	7,065,266	6,034,565
E-Mini Japanese Yen	6,250,000	2,023	6,166	1,072		
Mexican Peso	500,000	1,069,327	1,117,304	1,143,641	1,353,867	1,707,706
New Zealand Dollar	100,000	21,766	32,862	42,646	16,580	3,506
South African Rand	500,000	65,327	40,701	51,762	12,766	6,287
Swiss Franc	125,000	2,901,939	3,241,207	4,114,824	3,974,163	4,222,268
Australian Dollar	100,000	832,707	749,555	861,023	664,563	595,573
French Franc	250,000	17	44	6,745	72,562	112,520
Euro / British Pound	125,000 x Euro	127	973	3,332		
Euro / Japanese Yen	125,000 x Euro	98,970	4,289	2,018		
EuroYen LIBOR	100,000,000 JPY	17,474	7,924	3,869		
Euro / Swiss Franc	125,000 x Euro	182	2	398		
Nikkei 225	5 USD x Index	476,274	455,298	513,848	479,248	417,541
S&P 500 Index	500 USD x Index	22,478,152	22,467,859	27,003,387	31,430,523	21,294,584
E-Mini S&P	50 USD x S&P Index	39,434,843	19,211,355	10,953,551	4,466,032	885,825
S&P 500 Barra Growth Index	500 USD x Index	12,408	16,733	11,015	9,816	6,196
S&P 500 Barra Value Index	500 USD x Index	24,319	31,121	26,698	21,245	11,203
S&P MidCap 400 Index	500 USD x Index	378,526	332,438	326,117	310,008	262,017
Fortune E-50 Index	20 USD x Index	3,694	19,838			
NASDAQ 100 Index	500 USD x Index	5,586,750	5,094,042	2,360,938	1,063,328	807,604
E-Mini NASDAQ 100 Index	20 USD x Index	32,550,233	10,817,277	682,059		
Russell 2000 Index	500 USD x Index	714,259	508,726	363,041	276,662	182,717
E-Mini Russell 2000 Index	100 USD x Index	26,012				
Benzene	42,000 gal x Index	36				
Mixed Xylenes	42,000 gal x Index	6				
Goldman Sachs Commodity Index	250 USD x Index		1,002,673	926,933	854,264	773,088
HDD Weather	100 x HDD	131	67	336		
CDD Weather	100 x CDD		20			
Total		**315,971,885**	**195,106,383**	**168,013,357**	**183,627,443**	**159,975,955**

Kansas City Board of Trade (KCBT)

FUTURE	CONTRACT UNIT	2001	2000	1999	1998	1997
Wheat	5,000 bu	2,357,004	2,427,950	2,321,059	2,006,779	1,937,140
Value Line Index	100 USD x Index	17,773	9,954	1,264	4,485	14,047
Mini Value Line	100 USD x Index		3,962	31,377	76,345	154,784
ISDEX	100 USD x Index	356	4,740	3,186		
Total		**2,375,133**	**2,446,607**	**2,378,271**	**2,164,959**	**2,192,694**

Minneapolis Grain Exchange (MGE)

FUTURE	CONTRACT UNIT	2001	2000	1999	1998	1997
Wheat	5,000 bu	967,666	955,659	1,119,812	1,092,964	1,024,523
White Wheat	5,000 bu	227	1,495	4,786	15,209	14,284
Durum Wheat	5,000 bu	74	559	9,818	15,997	
Cottonseed	120 Tons	732	447			
Total		**968,699**	**958,420**	**1,134,945**	**1,125,194**	**1,040,594**

MidAmerica Commodity Exchange (MidAm)

FUTURE	CONTRACT UNIT	2001	2000	1999	1998	1997
Wheat	1,000 bu	52,285	77,477	132,392	133,200	130,968
Corn	1,000 bu	118,574	270,890	291,186	314,815	432,461
Oats	1,000 bu	1,892	2,711	3,509	5,451	4,916
Soybeans	1,000 bu	281,451	572,672	651,268	767,858	1,026,830
Soybean Meal New	20 tons	6,430	7,961	15,914	18,371	23,773
Soybean Oil	30,000 lbs	3,246	5,266	23,955	27,923	37,962
Live Cattle	20,000 lbs	6,529	8,326	16,285	18,883	16,316
Lean Hogs	20,000 lbs	8,968	16,047	31,827	18,597	1,312
New York Silver	1,000 oz	3,066	15,970	23,493	14,999	8,928
New York Gold	33.2 oz	3,023	10,637	23,662	14,060	15,161
Platinum	25 oz	96	1,038	1,162	1,582	4,248
T-Bonds	50,000 USD	50,936	550,714	1,058,816	1,537,286	1,513,925
T-Bills	500,000 USD	90	68	117	315	461
T-Notes (10 Year)	50,000 USD	1,909	9,183	33,364	39,458	49,700
T-Notes (5 Year)	50,000 USD	1	225	29	96	479
Eurodollars	500,000 USD	7,224	9,411	5,745	5,347	5,997
Australian Dollar	50,000	380	573	846	1,205	585
British Pound	12,500	6,200	12,078	17,871	23,929	28,094
Euro Currency	62,500	1,880	3,161	618		
Swiss Franc	62,500	10,999	34,532	29,039	33,599	47,504
Deutschemark	62,500	42	1,746	17,764	36,674	84,344
Japanese Yen	6,250,000	10,466	28,958	41,167	47,821	48,585
Canadian Dollar	50,000	7,185	9,905	13,865	18,358	14,090
Total		**582,872**	**1,649,549**	**2,433,894**	**3,081,181**	**3,500,791**

New York Board of Trade (NYBOT)*

FUTURE	CONTRACT UNIT	2001	2000	1999	1998	1997
Coffee C	37,500 lbs	2,199,371	2,134,961	2,659,233	2,095,030	2,294,181
Sugar #11	112,000 lbs	5,150,329	5,933,850	5,911,299	5,524,111	5,284,971
Sugar #14	112,000 lbs	116,733	122,976	138,661	157,987	158,431
Cocoa	10 metric tons	2,005,817	2,110,048	1,868,036	1,810,580	2,274,509
Cotton #2	50,000 lbs	2,259,665	2,597,757	2,448,087	3,200,830	2,837,280
Orange Juice Frozen Concentrate	15,000 lbs	577,496	712,204	793,882	914,614	1,029,861
Orange Juice Frozen Concentrate - Diff		15	1,003	886		
T-Note (5 Year)	100,000 USD	1,904	8,482	8,503	13,088	18,040
U.S. Dollar / Canadian Dollar	200,000 USD	1,854	2,825	3,406	3,726	830
U.S. Dollar / Swedish Krona	200,000 USD	2,564	2,423			
U.S. Dollar / Norwegian Krone	200,000 USD	746	58			
U.S. Dollar / Swiss Franc	200,000 USD	10,737	16,671	25,523	18,224	4,282
U.S. Dollar / Japanese Yen	200,000 USD	16,338	30,353	41,632	23,828	9,060
U.S. Dollar / British Pound	125,000 GBP	17,379	14,202	16,571	7,795	6,375
U.S. Dollar / South Arican Rand	100,000 USD	4,793	9,984	10,859	3,165	4,683
Canadian Dollar / Japanese Yen	200,000 CAD	18,865	5,380			
Australian Dollar / U.S. Dollar	100,000 AUD	2,640	44,307	40,711	7,310	5,393
Australian Dollar / Canadian Dollar	200,000 AUD	17,886	2,064			
Australian Dolar / New Zealand Dollar	200,000 AUD	12,673	15,333	26,088		
New Zealand Dollar / U.S. Dollar	100,000 NZD	24,426	23,866	70,717	30,622	9,499

New York Board of Trade (NYBOT)* (Continued)

FUTURE	CONTRACT UNIT	2001	2000	1999	1998	1997
Australian Dollar / Japanese Yen	200,000 AUD	31,250	32,390	18,538		
British Pound / Swiss franc	125,000 GBP	21,379	11,061	28,789	29,902	5,699
British Pound / Japanese Yen	125,000 GBP	42,651	85,530	69,207	46,584	9,629
Swiss Franc / Japanese Yen	200,000 CHF	15,196	13,662	20,988	6	
Euro		64,431	97,032	85,211	1,325	
Euro / U.S. Dollar, Small		2,299	6,508	2,337		
Euro / Australian Dollar	100,000 EUR	17,006	7,674			
Euro / Canadian Dollar	100,000 EUR	11,712	8,396			
Euro / Japanese Yen	100,000 EUR	294,733	278,119	192,987	356	
Euro / Swedish Krona	100,000 EUR	30,354	54,076	101,605	89	
Euro / British Pound	100,000 EUR	112,727	159,862	200,560	50	
Euro / Norwegian	100,000 EUR	4,488	2,461	10,452		
Euro / Swiss Franc	100,000 EUR	44,162	69,538	147,650	199	
U.S. Dollar Index	1,000 USD x Index	342,948	297,745	356,544	469,291	485,481
NYSE Composite Index	500 USD x Index	217,772	130,984	334,222	590,327	916,716
Russell 1000 Index	500 USD x Index	313,318	94,736	161,114		
PSE Tech 100	500 USD x Index	128	11,416	40,402	9,814	9,848
S&P Commodity Index	100 USD x Index	8,505				
Commodity Research Bureau Index	500 USD x Index	16,878	63,494	88,696	58,993	71,482
Total		**14,034,168**	**15,214,528**	**15,958,237**	**16,049,651**	**16,223,662**

New York Mercantile Exchange (NYMEX)

COMEX Division

FUTURE	CONTRACT UNIT	2001	2000	1999	1998	1997
Gold	100 oz	6,785,340	6,643,464	9,575,788	8,990,094	9,541,904
Silver	5,000 oz	2,569,198	3,117,017	4,157,500	4,094,616	4,893,520
High Grade Copper	25,000 lbs	2,856,641	2,778,124	2,852,962	2,483,610	2,356,170
Aluminum	44,000 lbs	43,089	46,099	27,978		
Eurotop 100 Index	100 USD x Price	976	4,800	25,181	50,619	47,427
Eurotop 300 Index	200 USD x Price	3,415	36,863	6,279		
Total		**12,258,659**	**12,626,367**	**16,645,688**	**15,618,939**	**16,839,021**

NYMEX Division

FUTURE	CONTRACT UNIT	2001	2000	1999	1998	1997
Palladium	100 oz	25,925	50,766	75,394	131,250	238,716
Platinum	50 oz	205,969	320,924	567,268	528,269	698,597
No. 2 Heating Oil, NY	1,000 bbl	9,264,472	9,631,376	9,200,703	8,863,764	8,370,964
Unleaded Gasoline, NY	1,000 bbl	9,223,510	8,645,182	8,701,216	7,992,269	7,475,145
Crude Oil	1,000 bbl	37,530,568	36,882,692	37,860,064	30,495,647	24,771,375
Brent Crude Oil	1,000 bbl	49,565				
Propane	42,000 gal	10,566	26,075	37,544	43,868	40,255
Natural Gas	10,000 MMBTU	16,468,355	17,875,013	19,165,096	15,978,286	11,923,628
Central Appalachian Coal (CAPP)	1,500 tons	2,209				
Mid-Columbia Electricity	736 Mwh	75				
Palo Verde Electricity	736 Mwh	109	21,477	51,852	139,738	155,977
California Oregon Border Electricity	736 Mwh	2	7,060	52,032	128,423	120,896
Total		**72,781,325**	**73,461,273**	**75,769,318**	**64,392,578**	**53,795,678**
Total**		**88,257,203**	**88,721,329**	**92,415,006**	**80,011,517**	**70,634,699**

Philadelphia Board of Trade (PBOT)

FUTURE	CONTRACT UNIT	2001	2000	1999	1998	1997
Australian Dollar	100,000			20	148	1,270
British Pound	62,500			92	235	2,543
Canadian Dollar	100,000			27		80
ECU	125,000			28		158
Swiss Franc	125,000			39	445	3,913
Japanese Yen	12,500,000			45	734	5,112
Total		**0**	**0**	**251**	**2,572**	**29,075**
Total Futures		**629,123,443**	**491,451,073**	**477,919,308**	**503,201,445**	**443,653,757**
Percent Change		**28.01%**	**2.83%**	**-5.02%**	**13.42%**	**11.64%**

* Includes the New York Futures Exchange, New York Cotton Exchange and Coffee, Sugar and Cocoa Exchange.

** Includes Commodity Exchange, Inc.

Options Traded on U.S. Securities Exchanges Volume Highlights

2001 in Comparison with 2000

2001 RANK	EXCHANGE	2001 CONTRACTS	%	2000 CONTRACTS	%	2000 RANK
1	Chicago Board of Options Exchange (CBOE)	306,667,851	42.84%	326,360,531	45.38%	1
2	American Stock Exchange (AMEX)	205,103,884	28.65%	207,714,296	28.88%	2
3	Pacific Stock Exchange (PSE)	102,701,752	14.35%	108,533,862	15.09%	3
4	Philadelphia Stock Exchange (PHLX)	101,373,433	14.16%	76,547,684	10.64%	4
	TOTAL	**715,846,920**	**100.00%**	**719,156,373**	**100.00%**	

Options Traded on U.S. Futures Exchanges Volume Highlights

2001 in Comparison with 2000

2001 RANK	EXCHANGE	2001 CONTRACTS	%	2000 CONTRACTS	%	2000 RANK
1	Chicago Mercantile Exchange (CME)	95,740,352	56.92%	36,007,913	34.94%	2
2	Chicago Board of Trade (CBT)	50,345,068	29.93%	43,866,151	42.56%	1
3	New York Mercantile Exchange (NYMEX)**	17,985,109	10.69%	17,987,598	17.45%	3
4	New York Board of Trade (NYBOT)*	3,857,721	2.29%	4,922,626	4.78%	4
5	Kansas City Board of Trade (KCBT)	243,356	0.14%	218,062	0.21%	5
6	Minneapolis Grain Exchange (MGE)	29,830	0.02%	42,658	0.04%	6
7	MidAmerica Commodity Exchange (MidAm)	9,887	0.01%	20,368	0.02%	7
	Total	**168,211,323**	**100.00%**	**103,065,376**	**100.00%**	

** Includes Commodity Exchange, Inc.

* Includes the New York Futures Exchange, New York Cotton Exchange and Coffee, Sugar and Cocoa Exchange.

Options Volume on U.S. Futures Exchange 1997-2001

Chicago Board of Trade (CBT)

Option	Contract Unit	2001	2000	1999	1998	1997
Wheat	5,000 bu	1,714,041	1,563,557	1,516,037	1,346,272	1,698,969
Corn	5,000 bu	4,864,294	5,135,111	4,205,325	4,267,274	4,963,603
Oats	5,000 bu	70,218	52,760	56,418	51,852	21,654
Soybeans	5,000 bu	3,829,236	3,890,510	4,792,245	3,845,804	5,339,936
Soybean Oil	60,000 lbs	672,284	490,666	801,367	752,627	381,193
Soybean Meal	100 tons	606,187	657,709	709,194	889,462	716,079
Rice	200,000 lbs	23,233	32,955	48,515	33,602	37,769
Silver	1,000 oz	4	22	38	154	68
T-Bonds	100,000 USD	13,478,771	17,267,458	34,680,068	39,941,672	30,805,885
T-Notes (10-year)	100,000 USD	19,983,876	10,629,021	9,738,808	9,296,742	6,032,088
T-Notes (5-year)	100,000 USD	4,681,604	3,733,542	2,537,044	3,184,609	2,105,792
T-Notes (2-year)	200,000 USD	44,185	3,824	1,780	2,780	4,268
Agency Debt (10-year)	100,000 USD	2,711	152,002			
Flexible U.S. T-Bonds		38,160	18,781	54,454	68,043	118,895
Flexible T-Notes (10-year)		45,700	24,670	6,150	10,520	15,910
Flexible T-Notes (5-year)		2,200	12,160	2,593	4,364	1,350
Dow Jones Industrial Index	10 USD x Index	288,364	200,379	229,560	245,398	156,132
Total		**50,345,068**	**43,866,151**	**59,413,936**	**64,050,508**	**52,642,632**

Chicago Mercantile Exchange (CME)

Option	Contract Unit	2001	2000	1999	1998	1997
Lean Hogs	40,000 lbs	171,472	161,931	231,273	206,014	210,429
Pork Bellies, Frozen	40,000 lbs	6,901	29,712	16,780	21,545	29,324
Butter	50,000 lbs	38	385	752	595	479
Fluid Milk	50,000 lbs	23,792	11,023	12,604	16,680	4,078
Mini BFP Milk	50,000 lbs	29	122	607	304	
Mini BFP Milk	100,000 lbs	2,836	263	387		
Class IV Milk	200,000 lbs	1,448	656			
Live Cattle	40,000 lbs	688,149	622,590	545,709	685,606	540,804
Feeder Cattle	44,000 lbs	186,247	132,086	130,410	170,857	161,100
Random Lumber	80,000 bd ft	25,752	19,413	24,745	18,928	19,826
Euroyen	100,000,000 JPY	2,225	9,756	41,073	38,208	41,577
Eurodollar (3-month)	1,000,000 USD	88,174,799	28,590,428	24,884,494	33,147,148	29,595,246
One Month LIBOR	3,000,000 USD	2,106	2,236	1,916	5,541	28,809
British Pound	62,500	147,205	174,928	208,921	241,720	986,950
Canadian Dollar	100,000	109,908	75,934	121,933	278,730	253,075
Deutschemark	125,000	727	6,329	140,522	734,678	1,411,110
Japanese Yen	12,500,000	839,069	567,896	1,100,130	1,942,417	1,661,417
Mexican Peso	500,000	5,331	5,741	8,133	25,948	186,594
Swiss Franc	125,000	119,051	125,360	178,433	281,354	591,509
Australian Dollar	100,000	30,050	10,337	9,509	9,133	25,465
Euro FX	125,000 EUR	655,991	371,737	167,078		
Nikkei 225	5 USD x Index	3,339	4,270	6,007	7,725	7,834
S&P 500 Index	500 USD x Index	4,381,924	4,352,249	4,603,946	4,986,687	4,734,950
E-Mini S&P	50 USD x S&P Index	21,777	18,814	54,480	20,629	8,661
S&P MidCap 400 Index	500 USD x Index	4,007	2,911	3,841	1,899	3,272
NASDAQ 100 Index	500 USD x Index	121,895	699,264	225,981	127,532	108,922
Russell 2000	500 USD x Index	10,941	8,047	1,230	2,656	2,849
Goldman Sachs Commodity Index	250 USD x Index	3,343	3,281	2,573	1,257	2,190
Total		**95,740,352**	**36,007,913**	**32,723,766**	**42,991,388**	**40,738,473**

Kansas City Board of Trade (KCBT)

Option	Contract Unit	2001	2000	1999	1998	1997
Wheat	5,000 bu	24,311	218,052	143,974	112,825	99,092
Mini Value Line	100 USD x Index	45	4	2,094	1,662	4,547
Total		**243,356**	**218,062**	**146,105**	**114,542**	**103,879**

Minneapolis Grain Exchange (MGE)

Option	Contract Unit	2001	2000	1999	1998	1997
American Spring Wheat	5,000 bu	29,112	41,441	53,246	41,702	40,383
Cottonseed	120 tons	718	778			
Total		**29,830**	**42,658**	**53,870**	**44,339**	**47,710**

MidAmerica Commodity Exchange (MidAm)

Option	Contract Unit	2001	2000	1999	1998	1997
Soft Red Winter Wheat	5,000 bu	832	4,023	1,813	3,121	4,491
Corn	1,000 bu	3,590	5,495	4,325	8,348	8,904
Soybeans	1,000 bu	5,116	8,500	10,705	11,603	19,594
Soybean Oil	30,000 lbs	4		6	7	3
Gold	33.2 troy oz	2	17	25	3	63
U.S. Treasury Bonds (30-year)	50,000 USD	343	2,333	2,095	2,646	1,282
Total		**9,887**	**20,368**	**18,969**	**25,728**	**34,337**

New York Board of Trade (NYBOT)**

Option	Contract Unit	2001	2000	1999	1998	1997
Coffee	37,500 lbs	799,506	909,251	1,369,021	974,690	1,272,767
Sugar #11	112,000 lbs	1,305,470	2,027,581	2,275,704	2,113,369	1,369,465
Flexible Sugar		12,200	0	5,200	9,930	155
Cocoa	10 metric tons	436,295	495,221	364,450	326,221	399,408
Cotton	50,000 lbs	1,025,578	1,027,002	706,589	1,127,326	648,154
Orange Juice Frozen Concentrate	15,000 lbs	170,756	237,673	351,763	464,773	457,143
U.S. Dollar Index	500 USD x Index	15,365	14,650	11,654	21,575	22,539
Euro		932	676	7,137		
Euro / British Pound	100,000 EUR	936	1,232	2,228		
Euro / Japanese Yen	100,000 EUR	685	1,492	5,200		
British Pound / Japanese Yen	125,000 GBP	16	0	291	20	
U.S. Dollar / British Pound	125,000 GBP	136	200	280	6	32
U.S. Dollar / Japanese Yen	12,500,000 JPY	867	0	2,431	1,811	1,225
NYSE Composite Index	500 USD x Index	78,053	93,912	112,052	93,343	81,038
Russell 1000 Index	500 USD x Index	9,905	48,245	69,990		
PSE Tech 100	500 USD x Index	130	59,931	204,682	37,339	8,801
Bridge/CRB Futures Index	500 USD x Index	891	3,306	8,868	5,844	5,835
Total**		**3,857,721**	**4,922,626**	**5,519,619**	**5,252,288**	**4,275,667**

New York Mercantile Exchange (NYMEX)*

COMEX Division

Option	Contract Unit	2001	2000	1999	1998	1997
Gold	100 oz	1,975,019	2,083,414	2,815,831	1,945,366	2,064,883
Silver	5,000 oz	483,386	579,085	725,885	818,053	842,923
High Grade Copper	25,000 lbs	50,826	65,043	160,857	153,332	133,603
Total		**2,509,231**	**2,727,542**	**3,703,215**	**2,916,751**	**3,041,409**

NYMEX Division

Option	Contract Unit	2001	2000	1999	1998	1997
Platinum	50 oz	1,813	7,065	11,146	14,183	31,139
Heating Oil	42,000 gal	704,972	1,385,968	695,558	669,725	1,147,034
Unleaded Gasoline	1,000 bbl	1,040,030	1,012,460	600,009	730,421	1,033,778
Crude Oil	1,000 bbl	7,726,076	7,460,052	8,161,976	7,448,095	5,790,333
Brent Crude Oil	1,000 bbl	741				
Natural Gas	10,000 MMBTU	5,974,240	5,335,800	3,749,454	3,115,765	2,079,607
Gas-Crude Oil Spread	1,000 bbl	14,992	16,348	46,281	22,575	41,867
Heating Oil-Crude Oil Spread	1,000 bbl	13,014	42,363	46,482	36,615	18,657
Total		**15,475,878**	**15,260,056**	**13,420,610**	**12,090,417**	**10,175,238**
Total*		**17,985,109**	**17,987,598**	**17,123,825**	**15,007,168**	**13,216,647**

		2001	2000	1999	1998	1997
TOTAL OPTIONS		**168,211,323**	**103,065,376**	**115,000,090**	**127,485,961**	**111,059,345**
PERCENT CHANGE		**63.21%**	**-10.38%**	**-9.79%**	**14.79%**	**8.91%**

* Includes Commodity Exchange, Inc.

** Includes the New York Futures Exchange, New York Cotton Exchange and Coffee, Sugar and Cocoa Exchange.

Volume U.S.

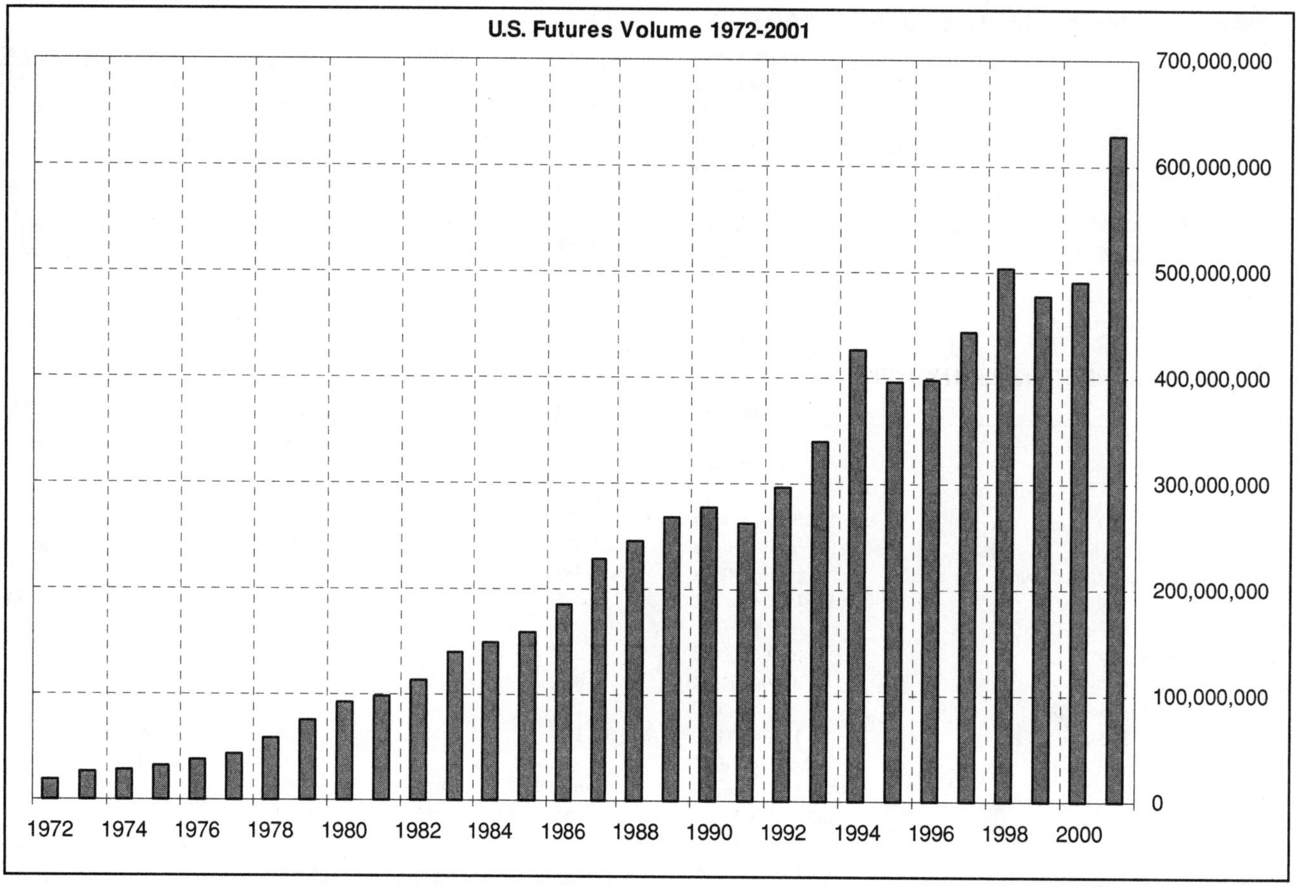

U.S. Futures Volume 1972-2001

700,000,000
600,000,000
500,000,000
400,000,000
300,000,000
200,000,000
100,000,000
0

1972 1974 1976 1978 1980 1982 1984 1986 1988 1990 1992 1994 1996 1998 2000

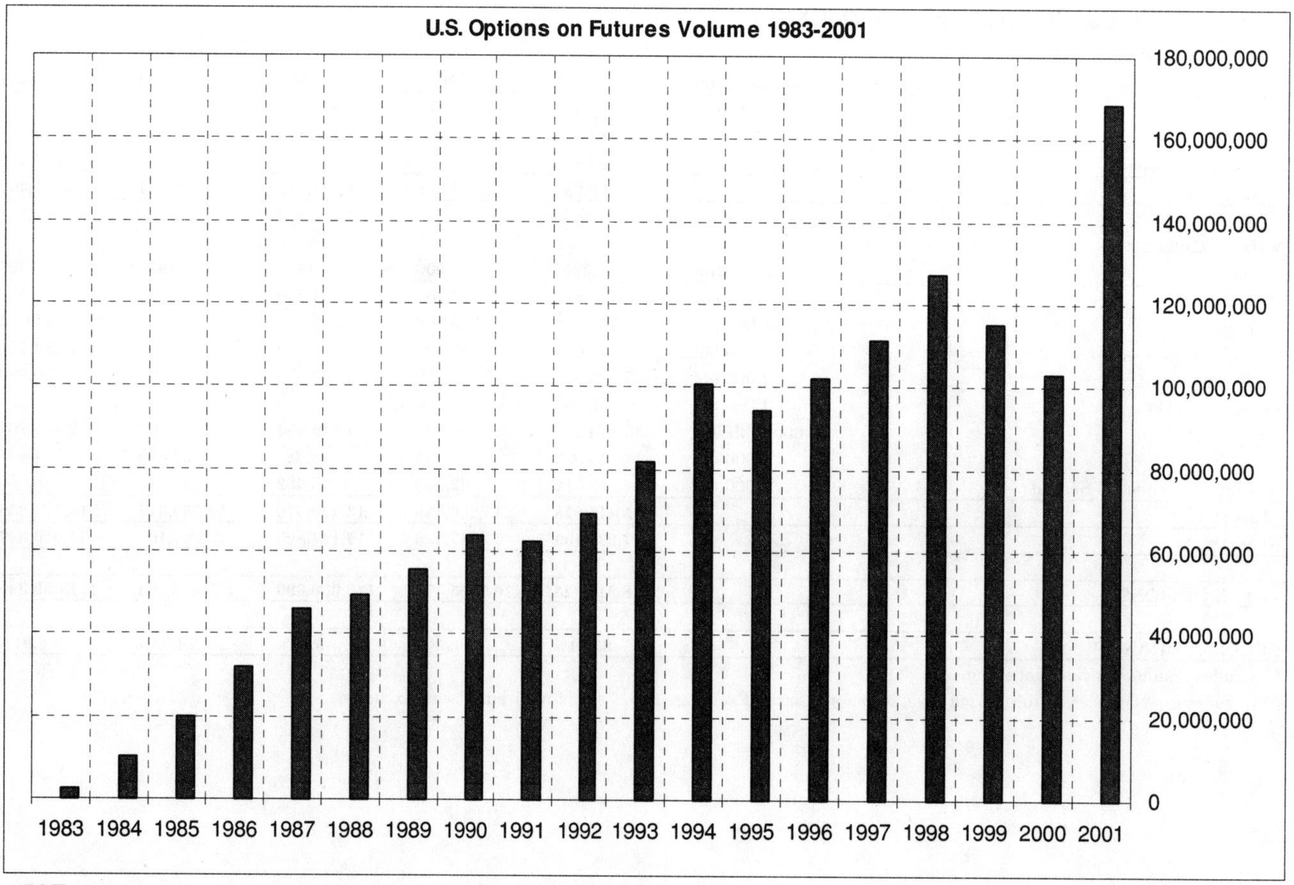

U.S. Options on Futures Volume 1983-2001

180,000,000
160,000,000
140,000,000
120,000,000
100,000,000
80,000,000
60,000,000
40,000,000
20,000,000
0

1983 1984 1985 1986 1987 1988 1989 1990 1991 1992 1993 1994 1995 1996 1997 1998 1999 2000 2001

Volume Worldwide

Agricultural Futures Markets (AFM), Netherlands

	2001	2000	1999	1998	1997
Live Hogs	32,437	32,020	43,051	45,705	57,069
Piglets	243	738	1,172	2,531	2,610
Eggs	3	300			
Potatoes	61,184	63,184	67,663	114,601	76,646
Potatoes Options	8,498	8,863	10,967	16,394	
Hogs Options	1,879	495			
Total	**104,244**	**105,600**	**122,853**	**179,231**	**136,325**

Amsterdam Exchanges (AEX), Netherlands

(formerly European Options Exchange)	2001	2000	1999	1998	1997
AEX Stock Index (FTI)	3,317,913	2,674,824	2,925,385	3,484,558	2,554,776
Light AEX Stock Index (FTIL)	8,211	20,700	12,445		
Amsterdam MidCap Index (FTM)	4,290	1,914	263		
FTSE Eurotop 100 Index (FETI)	253	2,112	292		
Euro / U.S. Dollar (FED)	2,346	989	167		
U.S. Dollar/Euro (FDE)	2,234	3,656	1,241	4,411	2,987
All Futures on Individual Equities	8,387	773			
Euro / U.S. Dollar (EDX) Options	29,760	30,835	17,398		
U.S. Dollar / Euro Options	39,790	63,560	87,249	273,455	270,088
Dutch Government Bond Options	10,937	22,515	77,619	208,994	286,808
EOE Stock Index Options	6,569,129	4,953,037	5,527,137	7,864,884	8,232,719
Light AEX Stock Index (AEXL) Options	50,241	37,782	38,872		
Eurotop 100 Options	2,358	0	19,763	33,586	12,127
FTSE sStars (STAR) Options	24	384	1,137		
FTSE Eurotop 100 Index (ETI) Options	5,210	9,940	11,017		
Amsterdam Information Technology Index (AIS) Options	53	1,573	514		
Amsterdam Financial Sector Index (AFS) Options	28	284	16,069		
Amsterdam MidCap Index (MID) Options	1,165	2,517	743		
Eurotop Bank Sector Index (EBS) Options	2	182	35		
Equity Options Options	56,348,323	50,345,697	40,653,520	52,741,082	36,340,078
Total	**63,057,020**	**58,184,322**	**49,431,139**	**64,756,919**	**48,669,669**

Wiener Borse - Derivatives Market of Vienna, Austria

(formerly the Austrian Futures & Options Exchange)	2001	2000	1999	1998	1997
ATX Index	271,741	431,048	598,981	618,358	566,459
CeCe (5 Eastern European Indices)	164,278	227,829	203,421	472,077	464,480
ATX Index Options	123,757	205,286	395,323	557,463	572,644
ATX LEOs (Long-term Equity) Options	274	2,154	7,971	11,421	4,693
CeCe (5 Eastern European Indices) Options	1,633	10,659	24,157	75,709	43,424
Equity Options	1,239,969	0	802,924	1,201,197	1,346,990
	1,801,652	**876,976**	**2,032,957**	**2,972,090**	**3,111,523**

Belgian Futures and Options Exchange (BELFOX), Belgium

	2001	2000	1999	1998	1997
Mini Bel 20 Index (MBEL)	2,166,420	23,814,060	4,888,140		
Mini Dow Jones Euro Stoxx 50 (MEUR)	728,700	5,704,990			
Bel 20 Index	543,501	780,301	823,244	664,360	551,044
Bel 20 Index Options	727,853	911,275	1,151,862	978,341	954,238
Equity Options	404,559	589,218	530,389	364,885	402,547
Total	**4,571,033**	**31,802,804**	**7,412,210**	**2,175,033**	**2,527,665**

Bolsa de Mercadorias & Futuros (BM&F), Brazil

	2001	2000	1999	1998	1997
Arabica Coffee	475,034	390,513	317,722	198,547	114,521
Live Cattle	92,365	149,795	123,442	88,054	109,261
Sugar Crystal	93,904	52,552	33,764	30,080	8,330
Cotton	15	306	5,115	17,007	13,689
Corn	4,588	8,084	10,432	15,949	18,907
Soybean Futures	83	2,257	13,424	13,489	16,082
Gold Forward	484	1,520	25	10	
Gold Spot	42,971	95,494	155,947	132,747	173,752
Anhydrous Fuel Alcohol	67,527	53,963			
Bovespa Stock Index Futures	5,151,572	7,000,335	5,551,918	9,926,890	14,914,692
Bovespa Mini Index	110,943				
Bovespa Volatilty Index	450				
Interest Rate	46,241,111	37,626,151	22,235,992	35,150,416	36,466,961
Interest Rate Swap	964,419	6,656,112	8,224,534	8,562,215	11,660,972
Interest Rate x Exchange Rate Swap	3,645,863	2,216,247	2,440,318	2,499,084	3,504,600
Interest Rate x Reference Rate Swap	27,953	33,753	80,140	83,256	139,929
Interest Rate x Inflation Index Swap (formerly Inflation)	99,900	67,468	17,163	4,496	10,324
Interest Rate x Ibovespa Swap	592	33	42	4,113	
Interest Rate x Ibovespa Index	800				
ID x U.S. Dollar Spread Futures	1,375,846	5,059,141	2,126,164	3,013,081	52,587
FRA on ID x US Dollar Spread	16,524,996				
ID Forward with Reset	602,431	370,747			
C-Bond	2,605	983	646	6,581	296,758
EI-Bond	407	1,617	2,074	703	4,060
U.S. Dollar	18,636,578	20,208,454	11,420,923	18,573,100	40,387,111
Mini U.S. Dollar	10,845	0	110		
Euro	170	33,753	80,140	83,256	139,929
Interest Rate x Inflation Index Swap (formerly Inflation)	99,900	67,468	17,163	4,496	10,324
Interest Rate x Ibovespa Swap	592	33	42	4,113	
Interest Rate x Ibovespa Index	800				
ID x U.S. Dollar Spread Futures	1,375,846	5,059,141	2,126,164	3,013,081	52,587
FRA on ID x US Dollar Spread	16,524,996				
ID Forward with Reset	602,431	370,747			
C-Bond	2,605	983	646	6,581	296,758
EI-Bond	407	1,617	2,074	703	4,060
U.S. Dollar	18,636,578	20,208,454	11,420,923	18,573,100	40,387,111
Mini U.S. Dollar	10,845	0	110		
Euro	170				
Gold on Actuals Options	156,447	119,512	283,221	88,932	141,880
Gold Exercise Options	58,316	34,114	35,634	41,928	81,542
U.S. $ Denominated Arabica Coffee Options	12,818	8,137	42,918	17,921	3,210
U.S. $ Denominated Arabica Coffee Exercise Options	1,130	1,041	4,856	1,103	1,256
Live Cattle Options	1,204	1,533		308	392
Bovespa Stock Options	41,210	5,365	26,020	103,860	359,846
Bovespa Stock Exercise Options	11,750	2,885	210	2,810	31,971
Interest Rate Options (IDI)	1,129,060	661,218	0	0	375,435
Interest Rate (IDI) Exercise Options	89,013	58,100	22,461	57,015	57,390
Fexible Bovespa Stock Index Options	273,888	116,976	257,870	333,582	618,424
U.S. Dollar on Actuals Options	1,211,601	1,328,215	694,483	3,405,413	7,211,258
U.S. Dollar Exercise Options	139,057	75,685	50,741	86,963	974,381
Flexible Currency Options	570,739	458,631	807,153	2,818,616	3,809,659
	97,870,685	**82,945,277**	**55,931,098**	**87,015,050**	**122,179,393**

Budapest Stock Exchange (BSE), Hungary

	2001	2000	1999	1998	1997
3-Year Hungarian Government Bond	1,800	500	12,230		
Budapest Stock Index (BUX) Futures	1,236,405	839,978	1,555,939	1,993,353	1,208,388
EUR / HUF	41,722	22,536	33,527	1	
JPY / HUF	3,084				
CHF / HUF	7,064	7,064	120	1,004	
GBP / HUF	1,000	1,000	150	1,602	
USD / HUF	116,176	74,790	25,106	144,368	55,116
All Futures on Individual Equities	879,049	456,510	181,031	71,158	
Budapest Stock Index (BUX) Options	9,076	8,516			
Total	**2,295,376**	**1,412,112**	**1,814,078**	**2,772,821**	**1,464,628**

Budapest Commodity Exchange (BCE), Hungary

	2001	2000	1999	1998	1997
Corn	15,733	41,956	48,918	37,941	77,992
Feed Wheat	2,403	726	48	858	13,693
Feed Barley	433	1,369	2,518	2,139	10,330
Wheat	14,987	21,345	65,823	2,011	
Extra Wheat	98				
Black Seed	1,101	845	7,351	9,623	4,448
Rapeseed	21	129	121		
Soybean	39	55	19		
TAX	44	17	2		
Ammonium Nitrate	17	67			
U.S. Dollar	425,125	486,860	470,550	1,730,165	1,097,502
Japanese Yen	226,639	232,844	101,884	183,118	852,629
EUR	1,840,127	1,306,688	596,258		
British Pound	15,426	42,380	17,103	42,454	201,974
Swiss Franc	63,010	38,901	72,500	389,118	849,185
3-Month BUBOR	7,585				
Corn Options	511	697	1,665	290	
Wheat Options	164	19	3,464	525	
EUR	11,000				
Total	**2,624,463**	**2,175,339**	**1,593,696**	**8,274,883**	**5,950,389**

EUREX, Frankfurt, Germany

	2001	2000	1999	1998	1997
DAX	14,686,359	11,524,330	12,876,982	6,937,139	6,623,287
FOX	74,819	109,822	741		
NEMAX 50	5,409,482	702,873			
Dow Jones Global Titans 50	871				
Dow Jones Euro STOXX 50	37,828,500	14,315,518	5,341,864	366,435	
Dow Jones Euro STOXX Banks	113,478				
Dow Jones Euro STOXX Healthcare	2,399				
Dow Jones Euro STOXX Technology	82,321				
Dow Jones Euro STOXX Telecom	47,967				
Dow Jones STOXX 50	452,830	355,801	326,136	94,771	
Dow Jones STOXX 600 Banks	11,259				
Dow Jones STOXX 600 Healthcare	11,968				
Dow Jones STOXX 600 Technology	5,152				
Dow Jones STOXX 600 Telecom	6,900				
Euro-BUND	178,011,304	151,326,295	121,311,878	2	
Euro-BOBL	99,578,068	62,502,582	45,481,843		
3-Month Euribor	663,980	1,224,877	3,031,138	378,420	
Euro-SCHATZ	92,637,630	42,822,290	17,748,784		
DAX Options	44,102,502	31,941,562	32,613,783	29,948,503	31,521,286
FOX Options	6,053	50,926	652		
NEMAX 50 Options	1,726,251	473,297			
Dow Jones Global Titans 50 Options	104				
Dow Jones Euro STOXX 50 Options	19,046,893	8,197,999	3,791,738	122,951	
Dow Jones Euro STOXX Banks Options	20,434				
Dow Jones Euro STOXX Healthcare Options	96				
Dow Jones Euro STOXX Technology Options	19,031				
Dow Jones Euro STOXX Telecom Options	9,677				
Dow Jones STOXX 50 Options	44,400	61,530	80,254	73,779	
Euro-BUND Options	22,054,064	26,291,123	24,940,113	5,000	
Euro-SCHATZ Options	10,075,031	1,954,183	450,836		
Euro-BOBL Options	6,188,962	2,436,491	1,787,840		
NEMAX 50 Component Equities Options	16,165,675	4,536,186	111,332		
Dow Jones Euro STOXX 50 Component Equities Options	984,468	294,917			
All Options on German Equities	240,918	9,905			
All Options on US Equities	38,196				
All Options on Individual Equities	79,875,125	48,748,287	36,123,317	30,853,782	9,667,248
	630,223,167	**409,883,020**	**339,426,590**	**209,550,981**	**112,164,106**

* Odd lots are a result of the Euro conversion and are not included in the total volume figures.

EUREX, Zurich, Switzerland

	2001	2000	1999	1998	1997
Swiss Market Index (SMI)	5,099,537	4,586,219	6,515,036	4,445,396	1,810,698
Swiss Government Bond (CONF)	416,883	479,350	577,030	722,066	638,638
Swiss Market Index (SMI) Options	3,179,143	3,474,369	3,669,386	3,394,098	4,316,384
Equity Options*	35,239,133	35,648,521	28,570,528	30,104,988	3,334,251
	674,157,863	**454,071,479**	**39,333,710**	**38,662,454**	**40,125,315**

* 1998 data reflects different contract size introduced in July. Not comparable with 1997 data.

Volume Worldwide

Helsinki Exchanges, Finland

(formerly the Finnish Options Market Exchange)	2001	2000	1999	1998	1997
STOX Stock Future	988,503	853,872	820,574	811,834	640,268
HEXTech Index	41	820,574	811,834	640,268	275,172
HEXTech Index Options	3040				
All Options on Individual Equitites (STOX)	152,052	324,526	1,263,363	693,310	1,699,591
Total	**1,143.636**	**1,207,016**	**2,635,112**	**2,814,089**	**5,513,479**

FUTOP Clearing Centre, Denmark

	2001	2000	1999	1998	1997
KFX Stock Index	459,007	995,934	1,093,917	289,424	252,571
KFX Stock Index Options	5,529	10,277	18,128	4,073	31,638
All Options on Individual Options	26,041	3,838	2,656	4,152	34,306
Total	**490,577**	**1,045,872**	**1,163,208**	**454,019**	**681,466**

International Petroleum Exchange (IPE), United Kingdom

	2001	2000	1999	1998	1997
Crude Oil	18,396,069	17,297,974	15,982,355	13,674,664	10,301,918
Gasoil	7,230,408	7,115,435	6,150,912	4,974,171	4,031,608
Electricity Baseload - Monthly	50				
Natural Gas - Seasons	1,005	50			
Natural Gas - Quarters	3,900	1,465			
Natural Gas BOM	2,570	2,555	4,270		
Natural Gas Daily (NBP)	1,540	5,440	12,000	3,160	
Natural Gas Monthly (NBP)	462,665	515,305	290,750	328,350	81,445
Crude Oil Options	252,217	452,284	495,798	337,999	250,176
Gasoil Options	60,240	100,631	104,813	104,523	68,195
	26,410,664	**25,491,139**	**23,042,833**	**19,422,867**	**14,733,342**

Italian Derivatives Market of the Italian Stock Exchange, Italy

	2001	2000	1999	1998	1997
MIB 30 Index	4,634,329	4,260,085	5,094,312	5,896,238	4,463,034
Mini FIB 30 Index	1,400,135	358,439			
MIDEX	743	2,044	5,144	30,072	
MIB 30 Index Options	2,716,271	2,843,986	2,236,241	1,616,635	1,159,059
Equity Options	8,329,533	5,875,138	1,947,931	1,296,791	2,444,424
Total	**17,081,011**	**13,339,692**	**9,283,628**	**8,839,736**	**8,066,517**

London Metal Exchange (LME), United Kingdom

	1999	1998	1997	1996	1995
High Grade Primary Aluminum	22,211,729	20,091,765	22,484,144	14,552,878	14,060,243
Aluminum Alloy	740,955	498,839	389,558	292,429	210,787
Copper - Grade A	16,789,674	15,699,702	15,099,842	18,484,367	17,530,263
Standard Lead	3,310,109	2,420,777	2,352,731	2,202,864	1,758,742
Primary Nickel	5,396,342	4,676,526	4,627,929	3,104,514	3,319,697
Special High Grade Zinc	7,341,620	5,742,948	7,390,436	4,852,942	5,241,931
Silver	1,773				
Tin	1,770,807	1,429,115	1,119,776	1,121,836	1,275,718
High Grade Primary Aluminum Options	1,502,276	909,526	1,659,879	1,030,703	1,241,596
Aluminum Alloy Options	1,037	1,031	535	242	96
Copper - Grade A Options	1,156,929	1,052,239	1,732,509	1,623,575	2,212,821
Standard Lead Options	114,498	36,862	34,531	30,992	22,262
Primary Nickel Options	250,823	119,406	60,645	54,646	83,637
Special High Grade Zinc Options	520,942	204,479	285,453	126,094	177,005
Tin Options	147,615	61,132	13,005	8,925	15,532
Primary Aluminum TAPOS	299,167	115,626	47,447		
Copper TAPOS	41,261	15,108	74,080		
Total	**61,597,557**	**53,075,081**	**57,372,500**	**47,487,007**	**47,150,330**

Korea Stock Exchange (KSE), Korea

	2001	2000	1999	1998	1997
KOPSI 200	31,502,184	19,666,518	17,200,349	17,893,592	3,252,060
KOPSI 200 Index Options	823,289,608	193,829,070	79,936,658	32,310,812	4,528,424
Total	**854,791,792**	**213,495,588**	**97,137,007**	**50,204,404**	**7,780,484**

Korea Futures Exchange (KFE), Korea

	2001	2000	1999
Korea Treasury Bonds	9,323,430	1,538,507	295,833
CD Interest Rate	1,410	2,801	349,812
KOSDAQ 50 Index	466,479		
U.S. Dollar	1,676,979	1,355,730	259,249
Gold	608	62,936	40,509
KOSDAQ 50 Index Options	85		
	11,468,906	**2,959,974**	**945,403**

London International Financial Futures Exchange (LIFFE), United Kingdom

(LCE merged with LIFFE in 1996)	2001	2000	1999	1998	1997
3-Month Short Sterling	34,945,053	22,606,948	27,272,559	33,750,746	20,370,846
3-Month Euroswiss	4,694,391	4,621,559	5,956,797	7,381,809	4,746,234
3-Month ECU	1,852	5,249	739,667	262,997	534,457
3-Month Euribor	91,083,198	58,016,852	35,657,690	1,269	
Long Gilt	6,710,557	5,350,705	8,421,533	16,185,316	19,651,565
2-Year Swapnote	686,450				
5-Year Swapnote	1,502,104				
10-Year Swapnote	1,967,221				
Japanese Government Bond	72,182	379,541	465,727	692,404	813,241
FTSE 100 Index	12,698,908	10,142,828	8,704,574	6,955,096	3,698,368
Mini FTSE 100 Index	129,283	29,765			
FTSE Eurotop 100 Index	130,824	153,792	139,552	42,058	
FTSE Eurotop 300 Index	33	0	1,780		
FTSE Eurobloc 100 Index	1,752	2,099	1,750		
MSCI Euro Index	124,202	77,140	41,746		
MSCI Pan-Euro Index	373,259	166,135	22,172		
FTSE Mid 250 Index	559	8,706	47,663	65,219	68,280
Barley	5,614	3,567	6,526	11,142	15,325
BIFFEX (Baltic Freight Index)	922	3,244	16,085	23,595	45,059
Cocoa #7	1,514,384	1,636,322	1,862,119	1,786,090	1,857,065
Robusta Coffee	1,547,838	1,470,980	1,565,708	1,290,049	1,544,193
Potatoes in Bulk	12,503	15,045	15,850	24,697	22,933
Wheat	95,676	87,387	100,127	98,501	128,411
White Sugar	898,261	907,399	990,595	945,896	686,302
London Monthy	5				
All Futures on Individual Equities	2,325,744				
3-Month Short Sterling Options	7,692,455	4,167,648	6,451,680	7,348,877	2,662,716
3-Month Sterling Mid-curve Options	427,975	127,080	112,735	35,480	
3-Month Euroswiss Options	82,145	68,922	89,777	154,477	31,390
3-Month Euribor Options	21,643,698	7,900,121	4,819,366		
3-Month Euribor Mid Curve Options	963,417	432,445	3,200		
Long Gilt Options	1,230	4,923	159,713	1,644,323	1,799,660
2-Year Swapnote Options	450				
5-Year Swapnote Options	1,730				
10-Year Swapnote Options	2,429				
FTSE 100 Index (ESX) Options	11,848,155	6,285,819	4,858,373	3,512,173	7,188,349
FTSE 100 Index (SEI) Options	320,461	531,389	843,100	1,001,428	
FTSE Eurotop 100 Index Options	28,100	3,010			
FTSE 100 Index FLEX Options	229,152	71,898	58,878	27,855	32,985
Barley Options	751	157	280	40	206
Cocoa Options	94,505	7,119	22,758	25,317	27,838
U.S. Dollar Coffee Options	80,197	119,200	186,155	159,557	184,975
Wheat Options	12,693	15,610	41,436	10,784	9,326
White Sugar Options	70,526	121,671	105,932	97,949	21,062
Equity Options	10,725,183	5,484,873	3,601,383	3,307,913	4,295,877
	215,748,027	**131,054,809**	**120,040,031**	**194,394,159**	**209,425,578**

Volume Worldwide

Commodity and Monetary Exchange of Malaysia, Malaysia

(formerly the KLCE and KLOFFE)	2001	2000	1999	1998	1997
Crude Palm Oil	479,799	308,622	388,105	353,545	935,595
3-Month KLIBOR	54,914	44,812	28,670		
KLSE Composite Index (FKLI)	287,528	366,942	436,678	771,244	382,974
KLSE Composite Index Options (FKLI)	564				
Total	**822,805**	**720,376**	**853,453**	**1,124,789**	**1,318,569**

Marche a Terme International de France (MATIF), France

	2001	2000	1999	1998	1997
Notional Bond	17,349,421	43,317,155	6,130,969	23,284,475	33,752,483
Euro 5-Year	621,814	0	114,946	2,825,479	2,100,683
3-Month Pibor	2,965	195,169	2,968,774	5,305,778	14,417,310
Wheat #2	57,159	33,038	43,193	41,091	
Corn	57,664	27,677	7,158		
Wine	68				
Rapeseed	135,655	115,840	137,244	102,897	74,387
Rapeseed Options	7,554	5,313	3,332		
	18,232,300	**43,706,067**	**9,588,766**	**35,595,438**	**62,102,581**

Marche des Options Negociables de Paris (MONEP), France

	2001	2000	1999	1998	1997
CAC 40 Stock Index 10 Euro	22,923,597	18,249,903	20,973,911		
Dow Jones Euro STOXX(SM) 50	887,447	999,596	437,447		
Dow Jones Euro STOXX	2,323				
Dow Jones STOXX 50	2,330	23,603	103,160		
Dow Jones STOXX (L&M)	1,606	6,243	1,131		
Dow Jones STOXX(SM) Sector Indices	624				
CAC 40 Index (Long Term) Options	107,251,388	84,036,775	75,652,724	2,752,536	3,285,383
DJ STOXX 50 Options	705	4,761	4,031	14,536	
Euro STOXX 50 Options	2,265	38,356	131,106	106,457	
Equity Options*	178,330,328	89,434,383	68,095,743	28,953,142	5,565,057
	309,402,613	**192,793,959**	**178,495,406**	**53,377,988**	**21,561,838**

*** 1998 data reflects different contract size introduced in July. Not comparable with 1997 data.**

**** Odd lots are a result of the Euro conversion and are not included in the total volume figures.**

MEFF Renta Fija (RF), Spain

	2001	2000	1999	1998	1997
10-Year Notional Bond	290,608	1,094,548	3,614,750	15,662,560	21,046,078
Total	**290,608**	**1,108,373**	**3,643,154**	**18,917,159**	**26,585,419**

MEFF Renta Variable (RV), Spain

	2001	2000	1999	1998	1997
IBEX 35 Plus Index	4,305,035	4,183,028	5,101,588	8,627,374	6,053,283
Mini IBEX 35 Index	22,423				
S&P Europe 350 Index	3,219				
S&P Financial Index	2,223				
S&P Technology Index	5,191				
S&P Telecommunications Index	4,037				
All Futures on Individual Equities	8,766,165				
IBEX 35 Plus Index Options	998,645	766,078	861,255	1,681,205	1,411,101
S&P Europe 350 Index Options	242				
S&P Financial Index Options	751				
S&P Technology Index Options	285				
S&P Telecommunications Index Options	391				
Equity Options	22,628,132	16,580,519	8,091,728	2,695,206	1,485,074
Total	**36,736,739**	**21,529,625**	**14,054,571**	**13,003,785**	**8,949,458**

Mercado a Termino de Buenos Aires, Argentina

	2001	2000	1999	1998	1997
Wheat	44,607	52,293	54,271	48,558	49,492
Corn	36,421	46,672	39,475	42,486	42,125
Sunflowerseed	8,440	26,910	34,080	23,576	19,312
Soybean	59,436	53,672	43,882	29,069	26,934
Argentine Wheat Index (ITA)	83				
Wheat Options	20,492	18,240	26,930	20,567	24,490
Corn Options	8,140	8,993	9,787	15,045	20,679
Sunflowerseed Options	1,764	1,807	6,104	9,957	9,805
Soybean Options	16,864	27,475	17,736	10,920	9,905
Argentine Wheat Index (ITA) Options	26				
Total	**196,273**	**236,062**	**232,265**	**200,178**	**202,742**

Mercato Italiano Futures (MIF), Italy

	2000	1999	1998	1997	1996
10-Year BTP	1,786	188,650	1,293,408	2,851,585	2,240,085
30-Year BTP		70			
Euribor	180	20,890			
Total	**1,966**	**209,610**	**1,440,543**	**3,156,181**	**2,439,089**

Montreal Exchange (ME), Canada

	2001	2000	1999	1998	1997
3 Month Bankers Acceptance	4,234,236	4,992,957	6,047,542	6,803,028	4,139,777
10 Year Canadian Government Bond	1,835,229	1,501,264	1,598,463	1,836,937	1,272,970
S&P Canada 60 Index	1,174,328	1,272,244	262,058		
All Futures on Individual Equities	17,206				
Canadian Government Bond (OGB) Options	12				
3-Month Bankers Acceptance Options	89,339	249,976	168,903	210,850	155,308
10-Year Canadian Government Bond Options	20,369	8,877	9,190	18,533	23,175
S&P Canada 60 Index Options	35,585	88,923	40,650		
i60 Index (XIU) Options	127,731	120,556			
Equity Options	5,099,894	4,753,495	1,439,476	1,375,274	1,016,945
	12,633,929	**12,988,514**	**9,592,717**	**10,292,532**	**6,660,052**

New Zealand Futures Exchange (NZFOE), New Zealand

	2001	2000	1999	1998	1997
3-Year Government Stock	62,521	3,867	2,356	18,240	43,967
10-Year Government Stock	32,319	8,024	2,853	9,948	17,265
90-Day Bank Bill	915,225	781,074	816,931	1,236,944	1,019,686
NZSE-10 Captial Share Price Index	637	1,087	1,842	2,138	3,038
New Zealand Electricity	150	450	1,564	3,092	4,596
90-Day Bank Bill Options	18,320	22,906	11,600	410	1,810
3-Year Government Stock Options	1,100				
10-Year Government Stock Options	200			20	
Equity Options	15,312	65,390	24,621	71,847	117,669
Total	**1,045,784**	**882,798**	**861,767**	**1,342,892**	**1,208,079**

OM Stockholm (OMS), Sweden

	2001	2000	1999	1998	1997
Interest Rate	7,033,675	5,371,720	8,002,707	9,356,221	12,704,397
OMX Index	14,906,505	11,477,162	11,931,352	9,265,510	2,163,560
All Futures on Individual Equities	1,468,018	2,144,767	1,129,453	533,508	288,841
Interest Rate Options	11,000	15,500	100	2,727	5,846
OMX Index Options	4,587,544	4,167,448	5,733,106	4,947,486	3,545,967
Equity Options	34,729,075	30,691,587	26,824,117	20,589,273	19,485,816
Total	**62,735,817**	**53,868,284**	**53,622,623**	**44,694,725**	**38,194,473**

Oslo Stock Exchange (OSE), Norway

	2001	2000	1999	1998	1997
OBr10	5,220	10,960	21,116	36,423	58,518
OBr5	8,310	2,521	8,224	31,332	33,422
Forwards	302,497	260,521	170,950	57,938	1,630
OBX	521,314	750,264	675,240	354,602	135,284
OBX Options	662,394	1,025,027	978,014	828,445	926,646
Equity Options	2,346,339	2,062,350	2,580,178	883,045	1,086,171
	3,846,074	**4,111,643**	**4,433,722**	**2,192,785**	**2,241,671**

Shanghai Futures Exchange, China

	2001	2000	1999	1998	1997
Copper	4,088,943	2,674,016	2,559,687	2,772,124	1,299,520
Aluminum	1,448,192	455,206	256,485	60,656	73,077
Rubber	73,200	1,000,299	318,096	391,009	
Total	**5,610,335**	**4,129,521**	**3,134,268**	**3,223,797**	**1,372,671**

Volume Worldwide

Singapore Exchange (SGX), Singapore

	2001	2000	1999	1998	1997
Eurodollar	17,684,054	10,083,633	8,999,879	9,837,115	7,400,058
Singapore Dollar Interest Rate	111,210	61,300	18,725		
Nikkei 225 Index	4,573,348	4,484,978	5,429,843	5,537,558	4,844,495
Nikkei 300 Index	29,439	38,304	34,273	95,255	129,695
Straits Times Index	20,023	47,106			
S&P CNX Nifty Index	1,800	20,403			
MSCI Singapore Index	488,489	479,486	291,527	27,727	
MSCI Taiwan Index	3,902,738	3,390,153	2,362,385	1,842,977	677,295
Brent Crude Oil	50	3,980	18,853	32,600	33,067
Euroyen TIBOR	2,711,826	7,149,469	6,777,548	8,757,516	9,624,680
Euroyen LIBOR	452,559	326,849	374,198		
5-Year Singapore Government Bond	79,246				
Japanese Government Bond	545,189	718,353	168,829	194,373	132,104
All Futures on Individual Equities	6,575				
Eurodollar Options	10				
Euroyen TIBOR Options	47,127	57,095	234,630	661,008	481,138
Euroyen LIBOR Options	2,000				
Japanese Government Bond Options	228	299	1,962	2,211	11,658
MSCI Taiwan Index Options	42,899	1,107	8,828	20,521	7,550
Nikkei 225 Index Options	291,052	708,498	1,137,716	838,891	628,222
	30,989,862	**27,571,963**	**25,863,140**	**27,861,162**	**24,090,285**

South African Futures Exchange (SAFEX), Africa

	2001	2000	1999	1998	1997
White Maize (WMAZ)	563,510	245,396			
Yellow Maize (YMAZ)	77,933	57,666			
WEAT	23,992	9,279			
SUNS	25,249	5,751			
WSEC	240	3,624			
YSEC	64	1,101			
All Share Index	8,044,557	5,817,231	6,037,573	4,620,298	2,599,489
Industrial Index	2,304,176	3,303,760	2,838,168	2,709,146	1,960,260
Financial Index (FINI)	10,585	25,788	80,497	80,229	
RESI	2,933	460	14,120		
Johannesburg Interbank Rate (JBAR)	4	2,350	6,092		
R 150	2,055	1,600	1,723	8,375	8,489
R 153	1,788	1,063	1,026	8,394	5,924
All Futures on Individual Equities	811,156	29,991	82,901		
White Maize (WMAZ) Options	269,887	116,714			
Yellow Maize (YMAZ) Options	27,785	12,117			
WEAT Options	8,694	3,429			
SUNS Options	5,775	1,904			
All Share Index Options	17,926,295	12,137,585	8,511,293	7,915,791	4,873,560
Industrial Index Options	337,289	898,320	973,633	713,337	1,282,555
Financial Index (FINI) Options	15,804	12,894	123,585	56,924	
R 150 Options	780	0	955	5,294	10,467
R 153 Options	9,449	3,099	2,720	5,957	20,085
Equity Options	5,705,719	1,992,579	82,576	152,960	75,360
	36,175,719	**24,389,674**	**18,683,450**	**16,266,370**	**11,583,654**

Taiwan Futures Exchange, Taiwan

	2001	2000	1999	1998	1997
TAIEX	2,844,707	1,339,908	971,578	277,909	
Mini TAIEX	413,343				
Taiwan Stock Exchange Electronic Sector Index	635,661	409,706	87,156		
Taiwan Stock Exchange Bank & Insurance Sector Index	452,541	177,175	18,938		
TAIEX Options	5,137				
Total	**4,351,389**	**1,926,789**	**1,077,672**	**277,909**	

Toronto Futures Exchange (TFE), Canada

(All trading has been moved to the Montreal Exchange)	2000	1999	1998	1997	1996
TSE 35 Index		374,525	440,851	317,408	155,652
TSE 100 Index		7,624	16,900	19,317	8,135
TSE 35 Options		250,960	388,273	431,623	254,199
Total		**633,109**	**846,024**	**768,399**	**418,831**

Sydney Futures Exchange (SFE), Australia

	2001	2000	1999	1998	1997
All Ordinaries Share Price Index	58,016	3,678,706	3,819,800	3,678,151	3,204,266
SPI 200	3,823,729	146,154			
Australian Dollar	40,654				
90-Day Bank Bills	9,108,108	7,700,381	7,184,423	7,735,231	5,918,447
3-Year Treasury Bonds	10,718,248	12,050,070	10,707,111	10,185,750	10,278,357
10-Year Treasury Bonds	5,296,233	4,981,880	5,345,640	5,640,716	5,819,677
NSW Electricity	125	832	4,670	6,797	1,191
NSW Peak Period Electricity	40	617	846		
VIC Electricity	30	421	2,130	4,615	1,129
VIC Peak Period Electricity	151	448	557		
Wheat	4,044	6,110	8,017	9,692	7,937
Fine Wool	2,385	3,063	4,106	2,041	
Broad Wool	944	417	699	496	
Barley	120	161			
Canola	556	971			
Sorghum	959	2,188			
Greasy Wool	8,621	11,126	16,108	11,507	10,127
All Futures on Individual Equities	12,545	8,817	8,658	9,026	29,157
All Ordinaries Share Price Index Options	11,478	1,028,665	1,237,294	847,375	896,340
SPI 200 Options	504,954	70,254			
90-Day Bank Bills Options	267,808	326,638	453,048	770,229	984,363
Overnight 90-Day Bank Bills Options	300	1,003			
3-Year Treasury Bond Options	301,782	319,383	289,196	223,842	418,081
Overnight 3-Year Treasury Bond Options	618,011	477,192	217,959	64,394	43,540
10-Year Treasury Bonds Options	36,341	104,948	242,732	354,311	545,359
Overnight 10-Year Treasury Bond Options	29,671	47,373	169,347	90,015	149,817
Wheat Options	6	120	561	2,040	1,740
Greasy Wool Options	20	3	30	47	11
Total	**35,845,879**	**31,299,021**	**29,793,333**	**29,936,275**	**28,409,539**

Winnipeg Commodity Exchange (WCE), Canada

	2001	2000	1999	1998	1997
Wheat	166,932	164,981	106,378	146,713	197,619
Flaxseed	72,476	101,216	78,433	115,552	140,756
Canola (Rapeseed)	2,424,973	1,858,773	1,685,756	1,557,358	1,387,675
Canola Meal	676				
Field Peas	1,195	15	4,520		
Western Barley	237,574	266,077	211,377	238,994	284,614
Wheat Options	243	210	115	537	250
Flaxseed Options	2,300	6,437	3,295	1,093	66
Western Barley Options	5,728	6,656	1,648	553	959
Canola Options	125,236	63,641	61,476	23,310	31,810
	3,037,333	**2,468,509**	**2,153,443**	**2,091,366**	**2,061,201**

Hong Kong Futures Exchange (HKFE), Hong Kong

	2001	2000	1999	1998	1997
Hang Seng Index	4,400,071	4,023,138	5,132,332	6,969,708	6,446,696
Mini Hang Seng Index	769,886	120,165			
MSCI China Free Index	3,141				
Hang Seng 100 Index	78	30,991	66,822	15,450	
Red Chip Index	533	3,801	30,753	170,385	143,078
Rolling Forex	4,226	3,279	9,042	17,146	251,226
1-Month HIBOR	14,315	12,075	9,726	4,405	
3-Month HIBOR	629,491	325,155	308,646	502,982	87,819
3-Year Exchange Fund Note	1,175				
All Futures on Individual Equities	7,756	3,322	5,696	4,082	4,453
Hang Seng Index Options	716,114	544,047	714,309	798,712	1,147,374
Hang Seng 100 Index Options	111	5,893	51,393	4,610	
Equity Options	4,002,655	4,188,702	2,197,972		
	10,549,552	**9,260,570**	**6,331,400**	**8,489,642**	**8,081,880**

Fukuoka Futures Exchange (FFE), Japan

(Formerly Kanmon Commodity Exchange)	2001	2000	1999	1998	1997
Red Beans	54,845	37,689	92,622	200,215	95,982
Imported Soybeans	122,429	307,676	498,795	572,570	1,382,063
Non-GMO Soybeans	1,478,070	1,284,179			
Refined Sugar	1,437	1,443	1,421	1,433	1,421
Corn	2,016,968	2,357,240	2,897,402	2,951,184	5,069,142
Broiler	2,693,858	2,443,593	1,203,656	5,069,142	4,346,586
	6,367,607	**6,431,820**	**4,693,896**	**3,725,402**	**6,548,608**

Volume Worldwide

Kansai Agricultural Commodities Exchange (KANEX), Japan

	1999	1998	1997	1996	1995
Red Beans	177,039	450,610	483,330	877,474	1,723,230
Imported Soybeans	1,245,358	1,513,589	4,022,023	2,656,174	1,695,414
Refined Sugar	2,842	2,866	2,842	2,876	2,886
Raw Sugar	462,427	558,075	643,742	577,641	730,582
Raw Silk (formerly at Kobe Raw Silk Exchange)	178,114	231,376	327,009	458,243	591,922
Kansai International Grain Index	376,660	60,008			
Raw Sugar Options	30,363	70,561	47,189	71,145	79,365
Total	**2,472,803**	**2,887,085**	**5,526,135**	**4,643,553**	**4,823,399**

Central Japan Commodity Exchange (CJCE), Japan

(formerly NGSE, NTE, and TDCE)	2001	2000	1999	1998	1997
Red Beans	29,614	45,297	147,511	188,937	241,008
Imported Soybeans	60,759	372,475	348,567	505,345	1,010,201
Non-GMO Soybeans	22,471	65,642			
Refined Sugar	345	1,443	1,421	1,433	1,421
Dried Cocoon	90,267	146,737	240,841	277,944	684,141
Cotton Yarn (40S)	307,768	344,006	183,945	114,877	126,684
Hen Egg	596,415	590,274	390,475		
Gasoline	14,392,478	11,048,071			
Kerosene	12,346,595	8,714,440			
Gasoline	11,048,071				
Kerosene	8,714,440				
	27,846,712	**21,328,867**	**1,327,024**	**1,131,738**	**2,108,766**

Osaka Securities Exchange(OSE), Japan

	2001	2000	1999	1998	1997
Nikkei 225 Index	9,516,875	7,426,478	9,067,883	8,191,130	7,484,182
Nikkei 300 Index	961,566	1,281,029	1,470,954	1,531,004	1,526,538
Nikkei 225 Index Options	6,953,222	5,715,856	5,753,760	5,230,046	4,910,359
Nikkei 300 Index Options	609	674	652	2,577	7,798
Equity Options Options	38,077	103,556	683,778	363,901	222,094
Total	**17,470,349**	**14,527,939**	**16,978,415**	**15,328,802**	**14,150,971**

Osaka Mercantile Exchange (OME), Japan

(formerly KRE and OTE)	2001	2000	1999	1998	1997
Cotton Yarn (20S)	113,074	183,568	189,240	583,851	1,245,452
Cotton Yarn (40S)	90,591	83,508	34,378	42,993	147,444
Rubber (RSS3)	710,872	1,404,451	1,546,297	2,835,126	1,200,850
Rubber (TSR20)	66,268	213,758			
Rubber Index	967,915	1,561,707	1,355,731	672,582	382,913
Aluminum	1,438,450	1,695,737	2,218,159	1,107,266	160,060
Total	**3,387,170**	**5,142,913**	**5,352,572**	**5,261,833**	**3,164,947**

Tokyo Commodity Exchange (TOCOM), Japan

	2001	2000	1999	1998	1997
Gold	9,791,711	7,841,692	16,011,962	9,373,909	8,871,965
Silver	660,864	558,770	966,838	1,679,647	792,844
Platinum	16,244,583	13,577,201	13,277,043	16,944,343	10,839,577
Palladium	117,098	1,007,307	5,832,649	5,194,391	3,817,892
Aluminum	735,366	543,015	710,782	305,436	567,175
Gasoline	16,441,056	14,370,266	3,973,668		
Kerosene	8,301,559	6,741,173	1,441,163		
Crude Oil	911,597				
Rubber	3,334,411	6,195,440	6,193,292	9,975,520	4,758,390
Total	**56,538,245**	**50,851,882**	**48,442,161**	**43,589,723**	**30,178,349**

Tokyo International Financial Futures Exchange (TIFFE), Japan

	2001	2000	1999	1998	1997
3-Month Euroyen TIBOR	7,624,711	17,077,791	14,572,255	21,162,012	25,523,583
3-Month Euroyen LIBOR	2,904	8,255	57,479		
U.S. Dollar /Japanese Yen	1,294	3,900	28,681	46,949	63,755
3-Month Euroyen Options	13,553	98,281	271,487	500,002	535,895
Total	**7,642,462**	**17,188,227**	**14,929,902**	**21,708,963**	**26,123,233**

Tokyo Grain Exchange (TGE), Japan

	2001	2000	1999	1998	1997
American Soybeans	1,740,613	2,355,163	3,279,175	3,820,850	9,966,257
Non-GMO Soybeans	3,342,542	2,875,667			
Soybean Meal	268,513				
Arabic Coffee	4,465,044	4,231,369	3,508,798	831,163	
Red Beans	1,093,922	680,751	1,378,169	1,953,618	2,542,760
Corn	10,341,897	8,341,227	8,107,879	7,267,045	13,840,721
Refined Sugar	2,874	2,886	2,842	2,886	2,842
Robusta Coffee	420,873	729,618	699,153	305,160	
Raw Sugar	1,031,530	1,561,657	1,042,427	789,778	1,279,550
American Soybean Options	19,040	84,819	79,955	97,599	263,990
Corn Options	52,012	113,888	141,578	201,269	44,220
Raw Sugar Options	37,544	85,957	153,285	143,434	186,698
Total	**22,816,404**	**21,063,002**	**18,393,261**	**15,412,802**	**28,127,038**

Tokyo Stock Exchange (TSE), Japan

	2001	2000	1999	1998	1997
5-Year Government Yen Bond	2,198	112,226	111,975	195,207	118,447
10-Year Government Yen Bond	7,377,641	9,909,127	9,727,855	10,784,966	11,873,549
TOPIX Stock Index	5,071,946	4,148,776	3,157,441	2,727,070	3,035,724
Electric Appliance Index	350	2,610	182	2,671	
Bank Index	13,298	50,545	25,719	1,127	
TOPIX Options	7,623	2,630	2,030	583	9,356
10-Year Government Yen Bond Options	1,062,235	1,271,887	1,137,319	1,848,851	2,002,357
Total	**13,535,291**	**15,528,865**	**14,162,760**	**15,563,087**	**17,072,250**

Yokohama Commodity Exchange (YCE), Japan

(formerly Maebashi Dried Cocoon & Yokohama Raw Silk Ex.)	2001	2000	1999	1998	1997
Raw Silk	602,727	789,795	704,657	371,732	658,176
Internaional Raw Silk	241,004	387,081			
Dried Cocoon	69,789	208,119	191,048	520,698	565,423
Potato	399,351				
Total	**1,312,871**	**1,384,995**	**895,705**	**892,430**	**1,223,599**

	2001	2000	1999	1998	1997
Total Futures	**1,171,633,033**	**952,905,056**	**781,797,938**	**798,107,856**	**750,548,594**
Percent Change	**22.95%**	**21.89%**	**-2.04%**	**6.34%**	**7.54%**
Total Options	**1,597,068,655**	**722,899,112**	**523,145,631**	**344,862,103**	**275,602,274**
Percent Change	**120.93%**	**38.18%**	**51.70%**	**25.13%**	**-1.22%**
Total	**2,768,701,688**	**1,675,804,168**	**1,304,943,569**	**1,142,969,959**	**1,026,150,868**
Percent Change	**65.22%**	**28.42%**	**14.17%**	**11.38%**	**5.21%**

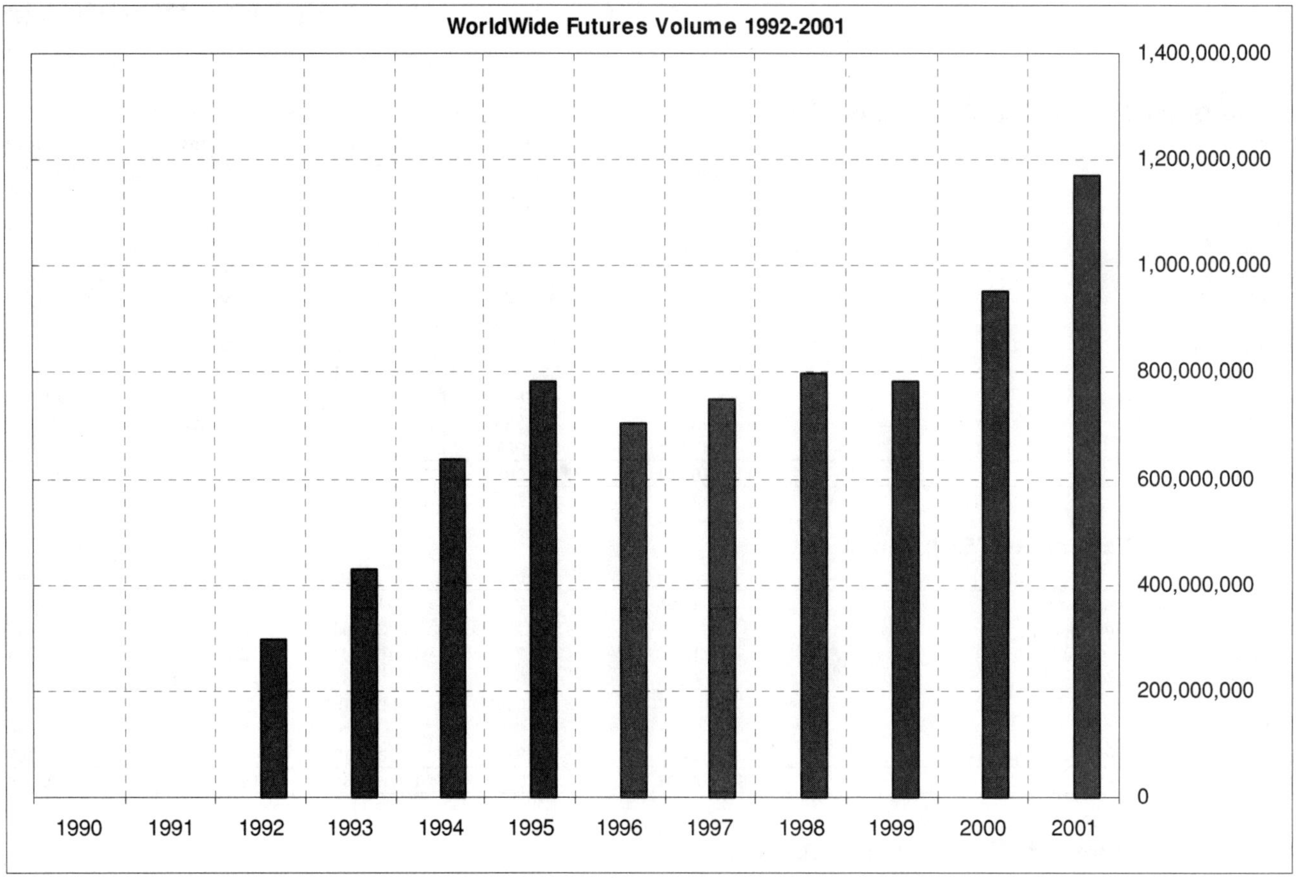

WorldWide Futures Volume 1992-2001

1,400,000,000
1,200,000,000
1,000,000,000
800,000,000
600,000,000
400,000,000
200,000,000
0

1990 1991 1992 1993 1994 1995 1996 1997 1998 1999 2000 2001

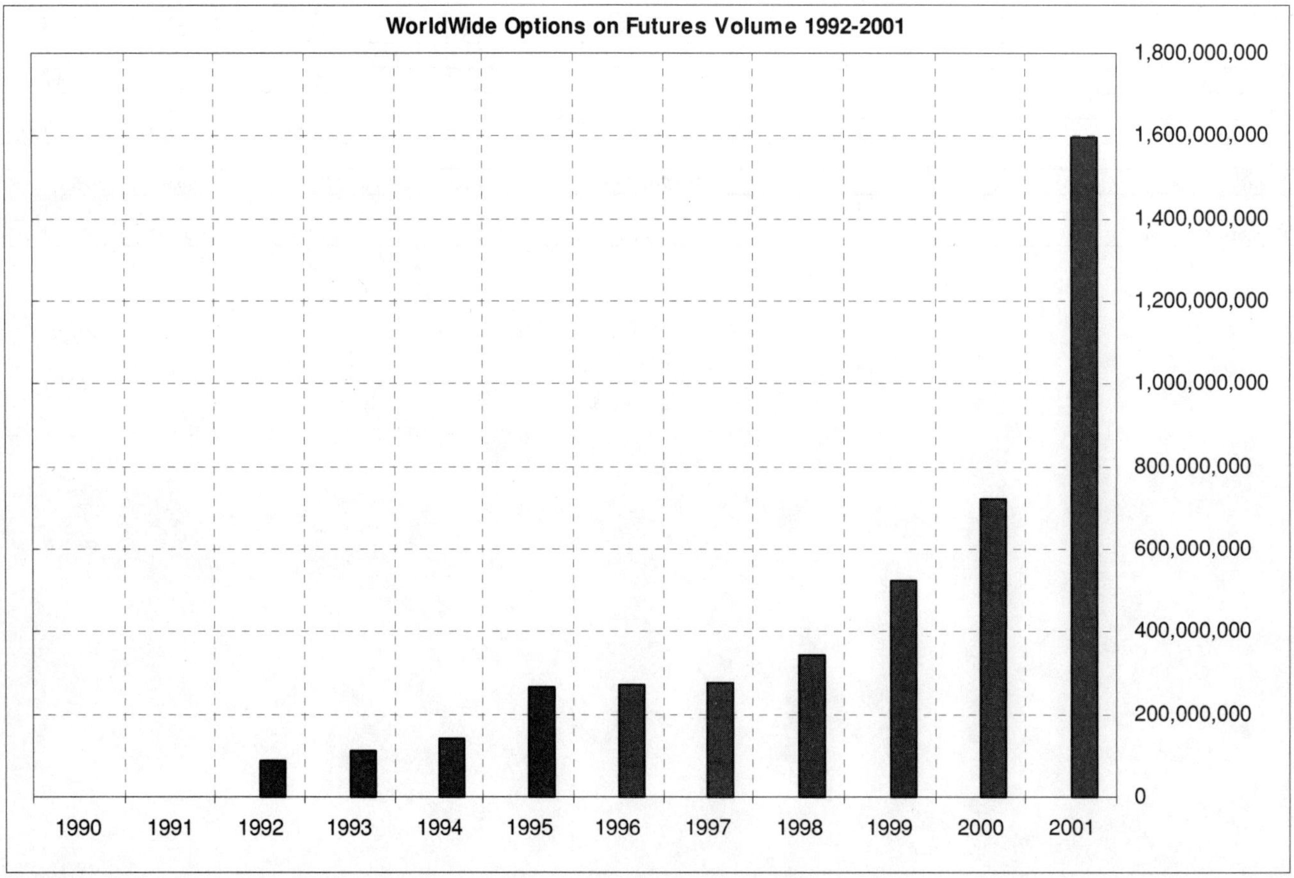

WorldWide Options on Futures Volume 1992-2001

1,800,000,000
1,600,000,000
1,400,000,000
1,200,000,000
1,000,000,000
800,000,000
600,000,000
400,000,000
200,000,000
0

1990 1991 1992 1993 1994 1995 1996 1997 1998 1999 2000 2001

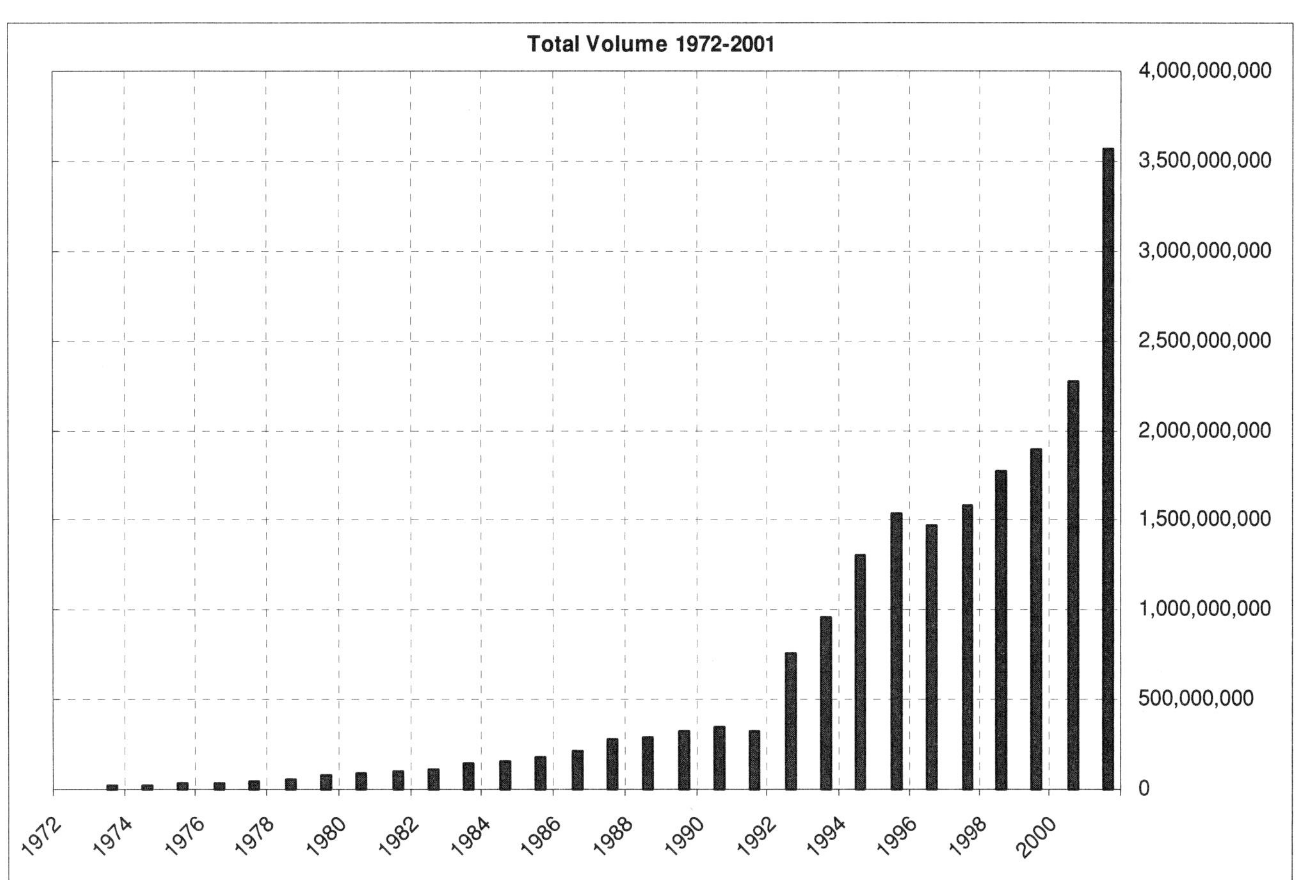
Total Volume 1972-2001
4,000,000,000
3,500,000,000
3,000,000,000
2,500,000,000
2,000,000,000
1,500,000,000
1,000,000,000
500,000,000
0
1972
1974
1976
1978
1980
1982
1984
1986
1988
1990
1992
1994
1996
1998
2000

Conversion Factors

Commonly Used Agricultural Weights and Measurements

Bushel Weights:
wheat and soybeans = 60 lbs.
corn, sorghum and rye = 56 lbs.
barley grain = 48 lbs.
barley malt = 34 lbs.
oats = 32 lbs.

Bushels to tonnes:
wheat and soybeans = bushels X 0.027216
barley grain = bushels X 0.021772
corn, sorghum and rye = bushels X 0.0254
oats = bushels X 0.014515

1 tonne (metric ton) equals:
2204.622 lbs.
1,000 kilograms
22.046 hundredweight
10 quintals

1 tonne (metric ton) equals:
36.7437 bushels of wheat or soybeans
39.3679 bushels of corn, sorghum or rye
45.9296 bushels of barley grain
68.8944 bushels of oats
4.5929 cotton bales (the statistical bale used by the USDA and ICAC contains a net weight of 480 pounds of lint)

Area Measurements:
1 acre = 43,560 square feet = 0.040694 hectare
1 hectare = 2.4710 acres = 10,000 square meters
640 acres = 1 square mile = 259 hectares

Yields:
wheat: bushels per acre X 0.6725 = quintals per hectare
rye, corn: bushels per acre X 0.6277 = quintals per hectare
barley grain: bushels per acre X 0.538 = quintals per hectare
oats: bushels per acre X 0.3587 = quintals per hectare

Commonly Used Weights

The troy, avoirdupois and apothecaries' grains are identical in U.S. and British weight systems, equal to 0.0648 gram in the metric system. One avoirdupois ounce equals 437.5 grains. The troy and apothecaries' ounces equal 480 grains, and their pounds contain 12 ounces.

Troy weights and conversions: 100 kilograms = 1 quintal
24 grains = 1 pennyweight
20 pennyweights = 1 ounce
12 ounces = 1 pound
1 troy ounce = 31.103 grams
1 troy ounce = 0.0311033 kilogram
1 troy pound = 0.37224 kilogram
1 kilogram = 32.1507 troy ounces
1 tonne = 32,151 troy ounces

Avoirdupois weights and conversions:
27 11/32 grains = 1 dram
16 drams = 1 ounce
16 ounces = 1 lb.
1 lb. = 7,000 grains
14 lbs. = 1 stone (British)
100 lbs. = 1 hundredweight (U.S.)
112 lbs. = 8 stone = 1 hundredweight (British)
2,000 lbs. = 1 short ton (U.S. ton)
2,240 lbs. = 1 long ton (British ton)
160 stone = 1 long ton
20 hundredweight = 1 ton
1 lb. = 0.4536 kilogram
1 hundredweight (cwt.) = 45.359 kilograms
1 short ton = 907.18 kilograms
1 long ton = 1,016.05 kilograms

Metric weights and conversions:
1,000 grams = 1 kilogram

1 tonne = 1,000 kilograms = 10 quintals
1 kilogram = 2.204622 lbs.
1 quintal = 220.462 lbs.
1 tonne = 2204.6 lbs.
1 tonne = 1.102 short tons
1 tonne = 0.9842 long ton

U.S. dry volumes and conversions:
1 pint = 33.6 cubic inches = 0.5506 liter
2 pints = 1 quart = 1.1012 liters
8 quarts = 1 peck = 8.8098 liters
4 pecks = 1 bushel = 35.2391 liters
1 cubic foot = 28.3169 liters

U.S. liquid volumes and conversions:
1 ounce = 1.8047 cubic inches = 29.6 milliliters
1 cup = 8 ounces = 0.24 liter = 237 milliliters
1 pint = 16 ounces = 0.48 liter = 473 milliliters
1 quart = 2 pints = 0.946 liter = 946 milliliters
1 gallon = 4 quarts = 231 cubic inches = 3.785 liters
1 milliliter = 0.033815 fluid ounce
1 liter = 1.0567 quarts = 1,000 milliliters
1 liter = 33.815 fluid ounces
1 imperial gallon = 277.42 cubic inches = 1.2 U.S. gallons = 4.546 liters

ENERGY CONVERSION FACTORS

U.S. Crude Oil (average gravity)
1 U.S. barrel = 42 U.S. gallons
1 short ton = 6.65 barrels
1 tonne = 7.33 barrels

Barrels per tonne for various origins

Abu Dhabi	7.624
Algeria	7.661
Angola	7.206
Australia	7.775
Bahrain	7.335
Brunei	7.334
Canada	7.428
Dubai	7.295
Ecuador	7.58
Gabon	7.245
Indonesia	7.348
Iran	7.37
Iraq	7.453
Kuwait	7.261
Libya	7.615
Mexico	7.104
Neutral Zone	6.825
Nigeria	7.41
Norway	7.444
Oman	7.39
Qatar	7.573
Romania	7.453
Saudi Arabia	7.338
Trinidad	6.989
Tunisia	7.709
United Arab Emirates	7.522
United Kingdom	7.279
United States	7.418
Former Soviet Union	7.35
Venezuela	7.005
Zaire	7.206

Barrels per tonne of refined products:

aviation gasoline	8.9
motor gasoline	8.5
kerosene	7.75
jet fuel	8
distillate, including diesel	7.46
residual fuel oil	6.45
lubricating oil	7
grease	6.3
white spirits	8.5
paraffin oil	7.14
paraffin wax	7.87
petrolatum	7.87
asphalt and road oil	6.06
petroleum coke	5.5
bitumen	6.06
LPG	11.6

(continued above)

Approximate heat content of refined products:
(Million Btu per barrel, 1 British thermal unit is the amount of heat required to raise the temperature of 1 pound of water 1 degree F.)

Petroleum Product	**Heat Content**
asphalt	6.636
aviation gasoline	5.048
butane	4.326
distillate fuel oil	5.825
ethane	3.082
isobutane	3.974
jet fuel, kerosene	5.67
jet fuel, naptha	5.355
kerosene	5.67
lubricants	6.065
motor gasoline	5.253
natural gasoline	4.62
pentanes plus	4.62

Petrochemical feedstocks:

naptha less than 401*F	5.248
other oils equal to or greater than 401*F	5.825
still gas	6
petroleum coke	6.024
plant condensate	5.418
propane	3.836
residual fuel oil	6.287
special napthas	5.248
unfinished oils	5.825
unfractionated steam	5.418
waxes	5.537

Source: U.S. Department of Energy

Natural Gas Conversions

Although there are approximately 1,031 Btu in a cubic foot of gas, for most applications, the following conversions are sufficient:

Cubic Feet					**MMBtu**
1,000	(one thousand cubic feet)	=	1 Mcf	=	1
1,000,000	(one million cubic feet)	=	1 MMcf	=	1,000
10,000,000	(ten million cubic feet)	=	10 MMcf	=	10,000
1,000,000,000	(one billion cubic feet)	=	1 Bcf	=	1,000,000
1,000,000,000,000	(one trillion cubic feet)	=	1 Tcf	=	1,000,000,000

Aluminum

The U.S. Geological Survey reported that world smelter production of aluminum in 2000 was 23.9 million metric tonnes, up 3 percent from the previous year. The U.S. was the world's largest producer of aluminum with production in 2000 estimated to be 3.7 million tonnes, down 2 percent from 1999. The next largest producer was Russia with 2000 output of 3.2 million tonnes, up 2 percent from 1999. Production by China was 2.6 million tonnes, up 6 percent from the previous year. Production by Canada was 2.4 million tonnes, down 1 percent from 1999. Other large aluminum producers include Australia, Brazil, and Norway. The U.S. production capacity was 4.3 million tonnes while Russia had capacity of 3.2 million tonnes. Other countries with large production capacities include China, Canada and Australia.

In the U.S., in 2000, 12 companies operated 23 primary aluminum reduction plants. Montana, Oregon, and Washington accounted for 33 percent of production. Of the U.S. domestic consumption, transportation accounted for 37 percent while container and packaging accounted for 24 percent of total use. Other users of aluminum were the building and construction industry, consumer durables and electrical industry.

U.S. primary production of aluminum in August 2001 was 212,000 tonnes, down 28 percent from the same month a year ago. In the January-August 2001 period, U.S. primary production of aluminum was 1.8 million tonnes, down 28 percent from the same period in 2000. For all of 2000, U.S. primary production of aluminum was 3.7 million tonnes.

There is substantial recovery of aluminum from secondary sources. In August 2001, secondary recovery of aluminum totaled 267,000 tonnes. Of the total, 162,000 tonnes came from new sources while 106,000 tonnes came from old sources. In the January-August 2001 period, aluminum recovered from secondary sources totaled 2.09 million tonnes, with 1.26 million tonnes from new sources and 829,000 tonnes from old sources. For all of 1999, secondary recovery of aluminum totaled 3.45 million tonnes of which 60 percent came from new sources and 40 percent from old sources.

U.S. imports for consumption of aluminum crude metal and alloys in July 2001 were 201,000 tonnes, up 12 percent from the previous month. In the January-July 2001 period, imports totaled 1.42 million tonnes. for all of 2000, metal and alloy imports totaled 2.49 million tonnes. Imports of aluminum plates, sheets and bars in July 2001 were 55,000 tonnes, the same as the previous month. In the January-July 2001 period, imports of plates, sheets and bars were 411,000 tonnes while for all of 2000 they were 791,000 tonnes. Total aluminum imports for consumption in July 2001 were 257,000 tonnes while in the January-July 2001 period they were 1.83 million tonnes. In 2000 imports totaled 3.28 million tonnes. The total new supply (primary production, secondary recovery and imports for consumption) in July 2001 were 730,000 tonnes. For 2000, the total new supply was 10.4 million tonnes.

U.S. exports of aluminum in July 2001 were 120,000 tonnes. In the January-July 2001 period exports were 924,000 tonnes. The major export destinations were Canada, Mexico, China and South Korea. Exports of aluminum scrap in July 2001 were 48,000 tonnes while in the January-July 2001 period they were 323,000 tonnes. U.S. stocks of July 2001 were 1.48 million tonnes.

Futures Markets

Aluminum futures and options are listed on the London Metals Exchange (LME), the New York Mercantile Exchange (NYMEX), the Shanghai Metal Exchange (SME), and the Tokyo Commodity Exchange (TOCOM).

World Production of Primary Aluminum In Thousands of Metric Tons

Year	Australia	Brazil	Canada	China	France	Germany	Norway	Russia	Spain	United Kingdom	United States	Venezuela	World Total
1992	1,236	1,193	1,972	1,100	418	603	838	2,700	359	244	4,042	561	19,532
1993	1,381	1,172	2,308	1,220	426	552	887	2,820	364	239	3,695	568	19,773
1994	1,317	1,185	2,255	1,450	437	505	857	2,670	338	231	3,299	585	19,211
1995	1,297	1,188	2,172	1,680	372	575	847	2,724	361	238	3,375	630	19,668
1996	1,372	1,195	2,283	1,770	380	576	863	2,874	362	240	3,577	629	20,800
1997	1,495	1,200	2,327	1,960	399	572	919	2,906	360	248	3,603	634	21,700
1998	1,627	1,208	2,374	2,340	424	612	996	3,005	362	258	3,713	585	22,600
1999[1]	1,718	1,250	2,390	2,530	455	634	1,020	3,146	364	272	3,779	570	23,600
2000[2]	1,769	1,277	2,373	2,550	441	644	1,026	3,245	366	305	3,668	570	24,000

[1] Preliminary. [2] Estimate. *Source: U.S. Geological Survey (USGS)*

Production of Primary Aluminum (Domestic and Foreign Ores) in the U.S. In Thousands of Metric Tons

Year	Jan.	Feb.	Mar.	Apr.	May	June	July	Aug.	Sept.	Oct.	Nov.	Dec.	Total
1992	344	320	343	330	342	330	339	340	330	343	335	347	4,042
1993	335	292	323	313	325	315	316	302	291	303	287	294	3,695
1994	293	261	286	269	277	268	275	274	267	277	270	280	3,299
1995	281	253	280	272	285	277	288	286	280	289	285	299	3,375
1996	301	283	303	293	303	293	301	302	292	304	295	305	3,577
1997	305	277	307	295	304	296	305	304	294	307	298	310	3,603
1998	309	280	312	305	316	307	319	318	309	315	307	317	3,713
1999	315	287	320	309	319	310	319	324	310	323	316	328	3,779
2000	329	308	327	316	327	299	296	296	291	300	289	291	3,668
2001[1]	256	220	232	225	229	215	214	212	206	214	208		2,652

[1] Preliminary. *Source: U.S. Geological Survey (USGS)*

ALUMINUM

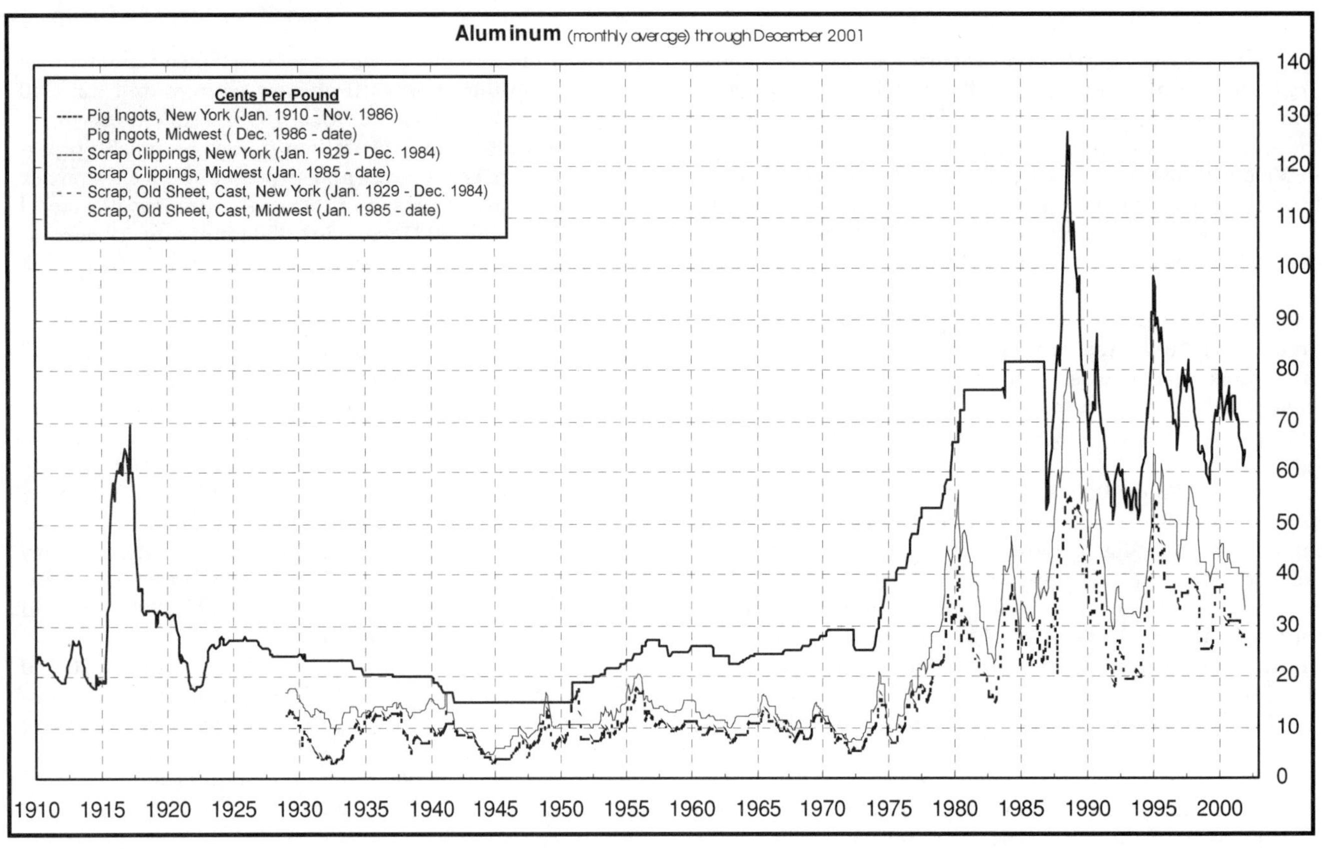

Salient Statistics of Aluminum in the United States In Thousands of Metric Tons

								Net Shipments[5] by Producers								
								Wrought Products				Castings				
Year	Net Import Reliance as a % of Apparent Consumption	Production Primary	Production Secondary	Primary Shipments	Recovery from Scrap OLd	Recovery from Scrap New	Apparent Consumption	Plate, Sheet, Foil	Rolled Structural Shapes[3]	Extruded Shapes[4]	All	Permanent Mold	Die	Sand	All	Total All Net Shipments
1991	E	4,121	2,286	6,354	1,320	969	5,043	3,787	311	1,096	5,300	168	575	97	864	6,156
1992	1	4,042	2,756	6,847	1,610	1,144	5,715	4,097	303	1,186	5,691	198	595	99	804	6,609
1993	19	3,695	2,944	7,326	1,630	1,312	6,612	4,030	297	1,300	5,770	225	645	103	994	6,770
1994	30	3,299	3,086	8,169	1,500	1,583	6,879	4,810	296	1,420	6,690	247	551	208	1,050	7,740
1995	23	3,375	3,189	8,258	1,510	1,684	6,295	4,900	526	1,540	7,130	442	627	207	1,440	8,580
1996	22	3,577	3,310	8,330	1,570	1,730	6,610	4,430	350	1,540	6,480	473	612	180	1,390	7,860
1997	23	3,603	3,550	8,880	1,530	2,020	6,720	4,710	315	1,610	6,800	468	670	153	1,410	8,210
1998	25	3,713	3,440	9,260	1,500	1,950	7,090	4,760	551	1,560	7,040	511	584	134	1,350	8,390
1999[1]	30	3,779	3,690	9,840	1,570	2,120	7,770	5,000	549	1,640	7,360	533	1,030	158	1,850	9,210
2000[1]	33	3,668	3,450	9,840	1,370	2,080	7,530	4,840	303	1,920	7,230	NA	NA	NA	NA	NA

[1] Preliminary. [2] To domestic industry. [3] Also rod, bar & wire. [4] Also rod, bar, tube, blooms & tubing. [5] Consists of total shipments less shipments to other mills for further fabrication. NA = Not available. E = Net exporter. *Source: U.S. Geological Survey (USGS)*

Supply and Distribution of Aluminum in the United States In Thousands of Metric Tons

Year	Apparent Consumption	Production Primary	Production From Old Scrap	Imports	Exports	Inventories December 31 Private	Inventories December 31 Government[2]	Year	Apparent Consumption	Production Primary	Production From Old Scrap	Imports	Exports	Inventories December 31 Private	Inventories December 31 Government[2]
1989	4,957	4,030	1,011	1,470	1,615	1,824	2	1995	6,295	3,375	1,505	2,975	1,610	2,099	57
1990	5,264	4,048	1,359	1,514	1,659	1,822	2	1996	6,610	3,577	1,570	2,810	1,500	1,860	57
1991	5,043	4,121	1,317	1,490	1,762	1,945	2	1997	6,720	3,603	1,530	3,080	1,570	1,860	[4]
1992	5,715	4,042	1,612	1,725	1,453	2,156	57	1998	7,090	3,713	1,500	3,550	1,590	1,930	----
1993	6,612	3,695	1,632	2,545	1,207	2,209	57	1999[1]	7,770	3,779	1,570	4,000	1,640	1,870	----
1994	6,879	3,299	1,503	3,382	1,365	2,149	57	2000[2]	7,530	3,668	1,370	3,910	1,760	1,550	----

[1] Preliminary. [2] Estimate. [3] National Defense Stockpile. [4] Less than 1/2 unit. Source: U.S. Geological Survey (USGS)

Aluminum Products Distribution of End-Use Shipments in the United States In Thousands of Metric Tons

Year	Building & Construction	Consumer Durables	Containers & Packaging	Electrical	Exports	Machinery & Equipment	Trans-portaion	Other	Total
1991	1,052	472	2,210	579	1,357	426	1,414	241	7,752
1992	1,144	523	2,259	587	1,236	448	1,591	256	8,045
1993	1,240	563	2,180	609	1,090	477	1,970	259	8,390
1994	1,400	647	2,270	682	1,200	572	2,310	276	9,360
1995	1,220	621	2,310	657	1,310	570	2,610	279	9,570
1996	1,330	655	2,180	671	1,290	569	2,640	291	9,610
1997	1,320	694	2,220	708	1,360	626	2,990	318	10,200
1998	1,390	725	2,270	714	1,260	629	3,250	273	10,500
1999	1,470	760	2,320	739	1,330	661	3,600	293	11,200
2000[1]	1,450	770	2,260	770	1,270	679	3,610	293	11,100

[1] Preliminary. *Source: U.S. Geological Survey (USGS)*

World Consumption of Primary Aluminum In Thousands of Metric Tons

Year	Brazil	Canada	China	France	Germany	India	Italy	Japan	Rep. of Korea	Russia	United Kingdom	United States	World Total
1991	354.2	408.2	938.0	725.9	1,360.9	430.2	670.0	2,431.6	383.5	2,409.0	412.4	4,137.2	18,778.2
1992	377.1	420.4	1,253.8	730.5	1,457.1	414.3	660.0	2,271.6	397.0	1,242.0	550.0	4,616.9	18,529.5
1993	378.9	492.5	1,339.9	667.2	1,150.7	475.3	554.0	2,138.3	524.8	657.0	540.0	4,877.1	18,122.6
1994	414.1	559.0	1,500.1	736.3	1,370.3	475.0	660.0	2,344.8	603.9	470.0	570.0	5,407.1	19,670.8
1995	500.6	611.9	1,941.6	743.8	1,491.3	581.0	665.4	2,335.6	675.4	476.0	620.0	5,054.8	20,480.9
1996	497.0	619.9	2,135.3	671.7	1,355.4	584.8	585.1	2,392.6	674.3	443.8	571.0	5,348.0	20,660.0
1997	478.6	628.2	2,260.3	724.2	1,558.4	553.4	671.0	2,434.3	666.3	469.2	583.0	5,390.0	21,855.0
1998	521.4	733.5	2,425.4	734.0	1,519.0	566.5	673.5	2,079.9	505.7	489.2	579.0	5,813.6	21,842.0
1999	463.1	773.7	2,926.0	786.0	1,520.0	548.0	735.0	2,099.7	814.0	563.0	581.0	6,203.3	23,580.0
2000[1]	520.0	812.0	3,533.0	777.0	1,632.0	548.0	780.0	2,223.0	823.0	759.0	576.0	5,833.0	24,774.0

[1] Preliminary. *Source: American Metal Market (AMM)*

Salient Statistics of Recycling Aluminum in the United States

Year	Percent Recycled	New Scrap[1]	Old Scrap[2]	Recycled Metal[3]	Apparent Supply	New Scrap[1]	Old Scrap[2]	Recycled Metal[3]	Apparent Supply
		In Thousands of Metric Tons				Value in Millions of Dollars			
1991	38	969	1,320	2,290	6,010	1,270	1,730	3,000	7,880
1992	40	1,140	1,610	2,760	6,870	1,450	2,040	3,500	8,710
1993	37	1,310	1,630	2,940	7,920	1,540	1,920	3,460	9,300
1994	36	1,580	1,500	3,090	8,460	2,480	2,360	4,840	13,300
1995	40	1,680	1,510	3,190	7,980	3,190	2,850	6,040	15,100
1996	40	1,730	1,570	3,310	8,340	2,730	2,480	5,200	13,100
1997	41	2,020	1,530	3,550	8,740	3,430	2,590	6,020	14,800
1998	38	1,950	1,500	3,440	9,040	2,810	2,160	4,970	13,100
1999	37	2,120	1,570	3,700	9,890	3,070	2,280	5,350	14,300
2000	36	2,080	1,370	3,450	9,610	3,420	2,260	5,670	15,800

[1] Scrap that results from the manufacturing process. [2] Scrap that results from consumer products. [3] Metal recovered from new plus old scrap.
Source: U.S. Geological Survey (USGS)

Producer Prices for Aluminum Used Beverage Can Scrap In Cents Per Pound

Year	Jan.	Feb.	Mar.	Apr.	May	June	July	Aug.	Sept.	Oct.	Nov.	Dec.	Average
1991	49.00	49.11	48.67	42.09	37.86	37.00	39.79	37.50	37.50	35.76	35.18	34.50	40.33
1992	35.38	38.32	40.73	43.91	44.40	41.50	41.50	41.69	39.93	38.07	38.00	38.68	40.18
1993	41.00	41.00	38.04	36.63	35.00	35.00	37.52	37.59	36.50	34.19	33.60	34.78	36.74
1994	38.45	43.08	42.50	46.60	45.50	48.98	56.40	56.00	56.00	62.64	70.40	71.00	53.13
1995	74.85	72.24	65.00	65.00	65.00	65.00	65.00	67.98	64.80	58.45	57.00	58.50	64.91
1996	57.73	56.00	56.24	58.90	59.00	49.70	47.50	49.25	50.20	48.50	49.03	53.50	52.96
1997	56.98	59.00	59.00	58.27	58.05	58.05	58.32	59.60	59.50	59.13	59.00	57.12	58.50
1998	54.53	57.00	57.00	52.95	49.85	47.09	45.50	44.50	46.21	44.50	44.50	46.14	49.15
1999	44.50	44.50	44.20	45.68	47.45	46.50	48.40	49.00	49.00	53.79	55.50	57.64	48.84
2000	58.58	62.90	61.50	56.85	54.50	54.50	56.50	57.00	57.00	56.20	53.50	53.50	56.88

Source: American Metal Market (AMM)

Average Price of Cast Aluminum Scrap (Crank Cases) in Chicago In Cents Per Pound

Year	Jan.	Feb.	Mar.	Apr.	May	June	July	Aug.	Sept.	Oct.	Nov.	Dec.	Average
1992	18.71	23.00	26.91	27.00	24.45	24.00	24.00	24.00	21.21	19.50	19.50	19.50	22.65
1993	19.50	19.50	19.50	19.50	19.50	19.50	20.79	21.00	20.62	20.00	20.00	20.00	19.95
1994	20.00	25.79	28.33	32.50	32.50	33.18	35.90	36.50	41.07	44.45	50.50	53.50	36.19
1995	53.53	54.08	49.02	48.50	44.41	42.50	43.76	45.80	45.05	39.27	37.50	37.50	45.08
1996	37.50	37.50	37.50	37.50	37.50	37.50	37.50	36.50	35.40	33.80	33.50	33.50	36.27
1997	36.09	36.50	36.50	36.50	36.50	36.50	36.50	39.36	38.60	38.50	38.50	38.07	37.34
1998	37.50	37.50	37.50	35.95	35.50	31.59	25.50	25.50	25.50	25.50	25.50	25.50	30.71
1999	25.50	25.50	25.50	25.50	26.45	29.23	36.83	37.50	37.50	37.50	37.50	37.50	31.87
2000	37.50	37.50	37.50	35.55	31.09	30.32	30.30	32.00	32.00	31.09	31.00	31.00	33.04
2001	31.00	31.00	31.00	31.00	31.00	31.00	28.29	28.00	28.00	28.00	26.40	26.00	29.25

Source: American Metal Market (AMM)

Aluminum Exports of Crude Metal and Alloys from the United States In Thousands of Metric Tons

Year	Jan.	Feb.	Mar.	Apr.	May	June	July	Aug.	Sept.	Oct.	Nov.	Dec.	Total
1992	50.8	43.8	49.7	38.6	33.6	39.8	50.0	50.3	40.4	82.1	50.5	73.5	603.1
1993	54.8	38.6	41.7	26.3	38.6	30.7	33.9	24.5	27.9	31.7	24.1	27.6	400.4
1994	22.1	18.3	28.3	17.9	37.5	30.5	30.6	38.3	40.3	24.8	26.1	24.1	338.9
1995	26.1	32.7	25.4	31.1	31.4	20.7	26.6	39.2	38.9	33.0	30.4	33.6	369.1
1996	23.1	27.9	31.2	34.3	46.2	54.3	36.3	33.7	30.2	40.3	33.2	26.2	416.9
1997	31.0	25.5	22.5	33.0	24.1	34.9	23.9	33.2	34.4	26.5	33.0	30.0	352.0
1998	21.2	21.4	21.8	17.4	22.6	21.8	20.9	21.5	28.0	23.9	20.4	24.7	265.6
1999	18.6	26.7	23.9	22.7	25.2	27.7	23.7	27.5	26.1	31.4	30.3	34.8	318.6
2000	18.7	27.2	30.2	21.9	24.4	22.4	20.5	24.2	20.5	20.7	20.7	21.6	273.0
2001[1]	19.6	16.1	18.9	14.7	16.8	15.6	12.4	14.5	12.6	18.9			192.1

[1] Preliminary. *Source: U.S. Geological Survey (USGS)*

Aluminum General Imports of Crude Metal and Alloys into the United States In Thousands of Metric Tons

Year	Jan.	Feb.	Mar.	Apr.	May	June	July	Aug.	Sept.	Oct.	Nov.	Dec.	Total
1992	100.7	93.1	97.1	94.6	96.3	87.8	82.4	103.4	94.3	108.4	100.5	96.8	1,155.4
1993	120.8	123.9	165.8	172.0	152.1	152.6	125.1	162.7	173.5	149.4	182.9	155.6	1,836.4
1994	200.2	157.8	282.0	206.9	251.9	179.3	202.8	198.3	160.0	183.4	240.1	222.2	2,484.9
1995	214.0	168.0	204.0	195.0	184.0	172.0	136.0	134.0	117.0	137.0	139.0	133.0	1,933.0
1996	158.0	150.0	148.0	188.0	176.0	169.0	139.0	149.0	136.0	170.0	147.0	180.0	1,910.0
1997	145.0	147.0	209.0	196.0	198.0	167.0	157.0	152.0	150.0	175.0	146.0	222.0	2,060.0
1998	220.0	204.0	202.0	200.0	189.0	243.0	170.0	204.0	198.0	198.0	189.0	177.0	2,394.0
1999	191.0	200.0	240.0	311.0	281.0	258.0	213.0	219.0	178.0	202.0	178.0	180.0	2,651.0
2000	246.0	213.0	206.0	211.0	233.0	234.0	250.0	206.0	189.0	186.0	181.0	137.0	2,490.0
2001[1]	193.0	200.0	237.0	197.0	209.0	179.0	201.0	198.0	252.0	220.0			2,503.2

[1] Preliminary. *Source: U.S. Geological Survey (USGS)*

Average Open Interest of Aluminum Futures in New York In Contracts

Year	Jan.	Feb.	Mar.	Apr.	May	June	July	Aug.	Sept.	Oct.	Nov.	Dec.
1999	----	----	----	----	1,032	1,461	1,875	1,984	1,767	1,244	625	615
2000	794	580	254	326	965	2,035	3,938	4,803	4,580	4,598	3,587	2,046
2001	2,446	3,173	3,450	3,529	3,269	3,724	3,891	3,459	2,753	3,728	3,644	3,276

Source: New York Mercantile Exchange (NYMEX), COMEX Division

Volume of Trading of Aluminum Futures in New York In Contracts

Year	Jan.	Feb.	Mar.	Apr.	May	June	July	Aug.	Sept.	Oct.	Nov.	Dec.	Total
1999	----	----	----	----	6,179	5,875	5,275	3,373	3,114	2,801	639	722	27,978
2000	1,224	2,394	1,664	1,901	3,859	3,566	6,295	3,767	5,993	6,365	5,055	4,016	46,099
2001	7,361	1,694	4,410	2,822	2,853	4,634	4,404	3,794	1,428	2,887	4,251	2,551	43,089

Source: New York Mercantile Exchange (NYMEX), COMEX Division

Antimony

Antimony is primarily a byproduct of the mining, smelting and refining of lead and silver-copper ores. In the U.S., one silver mine in Idaho produced antimony as a byproduct. Primary antimony metal and oxide was produced by five companies at processing plants that used foreign feedstock and a small amount of domestic feed materials. Antimony is used in the production of flame retardants, ceramics, glass, ammunition, and chemicals.

The world's largest producer of antimony by far is China which accounts for over 80 percent of the world supply. Other producers of antimony include Russia, Bolivia and South Africa. Because of the large production by China, other producers have had difficulty competing as prices have declined. In the January-May 2001 period, Chinese antimony production was put at 51,000 metric tonnes, up 29 percent from 2000, based on data from China.

The U.S. Geological Survey reports that U.S. production of primary smelter antimony in year 2000 was 20,900 tonnes. Nearly all smelter output is antimony trioxide. Data for 2001 was withheld. Secondary production of antimony in 2000 was 7,920 tonnes. Data was not available for 2001.

U.S. imports for consumption of antimony in the January-May 2001 period were 18,330 tonnes. For all of 2001, imports were 41,600 tonnes. Imports of antimony ore and concentrate in the January-May period were 1,637 tonnes. For 2000 they were 3,690 tonnes. The major suppliers were China and Australia. Imports of antimony metal in January-May 2001 were 4,270 tonnes and in 2000 they were 14,200 tonnes. The major suppliers of metal were China, Hong Kong, Mexico and Peru. Imports of antimony oxide in the first five months of 2001 were 12,400 tonnes. In 2000 they were 23,700 tonnes. The major suppliers were China, Mexico, Belgium and South Africa.

U.S. exports of metal, alloys and scrap in the first quarter of 2001 were 579 tonnes and for 2000 they were 1,080 tonnes. Antimony oxide exports in first quarter 2001 were 2,330 tonnes and in 2000 the total was 6,040 tonnes. U.S. consumption of primary antimony in the first half of 2001 was 7,840 tonnes. For 2000 consumption was 16,700 tonnes.

World Mine Production of Antimony (Content of Ore) In Metric Tons

Year	Australia	Bolivia	Canada	China[2]	Guatemala	Kyrgyzstan	Mexico[3]	Peru[4]	Russia	South Africa	Thailand	Turkey	World Total
1997	1,900	5,999	529	131,000	880	1,200	1,909	460	6,000	3,415	53	31	155,000
1998	1,800	4,735	428	97,400	440	150	1,301	460	4,000	4,243	199	30	117,000
1999[1]	2,300	2,790	357	89,600	440	100	273	460	4,000	5,278	59	180	108,000
2000[2]	1,800	2,800	364	100,000	450	150	52	460	4,500	5,000	84	360	118,000

[1] Preliminary. [2] Estimate. [3] Includes antimony content of miscellaneous smelter products. [4] Recoverable.
Source: U.S. Geological Survey (USGS)

Salient Statistics of Antimony in the United States In Metric Tons

		Production[3]			Imports for Consumption				Industry Stocks, December 31[3]				
		Primary[2]			Ore								
Year	Avg. Price cents/lb. CIF U.S. Ports	Mine	Smelter	Secondary (Alloys)[2]	Gross Weight	Antimony Content	Oxide (Gross Weight)	Exports (Oxide)	Metallic	Oxide	Sulfide	Other	Total[4]
1997	97.8	356	26,400	7,550	1,530	1,300	27,900	3,230	3,070	4,530	W	3,240	10,800
1998	71.8	489	24,000	7,710	2,640	2,020	23,000	3,270	2,920	4,610	W	3,060	10,600
1999[1]	62.7	450	23,800	8,220	3,590	2,870	23,100	3,190	2,430	5,780	W	2,720	10,900
2000[2]	65.5	W	20,900	7,920	4,630	3,690	28,500	6,040	2,570	4,880	W	2,860	10,300

[1] Preliminary. [2] Estimate. [3] Antimony content. [4] Including primary antimony residues & slag. W = Withheld proprietary data.
Source: U.S. Geological Survey (USGS)

Industrial Consumption of Primary Antimony in the United States In Metric Tons (Antimony Content)

	Metal Products						Non-Metal Products						
							Retardents						
Year	Ammunition	Antimonial Lead	Sheet & Pipe	Bearing Metal & Bearings	Solder	Total All Metal Products	Plastics	Total	Ceramics & Glass	Pigments	Plastics	Total	Grand Total
1997	W	1,180	W	45	226	2,600	6,610	7,560	1,080	824	1,230	3,310	13,500
1998	W	1,710	W	33	153	2,580	5,460	6,190	1,110	1,130	1,460	3,910	12,700
1999	W	1,110	W	29	136	2,440	6,370	7,140	1,120	1,020	1,580	3,940	13,500
2000[1]	W	864	W	42	136	2,700	8,920	9,930	862	620	1,960	4,110	16,700

[1] Preliminary. [2] Estimated coverage based on 77% of the industry. W=Withheld proprietary data. *Source: U.S. Geological Survey (USGS)*

Average Price of Antimony[1] in the United States In Cents Per Pound

Year	Jan.	Feb.	Mar.	Apr.	May	June	July	Aug.	Sept.	Oct.	Nov.	Dec.	Average
1998	80.00	80.00	80.00	80.00	74.38	71.25	66.25	61.50	62.50	65.00	65.00	65.00	70.91
1999	65.00	65.00	65.00	65.55	66.50	66.50	66.50	66.50	66.50	66.50	66.50	66.50	66.05
2000	66.50	66.50	66.50	66.50	66.50	66.50	68.38	69.00	84.40	91.00	91.00	91.00	74.48
2001	84.90	75.00	75.00	75.00	75.00	75.00	75.00	75.00	73.26	69.50	69.50	69.50	74.31

[1] Prices are for antimony metal (99.65%) merchants, minimum 18-ton containers, c.i.f. U.S. Ports. *Source: American Metal Market (AMM)*

Apples

The U.S. Department of Agriculture reported that U.S. apple bearing acreage in 2000 was estimated at 451,000 acres, down 2 percent from the 1999 acreage of 461,300. The state with the highest acreage was Washington with 172,000 acres, the same as in 1999. The second highest acreage state was New York with 55,000, also the same as in 1999. Michigan acreage was 50,500, down 4 percent from 1999. Other states with high apple bearing acreage include California, Pennsylvania and Virginia.

For 2000, the U.S. average yield per acre was 23,500 pounds, an increase of 2 percent from the previous year. The yield in 1998 was 24,900 pounds. The highest yielding state in 2000 was Washington with 33,100 pounds., an increase of 14 percent from 1999. The next highest yielding state was Idaho with 27,800 pounds, followed by Arizona with 24,400 pounds and California with 23,500.

U.S. commercial production in 2000 was estimated at 10.598 billion pounds, down less than 1 percent from the 1999 output of 10.63 billion pounds. The largest commercial apple producing state by far is Washington with 5.7 billion pounds, up 14 percent from 1999's crop of 5 billion pounds. The New York crop was 1.05 billion pounds, down 17 percent from 1999. Michigan's crop of 850 million pounds was down 29 percent from 1999.

World Production of Apples[3], Fresh (Dessert & Cooking) In Thousands of Metric Tons

Year	Argentina	Canada	France	Germany	Hungary	Italy	Japan	Netherlands	South Africa	Spain	Turkey	United States	World Total
1991-2	1,043	513	1,236	1,165	859	1,869	760	223	605	517	1,900	4,413	18,250
1992-3	947	564	2,398	3,228	666	2,394	1,039	640	633	1,095	2,100	4,798	35,443
1993-4	1,006	488	2,079	1,719	819	2,145	1,011	670	638	891	2,080	4,847	36,505
1994-5	1,146	554	2,166	2,080	610	2,153	989	590	577	739	2,095	5,217	37,712
1995-6	1,254	608	2,089	1,373	353	1,889	963	595	703	843	2,100	4,801	36,443
1996-7	1,300	513	2,047	1,878	552	2,025	899	490	639	894	2,200	4,714	40,825
1997-8	1,202	503	2,027	1,465	500	2,014	993	470	671	880	2,550	4,683	40,564
1998-9	1,316	523	1,794	1,980	482	2,243	879	507	675	722	2,450	5,283	42,477
1999-00[1]	829	582	2,166	1,936	470	2,196	928	575	709	887	2,500	4,799	43,179
2000-1[2]	----	522	2,140	2,428	530	2,165	863	510	----	719	2,500	4,845	----

[1] Preliminary. [2] Estimate. [3] Commercial crop. *Source: Foreign Agricultural Service, U.S. Department of Agriculture (FAS-USDA)*

Salient Statistics of Apples[2] in the United States

	Production		Growers Prices		Utilization of Quantities Sold — Processed[5]								Foreign Trade[4] — Domestic			
Year	Total	Utilized	Fresh cents/lb.	Processing $/ton	Fresh	Canned	Dried	Frozen	Juice & Cider	Other[3]	Avg. Farm Price cents/lb.	Farm Value Million $	Exports Fresh	Dried[5]	Imports Fresh & Dried[5]	Fresh Per Capita Consumption Lbs.
	Millions of Pounds												Metric Tons			
1991	9,707	9,637	25.1	171.0	5,447	1,311	299	286	2,194	100	17.9	1,727.0	530.1	44.2	143.9	18.2
1992	10,569	10,463	19.5	130.0	5,767	1,498	324	247	2,472	155	13.6	1,428.0	487.8	22.1	139.3	19.3
1993	10,685	10,574	18.4	107.0	6,124	1,335	366	282	2,382	85	12.9	1,363.8	662.9	19.2	130.9	19.2
1994	11,501	11,333	18.6	114.0	6,366	1,406	415	304	2,707	133	12.9	1,466.9	663.1	25.1	171.7	19.6
1995	10,578	10,384	24.0	159.0	5,840	1,292	334	305	2,538	78	17.0	1,767.0	565.0	24.6	196.1	18.9
1996	10,382	10,330	20.8	171.0	6,207	1,294	317	268	2,185	61	15.9	1,641.5	689.7	20.4	197.3	19.0
1997	10,324	10,254	22.1	130.0	5,815	1,499	267	349	2,145	180	15.4	1,575.4	539.1	18.0	173.6	18.4
1998	11,646	10,763	17.3	94.6	6,413	1,174	330	266	2,485	95	12.2	1,316.2	559.1	15.7	142.0	19.4
1999	10,631	10,447	21.3	128.0	5,995	1,319	263	271	2,473	126	15.0	1,552.6	610.8		164.2	19.0
2000[1]	10,649	10,383	17.9	103.0	6,258	1,151	248	194	2,418	115	12.9	1,553.5	637.6		163.9	17.9

[1] Preliminary. [2] Commercial crop. [3] Mostly crushed for vinegar, jam, etc. [4] Year beginning July. [5] Fresh weight basis.
Source: Economic Research Service, U.S. Department of Agriculture (ERS-USDA)

Price of Apples Received by Growers (for Fresh Use) in the United States In Cents Per Pound

Year	Jan.	Feb.	Mar.	Apr.	May	June	July	Aug.	Sept.	Oct.	Nov.	Dec.	Average
1992	24.6	24.8	24.3	24.1	25.0	25.2	28.6	33.3	27.1	21.2	19.4	19.9	24.8
1993	18.3	16.7	14.5	14.3	14.9	16.1	17.8	24.4	24.1	21.1	19.3	18.6	18.3
1994	18.7	17.8	16.6	15.5	14.3	13.5	19.4	29.0	20.8	19.2	16.4	19.2	18.4
1995	19.5	18.3	18.2	16.6	15.4	15.6	17.5	24.5	26.0	25.1	23.5	24.0	20.4
1996	25.4	24.2	25.1	22.6	21.9	21.9	23.3	25.2	30.2	24.6	23.2	22.6	24.2
1997	22.5	20.3	17.6	15.6	14.3	13.7	14.6	19.2	25.9	25.3	23.0	23.3	19.6
1998	21.9	20.8	20.5	19.4	17.8	16.3	12.7	13.8	22.6	22.1	17.5	14.9	18.4
1999	15.8	15.0	15.3	14.1	13.3	12.7	16.3	22.7	21.6	24.3	22.9	23.2	18.1
2000	21.8	20.3	19.8	19.3	17.8	16.1	16.2	19.5	23.3	21.8	18.5	18.1	19.4
2001[1]	15.8	15.2	14.2	15.8	15.4	15.3	14.4	16.9	18.7	24.2	23.3	22.4	17.6

[1] Preliminary. Source: Economic Research Service, U.S. Department of Agriculture (ERS-USDA)

Arsenic

The U.S. Geological Survey reported that no arsenic was removed from domestic ores in the United States. All arsenic metals and compounds used in the U.S. are imported. More than 95 percent of the arsenic consumed is in compound form, mostly as arsenic trioxide which in turn is converted into arsenic acid. Production of chromated copper arsenate, a wood preservative, accounts for over 90 percent of the domestic consumption of arsenic trioxide. Chromated copper arsenate is manufactured by three companies in the U.S.m while another company used arsenic acid to produce arsenical herbicide. Arsenic metal is used to produce nonferrous alloys, primarily lead-acid batteries.

One area where arsenic does seem to have a future is in the semiconductor industry. Very high-purity arsenic is used in the production of gallium arsenide. High speed and high frequency integrated circuits that use gallium arsenide have better signal reception and lower power consumption. It is estimated that 15 tonnes per year of high-purity arsenic is used in the production of semiconductor materials.

The largest market for arsenic in the U.S. is the production of arsenical wood preservatives. Demand for arsenic and arsenic compounds is therefore derived from the housing market and in particular home consumption. The addition of wooden decks to home would be an area where arsenic would find use though ongoing environmental concerns are likely to limit future use of arsenic. The U.S. Geological Survey reports that the U.S. is probably the world's largest consumer of arsenic. Demand for arsenic in the U.S. in 2000 was estimated at 34,000 metric tonnes, a substantial increase from the 1999 total of 22,000 tonnes. In the 1996-2000 period, U.S. estimated consumption of arsenic averaged 26,240 tonnes. In the u.S., three companies produced chromated copper arsenate, a wood preservative. Arsenic metal is used to produce principally lead alloys which are used in lead-acid batteries. Arsenic metal is used as an additive to improve corrosion resistance and tensile strength in copper alloys and as an additive to increase the strength of posts and grids in some lead-acid storage batteries.

World production of arsenic trioxide in 2000 was estimated to be 40,000 tonnes, up 3 percent from 1999 when production was estimated at 38,800 tonnes. The largest producer of arsenic trioxide in China with 2000 output of 16,000 tonnes, the same as in 1999. The next largest producer of arsenic trioxide in Chile with estimated output in 2000 of 8,000 tonnes. Other large producers include Ghana, Mexico, Kazakhstan, Russia, Belgium and France. It is estimated that world resources of copper and lead contain about 11 million tonnes of arsenic. Substantial resources of arsenic occur in copper ores in the Philippines and northern Peru and in copper-gold ores in Chile.

U.S. imports of arsenic metal in 2000 were 1,000 tonnes, a decrease of 23 percent from 1999. Imports of arsenic metal in the last five years have averaged about 890 tonnes. Imports or arsenic compounds in 2000 were 33,000 tonnes, up 49 percent from 1999. Total U.S. imports in 2000 were 34,000 tonnes. U.S. imports of arsenic metal in 2000 were 40 tonnes, down from 1,350 tonnes in 1999. Estimated consumption of arsenic in 2000 was 34,000 tonnes, up over 50 percent from 1999's total of 22,000 tonnes.

World Production of White Arsenic (Arsenic Trioxide) In Metric Tons

Year	Belgium	Bolivia	Canada[4]	Chile	China	France	Germany	Mexico	Namibia[3]	Peru	Phillip-pines	Russia[5]	World Total
1992	2,000	633	250	6,020	15,000	2,000	300	4,293	2,456	644	5,000	2,500	45,800
1993	2,000	663	250	6,200	14,000	3,000	300	4,447	2,290	391	2,000	2,000	42,100
1994	2,000	341	250	4,050	18,000	6,000	300	4,400	3,047	286	----	1,500	46,800
1995	2,000	362	250	4,076	21,000	5,000	250	3,620	1,661	285	----	1,500	47,000
1996	2,000	255	250	8,000	15,000	3,000	250	2,942	1,559	111	----	1,500	42,900
1997	2,000	282	250	8,350	15,000	2,500	250	2,999	1,297	103	----	1,500	41,600
1998	1,500	284	250	8,400	15,500	2,000	200	2,573	175	122	----	1,500	40,000
1999[1]	1,500	437	250	8,000	16,000	1,000	200	2,419	----	120	----	1,500	40,900
2000[2]	1,500	280	250	8,200	16,000	1,000	200	2,400	----	120	----	1,500	36,900

[1] Preliminary. [2] Estimate. [3] Output of Tsumeb Corp. Ltd. only. [4] Includes low-grade dusts that were exported to the U.S. for further refining. [5] Formerly part of the U.S.S.R.; not reported separately until 1992. *Source: U.S. Geological Survey (USGS)*

Salient Statistics of Arsenic in the United States In Metric Tons (Arsenic Content)

	Supply				Distribution		Estimated Demand Pattern						Average Price			
	Imports												Cents/Pound			
Year	Imports Metal	Imports Compounds	Industry Stocks Jan. 1	Total	Apparent Demand	Industry Stocks Dec.31	Agricultural Chemicals	Glass	Wood Preservatives	Non-Ferrous Alloys & Electric	Other	Total	Trioxide Mexican	Metal Chinese	Imports Trioxide[3]	Exports
1992	740	23,300	----	24,040	23,900	----	3,900	900	17,900	800	400	23,900	29	56	30,671	94
1993	767	20,900	----	21,667	21,300	----	3,000	900	16,200	800	400	21,300	33	44	27,500	364
1994	1,330	20,300	----	21,630	21,500	----	1,200	700	18,000	1,300	300	21,500	32	40	26,800	79
1995	557	22,100	----	22,657	22,300	----	1,000	700	19,600	600	400	22,300	33	66	29,000	430
1996	252	21,200	----	21,452	21,400	----	950	700	19,200	250	300	21,400	33	40	28,000	36
1997	909	22,800	----	23,709	23,700	----	1,400	700	20,000	900	300	23,700	31	32	30,000	61
1998	997	29,300	----	30,297	30,100	----	1,500	700	27,000	1,000	300	30,100	30	40	38,600	177
1999[1]	1,300	22,100	----	23,400	22,000	----	1,100	700	19,000	1,300	300	22,000	----	----	29,100	1,350
2000[2]	830	23,600	----	24,430	24,400	----	1,000	700	21,000	800	300	24,000	----	----	31,100	41

[1] Preliminary. [2] Estimate. [3] For Consumption. Source: U.S. Geological Survey (USGS)

Barley

World barley production since the late 1990's appears to be in an expansionary phase following a steady decline during much of the 1990's. World production in 2001/02 of 142 million metric tons compares with 134 million in 2000/01; a decade ago, production neared 170 million tons. Collectively, the EU is the largest producing area with 48.7 million tons forecast in 2001/01 vs. 51.2 million in 2000/01: Germany is the largest producer within the EU with about 13 million tons. Russia, the largest producer a decade ago, witnessed a halving of the crop to 10.6 million tons by 1999/00 but is forecast to produce almost 20 million tons in 2001/02. Canada's 2001/02 crop of 11.4 million tons trailed the 13.5 million ton crop of 2000/01. In the U.S., barley is the third largest produced feed grain; on worldwide basis U.S. production accounts for less than 5% of the total. World barley usage of 137.5 million tons in 2001/02 compares with 136.3 million in 2000/01. The 2001/02 world carryover of almost 25 million tons compares with 21 million a year earlier, the lowest since the mid-1990's.

The U.S. barley crop year begins June 1. Production peaked in the 1980's and has since declined sharply as producers found returns more favorable to wheat and sunflower crops. Barley production in 2001/02 of a record low 250 million bushels compares with 319 million bushels a year earlier. Planted acreage for the 2001/02 crop totaled only about 4.5 million acres vs. an annual average of about 7 million in the mid-1990's. North Dakota and Montana are the largest producing states.

U.S. total barley disappearance in 2001/02 of a record low 297 million bushels compares with 353 million in 2000/01. Feed and residual use was estimated at a record low 95 million bushels vs. 123 million a year earlier while industrial use, mostly for beer and alcohol was forecast at 172 million bushels, unchanged from 2000/01. Exports of 30 million were nearly half of 2000/01 while imports of 25 million bushels compare with 29 million, respectively, and mostly of malting quality barley from Canada. Carryover stocks on May 31, 2002 were estimated at only 84 million bushels vs. 106 million a year earlier.

World barley trade was forecast at 16.3 million tons in 2001/02 vs. 16.9 million in 2000/01. Collectively, the European Union is the largest exporter with at least a third of the total with Canada and Australia much of the balance. Importing countries are many, with Saudi Arabia the largest importer.

U.S. farmers' barley prices were forecast to average between $2.15-2.35 per bushel in 2001/02 vs. $2.11 in 2000/01.

Futures Markets

Barley futures and options are traded on the Winnipeg Commodity Exchange (WCE)and are quoted in Canadian dollars per ton. Futures are traded on the London International Financial Futures and Options Commodity Exchange (LIFFE) and on the Budapest Commodity Exchange.

World Barley Supply and Demand In Thousands of Metric Tons

	Exports						Imports			Utilization			Ending Stocks		
Year	Australia	Canada	EC-15	Total Non-US	U.S.	Total Exports	Saudi Arabia	Unaconted	Total Imports	Russia	U.S.	Total Utilization	Canada	U.S.	Total Stocks
1992-3	2,600	2,859	11,543	20,501	1,610	22,111	3,431	807	19,024	27,357	7,916	166,027	3,271	3,292	33,155
1993-4	4,232	3,789	10,055	20,414	1,550	21,964	4,308	384	20,285	26,824	9,053	168,997	3,376	3,023	33,236
1994-5	1,356	2,551	9,570	18,451	1,355	19,806	4,235	99	19,167	24,087	8,726	165,712	1,820	2,451	28,570
1995-6	3,375	2,596	8,654	18,347	1,182	19,529	3,876	214	19,172	17,566	7,635	150,965	1,749	2,168	19,700
1996-7	3,967	3,442	11,279	21,798	1,214	23,012	5,887	737	22,342	16,435	8,459	149,480	2,919	2,383	23,761
1997-8	2,838	1,897	2,990	11,755	1,071	12,826	4,026	483	12,826	16,494	6,879	146,037	2,459	2,596	32,137
1998-9	4,241	1,185	8,894	17,229	550	17,779	5,814	787	17,779	12,900	7,207	139,743	2,737	3,084	28,401
1999-00	2,870	1,806	10,458	17,941	852	18,793	5,900	169	18,793	11,441	6,752	133,105	2,838	2,424	23,139
2000-1[1]	3,600	1,956	5,900	14,731	1,059	15,790	4,400	156	15,790	13,007	6,432	136,637	2,454	2,314	21,511
2001-2[2]	4,500	1,000	4,500	15,480	650	16,130	4,500	250	16,130	14,350	5,813	139,251	1,700	1,826	24,033

[1] Preliminary. [2] Estimate. *Source: Foreign Agricutural Service, U.S. Department of Agriculture (FAS-USDA)*

World Production of Barley In Thousands of Metric Tons

Year	Australia	Canada	China	Denmark	France	Germany	India	Russia	Spain	Turkey	United Kingdom	United States	World Total
1992-3	5,460	11,032	4,665	2,974	10,580	12,196	1,700	26,989	6,105	6,500	7,350	9,908	166,068
1993-4	6,956	12,972	4,327	3,369	8,981	11,000	1,510	26,900	9,520	7,300	6,040	8,666	169,078
1994-5	2,913	11,690	4,411	3,446	7,646	10,902	1,310	27,000	7,596	6,500	5,945	8,162	161,046
1995-6	5,823	13,035	4,089	3,864	7,739	11,891	1,730	15,800	5,200	6,900	6,833	7,824	142,095
1996-7	6,696	15,562	4,000	3,953	9,540	12,074	1,510	15,900	9,600	7,200	7,780	8,544	143,541
1997-8	6,482	13,527	4,000	3,887	10,181	13,399	1,462	20,800	8,600	7,300	7,828	7,835	154,491
1998-9	5,987	12,709	2,656	3,565	10,591	12,512	1,680	9,800	10,902	7,500	6,630	7,667	136,007
1999-00	5,032	13,196	2,970	3,680	9,540	13,300	1,470	10,600	7,430	6,600	6,580	6,103	127,843
2000-1[1]	7,196	13,468	2,645	3,980	9,930	12,110	1,460	14,100	10,500	7,400	6,490	6,939	135,009
2001-2[2]	7,300	11,400	2,530	4,000	9,900	13,500	1,500	19,500	6,500	6,500	6,900	5,434	141,773

[1] Preliminary. [2] Estimate. *Source: Foreign Agricutural Service, U.S. Department of Agriculture (FAS-USDA)*

Barley Acreage and Prices in the United States

Year Begin-ning June 1	Acreage ----- 1,000 Acres ----- Planted	Harvested for Grain	Yield Per Harvested Acre -- Bushels --	Seasonal Prices: Received by Farmers[3] All	Feed[4]	Malting[4]	Portland No. 2 Western	Government Price Support Operations: National Average Loan Rate	Target Price	Put Under Support (mil. Bu.)	% of Production
				Dollars per Bushel							
1993-4	7,786	6,753	58.9	1.99	2.05	2.48	2.40	1.40	2.36	37.7	9.5
1994-5	7,159	6,667	56.2	2.03	2.02	2.75	2.51	1.54	2.36	28.2	7.5
1995-6	6,689	6,279	57.3	2.89	2.67	3.69	3.51	1.54	2.36	14.9	4.1
1996-7	7,094	6,707	58.5	2.74	2.32	3.18	3.07	1.55	NA	28.7	NA
1997-8	6,706	6,198	58.1	2.38	1.90	2.50	2.49	1.57	NA	32.8	NA
1998-9	6,337	5,864	60.0	1.98	1.23	2.30	1.96	1.56	NA	NA	NA
1999-00[1]	5,223	4,758	59.2	2.13	1.65	2.43	2.11	1.59	NA	NA	NA
2000-1[2]	5,864	5,213	61.1	2.11	1.76	2.34			NA	NA	NA

[1] Preliminary. [2] Estimate. [3] Excludes support payments. [4] Duluth through May 1998. *Source: Economic Research Service, U.S. Department of Agriculture (ERS-USDA)*

Salient Statistics of Barley in the United States In Millions of Bushels

Year Begin-ning June 1	Supply: Beginning Stocks	Production	Imports	Total Supply	Disappearance: Domestic Use: Food & Alcohol Beverages	Seed	Feed & Residual	Total	Exports	Total Disappearance	Ending Stocks: Gov't Owned	Privately Owned[3]	Total Stocks
1994-5	138.9	374.9	65.9	579.6	163.8	11.1	228.1	400.8	66.2	467.0	5.0	107.6	112.6
1995-6	112.6	359.4	40.7	512.7	160.1	11.7	178.9	350.7	62.4	413.1	4.2	95.4	99.6
1996-7	99.6	392.4	36.8	528.8	160.9	11.1	216.5	388.5	30.8	419.3	0	109.5	109.5
1997-8	109.5	360.0	40.3	509.6	161.6	10.4	144.0	316.0	74.4	390.3	0	119.2	119.2
1998-9	119.2	359.9	29.8	501.2	161.4	8.6	161.1	331.1	28.5	359.5	.3	141.4	141.7
1999-00	141.7	352.1	25.0	448.5	162.5	9.5	136.0	308.0	30.0	338.0	0	111.0	111.0
2000-1[1]	111.0	318.7	29.0	459.0	163.0	9.0	123.0	295.0	58.0	353.0	0	106.0	106.0
2001-2[2]	106.0	249.6	25.0	381.0			95.0		30.0	297.0	0	84.0	84.0

[1] Preliminary. [2] Estimate. [3] Uncommitted inventory. [4] Includes quantity under loan & farmer-owned reserve. *Source: Economic Research Service, U.S. Department of Agriculture (ERS-USDA)*

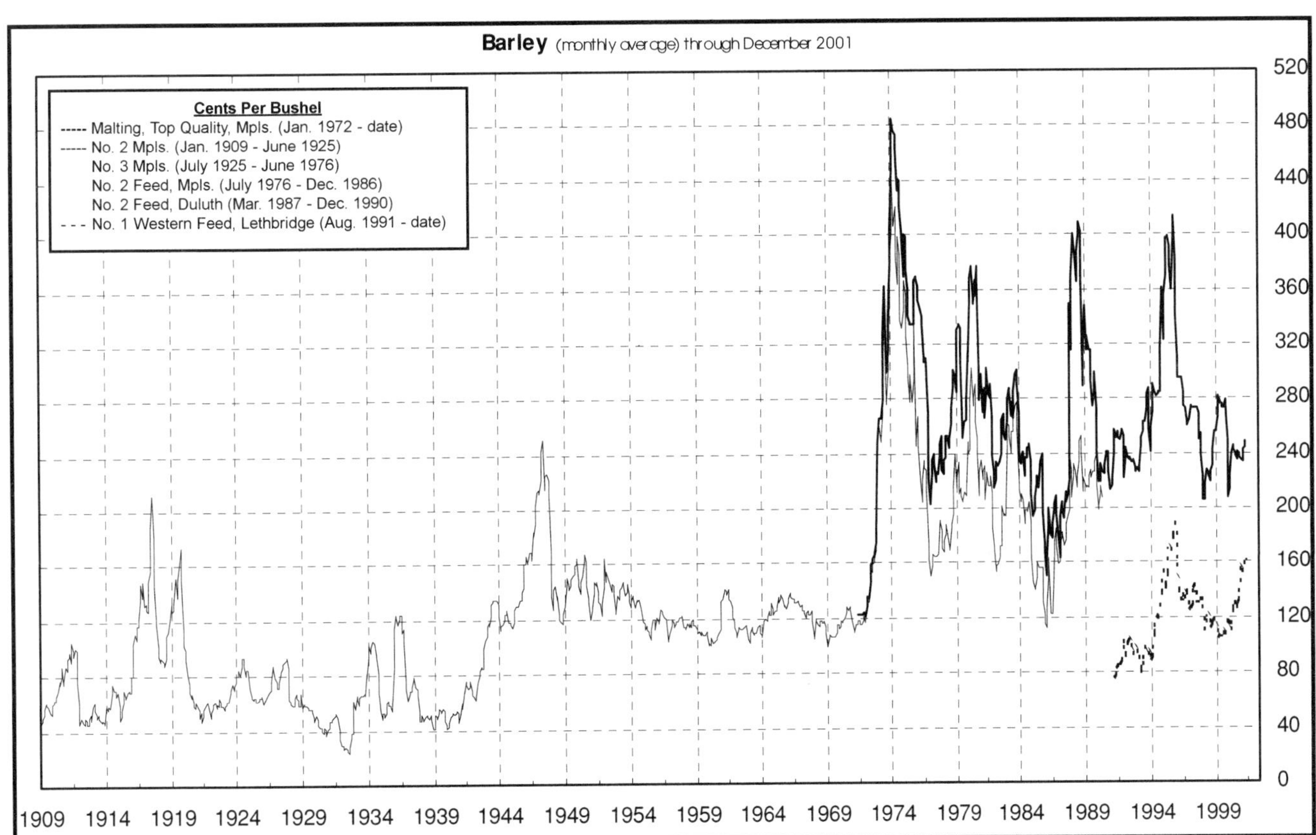

BARLEY

Average Price Received by Farmers for Feed[2] Barley in the United States In Cents Per Bushel

Year	June	July	Aug.	Sept.	Oct.	Nov.	Dec.	Jan.	Feb.	Mar.	Apr.	May	Average
1997-8	231	204	210	229	205	198	166	158	156	151	142	NQ	186
1998-9	182	162	149	140	146	147	155	158	160	149	154	162	155
1999-00	155	148	150	164	161	166	164	163	168	178	168	194	165
2000-1	173	171	150	154	171	187	190	180	177	176	172	191	174
2001-2[1]	177	163	153	171	186	179	174	166	176				172

[1] Preliminary. [2] Duluth No. 2 through May 1998. NQ = No quote. *Source: Economic Research Service, U.S. Department of Agriculture (ERS-USDA)*

Average Price Received by Farmers for All Barley in the United States In Cents Per Bushel

Year	June	July	Aug.	Sept.	Oct.	Nov.	Dec.	Jan.	Feb.	Mar.	Apr.	May	Average
1997-8	226	227	235	238	244	261	243	242	240	213	216	213	233
1998-9	193	201	207	201	191	205	203	189	190	200	178	182	195
1999-00	170	204	237	203	196	214	225	204	213	223	209	219	210
2000-1	204	270	223	181	197	215	222	200	210	207	205	213	212
2001-2[1]	198	200	242	224	230	231	216	210	219				219

[1] Preliminary. *Source: National Agricultural Statistical Service, U.S. Department of Agriculture (NASS-USDA)*

Average Open Interest of Western Feed Barley Futures in Winnipeg In Contracts

Year	Jan.	Feb.	Mar.	Apr.	May	June	July	Aug.	Sept.	Oct.	Nov.	Dec.
1997	22,718	19,290	15,080	14,620	14,385	12,291	10,023	13,641	12,909	13,147	14,473	13,576
1998	15,789	17,337	18,039	14,706	12,666	10,847	9,915	10,384	11,420	11,460	11,338	8,622
1999	8,231	10,635	10,579	9,713	8,333	8,993	10,348	11,959	13,206	15,014	15,662	15,031
2000	16,709	20,500	21,100	22,501	20,299	17,402	15,128	15,095	15,885	14,921	17,192	19,605
2001	19,453	20,515	19,163	19,458	16,020	15,778	16,475	17,202	16,926	13,577	11,407	10,480

Source: Winnipeg Commodity Exchange (WCE)

Volume of Trading of Western Barley Futures in Winnipeg In Contracts

Year	Jan.	Feb.	Mar.	Apr.	May	June	July	Aug.	Sept.	Oct.	Nov.	Dec.	Total
1997	30,608	30,298	25,910	23,511	17,228	18,912	15,615	21,993	23,291	29,418	31,629	16,201	284,614
1998	23,954	23,472	23,904	23,553	17,395	20,273	21,011	18,101	16,097	21,330	21,589	8,315	238,994
1999	15,463	17,539	13,853	17,179	8,911	16,294	17,936	15,837	29,141	16,662	26,445	16,117	211,377
2000	23,371	22,598	21,563	23,631	19,816	24,298	15,230	11,981	23,105	23,447	42,529	14,508	266,077
2001	26,836	18,732	16,962	24,993	26,361	20,465	20,849	20,137	19,735	21,276	14,926	6,302	237,574

Source: Winnipeg Commodity Exchange (WCE)

Bauxite

Bauxite is a naturally occurring, heterogeneous material comprised of one or more aluminum hydroxide minerals plus various mixtures of silica, iron oxide, titania, aluminosilicates, and other impurities in trace amounts.

Bauxite is the only raw material used in the production of alumina on a commercial scale in the United States. Bauxite is classified according to the intended commercial application, such as abrasive, cement, chemical, metallurgical, and refractory. Of all the bauxite mined, about 85 percent is converted to alumina for the production of aluminum metal, with an additional 10 percent going to nonmetal uses as various forms of specialty alumina. The remaining 5 percent is used in nonmetallurgical bauxite applications. Quantities of bauxite are also used to produce aluminum chemicals and in the steel industries.

The U.S. Geological Survey reported that 2000 world mine production of bauxite was 127 million metric tonnes, the same as in 1999. Mine production data in the U.S. was not available. The largest producer of bauxite is Australia with 49 million tonnes in 2000, up 1 percent from 1999. The next largest producer was Guinea with 15 million tonnes, the same as in 1999. Production by Brazil was 13.2 million tonnes, up 2 percent from 1999. Production by Jamaica was 11.2 million tonnes, down 4 percent from 1999. Other major producers include China, India and Venezuela. Estimated reserves of bauxite in the world are 25 billion tonnes. The largest reserves are in Guinea followed by Brazil and Australia.

Nearly all bauxite used in the U.S. came from imported sources. Virtually all of this production was used in nonmetallurgical products such as abrasives, chemicals, and refractories. Of the bauxite used in the U.S., about 95 percent was converted to alumina. The U.S. also imports about half of the alumina that is needed. U.S. bauxite import sources are Guinea, Jamaica, Brazil and Guyana while sources for imported alumina are Australia, Suriname and Jamaica.

U.S. imports of crude and dried bauxite in second quarter 2001 were 2.3 million tonnes. Imports in the first quarter were 2.25 million tonnes. The major suppliers of bauxite to the U.S. were Jamaica, Guinea and Brazil. Small amounts of bauxite were exported. In the first half of 2001, exports were 36,300 tonnes. The major destination was Canada.

U.S. imports of calcined bauxite for consumption for refractories in the first half of 2001 were 48,900 tonnes. Imports for other purposes were 95,200 tonnes. The major supplier was China. For all of 2000, calcined bauxite imports for refractories were 181,000 tonnes while for other purposes they were 129,000 tonnes. U.S. imports of alumina in first half 2001 were 1.48 million tonnes while for 2000 they totaled 3.82 million tonnes. The major suppliers were Australia, Suriname and Jamaica.

World Production of Bauxite In Thousands of Metric Tons

Year	Australia	Brazil	China	Greece	Guinea	Guyana[2]	Hungary	India	Jamaica[3]	Russia[3][4]	Sierra Leone	Suriname	World Total
1991	40,510	10,365	2,600	2,133	15,466	2,204	2,037	4,735	11,552	5,000	1,288	3,198	111,000
1992	39,746	9,366	2,700	2,078	13,800	2,376	1,721	4,898	11,302	4,578	1,250	3,250	105,000
1993	41,320	10,001	3,500	2,205	15,300	2,125	1,561	5,277	11,307	4,260	1,165	3,421	110,000
1994	41,733	8,673	3,700	2,196	13,300	1,732	836	4,809	11,564	3,000	735	3,772	106,000
1995	42,655	10,214	5,000	2,200	15,800	2,028	1,015	5,240	10,857	3,100	----	3,530	112,000
1996	43,063	10,998	6,200	2,452	15,600	2,475	1,044	5,757	11,863	3,300	----	3,695	117,000
1997	44,465	11,671	8,000	1,877	16,400	2,467	743	6,019	11,987	3,350	----	3,877	122,000
1998	44,553	11,961	8,200	1,823	15,000	2,267	1,138	6,102	12,646	3,450	----	3,890	122,000
1999[1]	48,416	13,839	8,500	1,883	15,000	2,359	935	6,712	11,688	3,750	----	3,715	128,000
2000[2]	53,802	14,000	9,000	1,991	15,000	2,404	1,047	7,366	11,127	4,200	----	3,610	135,000

[1] Preliminary. [2] Estimate. [3] Dry Bauxite equivalent of ore processed. [4] Formerly part of the U.S.S.R.; data not reported separately until 1992.

Source: U.S. Geological Survey (USGS)

Salient Statistics of Bauxite in the United States In Thousands of Metric Tons

			Consumption by Industry					Dry Equivalent			Stocks, December 31		
Year	Net Import Reliance as a % of Apparent Consumption	Average Price FOB Mine $ per Ton	Total	Alumina	Abrasive	Chemical	Refractory	Imports[3] (for Consumption)	Exports[3]	Consumption	Producers & Consumers	Government	Total
1991	100	15-18	12,204	11,383	204	218	328	11,871	51	12,204	2,620	18,477	21,097
1992	100	15-18	11,873	11,066	223	190	334	10,939	63	11,873	2,319	17,805	20,124
1993	100	15-24	11,917	11,002	203	225	429	11,621	90	12,200	1,590	16,938	18,500
1994	99	15-24	11,200	10,400	197	192	350	10,700	129	11,200	1,560	17,200	18,800
1995	99	15-18	10,900	10,100	133	201	394	10,100	108	10,900	1,730	16,300	18,100
1996	100	15-18	11,000	10,300	117	W	380	10,200	132	11,000	1,930	15,700	17,600
1997	100	15-18	11,500	10,700	98	W	466	10,700	85	11,500	2,260	14,300	16,500
1998	100	----	12,700	12,000	135	W	332	11,000	99	12,700	1,860	11,000	12,800
1999[1]	100	----	11,700	11,100	113	W	251	9,890	149	11,700	1,440	6,800	8,250
2000[2]	100	----	10,600	10,100	111	W	160	8,550	141	10,600	1,300	5,710	7,000

[1] Preliminary. [2] Estimate. [3] Including concentrates. W = Withheld to avoid disclosing company proprietary data.

Source: U.S. Geological Survey (USGS)

Bismuth

Bismuth finds a wide variety of uses ranging from pharmaceutical compounds, to glass ceramics, to chemicals and pigments. Bismuth is found in household pharmaceuticals and is used to treat stomach ulcers. There have been several new uses for bismuth as a nontoxic substitute for lead in various applications. These have included the use of bismuth in brass plumbing fixtures, ceramic glazes, crystalware, lubricating greases, pigments and solders. Of environment interest has ben the use of bismuth as a replacement for lead used in shot for waterfowl hunting and in fishing sinkers. Another new use has been in galvanizing to improve drainage characteristics of galvanizing alloys. Zinc-bismuth alloys have the same drainage properties as zinc-lead alloys. Bismuth has the advantage of being as durable as lead without being as hazardous. There is no domestic refiner production of primary bismuth in the U.S. now. About 40 percent of the bismuth used in the U.S. is used for pharmaceuticals and chemicals; about 39 percent is used in fusible alloys, solders and cartridges, 17 percent is used in metallurgical additives; and 2 percent in other uses.

World mine production of bismuth in 2000 was estimated at 3,780 metric tonnes, up 4 percent from 1999. The largest producer of bismuth was Mexico with 1,250 tonnes, the same as in 1999. The next largest producer was Peru with 1,000 tonnes, the same as the year before. Production by China was 500 tonnes, up 25 percent from the previous year. Other producers include Canada, Bolivia and Japan. World reserves of bismuth are currently estimated at 110,000 tonnes. World reserves of bismuth are usually located in lead deposits except in Chi na where it is found with tungsten ores and in Australia where it is found with copper-gold ores. Bismuth is rarely found in sufficient quantities to be mined as the principal product, except in Bolivia and possibly China.

Bismuth metal consumed in the U.S. in the second quarter of 2001 was 542 tonnes. In the first half of 2001 total metal consumed was 1,100 tonnes. For all of 2000, consumption of bismuth metal was 2,130 tonnes. In the first five months of 2001, bismuth metal consumed in chemicals was 410 tonnes while for 2000 the use was 861 tonnes.Use of bismuth metal in bismuth alloys in the first half of 2001 was 487 tonnes while for year 2000 the total was 889 tonnes. Use of the metal in metallurgical additives in the first half of 2001 was 179 tonnes and in 2000 the total was 346 tonnes. Other uses of bismuth metal in first half 2001 totaled 21.5 tonnes and in 2000 they were 34 tonnes.

U.S. imports for consumption of bismuth metal in the January-May 2001 period were 1,150 tonnes. Among the major suppliers were Belgium with 428 tonnes, China with 293 tonnes and Mexico with 252 tonnes. Other suppliers were the United Kingdom, Germany and Canada. For all of 2000, U.S. imports of bismuth metal were 241 tonnes. U.S. exports of bismuth metal, alloys waste and scrap in the first five months of 2001 were 277 tonnes. The major destinations were Belgium, Germany, Canada, the Netherlands and Mexico.

World Production of Bismuth In Metric Tons (Mine Output=Metal Content)

	Mine Output, Metal Content						Refined Metal						
Year	Canada	China	Japan	Mexico	Peru	Total	Belgium	China	Kazakhastan[3]	Japan	Mexico	Peru	Total
1991	65	1,040	138	651	610	3,230	800	1,260	70	461	500	377	3,820
1992	224	820	159	807	550	2,870	800	1,060	170	530	550	419	3,710
1993	144	740	149	908	1,300	3,550	950	1,050	180	497	650	937	4,390
1994	129	610	152	1,047	1,210	3,410	900	850	85	505	836	877	4,180
1995	187	740	177	995	900	3,430	800	800	33	591	924	581	3,840
1996	150	610	169	1,070	1,000	3,600	800	750	50	562	957	939	4,180
1997	196	550	165	1,642	1,000	4,490	800	760	50	550	990	774	4,070
1998	219	240	144	1,204	1,000	3,990	700	820	50	479	1,030	832	4,040
1999[1]	311	400	135	548	1,000	3,370	700	1,300	55	481	412	705	3,800
2000[2]	202	400	155	1,000	1,000	3,760	700	1,300	55	518	900	744	4,370

[1] Preliminary. [2] Estimate. [3] Formerly part of the U.S.S.R.; data not reported separately until 1992. *Source U.S. Geological Survey (USGS)*

Salient Statistics of Bismuth in the United States In Metric Tons

	Bismuth Consumed, By Uses							Imports from Metallic Bismuth from				
Year	Metallurgical Additives	Other Alloys & Uses	Fusible Alloys	Chemicals[3]	Total Consumption	Consumer Stocks Dec. 31	Exports of Metal & Alloys	Belgium	Mexico	Peru	Total	Dealer Price $ Per Pound
1991	341	26	271	789	1,427	247	75	345.1	535.0	169.8	1,411	3.00
1992	381	33	278	758	1,450	272	90	467.4	550.5	75.7	1,621	2.66
1993	232	59	256	750	1,300	323	70	275.1	479.1	117.2	1,330	2.50
1994	306	26	276	841	1,450	402	160	512.0	665.0	114.9	1,660	3.25
1995	257	27	544	1,320	2,150	390	261	636.0	444.0	10.9	1,450	3.85
1996	231	35	401	855	1,520	122	151	584.0	453.0	19.5	1,490	3.65
1997	252	31	593	655	1,530	213	206	691.0	601.0	163.0	2,170	3.50
1998	335	32	741	884	1,990	175	245	739.0	807.0	68.8	2,720	3.60
1999[1]	340	31	823	855	2,050	130	257	742.0	277.0	6.8	2,110	3.85
2000[2]	346	34	889	861	2,130	118	491	832.0	516.0	20.4	2,410	3.70

[1] Preliminary. [2] Estimate. [3] Includes pharmaceuticals. *Source: U.S. Geological Survey (USGS)*

Broilers

Federally inspected U.S. broiler production set new-year to year highs during the past decade. Production in calendar year 2001 of a record 31.2 billion pounds compares with 30.5 billion in 2000 and a forecast of 31.9 billion in 2002. In the late 1990's production averaged about 27 billion pounds. Fourth quarter 2001 broiler production of 7.8 billion pounds was 3.7% above a year earlier and is likely to hold at that level, if not higher, in the first quarter of 2002.. However, late 2001 export shipments were forecast to lag initial expectations. Late 2001 broiler chick placements averaged 142 million birds a week; chicks placed by mid-December are expected to reach slaughter size by late January. U.S. per capita consumption shows little sign of slowing, averaging 76.9 pounds in 2000, 76.7 in 2001 and estimated at 77.3 pounds in 2002, suggesting that the occasional publicity directed towards the need for proper cooking of poultry meat, notably at fast-food outlets, has not dampened consumption. The 12-city average broiler prices of 56.20 cents/lb in 2000 compares with 59.20 cents in 2001 and forecast to range between 57-61 cents in 2002. However, whole bird prices can be misleading as the sum of the parts can be greater than the whole bird: export demand can buoy leg parts while breast prices are more a function of domestic demand.

The steady gains in U.S. broiler production reflects strong foreign demand.. Exports in the first ten months of 2001 of 5.1 billion pounds compares with 4.6 billion in the like 2000 period, suggesting a pace that should carry above the record yearly total of 5.5 billion in The major importers are Russia (almost 2 billion pounds in 2001 vs. 1.3 billion in 2000), Hong Kong, Japan and Mexico, with the demand largely for leg parts. Although U.S. exports may face increasing global competition in the years ahead, inexpensive feed grain prices and an efficient industry should keep U.S. broilers export prices competitive.

Broiler Supply and Prices in the United States

Year & Quarters	Federally Inspected Slaughter: Number (Millions)	Average Weight (Pounds)	Liveweight Pounds (Mil. Lbs.)	Certified RTC Weight (Mil. Lbs.)	Total Production RTC[3] (Mil. Lbs.)	Per Capita Consumption RTC Basis (Mil. Lbs.)	Prices (Cents per Pound): Farm	Geogia Dock[4]
1996	7,546	4.78	36,034	36,336	26,124	81.4	38.67	61.09
1997	7,714	4.81	39,098	27,271	27,271	71.9	37.35	59.96
1998	7,825	4.86	38,016	27,832	27,863	72.6	39.81	59.81
1999	8,112	4.99	40,444	29,741	29,741	77.0	36.89	58.75
2000	8,239	5.00	38,417	30,397	30,495	77.4	35.20	58.14
2001[1]	8,320	5.03	41,858	30,920	31,143	76.4	39.58	62.08
I	2,011	5.02	10,102	7,469	7,547	18.9	37.00	60.48
II	2,118	5.04	10,678	7,884	7,926	19.2	40.00	61.37
III	2,117	4.97	10,521	7,770	7,831	19.5	42.33	63.61
IV	2,075	5.09	10,557	7,796	7,900	18.8	39.00	62.86

[1] Preliminary. [2] Estimate. [3] Total production equals federal inspected slaughter plus other slaughter minus cut-up & further processing condemnation. [4] Ready-to-cook basis. *Source: Economic Research Service, U.S. Department of Agriculture (ERS-USDA)*

Salient Statistics of Broilers in the United States

Year	Commercial Production: Number (Mil. Lbs.)	Liveweight (Mil. Lbs.)	Average: Liveweight Per Bird (Pounds)	Average Price (Cents/Lb.)	Value of Production (Mil. $)	Total Chickens[3] Supply and Distribution (In Millions of Pounds): Production: Federally Inspected	Other Chickens	Total	Storage Stocks January 1	Exports	Broiler Feed Ratio (Pounds)	Consumption: Total (Mil. Lbs.)	Per Capita[4] (Pounds)
1994	7,018	32,529	4.64	35.0	11,372	23,846	38	23,666	358	2,876	5.2	20,690	69.50
1995	7,326	34,222	4.66	34.4	11,762	25,021	39	24,827	458	3,894	5.1	20,832	68.80
1996	7,598	36,483	4.80	38.1	13,903	26,336	38	26,124	560	4,420	4.7	21,626	70.40
1997	7,764	37,541	4.84	37.7	14,159	27,271	35	27,041	641	4,664	6.3	22,416	71.90
1998	7,934	38,554	4.86	39.3	15,145	27,863	26	27,612	607	4,673	7.2	22,841	72.60
1999[1]	8,146	40,830	5.01	37.1	15,129	29,446	27	29,175	711	4,512	6.7	24,629	77.60
2000[2]	8,263	41,516	5.02	33.6	13,953						7.8		

[1] Preliminary. [2] Estimate. [3] Ready-to-cook. [4] Retail weight basis. *Source: Economic Research Service, U.S. Department of Agriculture (ERS-USDA)*

Average Wholesale Broiler[1] Prices RTC (Ready-to-Cook) (In Cents Per Pound)

Year	Jan.	Feb.	Mar.	Apr.	May	June	July	Aug.	Sept.	Oct.	Nov.	Dec.	Average
1995	51.14	51.73	52.32	51.51	52.94	55.88	58.76	61.74	61.48	58.79	61.08	58.87	56.35
1996	59.00	55.31	54.31	56.01	61.71	65.52	64.58	64.07	64.01	62.64	64.37	63.50	61.25
1997	61.99	59.53	58.41	59.77	58.53	59.05	63.04	63.25	59.86	55.39	54.62	52.25	58.81
1998	54.66	56.40	58.10	58.52	60.08	64.26	68.53	72.13	70.53	68.04	64.13	60.45	62.99
1999	59.33	58.23	56.79	55.08	60.02	60.33	59.46	57.65	57.15	54.87	59.52	58.42	58.07
2000	55.43	53.84	54.48	55.39	55.71	56.01	56.61	55.47	58.35	57.22	58.22	57.23	56.16
2001[2]	56.87	57.47	58.95	58.46	59.40	59.88	60.43	60.90	61.93	60.17	58.89	55.98	59.11

[1] 12-city composite wholesale price. [2] Preliminary. *Source: Economic Research Service, U.S. Department of Agriculture (ERS-USDA)*

Butter

U.S. butter production stalled in 2001, but forecast to recover in 2002, still well short of the record large 619,000 metric tons in 1992. Production in 2001 of 550,000 compares with expectations in 2002 of 580,000 tons. As a rule, any annual increase in output reflects the availability of milk supplies for butter production. Despite the expected increase in butter output, strong consumer demand should keep retail prices over a $1/pound. U.S. annual butter consumption fell during much of the 1990's, but has since rebounded from -- 555,000 tons in 1998 to 593,000 tons in 2000 and forecast at 598,000 tons in 2002. During the past few years consumption either exceeded or about equaled production. There is a definite production seasonality: January is the highest producing month and August the lowest. U.S. butter stocks, once mostly government owned, dropped sharply in the 1990's; from a high at year-end 1991 of 249,000 tons to 10,000 at year end 2001 and little change at yearend 2002. U.S. annual per capita butter is not high, averaging near 2 kilograms.

Butter production is derived directly from milk production. Butter manufacture is the third largest use of milk production, the first being milk as a fluid and then its conversion into cheese. California is the largest producing state followed by Wisconsin.

World butter production in 2001 of 5.7 million metric tons compares with 5.4 million in 2000, but forecast to reach a record large 6.1 million tons in 2002. The U.S. with almost 10% of the world's total is the largest producer followed by France and Germany, the three countries combined accounting for 1.4 million tons of 2001's production. India's 2001 output of 2.25 million tons compares with 1.95 million in 2000 and expected to reach a record large 2.6 million tons in 2002. India's production, however, is mostly Ghee, a butter-like substance ands consumed almost entirely in India. Russia's production which fell dramatically early in the 1990's appears to be recovering: production in 2001 of 280,000 tons compares with 265,000 in 2000 and perhaps 290,000 tons in 2002. China is not among the world's major producers even though their milk production is expanding. World consumption is growing: estimated at 5.5 million tons in 2001, vs. 4.9 million in 1999 and expected to reach 5.9 million in 2002. Among foreign nations, but exclusive of India, the world's largest consumer in 2001 with 2.25 million tons, was the U.S. at 587,000 tons and Germany with 542,000 tons. Russia, once the largest consumer now ranks fourth: 396,000 tons in 2001 vs. 514,000 tons five years earlier.

Global trade in butter is small. Exports were forecast at 674,000 tons in 2001 vs. 650,000 in 2000, almost two-thirds of which come from New Zealand and Australia. U.S. trade is insignificant, but on balance the U.S. is a net importer. Russia is the largest importer, estimated to take 110,000 tons in 2002 vs. 102,000 tons in 2001 and as little as 55,000 tons in 1999.

U.S. unsalted wholesale butter prices, 82% butterfat, are among the world's highest, averaging almost $4000 per metric tons in 2001 vs. a Northern European price of about $1300 per ton. Contributing to the high U.S. price is a government support program that in the second half of 2001 was pegged at $1,885 per ton.

Supply and Distribution of Butter in the United States In Millions of Pounds

	Supply				Distribution							93 Score AA Wholesale Price	
					Domestic Disappearance			Department of Agriculture					
Year	Production	Cold Storage Stocks[3] Jan. 1[5]	Imports	Total Supply	Total	Per Capita (Pounds)	Exports	Jan. 1 Stocks[4]	Dec. 31 Stocks[4]	Removed by USDA Programs	Total Use	California ($ per Pound)	Chicago ($ per Pound)
1991	1,337	417	4.740	1,759	1,101	4.4	107	373	511	442.8	1,209	1.2856	1.0182
1992	1,365	550	4.153	1,919	1,114	4.4	307	511	430	439.5	1,464	1.1386	.8427
1993	1,315	455	4.374	1,774	1,209	4.7	320	430	229	288.8	1,530	1.0612	.7693
1994	1,296	244	3.340	1,543	1,255	4.8	207	229	67	204.3	1,463	.9581	.7068
1995	1,264	80	1.536	1,348	1,186	4.5	140	67	----	78.5	1,329	----	.8188
1996	1,174	19	10.544	1,204	1,148	4.3	41	----	----	0	1,190	----	1.0824
1997	1,151	14	24.153	1,177	1,116	4.2	39	----	----	1	1,156	----	1.1625
1998	1,168	21	66.138	1,243	1,208	4.5	6	----	----	----	1,217	----	1.7764
1999[1]	1,277	26	22.046	1,337	1,305	4.8	4	----	----	----	1,312		
2000[2]	1,274	25											

[1] Preliminary. [2] Estimates. [3] Includes butter-equivalent. [4] Includes butteroil. [5] *Includes stocks held by USDA.*
Source: Economic Research Service, U.S. Department of Agriculture (ERS-USDA)

Commercial Disappearance of Creamery Butter in the United States In Millions of Pounds

Year	First Quarter	Second Quarter	Third Quarter	Fourth Quarter	Total	Year	First Quarter	Second Quarter	Third Quarter	Fourth Quarter	Total
1990	197.5	218.1	218.1	281.8	915.2	1996	325.6	301.8	237.5	310.3	1,180.0
1991	186.8	184.0	255.6	276.5	903.5	1997	302.7	250.7	265.8	287.6	1,109.0
1992	214.6	216.6	236.8	276.2	944.3	1998	289.0	276.3	255.3	308.6	1,137.0
1993	224.6	231.5	271.9	312.7	1,040.6	1999	299.3	316.4	318.3	374.8	1,308.8
1994	261.7	254.9	285.0	298.3	1,097.3	2000	300.8	286.9	332.3	380.6	1,300.6
1995	335.7	269.0	261.2	304.9	1,186.0	2001[1]	279.8	273.6	315.0	399.5	1,267.9

[1] Preliminary. *Source: Economic Research Service, U.S. Department of Agriculture (ERS-USDA)*

World (Total) Butter[3] Production In Thousands of Metric Tons

Year	Australia	France	Germany	India	Ireland	Netherlands	New Zealand	Poland	Russia	Ukraine	United Kingdom	United States	World Total
1991	111	496	555	1,020	146	196	269	220	729	376	132	606	5,667
1992	116	454	474	1,060	142	191	268	180	762	303	127	619	5,470
1993	131	444	480	1,110	135	184	276	180	732	312	152	596	5,493
1994	147	444	461	1,200	136	159	297	160	488	254	154	588	5,221
1995	138	453	486	1,300	150	132	280	163	419	219	130	573	5,173
1996	153	462	480	1,400	150	122	309	160	290	163	129	533	5,094
1997	147	466	442	1,470	145	134	307	178	280	109	139	522	5,073
1998	154	463	426	1,600	145	149	343	183	270	113	137	530	5,253
1999[1]	175	448	427	1,750	143	140	316	181	260	105	142	578	5,424
2000[2]	184	450	410	1,950	146	135	320	185	270	90	141	600	5,640

[1] Preliminary. [2] Forecast. [3] Factory (including creameries and dairies) & farm. *Source: Foreign Agricultural Service, U.S. Department of Agriculture (FAS-USDA)*

Production of Creamery Butter in Factories in the United States In Millions of Pounds

Year	Jan.	Feb.	Mar.	Apr.	May	June	July	Aug.	Sept.	Oct.	Nov.	Dec.	Total
1992	156.0	132.0	129.9	119.7	118.2	103.0	97.8	86.7	96.6	101.6	98.3	119.8	1,365.2
1993	147.3	127.2	131.6	121.8	116.4	102.3	86.2	80.7	86.3	97.8	97.3	120.3	1,315.2
1994	135.3	118.4	118.0	119.4	118.2	99.2	84.2	88.2	91.2	101.8	100.7	121.4	1,295.9
1995	135.6	121.7	127.3	120.6	119.4	98.4	85.0	76.0	80.2	93.5	90.5	112.4	1,260.7
1996	132.4	114.7	111.9	109.3	100.9	72.7	75.2	73.2	80.7	96.6	95.3	111.3	1,174.5
1997	127.6	108.6	105.4	118.3	102.7	82.0	80.0	68.8	79.3	83.3	89.1	106.0	1,151.3
1998	117.8	105.7	106.7	107.1	92.6	69.9	63.8	64.3	68.2	88.5	91.1	106.3	1,081.9
1999	123.3	111.5	113.7	106.4	104.7	86.0	75.8	66.1	78.8	93.0	90.4	117.2	1,166.8
2000[1]	139.9	128.2	121.0	111.7	108.9	89.1	85.4	83.7	89.9	103.9	100.4	111.6	1,273.6
2001[2]	129.4	110.2	101.9	106.0	109.1	86.9	79.9	76.8	88.7	111.0	101.3	123.4	1,224.6

[1] Preliminary. [2] Estimate. *Source: Economic Research Service, U.S. Department of Agriculture (ERS-USDA)*

Cold Storage Holdings of Creamery Butter on First of Month in the United States In Millions of Pounds

Year	Jan.	Feb.	Mar.	Apr.	May	June	July	Aug.	Sept.	Oct.	Nov.	Dec.
1992	539.4	565.4	624.8	645.3	678.7	712.6	747.0	755.8	705.7	608.1	541.7	487.6
1993	447.7	489.1	492.5	515.6	552.7	559.0	569.0	516.4	473.3	395.4	341.1	276.3
1994	234.7	251.0	243.2	253.5	265.7	281.4	275.1	245.9	206.6	163.4	124.6	84.5
1995	79.5	89.9	88.3	74.8	79.1	81.3	79.2	68.3	50.2	32.8	23.6	15.7
1996	18.6	25.5	33.7	48.7	39.8	34.0	29.7	31.7	27.3	21.4	20.5	17.6
1997	13.7	23.2	36.0	50.3	86.8	104.2	93.7	85.6	69.5	43.9	26.6	15.4
1998	20.8	34.2	44.2	55.9	67.4	72.7	60.6	51.0	41.1	34.1	31.2	28.7
1999	25.9	60.8	95.0	108.4	125.5	136.6	120.6	123.6	90.7	71.5	64.2	30.2
2000	25.1	82.4	107.8	114.0	126.9	138.2	145.8	136.9	101.3	85.0	58.3	27.3
2001[1]	24.1	68.4	86.1	96.2	112.3	138.0	153.5	151.1	110.9	100.8	57.9	53.9

[1] Preliminary. *Source: Agricultural Statistics Board, U.S. Department of Agriculture (ASB-USDA)*

Wholesale Price of 92 Score Creamery (Grade A) Butter, Central States[1] In Cents Per Pound

Year	Jan.	Feb.	Mar.	Apr.	May	June	July	Aug.	Sept.	Oct.	Nov.	Dec.	Average
1992	94.9	86.3	86.3	86.3	83.8	76.6	76.6	76.6	81.7	82.2	80.7	78.6	82.5
1993	75.3	75.3	75.3	75.3	75.3	76.2	73.5	74.6	74.3	74.2	73.6	69.7	74.4
1994	64.0	64.0	65.5	65.5	64.5	65.1	66.9	71.5	71.5	71.5	71.5	67.0	67.4
1995	64.0	65.5	66.5	66.5	66.5	69.9	74.5	79.5	80.9	95.4	103.5	74.4	75.6
1996	75.4	66.4	65.5	69.0	87.8	129.3	145.3	145.5	145.5	128.6	74.1	71.9	100.4
1997	81.9	98.4	106.3	95.6	86.1	105.5	102.7	102.5	101.6	135.3	148.8	120.1	116.2
1998	109.2	139.8	134.1	136.4	153.2	186.7	203.1	216.6	273.1	242.3	187.9	140.8	177.6
1999	144.4	133.1	130.3	103.9	111.0	147.7	134.7	141.4	135.8	113.8	109.6	94.2	125.0
2000	91.6	92.9	99.7	108.7	122.2	128.6	120.3	120.3	119.1	116.9	151.7	150.0	118.5
2001	122.3	138.1	154.9	174.7	190.4	197.4	192.4	204.5	219.7	151.9	135.2	130.2	167.6

[1] Data prior to June 1998 are for Grade AA in Chicago. *Source: Economic Research Service, U.S. Department of Agriculture (ERS-USDA)*

Cadmium

Cadmium is a rare chemical element that is the byproduct if the refining and smelting of zinc ores. The most common cadmium mineral is greenockite, which is almost always associated with the zinc ore mineral, sphalerite. It is estimated that at least 80 percent of the global cadmium output is the result of being a byproduct of primary zinc production. The remaining 20 percent comes from secondary sources and recycling of cadmium products. Because of low prices, the processing of many wastes for cadmium recovery is not economically viable. Cadmium is used primarily in iron and steel plating to protect them from corrosion. Due to the cost of waste disposal and problems with toxicity, the use of electroplating has decreased.

The U.S. Geological Survey reported that primary cadmium metal in the United States is produced by two companies, one located in Tennessee and one in Illinois. The metals is produced as a byproduct of smelting and refining zinc metal from sulfide ore concentrates. Secondary cadmium is recovered from used nickel-cadmium batteries by one company located in Pennsylvania. Consumption of cadmium has been declining over the last few year because of environmental concerns. In terms of the end uses of cadmium: some 75 percent is used in battery production with 13 percent used in pigments, 7 percent in coatings and plating, 4 percent went to stabilizers for plastics while nonferrous alloys and other uses took 1 percent. Cadmium recycling has been practical for nickel-cadmium batteries, some alloys and dust from electric arc furnaces. Due to environmental concerns, some nickel-cadmium batteries are being replaced by lithium-ion and nickel-metal hydride batteries. The higher cost of these substitutes limits their use. There is some substitution for cadmium in plating applications using zinc coatings. Cadmium pigments can be replaced with cerium sulfide.

World refinery production of cadmium in 2000 was estimated to be 19,300 metric tonnes, up 1 percent from 1999. The largest producer of cadmium was Japan with 2,550 tonnes, down 2 percent from the previous year. The next largest producer was Canada with 2000 output of 2,350 tonnes, up 69 percent from the previous year. Production by China was 2,250 tonnes, up 2 percent from 1999. Other producers of cadmium include Belgium, the U.S., Germany and Mexico. World cadmium reserves were estimated at 600,000 tonnes. There are large amounts of cadmium located in zinc deposits and in zinc-bearing coals in the Central United States.

U.S. refinery production of cadmium in 2000 was 1,200 tonnes, up slightly from the previous year. U.S. imports for consumption of cadmium metal in 2000 were 250 tonnes, down 15 percent from the previous year. Exports of cadmium metal, alloys, and scrap in 2000 were 40 tonnes, up from 20 tonnes the previous year. Shipments of cadmium from Government stockpile excesses in 2000 were 10 tonnes. U.S. apparent consumption of cadmium in 2000 was 1,270 tonnes, down 2 percent from 1999. Year end stocks at producers and distributors in 2000 were 1,040 tonnes, up 16 percent from the end of 1999.

World Refinery Production of Cadmium In Metric Tons

Year	Australia	Belgium	Canada	China	Finland	Germany	Italy	Japan	Kazakhstan[4]	Mexico	United Kingdom	United States[3]	World Total
1991	1,076	1,807	1,829	1,200	593	1,048	658	2,889	2,500	688	449	1,680	20,900
1992	1,001	1,549	1,963	1,150	590	961	742	2,986	1,000	602	383	1,620	19,800
1993	951	1,573	1,944	1,160	785	1,056	517	2,832	800	797	458	1,090	18,400
1994	910	1,556	2,173	1,280	548	1,145	475	2,629	1,097	646	469	1,010	18,200
1995	838	1,710	2,349	1,450	539	1,150	308	2,652	794	689	549	1,270	20,100
1996	639	1,579	2,537	1,570	648	1,150	296	2,344	800	784	541	1,530	18,900
1997	632	1,420	1,272	1,980	540	1,145	287	2,473	1,000	1,223	455	2,060	19,500
1998	585	1,318	1,361	2,130	520	1,020	328	2,337	1,450	1,218	440	1,240	19,200
1999[1]	462	1,400	1,390	2,150	500	1,100	360	2,567	1,061	1,352	547	1,190	19,700
2000[2]	552	1,400	1,390	2,200	550	1,000	350	2,472	1,060	1,350	500	1,890	19,700

[1] Preliminary. [2] Estimate. [3] Primary and secondary metal. [4] Formerly part of the U.S.S.R.; data not reported separately until 1992.
Source: U.S. Geological Survey (USGS)

Salient Statistics of Cadmium in the United States In Metric Tons of Contained Cadmium

Year	Net Import Reliance as a % of Apparent Consumption	Production (Metal)	Producer Shipments	Cadmium Sulfide Production	Production Other Compounds	Imports of Cadmium Metal[3]	Exports[4]	Apparent Consumption	Industry Stocks Dec. 31[5]	New York Dealer Price $ per Pound
1991	50	1,680	1,740	263	1,089	2,040	448	3,080	835	2.01
1992	50	1,620	2,080	270	1,073	1,960	213	3,330	868	.91
1993	64	1,090	1,320	303	731	1,420	38	2,940	579	.45
1994	3	1,010	1,290	170	898	1,110	1,450	1,040	423	1.13
1995	E	1,270	1,280	105	936	848	1,050	1,160	990	1.84
1996	32	1,530	1,310	119	720	843	201	2,250	1,140	1.24
1997	19	2,060	1,370	113	607	790	554	2,510	1,090	.51
1998	38	1,240	1,570	125	638	514	180	2,100	729	.28
1999[1]	9	1,190	1,020	64	604	294	20	1,850	893	.14
2000[2]	6	1,890	1,580	42	417	425	312	2,010	1,200	.16

[1] Preliminary. [2] Estimate. [3] For consumption. [4] Cadmium metal, alloys, dross, flue dust. [5] Metallic, Compounds, Distributors.
[6] Sticks & Balls in 1 to 5 short ton lots. E = Net exporter. *Source: U.S. Geological Survey (USGS)*

Canola (Rapeseed)

Canola prices, basis nearest Winnipeg futures, witnessed a sharp loss of more than $200 per metric ton during the second half of the 1990's before finding a bottom in 2000 around Canadian $250 per ton from which prices staged a $100 recovery into mid-summer of 2001: the strength apparently reflecting a smaller 2001 crop and lower than expected carryover.

World rapeseed production appears to have plateaued following a steady increase in production during the 1990's, the world crop (canola or rapeseed, the terms are interchangeable) in 2001/02 declined to 36.6 million metric tons from 37.6 million in 2000/01 and the record high 42.4 million in 1999/00 and a mid-1990's average of about 30 million. On a protein meal basis, rapeseed has been the world's second largest meal for some time, production of which totaled almost 21 million tons in 2001/02 vs. 21.5 million in 2000/01. For oil, however, rapeseed ranks third (after soybean and palm) with production of a 12.76 million tons in 2001/02 vs. a near record large 13.2 million in 2000/01. World rapeseed supplies in 2001/02 of about 38.4 million tons compares with over 40 million in 2000/01, the latter including a carry-in over more than 2 million tons.. The world 2001/02 (July/June) crush of 34.5 million tons compares with the previous year's 35.7 million and the record high 37 million in 1999/00. The ending world 2001/02 carryover is placed at 1.3 million tons, the smallest since 1997/98.

Collectively, the European Union is the largest producer with 8.6 million tons in 2001/02 vs. 9 million in 2000/01 and a late 1990's average of about 9 million tons. Germany is generally the largest producer within the EU. China is the largest single producer with a record large 11.7 million tons in 20001/02 vs. 11.4 million in 2000/01 and the late 1990's average of 9.4 million. Canada then follows with 5.0 million and 7.1 million, respectively. Although China continues to increase rapeseed acreage, average yield has failed to show much improvement and is almost 50% less than realized in Western Europe. In terms of protein meal consumption, E.U. 2001/02 meal consumption of 5.6 million tons is about one-fifth of soybean meal . E.U estimated rapeseed oil usage, however, in 2001/02 of 3.2 million tons is nearly 50% more than soybean oil. Between the two products, oil has shown the greater percentile growth in recent years. Foreign trade in rapeseed is a distant second to soybeans: exports of 7.7 million tons in 2001/02 compare with almost 10 million in 2000/01.

U.S. production of canola seed is small in absolute terms, but percentage wise increased rapidly in the 1990's. The crop is grown mostly in the Northern Plains states, Production in 2000/01 (June/May) of 2.2 million pounds in 2001/02 compares with 2.0 million in 2000/01. Acreage has grown, almost doubling from year to year at times during the 1990's. Harvested acreage in 2001 of about 1.56 million acres compares with 1.6 million in 2000. Contributing to the gains in U.S. production include: (1) government incentives to increase acreage; (2) development of better varieties that can be grown in the U.S.; and (3) the wider acceptance of canola oil in cooking owing to its lower content of saturated fats. Canola oil is said to be 94% saturated fat free, the lowest of any leading oil. Demand for canola meal has also grown sharply as a livestock feed.

U.S. Canola oil production (October/September) has hovered around 275,000 tons the past few years almost ten times more than in the early 1990'a. Meal production has also shown similar growth. For oil, the absolute gain in domestic usage nearly doubled in the 1990's, but the percentage gain in exports surpassed 1000%. Canola oil prices, basis New York, strengthened in the late 1990's, but significantly the average monthly price tends to remain very steady for protracted periods as it did for almost all the late 1990's at about 90 cents per pound. Canadian canola oilseed prices showed wide swings during that period, basis Vancouver. Rapeseed prices, basis Hamburg, in 20001/02 are forecast at $226 per metric ton vs. $202 in 2000/01 Rapeseed meal prices are forecast at $138 m/ton vs. $141, respectively. Rotterdam rapeseed oil in 2001/02 of $443 per ton compares with $372 m/ton and the 1990/91-99/00 average of $507. In the U.S., the average price for canola meal in 2000/01 of $139 per short ton vs. $117 a year earlier and as high as $192 in 1996/97, basis 36% Pacific Northwest.

Futures Markets

Canola futures and options are traded on the Winnipeg Commodity Exchange (WCE) and quoted in Canadian dollars per ton. Rapeseed futures are traded on the Marche a Terme International de France (MATIF).

World Production of Canola (Rapeseed) In Thousands of Metric Tons

Year	Austrlia	Canada	China	Czecho-slovakia	France	Germany	India	Pakistan	Poland	Sweden	United Kingdom	Former USSR	World Total
1989-90	78	3,209	5,435	387	1,748	1,893	4,125	233	1,586	370	953	401	21,891
1990-1	99	3,266	6,958	380	1,937	2,090	5,229	228	1,206	367	1,200	426	25,045
1991-2	170	4,224	7,436	445	2,270	3,030	5,863	219	1,043	252	1,300	313	28,214
1992-3	179	3,872	7,653	375	1,810	2,617	4,872	243	758	247	1,150	329	25,284
1993-4	305	5,480	6,940	377	1,550	2,848	5,390	225	594	313	1,136	211	26,734
1994-5	309	7,233	7,492	452	1,800	2,837	5,884	225	756	214	1,298	244	30,309
1995-6	557	6,436	9,777	662	2,700	3,127	6,000	255	1,377	215	1,330	252	34,434
1996-7	624	5,062	9,200	521	2,870	2,150	6,942	255	449	139	1,410	226	31,529
1997-8	856	6,392	9,578	575	3,400	2,867	4,935	286	595	118	1,523	223	33,222
1998-9[1]	1,690	7,643	8,300	680	3,700	3,388	4,900	292	1,099	124	1,569	366	35,854
1999-00[2]	2,426	8,798	10,132	854	4,400	4,212	5,110	279	1,132	162	1,733	475	42,138
2000-1[3]	1,650	7,119	11,000	904	3,600	3,550	3,700	297	959	115	1,200	535	37,098

[1] Preliminary. [2] Estimate. [3] Forecast. *Source: Economic Research Service, U.S. Department of Agriculture (ERS-USDA); The Oil World*

CANOLA

Volume of Trading of Canola Futures in Winnipeg In Contracts

Year	Jan.	Feb.	Mar.	Apr.	May	June	July	Aug.	Sept.	Oct.	Nov.	Dec.	Total
1992	57,429	54,546	57,174	38,674	87,638	75,018	50,157	72,971	79,034	93,692	99,577	73,805	839,715
1993	73,411	74,362	63,737	73,358	61,996	70,117	94,286	77,325	56,377	73,953	107,485	112,377	938,784
1994	119,691	103,517	85,125	100,923	111,962	79,307	83,903	95,712	54,893	87,350	101,727	96,797	1,120,907
1995	75,068	87,113	86,340	67,937	95,447	85,126	94,576	70,904	94,794	126,210	84,991	107,177	1,075,683
1996	99,542	95,034	76,704	128,169	148,189	103,892	135,652	87,896	108,490	161,894	90,105	110,453	1,346,020
1997	121,433	133,056	131,473	148,647	117,219	116,117	80,867	72,602	93,967	150,065	97,984	124,245	1,387,675
1998	100,926	144,309	110,708	140,789	130,551	121,829	107,816	89,457	121,573	181,002	127,120	181,278	1,557,358
1999	129,758	59,772	132,732	143,282	102,838	134,179	94,256	113,913	130,505	184,973	157,428	179,798	1,563,434
2000	137,528	182,744	163,038	169,807	168,164	152,358	79,071	91,762	146,890	208,639	154,727	204,045	1,858,773
2001	196,137	292,226	286,463	247,744	205,798	188,175	163,901	155,531	143,220	205,016	174,910	165,852	2,424,973

Source: Winnipeg Commodity Exchange (WCE)

Average Open Interest of Canola Futures in Winnipeg In Contracts

Year	Jan.	Feb.	Mar.	Apr.	May	June	July	Aug.	Sept.	Oct.	Nov.	Dec.
1992	15,943	17,556	20,559	21,410	23,727	28,885	26,013	25,674	28,049	32,724	35,693	37,375
1993	34,098	37,658	36,715	38,210	38,231	29,743	39,763	43,844	50,616	55,107	54,998	54,475
1994	50,335	55,280	54,899	58,012	60,567	55,434	54,733	57,044	57,049	54,375	55,045	49,475
1995	47,579	43,662	36,530	32,580	38,361	42,961	43,607	42,828	51,067	57,638	46,640	45,444
1996	42,646	43,808	45,126	47,989	54,228	52,176	49,387	40,619	42,242	52,273	53,121	54,323
1997	48,681	48,281	50,815	50,025	49,212	43,941	35,496	30,039	25,255	36,674	38,702	42,510
1998	35,864	46,678	49,161	48,683	56,163	60,285	57,627	51,462	53,919	56,651	51,426	60,663
1999	57,958	64,014	57,851	57,351	51,808	53,039	49,273	41,819	53,425	67,244	63,780	64,286
2000	59,057	65,545	65,296	66,253	65,855	59,673	46,813	51,367	59,342	72,618	64,862	65,170
2001	57,537	73,539	88,111	78,143	77,425	84,315	72,430	70,137	67,275	71,651	65,580	66,884

Source: Winnipeg Commodity Exchange (WCE)

World Supply and Distribution of Canola and Products In Thousands of Metric Tons

	Canola					Canola Meal					Canola Oil				
Year	Production	Exports	Imports	Crush	Ending Stocks	Production	Exports	Imports	Consumption	Ending Stocks	Production	Exports	Imports	Consumption	Ending Stocks
1991-2	28,214	4,675	4,734	25,557	1,045	15,662	3,367	3,389	15,569	445	9,314	2,076	2,049	9,194	468
1992-3	25,284	4,055	4,241	22,988	1,045	14,067	3,374	3,412	14,097	453	8,392	1,729	1,694	8,424	401
1993-4	26,731	5,153	5,317	21,636	888	15,005	3,040	3,509	15,254	447	9,119	2,239	2,203	9,064	420
1994-5	30,309	5,836	5,900	27,178	1,001	16,525	3,718	3,661	16,448	467	10,016	2,654	2,779	10,236	325
1995-6	34,434	5,978	5,795	30,393	1,681	18,467	4,322	4,108	18,138	582	11,128	2,596	2,563	10,970	450
1996-7	31,529	5,673	5,967	28,851	2,047	17,530	4,361	4,023	17,264	510	10,524	2,625	2,547	10,506	390
1997-8	33,222	6,902	6,757	31,192	1,081	18,839	4,581	4,417	18,741	444	11,420	3,024	2,691	11,037	440
1998-9[1]	35,854	9,154	9,096	32,001	2,232	19,166	3,777	3,804	19,322	315	11,845	2,873	2,639	11,563	488
1999-00[2]	42,138	10,979	10,986	37,173	3,953	22,306	4,362	4,283	22,167	375	13,646	2,966	2,743	13,242	669
2000-1[3]	37,098	9,821	9,723	35,507	2,291	21,302	4,002	4,029	21,402	302	13,153	2,756	2,690	13,141	615

[1] Preliminary. [2] Estimate. [3] Forecast. *Source: Economic Research Service, U.S. Department of Agriculture (ERS-USDA); The Oil World*

Salient Statistics of Canola and Canola Oil in the United States In Thousands of Metric Tons

	Canola							Canola Oil						
	Supply				Disappearance			Supply				Disappearance		
Year	Stocks June 1	Production	Imports	Total	Crush	Exports	Total[3]	Stocks June 1	Production	Imports	Total	Domestic	Exports	Total
1991-2	15	94	1	110	57	44	101	20	14	374	408	367	7	374
1992-3	6	72	12	90	35	47	82	34	24	396	454	415	7	422
1993-4	5	118	351	474	389	35	424	32	186	412	630	532	35	567
1994-5	43	209	286	538	413	103	516	63	137	430	630	535	70	605
1995-6	16	250	253	519	409	62	471	25	162	497	684	582	67	649
1996-7	40	219	259	518	395	79	474	35	155	502	692	529	133	662
1997-8	36	355	355	746	589	126	715	30	205	504	739	529	158	687
1998-9	19	710	310	1,039	698	246	944	52	250	503	805	603	123	726
1999-00[1]	77	621	242	940	722	136	858	79	279	534	892	667	129	796
2000-1[2]	50	917	190	1,157	758	210	968	96	296	533	925	699	126	825

[1] Preliminary. [2] Forecast. [3] Includes planting seed and residual. *Source: Economic Research Service, U.S. Department of Agriculture*

Wholesale Price of Canola Oil, Refined (Denatured), in Tanks in New York In Cents Per Pound

Year	Jan.	Feb.	Mar.	Apr.	May	June	July	Aug.	Sept.	Oct.	Nov.	Dec.	Average
1992	82.25	82.25	82.25	82.25	82.25	82.25	82.25	82.25	67.25	62.25	62.25	62.25	76.00
1993	62.25	62.25	62.25	62.25	55.88	53.75	53.25	53.00	53.00	52.00	52.50	50.00	56.00
1994	53.75	53.75	53.75	53.75	53.75	53.75	53.75	53.75	53.75	53.75	53.75	53.75	53.75
1995	53.75	53.75	53.75	53.75	53.15	50.75	50.75	50.75	50.75	50.75	50.75	50.75	51.95
1996	50.75	50.75	50.75	50.75	50.75	50.75	50.75	50.75	50.75	60.56	90.00	90.00	58.11
1997	90.00	90.00	90.00	90.00	90.00	90.00	90.00	90.00	90.00	82.00	82.00	82.00	88.00
1998	90.00	90.00	90.00	90.00	90.00	90.00	90.00	90.00	90.00	90.00	90.00	90.00	90.00
1999	80.00	80.00	80.00	80.00	80.00	80.00	80.00	80.00	80.00	80.00	80.00	80.00	80.00
2000	90.00	90.00	90.00	90.00	90.00	90.00	90.00	90.00	90.00	90.00	90.00	90.00	90.00
2001[1]	92.00	92.00	92.00	92.00	92.00	92.00	92.00	92.00	92.00	92.00			92.00

[1] Preliminary. *Source: Economic Research Service, U.S. Department of Agriculture (ERS-USDA)*

Average Price of Canola in Vancouver In Canadian Dollars Per Tonne

Year	Jan.	Feb.	Mar.	Apr.	May	June	July	Aug.	Sept.	Oct.	Nov.	Dec.	Average
1992	264.15	273.35	282.70	276.85	288.08	292.35	272.20	282.26	320.62	302.10	327.22	331.57	292.79
1993	344.22	329.26	328.67	325.06	318.85	319.23	331.29	322.85	311.29	311.66	331.44	366.37	328.35
1994	408.60	413.10	422.23	454.90	481.44	484.95	388.63	382.54	381.70	379.99	401.38	432.35	419.32
1995	431.85	440.41	456.13	425.40	404.27	414.31	426.49	405.94	405.89	413.29	416.03	423.77	421.98
1996	424.07	422.60	417.55	443.94	473.04	469.28	470.38	453.86	453.53	444.01	432.30	439.79	445.36
1997	441.96	441.68	457.95	448.09	446.00	428.47	395.58	400.68	390.38	398.81	419.12	410.21	423.24
1998	416.48	428.88	434.68	441.44	450.56	443.11	404.86	387.05	389.34	400.40	412.17	417.41	418.87
1999	402.74	368.17	363.24	362.16	353.21	356.53	317.36	305.73	302.93	302.68	297.76	287.62	335.01
2000	286.09	277.92	280.97	287.34	284.59	274.12	265.32	262.24	269.17	265.32	267.75	278.59	274.95
2001	279.07	285.05	302.04	299.59	310.00	320.79	356.98	368.33	351.01	332.16	328.99	334.53	322.38

Source: Winnipeg Commodity Exchange (WCE)

Cassava

Cassava, or tapioca root, is used primarily as an animal feed and as a foodstuff in tropical countries. Cassava has been viewed as a food that could be the solution to the hunger problems that exist in less developed countries. Technological advances have held the promise that there will be substantial increases in yields in the future. New strains of cassava root are being developed in Africa that could eventually be used in the fight against world hunger.

Cassava is grown in countries with tropical climates. It is a popular crop to produce since it is resistant to drought and relatively easy to grow. Cassava is a diet staple in many countries. In countries where the price of imported foodstuffs have risen there has been increased demand for locally produced foods like cassava.

For 2001, the Food and Agricultural Organization of the United Nations reported that world production of cassava was 175.6 million metric tonnes, an increase of less than 1 percent from 2000 when production was estimated to be 174.5 million tonnes. World harvested acreage was estimated at 16.5 million hectares. Acreage in 2000 was estimated at 16.4 million hectares.

The world's largest producer of cassava is Nigeria with 2001 production estimated at 33.9 million tonnes or 19 percent of the world total. harvested acreage in Nigeria was estimated to be 3.1 million hectares.

The next largest producer of cassava is Brazil. Production in year 2001 was estimated at 24.5 million tonnes, an increase of 5 percent from the previous year. Brazil's harvested acreage was estimated at 1.75 million hectares, an increase of almost 2 percent from the previous year.

The third largest producer of cassava is Thailand. Cassava production in Thailand in 2001 was estimated to be 18.3 million tonnes, down 3 percent from the previous season. Thailand's harvested acreage in 2001 was 1.15 million hectares. Thailand is the largest exporter of cassava with exports each season of about 6 million tonnes. Much of Thailand's exports go to Europe as animal feed. Exports have declined due in part to the effect mad cow disease has had in reducing herds. China also is a major buyer of Thailand's cassava. In addition to food and feed, cassava is used in alcohol, pharmaceuticals and cosmetics.

World Cassava Production In Thousands of Metric Tons

Year	Brazil	China	Ghana	India	Indonesia	Mozambique	Nigeria	Paraguay	Tanzania	Thailand	Uganda	Zaire	World Total
1993	21,837	3,403	4,500	5,413	16,799	3,511	29,900	2,656	6,833	20,203	3,139	20,835	163,002
1994	24,464	3,501	6,025	5,784	15,729	3,352	31,005	2,518	7,209	19,091	2,080	18,051	163,514
1995	25,423	3,501	6,612	5,929	15,442	4,178	31,404	3,054	5,969	17,388	2,224	17,500	165,436
1996	24,584	3,601	7,111	5,443	17,002	4,734	31,418	2,648	5,992	17,388	2,245	18,000	164,711
1997	24,305	3,651	7,000	5,868	15,134	5,337	30,409	3,155	5,700	18,084	2,291	----	164,373
1998	19,661	3,651	7,227	6,000	14,696	5,639	32,695	3,300	6,128	15,591	3,204	----	162,072
1999[1]	20,933	3,651	7,845	6,000	15,422	5,650	33,060	3,500	7,182	16,507	3,400	----	168,055

[1] Estimate. *Source: Food and Agriculture Organization of the United Nations (FAO-UN)*

Prices of Tapioca, Hard Pellets, F.O.B. Rotterdam U.S. Dollars Per Tonne

Year	Jan.	Feb.	Mar.	Apr.	May	June	July	Aug.	Sept.	Oct.	Nov.	Dec.	Average
1994	122	123	128	133	138	141	147	154	158	161	161	161	144
1995	164	170	180	178	174	176	183	176	178	184	182	178	177
1996	167	160	155	158	163	154	149	154	146	139	140	133	152
1997	133	118	112	108	114	110	100	97	100	102	102	100	108
1998	96	100	98	104	106	104	105	106	112	122	124	109	107
1999	104	102	101	102	108	104	99	102	100	99	100	97	102
2000	94	90	88	92	85	88	88	81	78	74	76	79	84
2001	83	80	77	78	80	82	84	84	87	83	84	84	82

Source: The Oil World

World Trade in Tapioca In Thousands of Metric Tons

	Exports					Imports						
Year	China	Indonesia	Thailand	Viet Nam	Total World Exports	China	EC-12[2]	Japan	Rep. of Korea	United States	Former USSR	Total World Imports
1993	269	936	6,707	29	8,090	149	6,449	151	658	60	8	8,376
1994	77	686	4,703	28	5,645	92	5,441	94	132	18	----	6,076
1995	10	481	3,297	1	3,860	362	2,924	16	140	----	----	3,590
1996	11	389	3,607	1	4,052	75	3,321	22	554	----	----	4,174
1997	11	247	4,155	26	4,477	242	3,413	15	455	----	----	4,475
1998	10	221	3,199	----	3,468	250	2,620	19	347	----	----	3,440
1999[1]	10	340	4,341	1	4,740	381	3,905	18	90	----	----	4,630

[1] Estimate. [2] Intra-EU trade is excluded. *Source: The Oil World*

Castor Beans

Castorseed beans are used to produce castor oil. The average castorseed bean contains from 35 percent to as much as 55 percent oil. The oil is removed from the bean by either pressing or solvent extraction. Castorseed oil is a valuable product in that it finds use in many other products. It is used in paint varnish as well as in the making of dibasic acids and plasticizers. Castor oil and its derivatives like dehydrated castor oil find use in a variety of products ranging from cosmetics and hair oils to printing inks, nylon plastics, greases and hydraulic fluids, dyeing acids and in textile finishing materials.

World production of castorseed beans has averaged a bit over a million metric tonnes per year. The trend has been slightly lower with production in the mid 1990's averaging 1.22 million tonnes while in the late 1990's it was closer to 1.1 million tonnes. The two major producers of castorseed are India and China. Between 1993 and 1999, India averaged 800,000 tonnes a year of output. China averaged about 214,000 tonnes per year. Smaller producers of castorseed include Brazil and Paraguay.

In the year from September 2001 to October 2002, castorseed production in India is expected to decline about 25 percent from 800,000 tonnes. While the crop was expected to decline, carryover stocks from 2000/01 were estimated to be between 250,000 and 300,000 tonnes. One characteristic of castorseed is that it does not require as much water as other crops and dry conditions in 2000/01 had led to increased castorseed plantings. In Gujaret, the largest castorseed production state, acreage planted in the new year was expected to be down 30 percent or more. Monsoon rains in Gujaret were good and that prompted producers to seed alternative crops like cotton.

World Production of Castorseed Beans In Thousands of Metric Tons

Crop Year	Brazil	China	Ecuador	India	Mexico	Paraguay	Pakistan	Philippines	Sudan	Tanzania	Thailand	Former U.S.S.R.	World Total
1993-4	45	280	13	700	1	15	7	7	6	3	22	4	1,135
1994-5	53	230	7	850	1	10	5	7	4	3	15	8	1,226
1995-6	33	165	5	930	1	9	9	7	2	3	16	3	1,214
1996-7	43	220	4	770	1	15	5	4	1	2	15	3	1,117
1997-8[1]	96	180	4	800	2	16	5	4	1	3	14	3	1,162
1998-9[2]	14	210	4	810	1	19	7	4	1	3	12	3	1,122
1999-00[3]	32	215	4	730	1	18	7	4	1	3	8	3	1,060

[1] Preliminary. [2] Estimate. [3] Forecast. *Sources: Foreign Agricultural Service, U.S.Department of Agriculture (FAS-USDA); The Oil World*

Castor Oil Consumption[2] in the United States In Thousands of Pounds

Year	Oct.	Nov.	Dec.	Jan.	Feb.	Mar.	Apr.	May	June	July	Aug.	Sept.	Total
1995-6	5,228	5,463	6,232	5,794	6,979	5,545	3,369	5,864	5,469	5,439	4,332	3,818	63,532
1996-7	3,921	4,460	4,555	3,738	4,679	4,256	4,476	4,006	3,851	3,855	3,763	5,050	50,610
1997-8	3,276	4,353	4,367	4,409	3,035	4,389	4,218	3,645	4,651	4,350	3,489	4,210	48,392
1998-9	2,348	3,579	3,740	3,323	4,197	5,004	5,218	4,639	4,396	4,471	4,465	4,494	49,874
1999-00	4,281	3,917	4,682	3,819	4,328	5,346	4,135	3,341	4,268	3,884	4,257	4,573	50,831
2000-1	2,694	4,601	2,386	3,975	2,896	3,209	3,159	3,840	3,112	3,050	4,686	2,257	39,865
2001-2[1]	4,127	2,346											38,838

[1] Preliminary. [2] In inedible products (Resins, Plastics, etc.). *Source: Bureau of the Census, U.S. Department of Commerce*

Castor Oil Stocks in the United States, on First of Month In Thousands of Pounds

Year	Oct.	Nov.	Dec.	Jan.	Feb.	Mar.	Apr.	May	June	July	Aug.	Sept.
1995-6	27,143	35,329	43,189	51,713	45,746	37,210	29,718	36,829	55,687	43,954	37,802	25,535
1996-7	23,831	38,785	41,016	31,755	23,630	15,157	7,200	24,164	14,166	27,754	17,426	20,656
1997-8	25,098	24,188	25,425	17,543	12,736	7,138	2,804	18,897	15,386	24,682	16,586	29,862
1998-9	40,018	46,809	36,881	35,668	31,961	22,252	13,771	11,950	5,568	13,952	34,956	25,944
1999-00	44,427	34,180	31,191	44,315	36,632	26,885	25,486	27,605	39,038	38,118	42,934	31,015
2000-1	32,585	35,858	30,058	24,728	32,566	35,186	24,808	51,808	57,910	48,415	40,279	59,461
2001-2[1]	53,083	45,933	23,973	38,459								

[1] Preliminary. *Source: Bureau of the Census, U.S. Department of Commerce*

Average Wholesale Price of Castor Oil No. 1, Brazilian Tanks in New York In Cents Per Pound

Year	Jan.	Feb.	Mar.	Apr.	May	June	July	Aug.	Sept.	Oct.	Nov.	Dec.	Average
1995	45.00	45.00	45.00	45.00	45.00	45.00	45.00	45.00	45.00	45.00	45.00	45.00	45.00
1996	43.50	41.50	41.50	41.50	41.50	41.50	41.50	41.50	41.50	41.50	41.50	41.50	41.67
1997	41.50	41.50	41.50	41.50	41.50	41.50	41.50	41.50	41.50	41.50	41.50	41.50	41.50
1998	41.50	41.50	41.50	41.50	41.50	48.00	48.00	48.00	48.00	48.00	48.00	48.00	45.29
1999	48.00	48.00	48.00	48.00	48.00	48.00	48.00	48.00	48.00	48.00	48.00	48.00	48.00
2000	47.00	47.00	47.00	47.00	47.00	47.00	47.00	48.00	48.00	48.00	48.00	48.00	47.42
2001	48.00	48.00	48.00	48.00	48.00	48.00	48.00	48.00	48.00	48.00			48.00

Source: Foreign Agricultural Service, U.S.Department of Agriculture (FAS-USDA)

Cattle and Calves

In early 2001 U.S. cattle prices, basis nearest Chicago futures prices, surged to more than $.80 a pound, their highest level since early 1993. The strength proved short lived, but not the downtrend that took hold that carried into yearend before finding support around $.65. In 2001, weather took a heavy toll on the domestic beef sector as the most severe winter since 1992/93 resulted in poor feedlot performance and sharply reduced slaughter weights. The second half of the year also saw drought and another round of record slaughter weights owing in part to longer days on feed, and extended the liquidation phase of the cattle cycle that began in 1995/96. The record heifer slaughter and, combined with the length of the biological lag, held down the beef cowherd expansion. Beef cow slaughter in 2001 was the largest since 1998 and along with large numbers of heifers on feed further brakes the cyclical expansionary phase from taking hold. Drawing from a smaller cattle inventory, it is expected that beef production will decline through 2004, particularly as heifers are retained for the breeding herd.

The world cattle inventory has shown relatively little growth during the past decade: the January 1, 2001 total of about 1,036 million head compares with 1,030 million a year earlier and ten years earlier. However, some large changes occurred since the early 1990's: notably the sharp decline in cattle numbers in the former USSR and increases in China. Russia's and the Ukraine's cattle inventory in early 2001 was estimated at only 36 million head vs. nearly 80 million head ten years earlier. In contrast, China's January 1, 2001 inventory of a record high 151 million head compares with 105 million a decade earlier. India, who held about 30% of the world's total cattle inventory on January 1, 2001--about 314 million head--appears to be slowly increasing its inventory following little expansion in the first half of the 1990's. Brazil had the second largest inventory in early 2001--about 151 million head vs. 146 million in 2000. The U.S. cattle inventory totaled around 110 million head in the 1980's, then cyclically declined to 96 million by early 1990 which was followed by an expansionary phase that peaked in the mid-1990's at around 104 million head. The January 1, 2001 inventory totaled about 97 million head. The three largest cattle inventory states are generally Texas, Kansas and Nebraska.

World beef consumption in 2000 showed little growth: 48.6 million metric tons vs. 48.2 million in 1999 and estimated at 48.6 million in 2001. European Union use in 2000 of 7.3 million tons was about unchanged from 1999 and it may prove no higher, if not lower, in 2001 depending upon the depth of latent consumer fears towards possible contaminated beef. China beef consumption in 2000 of a record high 5.3 million tons compares with 5 million in 1999 and estimated at 5.7 million in 2001. In the former USSR, consumption in 2000 fell to 2.8 million tons from 3.4 million in 1999, but forecast to hold at 2.8 million in 2001.

U.S. commercial cattle slaughter in 2001 of 35.3 million head compares with 36.2 million in 2000 of which steers comprised about half of the slaughter mix and heifers about a third. Dressed slaughter weights in late 2001 averaged a record large 760 pounds. U.S. beef production in 2001 of 26.1 billion pounds compares with 26.8 billion in 2000. U.S. per capita beef consumption had shown negative growth in recent years as consumers opt for less red meat in their diet; per capita use in 2001 of 68.4 pounds (retail weight) compares with 69.4 pounds in 2000 and a 2002 estimate of 66.6 pounds, the contraction in demand taking hold despite the industry's aggressive advertising stressing beef's high protein nutritional value and ease to prepare for the evening meal.

U.S. beef (and veal) exports in 2001 of 2.2 billion pounds compares with 2.5 billion in 2000 and forecast to slip under 2.2 billion in 2002. U.S. beef imports in 2001 of 3.2 billion pounds compare with 3.0 billion in 2000 and 3.24 billion forecast for 2002; Australia, New Zealand and Canada are the largest beef suppliers to the U.S. Live cattle is imported from Canada and Mexico.

Choice steer prices, basis Nebraska, in 2001 averaged $72.52 per cwt vs. $69.65 in 2000. Prices are forecast between $74-$78/cwt in 2002. On the retail level, choice beef prices in mid-2001 averaged around $3.40/lb, about 30 cents above a year earlier.

Futures Markets

Live cattle futures and options on futures are traded on the Chicago Mercantile Exchange (CME), the Bolsa de Mercadorias & Futures (BM&F), and the Midamerica Commodity Exchange (MidAm). Feeder cattle futures are traded on the CME and the BM&F, and feeder cattle options are traded on the CME.

World Cattle and Buffalo Numbers as of January 1 In Thousands of Head

Year	Argentina	Australia	Brazil	China	Colombia	France	Germany	India	Mexico	Russia	Ukraine	United States	World Total (Mil. Head)
1992	55,229	25,857	141,800	104,592	16,008	20,970	17,134	271,200	30,232	54,677	23,728	97,556	1,032
1993	55,577	25,182	149,000	107,840	16,391	20,383	16,207	271,255	30,649	52,226	22,457	99,176	1,031
1994	54,875	25,758	149,100	113,157	16,614	20,112	15,897	291,973	30,702	48,914	21,607	100,974	1,053
1995	54,207	25,736	149,315	123,317	17,556	20,524	15,962	293,922	30,191	43,296	19,624	102,785	1,058
1996	53,569	26,500	149,228	104,000	18,478	20,662	15,890	296,462	28,140	39,700	17,558	103,548	1,029
1997	51,696	26,780	146,110	110,318	19,038	20,557	15,760	299,802	26,822	35,800	15,313	101,656	1,026
1998	49,238	26,710	144,670	121,757	19,507	20,154	15,227	303,030	25,628	31,500	12,579	99,744	1,026
1999	49,437	26,578	143,893	124,354	20,621	20,097	14,942	306,967	24,859	28,600	11,722	99,115	1,025
2000[1]	49,832	26,716	146,272	126,983	21,700	20,197	14,657	312,572	23,715	27,000	10,627	98,198	1,031
2001[2]	50,052	27,003	150,853	130,000	22,663	20,518	14,557	313,774	22,500	25,500	10,000	97,309	1,037

[1] Preliminary. [2] Forecast. *Source: Foreign Agricultural Service, U.S. Department of Agriculture (FAS-USDA)*

Cattle Supply and Distribution in the United States In Thousands of Head

Year	Cattle & Calves on Farms January 1	Imports	Calves Born	Total Supply	Livestock Slaughter - Cattle and Calves: Commercial: Federally Inspected	Other[3]	All Commercial	Farm	Total Slaughter	Deaths on Farms	Exports	Total Disappearance
1991	96,393	1,939	38,583	139,861	33,285	841	34,126	242	34,368	4,247	311	38,927
1992	97,556	2,255	38,933	141,104	33,428	817	34,245	242	34,489	4,366	322	39,177
1993	99,176	2,499	39,369	142,750	33,752	767	34,519	233	34,746	4,630	153	39,529
1994	100,974	2,083	40,105	143,799	34,719	745	25,464	227	35,691	4,254	231	40,176
1995	102,755	2,786	40,264	145,805	36,272	798	37,069	225	37,294	4,382	95	41,771
1996	103,548	1,965	39,823	145,336	37,435	917	38,351	224	38,575	4,572	174	43,321
1997	101,656	2,046	38,961	142,663	37,101	792	37,893	218	38,111	4,676	282	43,069
1998	99,744	2,034	38,812	140,590	36,209	714	36,923	215	37,138	4,220	285	41,643
1999[1]	99,115	1,945	38,710	139,770	35,486	664	36,150	210	37,642		329	37,971
2000[2]	98,048	2,187			35,631	616	36,247				481	

[1] Preliminary. [2] Estimate. [3] Wholesale and retail. *Source: Economic Research Service, U.S. Department of Agriculture (ERS-USDA)*

Beef Supply and Utilization in the United States

Year/ Quarter	Beginning Stocks	Production: Commercial	Production: Total	Imports	Total Supply	Exports	Ending Stocks	Total Disappearance	Per Capita Disappearance: Carcass Weight	Per Capita Disappearance: Retail Weight
	Million Pounds								Pounds	
1997	377	25,384	25,490	2,343	28,210	2,136	465	25,609	96.7	67.2
I	377	6,112	6,149	536	7,062	455	387	6,220	23.3	16.2
II	387	6,419	6,435	716	7,538	513	425	6,600	24.7	17.1
III	425	6,603	6,636	576	7,741	600	430	6,811	25.4	17.6
IV	430	6,258	6,187	515	7,152	568	400	6,302	23.4	16.3
1998	465	25,653	27,134	2,642	29,775	2,171	465	25,536	94.5	68.1
I	465	6,215	6,680	644	7,324	500	375	6,317	23.4	16.7
II	375	6,463	6,838	682	7,520	537	316	6,451	23.9	17.2
III	316	6,638	6,954	685	7,639	563	323			17.5
IV	323	6,339	6,662	630	7,292	571	465			16.7
1999	296	26,386	27,579	2,874	30,453	2,329	302			67.4
I	296	6,399	6,695	628	7,323	564	309			16.7
II	309	6,627	6,936	812	7,748	557	293			17.7
III	293	6,838	7,131	742	7,873	593	294			17.2
IV	294	6,522	6,816	692	7,508	615	302			15.8
2000[1]	314	26,777	28,244	3,015	31,259	2,350	402			69.4
I	314	6,653	6,967	720	7,687	540	369			17.2
II	367	6,699	7,066	820	7,886	565	374			17.5
III	380	6,914	7,294	775	8,069	625	378			18.0
IV	406	6,511	6,917	700	7,617	620	412			16.7
2001[2]		25,574	25,574	3,080	28,654	2,550				68.4
I		6,204	6,204	735	6,939	620				16.5
II		6,675	6,675	840	7,515	635				17.2
III		6,620	6,620	785	7,405	650				17.4
IV		6,075	6,075	720	6,795	645				17.3

[1] Preliminary. [2] Forecast. *Source: Economic Research Service, U.S. Department of Agriculture (ERS-USDA)*

United States Cattle on Feed in 13 States In Thousands of Head

Year/ Quarter	Number on Feed[3]	Placed on Feed	Marketings	Other Disappearance	Year/ Quarter	Number on Feed[3]	Placed on Feed	Marketings	Other Disappearance
1998	11,155	19,476	18,878	712	2000[1]	11,475	25,348	24,100	925
I	11,155	4,931	5,706	262	I	11,475	6,107	6,150	250
II	10,118	1,563	2,033	72	II	11,182	5,656	6,187	262
II	9,161	6,606	5,857	163	III	10,389	7,043	6,269	147
IV	9,781	6,376	5,282	215	IV	11,016	6,542	5,494	266
1999	10,667	25,172	23,480	894	2001[2]	11,798	25,975	23,547	887
I	10,667	5,742	5,819	206	I	11,798	5,685	5,703	257
II	10,384	5,501	6,064	266	II	11,523	5,888	6,133	267
III	9,555	6,999	6,119	169	III	11,011	6,326	6,053	159
IV	10,276	6,930	5,478	253	IV	11,125	8,076	5,658	204

[1] Preliminary. [2] Estimate. [3] Beginning of period. *Source: Economic Research Service, U.S. Department of Agriculture (ERS-USDA)*

CATTLE AND CALVES

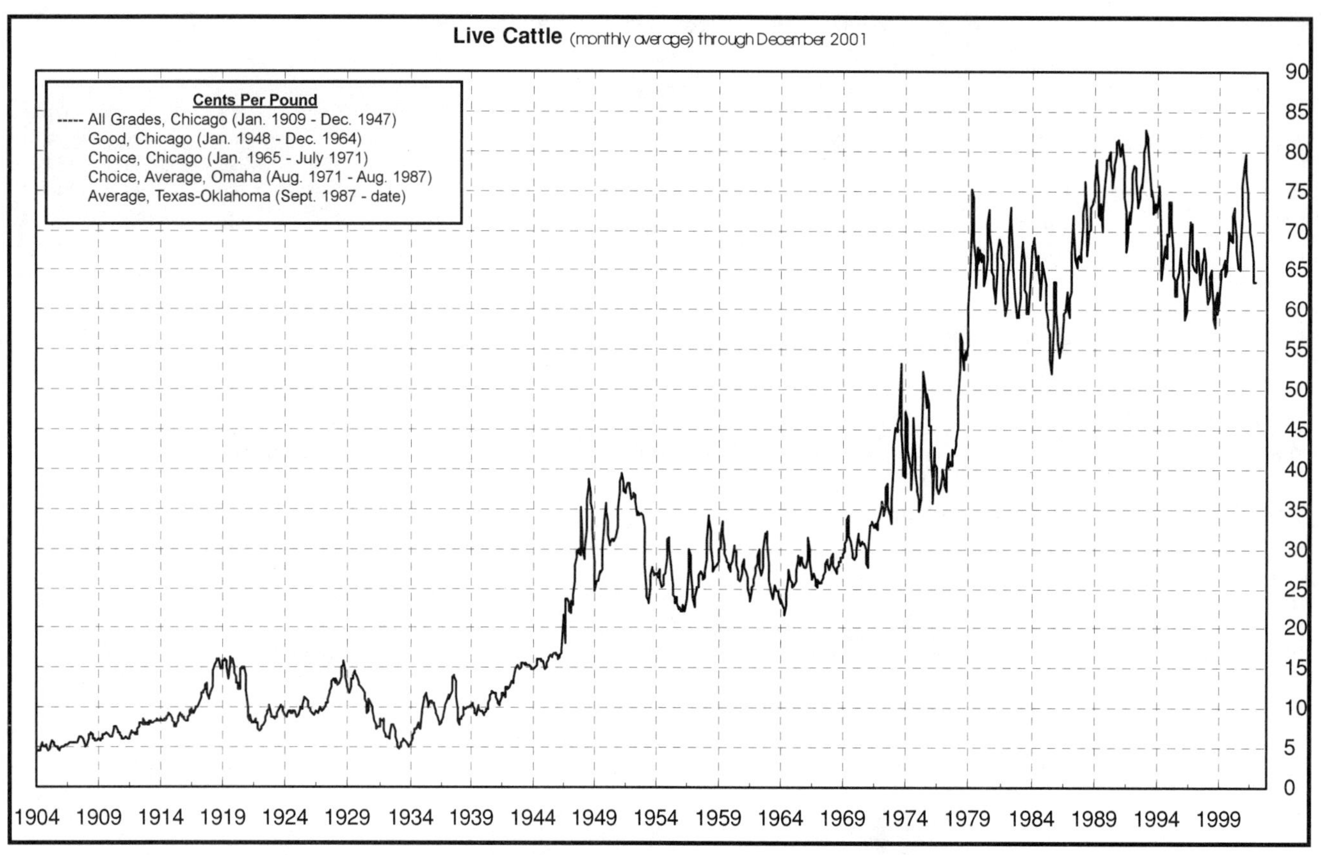

United States Cattle on Feed in 7 States, on First of Month In Thousands of Head

Year	Jan.	Feb.	Mar.	Apr.	May	June	July	Aug.	Sept.	Oct.	Nov.	Dec.
1992	8,397	8,223	8,195	8,058	7,868	7,876	7,377	7,050	7,018	7,565	8,704	8,984
1993	9,163	9,140	8,851	8,781	8,409	8,393	7,973	7,703	7,794	8,224	9,096	9,397
1994	8,256	8,139	7,981	7,960	7,772	7,511	6,910	6,841	6,949	7,295	7,988	8,198
1995	8,031	8,119	8,227	8,328	8,233	8,182	7,734	7,391	7,189	7,722	8,420	8,685
1996	8,667	8,304	8,152	8,286	7,758	7,253	6,578	6,337	6,612	7,486	8,534	9,003
1997	8,943	8,813	8,769	8,904	8,484	8,231	7,679	7,536	7,850	8,558	9,390	9,718
1998	9,455	9,180	8,835	8,607	8,295	8,289	7,825	7,706	7,750	8,376	9,190	9,404
1999	9,021	8,917	8,878	8,899	8,583	8,547	8,183	7,889	8,185	8,793	9,789	10,020
2000	9,752	9,885	9,695	9,593	9,391	9,411	8,959	8,812	8,972	9,502	10,192	10,213
2001[1]	10,076	10,222	10,012	9,859	9,563	9,660	9,466	9,387	9,383	9,613	10,231	10,203

[1] Preliminary. *Source: Economic Research Service, U.S. Department of Agriculture (ERS-USDA)*

United States Cattle Placed on Feedlots in 7 States In Thousands of Head

Year	Jan.	Feb.	Mar.	Apr.	May	June	July	Aug.	Sept.	Oct.	Nov.	Dec.	Total
1992	1,565	1,502	1,516	1,425	1,724	1,319	1,432	1,641	2,189	2,688	1,813	1,694	20,508
1993	1,641	1,262	1,626	1,326	1,801	1,430	1,513	1,865	2,148	2,494	1,878	1,490	20,474
1994	1,416	1,256	1,518	1,310	1,359	1,113	1,520	1,761	1,915	2,244	1,642	1,345	18,399
1995	1,631	1,532	1,681	1,403	1,673	1,356	1,404	1,653	2,173	2,278	1,804	1,446	20,034
1996	1,312	1,441	1,666	1,150	1,242	1,068	1,483	1,965	2,267	2,536	1,953	1,423	19,506
1997	1,663	1,552	1,694	1,296	1,612	1,224	1,751	2,111	2,278	2,454	1,826	1,304	20,765
1998	1,492	1,290	1,421	1,358	1,740	1,314	1,677	1,773	2,254	2,396	1,732	1,250	19,697
1999	1,681	1,563	1,741	1,443	1,733	1,515	1,565	2,085	2,345	2,629	1,823	1,408	21,531
2000	1,931	1,606	1,736	1,470	1,998	1,413	1,674	2,091	2,286	2,387	1,678	1,440	21,710
2001[1]	1,965	1,331	1,530	1,324	2,060	1,690	1,730	1,906	1,806	2,310	1,581	1,330	20,563

[1] Preliminary. *Source: Economic Research Service, U.S. Department of Agriculture (ERS-USDA)*

United States Cattle Marketings in 7 States In Thousands of Head

Year	Jan.	Feb.	Mar.	Apr.	May	June	July	Aug.	Sept.	Oct.	Nov.	Dec.	Total
1992	1,640	1,410	1,536	1,490	1,594	1,702	1,674	1,592	1,581	1,473	1,442	1,414	18,548
1993	1,534	1,441	1,585	1,572	1,681	1,743	1,702	1,692	1,652	1,546	1,469	1,431	19,048
1994	1,481	1,357	1,467	1,430	1,542	1,632	1,550	1,602	1,525	1,504	1,370	1,432	17,892
1995	1,484	1,372	1,513	1,437	1,667	1,754	1,698	1,815	1,594	1,529	1,478	1,412	18,753
1996	1,626	1,541	1,476	1,613	1,747	1,696	1,678	1,653	1,342	1,431	1,418	1,415	18,636
1997	1,728	1,554	1,497	1,648	1,785	1,732	1,852	1,755	1,528	1,545	1,429	1,499	19,552
1998	1,689	1,579	1,580	1,609	1,681	1,727	1,755	1,687	1,577	1,537	1,455	1,564	19,440
1999	1,738	1,560	1,668	1,681	1,696	1,835	1,816	1,747	1,682	1,570	1,530	1,601	20,124
2000	1,747	1,749	1,764	1,601	1,863	1,828	1,784	1,895	1,708	1,647	1,568	1,500	20,654
2001[1]	1,751	1,477	1,603	1,546	1,875	1,824	1,758	1,864	1,536	1,635	1,541	1,545	19,955

[1] Preliminary. *Source: Economic Research Service, U.S. Department of Agriculture (ERS-USDA)*

Quarterly Trade of Live Cattle in the United States In Head

	Imports					Exports				
Year	First Quarter	Second Quarter	Third Quarter	Fourth Quarter	Annual	First Quarter	Second Quarter	Third Quarter	Fourth Quarter	Annual
1992	599,255	505,568	389,417	801,025	2,255,265	97,683	100,282	74,827	48,998	321,790
1993	672,447	635,341	469,439	721,819	2,499,046	50,733	33,286	22,049	47,348	153,416
1994	569,466	540,845	386,596	585,597	2,082,504	51,803	43,115	62,729	73,144	230,791
1995	868,694	804,686	488,515	624,350	2,786,245	26,597	18,441	19,794	29,716	94,548
1996	605,648	467,059	391,633	501,108	1,965,448	33,906	42,796	42,757	54,848	174,307
1997	494,637	500,052	423,838	627,825	2,046,352	63,217	58,153	81,095	79,879	282,344
1998	538,018	503,547	373,451	618,993	2,034,009	69,824	63,459	53,145	98,781	285,209
1999	549,847	424,182	313,211	657,836	1,945,076	51,830	59,195	47,049	171,245	329,319
2000	580,174	537,009	346,087	724,016	2,187,286	117,889	67,895	72,028	223,430	481,242
2001[1]	700,239	612,645	444,637	679,194	2,436,715	111,549	75,152	297,069	194,683	678,453

[1] Preliminary. *Source: Economic Research Service, U.S. Department of Agriculture (ERS-USDA)*

CATTLE AND CALVES

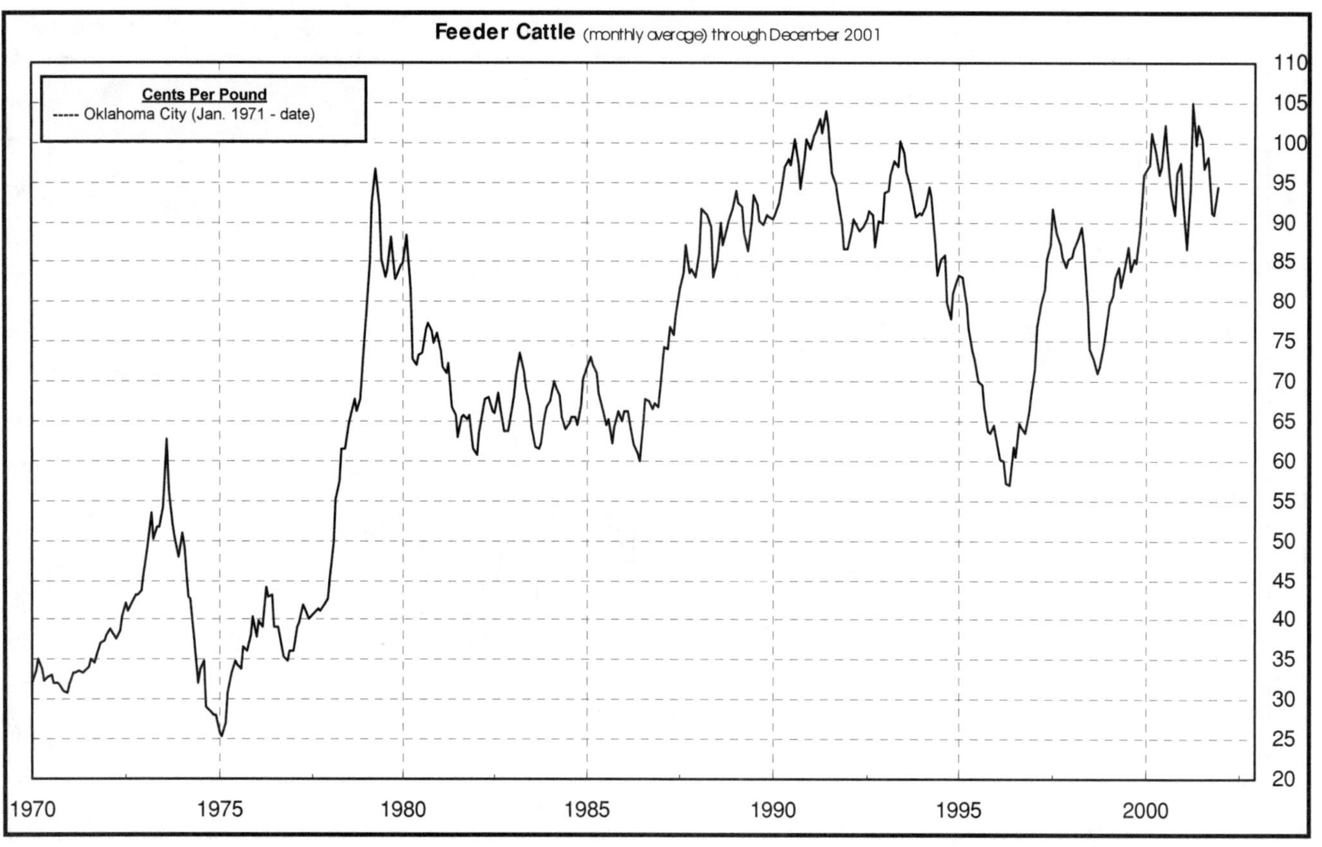

Average Slaughter Steer Price, Choice 2-4, Texas, 1100-1300 Lb. In Dollars Per 100 Pounds

Year	Jan.	Feb.	Mar.	Apr.	May	June	July	Aug.	Sept.	Oct.	Nov.	Dec.	Average
1995	71.97	72.55	70.23	66.63	63.72	63.74	62.54	62.18	63.23	64.44	67.51	66.34	66.26
1996	63.90	62.76	62.52	59.49	59.72	61.56	63.79	66.84	68.89	71.09	72.61	67.46	65.05
1997	65.51	65.48	68.21	68.32	67.49	64.07	64.77	65.96	66.22	67.08	67.21	65.53	66.32
1998	63.57	59.74	64.68	65.00	64.40	63.26	59.97	58.65	58.28	62.00	61.81	59.36	61.73
1999	60.65	62.01	64.63	65.19	64.41	65.51	64.05	65.26	66.06	69.58	70.31	69.05	65.56
2000	67.97	68.24	71.74	73.52	71.66	69.59	66.46	64.69	65.14	68.54	72.05	76.18	69.65
2001	78.49	79.58	79.26	75.92	75.72	73.76	71.66	70.16	69.16	66.68	64.71	64.00	72.43

Source: Economic Research Service, U.S. Department of Agriculture (ERS-USDA)

Average Price of Steers (Feeder) in Oklahoma City In Dollars Per 100 Pounds

Year	Jan.	Feb.	Mar.	Apr.	May	June	July	Aug.	Sept.	Oct.	Nov.	Dec.	Average
1995	73.60	73.79	70.64	67.54	64.27	63.91	61.81	61.95	63.80	64.89	67.94	66.14	66.69
1996	64.63	63.00	61.77	59.85	59.78	61.37	64.07	67.15	71.12	70.95	70.70	66.30	65.06
1997	65.07	65.35	67.44	67.66	67.36	63.53	63.80	65.19	66.04	66.93	67.66	65.91	66.00
1998	64.57	60.77	64.52	65.00	64.52	63.85	60.28	60.00	57.93	61.54	62.23	59.97	62.10
1999	61.46	63.17	64.75	65.34	65.00	66.15	64.51	65.29	66.05	69.63	70.28	69.01	65.89
2000	69.07	68.88	71.74	73.13	71.28	69.41	67.22	65.02	65.43	68.51	72.19	76.41	69.86
2001	78.79	79.40	79.44	76.50	74.94	72.64	70.71	69.07	68.75	66.30	63.60	63.62	71.98

Source: The Wall Street Journal

Federally Inspected Slaughter of Cattle in the United States In Thousands of Head

Year	Jan.	Feb.	Mar.	Apr.	May	June	July	Aug.	Sept.	Oct.	Nov.	Dec.	Total
1995	2,802	2,524	2,890	2,591	3,064	3,187	2,878	3,160	3,019	2,982	2,897	2,741	34,735
1996	3,046	2,855	2,834	3,039	3,257	3,078	3,080	3,148	2,693	3,074	2,801	2,800	35,721
1997	3,169	2,726	2,795	2,998	3,125	3,003	3,127	3,050	2,909	3,156	2,698	2,811	35,567
1998	2,977	2,691	2,838	2,872	2,906	3,050	2,987	2,987	2,938	2,991	2,717	2,834	34,787
1999	2,904	2,665	2,990	2,916	2,947	3,154	3,037	3,099	3,045	3,033	2,882	2,814	35,486
2000	2,878	2,883	3,078	2,735	3,128	3,191	2,918	3,211	2,984	3,082	2,879	2,665	35,631
2001[1]	2,947	2,533	2,867	2,667	3,152	3,075	2,898	3,193	2,758	3,103	2,854	2,726	34,771

[1] Preliminary. *Source: National Agricultural Statistics Board, U.S. Department of Agriculture (NASS-USDA)*

Average Open Interest of Live Cattle Futures in Chicago In Contracts

Year	Jan.	Feb.	Mar.	Apr.	May	June	July	Aug.	Sept.	Oct.	Nov.	Dec.
1992	79,638	97,500	97,222	90,823	83,112	68,135	67,828	62,656	61,783	60,761	63,945	67,125
1993	78,481	79,256	88,113	78,144	72,183	68,287	66,617	66,560	70,275	70,559	73,571	76,042
1994	87,923	87,578	83,949	70,287	72,851	75,470	76,663	72,988	73,391	67,924	74,152	68,600
1995	80,306	78,793	76,821	64,763	61,460	56,783	58,077	55,511	58,319	62,222	69,495	69,065
1996	72,870	83,064	91,348	97,315	97,911	96,320	96,547	93,557	92,804	88,467	88,062	87,305
1997	97,014	103,437	108,157	98,354	99,640	96,279	99,042	98,590	94,137	93,579	100,368	102,741
1998	105,559	102,036	101,264	88,257	88,167	87,493	86,776	86,874	95,013	102,636	108,263	106,156
1999	115,254	115,283	115,410	104,482	103,290	101,078	96,843	101,858	121,305	123,466	126,040	120,204
2000	128,918	123,980	123,925	122,596	117,834	106,196	116,266	120,526	123,945	123,517	131,773	132,239
2001	132,298	132,866	131,312	123,075	112,180	114,970	116,162	105,252	114,214	109,677	108,574	95,182

Source: Chicago Mercantile Exchange (CME)

Volume of Trading of Live Cattle Futures Chicago In Thousands of Contracts

Year	Jan.	Feb.	Mar.	Apr.	May	June	July	Aug.	Sept.	Oct.	Nov.	Dec.	Total
1992	413,170	322,538	353,793	319,051	275,933	263,919	268,914	230,971	195,950	227,879	203,806	246,694	3,319,618
1993	328,800	294,233	363,398	263,533	199,705	255,442	269,260	225,996	269,533	297,561	248,382	291,108	3,306,952
1994	280,820	291,834	262,399	264,242	372,913	363,935	318,198	317,127	270,048	308,879	275,875	254,626	3,580,896
1995	289,710	259,210	391,721	287,194	285,686	290,224	245,250	266,793	233,402	220,130	246,655	241,130	3,257,105
1996	312,018	275,399	333,200	457,536	385,875	303,091	319,815	299,498	278,083	339,419	312,577	309,681	3,926,192
1997	361,620	352,173	312,113	331,948	285,885	303,369	387,526	324,943	316,822	374,632	238,003	330,608	3,919,642
1998	355,728	400,210	327,169	400,584	296,651	321,370	334,424	369,604	370,282	373,207	318,152	349,125	4,216,506
1999	298,814	342,572	338,076	320,457	296,512	342,854	287,557	266,544	371,735	345,269	375,960	253,198	3,839,548
2000	347,290	323,524	356,258	236,494	302,001	244,755	248,377	293,450	277,913	293,972	397,879	359,599	3,681,512
2001	511,050	357,474	385,581	302,829	348,294	289,093	318,564	324,614	340,969	403,101	403,009	294,695	4,279,273

Source: Chicago Mercantile Exchange (CME)

CATTLE AND CALVES

Beef Steer-Corn Price Ratio in the United States

Year	Jan.	Feb.	Mar.	Apr.	May	June	July	Aug.	Sept.	Oct.	Nov.	Dec.	Average
1994	27.1	26.2	27.5	28.5	26.8	24.8	28.4	31.6	30.2	32.1	34.4	31.9	29.1
1995	32.6	32.3	30.5	28.2	26.3	25.2	23.5	23.5	23.0	22.3	22.7	21.1	25.9
1996	20.3	18.1	17.2	15.1	13.9	14.2	14.0	15.0	19.1	23.6	25.8	24.9	18.4
1997	24.2	24.6	24.3	24.3	25.4	25.4	27.0	26.6	26.6	26.5	27.1	26.5	25.7
1998	25.8	24.8	25.2	27.5	28.3	28.3	27.9	31.6	32.2	32.1	32.3	30.0	28.8
1999	30.2	31.0	31.8	32.4	32.8	33.9	37.5	37.8	38.3	41.5	41.7	38.9	35.7
2000	37.5	35.9	36.2	37.0	34.7	37.4	42.9	44.7	42.6	40.5	39.7	39.0	39.0
2001[2]	40.1	40.2	41.3	42.1	42.5	43.4	39.9	38.7	37.7	38.2	36.6	34.6	39.6

[1] Bushels of corn equal in value to 100 pounds of steers and heifers. [2] Preliminary. *Source: Economic Research Service, U.S. Department of Agriculture*

Farm Value, Income and Wholesale Prices of Cattle and Calves in the United States

	---- January 1 ----		Gross Income From	At Ohama[3]				Feeder Heifers at Oklahoma	Cows, Boning Utility	Cows, Commercial	Wholesale Prices, Central U.S.		
				Steers[3]		Heifers					Choice	Select	Cow[6],
Year	Per Head Dollars	Total Million $	C & C[2] Million $	Choice	Select	Select	Choice	City[5]	Sioux Falls[6]	Sioux Falls	700-850 lb.	700-850 lb.	Canner[7]
				Dollars per 100 Pounds									
1994	659	66,513	36,604	67.60	66.33	66.14	67.93	74.55	42.51	48.28	106.73	102.08	84.39
1995	615	63,185	34,349	65.64	63.94	63.69	65.46	64.43	35.58	39.03	106.09	98.45	68.67
1996	503	52,056	31,251	74.50	61.83	61.22	64.18	57.21	30.45	33.70	102.01	95.70	58.16
1997	525	53,383	36,322	65.92	63.85	63.36	65.66	72.04	34.27	36.14	102.56	95.92	64.30
1998	603	60,193	34,030	60.07	56.17	55.17	59.23	67.89	36.19	38.93	98.42	92.20	61.49
1999	594	58,834	----	65.64	----	----	65.68	71.90	38.40	40.61	110.91	103.07	66.51
2000[1]	683	67,011						82.23	41.71	44.45	117.45	108.83	72.57

[1] Preliminary. [2] Excludes interfarm sales & Gov't. payments. Cash receipts from farm marketings + value of farm home consumption. [3] 1,000 to 1,100 lb. [4] 1,000 to 1,200 lb. [5] 1992 to date are 700 to 750 lb., 1987 thru 1991 are 600 to 700 lb. [6] All weights. [7] & Cutter. *Source: Economic Research Service, U.S. Department of Agriculture (NASS-USDA)*

Average Price Received by Farmers for Beef Cattle in the United States In Dollars Per 100 Pounds

Year	Jan.	Feb.	Mar.	Apr.	May	June	July	Aug.	Sept.	Oct.	Nov.	Dec.	Average
1994	69.90	70.10	72.30	72.00	67.20	62.70	62.90	65.90	63.50	62.90	64.40	64.40	66.50
1995	67.50	68.70	66.90	63.80	60.80	60.90	59.50	59.40	59.10	58.80	60.70	60.60	62.20
1996	59.10	57.90	56.80	54.90	54.70	56.40	59.10	61.30	63.80	63.30	63.40	61.00	59.30
1997	61.40	61.90	64.80	64.80	65.10	62.30	62.80	63.90	63.60	63.30	63.30	62.90	63.30
1998	62.50	60.40	61.30	63.00	63.00	61.80	58.40	57.40	56.10	58.00	58.10	56.80	59.70
1999	59.00	60.60	62.40	62.70	62.10	63.70	62.60	63.50	63.80	66.20	66.20	66.60	63.28
2000	67.80	67.60	69.80	71.30	69.40	68.50	67.50	65.50	65.30	66.70	69.10	71.90	68.37
2001[1]	74.80	74.70	76.30	75.60	73.60	73.50	71.90	70.70	69.00	66.60	63.90	64.60	71.27

[1] Preliminary. *Source: National Agricultural Statistics Service, U.S. Department of Agriculture (NASS-USDA)*

Average Price Received by Farmers for Calves in the United States In Dollars Per 100 Pounds

Year	Jan.	Feb.	Mar.	Apr.	May	June	July	Aug.	Sept.	Oct.	Nov.	Dec.	Average
1994	93.90	94.90	97.60	95.80	89.40	84.80	83.80	84.40	80.00	78.20	81.00	81.90	87.10
1995	85.00	86.90	84.40	81.80	77.00	76.90	72.00	70.90	68.50	66.20	64.00	63.30	74.70
1996	61.80	60.20	59.40	55.10	54.40	55.10	56.80	59.30	61.00	60.10	61.20	61.80	58.90
1997	68.10	74.90	80.00	82.20	84.30	85.40	86.90	88.00	86.90	84.30	82.90	83.30	82.30
1998	86.60	88.70	89.80	90.80	88.90	81.70	76.60	76.90	74.10	75.70	77.50	80.20	82.30
1999	83.20	86.90	87.30	88.20	87.60	89.00	89.20	89.60	90.90	91.90	93.00	98.60	89.62
2000	103.00	105.00	109.00	111.00	107.00	104.00	106.00	106.00	103.00	102.00	106.00	106.00	105.67
2001[1]	108.00	109.00	112.00	111.00	111.00	109.00	107.00	106.00	106.00	99.20	96.40	100.00	106.22

[1] Preliminary. *Source: National Agricultural Statistics Board, U.S. Department of Agriculture (NASS-USDA)*

Federally Inspected Slaughter of Calves and Vealers in the United States In Thousands of Head

Year	Jan.	Feb.	Mar.	Apr.	May	June	July	Aug.	Sept.	Oct.	Nov.	Dec.	Total
1994	99	94	112	92	90	98	93	106	106	112	114	121	1,237
1995	121	104	118	96	114	115	111	121	119	124	125	125	1,393
1996	140	140	141	128	133	131	156	153	146	159	139	149	1,715
1997	143	122	128	126	114	115	131	123	133	137	121	142	1,534
1998	125	111	125	107	99	115	131	122	132	121	109	127	1,422
1999	103	98	115	95	87	102	109	115	117	102	100	110	1,252
2000	91	92	97	75	86	91	92	98	91	95	91	90	1,088
2001[1]	89	77	82	72	77	75	81	92	77	91	85	82	981

[1] Preliminary. *Source: Crop Reporting Board, U.S. Department of Agriculture (CRB-USDA)*

Cement

The U.S. Geological Survey reported that world production of cement in 2000 was 1.7 billion tonnes, up 6 percent from 1999. Cement is the binding agent in concrete and mortar, two construction materials. The production and consumption of cement is directly related to the level of activity in the construction industry. Almost all portland cement is used either is making concrete and mortars. Hydraulic cements are those that set and harden in water. In the U.S. in 2000, about 86 million tonnes or portland cement and 5 million tonnes of masonry cement were produced at a total of 116 plants. Most of the cement was used to produce concrete. Clinker, an intermediate product in cement manufacture, was produced at 109 plants.

By far the largest producer of cement in the world is China with 2000 output of 576 million tonnes, up less than one percent from the previous year. India is the second largest producer of cement with output in 2000 of 95 million tonnes, up 6 percent from 1999. U.S. production of cement in 2000 was 92.3 million tonnes, up 5 percent from the previous year. Production of cement by Japan in 2000 was 77.5 million tonnes, down 3 percent from 1999. Other large cement producers include South Korea, Brazil, Germany, Italy and Thailand.

U.S. shipments of portland and blended cement in August 2001 were 11.3 million tonnes, about the same as the year before. In the January-August 2001 period, shipments were 73.2 million tonnes. For all of 2000, shipments were 107.4 million tonnes. Masonry cement shipments in August 2001 were 435,399 tonnes, up 3 percent from a year ago. In the first eight months of 2001, shipments were 3.02 million tonnes while for all of 2000 they were 4.33 million tonnes.

Shipments of blended cement in August 2001 were 146,496 tonnes, down 10 percent from a year earlier. For all of 2000, shipments were 1.23 million tonnes. The major destinations were Oklahoma, Missouri, Nebraska, and Iowa. U.S. production of clinker in August 2001 was 7.12 million tonnes, up 2 percent from a year ago. In 2000, clinker production totaled 79.6 million tonnes. U.S. imports of clinker and hydraulic cement in July 2001 were 2.75 million tonnes. The major suppliers in 2001 were Canada, Thailand, China and Mexico.

World Production of Hydraulic Cement In Thousands of Short Tons

Year	Brazil	China	France	Germany	India	Italy	Japan	Rep. of Korea	Russia	Spain	Turkey	United States	World Total
1994	25,230	421,180	21,296	36,130	57,000	32,713	91,624	50,730	37,200	25,150	29,493	77,948	1,370,000
1995	28,256	475,910	19,692	33,302	62,000	33,715	90,474	55,130	36,500	26,423	33,153	76,906	1,445,000
1996	34,597	491,190	19,514	31,533	75,000	33,327	94,492	58,434	27,800	25,157	35,214	80,818	1,493,000
1997	38,096	511,730	19,780	35,945	80,000	33,721	91,938	60,317	26,700	27,632	36,035	84,255	1,547,000
1998	39,942	536,000	19,500	36,610	85,000	35,512	81,328	46,091	26,000	27,943	38,200	85,522	1,547,000
1999[1]	40,270	573,000	19,527	38,099	90,000	36,000	80,120	48,157	28,400	30,800	34,258	87,777	1,603,000
2000[2]	39,208	583,190	20,000	38,000	95,000	36,000	81,300	51,255	32,400	30,000	35,825	89,510	1,643,000

[1] Preliminary. [2] Estimate. *Source: U.S. Geological Survey (USGS)*

Salient Statistics of Cement in the United States

Year	Net Import Reliance as a % of Apparent Consumption	Production: Portland	Production: Others[3]	Production: Total	Capacity Used at (Portland Mills)	Shipments From Mills: Total	Shipments From Mills: Value[4]	Average Value (F.O.B. Mill)	Stocks at Mills Dec. 31	Exports	Apparent Consumption	Imports for Consumption[5] by Country: Canada	Japan	Mexico	Spain	Total
		------- Thousand Tons -------			%	Mil. Tons	Mil. $	$ per ton	--------- Million Tons ---------			-------- Thousands of Short Tons ---------				
1994	10	74,335	3,613	77,948	82.3	79,087	4,845	61.26	4,701	633	86,476	4,268	14	640	1,342	11,303
1995	11	73,303	3,603	76,906	81.2	78,518	5,329	67.87	5,814	759	86,003	4,886	[6]	850	1,501	13,848
1996	12	75,797	3,469	79,266	83.4	83,963	5,952	70.89	5,488	803	90,355	5,351	[6]	1,272	1,595	14,154
1997	14	78,948	3,634	82,582	84.7	90,359	6,637	73.46	5,784	791	96,018	5,350	[6]	995	1,845	17,596
1998	19	79,942	3,989	83,931	84.9	96,857	7,404	76.45	5,393	743	103,460	5,957	----	1,280	2,204	24,086
1999[1]	23	81,577	4,375	85,952	83.6	103,271	8,083	78.27	6,367	694	108,862	5,511	----	1,286	1,900	29,351
2000[2]	20	83,514	4,332	87,846	80.7	105,557	8,293	78.56	7,566	738	110,470	4,948	----	1,409	1,177	28,684

[1] Preliminary. [2] Estimate. [3] Masonry, natural & pozzolan (slag-line). [4] Value received F.O.B. mill, excluding cost of containers. [5] Hydraulic & clinker cement for consumption. [6] Less than 1/2 unit. *Source: U.S. Geological Survey (USGS)*

Shipments of Finished Portland Cement from Mills in the United States In Thousands of Metric Tons

Year	Jan.	Feb.	Mar.	Apr.	May	June	July	Aug.	Sept.	Oct.	Nov.	Dec.	Total
1996	3,913.3	4,312.7	5,234.1	6,801.6	7,621.3	7,395.1	7,749.4	8,193.4	7,178.3	8,276.7	6,011.4	4,763.3	77,550.0
1997	4,111.3	4,487.1	5,739.1	7,009.5	7,489.3	7,733.7	8,132.4	7,909.2	8,186.1	8,678.9	6,108.6	5,471.9	81,064.3
1998	4,552.0	4,559.7	5,867.4	7,009.7	7,420.2	8,095.1	8,295.6	7,963.3	8,089.5	8,404.6	6,640.5	6,059.4	82,956.8
1999	4,487.3	5,132.9	6,380.5	7,112.2	7,406.9	8,096.9	7,782.2	8,173.2	7,652.7	8,204.2	7,453.4	5,959.1	83,841.5
2000	4,765.5	5,343.1	7,196.9	6,930.2	8,448.2	8,391.5	7,843.8	8,982.3	7,860.8	8,474.2	6,587.0	4,865.5	84,980.3
2001[1]	5,107.6	5,088.8	6,684.6	7,800.7	8,511.6	8,401.8	8,336.8	8,858.5	7,521.8	8,964.2	7,363.0		90,152.0

[1] Preliminary. *Source: U.S. Geological Survey (USGS)*

Cheese

The steady annual gains in world cheese production shows little sign of abating. A record large 12.4 million metric tons were produced in 2001 and estimated at 12.7 million in 2002. U.S. production accounted for about 3.7 million tons and almost 3.9 million tons, respectively. France produces slightly less than half the U.S. total to rank in second place globally followed by Germany and Italy. Percentage-wise, Russia's production has nearly doubled since the late 1990's, but their total is still less than 10% of the U.S. World consumption is keeping pace with the new supply, totaling a record large 12.1 million tons in 2001 vs. and forecast to reach 12.3 million in 2002 with U.S. use, the world's largest, of 3.88 million and 4.0 million. France's annual usage in recent years has averaged about 1.40 million tons. Most of the world's cheese is consumed where produced. However, U.S. per capita cheese consumption, although at record highs, remains well below overall European use, which tops 20 kg in some countries, notably France.

World foreign trade of cheese is biased towards exports which topped for the first time slightly more than one million tons in 2000, and forecast at almost 1.1 million in 2002: annual imports in 2000-02 have averaged around 785,000 tons. New Zealand is the single largest exporter in 2001 with 255,000 tons and 270,000 tons expected in 2002. Collectively the European Union exported nearly half the world total with a record large 425,000 tons in 2001 and 428,000 in 2002.. However, EU cheese exports showed little percentile growth in recent years whereas Australia's and New Zealand's exports have increased by almost a third.. U.S. exports are small, averaging about 50,000 tons in 2000-02. The U.S. is a close second to Japan as the largest importer: 195,000 tons in 2001 vs. Japan's 200,000 tons. Ending 2001 world stocks of 1.61 million tons compares with 1.74 million a year earlier and forecast of 1.52 million tons at yearend 2002 with Italy accounting for 645,000 tons of the 2001 carryover.

Cheese is a multi-billion dollar a year industry in the U.S. with American and cheddar cheeses accounting for the largest individual varieties of both production and consumption. However, other varieties, mostly Italian, now have had a combined production that easily exceeds American cheese: 3.3 billion pounds of American in 2000 vs. 5.5 billion pounds of Italian cheeses. U.S. per-capita cheese consumption totals about 25 pounds.

Wholesale American cheese prices (40-pound blocks, Wisconsin) averaged about $1.16 per pound in 2000 vs. $1.42 in 1999. Northern European monthly average cheddar prices (40 pound blocks) in 2000 ranged from $1700 per metric ton $1900, strengthening during 2001 to as high as $2200 in late summer.

World Production of Cheese In Thousands of Metric Tons

Year	Argentina	Australia	Brazil	Canada	Denmark	France	Germany	Italy	Netherlands	New Zealand	United Kingdom	United States	World Total
1992	310	197	296	262	290	1,489	783	890	634	142	324	2,943	10,931
1993	350	211	310	271	321	1,509	821	885	637	145	331	2,961	10,895
1994	385	234	330	282	286	1,541	855	913	648	192	326	3,054	11,194
1995	370	241	360	277	311	1,579	875	942	680	197	354	3,138	11,345
1996	390	268	385	289	298	1,594	947	950	688	230	364	3,274	11,059
1997	415	285	405	329	290	1,645	990	985	693	240	368	3,325	11,388
1998	407	305	421	330	289	1,648	1,008	1,003	638	266	358	3,398	11,562
1999	446	320	434	331	285	1,658	1,006	969	643	245	361	3,603	11,826
2000[1]	432	367	445	329	305	1,680	1,046	1,000	690	270	330	3,775	12,232
2001[2]	420	395	460	337	315	1,685	1,060	1,000	690	283	350	3,900	12,500

[1] Preliminary. [2] Estimate. *Source: Foreign Agricultural Service, U.S. Department of Agriculture (FAS-USDA)*

Supply and Distribution of All Cheese in the United States In Millions of Pounds

	Supply						Distribution							
	Production					Cheese 40-lb. Blocks Wisconsin Assembly Points						Domestic Disappearance		
Year	Whole Milk[2]	All Cheese[3]	January 1 Commercial Stocks	Imports[4]	Total Supply	cents/lb.	Exports & Shipments[6]	Gov't - Dec. 31 Stocks	American Cheese Removed by USDA Programs	Total Disappearance	American Cheese Donated	Total	Per Capita
1991	2,769	6,055	458	301	6,806	124.41	72	23.1	76.9	6,393	60	6,321	25.01
1992	2,937	6,488	416	286	7,167	131.91	78	16.5	14.4	6,720	0	6,642	26.01
1993	2,957	6,528	470	321	7,303	131.52	87	2.2	8.3	6,853	0	6,766	26.24
1994	2,974	6,735	466	345	7,546	131.45	55	.9	6.9	7,094	0	6,994	26.82
1995	3,131	6,917	437	337	7,691	132.77	65	----	6.1	7,279	0	7,174	27.30
1996	3,281	7,218	412	338	7,968	149.14	71	----	4.6	7,478	0	7,364	27.70
1997	3,286	7,330	487	312	8,129	132.40	84	----	11.3	7,647	0	7,511	28.00
1998	3,326	7,502	480	344	8,326	158.10	82	----	8.2	7,790	0	7,673	28.40
1999	3,533	7,894	517	419	8,830	142.30	86	----	4.6	8,215			
2000[1]	3,634	8,255	621	386	9,262	116.20	88	----	28.0	8,552			

[1] Preliminary. [2] Whole milk American cheddar. [3] All types of cheese except cottage, pot and baker's cheese. [4] Imports for consumption. [5] Commercial. *Source: Economic Research Service, U.S. Department of Agriculture (ERS-USDA)*

Production of Cheese in the United States In Millions of Pounds

	American			Swiss,				Cream &				Total	Cottage Cheese		
Year	Whole Milk	Part Skim	Total	Including Block	Munster	Brick	Lim-burger	Neufchatel Cheese	Italian Varieties	Blue Mond	All Other Varieties	of All Cheese[2]	Lowfat	Curd[3]	Creamed[4]
1991	2,769	0.8	2,770	234.5	106.4	15.3	.7	446.7	2,328.6	34.3	118.5	6,055	321.1	490.9	497.9
1992	2,937	1.2	2,938	237.3	116.4	15.5	1.0	516.7	2,508.6	33.3	121.9	6,488	329.5	502.4	457.3
1993	2,957	3.7	2,961	201.4	117.5	12.5	.9	539.9	2,494.5	33.3	137.2	6,528	317.0	471.4	430.5
1994	2,974	24.7	2,999	221.2	113.6	12.2	.8	573.4	2,625.7	36.5	152.1	6,735	321.1	463.3	410.0
1995	3,131	24.0	3,155	221.7	109.1	10.4	.9	543.8	2,674.4	36.6	164.6	6,917	325.9	458.9	384.9
1996	3,281	NA	3,281	219.0	106.8	10.6	.7	574.7	2,812.4	38.3	106.7	7,218	329.9	448.3	360.4
1997	3,286	NA	3,286	207.6	100.2	8.5	.7	614.9	2,881.4	42.8	119.8	7,330	346.7	458.5	359.5
1998	3,315	NA	3,315	206.4	94.6	7.6	.9	621.3	3,004.7	5	166.0	7,492	361.2	465.8	366.8
1999	3,533	NA	3,533	221.0	80.3	8.1	.7	639.3	3,144.7	5	181.0	7,894	359.3	464.8	360.6
2000[1]	3,634	NA	3,634	229.3	81.5	8.6	.6	687.4	3,311.0	5	205.8	8,255	364.3	463.3	372.1

[1] Preliminary. [2] Excludes full-skim cheddar and cottage cheese. [3] Includes cottage, pot, and baker's cheese with a butterfat content of less than 4%. [4] Includes cheese with a butterfat content of 4 to 19 %. [5] Included in All Other Varieties. *Source: Economic Research Service, U.S. Department of Agriculture ERS-USDA)*

Wholesale Price of Cheese, 40-lb. Blocks, Wisconsin Assembly Points[2] In Cents Per Pound

Year	Jan.	Feb.	Mar.	Apr.	May	June	July	Aug.	Sept.	Oct.	Nov.	Dec.	Average
1992	125.4	119.0	119.8	131.9	140.0	141.3	141.8	142.0	136.9	132.4	129.4	123.2	131.9
1993	119.3	118.6	124.3	140.8	141.8	133.7	126.3	124.8	137.4	138.9	138.7	133.7	131.5
1994	132.2	134.2	140.0	143.3	125.7	120.2	129.1	132.2	135.6	135.4	127.9	121.3	131.5
1995	124.5	130.4	131.1	122.8	122.1	126.9	126.7	132.2	141.3	145.0	145.8	144.6	132.8
1996	139.3	139.3	140.9	145.1	151.8	151.5	158.2	167.6	145.5	162.3	133.9	126.0	146.8
1997	127.9	132.3	134.0	125.6	116.5	117.9	123.3	137.6	141.4	142.4	143.8	146.1	132.4
1998	144.5	144.7	138.8	129.7	123.0	151.3	162.6	166.9	171.0	183.5	188.7	192.5	158.1
1999	162.4	131.5	134.0	133.6	124.8	138.1	159.7	189.0	167.3	134.0	117.3	115.7	142.3
2000	114.6	111.6	112.2	110.7	110.6	120.0	125.2	125.5	133.4	109.4	107.5	113.0	116.1
2001[1]	110.3	120.0	131.9	140.5	160.3	166.8	168.5	171.8	173.9	139.7	126.4	129.1	144.9

[1] Preliminary. *Source: Economic Research Service, U.S. Department of Agriculture (ERS-USDA)*

Production[2] of Cheese in the United States In Millions of Pounds

Year	Jan.	Feb.	Mar.	Apr.	May	June	July	Aug.	Sept.	Oct.	Nov.	Dec.	Total
1992	514.1	497.1	542.7	534.7	550.9	549.8	541.8	534.6	528.3	558.2	547.5	571.6	6,488
1993	517.3	492.5	563.2	561.4	576.9	563.2	537.9	525.8	531.1	560.0	540.1	558.9	6,528
1994	538.3	505.8	591.8	554.3	590.4	558.7	550.7	562.4	565.5	574.5	559.3	578.3	6,730
1995	559.3	523.3	596.0	559.6	595.3	579.2	556.5	550.8	571.3	588.6	584.7	618.4	6,883
1996	590.0	576.0	625.4	606.0	636.5	595.8	582.2	589.5	584.5	612.2	595.5	623.9	7,218
1997	598.1	577.1	638.0	598.5	642.0	623.4	613.2	596.5	604.3	615.5	594.5	627.9	7,329
1998	617.2	574.3	646.7	636.9	650.4	639.9	607.9	596.4	583.8	633.2	637.8	667.4	7,492
1999	631.6	591.7	698.2	663.8	668.9	664.4	641.3	642.6	637.6	666.5	683.4	704.2	7,894
2000	692.9	649.5	714.8	694.0	730.4	695.7	687.6	683.8	653.8	688.5	675.0	688.4	8,255
2001[1]	686.6	632.2	714.1	675.1	708.8	682.3	679.1	663.4	644.5	683.0	686.2	704.3	8,160

[1] Preliminary. [2] Excludes cottage cheese. *Source: National Agricultural Statistics Service, U.S. Department of Agriculture (NASS-USDA)*

Cold Storage Holdings of All Varieties of Cheese in the United States, on First of Month Millions of Pounds

Year	Jan.	Feb.	Mar.	Apr.	May	June	July	Aug.	Sept.	Oct.	Nov.	Dec.
1992	415.4	440.9	445.9	449.0	449.7	455.9	465.2	496.2	487.3	449.7	441.1	462.0
1993	462.0	476.1	454.4	460.0	453.6	480.5	541.2	533.3	517.7	500.1	471.9	462.4
1994	465.2	495.2	473.6	473.3	487.9	513.4	521.4	506.3	474.7	453.0	448.3	434.2
1995	436.9	449.7	448.7	458.8	466.1	465.8	473.6	482.4	458.1	428.5	418.7	393.6
1996	412.1	441.3	466.4	490.9	525.5	541.8	542.8	536.6	506.9	495.8	494.6	480.2
1997	487.0	501.5	494.6	517.0	555.4	584.3	604.8	604.9	582.3	543.7	505.0	474.4
1998	480.4	509.3	521.5	533.1	557.6	568.5	583.7	595.8	576.8	553.0	522.7	494.5
1999	517.2	622.4	635.9	645.1	688.7	741.3	728.4	748.7	694.7	651.3	622.0	591.7
2000	621.3	728.1	757.2	765.1	794.0	811.4	828.1	870.3	839.9	780.9	732.0	696.0
2001[1]	707.8	709.9	723.9	711.6	711.8	712.1	739.2	752.6	721.2	708.7	672.2	631.3

Quantities are given in net weight. [1] Preliminary. *Source: National Agricultural Statistics Service, U.S. Department of Agriculture (NASS-USDA)*

Chromium

Chromite is the ore mineral of chromium. Chromium finds a wide range of uses in metals, chemicals, and refractories. Chromium enhances hardenability and resistance to corrosion and oxidation in iron, steel, and nonferrous alloys. Two of its applications are in the production of stainless steel and nonferrous alloys. It is also used in alloy steel, plating of metals, pigments, leather processing, surface treatments, catalysts, and refractories.

According to the U.S. Geological Survey, the U.S. consumes about 13 percent of world chromite ore production in various forms of imported materials, such as chromite ore, chromium chemicals, chromium ferroalloys and chromium metals. In the U.S., imported chromite was consumed by two chemical firms and two refractory firms to produce chromium chemicals and chromite-containing refractories, respectively. Consumption of chromium ferroalloys and metal was predominantly for the production of stainless and heat-resisting steel and superalloys, respectively.

World resources of chromite are estimated to exceed 11 billion metric tonnes of shipping-grade chromite, sufficient to meet demand for many years. About 95 percent of chromium resources are concentrated in southern Africa. World mine production of chromium in 2000 was estimated at 13.7 million tonnes, an increase of 200,000 tonnes from 1999. The world's largest producer of chromium was South Africa with 6.5 million tonnes, less than 1 percent more than in 1999. Other large producers include Turkey with 2000 output of 1.5 million tonnes, up 7 percent from 1999. Kazakhstan produced 1.6 million tonnes, unchanged from 1999. Production by India in 2000 was 1.4 million tonnes, up 7 percent from 1999. Other producers include Zimbabwe, Finland, and Brazil.

Chromium has no substitute in stainless steel which is the largest end use. Chromium is also used in superalloys, the major strategic end use. U.S. production of stainless steel in August 2001 was 162,000 tonnes. In the January-August 2001 period, production was 1.21 million tonnes. For all of 2000, stainless steel production was 2.19 million tonnes. U.S. stainless steel scrap consumption in August 2001 was 101,000 tonnes. In January-August 2001 it was 715,000 tonnes while for all of 2000 it was 1.22 million tonnes. U.S. imports for consumption of chromite ore in the first seven months of 2001 were 137,000 tonnes. For all of 2000 they were 268,000 tonnes. Total ferroalloy imports in the first seven months of 2001 were 182,000 tonnes while for all of 2000 they were 597,000 tonnes. Chromium metal imports in the first seven months of 2001 were 5,160 tonnes while for 2000 they were 9,940 tonnes. Imports of stainless steel in 2000 were 989,000 tonnes.

U.S. exports of stainless steel in January-July 2001 were 158,000 tonnes and in 2000 they were 264,000 tonnes. U.S. industry stocks of chromium ferroalloys and metal in August 2001 were 25,200 tonnes. The government stockpile of chromite ore in August 2001 was 561,000 tonnes. Chromium ferroalloy stocks in August 2001 were 873,000 tonnes while chromium metal stocks were 7,320 tonnes.

World Mine Production of Chromite In Thousands of Metric Tons (Gross Weight)

Year	Albania	Brazil	Cuba	Finland	India	Iran	Kazakhstan[3]	Madagascar	Philippines	South Africa	Turkey	Zimbabwe	World Total
1991	587	340	50	473	940	90	3,800	149	191	5,100	940	564	13,300
1992	322	449	10	499	1,080	130	3,500	161	66	3,360	759	522	11,100
1993	115	308	18	511	1,000	124	2,900	144	62	2,840	767	252	9,300
1994	118	360	29	573	909	354	2,100	90	76	3,640	1,270	517	10,400
1995	160	448	31	598	1,540	371	2,420	106	111	5,090	2,080	707	14,000
1996	144	408	37	582	1,363	130	1,190	137	107	5,078	1,279	697	11,600
1997	106	300	44	589	1,363	169	1,798	140	88	6,162	1,703	670	13,700
1998	102	301	49	610	1,311	314	1,603	104	54	6,480	1,404	605	13,400
1999[1]	71	420	36	635	1,473	311	2,405	100	20	6,817	770	654	14,100
2000[2]	70	400	40	640	1,500	310	2,607	100	15	6,621	1,000	640	14,400

[1] Preliminary. [2] Estimate. [3] Formerly part of the U.S.S.R.; data not reported separately unitl 1992. *Source: U.S. Geological Survey (USGS)*

Salient Statistics of Chromite in the United States In Thousands of Metric Tons (Gross Weight)

						Consumption by - Primary Conumer Groups -			-- Consumer Stocks, Dec. 31 --			- $ per Metric Ton -	
Year	Net Import Reliance as a % of Apparent Consumption	Production of Ferrochromium	Exports	Imports for Consumption	Reexports	Total	Metallurgical & Chemical	Refractory	Metallurgical & Chemical	Refractory	Total Stocks	South Africa[3]	Turkish[4]
1991	73	68	17	309	----	375	339	36	310	11	321	50	130
1992	73	61	16	324	----	362	335	27	308	13	321	60	110
1993	81	63	18	329	2	337	314	23	259	16	275	60	110
1994	75	67	31	272	----	322	302	20	250	17	266	60	110
1995	80	73	24	415	----	W	W	W	194	11	205	80	230
1996	79	37	47	361	----	W	W	W	165	8	173	80	230
1997	75	61	27	349	----	W	W	W	167	8	175	75	150
1998	80	W	55	383	----	W	W	W	W	W	159	68	145
1999[1]	80	W	53	475	----	W	W	W	W	W	130	63	145
2000[2]	78	W	86	453	----	W	W	W	W	W	W	60-65	140-150

[1] Preliminary. [2] Estimate. [3] Cr_2O_3, 44% (Transvaal). [4] 48% Cr_2O_3. W = Withheld. *Source: U.S. Geological Survey (USGS)*

Coal

U.S. coal production in November 2001 was 93 million short tons, up 3 percent from November 2000. Coal production east of the Mississippi River was 41.6 million tons while production west of the Mississippi River was 51.4 million tons. In the January-November 2001 period, U.S. coal production was 1.037 billion tons, up 5 percent from the same period in 2000. For 2001, production east of the Mississippi River was 485.8 million tons while west of the Mississippi production was 550.7 million tons. In the January-November 2001 period, the largest coal producing state was Wyoming with 337.4 million tons, up 8 percent from the year before. The next largest producer was West Virginia with 148.5 million tons, up 2 percent from 2000. Coal production by Kentucky was 120.5 million tons, down 1 percent from 2000. Pennsylvania coal production was 72.3 million tons, up 5 percent from the previous year.

The Energy Information Agency reported that in July 2001, receipts of coal by electric utilities totaled 66 million short tons, which was down about 2 million tons from July 2000. The decline was due to the sale and reclassification of plants in the nonutility sector. In the January-July 2001 period, receipts of coal by utilities totaled 447 million tons, down from 472 million tons in the same period of 2000.

Most electricity generated in the U.S. is from coal. In August 2001, U.S. electricity generation was 373.4 billion kilowatthours. Of the total, 50 percent was generated by coal. In the January-August 2001 period, U.S. electricity generation was 2.59 trillion kilowatthours and coal generated 1.33 trillion kilowatthours. In 1990, coal accounted for 53 percent of the electricity generated.

World Production[3] of Coal (Monthly Average) In Thousands of Metric Tons

Year	Australia	Canada	China	Czech-Rep.[4]	Ger-many	India	Indo-nesia	Kazak-hstan[5]	Poland	Russia[5]	Ukraine[5]	United Kingdom	United States
1992	14,594	2,693	91,278	1,532	6,013	19,490	1,760	10,546	10,960	16,123	ÑÑ	7,273	75,413
1993	14,746	2,943	96,177	1,532	5,347	20,503	2,300	9,323	10,873	16,200	9,545	5,683	71,473
1994	14,721	3,054	103,325	1,448	4,802	20,974	2,603	8,298	11,094	14,730	7,608	4,149	78,131
1995	15,921	3,216	113,394	1,431	4,905	22,131	3,460	6,626	11,349	14,743	6,796	4,420	78,091
1996	16,120	3,336	116,417	1,378	4,428	23,782	3,945	6,086	11,425	13,875	6,178	4,183	80,426
1997	17,235	3,435	114,402	1,339	4,267	24,688	4,340	6,268	11,427	13,317	6,293	4,041	82,398
1998	18,247	3,190	94,806	1,343	3,776	24,805	5,027	5,672	9,644	12,779	6,431	3,431	84,484
1999	18,751	3,043	80,200	1,193	3,657	24,349	5,892	4,644	9,301	13,799	6,804	3,090	82,704
2000[1]	25,292	2,817	70,782	1,238	3,111	25,979	4,862	6,084	8,598	14,292	6,708	2,600	81,306
2001[2]	27,337	2,872	75,818	1,279	2,584	26,356		6,120	8,581	15,328	7,078	2,531	86,804

[1] Preliminary. [2] Estimate. [3] All grades of anthracite and bituminous coal, but excludes recovered slurries, lignite and brown coal. [4] Formerly part of Czechoslovakia; data not reported separately until 1993. [5] Formerly part of the U.S.S.R.; data not reported separately until 1992.
NA = Not avaliable. *Source: United Nations*

Production of Bituminous & Lignite Coal in the United States In Thousands of Short Tons

Year	Alabama	Colorado	Illinois	Indiana	Kentucky	Montana	Ohio	Pennsyl-vania	Texas	Virginia	West Virginia	Wyoming	Total
1992	25,796	19,226	59,857	30,466	161,068	38,889	30,403	65,498	55,071	43,024	162,164	190,172	997,545
1993	24,768	21,886	41,098	29,295	156,299	35,917	28,816	55,394	54,567	39,317	130,525	210,129	945,424
1994	23,266	25,304	52,797	30,927	161,642	41,640	29,897	62,237	52,346	37,129	161,776	237,092	1,033,504
1995	24,640	25,710	48,180	26,007	153,739	39,451	26,118	61,576	52,684	34,099	162,997	263,822	1,032,974
1996	24,637	24,886	46,656	29,670	152,425	37,891	28,572	67,942	55,164	35,590	170,433	278,440	1,063,856
1997	24,468	27,449	41,159	35,497	155,853	41,005	29,154	76,198	53,328	35,837	173,743	281,881	1,089,932
1998	23,224	30,825	38,182	36,297	145,609	42,092	28,600	76,519	53,578	34,059	175,794	313,983	1,109,768
1999	19,504	29,989	40,417	34,004	139,626	41,102	22,480	76,368	53,071	32,181	157,919	337,119	1,095,474
2000[1]	19,736	28,992	34,525	27,696	135,333	38,794	22,229	78,512	50,398	31,605	155,820	347,442	1,082,307
2001[2]	18,321	32,151	33,132	38,660	129,642	36,915	24,862	74,624	47,831	32,817	161,061	367,687	1,114,909

[1] Preliminary. [2] Estimate. *Source: Energy Information Administration, U.S. Department of Energy (EIA-DOE)*

Production[2] of Bituminous Coal in the United States In Thousands of Short Tons

Year	Jan.	Feb.	Mar.	Apr.	May	June	July	Aug.	Sept.	Oct.	Nov.	Dec.	Total
1992	87,979	82,102	85,835	82,364	80,197	79,968	80,768	84,401	83,555	86,265	80,240	83,021	996,695
1993	80,508	76,341	84,782	79,329	73,759	80,949	70,771	76,209	79,705	80,628	79,404	79,905	942,290
1994	76,578	81,569	95,969	87,534	82,105	86,223	77,421	93,881	88,346	85,085	86,317	87,856	1,028,884
1995	88,351	83,893	93,020	80,092	83,291	84,210	79,511	88,035	89,052	90,573	86,779	81,292	1,032,974
1996	83,013	83,671	90,392	88,158	88,562	83,824	88,331	94,664	87,388	94,195	86,400	86,493	1,059,104
1997	92,425	88,028	92,265	87,909	94,296	86,382	88,666	89,319	92,298	94,562	83,344	94,913	1,085,254
1998	97,012	86,167	95,091	91,735	90,397	92,099	90,497	91,212	95,442	96,723	90,544	94,567	1,106,128
1999	90,928	92,015	98,672	88,630	84,436	89,734	87,759	92,600	92,248	89,146	90,885	92,450	1,089,503
2000	87,222	86,846	99,045	81,793	88,715	90,583	84,442	96,361	88,848	92,542	94,035	87,272	1,077,704
2001[1]	96,721	86,802	99,176	89,954	94,850	92,657	89,037	99,406	89,303	98,803	93,014	86,471	1,116,194

[1] Preliminary. [2] Includes small amount of lignite. *Source: Energy Information Administration, U.S. Department of Energy (EIA-DOE)*

Production[2] of Pennsylvania Anthracite Coal In Thousands of Short Tons

Year	Jan.	Feb.	Mar.	Apr.	May	June	July	Aug.	Sept.	Oct.	Nov.	Dec.	Total
1992	247	257	279	296	274	287	305	337	311	322	321	306	3,542
1993	272	266	290	175	305	358	222	277	351	603	315	271	3,705
1994	318	335	415	380	375	379	346	457	412	453	452	395	4,717
1995	304	304	372	332	335	353	307	396	428	445	388	347	4,682
1996	302	349	367	371	361	335	367	418	385	557	505	434	4,751
1997	351	366	492	374	351	390	407	423	415	448	384	415	4,678
1998	306	305	309	405	384	388	525	454	452	533	167	167	4,612
1999	355	369	389	354	459	402	343	436	479	414	407	406	4,808
2000	271	283	382	342	375	383	366	430	412	417	402	366	4,432
2001[1]	302	275	323	283	300	297	328	358	318	209	195	194	3,382

[1] Preliminary. [2] Represents production in Pennsylvania only. *Source: Energy Information Administration, U.S. Department of Energy (EIA-DOE)*

Salient Statistics of Coal in the United States In Thousands of Short Tons

				Exports						Losses &
Year	Production	Imports	Consumption	Brazil	Canada	Europe	Asia	Total	Total Ending Stocks[2]	Unaccounted For[3]
1991	995,984	3,390	887,621	7,052	11,178	65,520	21,788	108,969	200,682	3,731
1992	997,545	3,803	907,655	6,370	15,140	57,255	20,540	102,516	197,685	-5,826
1993	945,424	7,309	944,081	5,197	8,889	37,575	19,500	74,519	120,458	-13,924
1994	1,033,504	7,584	951,461	5,482	9,193	35,825	17,957	71,359	169,358	-2,743
1995	1,032,974	7,201	962,039	6,351	9,427	48,620	19,095	88,547	169,083	-7,863
1996	1,063,856	7,126	1,005,573	6,540	12,029	47,193	17,980	90,473	151,627	-7,351
1997	1,089,932	7,487	1,030,453	7,455	14,975	41,331	14,498	83,545	140,374	-5,017
1998	1,117,535	8,724	1,038,972	6,475	19,901	33,773	12,311	77,295	164,602	-14,309
1999	1,100,431	9,089	1,044,536	4,442	19,826	22,508	9,157	58,476	175,480	-6,439
2000[1]	1,075,500	12,513	1,080,194	4,536	18,769	24,969	6,702	58,489	129,149	-7,759

[1] Preliminary. [2] Producer & distributor and consumer stocks, excludes stocks held by retail dealers for consumption by the residential and commercial sector. [3] Equals production plus imports minus the change in producer & distributor and consumer stocks minus consumption minus exports.
Source: Energy Information Administraion, U.S. Department of Energy (EIA-DOE)

Consumption and Stocks of Coal in the United States In Thousands of Short Tons

	Consumtion								Stocks, Dec. 31[3]			
	Electric Utilities				Industrial		Residential		Consumer			Producers
Year	Anthracite	Bituminous	Lignite	Total	Coke Plants	Other Industrial[2]	and Commercial	Total	Electric Utilities	Coke Plants	Other Industrials	and Distributors
1991	994	691,275	79,999	772,268	33,854	75,405	6,094	899,067	157,876	2,773	7,061	32,971
1992	986	698,626	80,248	779,860	32,366	74,042	6,153	907,378	154,130	2,597	6,965	33,993
1993	951	732,736	79,821	813,508	31,323	74,892	6,221	943,467	111,341	2,401	6,716	25,284
1994	1,123	737,102	79,045	817,270	31,740	75,179	6,013	950,141	126,897	2,657	6,585	33,219
1995	978	749,951	78,078	829,007	33,011	73,055	5,807	962,038	126,304	2,632	5,702	34,444
1996	1,009	795,252	78,421	874,681	31,706	71,689	6,006	1,006,306	114,623	2,667	5,688	28,648
1997	1,014	821,823	77,524	900,361	30,203	71,515	6,463	1,030,145	98,826	1,978	5,597	33,973
1998	867	832,094	77,906	910,867	28,189	67,439	4,856	1,038,292	120,501	2,026	5,545	36,530
1999	686	815,909	77,525	894,120	28,108	64,738	4,879	1,044,536	128,493	1,943	5,569	39,475
2000[1]	NA	781,821	75,794	857,615	29,303	65,110	4,879	1,080,192	88,841	1,529	4,575	34,204

[1] Preliminary. [2] Including transportation. [3] Excludes stocks held at retail dealers for consumption by the residential and commercial sector.
Source: Energy Information Administration, U.S. Department of Energy (EIA-DOE)

Average Prices of Coal in the United States In Dollars Per Short Ton

	End-Use-Sector				Exports				End-Use-Sector				Exports		
Year	Electric Utilities	Coke Plants	Other Industrial[3]	Imports[4]	Steam	Metal-lurgical	Total Average[4]	Year	Electric Utilities	Coke Plants	Other Industrial[3]	Imports[4]	Steam	Metal-lurgical	Total Average[4]
1991	30.02	48.88	33.54	33.12	36.91	46.15	42.39	1996	26.45	47.33	32.32	33.45	34.09	45.49	40.76
1992	29.36	47.92	32.78	33.46	35.73	45.41	41.34	1997	26.16	47.36	32.41	34.32	32.45	45.47	40.59
1993	28.58	47.44	32.23	29.89	36.03	44.11	41.41	1998	25.64	46.06	32.30	32.29	30.27	44.53	38.92
1994	28.03	46.56	32.55	30.21	34.34	42.77	39.93	1999	24.72	45.85	31.59	30.77	29.91	41.91	36.50
1995	27.01	47.34	32.42	34.13	34.51	44.30	40.27	2000[1]	24.25	44.41	31.36	30.10	29.67	38.99	34.90

[1] Preliminary. [2] Estimate. [3] Manufacturing plants only. [4] Based on the free alongside ship (F.A.S.) value. NA = Not available.
Source: Energy Information Administration, U.S. Department of Energy (EIA-DOE)

Trends in Bituminous Coal, Lignite and Pennsylvania Anthracite in the U.S. In Thousands of Short Tons

	Bituminous Coal and Lignite							Pennsylvania Anthracite					All Mines
	Production				Labor Productivity								
Year	Underground	Surface	Total	Miners[1] Employed	Underground Short Tons Per Miner Per Hour	Surface	Average	Underground	Surface	Total	Miners[1] Employed	Labor Product. Short Tons Miner/Hr.	Labor Product. Short Tons Miner/Hr.
1990	424,119	601,449	1,025,570	131,310	2.54	5.94	3.83	427	3,080	3,506	1,687	1.03	3.83
1991	406,901	585,638	992,539	120,602	2.69	6.38	4.09	324	3,121	3,445	1,161	1.39	4.09
1992	406,815	587,248	994,062	110,196	2.93	6.59	4.36	424	3,058	3,483	1,217	1.33	4.36
1993	350,637	590,482	941,119	101,322	2.95	7.23	4.70	416	3,889	4,306	1,124	1.85	4.70
1994	399,103	634,401	1,033,504	97,500	3.19	7.67	4.98	343	4,278	4,621	1,183	1.93	4.98
1995	396,249	636,725	1,032,974	90,252	3.39	8.48	5.38	428	4,254	4,682	1,069	2.08	5.38
1996	409,849	654,007	1,063,856	83,462	3.57	9.05	5.69	391	4,360	4,751	1,171	1.92	5.69
1997	420,657	669,274	1,089,932	81,516	3.83	9.46	6.04	419	4,259	4,678	1,287	1.76	6.04
1998	417,728	699,807	1,117,535	85,418	3.84	9.85	6.22	408	4,823	5,231	1,281	2.04	6.20
1999	391,790	708,642	1,100,431	78,723				377	4,376	4,753	1,326	1.76	6.61

[1] Excludes miners employed at mines producing less than 10,000 tons. *Source: Energy Information Administration, U.S. Department of Energy (EIA-DOE)*

Average Mine Prices of Coal in the United States In Dollars Per Short Ton

	Average Mine Price by Method			Average Mine Prices by Rank						All Coal
Year	Underground	Surface	Total	Lignite	Subbituminous	Bituminous	Anthracite[1]	Bituminous & Lignite FOB Mines[2]	Anthracite FOB Mines[2]	CIF[3] Electric Utility Plants
1990	28.58	16.98	21.76	10.13	9.70	27.43	39.40	21.71	39.40	30.45
1991	28.56	16.60	21.49	10.89	9.68	27.49	36.34	21.45	36.34	30.02
1992	27.83	16.34	21.03	10.81	9.68	26.78	34.24	20.98	34.24	29.36
1993	26.92	15.67	19.85	11.11	9.33	26.15	32.94	20.56	37.80	28.58
1994	26.39	15.02	19.41	10.77	8.37	25.68	36.07	25.68	36.07	28.03
1995	26.18	14.25	18.83	10.83	8.10	25.56	39.78	25.56	39.78	27.01
1996	25.96	13.82	18.50	10.92	7.87	25.17	36.78	25.17	36.78	26.45
1997	25.68	13.39	18.14	10.91	7.42	24.64	35.12	24.64	35.12	26.16
1998	25.64	12.92	17.67	10.80	6.96	24.87	42.91	24.87	42.91	25.64
1999	24.33	12.37	16.63	11.04	6.87	23.92	35.13			24.72

[1] Produced in Pennsylvania. [2] FOB = free on board. [3] *CIF = cost, insurance and freight. W = Withheld data.*
Source: Energy Information Adminstration, U.S. Department of Energy (EIA-DOE)

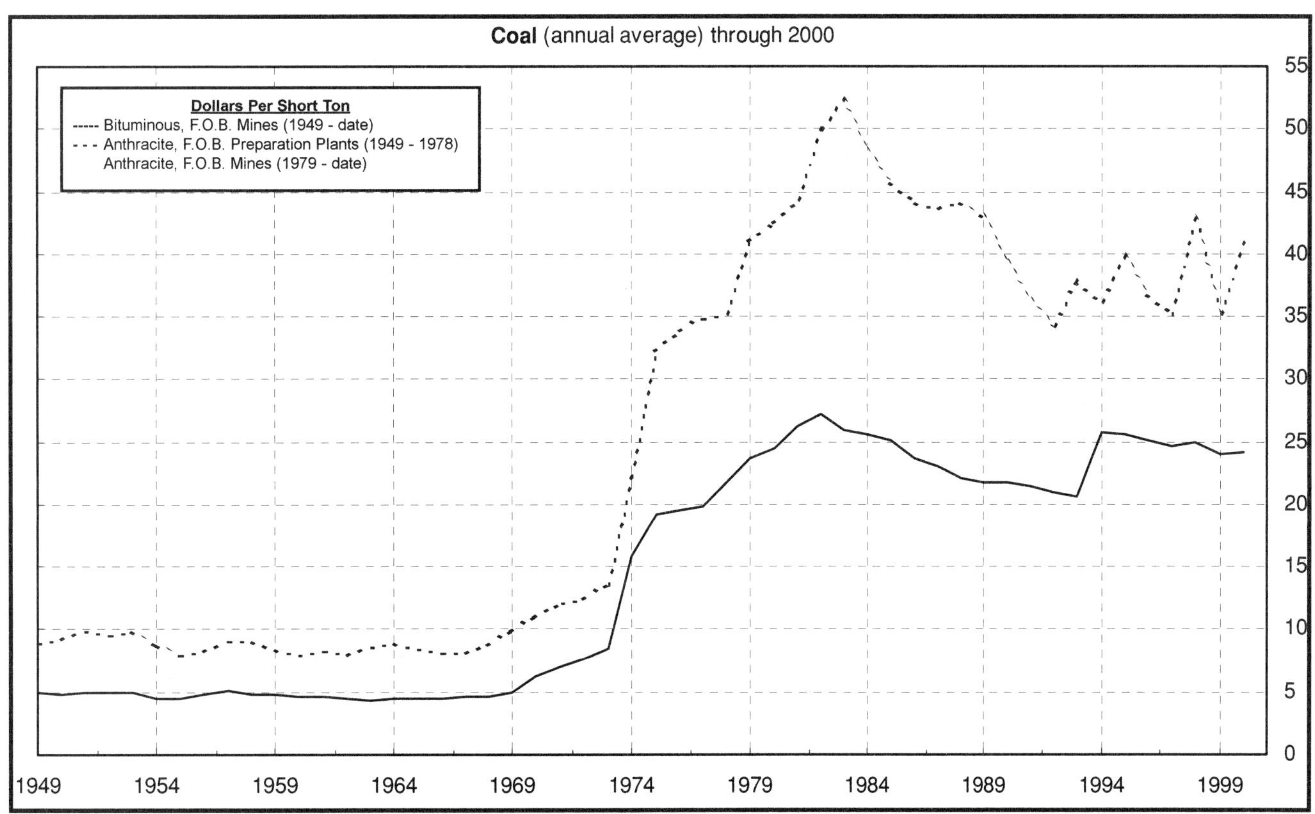

Cobalt

Cobalt is the strategic and critical metal with a variety of uses in industrial and military applications. It is found in the ores of iron and copper. Cobalt's largest use is in superalloys that are used in the manufacture of gas turbine aircraft engines. It is also used to make magnets, cemented carbides and diamond tools, catalysts for the petroleum and chemical industries, drying agents for paints, ground coats for porcelain enamels, pigments, battery electrodes, steelbelted radial tires, and magnetic recording media.

The U.S. Geological Survey reported that world mine production of cobalt in 2000 was 32,300 metric tonnes, up 8 percent from 1999. World cobalt production is forecast to increase as new projects in Australia and Uganda come on line. Adding to the cobalt supply are recycled scrap and sales from the U.S. Government's National Defense Stockpile. The largest producer of cobalt is the Congo with output of 7,000 tonnes in 2000., unchanged from 1999. Production by Australia was 5,700 tonnes, up 39 percent from 1999. The next largest producer was Canada with 5,000 tonnes, down 6 percent from 1999. Cobalt production by Russia was estimated at 4,000 tonnes, up 21 percent from 1999. Production by Zambia was 4,000 tonnes., down 15 percent from 1999. Other producers of cobalt include Cuba and New Caledonia.

World reserves of cobalt are estimated to be 4.7 million tonnes. the largest reserves are located in the Congo with 2 million tonnes. Cuba is estimated to have reserves of one million tonnes. Other countries with large reserves include Australia, Zambia and New Caledonia. The cobalt resources of the U.S. are estimated to be about 1.3 million tonnes. Most of those resources are located in Minnesota with other deposits in Alaska, California, Idaho and Montana.

U.S. reported consumption of cobalt materials in August 2001 was 601 tonnes. Consumption of cobalt metal in August 2001 was 283 tonnes, up 1 percent from a year ago. In the January-August 2001 period, consumption of cobalt metal was 2,390 tonnes, up 4 percent from 2000. For all of 2000, consumption was 3,460 tonnes. Consumption of cobalt oxide and other chemical compounds in the first eight months of 2001 was 1,040 tonnes, down 17 percent from 2000. For all of 2000, consumption was 1,850 tonnes. Consumption of cobalt scrap in January-August 2001 was 1,680 tonnes, down 6 percent from 2000. For 2000 scrap consumption was 2,680 tonnes. Use of cobalt in superalloys in 2000 totaled 3,580 tonnes while chemical and ceramic uses were 2,450 tonnes. use in magnetic alloys was 502 tonnes while use in steel was 137 tonnes.

U.S. reported stocks of cobalt materials in August 2001 were 720 tonnes, up 4 percent from the year before. Stocks of cobalt metal in August 2001 were 319 tonnes. U.S. government cobalt metal stocks were 8,260 tonnes, down 29 percent from the year before.

World Mine Production of Cobalt In Metric Tons (Cobalt Content)

Year	Australia	Botswana	Canada	Cuba	Finland (Refinery)	France (Refinery)	Japan (Refinery)	New Caledonia	Norway (Refinery)	Russia[3]	Congo[4]	Zambia	World Total
1991	1,400	208	5,274	1,100	1,503	123	185	800	1,983	5,800	9,900	6,994	33,300
1992	1,600	208	5,102	1,150	2,100	150	105	800	2,293	4,000	5,700	6,910	27,800
1993	1,900	205	5,108	1,061	2,200	144	191	800	2,414	3,500	2,459	4,840	21,900
1994	2,300	225	4,265	972	3,000	146	161	1,000	2,823	3,000	826	3,600	18,000
1995	2,500	271	5,339	1,591	3,610	161	227	1,100	2,804	3,500	1,647	5,908	24,500
1996	2,800	408	5,714	2,011	4,160	174	258	1,100	3,098	3,300	2,000	6,959	26,200
1997	3,000	334	5,709	2,082	5,000	159	264	1,000	3,417	3,300	3,500	6,037	27,200
1998	3,300	335	5,861	2,200	10,600	300	480	1,000	4,500	3,200	5,000	11,900	34,400
1999[1]	4,100	331	5,323	2,160	10,000	300	480	1,100	4,500	3,300	6,000	4,700	30,600
2000[2]	5,600	319	5,281	2,350	10,000	300	480	1,100	4,500	3,600	7,000	5,000	33,300

[1] Preliminary. [2] Estimate. [3] Formerly part of the U.S.S.R.; data not reported separately until 1992. [4] Formerly Zaire.

Source: U.S. Geological Survey (USGS)

Salient Statistics of Cobalt in the United States In Metric Tons (Cobalt Content)

					Consumption by End Uses											
Year	Net Import Reliance as a % of Apparent Consumption	Cobalt Secondary Production	Processors and Consumer Stocks Dec. 31	Imports for Consumption	Ground Coat Frit	Stainless & Heat Resisting	Catalysts	Superalloys	Tool Steel	Magnetic Alloys	Pigments	Drier in Paints, etc.[3]	Cutting & Wear-Resistant Material	Welding Materials	Total Apparent Uses	Price $ Per Pound[4]
1991	80	1,578	1,622	6,920	W	51	W	3,066	W	713	W	781	525	135	7,240	16.92
1992	76	1,613	840	5,760	257	26	949	2,697	47	670	197	745	522	128	6,590	22.93
1993	79	1,566	819	5,950	W	41	935	2,530	59	569	193	732	569	171	7,350	13.79
1994	81	1,570	914	6,780	W	41	871	2,810	84	698	198	809	723	312	8,730	24.66
1995	79	1,860	818	6,440	196	38	732	2,940	146	757	172	770	748	287	8,970	29.21
1996	76	2,280	770	6,710	391	38	652	3,360	95	719	191	733	722	347	9,380	25.50
1997	76	2,750	763	8,430	490	38	734	4,170	112	879	201	556	789	342	11,200	23.34
1998	73	3,080	750	7,670	W	38	W	4,060	96	771	W	W	844	421	11,500	21.43
1999[1]	73	2,720	738	8,150	W	W	W	3,830	W	794	W	W	755	291	10,700	17.02
2000[2]	74	2,550	780	8,770	W	W	W	3,800	W	544	W	W	760	1,020	11,700	15.16

[1] Preliminary. [2] Estimate. [3] Or related usage. [4] Annual spot for cathodes. W = Withheld proprietary data.

Source: U.S. Geological Survey (USGS)

Cocoa

Cocoa prices moved sharply higher in early 2001 as there were concerns in the market that political and social instability in the Ivory Coast would lead to a reduction in cocoa production and exports. The Ivory Coast is by far the world's largest producer and exporter of cocoa and any problems in that country that could effect the cocoa industry could be expected to increase prices. In addition to these concerns, the cocoa crops in West Africa overall appeared to be smaller than expected adding to the upward pressure on prices. In February 2001 cocoa prices had moved above $1,200 per metric tonne in trading on the New York Board of Trade. After that prices started to move lower. The problems in the Ivory Coast subsided which allowed prices to edge lower. Cocoa futures prices trended down reaching less than $900 per tonne in July 2001 before stabilizing around $1,000. In late 2001 prices once again rallied moving over $1,3000 on new concerns about the 2001/02 crops. In early 2002 there was not much fundamental evidence that the new crops would be much different than the 2000/01 crops.

The largest production area for cocoa is west Africa where about 60 percent of the world's cocoa is grown. Cocoa is a tropical crop found mostly in a zone that extends about 15 degrees north and 15 degrees south of the equator. Cocoa trees reach maturity in 5-6 years and can live 50 years or more. During the growing season the cocoa tree will produce thousands of flowers but only a few will develop into cocoa pods. The typical pattern is for a large crop or main crop to be followed by a smaller or midcrop. In West Africa the main crop harvest starts in the September-October period and can extend into the January-March period. That is followed by the harvest of the smaller midcrop which is usually of lower quality than the main crop.

The four major West African producers are the Ivory Coast, Ghana, Nigeria and Cameroon. The Ivory Coast produces about 40 percent of the world's cocoa. The next largest producer is Ghana with about 15 percent of the total. Outside of West Africa, the other major producers of cocoa are Indonesia, Brazil, Malaysia, Ecuador and the Dominican republic. Cocoa producers like Ghana and Indonesia have been making efforts to increase production while other producers like Malaysia have switched to other crops. Brazil, which had been one of the largest producers in the world, has seen its production reduced by witches' broom disease. Extensive efforts to control the disease appear to be paying off as the 2000/01 season saw an increase in cocoa production. If the disease has been successfully controlled, Brazil could emerge as a large cocoa producer in the future.

The 2001/02 season got underway in October with harvesting of the main crops in West Africa. In the Ivory Coast there have been a number of changes in the cocoa industry. the most important development has been that the cocoa industry has been liberalized or removed from the influence of the government. In the past the government had tried to protect local producers from low world prices by setting minimum prices. In 2001/02 there was an effort to establish a cocoa board that would set a minimum farmgate price. Additionally, there was an effort to put limits on how much of the crop each exporter could purchase so as to give smaller exporters a better chance to market the crop. The U.S.D.A.'s agricultural attache reported that the 2001/02 cocoa crop was projected to be 1.22 million metric tonnes with the main crop reaching 1.02 million tonnes and the midcrop 200,000 tonnes. Cocoa bean exports were forecast at a million tonnes. This would be higher than the 2000/01 crop of 1.18 million tonnes with a main crop of a million tonnes and a midcrop of 180,000 tonnes. Exports in 2000/01 were just under 900,000 tonnes. The quality of the 2001/02 crop appeared to be good at the beginning of the season but declined as the season progressed. The crop matured somewhat early meaning there would be little main crop cocoa harvested in the first quarter of 2002.

The Ghana cocoa crop in 2001/02 was expected to be larger than the 2000/01 crop. The Ghana Cocoa Board in late 2001 indicated that the crop would be 430,000 tonnes. The main crop was estimated at 400,000 tonnes and the midcrop at about 30,000 tonnes. If the crop turns out to be 430,000 tonnes, it would be about 9 percent larger than the previous year. Ghana has reported that cocoa was being smuggled into the neighboring Ivory Coast where prices were higher. There has also been an outbreak of black pod disease which could lower production by the end of the season. Nigeria's 2001/02 crop was expected to be 180,000 tonnes. the overall quality may be reduced because of heavy rain.

Malaysia has been producing less cocoa as other crops have replaced the cocoa trees. The Malaysian Cocoa Board indicated the crop in 2001 would be 80,000 tonnes which would be up about 14 percent from the previous year. Other estimates place the crop at less than a year ago due to heavy rains. Malaysia has a large capacity to process cocoa and imports cocoa to make up for small domestic production.

Futures Markets

Cocoa futures and options are traded at the CSCE Division of the New York Board of Trade (NYBOT) and on the London International Financial Futures and Options Exchange (LIFFE).

World Supply and Demand Cocoa In Thousands of Metric Tons

Crop Year Beginning October	Stocks Oct. 1	Production	Total Availability	Seasonal Grindings	Closing Stocks	Stock Change	Crop Year Beginning October	Stocks Oct. 1	Production	Total Availability	Seasonal Grindings	Closing Stocks	Stock Change
1985-6	531	1,962	2,474	1,877	597	65	1993-4	1,354	2,469	3,798	2,470	1,329	-25
1986-7	597	1,988	2,565	1,896	669	72	1994-5	1,329	2,352	3,657	2,482	1,175	-153
1987-8	669	2,194	2,841	2,003	838	169	1995-6	1,175	2,939	4,085	2,640	1,445	269
1988-9	838	2,460	3,273	2,118	1,155	317	1996-7	1,445	2,709	4,127	2,729	1,397	-48
1989-90	1,155	2,425	3,556	2,212	1,343	188	1997-8	1,397	2,655	4,026	2,779	1,246	-151
1990-1	1,343	2,510	3,828	2,351	1,476	133	1998-9[1]	1,246	2,829	4,047	2,713	1,334	88
1991-2	1,476	2,269	3,723	2,284	1,439	-38	1999-00[2]	1,334	3,027	4,331	2,938	1,393	59
1992-3	1,439	2,360	3,775	2,421	1,354	-85	2000-1[3]	1,393	2,783	4,149	2,940	1,208	-185

[1] Preliminary. [2] Estimate. [3] Forecast. [4] Obtained by adjusting the Gross World Crop for one percent loss in weight.
Source: E D & F Man Cocoa Ltd.

COCOA

World Production of Cocoa Beans In Thousands of Metric Tons

Crop Year Beginning October	Brazil	Cameroon	Colombia	Dominican Republic	Ecuador	Ghana	Indonesia	Ivory Coast	Malaysia	Mexico	Nigeria	Papua New Guinea	World Total
1991-2	310	108	47	48	83	243	169	748	217	51	110	41	2,269
1992-3	305	99	54	52	70	312	234	697	219	51	130	39	2,360
1993-4	276	97	49	59	79	255	251	887	204	39	142	31	2,469
1994-5	215	109	48	57	83	310	238	862	120	43	144	29	2,352
1995-6	222	117	45	55	103	404	284	1,265	116	30	163	35	2,939
1996-7	183	121	39	47	101	323	327	1,130	102	35	157	28	2,709
1997-8	173	114	38	60	28	409	331	1,113	57	30	165	26	2,655
1998-9[1]	138	121	39	24	72	398	393	1,197	79	25	198	35	2,829
1999-00[2]	124	112	37	34	92	435	412	1,404	39	22	168	40	3,027
2000-1[3]	135	115	38	37	95	440	400	1,140	35	30	170	38	2,783

[1] Preliminary. [2] Estimate. [3] Forecast. *Source: Foreign Agricultural Service, U.S. Department of Agriculture (FAS-USDA)*

World Consumption of Cocoa[4] In Thousands of Metric Tons

Year	Belgium	Brazil	Cote d'Ivoire	France	Germany	Italy	Malaysia	Netherlands	Singapore	United Kingdom	United States	Former U.S.S.R.	World Total
1991-2	46	216	108	67	306	62	87	294	51	153	307	25	2,284
1992-3	47	218	100	80	310	58	99	309	47	169	326	95	2,421
1993-4	50	210	110	95	310	65	103	331	52	170	317	90	2,470
1994-5	53	174	108	108	280	69	101	350	52	154	331	80	2,482
1995-6	54	183	130	111	270	73	96	385	56	191	345	80	2,640
1996-7	55	180	145	106	255	71	103	402	55	172	394	85	2,729
1997-8	55	188	195	107	240	72	94	425	51	174	399	85	2,779
1998-9[1]	55	191	210	124	197	72	109	415	41	166	406	55	2,713
1999-00[2]	55	202	230	142	215	73	116	437	50	167	439	75	2,938
2000-1[3]	55	202	270	148	225	73	102	440	45	159	435	75	2,940

[1] Preliminary. [2] Estimate. [3] Forecast. [4] Figures represent the grindings of cocoa beans in each country. *Source: Foreign Agricultural Service, U.S. Department of Agriculture (FAS-USDA)*

Raw Cocoa Grindings in Selected Countries In Metric Tons

Year	Total	First Quarter	Second Quarter	Third Quarter	Fourth Quarter	Total	First Quarter	Second Quarter	Third Quarter	Fourth Quarter
	Germany[2]					Netherlands				
1990	281,855	69,125	64,613	70,994	77,123	247,590	62,243	58,817	58,702	67,828
1991	290,703	73,172	72,396	70,934	73,661	274,741	64,299	71,643	63,973	74,826
1992	319,251	78,661	73,797	80,111	86,682	293,157	77,954	71,537	69,871	73,795
1993	298,681	74,119	69,805	74,010	80,747	320,060	78,338	75,548	81,183	84,991
1994	296,219	80,242	68,033	67,706	80,238	334,384	83,963	78,055	84,249	88,117
1995	258,817	69,441	56,478	61,523	71,375	355,492	91,314	85,248	85,311	93,619
1996	251,070	69,520	59,471	65,824	56,255	388,412	100,866	90,724	99,549	97,273
1997	245,244	61,379	57,402	65,233	61,230	407,340	102,338	100,132	101,817	103,053
1998	217,442	62,154	47,565	55,267	52,456	427,393	104,936	108,101	108,580	105,776
1999[1]	195,732	48,486	48,605	47,321	51,320	415,250	107,189	102,933	98,828	106,300
	United Kingdom					United States[3]				
1990	124,791	32,116	29,322	29,419	33,934	216,740	51,559	51,683	58,278	55,220
1991	148,191	32,902	36,016	41,863	37,410	255,781	51,191	64,365	66,544	73,681
1992	159,284	39,831	37,903	37,120	44,430	313,921	70,335	74,515	84,109	84,962
1993	171,343	44,575	41,975	37,496	47,297	321,905	78,968	77,720	84,593	80,624
1994	163,170	44,131	39,063	39,591	40,385	322,629	71,398	78,805	86,247	86,179
1995	159,877	43,410	35,348	34,431	46,688	338,401	78,835	78,886	87,360	93,320
1996	189,037	50,500	44,535	48,855	45,147	351,042	79,044	82,713	93,933	95,352
1997	173,522	44,059	42,702	41,180	45,581	397,895	95,435	97,223	105,984	99,253
1998	171,773	45,787	42,338	40,047	43,601	397,389	99,189	96,341	104,359	97,500
1999[1]	167,556	42,557	39,758	40,238	45,003	418,996	98,218	102,488	107,568	110,722

[1] Preliminary. [2] Beginning October 1990, includes former East Germany. [3] Data incomplete January 1984-March 1991, excludes one major processor. *Source: Foreign Agricultural Service, U.S. Department of Agriculture (FAS-USDA)*

Imports of Cocoa Butter in Selected Countries In Metric Tons

Year	Australia	Austria	Belgium	Canada	France	Germany	Italy	Japan	Nether-Lands	Sweden	Switzer-land	United Kingdom	United States
1990	10,025	6,047	22,125	8,830	28,539	49,999	6,187	15,686	34,529	5,855	16,306	34,604	92,165
1991	11,218	5,171	24,795	8,682	28,628	54,452	7,813	15,245	29,729	6,299	16,544	26,876	90,004
1992	10,697	5,249	31,836	10,706	28,560	44,906	8,431	15,835	29,999	5,885	17,422	26,300	99,509
1993	10,129	5,417	20,909	10,225	30,011	37,209	9,851	10,422	51,559	6,390	16,711	25,941	85,400
1994	13,030	5,410	34,061	11,551	36,698	59,170	9,173	15,937	43,192	7,079	17,242	35,453	54,550
1995	12,150	7,425	26,185	11,146	40,245	69,928	12,027	12,898	38,300	7,078	17,835	30,654	57,210
1996	14,316	7,124	23,771	12,166	47,349	69,298	11,178	16,096	39,193	5,698	18,690	32,781	68,761
1997	14,896	6,922	34,222	16,782	46,516	71,094	9,706	16,609	29,023	6,937	19,058	37,021	87,687
1998	16,305	5,984	25,722	16,941	43,610	76,057	8,957	15,363	28,523	7,403	19,857	32,951	65,306
1999[1]	22,573	5,363	42,278	17,323	49,722	70,323	8,281	17,824	35,602	6,884	21,278	39,648	80,475

[1] Preliminary. *Sources: E D & F Man Cocoa Limited*

Imports of Cocoa Liquor and Cocoa Powder in Selected Countries In Metric Tons

	Cocoa Liqour						Cocoa Powder						
Year	France	Germany	Nether-lands	Japan	United Kingdom	United States	Denmark	France	Germany	Italy	Japan	Nether-lands	United States
1990	35,146	1,860	9,875	3,123	1,713	25,047	3,014	12,244	21,294	11,418	6,284	6,446	58,280
1991	40,251	3,242	7,443	2,057	1,918	25,320	3,583	12,215	25,315	12,189	6,557	6,239	55,636
1992	45,056	2,540	7,130	2,246	3,611	24,255	3,291	14,896	27,745	14,469	6,067	9,412	56,089
1993	41,999	1,694	15,543	2,468	1,490	31,641	3,402	16,773	25,732	13,221	5,771	5,626	66,533
1994	42,392	2,682	14,913	2,312	4,443	26,846	3,625	19,215	28,806	12,884	6,461	10,078	67,207
1995	46,570	5,083	6,822	1,832	5,030	19,192	3,229	17,081	32,247	15,265	6,310	10,048	66,075
1996	62,938	7,437	9,926	2,133	5,069	15,357	3,711	18,398	36,211	15,006	13,069	6,678	68,658
1997	61,148	10,299	8,401	1,393	5,860	17,850	4,189	19,555	35,069	15,872	8,941	4,424	71,024
1998	70,883	9,121	12,534	1,144	3,813	21,894	3,865	19,533	32,479	17,122	8,779	3,746	84,211
1999[1]	74,721	13,833	25,639	1,421	4,396	12,823	3,676	19,342	33,404	16,464	9,779	NA	84,975

[1] Preliminary. NA = Not available. *Source: E D & F Man Cocoa Limited*

Imports of Cocoa and Products in the United States In Thousands of Metric Tons

Year	Jan.	Feb.	Mar.	Apr.	May	June	July	Aug.	Sept.	Oct.	Nov.	Dec.	Total
1992	83	66	62	55	50	60	52	60	67	67	64	69	755
1993	67	57	56	61	58	61	77	58	59	71	71	98	801
1994	67	68	56	61	49	51	49	58	58	61	45	48	672
1995	68	54	44	48	47	48	48	51	53	49	54	79	643
1996	90	87	90	80	55	49	62	53	53	60	60	86	821
1997	80	47	77	71	64	54	59	47	64	61	56	88	768
1998	86	105	90	71	55	65	65	62	72	63	54	77	865
1999	100	79	81	93	51	60	77	62	68	67	82	102	922
2000	111	128	101	91	70	67	70	70	86	76	59	69	998
2001[1]	108	97	77	47	68	61	80	78	76	87			935

[1] Preliminary. NA = Not available. *Source: Foreign Agricultural Service, U.S. Department of Agriculture (FAS-USDA)*

Visible Stocks of Cocoa in Port of Hampton Road Warehouses[1], at End of Month In Thousands of Bags

Year	Jan.	Feb.	Mar.	Apr.	May	June	July	Aug.	Sept.	Oct.	Nov.	Dec.
1992	1,588.3	1,892.1	2,233.1	2,236.2	2,236.9	2,204.8	2,150.8	2,087.4	1,982.4	2,018.6	2,043.9	2,188.5
1993	2,209.9	2,497.3	2,443.9	2,676.8	2,771.8	2,689.7	2,920.0	2,708.6	2,740.1	2,418.7	2,328.3	2,356.9
1994	2,329.6	2,441.1	2,443.9	2,522.9	2,533.1	2,460.2	2,445.4	2,335.0	2,308.4	2,360.2	2,306.9	2,253.7
1995	2,152.7	2,098.6	2,195.7	2,212.3	2,120.2	2,016.0	1,919.8	1,786.6	1,713.1	1,598.2	1,463.9	1,470.3
1996	1,439.8	1,492.8	1,458.0	1,549.6	1,561.7	1,493.9	1,412.3	1,315.4	1,239.6	1,338.9	1,108.1	1,116.2
1997	1,128.3	1,132.1	1,133.0	1,094.0	1,010.5	970.2	872.4	840.1	727.3	763.9	695.7	704.8
1998	726.5	693.4	841.9	842.5	811.6	764.7	714.3	712.3	795.4	801.9	705.9	673.0
1999	661.6	693.2	642.5	579.7	536.9	500.7	489.0	472.7	473.4	451.8	438.9	421.2
2000	469.7	448.4	571.7	583.4	711.1	672.4	720.3	925.2	921.4	839.7	762.9	816.0
2001	741.9	657.4	632.0	607.7	577.3	518.8	498.2	487.5	475.2	506.8	509.0	511.4

[1] Licensed and unlicensed warehouses approved by the CSCE. *Source: New York Board of Trade (NYBOT)*

COCOA

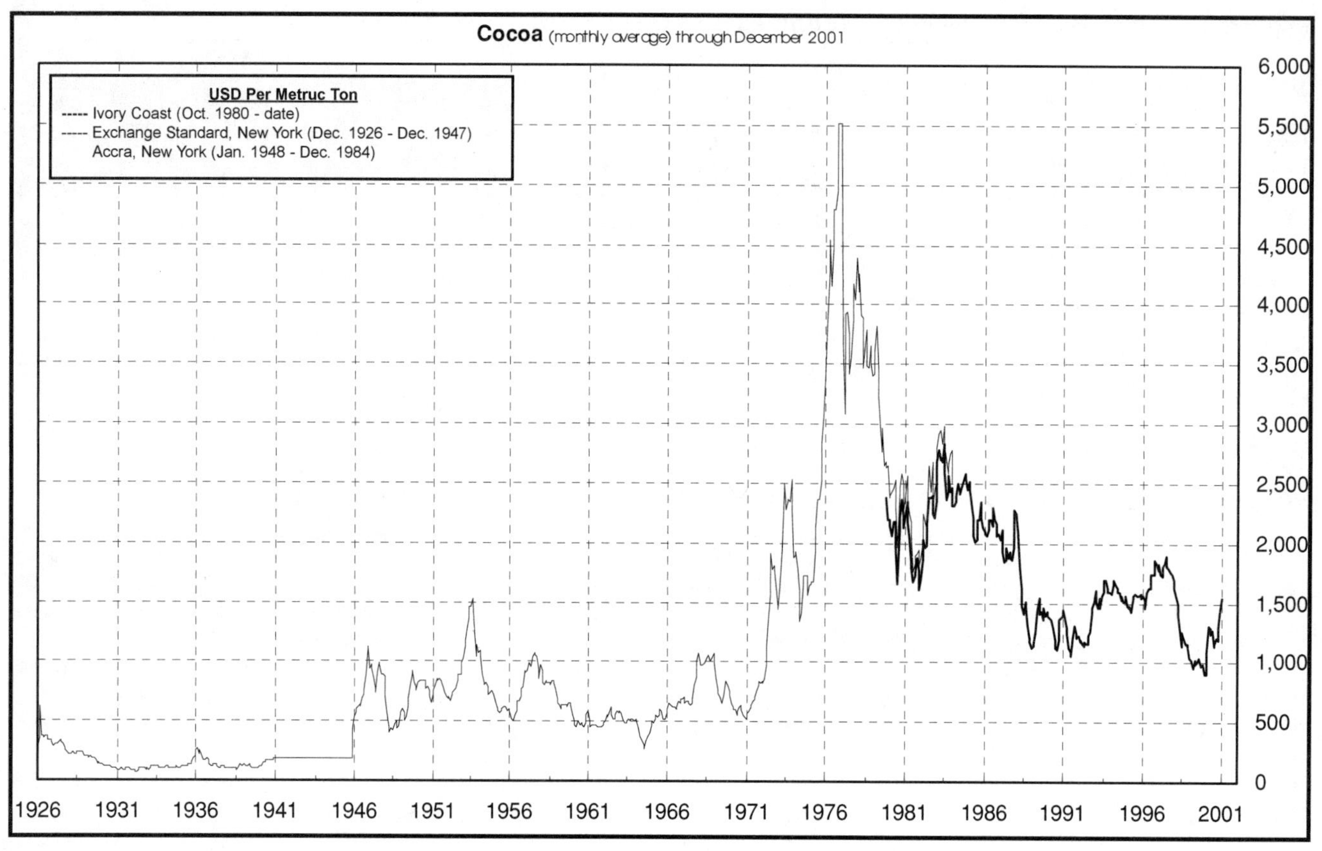

Visible Stocks of Cocoa in Philadelphia (Del. River) Warehouses[1], at End of Month In Thousands of Bags

Year	Jan.	Feb.	Mar.	Apr.	May	June	July	Aug.	Sept.	Oct.	Nov.	Dec.
1992	344.6	345.5	412.1	547.6	576.7	632.0	637.7	654.0	616.4	606.0	565.8	612.4
1993	562.2	589.8	603.9	606.0	653.1	678.0	665.7	648.9	600.6	611.5	685.2	781.8
1994	831.5	937.7	1,004.2	1,010.9	1,055.4	1,095.2	1,076.0	1,029.8	968.5	857.1	843.9	818.9
1995	807.5	1,034.3	1,038.9	1,020.2	963.7	924.3	860.7	759.2	852.2	727.0	666.0	735.6
1996	960.2	1,005.2	1,205.6	1,658.8	1,871.3	1,851.7	1,969.1	1,816.2	1,851.1	1,705.1	1,671.7	1,696.5
1997	1,753.0	1,634.4	1,579.6	1,641.0	1,578.7	1,625.9	1,696.2	1,637.6	1,530.9	1,491.8	1,414.2	1,394.0
1998	1,420.3	1,435.7	1,592.6	1,555.3	1,398.5	1,287.8	1,279.8	1,376.9	1,373.7	1,260.6	1,406.7	1,637.1
1999	1,763.0	1,832.8	1,982.7	2,217.8	2,019.4	1,999.6	2,084.6	2,133.4	2,144.1	2,015.5	1,774.4	1,608.5
2000	1,619.0	1,801.7	2,466.4	2,582.0	2,581.6	2,363.7	2,168.3	2,101.6	2,105.1	2,039.1	1,697.4	1,589.4
2001	1,844.0	2,082.3	2,173.3	1,960.0	1,785.9	1,610.4	1,391.6	1,543.0	1,391.3	1,131.4	1,303.2	1,682.1

[1] Licensed and unlicensed warehouses approved by the CSCE. *Source: New York Board of Trade (NYBOT)*

Visible Stocks of Cocoa in New York Warehouses[1], at End of Month In Thousands of Bags

Year	Jan.	Feb.	Mar.	Apr.	May	June	July	Aug.	Sept.	Oct.	Nov.	Dec.
1992	321.2	303.7	278.7	302.6	273.4	287.8	329.7	301.5	280.5	252.3	212.7	183.3
1993	150.9	144.1	122.0	125.0	119.8	119.8	119.8	119.8	119.8	118.6	132.4	187.7
1994	271.0	275.0	280.8	296.6	358.6	394.1	447.5	447.5	467.3	427.3	407.2	556.1
1995	560.5	634.5	559.2	539.4	510.4	561.1	579.3	595.4	459.9	598.7	679.7	598.7
1996	667.6	646.1	632.7	627.2	656.1	633.5	1,191.7	1,154.2	1,121.4	973.2	950.1	919.0
1997	984.7	981.3	945.0	1,250.0	1,574.4	1,524.7	1,512.8	1,348.0	1,217.3	1,073.7	1,020.0	980.4
1998	973.9	1,342.7	1,271.3	1,675.7	1,552.3	1,516.7	1,404.6	1,293.1	1,300.1	1,126.4	989.2	1,031.6
1999	1,085.0	1,089.3	1,083.1	1,134.1	1,139.4	1,114.3	1,093.5	974.5	941.9	821.7	847.5	1,573.1
2000	1,633.7	1,689.5	1,926.9	2,049.8	1,926.7	1,789.6	1,632.2	1,383.7	1,323.7	1,234.8	1,100.0	1,019.4
2001	1,005.6	1,173.8	1,119.6	1,024.9	967.5	906.6	776.2	758.5	657.6	687.4	750.8	1,196.2

[1] Licensed and unlicensed warehouses approved by the CSCE. *Source: New York Board of Trade (NYBOT)*

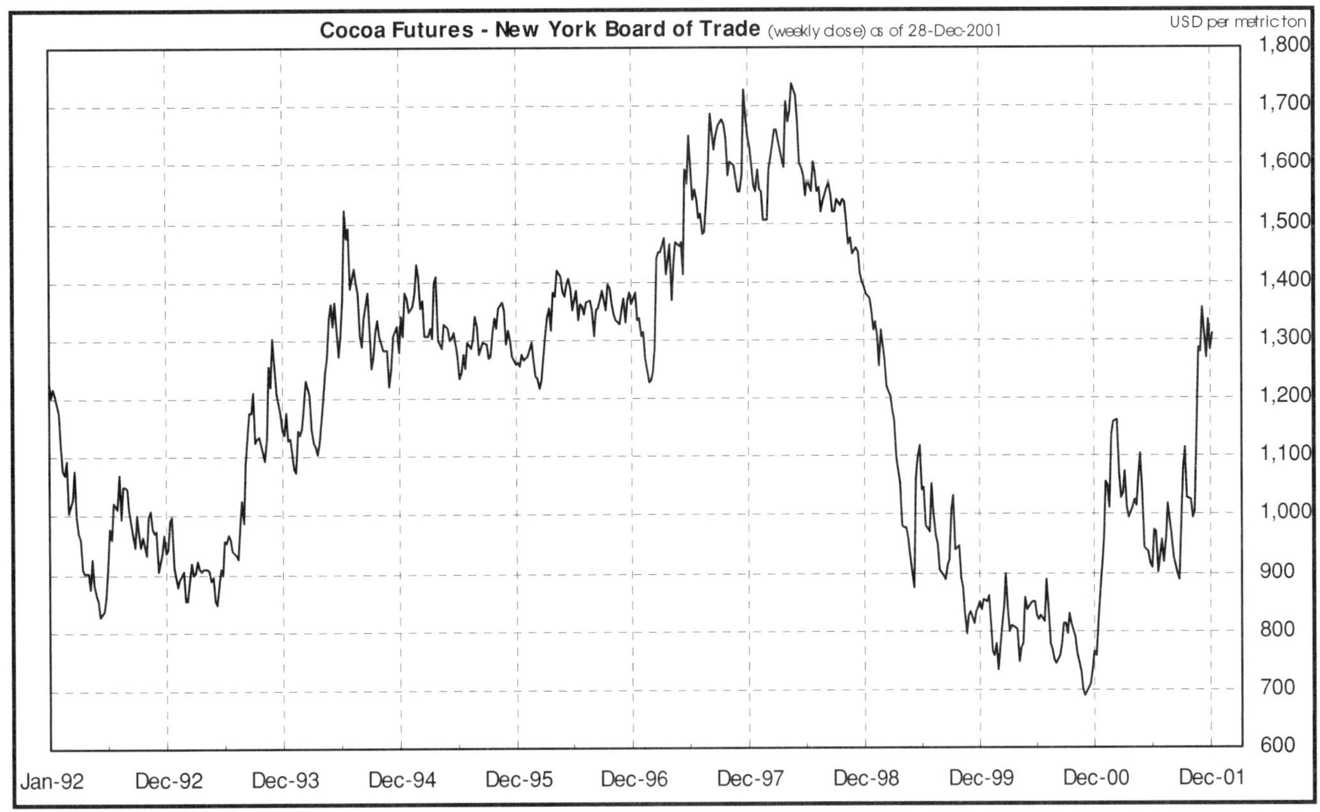

Average Open Interest of Cocoa Futures in New York In Contracts

Year	Jan.	Feb.	Mar.	Apr.	May	June	July	Aug.	Sept.	Oct.	Nov.	Dec.
1992	54,464	54,797	52,110	49,904	48,076	47,690	49,924	50,532	51,706	56,101	57,426	60,521
1993	64,886	68,307	69,464	68,533	71,802	71,792	87,011	83,057	88,000	94,844	96,507	91,573
1994	89,174	87,349	91,715	82,500	82,970	72,288	72,249	69,614	73,436	74,163	72,232	75,995
1995	78,873	80,786	82,299	78,435	80,547	75,496	74,975	65,794	68,547	72,758	76,680	79,844
1996	90,478	93,533	98,049	95,390	96,346	88,232	80,873	77,134	77,942	79,572	77,139	78,592
1997	86,960	90,589	96,771	96,956	94,651	97,385	101,815	101,138	106,487	108,263	99,544	97,009
1998	90,574	82,205	78,022	73,237	79,294	74,347	74,295	73,975	71,978	74,139	74,127	73,480
1999	77,067	72,324	69,221	65,856	71,990	75,195	70,787	69,939	74,572	79,770	89,035	92,609
2000	100,540	110,316	106,056	102,382	113,239	111,948	112,864	117,260	123,463	138,523	139,141	138,266
2001	132,711	119,459	114,036	102,275	107,008	1,111,224	104,473	99,280	92,235	96,204	93,088	92,326

Source: New York Board of Trade (NYBOT)

Volume of Trading of Cocoa Futures in New York In Contracts

Year	Jan.	Feb.	Mar.	Apr.	May	June	July	Aug.	Sept.	Oct.	Nov.	Dec.	Total
1992	122,576	119,375	94,131	116,804	66,185	135,373	104,660	145,815	113,589	109,888	137,815	95,024	1,397,235
1993	145,378	139,932	111,751	149,771	82,961	189,474	225,901	215,044	240,371	217,697	229,752	183,352	2,128,384
1994	178,303	190,804	205,623	188,004	267,188	251,300	193,883	241,340	142,589	183,975	210,635	164,917	2,417,006
1995	197,032	183,784	191,328	208,707	169,061	199,211	140,789	205,169	120,433	149,810	211,171	113,603	2,090,098
1996	177,720	226,701	213,189	242,988	164,749	183,544	159,070	164,719	107,634	167,227	185,226	128,809	2,121,576
1997	180,669	172,510	219,896	235,020	130,041	251,471	186,280	200,707	168,981	204,394	180,805	143,735	2,274,509
1998	175,844	145,311	171,333	192,120	143,602	183,719	131,642	156,737	115,066	125,320	155,280	114,606	1,810,580
1999	136,109	155,090	141,090	180,837	130,019	230,925	125,360	144,290	147,124	143,335	209,608	124,249	1,868,036
2000	156,812	231,562	232,803	186,837	147,072	267,470	124,906	191,849	111,740	174,216	186,515	98,266	2,110,048
2001	311,900	168,587	164,131	136,021	154,397	201,299	108,189	207,569	118,428	124,884	202,847	107,565	2,005,817

Source: New York Board of Trade (NYBOT)

Coconut Oil and Copra

The USDA lists copra as one of the seven major oilseeds despite the fact that the crop totals less than 2% of total global oilseed production. . Copra, dried coconut meat, is crushed or processed to yield coconut oil and copra meal. Coconut oil, an important ingredient in cosmetics and soap, is also used as food ingredient. As an edible oil, however, food stock use is shrinking, especially in the U.S., as the oil has a very high level of saturated fat--92%. U.S. coconut oil imports are mostly processed into inedible products.

Most of the world's copra crop is processed into coconut oil. Copra production in 2001/02, almost all of which is crushed, totaled 5.29 million metric tons compares with a record high 5.71 million in 2000/01. From the two most recent crops, 3.2 million tons and 3.42 million tons, respectively, of coconut oil were obtained. Copra meal output at 1.68 million tons compares with 1.82 million tons in 2000/01. Percentage wise, coconut oil accounts for only about 3 to 4% of the world's vegetable and marine oil, and meal less than 1%. The Philippines and Indonesia account for about two-thirds of world copra output; production of which is not only dependent on the weather, but the crop is also believed to have a well entrenched biological cycle that triggers relatively sharp swings in output. Indonesia's output since the mid-1990's has trended irregularly higher while in the Philippine's its been lower; but the combined total of both countries accounted for about 80% of world production in 2001, with the Philippines the larger producer. India's production has risen from a mid 1990's annual average of about 600,000 tons to over 740,000 tons by 2001.

Foreign trade in copra products is small: coconut oil exports in 2001/02 of 1.8 million tons compares with almost 2 million in 2000/01; meal exports were a shade hovered around a million tons in both years. World consumption of coconut oil in 2001/02 of 3.2 million tons about equals 2000/01 while meal usage of 1.7 million tons compares with 1.8 million, respectively. World carryover stocks of both products are also minimal: ending 2001/02 carryover of oil at 210,000 tons compares with 230,000 tons a year earlier while meal totals are about 111,000 tons and 140,000 tons, respectively.

U.S. crude coconut oil prices, basis tank cars, New York, has averaged near 30 cents per pound in recent years vs. a high for the 1990's of 42.4 cents in 1996. U.S. processors are not adverse to switching to palm oil should coconut oil's develop a wider than acceptable premium to palm oil. World copra meal prices, basis Rotterdam, in 2001/02 (October through September) are forecast to average $95 per metric ton vs. $92 in 2000/01 and the 1990/91-99/00 average of $127 per ton. The average Rotterdam coconut oil price in 2001/02 is forecast at $319 per metric ton vs. $323 a year earlier and the ten year average of $599 per ton.. Average Rotterdam copra seed prices of $199 per ton in 2001/02 compare with $208 in 2000/01 and ten-year average of $392 per ton.

World Production of Copra In Thousands of Metric Tons

Year	India	Indonesia	Ivory Coast	Malaysia	Mexico	Mozambique	New Guinea	Philippines	Sri Lanka	Thailand	Vanuatu	Vietnam	World Total
1992	440	1,110	65	82	200	72	117	1,845	70	65	24	220	4,624
1993	515	1,100	60	65	173	73	120	1,980	50	60	28	225	4,776
1994	592	1,270	65	60	216	74	104	1,930	104	100	27	210	5,072
1995	655	1,080	72	66	217	74	125	2,500	113	103	30	208	5,544
1996	720	1,155	75	60	204	75	178	1,725	75	61	33	210	4,880
1997	720	1,300	45	60	215	76	159	2,210	67	62	34	96	5,363
1998	735	970	43	52	200	76	150	2,270	95	90	37	123	5,147
1999[1]	720	860	42	52	153	73	146	1,250	90	87	35	100	3,878
2000[2]	660	1,200	45	55	140	73	160	2,000	95	90		102	4,955
2001[3]	740	1,300			135		162	2,180				100	5,313

[1] Preliminary. [2] Estimate. [3] Forecast. *Source: The Oil World*

World Supply and Distribution of Coconut Oil In Thousands of Metric Tons

	Production							Consumption						Ending Stocks		
Year	India	Indonesia	Malaysia	Philippines	Total	Exports	Imports	European Union	India	Indonesia	Philippines	United States	Total	Philippines	United States	Total
1991-2	274	701	33	1,110	2,848	1,343	1,321	513	285	380	257	409	2,880	115	85	420
1992-3	299	691	29	1,294	3,035	1,667	1,583	516	312	441	249	491	3,007	38	114	364
1993-4	343	704	32	1,242	3,009	1,361	1,437	547	346	337	294	483	2,962	181	74	457
1994-5	383	638	36	1,564	3,312	1,775	1,760	660	384	492	309	491	3,325	99	74	430
1995-6	397	612	35	1,206	2,912	1,374	1,405	606	396	373	306	427	3,005	100	38	368
1996-7	421	756	35	1,257	3,152	1,751	1,695	692	429	213	315	504	3,081	92	68	382
1997-8	439	652	40	1,628	3,451	2,122	2,117	777	437	185	302	540	3,230	32	178	598
1998-9[1]	432	458	52	780	2,352	1,039	1,166	580	447	113	293	461	2,762	56	69	311
1999-00[2]	397	674	50	1,152	2,923	1,550	1,564	605	424	157	313	478	2,875	75	70	373
2000-1[3]	445	760	47	1,331	3,244	1,767	1,761	660	465	206	341	527	3,133	95	86	478

[1] Preliminary. [2] Estimate. [3] Forecast. *Source: The Oil World*

Supply and Distribution of Coconut Oil in the United States In Millions of Pounds

	Rotterdam						Disappearance			Production of Coconut Oil (Refined)				
Year	Copra Tonne	Coconut Oil, CIF	Imports For Consumption	Stocks Oct. 1	Total Supply	Exports	Total Domestic	Edible Products	Inedible Products	Total	Oct.-Dec.	Jan.-Mar.	April-June	July-Sept.
	$ U.S.													
1992-3	292	446	1,162	187	1,349	15	1,082	202	692	650.5	156.0	158.8	166.6	169.1
1993-4	388	564	999	251	1,250	20	1,067	234	716	536.2	155.6	129.0	131.8	119.8
1994-5	432	656	1,100	163	1,263	18	1,082	247	694	546.8	137.5	142.7	144.3	122.3
1995-6	487	746	873	163	1,036	11	941	221	453	445.0	127.5	118.4	132.8	66.4
1996-7	452	693	1,188	83	1,271	11	1,111	120	471	324.2	77.0	61.5	101.5	84.2
1997-8	391	587	1,440	149	1,589	7	1,190	141	472	397.8	113.4	103.6	100.4	80.4
1998-9	468	748	791	392	1,183	11	1,021	144	380	363.2	89.6	82.9	99.3	91.4
1999-00	357	539	926	152	1,078	14	927	221	371	442.3	69.1	117.0	129.6	126.7
2000-1[1]			1,096	136	1,232	8	965	238	298	534.9	135.7	128.3	146.9	124.0
2001-2[2]			1,069	260	1,329	11	1,074	282	279	557.8	139.5			

[1] Preliminary. *Source: Bureau of Census, U.S. Department of Commerce*

Consumption of Coconut Oil in End Products (Edible and Inedible) in the U.S. In Millions of Pounds

Year	Jan.	Feb.	Mar.	Apr.	May	June	July	Aug.	Sept.	Oct.	Nov.	Dec.	Total
1992	72.5	70.6	76.5	70.7	78.7	74.8	65.2	70.6	77.4	75.8	76.2	66.4	875.4
1993	74.4	75.9	81.3	77.6	72.1	71.0	73.6	78.2	72.6	85.9	90.9	84.6	938.1
1994	74.4	77.4	77.5	80.4	86.6	88.8	76.0	88.4	65.1	74.6	85.1	95.0	969.3
1995	78.2	79.5	86.5	81.0	79.7	82.0	76.5	71.4	61.6	62.1	59.8	59.9	878.0
1996	47.0	54.3	60.1	60.2	68.6	54.6	55.1	47.9	44.9	49.6	50.3	47.9	640.7
1997	44.1	44.8	52.8	46.1	41.9	49.4	49.9	48.3	66.9	53.4	43.9	48.0	589.5
1998	51.5	48.1	59.4	54.3	54.5	47.0	49.3	50.3	53.7	49.4	50.0	42.1	609.6
1999	39.9	44.7	50.8	43.0	41.4	45.4	36.9	33.3	46.2	41.5	43.6	38.8	505.5
2000	49.4	44.0	52.7	54.6	51.4	56.5	49.1	56.2	54.7	44.1	44.3	43.0	600.0
2001[1]	44.3	40.6	45.5	42.5	48.3	43.3	46.5	45.6	48.4	50.3	44.4	45.5	545.1

[1] Preliminary. *Source: Bureau of Census, U.S. Department of Commerce*

Stocks of Coconut Oil (Crude and Refined) in the U.S., on First of Month In Millions of Pounds

Year	Jan.	Feb.	Mar.	Apr.	May	June	July	Aug.	Sept.	Oct.	Nov.	Dec.
1992	NA	266.3	274.2	239.7	211.2	173.7	178.3	141.1	187.1	187.7	225.1	278.8
1993	355.7	406.7	418.9	348.7	338.3	305.2	257.2	233.8	321.4	250.8	335.0	299.1
1994	291.7	316.5	284.5	251.5	237.6	199.9	151.4	163.7	156.0	164.1	166.2	152.9
1995	155.6	173.6	168.1	163.7	148.5	183.5	163.8	136.9	124.1	162.9	199.7	187.7
1996	164.7	229.1	200.4	217.7	173.6	175.9	171.5	116.7	113.8	84.0	78.6	65.0
1997	125.9	147.4	141.1	204.5	174.5	161.3	143.8	143.4	154.3	149.6	162.1	194.2
1998	274.2	332.4	344.5	337.4	318.8	300.6	366.3	424.6	434.4	392.6	431.8	447.3
1999	401.7	446.5	387.5	366.3	309.8	240.5	134.7	197.5	191.8	152.0	106.4	142.2
2000	93.6	123.6	100.1	99.6	102.3	104.0	137.7	163.6	161.4	136.4	178.1	161.6
2001[1]	245.4	280.3	357.8	276.5	286.9	194.3	254.4	260.9	246.4	259.7	234.1	231.3

[1] Preliminary. NA = Not available. *Source: Bureau of Census, U.S. Department of Commerce*

Average Price of Coconut Oil (Crude) Tank Cars in New York In Cents Per Pound

Year	Jan.	Feb.	Mar.	Apr.	May	June	July	Aug.	Sept.	Oct.	Nov.	Dec.	Average
1992	39.33	36.00	34.57	34.63	33.56	32.13	29.63	27.31	27.88	26.95	27.00	25.50	31.21
1993	24.94	24.37	23.65	23.13	24.13	24.95	25.35	25.61	24.44	23.88	26.69	34.25	25.45
1994	30.30	29.69	27.31	28.19	29.45	30.25	29.56	30.35	30.63	30.60	34.19	33.69	30.35
1995	32.50	32.00	31.13	31.00	30.50	35.00	37.90	35.63	35.00	36.00	37.88	33.69	34.02
1996	35.80	36.63	36.75	38.75	39.50	42.25	41.80	42.80	47.20	48.00	49.50	50.00	42.42
1997	44.20	44.00	42.88	42.50	42.50	35.00	36.50	36.50	37.00	37.25	37.25	37.25	39.40
1998	37.25	37.25	37.25	37.25	37.25	37.00	36.50	35.50	36.50	39.00	37.50	38.50	37.23
1999	35.38	35.00	34.00	34.06	38.25	42.13	39.83	36.08	46.00	35.02	40.73	41.43	38.16
2000	40.85	37.70	29.70	29.26	26.86	23.82	20.92	18.85	17.13	17.48	19.10	16.90	24.88
2001[1]	16.36	15.45	15.12	14.66	14.25	15.26	16.90	17.70	16.31	15.76	15.93	15.48	15.77

[1] Preliminary. *Source: Economic Research Service, U.S. Department of Agriculture (ERS-USDA)*

Coffee

Coffee prices moved lower in 2001 as a result of increased world production of coffee relative to consumption. Coffee prices have been trending lower since December 1999. Following a drought in Brazil which was alleviated by rains, prices moved lower in anticipation of increased Brazilian coffee production. The weather since late 1999 has been favorable in Brazil and in early 2002 it was expected that the next Brazilian crop would be large. How large was an important question for the market. The large decline in coffee prices appeared to be ending in late 2001 as prices on the New York Board of Trade approached 40 cents per pound for arabica coffee. It appeared that despite the fact that the fundamentals in the market had not improved very much, the market had already discounted most of not all of the negative news. Additionally, stocks of coffee in the U.S. had moved somewhat lower which was positive news.

One major development in the coffee market was the decision by the Association of Coffee Producing Countries (ACPC) to end the coffee retention plan. The plan was an attempt by the coffee producers to increase prices by withholding part of their exports from the market. The ACPC member countries agreed to hold 20 percent of their exports back from the market until prices had increased a set amount. The plan turned out to be unsuccessful as many countries in the ACPC were not able to withhold coffee from the export market due to the high cost of warehousing. Countries like Brazil and Colombia supported the plan but that was not enough to force prices higher and the plan was ended. It was interesting in that there was widespread support for the plan among coffee producers yet the producers were unable to fully implement it enough to increase prices. It was also interesting that countries that were not members of the ACPC like Vietnam and Mexico agreed to support the plan by holding some coffee off the market. The failure of the retention plan indicated that the producers were unable to implement a plan that they themselves could actually live with even though they were in agreement something needed to be done about low prices.

The basic problem in the coffee market from the perspective of producers is that there is more coffee being produced than is being consumed and this has allowed coffee stocks to increase. A number of countries are producing more and more coffee and they are exporting that coffee. This is acting to keep pressure on prices. The International Coffee Organization (ICO) reported that Brazil's coffee exports in November 2001 were 2.62 million bags, a considerable increase from the 1.68 million bags exported in November 2000. In the December 2000 to November 2001 twelve month period, Brazilian coffee exports were 22.92 million bags, an increase of 24 percent from the previous twelve month period. Brazil is the largest producer and exporter of coffee in the world. The ICO reported that Colombia's exports in November 2001 were 1.25 million bags, a 4 percent increase from a year before. In the December 2000 to November 2001 period, Colombia's exports were 9.79 million bags, up 6 percent from the previous twelve month period. The countries that has increased production the most in recent years and increased exports substantially is Vietnam. Vietnam produces robusta coffee. Vietnam has passed Colombia to become the second largest producer and exporter of coffee. The ICO reported that in November 2001, Vietnam exported 1.11 million bags, down from 1.18 million a year before. Exports in the last twelve months were 14.32 million bags, up 28 percent from the previous twelve month period.

Low prices for coffee are expected to reduce production and exports in the higher cost producing countries. Important producers and exporters of coffee are Mexico and Central America. the ICO reported that in November 2001, Mexico exported only 115,789 bags of coffee, down 63 percent from a year earlier. In the last twelve months, Mexico exported 3.34 million bags of coffee, down 38 percent from the prior twelve month period. Guatemala's exports in November 2001 were 91,162 bags, down 55 percent from a year ago. Exports in the last twelve months were down 12 percent from the same period a year before.

The U.S.D.A. in December 2001 released estimates of coffee production in the 2001/02 (October-September) season. The estimate of Brazilian coffee production was 33.7 million bags, the same estimate that the U.S.D.A. made in June 2001 and slightly below the 2000/01 crop of 34.1 million bags. Brazil produces both arabica and robusta coffees. Vietnam has been producing larger and larger coffee crops. The 2001/02 crop was estimated by the U.S.D.A. at 13.3 million bags, up 7 percent from the June estimate but some 11 percent less than the record 2000/01 crop of 15 million bags. Colombia's 2001/02 crop was estimated at 11 million bags, down 4 percent from the June estimate of 11.4 million bags but 5 percent more than the previous crop of 10.5 million bags. Colombia produces arabica coffee.

After Vietnam, the major producers of robusta coffee are Brazil and Indonesia. The U.S.D.A. estimated Indonesia's coffee crop in 2001/02 at 6.28 million bags, the same estimate as in June but some 3 percent less than the 2000/01 crop of 6.49 million bags. Mexico's crop of 5.5 million bags was expected to be 4 percent larger than the 2000/01 crop of 5.3 million bags. The Ivory Coast is the largest robusta coffee producer in Africa. The U.S.D.A. forecast the 2001/02 crop at 4.17 million bags, down 11 percent from the June estimate of 4.7 million bags and 4 percent less than the 2000/01 crop of 4.33 million bags. The 2001/02 Guatemalan crop was forecast at 3.83 million bags, down 23 percent from the June estimate and some 15 percent less than the 2000/01 crop of 4.49 million bags. The U.S.D.A. forecast world coffee production in 2001/02 at 115.8 million bags, down 2 percent from the June estimate of 117.7 million bags and 1 percent less that the 2000/01 crop of 117.4 million bags.

As 2002 progresses there will be a number of important developments to watch in the coffee market. maybe most important will be the size of the 2002/03 Brazilian coffee crop. That crop will be harvested starting in May. Brazilian production generally follows a two year cycle with the 2001/02 crop being a smaller crop so the new crop in Brazil has the potential to be a large crop. Based on previous production cycles, the crop could reach 40 million bags.

Futures Markets

Coffee futures are traded on the Bolsa de Mercadorias & Futuros (BM&F), the Tokyo Grain Exchange (TGE), the London International Financial Futures Exchange (LIFFE), and the CSCE Division of the New York Board of Trade (NYBOT). Options are traded on the BM&F, the LIFFE and the CSCE.

World Supply and Distribution of Coffee In Thousands of 60 Kilogram Bags (132.276 Lbs. Per Bag)

Crop Year	Beginning Stocks	Production	Imports	Supply	Total Exports	Bean Exports	Rst/Grn Exports	Soluble Exports	Domestic Use	Ending Stocks
1992-3	46,298	92,959	713	139,970	77,869	73,881	117	3,871	21,579	40,522
1993-4	40,522	92,406	585	133,513	76,284	71,779	108	4,397	22,928	34,301
1994-5	34,301	97,042	1,070	132,413	68,672	64,432	230	4,010	22,526	41,215
1995-6	41,215	88,946	1,079	131,240	74,103	69,021	231	4,851	24,049	33,088
1996-7	33,088	103,788	1,091	137,967	84,509	79,919	195	4,395	24,326	29,132
1997-8	29,132	97,413	1,220	127,765	77,947	73,261	193	4,493	25,119	24,699
1998-9	24,699	108,432	1,435	134,566	84,765	80,546	211	4,008	25,533	24,268
1999-00[1]	24,268	113,588	1,275	139,131	92,338	87,295	223	4,820	25,458	21,335
2000-1[2]	21,325	117,447	1,470	140,252	89,642	84,363	251	5,028	26,176	24,434
2001-2[3]	24,434	115,756	1,358	141,548	92,959	87,439	257	5,263	26,752	21,837

[1] Preliminary. [2] Estimate. [3] Forecast. *Source: Foreign Agricultural Service, U.S. Department of Agriculture (FAS-USDA)*

World Production of Green Coffee In Thousands of 60 Kilogram Bags (132.276 Lbs. Per Bag)

Crop Year	Brazil	Cameroon	Colombia	Costa Rica	El Salvador	Ethiopia	Guatemala	India	Indonesia	Ivory Coast	Mexico	Uganda	World Total
1992-3	24,000	837	14,950	2,620	2,894	3,500	3,584	2,700	7,350	2,500	4,180	2,800	92,894
1993-4	28,500	676	11,400	2,475	2,361	3,700	3,078	3,465	7,400	2,700	4,200	2,700	92,319
1994-5	28,000	401	13,000	2,492	2,314	3,800	3,500	3,060	6,400	3,733	4,030	3,100	97,024
1995-6	16,800	663	12,939	2,595	2,325	3,800	3,827	3,717	5,800	2,900	5,400	4,200	88,946
1996-7	28,000	1,432	10,779	2,376	2,498	3,800	4,141	3,417	7,900	5,333	5,300	4,297	103,788
1997-8	23,500	889	12,043	2,455	2,040	3,833	4,200	3,805	7,000	4,080	4,950	3,032	97,413
1998-9	35,600	1,114	10,868	2,459	1,860	3,867	4,300	4,415	6,950	2,217	5,010	3,640	108,432
1999-00[1]	30,800	1,370	9,512	2,688	2,612	3,833	4,364	4,870	6,660	5,700	6,193	3,097	113,588
2000-1[2]	34,100	1,505	10,500	2,502	1,624	3,683	4,494	5,020	6,495	4,333	5,300	3,200	117,447
2001-2[3]	33,700	1,550	11,000	2,560	1,700	3,800	3,827	5,000	6,280	4,166	5,500	3,200	115,756

[1] Preliminary. [2] Estimate. [3] Forecast. *Source: Foreign Agricultural Service, U.S. Department of Agriculture (FAS-USDA)*

World Exportable[4] Production of Green Coffee In Thousands of 60 Kilogram Bags (132.276 Lbs. Per Bag)

Crop Year	Brazil	Cameroon	Colombia	Costa Rica	El Salvador	Ethiopia	Guatemala	Indonesia	Ivory Coast	Kenya	Mexico	Uganda	World Total
1992-3	15,500	812	13,647	2,365	2,677	2,000	3,274	5,570	2,461	1,195	2,880	2,745	71,726
1993-4	19,100	611	9,700	2,225	2,131	2,200	2,777	5,535	2,661	1,208	2,900	2,640	69,678
1994-5	18,300	371	11,564	2,252	2,079	2,300	3,220	4,440	3,687	1,562	3,030	3,040	74,957
1995-6	6,300	563	11,439	2,360	2,055	2,300	3,527	3,750	2,852	1,789	4,340	4,140	65,393
1996-7	17,000	1,332	9,279	2,130	2,268	2,300	3,856	5,820	5,282	1,115	4,450	4,217	79,817
1997-8	12,000	789	10,483	2,150	1,805	2,250	3,850	5,360	4,025	1,005	3,955	2,952	72,772
1998-9	23,100	1,014	9,418	2,154	1,633	2,234	3,900	5,350	2,159	1,125	4,050	3,580	83,218
1999-00[1]	18,000	1,270	7,982	2,347	2,445	2,200	3,964	5,225	5,640	1,662	5,138	3,017	88,255
2000-1[2]	21,000	1,400	8,970	2,157	1,473	2,016	4,069	5,010	4,271	996	4,300	3,119	91,441
2001-2[3]	20,400	1,445	9,450	2,210	1,549	2,100	3,407	4,745	4,102	946	4,500	3,120	89,194

[1] Preliminary. [2] Estimate. [3] Forecast. [4] Marketing year begins in October in some countries and April or July in others. Exportable production represents total harvested production minus estimated domestic consumption. *Source: Foreign Agricultural Service, U.S. Department of Agriculture*

Green Coffee Imports in the United States In Thousands of 60 Kilogram Bags (132.276 Lbs. Per Bag)

Year	Brazil	Colombia	Costa Rica	Dominican Republic	Ecuador	El Salvador	Ethiopia	Guatemala	Indonesia	Mexico	Peru	Venezuela	Grand Total
1991	5,335	3,048	603	343	785	868	31	1,489	536	2,993	610	108	18,849
1992	4,253	4,852	662	254	753	1,344	23	1,812	581	3,042	526	104	21,673
1993	3,376	2,957	437	213	671	1,274	192	1,815	542	2,947	158	444	18,023
1994	2,850	2,372	325	207	969	376	215	1,403	558	2,516	249	295	14,913
1995	2,302	2,485	388	266	745	284	109	1,637	513	2,887	621	89	15,886
1996	1,852	3,011	482	255	665	401	137	1,748	1,246	3,734	441	445	17,947
1997	2,331	3,179	608	150	431	500	308	1,921	1,325	2,935	652	65	18,848
1998	2,688	3,410	771	164	347	501	183	1,563	1,273	2,471	771	146	18,998
1999	4,659	3,359	684	35	419	550	77	2,148	724	3,182	762	372	20,559
2000[1]	2,569	3,147	705	28	164	1,209	91	2,377	692	3,610	857	32	21,625

[1] Preliminary. *Source: Bureau of Census, U.S. Department of Commerce*

Monthly Green Coffee Imports in the United States In Thousands of 60 Kilogram Bags[2]

Year	Jan.	Feb.	Mar.	Apr.	May	June	July	Aug.	Sept.	Oct.	Nov.	Dec.	Total
1991	2,106	1,946	1,590	1,748	1,556	984	1,056	1,335	1,424	1,368	1,616	2,122	18,849
1992	2,262	1,944	2,125	1,698	1,534	1,795	1,806	1,692	1,644	1,615	1,508	2,050	21,673
1993	1,782	1,663	2,012	1,481	1,631	1,253	1,442	1,344	1,374	1,464	1,018	1,561	18,023
1994	1,538	1,152	1,409	1,077	1,082	1,151	1,195	1,560	1,266	1,127	1,103	1,213	14,872
1995	1,469	1,253	1,702	1,221	1,190	1,240	1,117	1,094	1,220	1,326	1,492	1,563	15,886
1996	1,824	1,657	1,753	1,395	1,444	1,236	1,329	1,341	1,364	1,279	1,485	1,828	17,936
1997	1,582	1,837	1,966	1,792	1,738	1,583	1,783	1,391	1,147	1,215	1,184	1,629	18,848
1998	1,747	1,893	1,827	1,587	1,540	1,412	1,386	1,478	1,369	1,499	1,423	1,837	18,998
1999	1,742	1,866	2,243	1,787	1,602	1,691	1,488	1,639	1,491	1,470	1,639	1,903	20,561
2000[1]	2,094	2,012	2,317	1,922	2,079	1,858	1,793	1,699	1,496	1,480	1,431	1,445	21,625

[1] Preliminary. [2] 132.276 pounds per bag. *Source: Bureau of the Census, U.S. Department of Commerce*

Average Price of Brazilian[1] Coffee in New York In Cents Per Pound

Year	Jan.	Feb.	Mar.	Apr.	May	June	July	Aug.	Sept.	Oct.	Nov.	Dec.	Average
1992	62.03	58.05	59.60	54.94	51.11	49.08	48.53	46.40	49.43	59.64	64.64	74.39	56.49
1993	67.13	66.34	62.60	54.92	57.26	55.70	65.76	73.25	75.58	71.65	74.20	74.51	66.58
1994	71.42	80.14	84.72	87.14	118.37	136.43	211.81	192.38	212.73	191.21	172.83	159.73	143.24
1995	162.81	161.07	171.48	166.54	161.72	145.22	139.68	149.54	130.26	127.23	125.33	110.46	145.95
1996	127.54	144.05	140.99	132.92	134.76	125.44	106.93	108.28	103.10	105.77	103.76	103.71	119.77
1997	127.28	160.21	179.75	183.73	209.62	184.21	158.52	158.25	167.77	152.12	149.07	171.12	166.80
1998	179.83	177.78	154.84	141.11	124.89	104.09	96.04	101.92	92.76	91.32	96.67	100.28	121.81
1999	99.43	91.72	88.90	86.14	96.29	91.69	78.13	76.67	70.43	78.74	98.41	109.47	88.84
2000	97.68	91.51	89.93	86.46	87.23	78.32	79.89	70.57	71.14	72.28	68.95	64.39	79.86
2001	62.38	62.50	60.35	55.11	57.19	51.86	46.43	46.49	42.42	38.63	42.28	41.60	50.60

[1] And other Arabicas. *Source: Coffee Publications, Inc.*

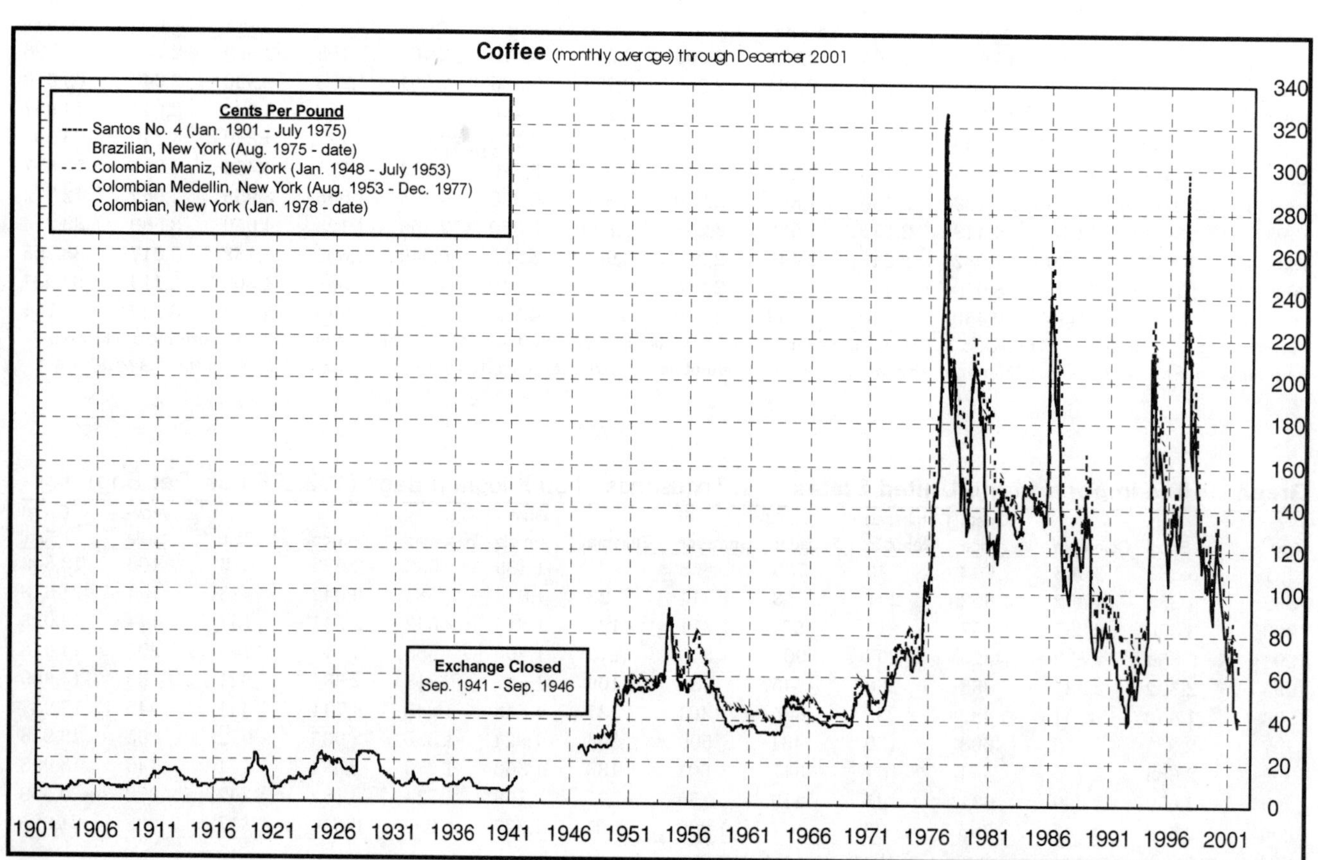

Average Monthly Retail [1] Price of Coffee in the United States In Cents Per Pound

Year	Jan.	Feb.	Mar.	Apr.	May	June	July	Aug.	Sept.	Oct.	Nov.	Dec.	Average
1994	253.0	252.9	251.5	251.6	253.5	259.8	334.1	448.0	445.8	445.0	448.2	438.2	340.1
1995	439.8	423.4	410.8	408.4	406.7	405.9	402.7	405.1	399.6	386.5	381.4	375.2	401.8
1996	357.7	359.0	355.0	352.7	344.4	343.8	338.0	339.0	333.3	334.4	328.3	330.7	343.0
1997	330.0	331.6	351.2	389.4	410.9	442.8	462.8	466.9	461.7	439.2	430.3	416.1	411.1
1998	402.5	397.3	403.3	395.9	387.8	378.6	377.1	370.4	362.0	350.3	348.2	344.6	376.5
1999	343.5	342.8	347.6	346.6	349.5	342.1	342.0	342.8	339.3	348.2	333.7	334.7	342.7
2000	365.4	367.7	363.3	358.4	353.1	343.1	344.6	344.4	333.9	331.7	324.3	321.2	345.9
2001	322.4	321.7	320.5	312.8	309.7	315.6	309.7	304.6	302.5	301.5	298.8	291.3	309.3

[1] Roasted in 13.1 to 20 ounce cans. *Source: Coffee Publications, Inc.*

Average Price of Colombian Mild Arabicas[1] in the United States In Cents Per Pound

Year	Jan.	Feb.	Mar.	Apr.	May	June	July	Aug.	Sept.	Oct.	Nov.	Dec.	Average
1994	85.85	93.04	93.23	97.53	133.90	151.85	222.75	210.57	231.52	206.07	186.96	173.94	157.27
1995	177.23	175.07	185.75	180.30	177.18	170.87	157.22	163.21	141.49	132.08	129.09	110.47	158.33
1996	119.08	134.94	160.60	134.31	142.56	133.25	135.39	137.68	123.30	127.77	129.41	126.41	133.73
1997	146.18	188.62	212.96	199.22	318.50	227.15	190.57	193.46	196.29	169.40	161.38	183.32	198.92
1998	184.21	190.59	166.07	158.17	146.33	135.83	125.03	129.45	117.56	115.01	121.74	123.96	142.83
1999	123.07	116.92	117.05	114.02	123.95	121.45	107.05	105.28	97.77	103.69	126.76	140.35	116.45
2000	130.13	124.73	119.51	112.67	110.31	100.30	101.67	91.87	89.98	90.25	84.01	75.81	102.60
2001	75.33	76.70	76.94	78.25	80.92	74.38	69.70	73.50	68.80	62.88	65.72	62.57	72.14

[1] ICO monthly and composite indicator prices on the New York Market, 1979 ICA Agreement basis. *Source: Coffee Publications, Inc.*

Average Price of Other Mild Arabicas[1] in the United States In Cents Per Pound

Year	Jan.	Feb.	Mar.	Apr.	May	June	July	Aug.	Sept.	Oct.	Nov.	Dec.	Average
1994	77.21	82.69	85.57	89.23	121.97	142.57	217.67	198.07	220.10	199.06	180.76	167.47	148.53
1995	171.74	168.71	178.22	172.81	168.63	151.56	143.83	151.41	131.87	125.38	123.23	103.99	149.28
1996	109.38	122.71	119.05	122.01	128.56	124.46	120.47	122.49	114.05	120.62	119.90	115.01	119.89
1997	131.83	167.20	193.82	204.43	264.50	212.55	186.52	185.17	184.38	161.45	154.15	174.25	185.02
1998	175.04	175.87	154.82	147.08	134.35	121.56	113.86	119.89	108.07	107.07	113.84	115.54	132.25
1999	110.99	103.24	103.23	99.69	109.10	104.21	90.85	87.64	81.06	92.22	112.74	123.56	101.54
2000	109.17	101.17	98.26	92.76	91.76	84.10	85.20	74.52	73.83	75.43	70.47	64.81	85.12
2001	64.98	67.00	65.88	65.68	68.94	63.79	58.47	59.68	57.71	56.23	58.96	55.63	61.91

[1] ICO monthly and composite indicator prices on the New York Market, 1979 ICA Agreement basis. *Source: Coffee Publications, Inc.*

Average Price of Robustas 1976[1] in the United States In Cents Per Pound

Year	Jan.	Feb.	Mar.	Apr.	May	June	July	Aug.	Sept.	Oct.	Nov.	Dec.	Average
1994	60.91	62.25	66.46	72.64	96.05	113.31	164.65	162.68	182.95	170.09	154.19	130.48	119.72
1995	132.26	135.22	146.83	145.47	141.89	129.53	120.89	131.28	116.41	114.15	112.79	94.72	126.79
1996	91.99	98.99	91.99	91.45	92.10	86.46	78.14	80.16	74.83	72.97	70.51	63.08	82.72
1997	67.66	76.65	81.31	78.48	95.74	91.94	82.52	76.92	77.43	76.90	78.20	84.65	80.70
1998	86.03	85.79	84.67	90.60	92.64	84.55	78.40	79.98	80.88	80.36	80.40	82.82	83.93
1999	81.65	77.68	72.70	68.89	68.28	66.20	62.28	63.80	60.44	59.25	64.10	66.40	67.64
2000	53.62	49.41	47.26	45.21	45.19	43.72	41.93	38.94	39.47	36.55	33.34	30.78	42.12
2001	31.00	31.96	30.96	28.59	29.71	29.33	27.59	25.86	23.79	21.26	22.03	23.57	27.14

[1] ICO monthly and composite indicator prices on the New York Market, 1979 ICA Agreement basis. *Source: Coffee Publications, Inc.*

Average Price of Composite 1979[1] in the United States In Cents Per Pound

Year	Jan.	Feb.	Mar.	Apr.	May	June	July	Aug.	Sept.	Oct.	Nov.	Dec.	Average
1994	69.17	72.37	76.11	81.19	108.42	127.91	191.44	181.53	202.39	185.64	168.12	149.14	134.45
1995	152.08	152.24	162.73	159.59	155.96	141.66	132.71	141.70	124.75	120.02	117.99	99.57	138.42
1996	100.33	110.50	105.89	107.09	110.24	105.79	99.97	102.73	96.52	98.56	97.14	90.04	102.07
1997	100.03	121.89	137.47	142.20	180.44	155.38	135.04	132.63	132.51	121.09	118.16	130.02	133.91
1998	130.61	130.78	119.93	119.66	114.23	103.84	97.32	101.25	95.82	95.01	98.26	100.73	108.95
1999	97.63	92.36	89.41	85.72	89.51	85.41	78.21	77.22	71.94	76.36	88.22	95.63	85.64
2000	82.15	76.15	73.49	69.53	69.23	64.56	64.09	57.59	57.31	56.40	52.18	48.27	64.25
2001	49.19	49.39	48.52	47.31	49.38	46.54	43.07	42.77	41.17	42.21	44.24	43.36	45.60

[1] ICO monthly and composite indicator prices on the New York Market, 1979 ICA Agreement basis. *Source: Coffee Publications, Inc.*

COFFEE

Average Open Interest of Coffee 'C' Futures in New York In Contracts

Year	Jan.	Feb.	Mar.	Apr.	May	June	July	Aug.	Sept.	Oct.	Nov.	Dec.
1992	47,042	51,183	48,961	51,979	59,275	58,304	59,096	58,401	56,446	59,808	57,527	58,257
1993	59,193	54,249	53,618	55,578	51,797	50,918	53,871	48,541	47,649	49,809	46,901	48,812
1994	54,796	50,230	53,713	57,226	58,574	54,589	43,056	35,052	35,800	34,258	31,046	31,134
1995	34,455	35,391	36,925	34,387	34,615	34,462	30,156	27,448	27,800	28,408	24,505	26,412
1996	28,430	28,224	28,127	28,793	28,394	25,096	26,188	25,799	23,929	26,202	27,599	27,201
1997	38,516	42,888	39,092	32,644	30,324	22,552	21,497	19,818	22,788	25,109	23,636	28,577
1998	30,042	30,539	30,211	32,617	36,345	36,651	37,531	30,074	30,429	32,940	31,677	32,816
1999	36,194	36,693	41,294	43,846	45,947	45,675	45,411	46,725	46,255	47,956	46,271	46,764
2000	47,829	50,620	50,565	53,662	49,692	50,293	45,513	40,177	40,133	42,906	43,187	45,086
2001	48,914	53,050	58,111	57,722	53,481	58,311	57,888	57,243	55,674	58,345	55,317	53,953

Source: New York Board of Trade (NYBOT)

Volume of Trading of Coffee 'C' Futures in New York In Contracts

Year	Jan.	Feb.	Mar.	Apr.	May	June	July	Aug.	Sept.	Oct.	Nov.	Dec.	Total
1992	153,332	199,420	174,662	188,232	156,944	164,586	177,493	182,741	163,214	108,707	211,678	199,374	2,152,383
1993	290,120	214,771	183,354	209,607	176,559	197,761	193,002	233,479	202,363	187,763	217,947	182,486	2,489,223
1994	188,508	219,455	208,113	284,734	380,119	304,542	210,479	196,685	159,574	177,424	184,172	142,713	2,658,073
1995	169,250	191,352	213,326	156,191	163,248	186,550	162,562	161,076	165,337	152,959	157,240	123,923	2,003,014
1996	203,369	186,526	152,797	197,442	137,454	158,929	171,800	196,991	136,054	196,696	135,305	166,213	2,039,576
1997	242,719	280,014	267,369	223,330	219,214	186,227	135,664	136,807	142,610	151,171	145,610	163,446	2,294,181
1998	155,774	194,435	186,712	194,732	157,935	189,768	165,868	189,047	156,556	172,956	197,776	133,471	2,095,030
1999	216,810	201,670	252,841	243,630	237,968	243,164	187,019	232,817	151,724	270,013	244,258	177,309	2,659,223
2000	158,962	232,174	166,970	224,266	177,753	218,467	198,975	175,868	119,304	163,399	187,230	111,593	2,134,961
2001	189,977	221,775	167,466	236,757	182,621	220,708	134,809	250,151	100,443	153,739	229,495	111,430	2,199,371

Source: New York Board of Trade (NYBOT)

Coke

Coke is the solid residue which remains when certain types of bituminous coals are heated to high temperatures out of contact with air. The residue is mostly carbon. High temperature coking produces coke for metallurgical use in blast furnaces. Coke is used to smelt iron.

U.S. coke and breeze stocks at coke plants on June 30, 2001 were 1.08 million short tons. Of the total, coke stocks were 963,000 tons. On March 31, 2001, coke and breeze stocks were 1.17 million tons with coke stocks 1.06 million. On June 30, 2000, coke and breeze stocks were 1.06 million tons with coke being 905,000 tons. Coal stocks at coke plants on June 30, 2001 were 1.63 million tons, down 14 percent from March 2001 and 11 percent less than a year earlier.

U.S. electric utility stocks of petroleum coke in August 2001 were 200,000 short tons which was up 27 percent from a year earlier. Consumption of petroleum coke to generate electricity at electric utilities in August 2001 was 177,000 tons, up 55 percent from the year before. In the January-August 2001 period, petroleum coke used to generate electricity was 847,000 tons. At nonutility power producers in August 2001, 338,000 tons of petroleum coke were used to generate electricity. In January-August 2001, that total was 2.8 million tons.

Salient Statistics of Coke in the United States In Thousands of Short Tons

	Coke and Breeze Production at Coke Plants								Producer and Distributor	Exports		Imports	
	By Census Division												
Year	Atlantic	Central	Central	Other	Total	Coke Total	Total	Consump-tion[2]	Stocks Dec. 31	Canada	Total	Japan	Total
1995	7,751	6,490	2,465	8,506	25,212	23,749	1,463	25,895	1,302	579	750	1,019	1,816
1996	7,729	5,863	2,445	8,440	24,477	23,075	1,402	23,974	1,323	491	1,121	811	1,111
1997	8,994	8,882	3,393	2,080	23,349	22,116	1,233	24,017	1,294	498	832	1,018	1,565
1998	6,371	9,224	2,922	2,766	21,283	20,041	1,242	23,108	933	830	1,129	2,062	3,834
1999	5,869	10,115	2,821	2,448	21,253	20,016	1,237	22,422	852	686	898	2,012	3,224
2000[1]	6,095	10,842	2,827	2,620	22,384	21,069	1,315	23,477	1,079	795	1,146	1,884	3,781

[1] Preliminary. [2] Equal to production plus imports minus the change in producer and distributor stocks minus exports.
Source: Energy Information Administration, U.S. Department of Energy (EIA-DOE)

Production of Petroleum Coke in the United States In Thousands of Barrels

Year	Jan.	Feb.	Mar.	Apr.	May	June	July	Aug.	Sept.	Oct.	Nov.	Dec.	Total
1995	19,079	17,117	18,556	18,519	19,774	19,949	19,527	19,722	19,184	19,292	19,349	19,887	229,955
1996	19,536	18,706	21,015	20,663	20,426	19,927	19,836	20,328	20,124	20,558	20,447	21,389	242,955
1997	19,798	17,594	20,603	21,274	22,210	21,052	21,619	22,229	21,630	21,782	20,313	21,827	251,931
1998	20,929	18,968	21,998	21,834	21,790	20,856	21,790	22,469	21,526	21,234	20,837	22,258	256,489
1999	22,312	20,084	22,148	21,444	21,410	20,943	21,741	22,180	21,249	22,166	21,695	22,866	260,238
2000	21,502	20,017	21,654	21,161	21,785	22,095	23,321	22,835	22,455	22,121	22,628	24,262	265,836
2001[1]	23,970	21,112	23,299	23,713	42,465	23,345	23,838	23,339	22,321	23,306	23,350	24,203	298,261

[1] Preliminary. *Source: Energy Information Administration, U.S. Department of Energy (EIA-DOE)*

Coal Receipts and Average Prices at Coke Plants in the United States

	Coal Receipts at Coke Plants					Average Price of Coal Receipts at Coke Plants				
	By Census Division, In Thousands of Short Tons					By Census Division, In Dollars per Short Ton				
Year	Middle Atlantic	East North Central	East South Central	Other	Total	Middle Atlantic	East North Central	East South Central	Other	Total
1995	10,959	8,489	3,183	10,405	33,036	46.11	47.47	48.42	W	47.34
1996	10,562	7,654	3,213	10,243	31,672	45.17	48.46	49.37	W	47.33
1997	11,555	10,825	4,290	2,880	29,550	47.05	49.12	47.72	W	47.61
1998	8,430	12,442	3,777	3,705	28,354	44.16	48.39	46.43	W	46.06
1999	7,784	13,524	3,571	3,276	28,155	44.33	47.74	45.28	W	45.85
2000[1]	7,971	14,008	3,564	2,612	28,155	42.89	45.70	45.08	W	44.41

[1] Preliminary. *Source: Energy Information Administration, U.S. Department of Energy (EIA-DOE)*

Coal Carbonized and Coke and Breeze Stocks at Coke Plants in the U.S. In Thousands of Short Tons

	Coal Carbonized at Coke Plants					Stocks at Coke Plants, Dec. 31						
	By Census Division					By Census Division						
Year	Middle Atlantic	East North Central	East South Central	Other	Total	Middle Atlantic	East North Central	East South Central	Other	Total	Total	Breeze Total
1995	10,858	12,345	3,257	6,551	33,011	191	589	81	577	1,438	1,302	136
1996	10,689	11,414	3,247	6,356	31,706	197	400	138	749	1,484	1,323	161
1997	11,655	11,366	4,299	2,883	30,203	297	509	159	465	1,430	1,294	135
1998	8,401	12,311	3,736	3,741	28,189	160	526	176	215	1,077	933	144
1999	7,799	13,404	3,584	3,321	28,108	69	500	157	277	1,003	852	150
2000[1]	8,129	13,959	3,645	3,570	29,303	148	628	188	258	1,222	1,079	143

[1] Preliminary. *Source: Energy Information Administration, U.S. Department of Energy (EIA-DOE)*

Copper

Copper metals and alloys have considerable commercial importance due to their electrical, mechanical and physical properties. Copper is used in alloys such as brass which is composed of zinc and copper. Copper for commercial purposes is obtained by the reduction of copper compounds in ores and by electrolytic refining.

After moving lower for much of 2001, copper prices rallied in the fourth quarter after a series of announced production cutbacks by large copper producers. World copper production had exceeded copper consumption by a large margin in 2001 and the announcements of production cuts promised to close that gap in 2002. A key question for the market is whether the production cutbacks will take place if copper prices increase as much as they did in late 2001. Another positive fundamental development for the copper market were some initial indications that the U.S. economy was close to a bottom. Various reports indicated that the economy was stating to show signs of turning the corner which would mean that demand for copper would improve. The major negative fundamental development in the copper market was a buildup in warehouse stocks of copper at the London Metals Exchange and the New York Commodity Exchange. In late 2001 there was little sign that these stocks were about to level off and decline. One positive development looking at year 2002 is China which continues to develop its infrastructure and telecommunications systems, both requiring more use of copper.

The U.S. Geological Survey reported that world mine production of copper in 2000 was 12.9 million metric tonnes. This was an increase of 2 percent from 2000. The largest producer of copper by far is Chile with year 2000 production of 4.5 million tonnes., up almost 3 percent from 1999. The U.S. is the second largest producer with output of 1.45 million tonnes, down 9 percent from 1999. Copper production by Indonesia was estimated to be 850,000 tonnes, up 15 percent from 1999. Another large producer is Australia with output of 760,000 tonnes, up over 3 percent from 1999. Other large producers include Canada, Peru, Russia and China.

U.S. mine production of copper in August 2001 was 112,000 tonnes. In the January-August 2001 period, mine production was 908,000 tonnes. Refinery production of copper in August 2001 was 129,000 tonnes, down from 132,000 tonnes in July. In the January-August 2001 period, refinery production was 1.06 million tonnes.

U.S. apparent consumption of copper in July 2001 was 145,000 tonnes. For 2000, consumption was 3.13 million tonnes. Consumption of refined copper in 2000 was 3.02 million tonnes while consumption of purchased copper-base scrap was 1.6 million tonnes. Refined copper stocks in August 2001 were 705,000 tonnes. U.S. imports of refined copper in 2000 were 1.06 million tonnes.

Futures Markets

Copper futures and options are traded on the London Metals Exchange (LME) and the New York Mercantile Exchange COMEX Division. Copper futures are traded on the Shanghai Futures Exchange (SHFE).

World Mine Production of Copper (Content of Ore) In Thousands of Metric Tons

Year	Australia	Canada[3]	Chile	China	Indonesia	Mexico	Peru	Poland	Russia[4]	South Africa	United States[3]	Zambia	World Total
1991	320.0	811.1	1,814.3	304	211.7	292.1	357.2	320.0	900	184.6	1,531	390.6	9,090
1992	378.0	768.6	1,932.7	334	280.8	279.0	345.6	331.9	699	176.1	1,760	429.5	9,470
1993	402.0	732.6	2,055.4	345	298.6	301.2	355.0	382.6	584	166.3	1,800	396.2	9,430
1994	415.6	616.8	2,219.9	396	322.2	294.7	395.9	378.0	573	160.1	1,820	373.2	9,490
1995	397.8	726.3	2,488.6	445	443.6	333.6	409.7	384.2	525	161.6	1,850	316.0	10,000
1996	547.3	688.4	3,115.8	439	507.5	340.7	484.2	421.9	523	152.6	1,920	334.0	11,000
1997	558.0	659.5	3,392.0	496	529.1	390.5	506.5	414.8	505	153.1	1,940	352.9	11,400
1998	607.0	705.8	3,686.8	486	780.8	384.6	483.3	436.2	500	166.0	1,860	315.0	12,100
1999[1]	739.0	620.1	4,391.2	520	766.0	381.2	536.4	464.0	530	144.3	1,600	270.0	12,700
2000[2]	829.0	634.2	4,602.4	590	1,012.1	364.6	553.9	456.2	570	137.1	1,440	241.2	13,200

[1] Preliminary. [2] Estimate. [3] Recoverable. [4] Formerly part of the U.S.S.R.; data not reported separately until 1992.
Source: U.S. Geological Survey (USGS)

Commodity Exchange Inc. Warehouse Stocks of Copper, on First of Month In Thousands of Short Tons

Year	Jan.	Feb.	Mar.	Apr.	May	June	July	Aug.	Sept.	Oct.	Nov.	Dec.
1992	33.7	34.8	29.5	28.2	30.3	32.4	31.8	36.0	40.4	51.7	70.1	73.8
1993	105.9	124.0	114.8	107.6	110.8	108.3	105.5	113.8	100.1	94.1	96.6	80.5
1994	74.0	56.7	49.8	37.2	31.6	30.4	36.0	37.4	28.5	17.9	20.3	21.5
1995	26.7	18.7	17.7	9.0	11.5	7.0	13.1	16.7	16.5	11.2	6.0	5.0
1996	23.7	12.1	12.4	13.9	20.7	13.2	7.6	17.7	22.1	21.7	30.8	36.2
1997	29.3	18.4	24.8	43.3	48.9	42.6	44.7	30.0	46.5	61.5	68.0	82.3
1998	91.9	101.8	113.7	112.6	106.5	83.0	62.5	55.7	56.1	67.7	70.7	75.8
1999	93.9	102.0	114.2	123.4	132.6	131.7	133.7	119.5	108.1	97.5	90.9	90.9
2000	92.3	95.7	95.9	95.9	85.7	75.0	73.6	72.0	62.8	62.3	63.4	64.9
2001	51.8	79.4	90.5	106.3	127.1	140.7	NA	NA	NA	NA	NA	248.3

Source: New York Mercantile Exchange (NYMEX), COMEX division

Salient Statistics of Copper in the United States In Thousands of Metric Tons

Year	New Copper Produced: From Domestic Ores: Mines	Smelters	Refineries	Foreign Ores[3]	Total New	Secondary Recovered[4]	Imports[3]: Unmanufactured	Imports[3]: Refined	Exports: Ore, Concentrate[6]	Exports: Refined[7]	Stocks, Dec 31: COMEX	Stocks, Dec 31: Primary Producers (Refined)	Stocks, Dec 31: Blister & Material in Solution	Apparent Consumption: Refined Copper (Reported)	Apparent Consumption: Primary & Old Copper[8]
1991	1,630	1,120	1,060	77	1,577	518	512	289	253	263	31	132	135	2,048	2,105
1992	1,760	1,180	1,110	96	1,710	555	593	289	266	177	96	205	166	2,178	2,311
1993	1,800	1,270	1,210	89	1,790	543	637	343	227	217	67	153	146	2,360	2,510
1994	1,850	1,310	1,280	64	1,840	500	763	470	261	157	24	119	167	2,680	2,690
1995	1,850	1,250	1,300	91	1,930	443	825	429	239	217	22	163	171	2,530	2,540
1996	1,920	1,300	1,290	147	2,010	428	961	543	195	169	27	146	173	2,610	2,830
1997	1,940	1,440	1,370	113	2,070	498	999	632	127	93	83	314	180	2,790	2,940
1998	1,860	1,490	1,290	238	2,140	466	1,190	683	37	86	85	532	160	2,890	3,030
1999[1]	1,600	1,090	1,110	196	1,890	381	1,280	837	63	25	83	565	138	2,980	3,130
2000[2]	1,440	W	865	163	1,590	363	1,350	1,060	107	94	59	334	122	3,030	3,110

[1] Preliminary. [2] Estimate. [3] Also from matte, etc., refinery reports. [4] From old scrap only. [5] For consumption. [6] Blister (copper content). [7] Ingots, bars, etc. [8] Old scrap only. *Source: U.S. Geological Survey (USGS)*

Consumption of Refined Copper[3] in the United States In Thousands of Metric Tons

Year	By-Products: Cathodes	Wire Bars	Ingots & Ingot Bars	Cakes & Slabs	Billets	Other[4]	By Class of Consumer: Wire Rod Mills	Brass Mills	Chemiacl Plants	Ingot Makers	Foundries	Miscellaneous[5]	Total Consumption
1991	1,854.9	W	24.7	33.3	W	135.4	1,591.8	458.5	0.9	3.4	12.7	25.3	2,048.3
1992	1,974.9	W	20.0	43.7	W	139.6	1,675.0	458.5	0.9	3.0	15.0	25.8	2,178.2
1993	2,130.0	W	37.7	55.5	W	136.0	1,819.1	503.0	0.9	2.2	10.2	27.6	2,360.0
1994	2,410.0	W	37.3	73.2	W	164.0	2,060.0	568.0	1.1	4.5	11.1	30.4	2,680.0
1995	2,250.0	W	31.3	75.9	W	181.0	1,950.0	533.0	1.1	7.7	15.6	31.4	2,530.0
1996	2,320.0	W	26.8	80.8	W	181.0	1,980.0	588.0	1.1	3.6	15.8	28.6	2,610.0
1997	2,490.0	W	29.4	81.1	W	194.0	2,140.0	597.0	1.0	4.2	16.6	29.9	2,790.0
1998	2,600.0	W	30.7	76.2	W	184.0	2,170.0	659.0	1.1	5.4	19.2	31.8	2,890.0
1999[1]	2,710.0	W	24.4	79.3	W	166.0	2,230.0	691.0	1.2	4.5	21.2	29.8	2,980.0
2000[2]	2,730.0	W	23.8	101.0	W	176.0	2,240.0	723.0	1.2	4.6	26.0	32.6	3,030.0

[1] Preliminary. [2] Estimate. [3] Primary & secondary. [4] 1991 to date include Wirebars and Billets. [5] Includes iron and steel plants, primary smelters producing alloys other than copper, consumers of copper powder and copper shot, and other manufacturers. W - Withheld proprietary data. *Source: U.S. Geological Survey (USGS)*

London Metals Exchange Warehouse Stocks of Copper, at End of Month In Thousands of Metric Tons

Year	Jan.	Feb.	Mar.	Apr.	May	June	July	Aug.	Sept.	Oct.	Nov.	Dec.
1992	308.6	302.7	296.4	279.7	265.4	259.1	246.8	275.2	299.7	317.8	327.0	315.8
1993	313.5	333.1	365.8	403.5	429.1	446.9	464.3	521.7	600.7	612.3	590.9	599.5
1994	597.6	554.5	504.3	446.4	379.0	350.9	338.9	367.8	359.3	333.1	318.4	302.2
1995	309.9	280.9	239.9	204.9	197.9	166.5	151.5	163.1	178.2	193.6	222.2	364.8
1996	355.1	348.4	322.3	303.9	309.7	263.0	227.6	275.5	240.7	122.1	96.1	119.6
1997	194.2	216.2	177.2	145.8	133.0	128.3	234.9	278.7	332.8	344.6	338.8	337.8
1998	365.7	376.0	339.5	262.3	261.8	249.3	260.9	307.7	414.2	460.6	511.9	590.1
1999	646.9	695.9	722.2	748.2	776.6	754.8	769.6	789.0	774.0	793.8	779.7	790.5
2000	807.3	824.1	755.4	697.8	605.7	553.4	487.8	449.2	401.5	380.9	349.4	357.4
2001[1]	349.9	327.9	400.5	445.2	431.3	464.7	651.9	661.2	729.0	737.2		

[1] Preliminary. *Source: American Bureau of Metal Statistics (ABMS)*

Copper Refined from Scrap in the United States In Thousands of Metric Tons

Year	Jan.	Feb.	Mar.	Apr.	May	June	July	Aug.	Sept.	Oct.	Nov.	Dec.	Total
1992	27.8	34.1	39.8	34.8	36.7	39.4	27.8	35.4	39.8	40.0	34.3	35.8	433.2
1993	38.1	45.9	38.9	37.8	36.4	41.1	35.0	37.6	37.4	43.0	35.4	32.2	459.8
1994	33.3	28.3	37.9	30.7	37.1	28.7	26.9	33.0	38.7	27.0	34.3	37.3	391.7
1995	30.9	30.6	36.0	32.7	33.7	28.2	18.7	25.1	25.4	25.0	26.2	24.4	319.0
1996	25.0	23.7	25.5	22.5	26.8	30.9	24.4	25.0	26.8	30.6	25.9	26.3	333.0
1997	35.9	30.0	36.4	32.6	35.4	30.8	26.4	28.4	34.3	36.5	24.6	29.3	383.0
1998	25.9	28.6	23.7	31.0	17.8	21.4	24.2	23.9	23.8	31.8	23.2	26.3	336.0
1999	20.1	21.8	23.7	17.6	16.2	17.5	21.2	18.2	21.3	21.0	17.7	20.0	230.0
2000	19.4	18.6	25.8	22.5	22.1	15.4	11.7	19.7	14.1	14.3	19.7	15.6	208.0
2001[1]	15.4	14.2	15.2	13.4	12.8	13.2	13.9	13.5	12.3	10.2			160.9

[1] Preliminary. *Source: U.S. Geological Survey (USGS)*

COPPER

Average Open Interest of Copper Futures in New York In Contracts

Year	Jan.	Feb.	Mar.	Apr.	May	June	July	Aug.	Sept.	Oct.	Nov.	Dec.
1992	47,109	47,929	48,700	45,114	39,986	48,129	47,065	38,397	37,041	41,658	44,927	45,541
1993	47,433	48,707	48,220	51,217	52,762	56,856	54,861	54,571	54,929	57,406	63,632	69,311
1994	65,518	65,446	66,177	59,346	63,825	60,383	51,616	46,855	56,344	59,060	59,158	51,078
1995	52,632	50,770	47,267	47,793	50,089	48,200	40,968	37,744	33,709	36,476	38,475	35,996
1996	47,771	45,706	42,732	46,771	47,284	52,558	56,564	56,549	55,408	58,124	61,031	55,807
1997	54,468	56,022	58,205	50,574	56,740	56,774	47,767	44,632	49,612	54,912	67,026	67,502
1998	69,607	72,302	67,154	68,670	65,033	66,002	63,271	61,116	60,520	62,944	67,984	76,846
1999	76,861	73,109	75,318	70,534	76,341	70,842	75,640	70,084	80,188	72,240	69,179	69,819
2000	82,289	73,778	68,026	75,520	69,531	63,786	71,389	79,565	83,546	73,609	74,161	70,349
2001	77,952	76,721	78,034	83,647	72,970	85,495	83,690	88,782	87,004	88,166	85,809	68,981

Source: New York Mercantile Exchange (NYMEX), COMEX division

Volume of Trading of Copper Futures in New York In Contracts

Year	Jan.	Feb.	Mar.	Apr.	May	June	July	Aug.	Sept.	Oct.	Nov.	Dec.	Total
1992	145,245	168,015	105,003	157,473	77,722	182,091	138,225	177,581	137,423	121,392	146,062	117,931	1,674,163
1993	152,387	148,388	132,705	212,086	160,751	181,427	165,727	169,428	222,099	133,364	203,729	182,538	2,064,629
1994	197,959	233,016	231,239	207,963	247,143	297,393	188,644	242,393	219,788	208,957	290,585	178,887	2,737,967
1995	242,760	267,883	232,229	242,302	195,554	274,587	167,836	213,110	169,689	181,945	185,141	146,378	2,519,414
1996	184,431	173,689	157,553	210,836	200,469	255,172	150,445	174,351	166,537	250,420	227,800	160,216	2,311,919
1997	193,543	221,504	190,000	218,607	164,728	238,918	191,609	198,156	197,746	202,615	203,376	135,368	2,356,170
1998	172,133	223,117	197,652	264,061	175,956	217,316	202,596	213,541	196,355	195,255	250,986	174,642	2,483,610
1999	159,147	288,394	230,716	296,162	224,221	319,157	244,567	267,325	220,958	193,628	231,399	177,288	2,852,962
2000	220,488	276,374	195,668	261,971	232,971	241,854	187,453	283,328	171,080	243,342	266,051	197,544	2,778,124
2001	240,588	246,052	247,722	279,348	260,697	317,001	159,394	298,639	129,622	190,469	337,589	149,520	2,856,641

Source: New York Mercantile Exchange (NYMEX), COMEX division

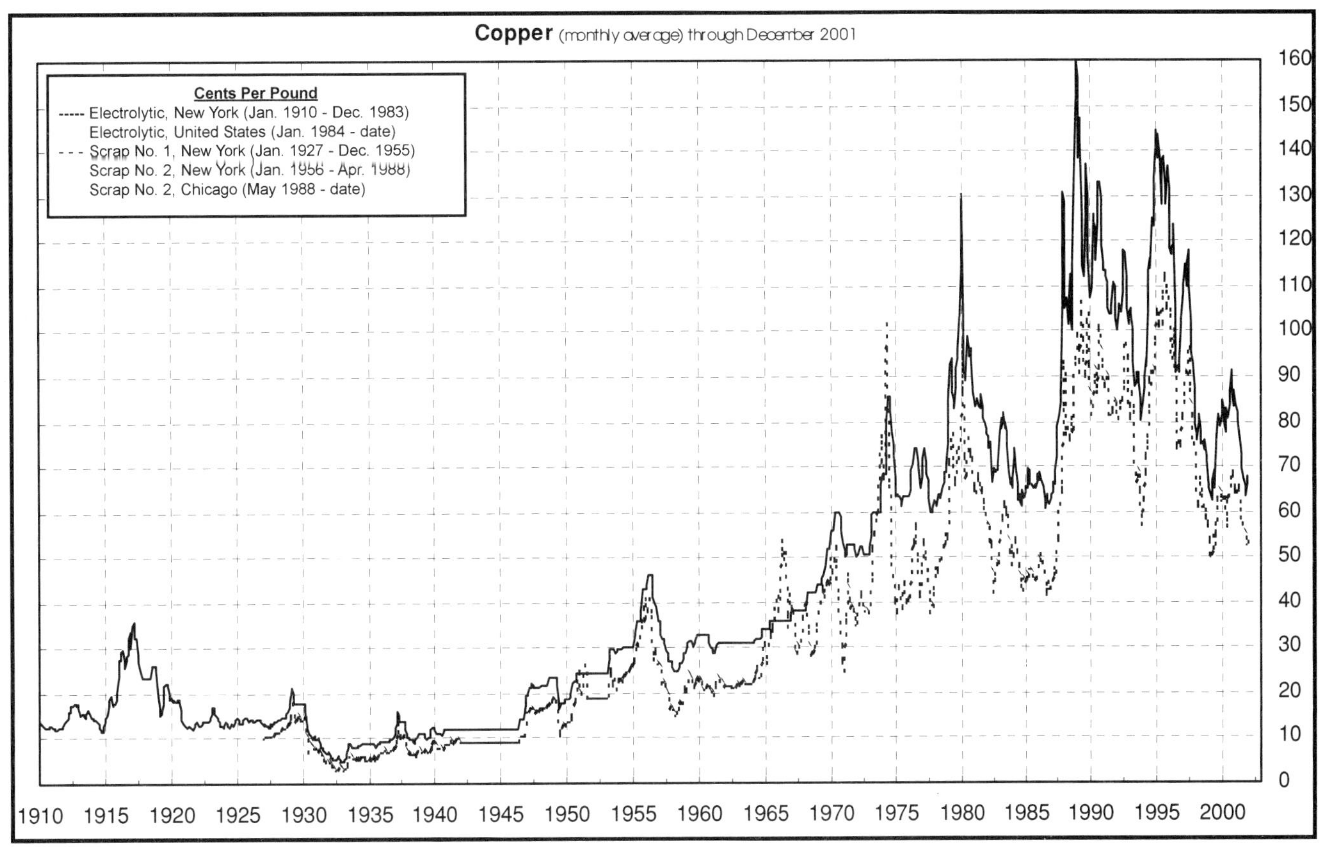

Producers' Price of Electrolytic (Wirebar) Copper, Delivered to U.S. Destinations In Cents Per Pound

Year	Jan.	Feb.	Mar.	Apr.	May	June	July	Aug.	Sept.	Oct.	Nov.	Dec.	Average
1992	108.16	112.52	113.56	112.35	112.56	116.74	125.66	124.30	119.39	112.09	108.23	111.13	114.72
1993	112.57	110.26	107.80	99.03	92.35	94.98	97.94	97.06	92.36	85.82	86.07	91.08	96.76
1994	95.65	99.13	101.76	99.87	112.30	120.58	123.68	121.38	132.53	130.91	141.92	148.86	119.05
1995	151.91	146.00	151.14	146.00	139.80	149.51	150.00	149.77	144.14	140.00	148.48	143.78	146.74
1996	130.09	128.75	130.20	131.29	135.33	116.55	103.63	104.14	102.51	101.80	112.58	114.78	117.86
1997	120.29	121.02	126.50	121.70	127.25	129.57	121.94	114.11	107.14	105.08	99.53	91.39	115.55
1998	88.88	87.52	91.69	93.54	90.02	86.90	87.37	85.30	87.62	84.26	83.51	78.30	87.09
1999	77.07	75.96	74.50	78.79	81.07	77.23	88.02	87.88	92.89	91.26	91.10	93.35	84.09
2000	96.83	94.41	91.63	89.32	94.80	92.74	95.81	98.67	103.49	99.63	95.25	98.92	95.96
2001	95.70	94.01	92.07	88.27	88.85	84.58	81.44	79.34	77.41	75.21	78.13	79.83	84.57

Source: American Metal Market (AMM)

Dealers' Buying Price of No. 2 Heavy Copper Scrap in Chicago[1] In Cents Per Pound

Year	Jan.	Feb.	Mar.	Apr.	May	June	July	Aug.	Sept.	Oct.	Nov.	Dec.	Average
1992	73.21	73.37	75.23	75.16	74.00	74.27	77.18	78.38	75.38	70.27	69.00	67.18	73.55
1993	67.95	67.00	67.00	62.95	55.12	53.59	56.33	54.18	52.67	49.10	47.00	48.00	56.74
1994	50.80	56.11	59.61	62.00	64.86	72.32	76.40	74.30	75.69	76.45	78.10	82.95	69.13
1995	89.48	90.79	89.39	91.75	85.91	88.73	92.32	92.65	92.70	90.64	92.00	92.00	90.70
1996	87.17	82.90	83.24	83.29	82.95	71.48	61.43	62.00	62.00	63.00	64.84	66.00	72.53
1997	68.73	71.63	77.50	79.18	77.33	78.19	72.64	70.24	65.67	63.74	61.31	58.43	70.38
1998	53.26	52.58	53.09	54.00	52.60	49.64	48.00	47.71	46.00	44.00	40.00	40.00	48.41
1999	36.32	36.00	36.00	36.00	39.60	41.77	41.00	45.09	46.19	48.00	48.00	48.67	41.90
2000	50.00	50.00	50.00	49.15	49.00	49.00	49.30	52.65	54.60	55.00	52.65	51.00	51.04
2001	51.62	49.16	49.00	49.81	50.00	50.00	49.14	44.00	44.00	43.48	41.45	41.47	46.93

Source: American Metal Market (AMM)

COPPER

Imports of Refined Copper into the United States In Thousands of Metric Tons

Year	Jan.	Feb.	Mar.	Apr.	May	June	July	Aug.	Sept.	Oct.	Nov.	Dec.	Total
1992	22.6	24.5	31.9	25.2	25.3	26.1	24.7	25.3	24.0	19.6	20.3	20.8	289.1
1993	21.8	25.6	28.2	35.9	29.5	26.9	30.6	28.3	22.5	31.6	32.2	30.5	343.4
1994	28.7	33.6	49.8	36.8	36.1	46.8	35.6	34.4	34.7	62.4	35.9	36.2	470.0
1995	34.9	30.0	37.1	36.9	36.5	37.9	31.5	31.8	28.7	38.7	44.4	40.3	429.0
1996	43.1	41.2	48.2	49.6	56.8	44.6	53.8	64.8	62.3	46.1	61.8	47.2	543.0
1997	55.4	48.0	43.6	43.6	61.0	42.0	53.1	73.3	53.8	55.0	53.4	42.0	632.0
1998	62.8	49.6	59.9	64.7	57.6	52.8	45.0	51.7	71.1	52.7	62.0	63.4	683.0
1999	64.7	53.2	68.1	59.9	62.3	63.8	73.0	84.5	90.3	81.0	59.0	77.5	837.0
2000	84.9	67.8	85.5	92.1	83.6	84.5	89.4	83.0	98.6	112.0	100.0	73.7	1,060.0
2001[1]	105.0	91.6	90.1	94.4	70.3	72.7	61.7	66.3	83.5				980.8

[1] Preliminary. *Source: U.S. Geological Survey (USGS)*

Exports of Refined Copper from the United States In Thousands of Metric Tons

Year	Jan.	Feb.	Mar.	Apr.	May	June	July	Aug.	Sept.	Oct.	Nov.	Dec.	Total
1992	21.7	18.4	10.8	12.3	11.7	12.0	9.3	13.0	13.6	24.1	14.1	16.1	176.9
1993	14.0	24.9	23.6	16.3	15.4	13.1	10.7	10.1	19.5	19.5	14.9	14.5	216.7
1994	13.0	10.2	10.7	6.8	14.8	9.1	15.6	10.9	15.4	15.9	13.1	21.1	157.0
1995	11.1	24.0	25.6	18.2	23.4	38.9	16.3	16.6	12.1	9.0	12.5	9.5	217.0
1996	13.7	16.5	12.7	12.3	10.8	10.7	15.7	17.7	14.5	16.4	12.8	16.0	170.0
1997	11.1	9.8	6.5	6.5	71.9	8.2	6.9	7.5	6.3	7.4	8.2	8.5	93.3
1998	6.2	12.1	12.2	7.5	7.8	6.4	7.5	6.4	5.8	5.0	3.6	6.2	86.2
1999	2.4	1.1	1.8	1.3	1.6	4.2	1.6	1.5	1.2	1.4	3.7	3.3	25.2
2000	1.6	5.3	22.0	12.2	18.1	12.8	6.7	4.4	2.9	4.3	1.2	2.1	93.6
2001[1]	1.2	.9	.8	1.9	1.0	.8	1.7	2.6	1.2				16.1

[1] Preliminary. *Source: U.S. Geological Survey (USGS)*

Stocks of Refined Copper in the United States, on First of Month In Thousands of Short Tons

Year	Jan.	Feb.	Mar.	Apr.	May	June	July	Aug.	Sept.	Oct.	Nov.	Dec.
1992	75.3	76.3	67.2	69.7	75.9	65.0	62.2	71.2	87.1	99.5	110.3	107.1
1993	135.4	152.7	144.3	132.3	146.0	153.6	137.1	151.0	128.4	117.2	124.6	107.1
1994	103.0	87.7	83.6	72.8	70.7	70.4	73.3	81.1	74.6	66.5	52.7	53.6
1995[2]	55.8	39.6	37.0	22.6	33.1	30.8	27.0	50.0	60.6	71.1	69.4	73.4
1996	120.0	131.4	125.5	123.1	126.3	107.9	102.8	106.2	104.7	68.0	76.0	77.5
1997	88.2	98.8	104.4	116.0	117.9	121.7	122.9	148.8	177.1	197.9	227.6	253.3
1998	281.5	282.2	312.7	315.7	304.5	308.6	306.2	319.0	334.1	367.4	407.2	444.6
1999	562.6	593.1	614.6	653.5	676.6	687.8	668.4	657.2	639.7	611.2	626.5	608.2
2000	619.2	620.8	619.5	582.9	537.0	508.8	467.8	418.0	397.7	394.3	379.1	344.2
2001[1]	383.8	408.4	416.2	481.9	552.6	585.7	626.7	733.1	767.4	895.6		

Recoverable copper content. [1] Preliminary. [2] New reporting method beginning January 1995, includes Comex, London Metal Exchange, and Refiners. Beginning January 1999, includes Consumers. *Source: American Bureau of Metal Statistics (ABMS)*

Stocks of Refined Copper Outside the United States, on First of Month In Thousands of Short Tons

Year	Jan.	Feb.	Mar.	Apr.	May	June	July	Aug.	Sept.	Oct.	Nov.	Dec.
1992	640.4	718.1	704.2	715.7	714.9	723.2	726.4	737.9	816.5	822.5	873.8	896.1
1993	757.1	765.9	789.6	817.2	885.1	912.2	910.4	943.8	1,040.3	1,124.3	1,133.9	1,106.1
1994	1,075.0	1,095.5	1,046.8	984.9	913.7	859.5	843.7	839.7	874.6	870.7	835.1	818.4
1995[2]	611.6	655.8	622.2	577.9	537.0	525.6	494.9	464.7	465.7	467.7	481.4	503.5
1996	560.2	566.0	552.5	517.5	498.7	563.9	507.9	476.6	544.4	499.5	391.8	362.0
1997	405.4	469.5	476.3	445.7	413.5	402.4	408.3	489.6	550.9	607.7	574.5	553.3
1998	580.8	512.4	487.3	438.1	371.1	368.0	335.7	324.0	387.2	468.0	506.9	509.0
1999	922.6	944.3	960.3	963.0	990.5	1,008.3	993.3	990.0	1,017.0	996.9	1,001.5	992.0
2000	983.8	1,034.9	1,040.7	1,011.4	988.6	880.9	866.0	857.3	837.0	826.7	784.1	764.8
2001[1]	616.2	814.8	788.0	799.6	871.7	867.3	959.1	1,166.9	1,235.7	1,374.2		

Recoverable copper content. [1] Preliminary. [2] New reporting method beginning January 1995, includes London Metal Exchange and Refiners. Beginning January 1999, also includes Shanghai Metal Exchange, Consumers and Other. *Source: American Bureau of Metal Statistics (ABMS)*

Production of Refined Copper in the United States In Thousands of Short Tons

Year	Jan.	Feb.	Mar.	Apr.	May	June	July	Aug.	Sept.	Oct.	Nov.	Dec.	Total
1992	139.9	135.6	150.6	142.8	123.0	138.5	140.3	150.1	146.9	155.3	156.8	153.7	1,734
1993	153.9	153.8	173.2	166.0	160.3	177.0	151.4	153.7	160.2	157.3	157.2	166.2	1,930
1994	160.9	150.1	167.8	157.2	165.5	160.4	148.9	165.6	162.1	157.3	153.3	159.8	2,360
1995	202.7	185.5	204.8	194.6	210.0	198.3	193.8	208.8	199.0	206.5	211.3	208.1	2,423
1996	210.8	197.6	209.7	212.4	213.5	193.4	206.1	199.5	198.8	223.1	199.3	212.0	2,476
1997	206.0	192.0	204.0	202.0	198.0	179.0	207.0	203.0	213.0	222.0	205.0	212.0	2,470
1998	214.0	204.0	216.0	209.0	197.0	188.0	197.0	203.0	201.0	217.0	207.0	217.0	2,490
1999	185.0	178.0	220.0	198.0	186.0	175.0	163.0	161.0	172.0	172.0	157.0	162.0	2,130
2000	157.0	149.0	173.0	144.0	161.0	146.0	134.0	149.0	141.0	140.0	147.0	154.0	1,800
2001[1]	152.0	140.0	153.0	143.0	152.0	152.0	145.0	143.0	138.0	132.0			1,740

Recoverable copper content. [1] Preliminary. *Source: U.S. Geological Survey (USGS)*

Stocks of Refined Copper in the United States, on First of Month In Thousands of Short Tons

Year	Jan.	Feb.	Mar.	Apr.	May	June	July	Aug.	Sept.	Oct.	Nov.	Dec.
1992	75.3	76.3	67.2	69.7	75.9	65.0	62.2	71.2	87.1	99.5	110.3	107.1
1993	135.4	152.7	144.3	132.3	146.0	153.6	137.1	151.0	128.4	117.2	124.6	107.1
1994	103.0	87.7	83.6	72.8	70.7	70.4	73.3	81.1	74.6	66.5	52.7	53.6
1995[2]	55.8	39.6	37.0	22.6	33.1	30.8	27.0	50.0	60.6	71.1	69.4	73.4
1996	120.0	131.4	125.5	123.1	126.3	107.9	102.8	106.2	104.7	68.0	76.0	77.5
1997	88.2	98.8	104.4	116.0	117.9	121.7	122.9	148.8	177.1	197.9	227.6	253.3
1998	281.5	282.2	312.7	315.7	304.5	308.6	306.2	319.0	334.1	367.4	407.2	444.6
1999	562.6	593.1	614.6	653.5	676.6	687.8	668.4	657.2	639.7	611.2	626.5	608.2
2000	619.2	620.8	619.5	582.9	537.0	508.8	467.8	418.0	397.7	394.3	379.1	344.2
2001[1]	383.8	408.4	416.2	481.9	552.6	585.7	626.7	733.1	767.4	895.6		

Recoverable copper content. [1] Preliminary. [2] New reporting method beginning January 1995, includes Comex, London Metal Exchange, and Refiners. Beginning January 1999, includes Consumers. *Source: American Bureau of Metal Statistics (ABMS)*

Deliveries of Refined Copper to Fabricators in the United States In Thousands of Short Tons

Year	Jan.	Feb.	Mar.	Apr.	May	June	July	Aug.	Sept.	Oct.	Nov.	Dec.	Total
1992	144.9	159.0	165.9	155.5	149.4	161.4	145.8	144.1	146.9	150.4	166.2	130.0	1,813
1993	142.9	165.3	201.6	170.4	162.5	209.6	144.8	191.4	178.9	164.3	194.8	182.7	2,109
1994	193.3	168.6	204.6	178.3	187.8	171.9	154.3	194.6	188.2	188.7	167.5	175.1	2,173
1995[2]	233.8	209.2	239.1	200.9	230.0	210.5	187.1	208.8	202.9	224.7	222.4	175.5	2,545
1996	221.6	227.2	240.0	242.2	270.7	222.1	233.8	246.8	277.5	239.7	240.6	231.9	2,896
1997	246.3	234.5	240.6	247.4	254.9	228.1	241.1	258.2	252.3	259.2	256.0	236.6	2,959
1998	284.5	248.4	288.1	289.2	278.7	258.0	252.4	242.1	260.7	232.0	251.9	220.0	3,106
1999	199.6	202.8	235.0	221.4	206.3	201.9	188.0	186.8	193.7	182.3	182.4	175.2	2,375
2000	166.8	161.3	176.3	157.0	173.7	161.3	145.2	149.7	150.6	154.8	149.8	162.7	1,909
2001[1]	166.1	150.8	167.4	148.4	167.6	165.2	162.7	154.0	151.6	160.7			1,913

Recoverable copper content. [1] Preliminary. [2] New reporting method beginning January 1995, includes crude copper deliveries.
Source: American Bureau of Metal Statistics (ABMS)

Deliveries of Refined Copper to Fabricators Outside the United States In Thousands of Short Tons

Year	Jan.	Feb.	Mar.	Apr.	May	June	July	Aug.	Sept.	Oct.	Nov.	Dec.	Total
1990	419.9	466.3	436.7	392.9	408.3	466.7	303.7	373.5	370.8	448.9	469.1	420.7	4,972
1991	405.0	404.4	391.5	361.2	406.3	433.5	368.5	323.4	420.7	499.1	391.4	483.4	4,807
1992	453.7	408.9	441.8	416.4	413.4	432.4	410.4	364.7	432.6	403.5	406.1	461.3	5,045
1993	427.9	392.9	452.3	361.7	422.2	442.6	384.4	347.9	387.5	414.8	463.4	458.5	4,956
1994	399.8	429.5	481.2	466.5	468.9	428.1	387.9	369.2	423.5	448.9	457.1	436.0	5,197
1995[2]	758.5	810.1	892.8	882.2	853.0	867.3	863.7	814.1	803.4	835.1	796.6	726.2	9,903
1996	875.2	859.4	934.3	907.2	816.7	950.7	908.3	817.4	911.5	1,056.0	922.7	918.3	10,878
1997	862.2	889.7	977.9	1,007.1	991.1	982.7	897.8	873.9	886.2	1,009.0	980.4	966.6	11,349
1998	1,091.7	973.8	1,062.0	1,055.5	995.7	1,014.8	986.8	924.8	913.3	987.9	982.1	1,023.0	12,011
1999[1]	314.5	745.5											6,360

Recoverable copper content. [1] Preliminary. [2] New reporting method beginning January 1995, includes crude copper deliveries.
Source: American Bureau of Metal Statistics (ABMS)

Corn

U.S. corn prices, basis nearby futures values, in calendar 2001 traversed a 45 cent range, bounded by $1.85 to about $2.30 cents/bushel. The action was in sharp contrast to 2000, which witnessed a mid-year 60-cent collapse. Although prices rallied in mid 2001, the recovery proved short lived and by yearend prices were hovering around $2, only a shade lower than a year earlier. On balance the first half of 2001 had a moderately bullish bias, which reversed course in the second half, a pattern that has basically persisted since 1998.

The U.S. 2001/02 corn crop was estimated at 9.5 billion bushels (242.5 million metric tons) vs. 10 billion in 2000/01 Harvested acreage in 2001 of a near record large 72.5 million acres compares with 72.7 million (79.5 million planted) in 2000. Average yield of about 138 bushels per acre compares with 137 bushels in 2000. Three states, Iowa, Illinois and Nebraska generally account for no less than a third of U.S. production.

Although crops of almost 10 billion bushels are no longer unusual, they are also not seen as burdensome if anticipated domestic and export demand reach expectations. Total domestic demand in 2001/02 of 7.8 billion bushels about equals 2000/01 while exports were put at 2.05 billion and 1.93 billion, respectively. Carryover stocks as of August 31, 2002 of 1.57 billion bushels compares with the year earlier 1.90 billion. The stock-to-use ratio in 2001/02 was forecast at about 16% and comparable to the previous season, but almost three times the very low 5% ratio of 1995/96: typically, the higher the ratio, the greater pressure on prices. In 2001/02 the average price received by farmers was forecast to range between $1.85-2.15 a bushel vs. the 2000/01 average of $1.85 and the 1995/96 record high of $3.24.

Corn is the leading U.S. feed grain with sorghums a distant second. The crop year encompasses September/August, but the international trade year is October/September. Animal feed usage in 2001/02 of 5.80 billion bushels compares with 5.89 billion in 2000/01. Food, seed, and industrial use (FSI) were estimated at a record high 2.03 billion bushel vs. 1.97 billion in 2000/01. The increases in FSI use during the past few years is not surprising considering that industrial demand for corn as a sweetener--High Fructose corn syrup (HFCS) continues to quicken, to another record high in 2001/02 of 543 million bushels from 537 million in 2000/01 and less than 500 million in the mid-1990's. Corn used to make fuel (ethanol) was estimated at a record high 680 million bushels in 2001/02 vs. 627 million in 2000/01.

The U.S. is the world's largest corn exporter, and Argentina a distant second. World importers are numerous, but the leaders are generally in Asia, paced by notably by Japan, then South Korea and Taiwan. U.S. exports in 2001/02 of a projected record large 2.1 billion bushels (52 million tons) compare with 1.9 billion in 2000/01. The 2001 estimate, however, could prove optimistic as actual shipments in the first few months of the year lagged outstanding sales. Moreover, exports to Japan in 2001/02 of 15.7 million tons, traditionally the largest purchaser of U.S. corn, have not yet recovered to normal levels in excess of 16 millions tons perhaps owing to lingering concerns about gene-altered U.S corn. U.S. corn imports are minimal, on average about 10 million bushels. World foreign trade in corn in 2001/02 of a near record large 74.1 million metric tons is marginally higher than initially forecast and compares with the record large 75.5 million in 2000/01, of which the U.S. accounted for about two-thirds in both years. However, in the mid-1990's the U.S. supplied about 80% of world exports. Argentina is forecast to export 10 million tons in 2001/02 vs. 12 million a year earlier, the decline reflecting a smaller crop owing to poor weather. South Korea's imports at 7 millions tons are a distant second to Japan, but also down from the 8.7 million tons imported in 2000/01. China imports relatively little corn, generally less than one-half a million tons, but is the third largest exporter in 2001/02 with an initial forecast 4 million tons, but could prove closer to 3 million tons vs. 7.3 million in 2000/01.

World corn production in 2001/02 of about 587 million metric tons, exceeded initial forecasts by 3 million tons, and compares with 586 million in 2000/01. China, since 1987/88 the second largest producer, produced 108 million tons in 2001/02 vs. 106 million in 2000/01 and record large 133 million in 1998/99. China's corn output has increased sharply from the 1980's when annual production averaged less than 100 million tons. The U.S. and China are forecast to produce about 60% of the world's corn in 2001/02; Brazil and Mexico combined should produce about 9%. The gains seen in China's production during much of the past decade reflects increases in per capita income and meat consumption and the need for more corn as a livestock feed. Global use in 2001/02 of a record large 615 million tons compares with 604 million in 2000/01. China's use of 124 million tons compares with 120 million in 2000/01, the seventh consecutive year in which China's use has topped 100 million tons. The U.S. is the largest consumer with almost a third of the total--199 million tons in both 2000/01 and 2001/02. Brazil is in third place with about 36 million tons. Ending world corn stocks are forecast to decrease during 2001/02 to 125 million tons from 153 million a year earlier, with almost half the total in China and the U.S. with about one-third.

U.S. #2 yellow corn prices vary with the location. Typically, Gulf port prices are about 30¢ per bushel higher than prices in Central Illinois while quotes at St. Louis run about 10¢-12¢ higher than Illinois prices. In mid- summer 2001, #2 yellow corn in Central Illinois averaged around $1.92/bu vs. $1.50 a year earlier; for the Gulf ports the average was around $2.30/bu vs. $1.91, respectively.

Futures Markets

Corn futures are traded on the Bolsa de Mercadorias & Futures (BM&F) in Brazil, the Budapest Commodity Exchange, the Marche a Terme International de France (MATIF), the Mercado a Termino de Buenos Aires in Argentina, The Kanmon Commodity Exchange (KCE) in Korea, the Tokyo Grain Exchange (TGE), the Chicago Board of Trade (CBOT), and the Mid-American Commodity Exchange (MidAm). Corn options are traded on the CBOT and the MidAm.

World Production of Corn or Maize In Thousands of Metric Tons

Crop Year	Argentina	Brazil	Canada	China	France	India	Italy	Mexico	Romania	South Africa	United States	Yugo-slavia	World Total
1992-3	10,200	29,200	4,883	95,380	14,872	9,992	7,413	18,631	6,829	9,997	240,719	6,650	538,665
1993-4	10,000	32,934	6,501	102,700	14,843	9,600	8,029	19,141	8,000	13,275	160,986	6,420	476,214
1994-5	11,360	37,440	7,043	99,280	12,640	8,884	7,320	17,005	8,500	4,866	255,295	7,415	560,288
1995-6	11,100	32,480	7,271	112,000	12,394	9,530	8,454	17,780	9,923	10,171	187,970	8,537	517,352
1996-7	15,500	35,700	7,380	127,470	14,432	10,612	9,547	18,922	9,610	10,136	234,518	8,293	592,172
1997-8	19,360	30,100	7,180	104,309	16,754	10,852	10,005	16,934	12,680	7,693	233,864	9,564	575,363
1998-9	13,500	32,393	8,952	132,954	15,204	10,680	8,600	17,788	8,000	7,724	247,882	8,386	605,689
1999-00[1]	17,200	31,641	9,161	128,086	15,643	11,470	10,020	19,240	10,500	10,563	239,549	10,500	607,075
2000-1[2]	15,500	41,536	6,827	106,000	16,470	11,840	10,140	17,700	4,500	7,500	251,854	4,500	585,593
2001-2[3]	11,500	36,000	8,200	108,000	16,500	11,300	10,000	18,000	8,400	8,500	241,485	8,400	583,077

[1] Preliminary. [2] Estimate. [3] Forecast. *Source: Foreign Agricultural Service, U.S. Department of Agriculture (FAS-USDA)*

World Supply and Demand of Course Grains In Millions of Metric Tons/Hectares

Crop Year Beginning Oct.1	Area Harvested	Yield	Pro-duction	World Trade	Total Con-sumption	Ending Stocks	Stocks as % of Con-sumption[3]
1992-3	325.9	2.67	871.6	93.4	844.5	218.7	25.9
1993-4	318.7	2.51	798.6	86.3	838.6	179.0	21.3
1994-5	324.0	2.69	871.3	98.4	859.6	190.6	22.2
1995-6	313.9	2.56	802.9	87.9	841.8	151.8	18.0
1996-7	322.7	2.82	908.5	91.2	875.0	185.3	21.2
1997-8	311.2	2.84	883.9	85.6	873.4	195.8	22.4
1998-9	307.2	2.89	889.0	96.5	870.1	214.7	24.7
1999-00	300.5	2.92	876.6	104.4	881.8	209.5	23.8
2000-1[1]	295.6	2.90	857.3	102.5	878.1	188.7	21.5
2001-2[2]	298.6	2.91	869.7	99.8	893.0	165.5	18.5

[1] Preliminary. [2] Estimate. [3] Represents the ratio of marketing year ending stocks to total consumption. *Source: Foreign Agricultural Service, U.S. Department of Agriculture (FAS-USDA)*

Acreage and Supply of Corn in the United States In Millions of Bushels

Crop Year Beginning Sept. 1[3]	Planted	Harvested For Grain	Harvested For Silage	Yield Per Harvested Acre	Carry-over, Sept. 1 On Farms	Carry-over, Sept. 1 Off Farms	Supply Beginning Stocks	Supply Pro-duction	Supply Imports	Supply Total Supply
	In Thousands of Acres			Bushels						
1992-3	79,311	72,077	6,069	131.5	605.0	494.8	1,100	9,477	7	10,584
1993-4	73,235	62,921	6,831	100.7	1,070.7	1,042.0	2,113	6,338	21	8,472
1994-5	79,175	72,887	5,601	138.6	395.4	454.7	850	10,051	10	10,910
1995-6	71,245	64,995	5,295	113.5	740.9	816.9	1,558	7,400	16	8,974
1996-7	79,229	72,644	5,607	127.1	196.6	229.3	426	9,233	13	9,672
1997-8	79,537	72,671	6,054	126.7	475.0	408.2	883	9,207	9	10,099
1998-9	80,165	72,589	5,913	134.4	640.0	667.8	1,308	9,759	19	11,088
1999-00	77,386	70,487	6,037	133.8	797.0	990.0	1,787	9,431	15	11,239
2000-1[1]	79,551	72,440	6,082	136.9	793.0	924.5	1,718	9,915	7	11,693
2001-2[2]	75,752	68,808	6,148	138.2	753.2	1,146.0	1,998	9,507	10	11,582

[1] Preliminary. 2 Estimate. *Source: Economic Research Service, U.S. Department of Agriculture (ERS-USDA)*

Production of Corn (For Grain) in the United States, by State In Million of Bushels

Year	Illinois	Indiana	Iowa	Kansas	Mich-igan	Minn-esota	Missouri	Nebraska	Ohio	South Dakota	Texas	Wis-consin	Total
1992	1,646.5	877.6	1,903.7	259.5	241.5	741.0	324.0	1,066.5	507.7	277.2	202.5	306.8	9,476.7
1993	1,300.0	712.8	880.0	216.0	225.5	322.0	166.5	785.2	360.8	160.7	212.8	216.2	6,336.5
1994	1,786.2	858.2	1,930.4	304.6	260.9	915.9	273.7	1,153.7	486.5	367.2	238.7	437.1	10,102.7
1995	1,130.0	598.9	1,402.2	244.3	249.6	731.9	149.9	854.7	375.1	193.6	216.6	347.7	7,373.9
1996	1,468.8	670.4	1,711.2	357.2	211.5	868.8	340.4	1,179.8	310.8	365.0	198.2	333.0	9,232.6
1997	1,425.5	701.5	1,642.2	371.8	255.1	851.4	299.0	1,135.2	475.7	326.4	241.5	402.6	9,206.8
1998	1,473.5	760.4	1,769.0	419.0	227.6	1,032.8	285.0	1,239.8	470.9	429.6	185.0	404.2	9,758.7
1999	1,491.0	748.4	1,758.2	420.2	253.5	990.0	247.4	1,153.7	403.2	367.3	228.3	407.6	9,437.3
2000	1,668.6	815.9	1,740.0	416.0	244.3	957.0	396.1	1,014.3	485.1	431.2	235.6	363.0	9,968.4
2001[1]	1,612.5	920.0	1,690.5	409.2	187.2	806.0	349.5	1,106.0	453.6	387.6	163.3	340.6	9,545.5

[1] Preliminary. *Source: National Agricultural Statistics Service, U.S. Department of Agriculture (NASS-USDA)*

Supply and Disappearance of Corn in the United States In Millions of Bushels

Crop Year Beginning Sept. 1	Supply: Beginning Stocks	Supply: Production	Supply: Imports	Supply: Total Supply	Disappearance – Domestic Use: Food, Alcohol & Industrial	Domestic Use: Seed	Domestic Use: Feed & Residual	Domestic Use: Total	Exports	Total Disappearance	Ending Inventory: Gov't Owned[3]	Ending Inventory: Privately Owned[4]	Ending Inventory: Total
1997-8	883	9,207	8.8	10,099	1,784	20.4	5,482	7,287	1,504	8,791	4.3	1,304	1,308
Sept.-Nov.	883	9,207	2.2	10,092	435	0	2,030	2,465	380	2,845	2.1	7,245	7,247
Dec.-Feb.	7,247	----	1.0	7,248	425	0	1,503	1,928	380	2,308	2.0	4,938	4,940
Mar.-May	4,940	----	3.6	4,944	450	19.7	1,084	1,553	350	1,904	2.0	3,038	3,040
June-Aug.	3,040	----	2.0	3,042	474	.7	865	1,340	394	1,734	4.3	1,304	1,308
1998-9	1,308	9,759	18.8	11,085	1,826	19.8	5,472	7,318	1,981	9,298	11.6	1,775	1,787
Sept.-Nov.	1,308	9,759	4.0	1,171	11,071	0	2,119	13,189	450	3,019	13.3	8,039	8,052
Dec.-Feb.	8,052	----	5.7	8,058	434	0	1,460	1,894	465	2,359	14.6	5,684	5,698
Mar.-May	5,698	----	7.2	5,706	476	19.0	1,097	1,592	497	2,089	14.6	3,602	3,616
June-Aug.	3,616	----	1.8	3,618	467	.8	795	1,263	568	1,831	11.6	1,775	1,787
1999-00	1,787	9,431	15.0	11,232	1,913	19.9	5,664	7,597	1,937	9,515	15.0	1,744	1,718
Sept.-Nov.	1,787	9,431	3.5	11,221	459	0	2,189	2,648	534	3,182	19.3	8,005	8,039
Dec.-Feb.	8,039	----	3.0	8,043	447	0	1,526	1,973	468	2,441	15.1	5,590	5,602
Mar.-May	5,602	----	6.0	5,607	512	0	1,059	1,571	451	2,021			3,586
June-Aug.	3,586	----	2.0	3,588	496	0	890	1,386	485	1,871			1,718
2000-1[1]	1,718	9,968	7.0	11,693	1,967		5,890	7,857	1,937	9,794			1,899
Sept.-Nov.	1,718	9,968	1.0	11,687	466		2,192	2,658	506	3,165			8,522
Dec.-Feb.	8,522	----	1.0	8,523	465		1,599	2,064	416	2,480			6,043
Mar.-May	6,043	----	3.0	6,046	524		1,142	1,666	456	2,122			3,924
June-Aug.	3,924	----	1.0	3,925	512		956	1,468	559	2,027			1,899
2001-2[2]	1,899	9,546	10.0	11,416	2,045		5,850	7,895	1,975	9,870			1,546
Sept.-Nov.	1,899	9,507	2.0	11,408	489		2,202	2,691	453	3,144			8,264

[1] Preliminary. [2] Estimate. [3] Uncommitted inventory. [4] Includes quantity under loan and farmer-owned reserve.
Source: Economic Research Service, U.S. Department of Agriculture (ERS-USDA)

Corn Production Estimates and Cash Price in the United States

Year	Corn for Grain Production Estimates (In Thousands of Bushels): Aug. 1	Sept. 1	Oct. 1	Nov. 1	Final	St. Louis No. 2 Yellow (Dollars Per Bushel)	Omaha No. 2 Yellow	Gulf Ports No. 2 Yellow	Kansas City No. 2 White	Chicago No. 2 Yellow	Average Farm Price[2]	Value of Production (Million Dollars)
1993-4	7,423,142	7,229,427	6,961,902	6,503,237	6,336,470	2.67	2.56	2.85	2.78	2.68	2.50	16,032
1994-5	9,214,420	9,257,170	9,602,340	10,010,310	10,102,735	2.51	2.33	2.78	2.91	2.43	2.26	22,992
1995-6	8,121,520	7,832,140	7,541,400	7,373,700	7,373,876	4.06	3.87	4.30	4.14	3.97	3.24	24,118
1996-7	8,694,628	8,803,928	9,012,148	9,265,288	9,293,435	2.90	2.70	3.07	3.09	2.84	2.71	25,149
1997-8	9,275,870	9,267,655	9,311,705	9,359,485	9,206,832	2.60	2.36	2.78	2.93	2.56	2.43	22,352
1998-9	9,592,089	9,737,949	9,743,399	9,836,069	9,758,685	1.99	1.88	2.35	2.51	2.06	1.94	18,922
1999-00	9,560,919	9,380,947	9,466,977	9,537,137	9,430,612	2.02	1.79	2.23	1.98	1.96	1.82	17,104
2000-1	10,369,369	10,362,374	10,191,817	10,053,942	9,968,358	1.85	1.85	2.27	2.03	1.98	1.85	18,499
2001-2[1]	9,266,397	9,238,356	9,429,543	9,545,513	9,506,840							19,209

[1] Preliminary. [2] Season-average price based on monthly prices weighted by monthly marketings. *Source: Economic Research Service, U.S. Department of Agriculture (ERS-USDA)*

Distribution of Corn in the United States In Millions of Bushels

Crop Year Beginning Sept. 1	Food, Seed and Industrial Use: HFCS	Glucose & Dextrose	Starch	Alcohol: Fuel	Alcohol: Beverage[3]	Seed	Cereal & Other Products	Total	Livestock Feed[4]	Exports (Including Grain Equiv. of Products)	Domestic Disappearance	Total Utilization
1993-4	444	223	223	458	106	20.1	118	1,571	4,680	1,328.3	6,293	7,621
1994-5	465	231	226	533	100	18.3	132	1,686	5,460	2,177.5	7,175	9,352
1995-6	482	237	219	396	125	20.2	133	1,592	4,693	2,227.8	6,301	8,528
1996-7	504	246	229	429	130	20.3	135	1,672	5,277	1,797.4	6,971	8,768
1997-8	513	229	246	481	133	20.4	182	1,784	5,482	1,504.4	7,266	8,771
1998-9	531	219	240	526	127	19.8	184	1,826	5,472	1,980.6	7,298	9,279
1999-00	540	222	251	566	130	20.3	185	1,893	5,664	1,937.3	7,557	9,495
2000-1[1]	537	221	248	628	130	20.0	185	1,948	5,775	2,000.0	7,735	9,735
2001-2[2]	548	220	250	690	131		186	2,025				

[1] Preliminary. [2] Estimate. [3] Also includes nonfuel industrial alcohol. [4] Feed and waste (residual, mostly feed). *Source: Economic Research Service, U.S. Department of Agriculture (ERS-USDA)*

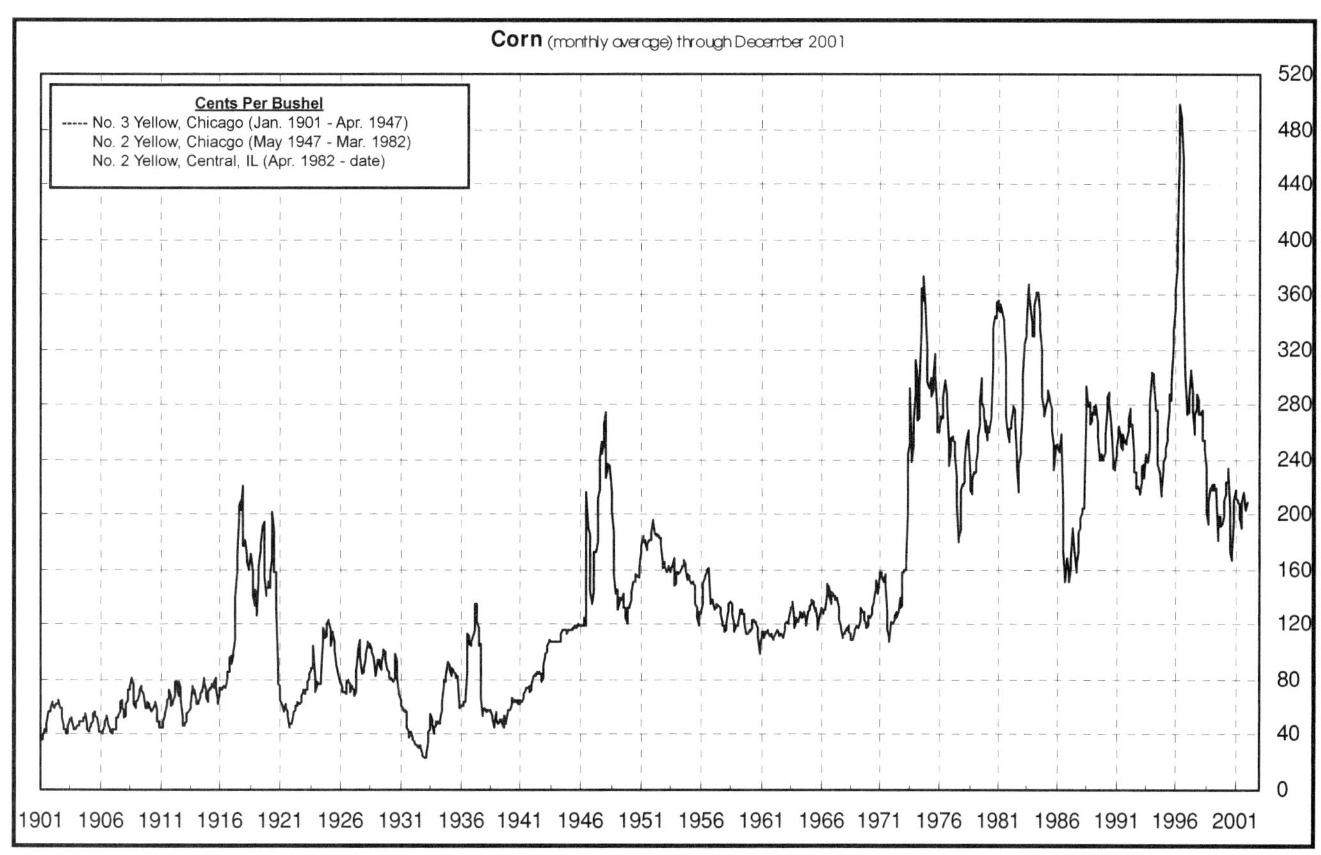

Average Cash Price of Corn, No. 2 Yellow in Central Illinois In Dollars Per Bushel

Year	Sept.	Oct.	Nov.	Dec.	Jan.	Feb.	Mar.	Apr.	May	June	July	Aug.	Average
1992-3	2.13	1.97	1.99	2.05	2.07	2.05	2.16	2.23	2.20	2.09	2.25	2.27	2.12
1993-4	2.22	2.27	2.63	2.81	2.89	2.83	2.76	2.61	2.58	2.61	2.19	2.13	2.54
1994-5	2.08	1.92	2.03	2.16	2.22	2.27	2.36	2.41	2.50	2.65	2.79	2.68	2.34
1995-6	2.83	3.12	3.22	3.36	3.53	3.71	3.92	4.47	4.86	4.74	4.70	4.48	3.91
1996-7	3.39	2.81	2.63	2.62	2.62	2.71	2.90	2.87	2.74	2.59	2.44	2.60	2.74
1997-8	2.61	2.66	2.70	2.60	2.60	2.58	2.59	2.41	2.37	2.29	2.16	1.86	2.45
1998-9	1.78	1.94	2.09	2.08	2.07	2.05	2.09	2.05	2.03	1.99	1.67	1.84	1.97
1999-00	1.81	1.72	1.82	1.84	1.95	2.03	2.08	2.09	2.15	1.83	1.53	1.49	1.86
2000-1	1.58	1.81	1.96	2.01	1.99	1.95	1.92	1.87	1.78	1.76	1.92	2.00	1.88
2001-2[1]	1.94	1.84	1.90	1.97									1.91

[1] Preliminary. *Source: Economic Research Service, U.S. Department of Agriculture (ERS-USDA)*

Average Cash Price of Corn, No. 2 Yellow at Gulf Ports[2] In Dollars Per Bushel

Year	Sept.	Oct.	Nov.	Dec.	Jan.	Feb.	Mar.	Apr.	May	June	July	Aug.	Average
1992-3	2.50	2.40	2.42	2.39	2.39	2.40	2.48	2.55	2.50	2.36	2.59	2.55	2.46
1993-4	2.57	2.68	2.94	3.08	3.22	3.14	3.05	2.88	2.81	2.85	2.51	2.44	2.85
1994-5	2.48	2.44	2.43	2.61	2.72	2.72	2.79	2.79	2.84	3.04	3.23	3.21	2.78
1995-6	3.32	3.57	3.63	3.76	4.00	4.18	4.34	4.80	5.17	4.99	5.07	4.73	4.30
1996-7	3.69	3.27	2.97	2.97	3.02	3.08	3.25	3.17	3.01	2.86	2.69	2.86	3.07
1997-8	2.88	3.05	2.98	2.89	2.90	2.88	2.89	2.71	2.69	2.64	2.55	2.24	2.78
1998-9	2.18	2.43	2.47	2.42	2.48	2.40	2.45	2.39	2.35	2.36	2.12	2.20	2.35
1999-00	2.21	2.17	2.17	2.21	2.36	2.42	2.42	2.43	2.43	2.13	1.91	1.91	2.23
2000-1	2.03	2.15	2.26	2.45	2.40	2.35	2.32	2.22	2.14	2.11	2.30	2.36	2.26
2001-2[1]	2.27	2.19	2.28	2.35									2.27

[1] Preliminary. [2] Barge delivered to Louisiana Gulf. *Source: Economic Research Service, U.S. Department of Agriculture (ERS-USDA)*

CORN

Weekly Outstanding Export Sales and Cumulative Exports of U.S. Corn In Thousands of Metric Tons

Marketing Year 1999/00 Week Ending	1999/00 Outstanding Sales	1999/00 Cumulative Exports	Marketing Year 2000-01 Week Ending	2000-01 Outstanding Sales	2000-01 Cumulative Exports	Marketing Year 2001-02 Week Ending	2001-02 Outstanding Sales	2001-02 Cumulative Exports
Sept. 2, 1999	8,647	475	Sept. 7 2000	7,856	825	Sept. 6 2001	7,090	567
9	8,841	1,333	14	7,509	1,848	13		
16	8,558	2,508	21	7,767	2,959	20		
23	8,224	3,543	28	6,994	4,390	27	7,018	3,780
30	8,037	4,398	Oct. 5	6,640	5,713	Oct. 4	6,862	4,552
Oct. 7	7,682	5,355	12	6,812	6,591	11	6,944	5,287
14	7,769	6,322	19	6,923	7,408	18	7,074	6,059
21	8,270	7,455	26	7,087	8,056	25	6,788	6,909
28	8,418	8,627	Nov. 2	6,671	9,087	Nov. 1	7,028	7,569
Nov. 4	8,508	9,266	9	6,622	9,650	8	6,838	8,566
11	8,756	10,254	16	6,366	10,563	15	6,824	9,261
18	8,836	11,180	23	6,224	11,144	22	6,603	10,131
25	8,387	12,191	30	6,146	12,159	29	7,635	10,618
Dec. 2	8,356	13,225	Dec. 7	6,664	12,954	Dec. 6	7,541	11,595
9	8,351	14,278	14	6,726	13,853	13	7,399	12,339
16	8,645	15,227	21	6,547	14,820	20	7,596	13,051
23	8,220	16,191	28	6,697	15,269	27	7,347	13,825
30	7,894	17,010	Jan. 4, 2001	6,253	15,898	Jan. 3 2002	6,830	14,456
Jan. 6, 2000	7,360	17,826	11	5,936	16,826	10	7,110	15,092
13	7,487	18,825	18	6,654	17,667	17	7,432	16,075
20	7,737	19,709	25	7,071	18,382	24	7,415	16,834
27	7,579	20,689	Feb. 1	7,569	18,913	31	7,944	17,637
Feb. 3	7,771	21,479	8	7,585	20,052	Feb. 7	8,339	18,278
10	7,408	22,367	15	7,576	20,800	14	8,530	19,260
17	7,423	23,246	22	7,303	21,728	21	8,410	20,187
24	7,517	24,282	Mar. 1	7,415	22,492	28		
Mar. 2	8,148	25,022	8	7,488	23,341	Mar. 7		
9	7,952	25,993	15	7,315	24,160	14		
16	7,537	26,940	22	6,439	25,448	21		
23	7,316	27,941	29	6,338	26,635	28		
30	7,249	28,833	Apr. 5	5,618	27,834	Apr. 4		
Apr. 6	7,132	29,674	12	5,216	28,787	11		
13	7,258	30,602	19	4,735	29,675	18		
20	7,405	31,698	26	5,168	30,510	25		
27	6,877	32,640	May 3	5,444	31,135	May 2		
May 4	6,817	33,432	10	5,620	31,846	9		
11	6,941	34,082	17	6,186	32,468	16		
18	6,979	34,970	24	6,164	33,266	23		
25	6,889	35,817	31	6,653	33,688	30		
June 1	7,063	36,584	June 7	7,364	34,243	June 6		
8	7,125	37,517	14	7,368	35,177	13		
15	7,250	38,348	21	7,448	36,139	20		
22	7,161	39,112	28	7,533	36,925	27		
29	7,227	39,854	July 5	7,384	37,918	July 4		
July 6	6,820	40,818	12	7,550	39,087	11		
13	6,716	41,731	19	7,934	39,922	18		
20	6,478	42,565	26	7,111	41,067	25		
27	6,116	43,477	Aug. 2	6,466	42,327	Aug. 1		
Aug. 3	5,766	44,337	9	5,807	43,635	8		
10	5,388	44,949	16	4,748	44,949	15		
17	4,296	46,181	23	3,731	46,025	22		
24	3,372	47,318	30	2,806	47,219	29		
31	2,006	48,760						

Source: Foreign Agricultural Service, U.S. Department of Agriculture (FAS-USDA)

Average Price Received by Farmers for Corn in the United States In Dollars Per Bushel

Year	Sept.	Oct.	Nov.	Dec.	Jan.	Feb.	Mar.	Apr.	May	June	July	Aug.	Average
1992-3	2.16	2.05	1.98	1.97	2.03	2.00	2.10	2.16	2.14	2.09	2.22	2.25	2.07
1993-4	2.21	2.28	2.45	2.67	2.70	2.79	2.74	2.65	2.60	2.61	2.29	2.16	2.50
1994-5	2.19	2.06	1.99	2.13	2.19	2.23	2.30	2.36	2.41	2.51	2.63	2.63	2.26
1995-6	2.69	2.79	2.87	3.07	3.09	3.37	3.51	3.85	4.14	4.20	4.43	4.30	3.53
1996-7	3.55	2.89	2.66	2.63	2.69	2.65	2.79	2.80	2.69	2.56	2.42	2.50	2.74
1997-8	2.52	2.54	2.51	2.52	2.56	2.55	2.54	2.41	2.34	2.28	2.19	1.89	2.40
1998-9	1.83	1.91	1.93	2.00	2.06	2.05	2.06	2.04	1.99	1.97	1.74	1.75	1.94
1999-00	1.75	1.69	1.70	1.82	1.91	1.98	2.03	2.03	2.11	1.91	1.64	1.52	1.84
2000-1	1.61	1.74	1.86	1.97	1.98	1.96	1.95	1.89	1.82	1.77	1.88	1.90	1.86
2001-2[1]	1.91	1.84	1.85	1.98	1.97	1.93							1.91

[1] Preliminary. *Source: Economic Research Service, U.S. Department of Agriculture (ERS-USDA)*

Corn Price Support Data in the United States

Crop Year Beginning Sept. 1	National Average Loan Rate[3]	Target Price	Placed Under Loan	% of Production	Acquired by CCC	Owned by CCC Aug. 31	CCC Inventory As of Dec. 31: CCC Owned	CCC Inventory As of Dec. 31: Under CCC Loan	Quantity Pledged (Thousands of Bushels)	Face Amount (Thousands of Dollars)
	--- Dollars Per Bushel ---		---------- Millions of Bushels ----------							
1990-1	1.57	2.75	1,071	13.5	285	371	214	1,071	1,071,040	1,616,948
1991-2	1.62	2.75	1,006	13.5	291	113	265	678	26,636	45,609
1992-3	1.72	2.75	1,646	17.4	0	56	125	1,021	15,245	28,947
1993-4	1.72	2.75	618	9.7	0	45	54	812	13,697	26,052
1994-5	1.89	2.75	2,002	19.8	0	-----	44	1,598	26,318	53,474
1995-6	1.89	2.75	970	9.2	0	-----	42	579	677,115	1,232,669
1996-7	1.89	NA	561	-----	0	-----	30	756	-----	-----
1997-8	1.89	NA	1,132	-----	19	-----	2	81	-----	-----
1998-9[1]	1.89	NA	823	-----	0	-----	-----	-----	-----	-----
1999-00[2]	1.89	NA	-----	-----	-----	-----	-----	-----	-----	-----

[1] Preliminary. [2] Estimate. [3] Findley or announced loan rate. *Source: National Agricultural Statistics Service, U.S. Department of Agriculture (NASS-USDA)*

U.S. Exports[1] of Corn (Including Seed), By Country of Destination In Thousands of Metric Tons

Year Beginning Oct. 1	Algeria	Canada	Egypt	Irael	Japan	Mexico	Rep. of Korea	Russia[3]	Saudi Arabia	Spain	Taiwan	Venezuela	Total
1991-2	776	330	1,058	369	13,480	1,006	1,508	1,309	602	1,273	4,998	552	40,608
1992-3	1,172	1,196	1,578	538	14,235	396	1,021	2,858	787	1,048	5,450	777	42,472
1993-4	1,095	574	1,402	268	11,923	1,678	631	2,259	851	1,102	5,015	751	33,015
1994-5	798	1,108	2,342	658	16,030	3,165	8,866	9	864	2,337	6,150	886	58,596
1995-6	507	736	1,854	625	14,900	6,268	7,333	50	844	1,156	5,600	479	52,660
1996-7	862	879	2,364	556	15,425	3,141	5,404	88	1,025	1,080	5,609	730	46,638
1997-8	829	1,404	1,951	141	13,957	4,423	3,364	1	883	141	3,488	645	37,755
1998-9	947	898	2,954	395	15,375	5,576	6,659	405	1,175	92	4,538	1,329	51,949
1999-00	1,099	1,080	3,542	748	14,939	4,910	2,822	491	1,197	16	4,989	1,146	49,378
2000-1[2]	1,180	2,793	4,116	621	14,091	5,929	3,109	26	1,003	0	4,875	1,152	48,115

[1] Excludes exports of corn by-products. [2] Preliminary. [3] Formerly part of the U.S.S.R.; data not reported separately until 1992. *Source: Economic Research Service, U.S. Department of Agriculture (ERS-USDA)*

Stocks of Corn (Shelled and Ear) in the United States In Millions of Bushels

Year	On Farms: Mar. 1	On Farms: June 1	On Farms: Sept. 1	On Farms: Dec. 1	Off Farms: Mar. 1	Off Farms: June 1	Off Farms: Sept. 1	Off Farms: Dec. 1	Total Stocks: Mar. 1	Total Stocks: June 1	Total Stocks: Sept. 1	Total Stocks: Dec. 1
1992	2,610.2	1,517.5	605.5	5,736.9	1,950.8	1,221.1	494.8	2,169.5	4,561.0	2,738.6	1,100.3	7,906.4
1993	3,630.0	2,216.5	1,070.7	3,803.0	2,048.2	1,492.9	1,042.3	2,133.5	5,678.2	3,709.4	2,113.0	5,936.5
1994	2,210.0	1,203.0	395.4	5,417.5	1,785.5	1,156.9	454.7	2,663.0	3,995.7	2,359.9	850.1	8,080.5
1995	3,502.0	2,072.0	740.9	3,960.0	2,089.7	1,342.9	816.9	2,145.8	5,591.7	3,414.9	1,557.8	6,105.8
1996	2,000.2	780.1	196.6	4,800.0	1,799.3	937.8	229.3	2,103.7	3,799.5	1,717.9	425.9	6,903.7
1997	2,870.0	1,501.0	475.0	4,822.0	1,624.1	995.6	408.2	2,424.8	4,494.1	2,496.6	883.2	7,246.8
1998	2,975.0	1,830.0	640.0	5,320.0	1,964.9	1,209.8	667.8	2,731.8	4,939.9	3,039.8	1,307.8	8,051.8
1999	3,570.0	2,257.0	797.0	5,195.0	2,128.4	1,359.2	990.0	2,844.4	5,698.4	3,616.2	1,787.0	8,039.4
2000	3,300.0	2,029.8	793.0	5,550.0	2,301.9	1,556.1	924.5	2,972.2	5,601.9	3,585.9	1,717.5	8,522.2
2001[1]	3,600.0	2,230.8	753.2	5,275.0	2,443.0	1,693.2	1,146.0	2,989.3	6,043.0	3,924.0	1,899.1	8,264.3

[1] Preliminary. *Source: National Agricultural Statistics Service, U.S. Department of Agriculture (NASS-USDA)*

CORN

Volume of Trading of Corn Futures in Chicago In Thousands of Contracts

Year	Jan.	Feb.	Mar.	Apr.	May	June	July	Aug.	Sept.	Oct.	Nov.	Dec.	Total
1992	901.2	1,002.6	952.2	868.6	938.2	1,015.2	865.6	795.0	688.6	688.4	996.2	644.4	10,356.6
1993	517.6	636.4	774.0	894.8	688.0	1,047.4	1,395.6	1,014.2	896.0	1,036.0	1,574.4	988.2	10,539.4
1994	1,251.4	1,035.6	1,045.6	1,108.8	1,079.2	1,455.0	747.6	601.8	615.0	703.0	1,025.4	861.4	11,529.8
1995	787.2	832.4	973.7	987.7	1,213.7	1,759.5	1,293.7	1,318.6	1,220.2	1,613.2	1,743.1	1,356.0	15,105.1
1996	1,992.2	1,819.6	1,607.6	2,655.2	2,085.2	1,545.1	1,590.5	1,144.6	1,183.4	1,435.7	1,514.7	1,046.3	19,620.2
1997	1,160.6	1,483.0	1,693.3	1,780.1	1,291.7	1,347.5	1,527.7	1,318.3	1,060.2	1,700.2	1,434.4	1,188.0	16,985.0
1998	1,250.2	1,276.5	1,432.8	1,620.3	1,148.5	1,771.0	1,415.3	1,231.4	1,126.3	1,319.3	1,217.2	986.6	15,795.5
1999	955.1	1,374.2	1,440.1	1,420.6	975.1	1,597.4	1,708.0	1,669.8	1,131.9	1,096.2	1,500.9	855.6	15,724.8
2000	1,502.2	1,580.9	1,713.1	1,386.3	1,789.7	1,830.7	1,178.3	1,291.8	1,057.4	1,256.1	1,612.8	986.1	17,185.4
2001	1,397.2	1,197.4	1,329.5	1,518.7	1,173.2	1,612.1	2,023.5	1,549.0	1,072.3	1,223.3	1,741.2	891.4	16,728.7

Source: Chicago Board of Trade (CBT)

Average Open Interest of Corn Futures in Chicago In Contracts

Year	Jan.	Feb.	Mar.	Apr.	May	June	July	Aug.	Sept.	Oct.	Nov.	Dec.
1992	254,195	294,957	285,429	260,527	230,359	232,189	211,221	219,796	208,613	239,888	262,345	244,803
1993	256,113	260,986	248,638	250,000	229,016	232,590	265,672	264,938	243,892	275,792	332,445	327,226
1994	346,077	336,342	327,539	305,722	262,621	246,308	215,081	208,990	212,983	243,678	262,849	250,646
1995	292,090	311,372	336,433	355,443	368,381	427,744	413,839	418,450	439,170	473,698	490,970	487,977
1996	500,837	508,496	469,697	453,707	403,118	350,066	304,265	298,894	302,170	326,373	332,809	306,256
1997	305,779	347,392	382,261	351,852	290,649	274,760	267,531	281,194	307,415	378,453	379,045	331,386
1998	328,020	341,444	358,221	366,657	337,703	327,237	297,894	318,162	321,992	332,337	342,868	322,157
1999	357,682	363,153	357,126	343,624	338,467	323,658	329,460	315,858	316,247	410,955	461,037	389,187
2000	445,999	478,892	482,080	487,758	476,891	445,018	391,967	387,289	356,583	397,966	454,920	414,851
2001	454,326	469,027	440,548	455,718	424,386	423,840	389,898	387,710	370,315	419,447	462,930	416,593

Source: Chicago Board of Trade (CBT)

Corn Oil

U.S. corn oil production (October/September) slipped in 2000/01 to 2.4 billion pounds from the record high 2.5 billion in 1999/00. The lower outturn reflected the sharp fall in price, from 17.8 cents/lb in 1999/00 to 13.5 cents. Domestic output also declined as a consequence of a reduced grind by dry corn millers whose sales suffered from concerns over the possible presence in their products of an unapproved, genetically modified corn variety. Production, however, is forecast to rise in 2001/02 to a record 2.55 billion pounds. Seasonally, production tends to peak around December and March and reaches a low in July.

Total 2000/01 domestic usage of a record 1.64 billion pounds compares with 1.4 billion in 1999/00 and forecast at 1.66 billion in 2001/02. Corn oil is cholesterol free which has enhanced its appeal among health conscious consumers. Exports totaled 0.9 billion pounds in 2000/01 vs. 0.97 billion in 1999/00 and forecast to drop further in 2001/02 to 0.93 billion pounds; the slippage reflecting large world supplies of competing vegetable oils. The European Union is a major importer of U.S. corn oil.. U.S. carryover stocks show considerable variation: estimated ending 2000/01 stocks of 117 million pounds compare with 267 million a year earlier, and slide to 102 million as of September 30, 2002.

Crude corn oil prices, basis wet/dry-milled Central Illinois, during 2000/01 were at record lows and compare with a 1990's high of almost 29 cents. Seasonally, prices tend to be highest around March/April and lowest late in the calendar year.

Supply and Disappearance of Corn Oil in the United States In Millions of Pounds

Crop Year Beginning Oct. 1	Supply: Stocks Oct. 1	Supply: Production	Supply: Imports	Supply: Total Supply	Disappearance: Baking and Frying Fats	Disappearance: Salad and Cooking Oil	Disappearance: Margarine	Disappearance: Total Edible Products	Disappearance: Domestic Disappearance	Disappearance: Exports	Disappearance: Total Disappearance
1995-6	241	2,139	11.0	2,391	82	434	79	595	1,298	977	2,275
1996-7	116	2,230	13.5	2,361	73	386	68	527	1,244	988	2,232
1997-8	129	2,335	28.1	2,492	W	375	W	492	1,272	1,118	2,390
1998-9	102	2,374	42.4	2,518	W	384	W	496	1,394	989	2,383
1999-00	135	2,501	17.5	2,654	W	498	W	586	1,417	970	2,387
2000-1[1]	267	2,403	27.3	2,698	W	W	W	689	1,638	944	2,581
2001-2[2]	117	2,550		2,692					1,665	925	2,590

[1] Preliminary. [2] Estimate. W = Withheld proprietary data. *Source: Economic Research Service, U.S. Department of Agriculture (ERS-USDA)*

Production[2] of Crude Corn Oil in the United States In Millions of Pounds

Year	Oct.	Nov.	Dec.	Jan.	Feb.	Mar.	Apr.	May	June	July	Aug.	Sept.	Total
1995-6	179.5	173.8	184.5	180.6	160.4	192.9	192.1	175.9	178.4	147.1	162.2	171.2	2,099
1996-7	183.8	182.3	208.2	172.5	170.9	209.9	188.3	182.5	184.3	174.0	180.6	182.2	2,220
1997-8	199.2	207.5	202.0	171.4	162.7	201.0	203.9	201.2	201.4	192.8	202.8	188.9	2,335
1998-9	209.2	199.4	189.2	182.9	177.0	201.0	201.1	205.3	205.7	194.8	212.5	196.3	2,374
1999-00	204.3	212.3	218.6	214.8	199.0	214.9	210.5	213.6	204.3	226.4	225.3	201.9	2,546
2000-1	208.6	192.7	190.4	198.9	180.5	201.6	200.7	206.2	204.0	205.7	211.1	203.2	2,404
2001-2[1]	196.0	203.3	206.5	200.1									2,418

[1] Preliminary. [2] Not seasonally adjusted. *Source: Bureau of the Census, U.S. Department of Commerce*

Consumption Corn Oil, in Refining, in the United States In Millions of Pounds

Year	Oct.	Nov.	Dec.	Jan.	Feb.	Mar.	Apr.	May	June	July	Aug.	Sept.	Total
1995-6	82.9	97.9	102.0	78.6	91.6	100.0	84.8	90.0	90.5	74.5	66.5	90.2	1,049
1996-7	82.0	83.0	84.7	69.7	71.0	79.5	71.4	76.1	80.4	86.9	90.8	58.5	934
1997-8	87.5	83.8	100.6	83.0	89.2	100.5	92.5	100.5	104.2	90.6	101.7	94.6	1,129
1998-9	106.6	104.4	105.0	82.0	W	102.0	94.6	101.7	104.3	90.1	97.0	103.5	1,190
1999-00	96.2	97.1	114.7	94.9	89.2	W	W	W	W	W	134.2	129.6	1,296
2000-1	136.2	112.2	129.3	106.7	122.6	118.7	111.9	140.4	W	W	W	W	1,467
2001-2[1]	W	W	W	W									

[1] Preliminary. W = Withheld proprietary data. *Source: Bureau of Census, U.S. Department of Commerce*

Average Corn Oil Price, Wet Mill in Chicago In Cents Per Pound

Year	Oct.	Nov.	Dec.	Jan.	Feb.	Mar.	Apr.	May	June	July	Aug.	Sept.	Average
1995-6	26.05	25.54	24.99	24.52	24.30	24.34	25.60	27.98	25.66	25.46	24.33	24.14	25.24
1996-7	22.67	21.96	22.27	23.39	23.97	24.38	24.60	24.66	24.82	25.34	25.36	25.15	24.05
1997-8	25.20	26.25	26.28	26.04	27.31	28.50	30.93	33.20	32.82	31.52	29.93	29.25	28.94
1998-9	29.46	29.65	29.88	29.15	26.58	23.01	23.08	22.96	22.95	22.43	22.41	22.08	25.30
1999-00	21.97	21.96	21.68	20.81	20.06	19.28	18.32	16.63	14.57	13.55	13.03	11.85	17.81
2000-1	10.52	10.37	10.54	10.25	11.06	11.91	13.76	14.84	15.94	17.28	18.73	17.30	13.54
2001-2[1]	17.18	18.30	22.45	20.54									19.62

[1] Preliminary. *Source: Economic Research Service,U.S. Department of Agriculture (ERS-USDA)*

Cotton

Cotton is a natural fiber that finds use in many products. These range from clothing to home furnishings to medical products. As a result, cotton is always in demand though its use is subject to the strengths and weaknesses of the overall economy. When the U.S. economy is contracting or in recession, use of cotton by textile mills slows substantially. When the economy is growing, use of cotton increases. A decline in interest rates which reduces the interest rate on mortgage loans will spur the housing sector and will in turn cause more cotton to be used in items like towels and sheets. At the same time, the reduction in interest rates and rising unemployment rates will cause consumers to spend less on items like clothing. The year 2001 saw just such a situation develop in the U.S. as the economy slowed, unemployment rates increased and interest rates declined. The result was that projected domestic use of cotton in the U.S. declined while at the same time the outlook for exports improved substantially.

In 2001, cotton prices declined. The U.S.D.A. in their December report indicated that the average prices for cotton in the August-October 2001 period was 35.7 cents per pound. That compared with the 2000/01 (August-September) season average price of 49.8 cents and the 1999/00 average price of 45 cents. The U.S.D.A. noted that cotton prices experienced greater weakness in terms of world prices that did grains and other crops. U.S. cotton prices in the first three months of the 2001/02 season were some 28 percent less than the average for the entire 2000/01 season. The decline in prices for crops like corn and soybeans has not been near as dramatic. Cotton prices have declined in part because of a global decline in demand for commodities which started in the mid-1990's. The problem for cotton has been compounded in that the world economy has slowed at the same time that production has increased. World use of cotton between 1999/00 and 2001/02 was largely flat while global production increased. Part of the reason for increased production was favorable weather.

For the 2001/02 season, U.S. planted acreage for cotton was 16.19 million acres, an increase of 4 percent from the 2000/01 season and some 9 percent more than in 1998/99. Even though cotton prices were weak during the planting period, acreage increased in part because prices of alternative crops were even weaker. Additionally, the government policies toward cotton provided more incentives to plant the crop. The result was an increase in acreage. Cotton acreage harvested in 2001/02 was 13.94 million acres, an increase of 7 percent from 2000/01 and up 4 percent from 1999/00. The implied acreage abandonment rate in 2001/02 was 14 percent.

The largest state in terms of harvested acreage was Texas with 4.32 million acres, down 2 percent from the previous season. Harvested acreage in Mississippi was 1.63 million acres, up 27 percent from the previous year. Georgia acreage was 1.49 million, up 10 percent from the prior season. The national average cotton yield in 2001/02 was 691 pounds per acre. This was up 9 percent from 2000/01 and up 14 percent from 1999/00. The highest yielding state was California with a cotton yield of 1,344 pounds per acre. This was followed by Arizona with a yield of 1,253 pounds. Both states use irrigation widely. The Texas yield was 460 pounds with Mississippi at 727 pounds and Georgia at 709 pounds.

U.S. cotton production in 2001/02 was forecast to be 20.06 million bales, up 17 percent from 2000/01 and 18 percent more than 1999/00. The largest producing state is Texas. The Texas crop was 4.13 million bales (480 pounds), up 4 percent from the previous year. Production in Mississippi was 2.47 million bales, up 44 percent from the previous season. California cotton production declined 5 percent to 2.42 million bales. Georgia production at 2.2 million bales was up 32 percent.

With season beginning stocks of 6 million bales and minor imports, the U.S. cotton supply in 2001/02 was estimated to be 26.08 million bales, up 23 percent from the previous season. Domestic use of cotton in the U.S. was forecast to be 7.9 million bales, a decline of 11 percent from the previous season and some 23 percent less than in 1999/00. Exports of cotton in 2001/02 were projected to be 9.8 million bales, up 45 percent from the previous season. and 45 percent more than in 1999/00. Total use of cotton is projected to be 17.7 million bales, up 13 percent from 2000/01 and 4 percent more than in 1999/00. Ending stocks of cotton are projected to be 8.4 million bales, up 40 percent from the previous year.

World cotton production in 2001/02 was forecast to be 96 million bales, up 8 percent from the previous season. Cotton production outside the U.S. was estimated to be 75.94 million bales, up 6 percent from the prior year. The largest producer of cotton is China with the current crop expected to be 23.50 million bales. India is also a large cotton producer with the 2001/02 crop expected to be 11.8 million bales. Central Asian cotton production was estimated at 7.19 million bales. A large portion of the crop is exported. Other producers of cotton include Australia, Brazil, Turkey, Argentina and Mexico.

Futures Markets

Cotton futures and options are traded on the New York Cotton Exchange, a division of the New York Board of Trade. Cotton futures are traded on the Bolsa de Mercadorias & Futuros (BM&F). Cotton yarn futures are traded on the Chuba Commodity Exchange (CCOM), the Osaka Mercantile Exchange (OME) and the Tokyo Commodity Exchange (TOCOM).

Supply and Distribution of All Cotton in the United States In Thousands of 480-Pound Bales

Crop Year Beginning Aug. 1	Acre: Planted (1,000 Acres)	Acre: Harvested (1,000 Acres)	Yield Lbs./acre	Supply: Beginning Stocks[3]	Supply: Production[4]	Supply: Imports	Supply: Total	Disappearance: Mill Use	Disappearance: Exports	Disappearance: Total	Unaccounted	Ending Stocks	Farm Price[5] (Cents per Lb.)	"A" Index Price[6] (Cents per Lb.)	Value of Production Million $
1992-3	13,240	11,143	699	3,704	16,219	1	19,923	10,250	5,201	15,451	190	4,662	54.9	56.87	4,273.9
1993-4	13,438	12,783	606	4,662	16,134	6	20,802	10,418	6,862	17,280	8	3,530	58.4	70.75	4,520.9
1994-5	13,720	13,322	708	3,530	19,662	20	23,212	11,198	9,402	20,600	38	2,650	72.0	92.66	6,796.7
1995-6	16,931	16,007	537	2,650	17,900	408	20,958	10,604	7,675	18,322	-27	2,609	76.5	85.61	6,574.6
1996-7	14,653	12,888	705	2,609	18,942	403	21,954	11,126	6,865	17,991	8	3,971	70.5	78.66	6,408.1
1997-8	13,898	13,406	673	3,971	18,793	13	22,777	11,349	7,500	18,849	-41	3,887	66.2	72.11	5,975.6
1998-9	13,393	10,684	625	3,887	13,918	443	18,248	10,401	4,344	14,745	436	3,939	61.7	58.97	4,119.9
1999-00	14,874	13,425	607	3,939	16,968	97	21,004	10,240	6,750	16,990	-92	3,922	46.8	52.85	3,836.5
2000-1[1]	15,517	13,053	632	3,922	17,188	15	21,125	8,882	6,763	15,645	522	6,002	51.0	57.25	4,780.7
2001-2[2]	16,194	14,140	685	6,002	20,175	10	26,187	8,100	9,400	17,500	-13	8,700			

[1] Preliminary. [2] Estimate. [3] Excludes preseason ginnings (adjusted to 480-lb. bale net weight basis). [4] Includes preseason ginnings.
[5] Marketing year average price. [6] Average of 5 cheapest types of SLM 1 3/32 staple length cotton *offered on the European market.*
Source: Economic Research Service, U.S. Department of Agriculture (ERS-USDA)

World Production of All Cotton In Thousands of 480-Pound Bales

Crop Year Beginning Aug. 1	Argentina	Brazil	China	Egypt	India	Iran	Mexico	Pakistan	Sudan	Turkey	United States	Uzbekistan	World Total
1992-3	666	2,113	20,700	1,620	10,775	464	147	7,073	276	2,635	16,218	5,851	82,505
1993-4	1,079	1,860	17,200	1,909	9,800	418	122	6,282	216	2,766	16,134	6,067	77,049
1994-5	1,608	2,526	19,900	1,170	11,148	762	460	6,250	400	2,886	19,662	5,778	85,857
1995-6	1,929	1,791	21,900	1,088	13,250	800	974	8,200	490	3,911	17,900	5,740	93,063
1996-7	1,493	1,286	19,300	1,568	13,918	825	1,078	7,323	460	3,600	18,942	4,813	89,589
1997-8	1,406	1,745	21,100	1,532	12,337	600	984	7,175	400	3,651	18,793	5,228	91,570
1998-9	920	2,100	20,700	1,050	12,883	638	1,039	6,300	250	3,860	13,918	4,600	84,879
1999-00	615	3,100	17,600	1,050	12,180	650	669	8,600	240	3,634	16,968	5,180	87,242
2000-1[1]	735	4,100	20,300	920	10,900	735	363	8,200	340	3,600	17,188	4,400	88,526
2001-2[2]	280	3,300	24,400	1,425	11,800	575	440	7,800	300	3,900	20,084	4,800	96,870

[1] Preliminary. [2] Estimate. *Source: Foreign Agricultural Service, U.S. Department of Agriculture (FAS-USDA)*

World Stocks and Trade of Cotton In Thousands of 480-Pound Bales

Crop Year Beginning Aug. 1	Beginning Stocks: United States	Beginning Stocks: Uzbekistan	Beginning Stocks: China	Beginning Stocks: World Total	Imports: Indonesia	Imports: Mexico	Imports: Russia	Imports: Turkey	Imports: World Total	Exports: United States	Exports: Uzbekistan	Exports: China	Exports: World Total
1992-3	3,704	2,133	11,934	37,580	1,989	656	2,650	1,070	26,945	5,201	5,500	684	25,579
1993-4	4,662	1,534	9,692	34,713	2,039	794	3,000	545	27,728	6,862	5,800	749	26,816
1994-5	3,530	1,006	5,251	26,758	2,075	580	2,159	1,060	30,618	9,402	5,006	183	28,452
1995-6	4,028	956	8,828	29,884	2,139	695	1,100	574	27,529	7,675	4,524	21	27,359
1996-7	2,609	1,304	14,052	36,614	2,147	900	1,000	1,150	28,763	6,865	4,550	10	26,494
1997-8	3,971	822	16,655	40,059	1,923	1,600	1,225	1,450	26,488	7,500	4,570	34	26,590
1998-9	3,887	635	19,955	43,684	2,329	1,488	850	1,139	25,248	4,344	3,812	681	23,649
1999-00	3,939	603	21,133	44,885	2,076	1,813	1,600	2,400	28,276	6,750	4,100	1,700	27,226
2000-1[1]	3,922	838	14,958	41,672	2,650	1,865	1,650	1,750	26,479	6,763	3,400	446	26,464
2001-2[2]	6,002	743	11,542	38,671	2,500	1,650	1,750	2,250	29,086	10,000	3,250	400	28,892

[1] Preliminary. [2] Estimate. *Source: Foreign Agricultural Service, U.S. Department of Agriculture (FAS-USDA)*

World Consumption of All Cottons in Specified Countries In Thousands of 480-Pound Bales

Year	Brazil	China	Egypt	France	Germany	India	Italy	Japan	Mexico	Pakistan	United States	Uzbekistan	World Total
1992-3	3,445	21,900	1,641	463	788	9,808	1,432	2,301	736	6,634	10,250	950	86,061
1993-4	3,950	21,400	1,343	516	781	9,840	1,594	2,071	838	6,725	10,418	800	85,453
1994-5	3,996	20,200	1,140	532	660	10,545	1,539	1,754	890	6,750	11,198	827	84,758
1995-6	3,904	19,700	1,010	484	606	11,977	1,539	1,529	1,100	7,200	10,647	873	86,040
1996-7	3,900	20,300	919	536	640	13,120	1,562	1,401	1,600	7,000	11,126	750	88,021
1997-8	3,400	19,600	1,033	505	650	12,675	1,612	1,400	1,950	7,187	11,349	850	87,157
1998-9	3,900	19,200	950	495	575	12,620	1,400	1,250	2,150	7,000	10,401	825	85,350
1999-00	4,100	22,200	850	500	650	13,500	1,300	1,280	2,400	7,650	10,241	850	91,812
2000-1[1]	4,350	23,500	750	425	600	13,550	1,330	1,150	2,100	8,100	8,882	1,100	91,954
2001-2[2]	4,200	24,250	750	425	575	13,200	1,300	1,100	1,900	8,200	7,300	1,300	91,700

[1] Preliminary. [2] Estimate. *Source: Foreign Agricultural Service, U.S. Department of Agriculture (FAS-USDA)*

COTTON

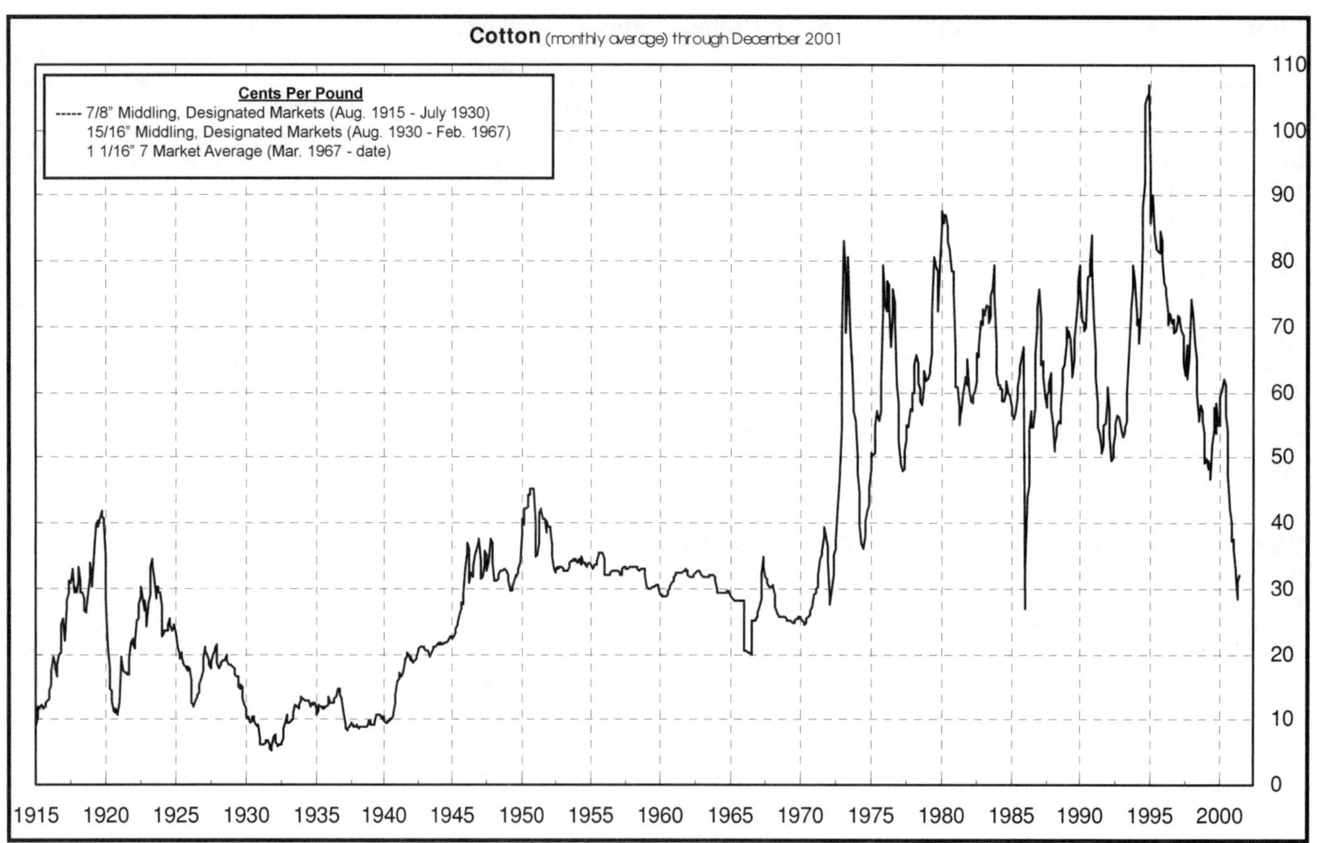

Average Spot Cotton Prices[2], C.I.F. Northern Europe   In U.S. Cents Per Pound

Crop Year Beginning Aug. 1	Argentina "C"[3] 1 1/16"	Australia M 1 3/32"	Cotlook Index A	Cotlook Index B	Egypt Giza[4] 81	Greece M 1 3/32"	Mexico[5] M 1 3/32"	Pakistan Sind/ Punjab[6]	Tanzania AR[7] Type 3	Turkey Izmir[8] 1 3/32"	U.S. Calif. ACALA SJV[9]	U.S. Memphis Terr.[10] M 1 3/32"	U.S. Orleans/ Texas [11] M 1 1/32"
1990-1	77.06	85.58	82.90	77.80	177.43	84.24	84.46	77.19	89.62	81.32	92.84	88.13	80.35
1991-2	55.08	65.97	63.05	58.50	128.10	65.90	68.19	58.14	68.90	74.66	74.47	66.35	63.41
1992-3	64.31	64.01	57.70	53.70	99.24	56.92	----	52.66	62.24	----	68.37	63.08	58.89
1993-4	80.20	72.81	70.60	67.30	88.35	58.81	----	54.42	69.83	59.80	77.55	72.80	69.78
1994-5	101.88	81.05	92.75	92.40	93.70	88.64	82.65	73.75	----	----	106.40	98.67	95.70
1995-6	82.98	93.75	85.61	81.06	----	84.95	94.94	81.86	96.20	90.38	103.49	94.71	90.37
1996-7	79.71	83.24	78.59	74.80	----	75.85	79.60	73.37	79.22	----	89.55	82.81	79.77
1997-8	69.96	77.49	72.19	70.69	----	72.03	81.70	72.93	84.04	----	85.11	78.12	74.74
1998-9	57.19	66.48	58.91	54.26	----	58.66	65.78	----	72.70	----	78.57	73.65	70.95
1999-00[1]	----	61.97	52.80	49.55	----	51.71	56.43	----	55.67	----	68.76	60.22	55.67

[1] Preliminary. [2] Generally for prompt shipment. [3] 1 1/32 prior to January 20, 1984; 1 1/16 since. [4] Dendera until 1969/70; Giza 67 1969/70 until December 1983; Giza 69/75/81 until November 1990; Giza 81 since. [5] S. Brazil Type 5, 1 1/32 prior to 1968-69; 1 1/16 until 1987/88; Brazilian Type 5/6, 1 1/16 since. [6] Punjab until 1979/80; Sind SG until June 1984; Sind/Punjab SG until January 1985; Afzal 1 until January 1986; Afzal 1 1/32 since. [7] No. 1 until 1978/79; No. 1/2 until February 1986; AR' Mwanza No. 3 until January 1992; AR' Type 3 since. [8] Izmir ST 1 White 1 1/16 RG prior to 1981/82; 1 3/32 from 1981/82 until January 1987; Izmir/Antalya ST 1 White -3/32 RG since. [9] SM 1 3/32 prior to 1975/76; SM 1 1/8 since. [10] SM 1 1/16 prior to 1981/82; Middling 1 3/32 since. [11] Middling 1 prior to 1988/89; Middling 1 1/32 since. *Source: International Cotton Advisory Committee*

Average Producer Price Index of Gray Cotton Broadwovens   Index 1982 = 100

Year	Jan.	Feb.	Mar.	Apr.	May	June	July	Aug.	Sept.	Oct.	Nov.	Dec.	Average
1992	116.9	116.8	116.7	116.7	116.8	117.5	117.3	117.3	117.2	116.9	117.1	117.2	117.0
1993	117.0	116.8	115.9	116.3	115.7	115.7	115.2	115.2	112.5	114.1	114.1	114.9	115.3
1994	109.9	110.8	115.4	115.7	114.9	114.9	115.0	117.5	117.6	118.9	117.2	118.0	116.2
1995	117.8	120.2	120.7	121.6	123.4	123.6	124.1	125.4	125.3	123.7	123.7	123.8	122.6
1996	123.6	123.7	122.0	122.0	121.1	120.7	120.7	119.9	119.7	120.4	120.0	120.4	121.2
1997	120.3	120.8	120.7	120.8	121.2	120.6	121.4	121.6	121.4	120.8	121.6	121.2	121.0
1998	122.8	122.0	122.1	121.5	121.8	120.8	120.0	119.1	118.8	118.1	117.3	117.8	120.2
1999	117.1	117.3	118.8	116.5	116.4	116.1	116.5	112.9	112.9	113.1	112.6	108.6	114.9
2000	112.1	111.1	106.9	108.2	108.6	107.7	108.3	108.8	110.1	110.2	112.3	112.3	109.7
2001[1]	112.8	113.1	113.1	112.7	112.8	112.9	113.2	112.9	112.9	112.3	111.2	111.3	112.6

[1] Preliminary. *Source: Bureau of Labor Statistics (0337-01), U.S. Department of Commerce*

Average Price of Strict Low Midd. 11/16,Cotton at Designated U.S. Mkts In Cents Per Pound (Net Weight)

Year	Aug.	Sept.	Oct.	Nov.	Dec.	Jan.	Feb.	Mar.	Apr.	May	June	July	Average
1992-3	57.56	53.49	49.47	49.98	51.85	53.72	55.38	56.45	56.17	56.37	54.38	54.35	54.10
1993-4	53.04	54.01	54.58	55.61	60.29	66.53	72.69	72.74	76.12	79.30	76.85	71.71	66.12
1994-5	70.32	71.10	67.58	72.00	81.92	88.11	91.89	104.20	104.94	105.38	106.96	93.26	88.14
1995-6	85.90	90.00	84.65	84.16	82.18	81.81	81.56	81.13	84.69	83.22	80.23	76.84	83.03
1996-7	76.15	75.24	72.21	70.12	71.98	70.53	70.53	71.12	69.09	69.30	71.03	71.83	71.59
1997-8	71.61	70.75	69.46	68.90	64.57	62.75	63.66	67.04	61.88	65.21	73.50	74.18	67.79
1998-9	71.87	71.75	67.61	64.95	59.88	56.20	55.46	58.17	57.01	55.54	53.74	49.23	60.12
1999-00	49.72	48.39	49.46	48.12	46.65	51.92	54.29	57.67	53.76	58.31	54.97	55.13	52.36
2000-1	59.33	60.62	60.54	62.16	61.04	56.66	54.10	47.22	42.19	40.02	37.38	37.48	51.56
2001-2[1]	36.05	33.22	28.42	31.23	32.21	32.13							32.21

[1] Preliminary. [2] Grade 41, leaf 4, staple 34, mike 35-36 and 43-49 , strength 23.5-26.4. *Source: Agricultural Marketing Service, U.S. Department of Agriculture (AMS-USDA)*

Average Spot Cotton, 1 3/32 , Price (SLM) at Designated U.S. Markets In Cents Per Pound (Net Weight)

Year	Aug.	Sept.	Oct.	Nov.	Dec.	Jan.	Feb.	Mar.	Apr.	May	June	July	Average
1992-3	59.08	54.99	50.96	51.41	53.37	55.24	56.86	58.30	58.03	58.23	56.24	56.22	55.74
1993-4	54.89	55.90	56.46	57.34	61.76	67.97	73.99	74.15	77.55	80.42	78.01	72.97	67.62
1994-5	71.46	72.42	68.82	73.38	83.41	89.92	94.25	106.66	107.50	107.93	109.52	96.31	90.13
1995-6	88.31	92.71	87.06	86.43	84.25	84.32	84.04	83.65	87.25	85.90	82.71	78.86	85.46
1996-7	77.97	76.92	73.90	71.74	75.75	72.53	72.86	73.60	71.23	71.38	73.25	74.04	73.76
1997-8	73.69	72.64	71.13	70.35	66.30	64.55	65.78	69.25	64.31	67.66	76.02	76.63	69.86
1998-9	73.93	73.75	69.90	67.18	62.18	58.56	58.27	61.34	60.33	58.89	56.85	52.61	62.82
1999-00	52.90	51.27	52.43	51.51	49.73	55.02	57.38	61.02	57.52	63.09	59.28	58.80	55.83
2000-1	62.60	63.62	63.13	65.08	64.73	60.18	57.18	50.08	44.94	42.54	39.88	39.96	54.49
2001-2[2]	38.88	36.11	31.55	34.03	34.82								35.08

[1] Preliminary. *Source: Agricultural Marketing Service, U.S. Department of Agriculture (AMS-USDA)*

Average Spot Prices of U.S. Cotton[1], Base Quality (SLM) at Designated Markets In Cents Per Pound

Crop Year Beginning Aug. 1	Dallas (East Tex.-Okl.)	Fresno (San Joaquin Valley)	Greenville (South-east)	Greenwood (South Delta)	Lubbock (West Texas)	Memphis (North Delta)	Phoenix Desert (South-west)	Average
1991-2	55.63	57.50	57.70	56.21	55.79	56.18	57.77	56.68
1992-3	53.78	52.84	56.73	55.03	53.53	55.03	51.61	54.10
1993-4[2]	66.22	65.04	67.46	67.04	65.92	67.04	64.16	66.13
1994-5	86.96	93.73	87.17	87.25	86.66	87.25	87.96	88.14
1995-6	80.89	87.40	83.86	83.76	80.64	83.76	80.90	83.03
1996-7	70.29	74.47	72.33	72.11	69.89	72.11	69.88	71.58
1997-8	65.93	71.79	68.60	68.36	65.88	68.36	65.63	67.79
1998-9	57.66	63.78	62.06	61.82	57.76	61.82	55.92	60.12
1999-00	50.49	56.67	53.81	53.34	50.12	53.34	48.79	52.36
2000-1[3]	51.03	52.45	52.63	52.32	50.71	52.32	49.47	51.56

[1] Prices are for mixed lots, net weight, uncompressed in warehouse. [2] 1993 prices are for mixed lots, net weight, compressed, FOB car/truck. [3] Preliminary. *Source: Agricultural Marketing Service, U.S. Department of Agriculture (AMS-USDA)*

Average Price[1] Received by Farmers for Upland Cotton in the United States In Cents Per Pound

Year	Aug.	Sept.	Oct.	Nov.	Dec.	Jan.	Feb.	Mar.	Apr.	May	June	July	Average
1992-3	52.7	52.8	53.9	52.7	54.3	53.0	53.8	56.3	55.1	54.4	53.6	53.7	53.7
1993-4	52.4	51.4	52.4	53.3	56.5	62.7	65.7	66.6	67.5	69.0	63.3	58.7	58.1
1994-5	66.8	65.9	66.2	68.5	73.3	78.7	80.2	82.6	77.6	76.2	86.5	80.1	72.0
1995-6	72.2	74.8	74.2	75.0	75.7	76.4	75.7	76.8	78.9	76.7	76.9	73.6	75.4
1996-7	71.9	71.6	71.5	69.7	69.3	67.9	68.1	69.3	67.6	68.3	67.1	67.5	69.3
1997-8	67.0	69.6	69.4	67.9	63.8	61.1	62.5	63.9	63.6	63.5	69.7	68.0	65.2
1998-9	66.0	66.2	65.9	64.6	60.6	58.1	55.6	55.1	55.6	55.0	54.6	53.8	60.2
1999-00	52.7	45.3	46.3	44.3	42.8	43.1	46.8	47.7	45.4	47.6	45.1	48.8	45.0
2000-1	51.4	50.6	55.5	58.0	57.8	52.1	48.5	41.1	42.6	40.9	39.2	38.9	49.8
2001-2[2]	36.0	38.5	34.5	29.5	32.2	29.0							33.3

[1] Weighted average by sales. [2] Preliminary. *Source: Agricultural Marketing Service, U.S. Department of Agriculture (AMS-USDA)*

COTTON

Purchases Reported by Exchanges in Designated U.S. Spot Markets[1] In Running Bales

Crop Year Beginning Aug. 1	Aug.	Sept.	Oct.	Nov.	Dec.	Jan.	Feb.	Mar.	Apr.	May	June	July	Market Total
1992-3	81,778	233,424	325,600	853,846	1,049,780	1,321,861	317,451	330,381	224,874	208,962	189,401	231,390	5,368,748
1993-4	143,237	173,896	321,119	1,071,518	1,213,655	500,246	602,766	318,008	234,331	318,244	83,083	40,699	5,020,802
1994-5	92,401	98,251	426,371	1,075,829	1,491,429	608,701	233,159	149,762	49,192	44,228	43,821	13,244	4,326,388
1995-6	60,442	38,855	73,857	209,279	381,943	765,502	153,758	241,197	225,797	73,459	59,042	31,324	2,314,455
1996-7	62,884	73,925	148,337	477,331	613,430	696,494	412,095	242,606	72,234	130,163	201,557	93,205	3,224,261
1997-8	48,504	106,503	323,400	367,010	617,470	655,432	482,625	396,946	92,072	210,906	105,139	39,647	3,445,654
1998-9	27,193	52,066	114,998	229,743	498,082	414,832	191,872	236,762	71,993	63,335	62,192	64,092	2,027,160
1999-00	83,564	95,241	195,370	320,434	517,579	744,400	294,843	189,460	89,473	129,879	49,012	33,942	2,743,197
2000-1	63,607	69,083	143,938	323,891	288,242	217,755	215,318	191,667	274,185	193,774	152,905	167,647	2,302,012
2001-2	118,000	94,697	214,785	644,860	225,869	289,778							3,175,978

[1] seven markets. *Source: Agricultural Marketing* Service, *U.S. Department of Agriculture (AMS-USDA)*

Production of Cotton (Upland and American-Pima) in the U.S. In Thousands of 480-Pound Bales

	Upland												Total
Year	Alabama	Arizona	Arkansas	California	Georgia	Louisiana	Mississippi	Missouri	North Carolina	South Carolina	Tennessee	Texas	American-Pima
1992	621	725	1,681	2,817	744	1,299	2,131	541	468	226	834	3,265	508.3
1993	469	790	1,094	2,918	733	1,105	1,550	376	429	204	545	5,095	369.3
1994	726	862	1,772	2,902	1,537	1,512	2,132	615	829	393	885	4,968	337.7
1995	492	793	1,468	2,312	1,941	1,375	1,841	513	798	376	724	4,460	367.6
1996	789	778	1,636	2,390	2,079	1,286	1,876	591	1,002	455	675	4,345	528.5
1997	550	847	1,683	2,191	1,919	986	1,821	565	930	410	662	5,140	548.0
1998	553	608	1,209	1,146	1,542	641	1,444	350	1,026	350	546	3,600	442.3
1999	625	716	1,428	1,580	1,567	901	1,731	472	816	281	595	5,050	674.3
2000[1]	543	791	1,425	2,210	1,663	911	1,711	540	1,429	379	710	3,940	389.1
2001[2]	890	730	1,825	1,850	2,200	1,030	2,470	710	1,550	410	960	4,100	628.0

[1] Preliminary. [2] Forecasted. *Source: Agricultural Statistics Board, U.S. Department of Agriculture (ASB-USDA)*

Cotton Production and Yield Estimates

	Forecast of Production (1,000 Bales of 480 Lbs.[1])						Actual	Forecasts of Yield (Lbs. Per Harvested Acre)						Actual
Year	Aug. 1	Sept. 1	Oct. 1	Nov. 1	Dec. 1	Jan. 1	Crop	Aug. 1	Sept. 1	Oct. 1	Nov. 1	Dec. 1	Jan. 1	Crop
1992	16,533	16,943	15,885	16,204	16,259	16,260	16,219	696	685	694	698	696	700	699
1993	18,545	17,867	17,014	16,297	16,284	16,176	16,134	668	645	614	594	597	607	606
1994	19,195	19,025	19,303	19,453	19,573	19,728	19,662	690	690	690	695	699	710	708
1995	21,811	20,266	18,771	18,838	18,236	17,971	17,900	663	615	574	567	551	540	537
1996	18,577	17,900	18,189	18,594	18,738	18,951	18,942	686	661	673	698	704	709	705
1997	17,783	18,418	18,410	18,848	18,819	18,977	18,793	637	658	665	673	672	686	673
1998	14,263	13,563	13,288	13,231	13,452	----	13,918	640	614	616	612	621	----	625
1999	18,304	17,535	16,430	16,531	16,875	----	16,968	649	621	588	592	604	----	607
2000	19,159	18,315	17,485	17,510	17,399	----	17,220	648	622	620	622	619	----	631
2001	20,003	19,992	20,072	20,175	20,064	----	20,084	670	679	681	685	691	----	698

[1] Net weight bales. *Source: Agricultural Statistics Board, U.S. Department of Agriculture (ASB-USDA)*

Supply and Distribution of Upland Cotton in the United States In Thousands of 480-Pound Bales

Crop Year	Area			Supply				Disappearance				
Beginning Aug. 1	Planted (1,000 Acres)	Harvested (1,000 Acres)	Yield Lbs./Acre	Beginning Stocks[3]	Production[4]	Imports	Total	Mill Use	Exports	Total	Ending Stocks	Farm Price5 Cents/Lb.
1992-3	12,977	10,863	694	3,583	15,710	1	19,294	10,190	4,869	15,059	4,456	53.7
1993-4	13,248	12,594	601	4,456	15,764	6	20,226	10,346	6,555	16,901	3,303	58.4
1994-5	13,552	13,156	705	3,303	19,324	18	22,645	11,109	8,978	20,087	2,588	72.0
1995-6	16,717	15,796	533	2,588	17,532	400	20,520	10,538	7,375	17,913	2,543	75.4
1996-7	14,376	12,612	701	2,543	18,413	403	21,359	11,020	6,399	17,419	3,920	69.3
1997-8	13,648	13,157	666	3,920	18,245	13	22,178	11,234	7,060	18,294	3,822	65.2
1998-9	13,064	10,449	619	3,822	13,476	431	17,729	10,254	4,056	14,310	3,836	60.2
1999-00	14,584	13,138	595	3,836	16,294	53	20,183	10,104	6,303	16,407	3,672	45.0
2000-1[1]	15,347	12,884	626	3,672	16,799	3	20,474	8,760	6,326	15,086	5,881	49.8
2001-2[2]	15,959	13,899	675	3,881	19,557	0	25,438	7,990	8,940	16,930	8,511	

[1] Preliminary. [2] Estimate. [3] Excludes preseason ginnings (adjusted to 480-lb. bale net weight basis). [4] Includes preseason ginnings. [5] Marketing year average price. [6] Average of 5 cheapest types of SLM 1 3/32 staple length cotton offered on the European market. *Source: Economic Research Service, U.S. Department of Agriculture (ERS-USDA)*

Average Open Interest of No. 2 Cotton Futures in New York In Contracts

Year	Jan.	Feb.	Mar.	Apr.	May	June	July	Aug.	Sept.	Oct.	Nov.	Dec.
1992	38,097	40,095	38,592	36,228	37,839	36,861	35,891	42,241	46,168	46,577	40,425	38,487
1993	41,946	38,657	38,576	33,641	33,012	34,057	32,118	33,872	37,393	36,479	38,567	45,975
1994	54,424	55,558	53,724	54,670	52,830	51,001	52,357	50,597	50,955	51,561	53,563	59,065
1995	71,353	75,100	79,090	71,488	71,714	68,159	65,656	69,653	69,528	65,768	38,475	35,996
1996	58,001	60,231	57,542	61,795	64,555	62,342	61,921	60,182	58,168	58,415	57,397	47,652
1997	59,909	65,392	72,130	76,779	73,464	70,296	73,893	79,309	87,134	92,430	89,150	87,120
1998	89,358	86,739	81,236	85,505	84,562	90,178	81,652	78,571	85,378	88,970	88,917	77,873
1999	79,598	75,794	62,857	60,384	61,470	66,789	68,975	65,690	63,976	60,369	63,746	61,474
2000	63,987	67,720	69,788	56,038	54,058	48,024	53,621	63,069	73,735	67,767	65,017	62,931
2001	71,849	73,383	71,389	70,407	66,680	64,032	61,183	65,257	65,496	59,777	56,896	58,156

Source: New York Board of Trade (NYBOT)

Volume of Trading of No. 2 Cotton Futures in New York In Contracts

Year	Jan.	Feb.	Mar.	Apr.	May	June	July	Aug.	Sept.	Oct.	Nov.	Dec.	Total
1992	134,531	134,184	149,711	167,778	173,128	153,194	105,534	142,323	144,844	129,680	161,194	105,157	1,701,258
1993	171,180	135,400	136,965	135,300	105,920	128,985	130,886	122,280	110,989	107,571	178,350	139,344	1,603,027
1994	210,011	207,421	210,363	252,614	179,591	208,945	161,688	128,879	140,574	179,604	205,936	203,021	2,289,998
1995	223,073	290,600	286,098	219,187	214,052	185,276	183,171	199,050	191,534	196,676	195,601	141,116	2,525,434
1996	215,882	196,225	147,393	251,786	236,684	264,047	131,183	177,430	166,629	229,305	229,281	128,010	2,373,855
1997	201,610	253,475	302,609	258,851	175,227	314,406	234,718	202,008	212,966	216,771	266,800	197,839	2,837,280
1998	221,308	289,222	310,075	362,688	218,595	407,922	226,138	230,752	195,690	303,849	272,775	161,816	3,200,830
1999	179,049	244,300	209,127	250,622	157,552	260,649	187,631	178,236	175,282	193,552	298,531	120,120	2,454,651
2000	270,792	279,566	248,017	220,222	232,947	272,023	147,878	175,707	154,735	172,875	242,013	180,982	2,597,757
2001	267,930	270,876	237,356	215,903	175,808	214,513	132,065	118,685	98,947	152,702	258,847	116,033	2,259,665

Source: New York Board of Trade (NYBOT)

Daily Rate of Upland Cotton Mill Consumption[2] on Cotton-System Spinning Spindles in the U.S.
In Thousands of Running Bales

Crop Year Beginning Aug. 1	Aug.	Sept.	Oct.	Nov.	Dec.	Jan.	Feb.	Mar.	Apr.	May	June	July	Average
1992-3	38.5	37.8	39.7	37.6	31.5	39.1	39.5	38.8	38.7	39.4	37.8	34.5	37.8
1993-4	39.8	38.4	39.4	36.4	31.4	36.9	37.9	39.0	39.3	39.5	40.4	40.3	38.2
1994-5	41.0	41.4	41.1	41.8	41.7	42.6	42.1	42.4	41.1	40.2	39.2	37.2	41.0
1995-6	38.8	39.4	37.6	38.1	37.9	37.5	38.1	39.5	39.4	39.6	40.5	39.8	38.9
1996-7	40.5	40.7	40.5	41.5	41.1	41.3	40.4	39.4	41.0	41.0	40.9	42.5	40.9
1997-8	40.7	42.4	42.0	42.4	43.9	41.8	41.7	41.1	40.5	40.8	40.0	41.5	41.6
1998-9	39.3	38.7	39.9	37.4	37.5	38.6	38.2	37.9	37.8	37.5	37.5	36.9	38.1
1999-00	36.5	36.9	37.7	38.1	38.1	36.8	37.5	37.6	37.5	37.0	38.1	36.5	37.4
2000-1	36.4	35.6	34.5	33.0	35.6	32.6	31.5	31.8	30.5	29.6	28.2	28.6	32.3
2001-2[1]	28.8	28.5	27.4	26.9	27.5	27.0							27.7

[1] Preliminary. [2] Not seasonally adjusted. *Source: Bureau of the Census: U.S. Department of Commerce*

Consumption of American and Foreign Cotton in the United States
In Thousands of Running Bales

Year	Aug.	Sept.	Oct.	Nov.	Dec.	Jan.	Feb.	Mar.	Apr.	May	June	July	Total
1992-3	776	950	799	756	792	788	796	976	778	792	951	694	9,846
1993-4	801	965	792	731	790	743	785	999	806	830	1,032	744	10,019
1994-5	870	1,070	873	838	897	858	878	1,097	847	842	999	681	10,750
1995-6	829	1,020	798	761	801	744	787	1,029	810	824	1,040	731	10,216
1996-7	847	1,028	829	816	858	810	819	1,014	834	840	1,044	781	10,519
1997-8	868	1,100	872	855	951	848	861	1,068	839	854	1,017	770	10,902
1998-9	835	1,013	834	758	796	979	795	983	777	793	970	678	10,210
1999-00	762	949	793	757	801	736	769	966	772	771	990	670	9,735
2000-1	766	929	741	663	749	661	657	837	641	628	727	510	8,510
2001-2[1]	616	751	600	521	563	546							7,193

[1] Preliminary. *Source: Bureau of the Census, U.S. Department of Commerce*

Exports of All Cotton[2] from the United States
In Thousands of Running Bales

Year	Aug.	Sept.	Oct.	Nov.	Dec.	Jan.	Feb.	Mar.	Apr.	May	June	July	Total
1991-2	219	126	239	396	674	961	725	791	787	535	430	466	6,349
1992-3	252	263	277	342	528	501	502	533	639	401	317	395	4,950
1993-4	287	248	345	405	571	738	512	743	761	854	770	626	6,860
1994-5	531	333	341	710	1,098	1,115	1,383	1,392	1,104	684	410	300	9,402
1995-6	315	245	452	733	1,230	1,262	1,295	777	576	343	263	183	7,675
1996-7	257	171	277	573	899	666	728	848	711	631	604	501	6,866
1997-8	458	299	400	581	774	734	777	888	669	477	574	571	7,202
1998-9	402	280	265	795	1,027	156	182	221	169	256	260	330	4,344
1999-00	254	146	167	455	654	658	736	978	708	659	508	479	6,402
2000-1[1]	430	336	382	435	541	564	614	720	568	692	NA	NA	6,338

[1] Preliminary. *Source: Foreign Agricultural Service, U.S. Department of Agriculture (FAS-USDA)*

U.S. Exports of American Cotton to Countries of Destination
In Thousands of 480-Pound Bales

Crop Year Beginning Aug. 1	Canada	China	Hong Kong	Indo-nesia	Italy	Japan	Rep. of Korea	Mexico	Philip-pines	Taiwan	Thai-land	United Kingdom	Total
1990-1	191	1,233	306	561	425	1,437	1,168	202	132	358	317	36	7,793
1991-2	181	792	335	739	240	1,107	1,024	213	181	380	368	60	6,646
1992-3	154	1	100	429	144	839	1,031	557	117	279	150	65	5,201
1993-4	165	1,183	314	653	96	790	976	653	168	356	277	65	6,862
1994-5	253	2,257	347	925	83	1,061	951	558	173	352	441	89	9,402
1995-6	294	1,847	223	794	115	940	769	618	144	255	331	85	7,675
1996-7	253	1,756	129	594	46	630	568	733	84	255	197	66	6,865
1997-8	288	737	151	464	85	637	712	1,447	53	376	220	13	7,202
1998-9[1]	281	71	245	241	29	421	382	1,355	58	251	82	6	4,328
1999-00[2]	245	146	318	573	61	424	307	1,503	71	474	256	4	6,402

[1] Preliminary. [2] Estimate. *Source: Foreign Agricultural Service, U.S. Department of Agriculture (FAS-USDA)*

Cotton[1] Government Loan Program in the United States

Crop Year Beginning Aug. 1	Support Price	Target Price	Put Under Support	% of Production	Acquired	Owned July 31	Crop Year Beginning Aug. 1	Support Price	Target Price	Put Under Support	% of Production	Acquired	Owned July 31
	-- Cents Per Lb. --		Ths Bales		----- Ths. Bales -----			-- Cents Per Lb. --		Ths Bales		----- Ths. Bales -----	
1991-2	50.77	72.9	6,312	36.6	8	[3]	1996-7	51.92	NA	3,340	18.1	0	0
1992-3	52.35	72.9	8,302	52.9	10	8	1997-8	51.92	NA	4,281	23.5	0	0
1993-4	52.35	72.9	7,721	49.0	3	14	1998-9	51.92	NA	4,724	36.8	31	3
1994-5	50.00	72.9	4,716	24.4	[3]	[3]	1999-00	51.92	NA	8,721	54.9	2	1
1995-6	51.92	72.9	3,478	19.8	0	0	2000-01[2]	51.92	NA				

[1] Upland. [2] Preliminary. [3] Less than 500 bales. NA = Not applicable. *Source: Economic Research Service, U.S. Department of Agriculture (ERS-USDA)*

Production of Cotton Cloth[1] in the United States In Millions of Square Yards

Year	First Quarter	Second Quarter	Third Quarter	Fourth Quarter	Total Year	Year	First Quarter	Second Quarter	Third Quarter	Fourth Quarter	Total Year
1992	1,154	1,172	1,130	1,144	4,600	1997	1,211	1,276	1,283	1,309	5,078
1993	1,150	1,144	1,071	1,039	4,403	1998	1,226	1,167	1,218	1,142	4,753
1994	1,073	1,125	1,131	1,143	4,473	1999	1,170	1,164	1,078	1,039	4,451
1995	1,169	1,137	1,090	1,093	4,488	2000	1,075	1,129	1,111	1,079	4,395
1996	1,182	1,230	1,198	1,187	4,796	2001[2]	1,070	998	897		3,953

[1] Cotton broadwoven goods over 12 inches in width. [2] Preliminary. *Source: Bureau of Census, U.S. Department of Commerce*

Cotton Ginnings[1] in the United States To: In Thousands of Running Bales

Crop Year	Aug. 1	Sept. 1	Sept. 15	Oct. 1	Oct. 15	Nov. 1	Nov. 15	Dec. 1	Dec. 15	Jan. 1	Jan. 15	Feb. 1	Total Crop
1992-3	14	446	740	1,664	4,046	7,584	10,296	12,597	14,083	14,944	15,311	15,527	15,786
1993-4	9	435	748	1,846	4,471	7,975	10,952	13,244	14,695	15,321	15,517	15,590	15,675
1994-5	113	680	943	2,324	5,002	8,878	12,479	15,587	17,465	18,438	18,842	19,028	19,127
1995-6	17	433	898	2,455	4,795	8,430	11,262	14,199	16,101	17,011	17,292	17,416	17,469
1996-7	48	342	637	2,146	4,780	8,876	11,906	14,623	16,528	17,681	18,101	18,308	18,439
1997-8	2	359	683	1,210	3,752	7,930	11,601	14,735	16,662	17,613	18,013	18,170	18,301
1998-9	146	523	739	2,056	4,265	7,359	9,366	11,310	12,558	13,160	13,376	13,458	13,534
1999-00	81	561	1,018	2,690	4,885	8,263	11,006	13,379	14,992	15,965	16,322	16,468	16,528
2000-1	245	842	1,454	3,264	5,930	9,221	11,546	13,657	15,364	16,097	16,518	16,648	16,742
2001-2[2]	99	609	802	2,007	4,562	8,748	12,522	15,498	17,727	18,672	19,242	19,587	

[1] Excluding linters. [2] Preliminary. *Source: National Agricultural Statistics Service, U.S. Department of Agriculture (NASS-USDA)*

Fiber Prices in the United States In Cents Per Pound

Year		Cotton[1] Actual	Cotton[1] Raw[5] Equivalent	Rayon[2] Actual	Rayon[2] Raw[5] Equivalent	Polyester[3] Actual	Polyester[3] Raw[5] Equivalent	Price Ratios[4] in Percent Cotton/Rayon	Price Ratios[4] in Percent Cotton/Polyester
1993		62.43	69.37	111.42	116.06	72.50	75.52	.60	.92
1994		78.69	87.43	103.00	107.29	74.92	78.04	.82	1.12
1995		100.76	111.95	118.67	123.61	88.83	92.53	.91	1.21
1996		86.24	95.83	118.00	122.92	81.10	84.48	.78	1.14
1997		76.29	84.77	115.00	119.79	69.50	72.40	.71	1.17
1998		74.21	82.45	110.25	114.84	62.50	65.11	.72	1.29
1999		61.45	68.28	98.92	103.04	51.67	53.82	.66	1.27
2000		64.06	71.17	97.58	101.65	57.08	59.46	.70	1.19
2001[6]		47.08	52.32	98.50	102.61	60.42	62.93	.52	.83
	Jan.	64.27	71.41	99.00	103.13	60.00	62.50	.69	1.14
	Feb.	61.25	68.06	99.00	103.13	60.00	62.50	.66	1.09
	Mar.	54.34	60.38	99.00	103.13	60.00	62.50	.59	.97
	Apr.	49.06	54.51	99.00	103.13	62.00	64.58	.67	.84
	May	47.92	53.24	99.00	103.13	62.00	64.58	.52	.82
	June	45.06	50.07	99.00	103.13	62.00	64.58	.49	.78
	July	44.83	49.81	99.00	103.13	62.00	64.58	.48	.77
	Aug.	43.83	48.70	99.00	103.13	62.00	64.58	.47	.75
	Sept.	40.43	44.92	98.00	102.08	60.00	62.50	.44	.72
	Oct.	36.26	40.29	98.00	102.08	59.00	61.46	.40	.66
	Nov.	37.44	41.60	97.00	101.04	58.00	60.42	.41	.69
	Dec.	40.32	44.80	97.00	101.04	58.00	60.42	.44	.74

[1] SLM-1 1/16 at group B Mill points, net weight. [2] 1.5 and 3.0 denier, regular rayon staples. [3] Reported average market price for 1.5 denier polyester staple for cotton blending. [4] Raw fiber equivalent. [5] Actual prices converted to estimated raw fiber equivalent as follows: cotton, divided by 0.90, rayon and polyester, divided by 0.96. [6] Preliminary. *Source: Economic Research Service, U.S. Department of Agriculture (ERS-USDA)*

Cottonseed and Products

Cottonseed production is directly related to the amount of cotton produce. When the cotton is harvested, it is ginned and the cottonseed is removed from the cotton fiber. The more cotton that is harvested the more cottonseed that is produced. The cotton seed is crushed too produce cottonseed meal and cottonseed oil. Cottonseed meal is used as a livestock ingredient while cottonseed oil is used in cooking. The largest cotton producers are the U.S., China and India.

The U.S. Department of Agriculture in December 2001 estimated U.S. cottonseed production at 7.53 million short tons, an increase of 17 percent from the 2000/01 season production of 6.44 million tons. For 1999/00, U.S. cottonseed production was 6.35 million tons. The U.S.D.A. estimate for 2001/02 was based on the three year average of cotton lint to seed ratio. Bales of cotton ginned in the U.S. in 2000 were 16.74 million while in 1999 they were 16.53 million.

U.S. cotton acreage in 2001/02 (August-September) was 16.19 million acres, an increase of 4 percent from 2000/01. Planted acreage in 2000/01 was up 4 percent from 1999/00. Harvested acreage in 2001/02 was 13.94 million. Cotton production was estimated at 20.06 million bales, up 17 percent from the previous year. The largest producing states for cotton and therefore cottonseed were Texas, Mississippi, California, Georgia, Arizona and North Carolina.

In the 2000/01 season, U.S. cottonseed stocks were 274,000 tons. With production of 6.44 million tons, the cottonseed supply was 7.01 million tons. Of the total, 2.85 million tons were crushed and some 180,000 tons were exported. Total use of cottonseed in 2000/01 was estimated at 6.73 million tons. The amount of cottonseed oil produced in 2000/01 was 910 million pounds, down 3 percent from the previous year. Cottonseed meal production was 1.31 million tons, down 8 percent from the year before.

World Production of Cottonseed In Thousands of Metric Ton

Crop Year	Argentina	Australia	Brazil	China	Egypt	Greece	India	Mexico	Pakistan	Turkey	United States	Former USSR	World Total
1992-3	275	528	800	8,024	571	410	4,740	50	3,080	905	5,652	3,557	31,914
1993-4	392	466	910	6,655	649	454	4,183	42	2,735	900	5,754	3,600	29,850
1994-5	638	474	980	7,727	411	574	4,709	187	2,959	930	6,898	3,380	33,129
1995-6	748	595	690	8,487	384	725	5,339	344	3,604	1,288	6,213	3,150	35,290
1996-7	564	859	568	7,481	560	540	5,890	421	3,230	1,259	6,480	2,561	34,490
1997-8	542	941	763	8,193	563	590	5,150	329	3,180	1,310	6,291	2,785	34,843
1998-9	337	1,012	924	8,012	379	665	5,420	363	2,990	1,284	4,867	2,577	32,818
1999-00[1]	241	983	1,144	6,817	375	730	5,500	220	3,500	1,360	5,764	2,950	33,500
2000-1[2]	310	1,045	1,200	6,300	310	640	5,300	110	3,100	1,340	6,380	2,900	32,860

[1] Preliminary. [2] Estimate. *Source: The Oil World*

Salient Statistics of Cottonseed in the United States In Thousands of Short Tons

Crop Year Beginning Aug. 1	Supply: Stocks	Supply: Production	Supply: Total Supply	Disappearance: Crush	Disappearance: Exports	Disappearance: Other	Disappearance: Total Disappearance	Farm Price $/Ton	Value of Production Mil. $	Products Produced: Oil Million Lbs.	Products Produced: Meal Thousand Sh. Tons
	In Thousands of Short Tons										
1993-4	365	6,343	6,708	3,470	157	2,649	6,276	113	714.4	1,119	1,563
1994-5	432	7,604	8,036	3,947	232	3,306	7,485	101	771.3	1,312	1,830
1995-6	551	6,849	7,399	3,882	114	2,886	6,882	106	731.0	1,229	1,748
1996-7	517	7,144	7,681	3,860	116	3,182	7,158	126	914.6	1,310	1,807
1997-8	523	6,935	7,553	3,885	149	2,957	6,990	121	835.4	1,224	1,769
1998-9	563	5,365	6,135	2,719	68	2,955	5,742	129	687.2	832	1,232
1999-00	393	6,354	7,055	3,079	198	3,505	6,781	89	565.5	939	1,390
2000-1[1]	274	6,436	7,084	2,674	235	3,751	6,660	105	656.4	818	1,291
2001-2[2]	424	7,533	8,130	3,000	300	4,250	7,550		651.3	945	1,350

[1] Preliminary. [2] Estimate. *Source: Economic Research Service, U.S. Department of Agriculture (ERS-USDA)*

Average Wholesale Price of Cottonseed Meal (41% Solvent)[2] in Memphis In Dollars Per Short Ton

Year	Jan.	Feb.	Mar.	Apr.	May	June	July	Aug.	Sept.	Oct.	Nov.	Dec.	Average
1993	164.40	149.40	153.50	149.00	143.10	153.00	170.30	178.50	193.75	173.10	181.00	180.00	165.75
1994	170.30	173.10	174.00	166.25	157.75	154.10	152.50	144.50	145.00	134.40	120.50	114.20	150.55
1995	106.75	97.50	100.30	98.10	92.75	108.75	116.90	116.50	137.60	153.25	165.00	185.80	123.27
1996	208.80	202.80	195.60	220.00	191.25	192.20	201.56	193.10	193.10	183.25	196.60	224.50	200.23
1997	207.20	183.75	189.10	189.10	193.75	190.30	170.75	176.25	192.00	189.10	189.10	190.50	188.41
1998	153.10	139.10	128.70	116.25	105.00	129.40	146.65	130.30	115.60	106.50	107.90	119.75	124.85
1999	110.60	101.25	106.90	110.90	108.75	114.50	115.00	100.65	111.92	111.83	112.00	124.20	110.71
2000	126.88	130.50	129.38	125.00	123.25	130.63	131.88	130.50	153.12	150.00	141.88	160.83	136.15
2001[1]	184.00	148.75	138.13	140.00	137.50	126.88	129.69	130.63	131.25	131.25	128.10	134.20	138.37

[1] Preliminary. *Source: Economic Research Service, U.S. Department of Agriculture (ERS-USDA)*

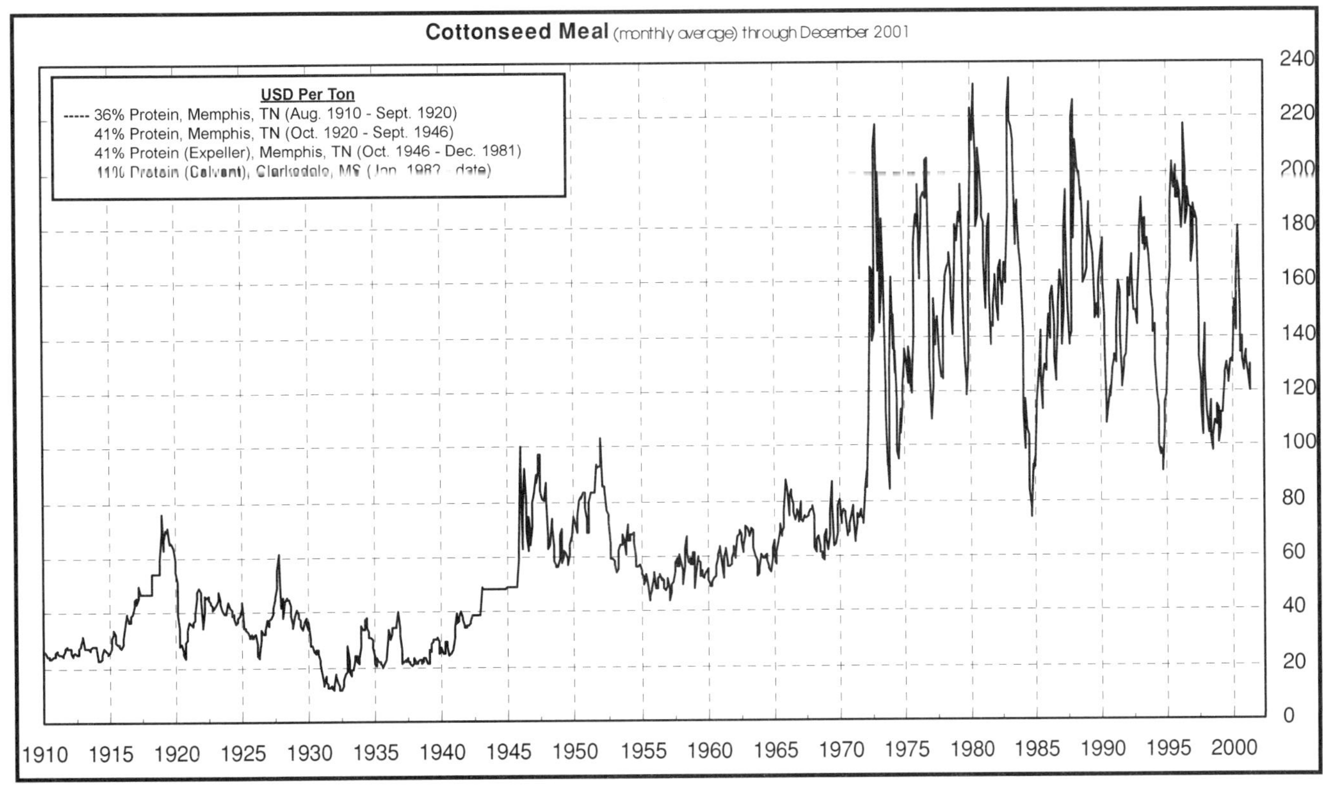

Supply and Distribution of Cottonseed Oil in the United States In Millions of Pounds

Crop Year Beginning Oct. 1	Supply: Stocks	Supply: Production	Supply: Imports	Supply: Total Supply	Disappearance: Domestic	Disappearance: Exports	Disappearance: Total	Per Capita Cunsump. of Salad & Cook Oils - In Lbs. -	Utilization Food Uses: Short-ening	Utilization Food Uses: Salad & Cooking Oils	Utilization Food Uses: Total	Prices: U.S.[3] (Crude) $/Met. Ton	Prices: Rott[4] (Cif) $/Met. Ton
1995-6	82	1,229	.3	1,311	996	221	1,217	27	218	235	497	575	613
1996-7	94	1,216	.3	1,310	1,012	232	1,244	26	271	265	556	564	590
1997-8	66	1,224	.1	1,291	1,004	208	1,212	29	208	184	414	663	693
1998-9	79	832	48.2	958	772	111	882	28	170	262	457	633	632
1999-00	76	939	8.1	1,023	833	141	974	29	166	251	525	474	496
2000-1[1]	49	818		867	644	131	775	35	161	185	384	352	428
2001-2[2]	92	945	5.0	1,042	818	135	953					347	411

[1] Preliminary. [2] Estimate. [3] Valley Points FOB; Tank Cars. [4] Rotterdam; US, PBSY, fob gulf. W = Withheld proprietary data.
Source: Economic Research Service, U.S. Department of Agriculture (ERS-USDA)

Consumption of Crude Cottonseed Oil in Refining in the United States In Millions of Pounds

Year	Oct.	Nov.	Dec.	Jan.	Feb.	Mar.	Apr.	May	June	July	Aug.	Sept.	Total
1995-6	76.1	91.8	89.7	94.5	87.2	92.2	83.4	77.3	55.5	56.2	64.3	54.4	922.5
1996-7	67.2	85.1	85.1	88.7	83.3	80.8	77.4	79.2	58.4	55.3	59.0	39.2	858.7
1997-8	73.1	73.1	77.2	85.0	75.7	70.2	72.1	57.1	51.9	54.9	57.5	30.1	778.1
1998-9	52.9	49.6	50.2	46.6	48.9	50.7	36.4	28.3	28.4	30.5	46.2	43.5	512.3
1999-00	51.9	57.3	61.5	60.0	58.1	67.8	62.0	52.7	43.2	22.7	45.8	37.2	620.1
2000-1	56.9	53.7	56.7	67.4	61.6	59.5	38.1	46.0	51.4	42.8	49.6	29.8	613.6
2001-2[1]	48.5	63.9	61.6										696.0

[1] Preliminary. *Source: U.S. Bureau of Census, U.S. Department of Commerce*

Exports of Cottonseed Oil (Crude and Refined) from the United States In Thousands of Pounds

Year	Jan.	Feb.	Mar.	Apr.	May	June	July	Aug.	Sept.	Oct.	Nov.	Dec.	Total
1995	18,808	43,454	48,471	34,500	28,775	22,692	18,490	11,973	13,741	9,896	30,268	13,223	294,291
1996	26,407	8,103	38,597	24,628	16,052	14,135	7,827	21,197	10,903	12,526	10,345	13,145	203,865
1997	25,722	26,835	22,647	22,230	30,319	9,535	25,207	24,717	8,919	15,351	24,217	8,164	243,863
1998	24,003	15,077	16,150	22,874	20,791	22,994	15,348	14,392	8,818	11,056	7,610	11,447	190,560
1999	11,541	10,235	7,780	11,387	6,328	7,161	8,725	8,111	9,275	11,060	12,313	23,025	126,941
2000	10,628	9,447	13,181	8,214	7,446	7,550	11,546	10,604	16,467	13,300	11,653	9,089	129,125
2001[1]	14,684	6,638	7,237	10,465	12,787	7,459	10,325	20,908	6,471	19,841			140,178

[1] Preliminary. *Source: Economic Research Service, U.S. Department of Agriculture (ERS-USDA)*

COTTONSEED AND PRODUCTS

Cottonseed Crushed (Consumption) in the United States In Thousands of Short Tons

Year	Aug.	Sept.	Oct.	Nov.	Dec.	Jan.	Feb.	Mar.	Apr.	May	June	July	Total
1993-4	182.9	162.6	300.4	391.4	375.0	391.0	335.2	358.6	265.7	257.7	239.4	210.2	3,470
1994-5	192.1	195.5	343.9	386.2	397.5	404.6	360.5	391.0	345.4	304.0	316.5	310.0	3,947
1995-6	264.4	245.5	337.1	386.7	362.4	402.3	373.5	381.4	349.6	325.2	223.7	209.2	3,861
1996-7	229.2	225.0	331.7	355.1	352.6	381.0	362.8	362.2	334.4	351.3	280.8	294.0	3,860
1997-8	244.4	178.6	329.7	374.5	371.3	428.4	352.3	370.8	359.1	309.1	278.8	277.6	3,875
1998-9	246.0	174.9	272.7	254.3	262.7	282.2	259.5	280.2	205.5	172.0	159.9	149.2	2,719
1999-00	166.8	230.7	281.6	302.5	296.4	297.7	300.1	301.8	265.5	250.8	227.7	156.9	3,079
2000-1	170.5	141.6	264.1	253.4	242.0	284.0	257.5	250.7	174.7	217.1	230.7	188.0	2,674
2001-2[1]	175.6	136.4	256.2	275.8	261.9	281.3							2,774

[1] Preliminary. *Source: Economic Research Service, U.S. Department of Agriculture* (ERS-USDA)

Production of Cottonseed Cake and Meal in the United States In Thousands of Short Tons

Year	Aug.	Sept.	Oct.	Nov.	Dec.	Jan.	Feb.	Mar.	Apr.	May	June	July	Total
1993-4	76.7	71.5	130.1	172.2	166.6	161.8	151.8	164.0	119.6	116.1	106.9	93.4	1,531
1994-5	90.6	89.4	154.2	171.5	176.9	184.1	162.2	174.3	154.2	137.4	143.9	137.2	1,776
1995-6	120.1	113.6	159.9	178.2	161.0	183.8	169.8	168.3	158.7	147.1	102.4	102.7	1,766
1996-7	100.9	99.1	146.1	161.5	158.2	174.5	164.6	162.1	152.2	160.7	128.6	123.2	1,732
1997-8	128.2	92.1	147.8	168.7	178.2	194.4	158.5	170.4	162.3	141.8	128.8	124.0	1,795
1998-9	114.7	77.1	118.7	115.9	122.5	130.2	114.8	127.2	90.6	75.6	75.6	71.0	1,234
1999-00	82.1	107.5	132.1	140.8	138.3	135.3	137.7	140.2	120.0	109.4	109.3	79.5	1,432
2000-1	74.1	79.3	134.1	121.4	117.1	136.0	118.9	120.3	83.4	101.0	114.3	89.7	1,290
2001-2[1]	83.9	70.8	118.5	126.5	118.2	129.0							1,294

[1] Preliminary. *Source: Bureau of Census, U.S. Department of Commerce*

Production of Crude Cottonseed Oil[2] in the United States In Millions of Pounds

Year	Aug.	Sept.	Oct.	Nov.	Dec.	Jan.	Feb.	Mar.	Apr.	May	June	July	Total
1993-4	59.1	51.7	93.5	122.2	117.5	124.7	99.9	119.6	85.3	85.2	78.4	69.8	1,107
1994-5	61.7	61.0	109.8	122.6	125.6	133.4	115.6	125.2	110.4	97.7	102.4	96.6	1,262
1995-6	87.8	84.3	105.2	121.6	111.6	130.9	121.4	125.6	110.4	101.9	73.3	76.7	1,251
1996-7	70.3	69.4	98.9	114.8	115.9	123.9	114.8	114.7	103.7	109.8	86.9	85.9	1,209
1997-8	80.6	66.0	97.8	120.3	119.6	136.4	111.1	115.5	112.7	96.1	87.3	88.8	1,232
1998-9	77.8	59.6	78.3	80.0	80.6	84.0	80.2	86.7	64.4	53.4	52.4	45.9	843
1999-00	56.1	69.6	88.3	95.4	94.2	93.4	93.2	93.8	82.6	75.7	70.2	49.2	962
2000-1	55.1	52.1	84.3	76.8	73.5	85.9	78.4	76.4	53.9	66.8	66.6	55.7	826
2001-2[1]	57.5	42.2	79.4	86.2	81.7	87.5							869

[1] Preliminary. [2] Not seasonally adjusted. *Source: Bureau of Census, U.S. Department of Commerce*

Production of Refined Cottonseed Oil in the United States In Millions of Pounds

Year	Aug.	Sept.	Oct.	Nov.	Dec.	Jan.	Feb.	Mar.	Apr.	May	June	July	Total
1993-4	65.1	54.6	79.4	109.1	100.6	107.2	93.4	107.8	66.9	71.6	70.0	72.2	998
1994-5	86.3	62.9	80.0	94.4	106.2	104.2	94.4	92.6	84.2	70.1	70.7	72.6	1,019
1995-6	80.5	69.0	74.0	89.5	86.9	91.7	84.6	89.8	81.7	75.0	53.8	54.5	931
1996-7	62.4	53.0	64.9	82.8	82.2	85.9	80.7	78.1	75.2	76.9	56.4	53.6	852
1997-8	57.4	38.1	48.3	71.0	74.8	82.2	73.1	68.2	69.8	55.2	50.3	53.0	741
1998-9	55.8	29.1	51.1	47.9	48.5	45.4	47.3	49.0	35.2	27.4	27.5	29.7	494
1999-00	44.8	42.4	50.4	55.6	59.5	58.3	56.7	65.8	60.0	51.0	41.9	22.0	608
2000-1	44.4	36.2	55.1	52.2	54.9	65.7	59.8	57.8	36.9	44.8	50.0	41.5	599
2001-2[1]	49.4	29.6	48.2	63.6	61.3								605

[1] Preliminary. *Source: Bureau of the Census, U.S. Department of Commerce*

Stocks of Cottonseed Oil (Crude and Refined) in the U.S., at End of Month In Millions of Pounds

Year	Aug.	Sept.	Oct.	Nov.	Dec.	Jan.	Feb.	Mar.	Apr.	May	June	July
1993-4	85.8	54.6	79.4	109.1	100.6	107.2	93.4	107.8	66.9	71.6	70.0	72.1
1994-5	112.4	105.6	103.5	117.0	114.7	122.2	150.5	129.9	120.8	95.7	96.9	92.2
1995-6	87.8	82.1	82.6	89.3	94.8	118.2	147.2	151.2	155.6	143.3	128.1	125.4
1996-7	101.2	94.1	97.5	102.5	106.0	120.9	133.7	137.5	131.7	116.1	103.4	85.9
1997-8	78.0	66.4	68.6	86.4	105.3	133.8	141.2	140.7	159.8	150.4	130.9	118.8
1998-9	97.3	78.6	89.1	110.0	85.5	109.5	113.3	125.3	126.0	112.0	100.7	83.7
1999-00	107.8	76.0	81.1	88.7	85.1	84.5	79.6	115.2	127.4	127.5	103.0	81.3
2000-1	59.9	49.0	66.5	75.2	95.0	109.5	134.4	139.9	133.5	123.5	126.8	114.0
2001-2[1]	97.7	91.8	113.8	112.9	111.5							

[1] Preliminary. *Source: Bureau of Census, U.S. Department of Commerce*

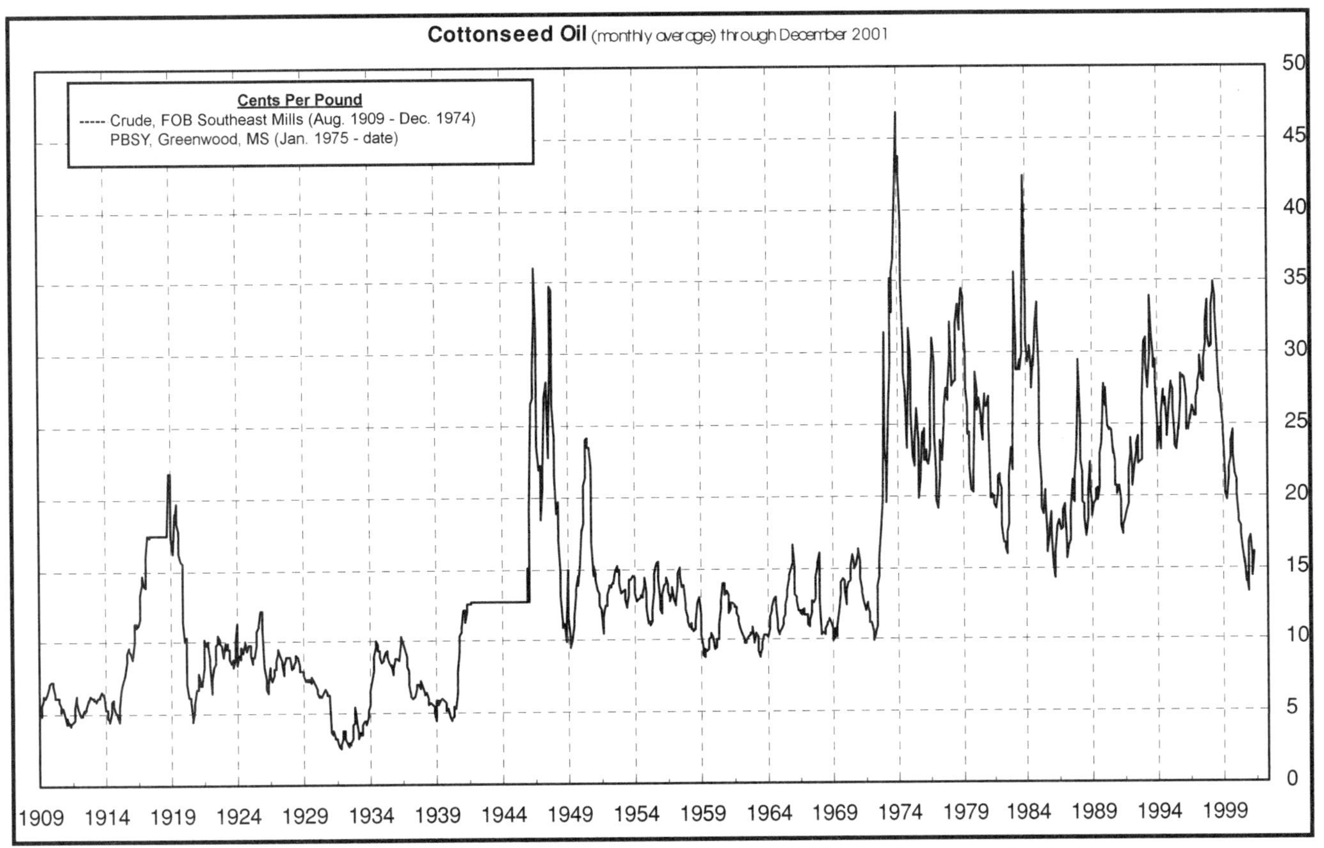

Average Price of Crude Cottonseed Oil, PBSY, Greenwood, MS.[1] in Tank Cars In Cents Per Pound

Year	Jan.	Feb.	Mar.	Apr.	May	June	July	Aug.	Sept.	Oct.	Nov.	Dec.	Average
1992	18.50	18.13	19.25	19.38	21.38	22.58	24.45	21.86	21.04	22.17	22.96	23.91	21.30
1993	24.09	22.03	22.24	22.55	22.70	26.76	30.74	30.45	28.98	24.79	26.69	30.39	26.03
1994	33.16	29.96	29.60	29.06	29.66	27.55	24.20	23.71	24.51	23.64	24.85	25.50	27.12
1995	28.70	29.95	27.14	27.61	27.51	30.04	30.63	30.26	28.61	27.61	26.27	26.10	26.36
1996	24.45	24.35	24.25	26.77	28.46	27.94	28.25	27.81	26.13	24.55	24.28	24.29	25.96
1997	25.21	25.44	26.18	25.10	25.19	25.01	26.53	27.11	28.03	28.47	29.11	26.78	26.51
1998	27.69	29.37	30.46	32.47	33.13	30.22	29.40	30.11	33.26	33.99	34.16	33.40	31.47
1999	31.72	28.21	26.27	24.39	24.25	25.19	24.70	21.39	20.22	20.15	19.69	21.25	23.95
2000	21.98	22.65	23.70	24.57	22.97	21.54	21.03	20.17	18.52	18.16	17.83	17.25	20.86
2001	16.24	15.20	15.53	14.03	14.53	13.27	16.78	17.18	15.78	14.44	15.91	16.07	15.41

[1] Data prior to 1995 are F.O.B. Valley Points, Southeastern mills. *Source: Economic Research Service, U.S. Department of Agriculture (ERS-USDA)*

Exports of Cottonseed Oil to Important Countries from the United States In Thousands of Metric Tons

Year	Canada	Dominican Republic	Egypt	Guate-mala	Japan	Mexico	Nether-lands	El Salvador	South Korea	Turkey	Vene-zuela	Total
1992	11.6	1.0	8.2	3.2	15.3	8.5	4.4	26.5	10.6	7.0	3.7	110.3
1993	11.1	.0	.0	.5	17.6	5.8	.2	30.8	6.6	.5	1.5	83.1
1994	10.8	.0	7.5	12.3	29.8	10.3	1.9	26.1	16.9	----	4.4	135.6
1995	12.0	----	10.3	1.9	17.9	5.7	1.4	37.8	19.2	----	2.8	137.7
1996	23.2	.0	----	1.7	15.8	3.3	----	20.6	7.2	----	.0	96.0
1997	28.0	.0	----	.4	11.3	2.5	4.2	25.3	1.9	2.5	----	110.6
1998	37.6	.1	----	----	6.0	6.1	----	16.1	2.1	----	.0	86.9
1999	37.5	----	----	----	4.2	5.4	.5	.8	.0	----	----	57.0
2000	40.2	.0	----	.0	7.6	7.9	.4	----	.1	----	----	58.5
2001[1]	26.0	.0	----	.5	6.5	8.5	3.1	4.8	2.5	----	----	64.5

[1] Preliminary. *Source: The Oil World*

Bridge/CRB Futures Index

The Bridge Commodity Research Bureau Futures Price Index was first calculated by Commodity Research Bureau, Inc. in 1957 and made its inaugural appearance in the 1958 CRB Commodity Year Book.

The Index originally consisted of two cash markets and 26 futures markets which were traded on exchanges in the U.S. and Canada. It included barley and flaxseed from the Winnipeg exchange; cocoa, coffee "B", copper, cotton, cottonseed oil, grease wool, hides, lead, potatoes, rubber, sugar #4, sugar #6, wool tops and zinc from New York exchanges; and corn, oats, wheat, rye, soybeans, soybean oil, soybean meal, lard, onions, and eggs from Chicago exchanges. In addition to those 26, the Index also included the spot New Orleans cotton and Minneapolis wheat markets.

Like the Bureau of Labor Statistics spot index, the Bridge/CRB Futures Price Index is calculated to produce an unweighted geometric mean of the individual commodity price relatives. In other words, a ratio of the current price to the base year average price. Currently, 1967 is the base year the Index is calculated against (1967 = 100).

The formula considers all future delivery contracts that expire on or before the end of the sixth calendar month from the current date, using up to a maximum of five contracts per commodity. However, a minimum of two contracts must be used to calculate the current price, even if the second contract is outside the six-month window. Contracts are excluded when in their delivery period.

The 2001 closing value of 190.61 was 16.34 percent lower than the 2000 close of 228.66. 12 of the 17 component commodities finished lower for the year.

Futures Markets

Futures and options on the CRB Futures Price Index are traded on the New York Board of Trade (NYBOT).

Bridge/CRB Futures Index Component Commodities by Group

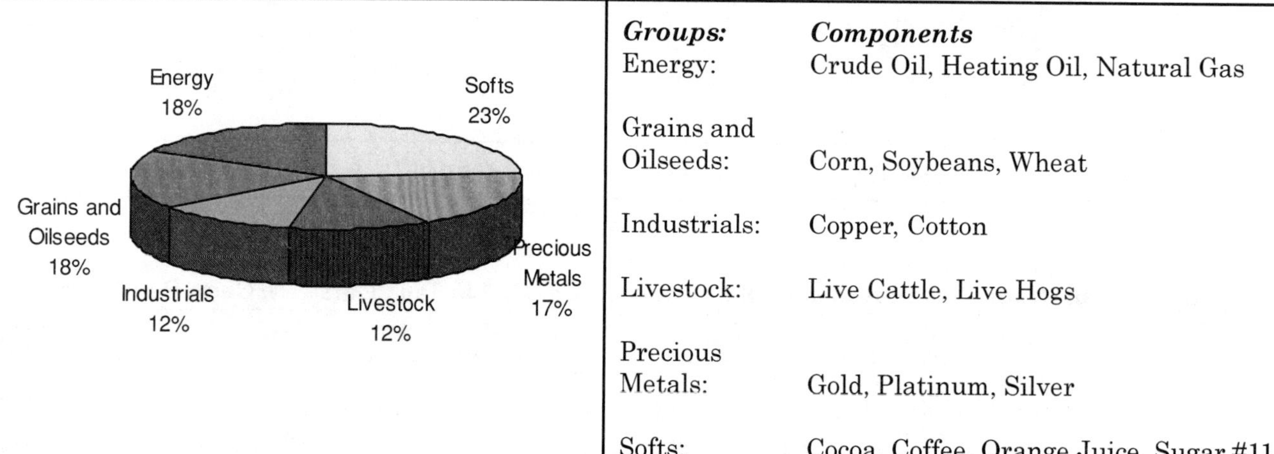

Groups:	*Components*
Energy:	Crude Oil, Heating Oil, Natural Gas
Grains and Oilseeds:	Corn, Soybeans, Wheat
Industrials:	Copper, Cotton
Livestock:	Live Cattle, Live Hogs
Precious Metals:	Gold, Platinum, Silver
Softs:	Cocoa, Coffee, Orange Juice, Sugar #11

The Bridge/CRB Futures Index is computed using a three-step process:

1) Each of the Index's 17 component commodities is arithmetically average using the prices for all of the designated contract months which expire on or before the end of the sixth calendar month from the current date, except that: a) no contract shall be included in the calculation whie in delivery; b) there shall be a minimum of two contract months for each component commodity (adding contracts beyond the six month window if necessary); c) there shall be a maximum of five contract months for each commodity (dropping the most deferred contracts to remain at five, if necessary). The result is that the Index extends six to seven months into the futures depending on where one is in the current month. For example, live cattle's average price on October 30, 1995 would be computed as follows:

$$\text{Cattle Average} = \frac{\text{Dec. '96 + Feb. '97}}{2}$$

2) These 17 component averages are then geometrically average by multiplying all of teh number together and taking the 17th root.

$$\text{Geometric Average} = 17\sqrt{\text{Crude Avg. * Heating Oil Avg. * Sugar Avg....}}$$

3) The resulting average is divided by 30.7766, the 1967 base-year average for these 17 commodities. That result is then multiplied by an adjustment factor of .8486. This adjustment factor is necessitated by the nine revisions to the Index since its inception in 1957. Finally, that result is multiplied by 100 in order to convert the Index into percentage terms:

$$\text{Bridge/CRB Futures Index} = \frac{\text{Current Geometric Average}}{\text{1967 Geometric Avg. (30.7766)}} * .8486 * 100$$

Average Open Interest of Bridge/CRB Futures Index in New York In Contracts

Year	Jan.	Feb.	Mar.	Apr.	May	June	July	Aug.	Sept.	Oct.	Nov.	Dec.
1992	1,435	1,472	1,185	1,347	1,311	1,087	951	1,179	1,075	1,226	1,283	1,406
1993	1,969	1,984	1,842	2,201	2,564	2,947	2,616	2,409	2,128	2,383	2,432	2,351
1994	2,607	3,146	2,680	2,691	2,339	2,698	3,838	5,146	4,562	4,942	4,535	2,800
1995	2,144	2,164	2,147	2,370	2,016	2,144	2,053	2,070	2,062	1,942	2,003	1,640
1996	1,934	1,826	1,753	2,355	1,881	1,890	1,562	1,345	1,596	1,853	1,861	1,866
1997	1,944	2,128	2,090	2,245	2,192	1,817	1,957	1,741	1,656	1,843	1,789	1,752
1998	1,679	1,557	1,626	1,509	1,641	1,895	1,832	1,719	1,839	2,162	2,639	2,787
1999	2,863	3,027	3,153	3,041	3,785	3,388	3,300	3,443	4,231	4,851	4,579	4,087
2000	3,487	3,525	3,271	3,117	3,155	2,737	2,104	1,640	1,551	1,632	1,544	1,438
2001	1,280	1,063	1,032	1,036	969	1,006	1,058	1,048	993	559	354	404

Source: New York Board of Trade (NYBOT)

Volume of Trading of Bridge/CRB Futures Index in New York In Contracts

Year	Jan.	Feb.	Mar.	Apr.	May	June	July	Aug.	Sept.	Oct.	Nov.	Dec.	Total
1992	4,895	6,031	4,136	5,697	5,496	4,487	4,162	4,617	3,874	3,183	5,277	4,400	56,255
1993	3,620	5,720	8,050	7,340	8,680	10,722	12,418	8,590	6,192	4,350	8,535	6,954	91,171
1994	6,956	7,473	10,085	10,274	11,298	14,652	10,560	8,967	7,445	6,575	10,186	5,515	109,986
1995	6,151	5,545	5,763	7,955	7,877	7,573	6,875	10,094	7,376	5,030	5,865	5,309	81,413
1996	7,490	6,041	6,428	10,784	9,526	5,543	7,476	5,816	6,311	6,527	5,990	3,181	81,113
1997	6,645	4,942	5,245	8,600	8,156	7,776	6,248	7,685	4,537	4,588	3,468	3,592	71,482
1998	7,659	4,623	3,953	3,890	2,933	5,634	3,394	4,578	5,101	4,013	8,814	4,401	58,993
1999	7,606	7,766	7,556	7,808	4,986	8,404	4,378	12,053	6,660	8,063	9,497	3,932	88,709
2000	14,975	6,760	3,941	7,582	7,402	8,924	2,023	3,973	1,333	2,122	3,254	1,205	63,494
2001	2,428	1,823	1,310	2,062	930	1,965	880	2,021	625	1,263	843	728	16,878

Source: New York Board of Trade (NYBOT)

Currencies

The U.S. dollar is the definitive focal point for the world's major currencies, a position that shows no sign of change any time soon. However, the action during 2001 was mixed in that the dollar gained dramatically against the J-Yen and to a lesser extent against the Canadian dollar: but a number of European stayed within relatively tight ranges against the dollar reflecting in part the broadening acceptance, and success, of the Euro as the continent's currency. Indeed, the euro is now viewed as the major step forward in the history of European integration. In theory, the single currency should make Europe a more efficient and therefore better place for capital investment. The euro in dollar terms was largely confined to a 10-cent range during 2001, starting the year near 95 cents, falling in mid-year to about 85 cents and closing out 2001 near 90 cents. Some of capital shift into European currencies during 2001 was not necessarily indicative of concern about the U.S. economy, but a perception that Europe's major economies were finally starting to come together. Still, Europe's longer-term economic growth rate is generally seen as +2.5% vs. closer to 3.5% in the U.S. In either case, on January 1, 2002 the euro notes and coins became legal tender in twelve nations with a combined population of 300 million and is expected to encompass 20 or more countries when it become fully operational, perhaps in 10 or 15 years.

Historically, a currency's value is largely determined by three variables: interest rate differentials, economic differentials and relative yield inside a country. For the U.S. the Federal Reserve's easier monetary policy during 2001 would have been expected to detract from the dollar's value, but the dollar retained much of its strength because the outlook for many countries was far from positive. Moreover, the Fed's policy which took short-term U.S. interest rates to a forty year low was seen as a positive for reversing the U.S. economy's slippage in 2001. Although the economy's recovery was suspect as the year drew to a close, there seemed to be little doubt that U.S. monetary and fiscal policy would remain stimulative.

Trading in the world's currencies exceeds $2 trillion per day. Most of the trading is via electronic transfers for central banks and commercial banks, but a growing portion of the trading is on organized exchanges where inter-day price swings often have speculative based roots that can exaggerate short term price swings. Annual trading in the IMM's J-Yen futures contract alone now exceeds several million contracts and not far behind with annual futures volume in the millions are the Swiss Franc and B-pound.

Japan's economy continued disappointing in 2001, as Japan's monetary and fiscal leaders seem reluctant to implement innovative policies. Indeed, Japan's government flooded the market with yen during 2001 with the rationalization that its needed if Japan's new government is to succeed. Its a questionable approach. In November 2001, Japan's industrial output fell a larger than expected 1.8% from October putting the industrial production index at 90.9, its lowest level since November 1987. Moreover, consumer retail spending and new home sales continued to slump, which helped to further weaken the yen's value against the dollar. Japan's export led economy was expected to shrink about 1% in 2001 and likely to see further shrinkage in 2002. Japan's economy may easily be worse in 2002 than it was in 2001 which if realized is likely to keep the yen on the defensive against the dollar, if not also against the key European currencies. The depreciating yen--it plunged nearly 20% against the dollar in the fourth quarter of 2001 is cause for problems around the world. U.S. manufacturers lobbied strongly in Washington in 2001 for the administration to brake the dollar's rise since its allows Japanese competitors to price their producers more aggressively in the U.S. Still, the U.S. is likely to maintain a hefty trade deficit against Japan, especially if the U.S. economy improves and consumer demand strengthens for Japanese cars and electronics.

The Canadian dollar peaked against the U.S. dollar at $1.04 in April 1974 and has fallen more or less steadily since then. In 2001 it lost 6.25% of its value and in late December reached a record low 62.3 American cents. Although the Canadian economy did not slow as much as the U.S. economy in 2001, it may not improve that much in 2002, which if realized is apt to further undermine the currency's value vis-à-vis the U.S. dollar. A test of the 60-cent level is not unrealistic in 2002.

Futures Markets

The Chicago Mercantile's International Monetary Market (IMM) trades futures and options on the British pound, Swiss franc, D-mark, J-yen, the Canadian, Australian and New Zealand dollars, and Mexican Peso. Chicago's MidAmerica Exchange (MidAm) trades smaller futures contracts on many of the IMM's currencies. The FINEX division of the New York Board of Trade (NYBOT) trades futures and options on a composite dollar index and also offers cross rate contracts: D-mark/J-yen, D-mark/French Franc and D-Mark/B-pound. Many currency contracts are also traded in Europe and Asia.

CRB Currency Futures Index 1977 = 100

Year	Jan.	Feb.	Mar.	Apr.	May	June	July	Aug.	Sept.	Oct.	Nov.	Dec.	Average
1992	136.15	133.37	129.33	129.78	132.13	135.42	139.83	142.26	140.65	136.30	129.70	129.91	134.57
1993	127.91	126.74	127.99	132.20	132.73	131.17	129.44	130.64	132.87	131.38	129.31	129.14	130.13
1994	128.54	129.57	130.89	130.57	132.23	134.18	137.60	137.51	139.78	141.94	140.29	137.85	135.08
1995	139.31	140.54	147.85	152.52	150.20	150.85	150.58	145.41	143.89	146.33	145.21	143.83	146.38
1996	141.69	141.01	141.12	139.61	138.11	138.37	139.53	140.52	139.51	138.74	139.92	137.47	139.63
1997	134.61	130.30	129.56	128.71	130.83	131.75	130.14	126.84	128.02	129.07	129.58	126.93	129.70
1998	125.06	126.10	125.65	124.96	124.33	122.86	121.89	120.65	126.18	130.98	128.86	130.69	125.68
1999	130.97	128.48	126.37	125.74	125.32	124.63	124.08	126.89	128.89	130.66	128.24	127.71	127.33
2000	127.65	124.37	124.01	123.43	119.42	122.54	121.59	119.04	117.11	115.99	114.89	117.55	120.63
2001	118.42	116.58	114.25	113.01	112.24	110.92	111.29	114.02	115.20	114.04	112.69	112.01	113.72

Average. *Source: Commodity Research Bureau (CRB)*

British Pound Futures - International Monetary Market (weekly close) as of 28-Dec-2001
USD/GBP
2.05
2.00
1.95
1.90
1.85
1.80
1.75
1.70
1.65
1.60
1.55
1.50
1.45
1.40
1.35
Jan-92
Dec-92
Dec-93
Dec-94
Dec-95
Dec-96
Dec-97
Dec-98
Dec-99
Dec-00
Dec-01

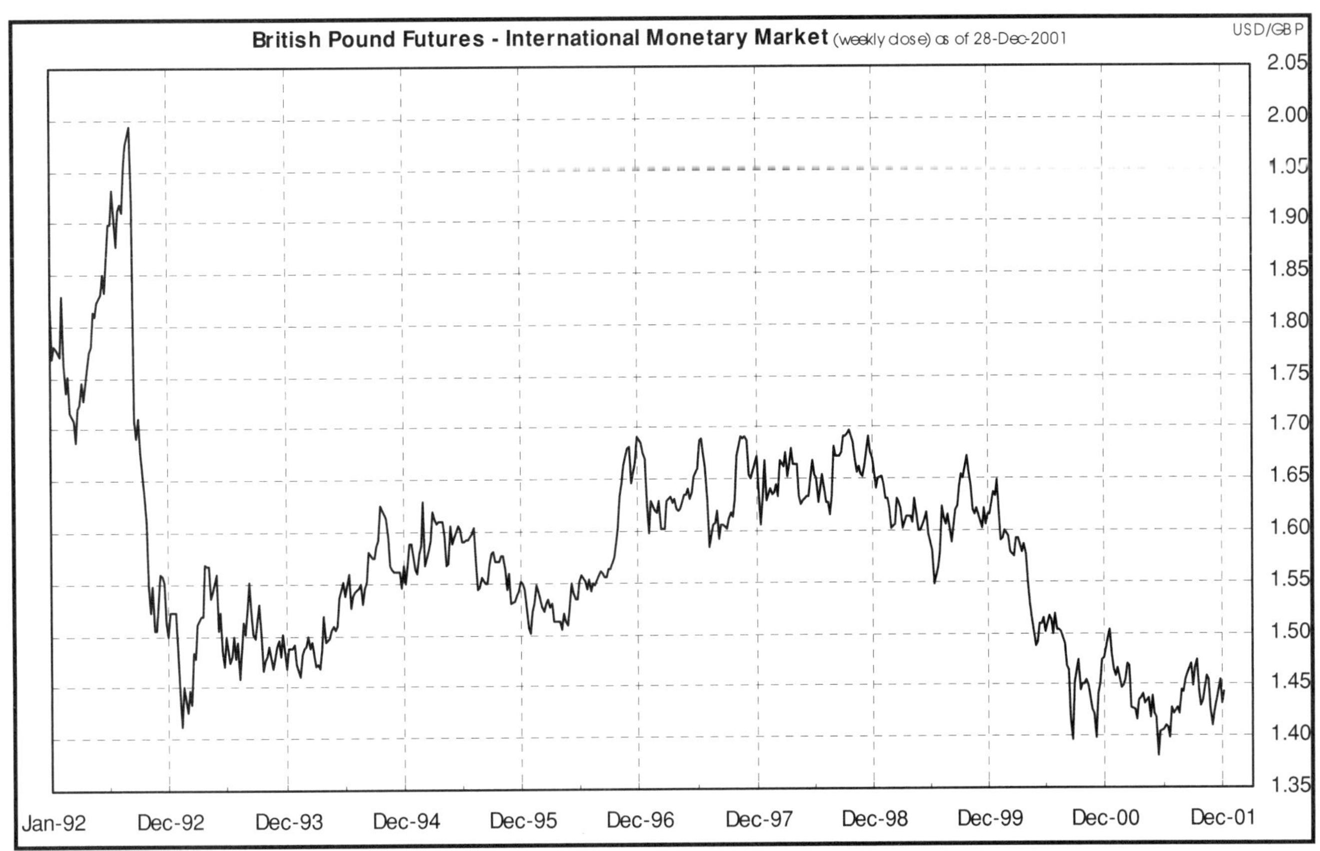

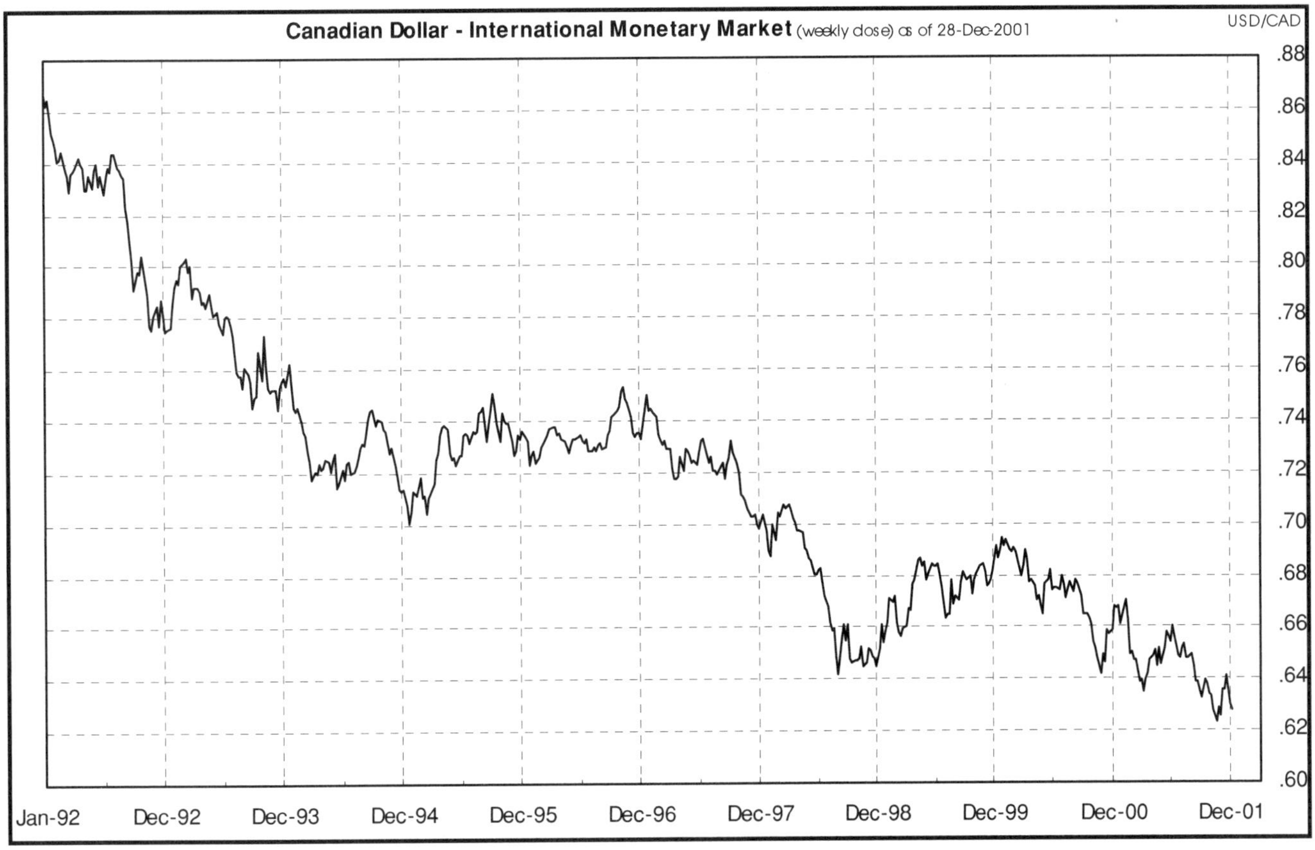

Canadian Dollar - International Monetary Market (weekly close) as of 28-Dec-2001
USD/CAD
.88
.86
.84
.82
.80
.78
.76
.74
.72
.70
.68
.66
.64
.62
.60
Jan-92
Dec-92
Dec-93
Dec-94
Dec-95
Dec-96
Dec-97
Dec-98
Dec-99
Dec-00
Dec-01

Euro FX Futures - International Monetary Market (weekly close) as of 28-Dec-2001
USD/EUR
1.45
1.40
1.35
1.30
1.25
1.20
1.15
1.10
1.05
1.00
.95
.90
.85
.80
Jan-92
Dec-92
Dec-93
Dec-94
Dec-95
Dec-96
Dec-97
Dec-98
Dec-99
Dec-00
Dec-01

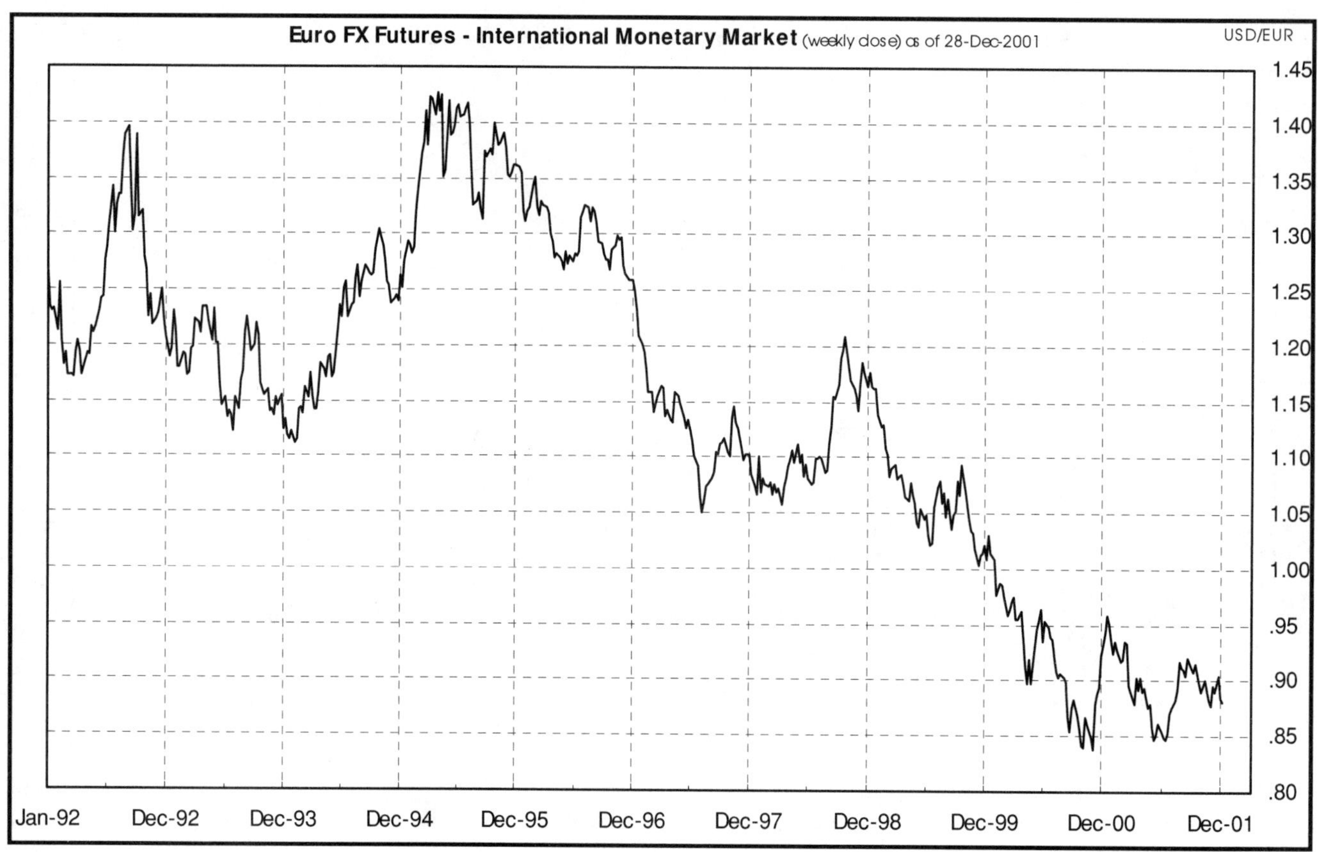

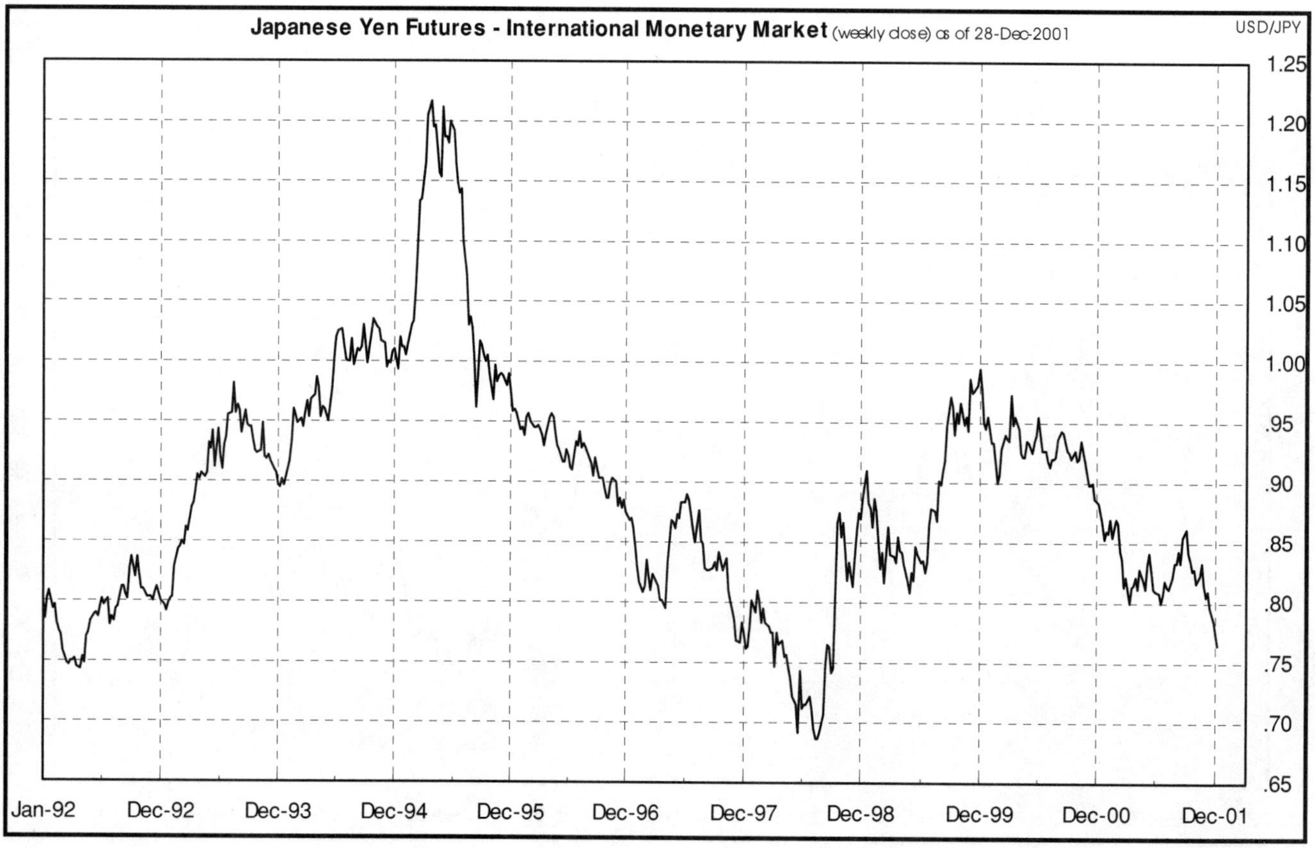

Japanese Yen Futures - International Monetary Market (weekly close) as of 28-Dec-2001
USD/JPY
1.25
1.20
1.15
1.10
1.05
1.00
.95
.90
.85
.80
.75
.70
.65
Jan-92
Dec-92
Dec-93
Dec-94
Dec-95
Dec-96
Dec-97
Dec-98
Dec-99
Dec-00
Dec-01

Swiss Franc Futures - International Monetary Market (weekly close) as of 28-Dec-2001
USD/CHF
.92
.88
.84
.80
.76
.72
.68
.64
.60
.56
.52
Jan-92
Dec-92
Dec-93
Dec-94
Dec-95
Dec-96
Dec-97
Dec-98
Dec-99
Dec-00
Dec-01

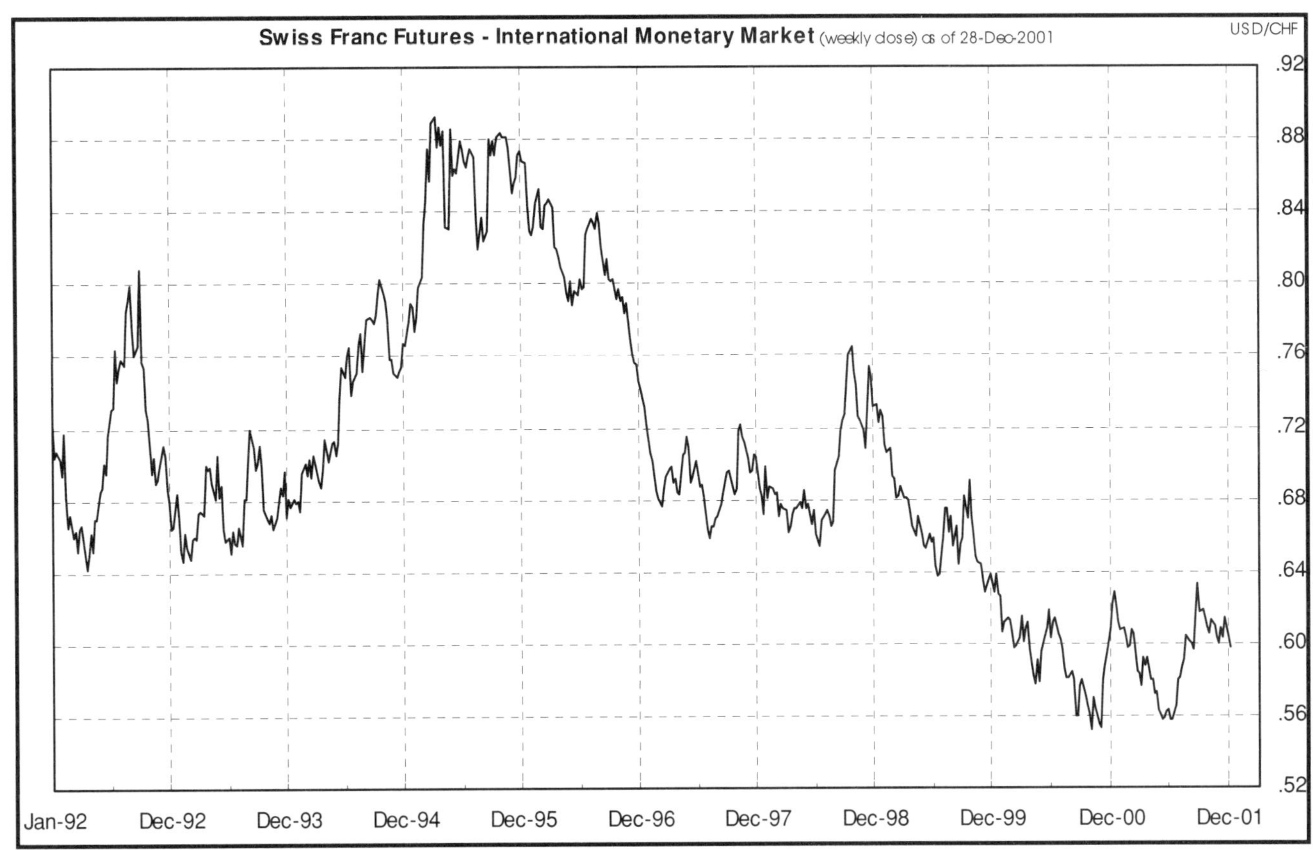

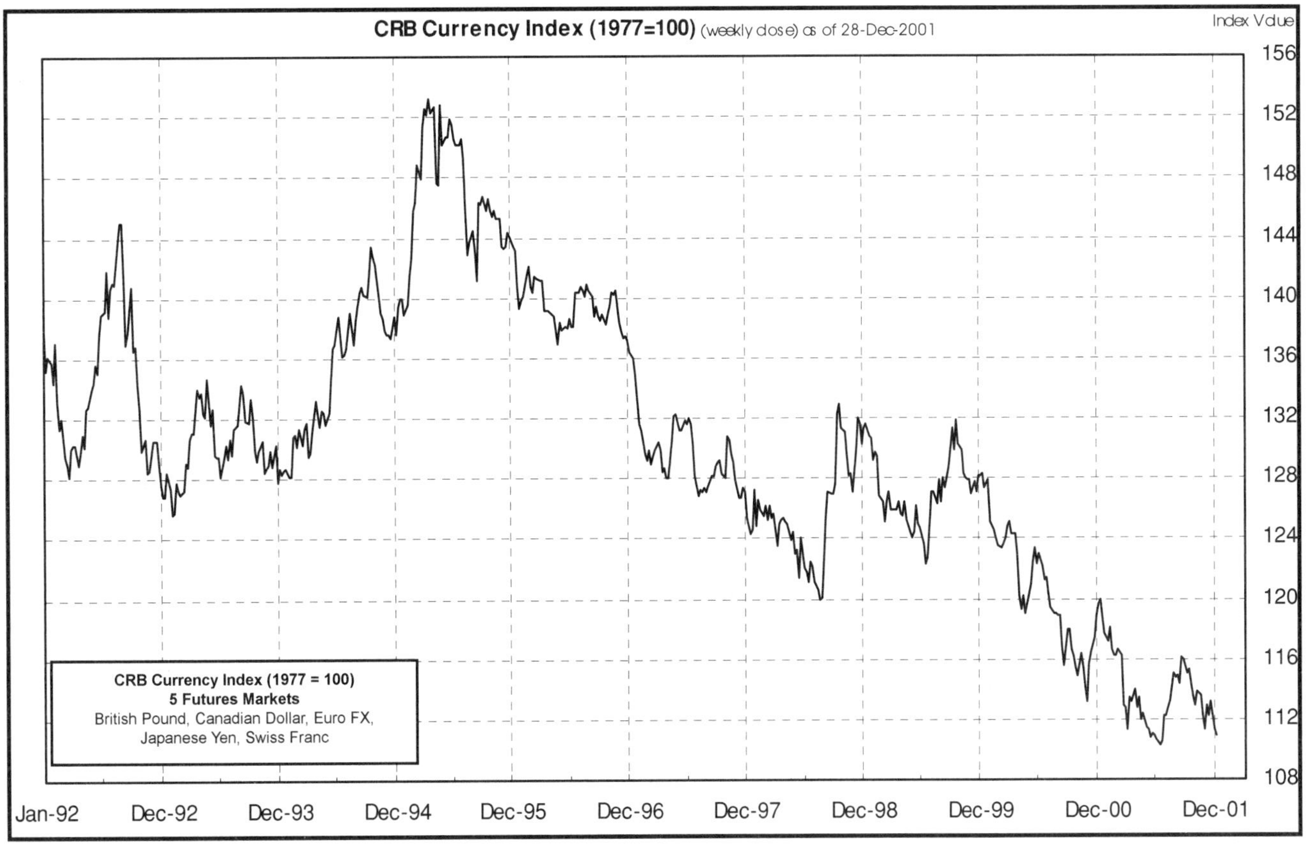

CRB Currency Index (1977=100) (weekly close) as of 28-Dec-2001
Index Value
156
152
148
144
140
136
132
128
124
120
116
112
108
CRB Currency Index (1977 = 100)
5 Futures Markets
British Pound, Canadian Dollar, Euro FX,
Japanese Yen, Swiss Franc
Jan-92
Dec-92
Dec-93
Dec-94
Dec-95
Dec-96
Dec-97
Dec-98
Dec-99
Dec-00
Dec-01

CURRENCIES

Canadian Dollars per U.S. Dollar

Year	Jan.	Feb.	Mar.	Apr.	May	June	July	Aug.	Sept.	Oct.	Nov.	Dec.	Average
1993	1.2774	1.2595	1.2467	1.2616	1.2686	1.2788	1.2817	1.3078	1.3210	1.3253	1.3166	1.3307	1.2896
1994	1.3175	1.3419	1.3645	1.3821	1.3805	1.3831	1.3818	1.3777	1.3536	1.3495	1.3649	1.3896	1.3656
1995	1.4120	1.3995	1.4065	1.3749	1.3607	1.3772	1.3609	1.3550	1.3495	1.3449	1.3525	1.3685	1.3718
1996	1.3664	1.3753	1.3651	1.3591	1.3690	1.3649	1.3687	1.3717	1.3691	1.3501	1.3382	1.3621	1.3633
1997	1.3484	1.3555	1.3727	1.3947	1.3793	1.3844	1.3769	1.3894	1.3865	1.3863	1.4127	1.4272	1.3845
1998	1.4407	1.4335	1.4159	1.4294	1.4449	1.4647	1.4865	1.5344	1.5212	1.5430	1.5400	1.5429	1.4831
1999	1.5189	1.4971	1.5174	1.4868	1.4614	1.4691	1.4877	1.4921	1.4772	1.4767	1.4671	1.4713	1.4852
2000	1.4480	1.4499	1.4600	1.4681	1.4944	1.4762	1.4778	1.4819	1.4841	1.5119	1.5425	1.5219	1.4847
2001	1.5021	1.5227	1.5579	1.5581	1.5403	1.5238	1.5294	1.5384	1.5665	1.5708	1.5934	1.5793	1.5486

Average. *Source: Bridge Information Systems, Inc.*

Euro per U.S. Dollar

Year	Jan.	Feb.	Mar.	Apr.	May	June	July	Aug.	Sept.	Oct.	Nov.	Dec.	Average
1993	1.2130	1.1856	1.1779	1.2214	1.2171	1.1828	1.1379	1.1253	1.1720	1.1587	1.1292	1.1285	1.1708
1994	1.1138	1.1183	1.1412	1.1390	1.1636	1.1819	1.2167	1.2182	1.2314	1.2559	1.2357	1.2129	1.1857
1995	1.2380	1.2536	1.3030	1.3292	1.3085	1.3196	1.3340	1.2939	1.2782	1.2987	1.2947	1.2757	1.2939
1996	1.2629	1.2543	1.2544	1.2430	1.2278	1.2386	1.2554	1.2686	1.2587	1.2532	1.2695	1.2416	1.2523
1997	1.2088	1.1592	1.1460	1.1396	1.1441	1.1309	1.0999	1.0694	1.0976	1.1190	1.1418	1.1114	1.1306
1998	1.0859	1.0896	1.0854	1.0931	1.1099	1.1015	1.0991	1.1041	1.1566	1.2015	1.1680	1.1746	1.1224
1999	1.1584	1.1202	1.0882	1.0700	1.0622	1.0385	1.0366	1.0603	1.0501	1.0705	1.0327	1.0117	1.0666
2000	1.0135	.9842	.9644	.9450	.9080	.9496	.9394	.9042	.8706	.8533	.8554	.9004	.9240
2001	.9380	.9208	.9085	.8931	.8747	.8536	.8616	.9023	.9123	.9062	.8882	.8913	.8959

Average. *Source: Bridge Information Systems, Inc.*

Japanese Yen per U.S. Dollar

Year	Jan.	Feb.	Mar.	Apr.	May	June	July	Aug.	Sept.	Oct.	Nov.	Dec.	Average
1993	124.94	120.77	116.99	112.22	110.10	107.29	107.57	103.74	105.41	107.00	107.78	109.89	111.14
1994	111.33	106.22	105.00	103.36	103.76	102.37	98.65	99.88	98.78	98.36	98.08	100.08	102.16
1995	99.67	98.14	90.40	83.59	84.96	84.55	87.22	94.72	100.49	100.76	101.93	101.84	94.02
1996	105.66	105.57	105.90	107.23	106.42	108.91	109.21	107.84	109.87	112.40	112.35	114.01	108.78
1997	117.93	122.90	122.72	125.66	118.93	114.25	115.30	117.90	120.85	121.06	125.35	129.62	121.04
1998	129.39	125.71	129.04	131.79	135.01	140.40	140.75	144.51	134.45	120.49	120.41	117.01	130.75
1999	113.23	116.62	119.49	119.73	121.88	120.69	119.38	113.16	107.00	105.94	104.62	102.64	113.70
2000	105.29	109.49	106.34	105.65	108.19	106.15	108.03	108.06	106.79	108.39	108.94	112.18	107.79
2001	116.83	116.17	121.44	123.64	121.66	122.38	124.45	121.29	118.64	121.35	122.39	127.72	121.50

Average. *Source: Bridge Information Systems, Inc.*

Swiss Francs per U.S. Dollar

Year	Jan.	Feb.	Mar.	Apr.	May	June	July	Aug.	Sept.	Oct.	Nov.	Dec.	Average
1993	1.4775	1.5197	1.5199	1.4572	1.4471	1.4767	1.5138	1.4947	1.4158	1.4421	1.4966	1.4629	1.4770
1994	1.4707	1.4558	1.4295	1.4363	1.4120	1.3723	1.3256	1.3176	1.2895	1.2636	1.2974	1.3275	1.3665
1995	1.2865	1.2694	1.1691	1.1362	1.1678	1.1564	1.1542	1.1958	1.1868	1.1444	1.1440	1.1624	1.1811
1996	1.1810	1.1942	1.1945	1.2194	1.2546	1.2574	1.2324	1.2022	1.2333	1.2583	1.2757	1.3296	1.2361
1997	1.3925	1.4543	1.4622	1.4614	1.4298	1.4419	1.4810	1.5123	1.4702	1.4507	1.4057	1.4393	1.4501
1998	1.4756	1.4616	1.4896	1.5050	1.4782	1.4951	1.5126	1.4927	1.4002	1.3376	1.3856	1.3600	1.4495
1999	1.3856	1.4273	1.4656	1.4972	1.5078	1.5359	1.5472	1.5092	1.5251	1.4891	1.5541	1.5827	1.5022
2000	1.5888	1.6326	1.6624	1.6638	1.7151	1.6422	1.6503	1.7146	1.7564	1.7727	1.7772	1.6778	1.6878
2001	1.6296	1.6681	1.6903	1.7115	1.7525	1.7842	1.7564	1.6791	1.6338	1.6337	1.6501	1.6569	1.6872

Average. *Source: Bridge Information Systems, Inc.*

U.S. Dollars per British Pound

Year	Jan.	Feb.	Mar.	Apr.	May	June	July	Aug.	Sept.	Oct.	Nov.	Dec.	Average
1993	1.5330	1.4383	1.4621	1.5465	1.5492	1.5090	1.4973	1.4928	1.5251	1.5027	1.4808	1.4904	1.5023
1994	1.4933	1.4787	1.4921	1.4832	1.5038	1.5261	1.5446	1.5421	1.5647	1.6073	1.5864	1.5582	1.5317
1995	1.5742	1.5727	1.6004	1.6087	1.5886	1.5960	1.5955	1.5668	1.5595	1.5782	1.5612	1.5411	1.5786
1996	1.5289	1.5376	1.5278	1.5159	1.5154	1.5417	1.5538	1.5501	1.5595	1.5863	1.6629	1.6660	1.5622
1997	1.6590	1.6258	1.6095	1.6285	1.6325	1.6457	1.6717	1.6044	1.6020	1.6331	1.6887	1.6606	1.6385
1998	1.6347	1.6402	1.6615	1.6720	1.6370	1.6509	1.6429	1.6355	1.6814	1.6933	1.6613	1.6713	1.6568
1999	1.6495	1.6269	1.6213	1.6085	1.6147	1.5957	1.5754	1.6051	1.6237	1.6570	1.6206	1.6131	1.6176
2000	1.6395	1.6007	1.5810	1.5807	1.5084	1.5102	1.5082	1.4885	1.4341	1.4509	1.4252	1.4657	1.5161
2001	1.4767	1.4522	1.4438	1.4350	1.4268	1.4025	1.4149	1.4376	1.4646	1.4520	1.4358	1.4422	1.4403

Average. *Source: Bridge Information Systems, Inc.*

Average Open Interest of Canadian Dollar Futures in Chicago In Contracts

Year	Jan.	Feb.	Mar.	Apr.	May	June	July	Aug.	Sept.	Oct.	Nov.	Dec.
1992	19,724	24,020	24,118	21,351	21,020	22,860	21,770	27,005	20,221	27,827	28,025	24,925
1993	20,410	24,376	25,877	23,639	27,438	29,784	29,385	45,397	40,639	43,476	32,469	28,879
1994	28,277	38,157	48,411	42,730	44,363	42,845	35,370	39,582	49,312	40,706	42,353	59,763
1995	55,863	44,677	33,706	45,394	47,832	36,677	44,930	42,629	49,526	43,032	40,047	40,592
1996	31,028	37,674	38,551	41,411	46,470	37,141	37,522	42,063	44,014	68,674	82,817	72,586
1997	55,949	56,600	72,803	82,732	73,747	57,243	43,937	59,112	56,387	59,265	75,027	74,221
1998	63,300	67,862	61,528	58,938	64,859	74,027	71,313	75,193	60,863	51,967	61,318	50,271
1999	50,061	71,819	63,782	73,773	84,885	71,923	65,877	71,458	61,994	58,749	59,941	51,967
2000	66,374	64,528	58,621	60,389	76,444	69,033	67,198	65,370	65,779	81,995	77,746	65,452
2001	54,369	58,660	72,051	64,550	65,407	62,489	54,742	54,580	73,647	71,610	82,083	67,578

Source: International Monetary Market (IMM), division of the Chicago Mercantile Exchange (CME)

Average Open Interest of Euro FX Futures in Chicago In Contracts

Year	Jan.	Feb.	Mar.	Apr.	May	June	July	Aug.	Sept.	Oct.	Nov.	Dec.
1998	----	----	----	----	1	1	1	1	1	0	7	7
1999	8,261	30,546	37,837	37,881	46,446	50,615	46,777	55,858	49,352	57,380	58,846	65,346
2000	63,124	68,413	61,180	59,110	67,644	63,361	57,723	69,561	77,617	73,314	79,577	92,730
2001	89,049	91,130	90,127	78,762	89,390	94,160	84,637	104,437	112,797	108,445	108,999	104,323

Source: International Monetary Market (IMM), division of the Chicago Mercantile Exchange (CME)

Average Open Interest of Japanese Yen Futures in Chicago In Contracts

Year	Jan.	Feb.	Mar.	Apr.	May	June	July	Aug.	Sept.	Oct.	Nov.	Dec.
1992	63,856	67,714	71,702	63,938	63,079	64,596	56,465	58,353	53,462	44,488	45,941	46,887
1993	50,066	70,195	81,979	76,696	82,028	81,103	72,186	80,780	73,002	83,097	84,812	95,817
1994	101,792	94,470	73,286	57,281	65,835	70,759	73,734	72,798	63,419	63,091	80,053	92,834
1995	86,569	86,852	77,649	63,379	67,644	56,285	48,680	63,463	73,830	67,336	73,335	70,268
1996	80,645	78,915	71,643	76,655	73,832	85,398	77,941	73,535	86,723	76,620	72,130	67,301
1997	73,391	82,542	78,466	81,117	85,984	73,322	62,488	82,369	96,468	90,080	130,606	121,001
1998	95,338	101,448	97,183	97,389	106,139	132,732	113,084	145,241	108,808	88,991	89,108	79,262
1999	78,767	81,859	96,271	87,829	118,819	120,681	118,329	136,826	115,884	82,657	87,869	87,595
2000	93,785	125,318	95,034	75,631	80,840	68,359	60,966	79,195	64,845	64,648	68,719	100,713
2001	89,680	90,652	109,536	96,244	89,377	82,838	93,430	107,588	102,710	75,096	97,368	137,756

Source: International Monetary Market (IMM), division of the Chicago Mercantile Exchange (CME)

Average Open Interest of Swiss Franc Futures in Chicago In Contracts

Year	Jan.	Feb.	Mar.	Apr.	May	June	July	Aug.	Sept.	Oct.	Nov.	Dec.
1992	24,653	33,640	42,825	36,230	38,269	36,668	30,159	33,707	33,167	34,767	45,428	44,901
1993	52,713	49,472	48,002	43,514	47,832	42,343	40,703	44,329	60,446	49,320	58,406	49,670
1994	41,914	46,280	44,134	37,450	42,071	49,162	45,223	43,746	44,495	39,587	51,539	55,424
1995	39,726	44,364	39,358	30,270	30,586	26,766	23,121	30,267	34,228	34,889	38,033	44,741
1996	42,280	42,902	36,924	39,233	46,810	44,848	38,300	40,298	43,695	47,613	53,581	59,405
1997	51,652	54,114	51,121	45,725	48,651	42,530	55,279	58,098	49,296	43,585	51,822	48,560
1998	57,740	46,160	67,722	67,303	63,477	77,564	85,984	70,569	81,465	57,413	44,810	43,436
1999	39,434	58,279	66,250	66,530	73,322	75,322	66,603	71,060	60,214	65,020	67,936	64,507
2000	55,660	69,983	57,703	41,732	46,159	41,727	36,894	50,595	57,439	47,313	48,870	55,982
2001	50,121	44,405	46,470	41,641	53,265	60,943	53,687	60,986	61,689	48,962	53,445	46,771

Source: International Monetary Market (IMM), division of the Chicago Mercantile Exchange (CME)

Average Open Interest of British Pound Futures in Chicago In Contracts

Year	Jan.	Feb.	Mar.	Apr.	May	June	July	Aug.	Sept.	Oct.	Nov.	Dec.
1992	21,578	28,215	22,882	31,595	36,426	35,529	27,160	28,041	30,137	30,330	33,121	27,935
1993	26,614	41,752	40,238	38,544	39,654	34,953	26,056	32,446	33,560	29,733	37,246	33,606
1994	39,223	43,878	35,554	44,725	46,577	41,801	37,633	34,988	40,751	42,648	49,684	65,834
1995	47,740	44,935	36,805	23,161	26,571	28,402	22,662	34,932	38,900	34,485	43,634	49,804
1996	40,315	50,106	52,349	54,954	52,573	61,461	55,080	50,862	53,868	51,934	62,128	47,652
1997	40,479	38,370	43,742	37,701	40,956	48,890	60,592	50,829	41,801	35,752	56,825	44,667
1998	33,616	31,282	38,712	41,256	47,303	55,511	39,156	49,645	63,756	53,458	54,004	53,578
1999	51,519	59,705	66,913	64,937	58,744	60,414	65,206	54,373	50,949	65,038	49,468	34,191
2000	37,192	45,329	51,645	41,488	51,965	43,009	30,766	36,320	42,781	30,978	34,627	32,913
2001	28,776	30,555	36,532	34,713	39,836	48,310	33,273	40,935	50,083	38,579	40,461	35,424

Source: International Monetary Market (IMM), division of the Chicago Mercantile Exchange (CME)

United States Merchandise Trade Balance In Millions of Dollars

Year	Jan.	Feb.	Mar.	Apr.	May	June	July	Aug.	Sept.	Oct.	Nov.	Dec.	Total
1992	-5,470	-2,178	-3,527	-5,772	-5,409	-6,718	-9,893	-10,218	-9,693	-9,706	-8,644	-7,276	-96,106
1993	-6,113	-5,905	-8,886	-8,428	-6,542	-11,749	-12,609	-11,949	-12,516	-12,638	-11,521	-9,115	-132,609
1994	-11,999	-13,573	-11,477	-13,405	-14,079	-14,009	-15,831	-14,232	-14,566	-14,926	-15,292	-13,272	-166,192
1995	-15,746	-14,221	-14,487	-16,051	-16,010	-15,862	-15,887	-13,415	-13,243	-13,108	-12,324	-12,600	-173,729
1996	-15,623	-12,911	-14,574	-15,897	-16,826	-14,839	-17,757	-16,759	-17,976	-15,320	-15,176	-17,695	-191,270
1997	-18,167	-16,780	-14,896	-16,505	-16,982	-15,610	-15,864	-16,909	-16,524	-16,270	-16,605	-16,962	-196,652
1998	-17,187	-18,331	-20,615	-20,860	-22,236	-20,404	-21,066	-22,291	-21,611	-20,990	-21,539	-21,059	-246,853
1999	-23,409	-25,233	-25,741	-25,851	-27,753	-30,381	-31,227	-30,518	-30,573	-31,576	-32,401	-32,255	-345,434
2000	-34,116	-34,708	-37,215	-36,934	-36,910	-37,827	-38,091	-36,839	-39,682	-40,205	-38,955	-39,360	-452,207
2001[2]	-39,126	-34,613	-38,781	-37,657	-34,449	-35,533	-35,838	-34,073	-35,531	-35,045	-33,969		-430,489

[1] Not seasonally adjusted. [2] Preliminary. *Source: Bureau of Economic Analysis, U.S. Department of Commerce (BEA)*

Index of Real Trade-Weighted Dollar Exchange Rates for Total Agriculture[2] 1990 = 100[3]

Year		Jan.	Feb.	Mar.	Apr.	May	June	July	Aug.	Sept.	Oct.	Nov.	Dec.
1994	U.S. Markets	77.0	77.0	97.1	97.4	97.0	96.9	95.3	95.2	94.3	93.8	94.2	96.7
	U.S. Competitors	78.3	78.3	107.3	107.6	105.7	104.5	101.5	101.2	100.1	98.4	99.1	100.5
1995	U.S. Markets	99.2	98.6	96.7	92.5	92.0	92.0	92.2	94.8	96.6	96.7	98.3	98.0
	U.S. Competitors	98.9	98.0	95.3	93.9	94.5	93.8	92.7	94.5	95.6	94.4	94.4	94.8
1996	U.S. Markets	99.4	99.2	99.4	99.4	99.4	100.1	100.4	99.4	100.1	101.1	100.8	101.5
	U.S. Competitors	96.0	96.0	96.3	97.0	97.9	97.5	96.7	96.2	96.8	97.4	96.5	97.8
1997	U.S. Markets	103.0	105.3	107.0	110.2	104.3	107.8	107.6	109.3	106.9	106.9	112.8	109.8
	U.S. Competitors	99.8	102.8	105.9	107.3	103.9	106.8	110.5	113.3	110.6	110.6	110.7	111.6
1998	U.S. Markets	115.9	114.6	117.1	115.2	115.1	117.6	117.5	119.8	118.5	113.8	114.9	118.6
	U.S. Competitors	117.2	115.6	115.5	114.2	114.8	116.3	117.1	116.3	112.3	109.0	113.9	117.9
1999	U.S. Markets	113.8	115.3	116.7	111.1	111.0	119.0	117.3	117.7	117.4	113.8	116.2	113.8
	U.S. Competitors	115.8	119.1	120.5	110.4	109.7	122.5	124.6	123.3	124.5	122.3	125.6	125.4
2000	U.S. Markets	115.2	116.8	119.4	120.6	117.5	123.2	123.2	119.0	121.0	123.1	126.8	126.5
	U.S. Competitors	126.1	128.5	130.9	132.9	132.2	133.6	133.7	137.0	140.8	143.7	144.0	138.9
2001[1]	U.S. Markets	123.6	124.9	128.3	128.2	127.5	129.5	129.3	126.4	128.2	128.8		
	U.S. Competitors	136.2	138.4	140.5	141.7	143.4	145.7	144.4	139.9	140.9	141.6		

[1] Preliminary. [2] Real indexes adjust nominal exchange rates for differences in rates of inflation, to avoid the distortion caused by high-inflation countries. A higher value means the dollar has appreciated. Federal Reserve Board Index of trade-weighted value of the U.S. dollar against 10 major currencies. Weights are based on relative importance in world financial markets. [3] 1988 thru February 1994; 1985 = 100; March 1994 to date; 1990 = 100. *Source: Economic Research Service, U.S. Department of Agriculture (ERS-USDA)*

United States Balance on Current Account[1] In Millions of Dollars

Year	First Quarter	Second Quarter	Third Quarter	Fourth Quarter	Annual
1992	859	-10,278	-19,226	-19,869	-48,514
1993	-6,650	-19,293	-27,830	-28,752	-82,525
1994	-16,427	-26,893	-38,521	-36,403	-118,244
1995	-22,292	-31,240	-34,179	-22,187	-109,898
1996	-16,189	-28,868	-45,125	-30,755	-120,937
1997	-25,437	-29,557	-43,819	-40,996	-139,809
1998	-34,168	-52,292	-70,949	-60,048	-217,457
1999	-57,263	-77,311	-97,787	-92,003	-324,364
2000	-94,278	-108,405	-124,549	-117,435	-444,667
2001[2]	-100,268	-107,843	-104,032		-416,191

[1] Not seasonally adjusted. [2] Preliminary. *Source: Bureau of Economic Analysis, U.S. Department of Commerce (BEA)*

Merchandise Trade and Current Account Balances In Billions of Dollars

	Merchandise Trade Balance					Current Account Balance				
Year	Canada	Germany	Japan	Switzerland	U.K.	Canada	Germany	Japan	Switzerland	U.K.
1993	10.2	41.2	139.4	1.7	-20.0	-21.7	-9.7	131.9	19.5	-15.9
1994	14.8	50.9	144.1	1.6	-17.0	-13.0	-24.3	130.3	17.5	-2.1
1995	25.8	65.1	132.1	.9	-18.5	-4.4	-20.7	111.2	21.4	-5.9
1996	31.1	70.6	83.7	.9	-20.4	3.4	-7.9	65.8	21.9	-.8
1997	17.2	72.0	101.6	-.3	-19.5	-10.0	-3.1	94.3	25.5	10.8
1998	12.8	79.7	122.4	-1.7	-34.1	-11.0	-4.6	120.8	25.8	-.2
1999	22.8	73.1	123.1	-.3	-43.4	-2.3	-19.3	106.9	29.9	-17.8
2000	34.4	64.1	124.8	-1.8	-45.5	12.6	-17.7	127.6	30.3	-21.5
2001[1]	36.5	69.4	117.1	-2.6	-49.9	15.7	-10.6	126.5	29.6	-26.8
2002[2]	37.7	80.6	130.7	-3.4	-52.3	16.7	-.3	143.0	31.2	-29.0

[1] Estimate. [2] Projection. *Source: Organization for Economic Cooperation and Development (OECD)*

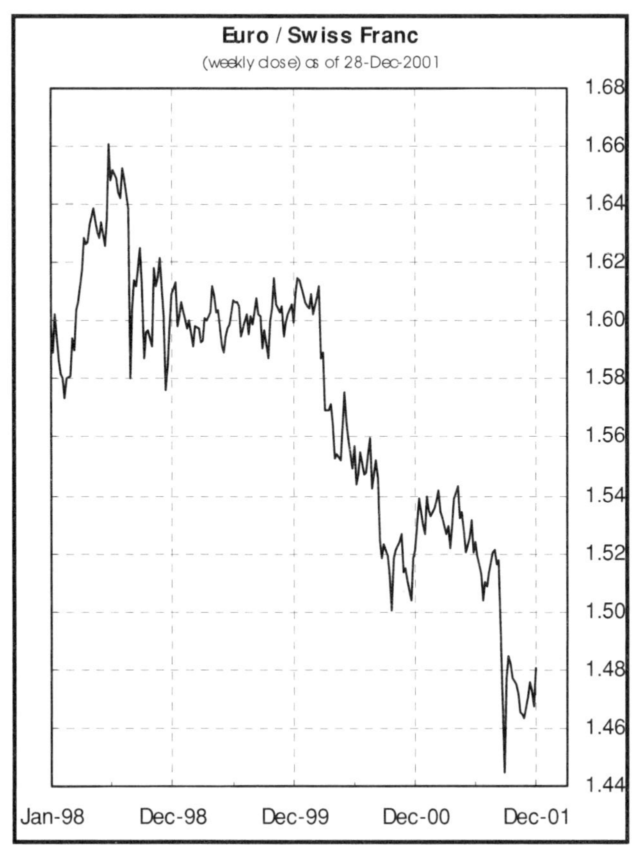
Euro / Swiss Franc
(weekly close) as of 28-Dec-2001
1.68
1.66
1.64
1.62
1.60
1.58
1.56
1.54
1.52
1.50
1.48
1.46
1.44
Jan-98
Dec-98
Dec-99
Dec-00
Dec-01

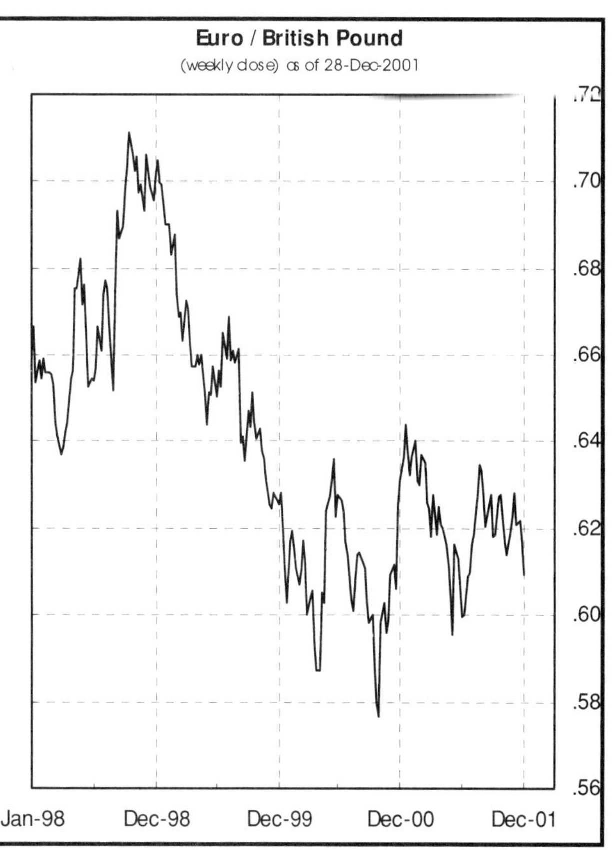
Euro / British Pound
(weekly close) as of 28-Dec-2001
.72
.70
.68
.66
.64
.62
.60
.58
.56
Jan-98
Dec-98
Dec-99
Dec-00
Dec-01

Japanese Yen / British Pound
(weekly close) as of 28-Dec-2001
250
240
230
220
210
200
190
180
170
160
150
140
Jan-98
Dec-98
Dec-99
Dec-00
Dec-01

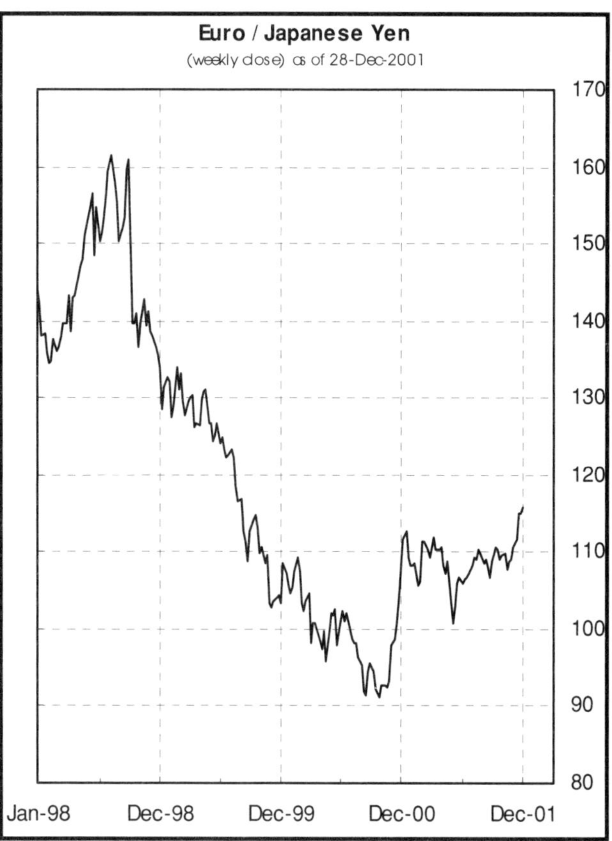
Euro / Japanese Yen
(weekly close) as of 28-Dec-2001
170
160
150
140
130
120
110
100
90
80
Jan-98
Dec-98
Dec-99
Dec-00
Dec-01

Diamonds

Natural gem-quality diamonds are among the rarest mineral materials. Diamonds have unique properties that give them value not only as gemstones but also as industrial materials. Diamonds are the strongest and hardest materials known and find use in drilling, cutting, grinding and polishing applications. Diamonds that do not meet gem-quality standards for clarity, color, size or shapes are used as industrial-grade diamonds.

The U.S. Geological Survey estimated that year 2000 world mine production of gem diamonds was 56.5 million carats, up 2 percent from 1999. The largest producer of gem diamonds was Botswana with 15 million carats, the same as 1999. Australia was the next largest producer with 14 million carats, unchanged from 1999.

The U.S. is the largest market for industrial diamonds. Industrial diamonds find particular use in the cutting edges of saws used to cut cement in highway construction. World mine production of industrial diamonds in 2000 was estimated to be 58.6 million carats, up 4 percent from 1999. The largest producer of industrial diamonds was Australia with 18.5 million carats, up 13 percent from 1999. Other larger producers are the Congo and Russia.

World Production of Natural Gem Diamonds In Thousands of Carats

Year	Angola	Australia	Botswana	Brazil	Central African Republic	China	Congo[3]	Ghana	Namibia	Russia	Sierra Leone	South Africa	World Total
1995	2,600	18,300	11,500	676	400	230	4,000	126	1,382	10,500	113	5,070	55,700
1996	2,250	18,897	12,388	200	350	230	3,300	142	1,402	10,500	162	4,400	55,200
1997	1,110	18,100	15,111	300	400	230	3,300	664	1,350	11,200	300	4,500	57,600
1998	2,400	18,400	14,772	300	330	230	5,080	649	1,390	11,500	200	4,300	60,800
1999[1]	3,700	13,403	16,000	300	400	230	4,120	518	1,550	11,500	450	4,000	59,200
2000[2]	5,400	12,014	19,700	300	400	230	3,500	178	1,520	11,600	450	4,300	62,600

[1] Preliminary. [2] Estimate. [3] Formerly Zaire. *Source: U.S. Geological Survey (USGS)*

World Production of Natural Industrial Diamonds[4] In Thousands of Carats

Year	Angola	Australia	Botswana	Brazil	Central African Republic	China	Congo[3]	Ghana	Russia	Sierra Leone	South Africa	Venezuela	World Total
1995	300	22,400	5,300	600	130	900	13,000	505	10,500	101	5,880	66	60,100
1996	250	23,096	5,000	600	120	900	18,940	573	10,500	108	5,550	73	66,200
1997	124	22,100	5,000	600	100	900	18,677	166	11,200	100	5,540	90	65,100
1998	364	22,500	5,000	600	200	900	21,000	160	11,500	50	6,460	17	69,300
1999[1]	400	16,381	5,350	600	150	920	16,000	128	11,500	150	6,020	36	58,200
2000[2]	600	14,684	4,950	600	150	920	14,200	712	11,600	150	6,480	40	55,600

[1] Preliminary. [2] Estimate. [3] Formerly Zaire. *Source: U.S. Geological Survey (USGS)*

World Production of Synthetic Diamonds In Thousands of Carats

Year	Belarus	China	Czech Republic	France	Greece	Ireland	Japan	Russia	South Africa	Sweden	Ukraine	United States	World Total
1995	25,000	15,500	5,000	3,000	1,000	60,000	32,000	80,000	60,000	25,000	8,000	115,000	440,000
1996	25,000	15,500	5,000	3,000	750	60,000	32,000	80,000	60,000	25,000	8,000	114,000	439,000
1997	25,000	16,000	5,000	3,500	750	60,000	32,000	80,000	60,000	25,000	8,000	125,000	451,000
1998	25,000	16,500	5,000	3,000	750	60,000	32,000	80,000	60,000	25,000	8,000	140,000	463,000
1999[1]	25,000	16,500	3,000	3,000	750	60,000	32,000	80,000	----	25,000	8,000	208,000	467,000
2000[2]	25,000	16,800	----	3,000	750	60,000	33,000	80,000	----	20,000	8,000	248,000	495,000

[1] Preliminary. [2] Estimate. *Source: U.S. Geological Survey (USGS)*

Salient Statistics of Industrial Diamonds in the United States In Millions of Carats

	Bort, Grit & Powder & Dust — Natural and Synthetic								Stones (Natural)						
	Production														
Year	Manufactured Diamond	Secondary	Imports for Consumption	Exports & Reexports	In Manufactured Products	Gov't Sales	Apparent Consumption	Price Value of Imports $ Per Carat	Secondary Production	Imports for Consumption	Exports & Reexports	Gov't Sales	Apparent Consumption	Price Value of Imports $ Per Carat	Net Import Reliance % of Consumption
1995	115.0	26.1	188.0	98.0	----	.2	231.0	.43	.3	4.1	.5	.3	4.2	6.62	86
1996	114.0	20.0	218.0	105.0	----	1.0	248.0	.46	.4	2.9	.5	.5	3.3	7.54	88
1997	125.0	10.0	254.0	126.0	----	.7	264.0	.43	.5	2.8	.6	1.2	3.9	7.69	87
1998	140.0	10.0	221.0	104.0	----	[3]	267.0	.44	.5	4.7	.8	.8	5.2	3.92	90
1999[1]	208.0	10.0	208.0	98.0	----	[3]	328.0	.44	.4	3.1	.7	.6	3.4	4.61	88
2000[2]	248.0	10.0	325.0	99.0	----	----	484.0	.37	.5	2.9	1.7	1.0	2.7	5.16	81

[1] Preliminary. [2] Estimate. [3] Less than 1/2 unit. *Source: U.S. Geological Survey (USGS)*

Eggs

Annual world egg production since the mid 1990's has continuously set new record highs. Production in 2001 of 815 billion eggs (68 billion dozen) compared with 802 billion in 2000 and almost 820 billion forecast for 2002. China produces and consumes almost half the world total egg supply; production of a record 387 billion eggs in 2001 compares with 381 billion in 2000 and forecasts of 395 billion in 2002 while consumption of 387 billion in 2001 compares with 380 billion in 2000 and a forecast of 394 billion in 2002. China's egg production and usage about doubled during the past decade. The U.S., the second largest producer with 2001 production of a record large 86 billion compares with 84 billion in 2000 and at least 87 billion forecast for 2002. However, there is a major difference between the two nations in respect to usage. Much of China's production is directly consumed as fresh brown eggs whereas in the U.S. about a third of production is processed and white eggs are favored for table use. Other major world producers include Mexico and the Russian Federation, each with about 35 billion eggs since calendar 2000.

U.S. consumption of 72.3 billion eggs in 2001 compares with the 71.1 billion in 2000 and a forecast of almost 74 billion in 2002. U.S. per capita egg consumption (including egg products) in 2001 of a record large 260 compares with 258 in 2000 and 262 in 2002 with part of the increase reflecting more eggs going to the breaking egg market. U.S. consumer preference continues to show signs of shifting to egg products for which eggs are broken relative to whole table eggs although per capita use is still biased towards the latter. Per capita use is much higher abroad: Japan is first followed by Taiwan, Mexico and China. Except for France, European per capita use runs under the U.S.

Foreign egg trade is small and skewed towards exports. The E.U. generally accounts for more than half of world exports--7.4 billion in 2001 vs. the world total of 12.8 billion, and the U.S. with 2.1 billion. Asia paced by Japan and Hong Kong import nearly half of the world total--3.3 billion in 2001 out of 8.2 billion. Collectively, the European Union is the largest importer with 3.6 billion in 2001. U.S shell egg exports totaled 94 million dozen in 2000 with Canada the primary destination. Exports in the first ten months of 2001 were running slightly under the 2000 owing in part to reduced shipments to Japan, whose total world imports in 2001 of 1.8 billion eggs compares with almost 2 billion in 2000.

There are definitive seasonal swings in U.S. egg production and table consumption. The table egg flocks typically reach a low in mid-summer, when heat stress is greatest on the birds and reduces the size of eggs produced by hens from large to medium. Larger egg production increases as the weather cools, reaching its average monthly high in the winter. However, table egg consumption tends to be highest in the summer when consumers have more time for leisurely meals. Thirty states account for most of U.S. production with Ohio, Iowa and California generally the largest producers.

The New York wholesale market price in 2001 averaged 67.80 cents per dozen vs. 68.90 cents in 2000. Prices are forecast to range between 62-67 cents in 2002. Retail prices in the second half of 2001 averaged around $.91/dozen, basis grade A, large.

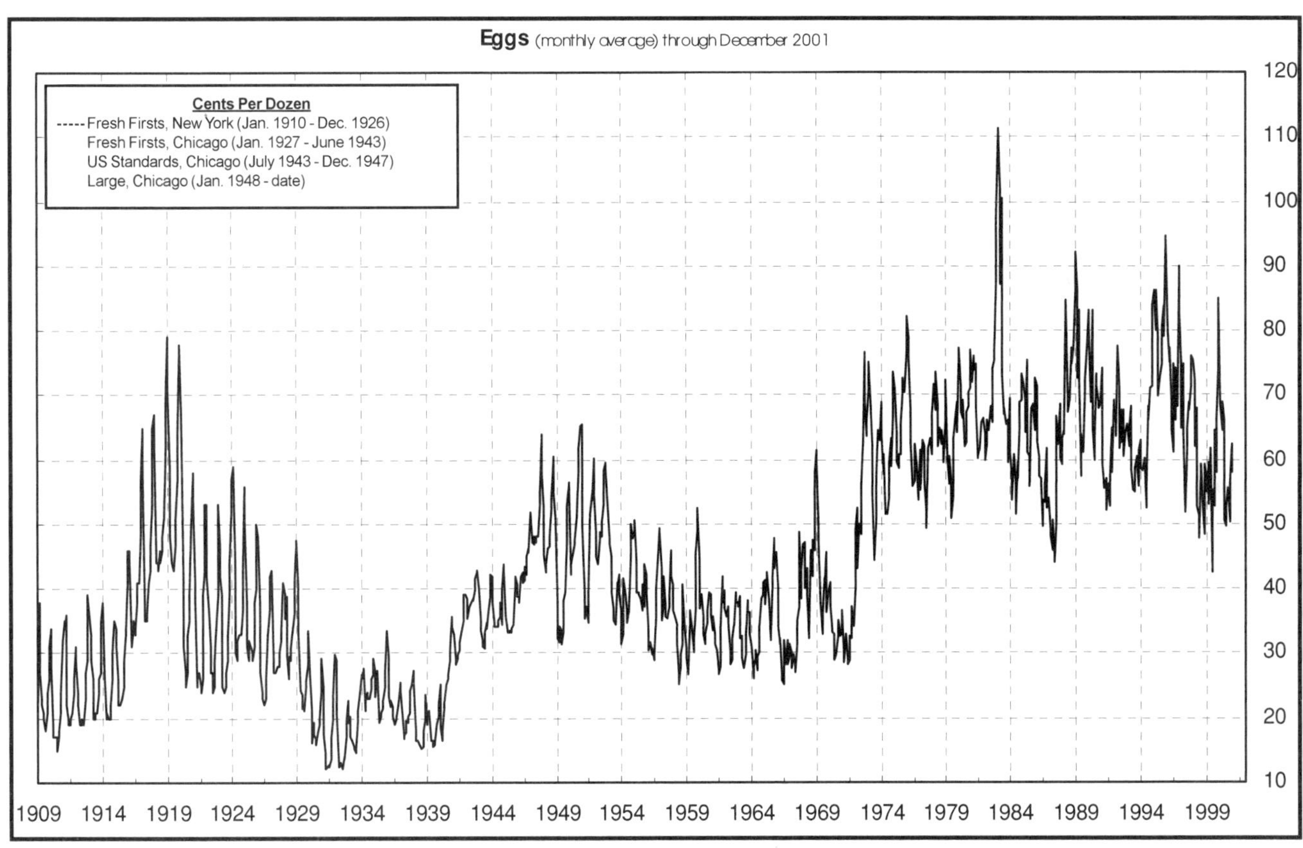

World Production of Eggs In Millions of Eggs

Year	Brazil	China	France	Germany	Italy	Japan	Mexico	Russia	Spain	Ukraine	United Kingdom	United States	World Total[3]
1992	14,190	230,980	15,375	15,165	11,454	42,911	19,650	42,900	8,675	13,445	10,699	70,860	541,859
1993	12,700	235,960	15,355	13,678	11,502	43,252	21,471	40,300	8,454	11,766	10,645	72,072	593,734
1994	13,460	281,010	16,370	13,960	11,599	43,047	25,896	37,400	9,670	10,145	10,620	74,136	643,045
1995	16,065	301,860	16,911	13,838	12,017	42,167	25,760	33,720	9,983	9,404	10,644	74,592	670,211
1996	15,932	253,680	16,500	13,922	11,923	42,786	26,045	31,500	8,952	8,763	10,668	76,536	631,846
1997	12,596	282,350	16,084	14,025	12,298	42,588	28,170	31,900	9,450	8,242	10,752	77,676	666,748
1998	13,636	307,760	16,900	14,164	12,433	42,117	29,898	33,000	9,084	8,269	10,812	79,896	695,281
1999	14,768	365,300	17,550	14,341	12,660	41,975	32,428	33,000	9,216	8,740	10,293	82,944	762,077
2000[1]	15,654	377,420	17,500	14,350	12,400	41,800	33,310	33,500	8,900	8,000	10,000	84,420	778,995
2001[2]	16,435	389,000	17,450	14,350	12,400	42,000	33,640	34,200	9,000	7,700	9,800	85,020	795,711

[1] Preliminary. [2] Forecast. [3] Selected countries. *Source: Foreign Agricultural Service, U.S. Department of Agriculture (FAS-USDA)*

Salient Statistics of Eggs in the United States

Year	-- Hens & Pullets -- On Farm Dec. 1[3]	Average Number During Year	Rate of Lay Per Layer During Year[4]	-------- Eggs -------- Total Produced	Price in Cents Per Dozen	Value of Production[5] Million Dollars	Total Egg Production	Imports[6]	Exports[6]	Used for Hatching	---- Consumption ---- Total	Per Capita Eggs[6]
	----- Thousands -----		(Number)	------- Millions -------			---------- Million Dozen ----------					(Number)
1991	279,325	275,451	252	69,465	67.6	3,915	5,779	2.3	154.5	708.6	4,938	234.6
1992	282,034	278,824	254	70,749	57.6	3,397	5,885	4.3	157.0	732.0	5,020	235.9
1993	290,626	284,770	253	71,936	63.4	3,800	5,960	4.7	158.9	769.6	5,082	236.2
1994	298,509	291,018	254	73,911	61.4	3,780	6,177	3.7	187.6	803.0	5,186	238.7
1995	298,753	293,854	253	74,591	62.4	3,880	6,216	4.1	208.9	847.2	5,167	235.7
1996	303,754	297,958	256	76,281	74.9	4,762	6,378	5.4	253.1	863.8	5,269	238.0
1997	312,137	304,230	255	77,532	70.3	4,540	6,473	6.9	227.8	894.7	5,359	240.0
1998	321,718	312,035	255	79,754	66.8	4,439	6,659	5.8	218.8	921.8	5,523	245.2
1999[1]	329,305	322,354	257	82,715	62.2	4,287	6,831	4.6	187.8	963.5	5,688	250.3
2000[2]	332,205	327,985	257	84,386	61.8	4,347	6,980	4.0	200.0	1,010.0	5,774	252.0

[1] Preliminary. [2] Forecast. [3] All layers of laying age. [4] Number of eggs produced during the year divided by the average number of all layers of laying age on hand during the year. [5] Value of sales plus value of eggs consumed in households of producers. [6] Shell-egg equivalent of eggs and egg products. *Source: National Agricultural Statistics Service, U.S. Department of Agriculture (NASS-USDA)*

Average Wholesale Price of Shell Eggs (Large) Delivered, Chicago In Cents Per Dozen

Year	Jan.	Feb.	Mar.	Apr.	May	June	July	Aug.	Sept.	Oct.	Nov.	Dec.	Average
1992	59.16	55.68	55.73	57.17	52.00	56.05	52.82	57.86	64.83	58.14	69.30	68.05	58.90
1993	65.65	63.61	77.50	71.07	61.90	67.64	62.79	67.59	60.64	64.21	65.55	65.55	66.14
1994	62.07	64.89	68.28	58.34	55.12	55.05	58.75	60.63	59.21	55.93	61.50	62.88	60.22
1995	58.55	58.24	60.22	59.87	52.50	56.84	68.10	65.93	71.10	71.34	83.93	86.35	66.08
1996	85.25	80.00	86.12	78.88	69.77	73.00	74.73	80.59	83.80	79.13	93.68	94.60	81.63
1997	79.77	75.18	77.25	68.55	64.40	61.02	74.66	66.07	74.26	68.39	89.87	82.68	73.51
1998	75.20	64.92	74.68	63.64	51.91	61.86	65.00	68.76	67.76	71.45	75.85	75.27	68.03
1999	72.34	62.13	67.85	52.74	51.35	47.86	58.40	59.30	52.86	48.38	59.26	56.38	57.40
2000	54.97	59.65	52.93	61.71	42.59	55.18	52.80	64.39	58.08	66.45	74.26	84.90	60.66
2001	68.52	64.45	69.00	66.12	50.61	49.81	52.83	55.46	50.21	57.41	62.50	58.05	58.75

Source: The Wall Street Journal

Total Egg Production in the United States In Millions of Eggs

Year	Jan.	Feb.	Mar.	Apr.	May	June	July	Aug.	Sept.	Oct.	Nov.	Dec.	Total
1992	5,951	5,558	6,042	5,832	5,918	5,693	5,908	5,919	5,753	6,019	5,920	6,163	70,860
1993	6,030	5,432	6,067	5,861	6,009	5,816	5,992	6,015	5,876	6,144	6,085	6,264	72,037
1994	6,186	5,598	6,320	6,073	6,189	5,992	6,205	6,272	6,125	6,377	6,265	6,516	74,121
1995	6,369	5,714	6,448	6,177	6,251	6,010	6,145	6,146	5,990	6,260	6,232	6,523	74,265
1996	6,398	5,954	6,495	6,243	6,340	6,169	6,440	6,447	6,235	6,495	6,409	6,696	76,321
1997	6,577	5,909	6,625	6,355	6,519	6,292	6,457	6,500	6,366	6,664	6,572	6,841	77,677
1998	6,766	6,109	6,869	6,603	6,665	6,456	6,720	6,694	6,480	6,791	6,723	7,047	79,923
1999	6,979	6,281	7,052	6,784	6,941	6,742	6,903	6,971	6,860	7,131	7,016	7,279	82,939
2000[1]	7,157	6,648	7,234	7,013	7,104	6,801	7,061	7,104	6,854	7,130	7,027	7,287	84,420
2001[2]	7,103	6,574	7,321	7,114	7,221	7,005	7,195	7,204	7,062	7,340	7,191	7,403	85,733

[1] Preliminary. [2] Estimate. *Source: National Agricultural Statistics Service, U.S. Department of Agriculture (NASS-USDA)*

Per Capita Disappearance of Eggs[4] in the United States In Number of Eggs

Year	First Quarter	Second Quarter	Third Quarter	Fourth Quarter	Total	Total Consumption (Million Dozen)	Year	First Quarter	Second Quarter	Third Quarter	Fourth Quarter	Total	Total Consumption (Million Dozen)
1991	46.7	43.8	45.1	47.0	182.6	3,844	1997	59.0	59.3	59.7	62.1	240.1	3,894
1992	45.1	44.1	44.4	46.7	180.3	3,838	1998	60.5	60.5	61.1	63.2	244.9	3,993
1993	46.1	44.0	43.8	46.0	179.7	3,825	1999	62.7	62.8	63.8	66.2	255.7	4,070
1994	45.0	43.0	43.9	46.0	177.9	3,864	2000[1]	64.5	64.0	64.2	65.6	258.2	4,124
1995	44.0	43.1	42.7	45.0	174.9	3,834	2001[2]	64.5	64.2	64.7	66.6	259.7	
1996	44.5	42.1	43.4	45.0	175.0	3,893	2002[3]	64.9	64.5	65.4	67.3	262.1	

[1] Preliminary. [2] Estimate. [3] Forecast *Source: Economic Research Service, U.S. Department of Agriculture (ERS-USDA)*

Egg-Feed Ratio[1] in the United States

Year	Jan.	Feb.	Mar.	Apr.	May	June	July	Aug.	Sept.	Oct.	Nov.	Dec.	Average
1992	8.4	7.8	7.4	7.6	6.7	7.0	7.3	8.1	9.6	9.3	11.2	11.1	8.4
1993	10.5	10.3	11.7	10.6	9.1	9.8	8.2	8.9	8.1	8.8	8.8	8.2	9.4
1994	7.9	8.0	8.4	7.7	7.2	7.0	8.0	9.0	9.2	8.9	10.3	9.9	8.5
1995	9.4	9.3	9.0	8.9	7.5	7.6	8.0	8.5	8.9	8.6	10.1	10.0	8.8
1996	9.8	8.7	9.1	7.9	6.5	6.7	6.3	6.9	8.1	9.3	11.3	12.5	8.6
1997	10.1	9.9	8.6	7.4	7.1	6.6	8.2	7.8	9.3	8.7	11.4	11.0	8.8
1998	10.1	8.3	9.4	8.5	6.7	8.0	7.9	10.8	10.7	11.3	12.6	12.8	9.7
1999	11.7	10.6	11.3	9.2	7.8	8.2	9.9	10.1	9.3	8.0	11.9	10.1	9.8
2000	8.9	11.3	8.0	9.9	6.4	9.5	9.2	12.9	10.3	12.2	13.1	15.0	10.6
2001[2]	10.9	11.4	11.7	11.5	8.4	8.5	7.8	8.4	8.5	10.7	11.5	9.3	9.9

[1] Pounds of laying feed equivalent in value to one dozen eggs. [2] Preliminary. *Source: Economic Research Service, U.S. Department of Agriculture (ERS-USDA)*

Total Eggs -- Supply and Distribution in the United States In Millions of Dozen

	Supply				Utilization			Consumption	
Year & Quarters	Beginning Stocks	Production	Imports[4]	Total Supply	Exports[4]	Eggs Used for Hatching	Ending Stocks	Total	Per Capita (Number)
1994 I	10.7	1,509	1.0	1,520	40.2	195.3	12.1	1,273	58.8
II	12.1	1,521	1.1	1,535	45.5	205.3	11.9	1,272	58.6
III	11.9	1,550	1.0	1,563	49.3	202.8	13.8	1,297	59.6
IV	13.8	1,597	.6	1,611	52.6	199.6	14.9	1,344	61.6
1995 I	14.9	1,549	1.1	1,565	45.5	207.1	14.9	1,297	59.4
II	14.9	1,545	1.2	1,561	50.1	214.1	17.9	1,279	58.4
III	17.9	1,533	1.0	1,552	47.0	213.0	13.0	1,279	58.3
IV	13.0	1,589	.8	1,602	66.4	212.9	11.2	1,312	59.6
1996 I	11.2	1,571	1.5	1,583	59.3	217.4	9.8	1,297	58.8
II	9.8	1,563	1.6	1,574	65.6	217.2	9.6	1,282	58.0
III	9.6	1,594	1.2	1,604	66.0	215.8	11.9	1,311	59.1
IV	11.9	1,632	1.0	1,645	62.2	214.3	8.5	1,360	61.2
1997 I	8.5	1,593	1.9	1,603	61.7	221.1	6.5	1,314	59.0
II	6.5	1,597	1.5	1,605	50.3	227.2	6.3	1,321	59.3
III	6.3	1,610	1.6	1,618	51.6	225.1	8.2	1,333	59.7
IV	8.2	1,673	1.9	1,683	64.2	221.3	7.4	1,390	62.1
1998[1] I	7.4	1,645	1.7	1,654	61.7	226.5	7.9	1,358	60.5
II	7.9	1,644	1.2	1,653	51.5	233.3	7.7	1,360	60.5
III	7.7	1,658	1.2	1,667	53.3	230.6	6.3	1,377	61.1
IV	6.3	1,712	1.8	1,720	52.3	231.4	8.4	1,428	63.2
1999[2] I	8.4	1,691	1.6	1,701	39.8	233.5	7.0	1,421	62.7
II	7.0	1,702	2.3	1,712	37.3	241.2	8.6	1,425	62.8
III	8.6	1,727	1.9	1,737	39.8	236.5	6.4	1,455	64.2
IV	6.4	1,765	1.8	1,773	42.0	235.0	5.0	1,491	65.8
2000[3] I	5.0	1,735	1.0	1,741	40.0	245.0	5.0	1,451	63.5
II	5.0	1,735	1.0	1,741	40.0	255.0	5.0	1,441	62.9
III	5.0	1,755	1.0	1,761	44.0	255.0	5.0	1,457	63.4
IV	5.0	1,805	1.0	1,811	46.0	250.0	5.0	1,510	65.6

[1] Preliminary. [2] Estimate. [3] Forecast. [4] Shell-egg equivalent of eggs and egg products. *Source: Economic Research Service, U.S. Department of Agriculture (ERS-USDA)*

Hens and Pullets of Laying Age (Layers) in the United States, on First of Month In Thousands

Year	Jan.	Feb.	Mar.	Apr.	May	June	July	Aug.	Sept.	Oct.	Nov.	Dec.
1992	280,697	279,274	279,117	279,009	276,757	275,645	275,179	275,091	274,010	279,233	280,183	282,034
1993	281,639	282,933	282,005	282,480	281,468	280,795	280,517	282,201	282,341	284,771	285,298	290,626
1994	290,413	289,625	290,416	290,979	289,125	288,398	287,454	288,484	292,116	294,576	295,719	298,509
1995	300,331	298,202	297,689	296,290	294,697	290,806	289,018	286,519	289,595	290,889	294,486	298,293
1996	299,261	298,320	298,348	298,029	295,123	293,740	294,044	296,612	296,911	298,433	299,910	303,754
1997	305,011	303,449	304,276	303,997	302,766	300,692	299,007	298,844	300,138	305,664	307,146	312,137
1998	311,593	312,111	314,322	313,833	309,945	309,235	309,049	308,747	309,706	312,807	316,840	321,718
1999	322,137	322,382	323,161	322,162	320,783	320,211	320,672	318,944	321,349	323,365	327,135	329,320
2000	328,307	328,767	330,876	330,807	327,597	325,012	324,843	326,240	325,212	327,219	329,092	332,410
2001[1]	332,107	335,449	336,056	337,096	336,379	333,115	331,632	331,505	332,867	336,076	336,536	338,233

[1] Preliminary. *Source: National Agricultural Statistics Service, U.S. Department of Agriculture (NASS-USDA)*

Eggs Laid Per Hundred Layers in the United States In Number of Eggs

Year	Jan.	Feb.	Mar.	Apr.	May	June	July	Aug.	Sept.	Oct.	Nov.	Dec.	Average
1992	2,176	2,036	2,216	2,148	2,186	2,110	2,196	2,204	2,125	2,200	2,140	2,226	2,164
1993	2,192	1,970	2,209	2,132	2,182	2,112	2,175	2,183	2,124	2,209	2,167	2,237	2,158
1994	2,199	1,987	2,246	2,160	2,204	2,142	2,222	2,230	2,152	2,227	2,180	2,176	2,177
1995	2,130	1,919	2,173	2,092	2,137	2,075	2,137	2,135	2,065	2,140	2,108	2,183	2,108
1996	2,141	1,996	2,178	2,105	2,153	2,099	2,180	2,172	2,094	2,171	2,124	2,199	2,134
1997	2,161	1,943	2,176	2,093	2,156	2,093	2,155	2,165	2,096	2,172	2,122	2,193	2,127
1998	2,169	1,950	2,187	2,117	2,153	2,088	2,175	2,165	2,082	2,157	2,109	2,190	2,129
1999	2,165	1,946	2,185	2,110	2,166	2,104	2,158	2,177	2,128	2,192	2,138	2,214	2,140
2000	2,178	2,016	2,186	2,130	2,177	2,093	2,169	2,181	2,101	2,173	2,125	2,193	2,144
2001[1]	2,128	1,943	2,178	2,105	2,160	2,100	2,165	2,169	2,102	2,179	2,128	2,187	2,129

[1] Preliminary. *Source: National Agricultural Statistics Service, U.S. Department of Agriculture (NASS-USDA)*

Egg-Type Chicks Hatched by Commercial Hatcheries in the United States In Thousands

Year	Jan.	Feb.	Mar.	Apr.	May	June	July	Aug.	Sept.	Oct.	Nov.	Dec.	Total
1992	32,496	31,950	36,490	35,755	38,513	34,568	32,265	28,349	28,760	32,843	27,718	31,612	391,319
1993	34,885	34,009	38,264	37,163	36,742	35,587	33,980	31,455	31,775	31,634	30,074	30,448	405,986
1994	33,236	31,086	33,489	35,657	35,322	31,985	29,613	31,295	31,587	32,066	26,075	30,166	381,577
1995	32,374	32,743	36,019	35,078	37,540	34,996	29,572	31,442	33,586	33,383	29,129	30,639	396,501
1996	31,580	34,608	36,890	35,740	38,028	33,017	31,920	31,782	31,930	32,319	30,947	32,879	401,640
1997	33,752	35,655	37,347	38,842	39,020	36,796	33,772	33,061	37,118	35,262	28,122	35,796	424,543
1998	37,168	34,597	40,604	39,057	39,206	39,323	35,576	33,398	37,959	34,667	31,217	35,501	438,273
1999	35,242	36,367	41,172	42,285	40,726	41,439	34,275	35,518	39,287	39,044	32,802	33,564	451,721
2000	34,178	34,656	38,874	36,649	41,182	37,265	33,237	34,324	36,316	36,077	32,290	34,690	429,738
2001[1]	37,976	38,198	40,109	41,691	42,579	40,601	37,903	35,162	36,594	36,501	31,649	31,504	450,467

[1] Preliminary. *Source: National Agricultural Statistics Service, U.S. Department of Agriculture (NASS-USDA)*

Cold Storage Holdings of Frozen Eggs in the United States, on First of Month In Millions of Pounds[1]

Year	Jan.	Feb.	Mar.	Apr.	May	June	July	Aug.	Sept.	Oct.	Nov.	Dec.
1992	16.0	20.0	19.2	19.7	18.8	18.9	21.1	19.5	20.2	20.0	21.7	18.7
1993	17.2	16.7	16.9	15.1	14.3	15.5	15.1	17.6	18.1	14.4	14.0	13.5
1994	13.7	14.8	15.8	15.6	16.3	15.2	15.4	19.0	19.7	17.8	20.0	19.1
1995	19.5	19.5	18.3	18.5	17.3	18.1	22.9	20.6	18.0	16.2	14.4	12.5
1996	13.8	15.6	16.2	12.4	11.5	11.4	11.7	13.5	15.0	14.9	12.6	10.4
1997	10.2	11.0	11.5	8.5	8.5	8.2	8.3	8.9	11.1	10.8	10.9	10.3
1998	9.7	12.0	12.3	10.4	9.2	12.9	10.2	11.8	9.0	8.2	9.0	9.3
1999	11.0	11.0	10.8	9.2	9.4	9.7	11.3	11.1	8.8	9.5	9.0	8.5
2000	10.1	17.6	14.8	14.0	12.8	13.5	14.1	14.4	14.9	14.4	16.6	15.4
2001[2]	15.0	16.9	15.5	14.6	15.9	15.8	14.4	16.7	17.8	17.4	8.8	7.3

[1] Converted on basis 39.5 pounds frozen eggs equals 1 case. [2] Preliminary. *Source: National Agricultural Statistics Service, U.S. Department of Agriculture (NASS-USDA)*

Electric Power

U.S. net generation of electric power by electric utilities in August 2001 was 373 billion kilowatthours. Of the total, 262 billion kilowatthours was generated by electric utilities and 111 billion kilowatthours by nonutility power producers. The August total was up almost 2 percent from August 2000. In the January-August 2001 period, U.S. net generation of electricity was 2.59 trillion kilowatthours with 1.83 trillion generated by electric utilities and 755 billion kilowatthours generated by nonutility power producers. In the same period of year 2000, 2.55 trillion kilowatthours were generated in the U.S. while in 1999 the total was 2.51 trillion kilowatthours. For all of 2000 net electricity generation was 3.8 trillion kilowatthours. In 1990 it was 3 trillion hours while in 1980 it was 2.29 trillion.

Electric power generation by nonutility power producers has been trending higher. For 2000 the total was 785 million kilowatthours, up 48 percent from the 1999 output of 531 billion kilowatthours. In 1990 the total output was 217 billion kilowatthours. Electric power generation by electric utilities appears to be leveling off. The total for 2000 was 3 trillion kilowatthours, down 5 percent from 1999. In 1998 the total was 3.21 trillion kilowatthours. Overall, electricity generation in the U.S. is trending higher. In 1973 the total output was 1.86 trillion kilowatthours.

Most of the electric power in the U.S. was generated using coal. In August 2001, coal generated 187 billion kilowatthours, half of the U.S. total. In the January-August 2002 period, coal generated 1.33 trillion kilowatthours of electricity, some 51 percent of the U.S. total. In 2000, coal's share of the total was 52 percent.

Other fossil fuels that are used to generate electricity are petroleum and natural gas. In August 2001, petroleum-generated electricity was 14.7 billion kilowatthours or 4 percent of the U.S. total. In the first eight months of 2001, petroleum generated 101 billion kilowatthours, some 4 percent of U.S. output. Natural gas generated 75 billion kilowatthours in August 2001, some 20 percent of the U.S. total. In January-August 2001, natural gas generated 421 billion kilowatthours, 16 percent of the U.S. total output. In 1990 the natural gas share of the U.S. total was 12 percent.

Nuclear power in January-August 2001 generated 515 billion kilowatthours or 20 percent of the U.S. total. In 2000 the nuclear electric power share was also 20 percent. In 1999 the share was 19 percent.

Renewable energy sources generate smaller amounts of electric power. In the January-August 2001 period, conventional hydroelectric power generated 152 billion kilowatthours, about 6 percent of the U.S. total. Geothermal electricity production in the period was 9.3 billion kilowatthours. Wood generated 26.4 billion kilowatthours, wind generated 5 billion kilowatthours and solar power generated 577 million kilowatthours in January-August 2001.

World Electricity Production (Monthly Average) In Millions of Kilowatt Hours

Year	Australia	Canada	China	Germany	India	Italy	Japan	Rep. of Korea	Russia[3]	South Africa	Ukraine[3]	United Kingdom	United States
1992	13,313	41,803	61,562	44,761	25,081	18,854	74,611	10,914	84,038	14,008	21,044	27,240	256,209
1993	13,646	42,591	67,723	37,722	26,961	18,566	75,559	12,036	79,716	14,548	19,159	26,834	266,410
1994	13,959	44,954	75,312	37,786	29,250	19,323	80,361	13,749	72,993	15,825	16,910	27,042	271,150
1995	14,449	45,208	81,979	38,207	31,675	20,228	82,490	15,388	71,669	16,016	16,193	27,970	279,820
1996	14,806	46,307	88,275	45,586	32,808	20,340	84,113	17,125	70,600	16,096	15,166	27,191	287,250
1997	15,256	47,929	91,277	45,133	35,105	20,898	86,676	18,704	69,511	16,108	14,834	27,012	291,185
1998	14,737	45,259	94,011	45,860	37,326	21,659	76,763	17,942	68,930	17,119	14,402	27,914	301,489
1999	15,399	46,496	100,345	45,973	39,766	22,136	76,755	19,944	70,611	16,961	14,342	28,095	308,964
2000[1]	15,712	48,500	109,426	45,178	41,705	22,986	78,391	22,200	73,117	17,557	13,601	28,484	315,994
2001[2]	15,531	49,436	112,485		41,998		78,060	23,268	52,837	17,582	14,745	30,256	304,748

[1] Preliminary. [2] Estimate. [3] Formerly part of the U.S.S.R.; data not reported separately until 1992. *Source: United Nations*

Installed Capacity, Capability & Peak Load of the U.S. Electric Utility Industry In Millions of Kilowatt Hours

	Installed Generating Capacity on December 31													Capacity	Total	
		Type of Prime Mover				Type of Ownership										
Year	Total Electric Utility Industry	Hydro	Gas, Turbine & Steam	Nuclear Power	Internal Combustion	Investor Owned	Cooperative	Subtotal Gov't	Municipal Utilities	Federal	Power Districts, State Projects	Capability at Winter Peak Load	Non-Coincident Winter Peak Load	Margin Non-Coincident Peak Load (%)	Electric Utility Industry Generation	Annual Peak Load Factor (%)
1990	735.1	87.2	531.1	108.0	8.7	568.8	26.3	139.9	40.1	65.4	34.4	696.8	484.0	20.4	2,808.2	60.4
1991	740.0	88.7	534.1	108.4	8.8	573.0	26.5	140.5	40.4	65.6	34.5	703.2	485.4	20.2	2,825.0	60.9
1992	741.7	89.7	534.5	107.9	9.6	572.9	26.0	142.7	41.6	66.1	35.0	707.8	493.0	21.1	2,797.2	61.1
1993	744.7	90.2	536.9	107.8	9.8	575.2	26.1	143.4	41.8	66.1	35.5	712.0	521.7	17.1	2,882.5	61.0
1994	746.0	90.3	537.9	107.9	9.9	574.8	26.4	144.7	42.0	66.3	36.4	715.1	518.3	16.7	2,910.7	61.2
1995	750.5	91.1	541.6	107.9	9.9	578.7	27.1	144.8	42.2	65.9	36.6	727.7	544.7	13.2	2,994.5	59.8
1996	756.5	91.0	546.6	109.0	9.9	582.2	27.2	147.1	43.0	67.2	36.9	740.5	545.1	14.9	3,073.1	61.0
1997	759.9	92.5	549.7	107.6	10.0	582.5	28.0	149.4	43.8	68.9	36.7	743.8	560.2	13.4	3,119.1	61.3
1998	728.3	91.2	522.1	104.8	10.2	531.3	32.5	164.5	50.5	68.7	45.3	835.3	652.4	12.0	3,212.2	62.0
1999[1]	678.0	89.8	476.3	102.3	9.6	483.7	34.6	159.6	50.2	68.7	40.7	848.9	656.3	10.3	3,173.7	61.2

[1] Preliminary. *Source: Edison Electric Institute (EEI)*

ELECTRIC POWER

Available Electricity and Energy Sales in the United States In Billions of Kilowatt Hours

	Net Generation										Sales to Ultimate Customers						
	Electric Utility Industry																
Year	Total[2]	Hydro	Natural Gas	Coal	Fuel Oil	Nu-clear	Other Source[3]	Total	Total Million $	Total	Resi-den-tial	Inter-depart-mental	Com-mercial	Indust-rial	Street & Highway Lighting	Other Public Auth.	Railways & Rail-roads
1986	2,487	290.8	248.5	1,386	136.6	414.0	11.5	2,599	152,481	2,360	820	5.2	629.0	819	15.0	61.9	4.7
1987	2,572	249.7	272.6	1,464	118.5	455.3	12.3	2,719	155,734	2,441	846	4.5	658.4	844	14.4	63.0	4.9
1988	2,704	222.9	252.8	1,541	148.9	527.0	12.0	2,879	162,449	2,561	886	4.2	697.8	882	14.6	64.6	5.1
1989	2,784	265.1	266.6	1,554	158.3	529.4	11.3	2,985	169,903	2,636	899	4.3	715.9	913	14.6	69.3	5.3
1990	2,808	279.9	264.1	1,560	117.0	576.9	10.7	3,041	176,929	2,705	916	4.2	738.9	932	15.2	72.8	5.3
1991	1,825	275.5	264.2	1,551	111.5	612.6	10.1	3,100	185,220	2,745	949	2.6	753.3	935	15.6	76.1	5.3
1992	2,797	239.6	263.9	1,576	88.9	618.8	10.2	3,107	187,399	2,744	929	2.6	755.7	949	15.8	77.2	5.2
1993	2,883	265.1	258.9	1,639	99.5	610.3	9.6	3,210	197,992	2,860	994	2.7	803.1	957	18.1	69.7	5.4
1994	2,911	243.7	291.1	1,635	91.0	640.4	8.9	3,283	202,597	2,936	1,008	3.0	833.5	990	18.5	70.6	5.8
1995	2,995	293.7	307.3	1,653	60.8	673.4	6.4	3,395	207,652	3,017	1,042	2.1	863.5	1,006	17.9	69.9	5.5
1996	3,073	324.5	262.3	1,737	67.0	674.7	7.2	3,473	212,390	3,103	1,082	2.5	887.1	1,028	18.0	70.3	5.3
1997	3,119	333.5	283.1	1,789	77.1	629.4	7.5	3,536	215,264	3,154	1,079	2.6	929.0	1,028	19.7	75.6	5.3
1998	3,212	304.4	309.2	1,807	110.2	673.7	7.2	3,726	218,491	3,256	1,128	NA	968.5	1,040	16.3	87.2	NA
1999[1]	3,174	293.9	296.4	1,768	86.9	725.0	3.7	3,743	215,647	3,250	1,141	NA	970.6	1,018	15.9	90.9	NA

[1] Preliminary. [2] Includes internal combustion. [3] Includes electricity produced from geothermal, wood, waste, wind, solar, etc. NA = Not available.
Source: Edison Electric Institute (EEI)

Electric Power Production by Electric Utilities in the United States In Millions of Kilowatt Hours

Year	Jan.	Feb.	Mar.	Apr.	May	June	July	Aug.	Sept.	Oct.	Nov.	Dec.	Total
1987	222,749	194,034	201,849	189,496	206,074	225,589	247,915	247,645	213,008	203,009	200,258	220,500	2,572,127
1988	237,897	216,937	214,013	196,000	208,371	232,747	257,461	267,693	220,179	210,608	209,593	232,752	2,704,250
1989	232,747	219,826	226,742	208,042	220,124	235,689	257,050	258,687	227,150	219,910	219,300	259,038	2,784,304
1990	237,289	212,880	226,034	211,070	222,908	249,175	266,375	268,527	237,017	224,694	213,748	237,434	2,808,151
1991	248,455	210,821	221,400	209,004	234,373	248,427	271,976	268,115	233,885	223,430	221,377	233,760	2,825,023
1992	243,970	217,761	224,665	210,837	220,355	236,842	266,148	255,203	234,760	221,289	221,263	244,126	2,797,219
1993	245,782	224,617	234,801	211,374	222,396	249,633	282,292	279,132	236,603	223,629	225,855	246,412	2,882,525
1994	261,697	225,011	231,544	214,817	227,703	263,859	278,149	274,645	237,663	227,972	224,745	242,906	2,910,712
1995	253,077	228,127	233,675	217,381	236,381	256,083	292,827	304,709	245,574	234,409	234,117	258,170	2,994,529
1996	268,713	245,388	247,989	226,423	251,570	268,644	289,329	290,458	250,672	240,674	241,077	258,138	3,077,442
1997	273,410	233,907	244,659	230,512	243,143	266,588	304,628	294,557	266,649	253,267	243,726	267,477	3,122,522
1998	265,435	235,340	256,575	232,457	265,077	291,029	317,521	312,538	279,198	251,380	239,089	266,532	3,212,171
1999	275,230	239,825	258,678	238,969	255,266	281,233	318,745	307,835	261,347	243,212	235,129	258,205	3,173,674
2000	265,991	237,324	241,397	227,031	253,890	268,128	279,421	286,682	245,137	228,389	226,765	255,229	3,015,383
2001[1]	238,967	202,716	214,773	199,971	219,021	236,477	256,716	262,393					2,746,551

[1] Preliminary. *Source: Energy Information Administration, U.S. Department of Energy (EIA-DOE)*

Use of Fuels for Electric Generation in the United States

	Consumption of Fuell									
Year	Coal (Thousand Short Tons)	Fuel Oil (Thousand Barels)[2]	Gas (Million Cubic Feet)	Total Fuel in Coal Equivalent[3] (Thousand Short Tons)	Net Generation by Fuels4 (Million Kilowatthour)	Pounds of Coal Per Kilowatthour (Pounds)	Cost of Fossil-fuel at Elec. Util. Cents/MBTU	Average Cost of Fuel Per Kiliowatthour (Cents)	Heat Rate BTU Per kilowatthour	Cost Per Million BTU Consumed (Cents)
1986	685,056	230,482	2,602,370	907,720	1,770,925	.989	175.0	1.92	10,423	184.5
1987	717,894	199,378	2,844,051	944,420	1,854,895	.981	170.6	1.84	10,354	177.7
1988	758,372	248,096	2,635,613	984,969	1,942,353	.984	164.3	1.76	10,328	170.7
1989	766,888	267,451	2,787,012	1,004,964	1,978,577	.987	167.5	1.79	10,312	174.0
1990	773,549	196,054	2,787,332	988,300	1,940,712	.997	168.9	1.80	10,366	174.1
1991	772,268	184,886	2,789,014	987,469	1,926,801	.996	160.3	1.75	10,322	169.6
1992	779,860	147,335	2,765,608	983,484	1,928,683	.990	159.0	1.72	10,340	166.6
1993	813,508	162,454	2,682,440	1,017,086	1,997,605	.993	159.5	1.72	10,351	166.6
1994	817,270	151,004	2,987,146	1,033,575	2,017,646	.999	152.6	1.59	10,425	152.6
1995	829,007	102,150	3,196,507	1,039,174	2,021,064	1.003	145.3	1.48	10,173	145.2
1996	874,681	113,274	2,732,107	1,063,755	2,066,666	1.007	151.9	1.55	10,176	151.9
1997	900,361	125,146	2,968,453	1,103,037	2,148,756	1.005	152.2	1.53	10,081	152.2
1998	910,867	178,614	3,258,054	1,147,317	2,226,860	.996	143.8	1.49	10,360	143.8
1999[1]	894,120	143,830	3,113,419	1,113,614	2,150,989	1.012	144.2	1.48	10,301	144.1

[1] Preliminary. [2] 42-gallon barrels. [3] Coal equivalents are calculated on the basis of Btu instead of generation data. [4] Excludes wood & waste fuels.
Source: Edison Electric Institute (EEI)

Fertilizer

The three primary fertilizer chemicals used in the United States are nitrogen, phosphorus and potassium. They provide basic nutrients to plants. The basic nitrogen fertilizer is ammonia which is comprised of nitrogen and natural gas. Nitrogen is required for proper nutrition and maturation of the plant. Phosphorus is produced from phosphate rock and in important in plant nutrition. Potash denotes a variety of mined and manufactured salts, all containing the element potassium in water soluble form. Potassium activates plant enzymes, aids photosynthesis in the leaves and increases disease resistance.

The U.S. Geological Survey reported that in 1999, world production of ammonia was 104 million metric tonnes. This was down 4 percent from 1999. The largest producer was China with 2000 output of 28 million tonnes, down 1 percent from 1999. U.S. production of ammonia was 13 million tonnes, up marginally from 1999. During 2000, ammonia in the U.S. was produced by 24 companies at 39 plants. There were shutdowns at some plants due to high natural gas prices. Over half of the total U.S. ammonia production capacity is in Louisiana, Oklahoma and Texas due to their large reserves of natural gas. The U.S. is the second largest producer and consumer of ammonia after China. The major derivatives of ammonia are urea, ammonium phosphate, ammonium nitrate, nitric acid and ammonium sulfate. The U.S. and China produce about 40 percent of the world's ammonia. Other large producers include India, Russia, Canada and Indonesia. Global resources of nitrogen from the atmosphere are unlimited.

About 88 percent of U.S. apparent domestic ammonia consumption was for fertilizer use including anhydrous ammonia for direct application, urea, ammonium nitrates, ammonium phosphates and other nitrogen compounds. Ammonia is also used to produce plastics, synthetic fibers and resins, explosives and other chemical compounds. U.S. apparent consumption of ammonia in 2000 was 16.5 million tonnes, up 1 percent from 1999. Imports for consumption in 2000 were 4 million tonnes, up 3 percent from 1999. Exports of ammonia in 2000 were 500,000 tonnes, down 11 percent from 1999. Producer stocks of ammonia at the end of 2000 were one million tonnes.

World mine production of potash in 2000 was estimated at 26.5 million tonnes, up 3 percent from 1999. The largest producer of potash was Canada with 9.2 million tonnes. The next largest producer was Belarus followed by Russia and Germany. The world's largest potash producers operated at reduced capacity due to potential oversupply. World potash reserves are estimated at 8.4 billion tonnes. There are no substitutes for potassium which is an essential plant nutrient.

U.S. production of potash in 2000 was 1.3 million tonnes, up 8 percent from 1999. The fertilizer industry used about 90 percent of potash sales and the chemical industry used about 10 percent. Over half of the potash was produced as potassium chloride. U.S. imports for consumption of potash in 2000 were 4.3 million tonnes, down 4 percent from 1999. The major supplier has been Canada. U.S. apparent consumption of potash in 2000 was 5 million tonnes, down 2 percent from 1999.

World mine production of phosphate rock in 2000 was 139 million tonnes, down 1 percent from 1999. The world's largest producer was the U.S. with 39.7 million tonnes, down 2 percent from 1999. The next largest producer was China with 26 million tonnes. Other large producers include Morocco and Russia.

World Production of Ammonia   In Thousands of Metric Tons of Contained Nitrogen

Year	Canada	China	France	Germany	India	Indo-nesia	Japan	Mexico	Nether-lands	Poland	Russia[3]	United States	World Total
1992	3,104	18,000	1,848	2,113	7,452	2,688	1,545	2,203	2,588	1,222	8,786	13,400	93,400
1993	3,410	19,000	1,871	2,100	7,176	2,888	1,471	1,758	2,472	1,163	8,138	12,600	91,600
1994	3,470	20,100	1,480	2,170	7,503	3,012	1,483	2,030	2,479	1,230	7,300	13,300	93,600
1995	3,773	22,600	1,470	2,518	8,287	3,336	1,584	1,992	2,580	1,726	7,900	13,000	100,000
1996	3,840	25,200	1,570	2,485	8,549	3,647	1,490	2,054	2,652	1,713	7,900	13,400	105,000
1997	4,081	24,800	1,757	2,470	9,328	3,770	1,509	1,448	2,478	1,824	7,150	13,300	103,000
1998	3,900	26,100	1,570	2,512	10,240	3,600	1,389	1,449	2,350	1,683	6,500	13,800	105,000
1999[1]	4,135	27,800	1,570	2,406	10,376	3,450	1,385	1,003	2,430	1,474	7,633	12,900	107,000
2000[2]	4,130	28,000	1,700	2,473	10,148	4,000	1,405	701	2,543	1,862	8,735	12,300	109,000

[1] Preliminary. [2] Estimate. [3] Formerly part of the U.S.S.R.; data not reported separately until 1992. *Source: U.S. Geological Survey (USGS)*

Salient Statistics of Nitrogen[3] (Ammonia) in the United States   In Thousands of Metric Tons

Year	Net Import Reliance as a % of Apparent Consumption	Production[3] (Fixed): Fertilizer	Production[3] (Fixed): Non-fertilizer	Production[3] (Fixed): Total	Imports[4] (Fixed)	Exports	Nitrogen[5] Compounds: Produced	Nitrogen[5] Compounds: Con-sumption	Stocks, Dec. 31: Ammonia	Stocks, Dec. 31: Fixed Nitrogen Com-pounds	Ammonia Con-sumption (Apparent)	Average Price ($ Per Tonne): Urea FOB Gulf[6] Coast	Average Price ($ Per Tonne): Urea FOB Corn Belt	Average Price ($ Per Tonne): Ammonium Nitrate: FOB Corn Belt	Average Price ($ Per Tonne): Ammonia FOB Gulf Coast
1993	17	11,300	1,320	12,620	2,657	378	10,000	10,100	852	1,600	15,100	139-141	141-165	138-149	121
1994	19	11,600	1,750	13,350	3,450	215	10,000	11,700	956	1,650	16,500	219-226	204-215	165-176	211
1995	15	11,600	1,410	13,010	2,630	319	10,400	10,700	959	1,580	15,300	217-222	220-235	162-170	191
1996	19	11,500	1,720	13,220	3,390	435	11,502	11,100	881	1,390	16,400	188-190	197-210	160-170	190
1997	16	11,400	1,900	13,300	3,530	395	11,441	11,300	1,530	2,220	15,800	102-103	125-135	122-125	173
1998	19	11,800	1,950	13,800	3,460	614	11,712	11,300	1,050	1,270	17,100	82-85	110-125	110-115	121
1999[1]	21	11,400	1,550	12,900	3,890	562	11,303	11,500	996	1,240	16,300	107-110	115-125	110-115	109
2000[2]	20	10,900	1,490	12,300	3,880	662	10,552	11,200	1,120	1,310	15,400	158-161	175-180	140-150	169

[1] Preliminary. [2] Estimate. [3] Anhydrous ammonia, synthetic. [4] For consumption. [5] Major downstream nitrogen compounds. [6] *Granular.*
E = Net exporter. *Source: U.S. Geological Survey (USGS)*

World Production of Phosphate Rock, Basic Slag & Guano   In Thousands of Metric Tons (Gross Weight)

Year	Brazil	China	Egypt	Israel	Jordan	Morocco	Russia[3]	Senegal	Syria	Togo	Tunisia	United States	World Total
1991	3,280	22,000	1,652	3,370	4,433	17,900	28,400	1,741	1,359	2,965	6,352	48,096	150,731
1992	2,825	21,400	2,000	3,595	4,296	19,145	11,500	2,284	1,266	2,083	6,400	46,965	139,000
1993	3,419	21,200	1,585	3,680	4,129	18,193	9,400	1,667	931	1,794	5,500	35,494	119,000
1994	3,937	24,100	632	3,961	4,217	19,764	8,000	1,587	1,203	2,149	5,699	41,100	127,000
1995	3,888	19,300	765	4,063	4,984	20,684	9,000	1,500	1,551	2,570	7,241	43,500	131,000
1996	3,823	21,000	808	3,839	5,355	20,855	8,300	1,340	2,189	2,731	7,167	45,400	135,000
1997	4,270	24,500	1,067	4,047	5,896	23,084	9,800	1,565	2,392	2,631	6,941	45,900	143,000
1998	4,421	25,000	1,076	4,067	5,925	23,587	10,100	1,478	2,496	2,250	7,901	44,200	144,000
1999[1]	4,300	20,000	1,018	4,128	6,014	22,767	11,400	1,800	2,084	1,700	8,006	40,600	137,000
2000[2]	4,900	19,400	1,020	4,110	5,506	21,568	11,100	1,800	2,166	1,370	8,339	38,600	133,000

[1] Preliminary. [2] Estimate. [3] Formerly part of the U.S.S.R.; data not reported separately until 1992. *Source: U.S. Geological Survey (USGS)*

Salient Statistics of Phosphate Rock in the United States   In Thousands of Metric Tons

									Avg. Price of Florida & N. Carolina $/Tonne - FOB Mine (-60% to +74%) -		
Year	Mine Production	Marketable Production	Value Million Dollars	Imports For Consumption	Exports	Apparent Consumption	Stocks, Dec. 31 (Producer)	Price - $ Avg. Per Metric Ton (FOB Mine)	Domestic	Export	Average
1991	154,485	48,096	1,109	552	5,082	40,177	10,168	23.06	22.67	31.69	23.69
1992	155,000	47,000	1,060	1,530	3,720	42,900	12,600	22.53	22.47	32.29	23.32
1993	107,000	35,500	759	534	3,200	38,300	9,220	21.38	21.26	28.51	21.89
1994	157,000	41,100	869	1,800	2,800	42,900	5,980	21.14	21.79	25.60	22.08
1995	165,000	43,500	947	1,800	2,760	42,700	5,710	21.75	21.29	28.35	21.75
1996	179,000	45,400	1,060	1,800	1,570	43,700	6,390	23.40	22.90	35.82	23.40
1997	166,000	45,900	1,080	1,830	335	43,600	7,910	24.50	24.40	34.80	24.50
1998	170,000	44,200	1,130	1,760	378	45,000	7,920	25.87	25.46	42.70	25.87
1999[1]	161,000	40,600	1,240	2,170	272	43,500	6,920	31.49	30.56	41.96	31.49
2000[2]	163,000	38,600	932	1,930	299	39,000	8,170	24.29	24.20	40.38	24.29

[1] Preliminary. [2] Estimate. *Source: U.S. Geological Survey (USGS)*

World Production of Marketable Potash   In Thousands of Metric Tons (K_2O Equivalent)

Year	Belarus[3]	Brazil	Canada	China	France	Germany	Israel	Jordan	Russia[3]	Spain	United Kingdom	United States	World Total
1991	----	101	7,406	32	1,129	3,855	1,320	818	8,560	585	495	1,749	26,136
1992	3,311	85	7,270	21	1,141	3,461	1,296	794	3,470	594	529	1,710	23,900
1993	1,947	168	3,836	25	890	2,861	1,309	822	2,628	661	555	1,510	20,400
1994	3,021	234	8,037	74	870	3,286	1,259	930	2,498	684	580	1,400	23,100
1995	3,211	215	9,066	80	799	3,278	1,330	1,075	2,800	760	582	1,480	24,800
1996	2,716	243	8,120	110	751	3,332	1,500	1,080	2,620	717	618	1,390	23,300
1997	3,247	280	8,989	115	725	3,423	1,488	868	3,400	640	565	1,400	25,200
1998	3,451	326	9,201	120	656	3,581	1,668	910	3,500	497	608	1,300	25,900
1999[1]	3,600	350	8,329	150	311	3,545	1,702	1,080	4,200	550	495	1,200	25,600
2000[2]	3,400	350	8,600	250	321	3,409	1,710	1,110	3,700	522	600	1,300	25,400

[1] Preliminary. [2] Estimate. [3] Formerly part of the U.S.S.R.; data not reported separately until 1992. *Source: U.S. Geological Survey (USGS)*

Salient Statistics of Potash in the United States   In Thousands of Metric Tons (K_2O Equivalent)

									---- $ Per Ton ----		
Year	Net Import Reliance as a % of Consumption	Production	Sales by Producers	Value Million Dollars	Imports For Consumption	Exports	Apparent Consumption	Producer Stocks Dec. 31	Avg. Value Per Ton of Product ($)	Avg. Value of K_2O Equiv.	Avg. Price[3] $ Per Tonne
1991	67	1,749	1,709	304.5	4,158	624	5,243	343	91.52	178.20	131.00
1992	68	1,710	1,770	334.0	4,250	663	5,350	283	96.45	189.36	134.00
1993	72	1,510	1,480	286.0	4,360	415	5,430	305	94.36	192.72	130.74
1994	76	1,400	1,470	284.0	4,800	464	5,810	234	95.93	193.50	125.34
1995	75	1,480	1,400	284.0	4,820	409	5,820	312	98.58	202.43	137.99
1996	77	1,390	1,430	299.0	4,940	481	5,890	265	101.08	208.57	134.07
1997	80	1,400	1,400	320.0	5,490	466	6,500	200	110.00	230.00	138.00
1998	80	1,300	1,300	330.0	4,780	477	5,600	300	115.00	250.00	145.00
1999[1]	80	1,200	1,200	280.0	4,470	459	5,100	300	110.00	230.00	150.00
2000[2]	70	1,300	1,200	290.0	4,600	367	5,600		110.00	230.00	157.50

[1] Preliminary. [2] Estimate. [3] Unit of K_2O, standard 60% muriate F.O.B. mine. *Source: U.S. Geological Survey (USGS)*

Fish

The U.S.D.A. reported that sales of catfish by growers to processors in 2000 were 594 million pounds, a decline of 1 percent from 1999. In August 2001, sales were 51.7 million pounds, down 3 percent from August 2000. The average price paid by processors for farm-raised catfish in 2000 was 75 cents-per-pound. In 1999 it was 73.7 cents. In the January-August 2001 period, the average price was 67.7 cents. Catfish sold by processors in 2000 were 297 million pounds, up just over 1 percent from the previous year. In the January-August 2001 period, catfish sold by processors were 204 million pounds. In 2000, the average price received by processors for all catfish was $2.379 per pound.

Catfish growers indicated that on July 1, 2001, their stocks of broodfish were 1.28 billion. The states surveyed were Alabama, Arkansas, Louisiana and Mississippi. The inventory was up less than 1 percent from 1999. The inventory of fingerling/fry was 1.82 billion, up 3 percent from 1999. Some 69 percent of the inventory was held in Mississippi. The stocker inventory on July 1, 2001 was 734.3 million, down 4 percent from 2000. Some 71 percent of the inventory was in Mississippi. The inventory of small foodsize catfish was 287.3 million, up 24 percent from 2000. Mississippi held 67 percent of the inventory. The inventory of medium foodsize catfish was 76.1 million, up 40 percent from the year before. Mississippi held 44 percent of the inventory. The inventory of large foodsize catfish was 6.17 million, up 54 percent from the previous year. Mississippi held 40 percent of the inventory.

U.S. imports of fresh Atlantic salmon in the January-June 2001 period were 154.5 million pounds, up 26 percent from 2000. Imports of fresh Pacific salmon in the first half of 2001 were 7.8 million pounds, down 18 percent from 2000. Imports of frozen Atlantic salmon in the first half of 2001 were 15.8 million pounds, up 8 percent from 2000. Imports of frozen Pacific salmon were 4.6 million pounds, down 15 percent from the same period in 2000. U.S. imports of frozen shrimp in the first half of 2001 were 270.2 million pounds, up 9 percent from the previous year. imports of fresh and frozen trout in first half 2001 were 3.7 million pounds, up 58 percent from 2000.

Fishery Products -- Supply in the United States In Millions of Pounds[2]

					Domestic Catch					Imports				
Year	Grand Total	For Human Food - Finfish	For Human Food - Shellfish[3]	For Industrial Use[4]	Total	% of Grand Total	For Human Food - Finfish	For Human Food - Shellfish[3]	For Industrial Use[4]	Total	% of Grand Total	For Human Food - Finfish	For Human Food - Shellfish[3]	For Industrial Use[4]
1990	16,349	10,120	2,542	3,687	9,404	57.5	5,747	1,294	2,363	6,945	42.5	4,373	1,248	1,324
1991	16,364	10,186	2,834	3,344	9,484	58.0	5,564	1,467	2,453	6,879	42.0	4,622	1,367	890
1992	16,106	10,297	2,945	2,864	9,637	59.8	6,182	1,436	2,019	6,469	40.2	4,115	1,509	845
1993	20,334	10,796	3,025	6,513	10,467	51.5	6,770	1,444	2,253	9,867	48.5	4,026	1,581	4,260
1994	19,309	10,719	2,995	5,595	10,461	54.2	6,612	1,324	2,525	8,848	45.8	4,107	1,671	3,070
1995	16,484	10,692	2,891	2,900	9,788	59.4	6,414	1,252	2,121	6,696	40.6	4,278	1,639	779
1996	16,474	10,699	2,927	2,848	9,565	58.1	6,205	1,271	2,089	6,909	41.9	4,494	1,656	759
1997	17,133	10,580	3,160	3,393	9,843	57.5	5,969	1,277	2,598	7,290	42.5	4,612	1,883	795
1998	16,898	10,837	3,338	2,723	9,194	54.4	5,935	1,238	2,021	7,704	45.6	4,901	2,100	702
1999[1]	17,378	10,831	3,630	2,916	9,339	53.7	5,490	1,341	2,507	8,039	46.3	5,341	2,289	409

[1] Preliminary. [2] Live weight, except percent. [3] For univalue and bivalues mollusks (conchs, clams, oysters, scallops, etc.) the weight of meats, excluding the shell is reported. [4] Fish meal and sea herring. *Source: Fisheries Statistics Division, U.S. Department of Commerce*

Fisheries -- Landings of Principal Species in the United States In Millions of Pounds

	Fish									Shelfish					
Year	Cod, Atlantic	Flounder	Halibut	Herring, Sea	Man-haden	Pollock	Salmon, Pacific	Tuna	Whiting	Clams (Meats)	Crabs	Lobsters (American)	Oysters (Meats)	Scallops (Meats)	Shrimp
1990	96	255	70	221	1,962	3,129	733	62	44	139	499	61	29	42	346
1991	93	405	66	230	1,977	2,873	783	36	37	134	650	63	32	40	320
1992	62	646	67	282	1,644	2,952	716	57	36	142	624	56	36	34	338
1993	51	599	63	216	1,983	3,258	888	55	36	148	604	57	34	19	293
1994	39	427	58	214	2,324	3,133	901	72	36	131	447	66	38	25	283
1995	30	423	45	265	1,847	2,853	1,137	14	34	134	364	66	40	20	307
1996	31	460	49	318	1,755	2,630	877	85	35	123	392	71	38	18	317
1997	29	566	70	348	2,028	2,522	568	83	34	114	430	84	40	15	290
1998	25	391	73	272	1,706	2,729	644	85	33	108	553	80	34	13	278
1999[1]	21	331	80	267	1,989	2,336	815	58	31	112	458	87	27	27	304

[1] Preliminary. *Source: National Marine Fisheries Service, U.S. Department of Commerce*

U.S. Fisheries: Quantity & Value of Domestic Catch & Consumption & World Fish Oil Production

	Disposition					For	For			Fish	World[2]
	Fresh &			For Meal,		Human	Industrial	Ex-vessel	Average	Per Capita	Fish Oil
	Frozen	Canned	Cured	Oil, Etc.	Total	Food	Products	Value[3]	Price	Cunsumption	Production
Year	Millions of Pounds							- Million $ -	- Cents/Lb. -	- Pounds -	- 1,000 Tons -
1993	7,744	649	115	1,959	10,467	8,214	2,253	3,471	33.2	14.9	1,184
1994	7,475	622	95	2,269	10,461	7,936	2,525	3,807	36.8	NA	1,470
1995	7,099	769	90	1,830	9,788	7,667	2,121	3,770	38.5	NA	1,302
1996	7,054	678	93	1,740	9,565	7,474	2,091	3,487	36.5	NA	1,337
1997	6,873	648	108	2,213	9,842	7,244	2,598	3,448	35.0	NA	1,214
1998	6,870	516	129	1,679	9,194	7,173	2,021	3,128	34.0	NA	892
1999[1]	6,416	712	133	2,078	9,339	6,832	2,407	3,467	37.1	NA	1,173

[1] Preliminary. [2] Crop years on a marketing year basis. [3] At the Dock Prices. *Source: Fisheries Statistics Division, U.S. Department of Commerce*

Imports of Seafood Products into the United States In Thousands of Pounds

	Fresh			Frozen								
	Atlantic	Pacific			Atlantic	Pacific					Canned	Prepared
Year	Salmon	Salmon	Shrimp	Trout	Salmon	Salmon	Shrimp	Oysters[2]	Mussels[3]	Clams[4]	Salmon	Shrimp[5]
1996	116,606	43,962	----	4,552	10,752	8,514	507,823	14,222	21,241	6,596	4,182	74,648
1997	150,135	38,999	----	5,403	14,956	25,662	572,111	14,531	26,903	5,703	3,675	76,213
1998	190,131	38,486	----	5,670	19,092	17,134	599,466	18,049	34,099	6,541	3,430	95,942
1999	217,948	26,467	----	5,259	24,222	16,596	617,089	18,325	34,969	7,537	5,627	114,191
2000	257,218	19,908	----	7,083	32,089	12,866	621,231	20,810	43,141	8,074	8,893	139,526
2001[1]	316,837	17,472	----	7,382	41,176	10,515	714,706	18,438	39,973	8,007	11,298	167,877

[1] Preliminary. [2] Oysters fresh or prepared. [3] Mussels fresh or prepared. [4] Clams, fresh or prepared. [5] Shrimp, canned, breaded or prepared.
NA = Not available. *Source: Bureau of the Census, U.S. Department of Commerce*

Exports of Seafood Products into the United States In Thousands of Pounds

	Fresh			Frozen								
	Atlantic	Pacific			Atlantic	Pacific					Canned	Prepared
Year	Salmon	Salmon	Shrimp	Trout	Salmon	Salmon	Shrimp	Oysters[2]	Mussels[3]	Clams[4]	Salmon	Shrimp[5]
1996	7,280	42,999	----	1,867	322	223,346	11,180	2,097	1,603	5,126	94,842	17,665
1997	7,504	25,529	----	1,709	322	152,516	11,967	2,890	1,157	4,916	81,407	14,826
1998	7,978	34,645	----	1,453	243	105,869	11,323	2,496	1,347	5,375	77,201	13,882
1999	10,717	40,683	----	1,697	182	157,278	13,607	2,727	1,861	5,240	113,556	13,153
2000	15,942	38,750	----	1,816	299	161,515	15,162	3,229	1,513	3,413	81,098	14,229
2001[1]	18,417	20,651	----	1,077	84	167,933	13,905	3,915	1,485	3,939	109,109	13,640

[1] Preliminary. [2] Oysters fresh or prepared. [3] Mussels fresh or prepared. [4] Clams, fresh or prepared. [5] Shrimp, canned, breaded or prepared.
NA = Not available. *Source: Bureau of the Census, U.S. Department of Commerce*

World Production of Fish Meal In Thousands of Metric Tons

										South		United	World
Year	Chile	Spain	Denmark	EU-12	FSU-12	Iceland	Japan	Norway	Peru	Africa	Thailand	States	Total
1992-3	1,091.2	97.9	300.1	544.0	355.0	197.7	395.0	250.8	1,767.3	128.3	352.8	352.5	6,258.6
1993-4	1,526.1	65.1	352.7	558.6	295.0	190.5	343.0	216.8	2,254.4	92.9	373.2	447.8	7,216.7
1994-5	1,549.7	70.1	363.4	573.1	198.3	173.8	239.0	225.0	2,052.6	95.8	385.2	338.3	6,847.0
1995-6	1,387.6	76.4	322.9	532.5	209.8	271.0	195.0	233.8	1,702.7	49.6	380.9	331.1	6,332.9
1996-7	1,209.9	75.0	334.6	540.6	183.7	272.5	180.0	259.7	2,150.5	52.6	383.2	345.0	6,601.1
1997-8[1]	708.5	77.0	317.2	526.6	195.3	221.6	167.0	296.7	697.2	89.3	405.2	341.0	4,652.8
1998-9[2]	837.5	76.0	319.1	530.7	150.6	240.6	180.0	254.0	1,597.4	72.0	393.0	345.0	5,605.9
1999-00[3]	1,000.0	76.0	320.0	531.4	153.0	275.0	180.0	290.0	2,100.0	83.0	400.0	378.0	6,400.0

[1] Preliminary. [2] Estimate. [3] Forecast. *Source: The Oil World*

World Production of Fish Oil In Thousands of Metric Tons

									South		United	World	Fish Oil
Year	Canada	Chile	China	Denmark	Iceland	Japan	Norway	Peru	Africa	FSU-12	States	Total	CIF[4]
1992-3	11.8	165.3	9.4	90.3	86.0	107.4	112.3	250.9	17.0	71.6	119.0	1,150.4	375
1993-4	9.9	280.0	9.4	112.0	96.5	93.3	122.7	426.5	8.5	52.7	141.2	1,473.5	332
1994-5	10.1	323.1	9.9	118.3	85.0	57.7	94.1	388.1	7.5	48.5	109.6	1,371.6	405
1995-6	10.6	280.2	12.0	120.0	120.5	45.8	93.7	410.0	3.7	43.0	110.4	1,363.4	461
1996-7	10.5	192.6	12.0	129.5	134.6	51.2	86.4	407.1	4.1	41.0	110.0	1,293.8	502
1997-8[1]	10.5	91.4	12.6	106.4	107.0	54.0	89.0	74.0	7.8	39.5	116.0	826.2	722
1998-9[2]	10.0	173.0	9.0	135.0	92.0	59.0	81.0	377.0	7.0	7.0	142.0	1,225.0	408
1999-00[3]	11.0	143.0	11.0	135.0	92.0	60.0	88.0	695.0	8.0	8.0	92.0	1,475.0	268

[1] Preliminary. [2] Estimate. [3] Forecast. [4] Any origin, N.W. Europe. NA = Not available. *Source: The Oil World*

Monthly Production of Catfish--Round Weight Processed, in the US In Thousands of Pounds (Live Weight)

Year	Jan.	Feb.	Mar.	Apr.	May	June	July	Aug.	Sept.	Oct.	Nov.	Dec.	Total
1993	40,327	40,277	43,521	39,920	37,030	35,496	37,086	37,706	37,072	39,472	36,557	34,549	459,013
1994	36,714	35,035	40,446	34,494	34,163	34,595	35,901	39,813	38,716	39,072	36,054	34,266	439,269
1995	38,807	38,515	42,200	36,588	37,030	36,047	35,800	38,827	37,634	39,156	34,119	31,863	446,886
1996	38,475	38,004	40,376	38,557	39,583	36,810	39,025	40,463	38,807	42,070	37,210	36,874	472,254
1997	42,409	45,067	48,431	45,721	43,409	42,282	43,376	44,154	43,472	46,275	40,137	40,216	524,949
1998	46,723	47,606	53,761	49,393	45,218	46,244	46,383	47,739	46,579	47,904	43,224	43,581	564,355
1999	48,723	48,891	56,310	46,830	47,703	48,445	50,074	50,372	50,414	52,407	48,118	48,341	596,628
2000	50,552	50,942	56,856	48,781	48,424	48,011	49,023	53,204	49,422	51,412	45,535	41,441	593,603
2001[1]	46,999	50,257	57,766	52,478	51,736	47,883	47,829	51,690	49,699	52,264	44,670	43,837	597,108

[1] Preliminary. *Source: Economic Research Service, U.S. Department of Agriculture ERS-USDA)*

Average Price Paid to Producers for Farm-Raised Catfish in the US In Cents Per Pound (Live Weight)

Year	Jan.	Feb.	Mar.	Apr.	May	June	July	Aug.	Sept.	Oct.	Nov.	Dec.	Average
1993	63.0	67.0	70.0	71.0	72.0	72.0	72.0	73.0	73.0	73.0	73.0	73.0	71.0
1994	74.0	77.0	79.0	80.0	80.0	80.0	80.0	80.0	80.0	77.0	77.0	77.0	78.4
1995	78.0	79.0	79.0	79.0	79.0	79.0	79.0	79.0	78.0	78.0	78.0	78.0	78.6
1996	77.0	78.0	78.0	78.0	79.0	79.0	79.0	78.0	77.0	76.0	75.0	73.0	77.3
1997	73.0	73.0	73.0	73.0	73.0	72.0	71.0	70.0	69.0	69.0	69.0	69.0	71.2
1998	69.0	73.0	78.0	79.0	79.0	78.0	76.0	74.0	73.0	71.0	70.0	70.0	74.2
1999	70.3	71.4	73.2	75.6	77.7	77.5	76.8	74.3	72.8	71.6	71.3	71.6	73.7
2000	74.4	78.8	78.9	78.9	78.5	78.6	76.0	74.1	72.7	71.0	69.6	68.2	75.0
2001[1]	69.3	69.6	69.7	69.4	68.7	66.9	65.6	62.4	61.0	59.6	56.6	55.4	64.5

[1] Preliminary. *Source: Economic Research Service, U.S. Department of Agriculture (ERS-USDA)*

Sales of Fresh Catfish in the United States In Thousands of Pounds

Year	Jan.	Feb.	Mar.	Apr.	May	June	July	Aug.	Sept.	Oct.	Nov.	Dec.	Total
Whole													
1998	3,700	4,049	4,308	3,856	3,421	3,340	3,342	3,270	3,332	3,431	3,152	3,254	42,455
1999	3,650	3,957	4,467	3,459	3,492	3,380	3,471	3,271	3,583	3,561	3,209	3,313	42,813
2000	3,496	3,396	4,031	3,655	3,483	3,581	3,491	3,545	3,246	3,504	2,971	2,993	41,392
2001[1]	3,516	3,242	4,260	3,644	3,271	3,166	3,233	3,204	3,174	3,294	2,865	2,803	39,672
Fillets[2]													
1998	4,292	4,784	5,130	4,634	4,371	4,220	4,542	4,622	4,626	4,588	4,092	3,975	53,876
1999	4,581	5,030	5,768	4,897	4,918	4,707	4,846	5,002	4,550	4,811	4,171	4,142	57,423
2000	4,686	4,853	5,957	5,206	5,099	4,792	4,650	4,899	4,650	5,283	4,355	4,099	58,529
2001[1]	4,884	6,112	6,751	5,709	5,587	5,122	5,191	5,313	5,264	5,273	4,463	4,489	64,158
Other[3]													
1998	1,499	1,712	1,721	1,509	1,395	1,453	1,246	1,369	1,314	1,345	1,117	1,081	16,761
1999	1,243	1,614	1,724	1,153	1,227	1,126	1,305	1,495	1,354	1,676	1,299	1,227	16,443
2000	1,429	1,437	1,685	1,547	1,364	1,299	1,340	1,438	1,332	1,473	1,271	1,198	16,813
2001[1]	1,443	1,292	2,156	1,309	1,282	1,298	1,375	1,436	1,449	1,430	1,223	1,252	16,945

[1] Preliminary. [2] Includes regular, shank and strip fillets; excludes breaded products. [3] Includes steaks, nuggets and all other products not reported.
Source: Economic Research Service, U.S. Department of Agriculture (ERS-USDA)

Prices of Fresh Catfish in the United States In Dollars per Pound

Year	Jan.	Feb.	Mar.	Apr.	May	June	July	Aug.	Sept.	Oct.	Nov.	Dec.	Average
Whole													
1998	1.52	1.57	1.63	1.61	1.65	1.60	1.60	1.63	1.59	1.59	1.56	1.52	1.59
1999	1.54	1.55	1.57	1.59	1.63	1.60	1.59	1.63	1.61	1.63	1.59	1.59	1.59
2000	1.63	1.67	1.69	1.70	1.68	1.63	1.65	1.70	1.67	1.64	1.62	1.58	1.66
2001[1]	1.59	1.68	1.63	1.65	1.65	1.62	1.59	1.55	1.53	1.49	1.42	1.37	1.56
Fillets[2]													
1998	2.71	2.75	2.85	2.86	2.86	2.85	2.84	2.82	2.78	2.78	2.75	2.73	2.80
1999	2.73	2.71	2.76	2.75	2.84	2.86	2.86	2.85	2.85	2.83	2.84	2.83	2.81
2000	2.82	2.87	2.89	2.88	2.88	2.90	2.90	2.88	2.85	2.83	2.83	2.81	2.86
2001[1]	2.80	2.79	2.80	2.80	2.80	2.78	2.77	2.75	2.69	2.63	2.60	2.55	2.73
Other[3]													
1998	1.61	1.65	1.72	1.78	1.78	1.76	1.79	1.71	1.72	1.69	1.73	1.69	1.72
1999	1.61	1.55	1.59	1.70	1.74	1.76	1.66	1.62	1.66	1.57	1.65	1.66	1.65
2000	1.66	1.69	1.69	1.66	1.71	1.71	1.72	1.69	1.62	1.68	1.71	1.68	1.69
2001[1]	1.64	1.68	1.57	1.64	1.69	1.64	1.61	1.57	1.52	1.59	1.59	1.53	1.61

[1] Preliminary. [2] Includes regular, shank and strip fillets; excludes breaded products. [3] Includes steaks, nuggets and all other products not reported.
Source: Economic Research Service, U.S. Department of Agriculture (ERS-USDA)

Flaxseed and Linseed Oil

U.S. flaxseed production shows wide year-to-year production swings on generally declining acreage, but average yield in recent years has a decidedly upward bias. Flaxseed (from which linseed oil is derived) is considered a minor U.S. oilseed. . Planted acreage in both 2000/01 and 2001/02 of 536,000 acres compares with 387,000 in 1999/00, the largest acreage since the mid-1980's. Average yield increased to a record 20.8 bushels per acre in 2000 from a mid-1990's average of about 16 bushels.

U.S. flaxseed production in 2000/01 (June/May) of 10.7 million bushels compares with 7.9 million the previous year and forecast at 10.9 million in 2001/02. The 1990's low were 1.6 million bushels in 1996/97. The U.S. crop is produced mostly in the Northern Plains states. Imports of flaxseed, mostly from Canada, the world's largest producer with about a third of global production, of 2.8 million bushels in 2000/01 compare with 6.6 million in 1999/00 and forecast at 3.0 million bushels in 2001/02. The U.S. has been a net importer of flaxseed since the late 1970's. Total 2000/01 supplies of 15.3 million bushels include a carryin of 1.8 million bushels vs. the previous crop year's total of 16.7 million. Disappearance in 2000/01 was forecast at 14 million bushels and ending carryover of 1.3 million bushels. Total usage in 2001/02 is also forecast at 14 million bushels.

U.S. domestic demand for linseed oil in 2000/01 of 150 million pounds is unchanged from the previous year; usage in 2001/02 is forecast at 147 million pounds. Exports in 2000/01 of a record 100 million pounds compare with 76 million in 1999/00 and are forecast at 90 million in 2001/02. The 2000/01 (and 2001/02) production of 234 million pounds is the highest since the early 1980's. Linseed oil is used as a drying agent in paint, but domestic use has at best stabilized in recent years due to the acceptance of water-based latex paints. Carryin stocks as of June 1, 2001 of 43 million pounds were 6 million pounds under a year earlier, but expected to rise to 45 million by the season's end. Linseed meal production in 2000/01 of 216,000 short tons is marginally over 1999/00, with a similar outturn in 2001/02. Meal usage in 2000/01 should about equal the total supply with carryover again holding near 5,000 tons.

The average price received by U.S. farmers for flaxseed in 200/01 of $3.30 per bushel compares with $3.79 in 1999/00 and a forecast of $3.30-4.30 in 2001/02. Linseed oil prices in 2000/01 of 36 cents/lb compare with 37.75 cents in 1999/00, basis Minneapolis. Linseed meal prices, basis Minneapolis, 34% protein, of $116.23 per short ton in 2000/01 compare with $93.77 in 1999/00 and a 2001/02 forecast of $78-$98.

Futures Markets

Flaxseed futures are traded on the Winnipeg Commodity Exchange (WCE). Prices are quoted in Canadian dollars per metric ton.

World Production of Flaxseed In Thousands of Metric Tons

Year	Argentina	Australia	Bangladesh	Canada	China	Egypt	France	Hungary	India	Romania	United States	Former USSR	World Total
1990-1	458	4	48	889	535	28	34	10	339	53	97	197	2,923
1991-2	341	5	55	635	410	24	26	13	292	23	158	140	2,458
1992-3	177	5	49	334	430	21	29	10	268	18	84	130	1,966
1993-4	112	8	49	627	410	22	27	4	330	28	88	120	2,191
1994-5	152	6	48	960	511	18	44	4	325	7	74	110	2,474
1995-6	149	15	49	1,105	420	16	27	4	308	5	56	113	2,518
1996-7	72	7	46	851	480	17	29	4	319	5	41	86	2,300
1997-8[1]	75	6	50	1,038	393	18	31	4	310	5	62	51	2,409
1998-9[2]	85	8	50	1,210	520	18	29	4	300	5	170	59	2,880
1999-00[3]	47	7	50	1,175	550	17	33	4	285	3	200	63	3,063

[1] Preliminary. [2] Estimate. [3] Forecast. *Source: The Oil World*

Supply and Distribution of Flaxseed in the United States In Thousands of Bushels

Crop Year Beginning June 1	Planted	Harvested	Yield Per Acre (Bushels)	Supply: Beginning Stocks	Supply: Production	Supply: Imports	Supply: Total Supply	Distribution: Seed	Distribution: Crush	Distribution: Exports	Distribution: Residual	Distribution: Total Distribution
	1,000 Acres											
1992-3	171	165	19.9	1,556	3,288	6,035	10,879	167	8,600	230	337	9,334
1993-4	206	191	18.2	1,545	3,480	5,118	10,143	144	8,650	126	69	8,989
1994-5	178	171	17.1	1,155	2,922	6,005	10,082	134	8,550	72	156	8,912
1995-6	165	147	15.0	1,170	2,212	7,248	10,681	78	9,000	119	203	9,451
1996-7	96	92	17.4	1,230	1,602	8,390	11,222	122	10,000	144	503	10,769
1997-8	151	146	16.6	453	2,420	9,636	10,808	272	10,500	174	382	9,627
1998-9	336	329	20.4	1,181	6,708	5,992	13,227	313	10,600	476	333	11,069
1999-00[1]	387	382	20.6	2,158	7,880	6,629	16,667	434	11,500	215	2,735	14,900
2000-1[2]	536	517	20.8	1,767	10,730	2,849	15,349	450	12,000	1,015	572	14,038
2001-2[3]	556	545	20.0	1,308	10,900	3,037	15,245	405	12,000	750	840	13,995

[1] Preliminary. [2] Estimate. [3] Forecast. *Source: Economic Research Service, U.S. Department of Agriculture*

Production of Flaxseed in the United States, by States   In Thousands of Bushels

Crop Year	Minne-sota	North Dakota	South Dakota	Other States	Total	Crop Year	Minne-sota	North Dakota	South Dakota	Other States	Total
1992	220	2,730	322	16	3,288	1997	96	1,997	252	75	2,420
1993	170	2,886	323	101	3,480	1998	432	5,817	294	165	6,708
1994	126	2,450	304	42	2,922	1999	300	6,867	357	340	7,864
1995	171	1,725	260	55	2,211	2000	198	9,975	361	196	10,730
1996	60	1,386	126	30	1,602	2001[1]	52	10,900	323	180	11,455

[1] Preliminary. *Source: National Agricultural Statistics Service, U.S. Department of Agriculture (NASS-USDA)*

Factory Shipments of Paints, Varnish and Lacquer in the United States   In Millions of Dollars

Year	First Quarter	Second Quarter	Third Quarter	Fourth Quarter	Total	Year	First Quarter	Second Quarter	Third Quarter	Fourth Quarter	Total
1992	2,852.3	3,464.1	3,308.7	2,816.4	12,441	1997	3,515.2	4,023.4	3,924.1	3,323.0	14,786
1993	2,894.1	3,600.5	3,448.9	2,993.7	12,937	1998	3,600.7	4,216.4	4,063.9	3,804.4	15,685
1994	3,039.8	3,783.0	3,736.2	3,240.8	13,800	1999	3,926.2	4,452.2	4,216.5	3,925.7	16,521
1995	3,330.3	3,838.0	3,814.5	3,423.4	14,406	2000	4,073.1	4,573.5	4,082.0	3,474.7	16,203
1996	3,438.6	4,161.9	3,954.9	3,428.9	14,984	2001[1]	3,899.9	4,666.6	4,398.0		17,286

[1] Preliminary. *Source: Bureau of the Census, U.S. Department of Commerce*

Consumption of Linseed Oil (Inedible Products) in the United States   In Millions of Pounds

Year	July	Aug.	Sept.	Oct.	Nov.	Dec.	Jan.	Feb.	Mar.	Apr.	May	June	Total
1994-5	10.7	10.8	12.3	12.2	9.0	10.0	12.6	8.2	11.4	8.1	10.0	9.7	124.9
1995-6	8.8	10.0	9.4	10.6	7.4	6.9	8.8	8.5	7.2	8.1	10.1	9.5	105.3
1996-7	9.0	10.8	7.8	6.0	6.7	6.1	6.7	7.1	6.3	8.3	8.9	8.5	92.3
1997-8	8.9	7.7	8.6	6.7	7.5	6.4	8.0	6.0	6.2	5.9	6.8	5.7	84.3
1998-9	7.2	6.8	6.4	5.6	4.6	6.6	5.9	4.7	6.8	6.4	5.6	7.9	74.6
1999-00	5.4	6.2	5.5	5.2	5.6	4.5	4.2	6.1	5.8	7.0	7.6	6.6	69.8
2000-1	6.5	7.2	7.3	7.5	6.5	5.7	8.0	6.7	7.7	7.6	9.3	9.4	89.3
2001-2[1]	9.6	8.4	9.2	7.4	5.3	5.0							89.5

[1] Preliminary. *Source: Bureau of the Census, U.S. Department of Commerce*

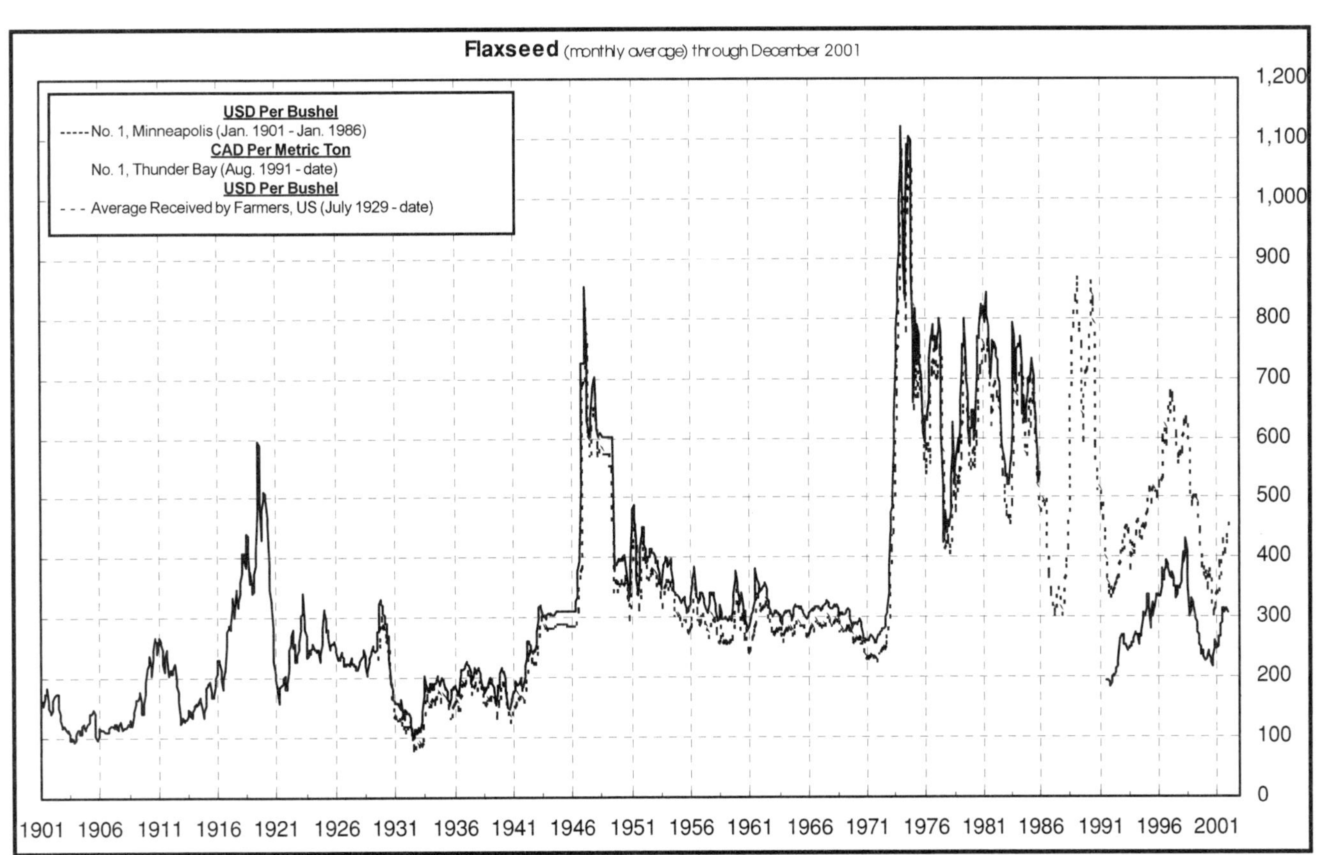

FLAXSEED AND LINSEED OIL

Supply and Distribution of Linseed Oil in the United States In Millions of Pounds

Crop Year Beginning June 1	Supply: Stocks June 1	Supply: Production	Supply: Total	Disappearance: Exports	Disappearance: Domestic	Disappearance: Total Disappearance	Average Price at Minneapolis Cents/Lb.
1992-3	40	172	212	8	150	158	31.5
1993-4	54	174	228	7	162	165	31.8
1994-5	63	171	235	24	166	190	33.7
1995-6	45	180	225	26	149	175	36.5
1996-7	50	200	250	66	149	215	36.0
1997-8	35	210	245	58	152	210	37.8
1998-9	35	212	247	63	139	202	37.5
1999-00	45	230	275	76	150	226	37.8
2000-1[1]	49	234	293	100	150	250	36.0
2001-2[2]	43	234	282	90	147	237	

[1] Preliminary. [2] Forecast. *Source: Economic Research Service, U.S. Department of Agriculture (ERS-USDA)*

World Production and Price of Linseed Oil In Thousands of Metric Tons

Year	Argentina	Bangladesh	Belgium	China	Egypt	Germany	India	Japan	United Kingdom	United States	Former USSR	World Total	Rotterdam Ex-Tank $/Tonne
1990-1	141.5	12.0	12.2	126.9	12.3	57.5	94.2	34.7	16.8	84.0	10.1	685.8	502
1991-2	114.0	13.5	14.7	111.0	11.3	56.1	83.8	31.9	27.0	87.9	9.1	637.9	377
1992-3	62.3	12.6	25.5	117.0	8.1	56.8	78.0	28.4	27.2	80.0	9.6	570.0	450
1993-4	32.2	12.7	28.8	121.8	8.6	77.2	90.7	30.7	35.2	78.7	11.2	617.9	476
1994-5	46.8	13.0	35.2	137.4	8.2	104.0	91.4	29.2	41.4	81.7	10.6	697.5	657
1995-6	47.5	13.0	44.3	125.1	8.0	72.0	88.1	30.0	28.9	80.0	12.7	665.3	579
1996-7	17.1	12.5	52.1	142.5	9.6	52.2	88.8	31.0	34.1	97.9	10.2	670.4	560
1997-8	24.1	13.4	54.7	120.0	10.9	66.9	87.5	31.3	35.1	100.7	7.9	683.7	686
1998-9[1]	24.5	13.4	60.8	150.0	14.6	74.1	85.5	26.5	34.3	99.5	10.9	729.3	575
1999-00[2]	13.6	13.3	54.1	153.1	14.6	80.9	85.7	28.8	32.3	114.3	11.9	748.1	413

[1] Preliminary. [2] Forecast. *Source: The Oil World*

Average Price Received by Farmers for Flaxseed in the United States In Dollars Per Bushel

Year	July	Aug.	Sept.	Oct.	Nov.	Dec.	Jan.	Feb.	Mar.	Apr.	May	June	Average
1992-3	3.70	3.68	4.12	4.09	4.08	4.24	4.11	4.46	4.52	4.40	4.42	4.45	4.19
1993-4	4.29	3.79	4.24	4.09	4.05	4.18	4.38	4.61	4.64	4.60	4.43	4.25	4.30
1994-5	4.28	4.52	4.54	4.49	4.51	4.71	4.76	4.94	5.13	5.10	4.91	5.03	4.74
1995-6	5.11	5.21	5.11	5.11	5.17	5.03	5.26	5.21	5.28	5.31	6.13	5.90	5.32
1996-7	6.19	6.15	5.89	6.49	6.38	6.77	6.43	6.74	6.66	6.43	6.45	5.99	6.38
1997-8	6.07	5.53	5.72	5.81	5.71	5.72	5.82	6.27	6.26	6.23	6.33	6.17	5.97
1998-9	6.17	5.45	5.09	4.86	4.97	5.00	5.05	5.05	4.94	4.93	4.89	4.38	5.07
1999-00	4.40	3.86	4.00	3.76	3.66	3.61	3.75	3.43	3.70	3.66	3.77	3.64	3.77
2000-1	3.25	3.05	3.10	3.17	3.39	4.45	3.42	3.40	3.90	3.67	3.91	4.02	3.56
2001-2[1]	4.28	4.09	4.10	4.21	4.36	4.67	4.65						4.34

[1] Preliminary. *Source: National Agricultural Statistics Service, U.S. Department of Agriculture (NASS-USDA)*

Stocks of Linseed Oil (Crude and Refined) at Factories and Warehouses in the US In Millions of Pounds

Year	July 1	Aug. 1	Sept. 1	Oct. 1	Nov. 1	Dec. 1	Jan. 1	Feb. 1	Mar. 1	Apr. 1	May 1	June 1
1992-3	34.6	35.5	29.7	41.3	49.1	47.7	39.9	44.2	45.1	49.1	42.8	43.1
1993-4	45.2	39.0	42.1	47.0	27.9	19.3	22.5	38.0	42.0	49.4	52.0	62.6
1994-5	60.3	56.5	49.4	60.6	48.1	39.3	38.6	38.9	31.0	35.7	37.9	44.8
1995-6	39.5	44.6	37.4	46.0	48.0	44.5	45.3	58.9	64.0	62.0	60.6	47.2
1996-7	51.3	50.9	59.0	46.1	38.8	41.8	49.2	48.1	53.9	50.5	44.5	45.6
1997-8	39.9	35.2	40.3	33.3	38.6	40.3	46.9	60.8	55.8	63.1	54.6	49.4
1998-9	49.6	45.3	38.5	55.4	35.7	44.5	53.2	68.2	54.6	68.2	65.3	76.2
1999-00	68.7	65.5	68.9	74.0	92.4	69.6	72.0	69.5	65.7	53.9	49.1	44.2
2000-1	39.5	42.5	41.3	54.3	58.7	87.0	61.6	50.1	50.5	51.2	39.2	44.8
2001-2[1]	29.1	30.2	22.6	38.4	32.4	29.9	33.4					

[1] Preliminary. *Source: Bureau of the Census, U.S. Department of Commerce*

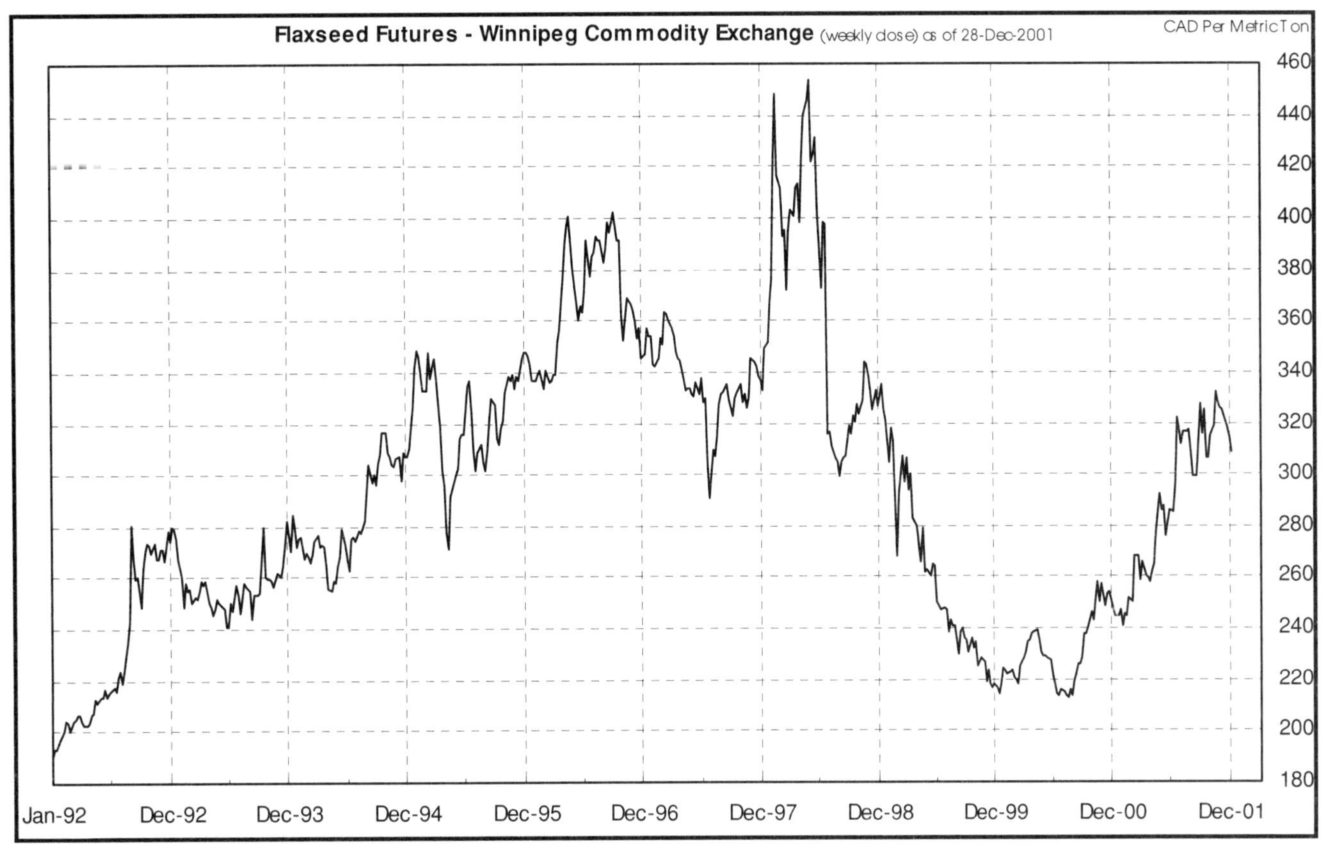

Wholesale Price of Raw Linseed Oil at Minneapolis in Tank Cars In Cents Per Pound

Year	July	Aug.	Sept.	Oct.	Nov.	Dec.	Jan.	Feb.	Mar.	Apr.	May	June	Average
1992-3	30.00	30.00	32.00	32.00	32.00	32.00	32.00	32.00	32.00	32.00	32.00	28.50	31.38
1993-4	32.00	32.00	32.00	32.00	32.00	32.00	32.00	32.00	32.00	32.00	32.00	32.00	32.00
1994-5	30.31	32.00	32.00	33.50	35.00	35.00	35.00	35.00	35.00	35.00	35.00	35.00	33.98
1995-6	35.00	35.50	37.00	37.00	37.00	37.00	37.00	37.00	37.00	37.00	37.00	37.00	36.71
1996-7	37.00	37.20	37.50	37.00	33.75	32.12	36.00	36.00	36.00	36.00	36.00	36.00	35.88
1997-8	36.00	36.00	36.00	37.00	37.00	37.00	36.00	36.00	36.00	36.00	37.00	37.00	36.42
1998-9	37.00	37.00	37.00	37.00	37.00	37.00	36.00	36.00	36.00	36.00	36.00	36.00	36.50
1999-00	36.00	36.00	36.00	36.00	36.00	36.00	36.00	36.00	36.00	36.00	36.00	36.00	36.00
2000-1	36.00	36.00	36.00	36.00	36.00	36.00	36.00	36.00	36.00	36.00	36.00	32.00	35.67
2001-2[1]	35.50	38.00	39.00	39.00									37.88

[1] Preliminary. *Source: Economic Research Service, U.S. Department of Agriculture (ERS-USDA)*

Average Open Interest of Flaxseed Futures in Winnipeg In Contracts

Year	Jan.	Feb.	Mar.	Apr.	May	June	July	Aug.	Sept.	Oct.	Nov.	Dec.
1992	5,620	6,772	7,864	7,984	7,786	7,321	6,299	6,553	5,623	4,860	6,734	5,979
1993	7,810	8,052	6,203	5,672	5,505	5,321	4,246	5,777	5,923	3,568	3,763	3,922
1994	6,118	6,201	5,946	5,519	4,683	3,945	4,301	4,654	4,997	3,077	4,888	5,251
1995	6,242	8,731	7,505	7,121	8,107	7,212	6,436	5,557	6,230	5,245	5,937	4,414
1996	6,059	6,056	4,402	5,192	6,970	4,435	3,102	2,989	3,257	3,438	4,326	5,119
1997	5,420	5,356	5,591	5,151	4,923	4,075	3,891	4,031	7,131	8,284	7,255	7,955
1998	10,059	10,190	9,707	8,540	6,480	6,874	6,030	6,767	7,421	7,221	7,564	5,828
1999	4,372	4,552	4,533	4,238	3,719	2,456	2,149	2,758	3,725	4,236	4,493	4,276
2000	4,365	4,907	5,588	6,218	5,066	3,696	3,152	3,585	3,936	4,666	4,922	4,914
2001	4,101	3,476	4,270	3,043	3,169	3,661	2,745	2,350	2,400	3,158	2,726	3,031

Source: Winnipeg Commodity Exchange (WCE)

Fruits

The U.S. Department of Agriculture estimated the U.S. 2001/02 orange crop at 287.9 million boxes, up less than 1 percent from the previous season's output of 285.4 million boxes. The 1999/00 crop was 300 million boxes. Florida is by far the largest producer of oranges. The U.S. Early, Midseason and Navel orange crop was forecast to be 165.4 million boxes, down 1 percent from the previous season. The Florida crop was forecast to be 131 million boxes, some 79 percent of the total. California production was 32 million boxes with Texas and Arizona producing smaller amounts. The Valencia orange crop was estimated at 122.5 million boxes. The Florida Valencia crop was forecast at 100 million boxes with the California crop at 22 million boxes.

The California and Arizona lemon crop for the 2001/02 season was forecast at 992,000 short tons, down 1 percent from the previous season. California production was forecast to be 874,000 tons which would be the largest crop since 1980/81. The Arizona crop of 118,000 tons would be 14 percent less than the 2000/01 crop of 137,000 tons. About 50 to 60 percent of the crop goes to the fresh market and the remainder is processed mostly into juice.

The Florida grapefruit crop was forecast to be 2.04 million short tons, an increase of 4 percent from the 2000/01 crop. The crop was divided into 850,000 tons of white grapefruit and 1.2 million tons of red and pink grapefruit. California grapefruit production was estimated to be 210,000 tons, down 8 percent from 2000/01. Texas grapefruit production was estimated at 312,000 tons, up 8 percent from the previous season.

The 2001/02 tangerine crop was estimated at 449,000 tons, an increase of 22 percent from the previous season. The largest tangerine producer is Florida with the new crop estimated at 332,000 tons, up 25 percent from the previous season. The California crop was estimated to be 94,000 tons, up 19 percent from the previous year. The Florida tangelo crop was forecast to be 104,000 tons, up 9 percent from a year ago.

The U.S. pecan crop for 2001/02 was forecast to be 141.1 million pounds (shelled basis), an increase of 53 percent from the previous year. Imports of pecans were forecast to be 26.3 million pounds. Total consumption of pecans was estimated to be 136.8 million pounds.

Commercial Production for Selected Fruits in the United States In Thousands of Short Tons

Year	Apples	Cherries[2]	Cranberries	Grapes	Grapefruit	Lemons	Nectarines	Oranges	Peaches	Pears	Pineapples	Prunes & Plums	Strawberries	Tangelos	Tangerines	Total All Fruits
1995	5,293	363	210	5,922	2,912	897	176	11,432	1,151	948	345	744	804	142	287	32,140
1996	5,191	290	234	5,554	2,718	992	247	11,426	1,052	821	347	952	813	110	349	30,904
1997	5,162	373	275	7,291	2,885	962	264	12,692	1,312	1,043	324	899	814	178	425	35,507
1998	5,823	371	272	5,820	2,593	897	224	13,670	1,200	970	332	559	820	128	360	34,582
1999	5,315	344	316	6,236	2,513	747	274	9,824	1,263	1,016	352	735	905	115	327	30,787
2000[1]	5,324	351	282	7,658	2,762	840	267	12,997	1,300	967	354	909	924	99	458	36,084

[1] Preliminary. [2] Sweet and tart. [3] Utilized production. *Source: Economic Research Service, U.S. Department of Agriculture (ERS-USDA)*

Utilized Production for Selected Fruits in the United States In Thousands of Short Tons

	Utilized Production				Value of Production			
	Citrus[2]	Noncitrus	Tree Nuts[3]	Total	Citrus[2]	Noncitrus	Tree Nuts[3]	Total
Year	In Thousands of Short Tons				In Thousands of Dollars			
1995	15,799	16,358	811	32,958	2,328,915	6,815,962	1,714,547	10,859,424
1996	15,712	16,103	831	32,646	2,517,394	7,265,788	1,663,574	11,446,756
1997	17,271	18,363	1,210	36,844	2,582,767	8,158,095	2,093,697	12,834,559
1998	17,770	16,545	908	35,223	2,600,066	7,257,288	1,365,349	11,222,703
1999	13,633	17,316	1,288	32,237	2,431,179	8,067,353	1,505,926	12,004,458
2000[1]	17,276	18,818	1,088	37,182	2,514,790	7,882,150	1,498,621	11,895,561

[1] Preliminary. [2] Year harvest was completed. [3] Tree nuts on an in-shell equivalent.

Annual Average Retail Prices for Selected Fruits in the United States In Dollars Per Pound

							Oranges	
Year	Red Delicious Apples	Bananas	Anjou Pears	Thompson Seedless Grapes	Lemons	Grapefruit	Navel	Valencias
1995	.835	.490	.774	1.551	1.136	.548	.625	.648
1996	.930	.490	.916	1.685	1.114	.574	.707	.703
1997	.907	.487	.985	1.712	1.154	.520	.592	.682
1998	.943	.494	1.089	1.589	1.198	.599	.565	.657
1999	.897	.491	.950	1.841	1.236	.612	.843	.947
2000[1]	.919	.501	.845	1.904	1.289	.610	.613	.610

[1] Estimate. *Source: Economic Research Service, U.S. Department of Agriculture (ERS-USDA)*

Utilization of Noncitrus Fruit Production, and Value in the U.S. 1,000 Short Tons (Fresh Equivalent)

Year	Utilized Production	Fresh	Processed: Canned	Dried	Juice	Frozen	Wine	Other	Value of utilized Production $1,000
1991	15,740	6,215	2,110	2,417	1,583	501	2,739	167	6,021,210
1992	17,124	6,317	2,386	2,369	1,743	584	3,256	261	6,036,615
1993	16,554	6,391	2,042	2,339	1,749	627	3,029	181	6,130,119
1994	17,339	6,710	2,090	2,816	1,886	665	2,711	228	6,268,176
1995	16,348	6,285	1,753	2,400	1,857	647	2,992	205	6,815,962
1996	16,103	6,313	1,873	2,275	1,582	604	3,043	180	7,265,788
1997	18,363	6,643	2,130	2,660	1,675	699	4,035	247	8,158,095
1998	16,545	6,505	1,845	1,911	1,786	713	3,315	198	7,257,288
1999	17,316	6,647	1,986	2,148	1,887	735	3,351	247	8,067,353
2000[1]	18,818	6,975	1,798	2,998	1,754	689	4,130	202	7,882,150

[1] Preliminary. *Source: Economic Research Service, U.S. Department of Agriculture (ERS-USDA)*

Average Price Indexes for Fruits in the United States

Year	Index of all Fruit and Nut Prices Received by Growers (1990-92=100)	Producer Price Index (1982 = 100): Fresh Fruit	Dried Fruit	Canned Fruits and Juices	Frozen Fruits and Juices	Consumer Price Index (1982-84 = 100): Fresh Fruit	Processed Fruit
1991	112	129.9	107.2	128.6	115.1	193.9	131.8
1992	99	84.0	109.9	134.6	125.7	184.2	137.7
1993	93	84.5	113.0	126.1	110.9	188.8	132.3
1994	90	82.7	116.1	126.0	111.9	201.2	133.1
1995	99	85.8	116.1	129.4	115.8	219.0	137.2
1996	118	100.8	119.1	137.5	123.9	234.4	145.2
1997	110	101.3	119.8	137.5	117.3	236.3	148.8
1998	113	90.5	119.3	138.6	ÑÑ	246.5	101.9
1999	117	103.2	116.2	130.0	ÑÑ	266.3	105.4
2000[1]	103	91.4	117.9	131.7	ÑÑ	258.3	108.1

[1] Estimate. *Source: Economic Research Service, U.S. Department of Agriculture (ERS-USDA)*

Fresh Fruit: Per Capita Consumption[1] in the United States In Pounds

Year	Citrus Fruit: Oranges	Tangerines and Tangelos	Lemons	Grapefruit	Total	Noncitrus Fruit: Apples	Apricots	Avacados	Bananas	Cherries	Cranberries
1991	8.46	1.38	2.60	5.87	19.07	18.18	.13	1.41	25.12	.40	.07
1992	12.91	1.94	2.54	5.95	24.36	19.25	.15	1.43	27.26	.53	.08
1993	14.24	1.87	2.65	6.23	25.97	19.17	.13	2.17	26.80	.43	.07
1994	13.06	2.11	2.68	6.12	24.97	19.58	.15	1.34	28.06	.53	.08
1995	11.97	2.01	2.87	6.07	24.13	18.94	.10	1.37	27.42	.29	.08
1996	12.77	2.19	2.90	5.93	25.23	18.97	.09	1.60	28.02	.41	.08
1997	14.16	2.57	2.80	6.28	27.47	18.42	.15	1.61	27.64	.61	.07
1998	14.91	2.21	2.51	6.05	27.34	19.38	.13	1.76	28.58	.53	.08
1999	8.57	2.26	2.67	5.87	20.95	18.95	.12	1.55	31.40	.64	.11
2000[2]	12.04	2.91	2.50	5.24	24.50	17.90	.16	1.97	29.17	.61	.14

[1] All data on calendar-year basis except for citrus fruits; apples, August; grapes and pears, July; grapefruit, September; lemons, August of prior year; all other citrus, November. [2] Preliminary. *Source: Economic Research Service, U.S. Department of Agriculture (ERS-USDA)*

Fresh Fruit: Per Capita Consumption[1] in the United States In Pounds

Year	Noncitrus Fruit Continued: Grapes	Kiwifruit	Mangos	Nectarines & Peaches	Pears	Pineapples	Papaya	Plums & Prunes	Strawberries	Total Noncitrus	Total Fruit
1992	7.19	.39	.68	6.03	3.14	2.00	.24	1.78	3.61	73.74	98.10
1993	7.05	.60	.90	5.89	3.38	2.05	.28	1.28	3.64	73.83	99.80
1994	7.32	.57	.98	5.47	3.48	2.04	.30	1.62	4.09	75.61	100.58
1995	7.52	.56	1.13	5.39	3.40	1.93	.37	.94	4.16	73.58	97.71
1996	6.93	.55	1.36	4.44	3.10	1.92	.55	1.45	4.38	73.86	99.09
1997	8.04	.49	1.46	5.61	3.45	2.38	.48	1.54	4.17	76.12	103.59
1998	7.29	.56	1.52	4.87	3.36	2.81	.47	1.20	4.00	76.54	103.88
1999	8.21	.56	1.66	5.49	3.41	3.10	.64	1.30	4.49	81.64	102.59
2000[2]	7.48	.57	1.80	5.55	3.29	3.30	.70	1.22	4.80	78.66	103.16

[1] All data on calendar-year basis except for citrus fruits; apples, August; grapes and pears, July; grapefruit, September; lemons, August of prior year; all other citrus, November. [2] Preliminary. *Source: Economic Research Service, U.S. Department of Agriculture (ERS-USDA)*

Gas

Natural gas prices were sharply higher in early 2001 and then spent the remainder of the year moving lower. The high prices of 2000 led to an increase in exploration for gas. Price returned to levels seen in early 2000. The major fundamental difference between the start of 2002 and 2001 is that the inventories of natural gas are much higher than the year before. Additionally, the U.S. economy has been slowing down leading to less demand for energy products. The start of the heating season in the Northeast U.S. has seen warmer temperatures leading to less use of natural gas for heating homes. By early 2002, more normal temperatures in the Northeast promised increased natural gas use. One effect of the September 11 events was to slow the economy even further leading to less energy use and lower prices.

The U.S. Energy Information Agency reported that in November 2001 , dry natural gas production in the U.S. was estimated to be 1.59 trillion cubic feet, up 2 percent from a year ago when production was 1.55 trillion cubic feet. In the January-November 2001 period, dry natural gas production in the U.S. was 17.87 trillion cubic feet, up almost 3 percent from the same period in 2000 and some 4 percent more than in 1999. For all of 2000, dry natural gas production was 18.99 trillion cubic feet. Gross withdrawals of natural gas in September 2001 were 1.99 trillion cubic feet, down 3 percent from the previous month. In September 2000 withdrawals were 1.98 trillion cubic feet. Natural gas repressuring in September 2001 was 280 billion cubic feet, down 3 percent from the previous month. A year ago repressuring was 279 billion cubic feet. For all of 2000, natural gas repressuring was 3.43 trillion cubic feet.

Marketed production (wet) of natural gas in November 2001 was 1.67 trillion cubic feet, down 3 percent from the previous month. A year ago marketed production was 1.64 trillion cubic feet.

Total natural gas consumption in November 2001 was 1.65 trillion cubic feet, down 14 percent from the same month a year ago. In the January-November 2001 period, total natural gas consumption in the U.S. was 19.33 trillion cubic feet. In the same period of 2000 it was 19.95 trillion cubic feet, a decline of 3 percent from 2001. For all of 2000, consumption was 22.55 trillion cubic feet while in 1999 it was 21.62 trillion. Natural gas delivered to consumers in the January-November 2001 period was 17.69 trillion cubic feet. Residential consumers took 4.18 trillion cubic feet and commercial consumers took 2.89 trillion cubic feet. Industrial consumers took delivery of 8.12 trillion cubic feet while electric utilities took 1.89 trillion.

Futures Markets

Natural gas futures and options are traded on the New York Mercantile Exchange (NYMEX). Futures are traded on the International Petroleum Exchange (IPE).

World Production of Natural Gas (Monthly Average Marketed Production[3]) (In Terajoule[4])

Year	Australia	Canada	China	Germany	Indonesia	India	Italy	Mexico	Netherlands	Romania	Rissia[5]	United Knigdom	United States
1992	67,696	397,229	50,052	51,911	165,761	43,297	57,117	95,688	240,043	61,470	1,743,167	176,661	1,614,941
1993	72,848	437,922	52,297	47,904	171,828	44,475	60,792	93,646	244,205	58,499	1,708,083	196,792	1,667,401
1994	87,178	480,577	57,036	52,911	190,775	55,355	64,122	95,250	207,317	51,720	1,657,151	214,710	1,703,771
1995	96,912	511,447	58,261	55,714	203,633	59,857	63,371	93,473	209,229	50,401	1,891,583	246,818	1,683,674
1996	99,461	530,891	72,609	60,925	248,574	85,092	63,436	106,214	236,803	48,023	1,844,954	293,536	1,706,758
1997	99,077	537,295	81,954	60,558	248,585	60,979	61,173	109,568	209,526	41,547	1,771,467	299,503	1,711,104
1998	95,265	538,273	72,074	59,072	274,281	64,262	60,159	179,213	198,554	32,932	1,665,726	314,506	1,693,542
1999	96,601	559,177	79,523	62,651	282,485	62,786	55,534	182,610	186,672	38,952	1,807,313	345,040	1,685,869
2000[1]	95,623	577,456	90,287	57,970	267,707	78,204	54,289	178,861	167,611	38,254	1,898,046	377,565	1,726,861
2001[2]		605,556	95,271	71,026		90,876		172,282		39,435	1,837,557	411,755	1,753,039

[1] Preliminary. [2] Estimate. [3] Compares all gas collected & utilized as fuel or as a chemical industry raw material, including gas used in oilfields and/or gasfields as a fuel by producers. [4] Terajoule = 10 to the 12th power Joule = approximately 10 to the 9th power BTU. [5] Formerly part os U.S.S.R., data not reported seperately until 1992. NA = Not available. *Source: United Nations*

Marketed Production of Natural Gas in the United States, by States (In Million Cubic Feet)

Year	Alaska	California	Colorado	Kansas	Louisiana	Michigan	Mississippi	New Mexico	Oklahoma	Texas	Wyoming	Total
1991	437,822	378,384	285,961	628,459	5,034,361	195,749	108,031	1,038,284	2,153,852	6,280,654	776,528	18,532,439
1992	443,597	365,632	323,041	658,007	4,914,300	194,815	91,697	1,268,863	2,017,356	6,145,862	842,576	18,711,808
1993	430,350	315,851	400,985	686,347	4,991,138	204,635	80,695	1,409,429	2,049,942	6,249,624	634,957	18,981,915
1994	555,402	309,427	453,207	712,730	5,169,705	222,657	63,448	1,557,689	1,934,864	6,353,844	696,018	19,709,525
1995	469,550	279,555	523,084	721,436	5,108,366	238,203	95,533	1,625,837	1,811,734	6,330,048	673,775	19,506,474
1996	480,828	286,494	572,071	712,796	5,240,747	245,740	103,263	1,554,087	1,734,887	6,449,022	666,036	19,750,793
1997	468,311	285,690	637,375	687,215	5,229,821	305,950	107,300	1,558,633	1,703,888	6,453,873	738,368	19,866,093
1998	466,648	315,277	696,321	603,586	5,287,870	278,076	108,068	1,501,098	1,644,531	6,318,754	761,313	19,645,554
1999	462,967	382,715	739,085	553,419	5,313,794	277,364	111,021	1,511,671	1,570,847	6,117,653	823,132	19,595,854
2000[1]	468,418	374,888	763,954	510,796	5,488,032	297,067	88,558	1,594,923	1,636,203	6,350,267	1,020,916	20,184,354

[1] Preliminary. *Source: Energy Information Administration, U.S. Department of Energy (EIA-DOE)*

World Production of Natural Gas Plant Liquids (Thousand Barrels per Day)

Year	Algeria	Canada	Mexico	Saudi Arabia	Russia	United States	Persian Gulf[2]	OAPEC[3]	OPEC[4]	World
1992	140	460	454	713	230	1,697	1,003	1,185	1,364	4,974
1993	145	506	459	704	220	1,736	1,040	1,238	1,435	5,180
1994	140	529	461	698	200	1,727	1,071	1,267	1,465	5,292
1995	145	581	447	701	180	1,762	1,106	1,301	1,506	5,485
1996	150	596	423	697	185	1,830	1,082	1,295	1,501	5,576
1997	160	636	388	712	195	1,817	1,152	1,384	1,589	5,721
1998	155	651	424	755	220	1,759	1,225	1,449	1,662	5,874
1999	190	653	439	666	231	1,850	1,152	1,411	1,648	5,984
2000	190	699	438	706	232	1,911	1,206	1,463	1,706	6,168
2001[1]	190	707	432	682	236	1,960	1,219	1,473	1,711	6,239

[1] Preliminary. [2] Bahrain, Iran, Iraq, Kuwait, Qatar, Saudi Arabia and the United Arab Emirates. [3] Organization of Arab Petroleum Exporting Countries. [4] Organization of Petroleum Exporting Countries. [5] Through 1991; Former USSR. *Source: Energy Information Administration, U.S. Department of Energy (EIA-DOE)*

Recoverable Reserves and Deliveries of Natural Gas in the United States (in Billions of Cubic Feet)

			Deliveries					Consumption		
Year	Gross Withdrawals	Recoverable Reserves of Natural Gas Dec. 31[2]	Residential	Commercial	Electric Utility Plants[3]	Industrial	Total Deliveries	Lease & Plant Fuel	Used as Pipeline Fuel	Heating Value BTU per Cubic Foot
1991	21,750	167,062	4,556	2,729	2,789	7,231	17,305	1,129	601	1,030
1992	22,132	165,015	4,690	2,803	2,766	7,527	17,786	1,171	588	1,030
1993	22,726	162,415	4,956	2,863	2,682	7,981	18,483	1,172	624	1,027
1994	23,581	163,837	4,848	2,897	2,987	8,167	18,899	1,124	685	1,028
1995	23,744	165,146	4,850	3,034	3,197	8,580	19,660	1,220	700	1,027
1996	24,114	166,474	5,241	3,161	2,732	8,870	20,006	1,250	711	1,027
1997	24,213	167,223	4,984	3,219	2,968	8,832	20,004	1,203	751	1,026
1998	24,108	NA	4,520	3,005	3,258	8,686	19,469	1,173	635	1,031
1999	23,823	NA	4,726	3,050	3,113	9,006	19,895	1,079	645	1,027
2000[1]	24,153	NA	4,992	3,226	6,043	9,512	20,772	1,130	644	1,027

[1] Preliminary. [2] Estimated proved recoverable reserves of dry natural gas. [3] Figures include gas other than natural (impossible to segregate); therefore, shown separately from other consumption. *Source: Energy Information Administration, U.S. Department of Energy (EIA-DOE)*

Gas Utility Sales in the United States by Types and Class of Service (In Trillions of BTUs)

			Class by Service					Revenue - Million $ From Sales to Customers					
Year	Total Utility Sales	Number of Customers (Millions)	Residential	Commercial	Industrial	Electric Generation	Other	Total	Residential	Commercial	Industrial	Electric Generation	Other
1992	9,907	56.1	4,694	2,209	1,959	813	231	46,178	26,702	10,865	5,837	2,077	698
1993	10,151	57.0	5,054	2,397	2,009	524	168	50,137	29,787	12,076	6,162	1,480	632
1994	9,248	57.9	4,845	2,253	1,690	420	159	49,852	30,552	12,276	5,529	1,170	597
1995	9,221	58.7	4,803	2,281	1,591	328	218	46,436	28,742	11,573	4,816	836	549
1996	9,532	59.8	5,198	2,395	1,519	271	148	51,115	32,021	12,726	5,039	783	545
1997	8,880	59.8	5,013	2,234	1,279	245	123	51,531	33,175	12,632	4,518	766	488
1998	8,630	60.4	4,828	2,157	1,153	336	117	47,930	31,333	11,523	3,779	899	391
1999[1]	8,889	64.0	4,865	2,087	1,200	644	69	48,423	31,472	11,133	3,883	1,664	272
2000[2]	9,052	64.1	4,941	2,116	1,382	522	91	59,667	37,446	13,648	6,011	2,058	504

[1] Preliminary. [2] Estimate. *Source: American Gas Association (AGA)*

Salient Statistics of Natural Gas in the United States

	Supply						Disposition				Average Price Delivered to Consumers						
Year	Marketed Production	Extraction Loss	Dry Production	Storage Withdrawals	Imports (Consumed)	Total Supply	Consumption	Exports	Added to Storage	Total Disposition	Wellhead Price	Imports	Exports	Residential	Commercial	Industrial	Electric Utilities
	In Billions of Cubic Feet										USD Per Thousand Cubic Feet						
1991	18,532	835	17,698	2,689	1,773	21,836	19,035	129	2,608	21,750	1.64	1.82	2.59	5.82	4.81	2.69	2.18
1992	18,712	872	17,840	2,724	2,138	22,360	19,544	216	2,555	22,132	1.74	1.85	2.25	5.89	4.88	2.84	2.36
1993	18,982	886	18,095	2,717	2,350	23,578	20,279	140	2,760	23,578	2.04	2.03	2.59	6.16	5.22	3.07	2.61
1994	19,710	889	18,821	2,508	2,624	24,207	20,708	162	2,796	24,207	1.85	1.87	2.50	6.41	5.44	3.05	2.28
1995	19,506	908	18,599	2,974	2,841	24,837	21,581	154	2,566	24,837	1.55	1.49	2.39	6.06	5.05	2.71	2.02
1996	19,812	958	18,854	2,911	2,937	25,635	21,967	153	2,906	25,635	2.17	1.97	2.97	6.34	5.40	3.42	2.69
1997	19,866	964	18,902	2,824	2,994	25,502	21,959	157	2,800	25,502	2.32	2.17	3.02	6.94	5.80	3.59	2.78
1998	19,961	938	19,024	2,377	3,152	24,859	21,262	159	2,904	24,859	1.96	1.97	2.45	6.82	5.48	3.14	2.40
1999[1]	19,805	973	18,832	2,772	3,586	25,055	21,703	163	2,598	25,055	2.19	2.24	2.61	6.69	5.33	3.10	2.62
2000[2]	20,002	1,016	18,987				22,723				3.69	3.95	4.10	7.76	6.59	4.48	4.38

[1] Preliminary. [2] Estimate. *Source: Energy Information Administration, U.S. Department of Energy (EIA-DOE)*

Average Open Interest of Natural Gas Futures in New York In Contracts

Year	Jan.	Feb.	Mar.	Apr.	May	June	July	Aug.	Sept.	Oct.	Nov.	Dec.
1992	24,718	28,661	29,851	33,626	41,456	49,642	49,829	57,346	68,306	77,034	80,349	74,569
1993	69,499	77,053	91,132	116,366	136,074	132,667	124,038	126,443	129,940	130,619	124,627	129,963
1994	127,254	128,336	118,480	119,908	120,894	120,956	111,044	135,652	156,238	145,766	139,471	139,054
1995	148,448	151,882	157,097	150,101	148,797	144,402	143,942	140,297	135,226	133,969	140,301	166,227
1996	155,024	150,521	149,809	159,132	147,616	156,959	151,913	135,191	138,657	144,944	147,854	151,498
1997	156,231	162,567	171,467	181,745	206,685	197,637	199,296	213,640	235,509	242,184	231,556	210,259
1998	192,652	198,853	203,402	251,344	255,837	264,517	255,878	273,350	275,868	252,827	236,292	240,832
1999	244,472	268,649	284,312	315,336	332,398	330,725	316,034	353,767	336,622	316,157	309,130	292,161
2000	262,845	266,826	295,176	313,739	342,455	347,353	330,604	339,025	373,654	369,448	389,363	377,470
2001	364,532	346,343	360,032	380,632	421,145	456,512	473,675	497,972	494,475	488,187	455,766	415,882

Source: *New York Mercantile Exchange (NYMEX)*

Volume of Trading of Natural Gas Futures in New York (In Thousands of Contracts)

Year	Jan.	Feb.	Mar.	Apr.	May	June	July	Aug.	Sept.	Oct.	Nov.	Dec.	Total
1992	89.0	45.4	77.9	98.9	137.5	116.4	156.0	192.2	268.7	300.0	213.5	227.6	1,923.2
1993	194.3	274.4	318.8	443.0	471.5	365.9	335.6	353.3	459.6	417.1	449.7	613.9	4,697.1
1994	667.6	470.9	373.5	344.7	411.1	465.8	438.8	724.2	578.7	594.2	621.9	721.8	6,413.2
1995	733.0	557.8	676.1	524.5	621.3	622.5	641.8	745.6	548.3	664.4	763.0	988.5	8,086.7
1996	887.2	655.7	694.6	620.0	590.7	681.3	829.0	628.8	679.1	924.4	802.8	820.4	8,813.9
1997	922.8	693.6	664.7	836.3	945.4	803.7	812.9	1,313.8	1,377.1	1,394.0	1,104.8	1,054.6	11,923.6
1998	1,005.6	1,089.1	1,193.5	1,625.9	1,245.2	1,568.8	1,310.4	1,237.0	1,656.3	1,339.5	1,243.1	1,464.0	15,978.3
1999	1,296.7	1,158.6	1,788.5	1,655.8	1,465.3	1,474.2	1,865.8	1,892.1	1,978.6	1,676.5	1,552.3	1,360.7	19,165.1
2000	1,388.8	1,470.9	1,505.0	1,179.3	1,822.2	1,853.7	1,331.4	1,483.9	1,510.2	1,594.9	1,759.5	975.1	17,875.0
2001	1,044.4	1,044.6	1,131.7	1,144.8	1,632.5	1,536.9	1,350.3	1,510.9	901.1	1,639.7	1,891.7	1,639.6	16,468.1

Source: *New York Mercantile Exchange (NYMEX)*

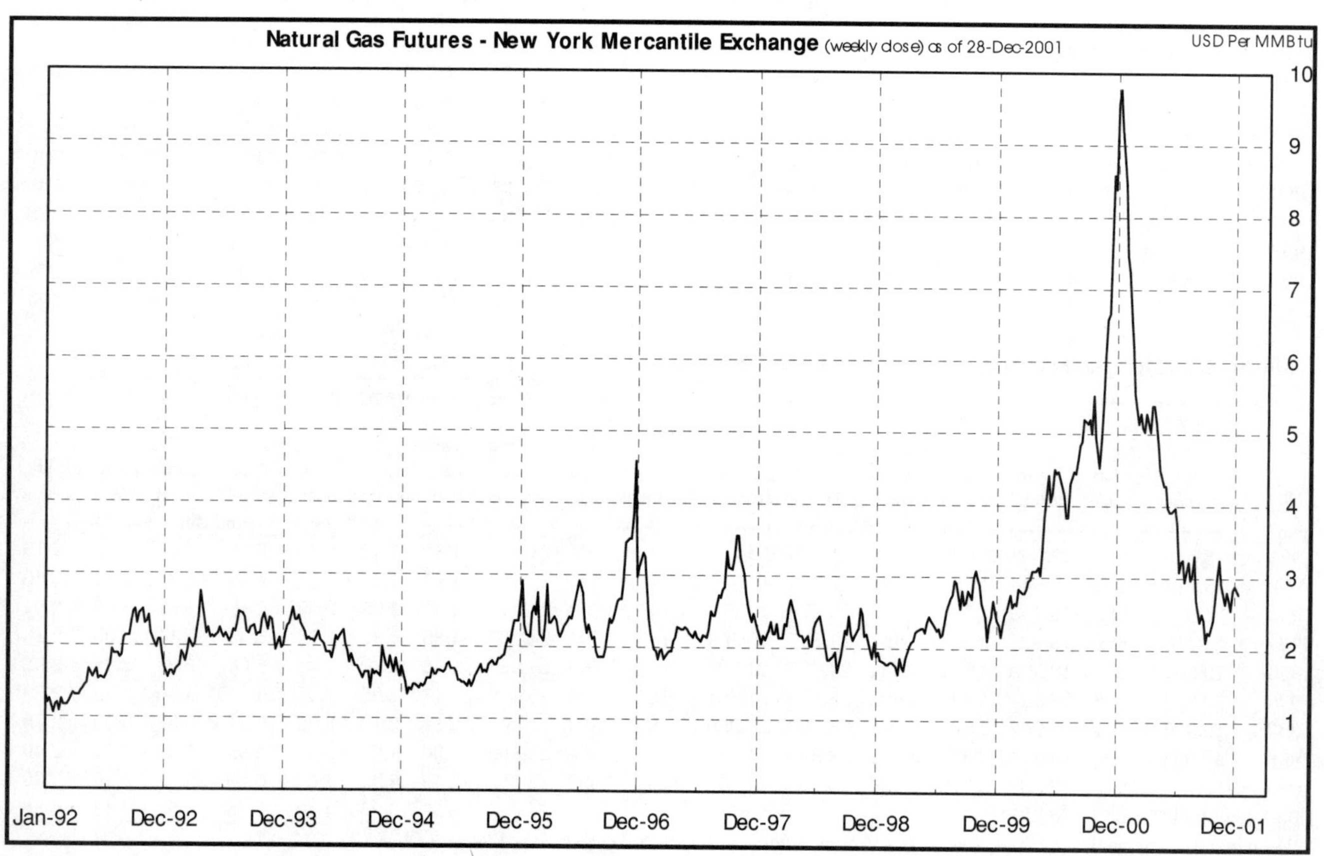

Gasoline

In year 2000, retail gasoline prices posted a substantial increase as the Organization of Petroleum Exporting Countries (OPEC) managed to adhere to production quota levels. There were other fundamental reasons for higher gasoline prices. One important reason was a decline in global stocks of petroleum which led to a surge in energy prices in everything from crude oil to heating oil to gasoline. Prices in 2000 peaked in October then started to decline with increased supplies. An OPEC decision to increase petroleum output seemed to be the primary reason for the decline in energy prices.

In 2001, the single important event was a decline in the U.S. economy as a recession promised to reduce the demand for energy products. The events of September 11 added to the bearish tone in the energy markets as these events caused a further slowing in the economy. Gasoline prices fell sharply in the wake of September 11 and by December 2001 retail gasoline prices were at the lowest level since March 1999. In some areas, gasoline prices had dropped to under $1.00 per gallon. Despite the low prices for gasoline, the combination of recession and growing unemployment reduced the demand for gasoline. OPEC members met again and agreed to reduce crude oil output which if effective should lead to higher gasoline prices in 2002. One critical element in the outlook has been whether non-OPEC countries like Russia will follow OPEC in terms of production cuts. The answer to that question could well determine the direction of gasoline prices as 2002 progresses.

U.S. production of finished motor gasoline in October 2001 was 8.51 million barrels per day. In October 2000, production was 8.03 million barrels per day. In the January-October 2000 period, production of finished motor gasoline averaged 8.3 million barrels per day., compared to 8.15 million barrels in the same period of 1999.

U.S. imports of finished gasoline in October 2001 were estimated at 454,000 barrels per day, down 16 percent from the previous month. In October 2000 imports were 381,000 barrels per day. In the January-October 2001 period, imports averaged 449,000 barrels per day. In the same period of 2000 they averaged 421,000 barrels while in 1999 the average was 402,000 barrels.

U.S. exports of motor gasoline in October 2001 were 148,000 barrels per day, up 29 percent from the previous month. In the January-October 2001 period, exports averaged 128,000 barrels per day. In 2000 that average was 136,000 barrels per day. Exports of gasoline have been increasing. In 1999 they averaged 111,000 barrels per day. In 1990 they average 55,000.

Total motor gasoline stocks in October 2001 were 207 million barrels. At the end of December 2000 they were 196 million barrels while at the end of 1999 they were 193 million.

Futures Markets

Unleaded gasoline futures and options are traded on the New York Mercantile Exchange (NYMEX.

Average Spot Price of Unleaded Gasoline in New York In Cents Per Gallon

Year	Jan.	Feb.	Mar.	Apr.	May	June	July	Aug.	Sept.	Oct.	Nov.	Dec.	Average
1992	53.04	55.14	54.10	59.75	63.48	64.51	59.94	62.06	61.63	60.81	58.22	53.24	58.83
1993	52.96	52.54	54.33	59.35	59.37	54.78	51.80	53.13	48.61	50.22	44.30	37.68	51.59
1994	42.40	43.75	44.04	48.98	50.62	52.84	54.52	55.61	46.53	51.14	52.32	46.87	49.14
1995	50.99	51.43	50.74	61.01	64.76	59.47	51.45	53.45	56.10	48.89	51.15	53.44	54.41
1996	50.70	53.26	58.56	69.17	65.10	58.03	61.65	61.17	62.43	65.52	69.23	68.58	61.95
1997	67.64	62.49	61.28	58.59	62.08	55.17	58.58	70.42	62.17	58.35	55.60	51.75	60.34
1998	47.85	45.14	44.13	46.98	48.26	43.95	42.29	40.14	42.70	43.71	36.78	30.92	42.74
1999	34.24	31.81	42.33	50.11	48.86	48.65	58.35	63.89	69.37	62.63	69.57	70.55	54.20
2000	70.43	81.30	89.11	73.15	89.06	96.18	86.76	86.97	96.04	94.71	93.94	73.66	85.94
2001	83.32	82.56	78.18	94.95	92.37	71.85	68.31	77.18	75.00	59.79	51.34	51.85	73.89

Source: *The Wall Street Journal*

Average Open Interest of Unleaded Regular Gasoline Futures in New York In Contracts

Year	Jan.	Feb.	Mar.	Apr.	May	June	July	Aug.	Sept.	Oct.	Nov.	Dec.
1992	124,896	117,155	108,388	89,775	79,680	80,394	81,110	76,741	71,264	68,059	71,110	77,508
1993	80,610	93,630	100,657	96,607	88,311	94,926	104,260	103,371	100,921	107,339	126,649	150,359
1994	135,366	120,204	118,977	122,092	96,525	89,854	86,401	76,213	67,881	70,258	71,245	63,679
1995	61,015	67,631	65,201	76,323	76,269	69,676	64,379	58,426	62,089	58,782	57,902	70,098
1996	64,561	64,990	70,100	71,895	66,172	52,882	55,394	55,618	57,119	59,993	58,416	62,760
1997	68,188	84,693	92,520	97,619	90,407	78,492	83,082	103,538	103,250	94,602	92,852	103,497
1998	106,353	102,656	108,667	117,521	107,235	100,792	89,846	86,902	85,188	81,991	87,306	103,079
1999	105,532	113,683	111,449	110,531	107,644	102,927	113,619	120,468	120,328	111,758	109,428	96,652
2000	89,049	103,586	105,448	105,133	103,831	96,772	80,886	66,598	74,735	80,446	88,509	92,041
2001	117,540	126,762	124,631	124,162	111,576	103,058	101,249	92,156	87,841	102,414	115,699	126,634

Source: *New York Mercantile Exchange (NYMEX)*

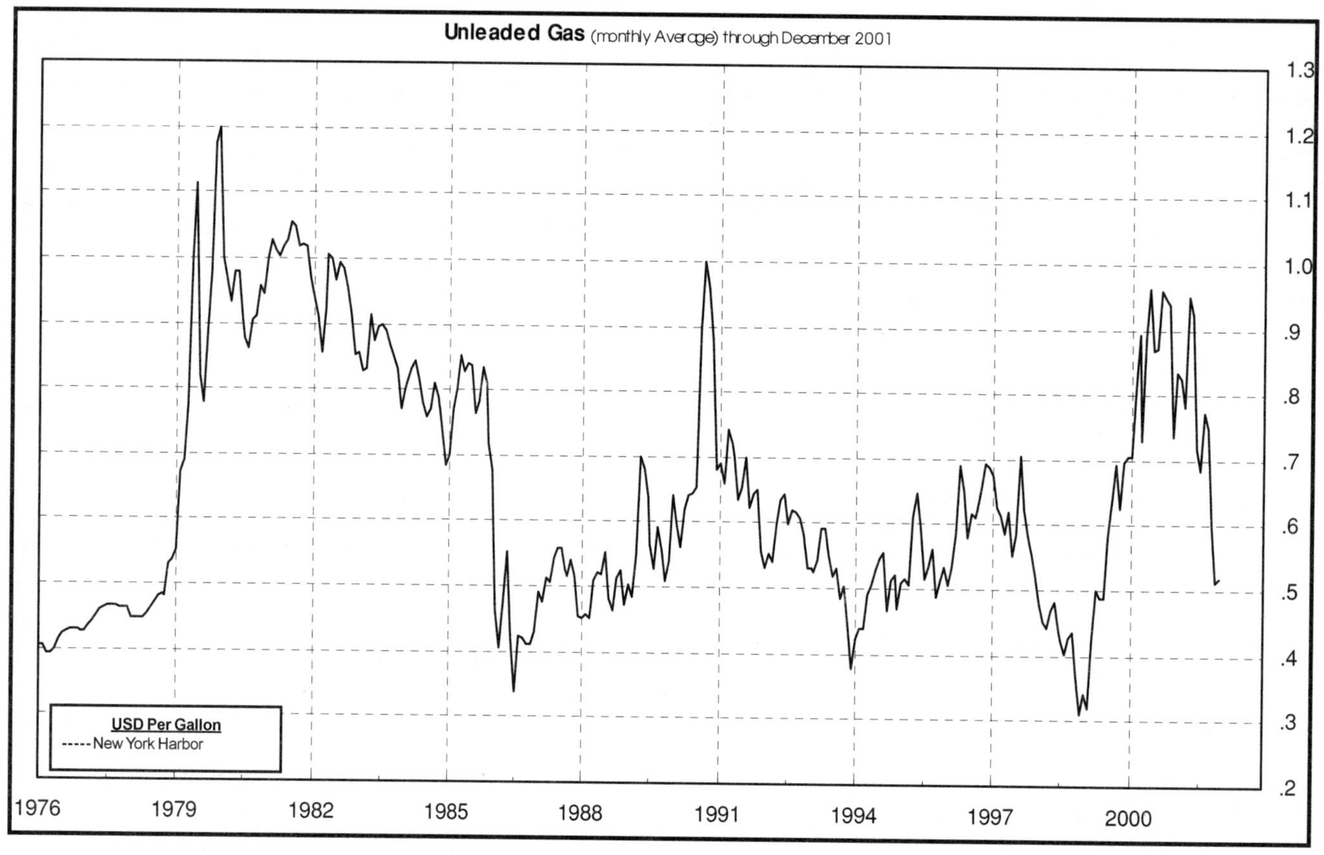

Volume of Trading of Unleaded Regular Gasoline Futures in New York In Contracts

Year	Jan.	Feb.	Mar.	Apr.	May	June	July	Aug.	Sept.	Oct.	Nov.	Dec.	Total
1992	565,922	558,476	604,678	668,490	580,088	620,114	600,897	545,520	469,844	563,856	435,847	461,025	6,674,757
1993	531,780	558,770	584,899	539,785	571,860	611,951	594,740	721,852	642,959	629,733	674,814	729,717	7,392,860
1994	634,027	526,505	615,594	677,891	636,990	673,034	601,980	748,415	569,384	684,670	582,359	519,987	7,470,836
1995	592,329	506,640	736,704	663,743	780,568	680,792	565,655	556,589	573,551	473,014	480,507	461,695	7,071,787
1996	543,818	449,537	570,341	676,193	623,347	467,953	533,793	463,830	469,036	527,553	487,624	499,314	6,312,339
1997	590,066	563,180	605,121	623,169	618,312	555,543	721,386	795,404	664,906	613,557	509,893	614,608	7,475,145
1998	613,643	612,266	766,430	789,293	681,052	753,120	680,551	591,985	654,247	670,159	577,799	601,724	7,992,269
1999	561,493	619,704	876,350	741,511	721,122	737,690	821,991	800,399	751,305	705,144	748,839	615,668	8,701,216
2000	693,610	721,890	921,642	730,022	927,541	838,537	650,632	677,207	641,169	635,690	612,112	595,130	8,645,182
2001	825,177	701,201	809,201	980,951	1,056,488	894,994	737,322	790,776	581,903	664,850	613,305	567,213	9,223,381

Source: New York Mercantile Exchange (NYMEX)

Production of Finished Motor Gasoline in the United States In Thousand Barrels per Day

Year	Jan.	Feb.	Mar.	Apr.	May	June	July	Aug.	Sept.	Oct.	Nov.	Dec.	Average
1992	7,013	6,726	6,683	6,954	7,092	7,198	7,195	6,817	7,071	7,198	7,323	7,411	7,058
1993	7,228	7,144	6,904	7,126	7,446	7,442	7,337	7,335	7,573	7,394	7,652	7,725	7,360
1994	7,097	6,790	6,760	7,195	7,348	7,455	7,380	7,432	7,385	7,151	7,849	7,867	7,312
1995	7,303	7,243	7,168	7,529	7,678	7,843	7,747	7,642	7,785	7,544	7,739	7,821	7,588
1996	7,333	7,303	7,242	7,475	7,724	7,820	7,811	7,696	7,585	7,496	7,835	7,784	7,647
1997	7,308	7,315	7,322	7,822	8,056	8,180	7,947	8,048	8,147	8,039	7,984	8,143	7,870
1998	7,749	7,485	7,591	8,029	8,057	8,372	8,287	8,200	8,029	7,995	8,263	8,395	8,082
1999	7,886	7,607	7,531	8,138	8,207	8,402	8,280	8,183	8,187	8,266	8,142	8,471	8,111
2000	7,798	7,658	8,032	8,130	8,398	8,550	8,320	8,251	8,358	8,031	8,394	8,298	8,186
2001[1]	7,903	7,781	7,963	8,447	8,648	8,625	8,428	8,265	8,383	8,410	8,321	8,211	8,282

[1] Preliminary. *Source: Energy Information Administration, U.S. Department of Energy (EIA-DOE)*

Disposition of Finished Motor Gasoline, Total Product Supplied in the U.S. In Thousand Barrels per Day

Year	Jan.	Feb.	Mar.	Apr.	May	June	July	Aug.	Sept.	Oct.	Nov.	Dec.	Average
1992	6,869	6,963	7,137	7,238	7,328	7,460	7,639	7,380	7,344	7,338	7,102	7,396	7,268
1993	6,639	7,112	7,389	7,435	7,585	7,700	7,785	7,864	7,607	7,382	7,533	7,661	7,476
1994	6,980	7,275	7,395	7,564	7,644	7,022	7,881	7,075	7,015	7,548	7,404	7,924	7,601
1995	7,163	7,481	7,788	7,651	7,894	8,220	7,888	8,187	7,786	7,781	7,866	7,742	7,789
1996	7,254	7,552	7,729	7,869	7,998	8,089	8,135	8,216	7,641	8,038	7,875	7,775	7,891
1997	7,312	7,651	7,808	8,067	8,128	8,260	8,471	8,195	8,004	8,166	7,955	8,093	8,017
1998	7,590	7,755	7,956	8,137	8,070	8,437	8,659	8,500	8,308	8,405	8,136	8,401	8,253
1999	7,701	8,031	8,128	8,506	8,420	8,886	8,942	8,579	8,305	8,542	8,240	8,859	8,431
2000	7,653	8,291	8,305	8,375	8,661	8,824	8,642	8,921	8,518	8,417	8,384	8,670	8,472
2001[1]	8,064	8,203	8,479	8,546	8,718	8,722	8,974	8,938	8,564	8,610	8,603	8,636	8,588

[1] Preliminary. *Source: Energy Information Administration, U.S. Department of Energy (EIA-DOE)*

Stocks of Finished Gasoline[2] on Hand in the United States, at End of Month In Millions of Barrels

Year	Jan.	Feb.	Mar.	Apr.	May	June	July	Aug.	Sept.	Oct.	Nov.	Dec.
1992	192.8	191.4	182.9	185.0	187.4	189.5	182.0	168.2	170.0	168.7	178.2	179.1
1993	197.8	201.9	189.0	184.0	186.8	184.2	176.8	166.7	171.2	175.6	182.6	187.1
1994	194.1	186.2	175.6	176.4	179.0	176.9	172.9	167.6	169.2	161.7	176.6	175.9
1995	182.7	180.0	167.8	167.1	167.1	163.5	166.0	154.6	158.9	155.6	155.6	161.3
1996	168.7	168.4	158.3	159.8	161.8	163.8	163.7	154.9	161.3	149.1	150.7	157.0
1997	164.9	161.3	153.8	152.0	157.8	163.9	150.6	149.6	158.1	158.0	161.1	166.1
1998	175.3	172.8	166.4	168.3	174.9	177.7	172.5	168.8	164.7	160.0	167.5	172.0
1999	185.2	178.4	167.8	168.9	176.5	172.3	163.6	158.6	159.2	158.8	160.5	151.6
2000	165.3	156.4	157.1	160.6	162.2	164.5	164.6	151.0	154.2	147.4	156.7	153.0
2001[1]	159.4	155.2	145.8	152.3	161.1	169.1	162.0	150.3	157.6	159.5	161.0	

[1] Preliminary. [2] Includes oxygenated and other finished. *Source: Energy Information Administration, U.S. Department of Energy (EIA-DOE)*

Average Refiner Price of Finished Motor Gasoline to End Users[1] in the U.S. In Cents Per Gallon

Year	Jan.	Feb.	Mar.	Apr.	May	June	July	Aug.	Sept.	Oct.	Nov.	Dec.	Average
1992	71.2	70.2	71.0	74.6	80.3	84.0	83.5	82.3	82.3	81.3	81.4	78.5	78.4
1993	76.9	76.1	75.7	77.8	80.1	79.8	77.6	76.2	74.9	75.3	72.5	68.0	75.9
1994	66.8	67.6	67.3	69.5	71.1	74.1	77.0	81.5	79.6	76.9	77.5	75.1	73.8
1995	74.5	73.3	73.1	77.3	83.4	83.9	80.0	76.9	75.8	73.6	71.8	73.0	76.5
1996	74.6	74.8	79.8	88.1	92.7	90.3	87.5	84.9	84.4	84.4	86.7	85.9	84.7
1997	86.6	86.1	84.3	83.9	84.5	83.3	81.5	86.8	87.2	84.3	81.6	77.8	83.9
1998	73.3	69.0	65.6	67.4	71.0	70.4	69.4	66.7	65.4	66.4	64.0	60.0	67.3
1999	59.2	56.8	65.1	79.0	78.2	75.6	80.6	86.5	88.8	87.1	88.4	90.3	78.1
2000	91.7	98.7	113.1	108.7	110.3	121.3	117.3	110.3	117.5	115.5	113.5	106.3	110.6
2001[2]	106.6	106.6	103.8	117.6	130.1	120.5	103.0	102.5	109.2	89.9			109.0

[1] Excludes aviation and taxes. [2] Preliminary. *Source: Energy Information Administration, U.S. Department of Energy (EIA-DOE)*

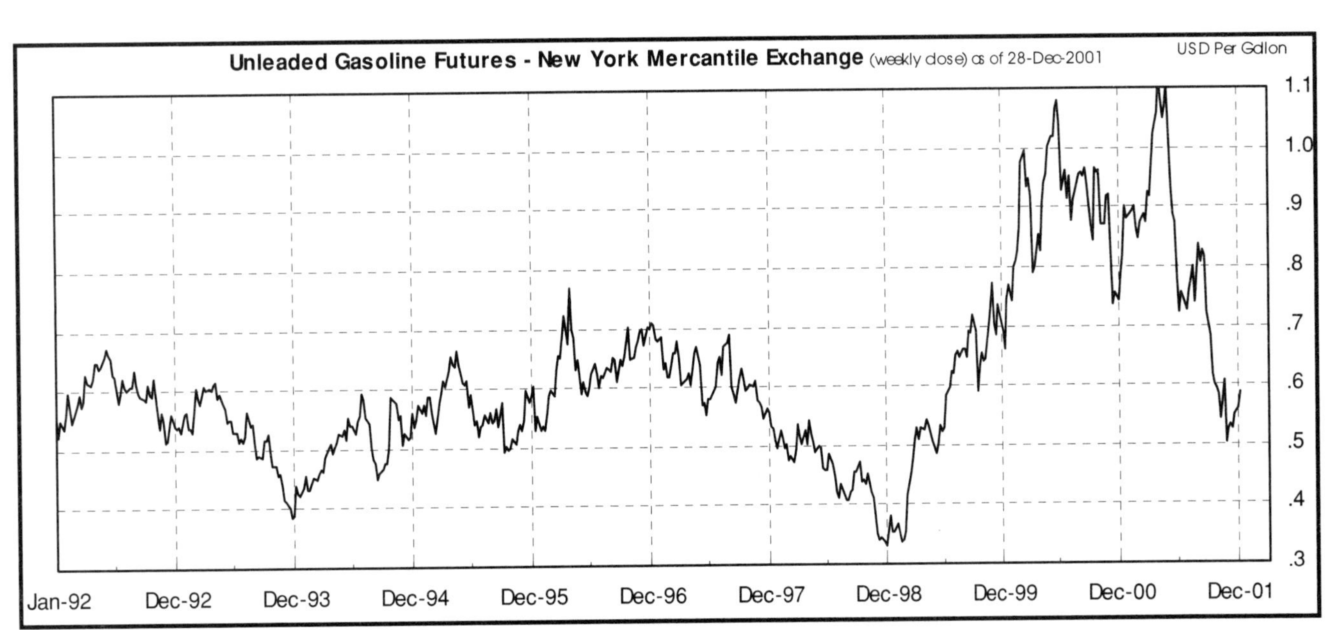

GASOLINE

Average Retail Price of Unleaded Premium Motor Gasoline[2] in the United States In Cents per Gallon

Year	Jan.	Feb.	Mar.	Apr.	May	June	July	Aug.	Sept.	Oct.	Nov.	Dec.	Average
1992	126.7	124.8	125.0	126.8	131.7	135.9	136.3	134.8	134.6	134.5	135.1	133.0	131.6
1993	131.3	130.1	129.4	130.4	131.9	132.1	130.5	129.4	128.2	132.3	130.5	126.8	130.2
1994	124.0	124.5	124.3	126.0	127.4	130.0	132.7	136.7	136.4	134.5	135.4	133.7	130.5
1995	132.4	131.6	130.6	132.5	138.3	141.1	138.4	135.2	133.2	131.5	129.2	129.0	133.6
1996	131.7	131.1	134.8	143.1	150.7	148.1	145.3	142.1	141.7	140.8	142.8	143.8	141.3
1997	144.1	143.4	141.5	141.3	140.9	141.1	138.8	143.3	145.8	142.6	139.7	136.3	141.6
1998	131.9	127.1	122.9	123.7	127.5	127.9	126.8	124.4	123.0	123.6	122.5	118.7	125.0
1999	117.1	115.5	118.6	136.7	137.0	133.9	137.8	144.1	146.8	146.4	145.4	148.6	135.7
2000	148.6	155.1	172.3	169.8	168.2	178.6	177.3	168.9	176.4	174.4	173.8	167.9	169.3
2001[1]	165.7	167.1	163.8	174.8	193.4	188.1	169.5	163.6	172.6	156.0	142.7		168.8

[1] Preliminary. [2] Including taxes. *Source: Energy Information Administration, U.S. Department of Energy (EIA-DOE)*

Average Retail Price of Unleaded Regular Motor Gasoline[2] in the United States In Cents per Gallon

Year	Jan.	Feb.	Mar.	Apr.	May	June	July	Aug.	Sept.	Oct.	Nov.	Dec.	Average
1992	107.3	105.4	105.8	107.9	113.6	117.9	117.5	115.8	115.8	115.4	115.9	113.6	112.7
1993	111.7	110.8	109.8	111.2	112.9	113.0	110.9	109.7	108.5	112.7	111.3	107.0	110.8
1994	104.3	105.1	104.5	106.4	108.0	110.6	113.6	118.2	117.7	115.2	116.3	114.3	111.2
1995	112.9	112.0	111.5	114.0	120.0	122.6	119.5	116.4	114.8	112.7	110.1	110.1	114.7
1996	112.9	112.4	116.2	125.1	132.3	129.9	127.2	124.0	123.4	122.7	125.0	126.0	123.1
1997	126.1	125.5	123.5	123.1	122.6	122.9	120.5	125.3	127.7	124.2	121.3	117.7	123.4
1998	113.1	108.2	104.1	105.2	109.2	109.4	107.9	105.2	103.3	104.2	102.8	98.6	105.9
1999	97.2	95.5	99.1	117.7	117.8	114.8	118.9	125.5	128.0	127.4	126.4	129.8	116.5
2000	130.1	136.9	154.1	150.6	149.8	161.7	159.3	151.0	158.2	155.9	155.5	148.9	151.0
2001[1]	147.2	148.4	144.7	156.4	172.9	164.0	148.2	142.7	153.1	136.2	126.3		149.1

[1] Preliminary. [2] Including taxes. *Source: Energy Information Administration, U.S. Department of Energy (EIA-DOE)*

Average Retail Price of All-Types[2] Motor Gasoline[3] in the United States In Cents per Gallon

Year	Jan.	Feb.	Mar.	Apr.	May	June	July	Aug.	Sept.	Oct.	Nov.	Dec.	Average
1992	113.5	111.7	112.2	114.3	119.7	123.9	123.8	122.1	122.2	121.9	122.3	120.1	119.0
1993	118.2	117.2	116.3	117.5	119.3	119.4	117.4	116.3	115.1	119.3	117.8	113.6	117.3
1994	110.9	111.4	110.9	112.8	114.3	116.7	119.9	124.3	123.7	121.2	122.2	120.3	117.4
1995	119.0	118.1	117.3	119.7	125.6	128.1	125.2	122.2	120.6	118.5	116.1	116.0	120.5
1996	118.6	118.1	121.9	130.5	137.8	135.4	132.8	129.8	129.3	128.7	130.8	131.8	128.8
1997	131.8	131.2	129.3	128.8	128.4	128.6	126.3	131.0	133.4	130.0	127.1	123.6	129.1
1998	118.6	113.7	109.7	110.6	114.6	114.8	113.4	110.8	109.1	109.9	108.6	104.6	111.5
1999	103.1	101.4	104.8	123.2	123.3	120.4	124.4	130.9	133.4	132.9	131.9	135.3	122.1
2000	135.6	142.2	159.4	156.1	155.2	166.6	164.2	155.9	163.5	161.3	160.8	154.4	156.3
2001[1]	152.5	153.8	150.3	161.7	181.2	173.1	156.5	150.9	160.9	144.2	132.4		156.1

[1] Preliminary. [2] Also includes types of motor oil not shown separately. [3] Including taxes. *Source: Energy Information Administration, U.S. Department of Energy (EIA-DOE)*

Average Refiner Price of Finished Aviation Gasoline to End Users[2] in the U.S. In Cents per Gallon

Year	Jan.	Feb.	Mar.	Apr.	May	June	July	Aug.	Sept.	Oct.	Nov.	Dec.	Average
1992	98.5	98.5	98.0	99.1	102.4	106.4	106.8	105.7	104.9	104.3	103.4	101.3	102.7
1993	100.3	99.9	99.4	100.7	102.2	102.5	99.7	98.8	98.2	98.0	95.7	91.2	99.0
1994	88.6	88.4	89.0	91.3	92.3	95.6	95.9	101.7	101.1	100.0	100.0	99.2	95.6
1995	99.6	99.8	99.0	101.3	105.8	106.4	101.8	99.2	101.3	96.8	95.4	96.0	100.5
1996	97.6	100.6	105.0	111.2	114.4	113.5	113.7	114.4	114.3	115.0	115.1	115.3	111.6
1997	113.7	114.9	113.8	114.7	115.7	114.6	112.5	114.6	115.6	113.9	113.0	107.7	113.8
1998	104.3	101.1	98.2	98.6	99.9	99.0	98.4	95.9	94.1	95.1	93.2	88.5	97.2
1999	87.1	85.1	90.1	101.4	104.2	104.1	107.9	113.2	115.4	117.6	116.4	119.6	105.9
2000	118.7	119.5	129.1	124.3	126.8	139.8	142.6	NA	138.2	134.9	134.9	126.1	130.6
2001[1]	128.5	130.3	124.5	132.8	146.5	145.1	134.6	136.3	142.5	125.4			134.7

[1] Preliminary. [2] Excluding taxes. *Source: Energy Information Administration, U.S. Department Energy (EIA-DOE)*

Gold

In the summer of 2001, gold prices on the COMEX Division of the New York Mercantile Exchange were trading in a range of about $270 to $280 per ounce. In the wake of the September 11 events, gold prices moved sharply higher approaching $300 per ounce. By early October 2001, gold prices started to move lower and by the end of the year were back near $270 to $280 per ounce. despite all of the events after September 11 and gold's reputation as a safe haven in times of uncertainty, gold prices did very little in terms of moving higher. The reason for this may very well be that there was little indication that there was any sign of inflation. Energy prices after the incident fell. The Federal Reserve aggressively lowered interest rates and the money supply expanded but gold prices were unable to mount a rally. Silver prices moved higher but gold was unable to follow. The steep decline in interest rates along with attempts to stimulate the economy could well mean that in year 2002 inflation will start to reappear. At the same time it is expected that the Federal Reserve will again start to increase interest rates at the first signs of inflation. One factor that could lead to inflation is energy. If prices for energy products begin to increase, gold prices could start to move higher.

In the gold sector itself, there continued to be a series of mergers and acquisitions among the gold producers. Canadian gold miner Barrick Gold acquired Homestake Mining. As 2002 got underway, Newmont Mining Corporation was ready to acquire Normandy Mining Ltd. That would make Newmont Mining the largest gold producer in the world. Another issue of importance in the gold market concerns hedging or forward selling of gold production. This activity, which is used by some mining firms, in effect protects against a decline in the price of gold. At the same time, it can prevent a gold producer from reaping the rewards of higher gold prices. There has been a trend toward less of this activity in hedging gold prices and that could lead to higher prices in 2002.

The U.S. Geological Survey reported that world mine production of gold in 2000 was 2,445 metric tonnes, down 4 percent from 1999. The world's largest producer of gold is South Africa with 2000 mine production of 440 tonnes., down 2 percent from 1999. The U.S. is the next largest producer with 2000 mine output of 330 tonnes, down 2 percent from the previous year. Production by Australia was estimated at 300 tonnes, down 1 percent from the previous year. Other large producers of gold include China, Canada, Peru, Indonesia and Russia.

World reserves of gold are estimated to be 48,000 tonnes. About 20 percent of the gold is a byproduct of another metal. South Africa has by far the largest reserves which are estimated at 19,000 tonnes. U.S. reserves of gold are estimated at 5,000 tonnes. It is estimated that 130,000 tonnes of gold have been mined. Of that total, about 20,000 tonnes have been lost, used up in industrial processes or otherwise unaccounted for. Of the remaining 110,000 tonnes, an estimated 33,300 tonnes are official stocks held by Central Banks and about 77,200 tonnes are held privately as coins, bullion and jewelry.

U.S. mine production of gold in 2000 was estimated to be 330 tonnes and over the last five years gold production has averaged 345 tonnes per year. In the u.S., gold was produced at about 60 major lode mines, a dozen or more large placer mines and numerous small placer mines. Gold is also recovered as a byproduct of processing base metals, mostly copper. Primary refinery production of gold in 2000 was 265 tonnes, the same as in 1999. secondary production of gold from new and old scrap in 2000 was 140 tonnes. The estimated uses of gold were jewelry and arts, 85 percent; electrical and electronics, 7 percent; dental, 3 percent; and other, 5 percent.

In August 2001, mine production of gold in the u.S. was 26,800 kilograms, down 9 percent from the previous month. In the January-August 2001 period, U.S. gold production was 222,000 kilograms. The largest gold producing state was Nevada. In August 2001, Nevada produced 20,800 kilograms. Gold production in Alaska in August 2001 was 1,370 kilograms while California production was 819 kilograms.

U.S. imports of gold in July 2001 were 15,300 kilograms. Of the total, 13,000 kilograms were refined bullion. The major suppliers of refined bullion were Canada and Brazil. July imports of gold waste and scrap were 2,500 kilograms. U.S. exports of gold in July 2001 were 20,300 kilograms. Exports of refined bullion were 12,900 kilograms. The major destinations were the U.K. and Switzerland.

Futures Markets

Gold futures are traded on the Bolsa de Mercadorias & Futuros (BM&F), the Tokyo Commodity Exchange (TOCOM), the Chicago Board of Trade (CBOT), the MidAmerica Commodity Exchange (MidAm), and the COMEX Division of the New York Mercantile Exchange. Gold options are traded on the BM&F, The Amsterdam Exchanges, (AEX-Optiebeurs), the MidAm and the COMEX.

World Mine Production of Gold In Kilograms (1 Kilogram = 32.1507 Troy Ounces)

Year	Australia	Brazil	Canada	Chile	China	Ghana	Indonesia	Papua N. Guinea	Russia[3]	South Africa	United States	Uzbekistan[3]	World Total
1991	234,218	89,578	176,552	28,879	120,000	26,311	16,879	60,780	260,000	601,110	294,062	----	2,190,000
1992	243,400	85,862	161,402	33,774	125,000	31,032	37,983	71,190	146,000	614,071	330,212	70,000	2,260,000
1993	247,196	69,894	152,929	33,638	130,000	38,911	42,097	61,671	149,500	619,201	331,000	70,000	2,280,000
1994	256,188	72,397	146,428	38,786	132,000	43,478	42,600	59,286	146,600	580,201	327,000	65,000	2,250,000
1995	253,504	64,424	152,032	44,585	140,000	53,087	64,031	53,405	132,170	523,809	317,000	65,000	2,230,000
1996	289,530	60,011	166,378	53,174	145,000	49,211	83,564	51,119	123,300	496,846	326,000	72,000	2,290,000
1997	314,500	58,488	171,479	49,459	175,000	54,662	86,927	45,418	124,000	491,680	362,000	81,700	2,450,000
1998	310,070	49,567	165,599	44,980	178,000	72,541	124,018	64,106	114,900	464,319	366,000	80,000	2,510,000
1999[1]	301,070	52,634	157,617	45,663	173,000	79,946	127,184	61,293	125,870	451,300	341,000	85,000	2,550,000
2000[2]	296,410	52,000	153,781	54,142	180,000	72,080	124,596	74,000	140,000	430,778	353,000	85,000	2,550,000

[1] Preliminary. [2] Estimate. [3] Formerly part of the U.S.S.R.; data not reported separately until 1992. *Source: U.S. Geological Survey (USGS)*

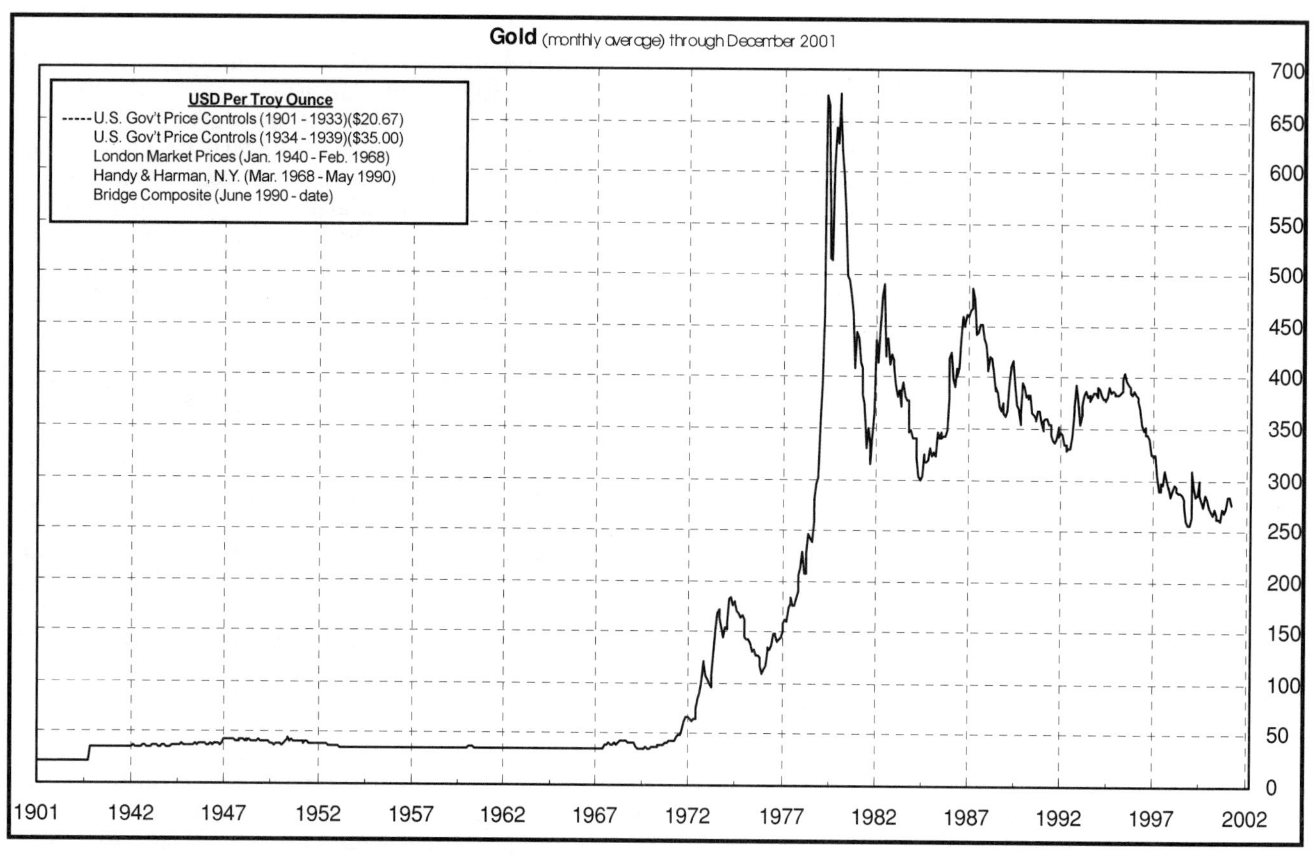

Salient Statistics of Gold in the United States In Kilograms (1 Kilogram = 32.1507 Troy Ounces)

			Refinery Production				---------- Stocks, Dec. 31 ---------				-------------- Consumption --------------			
Year	Mine Production	Value Million $	Domestic & Foreign Ores	Secondary (Old Scrap)	Exports (Excluding Coinage)	Imports for Consumption	Treasury Department[3]	Futures Exchange	Industry	Official World Reserves[4]	Dental	Industrial[5]	Jewelry & Arts	Total
1991	294,062	3,434.7	224,675	48,088	284,127	178,749	8,145,696	49,893	39,411	35,501	8,485	21,793	84,096	114,375
1992	330,212	3,662.4	283,951	53,396	368,851	174,341	8,145,000	46,453	36,713	35,100	6,543	20,360	83,508	110,410
1993	331,013	3,840.0	243,000	152,000	792,680	169,305	8,143,000	78,514	34,400	34,900	6,173	19,663	65,600	91,400
1994	327,000	4,050.0	241,000	148,000	471,000	114,000	8,142,000	49,100	32,700	34,800	5,430	17,013	53,700	76,100
1995	317,000	3,950.0	NA	NA	347,000	126,000	8,140,000	45,400	NA	34,600	NA	NA	NA	NA
1996	326,000	4,090.0	NA	NA	471,000	159,000	8,140,000	20,700	NA	34,400	NA	NA	NA	NA
1997	362,000	3,870.0	270,000	100,000	476,000	209,000	8,140,000	15,200	17,300	34,000	NA	NA	NA	137,000
1998	366,000	3,480.0	277,000	163,000	522,000	278,000	8,130,000	25,200	16,600	33,600	NA	NA	NA	219,000
1999[1]	341,000	3,070.0	265,000	143,000	523,000	221,000	8,170,000	37,900	14,700	33,500	----	----	----	245,000
2000[2]	353,000	3,180.0	197,000	81,600	547,000	223,000	8,140,000	52,900	9,300	33,000	----	----	----	183,000

[1] Preliminary. [2] Estimate. [3] Includes gold in Exchange Stabilization Fund. [4] Held by market economy country central banks and governments andinternational monetary orgainzations. [5] Including space and defense. *Source: U.S. Geological Survey (USGS)*

Monthly Average Gold Price (Handy & Harman) in New York In Dollars Per Troy Ounce

Year	Jan.	Feb.	Mar.	Apr.	May	June	July	Aug.	Sept.	Oct.	Nov.	Dec.	Average
1992	354.50	353.90	344.30	338.50	337.20	340.80	353.00	343.00	345.40	344.40	335.10	334.70	343.74
1993	329.00	329.40	330.10	341.90	366.70	371.90	392.40	378.50	354.90	364.20	373.50	383.70	359.67
1994	387.02	382.01	384.13	378.20	381.21	385.64	385.44	380.43	391.80	389.77	349.43	379.60	384.14
1995	378.55	376.51	382.12	391.11	385.46	387.56	386.40	383.63	382.22	383.14	385.53	387.42	384.22
1996	399.59	404.73	396.21	392.96	391.98	385.58	383.69	387.43	382.97	381.07	378.46	369.02	387.81
1997	355.10	346.71	351.67	344.47	343.75	340.75	324.08	324.03	322.74	324.87	307.10	288.65	331.16
1998	289.18	297.49	295.90	308.40	299.39	292.31	292.79	283.76	289.01	295.92	293.89	291.29	294.12
1999	287.05	287.22	285.96	282.45	276.94	261.31	255.81	256.56	265.23	310.72	292.74	283.69	278.81
2000	284.26	299.60	286.39	279.75	275.10	285.73	281.01	274.44	273.53	270.00	266.05	271.68	278.96
2001[1]	265.58	261.99	263.03	260.56	272.07	270.23	267.53	272.40	283.78	283.06	276.49		270.61

[1] Preliminary. *Source: U.S. Geological Survey (USGS)*

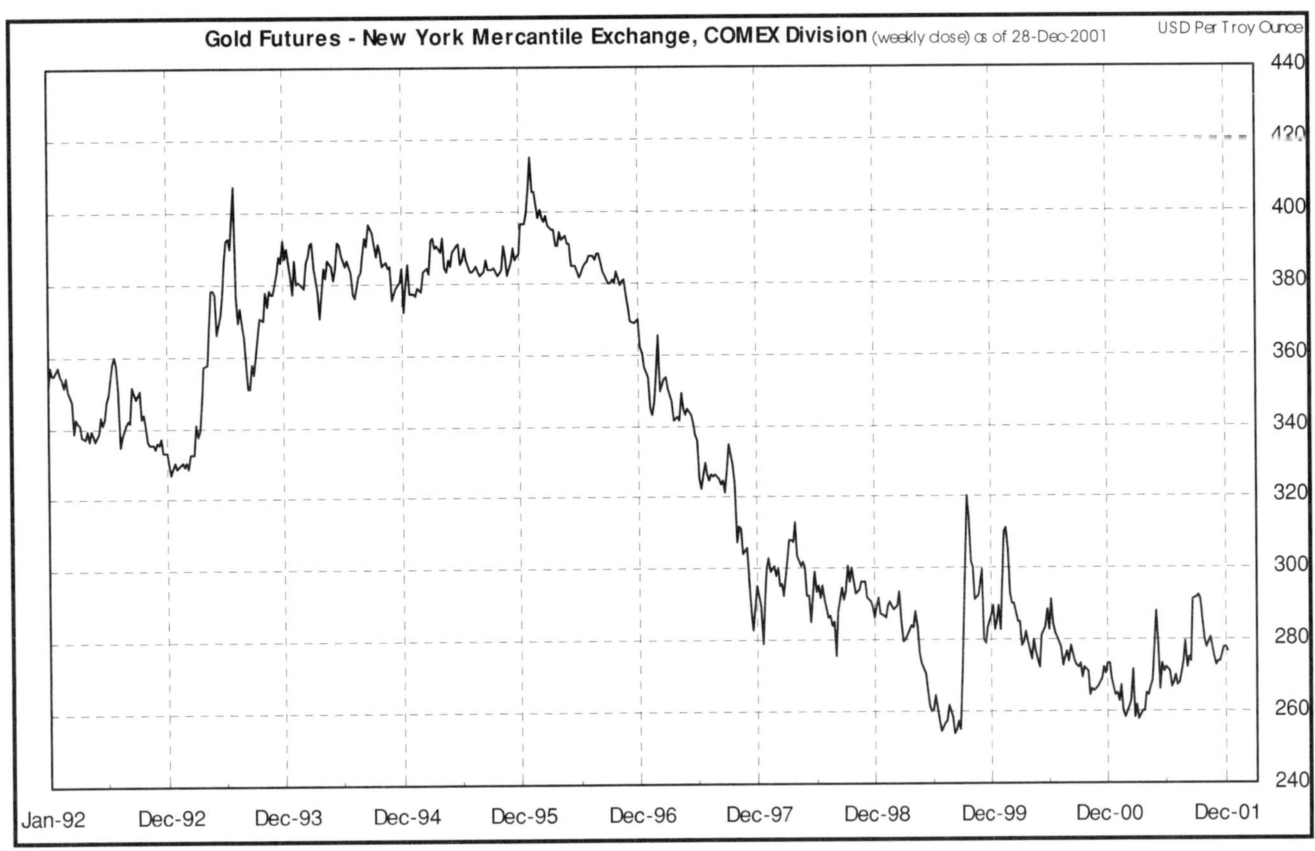

Average Open Interest of Gold in New York (NYMEX) In Thousands of Contracts

Year	Jan.	Feb.	Mar.	Apr.	May	June	July	Aug.	Sept.	Oct.	Nov.	Dec.
1992	106,110	103,319	109,796	106,485	109,947	98,127	111,039	102,239	102,376	102,232	109,965	100,328
1993	112,420	109,093	115,505	142,208	172,491	170,829	200,168	180,509	166,201	152,531	152,853	154,730
1994	156,045	139,354	146,269	144,386	147,738	146,255	148,915	155,641	167,981	166,041	166,536	178,998
1995	184,549	170,972	168,651	191,667	173,805	174,075	175,727	176,135	185,128	185,854	170,674	141,751
1996	210,695	226,160	203,968	201,826	203,056	192,423	185,374	159,435	185,907	192,606	187,145	185,994
1997	199,710	190,524	167,595	157,176	160,512	170,640	207,352	198,099	201,267	188,365	212,757	188,558
1998	180,994	171,507	183,358	180,267	158,157	172,250	169,180	192,623	183,351	186,680	164,304	153,063
1999	179,726	185,345	178,456	198,202	193,978	207,122	205,687	193,023	206,186	216,034	189,433	156,754
2000	149,606	158,026	160,325	155,188	162,516	144,099	133,087	126,893	132,731	132,546	134,630	113,830
2001	134,401	142,673	126,558	120,111	118,426	116,788	114,098	116,687	125,907	125,639	114,238	111,622

Source: New York Mercantile Exchange (NYMEX), COMEX division

Volume of Trading of Gold Futures in New York (NYMEX) In Thousands of Contracts

Year	Jan.	Feb.	Mar.	Apr.	May	June	July	Aug.	Sept.	Oct.	Nov.	Dec.	Total
1992	729.8	388.4	607.3	425.4	485.4	427.2	734.6	500.2	465.3	414.1	504.1	320.1	6,001.9
1993	506.0	446.2	661.4	640.4	1,140.7	809.6	1,171.7	808.8	728.9	565.2	892.3	533.2	8,904.4
1994	981.8	584.0	889.5	589.2	922.6	740.2	723.8	626.0	645.6	651.2	687.8	461.5	8,503.2
1995	881.9	420.0	1,087.5	613.0	777.0	588.1	669.9	500.5	495.5	387.7	982.5	378.1	7,781.6
1996	1,384.7	987.5	943.6	647.1	858.5	582.1	749.8	541.9	541.9	528.5	795.2	458.8	8,694.5
1997	1,102.8	830.2	899.4	508.5	762.1	522.7	1,147.5	667.8	715.8	988.0	808.8	588.1	9,541.9
1998	1,078.2	534.2	877.2	698.1	845.2	718.7	712.4	680.0	851.7	769.6	705.6	519.0	8,990.1
1999	860.8	517.4	1,147.6	561.1	1,069.6	573.6	964.3	709.6	1,067.3	993.8	674.7	436.1	9,575.8
2000	616.4	833.5	767.7	362.2	701.5	625.5	532.5	374.4	403.2	424.9	625.7	349.0	6,643.5
2001	755.2	483.3	766.6	438.1	971.6	481.4	578.3	547.4	341.0	481.4	573.6	367.4	6,785.3

Source: New York Mercantile Exchange (NYMEX), COMEX division

Commodity Exchange, Inc. (COMEX) Depository Warehouse Stocks of Gold In Thousands of Troy Ounces

Year	Jan. 1	Feb. 1	Mar. 1	Apr. 1	May 1	June 1	July 1	Aug. 1	Sept. 1	Oct. 1	Nov. 1	Dec. 1
1992	1,605	1,362	1,435	1,411	1,591	1,618	1,605	1,733	1,688	1,947	1,766	1,524
1993	1,507	1,340	1,365	1,426	1,383	2,231	2,247	2,448	2,437	2,425	2,349	2,552
1994	2,524	2,955	2,958	2,862	2,802	2,434	2,665	2,574	2,030	1,904	1,843	1,867
1995	1,577	1,498	1,386	1,360	1,391	1,488	1,505	1,608	1,448	1,745	1,395	1,315
1996	1,460	1,869	1,412	1,429	1,335	1,711	1,263	1,273	1,402	1,283	1,060	1,104
1997	666	837	583	1,000	946	878	850	914	733	894	615	761
1998	488	446	481	720	658	1,077	1,055	1,092	911	958	827	819
1999	809	809	731	1,032	896	876	818	936	1,198	928	874	1,195
2000	1,219	1,393	1,374	1,967	1,966	1,893	1,890	2,013	1,958	1,918	1,865	1,864
2001	1,612	1,775	1,649	1,302	826	825	NA	NA	NA	NA	NA	1,381

Source: New York Mercantile Exchange (NYMEX), COMEX division

Central Gold Bank Reserves In Millions of Troy Ounces

	Industrial Countries																
Year	Belgium	Canada	France	Germany	Italy	Japan	Netherlands	Switerland	United Kingdom	United States	Industrial Total	Developing Oil	Developing Non-Oil	IMF[2]	Bank for Int'l Settlements	World Total
1991	30.2	13.0	81.9	95.2	66.7	24.2	43.9	83.3	18.9	261.9	887.3	42.0	102.4	103.4	6.6	1,141.6
1992	25.0	9.9	81.9	95.2	66.7	24.2	43.9	83.3	18.6	261.8	877.4	42.0	100.3	103.4	6.8	1,129.9
1993	25.0	6.1	81.9	95.2	66.7	24.2	35.1	83.3	18.5	261.8	860.4	42.4	108.1	103.4	8.6	1,123.0
1994	25.0	3.9	81.9	95.2	66.7	24.2	34.8	83.3	18.4	261.7	856.9	42.4	106.6	103.4	7.0	1,116.2
1995	20.5	3.4	81.9	95.2	66.7	24.2	34.8	83.3	18.4	261.7	848.7	41.9	111.9	103.4	7.3	1,113.2
1996	15.3	3.1	81.9	95.2	66.7	24.2	34.8	83.3	18.4	261.7	840.1	42.5	115.5	103.4	6.6	1,108.2
1997	15.3	3.1	81.9	95.2	66.7	24.2	27.1	83.3	18.4	261.6	821.9	42.3	115.8	103.4	6.2	1,089.7
1998	9.5	2.5	102.4	119.0	83.4	24.2	33.8	83.3	23.0	261.6	809.0	41.6	115.7	103.4	6.4	1,076.1
1999	8.3	1.8	97.2	111.5	78.8	24.2	31.6	83.3	20.6	261.7	810.4	41.2	112.9	103.4	6.5	1,074.5
2000[1]	8.3	1.2	97.3	111.5	78.8	24.6	29.3	78.8	16.5	261.6	798.4	41.7	110.7	103.4	6.5	1,060.7

[1] Preliminary. [2] International Monetary Fund. *Source: American Metal Market (AMM)*

Mine Production of Recoverable Gold in the United States In Kilograms

Year	Arizona	California	Idaho	Montana	Nevada	Alaska	Colorado	South Dakota	New Mexico	Utah	Other States	Total
1991	6,195	30,404	3,348	13,715	178,488	3,200	3,181	16,371	W	W	41,055	295,957
1992	6,656	33,335	4,037	13,994	203,393	5,003	3,763	18,681	W	W	40,262	329,124
1993	2,710	35,800	4,324	14,300	211,000	2,780	W	19,200	995	W	39,891	331,000
1994	2,050	30,100	3,610	12,600	214,000	5,660	4,420	W	W	W	33,560	306,000
1995	1,920	25,600	8,850	12,400	210,000	4,410	W	W	W	W	53,820	317,000
1996	1,740	23,800	7,410	9,110	213,000	5,020	W	W	W	W	57,920	318,000
1997	2,140	24,200	7,490	10,200	243,000	18,400	W	16,400	W	W	40,170	362,000
1998	1,840	18,700	W	8,200	273,000	18,300	W	12,100	W	W	33,860	366,000
1999	786	17,500	W	7,540	9,310	16,200	W	10,300	W	W	279,364	341,000
2000[1]	442	17,200	W		230,000	15,600	W	8,230	W	W	81,528	353,000

[1] Preliminary. W = Withheld proprietary data, included in Other States. *Source: U.S. Geological Survey (USGS)*

Consumption of Gold, By End-Use in the United States In Kilograms

	Jewelry and the Arts					Industrial				
Year	Gold-Filled & Other	Electro-plating	Karat Gold	Total	Dental	Gold-Filled & Other	Electro-plating	Karat Gold	Total	Grand Total
1987	9,256	3,133	58,635	71,024	6,944	21,010	12,343	1,892	35,245	113,319
1988	7,598	1,469	57,959	67,027	7,576	21,034	15,088	1,104	37,226	111,836
1989	7,364	1,283	60,877	69,524	7,927	15,723	20,684	1,215	37,621	115,078
1990	8,132	429	69,952	78,514	8,700	12,725	17,251	1,020	30,996	118,216
1991	3,848	373	79,875	84,096	8,485	8,102	12,624	1,068	21,793	114,375
1992	3,546	581	79,381	83,508	6,543	8,802	10,476	1,082	20,360	110,410
1993	3,530	373	61,700	65,600	6,170	9,470	9,090	1,100	19,700	91,400
1994	3,650	369	49,700	53,700	5,430	7,450	9,470	96	17,000	76,100
1995	NA	NA	NA	NA	NA	NA	NA	NA	NA	NA
1996	NA	NA	NA	NA	NA	NA	NA	NA	NA	NA

[1] Preliminary. **Source: U.S. Geological Survey (USGS)**

Gold in British Pound
(weekly close) as of 28-Dec-2001
GBP Per Troy Ounce
210
205
200
195
190
185
180
175
170
165
160
155
150
Jan-98
Dec-98
Dec-99
Dec-00
Dec-01

Gold in Euro
(weekly close) as of 28-Dec-2001
EUR Per Troy Ounce
330
320
310
300
290
280
270
260
250
240
230
Jan-98
Dec-98
Dec-99
Dec-00
Dec-01

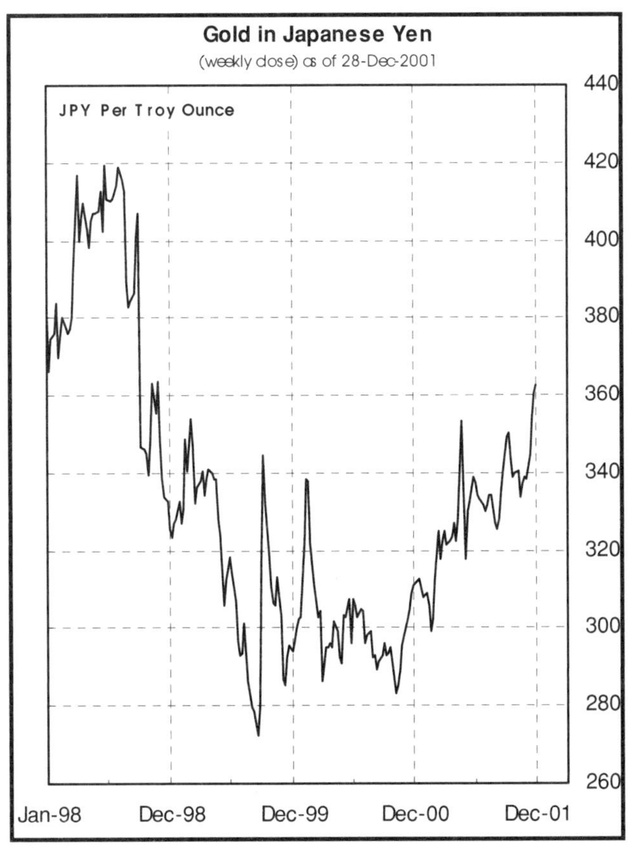
Gold in Japanese Yen
(weekly close) as of 28-Dec-2001
JPY Per Troy Ounce
440
420
400
380
360
340
320
300
280
260
Jan-98
Dec-98
Dec-99
Dec-00
Dec-01

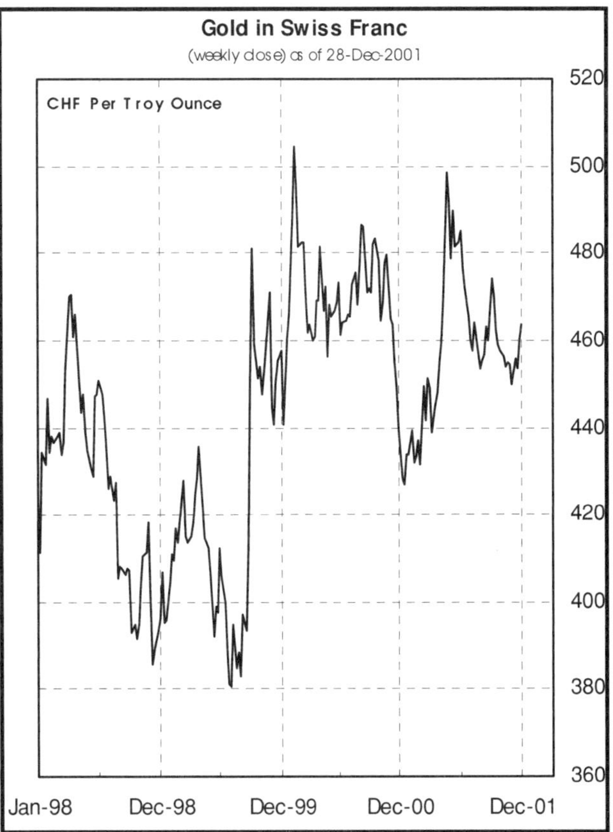
Gold in Swiss Franc
(weekly close) as of 28-Dec-2001
CHF Per Troy Ounce
520
500
480
460
440
420
400
380
360
Jan-98
Dec-98
Dec-99
Dec-00
Dec-01

Grain Sorghum

The U.S. is the world's largest producer of; grain sorghum (Milo), but within the U.S. feed grain complex holds a minor part. World production in 2001/02 of 55.3 million metric tons compares with 2000/01 production of 53.4 million. The U.S. produced about a fifth of the total with 13.7 million tons and 11.9 million, respectively.. However, unlike most of the world's sorghum producing nations who consume their production domestically, the U.S. generally consumes only about half and exports the balance.

India, the second largest producer, with an estimated 2001/02 crop of 7 million tons compares with 2000/01 production of 7.4 million. Significantly, India's sorghum acreage of 9.7 million hectares in 2001/02 accounts for about a quarter of the world's sorghum acreage, but India's average yield is consistently among the world's lowest; 0.72 mt/hectare vs. a world average of 1.36 and the U.S average of 3.841 mt/hectare. China's 2001/02 average yield was forecast at 2.87 mt/hectare on acreage of less than1 million hectare yielding a crop of 2.7 million tons vs. a yield of 2.90 mt/hectare and a crop of 2.64 million tons in 2000/01.

World sorghum trade is small; about 7.8 million tons in 2001/02, unchanged from 2000/01. The U.S. accounts for most of the exports--6.1 million tons in 2001/02 vs. 6.0 million in 2000/01--mostly to Japan and Mexico, generally the two largest importers. Argentina is the second largest exporter with 450,000 tons in 2001/02 vs. 900,000 a year earlier. The world 2001/02 carry-over is forecast at 4.0 million tons vs. 3.7 million a year earlier, almost a third of which will be in the U.S.

The U.S. sorghum crop year begins September 1. The three major producing states are usually Kansas, Texas and Nebraska. Total U.S. supplies in 2001/02 of 579 million bushels, includes production of 537 million bushels and a carry-in of 42 million vs. production of a record low 470 million bushels in 2000/01million bushels and a carry-in of 65 million bushels for a total supply of a record low 535 million bushels. No sorghum is imported into the U.S. Total disappearance in 2001/02 of 525 million bushels includes exports of 240 million and a like amount for feed and residual vs. 494 million in 2000/01. If the estimated use is realized it will place the August 31, 2002 carryover at 54 million bushels. The September-November quarter usually accounts for about half of the crop year's usage.

Sorghum prices received by farmers during 2001/02 are forecast between $1.85--$2.15/bushel vs. the 2000/01 average of $1.89.

World Supply and Demand Grain Sorghum In Thousands of Metric Tons

	Exports				Imports				Total	Utilization				Ending Stocks		
Year	Argentina	Non-U.S.	U.S.	Total	Japan	Mexico	Unaccounted	Total	Production	China	Mexico	U.S.	Total	Non-U.S.	U.S.	Total
1996-7	798	1,430	5,217	6,647	2,774	2,091	206	6,188	69,549	5,379	8,500	14,246	67,667	3,388	1,206	4,594
1997-8	1,373	1,656	5,164	6,820	2,769	3,340	75	6,820	58,947	3,650	8,940	10,670	59,039	3,260	1,242	4,502
1998-9	519	1,183	5,198	6,381	2,453	3,295	2	6,381	59,397	4,134	9,750	7,803	58,521	3,723	1,655	5,378
1999-00[1]	671	1,703	6,296	7,999	2,206	4,773	56	7,999	59,083	3,319	11,100	8,615	59,670	3,130	1,661	4,791
2000-1[2]	650	1,746	5,930	7,676	1,983	4,960	2	7,676	53,698	2,561	11,160	6,482	54,552	2,876	1,061	3,937
2001-2[3]	450	1,380	6,600	7,980	2,400	4,800	229	7,980	55,274	2,600	11,400	6,225	54,888	3,021	1,302	4,323

[1] Preliminary. [2] Estimate. [3] Forecast. *Source: Foreign Agricultural Service, U.S. Department of Agriculture (FAS-USDA)*

Salient Statistics of Grain Sorghum in the United States

	Acreage Planted[4] for All Purposes	Acreage Harvested	For Grain				For Silage			Sorghum Grain Stocks			
			Production 1,000 Bushels	Yield Per Harvested Acre Bushels	Price in Cents Per Bushel	Value of Production Million $	Acreage Harvested 1,000 Acres	Production 1,000 Tons	Yield Per Harvested Acre	Dec. 1 On Farms	Dec. 1 Off Farms	June 1 On Farms	June 1 Off Farms
Year	1,000 Acres	1,000 Acres								1,000 Bushels			
1996-7	13,097	11,811	795,274	67.3	234	1,986.3	423	4,976	11.8	144,590	322,767	38,815	80,329
1997-8	10,052	9,158	633,545	69.2	221	1,408.9	412	5,385	13.1	96,625	274,244	27,200	68,907
1998-9	9,626	7,723	519,933	67.3	166	905.5	308	3,526	11.4	95,900	239,416	27,400	88,680
1999-00[1]	9,288	8,544	595,166	69.7	157	937.4	320	3,716	11.6	90,300	259,136	27,300	99,606
2000-1[2]	9,195	7,723	470,070	60.9	189	822.6	265	2,863	10.8	74,300	187,681	19,000	57,411
2001-2[3]	10,252	8,584	514,524	59.9	185-215		336	3,728	11.1	72,400	240,937		

[1] Preliminary. [2] Estimate. [3] Forecast. NA = Not available. *Source: Economic Research Service, U.S. Department of Agriculture (ERS-USDA)*

Production of All Sorghum for Grain in the United States, by States In Thousands of Bushels

Year	Arkansas	Colorado	Illinois	Kansas	Louisiana	Mississippi	Missouri	Nebraska	New Mexico	Oklahoma	South Dakota	Texas	Total
1996	16,280	13,260	12,600	354,200	11,628	5,040	50,960	97,850	7,425	28,910	7,975	182,400	795,274
1997	11,100	6,000	10,465	265,200	6,600	2,475	36,800	60,750	9,988	22,500	11,360	185,850	633,545
1998	6,890	10,545	7,918	264,000	7,500	2,340	26,560	56,400	2,925	15,300	9,940	105,800	519,933
1999	9,750	8,610	9,215	258,400	19,270	4,872	22,010	42,770	7,425	18,000	4,640	185,850	595,166
2000	9,940	6,510	8,075	188,800	17,845	6,708	24,840	35,000	1,625	13,680	5,880	143,350	470,070
2001[1]	12,900	12,000	8,265	232,500	19,270	ÑÑ	21,620	37,800	9,000	14,700	9,300	143,000	536,755

[1] Preliminary. *Source: National Agricultural Statistics Service, U.S. Department of Agriculture (NASS-USDA)*

Grain Sorghum Quarterly Supply and Disappearance in the United States   In Millions of Bushels

Crop Year Beginning Sept. 1	Supply: Beginning Stocks	Supply: Production	Supply: Imports	Supply: Total Supply	Disappearance – Domestic Use: Food Alcohol & Industrial	Domestic Use: Seed	Domestic Use: Feed & Residual	Domestic Use: Total	Disappearance: Export	Disappearance: Total	Ending Stocks: Gov't Owned[3]	Ending Stocks: Privately Owned[4]	Ending Stocks: Total Stocks
1998-9	48.9	519.9	0	568.8	43.9	1.2	262.1	307.2	196.5	503.7	.3	64.9	65.2
Sept.-Nov.	48.9	519.9	0	568.8	15.0	0	178.0	193.0	40.5	233.5	.7	334.6	335.3
Dec.-Feb.	335.3	----	0	335.3	15.0	0	34.1	49.1	63.7	112.8	.7	221.7	222.4
Mar.-May	222.4	----	0	222.4	9.0	.6	45.4	55.0	51.4	106.4	.5	115.6	116.1
June-Aug.	116.1	----	0	116.1	4.9	.6	4.6	10.1	40.8	50.9	.3	64.9	65.2
1999-00	65.0	595.2	0	660.0	55.0	1.1	284.0	595.0	256.0	851.0	1.0	44.3	65.0
Sept.-Nov.	65.0	595.2	0	660.0	18.0	0	228.0	311.0	65.0	376.0	.7	347.7	349.0
Dec.-Feb.	349.0	----	0	349.0	18.0	0	29.0	124.0	77.0	201.0	.5	224.6	226.0
Mar.-May	226.0	----	0	226.0	13.0		22.0	99.0	64.0	163.0			127.0
June-Aug.	127.0	----	0	127.0	6.0		6.0	62.0	50.0	112.0			65.0
2000-1[1]	65.0	471.0	0	536.0	35.0		220.0	494.0	239.0	733.0			42.0
Sept.-Nov.	65.0	471.0	0	536.0	17.0		195.0	274.0	62.0	336.0			262.0
Dec.-Feb.	262.0	----	0	262.0	11.0		12.0	95.0	72.0	167.0			167.0
Mar.-May	167.0	----	0	167.0	4.0		24.0	91.0	63.0	154.0			76.0
June-Aug.	76.0	----	0	767.0	3.0		-11.0	35.0	42.0	77.0			42.0
2001-2[2]	42.0	515.0	0	556.0	45.0		200.0	505.0	260.0	765.0			51.0
Sept.-Nov.	42.0	515.0	0	556.0	15.0		163.0	243.0	65.0	308.0			313.0

[1] Preliminary. [2] Forecast. [3] Uncommitted inventory. [4] Includes quantity under loan & farmer-owned reserve. *Source: Economic Research Service, U.S. Department of Agriculture (ERS-USDA)*

Average Price of Sorghum Grain, No. 2, Yellow in Kansas City   In Dollars Per Hundred Pounds (Cwt.)

Year	Sept.	Oct.	Nov.	Dec.	Jan.	Feb.	Mar.	Apr.	May	June	July	Aug.	Average
1994-5	3.72	3.55	3.60	3.81	3.92	3.90	4.01	4.08	4.27	4.50	4.93	4.85	4.10
1995-6	5.08	5.45	5.68	6.19	6.39	6.58	6.81	7.79	8.17	7.79	7.24	6.74	6.66
1996-7	5.29	4.64	4.31	4.22	4.24	4.46	4.88	4.83	4.63	4.48	4.48	4.18	4.55
1997-8	4.13	4.36	4.30	4.26	4.33	4.36	4.40	4.10	4.09	4.03	4.03	3.74	4.18
1998-9	2.98	3.17	3.45	3.41	3.41	3.43	3.48	3.37	3.35	3.32	2.92	2.92	3.30
1999-00	2.97	2.71	2.75	2.87	3.20	3.28	3.51	3.53	3.75	3.18	2.71	2.76	3.10
2000-1	2.67	3.14	3.41	3.66	3.64	3.63	3.56	3.56	3.56	3.56	3.59	3.65	3.47
2001-2[1]	3.55	3.38	3.44										3.46

[1] Preliminary. *Source: Economic Research Service, U.S. Department of Agriculture (ERS-USDA)*

Exports of Grain Sorghum, by Country of Destination from the United States   In Metric Tons

Year Beginning Oct. 1	Canada	Ecuador	Ethiopia	Israel	Japan	Jordon	Mexico	South Africa	Spain	Sudan	Turkey	World Total
1994-5	3,713	0	0	214,073	1,987,738	0	2,543,696	0	398,339	12,304	0	5,652,585
1995-6	5,734	0	25,700	356,868	1,616,384	0	1,633,386	332	431,578	0	0	4,757,055
1996-7	3,347	0	10,020	456,271	2,207,304	0	2,091,131	0	125,827	8,000	138,590	5,210,569
1997-8	5,076	0	49,999	82,583	1,451,123	0	3,287,628	0	203,896	0	94	5,164,844
1998-9	3,484	0	0	92,335	1,480,220	0	3,290,663	0	196,110	0	101	5,194,028
1999-00[1]	4,061	0	0	167,816	1,045,253	0	4,773,760	12,857	178,829	0	0	6,297,344
2000-1[2]	4,170	0	0	82,776	853,211	0	4,861,700	0	0	0	0	5,863,626

[1] Preliminary. [2] Estimate. *Source: Economic Research Service, U.S. Department of Agriculture (ERS-USDA)*

Grain Sorghum Price Support Program and Market Prices in the United States

Year	Price Support Operations – Price Support: Quantity (Million Cwt.)	Price Support: % of Production (Million Cwt.)	Aquired by CCC (Million Cwt.)	Owned by CCC at Year End (Million Cwt.)	Basic Loan Rate ($ Per Bushel)	Target Price ($ Per Bushel)	Findley Loan Rate ($ Per Bushel)	Effective Base[3] Million Acres	Participation Rate[4] % of Base	No. 2 Yellow ($ Per Cwt.): Kansas City	Texas High Plains	Los Angeles	Gulf Ports
1993-4	8.2	2.6	0	1.4	1.89	2.61	1.63	13.5	81.6	4.37	4.95	----	4.90
1994-5	25.2	6.9	0	.4	1.89	2.61	1.80	13.5	81.1	4.10	4.75	----	4.62
1995-6	4.0	1.6	0	0	1.84	2.61	1.80	13.3	76.9	6.66	7.30	----	7.19
1996-7	11.4	2.6	0	0	[5]	NA	1.81	13.2	98.8	4.55	5.02	----	5.03
1997-8	9.8	2.8	.1	.1	[5]	NA	1.76	13.1	98.8	4.11	4.72	----	4.76
1998-9[1]	12.0	4.1	.6	.2	[5]	NA	1.74	13.6	98.8	3.29	3.78	----	3.97
1999-00[2]					[5]	NA	1.74	13.7	98.8	3.10	3.36	----	3.79

[1] Preliminary. [2] Estimate. [3] National effective crop acreage base as determined by ASCS. [4] Percentage of effective base acres enrolled in acreage reduction programs. [5] Beginning with the 1996-7 marketing year, target prices are no longer applicable. Source: Economic Research Service, U.S. Department of Agriculture (ERS-USDA)

Hay

Total U.S. hay production in 2001 (marketing year, May to April) of a record high 162 million short tons compares with the previous year's 152 million. The all hay yield of 2.54 tons per acre was realized in both 2001 and 2000. The acreage harvested of all hay in 2001of almost 64 million acres compares with 60 million in 2000. Alfalfa production of 81.6 million tons compares with 80.3 million in 2000 with average yield at 3.44 tons per acre vs. 3.48 tons in 2000. Hay is harvested in virtually all of the lower 48 states, but the top producing states are generally Texas, South Dakota, California and Minnesota. Yield show wide variance among the major producing states with California's yield nearly twice that of Texas., the effect of which holds California's production steady near 8.5 million tons while the Texas crop tends to show wide year to year swings. Other hay production in 2001 totaled 80.7 million tons vs. 71.8 million in 2000. Hay farm stocks are normally at their low in the spring and prices near their high while stocks are at their high and prices near their low following the fall harvest.

Domestic demand for hay and its price is derived from the number of Roughage consuming animal units (RCAU's), which have averaged annually about 90 million during the past few years. Despite the large number of animal units, the high hay production has prevented prices from sustaining any viable strength, especially relative to the $100 plus levels seen in early 1997.

Salient Statistics of All Hay in the United States

Crop Year Beginning May 1	Acres Harvested 1,000 Acres	Yield Per Acre Tons	Production (Millions of Tons)	Carryover May 1 (Millions of Tons)	Disappearance (Millions of Tons)	Supply Per Animal Unit (In Tons)	Disappearance Per Animal Unit (In Tons)	Animal Units Fed[3] Millions	Farm Price $ Per Ton	Farm Production Value Million $	Retail Price Paid by Farmers for Seed, April 15: Alfalfa (Certified) (Dollars Per Cwt.)	Timothy	Red Clover	Sudan-Grass
1995-6	59,629	2.59	154.2	20.8	154.2	2.24	1.97	78.1	82.2	11,042	274.00	71.00	134.00	51.80
1996-7	61,169	2.45	149.8	20.8	152.8	2.23	2.00	76.4	95.8	12,727	277.00	76.00	172.00	51.90
1997-8	61,084	2.50	152.5	17.4	148.1	2.27	1.98	74.9	100.0	13,250	282.00	73.00	184.00	51.40
1998-9	60,076	2.53	151.8	21.8	148.8	2.33	2.00	74.5	84.6	11,607	288.00	71.20	194.00	53.70
1999-00[1]	59,854	2.53	159.7	24.8	155.7	2.52	2.12	73.3	76.9	11,014	287.00	78.80	178.00	52.20
2000-1[2]	63,511	2.47	156.7	28.8	NA	2.49	NA	72.6	83.0	11,180	227.00	115.00	143.00	53.00

[1] Preliminary. [2] Estimate. [3] Roughage-consuming animal units fed annually. NA = Not available. *Source: Economic Research Service, U.S. Department of Agriculture (ERS-USDA)*

Production of All Hay in the United States, by States In Thousands of Tons

Year	California	Idaho	Iowa	Minnesota	Missouri	New York	North Dakota	Ohio	Oklahoma	South Dakota	Texas	Wisconsin	Total
1996	8,008	4,760	5,310	5,998	7,270	7,455	4,825	3,400	4,940	8,200	7,815	6,050	149,779
1997	8,408	4,730	5,190	6,398	7,340	6,790	4,375	3,850	5,108	7,810	10,955	6,353	152,536
1998	8,554	5,549	5,332	7,110	7,703	7,680	4,190	3,875	3,380	8,160	6,870	6,370	151,780
1999	8,782	5,132	5,970	7,130	7,225	7,700	5,511	3,060	5,000	9,440	13,135	7,510	159,707
2000	8,568	5,292	6,000	6,840	6,657	6,055	5,110	4,521	4,659	7,393	8,880	6,000	151,921
2001[1]	8,915	4,938	5,565	6,195	7,853	7,578	5,065	4,275	3,964	9,150	10,837	4,790	156,703

[1] Preliminary. *Source: Agricultural Statistics Board, U.S. Department of Agriculture (ASB-USDA)*

Hay Production and Farm Stocks in the United States In Thousands of Short Tons

Year	Production: Alfalfa & Mixtures	All Others	All Hay	Corn for Silage[1]	Sorghum Silage[1]	Farm Stocks: May 1	Dec. 1
1996	79,139	70,640	149,779	86,581	4,976	20,739	105,179
1997	78,535	74,001	152,536	97,192	5,385	17,424	103,044
1998	82,310	69,470	151,780	95,479	3,526	21,827	112,066
1999	84,385	75,322	159,707	95,633	3,716	24,817	108,922
2000	80,347	71,574	151,921	102,156	2,773	28,817	105,582
2001[2]	80,266	76,437	156,703	102,352	3,728	21,106	110,510

[1] Not included in all tame hay. [2] Preliminary. *Source: Agricultural Statistics Board, U.S. Department of Agriculture (ASB-USDA)*

Mid-Month Price Received by Farmers for All Hay (Baled) in the United States In Dollars Per Ton

Year	May	June	July	Aug.	Sept.	Oct.	Nov.	Dec.	Jan.	Feb.	Mar.	Apr.	Average[2]
1996-7	97.1	92.3	89.6	92.9	90.1	93.0	92.0	90.8	97.9	105.0	108.0	117.0	95.8
1997-8	118.0	108.0	98.4	99.0	103.0	103.0	101.0	97.7	98.1	97.2	97.5	101.0	100.0
1998-9	103.0	91.8	88.6	88.5	86.5	85.2	81.4	77.5	78.5	79.0	78.5	81.9	85.0
1999-00	91.6	81.7	78.4	77.4	74.5	73.7	74.0	71.1	71.8	72.6	74.8	78.2	76.7
2000-1	91.0	82.5	80.2	80.5	83.0	84.9	84.0	84.9	85.2	86.8	87.2	94.8	85.4
2001-2[1]	106.0	95.8	96.3	97.7	98.6	99.4	97.1	93.7	93.0				97.5

[1] Preliminary. [2] Marketing year average. *Source: Economic Research Service, U.S. Department of Agriculture (ERS-USDA)*

Heating Oil

In year 2000, prices for energy products were high. This was due in part to decisions by the Organization of Petroleum Exporting Countries (OPEC) to limit production and exports of petroleum. Prices for commodities like heating oil increased in 2000 and then declined in 2001. The price decline in 2001 was due to a slowing economy as well as mild weather in the late fall and early winter in the Northeast U.S., an area where much of the heating oil supply is used. OPEC members appear to have exceeded their production quotas leading prices lower while the events of September 11 slowed the economy even further leading to less use of energy products. One critical issue for OPEC has been that of petroleum production by countries that are not members. While OPEC has been somewhat successful in limiting production, oil production by countries outside of OPEC has been increasing. This, in effect, is acting to offset the OPEC production cutbacks. In late 2001 OPEC met and agreed to reduce production again. The outlook for energy prices will hinge in part on the extent to which the non-OPEC countries reduce production in support of the OPEC countries.

U.S. distillate fuel oil production in October 2001 was 3.85 million barrels per day. This represented as increase of 6 percent from the previous month and was some 2 percent more than a year earlier. The Energy Information Agency reported that in the ten month period of January-October 2001, distillate fuel oil production averaged 3.67 million barrels per day, an increase of 141,000 barrels per day or 4 percent from the same period in 2000. The production average in 2001 was nearly 9 percent more than in 1999 when production averaged 3.38 million barrels per day. For all of 2000, production averaged 3.58 million barrels per day. The higher price for heating oil seen in late 2000 led to increased production. In the December 2000 to February 2001 period, average daily production of distillate fuel oil was 3.7 million barrels per day. In the same period a year earlier, average production was 3.29 million barrels.

U.S. imports of distillate fuel oil in October 2001 were 289,000 barrels per day, down 16 percent from the previous month and some 12 percent more than a year ago. In the January-October 2001 period, imports of distillate averaged 381,000 barrels per day. In the same period in 2000, imports averaged 276,000 barrels, down 28 percent from 2001. In 1999 imports averaged 255,000 barrels. In response to the high prices in 2000, imports of distillate fuel oil surged. In December 2000, imports averaged 447,000 barrels per day, more than double the December 1999 average of 188,000 barrels per day. In January 2000, imports averaged 778,000 barrels, much above the year ago average of 218,000 barrels. In February 2001 imports averaged 668,000 barrels, up 31 percent from 2000.

U.S. exports of distillate fuel oil in October 2001 averaged 170,000 barrels per day, down 15 percent from the previous month and 33 percent less than a year ago. In the January-October 2001 period, exports of fuel oil averaged 155,000 barrels per day, down 11 percent from the same period in 2000 and 1 percent less than the same period in 1999. For all of 2000, imports averaged 173,000 barrels per day while for 1999 the average was 162,000 barrels.

Total distillate fuel oil in October 2001 was 3.82 million barrels per day, an increase of 3 percent from a year ago. In the January-October period, fuel oil supplied averaged 3.85 million barrels per day, an increase of 5 percent from a year ago and some 9 percent more than in 1999. For all of 2000, the daily supply of fuel oil was 3.72 million barrels.

U.S. ending stocks of distillate fuel oil in October 2001 were 128 million barrels. In January 2001 these stocks were 118 million barrels. In October 2001, stocks of fuel oil containing .05 percent sulfur and under were estimated at 70 million barrels while stocks with content of greater than .05 percent were estimated at 59 million barrels.

U.S. sales of distillate fuel oil in 2000 were 59.6 billion gallons, an increase of almost 4 percent from 1999. Sales to residential customers were 6.83 billion gallons, up 8 percent from 1999. Sales to commercial customers were 3.71 billion gallons, up 11 percent from 1999. Sales to industrial users were 2.33 billion gallons.

Futures Markets

Heating oil futures and options are traded on the New York Mercantile Exchange (NYMEX). In London, gasoil futures and options are listed on the International Petroleum Exchange (IPE).

Average Price of No. 2 Heating Oil In Cents Per Gallon

Year	Jan.	Feb.	Mar.	Apr.	May	June	July	Aug.	Sept.	Oct.	Nov.	Dec.	Average
1992	51.72	53.39	52.49	56.22	57.38	61.26	60.24	58.29	61.90	62.72	56.52	54.98	57.25
1993	53.14	56.02	58.13	55.49	54.53	52.62	49.74	50.70	51.96	54.00	50.30	43.47	52.51
1994	49.93	55.81	49.18	48.01	47.98	49.37	49.93	49.51	47.90	48.23	49.62	48.41	49.49
1995	47.98	47.64	45.95	49.40	50.31	47.75	46.65	49.14	50.21	48.89	51.89	57.76	49.46
1996	55.64	61.24	65.19	67.90	57.59	51.56	55.58	60.42	67.61	72.34	70.13	72.13	63.11
1997	69.90	61.15	54.83	57.74	56.31	52.32	53.11	54.02	53.19	57.24	56.23	51.09	56.43
1998	46.59	44.26	42.12	42.97	41.07	37.88	36.24	34.48	40.15	38.29	35.59	31.38	39.25
1999	33.41	30.48	38.74	43.07	41.68	43.36	50.02	54.81	60.27	58.34	64.89	67.36	48.87
2000	91.32	94.37	77.29	75.32	75.88	78.32	78.14	89.13	98.87	97.46	102.70	94.08	87.74
2001	84.30	78.55	74.17	78.02	77.11	75.74	69.88	73.41	71.65	62.63	54.37	52.60	71.04

Source: The Wall Street Journal

Average Open Interest of No. 2 Heating Oil Futures in New York In Contracts

Year	Jan.	Feb.	Mar.	Apr.	May	June	July	Aug.	Sept.	Oct.	Nov.	Dec.
1992	108,337	96,543	91,508	90,816	87,459	101,185	98,623	109,787	119,595	129,951	140,952	135,380
1993	130,536	125,603	130,438	107,363	102,708	113,898	131,816	142,054	166,253	172,940	175,781	199,299
1994	196,390	185,607	186,539	164,417	140,658	129,005	124,764	149,571	172,071	165,475	152,570	148,298
1995	128,664	112,508	118,700	121,974	115,501	122,163	136,722	140,214	149,934	152,244	139,232	138,596
1996	114,324	95,745	90,080	94,161	98,038	97,699	109,524	119,366	138,513	141,217	127,512	108,558
1997	100,333	105,223	122,149	139,981	135,523	141,864	151,403	149,243	151,407	141,008	126,528	145,153
1998	171,177	163,114	177,158	174,587	176,663	196,903	205,071	198,527	188,096	188,019	192,835	184,100
1999	167,686	160,388	166,472	172,127	170,842	168,307	182,383	188,726	192,883	179,040	165,334	146,997
2000	135,431	132,407	108,646	100,389	117,055	129,872	153,914	169,092	177,997	168,388	155,475	142,145
2001	138,980	127,219	120,899	127,395	130,328	141,436	149,577	145,605	145,692	155,540	162,392	153,850

Source: New York Mercantile Exchange (NYMEX)

Volume of Trading of No. 2 Heating Oil Futures in New York In Contracts

Year	Jan.	Feb.	Mar.	Apr.	May	June	July	Aug.	Sept.	Oct.	Nov.	Dec.	Total[1]
1992	815,199	574,007	550,113	592,056	586,707	601,067	645,020	663,743	625,675	709,532	808,201	807,142	8,005.5
1993	829,034	660,546	747,299	537,543	481,957	543,356	632,168	721,852	833,800	761,764	886,565	988,871	8,625.1
1994	1,085,683	875,714	766,788	631,664	629,295	723,677	612,316	783,181	706,822	721,375	652,257	798,063	8,986.8
1995	779,827	608,691	715,968	622,810	729,753	618,812	612,683	563,605	714,239	650,809	659,518	990,068	8,266.8
1996	977,235	768,075	666,168	586,471	530,858	402,004	530,230	624,402	766,517	1,014,238	724,975	750,704	8,341.9
1997	794,382	719,006	588,604	710,143	591,958	679,426	679,612	694,656	828,320	742,680	619,301	722,876	8,371.0
1998	793,567	641,818	776,422	578,430	688,490	904,881	720,232	683,047	748,235	768,220	766,543	793,879	8,863.8
1999	738,909	662,334	973,273	706,258	768,142	802,661	770,367	707,858	720,061	819,625	818,562	712,653	9,200.7
2000	913,985	770,322	645,175	556,134	673,281	705,881	662,964	1,004,401	954,872	878,135	938,967	927,259	9,631.4
2001	914,353	650,672	757,980	728,587	722,750	849,915	712,912	745,786	694,029	853,793	835,472	798,147	9,264.4

[1] In thousands of contracts. *Source: New York Mercantile Exchange (NYMEX)*

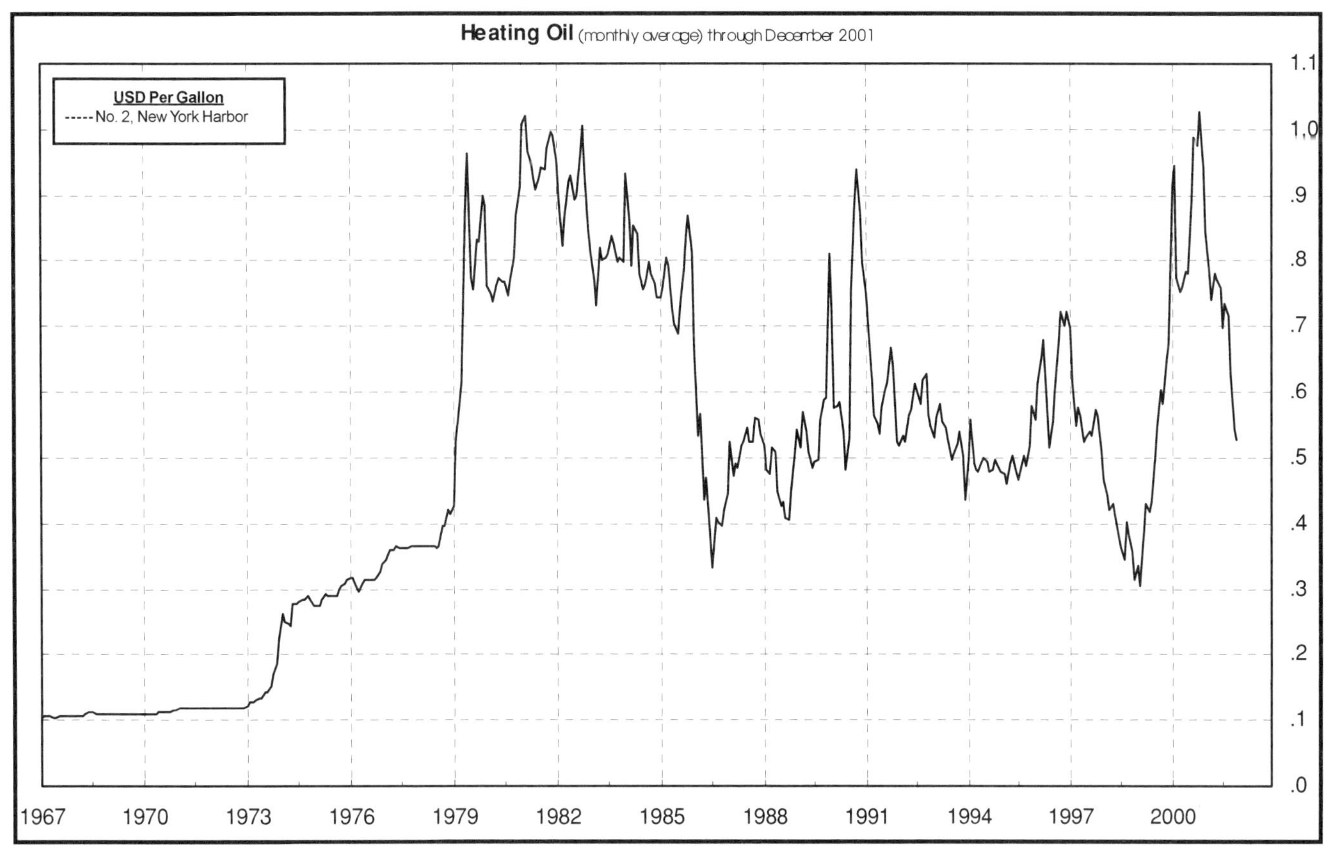

Stocks of Distillate and Residual Fuel in the United States, on First of Month In Millions of Barrels

Year	Jan.	Feb.	Mar.	Apr.	May	June	July	Aug.	Sept.	Oct.	Nov.	Dec.	Residual Fuel ----- Oil Stocks ----- Jan. 1	July 1
1992	143.5	126.7	108.8	97.7	92.1	96.4	104.5	114.6	122.8	127.8	136.8	146.3	49.9	40.9
1993	140.6	130.7	110.4	97.3	99.5	102.8	110.0	120.7	128.2	131.3	145.3	149.2	42.6	45.7
1994	140.9	117.5	102.9	99.4	102.6	112.4	119.5	134.2	138.6	144.7	146.0	147.3	44.2	39.4
1995	145.2	140.2	122.1	115.4	114.6	118.3	114.7	125.0	130.9	131.7	131.4	135.4	41.9	36.0
1996	130.2	113.8	97.3	89.7	90.1	95.7	101.6	106.8	110.3	115.0	114.7	121.8	36.8	34.8
1997	126.7	111.3	105.9	101.8	97.5	108.4	118.2	123.0	132.9	138.9	136.2	140.5	45.9	39.2
1998	139.0	133.1	127.9	124.4	125.7	136.8	139.1	148.8	150.5	152.5	147.5	154.6	40.4	39.8
1999	156.2	147.9	142.3	125.7	125.3	134.8	133.2	138.1	142.0	145.2	137.6	140.6	44.9	42.5
2000	124.1	106.7	105.2	96.0	100.1	105.4	106.4	112.9	111.0	115.3	116.5	121.1	35.8	37.0
2001[1]	118.0	118.2	117.2	105.0	1,055.0	107.4	114.4	125.1	122.0	126.5	128.6	138.8	36.2	42.7

[1] Preliminary. *Source: Energy Information Administration; U.S. Department of Energy (EIA-DOE)*

Production of Distillate Fuel Oil in the United States In Thousand Barrels per Day

Year	Jan.	Feb.	Mar.	Apr.	May	June	July	Aug.	Sept.	Oct.	Nov.	Dec.	Average
1992	2,818	2,661	2,749	2,930	2,933	2,995	3,067	2,865	2,983	3,251	3,240	3,179	2,974
1993	2,914	2,815	2,919	3,047	2,994	3,093	3,186	3,100	3,205	3,432	3,474	3,382	3,132
1994	3,114	3,018	3,096	3,249	3,317	3,285	3,191	3,187	3,285	3,203	3,270	3,232	3,205
1995	3,054	2,954	3,157	3,126	3,111	3,109	3,056	3,145	3,287	3,169	3,341	3,344	3,155
1996	3,110	3,145	3,110	3,305	3,258	3,291	3,139	3,295	3,403	3,626	3,665	3,558	3,325
1997	3,119	3,089	3,258	3,291	3,525	3,517	3,362	3,427	3,452	3,488	3,543	3,578	3,389
1998	3,323	3,280	3,397	3,468	3,560	3,520	3,569	3,482	3,399	3,215	3,438	3,431	3,424
1999	3,176	3,253	3,183	3,407	3,458	3,374	3,521	3,419	3,482	3,506	3,608	3,401	3,399
2000	3,123	3,348	3,342	3,533	3,650	3,481	3,520	3,678	3,844	3,774	3,785	3,872	3,580
2001[1]	3,606	3,621	3,487	3,651	3,656	3,702	3,838	3,653	3,637	3,788	3,948	3,802	3,699

[1] Preliminary. *Source: Energy Information Administration, U.S. Department of Energy (EIA-DOE)*

HEATING OIL

Imports of Distillate Fuel Oil in the United States   In Thousand Barrels per Day

Year	Jan.	Feb.	Mar.	Apr.	May	June	July	Aug.	Sept.	Oct.	Nov.	Dec.	Average
1994	161	276	318	226	202	182	164	211	193	159	166	187	203
1995	313	289	188	125	109	176	157	171	142	162	262	235	193
1996	243	271	253	258	215	185	194	195	187	246	192	253	224
1997	293	246	245	256	220	219	223	202	210	213	161	232	227
1998	195	213	237	209	185	202	229	181	203	239	179	245	210
1999	304	322	248	213	261	238	234	273	249	216	265	188	250
2000	218	510	260	234	316	258	199	234	283	259	332	447	295
2001[1]	778	668	343	302	330	311	250	215	346	282	242	221	357

[1] Preliminary. *Source: Energy Information Administration, U.S. Department of Energy (EIA-DOE)*

Exports of Distillate Fuel Oil in the United States   In Thousand Barrels per Day

Year	Jan.	Feb.	Mar.	Apr.	May	June	July	Aug.	Sept.	Oct.	Nov.	Dec.	Average
1994	332	235	220	252	289	168	220	193	140	256	211	284	234
1995	141	212	216	172	202	137	148	84	116	238	236	298	183
1996	216	256	139	166	176	81	134	182	256	300	171	206	190
1997	133	107	120	166	153	174	151	185	160	133	149	192	152
1998	131	120	135	168	227	152	124	105	133	139	110	108	138
1999	117	116	159	191	187	180	123	130	162	192	170	212	162
2000	132	112	211	178	127	149	132	253	194	255	191	135	173
2001[1]	97	116	101	139	181	167	162	216	201	153	189	158	157

[1] Preliminary. *Source: Energy Information Administration, U.S. Department of Energy (EIA-DOE)*

Disposition of Distillate Fuel Oil, Total Product Supplied in the U.S.   In Thousand Barrels per Day

Year	Jan.	Feb.	Mar.	Apr.	May	June	July	Aug.	Sept.	Oct.	Nov.	Dec.	Average
1994	3,698	3,581	3,307	3,116	2,912	3,062	2,663	3,063	3,133	3,066	3,180	3,203	3,162
1995	3,389	3,675	3,344	3,106	2,899	3,267	2,732	3,044	3,285	3,104	3,233	3,449	3,207
1996	3,681	3,722	3,453	3,385	3,118	3,194	3,046	3,184	3,178	3,575	3,460	3,434	3,368
1997	3,780	3,422	3,515	3,523	3,240	3,235	3,279	3,124	3,302	3,659	3,411	3,665	3,430
1998	3,566	3,598	3,606	3,465	3,268	3,574	3,294	3,446	3,377	3,547	3,320	3,484	3,461
1999	3,788	3,542	3,785	3,415	3,314	3,407	3,479	3,437	3,431	3,749	3,608	3,892	3,572
2000	3,818	3,794	3,693	3,455	3,681	3,549	3,369	3,726	3,786	3,712	3,829	4,250	3,722
2001[1]	4,281	4,208	4,124	3,811	3,727	3,615	3,580	3,754	3,629	3,850	3,662	3,802	3,837

[1] Preliminary. *Source: Energy Information Administration, U.S. Department of Energy (EIA-DOE)*

Production of Residual Fuel Oil in the United States   In Thousands Barrels per Day

Year	Jan.	Feb.	Mar.	Apr.	May	June	July	Aug.	Sept.	Oct.	Nov.	Dec.	Average
1994	809	852	859	846	860	779	807	838	800	755	835	871	826
1995	903	776	778	789	748	746	797	801	811	724	705	874	788
1996	774	776	701	671	732	731	646	732	713	693	712	753	719
1997	800	789	639	617	618	727	645	643	688	711	786	810	705
1998	765	672	790	857	766	739	778	782	749	676	753	805	762
1999	775	726	683	679	725	706	736	701	702	658	596	690	698
2000	640	627	649	620	640	679	741	760	702	747	778	768	696
2001[1]	815	743	749	817	786	783	639	622	656	699	680	660	721

[1] Preliminary. *Source: Energy Information Administration U.S. Department of Energy (EIA-DOE)*

Supply and Disposition of Residual Fuel Oil in the United States

	Supply		Disposition			Ending	Average
	Total Production	Imports	Stock Change	Exports	Product Supplied	Stocks Million	Sales to End Users[3]
Year	Thousand Barrels Per Day					Barrels	Cents per Gallon
1994	826	314	-6	125	1,021	42	35.2
1995	788	187	-13	136	852	37	39.2
1996	726	248	24	102	848	46	45.5
1997	708	194	-15	120	797	40	42.3
1998	762	275	12	138	887	45	30.5
1999	698	237	-25	129	830	36	37.4
2000	696	352	1	139	909	36	60.2
2001[1]	720	384	13	155	936	42	

[1] Preliminary. [2] Less than +500 barrels per day and greater than -500 barrels per day. [3] Refiner price excluding taxes.
Source: Energy Information Administration, U.S. Department of Energy (EIA-DOE)

Hides and Leather

The major producers of bovine hides and skins are the U.S., Brazil, Argentina and Russia. World production of hides and skins has been about 4.1 million metric tonnes. U.S. production is just over 20 percent of the total or about a million tonnes. U.S. production has been holding at about a million tonnes. After the U.S., the next largest producer is Brazil with just over 650,000 tonnes in 2000. The production trend in Brazil has been slightly higher. Argentina is the third largest producer with production of about 300,000 tonnes. Russian production of hides and skins has been trending lower. Other large producers include Mexico, Australia, France and Germany.

The U.S.D.A., in its summary export sales report for 2001 indicated that accumulated exports of whole cattle hides (excluding wet blues) totaled 23.1 million pieces, up from 22 million pieces in year 2000. The major export destination for cattle hides was the Republic of Korea which took 8.9 million pieces. This was down from the 9.99 million pieces they took in 2000. The next largest export destination was China which took 5.04 million pieces in 2001, almost double the 2000 total of 2.75 million. Taiwan took a total of 2.86 million pieces, down slightly from 3.05 million in 2000. Japan imported 1.62 million pieces, down from 1.71 million in 2000. Mexico also saw a decline taking 1.42 million pieces, down from 1.89 million in 2000.

U.S. exports of whole calf skins, excluding wet blues, in 2001 totaled 1.15 million pieces. In 2000, exports were 1.09 million pieces. By far the largest export destination was Italy with 1.05 million pieces, up from 986,400 in 2000. Other smaller importers were Japan, France, Canada and the United Kingdom.

Exports of kip skins, excluding wet blues, in 2001 were 944,300 pieces, up from 917,800 in 2000. The largest importer of kip skins was Italy with purchases in 2001 of 571,900 pieces, about the same as in 2000. Japan imported 274,400 pieces compared to 257,000 in 2000. Smaller importers included Mexico, the Republic of Korea and Germany.

U.S, exports of cattle wet blues-grain splits, whole or sided, in 2001 were 1.24 million prices, down from 1.94 million in 2000. The largest market was Taiwan which took 338,400 tonnes, well below the 712,000 in 2000. Mexico took 221,100, well above the 76,500 in 2000. Other importers were Hong Kong, the Republic of Korea, Spain and Japan.

World Production of Bovine Hides and Skins — In Thousands of Metric Tons

Year	Argentina	Australia	Brazil	Canada	Colombia	France	Germany	Italy	Mexico	Russia	United Kingdom	United States	World Total
1991	308	153	448	75	104	182	251	95	155	502	93	1,061	4,076
1992	298	162	442	77	88	180	205	98	160	466	88	1,073	3,983
1993	303	154	565	73	79	160	175	95	161	460	77	1,078	4,418
1994	305	152	573	74	77	151	158	93	166	350	81	942	4,073
1995	301	145	608	75	84	154	156	93	170	310	85	976	4,032
1996	306	145	615	81	88	158	164	92	160	280	90	994	4,072
1997	330	166	590	83	92	158	164	92	160	270	84	985	4,110
1998	285	171	622	83	93	148	152	90	170	235	86	987	4,116
1999[1]	300	162	637	88	92	145	149	90	170	210	85	1,002	4,130
2000[2]	295	152	667	89	92	148	139	91	175	200	83	993	4,139

[1] Preliminary. [2] Forecast. *Source: Foreign Agricultural Service, U.S. Department of Agriculture (FAS-USDA)*

Salient Statistics of Hides and Leather in the United States — In Thousands of Equivalent Hides

	New Supply of Cattle Hides				Wholesale Prices					Wholesale Leather			
	Domestic Slaughter				Cents Per Pound		Production			Indexes – Upper		Footwear	
Year	Federally Inspected	Uninspected[4]	Total Production	Net Exports	Heavy Native Cows[2]	Heavy Native Steers[3]	All U.S. Tanning	Cattle-hide	Value of Leather Exports $1,000	Men	Women	Production[5]	Exports
	Thousands of Equivalent Hides						In 1,000 Equiv. Hides			1982 = 100		Million Pairs	
1991	31,887	803	32,690	18,636	76.92	78.9	14,800	13,021	680,348	136.9	120.7	167,386	18,109
1992	32,094	780	32,874	17,810	81.71	75.9	15,900	14,474	705,038	140.5	124.2	168,451	21,401
1993	32,593	731	33,324	17,117	82.16	78.9	18,057	16,931	764,120	142.8	126.9	171,733	20,700
1994	33,483	713	34,196	16,259	94.99	87.3	18,842	18,117	811,951	144.7	127.2	163,000	22,505
1995	34,879	760	35,639	18,336	93.89	87.6	18,092	17,480	870,247	150.1	129.0	147,550	20,571
1996	36,583	177	36,760	18,626	92.15	86.4	18,769	18,135	950,510	152.4	132.1	127,315	23,726
1997	35,567	925	36,492	17,562	90.99	86.1	19,592	18,930	1,145,664	156.4	132.2	124,444	21,958
1998	34,787	850	35,637	15,937	75.45	69.5	20,297	19,706	1,289,547	158.0	132.4	108,536	19,009
1999	36,150	170	36,320	15,700	73.80	73.1	21,342	20,620	1,137,534	157.0	133.0	78,870	18,176
2000[1]	36,246	170	36,416	19,670	83.41	81.2	17,332	16,746	1,125,957	157.2	133.6		20,157

[1] Preliminary. [2] Central U.S., heifers. [3] F.O.B. Chicago. [4] Includes farm slaughter; diseased & condemned animals & hides taken off fallen animals. [5] Other than rubber. *Sources: Leather Industries of America (LIA); Bureau of Labor Statistics, U.S. Department of Commerce (BLS)*

Production of All Footwear (Shoes, Sandals, Slippers, Athletic, Etc.) in the U.S. In Millions of Pairs

Year	First Quarter	Second Quarter	Third Quarter	Fourth Quarter	Total	Year	First Quarter	Second Quarter	Third Quarter	Fourth Quarter	Total
1991	48.1	37.8	41.8	41.2	169.0	1996	33.2	31.8	29.7	33.2	128.0
1992	41.1	40.8	43.6	39.3	164.8	1997	31.4	33.1	28.6	30.6	124.4
1993	43.3	44.6	42.8	41.0	171.7	1998	32.8	31.8	29.3	28.6	108.5
1994	42.5	40.8	40.1	39.5	163.0	1999	26.7	26.1	24.5	21.7	78.6
1995	37.2	38.3	34.8	36.7	147.0	2000[1]	----	----	----	----	68.3

[1] Preliminary. *Source: Bureau of the Census, U.S. Department of Commerce*

Average Factory Price[2] of Footwear in the United States In Dollars Per Pair

Year	First Quarter	Second Quarter	Third Quarter	Fourth Quarter	Total	Year	First Quarter	Second Quarter	Third Quarter	Fourth Quarter	Total
1991	22.14	20.40	19.74	18.52	20.14	1996	23.65	22.78	22.14	20.38	22.07
1992	20.19	22.21	21.15	20.46	20.96	1997	22.42	21.56	22.21	22.24	22.11
1993	21.62	21.67	21.37	21.79	21.61	1998	24.39	24.21	20.27	19.78	21.84
1994	25.77	23.60	21.49	22.44	23.22	1999	23.33	22.70	19.90	19.50	21.19
1995	19.61	21.46	25.37	21.26	21.79	2000[1]	----	----	----	----	24.50

[1] Preliminary. [2] Average value of factory shipments per pair. *Source: Bureau of the Census, U.S. Department of Commerce*

Imports and Exports of All Cattle Hides in the United States In Thousands of Hides

	Imports		U.S. Exports - by Country of Destination										
Year	Total	From Canada	Total	Canada	Italy	Japan	Rep. of Korea	Mexico	Portugal	Romania	Spain	Taiwan	Thailand
1991	1,549	1,088	20,185	561	138	4,662	9,300	2,702	7	----	39	2,058	123
1992	1,536	1,457	19,347	684	107	4,647	8,589	2,729	100	4	30	1,823	160
1993	1,660	1,597	18,777	965	354	4,167	7,919	2,217	79	1	60	1,950	386
1994	1,731	----	17,990	995	309	3,133	7,472	1,553	168	72	141	2,491	332
1995	1,759	----	20,095	952	332	3,246	8,283	899	111	63	215	3,017	781
1996	1,702	----	20,328	1,149	522	2,372	7,956	2,123	64	171	189	2,871	455
1997	1,633	----	19,195	1,320	469	1,802	7,470	2,501	55	----	148	2,866	323
1998	1,930	----	17,867	1,126	1,164	1,407	4,897	2,846	91	----	440	2,701	336
1999	1,921	----	17,621	829	738	1,252	6,038	2,723	46	----	262	2,863	343
2000[1]	1,988	----	21,658	875	1,163	1,529	7,673	2,196	37	----	189	2,844	562

[1] Preliminary. *Source: Leather Industries of America*

Imports of Bovine Hides and Skins by Selected Countries In Metric Tons

Year	Brazil	Canada	Hong Kong	Italy	Japan	Mexico	Portugal	Rep. of Korea	Spain	Taiwan	Turkey	United States	World Total
1992	11	17	80	131	188	71	32	385	26	91	28	65	1,266
1993	21	26	81	141	188	71	39	372	35	94	37	57	1,426
1994	16	28	95	243	139	60	56	356	29	112	17	49	1,556
1995	33	35	100	250	152	30	43	342	42	112	43	57	1,715
1996	20	34	79	263	123	71	42	341	33	124	50	60	1,692
1997	13	39	64	254	114	96	37	323	44	140	68	60	1,985
1998	10	42	71	249	96	110	39	229	44	142	45	59	1,876
1999[1]	8	34	91	215	95	115	42	254	29	142	55	57	2,002
2000[2]	8	36	93	220	95	115	43	260	30	142	60	57	2,058

[1] Preliminary. [2] Forecast. *Source: Foreign Agricultural Service, U.S. Department of Agriculture (FAS-USDA)*

Exports of Bovine Hides and Skins by Selected Countries In Metric Tons

Year	Australia	Brazil	Canada	Germany	Hong Kong	Italy	Nether-lands	New Zealand	Poland	Russia	United Kingdom	United States	World Total
1992	144	71	74	38	75	9	66	31	17	28	19	610	1,261
1993	142	76	87	40	76	7	35	21	5	150	25	581	1,374
1994	96	84	79	24	93	10	37	22	2	216	22	455	1,271
1995	85	148	90	34	100	10	47	22	2	195	22	510	1,351
1996	93	174	97	33	72	20	47	28	3	212	24	506	1,423
1997	115	216	97	35	60	16	48	27	3	210	25	473	1,475
1998	111	220	86	31	69	24	32	28	6	202	17	443	1,400
1999[1]	115	230	83	28	90	7	30	30	7	190	15	436	1,389
2000[2]	108	250	85	31	92	8	25	30	7	170	15	427	1,399

[1] Preliminary. [2] Forecast. *Source: Foreign Agricultural Service, U.S. Department of Agriculture (FAS-USDA)*

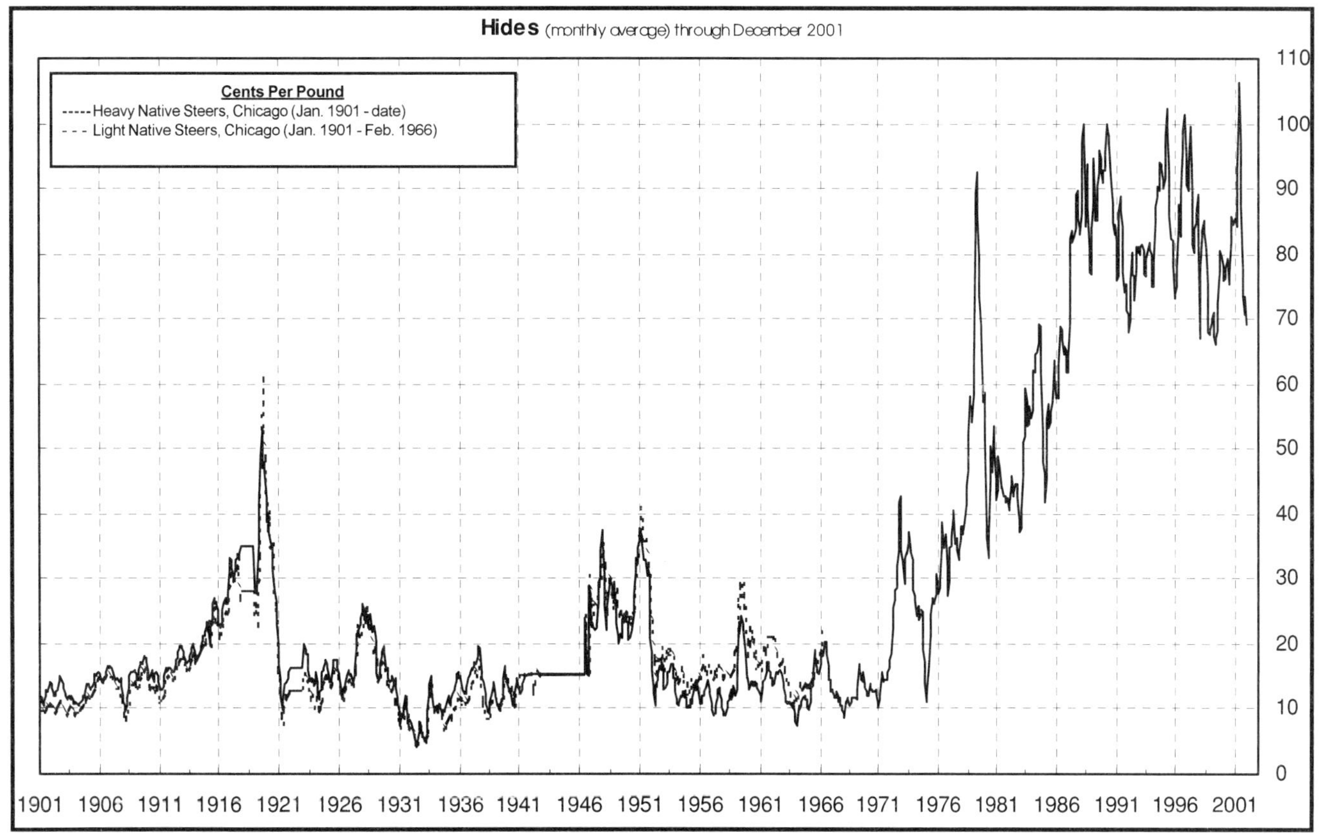

Utilization of Bovine Hides and Skins by Selected Countries In Metric Tons

Year	Argentina	Brazil	Colombia	Germany	Italy	Japan	Mexico	Rep. of Korea	Spain	Taiwan	Turkey	United States	World Total
1991	308	396	98	143	435	253	225	400	119	101	78	491	4,009
1992	298	382	97	129	435	229	231	400	98	91	90	528	3,977
1993	302	510	94	100	435	226	232	385	98	94	95	554	4,322
1994	304	505	96	83	550	200	226	374	94	112	85	536	4,282
1995	300	493	89	79	570	191	200	355	98	112	100	523	4,365
1996	308	461	91	80	615	165	230	353	95	124	110	548	4,332
1997	332	387	89	101	570	150	251	347	106	140	120	572	4,609
1998	285	412	91	100	540	135	275	265	108	142	100	603	4,584
1999[1]	300	415	89	102	500	130	280	280	104	142	110	623	4,707
2000[2]	285	425	89	103	505	130	285	283	108	142	120	623	4,774

[1] Preliminary. [2] Forecast. *Source: Foreign Agricultural Service, U.S. Department of Agriculture (FAS-USDA)*

Wholesale Price of Hides (Packer Heavy Native Steers) F.O.B. Chicago In Cents Per Pound

Year	Jan.	Feb.	Mar.	Apr.	May	June	July	Aug.	Sept.	Oct.	Nov.	Dec.	Average
1992	70.55	67.84	69.68	75.95	80.05	76.77	76.50	72.76	77.62	81.18	80.05	81.00	75.83
1993	79.82	81.05	81.48	81.44	80.35	76.95	76.62	79.27	80.52	81.76	80.81	79.83	79.99
1994	75.07	75.08	79.00	84.75	87.33	88.77	90.38	89.76	93.90	93.67	93.19	91.13	86.84
1995	90.10	91.42	97.99	102.32	99.64	92.45	85.74	82.46	82.45	82.16	78.02	73.02	88.15
1996	73.67	75.11	77.96	84.58	87.56	82.51	89.45	96.06	98.91	101.51	94.60	90.65	87.71
1997	89.77	93.47	99.44	99.40	89.44	81.45	80.20	83.92	84.86	86.35	89.20	82.61	88.34
1998	66.88	77.33	82.61	83.72	85.05	83.13	81.17	81.11	75.23	67.95	67.53	68.26	76.66
1999	69.42	69.97	70.84	67.36	65.96	66.89	68.17	72.41	77.52	80.43	79.67	78.00	72.22
2000	75.92	76.29	77.86	78.83	79.24	75.18	77.25	81.64	85.60	84.89	84.41	85.31	80.20
2001	85.33	84.12	93.02	102.64	106.19	97.31	87.59	77.28	73.51	70.58	73.30	69.16	85.00

Source: The Wall Street Journal

Hogs

The 2001 price action for U.S. hog prices, basis nearest Chicago futures, reflected similar action in 2000. In both years, prices worked higher during the first half and then broke sharply during the second half, more than erasing the earlier gains. By yearend 2001, prices were probing the mid-40 cent area vs. the mid-summer high near 75 cents. For the year, however, prices were expected to gain about $1 plus per cwt over the 2000 average of $44.70 as domestic and export demand supported prices. The outlook for 2002 is less positive due to a slackening economy and declining exports. Retail pork prices rose about 4% in 2001 with little gain forecast in 2002.

The world's hog inventory in 2001 of a near record 773 million head compares with 765 million in 2000. Record world pork production in 2001 of 83.2 million metric tons compares with 81.3 million in 2000 and forecasts of almost 85 million tons in 2002. World consumption of 83 million tons in 2001 compares with 81 million in 2000 and 84.5 million in 2002. China is the world's largest hog producer with more than half the total and the U.S. a distant second. China's January 1, 2001 inventory of a 440 million head compares with 430 million in 2000. In the U.S. the early 2001 total of 57.5 million head compares with 57.8 million a year earlier. Germany's 2001 inventory, the largest in the European Union, was estimated at 25.8 million head vs. 26 million in 2000. The decade long slide in Russia's and the Ukraine's hog inventory finally showed signs of bottoming in 2001 with a combined inventory of about 25 million head, almost unchanged from 2000, but still pales against the early 1990's inventory of over 50 million head.

The December 1, 2001 U.S. inventory of 58.8 million head was marginally under a year earlier. Of the total, 6.2 million head were kept for breeding vs. 6.3 million and the balance to be marketed. Farrowing during the December'01-February '02 period of 2.8 million head compare with 2.7 million in the like 2000/01 period, and which ultimately will represent about 46% of the breeding herd. Although the U.S. hog inventory is only about 8% of the world total, slaughter runs almost 10% and pork production somewhat higher. U.S. per capita pork use in 2001 of 51.8 pounds compares with 52.5 pounds in 2000 and a forecast of 51.7 pounds in 2002.

More than half the inventory share of U.S. hog marketing's now come from contract hog operations. In a contractual agreement, the contractor provides the hogs, feed, medication and supplies while the contractee provides the housing, utilities and labor. Most hog production still occurs in Corn Belt states, but Southern states have seen a dramatic growth in contractual operations in recent years. Still, most U.S. producers continue to raise hogs in farrow-to-finish operations. As of late 2001 the total number of hogs under contract, owned by operations with over 5,000 head total inventory, but raised by contractees, accounted for 33% of the total U.S. inventory vs. 30% in 2000.

Commercial U.S. hog slaughter in 2001 of 97.8 million head compares with 98 million in 2000 with an average dressed weight of about 195 pounds in both years. Pork production in 2001 of 19.1 billion pounds compares with 18.9 billion in 2000. Based upon the Fall 2001 hog inventory and breeding intentions, pork production in 2002 is forecast at 19.1 billion pounds.

The U.S. is the world's largest pork exporter: about 1.5 billion pounds in 2001 vs. 1.3 billion in 2000 and forecast of 1.4 billion in 2002. Japan, Russia, Canada and Mexico are generally the largest importers of U.S. pork. The U.S. imports pork products, mostly from Canada and Denmark, the total of which is generally less than one billion pounds. The U.S. also imports live hogs from Canada.

Midwest wholesale barrow and gilt hog prices during 2001 averaged about $45.86 per cwt vs. $44.70 in 2000 and forecast at $42-45 in 2002.

Futures Markets

Lean hog futures and options are traded on the Chicago Mercantile Exchange (CME) where futures settle to the CME lean hog Index (TM). Their proprietary index tracks the value of lean pork at select U.S. packing plants.

Live hog futures are traded on the Mid-America Commodity Exchange (MidAm) and the Agricultural Futures Markets (AFM) in the Netherlands.

Salient Statistics of Pigs and Hogs in the United States

	Pig Crop						Value of Hogs on Farms, Dec. 1					Hogs Slaughtered in Thousand Head				
	Spring[3]			Fall[4]								Commercial				
Year	Sows Farrowed (1,000 Head)	Pig Crop (1,000 Head)	Pigs Per Litter	Sows Farrowed (1,000 Head)	Pig Crop (1,000 Head)	Pigs Per Litter	$ Per Head	Total Million $	Hog Marketings Thousand Head	Quantity Produced (Live Wt.) Mill. Lbs.	Value of Production Mil. $	Federally Inspected	Other	Total	Farm	Total
1992	6,260	50,466	8.06	6,012	48,676	8.10	71.2	4,147	98,589	23,947	9,854	92,611	2,278	94,889	268	95,157
1993	6,034	49,084	8.14	5,976	48,216	8.07	74.9	4,340	98,351	23,693	10,628	90,933	2,135	93,068	229	93,296
1994	6,257	51,217	8.18	6,139	50,262	8.19	53.2	3,178	100,747	24,437	9,692	93,435	2,261	95,696	208	95,905
1995	6,046	50,077	8.28	5,843	48,739	8.35	70.7	4,115	102,684	24,426	9,829	94,203	2,123	96,325	210	96,535
1996	5,648	47,887	8.46	5,449	46,571	8.55	94.0	5,281	101,852	23,267	12,013	90,534	1,860	92,394	175	92,569
1997	5,595	48,393	8.65	5,885	51,190	8.70	82.0	4,986	104,301	23,979	12,552	90,228	1,733	91,960	165	92,125
1998	6,015	52,469	8.73	6,047	52,536	8.69	44.0	2,766	117,240	25,715	8,674	99,285	1,745	101,029	163	101,192
1999	5,877	51,519	8.77	5,764	50,835	8.82	72.0	4,254	121,137	25,791	7,766	99,739	1,806	101,544	141	101,685
2000[1]	5,683	50,087	8.81	5,727	50,660	8.85	76.0	4,534	118,418	25,717	10,791	96,436	1,519	97,955	125	98,079
2001[2]	5,618	49,472	8.81	5,684	50,001	8.80										

[1] Preliminary. [2] Estimate. [3] December-May. [4] June-November. *Source: Economic Research Service, U.S. Department of Agriculture (ERS-USDA)*

World Hog Numbers in Specified Countries as of January 1 In Thousands of Head

Year	Brazil	Canada	China	Denmark	France	Germany	Philip-pines	Poland	Russia	Spain	Ukraine	United States	World Total
1992	33,050	10,498	369,646	9,767	12,067	26,063	8,022	20,725	35,384	17,209	17,839	57,469	728,789
1993	31,050	10,577	384,210	10,345	13,015	26,514	7,954	21,059	31,520	18,260	16,175	58,202	740,758
1994	31,200	10,534	393,000	10,870	14,791	26,075	8,227	17,422	28,600	18,234	15,298	57,940	743,930
1995	31,338	11,291	414,619	10,864	14,593	24,698	8,941	19,138	24,859	18,295	13,946	59,738	758,461
1996	32,068	11,588	345,848	10,709	14,523	23,737	9,023	20,343	22,630	18,600	13,144	58,201	782,425
1997	31,369	11,480	362,836	11,081	14,968	24,283	9,750	17,697	19,500	18,651	11,236	56,124	695,133
1998	31,427	11,985	400,348	11,442	15,473	24,845	10,210	18,498	16,579	18,970	9,479	61,158	731,575
1999	31,427	12,409	422,563	11,991	15,869	26,299	10,398	19,275	16,400	21,715	10,083	62,206	762,206
2000[1]	31,860	12,242	430,198	11,914	15,991	26,043	10,764	18,224	16,100	22,597	10,073	59,342	765,288
2001[2]	31,840	12,027	440,000	12,125	15,911	25,862	11,715	16,500	15,600	22,700	10,000	59,848	773,188

[1] Preliminary. [2] Forecast. *Source: Foreign Agricultural Service, U.S. Department of Agriculture (FAS-USDA)*

Hogs and Pigs on Farms in the United States on December 1 In Thousands of Head

Year	Geargia	Illinois	Indiana	Iowa	Kansas	Minne-sota	Missouri	Nebraska	North Carolina	Ohio	South Dakota	Wis-consin	Total
1992	1,100	5,900	4,600	16,400	1,440	4,700	2,850	4,650	4,500	1,800	1,830	1,210	59,815
1993	1,000	5,450	4,300	15,000	1,350	4,750	3,000	4,300	5,400	1,630	1,750	1,170	57,904
1994	1,020	5,350	4,500	14,500	1,310	4,850	3,500	4,350	7,000	1,800	1,740	1,040	59,990
1995	900	4,800	4,000	13,400	1,230	4,950	1,100	4,050	8,200	1,800	1,450	900	58,264
1996	800	4,400	3,750	12,200	1,450	4,850	3,450	3,600	9,300	1,500	1,200	800	56,171
1997	520	4,700	3,950	14,600	1,530	5,700	3,550	3,500	9,600	1,700	1,400	740	61,158
1998	480	4,850	4,050	15,300	1,590	5,700	3,300	3,400	9,700	1,700	1,400	690	62,206
1999	480	4,050	3,250	15,400	1,460	5,500	3,150	3,000	9,500	1,480	1,260	570	59,342
2000	380	4,150	3,350	15,100	1,520	5,800	2,900	3,050	9,300	1,490	1,320	610	59,138
2001[1]	310	4,250	3,150	15,000	1,560	5,600	3,000	2,900	9,500	1,420	1,280	540	58,774

[1] Preliminary. *Source: National Agricultural Statistics Service, U.S. Department of Agriculture (NASS-USDA)*

Hog-Corn Price Ratio[1] in the United States

Year	Jan.	Feb.	Mar.	Apr.	May	June	July	Aug.	Sept.	Oct.	Nov.	Dec.	Average
1992	15.3	16.3	15.7	16.5	18.1	18.9	19.1	20.5	19.5	20.5	20.8	21.2	18.5
1993	20.3	22.0	22.1	21.0	21.9	23.0	20.6	21.0	21.6	20.6	17.3	15.1	20.5
1994	16.1	17.2	16.2	16.1	16.4	16.4	18.4	19.4	16.2	15.4	14.1	14.5	16.4
1995	16.8	17.5	16.4	15.1	15.3	16.8	17.6	18.5	18.0	16.4	13.9	14.2	16.4
1996	13.8	13.8	13.9	12.9	13.7	13.4	13.2	13.9	15.4	19.3	20.5	21.1	15.4
1997	20.0	19.9	17.7	19.2	21.6	22.6	24.3	22.1	20.0	18.6	18.0	16.5	20.0
1998	14.1	14.1	13.7	14.8	18.1	18.6	16.8	18.6	16.1	14.6	9.7	7.3	14.7
1999	12.8	13.5	13.6	14.8	18.4	17.3	18.2	20.7	19.4	20.2	19.6	19.6	17.3
2000	19.3	20.2	20.5	23.3	22.9	25.6	29.5	28.8	25.8	23.8	19.8	20.2	23.3
2001[2]	18.8	19.9	23.6	25.3	27.7	29.5	27.5	26.6	23.6	22.0	18.9	16.8	23.4

[1] Bushels of corn equal in value to 100 pounds of hog, live weight. [2] Preliminary. *Source: Economic Research Service, U.S. Department of Agriculture (ERS-USDA)*

Cold Storage Holdings of Frozen Pork[1] in the United States, on First of Month In Millions of Pounds

Year	Jan.	Feb.	Mar.	Apr.	May	June	July	Aug.	Sept.	Oct.	Nov.	Dec.
1992	311.1	341.2	364.0	372.2	362.6	344.9	319.0	307.0	266.7	297.3	306.8	316.7
1993	314.5	329.5	344.4	330.4	378.5	371.6	351.3	342.5	308.9	311.2	324.8	313.0
1994	299.2	348.8	356.9	393.1	429.7	437.6	410.8	393.7	364.0	352.7	385.4	383.2
1995	365.3	389.6	395.1	416.8	422.3	434.9	431.1	408.3	354.0	332.6	321.6	347.1
1996	334.8	382.2	385.5	352.9	385.5	381.3	351.8	322.7	322.9	340.3	333.3	316.4
1997	313.8	342.2	383.9	404.7	440.2	413.4	406.2	388.7	371.8	346.6	354.2	334.1
1998	346.4	446.1	464.5	458.8	487.0	477.4	426.8	414.6	392.6	388.9	411.9	443.4
1999	503.5	510.3	540.9	552.8	596.9	572.7	528.6	494.6	432.6	430.6	438.1	422.5
2000	415.4	481.4	523.5	534.7	532.1	537.9	495.5	478.5	455.6	439.5	438.6	445.6
2001[2]	411.5	472.5	468.3	431.9	432.6	421.2	374.1	339.5	332.6	366.9	430.3	432.5

[1] Excludes lard. [2] Preliminary. *Source: Economic Research Service, U.S. Department of Agriculture (ERS-USDA)*

HOGS

Average Price of Hogs, at Iowa/S Minn[2] In Dollars Per Hundred Pounds (Cwt.)

Year	Jan.	Feb.	Mar.	Apr.	May	June	July	Aug.	Sept.	Oct.	Nov.	Dec.	Average
1992	37.15	40.45	39.09	42.01	45.90	47.59	44.98	44.88	42.50	42.57	41.98	42.12	42.60
1993	41.66	44.57	46.76	45.46	47.10	48.52	46.38	48.67	48.40	47.27	42.76	40.38	45.66
1994	43.99	48.12	44.30	42.72	42.27	42.76	42.62	42.37	35.49	32.56	28.25	31.59	39.75
1995	37.82	39.09	37.94	35.88	37.35	43.03	47.18	49.46	48.67	45.42	40.02	43.80	42.14
1996	42.39	46.93	49.06	50.88	58.29	56.45	59.47	60.49	54.60	55.41	54.42	55.47	53.66
1997	52.96	51.36	48.52	54.41	57.84	57.43	58.89	54.17	49.45	46.12	44.86	40.33	51.36
1998	35.60	34.53	37.22	37.22	45.51	45.32	39.85	37.98	32.00	29.60	19.95	16.62	34.28
1999	28.58	29.65	28.25	31.69	38.45	35.39	32.84	38.56	35.71	35.84	35.34	37.70	34.00
2000	38.32	41.58	43.52	49.59	50.21	51.48	50.45	45.35	43.49	43.09	37.84	41.40	44.69
2001[1]	38.61	41.47	48.41	49.28	52.34	54.53	53.75	52.47	46.93	41.27	35.49	35.14	45.81

[1] Preliminary. [2] Data through December 1997 are for Sioux City. *Source: Economic Research Service, U.S. Department of Agriculture (ERS-USDA)*

Average Price Received by Farmers for Hogs in the United States In Cents Per Pound

Year	Jan.	Feb.	Mar.	Apr.	May	June	July	Aug.	Sept.	Oct.	Nov.	Dec.	Average
1992	36.8	40.2	39.1	41.0	45.1	46.7	44.6	44.1	42.1	42.0	41.1	41.7	42.0
1993	41.2	44.0	46.5	45.4	46.9	48.1	45.7	47.3	47.8	46.9	42.5	40.4	45.2
1994	43.5	47.9	44.4	42.7	42.7	42.7	42.2	41.8	35.4	31.8	28.0	30.9	39.5
1995	36.8	39.1	37.8	35.6	37.1	42.2	46.3	48.6	48.4	45.7	39.9	43.5	41.8
1996	42.6	46.5	48.7	49.7	56.8	56.4	58.6	59.7	54.7	55.6	54.4	55.6	53.3
1997	53.8	52.8	49.4	53.8	58.2	57.8	58.9	55.3	50.4	47.3	45.1	41.6	52.0
1998	36.0	35.9	34.9	35.6	42.4	42.5	36.9	35.2	29.5	27.8	18.9	15.0	32.6
1999	26.5	27.7	28.0	30.1	36.6	34.1	31.6	36.2	33.9	34.2	33.4	35.6	32.3
2000	36.8	39.9	41.7	47.4	48.3	48.9	48.3	43.8	41.6	41.4	36.8	39.8	42.9
2001[1]	37.2	39.1	46.0	47.8	50.4	52.2	51.7	50.6	45.1	40.5	35.0	33.3	44.1

[1] Preliminary. *Source: Economic Research Service, U.S. Department of Agriculture (ERS-USDA)*

Quarterly Hogs and Pigs Report in the United States, 10 States   In Thousands of Head

Year[2]	Inventory[3]	Breeding[3]	Market[3]	Farrowings	Pig Crop	Year[2]	Inventory[3]	Breeding[3]	Market[3]	Farrowings	Pig Crop
1992	45,735	5,610	40,125	10,202	82,497	1997	56,124	6,578	49,546	11,480	99,583
I	45,735	5,610	40,125	2,296	18,532	I	56,141	6,667	49,474	2,684	23,164
II	44,800	5,555	39,245	2,663	21,570	II	55,010	6,637	40,412	2,911	25,229
III	47,255	5,845	41,410	2,501	20,395	III	57,366	6,789	50,577	2,946	25,696
IV	49,175	5,840	43,335	2,398	19,351	IV	60,456	6,858	53,598	2,939	25,494
1993	58,202	7,109	51,093	11,982	97,050	1998	61,158	6,957	54,200	12,062	104,981
I	58,202	7,109	51,093	3,665	29,739	I	61,158	6,957	54,200	2,929	25,480
II	47,145	5,735	41,410	2,363	19,267	II	60,163	6,942	53,220	3,086	26,989
III	58,395	7,320	51,075	2,972	24,041	III	62,213	6,958	55,254	3,054	26,634
IV	59,030	7,130	51,900	2,982	24,003	IV	63,488	6,875	56,612	2,993	25,878
1994	57,904	7,130	50,739	12,376	101,400	1999	62,206	6,682	55,523	11,641	102,354
I	57,904	7,130	50,739	2,885	23,368	I	62,206	6,682	55,523	2,891	25,247
II	57,350	7,210	50,140	3,390	27,984	II	60,191	6,527	53,663	2,986	26,272
III	60,715	7,565	53,150	3,107	25,547	III	60,896	6,515	54,380	2,920	25,862
IV	62,320	7,415	54,905	2,997	24,517	IV	60,776	6,301	54,474	2,844	24,973
1995	59,990	7,060	52,930	11,847	98,516	2000	59,342	6,234	53,109	11,410	100,747
I	59,990	7,060	52,930	2,886	23,851	I	59,342	6,234	53,109	2,798	24,522
II	58,465	6,998	51,467	3,170	26,373	II	57,782	6,190	51,593	2,885	25,565
III	59,560	7,180	52,380	2,976	24,813	III	59,117	6,234	52,884	2,889	25,548
IV	60,540	6,898	53,642	2,815	23,479	IV	59,495	6,246	53,250	2,838	25,112
1996	58,264	6,839	51,425	11,114	94,458	2001[1]	59,138	6,270	52,868	11,302	99,473
I	58,264	6,839	51,425	2,735	23,054	I	59,138	6,270	52,868	2,748	23,963
II	55,741	6,701	49,040	2,930	24,833	II	57,524	6,232	51,292	2,870	25,509
III	56,038	6,682	49,356	2,718	23,244	III	58,603	6,186	52,417	2,838	25,029
IV	56,961	6,577	50,384	2,731	23,327	IV	58,992	6,158	52,834	2,846	24,972

[1] Preliminary. [2] Quarters are Dec. preceding year-Feb.(I), Mar.-May(II), June-Aug.(III) and Sept.-Nov.(IV). [3] Beginning of period.
Source: National Agricultural Statistics Service, U.S. Department of Agriculture (NASS-USDA)

Federally Inspected Hog Slaughter in the United States   In Thousands of Head

Year	Jan.	Feb.	Mar.	Apr.	May	June	July	Aug.	Sept.	Oct.	Nov.	Dec.	Total
1992	8,144	7,153	7,934	7,610	6,897	7,166	7,461	7,494	8,217	8,599	7,796	8,142	92,613
1993	7,649	6,921	7,958	7,840	6,988	7,338	7,010	7,473	7,763	7,857	7,952	8,184	90,993
1994	7,285	6,783	8,148	7,609	7,383	7,452	6,941	7,997	8,192	8,585	8,516	8,547	93,435
1995	7,882	7,157	8,628	7,379	8,012	7,731	6,918	8,083	7,752	8,358	8,424	7,881	94,203
1996	8,129	7,506	7,549	7,886	7,485	6,395	7,187	7,509	7,541	8,423	7,469	7,455	90,534
1997	7,610	6,836	7,437	7,590	6,971	6,859	7,169	7,197	7,872	8,625	7,601	8,461	90,228
1998	8,454	7,590	8,335	8,198	7,443	7,596	8,130	8,024	8,443	9,192	8,650	9,231	99,285
1999	8,373	7,746	8,945	8,386	7,303	8,176	7,778	8,256	8,501	8,806	8,750	8,719	99,739
2000	8,010	7,955	8,695	7,108	7,816	7,823	7,235	8,481	7,992	8,746	8,633	7,943	96,436
2001[1]	8,521	7,491	8,207	7,722	7,836	7,368	7,333	8,247	7,687	9,209	8,610	8,298	96,527

[1] Preliminary. *Source: National Agricultural Statistics Service, U.S. Department of Agriculture (NASS-USDA)*

Average Live Weight of all Hogs Slaughtered Under Federal Inspection   In Pounds Per Head

Year	Jan.	Feb.	Mar.	Apr.	May	June	July	Aug.	Sept.	Oct.	Nov.	Dec.	Average
1992	255	253	252	253	254	254	251	250	252	252	255	255	253
1993	254	253	253	254	254	256	254	252	252	254	257	258	254
1994	254	254	254	256	255	256	252	252	255	259	261	260	256
1995	258	256	257	258	258	258	256	253	252	255	259	258	257
1996	257	254	255	255	255	256	251	250	250	255	258	257	254
1997	257	256	256	256	256	257	253	252	255	257	261	260	256
1998	259	258	257	257	256	255	252	252	253	257	262	261	257
1999	259	259	259	260	260	260	257	254	256	259	262	262	259
2000	262	262	263	263	264	263	260	258	260	263	266	265	262
2001[1]	265	264	264	265	264	264	261	258	262	267	269	268	264

[1] Preliminary. *Source: Economic Research Service, U.S. Department of Agriculture (ERS-USDA)*

Average Open Interest of Lean Hog[1] Futures in Chicago In Contracts

Year	Jan.	Feb.	Mar.	Apr.	May	June	July	Aug.	Sept.	Oct.	Nov.	Dec.
1992	23,854	31,545	32,441	32,430	30,947	26,362	24,935	24,535	27,535	32,555	32,738	30,468
1993	27,210	25,620	28,264	24,139	22,581	19,840	19,026	20,761	20,544	20,051	21,167	24,096
1994	31,899	32,123	31,012	31,713	30,889	27,327	26,414	25,335	28,957	32,077	36,304	33,516
1995	36,705	30,958	30,736	28,035	28,294	28,729	29,959	31,599	34,183	31,312	31,519	35,127
1996	35,253	34,823	38,730	42,900	41,916	36,620	35,616	32,541	32,591	34,329	33,148	32,163
1997	33,105	33,953	31,289	34,071	41,978	37,398	36,141	33,712	31,483	36,928	39,363	39,394
1998	45,908	42,241	38,965	33,610	34,257	32,456	32,085	31,199	34,165	34,051	42,224	45,241
1999	46,003	44,211	43,803	48,277	55,951	52,398	54,723	49,915	53,055	54,089	54,432	50,691
2000	49,209	54,094	57,472	68,535	64,938	54,208	45,730	38,233	38,802	38,254	40,075	45,141
2001	41,425	41,892	48,381	45,296	41,910	45,715	51,661	47,760	42,072	36,983	32,821	27,687

[1] Data thru October 1995 are Live Hogs, November 1995 thru December 1996 are Live Hogs and Lean Hogs.
Source: Chicago Mercantile Exchange (CME)

Volume of Trading of Lean Hog[1] Futures in Chicago In Contracts

Year	Jan.	Feb.	Mar.	Apr.	May	June	July	Aug.	Sept.	Oct.	Nov.	Dec.	Total[2]
1992	135,226	136,997	140,411	138,248	116,738	131,209	148,754	102,165	116,565	149,458	117,023	123,298	1,556.1
1993	131,475	96,320	159,973	137,528	120,200	121,096	112,493	91,496	109,402	102,722	116,081	102,968	1,401.8
1994	144,701	96,736	146,934	93,105	127,381	144,373	116,181	122,058	110,697	128,980	150,744	172,132	1,554.0
1995	155,766	115,800	181,919	116,767	145,350	155,295	139,013	144,590	135,262	132,122	142,460	136,191	1,700.7
1996	177,299	138,002	150,117	216,476	208,696	177,359	185,872	157,540	158,077	203,789	170,586	152,098	2,095.9
1997	180,241	159,600	200,118	212,810	222,759	188,615	181,637	146,297	149,950	175,135	152,876	130,871	2,100.9
1998	180,241	182,698	174,752	132,952	155,737	167,767	185,427	157,973	164,964	173,163	218,950	241,767	2,136.3
1999	218,608	171,108	196,825	189,773	214,852	237,240	239,096	167,787	190,238	187,794	205,505	139,270	2,358.1
2000	175,399	186,352	231,532	158,765	218,222	235,036	172,725	145,849	146,240	142,240	153,043	146,404	2,111.8
2001	183,493	159,020	197,004	142,892	165,220	184,421	198,503	164,712	152,178	177,601	163,798	129,497	2,018.3

[1] Data thru October 1995 are Live Hogs, November 1995 thru December 1996 are Live Hogs and Lean Hogs. [2] In thousands of contracts.
Source: Chicago Mercantile Exchange (CME)

Honey

The world's honey production apparently peaked in the mid-1990's; the decline since reflects a contraction in the number of beekeepers and producing bee colonies. Also, the steady expansion of the more aggressive Africanized bees virtually erased honey production in some countries, notably Brazil. On a shorter term basis, weather can have a decisive impact on honey production if its effect harms the flowering plants the bees need to make honey.

China is the world's largest producer, with more than a third of total global production with average annual production at about 180,000 metric tons and apparently holding. U.S. production is a distant second followed by Argentina and Mexico. The latter two nations during the past decade increased output rather sharply, especially Argentina in absolute tonnage although Mexico showed a greater percentage gain. However, among the countries that until the mid-1990s showed at least annual production of more than 20,000 tons, but now report little, if any, production are Australia, Russia and Brazil.

U.S. honey production in 2000 from producers with five or more colonies totaled 221 million pounds, up 8% from 1999, but still 10 million pounds under the 1993 high of 231 million pounds. There were 2.63 million producing colonies in 2000, down 2% from 1999. Colonies, however, are not counted if honey was not harvested.. The annual yield per colony, which may be understated, shows wide variations, averaging 83.9 pounds in 2000 vs. 76.4 pounds in 1999 and annual average during the 1990's of about 75 pounds. Producer honey stocks of 86.2 million pounds as of December 15, 2000 compares with 79.4 million a year earlier and only 36 million a decade ago. Honey is produced is almost every state, but California is the leading producer with 30.8 million pounds in 2000 vs. 30.3 million in 1999. Other leading producing states include North and South Dakota, Florida and Minnesota.

The U.S. imports honey: 198 million pounds in 2000 vs. 183 million in 1999 and an average during the past decade of about 118 million pounds. Exports generally total less than 10 million pounds. Argentina is generally the largest exporter of honey to the U.S. followed by China at a distant second.

U.S. prices for the 2000 crop averaged 59.4 cents per pound, down 1% from 60.1 cents in 1999 and compare with a second half 1990's average of about 71 cents. Prices are based on retail sales by producers and sales to private processors and co-ops. At the state level, prices reflect the portions of honey sold retail, coop and private. At the U.S. level, prices for each color--ranging from white to amber--are derived by weighting quantities sold for each marketing channel. The total value of production in 2000 of $132 million compares with $126 million in 1999.

World Production of Honey In Metric Tons

Year	Argentina	Australia	Brazil	Canada	China	Germany	Japan	Mexico	Russia	United States	Total
1994	67,000	26,000	18,000	34,000	181,000	22,000	4,000	56,000	44,000	99,000	1,126,000
1995	70,000	19,000	18,000	31,000	182,000	37,000	4,000	49,000	44,000	95,000	1,148,000
1996	57,000	26,000	18,000	27,000	189,000	15,000	3,000	49,000	46,000	90,000	1,091,000
1997	70,000	27,000	18,000	31,000	215,000	15,000	3,000	54,000	49,000	89,000	1,148,000
1998	65,000	22,000	18,000	42,000	211,000	16,000	3,000	55,000	50,000	100,000	1,159,000
1999[1]	85,000	22,000	18,000	34,000	214,000	18,000	3,000	52,000	50,000	101,000	1,174,000

[1] Preliminary. *Source: Foreign Agricultural Service, U.S. Department of Agriculture (FAS-USDA)*

Salient Statistics of Honey in the United States In Millions of Pounds

Year	Number of Colonies (1,000)	Yield Per Colony Pounds	Stocks Jan. 1	Total U.S. Production	Imports for Consumption	Domestic Disappearance	Exports	Total Supply	Program Activity: Placed Under Loan	Program Activity: CCC Take Over	Program Activity: Net Gov't Expenditure[3] Mil. $	Domestic Avg. Price All Honey (Cents Per Pound)	National Avg. Price Support (Cents Per Pound)	Per Capita Consumption Pounds
1995	2,655	79.5	94.1	211.1	88.6	341.6	9.3	393.2	64.4	0	-9.3	68.5	50.0	1.0
1996	2,581	77.3	42.2	199.5	150.6	334.1	9.9	390.9	----	----	----	88.8	----	----
1997	2,631	74.7	47.0	196.5	167.4	328.8	8.9	406.8	----	----	----	75.2	----	----
1998	2,633	83.7	69.1	220.3	132.3	332.9	9.9	397.5	----	----	----	65.5	----	----
1999[1]	2,688	76.4	79.4	205.3										
2000[2]	2,634	83.9	86.2	221.0										

[1] Preliminary. [2] Forecast. [3] Fiscal year. *Source: Economic Research Service, U.S. Department of Agriculture (ERS-USDA)*

Production and Yield of Honey in the United States

Year	Production in Thousands of Pounds: California	Florida	Minnesota	North Dakota	South Dakota	Total	Value of Production $1,000	Yield per Colony in Pounds: California	Florida	Minnesota	North Dakota	South Dakota	Average
1995	39,060	19,780	13,530	23,760	2,040	210,516	144,203	93	86	82	108	85	79.5
1996	27,300	25,200	11,550	19,780	23,280	198,197	175,999	70	105	77	86	97	77.3
1997	31,500	16,080	10,585	24,500	15,600	196,536	147,795	75	67	73	100	65	74.7
1998	37,350	22,540	11,060	29,440	21,375	220,316	147,254	83	98	79	128	95	83.7
1999	30,300	23,256	11,890	26,775	23,296	205,250	126,075	60	102	82	105	104	76.4
2000[1]	30,800	24,360	13,500	33,350	28,435	221,005	132,205	70	105	90	115	121	83.9

[1] Preliminary. *Source: National Agricultural Statistics Service, U.S. Department of Agriculture (NASS-USDA)*

Interest Rates, U.S.

The Federal Reserve implemented a very aggressive easier monetary policy in 2001, dropping short-term rates to a forty year low in the wake of eleven rate cuts, each generally a 1/4 point (25 basis points). The fed's action apparently had a dual purpose: 1-to try and prevent slippage in the economy and 2- to correct the restrictive monetary policy of late 1999 and early 2000 which may have helped set the stage for the economy's weakness in 2001. Typically, the Fed's action takes about six months to filter into the economy, i.e. that the easier policy that began in January 2001 should have seen a buoyant effect taking hold by mid-summer. And it didn't happen, partly owing to factors that were beyond the Fed's scope to control as the September 11, terrorist attack, if not some deeper-rooted belief that Fed's policy in 2001 lacked its traditional clout. The U.S. economy was officially declared to have slipped into a recession in the first quarter of 2001, ending a near ten year record setting run of economic growth. By yearend, there were signs that the economy's contraction had bottomed, but there was little, if any, consensus as to how strong the recovery would be. Historically, the Fed's eleven rate cuts should have had a much greater effect on the economy than seen, even allowing for the lag time between action and effect, especially when viewed in the wake of supporting tax relief fiscal policy during 2001.

So what went wrong? The crack in the equities markets during 2000-01 likely had a greater negative effect than expected in that much of the paper wealth effect it helped to create in the 1990's was erased. Unemployment rose in 2001, nearing 6% by yearend and is expected to push over 6% in 2002. Inflation, however, was virtually non-existent which gave the Fed ample room to ease short-term rates. Ironically, long term rates failed to ease very much, suggesting that investors still opted for a net real return to capital of about 3% over the going inflation rate.

Unlike prior years when the markets' focused on long-term rates, notably the 30-year Treasury bond, in 2001 the attention focused on intermediate rates offered on notes. At yearend 2001 the 10 year T-note yield of 5.02% compared with 4.91% a year earlier; 3 month T-bills were at 1.71% vs. 5.70%; fed funds were at 1.63% vs. 6.67%, and the 30 year T-bond was at 5.46% vs. 5.34% respectively. The prime rate was at 4.75%, down from 9.50% and the discount rate was at 1.24% vs. 6.00% at yearend 2000.

In the Treasury debt market the ten-year note is now viewed as the benchmark Treasury security, replacing the 30-year bond. However, part of the treasury's reevaluation of what debt to issue and/or retire was based on prospects of continuing federal budget surpluses, a scenario that the war on terrorism has likely altered. The Fed may now have to worry whether its easier monetary policy of 2001 coupled with rising federal expenses may awaken inflationary pressures and set the stage for some monetary tightening in 2002.

Futures Markets

A futures (and options) contract exists for almost every maturity on the yield curve, as well as for municipal and commercial credit risks. Major U.S. contracts include Eurodollars on Chicago's International Monetary Market (IMM), and T-bonds, 10-year T-notes, 5-year T-notes and 2-year T-notes on the Chicago Board of Trade (CBOT). Futures are also traded in Chicago on municipal bonds, 30 day fed funds, one month LIBOR, and yield curve spreads. Smaller size contracts on some interest rate instruments are listed at the MidAmerica Commodity Exchange (MidAm).

U.S. Producer Price Index[2] (Wholesale, All Commodities) 1982 = 100

Year	Jan.	Feb.	Mar.	Apr.	May	June	July	Aug.	Sept.	Oct.	Nov.	Dec.	Average
1993	118.0	118.4	118.7	119.3	119.7	119.5	119.2	118.7	118.7	119.1	119.0	118.6	118.9
1994	119.1	119.3	119.7	119.7	119.9	120.5	120.7	121.2	120.9	120.9	121.5	121.9	120.4
1995	122.9	123.5	123.9	124.6	124.9	125.3	125.3	125.1	125.2	125.3	125.4	125.7	124.8
1996	126.3	126.2	126.4	127.4	128.1	128.0	128.0	128.3	128.2	128.0	128.2	129.1	127.7
1997	129.7	128.5	127.3	127.0	127.4	127.2	126.9	127.2	127.5	127.8	127.9	126.8	127.6
1998	125.4	125.0	124.7	124.9	125.1	124.8	124.9	124.2	123.8	124.0	123.6	122.8	124.4
1999	122.9	122.3	122.6	123.6	124.7	125.2	125.7	126.9	128.0	127.7	128.3	127.8	125.5
2000	128.3	129.8	130.8	130.7	131.6	133.8	133.7	132.9	134.7	135.4	135.0	136.2	132.7
2001[1]	140.0	137.4	135.9	136.4	136.8	135.5	133.4	133.4	133.4	130.2	130.1	128.0	134.2

[1] Preliminary. [2] Not seasonally adjusted. *Source: Bureau of Labor Statistics, U.S. Department of Commerce (BLS)*

U.S. Consumer Price Index[2] (Retail Price Index for All Items: Urban Consumers) 1982-84 = 100

Year	Jan.	Feb.	Mar.	Apr.	May	June	July	Aug.	Sept.	Oct.	Nov.	Dec.	Average
1993	142.6	143.1	143.6	144.0	144.2	144.4	144.4	144.8	145.1	145.7	145.8	145.8	144.5
1994	146.2	146.7	147.2	147.4	147.5	148.0	148.4	149.0	149.4	149.5	149.7	149.7	148.2
1995	150.3	150.9	151.4	151.9	152.2	152.5	152.5	152.9	153.2	153.7	153.6	153.5	152.4
1996	154.4	154.9	155.7	156.3	156.6	156.7	157.0	157.3	157.8	158.3	158.6	158.6	157.0
1997	159.1	159.6	159.8	160.0	160.1	160.4	160.6	160.9	161.3	161.6	161.8	161.9	160.6
1998	161.9	162.0	162.0	162.4	162.8	163.0	163.2	163.4	163.6	163.9	164.2	164.4	163.1
1999	164.6	164.8	165.1	166.2	166.2	166.2	166.7	167.2	167.8	168.1	168.4	168.8	166.7
2000	169.2	170.1	171.3	171.1	171.3	172.2	172.7	172.8	173.6	173.9	174.3	174.6	172.3
2001[1]	175.7	176.2	176.3	176.8	177.5	177.9	177.4	177.5	178.2	177.6	177.6	177.3	177.2

[1] Preliminary. [2] Not seasonally adjusted. *Source: Bureau of Labor Statistics, U.S. Department of Commerce (BLS)*

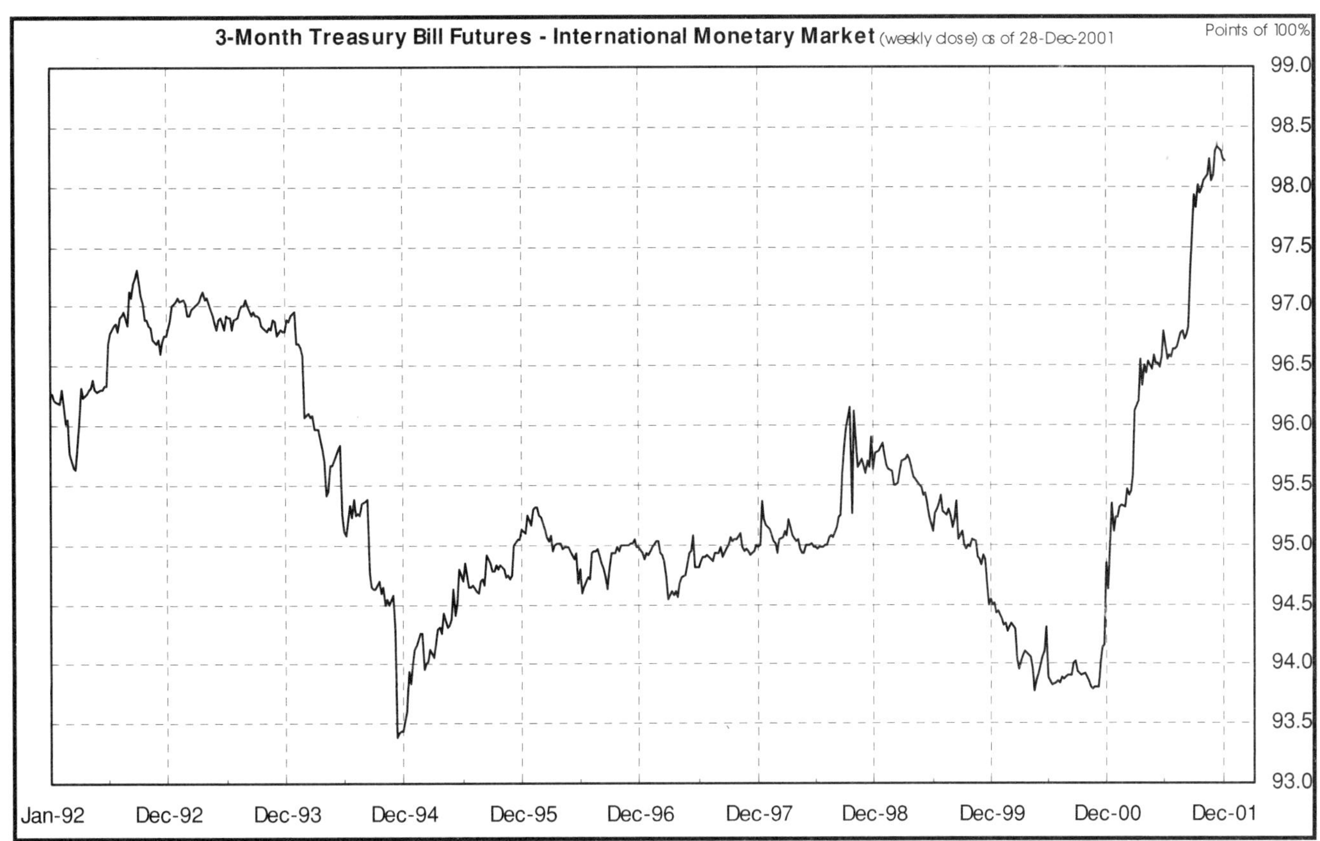

Average Open Interest of 13 Week[1] Treasury Bill Futures in Chicago   In Thousands of Contracts

Year	Jan.	Feb.	Mar.	Apr.	May	June	July	Aug.	Sept.	Oct.	Nov.	Dec.
1992	51,312	45,902	35,539	44,757	47,734	41,091	38,399	35,638	29,781	32,556	35,379	29,566
1993	32,544	35,756	32,556	39,115	40,724	34,614	30,895	34,177	28,983	30,121	33,800	30,996
1994	36,456	41,150	43,243	51,485	41,164	34,580	32,572	29,559	24,522	32,325	30,077	22,322
1995	21,065	26,289	33,420	35,873	34,608	25,930	20,534	19,195	18,929	16,781	16,384	11,279
1996	14,769	16,906	14,161	14,460	15,709	10,285	8,973	9,770	6,536	6,906	7,516	7,002
1997	8,114	9,793	9,968	10,390	10,048	8,949	8,425	9,760	7,899	9,497	11,223	10,679
1998	10,295	11,647	7,903	4,993	3,818	4,123	4,330	4,407	2,840	1,929	2,123	2,264
1999	2,179	2,998	2,720	1,523	2,367	1,586	690	909	471	476	1,033	2,321
2000	2,466	2,464	1,467	706	717	691	647	1,295	1,836	1,239	1,642	2,219
2001	1,936	2,789	3,410	2,272	2,519	2,065	1,472	2,474	1,666	1,338	1,770	1,445

[1] 90-day U.S. Treasury Bill. *Source: International Monetary Market (IOM), division of the Chicago Mercantile Exchange (CME)*

Volume of Trading of 13 Week[1] Treasury Bill Futures in Chicago   In Contracts

Year	Jan.	Feb.	Mar.	Apr.	May	June	July	Aug.	Sept.	Oct.	Nov.	Dec.	Total[2]
1992	143,844	137,933	144,984	115,861	106,459	106,107	85,838	76,187	102,992	127,015	106,450	833,921	1,337.1
1993	86,062	100,444	97,041	65,612	103,198	105,960	71,711	75,685	89,276	69,060	87,350	65,951	1,017.4
1994	59,771	136,974	115,874	104,387	99,385	89,399	53,725	60,937	77,599	57,428	81,192	83,820	1,020.5
1995	72,240	79,970	90,311	37,388	58,707	49,932	28,081	41,495	44,396	36,904	46,582	34,219	620.2
1996	31,957	36,039	36,514	17,897	16,574	25,193	11,984	19,383	19,783	10,835	10,397	14,342	250.9
1997	10,603	19,432	20,602	11,552	16,633	14,916	11,540	15,418	19,045	20,437	16,775	22,131	199.1
1998	18,492	14,290	14,434	9,470	9,394	7,558	3,411	7,629	5,172	4,761	3,855	5,714	104.2
1999	4,837	6,085	6,499	2,892	3,566	3,173	1,934	2,019	590	829	2,075	6,761	41.3
2000	1,621	886	3,201	379	789	1,320	394	1,721	1,228	596	3,231	1,397	16.8
2001	2,090	2,744	5,801	684	3,037	935	3,175	1,888	4,497	1,774	1,460	3,028	31.1

[1] 90-day U.S. Treasury Bill. [2] In thousands of contracts. *Source: International Monetary Market (IOM), division of the Chicago Mercantile Exchange*

Average Open Interest of 30-year U.S. Treasury Bond Futures in Chicago In Contracts

Year	Jan.	Feb.	Mar.	Apr.	May	June	July	Aug.	Sept.	Oct.	Nov.	Dec.
1992	343,156	353,782	318,737	313,742	346,542	347,293	370,850	427,723	385,645	364,250	362,231	321,706
1993	336,327	375,435	361,675	362,404	370,485	349,285	361,393	396,411	388,188	360,859	359,739	337,575
1994	380,057	422,902	454,539	500,790	497,296	421,286	441,884	451,462	447,924	436,684	449,642	397,554
1995	384,356	389,908	369,989	367,964	399,500	421,234	438,267	381,237	361,394	395,346	447,409	426,384
1996	382,001	403,403	395,338	381,926	413,944	443,644	464,145	471,203	420,622	409,950	463,731	479,086
1997	497,539	545,775	509,573	493,511	554,418	480,669	530,011	608,474	624,231	723,321	719,186	737,703
1998	744,894	764,309	766,233	806,559	888,215	1,040,659	1,084,889	1,061,223	837,986	769,932	782,677	662,025
1999	657,180	801,115	664,131	618,453	717,453	674,225	672,983	748,974	647,816	621,816	637,656	561,919
2000	637,023	612,298	530,957	503,412	434,771	390,928	394,075	440,437	402,156	399,880	443,282	445,386
2001	413,244	479,165	519,987	509,558	503,194	455,799	458,613	531,098	525,972	567,177	602,647	478,418

Source: Chicago Board of Trade (CBT)

Volume of Trading of 30-year U.S. Treasury Bond Futures in Chicago In Thousands of Contracts

Year	Jan.	Feb.	Mar.	Apr.	May	June	July	Aug.	Sept.	Oct.	Nov.	Dec.	Total
1992	7,523.4	6,270.1	6,793.4	4,810.1	5,417.7	4,828.8	6,081.0	6,085.5	5,953.3	6,870.7	5,287.8	4,083.0	70,004.8
1993	5,577.4	6,482.7	7,902.9	6,156.1	6,799.8	5,817.2	6,218.4	6,914.5	7,443.9	6,537.4	8,193.5	5,384.5	79,428.5
1994	7,287.8	8,430.2	10,836.7	9,557.4	9,999.0	9,804.0	6,987.0	7,910.0	7,913.0	7,004.0	8,533.0	5,699.0	99,960.0
1995	7,058.0	7,714.0	9,623.8	5,835.4	8,721.5	8,446.7	5,790.2	7,083.7	7,317.1	6,927.2	6,626.3	5,232.1	86,375.9
1996	7,528.6	8,781.4	7,199.3	6,010.6	7,932.3	6,520.6	6,422.1	6,625.8	6,926.1	6,772.4	7,297.7	6,708.4	84,725.1
1997	8,104.7	7,522.8	7,493.3	7,519.9	8,339.1	7,400.2	7,679.8	10,228.1	8,356.2	12,467.6	7,735.5	6,980.4	99,827.7
1998	9,595.3	9,368.1	9,763.9	8,516.7	9,054.1	10,208.6	8,070.9	12,024.8	11,159.2	10,698.1	8,155.0	5,609.2	112,224.1
1999	8,075.2	10,031.5	8,667.5	7,196.9	9,555.8	8,072.1	6,415.1	7,995.2	6,559.6	6,301.1	6,909.0	4,263.5	90,042.3
2000	7,966.4	8,157.4	5,378.6	5,282.3	5,972.9	4,458.6	3,080.0	4,709.9	4,529.2	4,460.4	5,072.8	3,682.3	62,750.8
2001	5,123.0	5,545.9	5,196.3	4,584.0	6,022.2	4,233.2	3,347.0	4,965.6	4,331.0	4,598.6	6,746.4	3,886.0	58,579.3

Source: Chicago Board of Trade (CBT)

Average Open Interest of 3-month Eurodollar Futures in Chicago In Thousands of Contracts

Year	Jan.	Feb.	Mar.	Apr.	May	June	July	Aug.	Sept.	Oct.	Nov.	Dec.
1992	1,129.8	1,213.7	1,244.6	1,269.1	1,377.2	1,382.7	1,434.1	1,549.9	1,537.0	1,537.6	1,547.0	1,418.7
1993	1,429.4	1,586.7	1,643.3	1,653.4	1,782.8	1,739.1	1,777.7	1,918.4	1,940.7	2,026.5	2,149.0	2,150.2
1994	2,300.5	2,529.5	2,568.1	2,627.3	2,734.3	2,565.2	2,599.1	2,703.8	2,699.6	2,561.2	2,660.3	2,606.3
1995	2,443.6	2,535.4	2,463.9	2,447.4	2,503.3	2,390.8	2,279.5	2,374.6	2,347.2	2,290.3	2,405.5	2,480.5
1996	2,519.4	2,638.6	2,511.4	2,483.5	2,571.8	2,590.1	2,504.4	2,485.5	2,392.4	2,349.7	2,378.2	2,225.7
1997	2,190.8	2,333.2	2,423.1	2,523.1	2,671.3	2,706.5	2,699.2	2,788.0	2,769.3	2,815.1	2,799.5	2,661.6
1998	2,713.4	2,821.5	2,797.9	2,892.6	3,089.0	3,093.9	3,027.7	3,223.0	3,359.9	3,303.4	3,297.4	3,000.1
1999	2,917.9	3,039.5	2,973.5	2,894.7	3,183.2	3,208.8	3,064.4	3,115.6	2,904.0	2,918.2	2,879.7	2,859.4
2000	2,971.3	3,261.4	3,138.7	3,156.6	3,331.7	3,272.1	3,160.3	3,225.7	3,181.8	3,067.2	3,201.1	3,349.7
2001	3,576.4	3,878.6	4,117.4	4,109.3	4,316.3	4,471.7	4,452.4	4,753.5	4,567.8	4,524.0	4,950.8	4,559.1

Source: International Monetary Market (IOM), division of the Chicago Mercantile Exchange (CME)

Volume of Trading of 3-month Eurodollar Futures in Chicago In Thousands of Contracts

Year	Jan.	Feb.	Mar.	Apr.	May	June	July	Aug.	Sept.	Oct.	Nov.	Dec.	Total
1992	5,365.7	4,418.5	5,582.8	4,942.2	4,819.0	4,602.6	5,357.8	4,016.3	4,705.2	6,691.6	5,461.3	4,568.1	60,531.1
1993	5,556.8	5,003.8	6,013.8	4,059.4	5,977.8	5,672.9	5,656.7	4,494.2	6,340.6	4,888.4	6,269.8	4,477.3	64,411.4
1994	6,074.8	8,745.3	9,468.9	9,639.2	11,494.0	9,348.0	7,810.0	7,128.0	7,641.0	7,992.0	9,715.0	9,766.0	104,823.0
1995	10,341.1	10,429.3	9,549.0	6,069.2	9,897.1	10,104.7	6,669.9	7,013.5	7,171.1	6,477.9	6,055.2	5,952.1	95,730.0
1996	7,485.7	9,267.2	9,526.3	6,872.4	7,413.7	7,415.0	8,323.2	6,967.5	8,232.5	7,014.5	5,056.9	5,308.1	88,883.1
1997	7,903.4	6,918.0	8,936.4	9,351.7	8,447.4	8,049.7	7,291.6	9,295.4	7,634.7	12,569.7	6,314.1	7,058.2	99,770.2
1998	10,908.0	7,861.4	8,842.1	9,488.4	7,202.4	8,349.5	5,452.3	9,811.3	13,593.9	11,756.9	9,627.8	6,578.5	109,472.5
1999	7,470.9	7,674.5	8,718.6	7,346.5	8,957.0	9,649.8	7,746.3	8,898.0	7,629.1	7,500.6	6,223.2	5,604.0	93,418.5
2000	8,379.6	9,723.0	10,197.8	10,171.8	10,261.3	9,791.3	7,384.8	7,009.6	8,204.6	9,276.4	7,561.4	10,152.3	108,115.0
2001	17,515.1	12,908.4	15,478.5	15,191.7	15,691.1	14,309.9	12,673.1	14,947.9	16,776.2	14,139.1	21,150.1	13,234.4	184,015.5

Source: International Monetary Market (IOM), division of the Chicago Mercantile Exchange (CME)

Average Open Interest of 10-year U.S. Treasury Note Futures in Chicago In Contracts

Year	Jan.	Feb.	Mar.	Apr.	May	June	July	Aug.	Sept.	Oct.	Nov.	Dec.
1992	119,739	114,521	106,497	102,862	112,666	126,228	143,924	158,831	179,045	191,725	199,990	195,705
1993	190,018	206,852	198,653	209,221	229,378	217,521	233,458	238,189	237,243	237,877	273,336	262,831
1994	264,848	258,643	300,080	328,821	294,091	254,612	232,373	253,233	273,564	277,313	301,000	271,992
1995	282,978	285,187	265,747	263,816	273,945	289,052	306,046	323,078	277,011	278,832	270,527	249,073
1996	260,374	297,850	285,501	319,234	331,032	293,416	302,330	326,391	291,208	284,581	313,298	303,702
1997	332,285	343,661	323,982	348,683	350,814	336,927	363,744	407,147	387,284	398,645	404,980	374,448
1998	430,335	507,986	474,916	494,417	533,214	513,369	512,173	604,862	555,268	482,928	508,299	503,533
1999	528,538	549,518	515,404	510,091	541,057	574,514	588,272	623,806	607,305	653,080	582,003	487,888
2000	595,180	653,822	571,932	615,618	621,361	583,900	608,358	602,068	547,582	564,606	555,189	508,888
2001	550,287	541,619	560,035	595,103	628,693	512,127	550,155	627,305	610,435	590,328	661,963	559,949

Source: Chicago Board of Trade (CBT)

Volume of Trading of 10-year U.S. Treasury Note Futures in Chicago In Thousands of Contracts

Year	Jan.	Feb.	Mar.	Apr.	May	June	July	Aug.	Sept.	Oct.	Nov.	Dec.	Total
1992	929.6	866.4	824.9	531.2	758.9	683.3	859.4	1,047.7	1,138.5	1,300.2	1,225.8	1,052.1	11,218.0
1993	1,134.6	1,286.3	1,763.1	1,089.5	1,341.4	1,390.6	1,147.0	1,390.7	1,523.7	1,279.5	1,926.6	1,328.2	16,601.2
1994	1,484.3	1,935.7	2,572.4	2,213.5	2,399.4	2,250.2	1,621.8	2,028.7	1,932.9	1,635.1	2,253.6	1,750.2	24,078.0
1995	1,752.6	1,978.8	2,458.7	1,368.2	2,236.5	2,495.8	1,588.9	2,028.7	1,859.0	1,459.7	1,730.8	1,487.6	22,445.4
1996	1,649.1	2,313.1	2,075.8	1,632.1	2,211.3	1,715.6	1,556.3	1,865.7	1,810.4	1,494.7	1,904.5	1,711.2	21,939.7
1997	1,780.5	1,939.9	2,051.8	1,703.2	2,025.6	1,942.3	1,509.6	2,535.9	2,062.5	2,593.7	1,825.6	1,991.2	23,961.8
1998	2,393.5	2,748.7	2,817.5	2,342.1	2,695.9	2,681.9	1,704.1	3,632.2	3,560.3	2,882.7	2,912.2	2,111.5	32,482.6
1999	2,269.1	3,562.1	2,993.8	2,145.3	3,519.3	3,153.0	2,438.5	3,735.6	2,508.7	2,470.9	3,201.5	2,048.0	34,045.8
2000	3,557.0	4,974.7	3,750.4	3,529.7	4,711.6	3,706.0	2,580.9	4,459.8	3,779.5	3,824.3	4,513.6	3,313.1	46,700.5
2001	4,632.8	4,915.3	4,500.5	4,299.4	5,483.3	4,083.8	3,493.1	5,683.1	4,389.7	4,144.8	7,270.1	4,689.8	57,585.8

Source: Chicago Board of Trade (CBT)

Average Open Interest of 5-Year U.S. Treasury Note Futures in Chicago In Contracts

Year	Jan.	Feb.	Mar.	Apr.	May	June	July	Aug.	Sept.	Oct.	Nov.	Dec.
1992	116,322	121,667	125,155	130,826	135,111	144,386	143,928	143,203	127,418	122,113	129,548	127,690
1993	139,207	150,443	152,711	158,607	169,234	152,262	152,403	160,258	159,754	154,501	181,492	206,914
1994	200,812	213,037	200,626	185,083	192,659	186,026	189,828	182,027	181,518	181,578	176,322	205,150
1995	206,539	210,192	199,357	200,087	213,531	189,332	176,329	173,897	163,419	162,121	177,915	171,023
1996	163,026	184,523	200,253	191,690	179,951	177,370	174,484	179,599	154,764	138,246	155,820	154,764
1997	176,691	208,928	219,540	235,543	227,882	225,691	226,306	225,792	234,309	233,480	248,377	257,886
1998	257,094	270,048	282,327	277,540	274,145	257,193	264,756	389,118	382,855	383,809	353,399	326,860
1999	290,373	268,561	247,526	246,916	311,106	348,627	325,348	341,495	298,861	328,581	272,628	288,523
2000	387,008	475,464	420,789	417,929	428,239	379,628	402,658	405,087	372,779	373,698	381,432	380,248
2001	377,692	391,989	374,481	376,929	436,278	421,968	460,960	483,252	451,429	463,247	554,640	491,105

Source: Chicago Board of Trade (CBT)

Volume of Trading of 5-Year U.S. Treasury Note Futures in Chicago In Thousands of Contracts

Year	Jan.	Feb.	Mar.	Apr.	May	June	July	Aug.	Sept.	Oct.	Nov.	Dec.	Total
1992	498.6	543.8	560.0	322.2	590.1	551.5	484.2	565.7	582.1	539.0	640.8	563.2	1,743.0
1993	539.5	673.1	886.0	447.6	755.9	753.8	506.4	711.3	753.8	472.6	908.0	715.8	2,096.4
1994	695.9	1,235.1	1,295.4	917.1	1,202.0	1,154.9	834.8	944.9	1,107.3	840.6	1,156.7	1,078.0	12,463.0
1995	988.5	1,296.2	1,386.9	783.4	1,291.1	1,402.9	828.6	1,100.5	1,008.7	769.6	996.0	784.7	12,637.1
1996	837.3	1,312.0	1,084.6	815.7	1,135.5	878.3	881.7	1,061.8	979.0	689.5	831.1	957.1	11,463.4
1997	927.5	1,156.7	1,271.1	984.4	1,190.6	1,143.8	761.4	1,244.6	1,243.7	1,314.1	1,068.1	1,182.8	13,488.7
1998	1,451.9	1,482.0	1,390.7	1,154.7	1,281.1	1,376.9	944.0	2,480.5	1,913.5	1,583.1	1,722.7	1,279.1	18,060.0
1999	1,119.7	1,553.6	1,336.6	1,115.0	1,906.4	1,543.9	1,166.4	2,163.6	1,034.1	1,245.2	1,606.6	1,192.8	16,983.8
2000	1,800.5	2,873.8	2,010.0	1,707.8	2,548.4	1,757.3	1,188.9	2,253.3	1,515.5	1,774.2	2,259.7	1,642.6	23,332.0
2001	2,422.8	2,591.5	2,281.2	2,062.8	3,221.5	2,264.0	1,702.0	2,697.4	2,617.3	2,525.7	4,052.5	2,683.6	31,122.4

Source: Chicago Board of Trade (CBT)

INTEREST RATES, U.S.

U.S. Federal Funds Rate In Percent

Year	Jan.	Feb.	Mar.	Apr.	May	June	July	Aug.	Sept.	Oct.	Nov.	Dec.	Average
1992	4.03	4.06	3.98	3.73	3.82	3.76	3.25	3.30	3.22	3.10	3.09	2.92	3.52
1993	3.02	3.03	3.07	2.96	3.00	3.04	3.06	3.03	3.09	2.99	3.02	2.96	3.02
1994	3.05	3.25	3.34	3.56	4.01	4.25	4.26	4.47	4.73	4.76	5.29	5.45	4.20
1995	5.53	5.92	5.98	6.05	6.01	6.00	5.85	5.74	5.80	5.76	5.80	5.60	5.84
1996	5.56	5.22	5.31	5.22	5.56	5.27	5.40	5.22	5.30	5.24	5.31	5.29	5.30
1997	5.25	5.19	5.39	5.51	5.50	5.56	5.52	5.54	5.54	5.50	5.52	5.50	5.46
1998	5.56	5.51	5.49	5.45	5.49	5.56	5.54	5.55	5.51	5.07	4.83	4.68	5.35
1999	4.63	4.76	4.81	4.74	4.74	4.76	4.99	5.07	5.22	5.20	5.42	5.30	4.97
2000	5.45	5.73	5.85	6.02	6.27	6.53	6.54	6.50	6.52	6.51	6.51	6.40	6.24
2001	5.98	5.49	5.31	4.80	4.21	3.97	3.77	3.65	3.07	2.49	2.09	1.82	3.89

Source: Bureau of Economic Analysis, U.S. Department of Commerce (BEA)

U.S. Municipal Bond Yield[1] In Percent

Year	Jan.	Feb.	Mar.	Apr.	May	June	July	Aug.	Sept.	Oct.	Nov.	Dec.	Average
1992	6.54	6.74	6.76	6.67	6.57	6.49	6.13	6.16	6.25	6.41	6.36	6.22	6.44
1993	6.16	5.86	5.85	5.76	5.73	5.63	5.57	5.45	5.29	5.25	5.47	5.35	5.61
1994	5.31	5.40	5.91	6.23	6.19	6.11	6.23	6.21	6.28	6.52	6.97	6.80	6.18
1995	6.53	6.22	6.10	6.02	5.95	5.84	5.92	6.06	5.91	5.80	5.64	5.45	5.95
1996	5.43	5.43	5.79	5.94	5.98	6.02	5.92	5.76	5.87	5.72	5.59	5.64	5.76
1997	5.72	5.63	5.76	5.88	5.70	5.53	5.35	5.41	5.39	5.38	5.33	5.19	5.52
1998	5.06	5.10	5.21	5.23	5.20	5.12	5.14	5.10	4.99	4.93	5.03	4.98	5.09
1999	5.02	5.03	5.10	5.08	5.18	5.37	5.36	5.58	5.69	5.92	5.86	5.95	5.43
2000	6.08	6.00	5.83	5.75	6.00	5.80	5.63	5.51	5.56	5.59	5.54	5.22	5.71
2001	5.10	5.18	5.13	5.27	5.29	5.20	5.20	5.03	5.09	5.05	5.04	5.25	5.15

[1] 20-bond average. *Source: Bureau of Economic Analysis, U.S. Department of Commerce (BEA)*

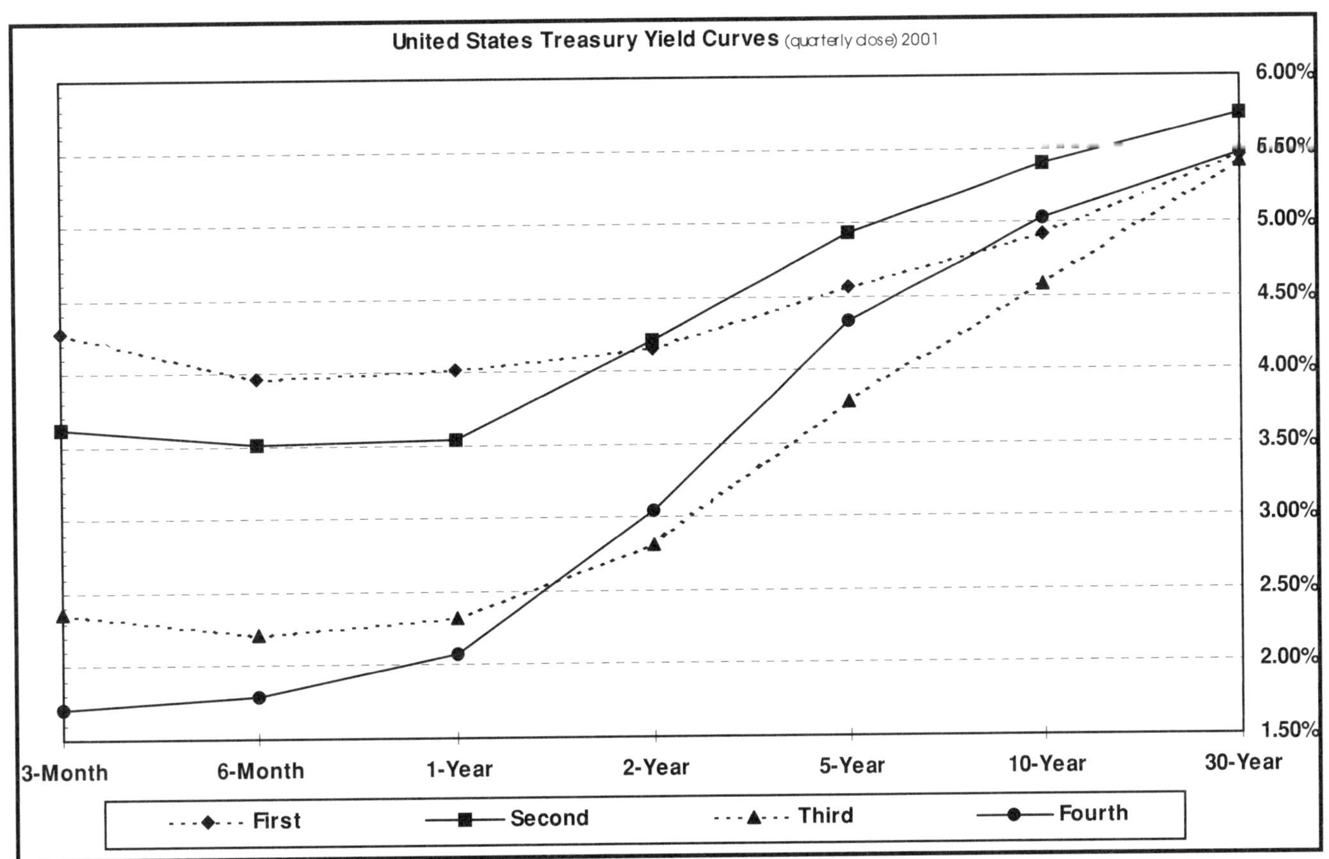

U.S. Industrial Production Index[1] 1992 = 100

Year	Jan.	Feb.	Mar.	Apr.	May	June	July	Aug.	Sept.	Oct.	Nov.	Dec.	Average
1992	97.5	98.1	98.9	99.6	100.0	99.7	100.4	100.1	100.5	101.3	101.9	101.9	100.0
1993	102.3	102.8	102.8	103.2	102.6	102.8	103.1	102.8	103.9	104.1	104.6	105.4	103.4
1994	105.7	106.2	107.0	107.4	108.1	108.6	109.1	109.2	109.3	109.9	110.6	111.6	108.6
1995	111.9	111.6	111.7	111.4	111.5	111.7	111.7	112.6	113.0	112.5	112.7	112.8	114.5
1996	112.4	113.8	113.2	114.3	114.8	115.5	115.5	115.8	116.0	116.2	120.6	120.9	119.5
1997	121.3	122.1	122.5	123.1	123.3	123.5	124.5	125.2	125.6	129.3	129.9	130.3	127.0
1998	130.3	130.2	130.7	131.3	131.9	130.6	130.5	132.4	131.9	134.1	133.8	133.8	132.4
1999	134.1	134.5	135.1	135.5	136.2	136.6	137.4	137.7	138.1	139.1	141.9	142.8	139.2
2000	143.6	144.3	145.2	146.3	147.2	147.9	147.6	148.7	148.8	146.3	145.8	145.1	145.7
2001[2]	143.9	143.5	142.9	142.0	141.6	140.3	140.4	140.0	138.5	137.5	136.9	136.7	140.4

[1] Total Index of the Federal Reserve Index of Quantity Output, seasonally adjusted. [2] Preliminary. *Source: Bureau of Economic Analysis, U.S. Department of Commerce (BEA)*

U.S. Gross National Product, National Income, and Personal Income In Billions of Constant Dollars[1]

	Gross Domestic Product					National Income					Personal Income				
Year	First Quarter	Second Quarter	Third Quarter	Fourth Quarter	Annual Average	First Quarter	Second Quarter	Third Quarter	Fourth Quarter	Annual Average	First Quarter	Second Quarter	Third Quarter	Fourth Quarter	Annual Average
1992	6,184	6,277	6,346	6,470	6,319	4,935	4,996	4,952	5,097	4,995	5,277	5,352	5,391	5,542	5,390
1993	6,522	6,597	6,656	6,796	6,642	5,150	5,233	5,259	5,366	5,252	5,466	5,595	5,630	5,749	5,610
1994	6,888	7,016	7,096	7,218	7,054	5,373	5,525	5,609	5,720	5,557	5,714	5,861	5,935	6,042	5,888
1995	7,298	7,343	7,433	7,529	7,401	5,775	5,834	5,920	5,978	5,877	6,110	6,163	6,226	6,305	6,201
1996	7,630	7,783	7,859	7,981	7,813	6,067	6,178	6,255	6,343	6,210	6,405	6,509	6,597	6,678	6,547
1997	8,124	8,280	8,391	8,479	8,318	6,455	6,556	6,676	6,787	6,618	6,792	6,879	6,979	7,098	6,937
1998	8,628	8,697	8,817	8,985	8,782	6,874	6,986	7,109	7,197	7,041	7,255	7,383	7,491	7,576	7,426
1999	9,093	9,161	9,297	9,523	9,269	7,327	7,393	7,481	7,647	7,462	7,631	7,720	7,819	7,939	7,777
2000	9,669	9,858	9,938	10,028	9,873	7,797	7,956	8,047	8,124	7,981	8,104	8,271	8,382	8,520	8,319
2001[2]	10,142	10,203	10,225	10,222	10,198	8,170	8,208	8,190		8,189	8,640	8,715	8,772	8,772	8,725

[1] Seasonally adjusted at annual rates. [2] Preliminary. *Source: Bureau of Economic Analysis, U.S. Department of Commerce (BEA)*

INTEREST RATES, U.S.

U.S. Money Supply M1[2] In Billions of Dollars

Year	Jan.	Feb.	Mar.	Apr.	May	June	July	Aug.	Sept.	Oct.	Nov.	Dec.	Average
1992	910.0	926.2	936.8	944.3	952.4	954.2	963.2	975.4	988.2	1,003.9	1,016.7	1,025.0	966.4
1993	1,032.0	1,034.0	1,038.4	1,047.8	1,067.5	1,075.4	1,084.7	1,094.5	1,104.2	1,114.3	1,123.6	1,129.8	1,078.9
1994	1,132.8	1,137.3	1,140.1	1,142.4	1,143.5	1,144.7	1,150.9	1,149.7	1,150.8	1,150.4	1,150.4	1,150.7	1,145.3
1995	1,150.3	1,148.4	1,147.1	1,150.4	1,145.1	1,142.7	1,145.0	1,144.0	1,141.6	1,135.7	1,133.1	1,129.0	1,142.7
1996	1,122.2	1,119.8	1,126.2	1,123.5	1,117.1	1,115.5	1,108.8	1,099.8	1,093.3	1,080.3	1,080.1	1,081.1	1,106.1
1997	1,080.8	1,078.8	1,075.0	1,068.3	1,064.3	1,065.4	1,065.6	1,071.1	1,063.5	1,061.9	1,069.2	1,076.0	1,069.6
1998	1,073.8	1,076.0	1,080.6	1,082.1	1,078.2	1,077.8	1,075.4	1,072.2	1,074.7	1,080.4	1,089.3	1,093.7	1,080.9
1999	1,096.0	1,094.3	1,101.4	1,107.2	1,101.7	1,100.1	1,099.5	1,098.7	1,096.1	1,102.5	1,109.6	1,123.0	1,101.5
2000	1,122.8	1,108.8	1,113.2	1,117.3	1,106.7	1,105.3	1,103.9	1,099.4	1,096.0	1,096.2	1,087.1	1,088.1	1,103.9
2001[1]	1,099.3	1,100.1	1,112.7	1,117.5	1,117.0	1,123.5	1,136.6	1,144.6	1,201.0	1,158.9	1,158.1	1,177.9	1,137.3

[1] Preliminary. [2] M1 -- This measure is currency, travelers checks, plus deposits at commercial banks and interest-earning checkable deposits at all depository institutions. *Source: Bureau of Economic Analysis, U.S. Department of Commerce (BEA)*

U.S. Money Supply M2[2] In Billions of Dollars

Year	Jan.	Feb.	Mar.	Apr.	May	June	July	Aug.	Sept.	Oct.	Nov.	Dec.	Average
1992	3,387.7	3,407.1	3,410.5	3,408.8	3,407.4	3,401.3	3,402.2	3,408.9	3,418.2	3,432.0	3,435.3	3,434.0	3,412.8
1993	3,431.3	3,424.0	3,420.4	3,423.6	3,447.6	3,452.9	3,452.7	3,456.8	3,463.6	3,469.7	3,480.2	3,486.6	3,450.8
1994	3,490.8	3,491.7	3,494.3	3,503.0	3,504.0	3,493.7	3,502.1	3,498.2	3,498.4	3,499.4	3,500.9	3,502.1	3,498.2
1995	3,506.3	3,506.1	3,506.7	3,519.1	3,534.9	3,562.9	3,583.1	3,604.4	3,620.1	3,629.8	3,639.3	3,655.0	3,572.3
1996	3,669.9	3,685.0	3,713.9	3,724.5	3,725.6	3,741.9	3,750.0	3,762.7	3,775.3	3,788.1	3,798.3	3,821.8	3,745.6
1997	3,840.7	3,853.3	3,868.9	3,890.0	3,892.5	3,908.0	3,922.5	3,954.8	3,979.3	3,999.3	4,023.6	4,046.4	3,931.5
1998	4,071.4	4,100.9	4,126.2	4,155.2	4,174.8	4,198.6	4,216.1	4,241.7	4,284.2	4,325.5	4,364.4	4,401.4	4,221.9
1999	4,422.4	4,538.5	4,463.4	4,490.4	4,513.0	4,530.9	4,552.8	4,570.5	4,590.0	4,608.8	4,614.6	4,643.7	4,526.2
2000	4,668.7	4,686.4	4,717.2	4,754.8	4,766.6	4,787.8	4,807.9	4,838.0	4,870.0	4,886.3	4,900.1	4,937.4	4,801.3
2001[1]	4,983.4	5,023.1	5,078.4	5,121.4	5,143.8	5,186.7	5,226.1	5,261.8	5,379.7	5,371.8	5,413.8	5,449.1	5,219.9

[1] Preliminary. [2] M2 -- This measure adds to M1 overnight repurchase agreements (RPs) issued by commercial banks and certain overnight Eurodollars (those issued by Caribbean branches of member banks) held by U.S. nonbank residents, general purpose and broker/dealer money market mutual funds shares (MMMF), and savings and small-denomination time deposits. *Source: Bureau of Economic Analysis, U.S. Department of Commerce (BEA)*

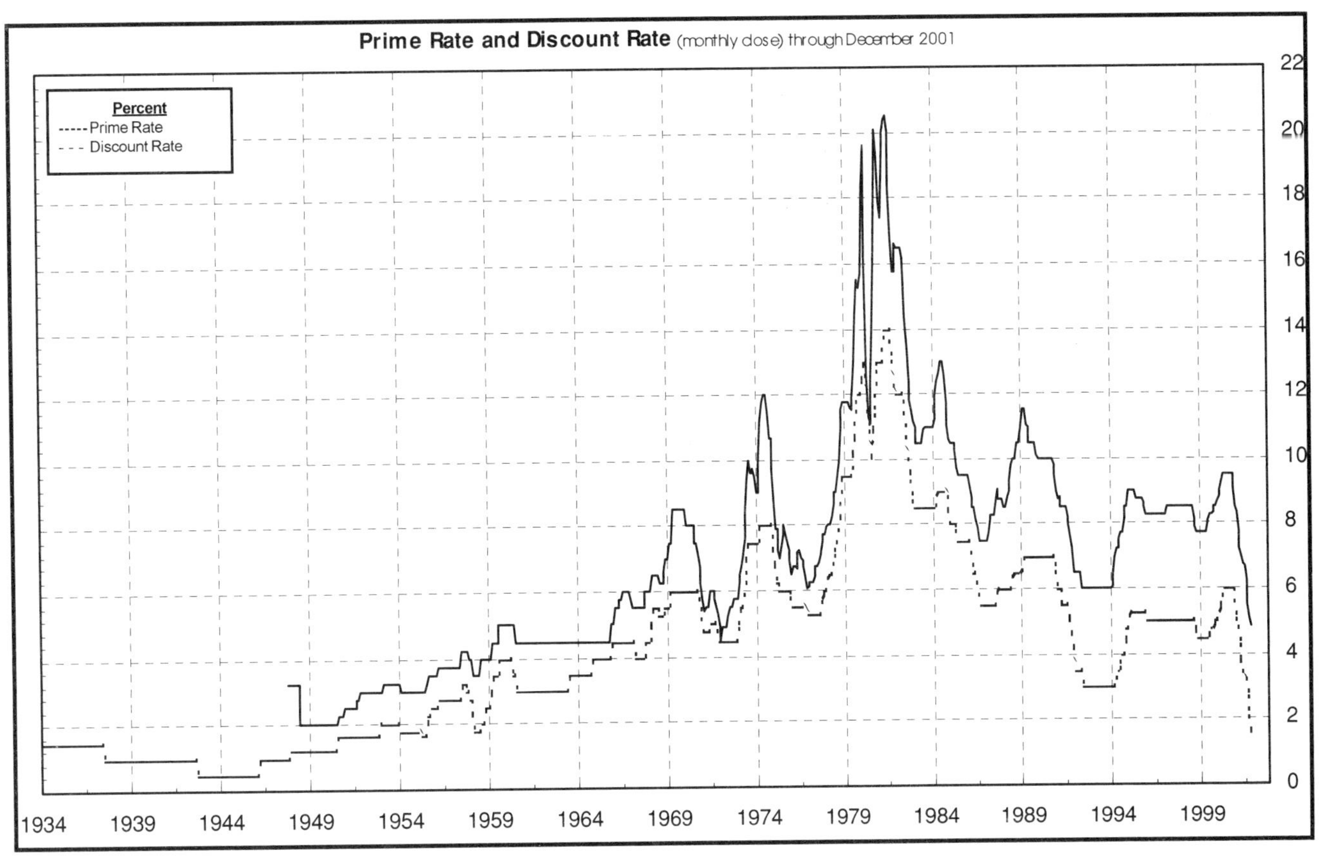

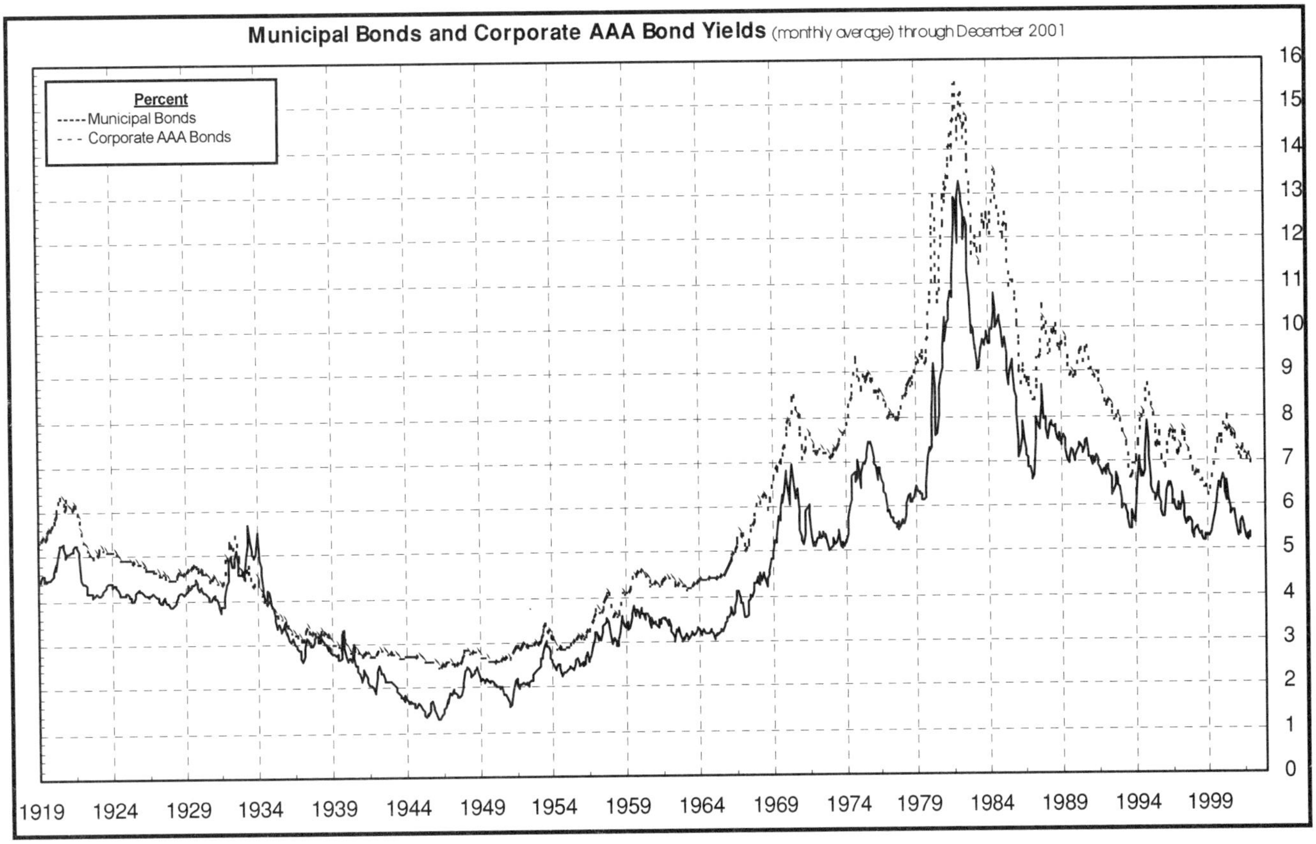

Municipal Bonds and Corporate AAA Bond Yields (monthly average) through December 2001

Percent
-----Municipal Bonds
- - - Corporate AAA Bonds

16 15 14 13 12 11 10 9 8 7 6 5 4 3 2 1 0

1919 1924 1929 1934 1939 1944 1949 1954 1959 1964 1969 1974 1979 1984 1989 1994 1999

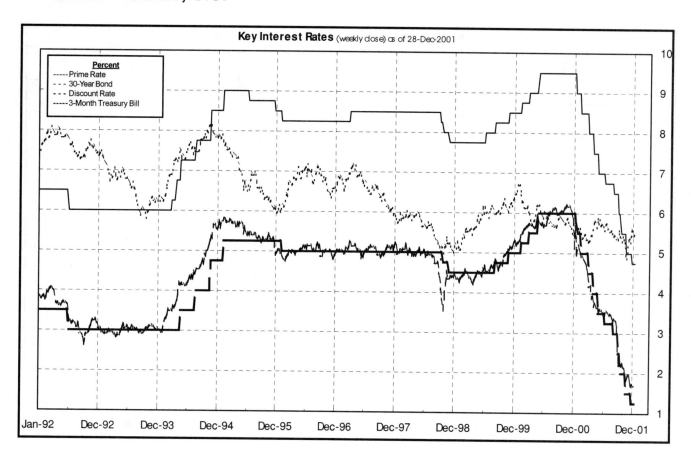

Key Interest Rates (weekly close) as of 28-Dec-2001

Percent
-----Prime Rate
- - - 30-Year Bond
- - - Discount Rate
-----3-Month Treasury Bill

10
9
8
7
6
5
4
3
2
1

Jan-92 Dec-92 Dec-93 Dec-94 Dec-95 Dec-96 Dec-97 Dec-98 Dec-99 Dec-00 Dec-01

2-Year Treasury Note Futures - Chicago Board of Trade (weekly close) as of 28-Dec-2001

Nominal Value

107
106
105
104
103
102
101
100
99
98
97
96

Jan-92 Dec-92 Dec-93 Dec-94 Dec-95 Dec-96 Dec-97 Dec-98 Dec-99 Dec-00 Dec-01

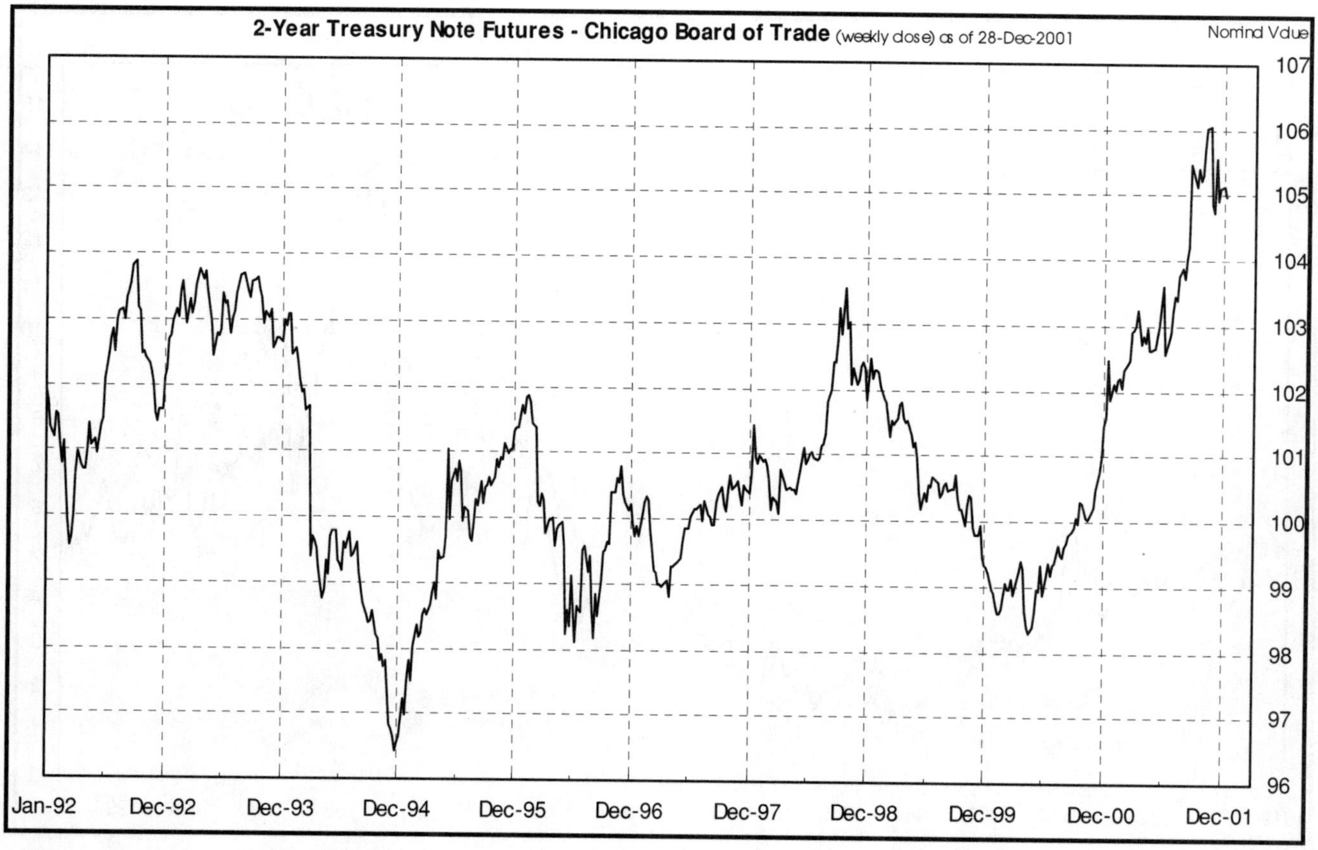

Interest Rates, Worldwide

Slowing world economies in 2001 triggered aggressive monetary easing by the key central banks, but it was U.S. Federal Reserve that set the pace with a series of eleven downward interest rate moves that carried U.S. short-term rates to a forty-year low. The overall 2001 action was in sharp contrast to a year earlier when the central banks followed a tight monetary policy on the assumption that the economies of at least some nations showed signs of overheating; a view that was partially abetted by bubbling equity markets. Since late 2000 and through 2001 the world's monetary pendulum swung the other way: the overriding concern focusing on trying to prevent the global economy from sinking into a recession, manifested in part by equities markets that declined very fast from historic highs set in early 2001. Inflationary fears, normally the nemesis of central banks, were glossed over as basic global supply/demand imbalances were not likely to trigger any upward pressure on prices; despite occasional, but short lived, bursts of oil (energy) related price increases. As 2001 drew to a close, a perception seemed to be taking hold that the global economy contraction, especially in the U.S., had run its course and further monetary easing was not necessary. However, considerable uncertainty also took hold as to the strength and staying power of the global recovery. U.S. economic growth in 2002 was seèn as again reaching to 3% plus vs. about 2 1/2% for Europe, but the outlook for Japan was at best murky. Meanwhile, the macroeconomics role of the central bank(s) is likely to take on greater importance in the years ahead. There are now almost 200 central banks, many of which are inclined to claim more independence from their national governments. The newly formed European Central Bank (ECB), representing in 2001 at least twelve European Union nations has been given a high degree of independence since no one government appoints all its members, and its creation is viewed as one of the most important structural reforms in the European economy. Over time, the bank will likely represent as many as twenty European nations.

Despite the ECB's short tenure, their monetary approach does not necessarily mirror the Federal Reserve as shown during 2001. The Fed's rates cuts were certainly not matched by the ECB and the reason is rooted in European fears of inflation, justified or not. The ECB did lower short terms rates in 2001 partially to help reverse the downward pressure on equity markets. Moreover, their action was abetted at times by other European central banks, as the Bank of England, which despite some reluctance joined with the ECB's easing in mid-September following the terrorist attack on the U.S., their second easing in as many months. The Bank of Japan also joined the collective move although their action was largely viewed as more symbolic than effective as Japan's interest rates are almost at zero anyway. The U.K.'s benchmark rate was trimmed in early August to 5% and cut again in mid-September to 4.75%, a forty year low despite signs that U.K. inflation rate was at the top end of the Bank of England's inflation ceiling of 2.5%. Still, the overall European action was seen as necessary as a means of restoring post September 11, 2001 confidence into the European economies and also to abet the Federal Reserve's easier monetary policy.

Ironically, the ECB showed signs of trying to maintain a stable monetary policy in late 2001, if not also into early 2002 despite a bleak European economic outlook through the first half of 2002. Gross domestic product in the euro zone in the last half of 2001 was minimal at best, if not flat. If economic growth fails to recover as expected in 2002, its likely that short term rates will be trimmed across the continent by as much as 50 basis points in the first quarter. Interest rates in emerging markets (includes much of Asia and South America, including Argentina), however, actually shot higher in 2001; the 2002 outlook is clouded since the longer term filtering down effect of the September 11, terrorist attack on trade and tourism is not discernible. Still, the difference between yields on emerging-market debt worldwide and comparable U.S. treasury securities of about 10% in 2001 was the highest in two years.

The U.S. economy dominates the world and it's not likely to lose that position. The Fed's rational for its sharp about face monetary policy in 2001 from 2000 largely reflected concern that the U.S. economy's decade long economic expansion had come to an end, and it did. The economy was officially declared in a recession as of the first quarter. The problem in 2001 was that the Fed's actions seemed to be have little effect on revitalizing the economy, notwithstanding the normal six-month or so lag between changes in monetary policy and desired economic effect. Although there were signs of a possible resurgence in late 2001, it was far from clear as to whether further fed easing might be necessary in 2002 even though key short term rates were not that far from zero. The Fed does have breathing room to ease since U.S. inflationary pressures are minimal, but any fresh action could rest more on developments in the equity markets. Another round of equity slippage could force the Fed's hand, although in theory, it should not.

Futures Markets

A number of actively traded interest rate futures markets are traded worldwide. The London International Financial Futures Exchange (LIFFE) trades contracts on 3-month Sterling prices and British long Gilts. LIFFE also offers futures on Euroswiss and Italian government bonds. The all-electronic Eurex exchange in Frankfurt trades a variety of Swiss and German government bonds as well as Euribors. Canadian Bankers Acceptances and 10-year Canadian government bonds are traded on the Montreal Exchange (ME). 3-year Australian Commonwealth T-bonds are traded on the Sydney Futures Exchange. Notional bond and PIBOR futures are traded on the Paris MATIF. Euroyen futures and Japanese yen government bonds are traded in Tokyo. Libor, eurodollars, and Brady bonds are traded on Chicago's Mercantile Exchange.. A Brady bond Index futures are traded on the CBOT. For a listing of other interest rate contracts see the volume section in the front of this Yearbook.

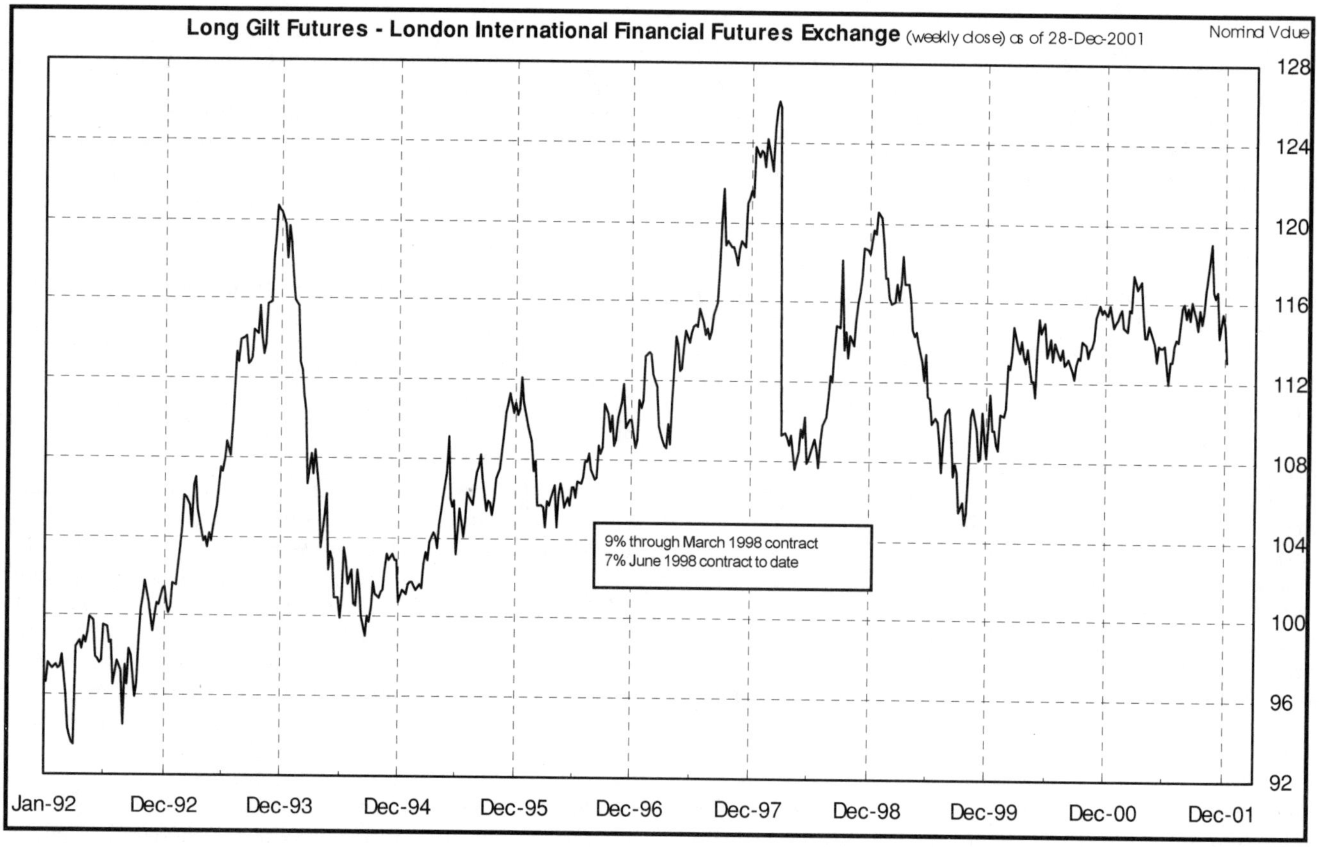

Long Gilt Futures - London International Financial Futures Exchange (weekly close) as of 28-Dec-2001

Nominal Value

9% through March 1998 contract
7% June 1998 contract to date

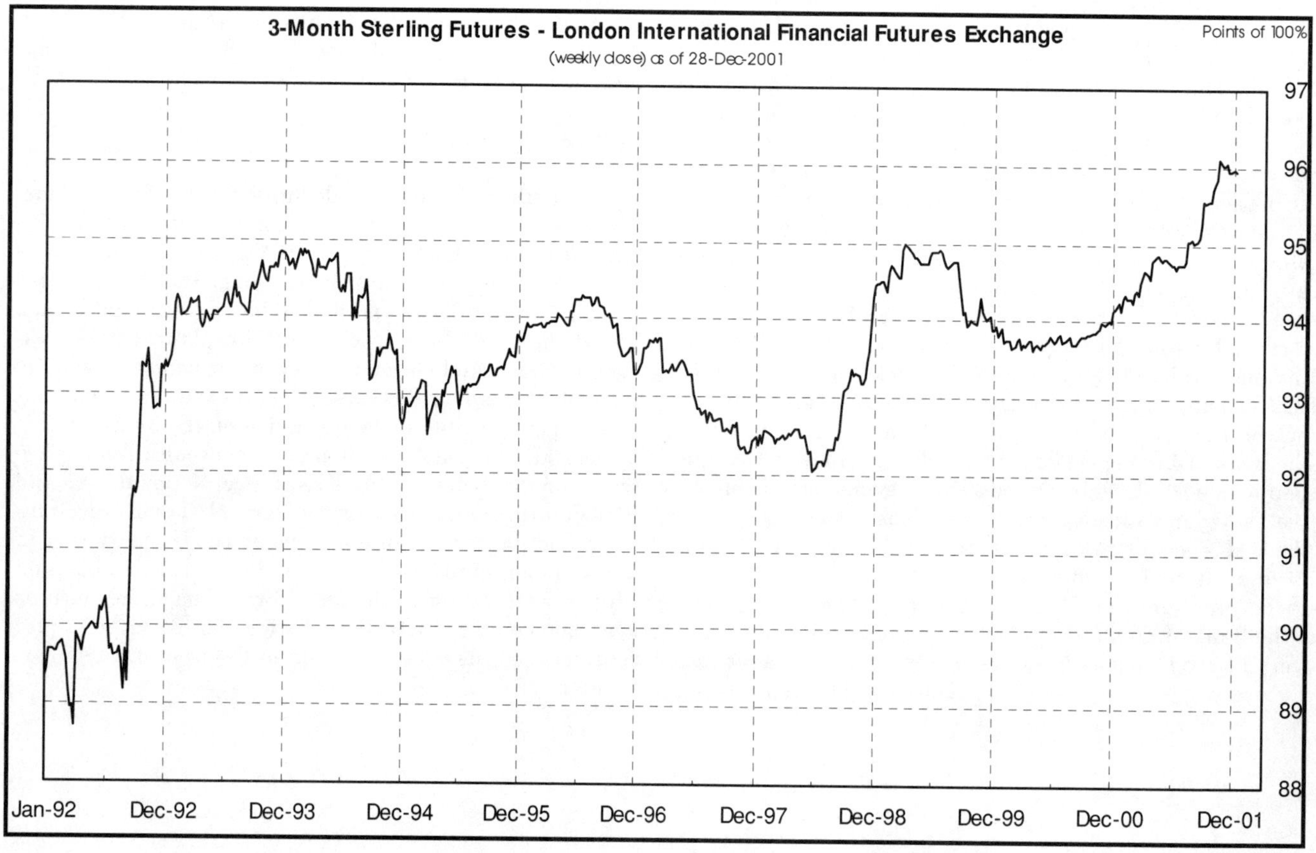

3-Month Sterling Futures - London International Financial Futures Exchange (weekly close) as of 28-Dec-2001

Points of 100%

10-Year Japanese Government Bond Futures - Tokyo Stock Exchange
(weekly close) as 28-Dec-2001
Nominal Value
145
140
135
130
125
120
115
110
105
100
Jan-92
Dec-92
Dec-93
Dec-94
Dec-95
Dec-96
Dec-97
Dec-98
Dec-99
Dec-00
Dec-01

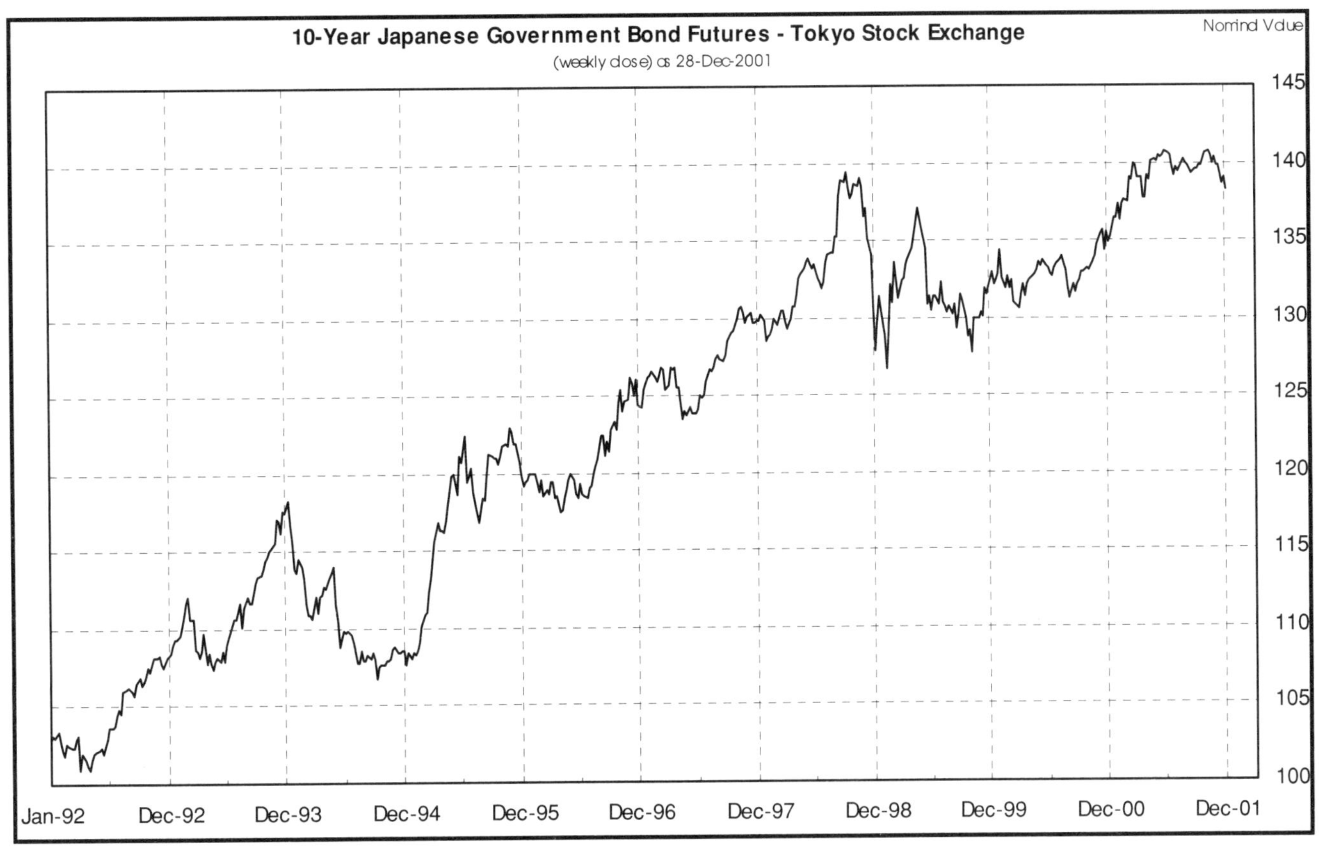

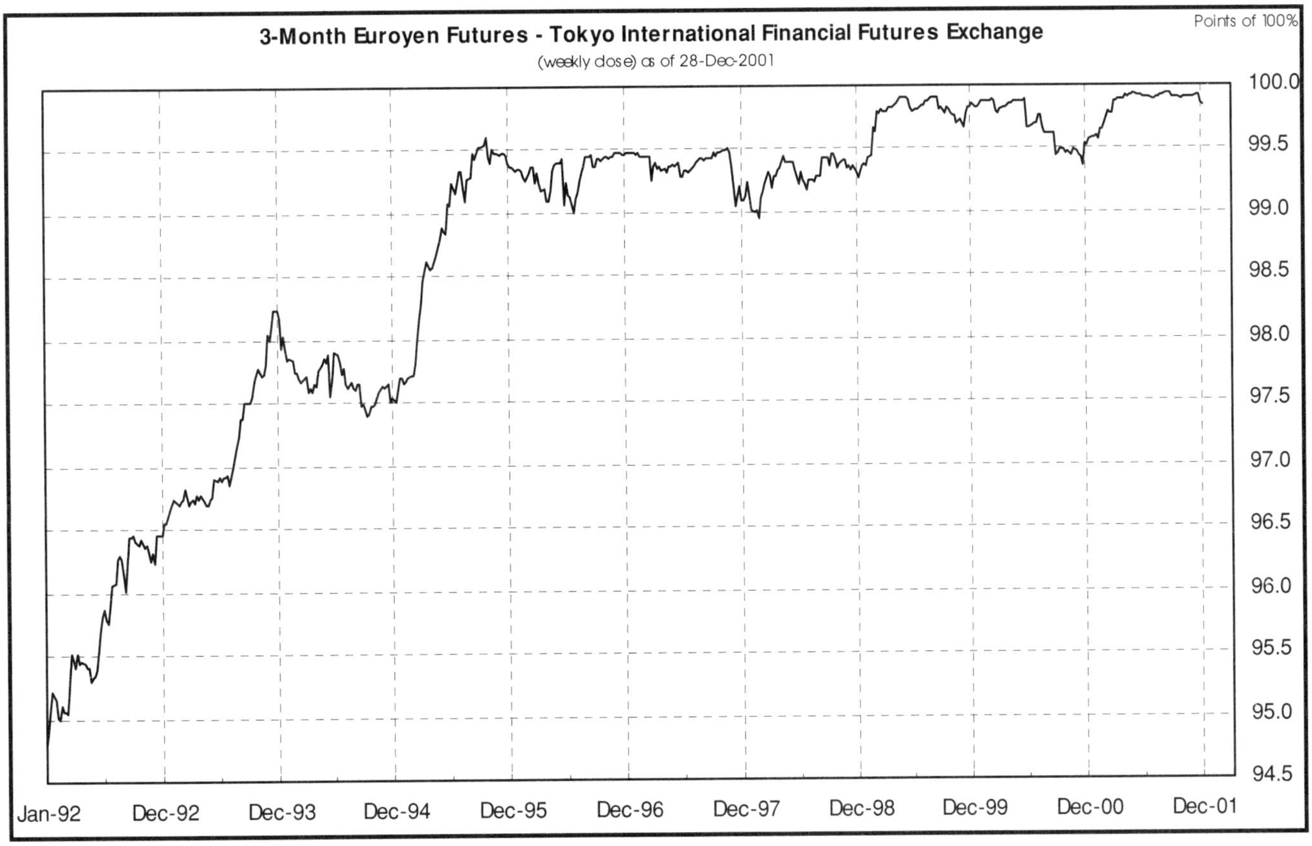

3-Month Euroyen Futures - Tokyo International Financial Futures Exchange
(weekly close) as of 28-Dec-2001
Points of 100%
100.0
99.5
99.0
98.5
98.0
97.5
97.0
96.5
96.0
95.5
95.0
94.5
Jan-92
Dec-92
Dec-93
Dec-94
Dec-95
Dec-96
Dec-97
Dec-98
Dec-99
Dec-00
Dec-01

10-Year Canadian Government Bond Futures - Montreal Exchange
(weekly close) as of 28-Dec-2001
Nominal Value
132
128
124
120
116
112
108
104
100
96
92
Jan-92
Dec-92
Dec-93
Dec-94
Dec-95
Dec-96
Dec-97
Dec-98
Dec-99
Dec-00
Dec-01

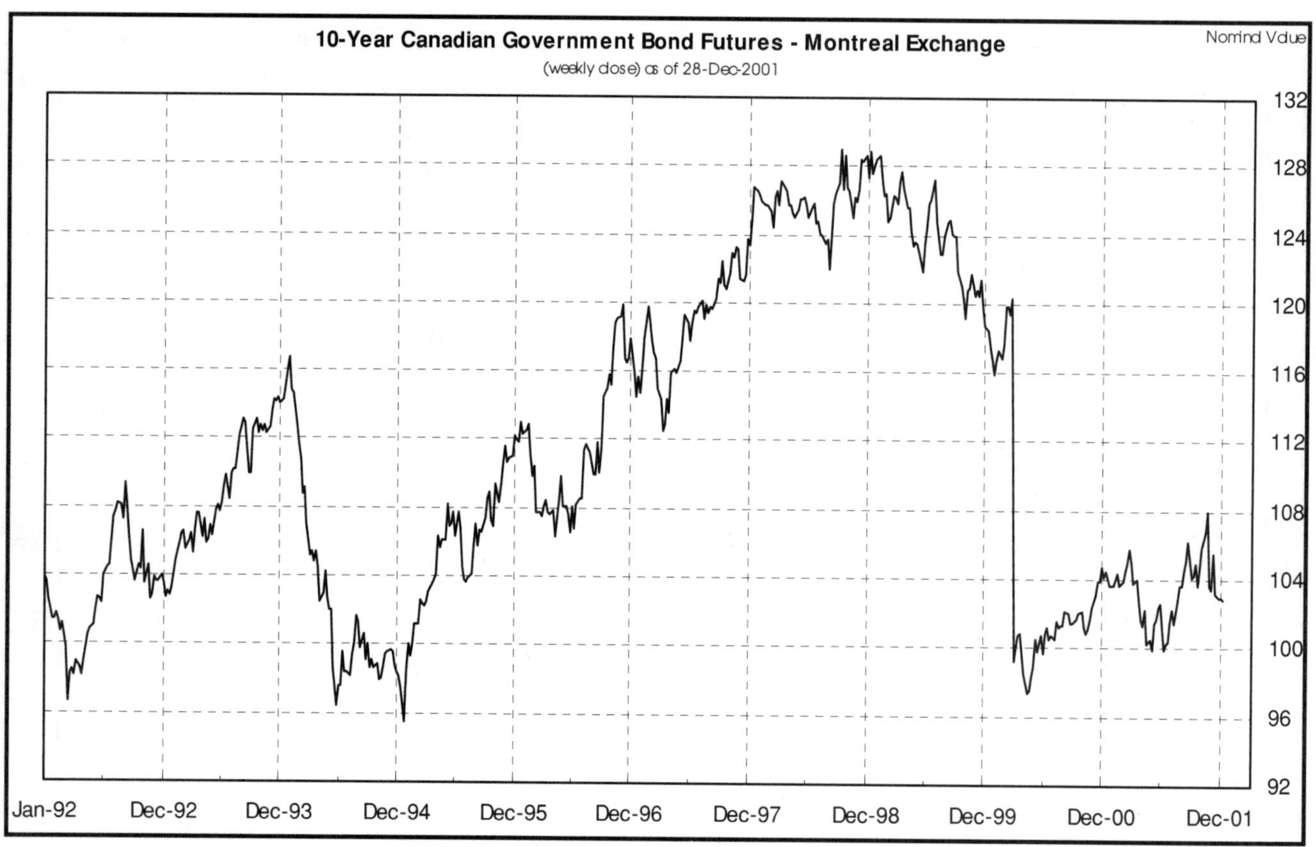

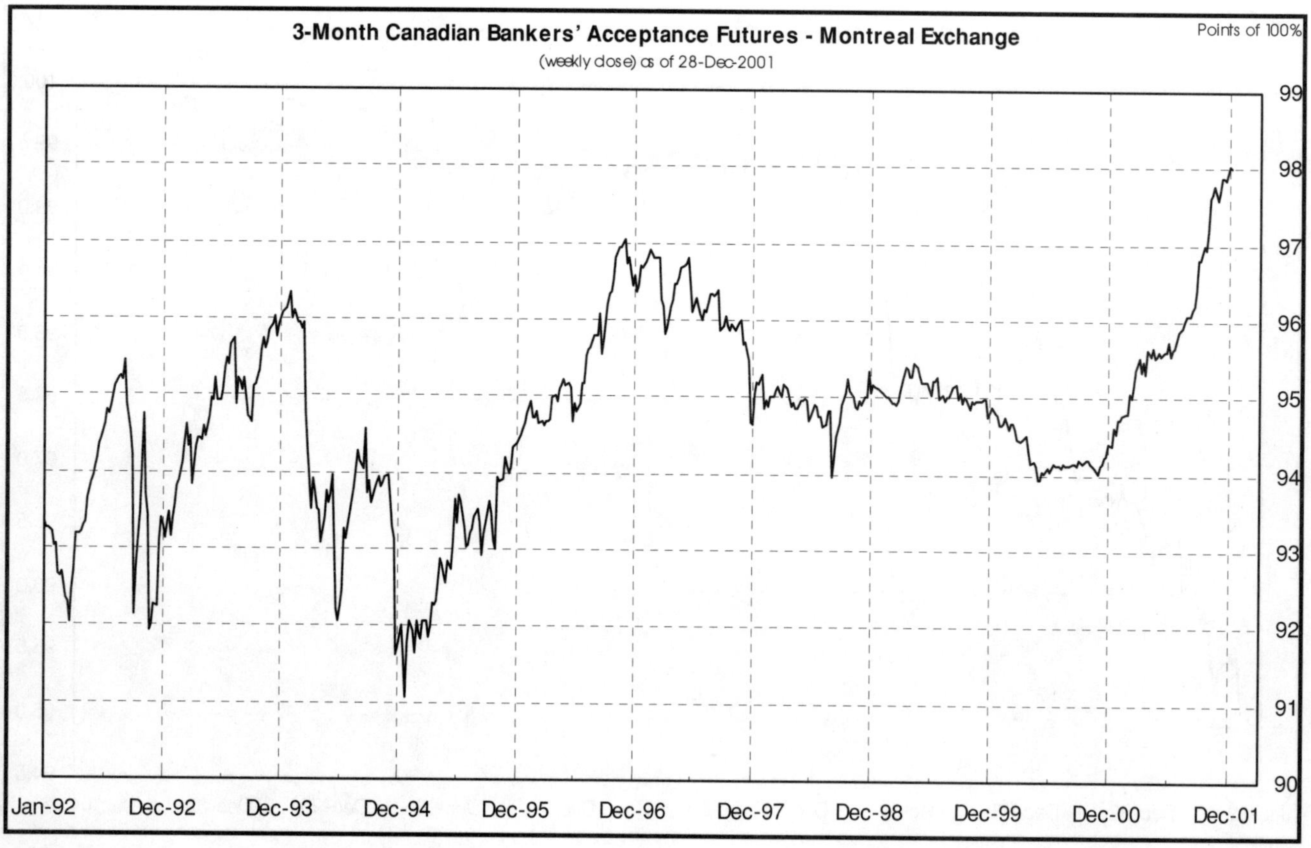

3-Month Canadian Bankers' Acceptance Futures - Montreal Exchange
(weekly close) as of 28-Dec-2001
Points of 100%
99
98
97
96
95
94
93
92
91
90
Jan-92
Dec-92
Dec-93
Dec-94
Dec-95
Dec-96
Dec-97
Dec-98
Dec-99
Dec-00
Dec-01

Australia -- Economic Statistics Percentage Change from Previous Period

Year	Real GDP	Nominal GDP	Real Private Consump-tion	Real Public Consump-tion	Grossed Fixed Invest-ment	Real Total Domestic Demand	Real Exports of Goods & Services	Real Imports of Goods & Services	Consumer Prices[1]	Unem-ployment Rate
1994	5.0	5.0	4.0	4.0	11.6	5.3	9.0	14.1	1.9	9.7
1995	4.4	6.0	5.0	3.6	3.2	4.8	5.1	8.1	4.6	8.5
1996	3.7	6.0	3.3	2.6	4.9	3.2	10.6	8.2	2.6	8.5
1997	3.8	5.4	3.9	1.6	11.0	3.4	11.5	10.3	.3	8.6
1998	5.6	5.7	4.6	4.0	7.5	7.0	-.3	5.9	.9	8.0
1999	4.7	5.7	5.2	5.3	6.5	5.7	4.6	9.5	1.5	7.2
2000	4.2	7.8	3.7	6.0	3.6	4.0	10.8	9.9		6.6
2001[2]	3.7	6.6	3.5	3.3	4.8	3.9	8.5	6.8		6.3
2002[3]	3.7	6.5	3.2	3.1	4.4	3.4	8.3	7.1		6.1

[1] National accounts inplicit private consumption deflator. [2] Estimate. [3] Projection. *Source: Organization for Economic Co-opertation and Development (OECD)*

Canada -- Economic Statistics Percentage Change from Previous Period

Year	Real GDP	Nominal GDP	Real Private Consump-tion	Real Public Consump-tion	Grossed Fixed Invest-ment	Real Total Domestic Demand	Real Exports of Goods & Services	Real Imports of Goods & Services	Consumer Prices[1]	Unem-ployment Rate
1994	4.7	5.9	3.1	-1.2	7.4	3.2	13.1	8.3	.2	10.3
1995	2.8	5.2	2.1	-.5	-1.9	1.7	9.0	6.2	2.2	9.4
1996	1.5	3.2	2.5	-1.4	5.8	1.4	5.9	5.8	1.6	9.6
1997	4.4	5.4	4.4	-1.2	15.4	6.2	8.8	15.1	1.6	9.1
1998	3.3	2.7	2.9	1.6	3.4	2.2	8.9	6.1	1.0	8.3
1999	4.5	6.2	3.5	1.3	10.1	4.2	10.0	9.4	1.7	7.6
2000	4.8	8.3	3.6	2.0	11.8	5.4	11.6	13.3		6.7
2001[2]	3.4	5.8	2.8	1.7	6.4	3.4	7.5	7.8		6.7
2002[3]	3.0	5.1	2.6	1.5	6.1	3.2	6.4	6.8		6.7

[1] National accounts inplicit private consumption deflator. [2] Estimate. [3] Projection. *Source: Organization for Economic Co-opertation and Development (OECD)*

France -- Economic Statistics Percentage Change from Previous Period

Year	Real GDP	Nominal GDP	Real Private Consump-tion	Real Public Consump-tion	Grossed Fixed Invest-ment	Real Total Domestic Demand	Real Exports of Goods & Services	Real Imports of Goods & Services	Consumer Prices[1]	Unem-ployment Rate
1994	1.8	3.6	.6	.6	1.5	1.8	7.9	8.5	1.7	12.2
1995	1.8	3.6	1.6	-.1	2.1	1.8	7.8	7.8	1.7	11.6
1996	1.1	2.6	1.3	2.2	-.1	.7	3.1	1.5	2.0	12.3
1997	1.9	3.1	.1	2.1		.6	12.1	7.1	1.2	12.4
1998	3.2	4.0	3.4	.3	6.6	3.9	7.7	11.3	.8	11.8
1999	2.9	3.3	2.3	2.5	7.2	2.9	3.8	3.8	.5	11.1
2000	3.3	4.2	2.6	1.3	6.0	3.0	12.8	12.5		9.7
2001[2]	2.9	4.6	2.3	1.3	4.6	2.5	8.7	8.1		8.8
2002[3]	2.5	4.8	2.2	1.3	4.8	2.5	7.4	8.1		8.2

[1] National accounts inplicit private consumption deflator. [2] Estimate. [3] Projection. *Source: Organization for Economic Co-opertation and Development (OECD)*

Germany[2] -- Economic Statistics Percentage Change from Previous Period

Year	Real GDP	Nominal GDP	Real Private Consump-tion	Real Public Consump-tion	Grossed Fixed Invest-ment	Real Total Domestic Demand	Real Exports of Goods & Services	Real Imports of Goods & Services	Consumer Prices[1]	Unem-ployment Rate
1994	2.3	4.9	1.0	2.4	4.0	2.3	7.6	7.4	2.8	8.2
1995	1.7	3.8	2.0	1.5	-.7	1.7	5.7	5.6	1.7	7.9
1996	.8	1.8	1.0	1.8	-.8	.3	5.1	3.1	1.4	8.6
1997	1.4	2.2	.7	-.9	.6	.6	11.3	8.4	1.9	9.5
1998	2.1	3.2	2.0	.5	3.0	2.4	7.0	8.6	.9	8.9
1999	1.6	2.5	2.6	-.1	3.3	2.4	5.1	8.1	.6	8.3
2000	3.0	2.9	1.7	1.0	2.4	1.9	12.6	9.1		7.7
2001[3]	2.7	3.7	2.6	.5	2.8	2.1	9.3	7.7		6.9
2002[4]	2.5	3.9	2.4	.6	2.7	2.1	7.4	6.5		6.3

[1] National accounts inplicit private consumption deflator. [2] Data are for Western Germany only, except for foreign trade statistics. [3] Estimate. [4] Projection. *Source: Organization for Economic Co-operation and Development (OECD)*

Italy -- Economic Statistics Percentage Change from Previous Period

Year	Real GDP	Nominal GDP	Real Private Consump-tion	Real Public Consump-tion	Grossed Fixed Invest-ment	Real Total Domestic Demand	Real Exports of Goods & Services	Real Imports of Goods & Services	Consumer Prices[1]	Unem-ployment Rate
1994	2.2	5.8	1.5	-.9	.1	1.7	9.8	8.1	4.1	11.2
1995	2.9	8.1	1.7	-2.2	6.0	2.0	12.6	9.7	5.2	11.7
1996	1.1	6.4	1.2	1.0	3.6	.9	.6	-.3	4.0	11.7
1997	1.8	4.3	3.0	.8	1.2	2.5	6.5	10.2	2.0	11.8
1998	1.5	4.2	2.3	.7	4.1	2.9	3.3	9.1	2.0	11.9
1999	1.4	2.9	1.7	.6	4.4	2.5	-.4	3.4	1.7	11.5
2000	2.8	4.7	2.0	1.2	6.9	2.2	9.5	7.6		10.8
2001[2]	2.7	4.9	1.8	1.1	4.7	2.2	9.3	8.1		10.1
2002[3]	2.6	4.7	2.3	1.2	5.2	2.7	7.6	8.4		9.4

[1] National accounts inplicit private consumption deflator. [2] Estimate. [3] Projection. *Source: Organization for Economic Co-opertation and Development (OECD)*

Japan -- Economic Statistics Percentage Change from Previous Period

Year	Real GDP	Nominal GDP	Real Private Consump-tion	Real Public Consump-tion	Grossed Fixed Invest-ment	Real Total Domestic Demand	Real Exports of Goods & Services	Real Imports of Goods & Services	Consumer Prices[1]	Unem-ployment Rate
1994	.6	.8	1.9	2.4	-.8	1.0	4.6	8.9	.7	2.9
1995	1.5	.8	2.1	3.3	1.7	2.3	5.4	14.2	-.1	3.1
1996	5.1	3.5	2.9	1.9	11.1	5.7	6.3	11.9	.1	3.4
1997	1.6	1.9	.5	1.5	-.8	.2	11.6	.5	1.7	3.4
1998	-2.5	-2.2	-.5	1.5	-7.4	-3.1	-2.5	-7.6	.6	4.1
1999	.2	-.7	1.2	1.3	-1.2	.5	1.9	5.3	-.3	4.7
2000	1.9	.3	1.6	.2	.6	1.3	13.6	10.5		4.7
2001[2]	2.3	1.9	2.1	.5	2.8	2.4	5.5	6.4		4.6
2002[3]	2.0	1.8	2.2	.6	1.2	1.8	5.3	4.2		4.6

[1] National accounts inplicit private consumption deflator. [2] Estimate. [3] Projection. *Source: Organization for Economic Co-opertation and Development (OECD)*

Switzerland -- Economic Statistics Percentage Change from Previous Period

Year	Real GDP	Nominal GDP	Real Private Consump-tion	Real Public Consump-tion	Grossed Fixed Invest-ment	Real Total Domestic Demand	Real Exports of Goods & Services	Real Imports of Goods & Services	Consumer Prices[1]	Unem-ployment Rate
1994	.5	2.2	1.0	2.0	6.5	2.7	1.8	7.9	.9	4.7
1995	.5	1.6	.6	-.1	1.8	1.8	1.6	5.1	1.8	4.2
1996	.3	.7	.7	2.0	-2.4	.4	2.5	2.7	.8	4.7
1997	1.7	1.5	1.4		1.5	1.3	8.6	7.6	.5	5.2
1998	2.3	2.6	2.2	.7	4.5	4.3	5.0	9.6		3.9
1999	1.5	2.1	2.2	-.4	1.8	1.4	5.9	5.5	.8	2.7
2000	3.3	4.4	2.1	.3	6.2	2.6	9.9	8.2		2.0
2001[2]	2.4	4.0	2.0	.3	4.6	2.4	6.6	6.7		1.8
2002[3]	2.0	3.9	1.9	.2	4.5	2.3	5.8	6.4		1.8

[1] National accounts inplicit private consumption deflator. [2] Estimate. [3] Projection. *Source: Organization for Economic Co-opertation and Development (OECD)*

United Kingdom -- Economic Statistics Percentage Change from Previous Period

Year	Real GDP	Nominal GDP	Real Private Consump-tion	Real Public Consump-tion	Grossed Fixed Invest-ment	Real Total Domestic Demand	Real Exports of Goods & Services	Real Imports of Goods & Services	Consumer Prices[1]	Unem-ployment Rate
1994	4.4	6.0	2.9	1.4	3.6	3.4	9.2	5.4	2.5	9.4
1995	2.8	5.4	1.7	1.6	2.9	1.8	9.5	5.5	3.4	8.5
1996	2.6	5.9	3.6	1.7	4.9	3.0	7.5	9.1	2.4	7.9
1997	3.5	6.5	3.9	-1.4	7.5	3.8	8.6	9.2	3.1	6.5
1998	2.6	5.7	4.0	1.1	10.1	4.6	2.6	8.8	3.4	5.9
1999	2.2	4.7	4.3	3.3	6.1	3.7	3.3	7.6	1.6	6.0
2000	3.0	5.0	3.5	1.8	2.4	3.4	7.8	8.5		5.5
2001[2]	2.6	5.1	2.4	4.3	3.8	2.9	7.2	7.5		5.4
2002[3]	2.3	5.0	2.2	3.3	3.0	2.6	6.0	6.1		5.5

[1] National accounts inplicit private consumption deflator. [2] Estimate. [3] Projection. *Source: Organization for Economic Co-opertation and Development (OECD)*

Iron and Steel

Iron is the least expensive and most widely used metal. Iron ore is used to make steel. In the U.S., about 97 percent of the iron ore is used in steelmaking. Iron and steel scrap is recycled material that is an important raw material for the production of new steel and cast iron products. The U.S. Geological Survey reports that the U.S. steel and foundry industries have been structured to recycle scrap and are therefore very dependent on scrap. In the U.S., it is estimated that 68 million metric tonnes of steel was recycled in steel mills and foundries in 2000. The automotive recycling industry recycles almost 13 million vehicles annually and that supplies more than 14 million tonnes of shredded steel scrap to the steel industry for recycling.

Iron and steel slags are coproducts of iron and steelmaking. In 2000 it was estimated that 19 million tonnes of domestic iron and steel slags were consumed. Iron or blast furnace slag accounted for 57 percent of the tonnage sold. Steel slags produced from open hearth, basic oxygen and electric arc furnaces accounted for the remainder. The uses of iron slag were for road bases, asphaltic aggregates, cement and concrete applications and fill. Steel slags are used mainly for road bases, asphaltic aggregates and fill.

U.S. raw steel production in July 2001 was reported to be 7.67 million tonnes, down 1 percent from the previous month and some 10 percent less than a year ago. In the January-July 2001 period, raw steel production totaled 54.5 million tonnes, down 12 percent from the same period in 2000. For all of 2000, raw steel production was 107 million tonnes.

U.S. exports of iron and steel scrap in June 2001 were 444,000 tonnes. In the January-June 2001 period, iron and steel scrap exports were 3.2 million tonnes. The major market was China which took 1.19 million tonnes. Other large export destinations were Canada, South Korea, Mexico, Taiwan, Malaysia and Turkey. Most iron and steel scrap is exported from the West Coast and Hawaii. Export locations on the West Coast are Los Angeles and San Francisco.

U.S. imports for consumption of iron and steel scrap in June 2001 were 246,000 tonnes. In the January-June 2001 period, imports were 1.57 million tonnes. The major suppliers were Canada, the United Kingdom, Sweden, Denmark, the Netherlands and Mexico. Stocks of iron and steel scrap held by consumers at the end of 2000 were 4.7 million tonnes, down 2 percent from the previous year. There is no government stockpile of iron and steel scrap.

World Production of Raw Steel (Ingots and Castings) In Thousands of Metric Tons

Year	Brazil	Canada	China	France	Germany	Italy	Japan	Rep. of Korea	Russia[3]	Ukraine[3]	United Kingdom	United States	World Total
1991	22,617	12,987	71,000	18,434	42,169	25,112	109,649	26,001	77,093	45,002	16,474	79,738	733,592
1992	23,934	13,933	80,935	17,972	39,711	24,835	98,132	28,055	67,029	41,759	16,212	84,322	719,679
1993	25,207	14,387	89,539	17,106	37,625	25,720	99,623	33,026	58,346	32,609	16,625	88,793	727,549
1994	25,747	13,897	92,613	18,031	40,837	26,151	98,295	33,745	48,812	24,081	17,286	91,244	725,108
1995	25,076	14,415	95,360	18,100	42,051	27,766	101,640	36,772	51,589	22,309	17,604	95,191	750,235
1996	25,237	14,735	101,237	17,633	39,793	23,910	98,801	38,903	49,253	22,332	17,992	95,535	749,991
1997	26,153	15,554	108,911	19,767	45,007	25,842	104,545	42,554	48,502	25,629	18,489	98,486	798,842
1998	25,760	15,930	114,588	20,126	44,046	25,714	93,548	39,896	43,822	24,445	17,315	98,658	777,229
1999[1]	24,996	16,235	123,954	20,200	42,062	24,738	94,192	41,042	51,510	27,453	16,298	97,427	788,151
2000[2]	27,865	16,594	127,326	20,956	46,376	26,721	106,444	43,107	59,098	31,373	15,155	101,517	847,113

[1] Preliminary. [2] Estimate. [3] Formerly part of the U.S.S.R.; data not reported separately until 1992. *Source: U.S. Geological Survey (USGS)*

Average Wholesale Prices of Iron and Steel in the United States

	No. 1 Heavy Melting Steel Scrap		Pittsburg Prices								
			Hot Rolled	Sheet Bars		Hot Rolled	Carbon Steel	Cold Rolled	Galvanized	Railroad Steel	Used Steel
Year	Pittsburg	Chicago	Sheet[2]	Hot Rolled	Cold Finished	Strip	Plates	Strip	Sheets	Scrap[3]	Cans[4]
	$ Per Gross Ton		Cents Per Pound							$ Per Gross Ton	
1991	95.18	95.19	22.88	20.60	25.75	23.15	24.50	38.86	35.35	129.69	89.00
1992	88.72	88.52	19.13	17.48	24.03	23.50	24.50	39.40	30.88	117.40	88.73
1993	116.30	115.26	20.99	18.44	23.83	23.50	25.12	39.40	30.90	142.18	91.79
1994	136.76	131.91	22.93	NA	25.70	23.50	27.61	39.40	32.24	169.00	102.33
1995	142.34	143.17	25.32	NA	25.70	24.88	29.98	39.40	34.47	NA	126.32
1996	137.28	136.07	23.94	NA	26.46	25.00	31.58	NA	35.05	NA	121.27
1997	133.38	139.40	18.12	NA	25.65	NA	32.00	NA	28.62	NA	108.13
1998	110.10	118.76	15.57	NA	25.50	NA	22.50	NA	24.11	NA	109.44
1999	97.86	102.49	14.74	NA	23.50	NA	14.00	NA	21.20	NA	68.94
2000[1]	103.75	96.12	15.67	NA	23.08	NA	15.69	NA	21.38	NA	82.23

[1] Preliminary. [2] 10 gauge; thru 1992,list prices;1993 to date, market prices. [3] Specialties scrap. [4] *Consumer buying prices.*
NA = Not available. *Source: American Metal Market (AMM)*

IRON AND STEEL

Salient Statistics of Steel in the United States In Thousands of Short Tons

Year	Pig Iron Production	Producer Price Index for Steel Mill Products (1982=100)	Raw Steel Production: By Type of Furnace: Basic Oxygen	Open Hearth	Electric[2]	Stainless	Carbon	Alloy	Total	Net Shipments Steel Mill Products	Total Steel Products: Exports	Imports
1992	52,224	106.4	57,642	----	35,308	1,993	82,458	8,498	92,949	82,241	5,016	19,033
1993	53,082	108.2	59,353	----	38,524	1,956	86,865	9,056	97,877	89,022	4,727	21,796
1994	54,426	113.4	61,028	----	39,551	2,022	89,535	9,022	100,579	95,084	4,852	32,705
1995	56,097	120.1	62,523	----	42,407	2,265	92,656	10,009	104,930	97,494	8,157	27,270
1996	54,485	115.7	60,433	----	44,876	2,061	93,649	9,599	105,309	100,878	6,168	32,115
1997	54,679	116.4	61,053	----	47,508	2,382	95,933	10,246	108,561	105,858	7,369	34,389
1998	53,164	113.8	59,686	----	49,067	2,214	97,054	9,484	108,752	102,420	5,520	41,520
1999	51,002	105.3	57,722	----	49,673	2,086	98,694	5,421	107,395	106,201	5,426	35,731
2000	52,787	108.4	59,485	----	52,756	2,104	102,141	5,379	111,903	109,050	6,529	37,957
2001[1]	46,424	101.3	52,204	----	47,118	2,003	90,782	6,537	99,322	99,448	6,144	30,080

[1] Preliminary. [2] Includes crucible steels. *Sources: American Iron & Steel Institute (AISI); U.S. Geological Survey (USGS)*

Production of Steel Ingots, Rate of Capability Utilization[1] in the United States In Percent

Year	Jan.	Feb.	Mar.	Apr.	May	June	July	Aug.	Sept.	Oct.	Nov.	Dec.	Average
1992	80.5	82.4	83.5	85.3	83.5	82.1	78.9	78.7	78.3	80.9	80.4	77.7	82.2
1993	84.8	89.0	87.0	87.4	88.3	87.5	86.9	86.2	87.7	90.2	86.3	85.9	89.1
1994	87.7	92.2	91.3	91.4	91.2	88.7	87.1	87.7	90.0	92.0	92.6	94.3	93.0
1995	93.8	95.6	96.0	92.9	91.6	90.1	86.8	88.3	93.6	90.3	92.1	90.2	91.7
1996	92.2	92.6	93.8	90.5	89.7	91.3	86.6	87.1	87.7	88.0	87.0	87.9	89.5
1997	85.3	89.3	89.6	89.2	87.9	87.0	85.1	86.4	91.2	86.9	89.6	86.3	89.4
1998	90.0	95.2	93.1	92.5	89.1	86.1	83.0	86.4	83.0	81.0	74.4	74.8	85.7
1999	77.2	79.5	81.7	81.8	81.7	79.7	79.4	82.8	82.3	88.2	89.1	88.5	82.7
2000	89.7	89.4	91.2	92.0	91.3	89.6	85.3	83.5	82.7	81.0	75.1	72.0	85.2
2001[2]	77.6	82.3	81.8	82.9	81.5	81.6	79.8	80.4	80.5	77.5	77.5	65.9	79.1

[1] Based on tonnage capability to produce raw steel for a full order book. [2] Preliminary. *Sources: American Iron and Steel Institute (AISI); U.S. Geological Survey (USGS)*

Production of Steel Ingots in the United States In Thousands of Short Tons

Year	Jan.	Feb.	Mar.	Apr.	May	June	July	Aug.	Sept.	Oct.	Nov.	Dec.	Total
1992	7,754	7,432	8,043	7,875	7,968	7,584	7,542	7,526	7,249	7,742	7,449	7,438	92,949
1993	7,942	7,528	8,148	7,926	8,278	7,937	8,066	8,001	7,878	8,409	7,786	8,008	97,877
1994	8,003	7,598	8,323	8,180	8,437	7,941	7,996	8,053	7,993	8,477	8,256	8,684	100,579
1995	8,918	8,211	9,131	8,548	8,696	8,286	8,308	8,455	8,668	8,685	8,574	8,678	103,142
1996	8,981	8,438	9,136	8,588	8,798	8,661	8,585	8,627	8,407	8,702	8,276	8,689	104,356
1997	8,735	8,266	9,175	8,882	9,048	8,662	8,692	8,818	9,006	9,128	9,116	9,071	107,488
1998	9,510	9,087	9,839	9,524	9,483	8,863	8,832	9,194	8,548	8,681	7,710	8,013	107,643
1999	8,422	7,837	8,854	8,643	8,914	8,413	8,619	8,993	8,650	9,574	9,357	9,604	105,882
2000	9,838	9,170	10,009	9,843	10,097	9,592	9,411	9,213	8,830	8,978	8,054	7,982	111,015
2001[1]	8,475	8,122	8,932	8,685	8,832	8,550	8,459	8,525	8,263	8,125	7,226	6,695	98,889

[1] Preliminary. *Source: American Iron and Steel Institute (AISI)*

Shipments of Steel Products[1] by Market Classifications in the United States In Thousands of Short Tons

Year	Appliances Utensils & Cutlery	Auto-motive	Con-tainers, Packaging & Shipping Materials	Cons-truction Including Maint.	Con-tractors Products	Electrical Equip-ment	Export	Machinery, Industrial Equipment & Tools	Oil and Gas	Rail Trans-portaion	Steel for Converting & Pro-cessing[2]	Steel Service Center & Dis-tributors	All Other[3]	Total Ship-ments
1992	1,503	11,092	3,974	9,536	2,694	2,136	2,650	1,951	1,454	1,052	9,226	21,328	13,645	82,241
1993	1,592	12,719	4,355	10,516	2,913	2,213	2,110	2,191	1,526	1,223	9,451	23,714	14,499	89,022
1994	1,736	14,753	4,495	10,935	3,348	2,299	1,710	2,427	1,703	1,248	10,502	24,153	15,775	95,084
1995	1,589	14,622	4,139	11,761	3,337	2,397	4,442	2,310	2,643	1,373	10,440	23,751	14,690	97,494
1996	1,713	14,665	4,101	15,561	5	2,401	2,328	2,410	3,254	1,400	10,245	27,124	15,676	100,878
1997	1,635	15,251	4,163	15,885	5	2,434	2,610	2,355	3,811	1,410	11,263	27,800	17,241	105,858
1998	1,729	15,842	3,829	15,289	5	2,255	2,556	2,147	2,649	1,657	9,975	27,751	16,741	102,420
1999	1,712	15,639	3,768	14,685	5	2,260	2,292	1,547	1,544	876	7,599	21,439	32,840	106,201
2000	1,530	14,697	3,684	14,763	5	2,039	2,752	1,513	2,268	994	7,753	22,537	35,093	109,624
2001[4]	1,675	12,767	3,193	16,339	5	1,694	2,281	1,210	2,134	720	7,462	23,887	26,086	99,448

[1] All grades including carbon, alloy and stainless steel. [2] Net total after deducting shipments to reporting companines for conversion or resale.
[3] Includes agricultural; bolts, nuts rivets & screws; forgings (other than automotive); shipbuilding & marine equipment; aircraft; mining, quarrying & lumbering; other domestic & commercial equipment machinery; ordnance & other direct military; and shipments of non-reporting companies.
[4] Preliminary. *Source: American Iron and Steel Institute (AISI)*

Net Shipments of Steel Products[1] in the United States — In Thousands of Short Tons

Year	Cold Finished Bars	Rails & Accessories	Wire Drawn	Tin Mill Products	Plates (Cut & Coils)	Sheet & Strip Galv. (Hot Dipped)	Hot Rolled Bars	Pipe & Tubing	Structural Shapes & Steel Piling	Reinforcing Bars	Hot Rolled Sheets	Cold Rolled Sheets	Carbon	Alloy	Stainless
1992	1,458	562	900	3,927	7,103	8,199	5,800	4,198	5,081	4,781	13,361	12,692	76,625	4,101	1,514
1993	1,580	679	802	4,123	7,538	9,712	6,339	4,445	4,973	5,033	14,873	12,758	83,106	4,381	1,534
1994	1,786	631	788	4,137	8,556	10,943	7,088	4,966	5,942	4,929	15,654	13,016	88,505	4,859	1,720
1995	1,782	630	654	3,942	9,043	11,329	6,902	5,437	6,278	5,048	16,978	12,347	90,485	5,115	1,894
1996	1,685	722	652	4,108	8,672	11,456	6,999	5,895	6,140	5,762	17,466	14,089	93,019	5,948	1,912
1997	1,809	875	619	4,057	8,855	12,439	8,153	6,548	6,029	6,188	18,221	13,322	97,509	6,282	2,067
1998	1,780	938	725	3,714	8,864	13,481	8,189	5,409	5,595	5,909	15,715	13,185	94,536	5,847	2,037
1999	1,775	646	611	3,771	8,200	14,870	8,078	4,772	5,995	6,183	17,740	13,874	98,694	5,421	2,086
2000	1,756	783	579	3,742	8,898	14,917	7,901	5,385	7,402	6,893	19,236	14,802	102,141	5,379	2,104
2001[2]	1,369	630	481	3,202	8,349	14,310	7,032	5,377	6,789	6,976	18,866	12,352	92,946	4,666	1,836

[1] All grades, including carbon, alloy and stainless steel. [2] Preliminary. *Source: American Iron and Steel Institute (AISI)*

World Production of Pig Iron (Excludes Ferro-Alloys) — In Thousands of Metric Tons

Year	Belgium	Brazil	China	France	Germany	India	Italy	Japan	Russia[4]	Ukraine[4]	United Kingdom	United States	World Total
1991	9,354	22,926	67,650	13,408	30,608	14,176	10,856	79,985	90,900	----	11,883	44,510	528,000
1992	8,533	23,152	75,890	13,051	27,399	15,126	10,462	73,144	45,824	34,663	11,542	47,400	524,000
1993	8,178	23,982	87,390	12,679	26,970	15,674	11,066	73,738	40,871	26,999	11,534	48,200	531,000
1994	8,974	25,177	97,410	13,293	29,923	17,808	11,157	73,776	36,116	21,200	11,943	49,400	544,000
1995	9,199	25,090	105,293	12,860	29,828	18,626	11,684	74,905	39,762	20,000	12,238	50,900	536,000
1996	8,628	23,978	107,225	12,108	30,012	19,864	10,347	74,597	36,061	18,143	12,830	49,400	549,000
1997	8,077	25,013	115,110	13,424	30,939	19,898	11,348	78,519	37,327	20,561	13,057	49,600	576,000
1998	8,730	25,111	118,600	13,603	30,162	20,194	10,704	74,981	34,827	20,840	12,574	48,200	572,000
1999[1]	8,472	25,060	125,390	13,854	27,931	20,139	10,509	74,520	40,854	21,937	12,399	46,300	576,000
2000[2]	8,472	27,723	131,030	13,621	30,846	21,321	11,223	81,071	44,618	25,700	10,989	47,900	612,000

[1] Preliminary. [2] Estimate. [3] Formerly part of the U.S.S.R.; data not reported separately until 1992. *Source: U.S. Geological Survey (USGS)*

Production of Pig Iron (Excludes Ferro-Alloys) in the United States — In Thousands of Short Tons

Year	Jan.	Feb.	Mar.	Apr.	May	June	July	Aug.	Sept.	Oct.	Nov.	Dec.	Total
1992	4,390	4,175	4,524	4,400	4,444	4,232	4,347	4,299	4,065	5,329	4,268	4,306	52,224
1993	4,503	4,503	4,454	4,328	4,555	4,351	4,522	4,504	4,367	4,652	4,218	4,514	53,103
1994	3,970	3,858	3,957	4,099	4,394	4,519	4,518	4,446	4,320	4,564	4,619	4,928	54,426
1995	4,820	4,453	4,916	4,568	4,674	4,499	4,576	4,688	4,727	4,687	4,738	4,762	56,115
1996	4,811	4,476	4,813	4,430	4,556	4,578	4,524	4,498	4,404	4,443	4,307	4,523	54,485
1997	4,489	4,243	4,713	4,440	4,690	4,452	4,420	4,443	4,605	4,662	4,717	4,861	54,680
1998	4,955	4,433	4,881	4,600	4,731	4,299	4,418	4,502	4,170	4,212	3,837	4,119	53,174
1999	4,140	3,802	4,257	4,157	4,352	4,045	4,204	4,280	4,167	4,572	4,447	4,722	51,145
2000	4,571	4,325	4,793	4,741	4,887	4,577	4,454	4,387	4,262	4,138	3,675	3,781	52,591
2001[1]	3,808	3,691	4,255	4,183	4,278	4,143	4,048	4,121	3,920	3,837	3,837	2,965	47,086

[1] Preliminary. *Source: American Iron and Steel Institute*

Salient Statistics of Ferrous Scrap and Pig Iron in the United States — In Thousands of Metric Tons

	Consumption: Ferrous Scrap & Pig Iron Charged To												Stocks -- Dec. 31 Ferrous Scrap & Pig Iron at Consumers		
	Mfg. of Pig Iron & Steel Ingots & Castings			Iron Foundries & Misc. Users			Mfg. of Steel Castings	All Uses							
Year	Scrap	Pig Iron	Total	Scrap	Pig Iron	Total	(Scrap)	Ferrous Scrap	Pig Iron	Grand Total	Imports of Scrap[2]	Exports of Scrap[3]	Scrap	Pig Iron	Total Stocks
1991	48,778	44,095	92,873	11,126	656	11,782	1,609	61,513	44,765	106,278	1,073	9,502	4,072	190	4,262
1992	50,144	47,263	97,407	11,444	619	12,063	1,640	63,228	47,894	111,122	1,316	9,262	3,752	181	3,933
1993	53,084	48,092	101,176	12,658	676	13,334	1,900	68,000	48,777	116,777	1,390	9,805	3,725	220	3,945
1994	53,801	50,257	104,057	14,000	1,000	15,000	2,000	70,000	51,000	121,000	1,740	8,813	4,100	400	4,500
1995	56,000	51,000	107,000	13,000	1,100	14,100	2,000	72,000	52,000	124,000	2,090	10,400	4,200	620	4,820
1996	56,000	50,000	106,000	13,000	1,100	14,100	2,700	72,000	52,000	124,000	2,600	8,440	5,200	600	5,800
1997	58,000	51,000	109,000	13,000	1,200	14,200	1,800	73,000	52,000	125,000	2,870	8,930	5,500	510	6,010
1998	58,000	49,000	107,000	13,000	1,200	14,200	2,000	73,000	50,000	123,000	3,060	5,570	5,200	560	5,760
1999	56,000	48,000	104,000	13,000	1,100	14,100	1,900	71,000	49,000	120,000	3,670	5,520	5,500	720	6,220
2000[1]	59,000	49,000	108,000	13,000	1,200	14,200	2,200	74,000	50,000	124,000	3,350	5,760	5,300	800	6,100

[1] Preliminary. [2] Includes tinplate and terneplate. [3] Excludes used rails for rerolling and other uses and ships, boats, and other vessels for scrapping. *Source: U.S. Geological Survey (USGS)*

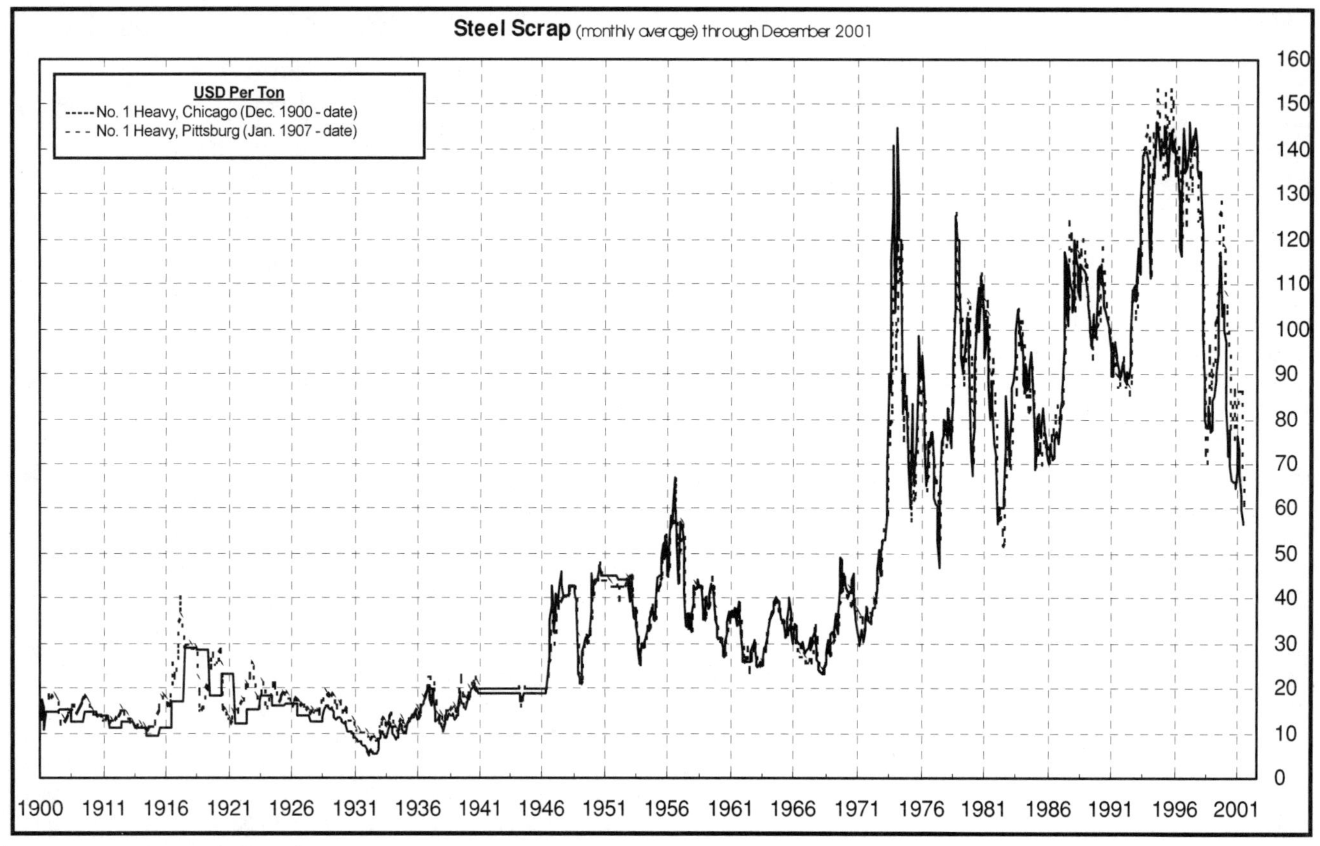

Consumption of Pig Iron in the U.S., by Type of Furnace or Equipment In Thousands of Metric Tons

Year	Open Hearth	Electric	Cupola	Basic Oxygen Process	Air & Other Furnace	Direct Casting	Total
1991	997	574	265	42,955	13	106	44,910
1992	----	429	215	47,194	7	49	47,894
1993	----	519	292	47,848	34	84	48,777
1994	----	1,700	520	49,138	4	39	51,401
1995	----	1,700	500	50,000	W	72	52,272
1996	----	2,200	530	49,000	W	42	52,000
1997	----	2,400	400	50,000	W	41	52,000
1998	----	4,000	590	46,000	W	36	50,000
1999[1]	----	3,100	520	45,000	W	W	49,000
2000[2]	----	2,900	530	47,000	W	W	50,000

[1] Preliminary. [2] Estimate. W = Withheld. *Source: U.S. Geological Survey (USGS)*

Wholesale Price of No. 1 Heavy Melting Steel Scrap in Chicago In Dollars Per Metric Ton

Year	Jan.	Feb.	Mar.	Apr.	May	June	July	Aug.	Sept.	Oct.	Nov.	Dec.	Average
1992	90.50	90.50	90.50	90.50	89.70	87.68	87.50	87.55	88.50	85.50	85.50	88.36	88.52
1993	98.34	109.50	109.50	106.50	106.50	111.27	118.50	114.18	113.50	125.88	131.50	138.00	115.26
1994	138.00	138.00	138.00	138.00	123.64	110.50	117.20	133.63	134.50	132.50	137.50	141.50	131.91
1995	152.05	147.50	140.20	141.50	144.50	141.64	141.50	149.76	144.90	141.50	136.50	136.50	143.17
1996	143.41	144.50	139.50	139.50	142.50	139.50	134.50	136.95	140.35	130.89	120.76	120.50	136.07
1997	131.14	143.50	139.70	132.59	136.50	136.50	143.50	146.50	139.60	139.63	142.50	142.50	139.51
1998	144.29	140.39	135.50	133.50	135.30	135.50	131.50	120.88	107.79	85.64	78.71	76.68	118.81
1999	89.66	101.50	90.89	90.50	100.00	104.32	100.98	105.95	106.50	106.50	113.40	120.17	102.49
2000	120.50	111.10	110.50	108.15	101.50	94.59	92.50	92.50	92.50	82.59	72.80	74.20	96.07
2001	83.55	74.50	74.50	74.50	73.23	72.50	75.93	76.50	76.50	72.54	67.50	67.50	74.17

Source: American Metal Market (AMM)

World Production of Iron Ore[3] In Thousands of Metric Tons (Gross Weight)

Year	Australia	Brazil	Canada	China	India	Maur-itania	Russia[4]	South Africa	Sweden	Ukraine[4]	United States	Vene-zuela	World Total
1991	117,134	151,500	39,307	176,070	56,880	10,246	199,000	29,075	19,328	----	56,761	21,296	955,618
1992	112,101	146,447	33,167	197,600	54,870	8,202	82,100	28,226	19,277	75,700	55,593	18,070	924,993
1993	120,534	150,000	31,830	234,660	57,375	9,360	76,100	29,385	18,728	65,500	55,676	16,871	953,316
1994	128,493	177,331	37,703	240,200	60,473	11,440	73,300	30,489	19,663	51,300	58,454	18,318	991,858
1995	142,936	183,839	38,560	249,350	65,173	11,610	78,300	31,946	19,058	50,400	62,501	18,955	1,034,539
1996	147,100	174,157	34,400	249,550	66,657	11,360	72,100	30,830	21,020	47,600	62,083	18,480	1,018,436
1997	157,766	184,970	37,277	268,000	69,453	11,700	70,900	33,225	21,893	53,000	62,971	18,503	1,068,727
1998	155,731	197,500	37,808	246,900	72,532	11,400	72,343	32,948	20,930	50,758	62,931	16,553	1,050,688
1999[1]	154,268	194,000	33,900	237,000	70,220	11,500	81,311	29,508	18,558	47,769	57,749	14,051	1,019,051
2000[2]	167,935	195,000	35,207	224,000	75,000	11,500	86,630	33,707	20,560	55,883	63,089	17,353	1,061,148

[1] Preliminary. [2] Estimate. [3] Iron ore, iron ore concentrates and iron ore agglomerates. [4] Formerly part of the U.S.S.R.; data not reported separately until 1992. *Source: U.S. Geological Survey (USGS)*

Salient Statistics of Iron Ore[3] in the United States In Thousands of Metric Tons

Year	Net Import Reliance as a % of Apparent Con-sumption	Production: Total	Production: Lake Superior	Production: Other Regions	Ship-ments	Value Million $ (at Mine)	Average Value $ at Mine Per Ton	Stocks -- Dec. 31: Mines	Stocks -- Dec. 31: Con suming Plants	Stocks -- Dec. 31: Lake Erie Docks	Imports	Exports	Con-sumption	Value Million $ Imports
1991	11	56,096	55,079	1,017	56,775	1,900.0	33.40	4,850	17,612	2,981	13,335	4,045	66,366	436.8
1992	12	55,593	55,018	575	55,600	1,550.0	27.90	3,780	16,100	2,980	12,500	5,060	75,100	396.0
1993	14	55,661	54,814	848	56,300	1,380.0	24.50	2,500	16,500	2,290	14,100	5,060	76,800	419.0
1994	18	58,215	57,848	367	57,600	1,410.0	24.49	2,790	16,300	2,230	17,500	4,980	80,200	499.0
1995	14	60,898	60,462	435	61,100	1,700.0	28.00	4,240	17,100	2,140	17,600	5,270	83,100	491.0
1996	14	62,132	61,748	383	62,200	1,750.0	28.07	4,650	18,800	2,260	18,400	6,260	79,600	556.0
1997	14	63,000	62,600	327	62,800	1,860.0	29.60	4,860	20,200	2,890	18,600	6,340	79,500	551.0
1998	17	62,900	62,591	327	63,200	1,970.0	31.14	6,020	20,500	4,080	16,900	6,000	78,200	517.0
1999[1]	17	57,410	57,410	NA	58,500	1,550.0	26.47	5,710	17,900	2,770	14,300	6,120	75,100	399.0
2000[2]	19				61,000	1,560.0	25.57	9,150	16,800	2,860	15,700	6,150	76,500	420.0

[1] Preliminary. [2] Estimate. [3] Usable iron ore exclusive of ore containing 5% or more manganese and includes byproduct ore. NA = Not available. *Source: U.S. Geological Survey (USGS)*

U.S. Imports (for Consumption) of Iron Ore[2] In Thousands of Metric Tons

Year	Australia	Brazil	Canada	Chile	Maur-itania	Peru	Sweden	Vene-zuela	Total
1991	----	2,481	7,299	103	459	157	51	2,763	13,335
1992	163	2,442	6,834	107	280	70	64	2,540	12,504
1993	254	2,872	7,442	68	206	1	60	3,170	14,097
1994	675	3,610	10,073	134	124	2	45	2,778	17,466
1995	570	4,810	9,050	57	317	54	47	2,500	17,600
1996	511	5,170	9,800	164	275	43	48	2,140	18,400
1997	742	4,970	10,000	228	----	252	149	2,090	18,600
1998	807	5,980	8,520	48	----	126	373	970	16,900
1999	694	5,540	6,860	69	----	63	421	327	14,300
2000[1]	755	6,090	7,990	135	----	40	250	349	15,700

[1] Preliminary. [2] Including agglomerates. *Source: U.S. Geological Survey (USGS)*

Total[1] Iron Ore Stocks in the United States, at End of Month In Thousands of Metric Tons

Year	Jan.	Feb.	Mar.	Apr.	May	June	July	Aug.	Sept.	Oct.	Nov.	Dec.
1992	24,527	23,162	20,922	20,550	21,501	22,492	23,046	21,721	22,735	23,190	23,433	22,856
1993	21,296	20,806	19,235	18,996	19,180	22,036	22,905	21,575	22,629	21,355	21,615	21,341
1994	19,013	17,816	15,950	14,880	15,251	16,592	17,864	18,931	20,554	20,760	21,552	21,339
1995	20,316	19,361	18,193	18,293	19,371	20,905	22,336	23,632	23,414	24,389	24,123	23,576
1996	22,277	20,744	19,779	20,104	23,426	21,822	22,445	23,663	24,116	24,866	25,465	25,701
1997	25,913	25,262	24,745	24,812	25,001	25,620	26,076	26,971	27,562	28,029	28,053	27,912
1998	27,977	26,317	24,039	25,251	25,576	26,197	27,605	29,037	30,301	30,095	30,199	30,624
1999	29,631	28,463	28,614	28,292	29,151	29,021	28,857	27,840	26,506	25,528	25,290	26,371
2000	24,885	24,810	23,556	23,714	24,032	24,613	24,993	26,278	26,815	27,530	27,987	28,779
2001[2]	27,583	26,059	24,553	24,425	23,528	21,683	20,722	20,142	20,065	19,689	18,691	

[1] All stocks at mines, furnace yards and at U.S. docks. [2] Preliminary. *Source: U.S. Geological Survey (USGS)*

Lard

Lard production is directly related to commercial hog production. The largest producers of hogs are the largest producers of lard. China is by far the largest producer of hogs with about 40 percent of world production. China's production of lard is nearly 3 million metric tonnes. The U.S. is the next largest producer followed by Germany. Other large producers include Russia, Poland, Spain and Brazil.

The Bureau of the Census reported that U.S. stocks of lard on January 1, 2001 were 27 million pounds, down 4 percent from the previous season. U.S. lard production was estimated at 1.06 billion pounds, down 4 percent from 1999. There are small imports of lard. The total supply of lard in 2000 was estimated to be 1.09 billion pounds, down 4 percent from the previous year.

In terms of usage, domestic use of lard in 2000 was estimated at 895 million pounds, down 6 percent from 1999. Lard finds use in baking and frying fats. The emphasis on healthier diets, which are much lower in fats, could limit the use of lard in certain foods. U.S. exports of lard in 2000 were 174 million pounds, an increase of 18 percent from the previous year. Exports of lard appear to be increasing. Use of lard, domestic use plus exports, in 2000 was 1.07 billion pounds, down 3 percent from the previous year.

Despite the trend toward consumption of healthier foods, per capita use of lard is not changing very much. For 2000, per capita use of lard was estimated to be 2.3 pounds. That was a decline of 8 percent from the previous year but the same level of use as seen in 1996 and 1997.

World Production of Lard In Thousands of Metric Tons

Year	Brazil	Canada	China	France	Germany	Italy	Japan	Poland	Romania	Spain	United States	Former USSR	World Total
1991-2	165.7	76.9	1,698.4	135.5	411.3	188.0	85.0	303.3	126.8	170.6	447.7	653.6	5,505.3
1992-3	175.5	77.0	1,767.6	142.9	418.2	192.1	85.8	283.6	119.6	185.8	445.0	534.1	5,487.7
1993-4	165.8	83.2	1,707.0	151.3	409.5	189.5	82.4	239.1	115.7	192.8	451.0	465.0	5,390.1
1994-5	181.6	86.3	1,931.8	153.2	404.8	191.3	83.8	267.9	106.9	196.7	471.2	414.0	5,640.7
1995-6	194.3	83.0	2,136.6	154.6	405.6	198.5	76.3	284.9	105.1	206.5	449.3	385.0	5,860.4
1996-7	199.4	83.1	2,400.2	157.3	396.5	197.6	74.1	259.4	96.3	211.8	437.0	359.3	6,048.8
1997-8[1]	210.8	88.1	2,624.8	162.3	413.4	194.0	67.9	266.6	87.4	229.9	478.9	332.6	6,358.6
1998-9[2]	224.0	97.4	2,728.3	169.0	454.1	202.8	66.4	270.9	80.8	260.6	501.7	308.8	6,596.2
1999-00[3]	236.2	105.1	2,823.8	164.6	436.2	197.6	65.0	264.9	81.5	260.1	490.3	303.9	6,675.7

[1] Preliminary. [2] Estimate. [3] Forecast. *Source: The Oil World*

Supply and Distribution of Lard in the United States In Millions of Pounds

	Supply			Disappearance						
Year	Production	Stocks Oct. 1	Total Supply	Domestic	Baking & Frying Fats	Margarine[2]	Exports	Total Disappearance	Direct Use	Per Capita (Lbs.)
1992-3	1,011.2	27.2	1,041.5	886.1	274.0	30.0	129.2	1,015.3	438.6	3.5
1993-4	1,014.7	26.2	1,043.6	890.4	251.0	39.0	118.8	1,009.2	573.0	3.4
1994-5	1,052.4	34.4	1,089.0	924.4	332.2	43.0	140.4	1,064.7	561.9	3.4
1995-6	1,012.6	24.3	1,038.8	921.8	295.9	33.0	94.3	1,016.1	593.0	3.5
1996-7	979.0	22.7	1,002.9	879.6	262.0	15.0	103.3	982.9	602.4	3.5
1997-8	1,064.7	19.9	1,086.7	924.6	285.0	17.0	121.8	1,046.4	623.3	3.4
1998-9	1,106.1	40.4	1,148.4	987.6	254.7	15.0	139.9	1,127.5	654.0	3.6
1999-00[1]	1,091.0	20.8	1,097.8	917.8	240.3	13.7	155.0	1,072.8	675.0	3.5
2000-1[2]	1,058.0	27.0	1,087.0	895.0		4.9	174.0	1,069.0	644.0	2.3

[1] Preliminary. [2] Forecast. [3] Includes edible tallow. NA = not avaliable. *Source: Economic Research Service, U.S. Department of Agriculture (ERS-USDA)*

Consumption of Lard (Edible and Inedible) in the United States In Millions of Pounds

Year	Jan.	Feb.	Mar.	Apr.	May	June	July	Aug.	Sept.	Oct.	Nov.	Dec.	Total
1993	40.1	34.4	45.9	36.8	38.2	38.8	32.6	38.4	41.8	44.0	43.0	40.3	474.3
1994	33.5	33.9	36.2	34.6	35.9	34.4	32.4	37.5	43.4	43.8	44.7	41.7	452.0
1995	37.5	34.7	41.2	36.2	42.2	44.4	34.9	35.9	35.9	40.1	38.9	36.8	458.7
1996	30.5	35.4	36.7	46.9	36.8	31.4	32.6	33.9	30.9	34.5	34.7	33.6	417.9
1997	26.5	30.5	31.0	36.5	39.9	36.2	36.1	35.0	37.4	39.0	41.5	40.4	429.8
1998	34.1	29.9	31.1	29.6	28.5	35.9	33.0	33.0	37.1	37.7	38.9	33.9	402.7
1999	34.6	30.2	28.8	31.1	30.5	32.9	28.9	33.0	29.2	31.2	31.3	30.3	372.1
2000	27.3	25.7	29.1	23.3	30.3	27.6	24.4	31.3	31.1	32.6	29.6	31.7	343.9
2001[1]	27.8	22.2	28.3	24.5	22.5	23.3	21.8	27.1	23.2	27.9	26.7	24.4	299.8

[1] Preliminary. *Source: Bureau of the Census, U.S. Department of Commerce*

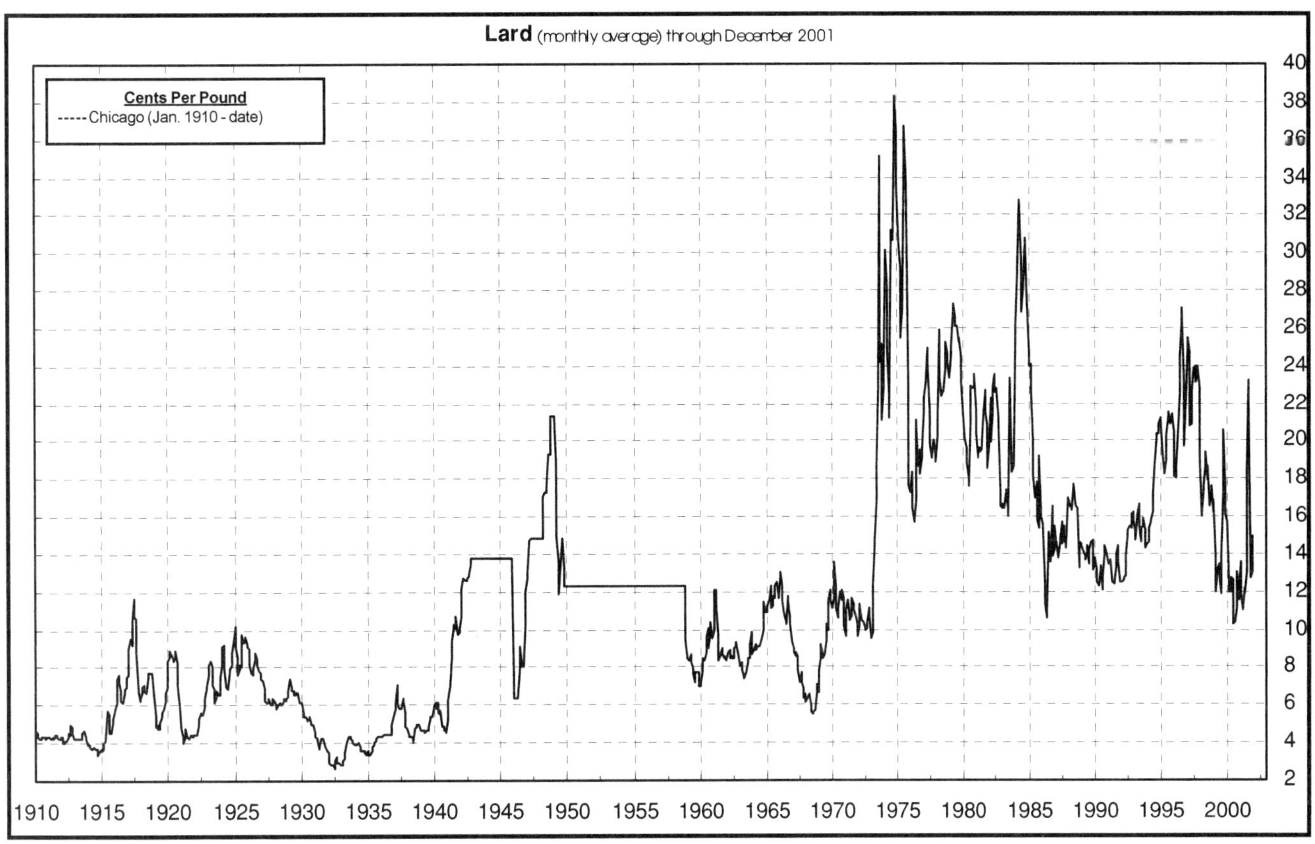

Average Wholesale Price of Lard, Loose, Tank Cars, in Chicago In Cents Per Pound

Year	Jan.	Feb.	Mar.	Apr.	May	June	July	Aug.	Sept.	Oct.	Nov.	Dec.	Average
1992	12.50	12.50	12.57	12.75	12.78	13.93	14.95	15.29	15.49	15.40	16.11	16.25	14.21
1993	15.83	15.03	14.70	16.15	16.67	15.50	14.64	15.42	15.50	15.93	15.26	14.31	15.41
1994	14.50	14.62	15.35	15.74	15.75	16.25	17.24	18.91	20.14	20.39	20.35	20.91	17.51
1995	21.21	21.13	19.25	18.34	18.25	19.02	20.25	21.30	21.48	20.90	21.38	21.35	20.32
1996	20.52	18.17	18.01	18.67	20.47	22.61	24.55	26.30	27.09	23.11	19.70	22.17	21.78
1997	24.93	25.47	24.69	20.82	20.94	22.68	23.83	23.95	23.14	23.41	23.97	22.85	23.39
1998	19.09	16.03	17.36	17.64	18.66	19.38	17.93	18.65	16.58	17.39	17.60	16.27	17.72
1999	16.89	13.91	11.98	13.12	13.43	12.98	11.87	13.89	17.44	20.55	17.74	16.12	14.99
2000	15.66	12.38	11.99	11.96	12.68	12.64	10.32	10.35	11.14	13.01	11.55	12.16	12.15
2001	13.60	11.90	11.00	12.15	11.84	13.00	18.44	23.20	22.12	12.77	13.06	14.94	14.84

Source: The Wall Street Journal

United States Cold Storage Holdings of all Lard[1], on First of Month In Millions of Pounds

Year	Jan.	Feb.	Mar.	Apr.	May	June	July	Aug.	Sept.	Oct.	Nov.	Dec.
1992	37.4	27.2	28.9	28.3	26.7	23.2	24.8	29.2	26.9	27.2	22.2	24.8
1993	22.7	25.9	27.2	24.0	22.8	25.8	31.1	27.4	23.6	26.2	24.6	30.1
1994	37.7	38.0	31.8	28.8	25.1	27.4	27.0	25.5	29.7	34.4	34.0	35.8
1995	40.6	50.3	46.4	43.0	36.8	27.1	25.8	22.1	30.2	24.3	19.9	21.6
1996	38.4	38.6	25.8	28.8	21.5	23.2	23.7	30.5	20.7	22.7	20.1	18.8
1997	18.9	16.3	18.5	19.2	18.9	18.7	23.0	23.2	21.5	19.9	21.3	19.7
1998	22.2	30.1	38.3	42.5	41.6	47.6	43.7	44.8	38.8	40.4	34.8	26.3
1999	28.4	30.4	30.6	34.0	27.1	39.9	30.7	25.5	29.4	20.8	19.1	22.8
2000	26.7	27.8	29.2	30.1	20.2	22.5	18.9	19.3	17.3	17.4	16.3	16.8
2001[2]	16.0	14.9	14.9	17.9	13.7	13.1	10.3	12.4	11.8	13.6	13.0	11.7

[1] Stocks in factories and warehouses (except that in hands of retailers). [2] Preliminary. *Source: Bureau of the Census, U.S. Department of Commerce*

Lead

Lead is used in a variety of products including batteries, fuel tanks, coverings for power and communications cables, cans and containers, solder for pipes and plumbing, as well as construction materials. By far the largest use of lead is in lead-acid batteries, which in the U.S. consume the overwhelming portion of the lead that is used. Lead and compounds that contain lead are very toxic and there has been an effort to reduce the use of lead. Some of the substitutes for lead include tin, iron, plastic and bismuth.

The U.S. Geological Survey reported that world mine production of lead in 2000 was 2.98 million metric tonnes, down 1 percent from 1999. The largest producer of lead was Australia with 2000 output of 630,000 tonnes, down 7 percent from the year before. Lead production by China was 560,000 tonnes, up 12 percent from 1999. U.S. production of lead was 480,000 tonnes, down 8 percent from a year earlier. In the U.S., there are seven lead mines in Missouri and lead-producing mines in Alaska, Idaho and Montana. Lead was consumed by about 150 manufacturing plants. Primary lead was processed at two smelter-refineries in Missouri and at a smelter in Montana. There were 27 plants that produced secondary lead. The transportation industries consume about 76 percent of the lead for batteries, fuel tanks, solder, wheel weights and bearings. Electrical, electronic and communications uses take about 22 percent of the lead. Other uses include ceramics, wire, foils and chemicals.

U.S. mine production (recoverable) of lead in July 2001 was 34,800 tonnes compared to 32,200 tonnes in June. In the first seven months of 2001, mine production was 258,000 tonnes. In 2000, production was 447,000 tonnes. Data on primary refinery production of lead in 2001 was not available but for all of 2000 it was 341,000 tonnes. Secondary refinery production of lead in July 2001 was 90,400 tonnes. Some 1,250 tonnes was recovered from copper-base scrap. In the January-July period, secondary production of lead was 638,000 tonnes. For all of 2000, secondary production was 1.11 million tonnes.

U.S. reported consumption of lead in July 2001 was 123,000 tonnes, down 1 percent from the previous month. In the January-July 2001 period, consumption was 896,000 tonnes while for all of 2000 it was 1.56 million tonnes. In the first seven months of 2001, lead consumed in producing ammunition, shot and bullets totaled 24,300 tonnes. Lead used in brass and bronze, billet and ingots was 2,140 tonnes. Lead used for cable covering, power and communications, calking lead and building construction was 2,440 tonnes. Lead used in casting metals was 4,190 tonnes while lead used for solder was 980 tonnes. Lead used in storage batteries was 813,000 tonnes in January-July 2001.

U.S. exports of lead ore and concentrates in January-June 2001 were 30,800 tonnes. Exports of bullion in the same period were 3,140 tonnes while exports of lead materials excluding scrap were 19,500 tonnes.

World Smelter (Primary and Secondary) Production of Lead In Thousands of Metric Tons

Year	Australia[3]	Belgium[4]	Canada[3]	China[2]	France	Germany	Italy	Japan	Mexico[3]	Spain	United Kingdom[3]	United States	World Total
1991	239.4	110.7	212.4	330.0	438.0	362.5	208.2	332.4	161.8	169.0	311.0	1,230	5,770
1992	232.0	116.3	252.9	365.0	284.1	354.3	186.3	330.2	177.0	120.0	346.8	1,220	5,230
1993	243.0	131.1	217.0	412.0	258.7	334.2	182.8	309.5	188.0	123.0	363.8	1,230	5,420
1994	237.0	123.5	251.6	467.9	260.5	331.7	205.9	292.2	171.0	140.0	352.5	1,280	5,360
1995	241.0	122.0	281.4	608.0	296.7	311.2	180.4	287.6	176.0	80.0	320.7	1,390	5,590
1996	228.0	125.0	309.4	706.0	302.8	238.1	209.8	287.4	160.0	86.0	345.6	1,400	5,630
1997	238.0	110.8	271.4	707.0	302.3	329.2	211.6	296.8	178.0	74.9	391.0	1,450	5,880
1998	206.0	91.5	265.5	757.0	318.0	380.2	199.3	302.1	173.0	90.0	348.9	1,450	5,940
1999[1]	272.8	103.2	262.9	918.0	279.0	373.6	215.3	293.4	121.0	96.0	348.1	1,460	6,130
2000[2]	251.8	118.0	282.9	1,030.0	258.0	415.0	235.0	312.1	160.0	120.0	337.2	1,470	6,460

[1] Preliminary. [2] Estimate. [3] Refinded & bullion. [4] Includes scrap. *Source: U.S. Geological Survey (USGS)*

Consumption of Lead in the United States, by Products In Metric Tons

											--- Storage Battery ---			
Year	Ammunition	Bearing Metals	Pipes, Traps & Bends[2]	Cable Covering	Calking Lead	Casting Metals	Other Metal Products[3]	Total Other Oxides[4]	Sheet Lead	Solder	Grids, Post, etc.	Oxides	Brass and Bronze	Total Consumption
1991	58,458	3,669	8,975	17,472	1,074	14,141	3,254	59,617	22,334	14,750	591,884	415,233	8,997	1,246,337
1992	64,845	4,785	11,652	15,992	1,045	17,111	3,024	63,225	21,006	13,518	629,147	373,185	9,175	1,236,571
1993	65,100	4,830	5,740	17,165	961	18,500	5,360	63,600	21,200	14,400	677,000	374,000	5,750	1,290,000
1994	62,400	5,560	3,370	16,000	764	18,900	5,330	62,700	21,500	12,200	797,000	425,000	6,320	1,450,000
1995	70,900	6,490	2,210	5,640	935	18,100	5,220	61,700	27,900	16,200	711,000	618,000	5,260	1,560,000
1996	52,100	4,350	1,810	W	767	18,900	5,220	62,100	19,400	9,020	635,000	706,000	5,460	1,540,000
1997	52,400	2,490	1,860	4,930	1,390	34,000	7,570	67,000	19,100	9,580	634,000	761,000	4,410	1,620,000
1998	52,800	2,210	3,130	4,630	1,350	32,600	8,160	53,400	15,500	10,900	685,000	742,000	3,460	1,630,000
1999	58,300	1,570	2,020	2,410	971	34,300	7,130	58,200	15,400	13,100	765,000	707,000	3,940	1,680,000
2000[1]	63,500	1,480	2,010	W	1,140	35,100	21,700	52,400	23,800	11,500	796,000	690,000	3,670	1,720,000

[1] Preliminary. [2] Including building. [3] Including terne metal, type metal, and lead consumerd in foil, collapsible tubes, annealing, plating, galvanizing and fishing weights. [4] Includes paints, glass and ceramic products, and other pigments and chemicals. W = Withheld proprietary data.
Source: U.S. Geological Survey (USGS)

Salient Statistics of Lead in the United States In Thousands of Metric Tons

Year	Net Import Reliance as a % of Apparent Consumption	Production of Refined Lead From: Domestic Ores[3]	Foreign Ores[8]	Total Primary	Total Value of Refined Million $	Secondary Lead Recovered: As Soft Lead	In Antimonial Lead	In Other Alloys	Total	Total Value of Secondary Million $	Stocks, Dec. 31: Primary	Consumer[4]	Average Price Cents Per Pound: New York	London[5]
1991	6	323.9	21.9	345.7	255.2	421.9	426.9	35.8	884.6	652.9	9.1	71.7	33.48	25.30
1992	10	284.0	20.8	304.8	235.9	452.9	424.5	23.1	916.3	709.1	20.5	82.3	35.10	34.50
1993	15	310.7	24.9	335.6	234.4	444.0	417.0	17.9	893.0	625.0	14.3	80.5	31.74	18.42
1994	19	328.0	23.4	351.4	288.0	527.0	371.0	16.1	931.0	763.0	9.3	68.8	37.17	24.83
1995	17	374.0	W	374.0	348.0	584.0	400.0	19.2	1,020.0	951.0	14.2	79.4	42.28	28.08
1996	17	326.0	W	326.0	351.0	625.0	420.0	9.2	1,070.0	1,150.0	8.1	72.1	48.83	31.22
1997	14	343.0	W	343.0	352.0	663.0	411.0	14.2	1,110.0	1,130.0	11.9	89.1	46.54	28.29
1998	21	337.0	W	337.0	336.0	667.0	417.0	16.1	1,120.0	1,110.0	10.9	77.9	45.27	23.96
1999[1]	20	350.0	W	350.0	337.0	635.0	444.0	18.1	1,110.0	1,070.0	12.3	78.7	43.72	22.78
2000[2]	24	341.0	W	341.0	328.0	651.0	428.0	36.8	1,130.0	1,090.0	18.6	104.0	43.57	20.57

[1] Preliminary. [2] Estimate. [3] And base bullion. [4] Also at secondary smelters. [5] LME data in dollars per metric ton beginning July 1993.
W = Withheld Proprietary data. E = Net exporter. *Source: U.S. Geological Survey (USGS)*

United States Foreign Trade of Lead In Thousands of Metric Tons

Year	Exports: Ore Concentrate	Unwrought Lead[3]	Wrought Lead[4]	Scrap	Ash & Residues	Imports for Consumption: Ores, Flue Dust or Fume & Mattes	Base Bullion	Pigs & Bars	Reclaimed Scrap, etc.	Value Million $	General Imports From: Ore, Flue Dust & Matte: Australia	Canada	Peru	Pigs & Bars: Canada	Mexico	Peru
1991	88.0	94.4	7.6	72.0	11.0	12.4	0.4	116.5	0.1	82.6	1.0	226.7	3.9	83.6	11.9	0.5
1992	72.3	64.3	5.3	63.2	2.1	5.3	0.2	190.7	0.2	120.6	----	239.9	21.2	124.7	56.1	9.8
1993	41.8	51.4	7.1	54.1	1.7	0.5	----	195.6	0.1	99.4	----	55.7	13.6	130.8	40.3	18.3
1994	38.7	48.2	5.3	88.1	20.6	0.5	0.6	230.8	0.1	146.6	0.5	0.2	----	159.0	31.9	25.6
1995	65.5	48.2	9.0	105.0	8.0	2.6	0.0	264.0	0.1	191.7	1.5	----	0.1	182.0	54.3	22.1
1996	59.7	44.0	16.7	85.3	19.4	6.6	0.0	268.0	0.2	217.0	----	4.4	----	192.0	56.9	17.1
1997	42.2	37.4	15.9	88.4	16.8	17.8	0.0	265.0	0.1	200.3	----	0.8	3.4	186.0	70.4	6.4
1998	72.4	24.1	15.4	99.2	9.0	32.7	0.5	267.0	[6]	191.9	2.4	6.5	18.5	181.0	63.6	11.4
1999[1]	93.5	23.4	13.9	117.0	1.4	12.3	0.1	311.0	----	196.5	0.1	1.2	8.8	198.0	27.2	6.9
2000[2]	117.0	21.4	27.2	71.6	11.3	31.2	0.1	356.0	0.0	217.2	----	[6]	10.8	216.0	18.4	1.8

[1] Preliminary. [2] Estimate. [3] And lead alloys. [4] Blocks, pigs, etc. [5] Formerly drosses & flue dust. [6] Less than 1/2 unit. NA = Not avaliable.
Source: U.S. Geological Survey (USGS)

Annual Mine Production of Recoverable Lead in the United States In Metric Tons

Year	Total	Idaho	Missouri	Montana	Other States	Missouri's % of Total
1991	465,931	W	351,995	W	113,936	76%
1992	397,923	W	300,589	W	97,334	76%
1993	353,607	W	276,569	W	77,800	78%
1994	363,443	W	290,738	9,940	63,100	80%
1995	386,000	W	359,000	8,350	18,200	93%
1996	426,000	W	397,000	7,970	21,200	93%
1997	448,000	W	412,000	9,230	26,600	92%
1998	481,000	W	439,000	7,310	35,100	91%
1999[1]	503,000	W	464,000	7,950	31,200	92%
2000[2]	457,000	W	416,000	W	41,000	91%

[1] Preliminary. [2] Estimate. W = Withheld, included in Other States. NA = Not Avaliable. *Source: U.S. Geological Survey (USGS)*

Mine Production of Recoverable Lead in the United States In Thousands of Metric Tons

Year	Jan.	Feb.	Mar.	Apr.	May	June	July	Aug.	Sept.	Oct.	Nov.	Dec.	Total
1992	36.0	34.0	34.0	31.2	31.5	32.4	33.8	32.5	32.5	33.3	30.8	31.7	392.7
1993	33.3	30.5	34.2	30.6	28.5	29.5	25.8	27.5	28.4	27.3	29.5	28.5	355.2
1994	27.6	28.8	33.0	31.3	32.4	29.1	29.4	30.4	31.2	28.0	31.7	29.9	363.4
1995	29.6	30.3	35.2	28.9	32.7	34.8	32.5	33.5	29.9	34.1	31.6	32.1	385.0
1996	36.9	36.4	35.6	35.9	37.5	33.8	35.6	34.1	26.9	35.2	33.6	35.7	426.0
1997	36.7	36.7	37.2	38.6	38.6	35.1	33.4	33.7	34.4	35.4	31.7	32.8	448.0
1998	37.4	35.4	37.8	37.3	35.7	34.7	34.3	35.6	36.1	40.3	37.8	39.2	449.0
1999	41.2	42.1	44.4	43.1	41.7	42.6	47.2	43.6	41.5	41.2	37.8	38.1	505.0
2000	35.1	36.7	43.0	37.5	37.4	37.8	33.0	36.8	36.8	32.4	38.8	36.9	447.0
2001[1]	39.0	37.8	39.4	33.7	35.0	32.2	38.2	39.6	32.4	39.2			439.8

[1] Preliminary. *Source: U.S. Geological Survey (USGS)*

LEAD

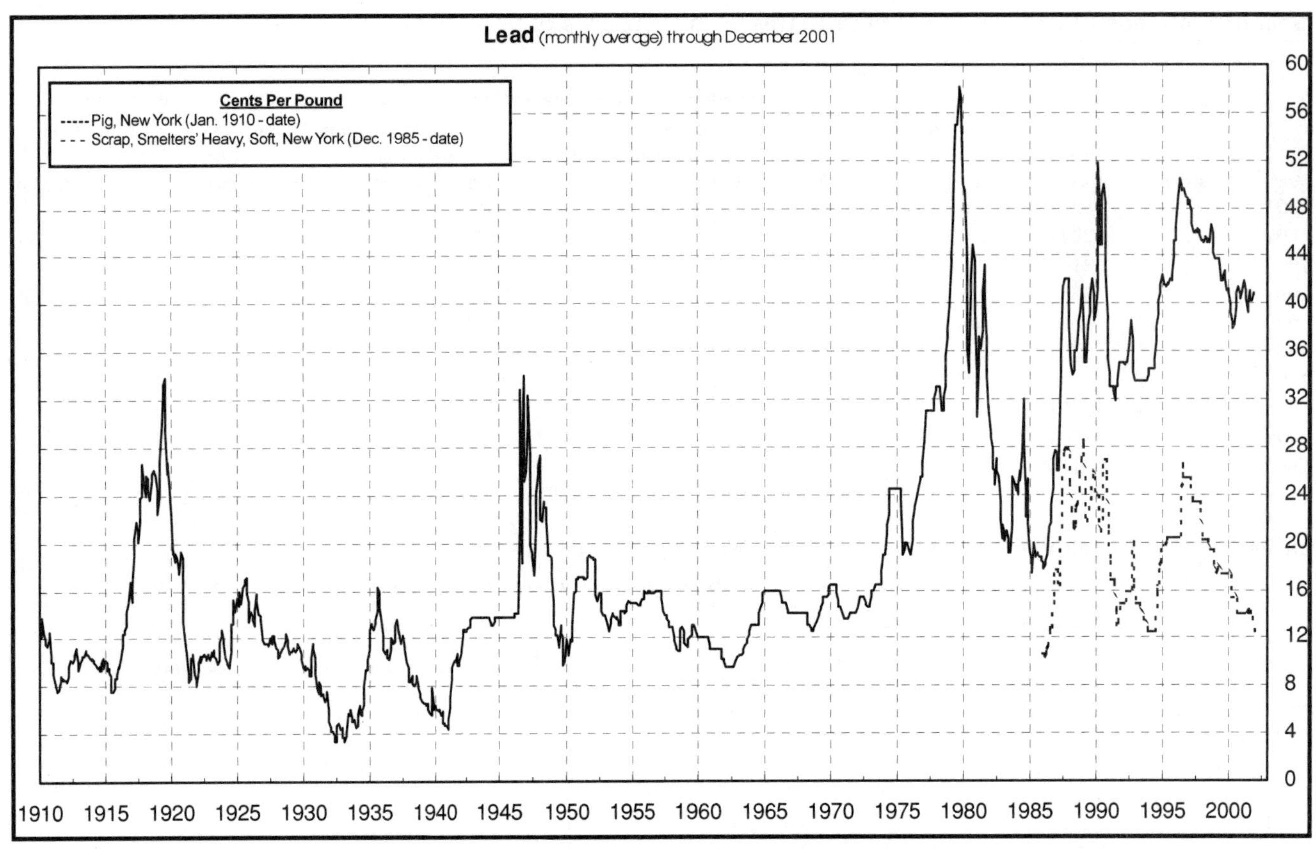

Average Price of Pig Lead, U.S. Primary Producers (Common Corroding)[1] In Cents Per Pound

Year	Jan.	Feb.	Mar.	Apr.	May	June	July	Aug.	Sept.	Oct.	Nov.	Dec.	Average
1992	35.00	35.00	35.00	35.00	35.00	35.00	36.91	40.00	40.00	36.64	32.63	32.00	35.68
1993	32.00	32.00	32.00	32.00	32.00	32.00	32.00	32.00	32.00	32.00	32.00	33.00	32.08
1994	34.00	34.00	34.00	34.00	34.00	35.73	37.70	38.00	40.00	42.00	43.70	44.00	37.59
1995	44.00	44.00	42.00	42.00	42.00	42.00	42.00	43.65	44.00	44.00	46.10	48.00	43.65
1996	48.00	49.50	50.96	52.00	52.00	52.00	50.29	49.18	50.00	50.00	50.00	50.00	50.33
1997	50.00	50.00	48.70	48.00	48.00	48.00	48.00	48.00	48.00	48.00	48.00	48.00	48.39
1998	48.00	48.00	48.00	48.00	48.00	48.00	48.00	48.00	48.00	48.00	45.47	45.00	47.54
1999	45.00	45.00	45.00	45.00	45.00	45.00	45.00	45.00	45.00	45.00	45.00	45.00	45.00
2000	45.00	45.00	45.00	45.00	45.00	45.00	45.00	45.00	45.00	45.00	45.00	45.00	45.00
2001	45.00	45.00	45.00	45.00	45.00	45.00	45.00	45.00	45.00	45.00	45.00	45.00	45.00

[1] New York Delivery. Source: American Metal Market (AMM)

Refiners Production[1] of Lead in the United States In Metric Tons

Year	Jan.	Feb.	Mar.	Apr.	May	June	July	Aug.	Sept.	Oct.	Nov.	Dec.	Total
1992	29,121	27,691	33,366	27,456	26,742	22,441	24,993	21,587	19,365	22,945	23,674	25,414	304,791
1993	29,627	26,693	30,197	27,578	29,814	28,253	16,734	22,817	32,725	31,220	27,953	31,312	335,014
1994	29,908	30,685	31,420	29,059	31,588	31,707	30,661	27,335	31,185	32,874	29,301	30,447	366,170
1995	32,100	29,100	32,600	32,300	32,600	28,300	31,000	29,300	30,600	34,200	30,100	31,500	374,000
1996	34,700	30,400	30,900	28,600	27,500	21,700	25,500	24,700	25,400	25,300	26,100	25,500	326,000
1997	28,800	28,500	31,900	30,400	30,800	28,700	25,900	28,000	21,600	30,500	29,000	28,700	343,000
1998	29,200	25,900	30,000	29,700	29,500	20,300	28,900	NA	NA	NA	NA	NA	337,000
1999	NA	NA	NA	NA	NA	NA	NA	NA	NA	NA	NA	NA	350,000
2000	NA	NA	NA	NA	NA	NA	NA	NA	NA	NA	NA	NA	341,000
2001[2]	NA	NA	NA	NA	NA	NA	NA	NA	NA	NA	NA		

[1] Represents refined lead produced from domestic ores by primary smelters plus small amounts of secondary material passing through these smelters. Includes GSA metal purchased for remelt. [2] Preliminary. *Source: U.S. Geological Survey (USGS)*

Total Stocks of Lead[1] in the United States at Refiners, at End of Month In Metric Tons

Year	Jan.	Feb.	Mar.	Apr.	May	June	July	Aug.	Sept.	Oct.	Nov.	Dec.
1992	9,774	15,785	21,682	25,220	28,940	26,490	26,634	22,347	17,736	14,971	14,796	20,543
1993	28,069	33,338	34,058	34,306	35,775	32,162	22,753	14,797	15,086	14,408	13,456	14,289
1994	11,964	12,633	12,048	11,445	11,598	10,251	12,368	9,256	8,897	10,650	0,060	9,271
1995	8,200	9,750	11,500	14,500	16,700	16,200	21,300	14,000	12,800	9,820	9,830	14,200
1996	15,000	15,000	15,000	15,000	15,000	19,600	19,900	14,200	12,200	7,060	7,830	8,160
1997	8,460	11,800	21,400	19,900	15,000	10,900	6,530	7,790	5,370	7,310	8,710	11,900
1998	13,000	15,900	18,700	20,900	11,400	11,400	13,700	NA	NA	NA	NA	10,900
1999	NA	NA	NA	NA	NA	NA	NA	NA	NA	NA	NA	12,300
2000	NA	NA	NA	NA	NA	NA	NA	NA	NA	NA	NA	18,600
2001[2]	NA	NA	NA	NA	NA	NA	NA	NA	NA	NA		

[1] Primary refineries. [2] Preliminary. *Source: U.S. Geological Survey (USGS)*

Total[1] Lead Consumption in the United States In Thousands of Metric Tons

Year	Jan.	Feb.	Mar.	Apr.	May	June	July	Aug.	Sept.	Oct.	Nov.	Dec.	Total
1992	102.5	99.3	108.3	98.5	96.0	103.5	94.8	104.8	106.6	105.4	98.2	92.9	1,215
1993	108.9	107.5	112.3	104.6	109.2	113.8	106.8	112.6	117.1	113.2	109.3	102.2	1,357
1994	107.0	115.2	112.8	111.6	113.5	115.2	114.3	115.5	115.9	121.2	118.7	113.0	1,384
1995	119.0	119.0	119.0	109.0	110.0	113.0	115.0	105.0	115.0	116.0	118.0	116.0	1,370
1996	107.0	100.0	106.0	111.0	113.0	106.0	104.0	146.0	140.0	147.0	163.0	143.0	1,530
1997	139.0	138.0	138.0	140.0	137.0	141.0	116.0	119.0	122.0	123.0	117.0	117.0	1,600
1998	116.0	115.0	119.0	128.0	127.0	129.0	128.0	128.0	129.0	129.0	134.0	125.0	1,550
1999	128.0	129.0	130.0	127.0	128.0	130.0	137.0	136.0	141.0	136.0	140.0	133.0	1,680
2000	139.0	139.0	139.0	139.0	140.0	140.0	135.0	141.0	139.0	139.0	136.0	132.0	1,660
2001[2]	134.0	135.0	133.0	130.0	138.0	136.0	135.0	136.0	142.0	145.0			1,637

[1] Represents total consumption of primary & secondary lead as metal, in chemicals, or in alloys. [2] Preliminary. *Source: U.S. Geological Survey (USGS)*

Lead Recovered from Scrap in the United States In Thousands of Metric Tons (Lead Content)

Year	Jan.	Feb.	Mar.	Apr.	May	June	July	Aug.	Sept.	Oct.	Nov.	Dec.	Total
1992	76.1	71.5	66.5	71.0	73.3	72.3	71.1	77.7	77.5	79.6	76.9	74.3	888.5
1993	71.1	76.8	71.7	80.2	78.9	72.5	70.3	76.6	76.3	77.0	77.9	79.3	903.6
1994	74.0	76.0	84.2	81.7	81.1	79.0	78.9	79.8	78.4	76.4	81.0	80.4	949.0
1995	82.5	80.8	84.4	72.8	73.7	72.5	79.9	71.5	82.3	80.0	82.3	82.1	945.0
1996	75.7	76.2	84.2	83.7	84.7	80.7	81.2	89.0	92.1	98.8	97.3	93.2	1,100.0
1997	88.0	89.8	91.7	86.0	88.2	85.7	86.7	94.7	97.3	96.2	95.2	91.7	1,110.0
1998	95.0	92.0	92.6	94.1	92.5	89.7	89.3	95.7	94.4	95.0	95.1	90.7	1,110.0
1999	89.5	89.1	88.9	91.0	90.2	91.1	81.3	91.9	91.6	93.5	91.4	93.1	1,110.0
2000	91.0	88.0	91.1	91.4	90.5	91.3	88.6	95.1	94.0	96.0	95.4	93.7	1,110.0
2001[1]	90.3	90.4	86.7	92.6	93.7	93.6	90.4	95.1	93.9	96.7			1,108.1

[1] Preliminary. *Source: U.S. Geological Survey (USGS)*

Domestic Shipments[1] of Lead in the United States, by Refiners In Thousands of Short Tons

Year	Jan.	Feb.	Mar.	Apr.	May	June	July	Aug.	Sept.	Oct.	Nov.	Dec.	Total
1988	33.5	29.5	39.2	33.0	41.4	44.7	32.0	34.7	33.7	43.0	38.5	35.5	438.7
1989	29.3	28.5	32.2	35.7	45.1	36.4	32.8	41.5	40.0	44.2	40.2	31.1	437.1
1990	39.3	33.9	39.1	33.5	38.4	32.9	32.6	38.9	36.6	38.9	37.9	31.7	433.7
1991	35.4	33.8	34.3	39.8	33.9	26.0	31.8	37.9	35.1	35.7	28.7	26.7	399.2
1992	31.3	23.9	30.4	26.3	25.6	27.2	27.3	28.7	26.3	28.5	26.3	21.7	323.5
1993	24.6	23.6	32.5	30.0	31.3	35.1	28.9	34.0	35.5	35.5	31.7	33.5	376.2
1994	35.9	32.8	35.2	32.7	34.7	36.7	31.6	33.4	34.8	34.3	34.0	33.3	409.3
1995	36.5	30.3	35.1	31.1	33.7	31.9	28.6	40.3	34.9	40.9	33.2	29.8	406.4
1996	37.2	32.4	29.5	30.2	29.4	26.7	27.7	33.5	30.1	33.5	28.1	27.6	366.0
1997[2]	31.5	27.8	24.7	35.2	39.2	36.1	33.4	29.4	26.4	31.5	30.4	28.1	377.8

[1] Includes GSA metal. [2] Preliminary. *Source: American Metal Market (AMM)*

Lumber & Plywood

The United States Department of Agriculture reported that U.S. exports of hardwood logs in the January-September 2001 period were 1.59 million cubic meters. This was up some 8 percent from the same period in 2000. For all of 2000, hardwood log exports totaled 1.98 million cubic meters. In 1996 exports were 1.18 million cubic meters. The major export destination was Canada. In the January-September 2001 period, Canada took 1.16 million cubic meters or some 73 percent of the U.S. exports. For all of 2000, Canada took 1.42 million cubic meters of hardwood logs. The next largest market was Japan which in the January-September 2001 period took 72,156 cubic meters. While Canada's imports of U.S. logs has been trending higher, Japan has been trending lower. Other large importers include Germany and Italy.

U.S. exports of hardwood lumber in the January-September 2001 period were 1.99 million cubic meters, down 12 percent from the same period in 2000. For all of 2000, exports were 2.95 million cubic meters. The largest market for U.S. exports is Canada. In the first nine months of 2001, Canada imported 699,502 cubic meters of hardwood lumber, some 35 percent of the U.S. total. Canada's imports were down 11 percent from the same period in 2000. For all of 2000, imports were 1.03 million cubic meters. Other large importers of U.S. hardwood lumber include Hong Kong, Mexico Spain and Italy. Among the species of hardwood lumber that were exports were red oak, while oak, maple and cherry. In the January-September 2001 period, exports of red oak were 423,499 cubic meters,. Exports of white oak were 400,486 cubic meters while maple exports were 283,281 cubic meters and cherry exports were 122,902 cubic meters.

U.S. exports of hardwood plywood in the first nine months of 2001 were 106,671 cubic meters. These were down 12 percent from a year ago. Exports for all of 2000 were 160,055 cubic meters. The largest market for U.S. exports was Canada which took 61,886 cubic meters in the January-September 2001 period, up 4 percent from a year earlier. For all of 2000, Canada took 76,349 cubic meters. The next largest market was Mexico which took 23,552 cubic meters in the first nine months of 2001, down 27 percent from the year before. For all of 2000, Mexico took 44,806 cubic meters. Canada and Mexico together take about 80 percent of the hardwood plywood exports from the United States. Other markets include Japan, the Cayman Islands and Israel.

U.S. export of softwood logs in the first nine months of 2001 were 5.06 million cubic meters, down 7 percent from a year ago. For all of 2000, exports were 7.40 million cubic meters. In 1996 exports were 10.65 million cubic meters. The major market for U.S. softwood logs was Japan. In January-September 2001 they took 2.48 million cubic meters, down 18 percent from the same period in 2000. For all of 2000 Japan imported 4.12 million cubic meters. Japan's imports have been trending lower . In the first none months of 2001, Canada imported 1.95 million cubic meters of softwood logs from the U.S., up 3 percent from the year before. For all of 2000, Canada took 2.48 million cubic meters. Other major markets include the Republic of Korea, Peoples Republic of China and Taiwan.

U.S. exports of softwood lumber in the January-September 2001 period were 18.74 million cubic meters, up 13 percent from the same period on 2000. For all of 2000, exports were 13.76 million cubic meters. Canada's imports in the first nine months of 2001 were 430,440 cubic meters, down 7 percent from a year ago. For all of 2000 imports were 631,403 cubic meters. In January-September 2001, Japan's imports were 338,253 cubic meters, down 33 percent from the same period in 2000. For 2000, Japan's imports were 649,499 cubic meters. Japan's imports have been trending lower. Other large importers of softwood lumber include Mexico, the Dominican Republic and Spain. In 2000, Mexico imported 316,567 cubic meters. The Dominican Republic imported 190,422 cubic meters while Spain imported 156,983 cubic meters.

Futures Markets

Lumber futures and options are traded on the Chicago Mercantile Exchange.

U.S. Housing Starts: Seasonally Adjusted Annual Rate In Thousands of Units

Year	Jan.	Feb.	Mar.	Apr.	May	June	July	Aug.	Sept.	Oct.	Nov.	Dec.	Average
1992	1,176	1,250	1,297	1,099	1,214	1,145	1,139	1,226	1,186	1,244	1,214	1,227	1,201
1993	1,210	1,210	1,083	1,258	1,260	1,280	1,254	1,300	1,343	1,392	1,376	1,533	1,292
1994	1,272	1,337	1,564	1,465	1,526	1,409	1,439	1,450	1,474	1,450	1,511	1,455	1,446
1995	1,407	1,316	1,249	1,267	1,314	1,281	1,461	1,416	1,369	1,369	1,452	1,431	1,354
1996	1,467	1,491	1,424	1,516	1,504	1,467	1,472	1,557	1,475	1,392	1,489	1,370	1,477
1997	1,355	1,486	1,457	1,492	1,442	1,494	1,437	1,390	1,546	1,520	1,510	1,566	1,474
1998	1,525	1,584	1,567	1,540	1,536	1,641	1,698	1,614	1,582	1,715	1,660	1,792	1,621
1999	1,804	1,738	1,737	1,561	1,649	1,562	1,704	1,657	1,628	1,636	1,663	1,769	1,676
2000	1,744	1,822	1,630	1,626	1,573	1,560	1,477	1,531	1,508	1,527	1,559	1,532	1,591
2001[1]	1,666	1,623	1,592	1,626	1,610	1,634	1,660	1,559	1,585	1,518	1,616	1,579	1,606

[1] Preliminary. Total Privately owned. Source: American Forest & Paper Association (AF&PA)

World Production of Industrial Roundwood by Selected Countries In Thousands of Cubic Meters

Year	Austria	Canada	Czech[3] Repulic	Finland	France	Germany	Japan	Poland	Russia[4]	Spain	Sweden	Turkey	United States
1991	12,535	159,039	13,770	31,616	33,754	29,823	27,938	14,334	275,300	12,988	47,600	5,502	388,310
1992	9,255	165,436	8,820	35,279	32,596	29,159	26,934	15,720	164,000	11,624	49,720	8,158	403,100
1993	9,107	169,770	9,706	37,758	29,563	29,357	25,570	15,940	136,030	11,419	50,200	9,408	401,520
1994	11,101	177,346	11,172	44,319	32,442	36,018	24,456	16,711	83,650	12,990	52,100	9,211	410,781
1995	10,746	183,113	11,716	45,799	33,561	36,914	22,897	17,677	83,050	12,997	59,800	10,745	408,948
1996	11,212	183,113	11,882	42,178	30,643	34,538	22,897	18,853	73,005	12,433	52,500	10,229	406,625
1997[1]	11,302	183,113	12,881	47,757	32,596	35,488	NA	20,097	88,410	12,433	56,400	9,773	416,092
1998[2]	10,858	183,113	13,171	49,638	33,070	36,441	NA	21,824	75,690	12,433	54,300	9,979	420,478

[1] Preliminary. [2] Estimate. [3] Formerly part of Czechoslovakia; data not reported separately until 1992. [4] Formerly part of the U.S.S.R.; data not reported separately until 1992. NA = Not available. *Source: Food and Agriculture Organization of the United Nations (FAO-UN)*

Lumber Production and Consumption in the United States In Millions of Board Feet

	Production						Domestic Consumption							
	Softwood						Softwood							
Year	California Redwood	Inland Region	Southern Pine	West Coast	Total	Total Hardwood	Inland Region	Southern Pine	West Coast	Softwood Imports	Total	U.S. Hardwood	Hardwood Imports	Total Lumber
1993	1,354	8,312	14,392	7,319	32,947	11,914	8,129	14,020	6,043	15,260	45,810	10,556	335	56,702
1994	1,474	8,097	15,010	7,902	34,107	12,311	7,856	14,618	6,833	16,380	48,104	11,127	394	59,625
1995	1,305	7,015	14,708	7,452	32,233	12,434	6,956	14,384	6,530	17,396	47,749	11,372	380	59,501
1996	1,371	7,079	15,262	7,745	33,266	NA	7,073	15,112	6,821	18,214	49,883	NA	NA	NA
1997	1,511	7,383	16,113	7,772	34,667	NA	7,180	15,993	7,012	18,002	50,863	NA	NA	NA
1998	1,391	7,298	16,151	7,797	34,677	NA	7,256	15,788	7,502	18,686	52,209	NA	NA	NA
1999	1,325	7,580	16,922	8,625	36,605	NA	7,445	16,525	8,115	19,178	54,262	NA	NA	NA
2000	1,320	7,078	16,672	8,782	35,967	NA	6,926	16,213	8,300	19,449	53,759	NA	NA	NA
I	367	1,999	4,349	2,371	9,654	NA	1,923	4,200	2,190	4,736	13,772	NA	NA	NA
II	359	1,842	4,469	2,317	9,548	NA	1,800	4,390	2,213	5,142	14,315	NA	NA	NA
III	322	1,614	4,123	2,000	8,563	NA	1,631	3,987	1,927	4,914	13,180	NA	NA	NA
IV	272	1,623	3,731	2,094	8,202	NA	1,572	3,636	1,970	4,657	12,492	NA	NA	NA
2001[1] I	284	1,657	3,818	2,181	8,437	NA	1,604	3,621	2,071	4,418	12,357	NA	NA	NA
II	309	1,730	4,279	2,378	9,239	NA	1,773	4,199	2,261	5,736	14,745	NA	NA	NA
III	339	1,692	4,149	2,287	8,996	NA	1,754	3,889	2,241	5,209	13,851	NA	NA	NA

[1] Preliminary. NA = Not available. *Source: American Forest & Paper Association (AFPA)*

Stocks (Gross) of Softwood Lumber in the United States, on First of Month In Millions of Board Feet

Year	Jan.	Feb.	Mar.	Apr.	May	June	July	Aug.	Sept.	Oct.	Nov.	Dec.
1992	4,616	4,603	4,567	4,608	4,730	4,731	4,678	4,606	4,418	4,419	4,365	4,263
1993	4,669	4,217	4,166	4,239	4,490	4,618	4,599	4,526	4,418	4,445	4,282	4,298
1994	4,207	4,512	4,656	4,816	4,883	4,649	4,738	4,432	4,349	4,539	4,235	4,294
1995	4,403	4,336	4,344	4,653	4,352	4,663	4,508	4,323	4,342	4,359	4,361	4,335
1996	4,293	4,435	4,459	4,357	4,251	4,153	4,156	4,038	3,918	3,965	3,939	3,906
1997	3,973	4,019	4,113	4,067	3,963	4,017	3,915	3,871	3,875	3,927	3,925	3,865
1998	3,884	3,970	4,048	4,062	4,158	4,084	NA	NA	NA	NA	NA	NA
1999	3,519	3,595	3,688	3,726	3,698	3,581	3,512	3,485	3,533	3,491	3,562	3,536
2000	3,639	3,704	3,811	3,887	3,960	2,738	3,902	3,936	3,878	3,848	3,957	3,875
2001[1]	3,919	3,864	4,013	3,951	4,095	3,955	NA	3,961	3,938	4,076	4,100	4,248

[1] Preliminary. NA = Not available. *Source: American Forest & Paper Association (AFPA)*

Lumber (Softwood)[2] Production in the United States In Millions of Board Feet

Year	Jan.	Feb.	Mar.	Apr.	May	June	July	Aug.	Sept.	Oct.	Nov.	Dec.	Total
1992	3,836	3,628	4,121	3,862	3,632	3,911	3,882	3,746	3,736	4,048	3,617	3,425	45,444
1993	3,545	3,596	3,954	3,809	3,555	3,787	3,685	3,930	3,824	4,103	3,883	3,576	45,247
1994	3,839	3,662	4,097	3,735	3,972	4,113	3,785	4,124	4,135	4,145	3,636	3,851	47,094
1995	4,084	3,577	3,931	3,675	3,805	3,897	3,641	3,866	3,757	4,105	3,549	3,297	45,184
1996	2,600	2,606	2,757	2,903	2,833	2,819	2,942	3,077	2,858	3,179	2,758	2,424	33,756
1997	3,012	2,791	2,866	3,149	2,890	3,027	3,097	2,889	2,905	3,094	2,536	2,487	34,743
1998	2,767	2,760	2,928	3,084	2,647	3,051	3,079	2,930	2,953	3,167	2,667	2,754	34,787
1999	2,783	2,921	3,190	3,227	3,071	3,318	3,115	3,054	2,992	3,096	2,954	2,795	36,516
2000	3,020	3,128	3,474	3,058	3,276	3,249	2,730	2,971	2,839	3,041	2,761	2,342	35,889
2001[1]	2,832	2,457	2,918	2,928	NA	3,032	2,812	3,240	2,743	3,188	2,740	2,373	34,105

[1] Preliminary. [2] Data prior to 1996 are Softwood and Hardwood. *Source: American Forest & Paper Association (AFPA)*

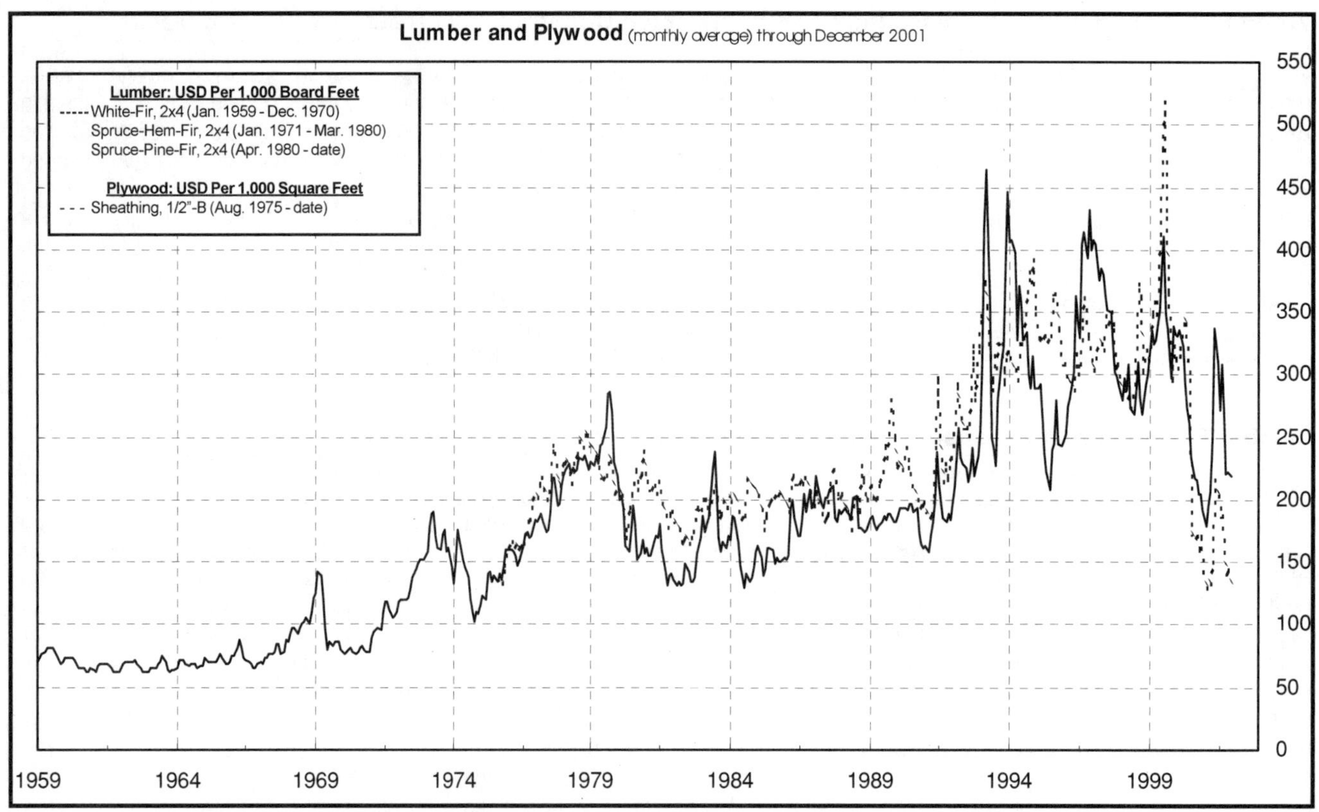

Lumber (Softwood)[2] Shipments in the United States In Millions of Board Feet

Year	Jan.	Feb.	Mar.	Apr.	May	June	July	Aug.	Sept.	Oct.	Nov.	Dec.	Total
1992	3,912	3,693	4,078	3,682	3,565	3,936	3,884	3,878	3,692	4,147	3,745	3,491	45,703
1993	3,575	3,649	3,852	3,563	3,402	3,759	3,721	3,997	3,724	4,211	3,798	3,617	44,868
1994	3,576	3,663	3,912	3,761	4,192	4,091	4,039	4,163	3,914	4,321	3,603	3,696	46,931
1995	3,971	3,584	3,855	3,831	3,765	4,026	3,826	3,870	3,760	4,055	3,478	3,367	45,388
1996	2,460	2,581	2,863	3,002	2,934	2,813	3,058	3,196	2,813	3,206	2,792	2,353	34,071
1997	2,966	2,697	2,890	3,253	2,834	3,126	3,139	2,885	2,852	3,096	2,598	2,461	34,797
1998	2,685	2,685	2,863	3,019	2,684	3,175	3,132	2,963	2,948	3,205	2,703	2,865	34,927
1999	2,689	2,829	3,177	3,227	3,071	3,383	3,141	3,004	3,037	3,021	2,944	2,691	36,214
2000	2,953	3,039	3,394	2,974	3,292	3,309	2,686	3,027	2,871	2,931	2,752	2,444	35,672
2001[1]	2,859	2,372	2,981	2,974	NA	2,961	2,936	3,279	2,644	3,166	2,732	2,355	34,101

[1] Preliminary. [2] Data prior to 1996 are Softwood and Hardwood. *Source: American Forest & Paper Association (AFPA)*

Imports and Exports of Lumber in the United States, by Type In Millions of Board Feet

	Imports[2]								Exports[2]						
	Software								Softwood						
Year	Cedar	Douglas Fir	Hemlock	Pine	Spruce	Total	Total Hardwood	Total Lumber	Douglas Fir	Hemlock	Ponderosa/White Pine	Southern Pine	Total	Total Hardwood	Total Lumber
1992	666.4	355.3	300.0	91.4	2,410.5	13,380.5	276.4	13,681.9	735.0	396.7	308.7	440.5	2,650.7	977.2	3,687.1
1993	615.3	327.6	354.9	84.6	3,104.1	15,259.9	335.0	15,625.4	664.9	340.4	273.3	339.6	2,376.4	1,008.9	3,468.9
1994	702.6	336.2	399.2	97.2	2,948.5	16,380.3	394.4	16,787.1	591.9	283.2	157.2	356.7	2,186.6	1,040.9	3,333.4
1995	768.0	395.4	258.1	97.1	2,827.7	17,395.3	379.7	17,786.9	637.9	227.0	106.7	334.6	1,987.5	1,100.5	3,192.5
1996	726.6	264.4	257.1	133.4	1,988.8	18,213.5	396.8	18,640.6	685.4	194.9	96.6	314.5	1,935.3	1,141.0	3,173.4
1997	586.1	263.9	249.8	314.2	1,040.4	18,014.3	464.5	18,505.9	435.8	104.6	122.1	299.3	1,820.0	1,281.4	3,189.0
1998	514.0	417.1	267.8	363.4	848.6	18,685.7	589.4	19,306.1	251.8	39.0	112.9	279.4	1,264.9	1,118.6	2,601.1
1999	590.5	426.0	259.0	448.7	802.8	19,177.8	708.4	19,903.4	248.6	53.6	140.3	326.0	1,430.6	1,241.7	2,867.3
2000	693.5	455.3	184.3	449.6	812.0	19,448.6	794.6	20,267.6	232.0	46.0	116.0	298.2	1,355.4	1,319.2	2,821.7
2001[1] I	187.2	90.5	45.5	95.6	177.1	4,417.3	171.2	4,592.6	45.9	6.4	22.4	68.8	283.0	306.8	627.6
II	193.8	125.3	75.6	100.0	211.1	5,736.5	144.3	5,883.4	55.0	4.9	23.8	51.2	253.3	314.8	615.7
III	182.2	130.8	67.9	101.0	213.0	5,208.7	166.1	5,377.5	54.7	5.0	21.9	46.9	239.7	295.3	581.5

[1] Preliminary. [2] Includes sawed timber, board planks & scantlings, flooring, box shook and railroad ties.
Source: American Forest & Paper Association (AFPA)

Average Open Interest of Random Lumber[1] Futures in Chicago In Contracts

Year	Jan.	Feb.	Mar.	Apr.	May	June	July	Aug.	Sept.	Oct.	Nov.	Dec.
1992	1,969	2,651	2,743	2,467	1,900	1,774	1,338	1,369	1,507	1,441	1,745	2,155
1993	2,194	2,432	2,163	2,055	2,302	2,658	2,254	2,141	2,011	2,080	2,140	2,721
1994	2,571	2,814	2,638	2,563	1,936	1,838	1,705	1,854	2,102	2,169	1,702	1,967
1995	1,757	1,923	2,142	2,509	2,742	3,252	2,896	2,918	2,809	3,039	2,626	2,940
1996	3,378	4,040	3,752	4,395	5,666	4,972	3,280	5,243	4,743	4,797	4,341	3,691
1997	3,745	3,211	3,048	3,337	2,895	3,137	2,767	3,119	3,267	4,006	3,606	4,068
1998	4,249	3,332	3,394	4,102	4,353	4,773	4,048	4,081	3,466	4,295	3,434	3,893
1999	4,864	5,497	4,698	4,456	4,927	6,405	6,263	4,882	3,457	3,704	2,963	2,868
2000	3,004	3,131	2,728	3,175	3,171	3,218	3,064	3,638	3,845	4,277	4,208	4,405
2001	4,605	4,494	3,654	3,644	3,867	3,733	2,612	2,949	2,148	2,102	2,173	2,416

[1] July 1995 thru March 1996, Lumber and Random Lumber. *Source: Chicago Mercantile Exchange (CME)*

Volume of Trading of Random Lumber[1] Futures in Chicago In Contracts

Year	Jan.	Feb.	Mar.	Apr.	May	June	July	Aug.	Sept.	Oct.	Nov.	Dec.	Total
1992	17,073	16,778	17,557	13,713	14,059	13,807	12,177	13,043	12,127	11,261	11,514	17,425	170,534
1993	14,915	15,080	14,808	14,661	14,241	15,308	13,287	13,358	12,400	13,248	18,150	18,728	178,184
1994	16,837	15,204	17,323	17,380	14,996	14,348	11,542	13,327	14,856	13,032	10,997	13,121	172,963
1995	12,150	12,909	15,088	12,139	14,536	20,126	13,766	16,919	15,718	18,981	15,551	14,803	182,686
1996	22,954	19,960	20,956	27,094	28,271	26,100	19,302	27,792	31,982	32,042	25,236	22,525	304,214
1997	28,561	20,946	21,071	24,624	18,248	24,797	20,308	18,503	21,736	24,416	15,131	21,977	260,318
1998	19,556	20,339	20,881	24,673	20,519	24,112	21,763	20,453	19,412	19,578	22,002	16,559	249,847
1999	25,962	22,184	28,151	22,618	23,835	30,410	30,791	25,683	24,177	18,125	20,802	15,118	287,856
2000	19,871	19,486	18,936	16,136	21,003	18,057	16,636	16,563	19,037	17,155	20,706	17,582	221,168
2001	21,567	15,076	24,561	22,458	23,681	18,878	15,210	16,440	12,882	11,608	11,989	12,490	206,840

[1] July 1995 thru March 1996, Lumber and Random Lumber. *Source: Chicago Mercantile Exchange (CME)*

Production of Plywood by Selected Countries In Thousands of Cubic Meters

Year	Austria	Canada	Finland	France	Germany	Italy	Japan	Poland	Romania	Russia	Spain	Sweden	United States
1994	150	1,834	700	594	397	427	4,865	124	97	890	210	85	17,380
1995	150	1,831	778	559	498	418	4,421	115	83	939	210	108	17,140
1996	150	1,814	869	537	512	402	4,421	109	83	972	210	119	16,975
1997	150	1,828	987	576	392	414	NA	118	81	968	125	113	15,987
1998	150	1,760	992	472	428	420	NA	178	76	1,094	125	114	15,732
1999[1]	150	1,760	1,000	480	400	430	NA	178	70	1,200	125	114	15,504
2000[2]	150	1,760	1,050	480	380	430	NA	185	70	1,335	125	114	15,019

[1] Preliminary. [2] Estimate. NA = Not available. *Source: Food and Agricultural Organization of the United Nations (FAO-UN)*

Imports of Plywood by Selected Countries In Thousands of Cubic Meters

Year	Austria	Belgium	Canada	Denmark	France	Germany	Italy	Japan	Netherlands	Sweden	Switzerland	United Kingdom	United States
1994	104	267	288	171	234	1,003	257	4,045	560	126	144	1,202	1,547
1995	116	146	353	188	260	1,177	323	4,394	552	112	136	1,127	1,791
1996	115	215	424	167	256	975	295	5,314	522	135	129	1,132	1,930
1997	120	313	428	196	310	1,083	312	5,326	484	184	138	947	1,973
1998	121	487	108	280	325	1,074	380	NA	530	145	143	963	2,150
1999[1]	123	500	125	250	332	1,070	370	NA	500	140	140	960	2,169
2000[2]	123	500	125	250	332	1,100	370	NA	500	140	140	960	2,107

[1] Preliminary. [2] Estimate. NA = Not available. *Source: Food and Agricultural Organization of the United Nations (FAO-UN)*

Exports of Plywood by Selected Countries In Thousands of Cubic Meters

Year	Austria	Baltic States	Belgium	Canada	Finland	France	Germany	Italy	Netherlands	Poland	Russia	Spain	United States
1994	158	143	134	511	627	193	131	108	102	66	568	67	1,346
1995	130	138	88	818	668	183	149	96	72	60	670	48	1,395
1996	150	187	88	870	794	214	135	117	64	53	612	77	1,384
1997	166	198	101	859	861	223	135	125	50	90	615	69	1,624
1998	180	NA	309	456	831	221	161	157	56	93	736	40	858
1999[1]	190	NA	325	570	850	230	140	130	50	95	800	40	902
2000[2]	190	NA	325	600	900	245	140	130	50	98	900	40	847

[1] Preliminary. [2] Estimate. NA = Not available. *Source: Food and Agricultural Organization of the United Nations (FAO-UN)*

Selected World Prices of Plywood

Year	Jan.	Feb.	Mar.	Apr.	May	June	July	Aug.	Sept.	Oct.	Nov.	Dec.	Average
Southeast Asia, Lauan, Wholesale Price, Spot Tokyo In U.S. Cents Per Sheet[1]													
1996	529.12	548.59	529.22	521.11	535.48	523.62	521.39	538.27	528.50	525.09	526.22	518.62	528.77
1997	500.31	479.63	489.39	485.57	511.91	524.85	512.10	500.68	480.05	454.68	438.61	424.25	483.50
1998	409.19	413.35	387.32	371.74	363.05	349.38	348.29	324.83	349.59	380.46	390.58	417.38	375.43
1999	441.27	420.34	418.38	434.22	426.27	430.68	426.82	441.49	458.03	462.25	468.20	477.41	441.30
2000	456.19	438.49	451.62	454.44	443.40	452.49	443.97	444.25	459.05	451.82			449.57
Canada, Export Unit Value, F.O.B. In Canadian Dollar Per Cubic Meter													
1992	426.14	409.62	373.22	396.94	387.59	395.95	354.61	373.58	385.20	395.29	410.59	353.95	388.56
1993	392.59	396.65	393.73	424.19	515.51	448.76	408.39	435.72	505.58	517.58	494.52	476.08	450.78
1994	442.04	574.74	553.92	553.81	542.95	458.48	472.29	510.01	526.42	454.20	462.90	499.71	504.29
1995	473.77	480.78											477.28
Finland, Export Unit Value, F.O.B. In Markka Per Cubic Meter													
1995	3,681	3,809	3,751	3,897	3,752	3,769	3,771	3,543	3,430	3,370	3,268	2,923	3,579
1996	3,084	2,548	3,129	3,296	3,075	3,225	3,070	3,003	3,245	3,036	3,264	2,900	3,060
1997	3,021	2,943	3,032	3,157	3,174	3,336	3,220	3,222	3,321	3,408	3,465	3,563	3,235
1998	3,488	3,565	3,573	3,774	3,567	3,698	3,542	3,374	3,486	3,474	3,426	3,022	3,505
United Kingdom, Import Unit Value, C.I.F. In Pound Sterling Per Cubic Meter													
1995	232.68	239.77	257.68	264.72	229.18	268.11	256.09	241.61	263.31	285.36	275.38	282.68	258.05
1996	238.86	249.65	224.40	273.23	256.16	275.38	269.36	247.83	253.37	261.66	260.77	293.42	258.67
1997	235.57	234.39	340.66	378.17	274.27	256.75	248.45	276.09	268.64	277.69	270.27	294.06	262.92
1998	188.51	229.59	230.75	237.89	215.24	207.63	209.45	204.69	200.66	206.68	206.01		212.46

[1] Sheet measurement = 1.2cm X 90.0cm X 1.80m. *Source: Food and Agricultural Organization of the United Nations (FAO-UN)*

Magnesium

Magnesium is one of the most abundant elements found in the Earth's crust and the third most plentiful element found in seawater. Magnesium compounds, primarily magnesium oxide, are used in refractory material in furnace linings for producing iron and steel, nonferrous metals, glass and cement. Magnesium oxide and other compounds are in the chemical, agricultural and construction industries. Magnesium metal's principal use is as an alloying addition to aluminum. These aluminum-magnesium alloys are used primarily in beverage cans. Magnesium alloys are used in structural components in machinery and automobiles. magnesium is also used to remove sulfur from iron and steel.

The U.S. Geological Survey estimated that world primary production of magnesium metal in 2000 was 234,000 metric tonnes excluding production in the United States. In 1999, global production was 277,000 tonnes. The U.S. is the world's largest producer of magnesium metal. In 1999, other large producers were Canada with 75,000 tonnes, China with 80,000 tonnes and Russia with 40,000 tonnes. Other large producers include Israel, France and Norway. The resources from which magnesium may be recovered are very large. Magnesium-bearing brines are estimated in the billions of tonnes. Magnesium can be recovered from seawater at many coastline locations. There are some substitutes for magnesium. Aluminum and zinc can substitute for magnesium castings and wrought products.

U.S. imports for consumption of magnesium metal in August 2001 were 1,410 tonnes, down 35 percent from the previous month. In the January-August 2001 period, imports of magnesium metal were 12,500 tonnes. For all of 2000, magnesium metal imports were 22,900 tonnes. Imports of magnesium waste and scrap in August 2001 were 840 tonnes compared to 573 tonnes the previous month. In the first eight months of 2001, waste and scrap imports were 6,890 tonnes and for all of 2000 they were 9,890 tonnes. Imports of magnesium alloys (magnesium content) in August 2001 were 3,590 tonnes, up 45 percent from the previous month. In January-August 2001, imports were 24,500 tonnes while for all of 2000 they were 56,300 tonnes. Imports of magnesium sheet, tubing, ribbons, wire, powder and other materials (magnesium content) in August 2001 were 102 tonnes. For all of 2000, imports were 2,300 tonnes. Total magnesium imports in January-August 2001 were 46,000 tonnes and for 2000 they were 91,400 tonnes.

U.S. exports of magnesium metal in the first eight months of 2001 were 3,760 tonnes. For 2000, metal exports were 7,300 tonnes. Exports of magnesium materials in the January-August 2001 period were 12,800 tonnes while for all of 2000 they were 23,800 tonnes.

World Production of Magnesium (Primary and Secondary) In Metric Tons

	Primary Production								Secondary Production				
Year	Brazil	Canada	China	France	Norway	Russia[4]	United States	World Total	Japan	United Kingdom	United States	Former USSR	World Total
1991	7,800	35,512	8,600	14,050	44,322	80,000	131,288	342,000	17,158	800	50,543	7,000	77,100
1992	7,300	25,800	10,600	13,660	30,404	40,000	137,000	295,000	12,978	800	57,000	6,500	78,900
1993	9,700	23,000	11,800	10,982	27,300	30,000	132,000	269,000	13,215	1,000	58,900	6,000	80,700
1994	9,700	28,900	24,000	12,280	27,635	35,400	128,000	282,000	19,009	1,000	62,100	5,000	88,700
1995	9,700	48,100	93,600	14,450	28,000	37,500	142,000	395,000	11,767	1,000	65,100	6,000	85,500
1996	9,000	54,000	73,100	14,000	37,800	35,000	133,000	378,000	8,175	1,000	71,200	6,000	88,000
1997	9,000	57,700	75,990	13,740	34,200	39,500	125,000	383,000	10,934	1,000	77,600	NA	91,100
1998	9,000	77,100	70,500	14,000	35,400	41,500	106,000	397,000	7,807	1,000	77,100	NA	87,500
1999[1]	9,000	80,000	120,000	14,000	35,000	45,000	W	342,000	7,735	500	86,100	NA	96,000
2000[2]	9,000	80,000	140,000	14,000	35,000	45,000	W	368,000	7,800	500	82,300	NA	92,200

[1] Preliminary. [2] Estimate. [3] Formerly part of the U.S.S.R.; data not reported separately until 1992. W = Withheld proprietary data.
Source: U.S. Geological Survey (USGS)

Salient Statistics of Magnesium in the United States In Metric Tons

	Production								Domestic Consumption of Primary Magnesium					
		Secondary							Structural Products					
Year	Primary (Ingot)	New Scrap	Old Scrap	Total	Total Exports[3]	Imports for Consumption	Stocks Dec. 31[4]	$ Price Per Pound[5]	Castings	Wrought	Total	Aluminum Alloys	Other Uses[6]	Total
1991	131,288	23,059	27,484	50,543	55,160	31,863	27,000	1.43	8,857	8,802	17,659	45,809	28,404	74,213
1992	136,947	26,191	30,854	57,045	51,951	11,844	13,000	1.46-1.53	10,223	8,843	19,066	41,003	33,758	74,761
1993	132,144	28,313	30,577	58,890	38,815	37,248	26,000	1.43-1.46	12,543	9,870	22,413	46,498	32,202	78,700
1994	128,000	32,500	29,600	62,100	45,200	29,100	20,030	1.63	15,676	7,690	23,366	61,100	27,900	89,000
1995	142,000	35,400	29,800	65,100	38,300	34,800	21,193	1.93-2.25	15,231	8,510	23,741	60,200	25,100	85,300
1996	133,000	41,100	30,100	71,200	40,500	46,600	25,000	1.70-1.80	16,400	8,080	24,480	52,300	25,500	77,800
1997	125,000	47,000	30,500	77,600	40,500	65,100	23,000	1.60-1.70	20,643	6,840	27,400	50,000	23,000	73,000
1998	106,000	45,200	31,800	77,100	35,400	82,500	27,000	1.52-1.62	27,057	7,100	34,157	52,000	20,900	72,900
1999[1]	W	52,000	34,200	86,100	29,100	90,700	W	1.40-1.55	49,181	9,380	58,561	57,800	14,900	72,700
2000[2]	W	52,200	30,100	82,300	23,800	91,400	W	1.23-1.30	29,457	2,120	31,577	55,400	17,400	72,800

[1] Preliminary. [2] Estimate. [3] Metal & alloys in crude form & scrap. [4] Estimate of Industry Stocks, metal. [5] Magnesium ingots (99.8%), f.o.b. Valasco, Texas. [6] Distributive or sacrificial purposes. W = Withheld proprietary data. *Source: U.S. Geological Survey (USGS)*

Manganese

Manganese is primarily used in the steel industry as an alloy. Manganese is essential to iron and steel production by virtue of its sulfur-fixing , deoxidizing, and alloying properties. Manganese increases the metal's hardness so virtually all steel contains some manganese. Steel making accounts for almost all manganese use although there are a variety of other uses for manganese. Manganese is used in aluminum alloys and in oxide form is used in dry cell batteries. Manganese is also used in plant fertilizers and animal feeds. Manganese ore, when converted to a metallic alloy with iron, forms the compound ferromanganese.

The U.S. Geological Survey estimated world mine production of manganese in 2000 at 7.45 million metric tonnes. This represented an increase of 7 percent from 1999. The largest producer of manganese was South Africa with output of 1.5 million tonnes, up 12 percent from the previous year. China was the next largest producer with 1.1 million tonnes, the same as in 1999. Production by Gabon was estimated at one million tonnes, up 4 percent from the previous year. Other large producers of manganese include the Ukraine, Australia, Brazil and India. World reserves of manganese are estimated to be 660 million tonnes with South Africa holding the largest reserves.

U.S. imports for consumption of manganese ore and dioxide in July 2001 were 30,600 tonnes. In the January-July 2001 period, imports of manganese ore and dioxide were 153,000 tonnes, down 7 percent from a year ago. U.S. imports for consumption of manganese ferroalloy and metal in July 2001 were 35,600 tonnes. In the first seven months of 2001, imports of ferroalloy and metal were 233,000 tonnes, down 27 percent from the same period in 2000. Among the major suppliers of manganese dioxide to the U.S. in 2001 were Australia, Ireland, South Africa and China. The major suppliers of unwrought manganese metal to the U.S. in 2001 were South Africa, China and Germany. Suppliers of other manganese metals were Russia, India and China.

U.S. imports of low carbon ferromanganese in the January-July 2001 period were 8,750 tonnes, gross weight. The major suppliers of low carbon ferromanganese were South Africa, Mexico, Italy and China. Imports of medium carbon ferromanganese in the same period were 28,500 tonnes, gross weight. Among the major suppliers were South Africa, Mexico, and China. Imports of high carbon ferromanganese in the first seven months of 2001 were 98,000 tonnes, gross weight. The major suppliers were South Africa, France, Australia, Brazil, and India. In July 2001, U.S. imports of low, medium and high carbon ferromanganese were 24,000 tonnes. Imports of silicomanganese in July 2001 were 21,400 tonnes, gross weight.

World Production of Manganese Ore In Thousands of Metric Tons (Gross Weight)

Year	Australia[2] 37-53[4]	Brazil 30-50	China 30	Gabon 50-53	Georgia[5] 29-30	Ghana 30-50	Hungary[3] 30-33	India 10-54	Mexico 27-50	Morocco 50-53	South Africa 30-48+	Ukraine[5] 29-30	World Total
1991	1,412	2,000	5,150	1,620	----	320	30	1,401	254	59	3,146	7,240	22,900
1992	1,251	1,703	5,300	1,556	500	276	18	1,810	407	44	2,464	5,819	21,800
1993	2,092	1,837	5,860	1,290	300	295	59	1,655	363	43	2,507	3,800	20,500
1994	1,920	2,199	3,570	1,436	150	270	55	1,632	307	31	2,851	2,979	18,000
1995	2,180	2,398	6,900	1,930	100	217	----	1,764	472	----	3,199	3,200	23,300
1996	2,109	2,506	7,600	1,983	97	448	----	1,797	485	----	3,240	3,070	24,300
1997	2,136	2,124	6,000	1,904	----	437	----	1,596	534	----	3,121	3,040	21,900
1998	1,500	2,149	5,300	2,092	----	537	----	1,557	510	----	3,044	2,226	20,100
1999	1,892	1,674	3,190	1,908	----	639	----	1,500	459	----	3,122	1,985	17,900
2000[1]	1,614	2,000	4,000	1,743	----	896	----	1,550	418	----	3,635	2,741	20,200

[1] Preliminary. [2] Metallurgical Ore. [3] Concentrate. [4] Ranges of percentage of manganese. [5] Formerly part of the U.S.S.R.; data not reported separately until 1992. *Source: U.S. Geological Survey (USGS)*

Salient Statistics of Manganese in the United States In Thousands of Metric Tons (Gross Weight)

Year	Net Import Reliance as a % of Apparent Consumption	Manganese Ore (35% or More Manganese): Imports for Consumption	Exports	Consumption	Stocks, Dec. 31[3]	Ferromanganese: Imports for Consumption	Exports	Consumption	Avg. Price Mn. Metallurgical Ore $ Lg. Ton Unit[4]	Silicomanganese: Exports	Imports
1991	100	234	66	473	275	320	15	346	3.72	2.9	258.3
1992	100	247	13	438	276	304	13	339	3.25	9.2	257.2
1993	100	232	16	389	302	347	18	341	2.60	9.4	316.0
1994	100	331	15	449	269	336	11	347	2.40	6.8	273.0
1995	100	394	15	486	309	310	11	348	2.40	7.8	305.0
1996	100	478	32	478	319	374	10	326	2.55	5.3	323.0
1997	100	355	84	510	241	304	12	337	2.44	5.4	306.0
1998	100	332	8	499	163	339	14	290	2.40	6.7	346.0
1999[1]	100	460	4	479	172	312	12	281	2.26	3.7	301.0
2000[2]	100	430	10	486	226	312	8	300	2.39	1.9	378.0

[1] Preliminary. [2] Estimate. [3] Including bonded warehouses; excludes Gov't stocks; also excludes small tonnages of dealers' stocks. [4] 46-48% Mn, C.I.F. U.S. Ports. *Source: U.S. Geological Survey (USGS)*

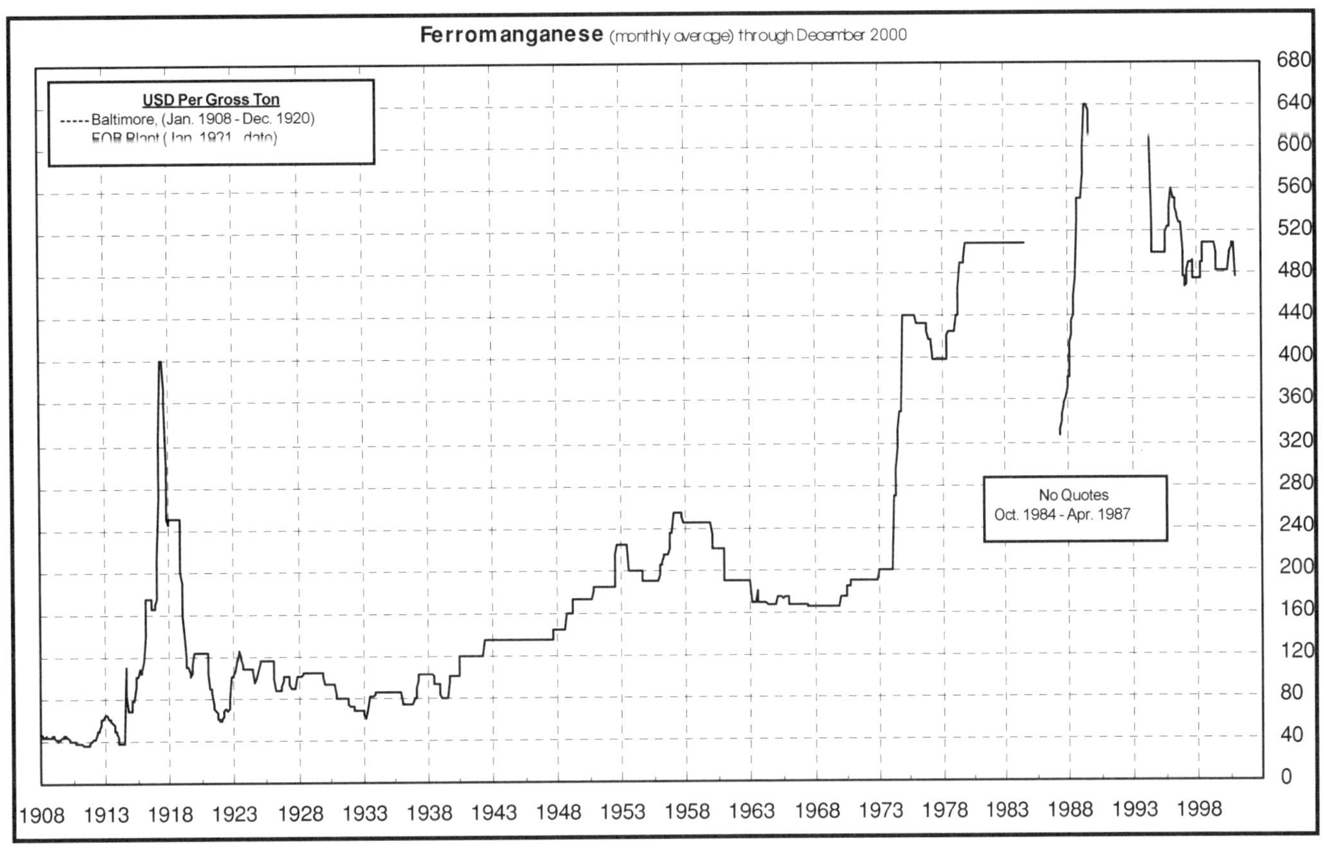

Imports[3] of Manganese Ore (20% or More Mn) in the United States In Metric Tons (Mn Content)

Year	Australia	Brazil	Gabon	Mexico	Morocco	South Africa	Total	Customs Value Thous. $
1991	16,485	2,583	79,997	4,673	44	----	117,255	40,332
1992	25,519	15,541	75,354	3,930	56	----	120,400	29,967
1993	30,171	5,573	66,659	7,317	43	6,006	115,770	24,927
1994	23,200	4,530	112,000	13,700	56	7,780	161,000	29,800
1995	31,600	7,080	104,000	23,600	37	13,100	187,000	33,300
1996	48,900	5,640	140,000	16,100	9	20,800	231,000	42,400
1997	16,400	9,100	99,400	30,100	37	----	156,000	30,800
1998	18,700	12,100	94,900	14,600	----	13,800	160,000	27,800
1999[1]	23,500	1	142,000	9,130	----	39,100	224,000	37,200
2000[2]	18,100	3,250	196,000	3,250	----	----	227,000	32,100

[1] Preliminary. [2] Estimate. [3] Imports for consumption. *Source: U.S. Geological Survey (USGS)*

Average Price of Ferromanganese In Dollars Per Gross Ton

Year	Jan.	Feb.	Mar.	Apr.	May	June	July	Aug.	Sept.	Oct.	Nov.	Dec.	Average
1991	610.00	610.00	610.00	610.00	610.00	610.00	610.00	610.00	610.00	610.00	610.00	610.00	610.00
1992	610.00	610.00	610.00	610.00	610.00	610.00	610.00	610.00	610.00	610.00	610.00	610.00	610.00
1993	610.00	610.00	610.00	610.00	610.00	610.00	610.00	610.00	610.00	610.00	610.00	610.00	610.00
1994	610.00	610.00	610.00	610.00	610.00	527.50	500.00	500.00	500.00	500.00	500.00	500.00	548.13
1995	500.00	500.00	500.00	500.00	500.00	500.00	500.00	518.75	525.00	525.00	542.50	560.00	514.27
1996	560.00	552.50	550.00	550.00	541.00	535.00	533.13	527.50	527.50	527.50	501.25	477.50	531.91
1997	477.50	467.50	470.00	482.50	490.00	490.00	490.00	492.50	475.00	475.00	475.00	475.00	480.00
1998	175.00	175.00	175.00	190.00	190.00	510.00	510.00	510.00	510.00	510.00	510.00	510.00	497.92
1999	510.00	510.00	510.00	510.00	510.00	498.75	482.50	482.50	482.50	482.50	482.50	482.50	495.21
2000	482.50	482.50	482.50	482.50	482.50	482.50	501.63	505.00	509.00	510.00	510.00	477.50	492.40

Domestic standard, high carbon, FOB plant, carloads. *Source: American Metal Market (AMM)*

Meats

U.S. commercial red meat production--the combined total of beef, veal, lamb and pork--during 2001 totaled a near record large 45.2 billion pounds vs. 45.7 billion in 2000. A further pullback, to 44.5 billion, is forecast for 2002. Red meat accounts for more than half of total U.S. meat production and poultry the balance: the combined annual total of 82.7 billion pounds in 2001 compares with 82.6 billion in 2000 and a forecast of 82.9 billion in 2002. Beef production in 2001 of 26.1 billion pounds compares with 26.8 billion in 2000 with pork production of 19.1 billion pounds vs. 18.9 billion, respectively. Forecasts for total 2002 beef output are 25.4 billion pounds and pork 19.1 billion. Poultry production in 2001 reached a record high 31.1 billion pounds vs. 30.5 billion in 2000 and forecast at 31.9 billion in 2002. U.S. veal and lamb production are insignificant.

Globally, however, more pork is produced than beef. China is the largest red meat producer, around 48 million metric tons-- (mostly pork, 42.4 million tons)-- in 2001, almost one-third of the world total with the U.S. second at about one-half of China's total output. However, U.S. beef production is double that of China. The decade long slide in red meat production in the former USSR finally shows some sign of abating, estimated at 3.2 million tons in 2001 about unchanged from 2000 and expected to hold at 3.2 million tons in 2002. In the European Union, beef production has slipped relative to pork owing largely to the mad cow disease that decimated herds in the late 1990's.

U.S. per capita beef consumption (retail weight) in 2001 of 68.4 pounds compares with 69.4 pounds in 2000 and a forecast of 66.6 pounds in 2002; pork use of 51.84 pounds compares with 52.5 in 2000 and 51.7 pounds forecast for 2002. The pork industry has aggressively advertised pork as a white, and not a red meat while the beef industry's advertising focuses on the ease (time wise) of preparing beef for dinner. For both meats, however, consumer preferences have shifted to foods containing less fat, which has benefited poultry at red meat's expense; per capita retail broiler and turkey consumption totaled a near record large 95 pounds in 2001 and is forecast at 95.2 pounds in 2002.

Choice steer market prices (basis Nebraska) averaged about $72.52/cwt. in 2001 vs. $69.65 in 2000; forecasts for 2002 are from $74 to $80/cwt. Hog barrow and gilt prices of $45.86/cwt. in 2001 compare with $44.70 in 2000 and estimates for 2002 of $42-45/cwt.

U.S. red meat imports in 2001 of 4.1 billion pounds compares with 4.0 billion in 2000 and forecasts of 4.2 billion in 2002 with beef imports accounting for almost two-thirds of the totals. U.S. red meat exports, again mostly beef, totaled 3.7 billion pounds in 2001 vs. 3.8 billion in 2000 and a forecast of 3.6 billion pounds in 2002.

World Total Meat Production[3] In Thousands of Metric Tons

Year	Argentina	Australia	Brazil	Canada	China[4]	France	Germany	Italy	Mexico	Russia	United Kingdom	United States	World Total
1992	2,602	2,810	5,620	2,107	29,406	3,997	4,994	2,648	2,626	6,748	2,297	18,589	116,309
1993	2,630	2,780	5,795	2,052	32,254	3,901	4,796	2,642	2,718	6,260	2,236	18,488	115,852
1994	2,682	2,807	7,030	2,132	36,968	3,868	5,092	2,618	2,852	5,659	2,323	19,361	124,693
1995	2,668	2,644	7,530	2,204	42,653	3,941	5,053	2,602	2,942	4,860	2,359	19,811	129,482
1996	2,636	2,650	7,750	2,226	36,947	3,973	5,161	2,668	2,832	4,487	2,088	19,634	123,100
1997	3,033	2,914	7,590	2,332	42,500	4,046	5,053	2,632	2,875	4,086	2,183	19,667	128,993
1998	2,648	2,973	7,830	2,488	45,982	4,065	5,244	2,595	2,852	3,775	2,367	20,541	134,134
1999	2,890	2,940	8,105	2,800	47,670	4,086	5,532	2,707	2,999	3,544	2,238	20,994	137,499
2000[1]	2,948	2,982	8,400	2,905	49,600	3,966	5,331	2,692	3,045	3,494	2,134	20,991	139,019
2001[2]	2,900	2,380	8,705	2,945	48,850	3,740	5,195	2,475	2,990	3,210	1,642	20,520	133,055

[1] Preliminary. [2] Forecast. [3] Data through 2000, includes beef, veal, pork, sheep and goat meat. Beginning 2001, excludes sheep and goat.
[4] Predominately pork production. *Source: Foreign Agricultural Service, U.S. Department of Agriculture (FAS-USDA)*

Production and Consumption of Red Meats in The United States

	Beef			Veal			Lamb & Mutton			Pork (Excluding Lard)			All Meats		
	Commercial Production	Consumption Total	Consumption Per Capita	Commercial Production	Consumption Total	Consumption Per Capita	Commercial Production	Consumption Total	Consumption Per Capita	Commercial Production	Consumption Total	Consumption Per Capita	Commercial Production	Consumption Total	Consumption Per Capita
Year	-- Million Pounds --		Lbs.[4]	- Million Pounds -		Lbs.[4]	- Million Pounds -		Lbs.[4]	-- Million Pounds --		Lbs.[4]	-- Million Pounds --		Lbs.[4]
1993	22,942	24,006	93.0	267	286	1.1	329	381	1.5	17,030	17,419	67.5	40,568	42,092	163.1
1994	24,278	25,124	96.4	283	290	1.2	304	345	1.3	17,658	17,829	68.4	42,523	43,588	167.3
1995	25,115	25,534	97.0	308	319	1.2	264	338	1.1	17,085	16,826	63.3	42,772	43,017	162.6
1996	25,419	25,863	97.4	378	378	1.4	268	334	1.1	17,117	16,795	63.3	43,182	43,370	163.2
1997	25,490	25,611	95.9	334	333	1.2	260	332	1.1	17,274	16,823	61.4	43,358	43,099	159.6
1998	25,760	26,305	93.3	262	265	1.0	251	360	1.0	19,011	18,309	65.3	45,284	45,239	160.6
1999	26,493	26,932	69.0	235	235	1.0	248	358	1.0	19,308	18,952	54.0	46,284	46,477	125.0
2000[1]	26,888	27,290	69.0	225	225	1.0	234	353	1.0	18,952	18,626	52.0	46,299	46,494	124.0
2001[2]	26,159	27,175	68.0	204	205	1.0	226	370	1.0	19,151	18,570	52.0	45,740	46,320	122.0
2002[3]	25,481	26,661	67.0	200	199	1.0	196	347	1.0	19,155	18,685	52.0	45,032	45,892	120.0

[1] Preliminary. [2] Estimate. [3] Forecast. [4] Data through 1998, are for Carcass weight. Beginning 1998, data are for Retail-weight basis.
Source: Economic Research Service, U.S. Department of Agriculture (ERS-USDA)

Total Red Meat Imports[3] (Carcass Weight Equivalent) of Principal Countries In Thousands of Metric Tons

Year	Canada	France	Germany	Hong Kong	Italy	Japan	Rep. of Korea	Nether- lands	Russia	Singa- pore	United Kingdom	United States	Total
1992	237	1,027	1,338	265	1,231	1,388	187	208	292	147	885	1,424	5,733
1993	292	1,010	1,319	280	1,139	1,480	134	207	227	150	889	1,410	6,118
1994	313	39	190	298	77	1,628	191	35	880	28	217	1,434	6,529
1995	283	39	150	223	37	1,840	239	25	1,084	28	294	1,284	6,465
1996	276	44	139	202	61	1,916	240	31	1,068	38	276	1,249	6,452
1997	311	47	132	238	64	1,727	276	56	1,129	36	293	1,383	6,707
1998	303	44	125	313	57	1,736	173	32	895	31	255	1,456	6,645
1999	325	53	135	329	61	1,885	365	25	1,235	39	256	1,730	7,792
2000[1]	343	53	138	391	61	2,008	454	21	735	38	260	1,865	7,951
2001[2]	345	19	72	436	56	1,955	440	32	875	32	164	1,851	7,797

[1] Preliminary. [2] Forecast. [3] Data through 2000, includes beef, veal, pork, sheep and goat meat. Beginning 2001, excludes sheep and goat.
Source: Foreign Agricultural Service, U.S. Department of Agriculture (FAS-USDA)

Total Red Meat Exports[3] (Carcass Weight Equivalent) of Principal Countries In Thousands of Metric Tons

Year	Argentina	Australia	Brazil	Canada	China	Denmark	France	India	Ireland	Nether- lands	New Zealand	United States	World Total
1992	301	1,510	470	453	195	1,657	864	110	643	1,491	884	789	7,484
1993	283	1,469	425	494	315	1,272	917	120	672	1,470	858	779	7,290
1994	379	1,495	417	521	256	550	352	138	347	133	934	984	8,138
1995	522	1,374	320	576	328	399	302	206	367	136	864	1,186	8,219
1996	472	1,299	330	658	274	387	290	220	305	195	875	1,294	8,361
1997	439	1,423	354	776	206	531	282	231	271	202	1,001	1,446	9,003
1998	292	1,588	449	848	241	490	214	263	308	150	987	1,546	8,898
1999	347	1,664	642	1,139	164	594	333	284	369	209	850	1,679	10,022
2000[1]	361	1,712	743	1,295	146	590	222	301	284	214	860	1,735	9,892
2001[2]	310	1,360	800	1,335	140	555	185	310	77	147	490	1,769	8,834

[1] Preliminary. [2] Forecast. [3] Data through 2000, includes beef, veal, pork, sheep and goat meat. Beginning 2001, excludes sheep and goat.
Source: Foreign Agricultural Service, U.S. Department of Agriculture (FAS-USDA)

United States Meat Imports by Type of Product In Metric Tons

	Beef and Veal			Lamb, Mutton	Pork							
Year	Fresh, Chilled & Frozen	Canned, Including Sausage	Other Pre- pared or Preserved	and Goat, Except Canned	Fresh and Frozen	Canned[2]	Other Pre- pared or Preserved	Sausage, All Types	Mixed Sausage	Other Meats[3]	Variety Meats, Fresh or Frozen	Total
1991	709,997	60,511	12,929	19,100	215,933	82,342	16,948	2,144	1,534	22,979	18,266	1,162,683
1992	728,922	64,303	10,641	23,853	185,672	61,005	16,553	2,453	1,674	19,225	20,059	1,134,360
1993	719,377	59,786	14,559	24,468	207,652	75,434	17,686	2,689	1,368	18,679	25,298	1,166,996
1994	714,450	61,575	13,335	23,276	209,026	75,443	17,577	2,237	1,899	18,724	27,407	1,164,949
1995	641,916	52,012	13,528	29,919	194,386	61,904	15,571	2,553	1,935	19,550	25,972	1,059,246
1996	640,652	53,388	13,616	33,097	183,555	55,247	15,277	2,418	1,639	21,934	32,472	1,053,295
1997	732,933	51,538	12,064	37,871	191,045	56,353	14,632	2,466	1,608	25,852	44,162	1,170,524
1998	822,883	54,288	14,902	51,695	217,192	61,137	14,658	2,861	786	23,669	46,908	1,310,979
1999[1]	880,582	66,500	16,566	50,293	266,197	62,209	21,668	3,066	578	78,659	51,504	1,497,822

[1] Preliminary. [2] Includes canned hams, shoulders and bacon; not specified elsewhere. [3] Mostly mixed lucheon meats.
Source: Foreign Agricultural Service, U.S. Department of Agriculture (FAS-USDA)

United States Meat Exports by Type of Product In Metric Tons

	Beef and Veal			Pork								
							Other Pork Prepared or Preserved					
Year	Fresh, Chilled & Frozen	Prepared and Preserved	Lamb and Mutton, Fresh or Frozen	Fresh, Chilled & Frozen	Hams & Shoul- ders, Cured	Bacon	Not Canned	Canned	Sausage, Bologna & Frank- furters	Variety Meats, Fresh, Chilled & Frozen	Other Meats[2]	Total
1991	395,830	10,255	3,798	76,378	4,696	5,469	6,180	1,263	24,021	281,034	61,380	870,304
1992	436,534	12,061	3,278	116,582	8,181	7,376	5,812	2,347	22,817	303,700	57,144	975,832
1993	410,635	14,477	3,608	129,041	5,032	7,088	4,761	2,350	34,200	338,408	45,938	995,538
1994	517,458	13,419	3,766	149,414	8,434	12,081	4,472	2,973	46,906	375,029	34,694	1,168,646
1995	581,798	13,651	2,511	228,071	12,066	13,823	6,265	3,613	56,853	447,837	34,113	1,400,601
1996	597,605	14,577	2,478	268,032	9,748	15,843	7,560	5,330	92,503	469,782	42,260	1,525,718
1997	675,994	15,227	2,545	285,805	9,018	12,362	9,230	7,691	122,248	424,724	58,469	1,623,313
1998	698,453	17,966	2,528	356,140	11,825	13,627	9,895	8,442	98,712	447,649	46,706	1,711,943
1999[1]	784,642	19,323	2,219	386,402	12,593	17,729	9,237	8,339	64,048	476,938	37,549	1,819,019

[1] Preliminary. [2] Includes sausage ingredients, cured (excluding canned);meat and meat products canned; and baby food, canned.
Source: Foreign Agricultural Service, U.S. Department of Agriculture (FAS-USDA)

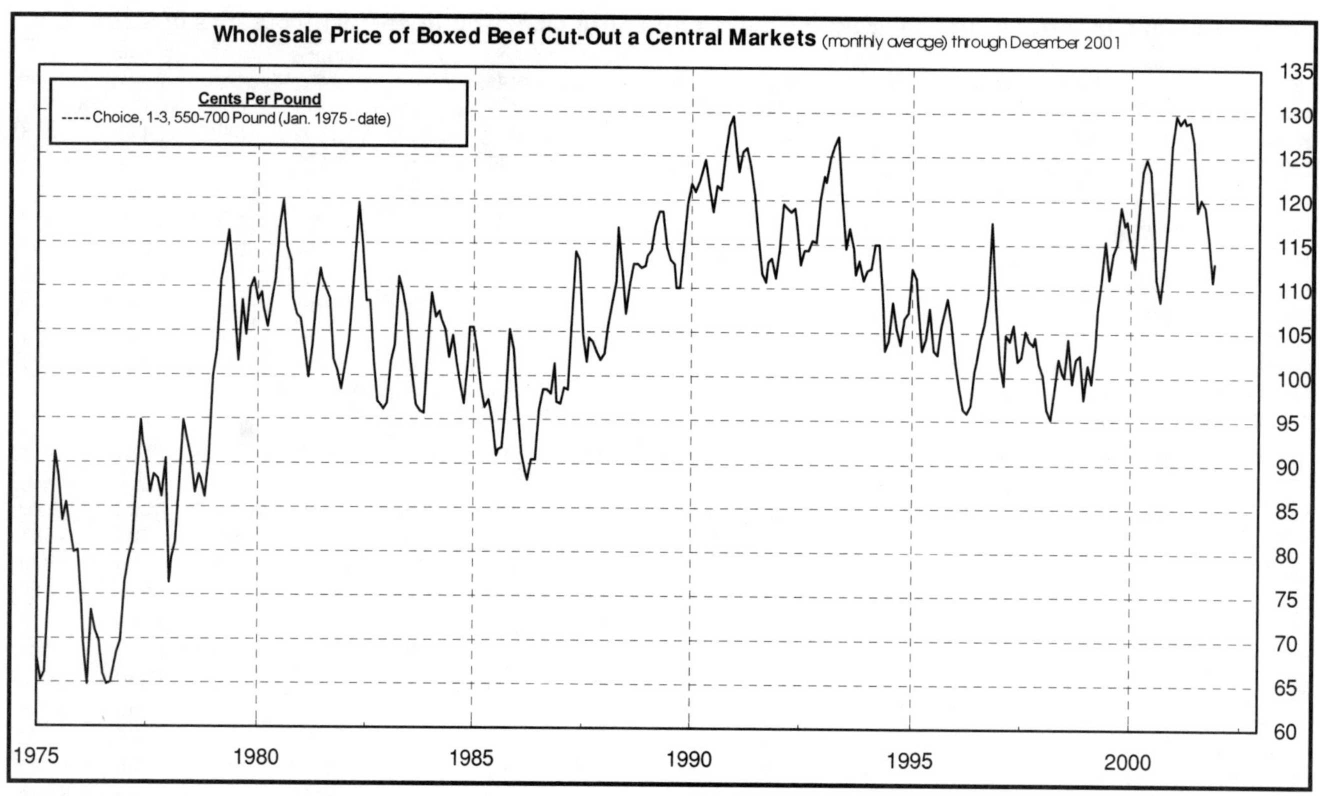

Exports and Imports of Meats in the United States (Carcass Weight Equivalent)[4] In Millions of Pounds

	Exports				Imports			
Year	Beef and Veal	Lamb and Mutton	Pork[4]	All Meat	Beef and Veal	Lamb and Mutton	Pork[4]	All Meat
1992	1,324	8	420	1,752	2,440	50	645	3,135
1993	1,275	8	446	1,730	2,401	53	740	3,194
1994	1,611	9	549	2,169	2,369	49	743	3,161
1995	1,821	6	787	2,614	2,103	64	664	2,832
1996	1,877	6	970	2,853	2,073	73	620	2,764
1997	2,136	5	1,044	3,185	2,343	83	634	3,061
1998	2,171	6	1,229	3,407	2,643	112	705	3,461
1999	2,417	5	1,278	3,700	2,874	113	827	3,813
2000[1]	2,510	6	1,292	3,808	3,076	131	967	4,174
2001[2]	2,530	4	1,315	3,849	3,080	135	985	4,200

[1] Preliminary. [2] Estimate. [3] Forecast. [4] Includes meat content of minor meats and of mixed products. *Source: Economic Research Service, U.S. Department of Agriculture (FAS-USDA)*

Average Wholesale Prices of Meats in the United States In Cents Per Pound

	Composite Retail Price		Wholesale Value[4]									
Year	of Beef, Choice, Grade 3	of Pork[3]	Beef	Pork	Net Farm Value of Pork[5]	Cow Beef Canner & Cutter, Central US	Boxed Beef Cut-out, Choice 1-3, Central US, 550-700 Lbs.	Pork Carcass Cut-out, US No. 2	Lamb Carcass, Choice-Prime, East Coast, 55-65 Lbs.	Pork Loins, Central US, 14-18 Lbs.	Skinned Ham, Central US, 20-26 Lbs.[6]	Pork Bellies, Central US, 12-14 Lbs.
1993	293.40	197.60	182.50	102.90	72.50	95.43	118.74	62.19	143.97	107.47	67.85	41.62
1994	282.90	198.10	166.70	98.90	62.90	84.39	108.47	57.29	147.62	101.50	58.12	40.00
1995	284.30	194.80	163.90	98.80	66.70	68.22	106.68	59.98	163.45	107.74	58.56	43.04
1996	280.20	220.90	158.10	117.20	84.60	58.18	103.09	72.39	177.58	118.49	72.41	69.97
1997	279.53	231.54	----	----	----	64.30	103.26	70.87	178.99	108.06	62.75	71.41
1998	277.12	239.18	----	----	----	61.33	99.82	52.80	156.75	99.75	44.75	51.94
1999	287.77	241.44	----	----	----	66.51	111.06	53.45	170.29	100.38	45.18	57.12
2000[1]	306.42	258.19	----	----	----	72.57	117.51	64.07	177.78	117.13	52.02	77.46
2001[2]	338.58	269.43	----	----	----	79.50	122.61	66.85	148.96	116.97	56.86	78.61

[1] Preliminary. [2] Estimate. [3] Sold as retail cuts (ham, bacon, loin, etc.). [4] Quantity equivalent to 1 pound of retail cuts. [5] Portion of gross farm value minus farm by-product allowance. [6] Prior to 1995, 17-20 pounds. *Source: Economic Research Service, U.S. Department of Agriculture (ERS-USDA)*

Average Wholesale Price of Boxed Beef Cut-Out[1], Choice, at Central Markets   In Cents Per Pound

Year	Jan.	Feb.	Mar.	Apr.	May	June	July	Aug.	Sept.	Oct.	Nov.	Dec.	Average
1992	114.38	119.65	119.14	118.66	119.18	117.53	112.79	114.36	114.40	115.51	115.26	119.95	116.73
1993	122.69	122.13	124.80	126.12	127.19	120.52	114.48	116.73	114.65	111.52	113.26	110.83	118.74
1994	112.11	112.23	115.03	111.08	108.85	102.02	104.10	100.00	105.40	103.03	100.00	107.22	108.47
1995	112.17	111.12	107.87	103.03	104.21	107.65	103.03	102.55	105.82	107.77	108.88	106.08	106.68
1996	101.71	98.86	96.36	96.01	96.90	100.70	101.53	104.43	105.93	109.10	117.53	108.03	103.09
1997	101.90	98.98	104.87	104.17	105.97	101.83	102.38	105.14	104.06	103.72	104.63	101.50	103.26
1998	100.26	96.27	95.34	98.32	102.09	100.38	99.96	104.28	99.28	102.08	102.61	97.49	99.86
1999	101.37	99.37	103.62	107.55	110.89	115.39	111.14	114.00	115.13	119.21	117.38	117.71	111.05
2000	114.74	112.59	118.42	123.45	124.88	123.30	115.85	111.20	108.68	112.58	118.05	126.41	117.51
2001[2]	129.78	128.87	129.58	128.93	129.03	126.82	118.93	120.20	119.30	115.93	110.95	113.04	122.61

[1] Choice 1-3, 550-700 pounds. [2] Preliminary. *Source: Economic Research Service, U.S. Department of Agriculture (ERS-USDA)*

Production (Commercial) of All Red Meats in the United States   In Millions of Pounds (Carcass Weight)

Year	Jan.	Feb.	Mar.	Apr.	May	June	July	Aug.	Sept.	Oct.	Nov.	Dec.	Total
1992	3,623	3,090	3,376	3,259	3,237	3,423	3,441	3,406	3,560	3,656	3,289	3,434	40,794
1993	3,304	3,012	3,396	3,299	3,212	3,481	3,342	3,504	3,516	3,499	3,449	3,554	40,568
1994	3,366	3,126	3,591	3,382	3,431	3,615	3,361	3,756	3,720	3,795	3,666	3,714	42,523
1995	3,560	3,210	3,751	3,304	3,758	3,798	3,424	3,860	3,697	3,795	3,748	3,553	43,458
1996	3,823	3,519	3,512	3,690	3,767	3,439	3,585	3,707	3,396	3,827	3,435	3,432	43,132
1997	3,735	3,278	3,444	3,592	3,571	3,492	3,657	3,619	3,665	4,005	3,453	3,715	43,226
1998	3,836	3,476	3,726	3,701	3,582	3,732	3,781	3,770	3,827	4,033	3,725	3,945	45,134
1999	3,833	3,535	4,016	3,824	3,604	3,940	3,781	3,913	3,933	4,002	3,895	3,862	46,138
2000	3,784	3,767	4,044	3,460	3,878	3,941	3,644	4,113	3,861	4,096	3,919	3,619	46,126
2001[1]	3,935	3,761	3,761	3,506	3,881	3,758	3,643	4,060	3,664	4,264	3,970	3,813	46,016

[1] Preliminary. *Source: Economic Research Service, U.S. Department of Agriculture (ERS-USDA)*

Cold Storage Holdings of All[1] Meats in the United States, at End of Month   In Millions of Pounds

Year	Jan.	Feb.	Mar.	Apr.	May	June	July	Aug.	Sept.	Oct.	Nov.	Dec.
1992	707.9	690.5	725.4	706.8	692.2	665.3	646.0	595.6	613.4	637.8	626.6	615.1
1993	649.4	654.6	652.9	692.0	671.0	660.8	664.2	650.7	671.7	702.4	720.3	726.7
1994	807.7	800.5	842.5	858.0	837.5	822.6	816.2	771.9	788.5	822.7	827.5	802.0
1995	838.7	833.8	834.0	852.7	831.2	820.8	803.6	733.4	711.3	732.3	757.0	749.7
1996	779.5	781.6	729.3	748.6	716.2	687.9	642.7	657.4	678.4	655.5	627.1	621.3
1997	655.9	669.9	719.5	752.5	719.7	742.9	726.3	731.5	728.2	739.1	741.0	722.4
1998	802.8	825.8	816.3	849.3	814.3	771.0	747.2	728.2	738.8	794.9	794.1	821.0
1999	833.0	863.1	883.5	936.4	901.2	843.9	810.4	834.9	746.3	780.3	750.5	748.3
2000	853.1	913.9	934.3	951.3	963.5	926.7	896.2	881.0	871.1	868.0	883.0	836.2
2001[2]	909.5	852.6	787.5	771.4	772.5	742.2	713.2	732.6	775.3	847.2	879.1	940.1

[1] Includes beef and veal, mutton and lamb, pork and products, rendered pork fat, and miscellaneous meats. Excludes lard. [2] Preliminary.
Source: Economic Research Service, U.S. Department of Agriculture (ERS-USDA)

Cold Storage Holdings of Frozen Beef in the United States, on First of Month   In Millions of Pounds

Year	Jan. 1	Feb. 1	Mar. 1	Apr. 1	May 1	June 1	July 1	Aug. 1	Sept. 1	Oct. 1	Nov. 1	Dec. 1
1992	315.9	329.1	298.9	313.7	302.1	303.5	299.4	294.1	288.9	275.2	291.2	275.9
1993	272.8	286.4	279.9	293.9	276.7	262.1	271.7	285.3	307.5	326.8	344.4	376.3
1994	401.0	430.2	414.4	423.2	399.5	367.9	379.4	388.9	377.2	406.8	410.6	419.5
1995	411.2	420.3	407.7	385.4	392.2	359.1	352.3	359.3	344.9	347.7	381.6	381.4
1996	389.6	367.9	362.6	347.3	335.6	307.4	306.7	291.1	305.2	312.2	295.9	288.1
1997	284.9	290.3	261.7	290.4	285.4	278.7	305.6	302.8	324.6	349.1	351.6	378.2
1998	350.2	331.1	334.9	329.7	335.5	310.2	316.5	303.0	306.7	323.1	358.2	328.2
1999	296.4	301.1	300.1	309.2	316.8	306.7	293.1	292.7	377.9	294.4	322.5	308.9
2000	314.2	350.9	369.0	378.2	396.1	401.1	405.1	391.5	398.8	405.7	404.4	411.8
2001[1]	401.7	411.4	360.2	332.6	315.3	325.4	340.8	347.1	373.2	382.8	393.6	426.0

[1] Preliminary. *Source: Economic Research Service, U.S. Department of Agriculture (ERS-USDA)*

Mercury

Since 1990, recycled mercury-containing devices accounted for virtually all domestic mercury production in 2000. Domestic mines no longer produce mercury as their primary product. Owing largely to strict regulations controlling mercury discharges to the environment. Both U.S. primary mercury production and usage have declined steadily since the 1970's reflecting a trend of finding substitutes for mercury rather than develop large-scale recycling programs. On a global basis as well, secondary mercury now accounts for a large part of supply.

Mercury is the only common metal that is liquid at room temperatures. It is also highly toxic, and perhaps a greater contaminant than lead because mercury can exist in vapor form: despite global efforts to confine mercury it is believed that airborne mercury, called methyl mercury, is now as much as three to six times greater than it was in pre-industrial times--its formed from the mercury discharged into the air from industrial plants. In the U.S., prime virgin mercury is produced as a by-product of gold mining operations from fewer than ten mines in California, Nevada and Utah.

World production of mercury is largely limited to four main countries and a few marginal producers. World production in 2000 of a near record low 1,640 metric tons compares with 1,630 in 1999 and nearly 3,000 tons in 1997. (One ton equals 29+ flasks of 76 pounds each.) Kyrgyzstan's, now the world's largest producer, produced 550 tons in 2000 vs. 620 tons in 1999, most of which is exported, primarily to China. Algeria and China produced 240 tons and 200 tons in 2000, respectively, unchanged from 1999. During 1996-98, China's annual mercury production averaged over 500 tons. Spain, once the world's largest producer, with almost 1,500 tons in the mid-1990's, produced only 500 tons in 2000 vs. 433 tons in 1999. World mercury resources are estimated at nearly 600,000 tons, mostly in Kyrgyzstan, Ukraine and Spain, with the total viewed as sufficient to last at least a century, based on declining world usage rates.

Mercury is a recoverable metal. U.S. secondary production in the mid-1990's totaled about 400 tons , but recent annual totals are not available. Tight EPA restrictions banning landfill disposal and/or transport of mercury-containing wastes has encouraged more efficient recovery methods, especially from fluorescent lamps. The U.S. government has a mercury stockpile of about 4435 tons, authorized for disposal but with tight restrictions as to how much if any, can be sold each year. Reportedly, the goal is to reduce the inventory to zero, but the timeframe is uncertain. Disposal of 690 tons was apparently planned for fiscal 2000.

Chlorine and caustic soda manufacture now accounts for the largest domestic use of mercury with about 50% of the total and electrical applications about 25%. Substitutes for mercury include lithium and composite ceramic materials.

U.S. foreign trade in mercury is small. Imports of 103 tons in 2000 compare with 62 tons in 1999 while exports were 178 tons and 181 tons, respectively.

Mercury is sold in 34.5-kilogram flasks. The average free market price in 2000 of $155/flask compares with $140 in 1999.

World Mine Production of Mercury In Metric Tons (1 tonne = 29.008216 flasks)

Year	Algeria	China	Finland	Kyrgyz-stan[3]	Mexico	Spain	Tajik-istan[3]	Turkey	Ukraine[3]	United States	World Total
1992	476	580	75	350	21	36	100	5	100	64	1,960
1993	459	520	98	1,000	12	64	80	----	50	W	2,390
1994	414	470	83	379	12	393	55	----	50	W	1,960
1995	292	780	90	380	15	1,497	50	----	40	W	3,190
1996	368	510	88	584	15	862	45	----	30	W	2,560
1997	447	830	63	610	15	863	40	----	25	W	2,950
1998	224	230	54	620	15	675	35	----	20	NA	1,950
1999[1]	240	200	40	620	15	433	35	----	NA	NA	1,630
2000[2]	240	200	45	550	25	500	40	----	NA	NA	1,640

[1] Preliminary. [2] Estimate. [3] Formerly part of the U.S.S.R.; data not reported separately until 1992. W = Withheld to avoid disclosing company proprietary data. NA = Not available. *Source: U.S. Geological Survey (USGS)*

Salient Statistics of Mercury in the United States In Metric Tons

Year	Priducing Mines	Secondary Production: Industrial	Secondary Production: Govern-ment[3]	Secondary Production: NDS[4] Shipments	Consumer & Dealer Stocks, Dec. 31	Industrial Demand	Exports	Imports
1992	9	176	103	267	436	621	977	92
1993	9	350	----	543	384	558	389	40
1994	7	466	----	86	469	483	316	129
1995	8	534	----	----	321	436	179	377
1996	6	446	----	----	446	372	45	340
1997	5	389	----	----	203	346	134	164
1998	NA	NA	----	----	NA	NA	63	128
1999[1]	NA	NA	----	----	NA	NA	181	62
2000[2]	NA	NA	----	----	NA	NA	178	103

[1] Preliminary. [2] Estimate. [3] Secondary mercury shipped from the Department of Energy. [4] National Defense Stockpile. NA = Not available.
Source: U.S. Geological Survey (USGS)

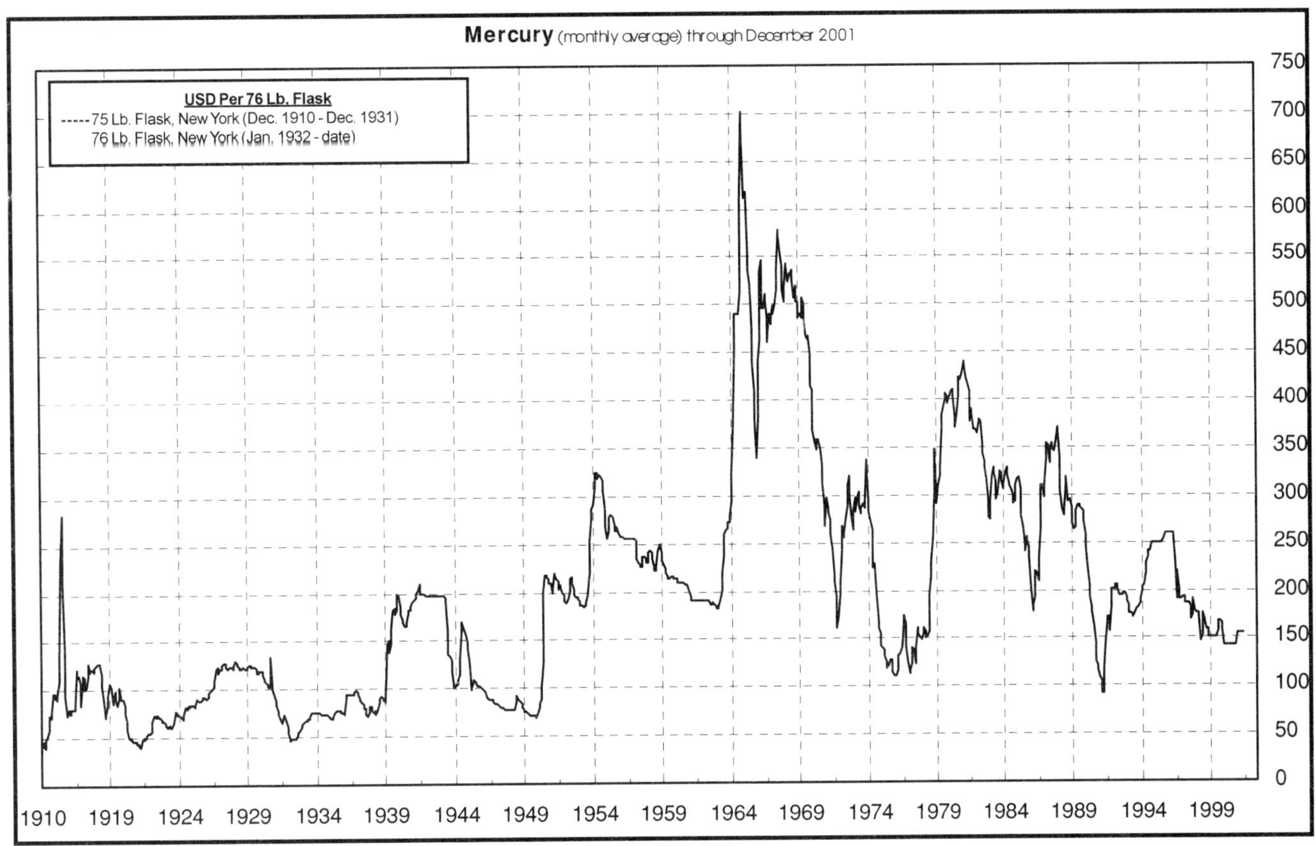

Average Price of Mercury in New York In Dollars Per Flask of 76 Pounds (34.5 Kilograms)

Year	Jan.	Feb.	Mar.	Apr.	May	June	July	Aug.	Sept.	Oct.	Nov.	Dec.	Average
1992	162.86	177.24	180.00	180.00	190.63	202.50	202.50	203.45	207.50	207.50	207.50	207.50	194.10
1993	207.50	207.50	207.50	207.50	207.50	201.30	191.00	191.00	185.00	185.00	181.00	175.00	195.57
1994	175.00	175.00	179.78	180.00	180.95	186.64	196.50	200.00	203.10	205.00	217.50	230.71	194.18
1995	235.00	240.00	241.30	250.00	250.00	250.00	250.00	250.00	250.00	250.00	250.00	250.00	247.19
1996	250.00	250.00	261.67	268.33	265.00	265.00	265.00	265.00	265.00	265.00	262.63	235.48	259.84
1997	233.98	232.76	228.88	228.64	220.00	199.05	200.00	198.10	190.83	198.83	191.47	187.00	209.13
1998	187.00	187.00	187.00	187.00	187.00	181.55	175.00	175.00	175.00	175.00	175.00	175.00	180.55
1999	175.00	152.63	150.00	150.00	150.00	150.00	150.00	150.00	150.00	150.00	150.00	150.00	152.09
2000	150.00	157.88	167.50	167.50	167.50	158.23	142.00	142.00	142.00	142.00	142.00	142.00	151.72
2001	142.00	142.00	142.00	142.00	142.00	143.71	154.00	154.00	154.00	154.00	154.00	154.00	148.14

Source: American Metal Market (AMM)

Mercury Consumed in the United States In Metric Tons

Year	Batteries[3]	Chlorine & Caustic Soda	Catalysts, Misc.	Dental Equip.	Electrical Lighting[3]	General Lab Use	Measuring Contraol Instrument	Paints	Wiring Devices & Switches[3]	Other Uses	Total
1988	448	354	86	53	31	26	77	197	176	55	1,503
1989	250	379	40	39	31	18	87	192	141	32	1,212
1990	106	247	29	44	33	32	108	14	70	38	720
1991	18	184	26	41	39	30	90	6	71	49	554
1992	13	209	20	42	55	28	80	-----	82	92	621
1993	10	180	18	35	38	26	65	-----	83	103	558
1994	6	135	25	24	27	24	53	-----	79	110	483
1995	-----	154	-----	32	30	-----	43	-----	84	93	436
1996[1]	-----	136	-----	31	29	-----	41	-----	49	86	372
1997[2]	-----	160	-----	40	29	-----	24	-----	57	36	346

[1] Preliminary. [2] Estimate. W = Withheld proprietary data. *Source: U.S. Geological Survey (USGS)*

Milk

U.S. monthly milk production in late 2001 finally made it back to year earlier levels following almost a year of lower output. Ironically, the relatively high milk prices and low concentrate feed prices during 2001 normally would have been conducive growth in milk production, but very tight supplies of replacement heifers and high quality forage curtailed bringing new facilities into full operations. However, the high prices also had the effect of slowing the rate of dairy farm exits.

Milk production dipped in 2001 to 165.4 billion pounds, but forecast to rise to record high 170 billion in 2002. U.S. milk production is at least twice at high as any other country. The U.S. 2001 milk cow inventory at 9.1 million head was marginally lower than 2000 with a further modest reduction likely in 2002. In the mid 1990's the inventory averaged about 9.4 million head. The annual average of milk cows in the twenty key producing states in 2000 of 7,799,000 head compares with about 7,735,000 in 2001. Farmers received an average of $15/cwt of milk in 2001; prices are expected to decline less than $2/cwt in 2002, but still remain about $1/cwt over calendar 2000. For 2000, the U.S. Class 111, 3.5% fat (Basic Formula Prices--BFP) milk price, averaged $9.74 per cwt vs. the 2001 average of about $13.05 and forecasts of $11.25 to $12.05/cwt in 20002. Retail milk prices generally show more variance than wholesale values largely due to differences in transportation and marketing costs. The retail fluid milk price index for 2000 was at 107.8 (December '97=100).

Politics remains deeply imbedded with U.S. milk prices. At issue most of the time is a convoluted Federal milk-pricing system devised in 1937 to insure that fresh milk was available in all parts of the country with the minimum price that farmers can charge for milk fixed monthly by the USDA. At the time the country was divided into 31 regions and the set price is higher the further the regions are from Wisconsin, effectively making retail prices in the East higher than in the Midwest. Dairy technology and improved refrigeration have basically made the old system obsolete.

The milk industry continues to aggressively advertise milk as a beverage in an effort to bolster U.S. fluid milk consumption; the expected positive results so far are questionable. U.S. fluid milk usage in 2000 of 26.9 million metric tons is marginally under 1999 and forecast to slip further in 2001 and 2002 to 26.8 million tons. About half of U.S. adults over age 35 are believed to have eliminated milk from their diets. Moreover, consumer milk patterns have changed with plain whole milk sales slipping while low fat and skim milk sales increased. California and Wisconsin are the two largest producing states. Seasonally, milk production is highest during the April-June quarter.

The world's cow 2002 milk production of 382.6 million metric tons compares with 378.5 million in 2001. Russia is among the largest producers with 33 million tons in 2002. With France and Germany in producing 25 million and 28 million tons, respectively. The world's milk cow inventory of 122.9 million head in 2002 compares with 122.9 million in 2001, the largest number of which is in India with about 36 million head.

Futures Markets

BFP milk futures and options are traded on the New York Board of Trade (NYBOT). Fluid milk futures and options are traded on the Chicago Mercantile Exchange (CME).

World Fluid Milk Production (Cow's Milk) In Thousands of Metric Tons

Year	Brazil	France	Germany	India	Italy	Netherlands	New Zealand	Poland	Russia	Ukraine	United Kingdom	United States	World Total
1994	16,700	25,322	27,866	31,000	10,365	10,964	9,719	11,822	42,800	18,138	14,920	69,701	378,408
1995	18,375	25,413	28,621	32,500	10,500	11,294	9,684	11,420	39,300	17,181	14,700	70,440	380,729
1996	19,480	25,083	28,776	33,500	10,800	11,013	10,405	11,690	35,800	16,000	14,640	69,857	364,321
1997	20,600	24,893	28,702	34,500	10,818	10,922	11,500	11,980	34,100	13,650	14,857	70,802	365,609
1998	21,630	24,793	28,378	35,500	10,736	11,000	11,640	12,500	33,000	13,800	14,218	71,373	368,028
1999	21,700	24,892	28,400	36,000	10,444	11,174	11,070	12,068	32,000	13,140	14,584	73,805	371,572
2000[1]	22,134	24,890	28,400	36,250	10,350	10,800	12,835	11,800	31,900	12,200	14,200	76,370	375,676
2001[2]	22,800	24,890	28,400	36,400	10,350	10,500	13,348	12,000	32,000	12,000	14,300	76,975	378,823

[1] Preliminary. [2] Forecast. *Source: Foreign Agricultural Service, U.S. Department of Agriculture (FAS-USDA)*

Milk-Feed Price Ratio[1] in the United States In Pounds

Year	Jan.	Feb.	Mar.	Apr.	May	June	July	Aug.	Sept.	Oct.	Nov.	Dec.	Average
1994	2.61	2.51	2.52	2.51	2.36	2.42	2.61	2.72	2.81	2.92	2.96	2.81	2.65
1995	2.77	2.73	2.71	2.60	2.52	2.48	2.40	2.50	2.56	2.62	2.69	2.56	2.59
1996	2.59	2.42	2.35	2.17	2.10	2.17	2.19	2.28	2.64	2.98	2.85	2.70	2.45
1997	2.44	2.35	2.27	2.14	2.07	2.12	2.24	2.35	2.44	2.63	2.73	2.80	2.38
1998	2.75	2.77	2.73	2.70	2.58	2.89	3.00	3.60	3.98	4.18	4.22	4.27	3.31
1999	4.09	3.67	3.57	2.97	2.89	3.17	3.61	3.85	4.09	3.96	3.87	3.24	3.58
2000	3.07	2.94	2.91	2.84	2.63	2.96	3.29	3.38	3.34	3.12	3.03	3.04	3.05
2001[2]	3.08	3.02	3.25	3.32	3.38	3.73	3.60	3.62	3.76	3.54	3.26	3.01	3.38

[1] Pounds of 16% protein mixed dairy feed equal in value to one pound of whole milk. [2] Preliminary. *Source: Economic Research Service, U.S. Department of Agriculture (ERS-USDA)*

Salient Statistics of Milk in the United States In Millions of Pounds

Year	Number of Milk Cows on Farms[3] (Thousands)	Supply: Production: Per Cow[4] (Pounds)	Supply: Production: Total[4]	Supply: Beginning Stocks[5]	Supply: Imports	Supply: Total Supply	Utilization: Exports[5]	Utilization: Domestic: Fed to Calves	Utilization: Domestic: Humans	Utilization: Total Use	Average Farm Price Received Per Cwt.: All Milk, Wholesale	Average Farm Price Received Per Cwt.: Milk Eligible for Fluid Market	Average Farm Price Received Per Cwt.: Milk, Manufacturing Grade	Per Capita Consumption[6] (Fluid Milk in Lbs.)
1994	9,494	16,179	153,602	9,570	2,880	166,052	5,725	1,267	152,687	160,292	13.01	13.02	11.85	226
1995	9,466	16,405	155,292	5,760	2,935	163,987	4,321	1,216	153,600	159,819	12.74	12.78	11.78	223
1996	9,372	16,433	154,006	4,168	2,944	161,118	2,061	1,175	152,556	156,404	14.88	14.95	13.38	224
1997	9,252	16,871	156,091	4,714	2,900	163,705	2,094	1,138	154,816	158,048	13.34	13.38	12.18	221
1998	9,154	17,189	157,441	4,887	3,813	166,141	1,408	1,162	157,352	159,922	14.37	14.41	12.78	219
1999[1]	9,156	17,771	162,711	5,302	4,447	172,460	1,303	1,134	163,316	165,753	12.33	12.38	10.53	219
2000[2]	9,210	18,204	167,658		4,496						14.93	14.98	13.57	

[1] Preliminary. [2] Estimate. [3] Average number on farms during year including dry cows, excluding heifers not yet fresh. [4] Excludes milk sucked by calves. [5] Government and commercial. [6] Product pounds of commercial sales and on farm consumption. *Source: Economic Research Service, U.S. Department of Agriculture (ERS-USDA)*

Utilization of Milk in the United States In Millions of Pounds (Milk Equivalent)

Year	Butter from Whey Cream	Creamery Butter[2]	Cheese[3]	Cottage Cheese (Creamed)	Canned Milk[4]	Bulk Condensed Whole Milk: Unsweetened	Bulk Condensed Whole Milk: Sweetened	Dry Whole Milk Products	Ice Cream[5]	Other Frozen Dairy Products	Other Manufactured Products[6]	Used on Farms: Farm-Churned Butter	Used on Farms: Total
1994	4,592	29,127	51,143	524	1,184	205	277	1,227	2,083	13,182	216	394	1,657
1995	4,735	28,388	52,587	494	1,049	203	254	1,262	2,053	13,041	252	340	1,556
1996	4,911	26,187	53,937	461	1,013	242	266	983	2,058	13,190	217	301	1,476
1997	4,966	25,714	55,719	NA	1,208	227	314	898	2,112	13,859	686	256	1,394
1998	5,094	26,211	56,827	NA	1,017	222	186	1,050	2,151	14,301	697	244	1,406
1999[1]	5,392	28,604	60,221	NA	1,036	216	171	867	2,243	14,265	684	233	1,367

[1] Preliminary. [2] Excludes whey butter. [3] American and other. [4] Includes evaporated and sweetened condensed. [5] Milk equivalent of butter and condensed milk used in ice cream. [6] Whole milk equivalent of dry cream, malted milk powder, part-skim milk, dry or concentrated ice cream mix, dehydrated butterfat and other miscellaneous products using milkfat. *Source: National Agricultural Statistics Service, U.S. Department of Agriculture (NASS-USDA)*

Milk Production[1] in the United States In Millions of Pounds

Year	Jan.	Feb.	Mar.	Apr.	May	June	July	Aug.	Sept.	Oct.	Nov.	Dec.	Total
1995	13,147	12,142	13,640	13,343	13,875	13,302	13,152	12,793	12,381	12,716	12,297	12,804	155,423
1996	13,085	12,431	13,537	13,230	13,576	12,832	12,809	12,624	12,241	12,714	12,324	12,928	154,331
1997	13,126	12,141	13,694	13,406	13,902	13,375	13,319	13,059	12,427	12,814	12,362	12,977	156,602
1998	13,282	12,188	13,694	13,510	14,015	13,296	13,162	12,942	12,415	12,956	12,611	13,370	157,441
1999	13,628	12,607	14,270	13,938	14,458	13,633	13,444	13,357	12,970	13,412	13,140	13,854	162,711
2000	14,263	13,606	14,761	14,390	14,791	14,008	14,117	13,798	13,246	13,708	13,212	13,758	167,658
2001[2]	13,998	12,894	14,375	14,078	14,646	13,957	13,877	13,564	13,129	13,611	13,305	13,902	165,336

[1] Excludes milk sucked by calves. [2] Preliminary. *Source: Economic Research Service, U.S. Department of Agriculture (ERS-USDA)*

Average Price Received by U.S. Farmers for All Milk (Sold to Plants) In Dollars Per Hundred Pounds (Cwt.)

Year	Jan.	Feb.	Mar.	Apr.	May	June	July	Aug.	Sept.	Oct.	Nov.	Dec.	Average
1995	12.60	12.60	12.70	12.30	12.30	12.10	12.00	12.40	12.80	13.40	14.00	13.90	12.76
1996	14.00	13.80	13.70	13.90	14.30	14.80	15.40	15.90	16.50	16.40	15.20	14.30	14.85
1997	13.40	13.50	13.50	13.20	12.70	12.20	12.10	12.70	13.10	14.10	14.70	14.80	13.33
1998	14.70	14.70	14.40	14.00	13.30	14.10	14.20	15.50	16.70	17.70	17.80	18.00	15.43
1999	17.40	15.50	15.00	12.60	12.70	13.10	13.80	15.10	15.70	14.90	14.40	12.20	14.37
2000	12.00	11.80	11.90	11.90	12.00	12.30	12.60	12.50	12.90	12.50	12.60	13.00	12.33
2001[1]	13.20	13.00	13.90	14.40	15.40	16.10	16.20	16.40	17.00	15.70	14.40	13.40	14.93

[1] Preliminary. *Source: Economic Research Service, U.S. Department of Agriculture (ERS-USDA)*

Average Farm Price of Milk Eligible for Fluid Market In Dollars Per Hundred Pounds (Cwt.)

Year	Jan.	Feb.	Mar.	Apr.	May	June	July	Aug.	Sept.	Oct.	Nov.	Dec.	Average
1995	12.70	12.60	12.60	12.30	12.30	12.20	12.10	12.50	12.80	13.40	14.00	14.00	12.79
1996	14.00	13.90	13.70	13.90	14.30	14.90	15.50	16.00	16.60	16.40	15.30	14.40	14.91
1997	13.40	13.50	13.60	13.20	12.80	12.30	12.20	12.80	13.10	14.10	14.70	14.80	13.38
1998	14.70	14.80	14.50	14.00	13.30	14.10	14.20	15.50	16.80	17.80	17.80	18.10	15.47
1999	17.50	15.60	15.10	12.60	12.80	13.20	13.90	15.00	15.70	15.00	14.50	12.30	14.43
2000	12.00	11.90	12.00	11.90	12.10	12.30	12.60	12.50	13.00	12.60	12.60	13.10	12.38
2001[1]	13.20	13.10	13.90	14.50	15.40	16.20	16.30	16.50	17.00	15.70	14.50	13.40	14.98

[1] Preliminary. *Source: Economic Research Service, U.S. Department of Agriculture (ERS-USDA)*

Molasses

Molasses is a heavy, viscous fluid produced as a byproduct of raw sugar refining. Molasses is the syrup remaining from the crystallization of sugar from cane and beet juice. It is separated from the sugar by centrifuging. Blackstrap molasses has had all the sugar removed. About 50 gallons of molasses is produced for each ton of raw sugar refined. Molasses contains about 33 percent sucrose. Syrups produced from molasses are often used in sweeteners for the candy and baking industries.

U.S. supplies of molasses are about three million metric tonnes per year. Of this total, a third comes from mainland sugar mills, a quarter from beet sugar refiners, and smaller amounts from Hawaiian cane and cane refiners. Beet molasses is used primarily as a livestock feed and a yeast by the pharmaceutical industry. To some extent, an individual country's production of molasses is related to the degree to which it refines sugar. Some countries produce and export raw sugar. Other countries produce raw and refined sugar which means they produce more molasses due to refining.

In Mexico, one of the largest sugar producers in the world, the government seized 27 sugar mills in late 2001. The government has been attempting to restructure the sugar industry which has been plagued by debt. As part of that process, the Mexican government in early February 2002 announced that they would hold an auction to pre-sell or forward sell 789,330 tonnes of sugar molasses. The aim of the auction was apparently to help ensure that sugar as well as sugar products are exported and now allowed to become stocks that will act to pressure domestic prices. In addition to this, Mexico also has a 275,000 tonnes duty-free export quota for molasses in a free trade agreement with the European Union.

In early 2002, U.S. prices for sugarcane molasses were higher than a year earlier. One development was that the Mexican government imposed a 20 percent tax on soft drinks using high fructose corn syrup instead of cane sugar. In early February 2002, cane blackstrap feed molasses in New Orleans was prices at $70.00 to $75.00 per short ton compared to $55.00 to $60.00 per short ton in February 2001.

World Production of Sugarcane, by Selected Countries In Thousands of Metric Tons

Crop Year	Australia	Brazil	China	Cuba	India	Indonesia	Mexico	Pakistan	Philip-pines	South Africa	Thailand	United States	World Total
1990-1	25,140	75,000	57,620	67,500	135,494	28,074	36,000	22,604	18,600	18,083	40,563	24,018	707,497
1991-2	21,306	87,000	67,898	62,000	148,814	28,100	35,300	24,796	22,816	20,078	47,505	26,272	753,303
1992-3	29,400	90,000	73,011	47,150	123,985	32,000	39,700	27,276	23,850	12,955	34,711	26,264	719,671
1993-4	31,951	91,000	63,549	46,000	116,638	33,000	34,100	34,182	22,753	11,244	37,569	26,680	706,433
1994-5	34,860	110,000	60,300	39,000	159,593	30,545	40,134	34,193	18,415	15,683	50,459	25,485	783,373
1995-6	37,378	93,000	65,417	45,500	184,708	30,000	42,300	28,151	22,774	16,750	57,693	25,835	842,937
1996-7[1]	39,878	101,000	68,500	45,000	147,858	28,600	42,000	25,580	23,500	22,512	59,000	24,055	845,645
1997-8[2]	40,878	105,000	69,400	45,500	137,184	29,000		31,600			60,000		

[1] Preliminary. [2] Estimate. *Source: Economic Research Service, U.S. Department of Agriculture (ERS-USDA)*

World Production of Sugarbeet, by Selected Countries In Thousands of Metric Tons

Year	Belgium-Luxembourg	China	France	Germany	Italy	Poland	Russia	Spain	Turkey	Ukraine	United Kingdom	United States	World Total
1990-1	6,857	14,525	25,520	30,366	11,600	16,721	31,091	7,358	13,986	44,265	8,000	24,959	303,149
1991-2	6,043	16,289	24,403	25,926	11,400	11,412	24,280	6,679	15,474	36,168	7,672	25,485	277,368
1992-3	6,174	15,069	26,491	27,177	14,762	11,052	25,548	7,234	15,563	28,783	9,180	26,438	274,751
1993-4	6,120	11,938	25,514	28,606	10,510	15,621	25,468	8,622	15,463	33,717	8,988	23,813	272,746
1994-5	5,729	12,406	23,943	24,211	11,905	11,630	13,945	8,100	12,757	28,138	8,360	29,024	247,798
1995-6	6,291	13,984	25,121	26,049	12,932	13,309	19,110	7,450	10,989	28,000	8,360	25,460	257,984
1996-7[1]	6,100	13,900	24,400	27,000	11,150	17,460	16,500	7,700	14,383	25,500	8,432	24,104	254,335
1997-8[2]	6,000	14,000	24,500	26,500	12,500	14,000	17,000	6,800	15,100	25,400	8,400	26,134	256,393

[1] Preliminary. [2] Estimate. *Source: Economic Research Service, U.S. Department of Agriculture (ERS-USDA)*

U.S. Annual Average Prices of Molasses, by Types (F.O.B. Tank Car or Truck) In Dollars Per Short Ton[2]

	Blackstrap							Beet Molasses	
Year	New Orleans	South Florida	Baltimore	Upper Mississippi	Savannah	California Ports[3]	Houston	Montana, Wyoming & Nebraska	Red River Valley[4]
1992	61.27	68.36	80.41	92.95	76.70	78.43	63.75	67.81	57.50
1993	55.48	62.36	76.03	89.26	70.00	74.24	57.12	72.63	64.44
1994	65.53	72.23	85.94	91.97	79.23	83.31	69.86	-----	-----
1995	72.00	79.92	86.30	99.11	87.48	90.30	76.37	-----	-----
1996	74.88	83.07	91.27	104.71	92.55	97.11	79.41	-----	-----
1997	58.14	68.00	76.84	90.69	77.51	83.38	62.13	-----	-----
1998	46.35	59.92	63.37	78.00	68.75	69.30	48.85	-----	-----
1999[1]	33.77	49.15	51.06	65.50	56.63	58.32	36.30	-----	-----

[1] Preliminary. [2] To convert dollars per short ton to cents per gallon divide by 171. [3] Los Angeles and Stockton. [4] North Dakota and Minnesota.
Source: Agricultural Marketing Service, U.S. Department of Agriculture (AMS-USDA)

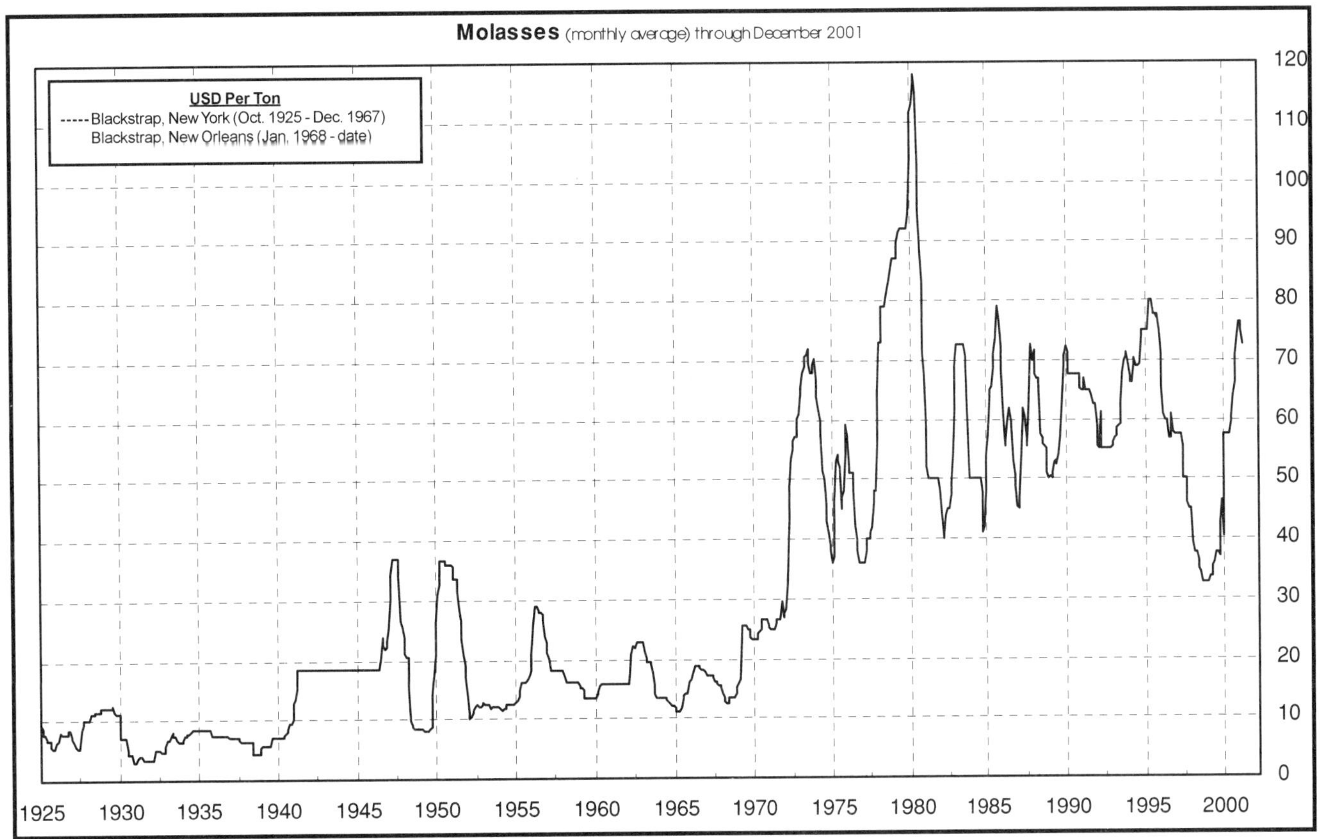

Salient Statistics of Molasses[3] in the United States In Metric Tons

	Production						Inedible Imports From						Production of Edible
		Mainland				In Shipments							Total Molasses
			Refiners										
Year	Hawaii	Mainland Hills[4]	Black-strap	Beet	Puerto Rico	From Hawaii	Total Imports	Brazil	Dominican Republic	Mexico	Mainland Exports[5]	U.S. Supply	(1,000 Gallons)
1989	218,009	808,355	122,786	974,179	34,864	169,270	926,870	107,109	147,235	75,634	293,535	2,707,925	1,990
1990	228,968	741,749	105,124	948,820	24,959	214,045	1,078,924	70,986	145,543	88,401	212,263	2,876,399	1,405
1991	188,252	807,652	126,000	1,165,962	27,882	184,337	1,258,637	10,342	137,271	235,244	242,635	3,299,953	1,825
1992	182,849	782,566	123,000	950,312	25,097	183,657	1,115,863	0	127,500	117,722	282,098	2,873,300	1,460
1993	187,915	831,661	113,000	692,465	22,802	190,371	1,040,858	0	163,180	47,596	255,907	2,612,448	1,480
1994	180,884	824,453	114,000	1,200,000	18,531	151,172	1,556,640	0	121,320	197,753	277,098	3,459,167	1,500
1995	146,000	886,826	114,000	1,040,000	16,156	146,000	1,048,726	0	132,983	172,177	274,868	2,960,684	1,500
1996[1]	-----	NA	NA	NA	-----	NA	NA	-----	-----	-----	NA	NA	0
1997[2]	-----	900,000	100,000	1,200,000	-----	100,000	1,583,755	-----	-----	-----	300,000	3,583,755	0

[1] Preliminary. [2] Estimate. [3] Feed and industrial molasses. [4] Includes high-test molasses from frozen cane. [5] Excluding exports from Hawaii and Puerto Rico. NA = Not available. *Source: Agricultural Marketing Service, U.S. Department of Agriculture (AMS-USDA)*

Wholesale Price of Blackstrap Molasses (Cane) at New Orleans In Dollars Per Short Ton

Year	Jan.	Feb.	Mar.	Apr.	May	June	July	Aug.	Sept.	Oct.	Nov.	Dec.	Average
1992	65.00	65.00	65.00	65.00	63.75	62.50	62.50	62.50	58.75	55.31	55.00	55.00	61.27
1993	55.00	55.00	55.00	55.00	55.00	55.00	55.00	55.25	55.31	56.25	56.75	57.19	55.48
1994	57.75	57.50	59.38	62.50	68.00	70.00	70.63	71.25	69.38	67.50	66.25	66.25	65.53
1995	69.00	70.31	68.75	68.75	68.75	69.38	74.25	75.00	75.00	75.00	75.00	75.00	72.00
1996	80.00	80.00	80.00	78.00	77.50	77.50	77.50	77.50	75.00	70.00	65.63	60.75	74.88
1997	60.00	60.00	59.00	56.56	56.88	60.31	57.50	57.50	57.50	57.50	57.50	57.50	58.14
1998	57.50	55.63	51.00	50.00	50.00	46.00	45.00	45.00	45.00	37.50	37.50	37.50	46.35
1999	37.50	36.25	35.00	34.38	32.50	32.50	32.50	32.50	32.50	32.50	33.75	33.75	33.80
2000	35.25	36.11	37.50	37.50	37.50	37.12	42.75	46.25	40.35	57.50	57.50	57.50	43.57
2001[1]	57.50	57.50	59.38	60.25	63.75	66.25	70.75	73.75	76.25	76.25	75.00	72.50	67.43

[1] Preliminary. *Source: Agricultural Marketing Service, U.S. Department of Agriculture (AMS-USDA)*

Molybdenum

Molybdenum is a silver-gray metal used principally as an alloying agent in cast irons, steels, and superalloys. It is used to enhance strength, toughness, and wear resistance. There is little substitution for molybdenum as an alloying element in steels and cast irons. Because of the availability and versatility of the metal, new materials are being developed that benefit from the alloying properties. In the form of molybdic acid or ferromolybdenum, it is combined with or added to chromium, manganese, nickel, tungsten, and other alloy metals. Molybdenum also finds use as a refractory metal in chemical applications.

The U.S. Geological Survey reported that year 2000 world mine production of molybdenum was estimated at 112,000 metric tonnes, down 8 percent from 1999. The largest producer of molybdenum was the U.S. with 2000 production estimated at 32,1000 tonnes, down 25 percent from the year before. In 1998 production was 53,300 tonnes. In the U.S., molybdenum ore was produced at a mine in Idaho and there were five mines where molybdenum was recovered as a byproduct. The next largest producer of the metal in 2000 was China with output of 28,000 tonnes. Molybdenum production by Chine was 27,000 tonnes. Other producers include Canada, Mexico and Peru. World reserves of molybdenum are estimated at 5.5 million tonnes. The U.S. has the largest reserves of molybdenum.

U.S. production of molybdenum concentrate in August 2001 was 2,600 tonnes. In the January-August 2001 period, production was 24,600 tonnes. For all of 2000, production was 40,900 tonnes. Domestic shipments of molybdenum, including metal powder, molybdic oxides and other in August 2001 were 1,580 tonnes and in the first eight months of 2001 were 14,700 tonnes. For all of 2000, shipments were 15,800 tonnes. U.S. gross production of molybdenum products in August 2001 was 4,480 tonnes. In the January-August 2001 period production was 30,200 tonnes and for all of 2000 it was 42,900 tonnes. U.S. internal consumption of molybdenum production in the January-August 2001 period was 18,100 tonnes while for 2000 it was 23,200 tonnes.

U.S. exports of molybdenum ores and concentrates in July 2001 were 2,510 tonnes. In the January-July 2001 period, exports were 17,500 tonnes, while for all of 2000 they were 23,600 tonnes. The major market for these exports was the Netherlands followed by the United Kingdom and Belgium. U.S. exports of ferromolybdenum in January-July 2001 were 442 tonnes. For 2000, exports were 742 tonnes. The major destination for ferromolybdenum was Canada followed by Mexico and Japan.

World Mine Production of Molybdenum In Metric Tons (Contained Molybdenum)

Year	Bulgaria	Canada[3]	Chile	China	Iran	Kazakhstan[4]	Mexico	Mongolia	Peru	Russia[4]	United States	Uzbekisten[4]	World Total
1991	120	11,329	14,434	13,200	395	----	1,716	1,716	3,031	16,000	53,364	----	115,000
1992	120	9,405	14,500	19,200	1,320	700	1,458	1,610	3,220	10,800	49,700	700	114,000
1993	120	9,700	14,899	18,300	700	600	1,705	2,050	2,980	10,300	36,800	700	99,200
1994	100	10,250	16,028	21,400	670	100	2,610	2,066	2,765	4,000	46,800	500	108,000
1995	400	9,113	17,889	33,000	560	75	3,883	1,822	3,411	3,000	60,900	400	136,000
1996	400	8,789	17,415	29,600	560	100	4,210	2,201	3,711	2,000	56,000	500	127,000
1997	----	7,612	21,339	33,300	600	100	4,842	1,992	3,835	2,000	60,100	500	138,000
1998	----	7,991	25,298	30,000	1,400	100	5,949	1,993	4,344	2,000	53,300	350	135,000
1999[1]	----	6,250	27,270	29,700	1,600	110	7,961	1,953	5,470	2,400	42,400	350	128,000
2000[2]	----	6,833	29,100	28,900	1,600	600	6,886	1,336	7,193	2,400	41,100	350	129,000

[1] Preliminary. [2] Estimate. [3] Shipments. [4] Formerly part of the U.S.S.R.; data not reported separately until 1992.
Source: U.S. Geological Survey (USGS)

Salient Statistics of Molybdenum in the United States In Metric Tons (Contained Molybdenum)

	Concentrate							Primary Products[4]							
		Shipments						Net Production				Shipments			
Year	Production	Total (Includes Exports)	Value Million $	For Exports	Consumption	Imports For Consumption	Stocks, Dec. 31[3]	Grand Total	Molybolic Oxide[5]	Molybolic Metal Powder	Price Average Value $ / Kg.[6]	To Domestic Destinations	Oxide for Exports (Groos Weight)	Consumption	Producer Stocks, Dec. 31
1991	53,364	53,607	249.9	22,424	32,998	161	5,291	20,782	18,739	2,043	5.27	19,105	1,571	16,901	9,422
1992	49,700	43,100	189.9	33,439	15,200	831	11,900	13,880	11,916	1,964	4.85	17,300	557	17,200	7,480
1993	36,800	39,200	165.1	28,280	13,800	3,400	11,200	11,989	10,697	1,292	5.13	16,000	1,042	17,700	6,150
1994	46,800	46,000	284.0	14,568	17,200	2,280	5,510	16,000	14,900	1,070	4.60	21,400	2,240	19,100	3,940
1995	60,900	61,700	651.0	18,600	25,500	5,570	5,390	22,900	20,900	1,970	17.50	24,000	2,840	19,900	4,820
1996	56,000	35,800	456.0	19,700	24,500	5,480	2,470	24,100	20,400	1,970	8.30	24,100	1,790	20,900	5,780
1997	60,100	32,100	406.0	20,000	24,300	6,330	3,660	25,900	22,700	2,000	9.46	25,900	1,240	20,000	6,500
1998	53,300	52,100	200.0	----	35,900	6,570	6,270	33,900	31,600	2,270	5.90	38,000	1,100	18,800	7,780
1999[1]	42,400	42,800	251.0	----	34,500	6,390	4,580	19,200	17,400	1,880	5.90	39,000	1,130	18,700	5,340
2000[2]	41,100	35,600	232.0	----	33,800	6,120	4,030	19,700	17,500	2,190	5.90	34,600	1,190	18,600	5,360

[1] Preliminary. [2] Estimate. [3] At mines & at plants making molybdenum products. [4] Comprises ferromolybdenum, molybdic oxide, & molybdenum salts & metal. [5] Includes molybdic oxide briquets, molybdic acid, molybdenum trioxide, all other. [6] U.S. producer price per kilogram of molybdenum oxide contained in technical-grade molybdic oxide. W = Withheld proprietary data. *Source: U.S. Geological Survey (USGS)*

Nickel

Nickel is used in the production of stainless steel and other corrosion-resistant alloys. About one-fifth of the nickel produced in the U.S. is used in the plating of hard, tarnish-resistant, polishable surfaces. Elemental nickel is used to make nickel-based corrosion resistant alloys. Nickel is used in coins to replace silver, in rechargeable batteries, and in electronic circuity. Nickel-based alloys are used in wire, bars, sheets, and in tubular forms. Nickel plating techniques, like electroless coating or single-slurry coating, are employed in such applications as turbine blades, helicopter rotors, extrusion dies, and rolled steel strip. By far, the largest use of nickel is in stainless steel production. About two-thirds of the primary nickel consumed in the world goes into stainless steel production.

The U.S.Geological Survey reported that world mine production of nickel in 2000 was 1.23 million metric tonnes, up 10 percent from 1999. The world's largest producer of nickel was Russia with 2000 production of 265,000 tonnes, up 2 percent from 1999. The next largest producer was Canada with 2000 output of 194,000 tonnes, up 3 percent from the previous year. Other large producers include Australia, New Caledonia, Indonesia, Cuba and Colombia. Estimated world reserves of nickel in 2000 were 49 million tonnes. The largest reserves were located in Australia, Russia, Canada, and Cuba. There are extensive deep-sea resources of nickel in manganese crusts and modules covering large areas of the ocean floor.

U.S. reported consumption of nickel in August 2001 was 7,210 tonnes. In the January-August 2001 period, consumption was 58,700 tonnes. Consumption of nickel in 2000 was 103,000 tonnes. In the first eight months of 2001, consumption of nickel for stainless and heat resisting steel was 19,500 tonnes. Use of nickel in super-alloys was 11,300 tonnes. Other uses for nickel include steel alloys, chemicals and electroplating.

U.S. imports of nickel in July 2001 were 12,000 tonnes, nickel content. In the January-July 2001 period, imports of nickel were 91,800 tonnes. For all of 2000, nickel imports were 167,000 tonnes. The major suppliers of nickel to the U.S. in 2001 were Canada, Australia, Norway, Russia, Finland and the Dominican Republic. U.S. exports of nickel in the January-July 2001 period were 37,700 tonnes. For all of 2000, exports were 58,100 tonnes. Most of the exports were in the form of stainless steel scrap and waste and scrap.

U.S. ending stocks of ferrous scrap in August 2001 were 2,810 tonnes while stocks of nonferrous scrap were 113 tonnes. Total nickel scrap stocks were nearly 3,000 tonnes. In August 2000, stocks of nickel cathodes, pellets, briquets and powder were 2,270 tonnes. Stocks of ferronickel were 645 tonnes.

World Mine Production of Nickel In Metric Tons (Contained Nickel)

Year	Australia[3]	Botswana	Brazil	Canada	China	Dominican Republic	Greece	Indonesia	New Caledonia	Phillip-pines	Russia	South Africa	World Total
1991	69,000	23,500	26,400	192,259	31,000	29,062	19,300	71,681	114,492	13,658	245,000	27,700	991,000
1992	57,683	23,000	29,372	186,384	32,800	42,641	17,000	77,600	113,000	13,022	280,000	28,400	1,010,000
1993	64,717	23,000	32,154	188,080	30,700	37,423	12,940	65,757	97,092	7,663	244,000	29,868	926,000
1994	78,962	19,041	27,706	149,886	36,900	50,146	18,821	81,175	97,323	9,895	240,000	30,751	932,000
1995	98,467	21,107	29,124	181,820	41,800	46,523	19,947	88,183	119,905	15,075	251,000	29,803	1,040,000
1996	113,134	21,910	25,245	192,649	43,800	45,168	21,600	87,911	122,486	14,539	230,000	33,861	1,060,000
1997	123,372	19,860	31,936	190,529	46,600	49,152	18,419	71,127	136,467	18,137	260,000	34,830	1,120,000
1998	143,513	21,700	36,764	208,201	48,700	40,311	16,985	74,063	125,319	12,840	250,000	36,679	1,130,000
1999[1]	127,000	33,733	41,522	186,236	49,500	39,997	16,050	89,111	110,062	14,300	260,000	36,200	1,120,000
2000[2]	168,300	34,465	45,317	190,728	51,100	39,943	19,535	98,200	127,493	23,500	270,000	36,616	1,250,000

[1] Preliminary. [2] Estimate. [3] Content of nickel sulfate and concentrates. *Source: U.S. Geological Survey (USGS)*

Salient Statistics of Nickel in the United States In Metric Tons (Contained Nickel)

	Net Import Reliance as a % of Apparent	--- Production ---		---- Nickel Consumed[1], By Uses ----									Stocks, ---- Dec. 31 ----		Primary & Secondary Nickel		Avg. Price
Year	Con-sumption	Plant[4]	Secon-dary[5]	Alloy Sheets	Cast Irons	Copper Base Alloys	Electro-plating Anodes	Nickel Alloys	Stainless & Heat Re-sisting Steels	Super Alloys	Chem-icals	Apparent Con-sumption	At Con-sumers' Plants	At Pro-ducer Plants	Exports	Imports	LME[6] $/Lb.
1991	67	7,065	53,521	5,536	1,185	6,938	15,474	16,882	84,292	13,787	1,363	156,663	15,940	11,794	36,902	138,210	3.70
1992	59	8,960	55,871	4,988	1,202	6,313	16,538	15,946	83,460	10,872	51	159,373	17,480	10,140	33,860	128,510	3.18
1993	63	4,880	54,702	4,940	805	6,078	16,611	17,004	87,300	10,783	1,170	158,000	14,430	15,700	33,180	132,710	2.40
1994	64	----	58,590	5,930	499	7,940	15,500	20,500	88,700	11,700	2,670	164,000	11,000	10,200	41,920	133,070	2.88
1995	60	8,290	64,600	9,570	491	8,510	15,600	21,800	103,000	14,100	5,210	181,000	12,300	12,700	51,550	156,930	3.73
1996	59	15,100	59,300	6,240	563	7,300	16,200	19,700	94,000	12,600	5,310	183,000	12,900	13,300	46,700	150,060	3.40
1997	56	16,000	68,400	9,290	654	6,530	15,900	19,400	105,000	19,000	3,720	191,000	16,100	12,600	56,500	158,000	3.14
1998	64	4,290	63,100	9,590	908	7,470	16,400	17,500	93,000	18,600	1,970	186,000	15,800	13,100	43,540	157,920	2.10
1999[2]	63	----	71,000	8,100	495	10,500	15,400	15,200	102,000	18,900	1,580	190,000	9,920	12,700	38,840	148,480	2.73
2000[3]	58	----	83,900	7,700	168	9,960	15,700	18,200	108,000	19,400	991	189,000	14,300	12,300	58,050	166,700	3.92

[1] Exclusive of scrap. [2] Preliminary. [3] Estimate. [4] Smelter & refinery. [5] From purchased scrap (ferrous & nonferrous). W = Withheld proprietary data. NA = Not avaliable. *Source: U.S. Geological Survey (USGS)*

Oats

Oats prices, basis Chicago futures, scored solid gains during 2001, reaching their highest level since the mid-1990's at about $2.45 per bushel. The bullish action followed a few years of sideways price action, but with apparent underlying technical and/or psychological support near $1 per bushel that served to check the pressure on prices that perhaps set the stage for the move in 2001.

Within the worldwide feed grain complex, oats production is the smallest crop although there are signs that the crop's long-term slippage outside the U.S. may be ending. The U.S. 2001/02 crop (June to May) of a record low 117 million bushels compares with the previous year's 150 million; the lower supply setting contributing to the price strength during calendar 2001. U.S. production in the first half of the 1990's averaged over 250 million bushels.. U.S. oats acreage in 2001/02 of about 2 million acres is the smallest on record: by comparison, in the first half of the 1990's harvested acreage averaged almost 5 million acres. Average yield, however, has held steady, averaging around 60 bushels/acre. North Dakota is generally the largest producing state with Minnesota close by. Imports, mostly from Canada help complement U.S. supplies, were forecast at 90 million bushels in 2001/02 vs. 106 million in 2000/01.

U.S. oats 2001/02 carry-in stocks as of June 1, 2001 of 73 million bushels compare with 76 million a year earlier. The total domestic supply for 2001/02 of a record low 280 million bushels compares with 332 million in 2000/01. Disappearance was estimated at 225 million bushels vs. 259 million in 2000/01. Feed and residual use was forecast at 155 million bushels in 2001/02 vs. 189 million in 2000/01: feed/seed/industrial use was placed at 68 million, unchanged from 2000/01. U.S. oats exports are insignificant. Carryover stocks on May 31, 2002 are forecast at a record low 55 million bushels. The average farm price for 2001/02 was forecast at $1.30-1.40/bus vs. $1.10 in 2000/01 and $1.96 in 1996/97, the highest farm price of the 1990's.

World oats production fell to 24 million tons in 1999/00 vs. an average of about 30 million metric tons in the mid-1990's. Production in 2001/02 was forecast at 26.3 million tons owing to greater acreage and/or higher yields. Globally, average yield show wide divergence, from as low as 1 ton per acre at times in Russia to almost 5 tons per acre in Western Europe. Still, Russia is one of the largest producers owing to the large acreage devoted to oats, and their output has increased--from 4.4 million tons in 1999/00 to 7 million in 2001/02. Among the few major producers Canada has shown steadiness in production during the past decade; averaging about 3.5 million tons although yields in 2001/02 dropped production to about 2.8 million tons.

Most of the world's oats production is consumed domestically and world trade is small. In 2001/01 exports were forecast at only 1.75 million tons vs. 2.2 million in 2000/01 with Canada accounting for more than half the total. Importing nations are more numerous, but the U.S. is the consistent leader with 1.3 million tons in 2001/02 vs. 2.2 million in 200/01.

Futures Markets

Oat futures and options are traded on the Chicago Board of trade (CBOT) and the Winnipeg Commodity Exchange (WCE). Oats futures are traded on the Mid-America Commodity Exchange (MidAm).

World Production of Oats In Thousands of Metric Tons

Year	Argentina	Australia	Canada	China	France	Germany	Italy	Poland	Sweden	Turkey	United States	Ex-USSR	World Total
1992-3	600	1,966	2,829	640	700	1,314	333	1,229	807	280	4,271	14,121	33,894
1993-4	436	1,651	3,549	640	713	1,731	372	1,500	1,295	280	3,001	15,004	35,370
1994-5	357	924	3,638	600	681	1,663	355	1,243	991	300	3,322	13,903	32,967
1995-6	260	1,875	2,858	640	617	1,421	301	1,495	947	275	2,338	10,843	28,663
1996-7	310	1,653	4,361	600	622	1,606	350	1,581	1,200	275	2,224	10,430	30,637
1997-8	517	1,634	3,485	400	564	1,599	311	1,630	1,275	280	2,428	11,560	30,903
1998-9	383	1,880	3,958	650	658	1,279	280	1,460	1,136	310	2,409	6,490	25,911
1999-00[1]	400	1,120	3,640	600	550	1,340	350	1,450	1,200	250	2,120	5,740	24,000
2000-1[2]	380	1,130	3,390	600	500	1,090	370	1,070	1,300	250	2,170	7,500	25,690
2001-2[3]	350	1,380	2,770	600	450	1,100	350	1,300	1,150	250	1,700	8,800	26,290

[1] Preliminary. [2] Estimate. [3] Forecast. *Source: Foreign Agricultural Service, U.S. Department of Agriculture (FAS-USDA)*

Official Oats Crop Production Reports in the United States In Thousands of Bushels

Year	July 1	Aug. 1	Sept. 1	Oct. 1	Dec. 1	Final	Year	July 1	Aug. 1	Sept. 1	Oct. 1	Dec. 1	Final
1990	374,457	365,337	365,337	358,288	----	357,654	1996	154,968	157,663	----	----	----	153,245
1991	280,016	259,666	259,666	242,526	----	243,851	1997	182,672	187,127	----	----	----	167,246
1992	256,381	276,381	----	----	----	294,229	1998	183,201	177,211	----	----	----	165,981
1993	262,860	249,830	249,830	208,138	----	206,770	1999	----	162,096	----	----	----	146,218
1994	248,151	247,753	247,753	229,717	----	229,008	2000	151,380	152,745	----	----	----	149,545
1995	181,508	186,167	186,167	----	----	162,027	2001[1]	132,150	135,445	----	----	----	116,856

[1] Preliminary. *Source: National Agricultural Statistics Service, U.S. Department of Agriculture (NASS-USDA)*

Oat Stocks in the United States In Thousands of Bushels

	On Farms				Off Farms				Total Stocks			
Year	Mar. 1	June 1	Sept. 1	Dec. 1	Mar. 1	June 1	Sept. 1	Dec. 1	Mar. 1	June 1	Sept. 1	Dec. 1
1992	98,150	61,000	199,900	161,200	76,735	66,721	94,717	81,292	174,885	127,721	294,617	242,492
1993	110,250	66,130	161,000	124,200	64,875	47,063	58,004	69,517	175,125	113,193	219,004	193,717
1994	85,050	53,940	144,300	113,400	61,502	51,583	75,551	78,664	146,552	105,523	219,851	192,064
1995	78,400	46,750	107,200	87,200	70,575	53,848	72,967	65,804	148,975	100,598	180,167	153,004
1996	57,350	32,600	93,400	80,650	55,268	33,708	38,716	45,218	112,618	66,308	132,116	125,868
1997	56,200	33,100	107,950	83,200	39,362	33,576	48,972	61,051	95,562	66,676	156,922	144,251
1998	58,800	34,500	110,300	81,500	52,418	39,498	51,502	61,835	111,218	73,998	161,802	143,335
1999	61,700	40,700	97,300	79,800	50,850	40,678	51,151	53,872	112,550	81,378	148,451	133,672
2000	53,300	36,000	101,200	86,900	48,500	40,031	49,177	57,237	101,800	76,031	150,377	144,137
2001[1]	55,800	32,050	74,800	58,100	54,128	40,677	41,592	56,120	109,928	72,727	116,392	114,220

[1] Preliminary. *Source: National Agricultural Statistics Service, U.S. Department of Agriculture (NASS-USDA)*

Supply and Utilizationof Oats in the United States In Millions of Bushels

Year	Acreage Planted (1,000 acres)	Acreage Harvested (1,000 acres)	Yield Per Acre (Bushels)	Pro-duction	Imports	Total Supply	Feed & Residual	Food, Alcohol & Industrial	Seed	Exports	Total Use	Ending Stocks	Farm Price	Findley Loan Rate	Target Price
				In Millions of Bushels									Dollars Per Bushel		
1992-3	7,943	4,496	65.4	294.2	55.0	476.9	263.1	77.4	17.8	5.7	363.7	113.2	1.32	.88	1.45
1993-4	7,937	3,803	54.4	206.7	106.8	426.7	230.2	73.0	15.0	3.0	321.2	105.5	1.36	.88	1.45
1994-5	6,637	4,008	57.1	228.8	93.2	427.6	242.6	70.0	13.4	1.0	327.0	100.6	1.22	.97	1.45
1995-6	6,225	2,952	54.6	161.1	80.5	342.2	194.9	67.0	12.0	2.1	275.9	66.3	1.67	.97	1.45
1996-7	4,638	2,655	57.7	153.2	97.5	317.1	171.7	63.0	13.1	2.5	250.4	66.7	1.96	1.03	NA
1997-8	5,068	2,813	59.5	167.2	98.4	332.3	184.6	59.0	12.6	2.1	258.3	74.0	1.60	1.11	NA
1998-9	4,892	2,755	60.2	166.0	108.0	347.7	195.6	57.0	12.0	1.7	266.3	81.4	1.10	1.11	NA
1999-00	4,670	2,453	59.6	146.2	99.0	326.0	180.0	56.8	11.2	1.8	250.0	76.0	1.12	1.13	NA
2000-1[1]	4,477	2,329	64.2	149.5	106.0	332.0	189.0			1.7	259.0	73.0	1.10	1.16	NA
2001-2[2]	4,403	1,905	61.3	116.9	100.0	290.0	155.0			3.0	228.0	62.0	1.45-1.55	1.16	NA

[1] Preliminary. [2] Forecast. NA = Not available. *Source: Economic Research Service, U.S. Department of Agriculture (ERS-USDA)*

Production of Oats in the United States, by States In Thousands of Bushels

Year	Illinois	Iowa	Michigan	Minnesota	Nebraska	New York	North Dakota	Ohio	Penn-slyvania	South Dakota	Texas	Wisconsin	Total
1992	7,930	25,125	8,400	35,000	15,400	7,700	37,400	12,070	13,735	42,900	5,720	34,410	294,229
1993	4,590	9,000	7,150	23,750	6,880	6,510	37,100	9,000	10,000	26,520	7,420	24,150	206,770
1994	5,490	26,660	6,270	24,750	7,500	7,040	33,550	6,720	8,480	31,360	5,200	25,380	229,008
1995	5,360	14,625	5,130	18,000	4,500	5,310	21,600	6,900	9,440	11,500	5,040	18,700	162,027
1996	4,620	12,920	3,600	15,120	7,455	3,850	19,000	5,130	7,560	21,600	3,400	17,400	153,245
1997	5,550	16,790	4,880	17,400	5,850	5,850	18,700	6,660	8,990	14,850	6,760	20,160	167,246
1998	3,920	10,915	4,800	19,530	5,320	6,510	25,200	6,500	8,480	20,100	6,890	18,300	165,981
1999	4,260	11,375	4,875	17,700	4,650	4,760	16,830	7,000	7,975	12,800	4,840	18,600	146,193
2000	4,015	12,060	4,800	22,320	1,890	3,900	19,845	6,840	8,265	13,420	4,300	19,040	149,545
2001[1]	3,200	9,100	3,520	12,600	3,660	5,520	14,880	6,205	7,475	7,800	7,200	12,480	116,856

[1] Preliminary. *Source: National Agricultural Statistics Service, U.S. Department of Agriculture (NASS-USDA)*

Average Cash Price of No. 2 Heavy White Oats in Toledo In Dollars Per Bushel

Year	June	July	Aug.	Sept.	Oct.	Nov.	Dec.	Jan.	Feb.	Mar.	Apr.	May	Average
1991-2	1.14	1.24	1.29	1.28	1.31	1.30	1.34	1.41	1.58	1.61	1.48	1.50	1.37
1992-3	1.46	1.47	1.46	1.58	1.54	1.58	1.55	1.54	1.49	1.43	1.53	1.50	1.51
1993-4	1.42	1.50	1.49	1.43	1.41	1.38	1.37	1.43	1.40	1.37	1.37	1.25	1.40
1994-5	1.35	1.26	1.26	1.32	1.35	1.28	1.27	1.34	1.45	1.43	1.48	1.59	1.37
1995-6	1.65	1.76	1.83	1.90	1.76	1.91	2.21	2.14	2.06	2.17	2.32	2.05	1.98
1996-7	NQ	2.45	2.34	2.19	2.02	1.96	1.96	1.99	2.16	2.26	2.12	2.08	2.14
1997-8	2.12	1.79	1.84	1.80	1.77	NQ	NQ	NQ	NQ	NQ	NQ	NQ	1.86
1998-9	NQ	NQ	NQ	NQ	NQ	NQ	NQ	NQ	NQ	NQ	NQ	NQ	NQ
1999-00	NQ	NQ	NQ	NQ	NQ	NQ	NQ	NQ	NQ	NQ	NQ	NQ	NQ
2000-1[1]	NQ	NQ	NQ	NQ	NQ	NQ	NQ	NQ					

[1] Preliminary. NQ = No quotes. *Source: Economic Research Service, U.S. Department of Agriculture (ERS-USDA)*

Volume of Trading in Oats Futures in Chicago In Contracts

Year	Jan.	Feb.	Mar.	Apr.	May	June	July	Aug.	Sept.	Oct.	Nov.	Dec.	Total
1992	31,020	84,020	42,260	47,060	42,020	54,540	22,200	40,160	25,100	16,580	35,220	19,400	459,580
1993	20,480	26,500	26,060	63,140	33,420	43,120	33,300	32,080	26,880	40,780	72,320	37,260	455,340
1994	47,980	57,060	39,800	53,820	34,300	69,760	20,760	39,340	28,840	24,900	56,940	19,680	493,180
1995	13,512	37,014	29,490	45,536	34,116	107,082	29,862	45,677	31,676	38,641	52,321	47,005	511,932
1996	61,451	52,079	34,608	77,395	47,161	34,498	38,960	33,316	30,801	37,579	37,856	16,154	501,858
1997	34,238	51,608	39,607	41,988	27,028	29,632	25,473	26,486	21,241	42,630	38,187	19,214	397,332
1998	21,150	51,247	25,551	65,381	23,490	55,376	29,870	42,156	27,131	31,426	51,172	18,924	442,874
1999	23,747	35,706	43,671	44,974	22,399	40,722	35,812	27,928	17,893	16,155	42,029	20,370	371,406
2000	27,073	43,332	29,707	31,653	38,647	50,461	30,885	42,814	21,846	21,476	48,890	15,406	402,190
2001	26,377	38,040	24,903	41,482	20,516	41,926	50,440	22,883	31,252	50,580	53,578	38,877	438,520

Source: Chicago Board of Trade (CBT)

Average Open Interest of Oats in Chicago In Contracts

Year	Jan.	Feb.	Mar.	Apr.	May	June	July	Aug.	Sept.	Oct.	Nov.	Dec.
1992	9,555	15,499	15,359	15,052	15,329	14,773	12,759	11,100	9,869	9,178	8,781	7,287
1993	7,398	7,739	7,655	11,579	13,357	12,020	10,894	11,381	11,171	14,116	20,057	20,547
1994	21,193	20,137	20,194	19,882	18,312	14,575	11,710	13,923	14,743	16,266	15,354	13,376
1995	13,133	13,231	13,000	15,426	16,054	13,611	11,019	11,348	11,012	11,970	12,542	13,003
1996	13,253	14,095	14,231	14,497	13,897	11,697	11,336	11,803	11,457	11,918	11,150	8,550
1997	8,088	9,650	12,649	11,024	9,830	9,395	8,131	8,606	8,618	10,953	11,816	10,964
1998	12,782	15,368	16,553	17,748	17,441	16,437	14,255	15,052	14,771	16,263	18,466	17,048
1999	17,126	17,019	16,677	15,398	13,491	12,705	11,927	11,670	9,802	10,638	12,754	12,360
2000	15,343	17,521	17,719	18,183	176,686	16,178	15,550	15,225	13,176	13,985	14,377	14,119
2001	14,093	15,060	14,873	14,962	14,875	13,695	11,861	11,707	10,059	12,111	14,453	12,142

Source: Chicago Board of Trade (CBT)

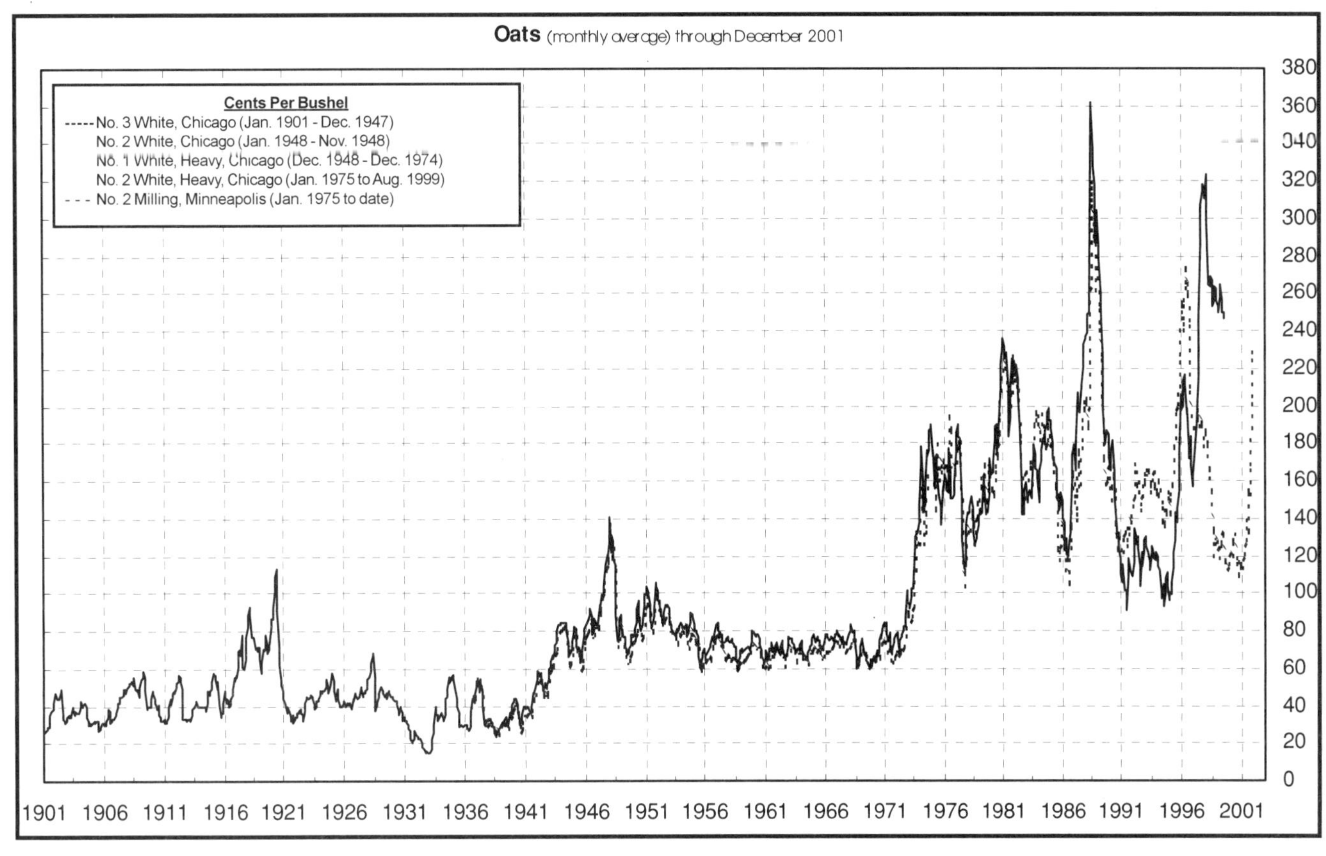

Average Cash Price of No. 2 Heavy White Oats in Minneapolis In Dollars Per Bushel

Year	June	July	Aug.	Sept.	Oct.	Nov.	Dec.	Jan.	Feb.	Mar.	Apr.	May	Average
1991-2	1.25	1.33	1.38	1.35	1.41	1.42	1.49	1.50	1.68	1.66	1.57	1.59	1.47
1992-3	1.55	1.49	1.45	1.58	1.52	1.59	1.63	1.66	1.63	1.63	1.66	1.57	1.58
1993-4	1.54	1.63	1.63	1.66	1.56	1.51	1.56	1.57	1.52	1.55	1.46	1.37	1.55
1994-5	1.47	1.36	1.44	1.44	1.44	1.41	NQ	1.46	1.42	1.54	1.62	1.76	1.36
1995-6	1.73	1.92	1.96	2.04	2.11	2.63	2.50	2.40	2.31	2.47	2.56	2.68	2.28
1996-7	2.11	2.48	2.36	2.08	2.06	1.87	1.86	1.89	1.94	1.99	1.88	1.81	2.03
1997-8	1.89	1.76	1.80	1.78	1.75	1.65	1.71	1.68	1.59	1.65	1.54	1.58	1.70
1998-9	1.52	1.42	1.21	1.30	1.29	1.32	1.31	1.33	1.26	1.35	1.36	1.39	1.34
1999-00	1.34	1.25	1.20	1.17	1.20	1.20	1.28	1.21	1.19	1.34	1.45	NQ	1.26
2000-1[1]	NQ	NQ	NQ	NQ	NQ	NQ	NQ	NQ					

[1] Preliminary. NQ = No quote. *Source: Economic Research Service, U.S. Department of Agriculture (ERS-USDA)*

Average Price Received by U.S. Farmers for Oats In Dollars Per Bushel

Year	June	July	Aug.	Sept.	Oct.	Nov.	Dec.	Jan.	Feb.	Mar.	Apr.	May	Average
1992-3	1.38	1.32	1.23	1.28	1.31	1.35	1.36	1.42	1.42	1.43	1.45	1.51	1.32
1993-4	1.43	1.36	1.32	1.31	1.33	1.39	1.42	1.42	1.42	1.39	1.32	1.49	1.36
1994-5	1.31	1.20	1.16	1.18	1.21	1.18	1.18	1.22	1.22	1.33	1.36	1.41	1.22
1995-6	1.38	1.52	1.48	1.43	1.50	1.72	1.91	1.93	1.96	2.04	2.13	2.48	1.46
1996-7	2.17	2.13	2.00	1.83	1.84	1.85	1.72	1.83	1.81	1.91	1.87	1.86	1.96
1997-8	1.81	1.68	1.57	1.47	1.62	1.66	1.57	1.60	1.60	1.64	1.61	1.53	1.61
1998-9	1.39	1.19	1.02	1.07	1.09	1.10	1.19	1.20	1.20	1.20	1.18	1.31	1.18
1999-00	1.22	1.08	.97	1.08	1.06	1.12	1.18	1.20	1.27	1.28	1.35	1.31	1.18
2000-1	1.24	1.07	.93	.95	1.08	1.22	1.14	1.21	1.27	1.24	1.28	1.28	1.16
2001-2[1]	1.38	1.33	1.26	1.39	1.65	1.82	1.90	1.84					1.57

[1] Preliminary. *Source: National Agricultural Statistics Service, U.S. Department of Agriculture (NASS-USDA)*

Olive Oil

Olive and olive oil production is very cyclical. This is fairly typical of tree crops which can follow a biennial production cycle. In that cycle, a large crop is followed by a small crop which in turn is followed by a large crop. Individual countries can have biennial cycles that run counter to another country. Weather can cause the cycle to be even more pronounced.

Olive oil production data from the newsletter, Oil World, illustrates the production cycle. In 1994/95, world production was 1.96 million metric tonnes. In 1995/96 that has declined to 1.6 million tonnes. In the following 1996/97 season, production was back up to 2.77 million tonnes. Olive oil production in Turkey in 1994/95 was 181,500 tonnes. The following season that fell to 45,500 tonnes and then in 1996/97 it rebounded to 222,000 tonnes.

The world's largest producers of olive oil are Spain followed by Italy, Greece, Turkey, Syria and Tunisia. The Agricultural Ministry of Spain, which has the largest olive oil industry, reported that in the 2000/01 season that ended in October, olive oil production was 1.03 million tonnes which was up some 16 percent from the average production of the last three seasons. Olive oil exports in the season that ended at the end of October were a record 477,200 tonnes, up over 30 percent from recent seasons. Domestic consumption of olive oil was reported to have increased by 8 percent from the previous year and olive oil stocks were 137,000 tonnes.

A Turkish official reported that Turkey's olive oil production in the 2000/01 season was projected to decline to 65,000 tonnes from 180,000 tonnes produced in 2000/01. Domestic consumption of olive oil in Turkey is estimated to be about 80,000 tonnes. Exports in 2000/01, which was a cyclically large season, were 93,000 tonnes. The harvest begins in November and ends in January.

World Production of Olive Oil (Pressed Oil) In Thousands of Metric Tons

Year	Algeria	Argentina	Greece	Italy	Jordan	Libya	Morocco	Portugal	Spain	Syria	Tunisia	Turkey	World Total
1993-4	21.0	8.5	275.0	451.5	9.5	8.0	45.5	36.1	593.2	71.0	251.0	55.0	1,875.2
1994-5	14.0	10.0	389.8	464.4	15.0	6.5	50.0	36.2	547.0	101.5	106.5	181.5	1,963.6
1995-6	23.0	11.5	362.0	540.0	15.5	4.0	40.0	48.6	320.0	84.0	64.5	45.5	1,598.4
1996-7	46.0	12.0	469.8	317.0	25.5	10.0	121.0	48.8	1,027.5	138.0	288.5	222.0	2,771.6
1997-8	6.5	8.5	405.0	585.0	16.0	6.0	75.0	45.5	1,212.0	78.0	99.0	40.0	2,615.5
1998-9[1]	39.5	7.0	511.0	428.8	23.5	8.0	70.0	41.6	804.0	129.0	231.0	188.0	2,521.2
1999-00[2]	25.0	7.0	378.0	669.6	8.0	7.0	45.0	45.4	667.0	90.0	215.5	77.0	2,273.9
2000-1[3]	31.0	3.0	443.0	445.0	20.0	4.0	40.0	44.0	1,022.0	183.0	163.0	210.0	2,668.0

[1] Preliminary. [2] Estimate. [3] Forecast. *Source: The Oil World*

World Imports and Exports of Olive Oil (Pressed Oil) In Thousands of Metric Tons

	Imports							Exports					
Year	Australia	Brazil	Italy	Japan	Spain	United States	World Total	Greece	Italy	Spain	Tunisia	Turkey	World Total
1993-4	15.5	18.2	85.8	6.2	46.3	123.9	399.2	8.6	118.2	58.2	166.2	8.7	402.4
1994-5	18.0	23.2	122.6	8.3	68.0	127.6	456.9	9.1	111.4	56.6	141.4	53.2	438.5
1995-6	16.7	18.8	47.0	16.1	26.4	113.6	318.4	7.8	98.0	54.4	33.1	28.9	307.9
1996-7	19.0	26.5	108.1	24.3	35.2	148.1	460.2	10.7	136.8	72.0	101.4	46.6	462.6
1997-8	17.7	28.9	89.4	35.5	28.0	161.0	467.7	14.4	140.2	82.0	126.8	42.2	474.3
1998-9[1]	23.7	23.0	150.4	28.1	76.8	169.9	580.9	20.0	141.6	70.9	174.4	92.1	577.6
1999-00[2]	25.4	24.1	110.0	30.0	45.2	171.0	526.5	18.0	180.0	92.0	130.0	36.7	528.4
2000-1[3]	27.0	28.0	90.0	32.0	15.0	200.0	535.0	19.0	147.0	120.0	115.0	75.0	539.0

[1] Preliminary. [2] Estimate. [3] Forecast. *Source: The Oil World*

World Consumption and Ending Stocks of Olive Oil (Pressed Oil) In Thousands of Metric Tons

	Consumption							Ending Stocks					
Year	Brazil	Morocco	Syria	Tunisia	Turkey	United States	World Total	Greece	Italy	Spain	Syria	Turkey	World Total
1993-4	18.2	53.5	82.0	66.8	63.4	119.9	2,016.3	32.0	224.4	189.3	19.0	14.0	667.3
1994-5	23.2	46.7	93.4	42.1	71.4	120.8	2,053.5	45.6	133.9	223.0	28.0	71.0	595.8
1995-6	18.8	32.9	98.5	32.4	64.7	110.5	1,884.6	30.9	81.4	88.4	12.0	23.0	320.1
1996-7	26.5	57.2	103.9	89.1	83.4	130.9	2,269.3	115.0	43.6	250.0	50.0	115.0	820.0
1997-8	28.9	61.3	105.6	61.0	82.9	154.8	2,381.5	122.0	196.3	529.0	24.0	35.0	1,047.4
1998-9[1]	23.0	64.5	108.9	60.9	77.0	160.9	2,392.4	190.0	163.6	600.0	45.0	55.0	1,179.5
1999-00[2]	24.1	57.0	114.6	75.3	75.4	167.3	2,464.2	150.0	210.0	490.0	22.0	20.0	987.4
2000-1[3]	28.0	53.0	114.0	70.0	95.0	200.0	2,695.0						

[1] Preliminary. [2] Estimate. [3] Forecast. *Source: The Oil World*

Onions

The U.S.D.A. reported that summer storage onion harvested acreage in 2001 was 124,790 acres, down 4 percent from 2000 and down 8 percent from 1999. California is by far the largest producing state with acreage in 2001 of 29,000, down 20 percent from 2000 and down 25 percent from 1999. The next largest producing state is Oregon with harvested acreage of 18,400, up 4 percent from 2000. Other large producers include Washington, Colorado and New York. U.S. summer non-storage onion acreage in 2001 was estimated to be 20,600, down 4 percent from 2000 but up 43 percent from 1999. Spring onion acreage was 36,000.

Yields for summer 2001 storage onions vary widely. Yields in Idaho were 630 hundredweight per acre while yields in Minnesota were 260 hundredweight. The California yield was 430 hundredweight in 2001, down 3 percent from 2000 and down 1 percent from 1999. The average yield for 2001 was 452 hundredweight per acre, down 2 percent from 2000 and 2 percent less than in 1999.

U.S. production of storage summer onions in 2001 was forecast at 46.36 million hundredweight, down 9 percent from 2000 and down 17 percent from 1999. California production was forecast at 12.56 million hundredweight, down 22 percent from 2000 and 26 percent less than in 1999. Oregon production was 9.88 million hundredweight, down 2 percent from 2000 and 19 percent less than in 1999. U.S. spring onion production in 2001 was 11 million hundredweight.

Salient Statistics of Onions in the United States

Crop Year	Harvested Acres	Yield Per Acre	Production 1,000 Cwt.	Price Per Cwt.	Farm Value $1,000	Jan. 1 Pack Frozen	Annual Pack Frozen	Imports Canned	Exports (Fresh)	Imports (Fresh)	Per Capita[3] Utilization -- Lbs., Farm Weight -- All	Fresh
						In Millions of Pounds						
1996	166,210	386	64,106	10.50	604,789	48.8	259.5	3.6	586.3	625.2	19.6	18.7
1997	165,910	414	68,769	12.60	769,974	40.8	230.1	3.8	600.9	576.0	20.0	19.1
1998	171,340	393	67,282	13.80	838,441	42.2	270.9	3.5	628.8	598.5	19.4	18.3
1999	173,400	424	73,562	9.78	635,128	40.3		5.2	667.7	583.9	21.6	18.6
2000[1]	166,170	432	71,721	11.20	732,283	58.3			675.0	590.0	19.4	18.3
2001[2]	160,790	419	67,386									

[1] Preliminary. [2] Forecast. [3] Includes fresh and processing. *Source: Economic Research Service, U.S. Department of Agiculture (ERS-USDA)*

Production of Onions in the United States In Thousands of Hundredweight (Cwt.)

Year	Spring: Arizona	California	Texas	Total (All)	Summer: California	Colorado	Idaho	Michigan	Minnesota	New Mexico	New York	Oregon (Malheur)	Texas	Total (All)	Grand Total
1996	760	2,736	4,030	9,290	13,330	5,200	5,590	1,798	114	3,266	2,736	7,080	924	52,079	61,369
1997	746	3,204	1,661	9,087	13,772	5,355	5,658	1,568	180	----	3,660	7,440	----	58,120	68,769
1998	1,175	4,050	2,907	10,356	14,388	6,080	4,640	1,092	150	----	3,750	6,120	----	55,668	66,024
1999	1,635	3,212	3,620	11,222	16,965	5,438	5,530	1,080	118	----	3,528	8,643	----	62,340	73,562
2000	1,376	3,089	4,185	11,812	16,154	4,083	4,810	945	19	----	4,674	6,960	----	59,909	71,721
2001[1]	1,290	2,544	4,615	11,014	12,556	5,148	4,725	952	53	----	4,064	6,384	----	57,020	68,034

[1] Preliminary. *Source: Agricultural Statistics Board, U.S. Department of Agiculture (ASB-USDA)*

Cold Storage Stocks of Frozen Onions in the United States, on First of Month In Thousands of Pounds

Year	Jan.	Feb.	Mar.	Apr.	May	June	July	Aug.	Sept.	Oct.	Nov.	Dec.
1996	35,354	35,819	31,784	32,782	27,670	29,200	27,511	27,536	27,659	30,288	27,889	32,261
1997	30,481	29,255	32,227	31,811	29,693	28,061	29,314	28,520	27,336	26,908	29,831	30,513
1998	31,187	28,724	27,710	24,428	23,443	22,787	22,179	21,468	18,755	24,553	27,070	25,965
1999	24,596	24,665	27,280	27,972	33,113	35,809	35,605	33,171	31,675	31,338	35,573	41,677
2000	41,236	40,730	44,029	45,874	52,691	55,340	53,537	42,910	40,792	34,318	37,408	39,909
2001[1]	40,420	39,717	39,407	36,925	36,503	38,709	38,277	29,943	28,912	26,133	27,726	28,739

[1] Preliminary. *Source: National Agricultural Statistics Service, U.S. Department of Agiculture (NASS-USDA)*

F.O.B. Price Received by Growers for Onions in the United States In Dollars Per Hundred Pounds (Cwt.)

Year	Jan.	Feb.	Mar.	Apr.	May	June	July	Aug.	Sept.	Oct.	Nov.	Dec.	Season Average
1996	10.70	10.10	8.11	8.86	9.54	11.10	12.10	12.60	12.70	11.50	10.40	10.20	10.50
1997	9.71	7.91	8.15	14.80	13.20	16.40	14.20	13.40	10.10	9.00	10.30	10.90	12.60
1998	10.50	14.00	19.40	19.20	15.80	14.00	19.10	14.00	12.90	12.70	14.00	16.00	13.80
1999	16.10	13.00	10.00	14.60	13.00	15.00	15.70	13.10	10.10	8.21	7.50	6.97	9.78
2000	5.88	4.89	4.40	9.99	12.50	12.10	13.30	12.20	10.70	10.20	11.00	11.30	11.20
2001[1]	13.90	14.10	15.60	21.00	19.00	17.60	16.80	14.80	13.20	10.40			

[1] Preliminary. *Source: Economic Research Service, U.S. Department of Agiculture (ERS-USDA)*

Oranges and Orange Juice

The world's largest producers of oranges and frozen concentrated orange juice (FCOJ) are Brazil and the United States. Brazil in recent years has passed the U.S. to become the largest producer of FCOJ. Brazilian production is concentrated in Sao Paulo where about 95 percent of the citrus trees are grown. The domestic market in Brazil prefers fresh oranges that are squeezed for juice. Other oranges are processed from FCOJ and sent to export markets in the U.S., Europe and Asia. The U.S. and Brazil produce about 60 percent of the world's oranges. Other countries that produce oranges are Mexico and Spain.

In November 2001, the U.S.D.A. released a report on the Brazilian citrus outlook prepared by the Department's agricultural attache in Sao Paulo. For the marketing year 2001/02 (July-June), the crop was estimated at 346 million boxes, down 74 million boxes from the previous season. The decline of 18 percent has caused orange prices in Sao Paulo to increase sharply. Orange production for the commercial area of Sao Paulo and western Minas Gerais was estimated at 286 million boxes. The harvest is expected to extend into January 2002. There was been no estimate of the 2002/03 orange crop though the trees were reported to have had an excellent flowering.

The agricultural attache estimated Brazilian 2001/02 FCOJ production at 960,000 metric tonnes which was down 220,000 tonnes from the previous season. The decline was due to a reduction in the number of oranges available for processing. Brazilian exports of FCOJ in the 2001/02 season were forecast at 1.055 million tonnes, down 210,000 tonnes from the previous season. The decline was also due to less availability of oranges for processing.

The U.S.D.A. forecast the 2001/02 U.S. orange crop at 287.95 million boxes, up less than 1 percent from the 2000/01 season. The California crop was estimated at 54 million boxes, down 8 percent from 2000/01. The California Early, Midseason and Navel orange crop was estimated at 32 million boxes while the Valencia crop was estimated at 22 million boxes. Texas and Arizona produce smaller amounts of oranges.

The Florida 2001/02 crop was forecast at 231 million boxes, up 3 percent from the previous season. The Early, Midseason and Navel orange crop was estimated at 131 million boxes, up 2 percent from the previous year. The Valencia crop was estimated at 100 million boxes, up 5 percent from last season. The juice yield was estimated at 1.55 gallons per box, down 2 percent from a year ago.

Futures Markets

Frozen concentrated orange juice futures and options are traded on the NYCE division of the New York Board of Trade (NYBOT).

World Production of Oranges In Thousands of Metric Tons

Year	Argentina	Australia	Brazil	Egypt	Greece	Italy	Mexico	Morocco	South Africa	Spain	Turkey	United States	World Total
1989-90	750	458	12,036	1,397	932	2,067	1,900	775	697	2,400	740	7,083	33,361
1990-1	600	485	12,362	1,574	819	1,760	2,300	1,103	648	2,590	735	7,222	33,938
1991-2	640	595	14,974	1,694	820	1,842	2,100	780	680	2,651	830	8,175	38,193
1992-3	660	578	14,484	1,771	1,042	2,111	2,913	874	712	2,926	820	10,074	41,582
1993-4	746	651	13,710	1,324	854	2,100	3,174	916	739	2,509	840	9,462	39,595
1994-5	712	416	16,520	1,513	865	1,710	3,500	657	770	2,644	920	10,641	43,539
1995-6	703	589	16,973	1,360	838	1,770	2,600	870	850	2,440	880	10,454	43,066
1996-7[1]	640	543	16,450	1,360	850	1,770	2,600	870	850	2,440	880	10,747	42,932
1997-8[2]	841	556	18,972	1,613	946	2,100	3,917	774	895	2,200	890	11,605	48,296
1998-9[3]	921	421	15,912	1,350	985	2,057	3,920	1,131	961	2,744	740	12,495	46,796

[1] Preliminary. [2] Estimate. [3] Forecast. NA = Not available. *Source: Foreign Agricultural Service, U.S. Department of Agriculture (FAS-USDA)*

Salient Statistics of Oranges & Orange Juice in the United States

	Production[4]					Florida Crop Processed				Frozen Concentrated Orange Juice - Florida			
Year	California	Florida	Total U.S.	Farm Price $ Per Box	Farm Value Million $	Frozen Concentrates	Chilled Products	Total Processed	Yield Per Box Gallons[5]	Carry-in	Pack	Total Supply	Total Season Movement
	Million Boxes					Million Boxes				In Millions of Gallons (42 Deg. Brix)			
1991-2	67.4	139.8	209.6	7.4	1,545.2	90.6	37.0	139.8	1.6	31.8	211.7	243.5	212.6
1992-3	66.8	186.6	255.8	5.8	1,489.9	128.3	47.2	186.6	1.6	31.0	292.0	322.9	269.4
1993-4	63.6	174.4	240.5	6.4	1,541.3	111.7	51.0	174.4	1.6	53.5	261.7	315.2	256.6
1994-5	56.0	205.5	263.6	6.1	1,624.1	144.7	54.8	199.8	1.5	58.6	274.2	332.8	290.4
1995-6	58.0	203.3	263.9	6.9	1,821.6	132.9	64.5	197.7	1.5	42.4	284.5	326.9	285.7
1996-7	64.0	226.2	293.0	6.2	1,836.7	153.8	65.7	220.4	1.6	41.2	301.7	342.9	273.9
1997-8	69.0	244.0	315.5	6.1	1,965.4	160.9	74.8	236.6	1.6	69.7	298.8	368.4	263.8
1998-9[1]	36.0	186.0	224.6	7.4	1,687.9	97.2	80.1	175.1	1.6	104.7	108.4	213.1	209.1
1999-00[2]	64.0	233.0	299.8	5.6	1,666.1	134.2	90.1	223.6	1.5	105.2	161.4	266.6	239.7
2000-1[3]	59.0	223.3	285.4	5.6	1,636.3	124.1	89.6	213.7	1.6	112.6	146.4	259.0	229.8

[1] Preliminary. [2] Estimate. [3] Forecast. [4] Fruit ripened on trees, but destroyed prior to picking not included. [5] *42 deg. Brix equivalent.*
Source: Economic Research Service, U.S. Department of Agriculture (ERS-USDA); Florida Department of Citrus

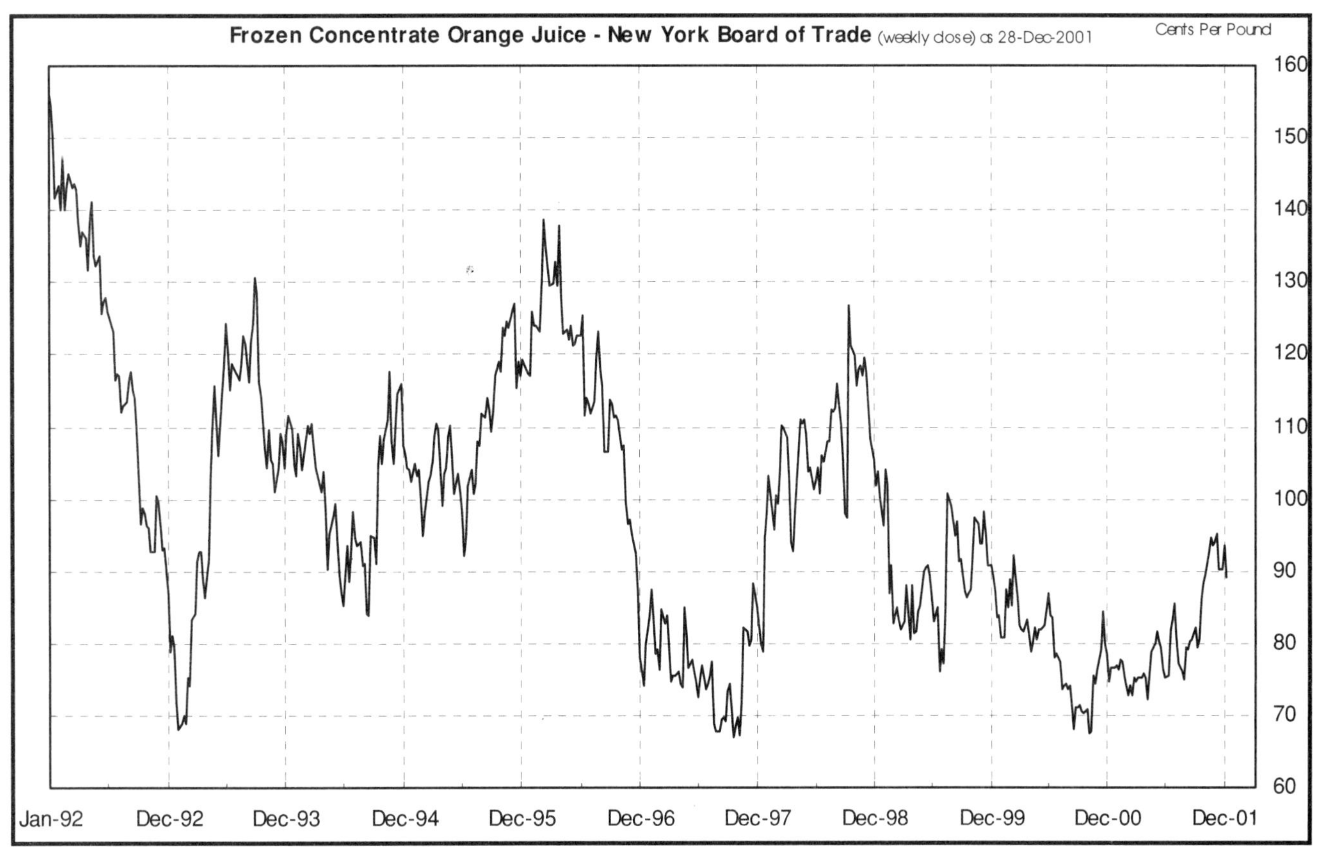

Average Open Interest of Frozen Concentrated Orange Juice Futures in New York In Contracts

Year	Jan.	Feb.	Mar.	Apr.	May	June	July	Aug.	Sept.	Oct.	Nov.	Dec.
1992	9,095	10,033	9,872	11,309	10,791	9,776	10,109	12,132	11,910	14,224	16,669	17,455
1993	17,733	18,199	19,030	20,210	18,525	19,267	20,000	18,899	18,287	18,825	18,422	20,367
1994	17,544	18,137	19,073	21,607	21,450	23,530	24,829	21,874	22,739	23,385	26,859	26,413
1995	27,439	25,885	26,407	30,172	27,057	26,844	23,537	17,881	20,918	22,460	26,303	24,202
1996	22,943	21,670	25,232	23,788	21,724	20,934	20,159	19,834	18,029	18,000	22,513	26,405
1997	29,171	26,929	26,331	28,955	29,868	33,639	31,799	34,339	36,057	40,365	41,811	46,169
1998	38,885	37,893	36,843	33,146	35,749	32,608	25,503	26,394	28,017	26,506	21,984	24,562
1999	25,917	28,965	28,707	31,199	26,669	28,362	28,087	30,021	28,922	27,498	26,893	25,887
2000	23,727	24,647	19,684	22,475	23,456	27,087	27,386	30,272	30,090	32,328	30,192	30,757
2001	28,852	28,011	28,073	27,794	24,199	24,428	22,591	22,073	17,789	18,026	21,506	19,275

Source: New York Board of Trade (NYBOT)

Volume of Trading of Frozen Concentrated Orange Juice Futures in New York In Contracts

Year	Jan.	Feb.	Mar.	Apr.	May	June	July	Aug.	Sept.	Oct.	Nov.	Dec.	Total
1992	30,508	28,177	21,371	31,725	21,253	22,473	21,877	27,208	26,912	29,604	33,133	44,979	339,230
1993	43,634	46,067	58,298	52,554	53,566	60,330	49,415	52,381	56,838	63,808	44,167	58,073	640,131
1994	46,166	51,123	43,075	55,955	48,236	60,110	37,069	55,711	52,209	73,155	54,978	76,037	653,824
1995	50,875	66,370	51,292	78,288	32,607	80,165	41,357	67,528	38,781	64,904	45,688	71,077	688,932
1996	59,666	82,057	46,272	65,752	62,247	44,827	40,884	58,346	44,239	40,680	39,291	70,676	654,937
1997	84,982	89,875	66,340	82,772	62,890	78,690	47,242	118,286	55,081	108,413	100,941	134,349	1,029,861
1998	96,020	81,554	66,235	101,651	70,909	79,319	48,844	85,544	81,187	98,639	29,541	75,171	914,614
1999	64,149	92,868	40,027	92,522	49,180	78,627	48,177	99,531	49,323	71,914	42,532	68,734	797,584
2000	45,680	78,532	33,617	71,024	50,475	80,372	46,548	67,312	38,485	64,831	45,966	89,362	712,204
2001	46,655	66,561	27,994	63,012	38,447	66,773	40,870	64,860	22,246	68,364	23,376	48,338	577,496

Source: New York Board of Trade (NYBOT)

ORANGES AND ORANGE JUICE

Cold Storage Stocks of Orange Juice Concentrate in the U.S., on First of Month — In Millions of Pounds

Year	Jan.	Feb.	Mar.	Apr.	May	June	July	Aug.	Sept.	Oct.	Nov.	Dec.
1992	828.4	1,130.7	1,150.0	1,102.9	1,269.3	1,294.8	1,143.8	978.0	874.9	741.9	665.5	638.0
1993	892.9	1,135.9	1,282.8	1,297.5	1,440.9	1,462.3	1,351.8	1,147.0	1,029.6	875.7	813.3	890.9
1994	955.5	1,248.9	1,429.0	1,273.8	1,499.6	1,615.2	1,521.8	1,449.1	1,257.5	1,119.6	1,026.1	1,055.9
1995	1,353.1	1,704.0	1,685.1	1,773.3	1,864.6	1,833.8	1,631.6	1,424.1	1,233.7	1,038.3	830.3	897.7
1996	1,050.6	1,295.4	1,353.0	1,322.3	1,443.9	1,596.9	1,535.0	1,423.6	1,238.6	965.6	732.7	691.0
1997	1,069.4	1,522.6	1,677.6	1,752.9	1,993.4	2,176.0	1,977.7	1,761.8	1,571.8	1,287.8	1,140.9	1,214.4
1998	1,503.4	1,945.9	2,029.7	2,025.0	2,487.0	2,627.5	2,457.7	2,249.0	2,025.1	1,803.9	1,470.7	1,540.2
1999	1,791.9	1,999.4	2,204.2	2,191.3	2,485.7	2,115.6	1,969.7	1,823.0	1,618.5	1,443.4	1,182.0	1,102.7
2000	1,330.7	1,540.6	1,632.7	1,857.9	1,812.5	1,965.6	2,037.9	1,843.7	1,457.7	1,346.6	1,169.4	1,202.0
2001[1]	1,382.0	1,610.9	1,825.1	1,735.5	1,880.4	2,061.8	2,035.6	1,913.2	1,691.1	1,537.7	1,405.5	1,406.7

[1] Preliminary. *Source: Agricultural Statistics Board, U.S. Department of Agriculture (ASB-USDA)*

Retail and Nonretail Sales of Orange Juice in the United States — In Millions of SSE Gallons

Year	Retail Sales	% Change[2]	Nonretail Sales	% Change[2]	Apparent Con-sumption	% Change[2]	Per Capita Con-sumption	% Change[2]
1990-1	754	7.5%	296	-6.6%	1,146	6.2%	4.5	4.7%
1991-2	750	-.6%	268	-9.5%	1,112	-3.0%	4.3	-4.4%
1992-3	808	7.7%	371	38.4%	1,328	19.4%	5.1	18.6%
1993-4	804	-.5%	----	----	1,368	3.0%	5.2	2.0%
1994-5	807	.4%	----	----	1,355	-1.0%	5.1	-1.9%
1995-6	838	3.8%	----	----	1,363	.6%	4.9	-3.9%
1996-7	825	-1.5%	----	----	1,320	-3.1%	NA	NA
1997-8	855	3.6%						
1998-9	840	-1.7%						
1999-00[1]	858	2.0%						

[1] Estimate. [2] Percentage change from previous period. *Source: Florida Department of Citrus*

Producer Price Index of Frozen Orange Juice Concentrate — 1982 = 100

Year	Jan.	Feb.	Mar.	Apr.	May	June	July	Aug.	Sept.	Oct.	Nov.	Dec.	Average
1992	135.1	134.7	134.7	134.3	126.2	118.5	115.5	114.5	112.5	106.5	104.2	98.8	119.6
1993	91.6	88.8	88.2	89.0	89.3	97.5	104.5	104.5	104.7	104.7	107.9	107.9	98.2
1994	107.9	104.8	104.2	104.2	102.7	101.2	100.2	100.1	99.9	99.8	100.7	100.5	102.2
1995	107.4	105.4	107.6	107.6	109.1	109.1	109.1	105.3	101.0	101.6	106.1	107.3	106.4
1996	109.4	112.5	117.2	119.5	119.5	119.5	115.3	113.6	113.6	112.8	112.8	108.8	114.5
1997	106.9	106.9	106.0	107.6	107.7	107.3	105.3	105.8	102.7	101.4	95.0	94.2	103.9
1998	94.9	101.2	104.1	103.2	108.8	109.1	109.5	109.6	109.5	110.2	119.1	121.2	108.4
1999	119.7	118.6	118.0	115.5	113.3	113.2	112.5	111.3	112.4	112.5	113.1	112.4	114.4
2000	110.0	108.9	108.0	107.1	106.9	106.6	105.4	104.8	101.5	100.4	99.8	99.1	104.9
2001[1]	98.9	99.2	98.3	96.8	96.8	97.4	97.3	97.2	97.3	97.3	99.6	102.4	98.2

[1] Preliminary. *Source: Bureau of Labor Statistics, U.S. Department of Labor (BLS)*

Average Price of Oranges (Equivalent On-Tree) Received by Growers in the U.S. — In Dollars Per Box

Year	Jan.	Feb.	Mar.	Apr.	May	June	July	Aug.	Sept.	Oct.	Nov.	Dec.	Average
1992	5.90	6.02	5.81	6.14	6.16	4.26	1.85	1.02	1.05	2.43	4.10	3.67	4.03
1993	3.37	3.21	3.41	4.00	4.03	4.09	5.02	7.25	11.85	11.40	6.15	4.00	5.65
1994	3.76	3.90	4.66	4.83	5.04	4.94	4.08	4.24	3.44	2.92	3.44	3.43	4.06
1995	3.43	3.59	4.22	4.61	4.90	5.63	7.44	7.30	7.26	7.90	3.57	3.55	5.28
1996	3.97	4.39	5.20	6.11	6.63	6.72	6.97	8.15	13.70	10.94	4.17	3.52	6.71
1997	3.59	3.67	4.82	4.68	4.74	4.62	6.48	7.45	7.15	4.48	3.09	3.14	4.83
1998	3.14	3.55	5.05	5.44	5.70	6.05	6.77	5.56	6.03	6.38	5.37	4.99	5.34
1999	4.98	5.71	6.03	6.09	7.40	9.90	7.54	11.48	10.41	9.88	4.29	3.56	7.27
2000	3.55	3.43	3.82	4.36	4.67	4.70	3.35	2.17	0.32	1.50	2.69	2.46	3.09
2001[1]	2.44	3.29	4.13	5.02	4.80	4.30	6.23	5.57	6.53	5.12	3.19	3.44	4.51

[1] Preliminary. *Source: Economic Research Service, U.S. Department of Agriculture (ERS-USDA)*

Palm Oil

Palm oil is the world's second largest vegetable oil crop, after soybeans, but first in foreign trade. Palm oil now accounts for almost half the international trade of the world's major vegetable oils vs. about a third in the late 1990's. Palm oil is a tropical oil, but competes directly with other cooking oils such as soybean and sunflower oils that are grown in more temperate climates. Almost half of the world's production comes from Malaysia and about a third from Indonesia. However, over the longer term Indonesia may be able to close the gap against Malaysia, assuming no adverse political/economic developments that hamper anticipated new investment in palm oil plantations.

Palm oil production in 2001/02 (October/September) of a record 24.6 million metric tons compares with 23.7 million in 2000/01/. About two-thirds of the world's production is exported. Estimated consumption at a record large 25.1 million tons in 2001/02 compares with 16.3 million in 2000/01 and annual usage of 12 million tons in the late 1990's. Palm oil exports go mostly to Europe, the world's largest importer of crude vegetable oils. World palm oil stocks were estimated at 2.54 million tons at yearend 2001/02 (September) vs. 2.83 million a year earlier.

Malaysia's 2001/02 production was forecast at a record large 12.2 million metric tons vs. 11.9.million in 2000/01. Ten years earlier, production averaged around 6 million tons. Assuming the 2001/02-crop forecast is realized, Malaysia's exports may total a record 10.7 million tons vs10.5 million in 2000/01. Carryover stocks are expected to decline to 1.06 million tons as of September 2002 vs. 1.2 million a year earlier, still well above the 800,000-ton average in the mid-1990's. Palm kernel production is likewise concentrated in Southeast Asia; the 2001/02 world crop of 7.24 million tons compares with 6.9 million in 2000/01.

World palm oil crop year prices tend to have wide year-to-year variance. Forecasts for the 2001/02 year are centered on $264/metric ton vs. $235 in 2000/01, basis Malaysia, FOB. During the past decade, prices reached a high of f $651/mt in 1994/95. The 2000/01 price was the decade's lowest average.

Futures Markets

Crude Palm Oil and crude Palm Kernel Oil are traded on the Kuala Lumpur Commodity Exchange (KLSE).

World Palm Oil Statistics In Thousands of Metric Tons

Crop Year	Production: Colombia	Production: Indonesia	Production: Ivory Coast	Production: Malaysia	Production: Nigeria	Production: Thailand	Production: World Total	Imports: China	Imports: Pakistan	Imports: World Total	Exports: Indonesia	Exports: Malaysia	Exports: World Total
1994-5	391	4,144	282	7,771	661	346	15,073	1,786	1,215	10,674	1,904	6,728	10,573
1995-6	393	4,587	277	8,264	667	369	16,152	1,178	1,166	10,558	2,082	6,896	10,582
1996-7	440	5,078	250	9,000	678	386	17,487	1,851	1,020	11,729	2,419	7,794	11,875
1997-8	439	5,086	276	8,509	688	363	17,018	1,490	1,210	11,866	2,301	7,847	11,630
1998-9[1]	465	5,920	281	9,759	713	458	19,307	1,433	1,053	12,846	3,118	8,482	13,090
1999-00[2]	502	6,704	288	10,432	735	502	20,956	1,329	1,090	14,823	3,758	9,175	14,649
2000-1[3]	517	7,256	287	11,170	748	525	22,397	1,510	1,150	15,949	4,182	10,050	15,940

[1] Preliminary. [2] Estimate. [3] Forecast. *Source: The Oil World*

Supply and Distribution of Palm Oil in the United States In Thousands of Metric Tons

Year Beginning Oct. 1	Stocks Oct. 1	Imports	Total Supply	Consumption: Edible Products	Consumption: Inedible Products	Consumption: Total End Products	Total Disappearance	Exports	Prices: U.S. Import Value[4]	Prices: Malaysia, F.O.B., RBD	Prices: Palm Kernal Oil, Malaysia, C.I.F. Rotterdam
				In Millions of Pounds					U.S. $ Per Metric Ton		
1995-6	7.4	106.9	114.3	6.7	103.9	110.6	91.1	9.2	511	545	729
1996-7	14.0	146.4	160.4		91.8	91.8	134.8	4.2	432	544	680
1997-8	21.4	128.0	149.4		93.8	93.8	155.0	4.4	464	640	653
1998-9[1]	29.0	128.8	157.8		72.4	72.4	173.0	5.2	ÑÑ	514	725
1999-00[2]	34.0	160.0	194.0		55.0	55.0	202.0	4.9		371	
2000-1[3]	35.0				36.0	36.0					

[1] Preliminary. [2] Estimate. [3] Forecast. [4] Market value in the foreign country, excluding import duties, ocean freight and marine insurance.
Sources: The Oil World; Economic Research Service, U.S. Department of Agriculture (ERS-USDA)

Average Wholesale Palm Oil Prices, CIF, Bulk, U.S. Ports In Cents Per Pound

Year	Jan.	Feb.	Mar.	Apr.	May	June	July	Aug.	Sept.	Oct.	Nov.	Dec.	Average
1995	34.26	33.82	36.18	35.56	32.80	33.06	33.68	32.59	30.86	31.45	31.96	30.00	33.02
1996	27.08	26.52	26.33	27.52	28.57	25.43	24.78	24.46	27.24	26.13	26.95	27.45	26.54
1997	28.68	29.25	28.00	28.18	28.93	27.25	26.17	25.55	25.37	27.33	27.28	25.05	27.25
1998	29.30	29.59	30.53	32.10	31.11	31.42	32.33	33.14	33.14	33.06	33.30	34.00	31.92
1999	31.06	28.58	25.52	25.52	24.50	21.30	18.15	18.70	21.00	20.00	20.00	20.00	22.86
2000	18.65	17.66	17.73	18.21	18.12	16.52	16.85	16.23	15.90	13.19	13.56	12.75	16.28
2001	18.05	18.05	13.50	13.50	12.50	13.00	15.50	18.00	16.75	15.60			15.45

Source: Economic Research Service, U.S. Department of Agriculture (ERS-USDA)

Paper

The paper and paperboard industries are affected by a number of economic factors. As the economy strengthens, the amount of paper consumed increases. As the economy weakens, paper use declines. From 2001 to 2002, the U.S. economy was in decline though the decline does not appear to have been that severe. With the economy strengthening in 2002, use of paper should begin to increase. It is difficult to ascertain the impact of the events of September 2001 on the paper industry. There may well have been some increase in use of newsprint following the incident while the overall economy was slowed even more. It is also of interest to note that with ever increasing use of the internet, there continues to be strong demand for paper products like magazines, coupons and advertising inserts.

The U.S. is by far the world's largest producer of paper and paperboard. U.S. production has averaged about 80 million metric tonnes per year. Other large producers of paper and paperboard are Japan, Canada, Germany, Finland and Sweden. The largest producer of newsprint is Canada. Production in 2000 averaged 774,300 tonnes per month or 9.3 million tonnes per year. The U.S. was the second largest newsprint producer while Japan was the third largest. Other large newsprint producers include Sweden, South Korea and China.

Production of Paper and Paperboard by Selected Countries In Thousands of Metric Tons

Year	Austria	Canada	Finland	France	Germany	Italy	Japan	Netherlands	Russia	Spain	Sweden	United Kingdom	United States
1993	3300	17,528	9,990	7,975	13,034	6,019	27,764	2,855	4,459	3,348	8,781	5,406	77,167
1994	3603	18,349	10,909	8,701	14,457	6,705	28,527	3,011	3,412	3,503	9,284	5,829	80,948
1995	3599	18,713	10,942	8,619	14,827	6,810	59,664	2,967	4,073	3,684	9,159	6,093	85,526
1996	3653	17,472	10,441	8,556	14,733	6,954	30,014	2,987	3,224	3,684	9,018	6,188	81,971
1997	3816	17,976	12,149	9,143	15,953	8,032		3,159	3,342	3,684	9,756	6,479	76,449
1998[1]	4009	17,541	12,703	9,058	16,311	8,246		3,180	3,540	3,684	9,879	6,477	75,812

[1] Preliminary. *Source: Food and Agriculture Organization of the United Nations (FAO-UN)*

Production of Newsprint by Selected Countries (Monthly Average) In Thousands of Metric Tons

Year	Australia	Brazil	Canada	China	Finland	France	Germany	India	Japan	Rep. of Korea	Russia	Sweden	United States
1994	33.5	21.9	776.8	60.1	120.5	70.3	124.9	22.9	247.7	72.8	86.5	201.3	582.0
1995	37.4	23.5	768.8	72.1	118.8	74.2	143.8	26.3	258.2	79.0	121.4	195.5	529.3
1996	36.5	23.1	751.3	79.6	110.6	65.2	131.0	24.8	261.7	108.7	103.8	190.2	525.3
1997	34.0	22.1	767.1	68.7	122.5	65.3	134.8	23.3	266.0	132.7	99.8	200.9	545.3
1998	33.9	22.7	718.6	70.8	123.6	75.7	148.0	28.8	272.0	141.7		206.9	
1999[1]	31.8	20.2	767.0	93.4	124.2			32.4	274.6	144.8		208.2	
2000[2]	32.5	21.9	774.3	117.3	112.6			47.1	283.7	151.9		211.2	

[1] Preliminary. [2] Estimate. *Source: United Nations*

Index Price of Paperboard 1982 = 100

Year	Jan.	Feb.	Mar.	Apr.	May	June	July	Aug.	Sept.	Oct.	Nov.	Dec.	Average
1995	165.3	171.2	172.3	183.8	188.2	188.4	189.9	190.6	190.3	188.8	185.7	182.2	183.1
1996	175.7	172.6	166.6	161.8	154.0	150.6	148.0	145.5	145.6	146.6	146.9	147.6	155.1
1997	147.1	144.2	139.7	137.2	136.8	137.5	137.8	143.8	148.4	150.1	154.4	156.1	144.4
1998	155.9	156.1	156.0	155.2	154.2	153.7	152.2	150.9	149.0	146.9	144.7	143.6	151.6
1999	142.2	142.3	146.4	148.1	149.3	149.5	154.5	158.6	161.0	162.1	162.2	162.3	153.2
2000	163.1	163.6	173.6	176.6	180.4	180.3	180.9	181.2	180.9	180.4	180.2	179.5	176.7
2001[1]	179.4	176.6	175.8	175.2	174.1	172.4	172.3	169.8	168.5	166.3	166.1	166.7	171.9

[1] Preliminary. *Source: Bureau of Labor Statistics, U.S. Department of Commerce (BLS) (0914)*

Index Price of Wood Pulp, Bleached Suphate Softwood 1982 = 100

Year	Jan.	Feb.	Mar.	Apr.	May	June	July	Aug.	Sept.	Oct.	Nov.	Dec.	Average
1994	106.7	106.9	109.6	113.5	113.4	118.0	119.4	124.3	130.3	137.1	141.4	142.2	121.9
1995	150.9	153.0	187.5	193.0	202.4	215.2	217.8	223.3	218.8	223.3	217.0	212.7	201.2
1996	195.0	175.4	155.5	123.5	111.1	120.1	126.9	129.0	129.4	130.3	129.3	131.5	138.1
1997	129.6	125.9	123.9	119.0	121.8	123.9	130.9	134.4	135.7	135.7	136.8	136.2	129.5
1998	132.0	131.3	127.8	118.7	118.0	122.8	125.7	122.8	117.2	113.7	111.9	111.4	121.1
1999[1]	103.2	102.6	102.4	100.8	101.1	102.3	112.5	115.6	117.9	117.1	121.2	126.5	110.3
2000[1]	No data available for this year.												

[1] Preliminary. *Source: Bureau of Labor Statistics, U.S. Department of Commerce (BLS) (0911-0211)*

Index Price of Shipping Sack Paper[2] 1982 = 100

Year	Jan.	Feb.	Mar.	Apr.	May	June	July	Aug.	Sept.	Oct.	Nov.	Dec.	Average
1994	151.3	150.9	154.3	154.5	159.3	163.9	169.9	170.3	176.6	178.2	184.9	185.5	166.6
1995	190.4	204.5	209.5	212.0	221.5	224.2	224.2	224.2	224.0	223.4	212.8	207.3	214.8
1996	205.2	202.2	201.5	194.7	194.3	193.1	189.9	185.7	183.0	183.0	185.0	185.8	192.0
1997	185.8	186.4	186.7	186.5	184.3	184.1	183.9	188.1	182.0	188.5	196.9	197.6	187.6
1998	197.1	197.2	197.2	197.2	196.3	196.3	194.4	194.4	194.4	194.4	194.4	194.4	195.6
1999[1]	194.4	194.4	194.4	199.7	201.7	203.2	203.2	207.8	208.4	208.0	208.4	208.4	202.7
2000[1]	No data available for this year.												

[1] Preliminary. [2] Unbleached kraft. *Source: Bureau of Labor Statistics, U.S. Department of Commerce (BLS) (0913-0307)*

Producer Price Index of Standard Newsprint 1982 = 100

Year	Jan.	Feb.	Mar.	Apr.	May	June	July	Aug.	Sept.	Oct.	Nov.	Dec.	Average
1995	135.8	134.6	140.1	147.4	152.3	164.8	166.1	166.1	174.5	186.2	186.2	186.2	161.8
1996	186.2	186.2	185.2	182.7	173.5	164.4	157.4	148.7	145.7	133.1	127.3	123.1	159.5
1997	121.1	120.9	123.1	128.6	135.9	137.2	138.6	139.4	139.4	139.4	141.3	141.8	133.9
1998	142.2	142.5	141.8	142.3	140.0	140.3	143.4	143.1	144.6	147.6	147.6	145.0	143.4
1999	143.0	135.9	128.1	125.0	117.8	117.7	110.3	111.7	111.4	NA	NA	NA	122.3
2000	117.2	116.8	116.5	118.3	123.1	127.1	127.6	130.7	131.5	139.4	141.2	140.5	127.5
2001[1]	140.6	141.4	143.0	150.9	146.8	148.5	146.6	142.4	134.0	129.7	120.1	117.4	138.5

[1] Preliminary. NA = Not available. *Source: Bureau of Labor Statistics, U.S. Department of Commerce (BLS) (0913-02)*

Index Price of Coated Printing Paper, No. 3 1982 = 100

Year	Jan.	Feb.	Mar.	Apr.	May	June	July	Aug.	Sept.	Oct.	Nov.	Dec.	Average
1994	122.0	122.1	121.8	122.2	121.6	121.6	121.6	125.2	130.7	131.7	132.9	136.3	125.8
1995	139.5	145.8	150.2	153.1	147.7	152.0	159.3	159.3	160.4	160.3	160.3	160.3	154.0
1996	160.2	159.7	159.4	159.2	155.6	153.5	153.0	152.5	152.2	151.8	151.9	152.9	155.2
1997	152.7	153.1	152.9	153.2	153.2	154.6	154.5	154.5	153.2	153.3	153.2	153.3	153.5
1998	153.8	154.7	154.2	154.2	154.1	154.0	154.0	153.8	151.9	151.5	151.5	151.9	153.3
1999[1]	151.1	150.8	149.4	149.4	152.4	152.0							150.9
2000[1]	No data available for this year.												

[1] Preliminary. *Source: Bureau of Labor Statistics, U.S. Department of Commerce (BLS) (0913-0113)*

International Paper Prices--Export Unit Value

Year	Jan.	Feb.	Mar.	Apr.	May	June	July	Aug.	Sept.	Oct.	Nov.	Dec.	Average
NEWSPRINT - Finland	In Markka Per Metric Ton												
1995	2,563	2,589	2,577	2,614	2,598	2,667	3,037	3,122	3,172	3,187	3,214	3,191	2,885
1996	3,320	3,412	3,438	3,463	3,442	3,362	3,265	3,110	3,010	3,709	2,899	2,841	3,207
1997	2,741	2,662	2,669	2,667	2,701	2,602	2,642	2,709	2,736	2,697	2,706	2,755	2,694
1998	2,852	2,843	2,858	2,896	2,890	2,839	2,858	2,870	2,847	2,809	2,755	2,748	2,838
PRINTING AND WRITING - Finland	In Markka Per Metric Ton												
1995	3,816	3,897	3,905	4,066	4,165	4,284	4,473	4,416	4,439	4,555	4,569	4,400	4,235
1996	4,556	4,555	4,503	4,374	4,265	4,069	3,871	3,743	3,644	3,644	3,667	3,654	4,027
1997	3,620	3,579	3,648	3,651	3,698	3,656	3,620	3,649	3,725	3,738	3,799	3,803	3,687
1998	4,029	4,068	4,097	4,155	4,104	4,070	4,060	4,042	4,003	3,951	3,884	3,841	4,029

Source: Food and Agricultural Organization of the United Nations (FAO-UN)

International Paper Prices--Import Unit Value

Year	Jan.	Feb.	Mar.	Apr.	May	June	July	Aug.	Sept.	Oct.	Nov.	Dec.	Average
NEWSPRINT - United Kingdom	In British Pounds Per Metric Ton												
1995	344	353	348	363	376	384	428	465	470	473	469	241	393
1996	498	534	529	514	518	513	504	476	461	412	435	427	485
1997	439	400	394	380	372	380	200	385	374	368	373	377	370
1998	379	367	367	370	357	361	360	357	364	360	359		364
PRINTING AND WRITING - United Kingdom	In British Pounds Per Metric Ton												
1995	613	571	611	617	643	619	670	698	718	713	675	684	653
1996	709	776	683	639	661	635	607	919	664	631	629	684	686
1997	606	561	580	561	554	530	555	549	594	559	602	565	568
1998	535	540	540	530	550	516	514	494	532	511	513		525

Source: Food and Agricultural Organization of the United Nations (FAO-UN)

Peanuts and Peanut Oil

World peanut (groundnut) acreage has increased almost 10% since the late 1990's, with a smaller percentage gain in yield, the effect of which lifted raw production to a record high in 2000/01--31.2 million metric tons--and forecasts of even larger production in 2001/02--33.8 million tons. Still, peanuts remain fourth in production among the world's major oilseeds. On a shelled basis the totals would be about 25% lower.

China is the world's largest producer with a record large 14.4 million tons in 2000/01 and forecasts of a larger crop in 2001/02. China's late 1990's average crop was 10.9 million tons. India's 2001/02 crop is forecast at 7.8 million tons compares with 5.7 million in 2000/01. The two countries produce more than half of the world's crop with the U.S. a distant third--1.48 million tons in 2000/01 and perhaps 1.90 million in 2001/02. India's 2000/01 peanut acreage is nearly twice that of China: 8.1 million hectare vs. 4.9 million, respectively, but India's average yield is about a third of China's yield; .70 tons/hectare vs. 2.97 tons: acreage and yield forecasts for 2001/02 are about the same. Generally, the U.S. has the highest world yield. Foreign trade and world carryover in peanuts is small as most of the crop is consumed locally. World imports during 2000/01 of 1.50 million tons were marginally above 1999/00 and with little change expected during 2001/02. The world's peanut crush is among the smallest of the major oilseeds; 14.2 million tons in 2000/01 vs. 13.7 million in 1999/00, each about a tenth of the soybean crush. More of the world's peanut crop is allocated to meal production than oil, production of which totaled 5.5 million tons in 2000/01 vs. 5.3 million in 1999/00, but forecast at 6 million tons in 2001/02. As a rule, meal production about equals consumption. Peanut oil production in 2000/01 of 4.3 million tons compares with 4.2 million in 1999/00, and estimated at 4.8 million in 2001/02. Foreign trade in meal and oil is small and carryover stocks are generally insignificant.

The average world peanut oilseed prices in 12000/01 (October/September) of $888 per metric ton, basis Rotterdam, compares with $820 in 1999/00 and a 1990's average of $991 per ton. Rotterdam meal prices in the 1990's averaged $165 per metric ton; oil prices of $685 per ton in 2000/01 compare with $744 in 1999/00 and ten-year average of $866. In the U.S., the average price for peanut meal, basis southeast mills FOB during 2000/01 averaged $123 per ton vs. $122 in 1999/00 and the 1990's average of $187; peanut oil prices averaged $768 per ton, $780 and $865, respectively. For 2001/02, U.S. meal prices are forecast at $125 per ton and oil at $739 per ton.

In the U.S., the 2001/02 crop (August/July) of 4.16 billion pounds compares with a poor weather crop of 3.27 billion in 2000/01. U.S. peanut production is largely concentrated in the Southeastern states. Peanuts are also grown in the Southern Plains States where irrigation may be needed and production costs run higher, but not necessarily realized yield per acre. The average yield for the 2001 crop of 2,990 pounds per acre compares with 2,444 pounds in 2000 while the acreage harvested of 1.39 million acres compares with 1.34 million, respectively. Georgia is the largest producing state with at least a third of total production (1.6 billion pounds in 2001) followed by Texas, North Carolina and Alabama. Georgia's harvested acreage in 2001 of 477,000 acres compares with 492,000 in 2000, but average yield jumped to 3350 pounds/acre from 2700 pounds.

Total supplies in 2001/02 of 5.5 billion pounds compares with 4.7 billion for 2000/01 and includes an August 1, 2001 carryin of about 1.12 billion pounds vs 1.23 billion a year earlier. U.S. peanut imports have seen wide swings at times and were as low as 2 million per year in the early 1990's to 204 million in 2000/01.

Total U.S. peanut disappearance in 2001/02 of 4.1 billion pounds compares with 4.6 billion in 2000/01. The crush was forecast at 800 million pounds vs. 548 million, and exports at 775 million pounds vs. 519 million, respectively; most of which goes to Canada followed by the Netherlands and U.K. As a direct food, a near record high 2.25 billion pounds were forecast for 2001/02 vs. 2.2 billion in 2000/01. Still, peanut use as a direct foodstuff has been basically static during the past decade, apparently reflecting reduced demand for peanut butter and a drop in snack peanut based candies.

Futures Market

Peanut futures are traded on the Beijing Commodity Exchange (BCE).

World Production of Peanuts (in the Shell) In Thousands of Metric Tons

Year	Argentina	Burma	China	India	Indonesia	Nigeria	Senegal	South Africa	Sudan	Thailand	United States	Zaire	World Total
1992-3	233	433	5,953	8,854	913	250	579	172	390	162	1,943	380	22,993
1993-4	208	389	8,420	7,760	865	500	620	190	390	136	1,539	380	24,229
1994-5	238	445	9,682	8,255	1,085	650	720	105	390	150	1,927	581	27,366
1995-6	462	501	10,200	7,400	1,055	800	827	193	370	147	1,570	585	27,467
1996-7	300	593	10,140	9,024	985	950	646	140	370	147	1,661	570	28,958
1997-8	625	559	9,648	7,580	990	1,250	506	97	370	130	1,605	400	27,289
1998-9	340	540	11,886	7,450	930	1,430	541	138	370	135	1,798	410	29,765
1999-00	420	560	12,640	5,500	1,020	1,450	760	170	370	150	1,740	400	29,060
2000-1[1]	360	640	14,440	5,700	970	1,470	920	260	370	150	1,480	380	31,170
2001-2[2]	380	640	14,500	7,800	1,000	1,490	950	150	370	150	1,920	380	33,760

[1] Preliminary. [2] Estimate. *Source: Foreign Agricultural Service, U.S. Department of Agriculture (FAS-USDA)*

Salient Statistics of Peanuts in the United States

Crop Year	Agreage Planted	Acreage Harvested for Nuts	Average Yield Per Acre In Lbs.	Production 1,000 Lbs.	Season Farm Price Cents/Lb.	Farm Value Million Dollars	Exports Unshelled	Exports Shelled	Imports Unshelled	Imports Shelled
	----- 1,000 Acres -----						----- Thousand Pounds (Year Beginning August 1) -----			
1992-3	1,686.6	1,669.1	2,567	4,284,416	30.0	1,285.4	951,000	611,250	2,000	2,000
1993-4	1,733.5	1,689.8	2,008	3,392,415	30.4	1,030.9	555,000	352,500	2,000	1,420
1994-5	1,641.0	1,618.5	2,624	4,247,455	28.9	1,229.0	878,000	583,142	74,000	55,385
1995-6	1,537.5	1,517.0	2,282	3,461,475	29.3	1,013.3	826,000	564,021	153,000	108,303
1996-7	1,401.5	1,380.0	2,653	3,661,205	28.1	1,029.8	668,000	440,438	127,000	95,041
1997-8	1,434.0	1,413.8	2,503	3,539,380	28.3	1,001.6	682,000	455,264	141,000	101,792
1998-9	1,521.0	1,467.0	2,702	3,963,440	28.4	1,126.0	562,000	----	155,000	----
1999-00	1,534.5	1,436.0	2,667	3,829,490	25.4	971.6	727,000	----	178,000	----
2000-1[1]	1,536.8	1,336.0	2,444	3,265,505	27.4	896.1	519,000	----	204,000	----
2001-2[2]	1,543.0	1,400.5	3,027	4,239,450	23.4	1,003.0	775,000	----	178,000	----

[1] Preliminary. [2] Estimate. *Source: Economic Research Service, U.S. Department of Agriculture (ERS-USDA)*

Supply and Disposition of Peanuts (Farmer's Stock Basis) & Support Program in the United States

Crop Year	Production	Imports	Stocks Aug. 1	Total	Exports	Crushed fior Oil	Seed, Loss & Residual	Food	Total Disappearance	Support Price	Additional	Amount Put Under Support Quantity	Amount Put Under Support % of Production
	Supply				Disposition					Government Support Program			
	In Millions of Pounds									---- Cents per Lb. ----		Mil. Lbs.	
1993-4	3,392	2	1,350	4,744	553	670	372	2,088	3,683	33.37	6.6	324	9.6
1994-5	4,247	74	1,061	5,382	878	982	316	2,009	4,184	33.92	6.6	820	19.3
1995-6	3,461	153	1,198	4,812	826	999	238	1,993	4,054	33.92	6.6	818	24.0
1996-7	3,661	127	758	4,546	668	692	363	2,029	3,750	30.50	6.6	320	8.7
1997-8	3,539	141	795	4,475	682	544	303	2,099	3,627	30.50	6.6	417	11.8
1998-9	3,963	155	848	4,966	562	460	374	2,153	3,574	30.50	8.8	----	----
1999-00	3,829	178	1,392	5,399	727	713	493	2,233	4,166	30.50	8.8	----	----
2000-1[1]	3,266	204	1,233	4,703	519	548	341	2,179	3,588	30.50	6.6	----	----
2001-2[2]	4,157	178	1,116	5,451	775	800	286	2,250	4,111	30.50	6.6	----	----

[1] Preliminary. [2] Estimate. *Source: Economic Research Service, U.S. Department of Agriculture (ERS-USDA)*

Production of Peanuts (Harvested for Nuts) in the United States, by States In Thousands of Pounds

Year	Alabama	Florida	Georgia	New Mexico	North Carolina	Oklahoma	South Carolina	Texas	Virgina	Total
1992	591,180	202,510	1,820,465	58,236	406,980	236,180	32,500	680,150	256,215	4,284,416
1993	473,220	194,880	1,383,545	56,680	299,585	233,580	24,500	550,175	176,250	3,392,415
1994	446,220	207,480	1,862,630	51,660	485,465	261,000	36,250	605,570	291,180	4,247,455
1995	483,360	193,590	1,414,880	43,000	347,040	201,880	30,800	540,000	206,925	3,461,475
1996	449,805	236,160	1,433,770	37,950	367,500	195,210	32,550	689,000	219,260	3,661,205
1997	372,490	228,060	1,333,830	46,710	329,640	184,800	30,450	822,150	191,250	3,539,380
1998	432,415	233,100	1,511,655	62,040	397,155	159,750	28,175	917,900	221,250	3,963,440
1999	448,050	260,380	1,400,800	61,600	298,840	189,600	25,300	926,800	218,120	3,829,490
2000	271,180	213,710	1,328,400	54,990	338,250	120,600	29,500	698,500	210,375	3,265,505
2001[1]	510,300	261,000	1,597,950	67,200	369,000	165,000	30,450	924,000	232,500	4,157,400

[1] Preliminary. *Source: Agricultural Statistics Board, U.S. Department of Agriculture (ASB-USDA)*

Supply and Reported Uses of Shelled Peanuts and Products in the United States In Thousands of Pounds

Crop Year Beginning Aug. 1	Shelled Peanuts --- Stocks, Aug. 1 --- Edible	Oil Stock[2]	Shelled Peanuts ------- Production ------- Edible	Oil Stock[2]	Reported Used (Shelled Peanuts -- Raw Basis) Edible Grades Used In Candy[3]	Snacks[4]	Sandwich Spread	Butter[5]	Other Products	Total	Shelled Peanuts Crushed[6]	Crude Oil Production	Cake & Meal Production
1992-3	871,207	57,829	2,376,782	533,641	328,324	352,775	----	797,910	24,981	1,503,990	669,942	285,904	377,301
1993-4	679,639	42,054	1,748,734	425,710	362,418	348,867	----	727,006	36,301	1,474,592	503,674	212,216	292,093
1994-5	752,814	57,188	1,741,824	511,635	349,630	301,548	----	709,823	36,854	1,397,855	738,221	314,189	415,394
1995-6	370,431	58,188	1,253,451	491,818	350,663	277,089	----	728,076	32,015	1,387,843	751,281	320,909	420,919
1996-7	498,954	126,318	1,692,581	305,674	360,846	290,102	----	727,531	33,825	1,412,304	520,413	220,877	294,590
1997-8	509,476	41,000	1,694,016	290,882	351,017	306,908	----	760,230	35,471	1,453,626	409,249	175,853	228,276
1998-9	788,877	16,454	2,186,629	286,060	380,177	349,806	----	744,706	22,131	1,496,820	345,825	145,254	192,425
1999-00	778,671	70,391	2,157,828	448,875	354,953	394,121	----	772,104	20,227	1,541,405	536,164	228,839	291,491
2000-1[1]	707,524	14,463	1,939,736	344,582	355,694	358,205	----	753,241	19,974	1,487,114	411,734	178,523	230,099

[1] Preliminary. [2] Includes straight run oil stock peanuts. [3] Includes peanut butter made by manufacturers for own use in candy. [4] Formerly titled Salted Peanuts. [5] Includes peanut butter made by manufacturers for own use in cookies and sandwiches, but excludes peanut butter used in candy. [6] All crushings regardless of grade. *Source: National Agricultural Statistics Service, U.S. Department of Agriculture (NASS-USDA)*

PEANUTS AND PEANUT OIL

Shelled Peanuts (Raw Basis) Used in Primary Products, by Type In Thousands of Pounds

	Virginia				Runner				Spanish			
Year	Candy[2]	Snack Peanuts	Peanut Butter[3]	Total	Candy[2]	Snack Peanuts	Peanut Butter[3]	Total	Candy[2]	Snack Peanuts	Peanut Butter[3]	Total
1992-3	49,223	124,875	92,355	275,895	259,498	203,732	674,962	1,152,775	19,603	24,168	30,593	75,320
1993-4	44,889	99,381	63,270	222,641	298,325	227,286	365,047	1,179,396	19,204	22,200	28,689	72,555
1994-5	26,857	97,389	51,354	190,916	302,697	185,377	644,711	1,152,110	20,076	18,782	13,758	54,829
1995-6	25,176	93,041	71,310	203,183	304,285	169,142	634,350	1,123,719	21,202	14,906	22,416	60,941
1996-7	24,158	91,882	64,274	193,166	318,924	176,851	634,387	1,149,347	17,764	21,369	28,870	69,791
1997-8	48,428	80,309	59,228	182,100	302,791	206,718	676,839	1,206,946	19,798	19,581	24,163	64,580
1998-9	36,178	99,401	57,864	196,935	321,838	234,486	670,705	1,244,748	22,161	15,919	16,137	55,137
1999-00	23,173	100,384	73,926	200,804	315,467	278,440	690,564	1,300,393	16,313	15,297	7,614	40,208
2000-1[1]	19,132	99,755	102,052	224,210	320,210	245,286	643,229	1,224,585	16,352	13,164	7,960	38,319

[1] Preliminary. [2] Includes peanut butter made by manufacturers for own use in candy. [3] Includes peanut butter made by manufacturers for own use in cookies and sandwiches, but excludes peanut butter used in candy. *Source: National Agricultural Statistics Service, U.S. Department of Agriculture (NASS-USDA)*

Production, Consumption, Stocks and Foreign Trade of Peanut Oil in the U.S. In Millions of Pounds

Crop Year Beginning Aug. 1	Production: Crude	Production: Refined	Consumption: In Refining	Consumption: In End Products	Stocks Dec. 31: Crude	Stocks Dec. 31: Refined	Imports for Consumption	Exports
1993-4	212.2	155.2	163.7	149.1	6.5	3.9	11.0	61.0
1994-5	319.9	120.0	126.1	118.9	5.0	2.8	5.0	21.5
1995-6	329.0	125.7	129.9	126.0	19.9	2.8	3.2	47.8
1996-7	233.9	133.5	138.9	138.4	85.6	2.8	1.6	35.1
1997-8	144.3	104.0	111.6	121.6	42.6	3.0	6.6	8.8
1998-9	172.9	118.3	123.7	180.1	47.2	3.8	30.3	4.3
1999-00	262.9	195.9	238.9	260.4	19.7	1.7	9.6	5.8
2000-1[1]	222.1	206.3	258.9		23.1	1.9	19.5	5.5
2001-2[2]	182.1	118.9	406.5		15.2	1.7		

[1] Preliminary. [2] Forecast. *Source: Bureau of the Census, U.S. Department of Commerce*

Production of Crude Peanut Oil in the United States In Millions of Pounds

Year	Jan.	Feb.	Mar.	Apr.	May	June	July	Aug.	Sept.	Oct.	Nov.	Dec.	Total
1992	28.0	26.8	42.5	40.9	39.8	40.6	37.3	31.3	35.1	24.2	19.2	15.6	381.3
1993	16.9	17.0	24.1	28.8	23.3	29.0	25.6	22.5	3.6	8.6	16.4	14.6	230.4
1994	18.1	18.3	21.2	18.7	25.6	15.4	21.7	16.8	17.2	11.9	18.4	24.2	227.5
1995	27.9	28.6	42.7	36.9	39.2	29.2	26.9	26.3	17.4	13.2	19.5	24.3	332.0
1996	29.2	31.9	36.8	36.8	36.7	33.3	31.4	31.5	27.1	21.1	20.6	21.8	358.2
1997	19.9	16.1	18.8	17.9	13.3	15.9	9.9	12.1	6.1	12.2	11.6	14.0	167.7
1998	16.0	14.5	14.3	13.0	10.8	10.0	9.5	6.3	5.8	6.9	13.6	13.9	134.5
1999	16.2	18.2	15.8	18.2	16.4	20.7	20.8	17.8	16.3	13.5	22.6	22.7	219.2
2000	35.2	32.1	27.4	31.9	30.4	28.0	24.1	28.8	21.5	25.4	16.4	15.2	316.3
2001[1]	17.3	15.7	20.1	15.3	12.4	19.1	16.3	16.7	12.9	17.1	13.8	15.4	192.2

[1] Preliminary. *Source: Bureau of the Census, U.S. Department of Commerce*

Average Price of Peanut Meal 50% Southeast Mills In Dollars Per Short Ton

Year	Oct.	Nov.	Dec.	Jan.	Feb.	Mar.	Apr.	May	June	July	Aug.	Sept.	Average
1992-3	163.33	170.00	173.13	180.00	175.83	165.00	161.50	165.63	171.25	200.00	213.75	210.63	172.90
1993-4	196.00	197.00	200.00	209.00	207.50	198.75	191.00	187.50	163.75	164.00	153.75	114.80	194.91
1994-5	151.25	147.50	127.00	105.00	107.50	119.00	125.00	123.75	134.00	138.75	136.25	142.00	128.94
1995-6	132.50	175.00	204.00	220.00	215.00	210.00	210.00	212.00	210.00	224.25	227.00	192.80	202.70
1996-7	170.00	146.13	172.67	221.00	228.13	225.00	233.75	222.00	235.00	220.00	213.00	210.00	232.00
1997-8	210.00	210.00	210.00	210.00	210.00	210.00	210.00	210.00	210.00	210.00	207.50	205.00	209.60
1998-9	161.00	100.00	103.75	105.00	102.50	91.25	94.50	93.75	100.00	100.00	105.00	102.50	104.94
1999-00	98.00	103.00	103.00	104.00	104.75	110.00	115.00	115.00	119.60	118.00	118.00	118.00	108.15
2000-1	118.00	118.00	118.00	142.50	120.00	118.00	110.75	112.50	NA	123.50	130.50	126.25	121.64
2001-2[1]	115.00	111.25	100.00	102.50									107.19

[1] Preliminary. NA = Not available. *Source: Agricultural Marketing Service, U.S. Department of Agriculture (AMS-USDA)*

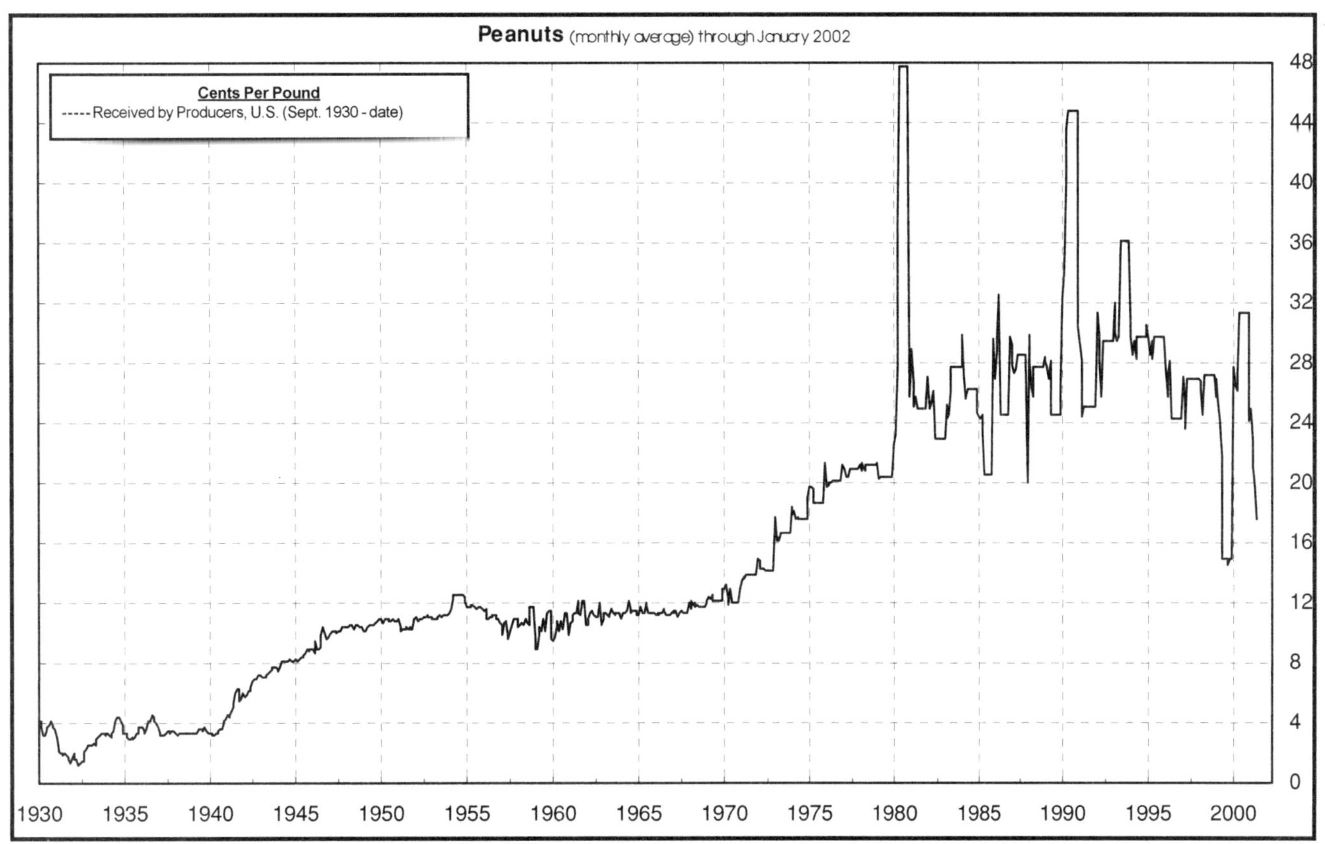

Average Price Received by Producers for Peanuts (in the Shell) in the U.S. In Cents Per Pound

Year	Aug.	Sept.	Oct.	Nov.	Dec.	Jan.	Feb.	Mar.	Apr.	May	June	July	Average[1]
1992-3	NQ	31.3	29.9	28.2	25.7	29.5	NQ	NQ	NQ	NQ	NQ	NQ	30.0
1993-4	NQ	32.0	30.0	29.5	29.7	36.1	NQ	NQ	NQ	NQ	NQ	NQ	30.4
1994-5	NQ	30.6	28.6	25.9	25.8	25.7	NQ	NQ	NQ	NQ	NQ	NQ	27.9
1995-6	30.6	29.7	28.6	29.5	28.3	29.8	NQ	NQ	NQ	NQ	NQ	NQ	29.4
1996-7	NQ	27.6	25.8	27.1	28.1	24.3	NQ	NQ	NQ	NQ	NQ	NQ	26.6
1997-8	23.3	27.1	25.4	25.0	30.7	24.7	NQ	NQ	NQ	NQ	NQ	NQ	26.0
1998-9	NQ	26.8	26.3	24.6	27.2	NQ	NQ	NQ	NQ	NQ	NQ	NQ	26.2
1999-00	25.7	27.0	25.4	24.1	21.8	14.9	NQ	NQ	NQ	NQ	NQ	NQ	23.2
2000-1	NQ	27.7	26.5	26.1	27.3	31.4	NQ	NQ	NQ	NQ	NQ	NQ	27.8
2001-2[2]	24.1	24.9	22.8	21.1	19.7	17.6							21.7

[1] Weighted average by sales. [2] Preliminarly. NQ = No quote. *Source: National Agricultural Statistics Service, U.S. Department of Agriculture (NASS-USDA)*

Average Price of Domestic Crude Peanut Oil (in Tanks) F.O.B. Southeast Mills In Cents Per Pound

Year	Oct.	Nov.	Dec.	Jan.	Feb.	Mar.	Apr.	May	June	July	Aug.	Sept.	Average
1992-3	23.63	25.58	30.30	30.88	27.17	26.00	27.50	30.00	30.20	33.00	39.50	35.93	29.97
1993-4	40.20	43.33	43.17	46.10	46.12	44.50	43.40	44.25	43.75	44.00	45.00	43.10	43.91
1994-5	46.00	50.88	53.80	50.25	41.83	41.00	41.25	40.25	39.00	39.13	41.50	41.30	43.85
1995-6	42.50	41.63	39.20	37.25	36.00	36.60	39.25	42.80	43.00	43.00	42.60	40.80	40.39
1996-7	41.50	39.20	40.75	43.50	43.88	44.75	45.00	46.20	47.88	48.06	48.00	47.25	44.66
1997-8	49.63	51.00	51.25	51.60	51.00	51.00	50.00	47.20	45.50	44.00	43.75	43.88	48.32
1998-9	45.40	45.00	44.25	44.00	39.75	34.75	35.20	35.00	37.75	39.00	38.75	38.00	39.74
1999-00	40.40	41.00	35.40	33.00	32.50	31.60	33.00	36.25	36.00	35.63	35.00	34.90	35.39
2000-1	34.63	35.50	36.40	37.25	37.00	35.90	34.00	33.00	33.00	33.00	34.00	34.00	34.81
2001-2[1]	36.25	37.00	37.00	35.00									36.31

[1] Preliminary. *Source: Agricultural Marketing Service, U.S. Department of Agriculture (AMS-USDA)*

Pepper

In a report released in late 2001 by the International Pepper Community (IPC), it was noted that world exports of pepper are expected to continue increasing. Exports have been on the increase in recent years as a result of increased production and surplus stocks. Countries that have increased production and exports of pepper include Vietnam and Brazil. Even smaller exporters like China and Sri Lanka have increased their exports of pepper. One notable exception has been India where the domestic market has taken more pepper. India's pepper prices are higher and that has acted to limit exports.

The largest exporter of pepper is Vietnam. Exports in 2001 were estimated at 53,000 metric tonnes, up 47 percent from 2000 when exports were 36,465 tonnes. Vietnam's pepper prices are more favorable and that brings buying interest. the IPC projects that for 2002, Vietnam will see an increase of 5 percent from 2001 with exports forecast at 56,000 tonnes. Pepper exports by Brazil in 2001 were estimated at 34,000 tonnes, an increase of 67 percent from the previous year. The IPC reported that Brazilian pepper exports in 2002 were expected to increase another 24 percent to 42,000 tonnes. Another major exporter is Indonesia. Pepper exports in 2001 were estimated at 45,000 tonnes, a decline of 30 percent from 2000. For 2002, Indonesia was expected to export 45,000 tonnes of pepper.

Among the smaller exporters, Malaysia exported 26,000 tonnes in 2001, an increase of 14 percent from 2000. Exports in 2002 are projected to be 24,000 tonnes. India exported 25,000 tonnes of pepper in 2001, an increase of 14 percent from the previous year. In 1999 exports were 47,319 tonnes. For 2001 India is expected to export 25,000 tonnes. In 2001, China exported 4,000 tonnes of pepper while in 2002 exports are expected to increase 50 percent to 6,000 tonnes. Sri Lanka had 2001 exports of 4,500 tonnes. For 2002 exports are expected to increase 56 percent to 7,000 tonnes. According to the IPC, world pepper exports in 2001 were 193,800 tonnes, an increase of 12 percent from 2000. For 2002, world exports of pepper are expected to be 207,052 tonnes. The increase is accounted for mostly by Brazil.

The IPC reported that in the January-September 2001 period, U.S. imports of pepper were 34,187 tonnes, an increase of 4 percent from the year before. The increase was not expected to continue due to the slowdown in the economy. Imports were 3,345 tonnes in September while a year ago in the same month they were 5,084 tonnes.

World Exports of Pepper (Black and White) and Prices in the United States — In Metric Tons

	Exports (In Metric Tons)								New York Spot Prices (Cents Per Pound)				
									Indonesian			Indian	
Year	Brazil	India	Indonesia	Madagascar	Malaysia	Mexico	Sri Lanka	Vietnam	Lampong Black	Muntok White	Brazilian Black	Malabar Black	Tellicherry[2]
1991	47,553	18,735	49,667	1,844	25,458	1,861	2,058	16,252	71.1	70.1	67.1	67.1	117.8
1992	26,277	22,684	62,136	1,948	22,919	3,636	2,143	22,347	56.1	70.8	54.7	54.7	86.1
1993	26,254	47,677	27,684	2,001	16,737	2,430	5,032	20,138	62.5	114.6	62.3	62.3	84.0
1994	22,231	36,536	36,036	2,066	23,275	2,615	1,850	16,000	95.3	151.9	95.0	95.0	110.7
1995	22,158	25,270	57,781	1,274	14,869	3,085	2,082	17,900	116.8	182.3	116.8	116.8	150.9
1996	24,178	47,211	36,849	1,570	28,124	4,200	2,612	25,300	114.8	178.9	114.8	114.8	140.0
1997	13,962	40,000	33,386	894	29,000	4,210	3,485	24,713	206.7	304.6	206.7	206.7	225.8
1998[1]	17,249	32,000	38,723	339	18,717	3,365	3,485	15,000	239.5	356.5	239.5	239.5	286.6
1999[1]									254.5	334.9	254.5	254.5	296.3
2000[1]									228.1	227.1	228.1	228.1	282.6

[1] Preliminary. [2] Extra bold. *Source: Foreign Agricultural Service, U.S. Department of Agriculture (FAS-USDA)*

United States Imports of Unground Pepper from Specified Countries — In Metric Tons

	Black Pepper							White Pepper					
Year	Brazil	India	Indonesia	Malaysia	Singapore	Sri Lanka	Total	Brazil	China	Indonesia	Malaysia	Singapore	Total
1991	15,069	2,308	11,330	8,154	391	396	38,860	2	7	4,938	37	96	5,174
1992	6,601	9,892	20,768	2,073	52	310	40,590	51	2	5,089	29	261	5,544
1993	4,580	21,985	7,666	209	----	539	35,969	322	114	4,304	137	363	5,481
1994	8,215	21,097	11,877	829	90	386	43,011	312	756	3,974	228	302	6,102
1995	3,165	10,836	19,630	268	30	327	34,465	414	280	4,037	164	211	5,266
1996	4,267	18,350	17,213	1,084	101	411	41,602	519	54	4,370	150	391	5,765
1997	4,328	23,404	13,610	2,203	678	285	45,319	75	522	3,755	199	750	5,751
1998	5,806	15,540	13,045	422	185	578	36,508	32	108	4,571	195	203	5,393
1999	7,093	24,931	8,429	2,392	525	441	47,591	32	451	5,202	420	342	6,789
2000[1]	7,853	10,981	15,713	4,148	306	516	43,479	15	210	6,345	185	215	7,311

[1] Preliminary. *Source: Foreign Agricultural Service, U.S. Department of Agriculture (FAS-USDA)*

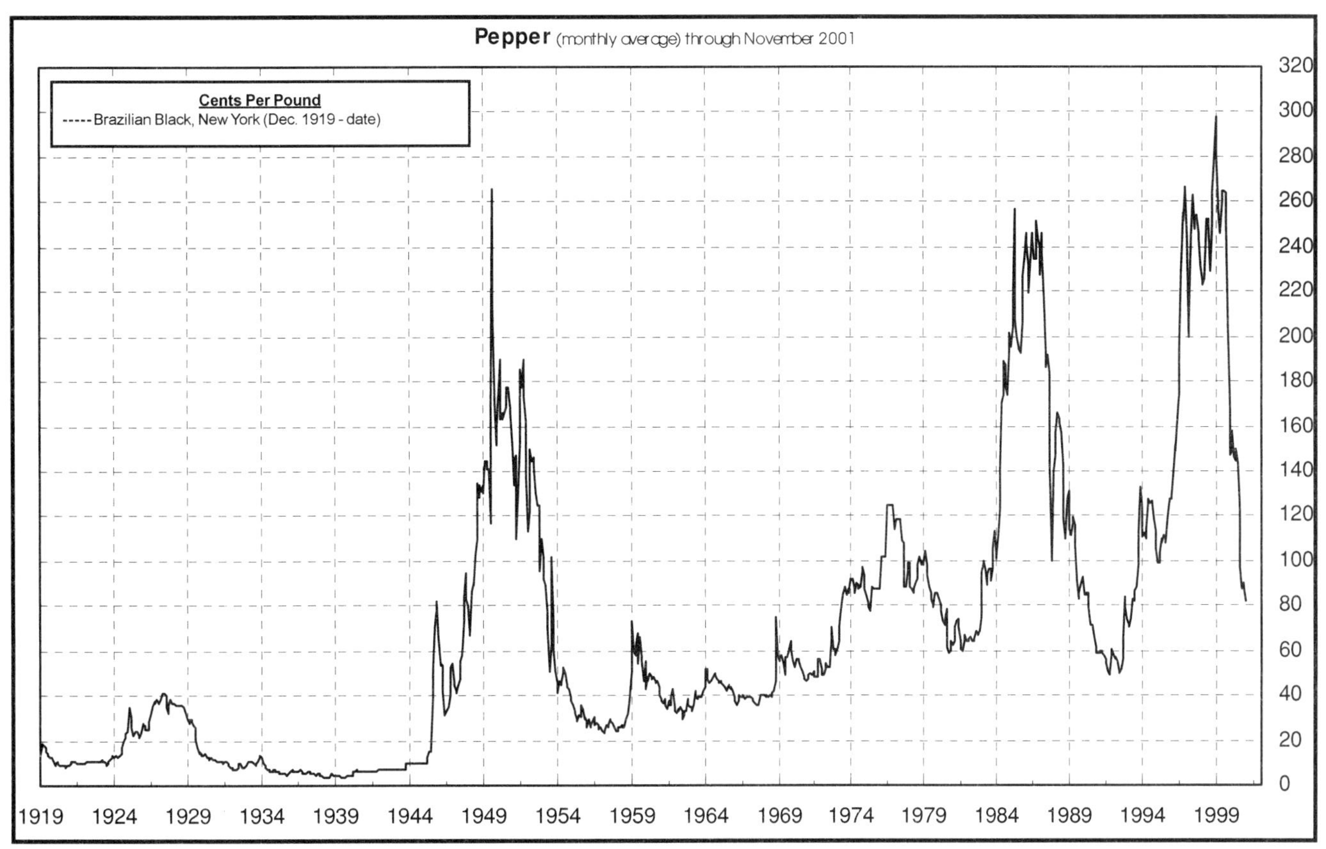

Average Black Pepper in New York (Brazilian) In Cents Per Pound

Year	Jan.	Feb.	Mar.	Apr.	May	June	July	Aug.	Sept.	Oct.	Nov.	Dec.	Average
1992	55.6	54.5	56.0	55.3	54.0	54.0	50.8	49.0	50.0	57.8	61.0	58.0	54.7
1993	56.0	56.5	54.3	51.2	50.0	51.5	55.8	64.8	84.0	79.0	74.2	70.8	62.3
1994	69.3	74.3	82.0	82.8	82.0	86.5	87.8	97.8	112.2	131.5	123.5	110.4	95.0
1995	111.0	110.0	114.2	124.8	127.3	126.0	127.0	126.3	118.2	113.5	104.8	99.0	116.8
1996	99.3	103.3	109.2	108.3	111.2	109.5	108.0	119.8	126.5	127.5	127.6	128.0	114.8
1997	138.6	151.8	149.0	161.8	173.4	193.8	229.5	255.0	251.3	264.8	266.3	245.0	206.7
1998	199.4	205.5	243.8	262.8	262.8	247.5	253.0	253.8	246.3	243.0	231.3	225.0	239.5
1999	222.5	225.8	252.5	248.0	252.5	250.0	229.0	249.3	263.8	282.0	297.5	281.0	254.5
2000	260.0	256.3	246.0	260.0	265.0	265.0	263.8	252.5	205.0	167.5	147.5	149.0	228.1
2001	157.5	146.3	144.0	150.0	143.8	123.0	97.3	87.0	90.0	89.3	81.6		119.1

Source: Foreign Agricultural Service, U.S. Department of Agriculture (FAS-USDA)

Average White Pepper in New York (Indonesian)[1] In Cents Per Pound

Year	Jan.	Feb.	Mar.	Apr.	May	June	July	Aug.	Sept.	Oct.	Nov.	Dec.	Average
1992	70.0	70.0	70.0	70.0	68.0	65.0	64.2	65.0	72.7	79.2	78.5	77.4	70.8
1993	79.0	89.0	85.3	84.0	81.3	87.3	97.0	121.5	181.3	172.6	154.7	142.4	114.6
1994	144.5	139.5	141.3	140.8	137.0	143.3	143.4	156.3	159.2	167.5	176.5	173.0	151.9
1995	179.5	175.8	168.0	181.3	195.0	184.2	187.5	190.8	191.0	182.0	178.5	174.2	182.3
1996	174.5	177.5	181.6	179.5	172.6	164.8	154.0	169.6	181.5	193.5	191.8	205.8	178.9
1997	256.0	264.5	255.0	250.0	241.0	248.8	280.3	324.0	332.5	362.0	433.8	407.5	304.6
1998	348.0	346.3	362.5	390.0	393.0	358.8	354.0	356.3	348.8	340.0	340.0	340.0	356.5
1999	361.3	355.0	365.0	355.0	352.5	335.0	310.0	313.8	325.0	327.0	316.3	303.0	334.9
2000	295.0	293.8	264.0	253.8	246.3	242.0	226.3	227.5	205.0	171.3	150.0	150.0	227.1
2001	159.0	151.3	144.0	133.8	130.0	127.0	122.5	129.6	128.0	125.5	120.0		133.7

[1] Muntok White. *Source: Foreign Agricultural Service, U.S. Department of Agriculture (FAS-USDA)*

Petroleum

After high prices in the energy complex in year 2000, prices trended lower in 2001. The high prices seen in 2000 led to more conservation as well as more exploration and development. That, in turn, led to a decline in prices for energy products like gasoline and heating oil. The events of September 11 were followed by a sharp decline in crude oil prices. Prices for crude oil on the New York Mercantile Exchange (NYMEX) had been about $28 per barrel. After September 11 they fell to about $21 per barrel. After some stability in October, prices again declined and by mid November 2001 crude oil prices on the NYMEX were under $18 per barrel. The decline in crude oil prices was due in part to a slowdown in the U.S. economy as well as other economies.

In response to the decline in crude oil prices, the Organization of Petroleum Exporting Countries (OPEC) met and agreed to cut daily production by 1.5 million barrels. New output quotas for 10 OPEC members were set with no quota for Iraq. OPEC had expected that non-OPEC oil exporters like Russia would contribute to the cuts by reducing daily production by 500,000 barrels. The non-OPEC cuts were somewhat less than 500,000 barrels and crude oil prices moved lower as there remained questions as to the extent of compliance in the cuts by both OPEC and non-OPEC countries.

The U.S. Energy Information Agency reported that U.S. domestic field production of crude oil in November 2001 was 5.87 million barrels per day, up from 5.81 million barrels per day in October 2001. A year before, production averaged 5.83 million barrels. In the January-November 2001 period, crude oil production averaged 5.84 million barrels per day. In the same period in 2000, production averaged 5.82 million barrels while in 1999 the average was 5.87 million barrels. U.S. field production of crude oil has been trending lower for several year. In 2000 production averaged 5.82 million barrels per day. In 1995 production averaged 6.56 million barrels while in 1990 it was 7.35 million barrels. In 1986 average production each day was 8.68 million barrels.

The year 2001 saw an active debate over the merits of opening more of Alaska to exploration and drilling for oil. In November 2001, Alaskan oil production averaged 1.04 million barrels per day, up 16 percent from the previous month and some 5 percent more than a year ago. In the January-November 2001 period, Alaskan production averaged 963,000 barrels per day. In 1999 production averaged 1.05 million barrels per day. Production of oil in Alaska has been steadily declining. In 1998 production was 2.02 million barrels per day. By 1995 that had fallen to 1.48 million barrels. For all of 2000, production was 970,000 barrels per day.

U.S. imports of crude oil in November 2001 averaged 9.17 million barrels per day, up 1 percent from the previous month. In November 2000, imports averaged 8.91 million barrels per day. In the January-November 2001 period, imports of crude oil averaged 9.18 million barrels per day. In the same period of 2000, imports of crude oil averaged 9.06 million barrels per day while in 1999 they averaged 8.78 million barrels. The trend in the U.S. is for increased imports of crude oil. In 1988 imports averaged 5.11 million barrels per day. For all of 2000, crude oil imports averaged 9.07 million barrels per day.

The U.S. exports small amounts of crude oil. In November 2001, exports averaged 31,000 barrels per day. In the January-November 2001 period, exports averaged 26,000 barrels per day. That was well down from the same period in 2000 when exports averaged 53,000 barrels per day. In 1999 the average was 116,000 barrels.

U.S. stocks of crude oil at the end of November 2001 were 859 million barrels. At the end of November 2000, stocks were 834 million barrels. Stocks of oil in the past have been close to those levels. In 1990 stocks were 908 million barrels. Stocks of oil in the Strategic Petroleum Reserve in November 2001 were 547 million barrels.

Futures Markets

Futures and options on light sweet crude oil are traded on the New York Mercantile Exchange (NYMEX). Other energy products traded there include heating oil, unleaded gasoline and natural gas. London's International Petroleum Exchange (IPE) trades Brent crude oil futures and options. The IPE also trades gasoil, natural gas and fuel oil. The Singapore International Monetary Exchange Ltd. (SIMEX) trades Brent crude oil futures.

World Production of Crude Petroleum In Thousands of Barrels Per Day

Year	Canada	China	Indo-nesia	Iran	Kuwait	Mexico	Nigeria	Russia[3]	Saudi Arabia	United Kingdom	United States	Vene-zuela	World Total
1992	1,605	2,845	1,504	3,429	1,058	2,669	1,943	7,632	8,332	1,825	7,171	2,371	60,213
1993	1,679	2,890	1,511	3,540	1,852	2,673	1,960	6,730	8,198	1,915	6,847	2,450	60,236
1994	1,746	2,939	1,510	3,618	2,025	2,685	1,931	6,135	8,120	2,375	6,662	2,588	60,991
1995	1,805	2,990	1,503	3,643	2,057	2,618	1,993	5,995	8,231	2,489	6,560	2,750	62,335
1996	1,837	3,131	1,547	3,686	2,062	2,855	2,188	5,850	8,218	2,568	6,465	3,053	63,711
1997	1,893	3,200	1,520	3,664	2,083	3,023	2,317	5,920	8,562	2,517	6,452	3,315	65,690
1998	1,981	3,198	1,518	3,634	2,085	3,070	2,153	2,854	8,389	2,616	6,252	3,167	66,921
1999	1,907	3,206	1,472	3,557	1,898	2,906	2,130	6,079	7,833	2,684	5,881	2,826	65,870
2000[1]	1,977	3,249	1,466	3,719	2,126	3,012	2,144	6,479	8,404	2,475	5,822	2,949	68,200
2001[2]	2,021	3,303	1,375	3,745	2,034	3,113	2,253	7,030	8,071	2,286	5,837	2,892	68,136

Includes lease condensate. [1] Preliminary. [2] Estimate. [3] Formerly part of the U.S.S.R.; data not reported separately until 1992.

Source: Energy Information Administration, U.S. Department of Energy (EIA-DOE)

Refiner Sales Prices of Residual Fuel Oil   In Cents Per Gallon

Year	Jan.	Feb.	Mar.	Apr.	May	June	July	Aug.	Sept.	Oct.	Nov.	Dec.	Average
1996	49.9	42.8	47.1	48.3	45.0	40.4	41.4	42.0	42.8	47.9	49.1	51.4	45.7
1997	46.2	43.7	39.6	37.6	36.6	39.4	38.5	39.4	40.1	44.6	46.5	38.7	41.5
1998	35.2	30.7	29.4	32.0	31.0	29.3	30.7	26.0	20.0	31.0	27.3	21.0	20.0
1999	27.5	21.8	27.2	30.9	34.6	35.0	38.6	44.8	49.8	47.3	48.5	50.3	38.2
2000	55.3	59.2	53.2	52.3	58.9	65.8	65.1	61.5	71.9	73.7	71.3	66.6	62.7
2001[1]	64.5	61.9	57.2	57.3	58.2	53.0	50.0	50.4	51.2	45.3			54.9

Sulfur 1% or less, excluding taxes. [1] Preliminary. *Source: Energy Information Administration, U.S. Department of Energy (EIA-DOE)*

Refiner Sales Prices of No. 2 Fuel Oil   In Cents Per Gallon

Year	Jan.	Feb.	Mar.	Apr.	May	June	July	Aug.	Sept.	Oct.	Nov.	Dec.	Average
1996	56.8	58.9	62.8	67.5	61.1	53.7	57.1	62.1	68.7	72.7	71.4	71.2	63.9
1997	69.8	64.5	57.7	58.6	58.8	54.5	53.8	55.3	54.3	59.0	58.4	53.4	58.9
1998	48.9	47.7	44.9	44.9	43.4	39.9	38.8	36.9	41.8	41.2	38.9	34.6	42.2
1999	36.3	33.1	39.8	44.7	43.8	44.7	51.2	56.2	60.9	61.0	66.2	67.8	49.3
2000	84.1	92.4	79.6	76.4	78.4	80.3	81.0	88.3	100.9	98.8	100.4	94.1	88.6
2001[1]	90.3	82.5	76.3	79.2	82.7	79.3	72.8	77.0	79.0	68.5			78.8

Excluding taxes. [1] Preliminary. *Source: Energy Information Administration, U.S. Department of Energy (EIA-DOE)*

Refiner Sales Prices of No. 2 Diesel Fuel   In Cents Per Gallon

Year	Jan.	Feb.	Mar.	Apr.	May	June	July	Aug.	Sept.	Oct.	Nov.	Dec.	Average
1996	56.2	57.9	61.9	70.1	67.0	59.1	60.0	64.9	71.7	75.4	73.2	71.0	65.9
1997	69.9	67.8	62.5	61.7	60.7	56.5	55.8	58.9	57.8	61.7	61.5	55.0	60.6
1998	49.6	48.3	45.8	48.2	47.0	43.6	42.6	41.4	45.6	45.5	41.4	35.6	44.4
1999	36.2	35.1	43.2	48.8	47.9	50.4	56.4	61.6	64.9	65.0	69.9	70.5	54.6
2000	77.7	85.2	85.1	79.9	81.4	82.4	83.6	92.1	105.0	104.0	103.2	93.8	89.8
2001[1]	90.7	85.8	78.1	82.6	89.8	85.3	75.5	80.8	84.1	71.4			82.4

Excluding taxes. [1] Preliminary. *Source: Energy Information Administration, U.S. Department of Energy (EIA-DOE)*

Refiner Sales Prices of Kerosine-Type Jet Fuel   In Cents Per Gallon

Year	Jan.	Feb.	Mar.	Apr.	May	June	July	Aug.	Sept.	Oct.	Nov.	Dec.	Average
1996	60.3	57.2	59.6	65.3	62.2	57.5	59.6	64.5	71.6	73.6	72.2	73.0	64.6
1997	73.5	71.4	61.8	60.5	59.4	58.1	56.8	59.4	58.8	61.3	61.3	55.6	61.2
1998	53.4	50.2	45.7	46.6	46.9	43.5	43.8	42.9	44.6	45.8	43.1	36.5	45.0
1999	37.3	35.2	39.5	46.6	46.8	48.6	53.7	59.1	62.7	63.8	66.5	72.1	53.3
2000	80.4	83.6	83.4	77.4	77.9	79.9	83.6	87.9	105.1	104.4	105.1	99.0	88.0
2001[1]	88.2	86.8	80.5	79.5	83.5	82.6	75.9	77.6	80.7	68.9			80.4

Excluding taxes. [1] Preliminary. *Source: Energy Information Administration, U.S. Department of Energy (EIA-DOE)*

Refiner Sales Prices of Propane   In Cents Per Gallon

Year	Jan.	Feb.	Mar.	Apr.	May	June	July	Aug.	Sept.	Oct.	Nov.	Dec.	Average
1996	41.6	44.1	41.1	37.8	36.2	36.2	36.9	38.9	45.3	51.1	58.0	67.7	46.1
1997	59.9	44.7	41.3	37.7	36.9	36.4	35.9	37.5	39.5	41.1	39.6	37.5	41.6
1998	35.4	33.1	31.2	30.3	29.3	26.6	25.7	25.7	26.3	27.6	27.7	25.7	28.8
1999	26.5	26.1	26.8	28.7	29.1	29.1	34.7	38.3	42.6	43.7	42.6	41.8	34.2
2000	49.4	60.2	52.9	48.8	49.3	53.9	54.8	60.3	65.9	64.3	63.3	76.7	59.5
2001[1]	86.4	66.9	60.1	58.6	56.2	48.7	43.6	45.6	46.4	46.1			55.9

Consumer Grade, Excluding taxes. [1] Preliminary. *Source: Energy Information Administration, U.S. Department of Energy (EIA-DOE)*

Supply and Disposition of Crude Oil in the United States   In Thousands of Barrels Per Day

	Supply						Stock		Disposition		Ending Stocks		
	Field Production		Imports			Unaccounted for Crude Oil	Withdrawal[3]		Refinery				Other
Yearly Average	Total Domestic	Alaskan	Total	SPR[2]	Other		SPR[2]	Other	Inputs	Exports	Total	SPR[2]	Primary
	In Thousands of Barrels Per Day										In Millions of Barrels		
1994	6,662	1,559	7,063	12	7,051	266	13	5	13,866	99	929	592	337
1995	6,560	1,484	7,230	0	7,230	193	0	-93	13,973	95	895	592	303
1996	6,465	1,393	7,508	0	7,508	215	-71	-53	14,195	110	850	566	284
1997	6,452	1,296	8,225	0	8,225	145	-7	57	14,662	108	868	563	305
1998	6,252	1,175	8,706	0	8,706	115	22	52	14,889	110	895	571	324
1999	5,881	1,050	8,731	8	8,722	191	-11	-107	14,804	118	852	567	284
2000	5,822	970	9,071	8	9,062	155	-73	3	15,067	50	826	541	286
2001[1]	5,848	970	9,136	10	9,126	263	25	56	15,141	25	860	550	311

[1] Preliminary. [2] Strategic Petroleum Reserve. [3] A negative number indicates a decrease in stocks and a positive number indicates an increase.

Note: Crude oil includes lease condensate. Stocks of Alaskan crude oil in transit were included beginning in January 1981.

Source: Energy Information Administration, U.S. Department of Energy (EIA-DOE)

Crude Petroleum Refinery Operations Ratio[1] in the United States In Percent of Capacity

Year	Jan.	Feb.	Mar.	Apr.	May	June	July	Aug.	Sept.	Oct.	Nov.	Dec.	Average
1992	83.0	81.0	85.0	86.0	89.0	92.0	92.0	89.0	91.0	89.0	90.0	88.0	87.9
1993	87.0	87.0	89.0	91.0	93.0	95.0	95.0	93.0	93.0	92.0	92.0	91.0	91.5
1994	89.8	88.7	87.6	92.4	95.4	95.8	95.5	96.4	94.4	89.8	92.7	92.6	92.6
1995	89.6	87.9	86.7	90.5	94.0	95.6	94.0	94.0	95.6	90.5	92.1	93.3	92.0
1996	90.6	89.1	90.6	93.7	94.4	95.4	93.9	95.0	95.5	94.6	94.7	94.3	93.5
1997	89.3	87.3	90.7	92.6	97.3	97.7	97.1	98.6	99.7	96.7	95.6	97.2	95.0
1998	93.3	91.3	94.4	96.4	97.1	98.9	99.2	99.8	95.0	89.7	94.7	95.1	95.4
1999	90.4	90.0	90.9	94.6	93.9	93.5	94.9	95.5	94.1	91.1	92.0	90.4	92.7
2000	85.7	86.4	89.8	92.6	94.7	96.2	96.9	95.9	94.3	92.4	92.7	94.0	92.6
2001[2]	90.0	90.4	89.3	94.8	96.3	95.5	93.9	93.5	91.8	91.2	91.3		92.5

[1] Based on the ration of the daily average crude runs to stills to the rated capacity of refineries per day. [2] Preliminary.
Source: Energy Information Administration, U.S. Department of Energy (EIA-DOE)

Crude Oil Refinery Inputs in the United States In Thousands of Barrels Per Day

Year	Jan.	Feb.	Mar.	Apr.	May	June	July	Aug.	Sept.	Oct.	Nov.	Dec.	Average
1992	12,923	12,486	13,083	13,260	13,679	14,059	13,953	13,426	13,714	13,584	13,547	13,194	13,411
1993	12,938	12,865	13,200	13,538	13,829	14,129	14,136	13,844	13,841	13,729	13,686	13,571	13,613
1994	13,286	13,130	12,985	13,809	14,272	14,351	14,344	14,491	14,234	13,529	13,968	13,951	13,866
1995	13,604	13,365	13,480	13,817	14,303	14,553	14,403	14,276	14,402	13,598	13,833	14,011	13,973
1996	13,708	13,529	13,755	14,263	14,401	14,535	14,319	14,423	14,483	14,276	14,276	14,194	14,195
1997	13,632	13,425	14,047	14,283	15,083	15,139	14,958	15,217	15,297	14,790	14,654	14,898	14,662
1998	14,313	14,034	14,590	14,961	15,104	15,368	15,496	15,660	14,854	14,001	14,769	14,832	14,889
1999	14,442	14,309	14,498	15,094	14,973	14,959	15,237	15,299	15,107	14,589	14,704	14,410	14,804
2000	13,779	14,028	14,613	15,053	15,494	15,643	15,819	15,640	15,407	15,029	15,023	15,232	15,067
2001[1]	14,797	14,813	14,643	15,537	15,766	15,651	15,364	15,267	15,055	15,001	14,968	14,816	15,140

[1] Preliminary. *Source: Energy Information Administration, U.S. Department of Energy (EIA-DOE)*

Production of Major Refined Petroleum Products in Continental United States In Millions of Barrels

			Fuel Oil					Natural		Liquified Gasses		
Year	Asphalt	Aviation Gasoline	Distillate	Residual	Gasoline	Jet Fuel	Kero-sene	Gas Plant Liquids	Lubri-cants	Total	at L.P.G.[2]	at L.P.G.[3]
1992	153.0	7.9	1,088.4	326.1	2,591.0	512.0	14.8	668.0	57.5	721.9	499.7	222.2
1993	165.6	7.9	1,139.7	303.9	2,644.3	518.8	17.5	631.2	58.4	849.4	633.5	215.9
1994	164.8	7.9	1,169.7	301.4	2,621.0	528.4	21.1	630.2	62.1	734.2	511.1	223.2
1995	170.4	7.8	1,151.7	287.6	2,722.4	516.8	19.2	643.2	63.7	759.9	521.1	238.8
1996	167.8	7.3	1,213.6	265.5	2,768.6	554.5	22.8	669.8	63.3	789.1	546.7	242.5
1997	177.0	7.2	1,238.0	258.3	2,826.1	567.3	23.9	663.3	65.9	799.4	547.3	252.2
1998	179.7	7.3	1,248.6	278.0	2,865.3	554.6	28.6	639.9	67.2	771.2	526.3	244.9
1999	184.3	7.5	1,240.8	254.8	2,896.0	571.3	24.4	675.1	66.8	811.0	564.5	246.5
2000	180.6	6.2	1,189.9	234.3	2,664.0	536.6	20.4	649.4	60.9	788.0	545.5	242.5
2001[1]	177.3	6.5	1,348.4	262.8	2,913.0	558.2	26.7	680.3	64.1	810.1	569.1	241.0

[1] Preliminary. [2] Gas processing plants. [3] Refineries. *Source: Energy Information Administration, U.S. Department of Energy (EIA-DOE)*

Stocks of Petroleum and Products in the United States on January 1 In Millions of Barrels

			Refined Products											
						Fuel Oil							Motor Gasoline	
Year	Crude Petroleum	Strategic Reserve	Total	Asphalt	Aviation Gasoline	Distillate	Residual	Finished Gasoline	Jet Fuel	Kero-sene	Liduified Gases[2]	Lubri-cants	Total	Finished[3]
1992	893.1	568.5	576.7	22.3	1.6	143.5	49.9	183.3	48.8	5.8	92.3	12.3	219	182
1993	892.9	574.7	549.1	17.7	1.6	140.6	42.6	179.1	43.1	5.7	88.7	13.3	216	178
1994	922.5	587.1	465.8	19.1	1.8	140.9	44.2	185.7	40.4	4.1	106.6	11.8	226	187
1995	928.9	591.7	468.0	18.6	2.3	145.2	41.9	175.9	46.8	8.0	108.0	11.5	215	176
1996	895.0	591.6	401.2	26.3	2.2	106.3	34.8	162.8	38.4	4.0	99.2	11.7	206	161
1997	868.1	565.8	452.6	22.3	1.7	139.0	40.4	166.1	43.9	7.3	89.5	13.2	203	157
1998	868.1	563.4	451.6	22.1	1.7	138.4	40.5	166.4	44.0	7.3	95.2	12.9	166	166
1999	851.7	567.2	407.1	16.9	1.6	125.5	35.8	154.1	40.5	4.9	89.3	11.8	172	154
2000	836.7	547.5	415.7	21.4	1.4	121.1	38.9	157.4	42.3	5.3	114.6	11.2	193	157
2001[1]	862.1	550.2	445.6	20.6	1.5	143.8	41.0	161.3	41.9	5.4	121.4	13.8	207	161

[1] Preliminary. [2] Includes ethane & ethylene at plants and refineries. [3] Includes oxygenated. *Source: Energy Information Administration, U.S. Department of Energy (EIA-DOE)*

Stocks of Crude Petroleum in the United States, on First of Month In Millions of Barrels

Year	Jan.	Feb.	Mar.	Apr.	May	June	July	Aug.	Sept.	Oct.	Nov.	Dec.
1992	893.1	909.7	914.8	907.1	916.5	912.0	894.6	902.2	898.3	893.5	906.2	899.4
1993	892.9	902.0	908.1	914.7	930.4	935.0	935.1	935.2	919.6	906.4	916.5	924.1
1994	922.5	925.3	922.6	932.6	930.6	922.7	919.6	921.2	920.2	[illegible]	904.9	[illegible]
1995	922.2	920.8	931.0	929.4	924.1	919.6	907.3	899.5	897.5	902.8	910.6	894.9
1996	894.9	894.7	892.9	888.8	889.7	889.7	898.9	891.3	890.8	875.8	881.5	869.1
1997	849.7	865.9	862.1	877.6	883.9	890.5	885.3	873.0	864.2	866.6	879.3	886.9
1998	868.1	884.3	885.7	899.8	914.6	916.1	896.4	902.6	893.5	873.0	897.4	906.2
1999	894.4	896.6	897.4	908.0	902.3	914.8	902.8	906.0	889.1	878.0	875.7	866.2
2000	851.6	852.4	855.2	866.5	873.2	864.1	859.5	852.6	858.7	848.2	842.4	833.9
2001[1]	826.2	835.9	822.1	846.8	867.8	868.9	848.9	854.7	849.6	851.8	856.7	857.0

[1] Preliminary. *Source: Energy Information Administration; U.S. Department of Energy (EIA-DOE)*

Production of Crude Petroleum in the United States In Thousands of Barrels Per Day

Year	Jan.	Feb.	Mar.	Apr.	May	June	July	Aug.	Sept.	Oct.	Nov.	Dec.	Average
1992	7,361	7,389	7,348	7,293	7,169	7,167	7,131	6,922	7,030	7,126	7,024	7,103	7,171
1993	6,961	6,943	6,974	6,881	6,847	6,795	6,688	6,758	6,712	6,839	6,912	6,858	6,847
1994	6,817	6,770	6,746	6,612	6,688	6,611	6,501	6,544	6,609	6,658	6,628	6,760	6,662
1995	6,682	6,794	6,600	6,604	6,629	6,579	6,449	6,447	6,416	6,421	6,585	6,530	6,560
1996	6,495	6,577	6,571	6,444	6,394	6,458	6,338	6,360	6,482	6,481	6,476	6,506	6,465
1997	6,402	6,514	6,452	6,441	6,474	6,442	6,409	6,347	6,486	6,467	6,459	6,531	6,452
1998	6,541	6,476	6,408	6,483	6,347	6,267	6,194	6,203	5,789	6,143	6,140	6,043	6,252
1999	5,963	5,966	5,883	5,887	5,875	5,760	5,798	5,780	5,804	5,947	5,960	5,959	5,881
2000	5,784	5,852	5,918	5,854	5,847	5,823	5,739	5,789	5,758	5,809	5,833	5,855	5,822
2001[1]	5,836	5,840	5,878	5,854	5,859	5,799	5,806	5,823	5,829	5,812	5,946	5,894	5,848

[1] Preliminary. *Source: Energy Information Administration, U.S. Department of Energy (EIA-DOE)*

U.S. Foreign Trade of Petroleum and Products In Thousands of Barrels Per Day

	Exports		Imports						Exports		Imports				
Year	Total[2]	Petroleum Products	Crude	Petroleum Products	Distillate Fuel Oil	Residual Fuel Oil	Net Imports[3]	Year	Total[2]	Petroleum Products	Crude	Petroleum Products	Distillate Fuel Oil	Residual Fuel Oil	Net Imports[3]
1982	815	579	3,488	1,325	93	776	4,298	1992	950	861	6,083	1,805	216	375	6,938
1983	739	575	3,329	1,722	174	699	4,312	1993	1,003	904	6,787	1,833	184	373	7,618
1984	722	541	3,426	2,011	272	681	4,715	1994	942	843	7,063	1,933	203	314	8,054
1985	781	577	3,201	1,866	200	510	4,286	1995	949	855	7,230	1,605	193	187	7,886
1986	785	631	4,178	2,045	247	669	5,439	1996	981	871	7,508	1,971	230	248	8,498
1987	764	613	4,674	2,004	255	565	5,914	1997	1,003	896	8,225	1,936	228	194	9,158
1988	815	661	5,107	2,295	302	644	6,587	1998	945	835	8,706	2,002	210	275	9,764
1989	859	717	5,843	2,217	306	629	7,202	1999	940	822	8,731	2,122	250	237	9,912
1990	857	748	5,894	2,123	278	504	7,161	2000	1,040	990	9,071	2,389	295	352	10,419
1991	1,001	885	5,782	1,844	205	453	6,626	2001[1]	971	946	9,136	2,471	355	384	10,636

[1] Preliminary. [2] Includes crude oil. [3] Equals imports minus exports. *Source: Energy Information Administration, U.S. Department of Energy (EIA-DOE)*

Domestic First Purchase Price of Crude Petroleum at Wells[1] In Dollars Per Barrel

Year	Jan.	Feb.	Mar.	Apr.	May	June	July	Aug.	Sept.	Oct.	Nov.	Dec.	Average
1992	13.99	14.04	14.12	15.36	16.38	17.96	17.80	17.07	17.20	17.16	16.00	14.94	15.99
1993	14.70	15.53	15.94	16.15	16.03	15.06	13.83	13.75	13.39	13.72	12.45	10.38	14.25
1994	10.49	10.71	10.94	12.31	14.02	14.93	15.34	14.50	13.62	13.84	14.14	13.43	13.19
1995	14.00	14.69	14.68	15.84	15.85	15.02	14.01	14.13	14.49	13.68	14.03	15.02	14.62
1996	15.43	15.54	17.63	19.58	17.94	16.94	17.63	18.29	19.93	21.09	20.20	21.34	18.46
1997	21.76	19.38	17.85	16.64	17.24	15.90	15.91	16.21	16.44	17.68	16.84	15.06	17.23
1998	13.48	12.16	11.53	11.64	11.49	10.00	10.46	10.18	11.28	11.32	9.65	8.05	10.87
1999	8.57	8.60	10.76	12.82	13.92	14.39	16.12	17.58	20.03	19.71	21.35	22.55	15.56
2000	23.53	25.48	26.19	23.20	25.58	27.62	26.81	27.91	29.72	29.65	30.36	24.46	26.72
2001[2]	24.58	25.27	23.02	23.41	24.06	23.43	22.94	23.08	22.37	18.68			23.08

[1] Buyers posted prices. [2] Preliminary. *Source: Energy Information Administration, U.S. Department of Energy (EIA-DOE)*

Volume of Trading of Crude Oil Futures in New York In Thousands of Contracts

Year	Jan.	Feb.	Mar.	Apr.	May	June	July	Aug.	Sept.	Oct.	Nov.	Dec.	Total
1992	2,096.6	1,629.9	1,619.8	1,888.6	1,884.7	2,005.7	1,796.3	1,530.9	1,540.7	1,796.8	1,542.1	1,777.5	21,109.6
1993	2,138.9	1,783.6	1,812.7	1,531.4	1,641.5	2,018.5	2,616.2	2,200.3	2,679.5	1,945.2	2,378.4	2,122.4	24,868.6
1994	2,295.6	1,933.0	2,227.7	2,381.7	2,602.3	2,575.8	2,186.5	2,543.6	1,897.5	2,194.5	2,195.9	1,778.2	26,812.3
1995	2,133.5	1,657.3	2,289.8	2,220.1	2,408.9	2,172.4	1,749.3	1,793.8	1,968.0	1,834.6	1,739.1	1,647.2	23,614.0
1996	2,260.1	1,928.3	2,399.3	2,489.9	2,161.3	1,601.7	1,732.1	1,657.0	1,912.6	2,098.0	1,643.1	1,604.3	23,487.8
1997	1,949.9	1,973.7	2,086.6	2,033.7	2,134.9	2,098.6	2,221.4	2,053.7	2,027.5	2,574.0	1,770.2	1,847.2	24,771.4
1998	2,468.3	2,208.3	2,902.8	2,451.1	2,603.6	3,079.5	2,375.0	2,066.7	2,617.8	2,592.4	2,552.9	2,577.3	30,495.6
1999	2,533.6	2,326.0	3,767.7	3,166.8	3,037.9	3,306.8	3,471.3	3,354.8	3,388.4	3,571.2	3,465.1	2,470.4	37,860.1
2000	3,139.0	3,076.6	3,380.2	2,578.9	3,001.8	3,232.2	2,749.7	3,149.3	3,712.0	3,418.0	2,824.5	2,620.5	36,882.7
2001	3,035.0	2,855.2	3,448.7	3,312.1	3,468.5	3,572.4	3,170.1	3,315.8	2,773.2	2,912.7	3,210.3	2,454.6	37,528.5

Source: New York Mercantile Exchange (NYMEX)

Average Open Interest of Crude Oil Futures in New York In Contracts

Year	Jan.	Feb.	Mar.	Apr.	May	June	July	Aug.	Sept.	Oct.	Nov.	Dec.
1992	310,763	331,050	316,544	340,315	335,545	364,155	331,972	316,066	314,446	301,381	308,467	330,134
1993	352,316	369,180	385,768	381,954	384,309	396,832	423,041	428,418	404,172	397,121	404,046	427,756
1994	427,705	438,929	424,462	410,974	427,071	414,257	409,251	396,657	395,194	413,206	388,932	391,151
1995	373,798	379,329	353,805	364,929	350,826	346,051	357,718	343,636	342,360	334,170	329,786	348,954
1996	389,935	400,236	427,306	460,841	424,994	376,164	367,405	364,458	395,358	410,387	385,415	368,331
1997	365,522	384,737	408,751	409,719	401,663	397,245	411,292	424,529	405,389	419,821	404,597	424,333
1998	424,810	445,167	468,438	463,961	450,611	467,998	476,516	486,499	486,047	481,657	487,175	501,591
1999	501,655	524,677	581,072	611,727	594,032	582,058	601,212	584,962	622,257	595,743	564,488	531,567
2000	512,049	519,090	513,359	467,259	453,042	462,476	432,571	416,934	461,298	478,242	479,008	438,118
2001	432,892	437,188	432,627	419,904	442,950	462,321	451,005	461,851	434,967	430,774	435,178	436,332

Source: New York Mercantile Exchange (NYMEX)

Plastics

Plastics are one of the most important materials in the U.S. for industrial and commercial purposes. The most important developments in the plastics industry have occurred since 1910. The period 1930-40 saw the initial commercial development of the major thermoplastics used today. These include polyvinyl chloride, low density polyethylene, polystyrene, and polymethyl methacrylate. World War II brought plastics into great demand as substitutes for material that was in short supply, such as natural rubber. In the U.S., the production of synthetic rubbers led to the development of more plastics materials. New materials that have been developed are competing with older plastics and other materials like wood. The demand for plastics continues to increase.

The American Plastics Council reported sales and production of plastic resins in year 2000 showed little growth. It was reported that resin sales and captive (internal) use grew to 103.2 billion pounds in 2000, less than 1 percent more than 1999. Resin production was only slightly higher than 1999 at 100.1 billion pounds. Export sales of the major plastic resins increased in 2000 by almost 15 percent from 1999 due to strong economic growth, particularly in Asia and Latin America. Sales of major resins domestically were down just over 2 percent. Early in 2000, resin sales appeared to be very good but by the second half of 2000 inventories had been down while economic growth slowed and energy and feedstock prices increased. In comparison, 1999 was a strong growth year for plastic resins. In 2001, U.S. economic growth was sluggish at best.

Sales and captive use for the major commodity thermoplastic resins (including polyethylene, polypropylene, polystyrene and polyvinyl chloride) declined nearly 1 percent in 2000. Production also declined by nearly 1 percent compared to 1999. These resins comprise nearly 70 percent of the total volume of plastic resins that are sold to and exported from the U.S. each year. Polyethylene sales increased just under 2 percent in 2000, much less than the growth in the U.S. economy. Domestic sales of polyethylene decreased almost 2 percent in 2000 while exports were up over 20 percent. Polypropylene sales growth in 2000 was the lowest since 1982, gaining 1 percent in sales and use. Production increased less than 2 percent. Sales in the U.S. and Canada declined slightly.

After increasing for 17 years, polyvinyl chloride production declined in 2000. Domestic production was down just over 3 percent. Exports did improve in the last quarter of 2000.

Plastics Production by Resin in the United States In Millions of Pounds

	Thermosets				Thermoplastics										
Year	Polyester Unsat-urated	Phenlic	Epoxy	Total Thermo-sets	Thermo-plastic Polyester	Polyvinyl Chloride	Poly-styrene	Poly-propylene	Nylon	Low Density Polye-thylene[1]	High Density Polye-thylene	Total Thermo-plastics	Total Selected Plastics	Other Plastics	Total Plastics
1991	1,075	2,658	497	5,909	2,115	9,164	4,954	8,330	576	11,582	9,213	47,146	53,055	9,731	62,786
1992	1,175	2,923	457	6,335	2,413	9,989	5,096	8,421	668	11,917	9,808	49,751	56,086	10,285	66,371
1993	1,264	3,078	512	6,868	2,549	10,257	5,382	8,628	768	12,067	9,941	51,159	58,027	10,777	68,854
1994	1,468	3,229	601	7,513	3,196	11,712	5,848	9,539	943	12,600	11,117	56,794	64,307	11,664	75,971
1995	1,577	3,204	632	7,519	3,785	12,295	5,656	10,890	1,020	12,886	11,211	59,331	66,850	11,834	78,684
1996	1,557	3,476	662	8,129	4,031	13,220	6,065	11,991	1,103	14,145	12,373	64,526	72,655	11,640	84,295
1997	1,621	3,734	654	8,647	4,260	14,084	6,380	13,320	1,222	14,579	12,557	67,872	76,519	12,287	88,806
1998	1,713	3,940	639	9,163	4,423	14,502	6,237	13,825	1,285	14,805	12,924	71,209	78,659	13,026	91,685
1999	2,985	4,388	657	8,030	6,735	14,912	7,075	15,493	1,349	15,807	13,864	78,457	86,487	13,467	99,954
2000	3,169	4,353	693	8,215	7,029	14,442	6,844	15,739	1,281	15,526	13,968	78,078	86,293	13,760	100,053

[1] Includes LDPE and LLDPE. *Source: The Society of the Plastics Industry, Inc. (SPI)*

Total Resin Sales and Captive Use by Important Markets In Millions of Pounds (Dry Weight Basis)

Year	Adhesive, Inks & Coatings	Building & Con-struction	Consumer & Indust-rial	Electrical & Elec-tronics	Exports	Furniture & Fur-nishings	Industrial & Mach-inary	Pack-aging	Trans-portation	Other	Total
1991	1,391	10,650	5,689	2,896	7,418	2,255	587	16,723	2,328	6,616	56,553
1992	1,723	11,876	6,093	2,766	6,950	2,559	617	18,284	2,817	6,877	60,562
1993	1,572	12,885	6,015	2,981	6,632	2,759	768	19,569	3,221	7,234	63,636
1994	1,789	14,715	9,266	3,325	6,889	3,118	836	19,551	3,795	7,515	70,799
1995	1,795	13,551	8,921	2,872	7,162	3,189	805	17,107	3,376	7,421	66,200
1996	1,833	15,413	9,662	3,022	7,997	3,468	965	18,691	3,469	8,701	73,221
1997	2,019	16,273	10,505	3,021	8,839	3,721	938	19,192	3,603	8,884	76,995
1998	2,038	17,217	11,184	3,036	8,397	3,995	933	19,454	3,788	9,460	79,501
1999	2,065	19,072	11,802	3,256	8,622	3,587	1,043	21,270	3,836	10,446	84,999
2000	2,038	18,859	11,662	3,222	9,692	3,735	1,023	21,348	4,070	11,525	87,174

[1] Included in other. *Source: The Society of the Plastics Industry, Inc. (SPI)*

PLASTICS

Average Producer Price Index of Plastic Resins and Materials (066) in the United States (1982 = 100)

Year	Jan.	Feb.	Mar.	Apr.	May	June	July	Aug.	Sept.	Oct.	Nov.	Dec.	Average
1995	142.5	144.1	145.9	148.5	149.0	148.9	147.0	144.8	142.7	139.2	135.8	132.2	143.4
1996	129.9	128.4	128.4	127.7	130.6	132.1	133.2	135.2	137.9	138.0	138.0	137.7	133.1
1997	137.0	137.5	138.7	138.9	139.1	139.6	139.3	137.4	136.0	135.9	134.6	133.9	137.3
1998	134.0	132.2	131.0	130.7	128.8	126.8	125.0	123.7	119.6	118.6	117.1	115.9	125.3
1999	115.9	115.8	117.3	118.6	122.1	123.1	127.9	130.0	133.8	135.6	135.8	134.3	125.8
2000	133.2	135.7	139.4	143.7	147.4	147.8	146.4	146.3	142.4	140.7	138.8	137.3	141.6
2001[1]	137.8	139.3	141.4	141.9	139.9	137.6	135.1	131.3	129.1	130.8	128.8	125.2	134.9

[1] Preliminary. *Source: Bureau of Labor Statistics, U.S. Department of Commerce (BLS)*

Average Producer Price Index of Thermoplastic Resins (0662) in the United States (1982 = 100)

Year	Jan.	Feb.	Mar.	Apr.	May	June	July	Aug.	Sept.	Oct.	Nov.	Dec.	Average
1995	143.1	145.0	147.1	150.3	151.0	151.2	148.7	146.2	143.7	139.6	135.5	131.1	144.4
1996	128.4	126.7	126.8	125.9	129.4	131.1	132.5	134.8	137.8	137.9	137.9	137.6	132.2
1997	136.7	137.3	138.6	138.8	139.0	139.7	139.3	137.0	135.5	135.3	133.8	133.0	137.0
1998	133.0	130.7	129.5	129.2	127.0	124.7	122.5	121.0	116.4	115.3	113.7	112.2	122.9
1999	112.3	112.5	114.4	116.1	120.4	121.6	127.5	129.9	134.5	136.7	137.0	135.2	124.9
2000	133.8	136.0	140.4	145.2	149.3	149.6	147.6	147.4	142.7	140.3	137.9	136.0	142.2
2001[1]	136.3	138.0	140.2	140.8	138.4	135.7	133.1	128.6	126.5	128.3	126.6	122.5	132.9

[1] Preliminary. *Source: Bureau of Labor Statistics, U.S. Department of Commerce (BLS)*

Average Producer Price Index of PE Resin, Low, Film & Sheeting (0662-0301) in the United States

Year	Jan.	Feb.	Mar.	Apr.	May	June	July	Aug.	Sept.	Oct.	Nov.	Dec.	Average
1993	NA	151.4	145.6	141.8	135.5	137.1	132.2	136.6	129.2	128.4	127.6	127.4	135.7
1994	121.6	119.4	119.3	120.8	127.6	134.5	136.3	140.8	146.6	155.4	172.8	182.2	139.8
1995	188.5	196.0	202.0	210.6	215.4	211.1	205.7	194.4	185.0	173.4	167.5	157.4	192.3
1996	146.4	139.9	137.6	139.5	147.6	158.8	166.0	165.3	190.1	195.2	195.9	196.6	164.9
1997	191.8	189.0	189.7	193.8	196.8	199.4	197.9	201.0	190.2	185.1	182.5	177.2	191.2
1998	181.3	181.0	168.7	NA	159.1	162.9	158.0	152.8	NA	NA	NA	NA	166.3
1999[1]	No data available for this year.												

1982=100. [1] Preliminary. NA = Not available. *Source: Bureau of Labor Statistics, U.S. Department of Commerce (BLS)*

Average Producer Price Index of Styrene Plastics Materials (0662-06) in the United States (1982 = 100)

Year	Jan.	Feb.	Mar.	Apr.	May	June	July	Aug.	Sept.	Oct.	Nov.	Dec.	Average
1995	129.0	127.0	132.5	134.7	135.9	137.5	135.1	133.2	132.1	130.1	127.9	126.1	131.8
1996	125.7	123.5	125.0	118.3	120.1	122.7	123.4	123.3	123.6	122.8	122.0	120.9	122.6
1997	120.6	123.1	123.0	121.6	121.6	121.6	122.7	117.7	118.0	116.5	113.5	113.7	119.5
1998	113.3	113.9	115.5	114.9	114.1	112.8	111.3	111.2	107.6	107.9	107.1	106.3	111.3
1999	103.5	102.4	103.5	104.7	103.0	102.3	103.1	101.5	101.4	99.8	99.4	100.5	102.1
2000	103.0	104.3	110.5	113.0	116.2	116.9	118.5	116.5	115.0	114.1	112.1	110.4	112.5
2001[1]	110.5	109.2	107.9	108.0	101.8	99.9	97.6	95.7	93.9	90.9	88.9	88.0	99.4

[1] Preliminary. *Source: Bureau of Labor Statistics, U.S. Department of Commerce (BLS)*

Average Producer Price Index of Thermosetting Resins (0663) in the United States (1982 = 100)

Year	Jan.	Feb.	Mar.	Apr.	May	June	July	Aug.	Sept.	Oct.	Nov.	Dec.	Average
1995	144.3	145.1	145.4	145.2	144.7	143.5	144.0	143.5	142.9	142.3	142.4	142.1	143.8
1996	141.8	141.9	141.2	141.3	141.4	141.2	140.6	141.5	141.7	142.0	142.0	142.2	141.6
1997	142.1	142.3	142.7	143.1	143.2	143.0	142.8	142.9	143.0	143.1	142.9	142.9	142.8
1998	143.6	144.0	143.2	142.9	142.6	142.7	142.5	142.2	141.2	140.9	140.1	140.3	142.2
1999	139.9	138.1	137.7	137.4	136.9	136.5	136.2	136.5	136.5	136.5	136.3	136.2	137.0
2000	136.8	141.1	141.3	142.8	144.9	146.0	147.6	147.8	147.5	149.5	150.3	151.0	145.6
2001[1]	152.1	152.9	154.5	154.4	154.2	154.2	152.3	151.3	149.0	150.2	146.5	145.5	151.4

[1] Preliminary. *Source: Bureau of Labor Statistics, U.S. Department of Commerce (BLS)*

Average Producer Price Index of Phenolic & Tar Acid Resins (0663-02) in the United States (1982 = 100)

Year	Jan.	Feb.	Mar.	Apr.	May	June	July	Aug.	Sept.	Oct.	Nov.	Dec.	Average
1993	128.5	130.3	130.5	131.4	133.7	134.1	133.9	132.8	133.1	132.1	132.0	132.9	132.1
1994	133.0	130.9	129.7	131.3	134.1	135.9	139.2	143.7	147.2	154.7	161.0	161.5	141.9
1995	164.6	166.4	165.1	162.5	158.6	153.5	152.0	148.5	147.7	146.2	143.2	142.6	154.2
1996	142.7	142.6	141.9	142.2	143.1	143.4	143.2	147.2	148.7	149.1	149.8	150.5	145.4
1997	150.5	151.2	150.9	152.7	152.9	152.6	151.9	152.7	153.1	152.5	151.9	151.8	152.0
1998	153.1	154.9	153.0	151.0	148.7	148.8	148.5	149.0	142.8	141.7	140.6	138.6	147.6
1999[1]	No data available for this year.												

[1] Preliminary. *Source: Bureau of Labor Statistics, U.S. Department of Commerce (BLS)*

Platinum-Group Metals

Prices in the platinum-group metals in late 2001 moved higher only to move lower as late 2000 got underway. In early 2001, platinum prices had moved to a multiyear high. Even more impressive was palladium which is used extensively in pollution control devices. Palladium had reached over $1,000 per ounce on concerns about the ability of Russia to deliver on contracted sales of the metal. Russia is the largest producer of palladium and the second largest producer of platinum. Since 1997, the focus of the market for the platinum-group metals has been on Russia early in the year as decisions are made regarding export quotas and licences for these metals. There have been efforts in Russia to streamline the process for determining quotas and issuing licenses to reduce the uncertainty surrounding this issue. Russia appeared to stop selling palladium into the spot market in the second half of 2001 due to low prices. The Russian firm Norilsk Nickel is the world's largest producer of palladium. The firm has a ten year export quota on the metal. In early 2002, the Russian government granted the from a five year export quota for platinum and a one year export quota for rhodium. In the past Norilsk Nickel received one year quotas for platinum. The firm indicated that it would look for ways of stabilizing prices fluctuations.

The U.S. Geological Survey reported that world mine production of platinum in 2000 was 178,000 kilograms or 178 metric tonnes. That was an increase of 5 percent from 1999 when world platinum production was 169,000 kilograms. The largest producer of platinum by far was South Africa with 2000 production estimated at 140,000 kilograms, up 7 percent from 1999 when production was 131,000 kilograms. The next largest producer was Russia with production in 2000 of 26,000 kilograms, down 4 percent from the previous year. Platinum production by Canada in 2000 was estimated at 5,500 kilograms, up 1 percent from 1999. U.S. mine production of platinum in 2000 was estimated at 3,050 kilograms, up 4 percent from 1999. The U.S. has one primary producer of platinum-group metals located in Montana. Some small quantities of platinum-group metals are recovered in copper refining. World reserves of platinum-group metals are estimated to be 71 million kilograms. The largest reserves by far are held by South Africa and are estimated to be 63 million kilograms. World production of platinum-group metals is expected to increase especially in South Africa.

World mine production of palladium in 2000 is estimated to be 177,000 kilograms, an increase of 2 percent from 1999. Russia is the largest producer of palladium with 2000 production estimated to be 86,000 kilograms, an increase of 1 percent from 1999. South Africa is the next largest producer of palladium with 2000 production of 65,000 kilograms, up 3 percent from 1999. U.S. production of palladium in 2000 was 10,000 kilograms, a 2 percent increase from 1999. Palladium production by Canada in 2000 was 8,800 kilograms, an increase of 2 percent from the previous year.

Most platinum-group metals are consumed by the automotive industry. The metals are used as oxidation catalysts in air pollution abatement devices to remove odors, vapors and carbon monoxide. In the past when palladium prices were lower than platinum, there was substitution of palladium for platinum in catalytic converters. Palladium is less resistant than platinum to poisoning by sulfur and lead. In 2001, palladium prices moved over $1,000 per ounce. This likely led to the substitution of other metals for palladium. An automobile producer reported holding an inventory of platinum-group metals that had declined in value leading to ideas that these metals could be sold into the market. That possibility led to further pressure on prices in late 2001. The platinum-group metals also find use as chemical catalysts. Platinum alloys find use in jewelry, while both platinum and palladium are used in dentistry. Platinum jewelry is popular in Japan and China. China is reported to be the largest market for platinum jewelry which finds the most use in bridal wear. The metals find use in medicine and cancer chemotherapy. Platinum also is used in the manufacture of computer storage disks.

Iridium is used in process catalysts and it has also found use in some autocatalysts. Iridium and ruthenium are used in the production of polyvinyl chloride. Rhodium finds use in the automotive industry in pollution control devices. Palladium has replaced rhodium to some extent. As the standards for allowable levels of pollution are lowered, the use of palladium increases.

U.S. mine production of platinum in 2000 was estimated at 3,050 kilograms, an increase of 4 percent from 1999. Production has about doubled since 1995. There is only one primary platinum-group metal producer in the U.S. with its main mine in Montana. There are tow companies that recover platinum-group metals as byproducts of copper refining. More than 110,000 kilograms of platinum-group metals were used by the automotive industry in the manufacture of catalysts.

In July 2001, U.S. imports for consumption of platinum sponge were 5,940 kilograms, an increase of 3 percent from the previous month. In the January-July 2001 period, imports of platinum sponge were 39,700 kilograms while for all of 2000 they were 68,000. Imports of other unwrought platinum in July 2001 were 446 kilograms. For January-July 2001, imports totaled 2,720 kilograms while for all of 2000 they were 3,870 kilograms.

Unwrought palladium imports in July 2001 were 12,300 kilograms while in January-July 2001 they were 108,000 kilograms. For all of 2000 they were 154,000 kilograms. In 2000 iridium imports were 2,700 kilograms. Imports of unwrought osmium were 133 kilograms while imports of i=unwrought ruthenium were 20,800 kilograms. Imports of rhodium in 2000 were 18,200 kilograms.

Futures Markets

Platinum and palladium futures and options are traded on the New York Mercantile Exchange (NYMEX). In Japan, platinum and palladium futures are listed on the Tokyo Commodity Exchange (TOCOM).

PLATINUM-GROUP METALS

World Mine Production of Platinum In Kilograms

Year	Australia	Canada	Colombia[3]	Finland	Japan	Russia	Serbia/ Montenegro	South Africa	United States	Zimbabwe	World Total
1992	100	4,800	1,956	60	629	28,000	19	94,900	1,650	9	132,000
1993	100	5,000	1,722	60	661	20,000	10	109,000	2,050	4	139,000
1994	100	6,000	1,084	60	691	15,000	10	114,000	1,960	7	139,000
1995	100	5,945	973	60	730	27,000	10	102,000	1,590	7	139,000
1996	100	5,155	672	62	816	25,000	10	105,000	1,840	100	139,000
1997	100	4,813	409	60	693	25,000	10	115,861	2,610	345	150,000
1998	100	5,640	437	50	533	25,000	10	116,483	3,240	2,730	154,000
1999[1]	100	5,442	440	50	737	27,000	5	130,745	2,920	479	168,000
2000[2]	100	5,450	440	50	782	30,000	5	114,434	3,110	150	155,000

[1] Preliminary. [2] Estimate. [3] Placer platinum. *Source: U.S. Geological Survey (USGS)*

World Mine Production of Palladium and Other Group Metals In Kilograms

Year	Palladium: Australia	Canada	Finland	Japan	Russia	Serbia/ Montenegro	South Africa	United States	Zimbabwe	World Total	Other Group Metals: Russia	South Africa	World Total
1992	400	5,800	100	986	70,000	130	41,000	5,440	19	124,000	6,000	17,000	24,300
1993	400	6,000	100	1,183	50,000	72	48,000	6,780	11	113,000	4,000	19,000	24,400
1994	400	7,000	100	1,277	40,000	50	47,800	6,440	17	103,000	3,000	22,100	27,100
1995	400	9,319	95	2,174	85,000	50	51,000	5,260	17	153,000	3,600	29,797	34,200
1996	400	8,082	182	2,182	80,000	50	52,600	6,100	120	150,000	3,500	30,363	34,800
1997	400	7,545	180	1,899	80,000	50	55,675	8,430	245	154,000	3,500	24,930	29,100
1998	400	8,905	150	4,151	80,000	50	56,608	10,600	1,855	163,000	3,500	27,052	31,500
1999[1]	400	8,592	150	5,354	85,000	25	63,600	9,800	342	173,000	3,700	30,300	34,700
2000[2]	400	8,600	150	4,712	94,000	25	55,888	10,300	70	174,000	4,100	31,522	36,400

[1] Preliminary. [2] Estimate. *Source: U.S. Geological Survey (USGS)*

Platinum-Group Metals Sold to Consuming Industries in the United States In Kilograms

Year	Automotive: Platinum	Automotive: Other[3]	Chemical: Platinum	Chemical: Other[3]	Electrical: Platinum	Electrical: Other[3]	Dental & Medical: Platinum	Dental & Medical: Other[3]	Jewelry & Decorative: Platinum	Jewelry & Decorative: Other[3]	Petroleum: Platinum	Petroleum: Other[3]	All Platinum-Group Metals: Platinum	Palladium	Other[3]	Total
1991	18,643	5,338	861	1,749	3,910	14,428	598	4,918	626	500	3,163	181	31,112	25,747	5,738	62,597
1992	20,503	5,860	1,716	2,297	2,922	15,738	640	5,386	881	1,417	1,036	790	31,095	28,935	6,816	66,846
1993	19,446	10,124	2,364	3,121	2,125	12,699	687	5,562	1,024	1,422	1,204	709	29,879	26,840	8,544	65,063
1994	21,756	11,413	3,104	1,889	2,790	7,961	902	5,092	1,345	824	1,581	422	34,044	21,509	7,387	62,940
1995	27,990	12,440	2,022	2,395	4,510	18,225	778	6,158	1,337	1,431	3,421	871	43,524	45,188	----	88,712
1996	28,550	19,282	2,115	2,457	4,541	17,665	778	6,285	1,493	1,493	3,514	902	44,489	45,157	----	89,646
1997	28,923	20,402	2,239	2,426	4,945	19,997	840	6,376	2,115	1,617	3,390	871	46,184	50,227	----	96,411
1998[1]	29,483	26,528	2,301	2,488	5,194	20,215	902	6,376	2,333	1,617	3,390	809	47,396	61,827	----	109,223
1999[2]	31,100	29,390	2,364	2,519	5,443	21,148	933	6,065	2,644	1,679	3,514	NA	49,844	64,470	----	114,314

[1] Preliminary. [2] Estimate. [3] Includes Palladium, iridium, osmium, rhodium, and ruthenium. *Sources: U.S. Geological Survey (USGS); American Metal Market (AMM)*

Salient Statistics of Platinum and Allied Metals[3] in the United States In Kilograms

Year	Net Import Reliance as a % of Apparent Consumption	Mine Production: Platinum	Mine Production: Palladium	Refinery Production (Secondary)	Total Refined	Refiner, Importer & Dealer Stocks as of Dec. 31: Platinum	Palladium	Other[4]	Total	Imports for Consumption: Refined	Total	Exports: Refined	Total	Apparent Consumption
1992	87	1,650	5,440	64,309	64,309	14,187	10,641	2,118	26,946	129,419	132,006	31,060	57,830	109,469
1993	89	2,050	6,780	65,792	65,792	10,263	8,324	176	18,763	148,790	153,165	43,798	78,486	123,273
1994	91	1,960	6,440	63,000	63,000	10,304	9,345	123	19,772	167,681	170,907	46,259	88,561	127,000
1995	----	1,590	5,260	NA	NA	----	----	----	----	214,143	220,613	41,825	50,575	----
1996	84	1,840	6,100	NA	NA	----	----	----	----	248,860	255,880	39,709	48,836	----
1997	84	2,610	8,430	NA	NA	----	----	----	----	253,114	258,424	67,656	81,249	----
1998	94	3,240	10,600	NA	NA	----	----	----	----	297,961	303,351	52,715	73,162	----
1999[1]	----	2,920	9,800	28,400	28,400	----	----	----	----	----	----	----	----	----
2000[2]	83	3,110	10,300	31,000	31,000	----	----	----	----	----	----	----	----	----

[1] Preliminary. [2] Estimate. [3] Includes platinum, palladium, iridium, osmium, rhodium, and ruthenium. [4] Includes iridium, osmium, rhodium, and ruthenium. W = Withheld proprietary data. *Source: U.S. Geological Survey (USGS)*

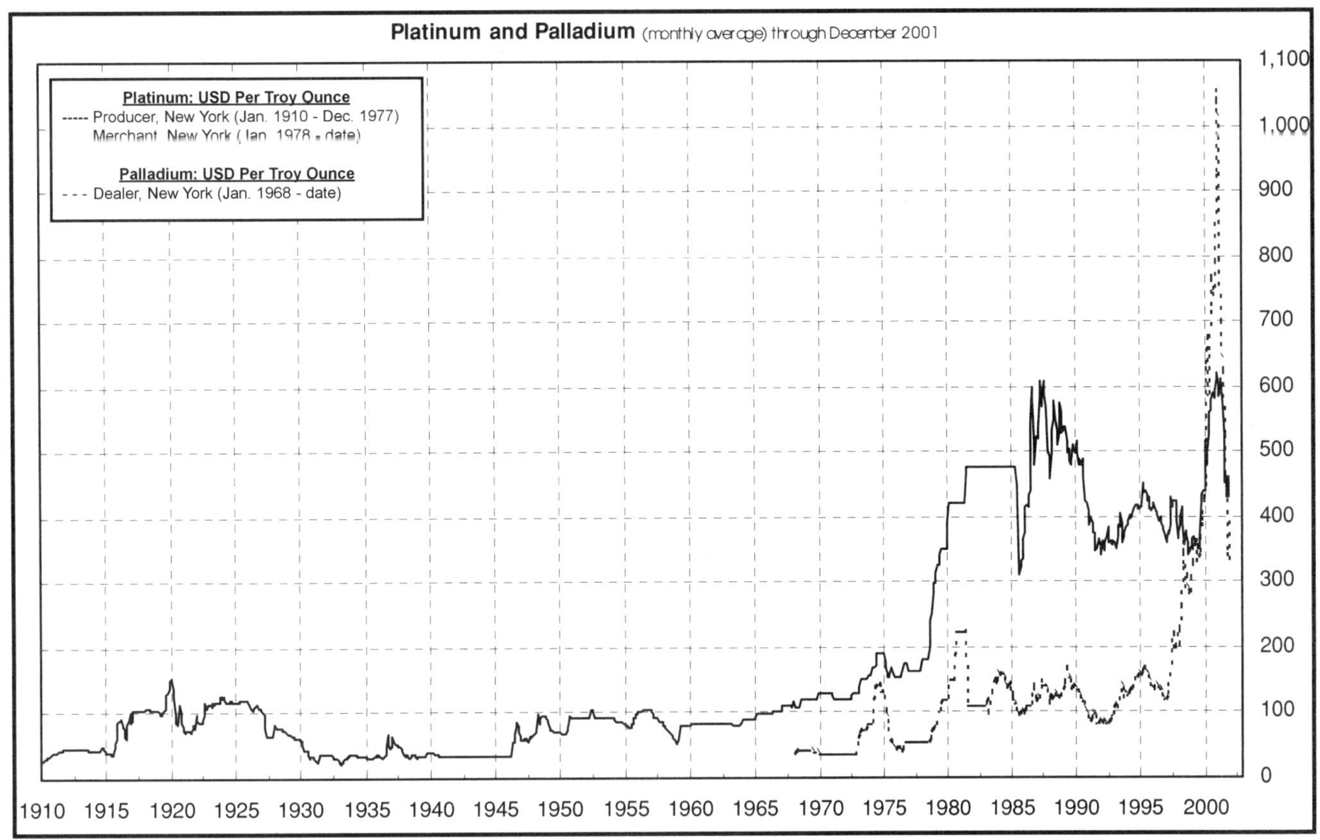

Average Merchant's Price of Platinum in the United States In Dollars Per Troy Ounce

Year	Jan.	Feb.	Mar.	Apr.	May	June	July	Aug.	Sept.	Oct.	Nov.	Dec.	Average
1992	341.88	362.97	356.84	347.73	354.75	368.17	378.89	360.20	361.60	359.75	355.81	361.98	359.21
1993	359.99	361.53	349.31	365.98	385.50	384.54	401.10	394.69	365.29	369.19	376.98	383.85	374.75
1994	390.30	393.95	398.29	400.38	395.41	401.42	408.25	411.91	415.93	421.11	415.73	408.83	405.13
1995	414.27	415.22	415.37	446.24	439.02	436.58	435.21	425.61	430.31	414.49	413.55	410.17	424.67
1996	416.59	421.45	412.39	405.71	402.86	393.18	392.00	400.97	391.43	385.53	383.92	372.97	398.24
1997	360.13	362.35	382.82	371.18	385.20	427.12	409.93	423.48	424.00	428.59	396.68	369.55	395.42
1998	375.30	390.56	396.18	412.82	392.60	357.38	379.34	372.24	361.40	347.27	348.42	352.76	373.85
1999	353.53	361.55	370.80	357.30	354.75	357.75	350.30	352.24	365.62	421.52	436.48	438.00	376.44
2000	432.95	517.02	478.28	493.53	519.57	557.45	558.53	572.76	592.53	576.91	592.73	608.28	541.49
2001[1]	620.00	600.84	584.45	593.16	610.18	579.10	529.48	451.75	460.00	430.61	429.17	461.79	529.21

[1] Preliminary. *Source: American Metal Market (AMM)*

Average Dealer[1] Price of Palladium in the United States In Dollars Per Troy Ounce

Year	Jan.	Feb.	Mar.	Apr.	May	June	July	Aug.	Sept.	Oct.	Nov.	Dec.	Average
1992	82.96	86.04	84.50	83.71	82.90	80.98	86.49	86.04	90.67	95.07	95.01	104.88	88.27
1993	110.39	112.57	106.22	113.79	119.94	125.36	139.74	137.37	121.95	130.04	123.62	125.60	122.22
1994	124.40	130.92	132.43	133.22	135.76	137.03	145.28	151.83	152.99	154.90	158.10	153.80	142.56
1995	156.67	157.53	161.18	170.91	160.87	158.59	156.27	138.81	143.76	137.36	135.57	132.37	150.83
1996	130.47	138.77	138.77	137.10	132.83	129.70	132.69	128.12	122.55	118.35	118.21	117.91	128.79
1997	121.48	134.26	151.13	152.75	167.52	203.62	176.84	210.90	190.17	206.52	209.93	200.70	177.15
1998	222.55	237.25	258.01	310.81	353.58	284.34	307.53	287.48	283.88	277.89	281.82	306.73	284.32
1999	317.28	351.38	351.78	358.83	330.70	339.84	333.17	341.64	358.55	387.05	400.38	420.17	357.50
2000	447.45	607.33	687.72	580.00	574.89	640.80	686.63	759.63	731.15	734.91	778.73	887.33	676.55
2001[2]	1054.10	984.37	792.68	699.15	663.41	619.67	525.90	459.83	444.47	340.52	333.14	405.95	610.27

[1] Based on wholesale quantities, prompt delivery. [2] Preliminary. *Source: U.S. Geological Survey (USGS)*

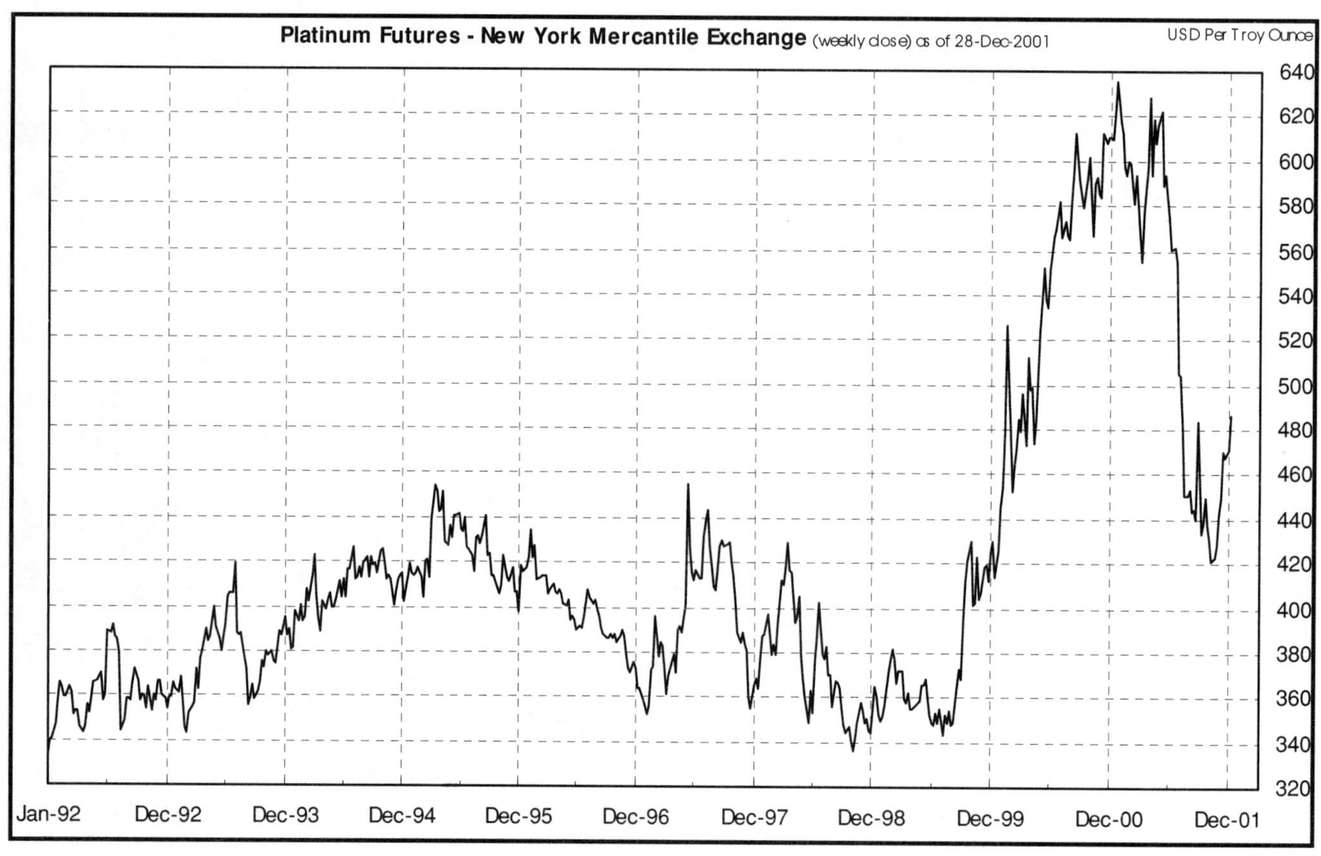

Volume of Trading of Platinum Futures in New York In Contracts

Year	Jan.	Feb.	Mar.	Apr.	May	June	July	Aug.	Sept.	Oct.	Nov.	Dec.	Total
1992	47,875	38,332	54,104	29,294	37,660	81,984	60,973	50,632	51,797	28,500	42,300	53,800	577,300
1993	29,400	55,555	61,425	50,603	65,778	72,535	59,751	56,399	58,552	36,965	43,998	60,269	651,222
1994	48,259	65,297	94,426	62,600	65,140	88,300	84,182	75,409	92,439	60,878	77,264	81,611	895,805
1995	61,400	38,594	131,294	69,892	60,382	75,353	53,422	62,451	98,837	55,919	56,339	82,810	846,693
1996	80,545	70,260	86,258	54,151	47,929	88,806	53,312	53,654	90,140	47,116	41,970	88,327	802,468
1997	60,515	83,325	86,242	57,719	67,000	72,481	37,836	36,391	62,462	46,188	28,913	58,625	698,597
1998	38,198	35,538	65,871	36,169	36,208	47,464	35,223	27,505	58,302	44,381	42,658	60,752	528,629
1999	37,700	53,698	68,350	36,900	26,507	75,444	57,536	36,115	102,196	30,637	32,176	40,009	597,268
2000	33,226	31,352	35,013	28,057	22,741	47,197	16,527	14,739	36,643	12,122	12,662	30,645	320,924
2001	19,278	12,885	31,617	14,961	15,714	23,245	14,494	12,477	17,040	9,957	11,401	22,890	205,959

Source: New York Mercantile Exchange (NYMEX)

Average Open Interest of Platinum Futures in New York In Contracts

Year	Jan.	Feb.	Mar.	Apr.	May	June	July	Aug.	Sept.	Oct.	Nov.	Dec.
1992	15,464	14,231	14,272	14,130	15,353	19,070	20,402	18,444	17,574	14,079	13,532	14,282
1993	11,889	14,315	12,990	15,490	19,641	17,919	20,931	18,892	16,883	15,690	16,658	19,633
1994	18,779	19,655	21,673	22,834	21,880	22,835	24,804	25,049	24,245	24,159	26,287	26,661
1995	23,285	23,058	23,470	23,657	20,984	21,533	20,801	25,288	23,489	24,498	22,137	21,534
1996	23,130	21,535	23,156	25,081	26,343	27,720	25,861	25,455	28,511	28,305	27,423	29,143
1997	25,890	26,092	22,364	16,568	18,933	18,440	13,280	14,180	13,639	13,466	12,396	13,501
1998	10,791	10,932	13,220	13,559	12,048	11,471	10,607	9,733	11,950	14,601	15,709	13,289
1999	12,311	14,481	16,493	11,471	12,256	12,436	14,703	13,777	15,014	14,892	13,402	12,017
2000	10,858	10,952	9,218	8,484	9,057	10,585	9,566	9,731	9,716	8,106	8,163	8,507
2001	8,449	7,311	6,855	6,715	7,436	5,751	6,210	5,996	5,646	5,395	6,102	6,033

Source: New York Mercantile Exchange (NYMEX)

Volume of Trading of Palladium Futures in New York In Contracts

Year	Jan.	Feb.	Mar.	Apr.	May	June	July	Aug.	Sept.	Oct.	Nov.	Dec.	Total
1992	7,217	7,323	3,429	2,833	8,011	2,881	4,965	6,752	5,066	5,359	6,461	7,912	68,209
1993	7,708	14,461	8,057	10,034	12,190	7,368	7,043	13,356	6,977	9,220	12,477	4,790	113,681
1994	8,250	14,953	6,067	6,676	15,481	6,514	9,024	21,741	15,690	9,603	21,384	8,390	143,773
1995	10,684	17,092	21,001	12,775	17,413	9,615	11,816	18,948	9,754	9,320	16,662	11,633	166,713
1996	13,725	33,519	11,931	16,416	27,467	8,989	9,896	23,740	10,721	8,149	28,870	12,187	205,610
1997	13,908	43,160	22,796	21,604	36,422	17,647	18,097	18,751	8,331	13,094	13,143	11,763	238,716
1998	11,506	17,786	18,678	14,042	17,942	7,370	4,241	8,737	6,214	4,962	12,839	6,933	131,250
1999	3,092	11,614	4,082	7,097	8,890	3,411	5,053	6,868	5,826	3,722	10,670	5,069	75,394
2000	4,584	13,976	2,803	1,833	7,034	2,622	3,120	5,169	2,523	2,460	3,041	1,601	50,766
2001	2,171	6,090	1,397	1,121	3,325	1,013	1,173	3,221	523	1,255	3,261	1,375	25,925

Source: New York Mercantile Exchange (NYMEX)

Average Open Interest of Palladium Futures in New York In Contracts

Year	Jan.	Feb.	Mar.	Apr.	May	June	July	Aug.	Sept.	Oct.	Nov.	Dec.
1992	3,984	4,071	4,101	4,206	4,137	3,852	3,762	3,362	3,041	2,982	2,901	3,246
1993	3,718	4,213	4,365	4,897	5,312	4,513	4,655	5,080	4,360	4,495	4,472	4,484
1994	4,626	4,995	4,672	4,303	5,116	4,530	5,807	6,851	6,625	6,511	7,726	6,917
1995	7,484	7,579	7,102	7,231	6,519	6,413	6,739	6,852	5,950	6,120	6,486	6,090
1996	6,365	7,539	6,682	7,099	8,713	8,143	7,977	8,805	8,129	7,971	8,227	7,727
1997	8,291	10,946	10,528	9,759	9,947	7,072	5,538	4,973	3,822	4,282	4,291	4,030
1998	4,062	4,873	5,220	5,369	4,371	4,219	4,166	3,488	2,959	3,048	2,938	2,700
1999	2,846	3,234	2,957	3,015	2,796	2,757	2,823	2,496	2,755	3,210	3,301	3,045
2000	3,129	3,101	2,367	2,359	2,628	2,015	2,118	1,974	1,757	1,905	1,859	1,837
2001	1,828	1,666	1,525	1,577	1,613	1,385	1,420	1,318	1,383	1,286	1,477	1,244

Source: New York Mercantile Exchange (NYMEX)

Pork Bellies

Although traders' enthusiasm towards the Chicago pork belly futures market has waned in recent years, wide price swings are still the rule and calendar 2001 was no exception. Prices, basis nearest futures contract, started the year rather subdued, trading within a tight 10 cents/lb range during the first quarter, but rallied about 25 cents in early spring almost $1/lb. Towards mid-year much of the gain was lost, before another rally took hold that briefly carried carried through $1, the highest price seen since 1996, but it too failed to hold. By year-end, futures were back in a trading range, but about 10 cents higher than a year earlier.

Pork bellies, more commonly known as bacon, are obtained from the underside of a hog. A hog has two bellies, generally weighing about 8-18 pounds, depending on the hog's commercial slaughter weight. Slaughter weights now average about 255 pounds per head, equal to a dressed weight of about 190 pounds. Bellies account for about12% of a hog's live weight, but represent a somewhat larger percentage of the total cutout value of the realized pork products. Frozen bellies deliverable against futures generally weigh between 12-14 pounds.

There are definitive seasonalities for pork bellies. Bellies are storable and the movement into cold storage builds early in the calendar year, peaking about mid-year. Net withdrawals from storage then carry stocks to a low around October. The cycle then starts again. Retail bacon demand also follows an time worn trend; peaking in the summer when consumer preference shifts to lighter foods and tapering off to a low during the winter months. While demand patterns would suggest the highest prices in the summer and the lowest in the winter, just the opposite is not unusual. Such contra-seasonal price moves can be partially attributed to supply logistics, notably the availability of frozen storage stocks deliverable against futures at exchange (CME) approved warehouses. When stocks prove either too large or small the underlying demand variables for bacon can be relegated to the backburner as a market making variable. The fact that no contract months are traded between August and the following February adds to the midsummer futures price distortion, as seen in 2001.

Belly prices (cash and futures) are sensitive to the inventory in cold storage and to the weekly net movement in and out of storage which afford some insight to demand although a better measures is the weekly quantity of bellies being sliced into bacon. Higher prices tend to encourage placing more supply into storage by discouraging retail bacon demand. Bacon is not a necessary foodstuff, but demand can be buoyed by favorable consumer disposable income. However, dietary standards have changed dramatically in recent years that do not favor the consumption of high fat and salt content food--like bacon. The U.S. economy weakened in 2001, which would have been expected to ease consumer bacon demand, but retail prices held firm, averaging in the second half of 2001 near $3.40/lb vs. about $3.20 a year earlier.

U.S. foreign trade in bacon as a processed product is small. Imports are largely from Denmark and exports go to Eastern Europe.

Futures markets

Frozen pork belly futures and options are traded on the Chicago Mercantile Exchange (CME). Futures are also listed on the CME in fresh pork bellies.

Average Retail Price of Bacon, Sliced In Dollars Per Pound

Year	Jan.	Feb.	Mar.	Apr.	May	June	July	Aug.	Sept.	Oct.	Nov.	Dec.	Average
1992	1.96	1.95	1.92	1.92	1.90	1.93	1.95	1.94	1.93	1.89	1.85	1.86	1.92
1993	1.87	1.84	1.80	1.89	1.91	1.95	2.00	1.95	1.98	1.99	2.01	2.02	1.93
1994	2.04	2.02	2.02	2.06	1.99	1.99	2.00	1.99	1.97	1.97	1.92	1.89	1.99
1995	1.93	1.93	1.91	1.89	1.92	1.90	1.91	1.97	2.04	2.12	2.16	2.17	1.99
1996	2.14	2.20	2.20	2.24	2.35	2.49	2.54	2.68	2.81	2.72	2.66	2.64	2.47
1997	2.66	2.65	2.66	2.66	2.63	2.69	2.72	2.76	2.75	2.73	2.67	2.61	2.68
1998	2.64	2.62	2.54	2.44	2.44	2.46	2.52	2.51	2.58	2.57	2.62	2.58	2.54
1999	2.52	2.52	2.51	2.45	2.47	2.50	2.50	2.93	2.58	2.57	2.66	2.75	2.58
2000	2.75	2.87	2.93	2.95	3.01	3.13	3.17	3.20	3.21	3.07	3.05	3.03	3.03
2001[1]	2.99	3.07	3.16	3.11	3.26	3.25	3.32	3.47	3.49	3.34	3.30	3.30	3.25

[1] Preliminary. *Source: Economic Research Service, U.S. Department of Agriculture (ERS-USDA)*

Frozen Pork Belly Storage Stocks in the United States, on First of Month In Thousands of Pounds

Year	Jan.	Feb.	Mar.	Apr.	May	June	July	Aug.	Sept.	Oct.	Nov.	Dec.
1992	71,318	76,894	75,925	85,095	96,653	92,677	78,646	54,544	26,854	21,973	26,044	49,970
1993	70,576	65,280	65,919	66,064	79,430	77,903	70,251	46,630	20,811	10,964	14,345	33,563
1994	53,168	55,999	54,921	63,099	72,230	79,018	73,583	57,747	30,636	18,260	22,656	40,725
1995	61,073	62,776	64,228	78,975	78,539	77,919	67,607	47,055	17,435	6,255	13,478	37,092
1996	47,587	46,498	46,381	47,655	57,174	63,522	56,767	28,533	18,996	12,702	16,206	30,943
1997	37,930	38,030	44,277	54,767	54,015	55,274	52,274	33,657	18,346	11,148	14,408	25,365
1998	44,763	55,249	55,368	54,441	58,600	59,462	52,010	31,433	14,786	9,452	16,440	41,711
1999	72,657	82,605	93,323	106,194	109,521	108,257	93,383	69,675	34,814	19,273	22,489	26,170
2000	40,300	43,802	49,983	60,527	63,461	68,292	60,097	50,515	33,005	21,341	20,589	38,674
2001[1]	47,099	50,728	47,154	45,440	43,878	46,029	39,552	24,996	12,754	8,960	28,209	36,290

[1] Preliminary. *Source: National Agricultural Statistics Service, U.S. Department of Agriculture (NASS-USDA)*

Weekly Pork Belly Storage Movement

2000 Week Ending	Stocks[1] In Thousands of Pounds In	Out	On Hand	Net Move-ment	2001 Week Ending	Stocks[1] In Thousands of Pounds In	Out	On Hand	Net Move-ment
Jan. 1	3,988	31	17,214	3,957	Jan. 6	1,337	161	34,959	1,176
8	1,955	0	19,169	1,955	13	1,239	404	35,794	835
15	520	511	19,178	9	20	580	524	35,850	56
22	916	499	19,595	417	27	309	696	35,463	-387
29	406	308	19,693	98	Feb. 3	227	872	34,817	-645
Feb. 5	2,120	765	21,048	1,355	10	195	748	34,264	-553
12	417	309	21,156	108	17	115	719	33,660	-604
19	441	448	21,149	-7	24	1,270	643	34,287	627
26	1,026	320	21,855	706	Mar. 3	656	477	34,466	179
Mar. 4	2,394	0	24,249	2,394	10	174	849	33,791	-675
11	1,574	79	25,744	1,495	17	114	598	33,307	-484
18	2,095	47	27,792	2,048	24	120	648	32,779	-528
25	946	409	28,329	537	31	493	447	32,825	46
Apr. 1	965	101	29,193	864	Apr. 7	220	1,410	31,635	-1,190
8	208	207	29,194	1	14	498	420	31,713	78
15	753	233	29,714	520	21	359	235	31,837	124
22	1,413	111	31,017	1,302	28	561	286	32,112	275
29	1,387	167	32,237	1,220	May 5	629	104	32,637	525
May 6	2,446	4	34,679	2,442	12	814	429	33,022	385
13	1,009	480	35,208	529	19	1,147	534	33,635	613
20	1,237	8	36,437	1,229	26	1,591	217	35,009	1,374
27	823	166	37,094	657	June 2	937	470	35,476	467
June 3	1,363	415	38,042	948	9	51	250	35,277	-199
10	583	290	38,335	293	16	381	1,348	34,310	-967
17	193	847	37,681	-654	23				
24	356	2,118	35,919	-1,762	30				
July 1	246	2,928	33,237	-2,682	July 7				
8	1,124	732	33,629	392	14				
15	43	2,331	31,341	-2,288	21				
22	310	1,787	29,864	-1,477	28				
29	84	1,639	28,309	-1,555	Aug. 4				
Aug. 5	55	1,524	26,840	-1,469	11				
12	0	2,981	23,859	-2,981	18	123	2,580	9,389	-2,457
19	167	2,666	21,360	-2,499	25	532	2,406	7,515	-1,874
26	307	2,447	19,220	-2,140	Sept. 1	476	1,763	6,228	-1,287
Sept. 2	15	2,855	-17,030	-2,840	8	99	1,364	4,963	-1,265
9	1,510	1,972	18,262	-462	15	165	823	4,305	-658
16	675	886	18,051	-211	22	165	617	3,853	-452
23	871	2,351	16,571	-1,480	29	193	368	3,678	-175
30	128	1,621	15,078	-1,493	Oct. 6	1,016	245	4,449	771
Oct. 7	42	1,800	13,320	-1,758	13	2,014	210	6,253	1,804
14	833	524	13,629	309	20	3,579	114	9,718	3,465
21	1,509	905	14,233	604	27	4,159	280	13,597	3,879
28	135	754	13,614	-619	Nov. 3	4,186	656	17,127	3,530
Nov. 4	693	593	13,714	100	10	2,085	739	18,473	1,346
11	4,224	770	17,168	3,454	17	2,382	1,099	16,719	1,283
18	3,001	809	19,360	2,192	24	2,350	385	20,973	1,965
25	3,930	1,474	1,817	2,456	Dec. 1	1,301	514	21,760	787
Dec. 2	2,724	396	24,145	2,328	8	789	522	22,027	267
9	4,407	1,004	27,548	3,403	15	829	207	22,649	622
16	4,089	828	30,809	3,261	22	2,259	195	24,713	2,064
23	2,382	322	32,869	2,060	29				
30	987	73	33,783	914					

[1] 57 Chicago and Outside Combined Chicago Mercantile Exchange approved warehouses. *Source: Chicago Mercantile Exchange (CME)*

PORK BELLIES

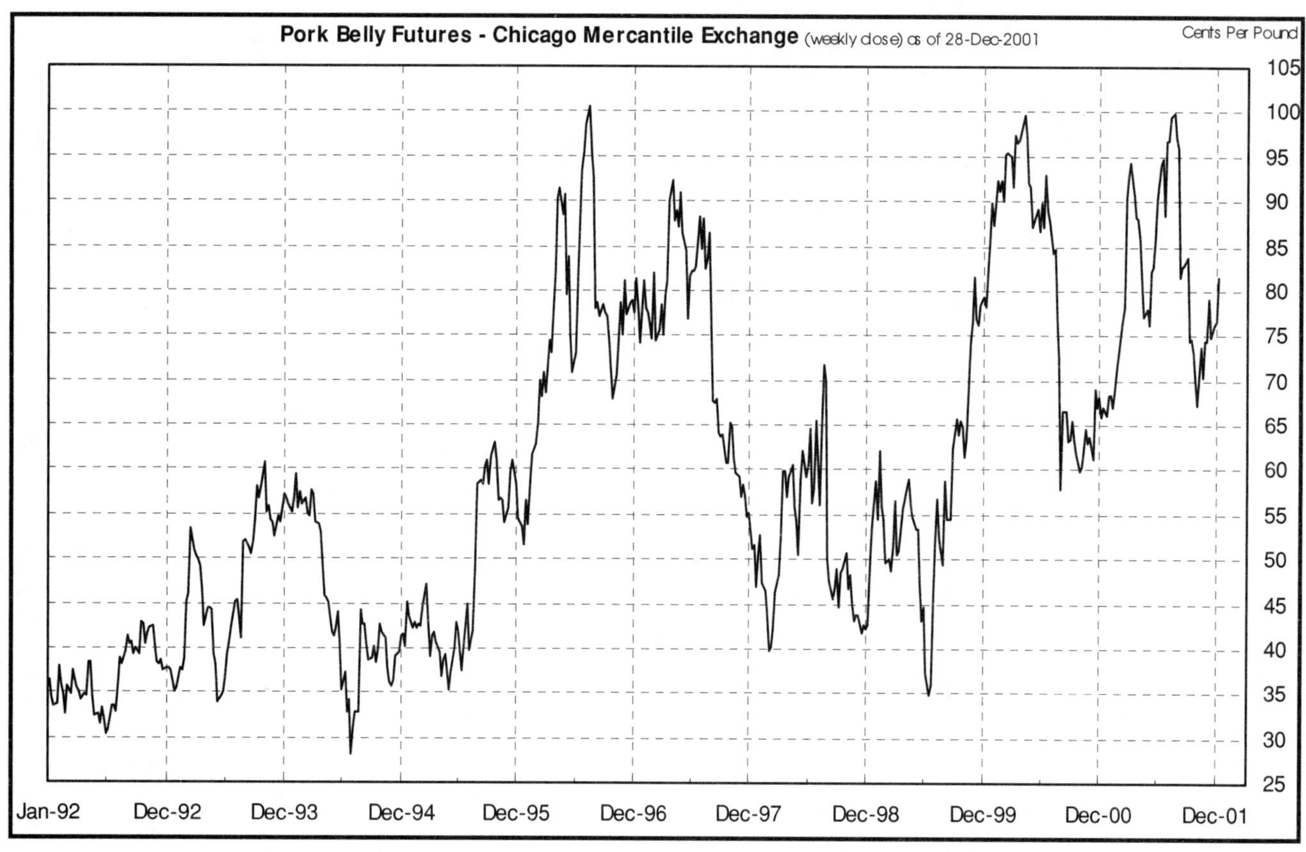

Average Open Interest of Pork Belly Futures in Chicago In Contracts

Year	Jan.	Feb.	Mar.	Apr.	May	June	July	Aug.	Sept.	Oct.	Nov.	Dec.
1992	12,521	12,195	11,901	12,345	12,497	13,598	12,623	7,149	6,540	7,033	9,251	10,953
1993	10,623	9,244	8,283	8,626	10,096	11,092	9,031	5,427	4,644	7,241	8,701	9,121
1994	11,053	10,426	9,375	9,894	8,092	8,248	7,836	7,841	8,398	10,072	10,141	10,216
1995	10,294	9,080	7,809	7,367	8,017	7,036	5,666	4,271	6,246	7,007	7,103	7,282
1996	7,094	8,028	10,521	10,753	10,018	8,136	6,432	6,296	6,056	6,395	6,050	6,480
1997	7,504	7,930	7,260	7,165	8,950	7,203	5,905	4,791	5,242	7,520	8,302	9,009
1998	9,187	9,145	9,082	7,825	6,786	5,406	4,185	3,493	2,933	3,841	4,987	7,085
1999	7,217	6,192	4,623	5,113	6,030	6,639	5,003	2,415	2,320	3,206	4,011	4,868
2000	5,872	6,011	6,320	6,563	5,836	5,306	3,650	1,877	1,860	2,093	2,409	2,610
2001	2,719	2,908	2,935	3,138	2,808	2,354	2,526	2,579	2,695	2,321	2,441	2,451

Source: Chicago Mercantile Exchange (CME)

Volume of Trading of Pork Belly Futures in Chicago In Contracts

Year	Jan.	Feb.	Mar.	Apr.	May	June	July	Aug.	Sept.	Oct.	Nov.	Dec.	Total
1992	80,697	79,700	67,470	57,565	73,137	73,081	78,588	54,663	39,839	64,248	60,724	54,440	784,152
1993	77,380	62,871	63,988	62,403	62,400	70,124	65,496	42,613	37,992	47,780	60,163	49,099	698,799
1994	60,316	67,250	58,183	53,839	56,575	58,424	50,450	47,626	38,375	45,525	49,280	47,803	633,646
1995	62,994	54,330	59,324	43,501	49,453	53,571	45,869	36,623	31,112	35,444	47,061	42,631	561,913
1996	48,563	56,623	61,669	61,703	61,868	55,337	55,121	45,399	39,182	48,973	42,709	35,502	612,649
1997	60,761	53,604	56,750	76,072	62,190	54,043	55,043	36,153	31,154	44,277	31,663	33,609	595,319
1998	41,894	50,105	47,249	61,910	36,058	48,913	41,133	33,832	24,006	30,538	30,093	35,521	481,252
1999	39,925	36,293	33,322	31,558	31,321	45,030	36,513	23,536	16,544	20,392	28,920	24,955	368,309
2000	37,650	38,943	39,061	31,464	40,311	31,229	25,051	17,875	10,711	11,854	11,737	13,690	309,576
2001	15,861	16,200	16,675	18,274	18,708	16,989	20,187	18,823	12,719	12,905	15,984	13,034	196,359

Source: Chicago Mercantile Exchange (CME)

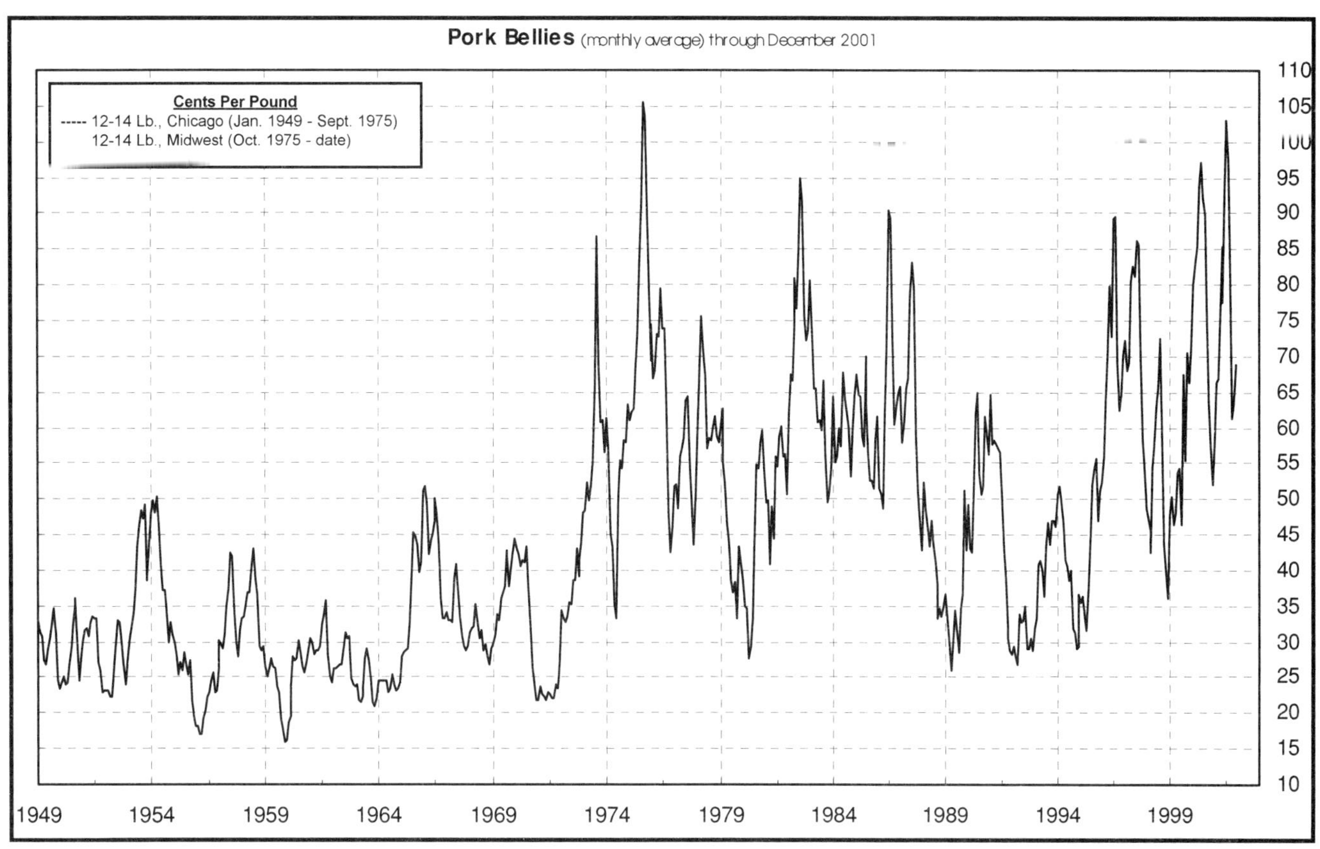

Average Price of Pork Bellies (12-14 Pounds) Midwest In Cents Per Pound

Year	Jan.	Feb.	Mar.	Apr.	May	June	July	Aug.	Sept.	Oct.	Nov.	Dec.	Average
1992	28.05	29.44	28.01	26.93	34.09	32.78	32.77	35.13	29.09	29.13	30.48	28.80	30.39
1993	31.97	33.22	41.28	41.19	39.86	36.24	44.51	46.68	43.82	47.25	47.21	46.21	41.62
1994	50.63	51.66	49.68	46.84	41.40	40.39	38.64	39.60	31.50	31.33	29.09	29.29	40.00
1995	36.03	35.80	36.30	33.83	31.70	37.94	43.10	52.42	54.43	56.20	47.28	51.45	43.04
1996	52.33	56.33	64.50	69.86	79.50	72.64	89.49	88.40	68.12	63.07	65.27	70.07	69.97
1997	72.04	68.42	59.05	80.54	82.58	80.68	86.70	85.43	72.25	57.97	53.77	47.52	70.58
1998	43.00	45.89	42.28	54.65	57.87	63.10	68.46	72.99	57.49	42.05	39.13	36.31	51.94
1999	48.80	50.76	46.51	49.23	53.76	53.41	47.78	67.29	57.87	70.83	67.81	71.37	57.12
2000	80.45	82.40	85.00	93.70	97.85	91.99	90.38	75.64	63.94	57.83	51.97	58.36	77.46
2001[1]	66.61	66.68	78.04	85.80	77.91	91.50	102.42	98.39	81.91	61.30	63.68	69.13	78.61

[1] Preliminary. *Source: Economic Research Service, U.S. Department of Agriculture (ERS-USDA)*

Average Price of Pork Loins (12-14 lbs.)[2] Central, U.S. In Cents Per Pound

Year	Jan.	Feb.	Mar.	Apr.	May	June	July	Aug.	Sept.	Oct.	Nov.	Dec.	Average
1992	96.89	99.13	94.10	98.65	108.94	113.94	108.22	111.18	102.98	96.98	89.64	96.22	101.41
1993	98.22	100.05	100.61	107.61	111.16	122.28	113.40	116.73	116.74	111.85	98.68	92.33	107.47
1994	103.90	110.75	100.45	101.89	103.99	103.84	109.79	112.86	105.34	95.65	80.00	89.50	101.50
1995	96.94	102.20	95.30	93.33	103.50	118.81	124.65	127.98	117.63	108.23	93.94	110.39	107.74
1996	110.00	116.43	120.49	119.70	131.61	115.73	126.16	118.18	112.28	115.40	115.39	120.45	118.49
1997	112.50	109.50	106.58	117.16	125.68	116.28	122.53	119.28	112.07	99.68	85.99	79.44	108.89
1998	76.50	103.03	104.56	102.51	130.64	113.13	106.51	105.90	97.23	99.63	79.90	72.49	99.34
1999	105.82	92.35	83.47	99.35	107.44	97.62	105.72	111.55	104.99	98.98	94.64	102.75	100.39
2000	99.29	110.66	110.06	127.48	115.38	132.53	131.73	120.45	119.22	119.90	104.19	114.68	117.13
2001[1]	110.80	114.32	128.53	117.98	130.72	132.33	126.41	121.22	116.21	108.69	97.87	98.50	116.97

[1] Preliminary. *Source: Economic Research Service, U.S. Department of Agriculture (ERS-USDA)*

Potatoes

Potatoes are the largest vegetable crop grown in the U.S. The value of all potato production in 2000 was estimated at $2.59 billion, down 6% from 1999, but the average price, at $5.08 per cwt, fell 69 cents from 1999. Total potato production in 2000 of a record large 514 million cwt compares with 478 million in 1999, up 7%. Harvested acreage in 2000 of 1.35 million acres (planted 1.38 million) was only 1% above1999, but average yield reached a record high 381 cwt per acre, up 22% from the 359 cwt. realized in 1999.

Total 2000 consumption (sales) of a record of a 465 million cwt compares with 437 million in 1999. Non-sales, i.e., seed use, shrinkage and loss in 2000 of 49 million cwt. compares with 41 million in 1999. Total domestic food stock usage of a record large 288 million cwt. compares with 275 million in 1999 and the previous record 284 million in 1996; included in the 2000 total was 147 million cwt. allocated to frozen french fry production vs. 140 million in 1999 and a relatively low 132 million in 1997. Table stock usage of 139 million cwt in 2000 compares with 134 million in 1999. For a time in the mid-1990's, the U.S. consumer's affinity for deep-fried processed potatoes slackened apparently owing to nutritional concerns--but the latter appears to have run its course. Moreover, some of the slack in usage was offset by increased demand for fresh potatoes, i.e. table stock.

Potatoes are grown in all fifty states. The crop, however, is divided into four, but not necessarily distinct, seasonal groups based on harvest time: a crop year is associated with the calendar year in which the harvest is accomplished.. The fall crop, consisting of about two dozen states, accounts for 85-90% of total production and is usually harvested from September through November. The winter crop is the smallest and harvested only in Florida and California from January into March. The spring and summer crops tend to be fairly close in size. The seasonal disparities reflect major differences in planted acreage and realized yield, which is consistently higher in the fall producing states. The marketing season follows the harvest, but the movement of the fall crop can extend into the following July with supplies drawn from storage. The inventoried fall crop can serve as a supply buffer in the event the spring and summer crop are short. However, large fall stocks can also prove a depressant on prices should earlier crops prove large. Generally about one-third of farm marketing's occur during September and October.

Idaho is the nation's largest producer with a 2000 fall crop of a record large 152 million cwt. vs. 133 million in 1999 and the previous record 143 million cwt in 1996. Washington's crop, at distant second, of 105 million cwt compares with 95 million in 1999. As usual, Washington's average yield was the nation's highest, 600 cwt. per acre in 2000 compared to Idaho's average of 369 cwt.. Maine's crop, once the largest producing fall state, totaled only 17.9 million cwt. in 2000 vs. 17.8 million in 1999 with an average yield per acre in both years of about 282 cwt. Maine's decline largely reflects the wide variety of potatoes grown in the state--about 80-- whereas in Idaho production is focused on one type of baking potato, the Russet Burbank, which has enhanced marketing consistency and consumer preference.

About 56% of the 2000 crop was processed, either into frozen products or as a direct consumer food, such as potato chips vs. 57% of the 2000 crop. In 2000 there were 98 chip processing plants vs. 108 n 1999. Frozen french fries account for about 29% (147 million cwt) of the nation's total potato crop in 2000 with chips accounting for almost 10% (52 million cwt.) and dehydrated potatoes another 11% (55 million cwt.). Generally about 1% of the total crop has been used for seed, but the percentage slipped to .0.7%, 3.8 million cwt in 2000. However, nearly 44 million cwt were considered lost, mostly owing to shrinkage, a sizable increase from previous years when it averaged about 40 million cwt.

Foreign trade in U.S. is small: Japan imports processed potatoes, mostly french fries, while Canada exports fresh potatoes which are used mostly for seed.

Salient Statistics of Potatoes in the United States

Crop Year	Acreage: Planted (1,000 Acres)	Acreage: Harvested (1,000 Acres)	Yield Per Harvested Acre (Cwt.)	Total Production (In Thousands of Cwt.)	Farm Disposition — Used Where Grown: Seed & Feed	Farm Disposition — Used Where Grown: Shrinkage & Loss	Sold[2]	Farm Price ($/Cwt.)	Value of Production[3] (Million $)	Value of Sales (Million $)	Stocks on Jan. 1 (1,000 Cwt.)	Foreign Trade[5]: (Fresh) Domestic Exports (Millions of Lbs.)	Foreign Trade[5]: Imports (Millions of Lbs.)	Consumption[5] Per Capita — In Pounds: Fresh	Consumption[5] Per Capita — In Pounds: Total
1992	1,339	1,315	323	425,367	5,925	33,807	385,637	5.52	2,336	2,129	215,990	537,939	273,515	48.6	130.7
1993	1,385	1,317	326	428,693	5,931	30,152	392,610	6.17	2,637	2,424	217,300	539,345	541,382	50.6	137.8
1994	1,416	1,380	339	467,054	5,878	37,166	424,010	5.58	2,590	2,367	238,560	655,026	405,899	50.2	138.3
1995	1,398	1,372	323	443,606	5,745	29,530	408,331	6.77	2,992	2,762	223,550	583,938	458,926	49.9	138.8
1996	1,455	1,426	350	499,254	6,221	41,222	451,190	4.91	2,425	2,220	261,320	564,010	690,768	50.7	147.2
1997	1,384	1,354	345	467,091	5,475	32,183	429,433	5.64	2,623	2,421	246,550	670,270	512,321	49.4	144.0
1998	1,417	1,388	343	475,771	5,766	35,454	434,551	5.56	2,635	2,416	246,230	650,917	737,223	47.9	140.8
1999	1,377	1,332	359	478,216	5,569	35,531	437,116	5.77	2,746	2,522	239,910	598,574	610,538	49.2	139.8
2000	1,384	1,348	381	513,621	5,288	43,688	464,645	5.08	2,591	2,360	275,270	644,190	502,706	50.8	146.2
2001[1]	1,267	1,241	358	444,766				6.60	2,934		233,420	555,829	420,167	48.5	144.0

[1] Preliminary. [2] For all purposes, including food, seed processing & livestock feed. [3] Farm weight basis, excluding canned and frozen potatoes.

Source: Economic Research Service, U.S. Department of Agriculture (ERS-USDA)

Cold Storage Stocks of All Frozen Potatoes in the United States, on First of Month — In Millions of Pounds

Year	Jan.	Feb.	Mar.	Apr.	May	June	July	Aug.	Sept.	Oct.	Nov.	Dec.
1992	980.8	996.5	1,036.3	1,082.7	1,077.6	1,137.3	1,131.4	966.4	948.7	949.1	1,067.1	1,038.7
1993	963.2	971.2	1,028.2	1,046.6	912.7	979.5	989.8	932.8	902.8	1,019.5	1,184.7	1,130.7
1994	1,006.4	1,019.9	1,057.1	1,054.4	1,050.5	1,118.9	1,000.0	979.0	1,028.2	1,108.7	1,189.0	1,163.5
1995	1,096.6	1,156.0	1,179.9	1,169.0	1,138.0	1,125.4	1,116.5	992.4	992.6	1,145.3	1,225.6	1,174.5
1996	1,123.7	1,147.2	1,172.5	1,164.6	1,112.1	1,076.4	1,059.7	907.1	957.8	1,124.9	1,225.2	1,146.3
1997	1,098.4	1,111.5	1,180.1	1,177.1	1,195.8	1,213.3	1,271.4	1,214.3	1,130.8	1,270.0	1,354.7	1,313.5
1998	1,163.5	1,147.2	1,235.7	1,278.3	1,225.1	1,282.8	1,316.5	1,234.7	1,204.5	1,266.8	1,341.0	1,290.5
1999	1,151.3	1,219.7	1,272.9	1,278.8	1,236.2	1,255.5	1,234.1	1,142.3	1,169.8	1,235.5	1,307.8	1,254.5
2000	1,165.4	1,140.9	1,270.1	1,283.4	1,239.4	1,250.4	1,186.3	1,180.3	1,185.7	1,291.5	1,351.5	1,285.9
2001[1]	1,189.7	1,179.5	1,254.7	1,220.9	1,280.4	1,270.4	1,355.1	1,282.6	1,197.5	1,323.2	1,338.5	1,297.4

[1] Preliminary. *Source: Agricultural Statistics Board, U.S. Department of Agriculture (ASB-USDA)*

Potato Crop Production Estimates, Stocks and Disappearance in the United States — In Millions of Cwt.

	Crop Production Estimates				Total Storage Stocks[2]							Fall Crop				
	Total Crop			Fall Crop			Following Year					1,000 Cwt.				
Year	Oct. 1	Nov. 1	Dec. 1	Oct. 1	Nov. 1	Dec. 1	Jan. 1	Feb. 1	Mar. 1	Apr. 1	May 1	Production	Disappearance (Sold)	Dec. 1 Stocks	Average Price $/Cwt.	Value of Sales $ 1,000
1992	----	425.4	----	----	372.4	246.8	216.0	184.6	152.8	115.8	75.0	368,516	341,209	246,820	5.17	1,762,984
1993	----	428.7	----	----	372.4	249.4	217.3	185.5	153.4	115.2	72.9	376,954	353,052	249,710	5.65	1,981,017
1994	----	467.9	----	----	412.4	273.3	238.6	202.5	169.6	129.8	87.6	410,839	380,818	273,290	5.06	1,914,311
1995	----	444.8	----	----	402.4	256.7	223.6	189.4	156.0	115.9	75.9	394,785	370,679	256,710	6.43	2,372,983
1996	----	491.5	----	----	447.9	295.1	261.3	226.1	189.2	147.6	103.2	443,704	408,247	295,100	4.35	1,772,037
1997	----	459.4	----	----	417.5	278.8	246.6	212.6	175.9	134.2	92.8	413,513	387,089	278,830	5.20	2,011,004
1998	----	471.0	----	----	429.0	280.9	246.2	209.6	173.7	131.2	87.9	423,170	392,922	280,910	5.07	1,994,030
1999	----	481.5	----	----	435.6	275.1	239.9	207.2	169.6	128.4	86.9	420,567	390,210	275,100	5.29	2,064,564
2000	----	509.4	----	----	463.4	310.3	275.3	234.3	197.7	153.5	109.2	467,504	420,279	310,300	4.55	1,910,833
2001[1]	----	441.8	----	----	400.7	266.5	233.4	201.8	167.9			400,727		266,520		

[1] Preliminary. [2] Held by growers and local dealers in the fall producing areas. *Source: Agricultural Statistics Board, U.S. Department of Agriculture*

Production of Potatoes by Seasonal Groups in the United States — In Thousands of Cwt.

	Winter	Spring			Summer			Fall								
Year	Total	California	Florida	Total	New Mexico	Virginia	Total	Colorado	Idaho	Maine	Minnesota	North Dakota	Oregon	Washington	Wisconsin	Total
1992	2,998	7,238	7,750	21,535	952	1,980	21,309	22,110	127,050	24,300	16,080	27,690	21,075	69,300	25,160	379,525
1993	2,552	7,508	6,068	19,654	1,290	1,760	14,922	25,270	126,192	19,890	14,780	21,090	23,103	88,500	22,588	385,935
1994	2,372	7,790	8,588	22,646	1,088	1,425	17,381	25,795	138,801	18,375	20,035	28,200	27,514	88,920	25,740	419,645
1995	2,473	6,230	7,830	20,193	1,344	2,040	17,931	23,808	132,657	17,160	20,790	25,410	24,788	80,850	26,000	403,009
1996	3,273	7,538	7,765	22,417	1,404	1,463	19,176	29,175	142,800	21,175	24,600	28,820	30,124	94,990	33,150	454,388
1997	3,431	8,073	7,150	22,299	1,248	1,268	18,171	24,993	140,314	19,080	20,440	22,000	27,319	88,160	30,175	423,190
1998	2,980	6,198	7,358	21,121	962	1,380	18,933	25,360	138,000	18,060	21,170	28,670	26,229	93,225	30,895	432,737
1999	4,070	7,600	8,820	25,327	1,247	1,050	18,972	25,762	133,330	17,813	18,020	26,400	28,020	95,200	34,000	429,847
2000	4,960	7,426	6,343	21,921	1,050	1,292	19,236	27,972	152,320	17,920	21,240	26,950	30,683	105,000	33,800	467,504
2001[1]	4,115	6,045	7,970	21,814	770	1,386	17,503	21,357	127,980	16,120	19,380	25,680	20,900	94,400	31,955	400,730

[1] Preliminary. *Source: Agricultural Statistics Board, U.S. Department of Agriculture (ASB-USDA)*

Production of Potatoes by Seasonal Groups in the United States — In Thousands of Cwt.

	Winter	Spring			Summer			Fall								
Year	Total	California	Florida	Total	New Mexico	Virginia	Total	Colorado	Idaho	Maine	Minnesota	North Dakota	Oregon	Washington	Wisconsin	Total
1992	2,998	7,238	7,750	21,535	952	1,980	21,309	22,110	127,050	24,300	16,080	27,690	21,075	69,300	25,160	379,525
1993	2,552	7,508	6,068	19,654	1,290	1,760	14,922	25,270	126,192	19,890	14,780	21,090	23,103	88,500	22,588	385,935
1994	2,372	7,790	8,588	22,646	1,088	1,425	17,381	25,795	138,801	18,375	20,035	28,200	27,514	88,920	25,740	419,645
1995	2,473	6,230	7,830	20,193	1,344	2,040	17,931	23,808	132,657	17,160	20,790	25,410	24,788	80,850	26,000	403,009
1996	3,273	7,538	7,765	22,417	1,404	1,463	19,176	29,175	142,800	21,175	24,600	28,820	30,124	94,990	33,150	454,388
1997	3,431	8,073	7,150	22,299	1,248	1,268	18,171	24,993	140,314	19,080	20,440	22,000	27,319	88,160	30,175	423,190
1998	2,980	6,198	7,358	21,121	962	1,380	18,933	25,360	138,000	18,060	21,170	28,670	26,229	93,225	30,895	432,737
1999	4,070	7,600	8,820	25,327	1,247	1,050	18,972	25,762	133,330	17,813	18,020	26,400	28,020	95,200	34,000	429,847
2000	4,960	7,426	6,343	21,921	1,050	1,292	19,236	27,972	152,320	17,920	21,240	26,950	30,683	105,000	33,800	467,504
2001[1]	4,115	6,045	7,970	21,814	770	1,386	17,503	21,357	127,980	16,120	19,380	25,680	20,900	94,400	31,955	400,730

[1] Preliminary. *Source: Agricultural Statistics Board, U.S. Department of Agriculture (ASB-USDA)*

POTATOES

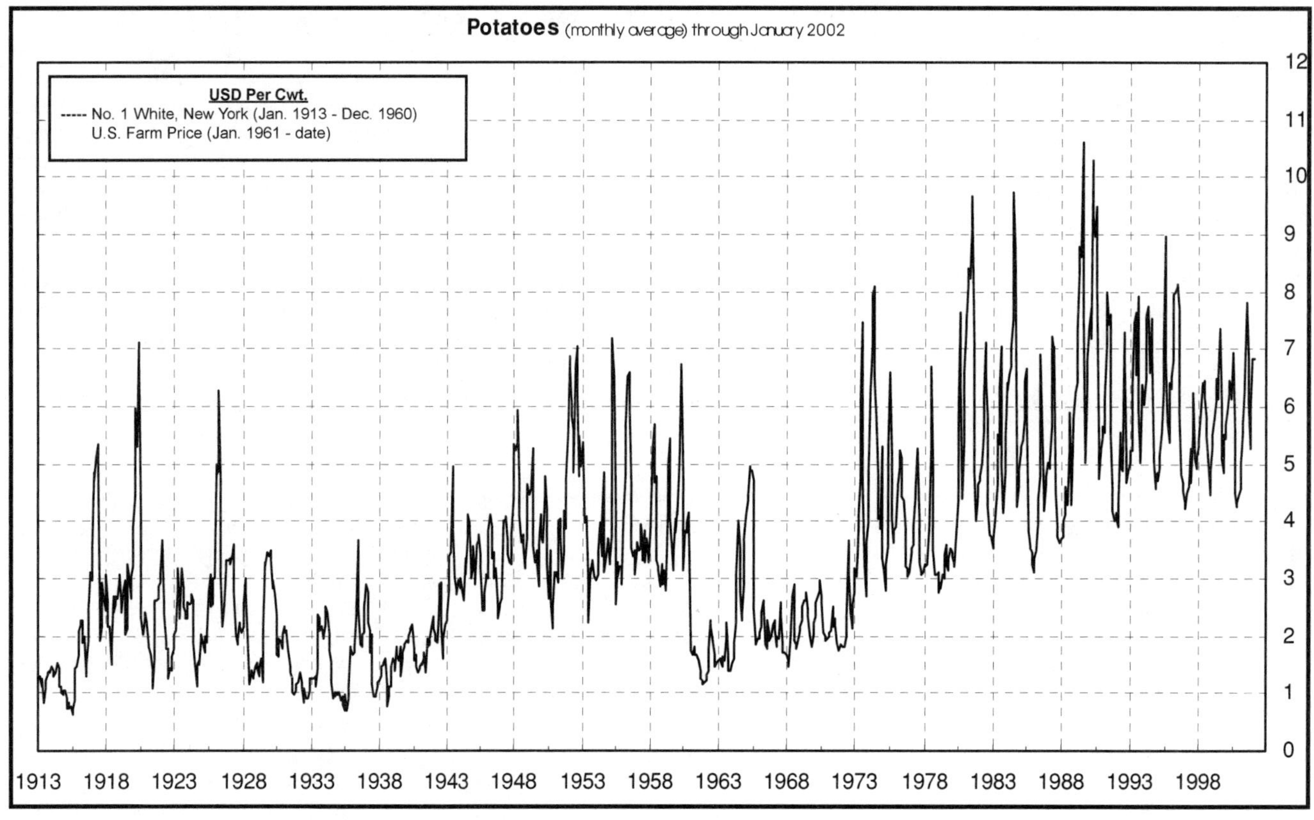

Per Capita Utilization of Potatoes in the United States In Pounds (Farm Weight)

			Processing				
Year	Total	Fresh	Freezing	Chips & Shoe-string	Dehy-drating	Canning	Total
1992	130.6	48.6	50.1	17.2	12.9	1.8	82.0
1993	137.7	50.5	53.9	17.8	13.8	1.7	87.2
1994	138.3	50.2	56.3	16.7	13.4	1.7	88.1
1995	138.8	49.9	56.9	16.6	13.4	2.0	88.9
1996	147.2	50.7	61.1	16.7	16.9	1.8	96.5
1997	144.0	49.4	60.4	16.2	16.2	1.8	94.6
1998	141.0	47.9	59.1	15.1	17.2	1.5	93.1
1999	139.8	49.2	59.5	16.3	13.0	1.8	90.6
2000[1]	147.9	51.1	60.4	17.0	17.5	1.9	96.8
2001[2]	144.4	49.3	60.1	16.3	16.9	1.8	95.1

[1] Preliminary. [2] Forecast. *Source: Agricultural Statistics Board, U.S. Department of Agriculture (ASB-USDA)*

Average Price Received by Farmers for Potatoes in the United States In Dollars Per Cwt.

Year	Jan.	Feb.	Mar.	Apr.	May	June	July	Aug.	Sept.	Oct.	Nov.	Dec.	Season Average
1992	4.07	4.08	4.64	5.16	4.43	4.71	7.00	6.64	4.89	4.55	4.90	5.06	5.52
1993	5.15	5.29	6.06	7.19	7.18	6.45	7.61	6.05	5.12	4.96	6.40	6.12	6.17
1994	6.04	6.37	7.75	6.68	6.62	6.80	7.38	6.25	4.95	4.57	4.77	4.85	5.56
1995	4.83	4.97	5.37	5.41	5.86	7.12	8.75	6.64	5.76	6.30	6.39	6.33	6.75
1996	6.65	6.92	7.51	7.82	8.09	8.16	7.79	5.58	4.92	4.75	4.44	4.28	4.91
1997	4.22	4.56	4.64	4.67	5.31	5.67	5.66	6.31	5.08	4.93	5.12	5.36	5.64
1998	5.40	5.94	6.41	6.27	6.45	6.16	5.81	5.46	4.97	4.47	4.86	5.30	5.56
1999	5.50	5.75	6.12	6.50	6.13	6.54	7.35	6.02	5.09	4.86	5.52	5.44	5.77
2000	5.68	5.92	6.26	6.46	6.31	6.14	6.93	5.56	4.49	4.27	4.31	4.48	4.95
2001[1]	4.56	5.02	5.56	5.71	6.31	6.47	7.83	6.84	6.05	5.28	5.97	6.85	

[1] Preliminary. *Source: Agricultural Statistics Board, U.S. Department of Agriculture (ASB-USDA)*

Potatoes Processed[1] in the United States, Eight States In Thousands of Cwt.

States	Storage Season	to Dec. 1	to Jan. 1	to Feb. 1	to Mar. 1	to Apr. 1	to May 1	to June 1	Entire Season
Idaho and	1992-3	22,180	29,080	35,710	42,800	50,090	57,090	----	80,570
Oregon-	1993-4	24,090	30,540	37,150	44,720	53,070	61,440	----	85,780
Malheur	1994-5	26,620	34,230	42,330	49,890	57,990	66,680	----	90,300
Co	1995-6	27,310	35,040	43,260	51,530	59,060	66,690	----	89,250
	1996-7	31,060	38,210	45,420	54,640	62,570	70,720	----	96,970
	1997-8	26,880	33,950	41,050	49,470	57,620	65,750	----	91,450
	1998-9	27,510	34,700	42,670	51,210	60,040	68,550	76,410	92,860
	1999-00	27,970	34,490	40,790	49,220	57,820	66,080	74,110	88,210
	2000-1	29,290	35,720	43,470	50,580	58,910	66,760	75,270	93,460
	2001-2	20,940	27,330	33,620	40,860				
Maine[2]	1992-3	1,195	1,630	2,205	2,720	3,390	4,020	----	5,055
	1993-4	1,350	1,720	2,210	2,505	2,890	3,275	----	4,555
	1994-5	1,505	1,840	2,265	2,540	2,985	3,330	----	4,770
	1995-6	1,455	1,850	2,430	2,850	3,435	3,965	----	5,725
	1996-7	1,790	2,115	2,820	3,280	3,820	4,420	----	6,495
	1997-8	1,250	1,720	2,265	2,735	3,355	3,900	----	5,870
	1998-9	1,430	1,935	2,530	2,985	3,595	4,180	4,705	5,945
	1999-00	1,270	1,700	2,385	3,070	3,765	4,560	5,150	6,670
	2000-1	1,845	2,475	3,105	3,695	4,225	4,760	5,340	7,015
	2001-2	1,935	2,420	3,080	3,665				
Wash. &	1992-3	26,840	31,550	35,950	41,670	46,530	51,630	----	63,510
Oregon-	1993-4	28,260	33,350	39,010	45,020	51,290	57,180	----	70,690
Other	1994-5	28,670	33,480	39,120	46,070	52,940	59,540	----	76,780
	1995-6	30,000	35,170	39,460	45,280	51,730	57,360	----	70,250
	1996-7	31,670	36,660	41,700	48,740	55,570	62,320	----	80,970
	1997-8	28,580	33,990	38,690	46,400	53,720	59,780	----	76,930
	1998-9	33,630	38,890	45,650	53,290	60,930	67,180	74,190	83,730
	1999-00	33,320	39,620	45,500	53,350	61,080	67,230	74,840	83,210
	2000-1	34,770	40,970	47,720	55,250	62,860	69,850	78,010	91,130
	2001-2	29,270	35,310	40,540	47,910				
Other	1992-3	7,140	9,220	11,265	13,305	15,550	17,555	----	25,070
States[3]	1993-4	7,605	9,515	11,605	13,720	16,080	18,705	----	25,690
	1994-5	9,725	13,110	15,630	18,260	21,115	24,060	----	32,260
	1995-6	12,650	15,630	18,815	21,985	25,510	28,610	----	33,580
	1996-7	13,720	17,000	20,645	24,085	27,650	30,830	----	43,100
	1997-8	11,645	13,960	17,115	19,905	23,515	26,365	----	37,842
	1998-9	11,570	14,465	18,030	20,850	24,850	28,190	31,365	39,865
	1999-00	12,455	15,035	17,950	20,855	24,305	27,220	30,410	36,435
	2000-1	12,665	16,215	18,975	22,095	25,410	28,695	31,765	39,020
	2001-2	12,715	15,905	18,765	21,915				
Total	1992-3	57,355	71,480	85,130	100,495	115,560	130,295	----	174,205
	1993-4	61,305	75,125	89,975	105,965	123,330	140,600	----	186,715
	1994-5	66,520	82,660	99,345	116,760	135,030	153,610	----	204,110
	1995-6	71,415	87,690	103,965	121,645	139,735	156,625	----	198,805
	1996-7	78,240	93,985	110,585	130,745	149,610	168,290	----	227,535
	1997-8	68,355	83,620	99,120	118,510	138,210	155,795	----	212,092
	1998-9	74,140	89,990	108,880	128,335	149,415	168,100	186,670	222,400
	1999-00	75,015	90,845	106,625	126,495	146,970	165,090	184,510	214,525
	2000-1	78,570	95,380	113,270	131,620	151,405	170,065	190,385	230,625
	2001-2	64,860	80,965	96,005	114,350				

[1] Total quantity received and used for processing regardless of the state in which the potatoes were produced. Excludes quantities used for potato chips in Maine, Michigan, Minnesota, North Dakota or Wisconsin. [2] Includes Maine grown potatoes only. [3] Michigan, Minnesota, North Dakota and Wisconsin. *Source: National Agricultural Statistics Service, U.S. Department of Agriculture (NASS-USDA)*

Rayon and Other Synthetic Fibers

World Cellulosic Fiber Production In Thousands of Metric Tons

Year	Austria	Brazil	China	Czech Republic	Finland	Germany	India	Japan	Taiwan	United Kingdom	United States	Ex-USSR	World Total
1992	128.3	54.2	249.1	39.3	56.0	139.9	219.9	254.4	139.3	65.0	224.5	292.3	2,327
1993	131.2	56.7	276.2	41.0	56.5	125.1	238.9	244.4	130.8	67.2	244.5	258.3	2,089
1994	134.3	58.6	336.0	33.7	58.5	138.1	239.7	218.9	149.3	67.0	225.0	189.8	2,308
1995	139.4	53.1	435.0	35.0	57.5	143.5	262.1	212.7	139.6	67.1	226.0	188.4	2,423
1996	145.0	34.4	432.0	31.4	49.8	143.6	251.9	198.2	144.7	62.3	213.1	127.3	2,270
1997	145.0	36.4	450.0	27.3	62.0	155.0	242.4	184.1	148.4	70.0	208.1	401.2	2,314
1998	----	29.2	451.5	26.9	----	----	264.4	164.5	142.6	----	165.5	----	2,238
1999	----	34.6	472.1	17.6	----	----	248.5	135.5	143.7	----	134.7	----	2,084
2000[1]	----	36.4	545.9	7.1	----	----	297.5	139.4	141.5	----	158.8	----	2,212
2001[2]	----	38.8	633.0	9.2	----	----	385.7	207.9	148.3	----	172.5	----	2,957

[1] Preliminary. [2] Producing capacity. *Source: Fiber Economics Bureau, Inc. (FEB)*

World Noncellulosic Fiber Production (Except Olefin) In Thousands of Metric Tons

Year	Brazil	China	West Germany	India	Italy/ Malta	Japan	Rep. of Korea	Mexico	Spain	Taiwan[3]	United States[4]	Ex-USSR	World Total
1992	220.2	1,733.7	817.3	530.5	589.9	1,448.8	1,451.4	425.3	257.0	2,042.6	2,980.6	744.8	16,161
1993	233.3	1,871.9	758.8	608.9	551.6	1,365.1	1,592.0	406.5	240.3	2,121.0	3,039.0	669.8	16,585
1994	243.2	2,119.0	807.6	681.1	599.9	1,394.0	1,825.0	484.4	273.6	2,301.5	3,250.3	658.1	17,939
1995	227.4	2,283.7	771.3	738.0	551.3	1,400.0	1,858.2	516.6	252.3	2,410.5	3,238.9	636.1	18,377
1996	229.6	2,729.6	----	916.4	----	1,399.0	2,025.2	584.6	----	2,561.0	3,284.1	1,359.8	19,765
1997	248.3	3,527.2	----	1,240.7	----	1,433.6	2,403.3	612.7	----	2,932.4	3,420.0	----	22,396
1998	268.6	4,406.8	----	1,361.3	----	1,363.6	2,446.0	591.1	----	3,111.5	3,222.7	----	23,278
1999	292.6	5,235.1	----	1,486.1	----	1,299.7	2,592.8	578.9	----	2,927.9	3,169.5	----	24,514
2000[1]	314.9	6,038.7	----	1,501.5	----	1,307.9	2,681.5	600.4	----	3,120.7	3,166.9	----	26,011
2001[2]	388.2	7,812.0	----	1,996.7	----	1,781.0	3,089.2	773.5	----	3,920.3	3,502.0	----	32,455

[1] Preliminary. [2] Producing capacity. [3] Beginning 1995; data for S. Korea and Taiwan. [4] Beginning 1995; data for USA and Canada.
Source: Fiber Economics Bureau, Inc. (FEB)

World Production of Synthetic Fibers In Thousands of Metric Tons

	Noncellulosic Fiber Production (Except Olefin)														
	By Fibers				World Total			Glass Fiber Production							Cigarette
Year	Acrylic & Mod-acrylic	Nylon & Aramid	Polyester	Other Fibers[3]	Yarn & Monofil-aments	Staple, Tow & Fiberfill	Total	Europe	Japan	Other Americas	United States	Total	China	Ex-USSR	Tow Pro-duction
1992	2,365	3,723	9,916	155	7,971	8,188	16,159	442	307	83	700	1,652	75	84	475
1993	2,314	3,684	10,411	178	8,399	8,188	16,587	508	312	86	794	1,865	77	69	482
1994	2,543	3,706	11,468	222	9,087	8,852	17,939	545	313	87	959	2,235	78	54	536
1995	2,446	3,740	11,945	247	9,684	8,693	18,377	567	318	96	981	2,308	85	55	550
1996	2,604	3,858	13,047	256	10,529	9,236	19,765	585	316	94	996	2,387	98	25	584
1997	2,706	4,028	15,406	256	12,093	10,303	22,396	610	328	100	1,007	2,431	75	27	608
1998	2,668	3,794	16,549	267	12,971	10,308	23,278	660	300	96	1,018	2,416	60	30	554
1999	2,513	3,828	17,879	294	13,682	10,832	24,514	674	300	96	1,126	2,538	60	30	544
2000[1]	2,669	4,118	18,912	312	14,698	11,313	26,011	728	280	96	1,143	2,580	60	28	543
2001[2]	3,287	5,279	23,433	456	18,807	13,648	32,455	750	290	100	1,200	2,675	60	25	-----

[1] Preliminary. [2] Producing capacity. [3] Alginate, azion, spandex, saran, etc. *Source: Fiber Economics Bureau, Inc. (FEB)*

Artificial (Cellulosic) Fiber Distribution in the United States In Millions of Pounds

	Yarn & Monofilament					Staple & Tow					Glass
	Producers' Shipments				Domestic	Producers' Shipments				Domestic	Fiber
Year	Domestic	Exports	Total	Imports	Con-sumption	Domestic	Exports	Total	Imports	Con-sumption	Ship-ments
1992	182.9	35.1	218.0	32.1	215.0	260.7	6.9	267.6	85.6	346.3	1,629.7
1993	196.5	31.5	228.0	40.4	236.9	273.6	10.3	283.9	89.5	363.1	1,780.6
1994	190.3	32.9	223.2	32.9	223.2	252.3	30.7	283.0	65.7	318.0	2,114.0
1995	169.3	41.5	210.8	34.0	203.3	259.8	28.7	288.5	40.8	300.6	2,163.0
1996	169.0	49.6	218.6	39.3	208.3	225.3	20.0	245.3	35.3	260.6	2,196.0
1997	145.9	41.2	187.1	42.9	188.8	205.3	60.1	265.4	51.6	256.9	2,275.0
1998	111.2	32.7	143.9	38.1	149.3	184.4	31.4	215.8	47.4	231.8	
1999	85.3	30.0	115.4	28.3	113.6	168.8	29.9	198.7	47.5	216.3	
2000[1]	76.3	37.8	114.0	23.2	99.4	162.3	69.3	231.5	37.5	199.7	

[1] Preliminary. *Source: Fiber Economice Bureau, Inc. (FEB)*

Man-Made Fiber Production in the United States In Millions of Pounds

	Artificial (Cellulosic) Fibers -- Rayon & Acetate			Synthetic (Noncellulosic) Fibers											
				Yarn & Monofilament				Staple & Tow							
Year	Filament Yarn & Monofilament	Staple & Tow	Total Cellulosic	Nylon	Polyester	Olefin	Total Yarn	Nylon	Polyester	Acrylic & Modacrylic	Olefin	Total Staple	Total Noncellulosic	Total Manufactured Fibers	Total Glass Fiber
1992	220	275	495	1,652	1,269	1,496	4,417	904	2,307	439	474	4,124	8,541	9,068	1,953
1993	227	278	505	1,700	1,284	1,631	4,615	959	2,273	433	483	4,148	8,763	9,296	2,061
1994	225	273	498	1,805	1,492	1,839	5,136	935	2,366	442	549	4,292	9,428	9,957	2,159
1995	208	290	498	1,829	1,597	1,870	5,296	874	2,290	432	521	4,117	9,413	9,948	2,282
1996	219	245	464	1,917	1,571	1,951	5,438	883	2,260	465	610	4,217	9,655	9,979	2,326
1997	187	266	453	2,039	1,644	2,058	5,740	797	2,446	461	623	4,327	10,068	10,465	2,408
1998	144	216	360	1,887	1,541	2,212	5,640	799	2,357	346	712	4,214	9,854	10,314	2,490
1999	115	199	314	1,896	1,595	2,278	5,769	787	2,232	316	797	4,132	9,901	10,263	2,570
2000[1]	114	231	345	1,873	1,509	2,406	5,787	733	2,295	339	816	4,183	9,970	10,236	2,738
2001[2]		153	153	1,595	1,170	2,233	4,997	606	1,912	302	721	3,540	8,536		2,638

[1] Preliminary. [2] Estimate. *Source: Fiber Economics Bureau, Inc. (FEB)*

Domestic Distribution of Synethic (Noncellulosic) Fibers in the United States In Millions of Pounds

	Yarn & Monofilament								Staple & Tow								
	Producers' Shipments								Producers' Shipments								
	Domestic								Domestic								
Year	Nylon	Polyester	Olefin	Total	Exports	Total	Imports	Domestic Consumption	Nylon	Polyester	Acrylic & Modacrylic	Olefin	Total	Exports	Total	Imports	Domestic Consumption
1992	1,570.1	1,229.6	1,496.1	4,295.8	194.8	4,490.6	209.3	4,505.1	891.7	2,202.1	322.3	441.0	3,857.1	267.2	4,124.3	397.7	4,255.0
1993	1,612.7	1,228.4	1,631.5	4,472.6	174.6	4,647.2	295.8	4,768.4	907.9	2,157.8	333.0	468.2	3,866.9	297.1	4,164.0	509.0	4,375.9
1994	1,700.0	1,402.8	1,838.2	4,941.0	204.9	5,145.9	377.7	5,318.7	911.7	2,221.3	319.6	489.0	3,941.6	390.9	4,332.5	622.9	4,564.5
1995	1,741.4	1,439.8	1,870.3	5,051.5	259.0	5,310.5	393.6	5,445.1	828.5	2,100.4	266.1	458.0	3,653.0	398.7	4,051.7	624.9	4,277.9
1996	1,801.2	1,428.5	1,954.4	5,183.9	250.7	5,434.6	482.0	5,665.9	843.8	2,015.8	287.9	514.9	3,662.4	465.2	4,127.6	607.7	4,270.1
1997	1,877.1	1,528.4	2,015.4	5,420.9	238.5	5,659.4	589.0	6,009.0	757.2	2,249.7	288.6	541.9	3,837.4	391.9	4,229.3	672.8	4,510.2
1998	1,790.4	1,425.7	2,166.9	5,383.0	218.1	5,601.1	637.3	6,020.3	762.8	2,105.0	267.3	596.4	3,731.5	340.2	4,071.7	777.4	4,508.9
1999	1,758.9	1,463.4	2,251.0	5,473.3	243.9	5,717.2	719.2	6,192.5	756.4	2,078.0	232.5	725.5	3,792.4	337.8	4,130.2	788.0	4,580.4
2000[1]	1,718.5	1,416.6	2,332.5	5,467.6	250.4	5,718.0	789.9	6,257.5	674.1	2,063.9	243.8	757.3	3,739.0	299.9	4,038.9	726.7	4,465.7

[1] Preliminary. *Source: Fiber Economice Bureau, Inc. (FEB)*

Mill Consumption of Fiber & Products and Per Capita Consumption in the U.S. In Millions of Pounds

	Cellulosic Fibers				Noncellulosic Fibers								Per Capita[4] Mill Consumption (Lbs.)				
Year	Yarn & Monofilament	Staple & Tow	Net Waste	Total Cellulosic	Noncellulosic	Net Waste	Total Noncellulosic	Total Manufactured Fibers[2]	Cotton	Wool	Other Fibers[3]	Grand Total	Man-made Fibers[2]	Cotton	Wool	Other Fibers[3]	Total All Fibers
1992	215.0	346.3	-3.6	557.7	8,760.1	181.1	8,941.2	9,498.9	4,920.7	171.5	76.7	14,667.8	41.5	28.5	1.3	2.5	73.7
1993	236.9	363.1	-5.6	594.4	9,144.3	189.8	9,334.1	9,928.5	5,000.0	179.5	74.0	15,182.0	43.2	29.5	1.4	2.7	76.7
1994	223.2	318.0	-21.4	519.8	9,883.2	102.4	9,985.6	10,505.5	5,374.8	171.9	54.8	16,107.0	44.5	30.9	1.4	2.7	79.5
1995	203.3	300.6	-22.7	481.2	9,936.9	76.3	10,013.2	10,494.4	5,110.3	161.8	65.6	15,832.1	44.4	29.8	1.4	2.5	78.1
1996	208.2	260.7	-12.8	456.1	10,215.1	99.8	10,314.9	10,771.0	5,339.5	164.4	46.0	16,320.9	45.1	30.2	1.4	1.8	78.5
1997	188.8	256.9	-18.4	427.3	10,335.7	100.4	10,436.1	10,863.4	5,447.6	164.4	42.8	16,518.2	45.8	32.5	1.4	2.0	81.8
1998	149.3	231.8	-18.5	362.6	10,530.4	162.9	10,693.3	11,055.9	4,993.4	125.7	44.6	16,219.6	47.4	33.6	1.3	1.8	84.0
1999	113.6	216.3	-13.3	316.6	10,701.4	176.9	10,878.3	11,194.9	4,914.1	85.3	40.9	16,235.2	48.5	35.1	1.2	1.9	86.7
2000[1]	99.4	199.7	-15.1	284.0	10,830.9	190.4	11,021.3	11,305.3	4,409.2	82.9	38.8	15,836.2	49.5	34.6	1.3	2.2	87.6

[1] Preliminary. [2] Excludes Glass Fiber. [3] Includes silk, linen, jute and sisal & others. [4] Mill consumption plus inports less exports of semimanufactured and unmanufactured products. *Source: Fiber Economics Bureau, Inc. (FEB)*

Producer Price Index of Grey Synthetic Broadwovens (1982 = 100)

Year	Jan.	Feb.	Mar.	Apr.	May	June	July	Aug.	Sept.	Oct.	Nov.	Dec.	Average
1989	114.3	112.0	112.2	112.2	112.1	113.1	114.7	115.0	115.0	115.8	115.9	115.3	114.0
1990	115.6	115.7	115.6	115.7	115.5	115.6	115.7	115.2	115.3	115.6	115.8	116.1	115.6
1991	115.7	114.7	114.4	114.1	114.3	113.9	114.8	116.4	116.5	116.5	116.8	118.2	115.5
1992	119.0	119.9	120.3	120.9	121.8	122.0	122.6	122.0	121.7	120.8	119.4	119.9	120.9
1993	119.6	119.1	119.1	119.2	117.1	118.4	118.0	118.0	116.9	117.3	115.2	114.5	117.7
1994	113.5	112.8	112.9	113.2	113.2	113.3	113.1	113.3	114.1	111.8	112.9	113.8	113.2
1995	114.8	116.8	116.7	116.3	116.6	117.1	115.4	114.8	116.9	116.4	114.7	116.2	116.1
1996	114.3	114.1	116.9	117.9	116.8	115.7	116.1	117.1	116.9	117.2	116.6	117.0	116.4
1997	117.9	118.3	118.3	117.9	118.4	119.0	118.8	118.5	119.4	118.7	117.6	119.6	118.5
1998[1]	120.1	120.4	119.7	120.2	119.8	119.7	118.0	118.1	116.7	114.2	115.1	115.0	118.1

[1] Preliminary. *Source: Bureau of Labor Statistics, U.S. Department of Commerce (BLS) (0337-03)*

Rice

Rice, the world's second most popular foodstuff after wheat, is generally consumed where it is produced. Global milled rice trade in calendar 2002 of 23 million metric tons was marginally lower than 2001, but about 15% below the record high 27.6 million tons in 1998. U.S. 2002 exports estimated at 2.7 million tons compare with 2.65 million in 2001 and 3.2 million in 1998.. The U.S. ranks third among the top exporters.

Asia accounts for most of the world's exports with Thailand the largest exporter at a near record 7 million tons in 2002. China's exports have fallen in recent years, from 3.7 million in 1998 to about 2 million in 2001 and 2002. Vietnam is now the second largest exporter: 4 million tons in 2002. Importing nations are numerous, with only three nations forecast to import one million tons or more in 2002; Indonesia is consistently the largest importer although the total has dropped of late with only 1.6 million in 2002 vs. 5.8 million tons in 1998. On a regional basis, the Middle east tends to be the largest importer, notably Iran.. For U.S. rice exports, the Western hemisphere is the primary destination and is generally higher priced than Asian rice.

World rice stocks have fallen; carryover for the 2001/02 marketing year of about 126 million tons compares with 137 million a year earlier. China generally holds more than half of carryover supplies. World rough rice production in 2001/02 of 586 million tons (393 million, milled) compares with 589 million (395 million, milled) in 2000/01 and record high 607 million in 1999/00. World consumption of a record high 404.6 million tons (milled) in 2001/02 compares with 401 million in 2000/01. China is the largest producer and consumer and India is second. China's production has slipped since the late 1990's, but could quicken in the years ahead reflecting a possible change in traditional planting methods. Previously, a single rice variety was used that was often susceptible to disease, but increasing use of a mixture of rice varieties that offers resistance to fungus could , it is believed, nearly doubled average yield.

Estimated U.S. rice production in 2001/02 (August-July) of a record large 209.7 million cwt compares with previous year's 190.9 million cwt, the increase reflecting federal subsidies that abetted larger planted acreage of 3.3 million acres vs. 3.1 million in 2000/01 and an average yield 6,374 pounds/acre vs. 6,281 pounds in 200/01. Domestic use was put at a near record high 121 million cwt in 2001/02 vs. 117.2 million in 2000/01. Carryover stocks for the 2001/02 season were forecast at a record large 42.2 million cwt vs. 28.5 million a year earlier.

The U.S. average farm price in 2001/02 was forecast at $4.00-$4.50 per cwt vs. $5.56 in 2000/01 and farm prices that averaged over $9 per cwt in the late 1990's.

Futures Markets

Rough rice futures and options are traded on the Chicago Board of trade (CBOT).

World Rice Supply and Distribution In Thousands of Metric Tons

	Imports							Utilization			Ending Stocks		
Year	Brazil	Indonesia	European Union	Iran	Saudi Arabia	Unaccounted	Total	China	India	Total	China	India	Total
1996-7	849	839	1,761	1,288	814	1,621	17,815	131,954	81,212	379,302	88,500	9,500	115,558
1997-8	1,555	5,765	1,791	844	775	997	27,670	132,517	77,552	379,664	93,000	10,500	126,282
1998-9	781	3,729	3,729	1,313	750	1,638	24,925	133,570	81,154	387,345	96,000	12,000	133,066
1999-00[1]	700	1,500	1,500	1,100	992	1,877	22,896	133,763	82,450	398,505	98,500	17,716	143,014
2000-1[2]	500	1,300	1,800	1,000	900	2,050	23,705	134,336	83,500	402,999	94,225	18,916	137,009
2001-2[3]	500	1,600		1,250	875	1,117	22,514	134,610	85,000	404,200	85,125	20,616	125,417

[1] Preliminary. [2] Estimate. [3] Forecast. *Source: Foreign Agricultural Service, U.S. Department of Agriculture (FAS-USDA)*

World Production of Rough Rice In Thousands of Metric Tons

Year	Bangladesh	Brazil	Burma	China	India	Indonesia	Japan	Rep. of Korea	Pakistan	Philippines	Thailand	Vietnam	World Total
1996-7	28,326	9,504	15,517	195,100	121,980	49,360	12,930	7,123	6,461	11,177	20,700	27,277	563,461
1997-8	28,296	8,462	15,345	200,700	123,822	49,237	12,532	7,365	6,500	9,982	23,500	28,930	574,365
1998-9	29,784	11,582	16,000	198,714	129,013	50,400	11,201	6,800	7,012	10,268	23,620	30,467	585,712
1999-00[1]	34,602	11,424	17,000	198,480	134,233	52,919	11,470	7,066	7,735	11,957	25,000	31,706	607,545
2000-1[2]	36,547	10,385	18,571	187,909	129,463	50,633	11,863	7,197	7,051	12,515	25,500	31,020	591,159
2001-2[3]	34,503	11,000	17,000	181,000	133,513	51,424	11,332	7,503	5,611	12,692	25,500	31,212	584,865

[1] Preliminary. [2] Estimate. [3] Forecast. *Source: Foreign Agricultural Service, U.S. Department of Agriculture (FAS-USDA)*

World Exports of Rice (Milled Basis) In Thousands of Metric Tons

Year	Argentina	Australia	Burma	China	European Union	Guyana	India	Pakistan	Thailand	Uruguay	Vietnam	United States	World Total
1996-7	530	657	15	938	1,408	262	2,100	1,834	5,216	645	3,327	2,488	20,154
1997-8	599	547	94	3,734	1,388	249	4,666	1,994	6,367	628	3,776	3,156	27,670
1998-9	654	667	57	2,708	1,343	252	2,752	1,838	6,679	681	4,555	2,648	24,925
1999-00[1]	473	617	159	2,951	1,362	167	1,449	2,026	6,549	642	3,370	2,756	22,896
2000-1[2]	275	575	500	1,700	1,372	175	1,600	2,100	7,500	700	3,600	2,650	23,705
2001-2[3]	250	700	500	1,500		150	2,300	1,100	7,000	650	4,000	2,750	22,514

[1] Preliminary. [2] Estimate. [3] Forecast. *Source: Foreign Agricultural Service, U.S. Department of Agriculture (FAS-USDA)*

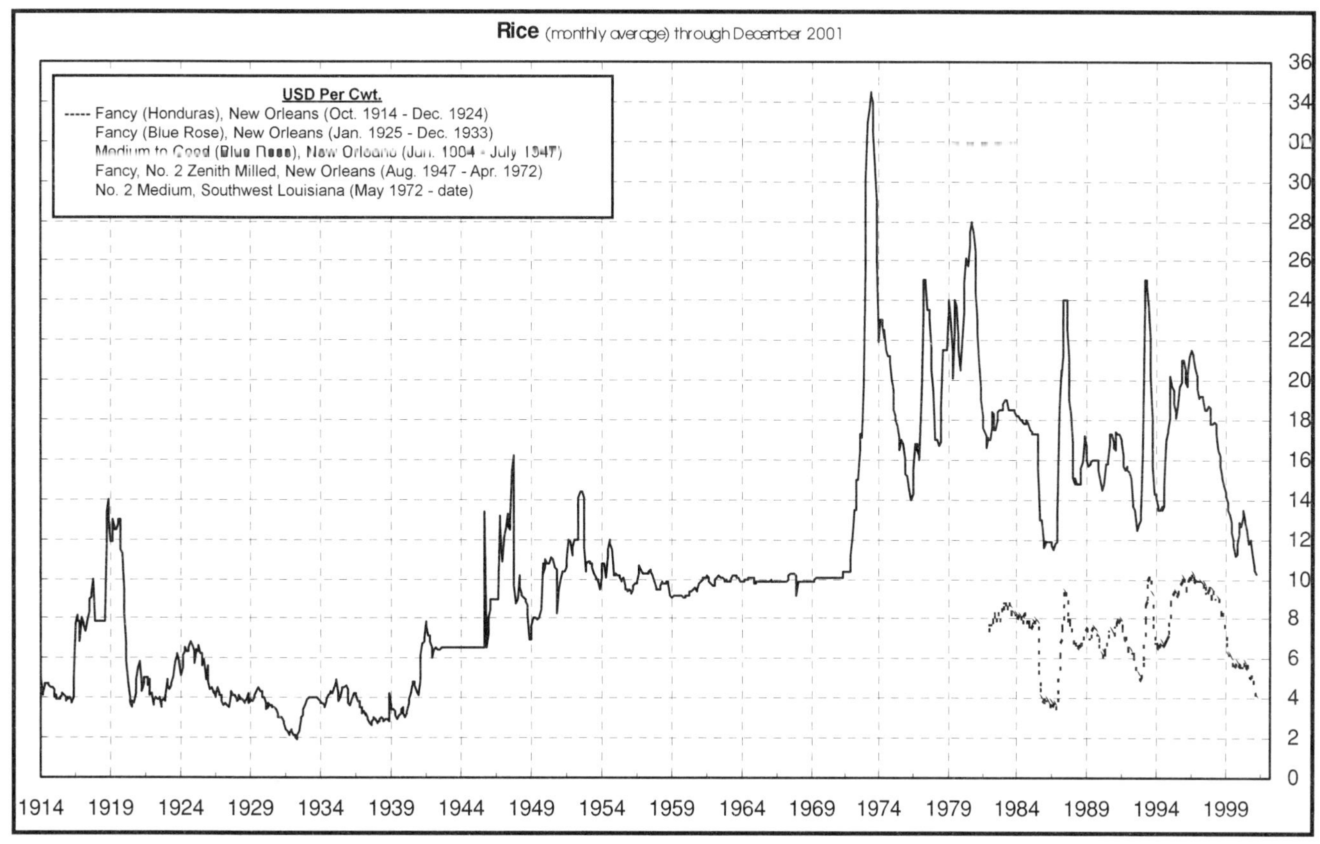

Average Wholesale Price of Rice No. 2 (Medium)[1] Southwest Louisiana In Dollars Per Cwt. Bagged

Year	Aug.	Sept.	Oct.	Nov.	Dec.	Jan.	Feb.	Mar.	Apr.	May	June	July	Average
1992-3	14.50	14.00	14.50	14.15	13.40	13.40	13.00	12.80	12.40	11.94	12.00	12.00	13.15
1993-4	12.25	12.45	15.65	21.95	24.00	24.00	23.88	23.80	24.00	23.70	22.00	20.00	20.65
1994-5	18.30	15.88	15.00	15.00	14.00	13.80	14.16	14.38	14.38	14.70	14.75	14.55	14.91
1995-6	15.44	17.50	20.25	20.13	20.00	20.00	19.88	19.25	19.13	19.38	19.40	19.50	19.15
1996-7	19.50	19.50	19.25	19.25	19.00	18.81	19.19	19.25	19.25	19.25	18.40	19.00	19.14
1997-8	18.25	18.35	18.63	19.00	19.00	19.00	19.00	18.20	18.00	18.13	18.50	18.50	18.55
1998-9	18.35	18.75	19.00	19.00	20.00	20.00	20.00	20.00	20.00	20.00	20.00	20.00	19.59
1999-00	18.60	17.50	14.88	14.70	14.67	14.35	14.00	13.83	13.75	13.40	12.50	12.63	14.57
2000-1	13.00	12.34	12.48	12.41	12.38	12.38	12.25	12.00	11.82	11.53	11.25	11.25	12.09
2001-2[2]	11.06	11.50	11.50	11.50	11.08								11.33

[1] U.S. No. 2 -- broken not to exceed 4%. [2] Preliminary. *Source: Economic Research Service, U.S. Department of Agriculture (ERS-USDA)*

Average Price Received by Farmers for Rice (Rough) in the United States In Dollars Per Cwt.

Year	Aug.	Sept.	Oct.	Nov.	Dec.	Jan.	Feb.	Mar.	Apr.	May	June	July	Average[2]
1992-3	6.60	6.41	6.40	6.42	6.39	6.36	6.06	5.64	5.52	5.24	5.02	4.92	5.89
1993-4	5.19	5.21	6.10	8.06	8.91	8.98	10.10	10.20	9.93	10.00	8.88	7.80	7.98
1994-5	6.87	6.89	6.47	6.53	6.56	6.78	6.71	6.64	6.70	6.75	7.03	7.17	6.78
1995-6	7.64	7.95	8.77	9.12	9.36	9.33	9.10	9.31	9.34	9.69	9.74	9.68	9.15
1996-7	10.10	10.00	9.66	9.41	9.82	9.95	10.10	10.20	10.30	10.20	9.90	10.00	9.96
1997-8	9.94	9.92	10.00	9.82	9.77	9.57	9.75	9.67	9.40	9.38	9.58	9.58	9.70
1998-9	9.01	9.42	9.31	9.02	9.10	9.09	9.02	8.93	8.49	8.21	8.25	8.26	8.89
1999-00	6.94	5.78	5.97	6.02	6.08	6.02	5.88	5.71	5.75	5.63	5.80	5.65	5.93
2000-1	5.60	5.72	5.61	5.63	5.60	5.84	5.72	5.55	5.59	5.15	5.01	5.25	5.56
2001-2[1]	5.10	4.78	4.36	4.08	4.09								4.48

[1] Preliminary. [2] Weighted average by sales. *Source: Economic Research Service, U.S. Department of Agriculture (ERS-USDA)*

Salient Statistics of Rice, Rough & Milled (Rough Equivalent) in the United States   In Millions of Cwt.

Crop Year Beginning Aug. 1	Supply: Stocks Aug. 1	Supply: Pro-duction	Supply: Imports	Supply: Total Supply	Disappearance: Domestic: Food	Domestic: Brewers	Domestic: Seed	Domestic: Total	Resi-dual	Exports	Total Disap-pearance	CCC Stocks July 31	Government Support Program: Put Under Price Support	Loan Rate ($ Per Cwt.): Rough[3]: Long	Rough[3]: Medium	Rough[3]: All Classes	Milled Long
1996-7	25.0	171.6	10.5	207.2	81.0	15.8	3.9	101.6	2.0	78.3	179.9	0	68.9	6.68	6.17	6.50	10.77
1997-8	27.2	183.0	9.3	219.5	84.2	16.0	4.1	103.3	.2	87.7	191.6	0	67.6	6.67	6.14	6.50	10.69
1998-9	27.9	184.4	10.6	223.0	87.3	16.0	4.4	114.0	11.4	86.8	200.9	0	80.2	6.67	6.14	6.50	10.71
1999-00	22.1	206.0	10.1	238.2	90.1	16.0	4.0	121.4	6.5	88.9	210.7	0	107.6	6.67	6.12	6.50	10.66
2000-1[1]	27.5	190.9	10.9	229.2	113.1	[4]	4.1	117.2	[4]	83.5	200.7	0		6.66	6.12	6.50	10.71
2001-2[2]	28.5	213.0	11.0	252.5	118.0	[4]	4.1	122.1	[4]	88.0	210.1	0		6.67	6.09	6.50	10.69

[1] Preliminary. [2] Forecast. [3] Loan rate for each class of rice is the sum of the whole kernels' loan rate weighted by its milling yield (average 56%) and the broken kernels' loan rate weighted by its milling yield (average 12%). Source: Economic Research Service, U.S. Department of Agriculture (ERS)

Acreage, Yield, Production and Prices of Rice in the United States

Crop Year	Acreage Harvested (1,000 Acres): Southern States	Acreage: California	Acreage: United States	Yield Per Harvested Acre (In Lbs.): California	Yield: United States	Production (1,000 Cwt.): Southern States	Production: California	Production: United States	Value of Production $1,000	Wholesale Prices ($ Per Cwt.): Arkansas[2]	Wholesale Prices: Houston[3]	Milled Rice, Average C.I.F. at Rotterdam ($ Per Metric Ton): U.S. No. 2[4]	Thai "A"[5]	Thai "B"[5]
1996-7	2,304	500	2,804	7,490	6,120	134,140	37,459	171,599	1,690,270	19.02	20.95	428	----	380
1997-8	2,587	516	3,103	8,250	5,897	140,446	42,546	182,992	1,756,136	18.14	19.61	417	----	345
1998-9	2,799	458	3,257	6,850	5,663	153,057	31,386	184,443	1,654,157	19.04	18.05	368	----	333
1999-00	3,007	505	3,512	7,270	5,866	169,337	36,690	206,027	1,231,207	15.01	15.33	272	----	278
2000-1	2,491	548	3,039	7,940	6,281	147,351	43,521	190,872	1,049,961	11.75	14.92	274	----	234
2001-2[1]	2,819	471	3,290	8,200	6,374	171,087	38,622	209,709	895,757	11.30	13.89	226	----	226

[1] Preliminary. [2] F.O.B. mills, Arkansas, medium. [3] Houston, Texas (long grain). [4] Milled, 4%, container, FAS. [5] SWR, 100%, bulk.
NA = Not available. *Source: Economic Research Service, U.S. Department of Agriculture (ERS-USDA)*

U.S. Exports of Milled Rice, by Country of Destination   In Thousands of Metric Tons

Year Beginning October	Canada	Haiti	Iran	Ivory Coast	Jamaica	Mexico	Nether-lands	Peru	Saudi Arabia	South Africa	Switzer-land	United Kingdom	Total
1995-6	172.2	149.6	24.5	61.3	63.1	359.1	113.9	97.8	141.5	169.9	80.3	85.4	2,826
1996-7	163.7	178.7	0	35.6	27.4	381.3	54.0	35.1	150.9	108.5	64.2	101.0	2,561
1997-8	175.8	160.0	0	32.3	26.7	413.7	54.6	149.3	123.1	74.4	22.8	105.9	3,309
1998-9	174.9	219.9	0	13.9	17.4	353.7	44.0	103.9	113.0	77.9	25.0	110.3	3,076
1999-00	181.1	221.0	0	21.1	38.2	525.8	50.6	19.5	164.8	70.6	30.2	141.9	3,307
2000-1[1]	183.3	212.4	0	22.2	32.0	516.0	50.8	1.0	158.4	65.9	33.2	104.7	3,158

[1] Preliminary. *Source: Economic Research Service, U.S. Department of Agriculture (ERS-USDA)*

U.S. Rice Exports by Export Program   In Thousands of Metric Tons

Fiscal Year	PL 480	Section 416	CCC Credit Pro-grams[2]	CCC African Reliel Exports	EEP[3]	Export Pro-grams[4]	Exports Outside Specified Export Programs	Total U.S. Rice Exports	% Export Programs as a Share of Total Exports
1996	179	0	141	0	23	214	2,613	2,826	8
1997	115	0	80	0	0	129	2,431	2,560	5
1998	183	0	499	0	0	194	3,116	3,310	6
1999	515	0	192	0	0	561	2,505	3,066	18
2000	216	147	225	0	0	394	2,913	3,307	12
2001[1]	144	0		0	0	205	2,953	3,158	7

[1] Preliminary. [2] May not completely reflect exports made under these programs. [3] Sales not shipments. [4] adjusted for estimated overlap between CCC export credit and EEP shipments. *Source: Economice Research Service, U.S. Department of Agriculture (ERS-USDA)*

Production of Rice (Rough) in the United States, by Type and Variety   In Thousands of Cwt.

Year	Long Grain	Medium Grain	Short Grain	Total	Year	Long Grain	Medium Grain	Short Grain	Total
1992	128,015	50,633	1,010	179,658	1997	124,485	57,091	1,416	182,992
1993	103,064	51,873	1,173	156,110	1998	139,328	43,404	1,711	184,443
1994	133,445	63,390	944	197,779	1999	151,863	50,540	3,624	206,027
1995	121,730	51,241	900	173,871	2000	128,756	59,514	2,602	190,872
1996	113,629	56,901	1,069	171,599	2001[1]	162,260	45,584	1,865	209,709

[1] Preliminary. *Source: National Agricultural Statistics Service, U.S. Department of Agriculture (NASS-USDA)*

Rubber

According to the International Rubber Study Group, world production of natural rubber in 2000 was 6.81 million metric tonnes. That represented a decline of less than one percent from 1999. Estates production of natural rubber in 2000 was 1.61 million tonnes, an increase of less than one percent from 1999. Smallholdings production of rubber was 5.2 million tonnes, down less than one percent from 1999. In the January-April 2001 period, world production of natural rubber was 2.38 million tonnes. Estates production of rubber in the same period was 540,000 tonnes and smallholdings production was 1.84 million tonnes.

World consumption of natural rubber in 2000 was 7.34 million tonnes, an increase of 10 percent from 1999. In the January-April 2001 period, consumption of natural rubber was 2.38 million tonnes. Producer stocks of natural rubber at the end of April 2001 were 720,000 tonnes, up 12 percent from the previous year. At the end of 2000, producer stocks were 680,000 tonnes. Consumer reported stocks of rubber at the end of April 2001 were 418,000 tonnes, up 6 percent from the year before. Consumer stocks at the end of 2000 were 450,000 tonnes. Stocks afloat in April 2001 were 300,000 tonnes, down 55 percent from a year earlier. At the end of 2000, rubber stocks afloat were 340,000 tonnes. World stocks of natural rubber in April 2001 were 2.06 million tonnes, down 5 percent from a year ago.

World production of synthetic rubber in 2000 was 10.8 million tonnes, up 5 percent from 1999. Production of synthetic rubber in the January-April 2001 period was 3.64 million tonnes. Global consumption of synthetic rubber in 2000 was 10.7 million tonnes, up 5 percent from the previous year. In the first four months of 2001, world consumption of synthetic rubber was 3.49 million tonnes.

Reported world stocks of synthetic rubber at the end of April 2001 were 1.26 million tonnes. At the end of April 2000, stocks were 1.11 million tonnes. Russian Federation stocks of synthetic rubber in April 2001 were 230,000 tonnes. A year earlier they were 210,000 tonnes. China's stocks of synthetic rubber at the end of April 2001 were 130,000 tonnes, unchanged from the previous year. Stocks elsewhere in April 2001 were 810,000 tonnes, up 4 percent from the year before. Synthetic rubber stocks afloat were 300,000 tonnes in April, up 3 percent from the year before. Total world stocks of synthetic rubber in April 2001 were 2.73 million tonnes, up 8 percent from the year before. Stocks at the end of 2000 were 2.58 million tonnes.

U.S. consumption of natural and synthetic rubber in 2000 was 3.35 million tonnes. up 4 percent from 2000. In the first four months of 2001, U.S. consumption of natural and synthetic rubber was 975,000 tonnes. China's consumption of natural and synthetic rubber in 2000 was 2.53 million tonnes, up 19 percent from the year before. Japan's consumption in 2000 was 1.89 million tonnes, up 1 percent from the previous year. Russian Federation consumption of rubber in 2000 was 515,500 tonnes, up 14 percent from 1999. Consumption of rubber by Germany in 2000 was 889,000 tonnes, up 7 percent from the previous year. Rubber consumption by India in 2000 was 809,000 tonnes, up 3 percent from the previous year. Rubber consumption by Canada was 383,000 tonnes, up 6 percent from the previous year. Other large users include France, Italy and South Korea.

The U.S, stockpile of natural rubber held in the national Stockpile Center in April 2001 was 69,200 tonnes, the same as the previous year. Stocks of natural rubber held by India were 179,000 tonnes while stocks held by Japan were 88,700 tonnes. U.S. reported stocks of synthetic rubber in April 2001 were 476,000 tonnes, up 18 percent from the year before. Stocks of synthetic rubber in Japan in April 2001 were 437,100 tonnes while stocks in France were 240,100 tonnes.

The major producers of natural rubber are Thailand, Indonesia and Malaysia. Thailand's production of natural rubber in 2000 was 2.35 million tonnes, up 9 percent from a year ago. Production of natural rubber in Malaysia in 2000 was 615,400 tonnes, down 20 percent from a year ago. Indonesia's production of natural rubber in 2000 was 1.26 million tonnes, down 3 percent from the year before. Production of rubber by India was 629,000 tonnes, up 1 percent from a year ago. Natural rubber production by China was 445,000 tonnes, down 3 percent from the previous year. Production by Vietnam in 2000 was 269,000 tonnes, up 17 percent from the year before.

Futures Markets

Natural Rubber and Rubber Index futures are traded on the Osaka Mercantile Exchange (OME). Rubber futures are traded on the Shanghai Metal Exchange (SME) and the Tokyo Commodity Exchange (TOCOM).

U.S. Imports of Natural Rubber (Includes Latex & Guayule) In Thousands of Metric Tons

Year	Jan.	Feb.	Mar.	Apr.	May	June	July	Aug.	Sept.	Oct.	Nov.	Dec.	Total
1992	77.5	75.2	84.7	64.7	79.0	73.8	80.5	77.2	73.9	81.3	68.1	77.5	913.4
1993	95.3	79.9	93.9	86.3	74.1	81.2	83.6	77.8	69.2	73.4	86.0	86.9	987.6
1994	87.5	74.7	102.6	78.9	88.3	77.8	66.7	85.0	78.8	89.3	70.0	76.0	975.6
1995	81.7	86.9	102.3	90.2	94.1	93.4	78.0	81.0	81.5	89.2	79.1	68.7	1,026.1
1996	105.4	86.1	82.2	90.6	65.1	70.4	79.0	81.0	82.1	113.6	73.5	85.0	1,014.0
1997	94.2	92.0	93.9	88.2	93.0	65.1	76.8	90.1	87.5	86.8	87.6	89.0	1,044.2
1998	104.4	76.6	102.8	81.0	98.0	92.9	96.4	100.8	123.2	104.8	84.5	111.4	1,176.8
1999	91.8	90.7	93.4	101.6	84.8	80.0	76.6	112.2	88.7	127.5	83.1	85.9	1,116.3
2000	127.4	88.2	114.1	107.9	114.9	120.1	65.9	96.2	79.2	96.2	92.2	89.3	1,191.6
2001[1]	85.2	69.1	93.9	80.0	74.9								967.4

[1] Preliminary. *Source: International Rubber Study Group (IRSG)*

World Production[1] of Rubber In Thousands of Metric Tons

	Natural								Synthetic				
Year	China	India	Indo-nesia	Malaysia	Sri Lanka	Thailand	Vietnam	World Total	Ger-many	Japan	United States	Russia[3]	World Total
1991	296.4	360.2	1,284.0	1,255.7	103.9	1,341.2	87.0	5,160	504.4	1,377.3	2,050.0	2,125.3	9,290
1992	309.3	383.0	1,387.0	1,173.2	106.1	1,531.0	114.0	5,440	544.7	1,389.9	2,300.0	1,610.5	9,300
1993	326.1	428.1	1,300.5	1,074.3	104.2	1,553.4	114.0	5,310	569.7	1,309.8	2,180.0	1,102.5	8,600
1994	374.0	464.0	1,358.5	1,100.6	105.3	1,717.9	156.0	5,720	621.6	1,349.0	2,390.0	631.9	8,870
1995	424.0	499.6	1,454.5	1,089.3	105.7	1,804.8	155.0	6,070	480.0	1,497.6	2,530.0	836.9	9,480
1996	430.0	540.1	1,527.0	1,082.5	112.5	1,970.4	220.0	6,440	548.1	1,519.9	2,486.0	775.1	9,760
1997	444.0	580.3	1,504.8	971.1	105.8	2,032.7	212.0	6,460	555.1	1,591.5	2,589.0	724.9	10,080
1998	450.0	591.1	1,714.0	885.7	95.7	2,075.9	218.0	6,840	619.0	1,520.1	2,600.0	621.0	9,880
1999	460.0	620.1	1,599.2	768.9	96.6	2,154.6	230.0	6,810	720.1	1,576.7	2,354.0	737.0	10,300
2000[2]	445.0	629.0	1,556.0	615.4	87.6	2,346.4	269.0	6,810	831.6	1,591.7	2,385.0	792.6	10,790

[1] Including rubber in the form of latex. [2] Preliminary. [3] Formerly part of the U.S.S.R., data reported separately until 1992.
Source: International Rubber Study Group (IRSG)

World Consumption of Natural and Synthetic Rubber In Thousands of Metric Tons

	Natural							Synthetic					
Year	Brazil	France	Ger-many	Japan	United Kingdom	United States	World Total	France	Ger-many	Japan	United Kingdom	United States	World Total
1991	122.8	183.0	210.7	689.5	119.0	755.8	5,060	342.0	502.0	1,118.5	201.0	1,768.1	9,220
1992	123.4	179.0	212.8	685.4	124.5	910.2	5,320	365.4	506.0	1,080.6	231.0	1,959.6	9,360
1993	131.7	168.5	174.9	631.0	119.0	966.7	5,430	314.7	488.0	1,022.0	211.0	2,001.0	8,630
1994	144.7	179.8	186.4	639.8	135.0	1,001.7	5,650	400.1	512.2	1,026.2	220.0	2,117.6	8,820
1995	155.2	176.0	211.7	692.0	118.0	1,003.9	5,950	430.2	426.4	1,085.0	226.0	2,172.0	9,270
1996	155.0	182.2	193.0	714.5	111.0	1,001.7	6,110	436.1	478.0	1,124.5	230.0	2,186.6	9,590
1997	160.0	192.3	212.0	713.0	119.0	1,044.1	6,460	416.2	501.0	1,163.0	235.0	2,322.7	10,000
1998	160.0	223.0	247.0	707.3	139.0	1,157.4	6,540	451.4	569.0	1,115.7	177.0	2,354.4	9,880
1999	170.0	252.7	226.0	734.2	130.0	1,117.0	6,660	434.3	604.0	1,132.9	189.0	2,113.0	10,180
2000[1]	210.0	308.6	250.0	751.8	131.0	1,191.0	7,340	481.5	639.0	1,137.5	193.0	2,163.0	10,730

[1] Preliminary. *Source: International Rubber Study Group (IRSG)*

World Stocks[1] of Natural & Synthetic Rubber (by Countries) on January 1 In Thousands of Metric Tons

		In Producing Countries							In Consuming Countries (Reported Stocks)				
Year	Total Synthetic	Africa	Indo-nesia	Malaysia	Sri Lanka	Thai-land	Vietnam	Total Natural	Brazil	India	Japan	United States	Total
1992	963	18.4	110	196.1	17.3	89.3	9.0	500	6.0	106.0	92.7	109.4	443
1993	1,004	19.6	110	187.2	16.0	89.0	12.0	560	17.0	90.9	82.9	108.0	442
1994	949	21.6	110	159.2	17.2	115.6	12.0	570	25.0	96.4	85.4	71.3	410
1995	915	17.0	110	187.0	16.5	96.5	19.0	480	17.0	94.1	72.9	45.2	363
1996	988	21.0	110	175.6	17.0	113.0	20.0	490	13.0	127.4	77.1	67.1	414
1997	1,057	20.5	70	190.3	17.6	147.7	28.0	510	16.0	123.4	86.8	79.3	430
1998	1,081	25.5	40	209.5	17.9	159.4	28.0	510	14.0	157.0	87.2	57.2	386
1999	1,116	27.6	30	234.2	18.6	209.5	36.0	750	35.0	194.0	58.0	70.4	428
2000	1,103	28.7	33	236.6	18.6	250.9	16.0	880	34.0	215.1	79.1	46.0	443
2001[1]	1,170	31.0	110	212.7	18.7	188.6	13.0	680	36.0	203.3	95.2	46.6	450

[1] Preliminary. *Source: International Rubber Study Group (IRSG)*

Net Exports of Natural Rubber from Producing Areas In Thousands of Metric Tons

Year	Cam-bodia	Guat-emala[4]	Indo-nesia	Liberia	Malaysia	Nigeria	Sri Lanka	Thai-land	Vietnam	Other Africa[2]	Other Asia[3]	World Total
1991	21.0	14.3	1,220.0	32.0	1,041.2	63.0	76.4	1,231.9	62.9	126.0	44.0	3,890
1992	20.0	15.7	1,268.1	30.0	939.1	70.4	78.6	1,412.9	80.9	135.0	25.9	4,010
1993	21.0	16.9	1,214.3	45.0	769.8	79.7	69.6	1,396.8	96.7	136.0	32.6	3,880
1994	32.0	22.3	1,244.8	10.0	782.1	49.6	69.1	1,605.0	135.5	145.0	28.9	4,250
1995	30.0	23.2	1,323.8	13.0	777.5	99.2	68.2	1,635.5	138.1	140.0	31.1	4,340
1996	31.0	29.2	1,434.3	30.0	709.7	48.8	72.1	1,763.0	194.5	167.0	41.0	4,590
1997	32.0	28.3	1,403.8	67.2	586.8	53.0	61.4	1,837.1	194.2	186.0	38.0	4,570
1998	33.0	25.2	1,641.2	75.0	424.9	74.0	41.4	1,839.4	190.6	182.0	39.0	4,710
1999	34.0	26.7	1,494.6	100.0	435.5	38.0	42.7	1,886.3	230.0	206.0	38.3	4,670
2000[1]	35.0	30.0	1,379.6	127.0	196.4	43.0	32.6	2,166.2	256.0	202.0	38.6	4,970

[1] Preliminary. [2] Includes Cameroon, Cote d'Ivoire, Gabon, Ghana and Zaire. [3] Includes Myanmar, Papua New Guinea and the Philippines.
Source: International Rubber Study Group (IRSG)

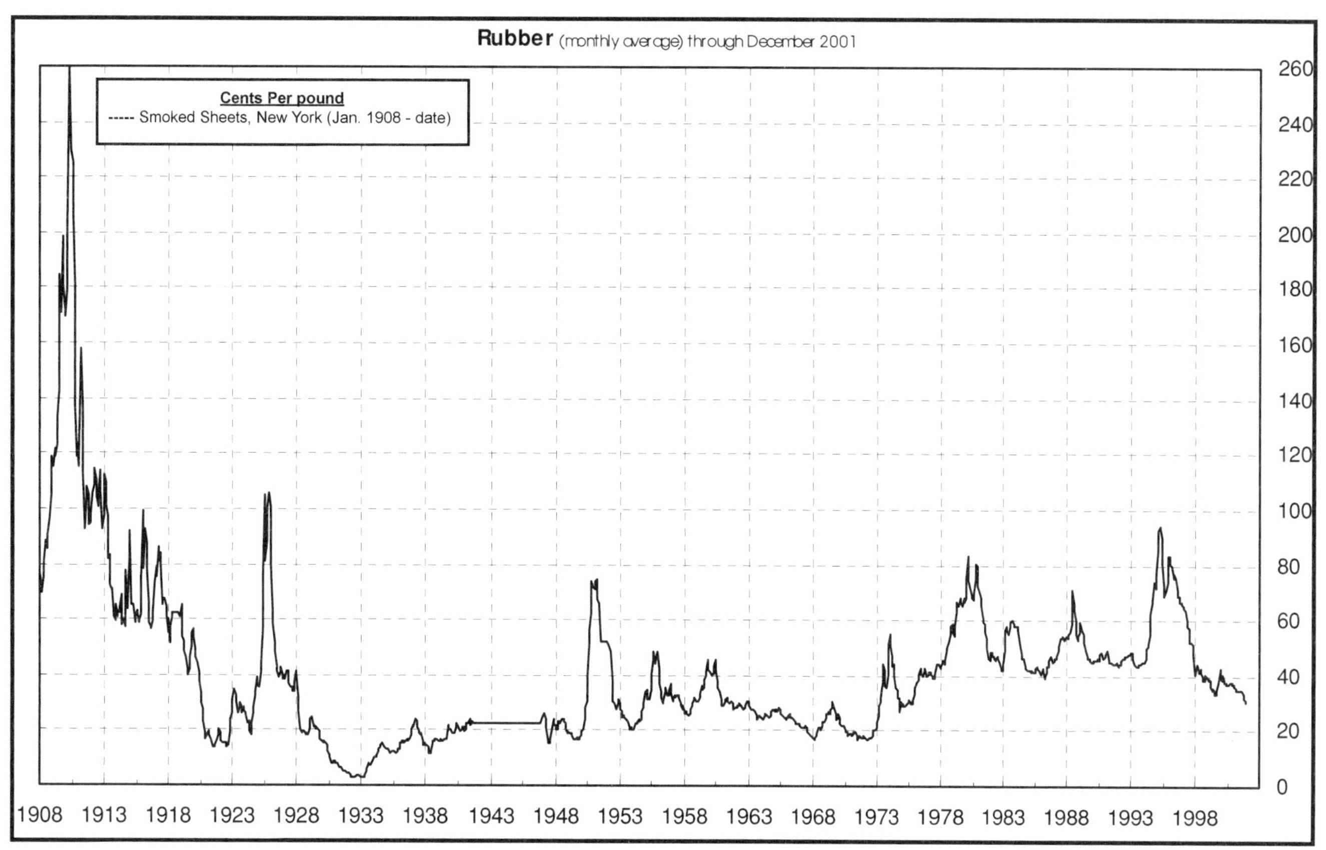

Average Spot Crude Rubber Prices (Smoked Sheets1) in New York   In Cents Per Pound

Year	Jan.	Feb.	Mar.	Apr.	May	June	July	Aug.	Sept.	Oct.	Nov.	Dec.	Average
1992	43.11	43.95	44.50	45.86	46.41	46.57	46.78	47.05	46.86	47.83	48.00	48.03	46.25
1993	48.51	48.30	46.41	44.15	43.78	43.78	43.30	43.85	44.54	44.23	44.90	44.70	45.04
1994	44.92	46.11	49.62	50.83	51.43	55.13	62.49	66.35	67.15	73.51	71.76	77.35	59.72
1995	85.68	92.61	94.15	93.43	89.50	80.57	72.13	68.54	70.70	73.59	83.19	83.39	82.29
1996	80.25	79.90	79.76	75.08	76.99	75.10	71.03	69.13	68.75	66.32	66.32	66.14	72.90
1997	65.06	64.76	63.53	59.97	57.71	57.30	51.96	52.45	51.89	51.36	47.99	40.53	55.38
1998	40.21	43.96	41.70	41.23	42.65	41.28	40.03	38.58	38.62	40.26	39.96	38.20	40.56
1999	38.99	38.58	36.34	34.98	35.75	34.64	33.60	33.63	34.45	37.58	42.57	38.88	36.67
2000	38.16	40.36	38.17	37.80	37.76	37.07	36.65	37.90	37.35	37.61	37.02	36.90	37.73
2001	35.98	35.66	34.78	34.50	34.80	35.00	34.80	34.48	33.07	31.98	31.14	30.35	33.88

[1] No. 1, ribbed, plantation rubber. *Source: The Wall Street Journal*

Natural Rubber Prices in London   In British Pounds Per Metric Ton

Year	Jan.	Feb.	Mar.	Apr.	May	June	July	Aug	Sept.	Oct.	Nov.	Dec.	Average
Buyers' Price RSS 1 (CIF)													
1998	464.6	516.9	470.7	473.3	487.0	461.5	473.8	456.6	469.3	490.2	487.7	464.6	476.1
1999	495.8	463.3	430.0	414.4	442.4	435.7	410.2	404.5	419.9	455.4	509.8	484.7	446.4
2000	462.0	518.2	487.6	496.0	500.5	501.8	494.5	529.5	526.2	537.4	518.4	502.4	506.2
2001	490.5	494.0	477.3	479.9	498.8	509.5	493.3						491.9
Buyers' Prices RSS 3 (CIF)													
1998	416.0	500.3	445.5	465.6	480.7	451.0	466.3	439.1	454.3	478.0	467.1	430.0	457.6
1999	466.4	451.6	417.9	394.0	418.8	425.3	391.1	384.8	398.6	439.0	489.5	453.3	427.1
2000	440.0	498.5	464.8	481.0	483.0	479.3	472.0	509.5	507.3	519.9	498.4	477.9	486.0
2001	464.2	467.3	450.2	455.6	482.5	497.3	477.3						470.6
Sellers' Prices SMR 20 (CIF)													
1998	477.5	539.4	485.0	487.0	495.0	438.8	417.0	396.3	403.0	416.9	409.4	401.0	445.6
1999	414.4	411.9	380.5	375.0	396.9	393.5	373.8	388.8	417.0	453.1	518.8	480.0	415.8
2000	471.9	504.4	472.5	466.3	465.0	447.5	435.0	477.0	478.1	486.3	487.0	483.8	472.9
2001	468.8	461.3	433.8	411.9	414.5	418.8	416.3						432.2

Source: International Rubber Study Group (IRSG)

Consumption of Natural Rubber in the United States In Thousands of Metric Tons

Year	Jan.	Feb.	Mar.	Apr.	May	June	July	Aug.	Sept.	Oct.	Nov.	Dec.	Total
1992	83.4	63.3	85.9	66.9	80.6	78.6	82.6	79.5	70.2	84.6	64.4	70.2	910.2
1993	96.3	76.0	93.4	93.4	67.9	76.8	77.3	84.9	72.0	73.6	82.9	72.2	966.7
1994	92.8	84.9	93.1	82.7	89.6	84.6	76.2	87.8	74.8	90.1	66.4	78.7	1,001.7
1995	70.5	75.8	98.4	90.3	92.2	93.3	85.0	82.7	83.1	89.9	81.4	61.3	1,003.9
1996	102.5	85.8	81.2	87.9	65.6	76.7	81.9	88.1	83.3	108.4	72.1	68.2	1,001.7
1997	94.2	92.0	93.9	88.2	93.0	65.1	76.8	90.1	87.5	86.8	87.5	89.0	1,044.1
1998	104.4	76.6	102.7	81.0	98.0	92.9	96.4	91.7	119.1	104.8	78.4	111.4	1,157.4
1999	92.0	92.0	93.0	88.0	88.0	88.0	92.0	92.0	92.0	100.0	100.0	100.0	1,117.0
2000	110.0	110.0	110.0	114.0	114.0	114.0	80.0	80.0	80.0	93.0	93.0	93.0	1,191.0
2001[1]	80.0	85.0	85.0	80.0									990.0

[1] Preliminary. *Source: International Rubber Study Group (IRSG)*

Stocks of Natural Rubber in the United States, on First of Month In Thousands of Metric Tons

Year	Jan.	Feb.	Mar.	Apr.	May	June	July	Aug.	Sept.	Oct.	Nov.	Dec.
1992	109.4	103.6	112.7	110.4	107.5	105.9	101.1	99.0	96.7	100.3	97.0	100.7
1993	108.0	49.4	53.3	53.7	46.7	52.9	57.3	63.6	56.5	53.7	53.4	56.5
1994	71.3	65.9	55.7	65.2	61.4	60.0	53.2	43.8	41.0	45.0	44.2	47.8
1995	45.2	56.4	67.5	71.4	71.2	72.6	73.0	66.0	64.4	62.8	62.1	59.8
1996	67.1	70.0	70.3	71.2	73.9	73.4	67.1	64.2	57.2	56.0	61.1	62.4
1997	79.3	74.2	74.2	76.9	77.5	62.2	55.2	53.6	52.1	51.2	52.4	55.2
1998	57.2	61.2	65.5	63.5	60.9	66.7	53.6	57.9	54.7	58.3	58.9	66.5
1999	70.4	68.0	66.0	64.0	62.0	60.0	58.0	56.0	54.0	52.0	50.0	48.0
2000	46.0	69.2	69.2	69.2	69.2	69.2	69.2	69.2	69.2	69.2	69.2	69.2
2001[1]	69.2	69.2	69.2	69.2								

[1] Preliminary. *Source: International Rubber Study Group (IRSG)*

Stocks of Synthetic Rubber in the United States, on First of Month In Thousands of Metric Tons

Year	Jan.	Feb.	Mar.	Apr.	May	June	July	Aug.	Sept.	Oct.	Nov.	Dec.
1992	403.7	386.0	381.2	383.9	393.2	389.2	372.8	382.7	382.1	375.1	378.6	401.1
1993	406.9	345.9	345.7	346.0	340.5	351.8	342.1	341.6	333.6	326.4	319.9	321.4
1994	331.1	313.3	313.3	307.9	306.0	314.2	302.5	323.2	318.5	304.6	299.4	299.5
1995	305.4	307.4	302.8	293.5	319.4	315.6	325.9	349.2	355.7	354.6	347.0	351.5
1996	366.2	355.3	342.0	354.8	365.4	360.0	367.0	377.3	366.0	362.8	354.1	370.6
1997	400.5	400.4	408.4	412.7	411.9	403.5	393.1	376.9	378.4	364.4	365.2	377.7
1998	377.7	382.2	375.7	379.5	387.5	402.8	394.6	406.8	394.2	398.7	395.7	396.5
1999	409.3	404.0	404.0	406.0	399.0	420.0	410.0	419.0	413.0	390.0	391.0	389.0
2000	406.0	416.0	413.0	402.0	405.0	416.0	409.0	418.0	400.0	412.0	407.0	419.0
2001[1]	443.0	467.0	487.0	483.0	476.0							

[1] Preliminary. *Source: International Rubber Study Group (IRSG)*

Production of Synthetic Rubber in the United States In Thousands of Metric Tons

Year	Jan.	Feb.	Mar.	Apr.	May	June	July	Aug.	Sept.	Oct.	Nov.	Dec.	Total
1992	180.0	190.0	200.0	210.0	200.0	190.0	190.0	200.0	210.0	200.0	195.0	175.0	2,300
1993	120.0	160.0	220.0	190.0	200.0	180.0	190.0	180.0	180.0	180.0	190.0	180.0	2,180
1994	180.0	180.0	210.0	200.0	210.0	200.0	200.0	210.0	190.0	210.0	200.0	200.0	2,390
1995	220.0	200.0	210.0	210.0	240.0	220.0	210.0	230.0	210.0	200.0	200.0	190.0	2,530
1996	200.0	190.0	220.0	210.0	200.0	210.0	200.0	210.0	200.0	210.0	220.0	216.0	2,486
1997	220.0	200.0	220.0	230.0	220.0	200.0	220.0	220.0	230.0	210.0	210.0	203.0	2,589
1998	230.0	200.0	230.0	220.0	240.0	210.0	220.0	210.0	230.0	210.0	200.0	210.0	2,610
1999	200.0	181.0	209.0	195.0	205.0	190.0	199.0	192.0	180.0	204.0	197.0	202.0	2,354
2000	202.0	202.0	214.0	193.0	216.0	202.0	198.0	187.0	193.0	197.0	194.0	184.0	2,382
2001[1]	204.0	189.0	178.0	168.0									2,217

[1] Preliminary. *Source: International Rubber Study Group (IRSG)*

Consumption of Synthetic Rubber in the United States In Thousands of Metric Tons

Year	Jan.	Feb.	Mar.	Apr.	May	June	July	Aug.	Sept.	Oct.	Nov.	Dec.	Total
1992	167.8	159.5	174.7	158.9	162.6	184.2	154.5	177.7	180.2	171.5	155.1	148.2	1,960
1993	161.3	154.4	189.4	172.8	164.5	173.6	166.0	173.9	162.0	169.4	162.3	151.4	2,001
1994	177.7	160.8	191.8	173.0	173.5	187.5	164.9	187.1	176.0	178.0	175.7	170.8	2,118
1995	188.6	182.2	194.3	179.1	212.7	188.7	160.0	190.7	182.4	178.1	169.7	145.5	2,172
1996	188.0	173.7	186.9	176.8	184.9	178.5	177.0	197.3	182.9	201.0	177.8	165.5	2,187
1997	191.7	181.4	190.0	187.9	192.2	187.7	205.9	208.0	204.2	203.0	181.9	188.8	2,323
1998	196.5	192.5	214.8	194.4	199.8	201.4	192.0	204.5	202.2	200.3	181.2	174.8	2,354
1999	164.0	166.0	195.0	178.0	170.0	186.0	177.0	176.0	191.0	171.0	178.0	161.0	2,113
2000	173.0	185.0	202.0	178.0	194.0	196.0	177.0	189.0	172.0	182.0	168.0	147.0	2,163
2001[1]	171.0	151.0	168.0	155.0									1,935

[1] Preliminary. *Source: International Rubber Study Group (IRSG)*

U.S. Exports of Synthetic Rubber In Thousands of Metric Tons

Year	Jan.	Feb.	Mar.	Apr.	May	June	July	Aug.	Sept.	Oct.	Nov.	Dec.	Total
1992	52.3	55.1	51.3	59.1	58.2	51.6	46.5	52.8	58.0	51.4	48.1	39.7	624.1
1993	47.1	34.1	57.7	47.4	52.4	46.9	46.9	43.8	48.8	46.6	49.0	41.9	562.6
1994	48.8	46.4	55.4	57.0	52.4	49.6	50.2	62.8	60.7	59.9	56.9	55.0	655.1
1995	54.9	51.6	62.7	55.6	58.6	58.6	50.0	54.9	53.0	60.4	53.9	52.6	666.8
1996	61.1	57.7	64.0	68.0	48.2	66.8	62.3	57.1	63.9	65.2	58.6	58.6	731.5
1997	63.1	58.2	57.5	74.2	66.9	61.6	64.1	70.0	65.6	65.6	63.0	58.7	768.5
1998	61.1	60.8	62.8	59.8	66.9	61.8	60.1	64.4	63.7	62.3	59.2	59.2	742.1
1999	57.6	63.3	65.0	70.5	64.7	66.0	61.5	68.2	65.1	79.0	70.2	65.7	796.8
2000	64.3	73.4	83.8	70.2	73.2	72.3	72.4	78.6	78.6	75.2	73.3	70.7	886.0
2001[1]	74.6	67.3	76.4	78.2	75.1								891.8

[1] Preliminary. *Source: International Rubber Study Group (IRSG)*

Production of Tyres (Car and Truck) in the United States In Thousands of Units

Year	First Quarter	Second Quarter	Third Quarter	Fourth Quarter	Total	Year	First Quarter	Second Quarter	Third Quarter	Fourth Quarter	Total
1983	45,859	47,451	45,370	47,353	186,923	1992	57,890	57,319	57,554	57,487	230,250
1984	53,369	53,588	50,957	51,463	209,375	1993	61,809	60,752	57,702	57,184	237,447
1985	54,460	49,385	46,468	46,610	196,923	1994	63,586	63,331	57,018	59,442	243,696
1986	49,240	45,687	46,855	48,507	190,289	1995	63,800	63,800	63,800	63,754	255,521
1987	51,205	50,210	49,723	51,839	202,978	1996	64,000	64,000	64,000	63,700	255,723
1988	54,677	52,986	51,195	52,493	211,351	1997	----	----	----	----	263,860
1989	56,716	56,626	50,086	49,444	212,870	1998	----	----	----	----	270,905
1990	55,915	53,856	51,163	49,729	210,663	1999	----	----	----	----	267,652
1991	51,296	52,796	49,183	51,115	202,391	2000[1]	----	----	----	----	276,763

[1] Preliminary. [2] Estimate. *Source: International Rubber Study Group IRSG)*

U.S. Foreign Trade of Tyres (Car and Truck) In Thousands of Units

	Imports					Exports				
Year	First Quarter	Second Quarter	Third Quarter	Fourth Quarter	Total	First Quarter	Second Quarter	Third Quarter	Fourth Quarter	Total
1991	12,011	13,008	11,320	10,158	46,497	6,407	6,388	6,623	6,342	25,760
1992	10,760	12,496	11,850	12,285	47,391	6,243	6,475	7,125	6,646	26,489
1993	11,519	13,045	12,688	13,036	50,288	7,266	6,930	7,163	7,133	28,492
1994	13,809	15,352	14,906	14,774	58,841	7,444	8,035	7,945	8,678	32,102
1995	14,883	14,977	13,762	12,718	56,340	8,438	8,502	8,478	9,174	34,592
1996	13,163	13,864	12,543	13,186	52,756	8,244	10,013	8,672	9,401	36,330
1997	13,359	14,487	15,314	16,064	59,224	9,466	11,386	10,456	11,085	42,393
1998	17,046	17,728	18,016	19,346	72,136	12,840	10,678	10,018	10,372	43,908
1999[1]	19,471	22,295	22,194	23,784	87,744	9,874	9,580	10,480	10,537	40,471
2000[2]	24,200	24,698	23,561	22,123	94,582	11,200	10,200	10,200	10,100	41,700

[1] Preliminary. [2] Estimate. *Source: International Rubber Study Group (IRSG)*

Rye

World rye production declined by almost a third since the early 1990's, largely owing to a sharp drop in Russia's production. In the U.S., rye is a minor crop with an annual outturn about half of what it was in the 1980's. Still, there is a relatively large variation in domestic year-to-year production, ranging during the past decade from a high of 12.2 million bushels in 1998 to a record low 7 million in 2001. Production in 2000 totaled 8.4 million bushels. The U.S. is a net importer of rye, importing at times almost half of domestic production. The major producing states are generally the Dakotas, Oklahoma and Georgia. The crop year encompasses June to May. Although average yield appears to have steadied in recent years, the area planted to rye continues to slip with only a record low 103,200 hectares harvested in 2001 vs.. 119,790 in 2000 and as much as 155,000 in 1999.

In the U.S. rye is used as an animal feed and as an ingredient in bread and some whiskeys. About a third of the total supply is used as a feedstuff, an equal quantity as a foodstuff and the balance as seed and for whisky. U.S. rye exports are minimal as are carryover stocks. The contraction in U.S. supply/demand reflects a seemingly deep-rooted lack of interest towards the grain by producers and consumers alike.

World production in 2001/02 of 23.4 million metric tons exceeded initial estimates and compares with the record low 19 million tons in 2000/01. Average yield in 2001/02 was forecast at 2.42 mt/hectare vs. 2.03 mt/hectare in 2000/01. World 2001/02 acreage was estimated at 9.64 million hectares vs. 9.34 million a year earlier. Eastern Europe is the major producing area with almost half of the world's crop. Poland has recently vied with Germany as the largest producer, about 5 million tons each in 2001/02, but Russia recovered the top spot in 2001/02 with a 7 million ton crop vs. 5.5 million in 2000/01. Canada, whose output is not much larger than the U. S., but realizes a higher average yield, exports most of its crop to the U.S., about 75,000 tons annually in recent years, and Canada is considered a major global exporter.

World trade in 2001/02 (October/September) of 1.4 million metric tons is about unchanged from 2000/01, but percentage wise well above the paltry 662,000 tons in 1997/98. Importing nations show wide year-to-year variance. China's 2001/02 imports of 50,000 tons is twice that of 2000/01, but well under the 367,000 tons in 1998/99. South Korea's 2001/02 imports of 150,000 tons compares with only 60,000 in 2000/01 and only 4,000 in 1997/98. Japan, however, is forecast to import 400,000 tons in 2001/02. The largest exporter is the European Union with 0.9 million tons in 2001/02, down 200,000 tons from a year earlier. Russia's exports in 2001/02 of 50,000 tons is about unchanged from the previous two crop years. but compares very favorably with the late 1990's when exports were virtually nil.

World Production of Rye In Thousands of Metric Tons

Year	Austria	Canada	Czech Republic[5]	Denmark	France	Germany	Poland	Russia[4]	Spain	Turkey	Ukraine[4]	United States	World Total
1992-3	278	278	240	308	205	2,422	3,981	13,887	230	240	1,156	291	28,661
1993-4	290	319	260	323	189	2,984	5,000	9,151	300	230	1,180	263	26,029
1994-5	319	397	281	380	182	3,451	5,300	6,000	217	250	941	288	21,571
1995-6	314	310	262	500	198	4,521	6,287	4,100	174	255	1,208	256	21,939
1996-7	151	309	204	343	225	4,214	5,652	5,900	295	245	1,100	227	22,050
1997-8	207	320	259	453	207	4,580	5,300	7,500	212	235	1,348	207	24,433
1998-9	236	398	261	538	216	4,775	5,664	3,300	207	237	1,140	309	20,306
1999-00[1]	220	390	200	250	190	4,330	5,180	4,800	220	250	920	280	19,290
2000-1[2]	170	260	150	260	160	4,150	4,000	5,450	240	250	970	210	18,990
2001-2[3]	170	190	150	330	130	5,000	4,900	7,000	240	250	1,800	180	23,260

[1] Preliminary. [2] Estimate. [3] Forecast. [4] Formerly part of the U.S.S.R.; data not reported separately until 1992. [5] Formerly part of Czechoslovakia; data not reported separately until 1992. *Source: Foreign Agricultural Service, U.S. Department of Agriculture (FAS-USDA)*

Production of Rye in the United States In Thousands of Bushels

Year	Georgia	Kansas	Michigan	Minnesota	Nebraska	North Dakota	Oklahoma	Penns-ylvania	South Carolina	South Dakota	Texas	Wisconsin	Total
1992	1,560	130	496	720	1,040	1,496	798	720	675	1,666	280	330	11,952
1993	1,380	693	420	667	500	1,050	660	340	380	1,600	363	260	10,340
1994	1,890	325	442	810	546	700	945	320	600	1,485	435	875	11,341
1995	1,155	400	544	609	480	726	810	330	440	1,650	380	480	10,064
1996	1,820	150	351	480	323	528	975	216	520	1,476	190	384	8,936
1997	1,430	300	450	400	240	513	1,080	400	250	728	330	432	8,132
1998	1,050	375	420	837	288	2,562	1,540	495	400	1,400	400	360	12,161
1999	1,050	300	756	775	405	1,517	1,045	600	500	1,012	450	384	11,038
2000	1,170	[2]	[2]	[2]	[2]	704	1,470	[2]	[2]	546	[2]	[2]	8,386
2001[1]	875	[2]	[2]	[2]	[2]	340	1,150	[2]	[2]	350	[2]	[2]	6,971

[1] Preliminary. [2] Estimates not published beginning in 2000. *Source: Agricultural Statistics Board, U.S. Department of Agriculture (ASB-USDA)*

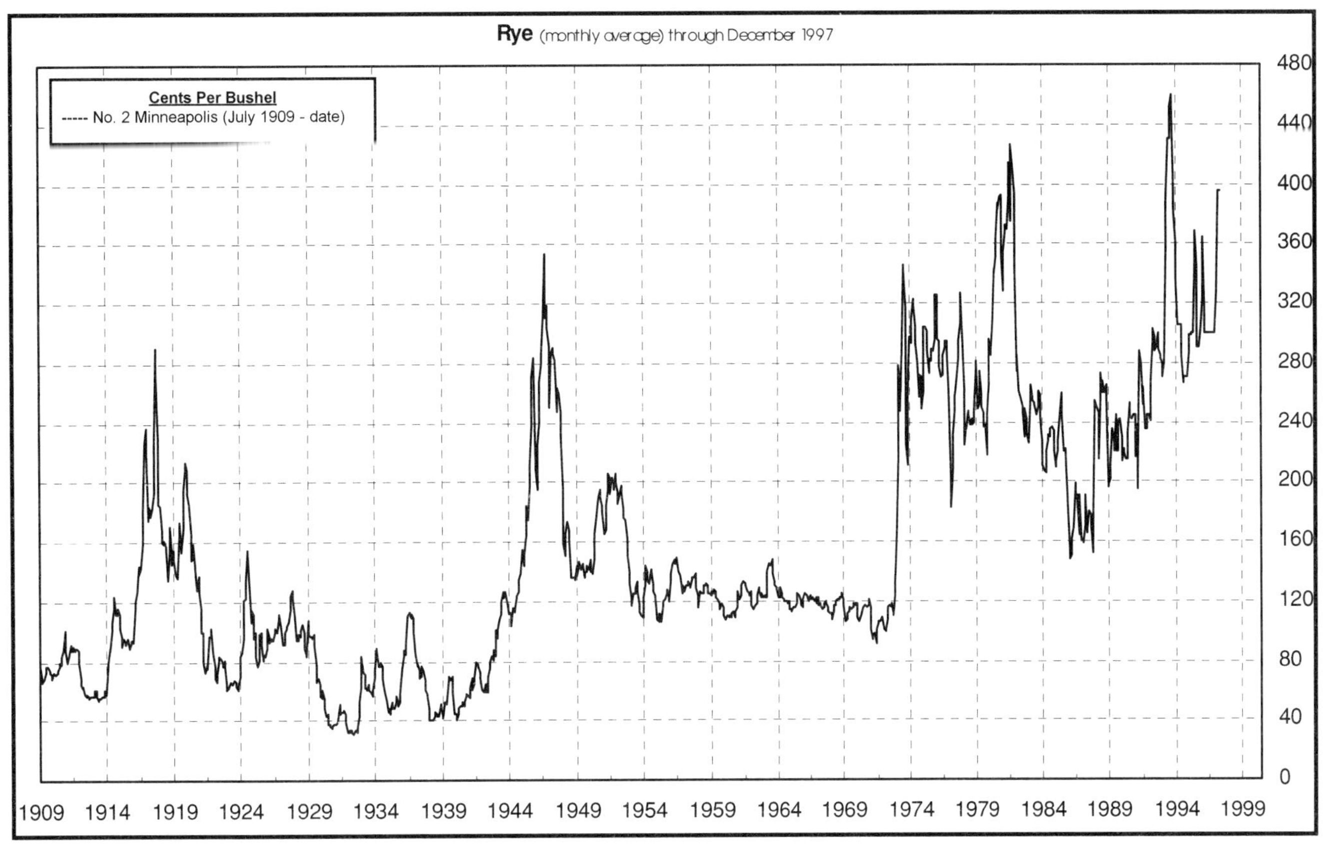

Salient Statistics of Rye in the United States In Thousands of Bushels

Crop Year Beginning June 1	Supply: Stocks June 1	Supply: Production	Supply: Imports	Supply: Total Supply	Domestic Use: Food	Domestic Use: Industry	Domestic Use: Seed	Domestic Use: Feed & Residual	Domestic Use: Total	Exports	Total Disappearance	Acreage: Planted (1,000 Acres)	Acreage: Harvested for Grain (1,000 Acres)	Yield Per Harvested Acre Bushels
1992-3	1,523	11,952	3,099	16,100	3,419	2,000	3,000	6,065	14,484	14	14,498	1,582	406	29.4
1993-4	1,555	10,340	4,607	16,502	3,538	2,000	3,000	6,977	15,515	16	15,531	1,493	381	27.1
1994-5	971	11,341	4,386	16,698	3,312	2,000	3,000	6,900	15,212	35	15,247	1,613	407	27.9
1995-6	1,451	10,064	3,760	15,275	3,318	2,000	3,000	6,018	14,336	41	14,377	1,602	385	26.1
1996-7	898	8,936	4,327	14,161	3,459	2,000	3,000	4,916	13,375	32	13,407	1,457	345	25.9
1997-8	754	8,132	5,562	14,448	3,298	3,000	2,000	5,306	13,604	80	13,684	1,400	316	25.7
1998-9	764	12,161	3,322	16,247	3,639	3,000	3,000	4,392	14,031	33	14,064	1,566	418	29.1
1999-00[1]	2,400	11,038	3,400	16,838	3,300	3,000	3,000	5,700	15,000	300	15,300	1,582	383	28.8
2000-1[2]	1,600	8,386	4,000	13,986	3,300	3,000	3,000	3,100	12,400	300	12,600	1,329	296	28.3
2001-2[3]		6,971										1,328	255	27.3

[1] Preliminary. [2] Estimate. [3] Forecast *Source: Economic Research Service, U.S. Department of Agriculture (ERS-USDA)*

Average Price of Cash Rye No. 2 in Minneapolis In Cents Per Bushel

Year	July	Aug.	Sept.	Oct.	Nov.	Dec.	Jan.	Feb.	Mar.	Apr.	May	June	Average
1992-3	245	241	267	295	303	298	288	290	300	289	285	282	282
1993-4	280	270	280	354	387	427	430	430	452	460	400	383	372
1994-5	360	336	305	305	305	305	285	267	270	270	270	270	296
1995-6	287	298	299	300	300	350	368	346	290	290	290	304	310
1996-7	325	364	314	300	300	300	300	300	300	300	300	300	309
1997-8	300	327	395	395	395	395	NQ	NQ	NQ	NQ	NQ	NQ	382
1998-9	NQ	NQ	NQ	NQ	NQ	NQ	NQ	NQ	NQ	NQ	NQ	NQ	NQ
1999-00	NQ	NQ	NQ	NQ	NQ	NQ	NQ	NQ	NQ	NQ	NQ	NQ	NQ
2000-1	NQ	NQ	NQ	NQ	NQ	NQ	NQ	NQ	NQ	NQ	NQ	NQ	NQ
2001-2[1]	NQ	NQ	NQ	NQ	NQ	NQ	NQ						

[1] Preliminary. NQ = No quote. *Source: Agricultural Marketing Service, U.S. Department of Agriculture (AMS-USDA)*

Salt

Salt or sodium chloride, is a basic commodity with many uses. Salt is added to food to enhance flavor and is used to remove ice in winter. Salt is used in the manufacture of caustic soda and as a feedstock for chlorine. Salt is produced by a number of methods including solar evaporation, vacuum pan, mined as rock salt, and taken from the ocean as brine. There are no economic substitutes for salt. Calcium chloride or calcium magnesium acetate, hydrochloric acid, and potassium chloride can be substituted for salt in deicing, certain chemical processes and food flavoring, although at a higher cost.

The U.S. Geological Survey estimated that world production of salt in 1999 was 200 million metric tonnes, an increase of 8 percent from the previous year. The U.S. was the largest producer of salt with production of 41.4 million tonnes, up slightly from 1998. The next largest producer of salt was China with 31 million tonnes, up less than 1 percent from the previous year. Salt production by Germany was down 3 percent at 15.2 million tonnes. Production by Canada was 13.4 million tonnes, up less than 1 percent from the previous year. Other large producers of salt are India, Australia, Mexico, France and Brazil. World resources and reserves of salt are practically unlimited. Rock salt and salt from brine are readily available in the U.S. as well as other countries.

U.S. salt production in 1999 was just over 41 million tonnes. A major development had been the closure of a large salt mine in New York. Some of this loss was made up with the opening of a new mine in New York and the reopening of a rock salt mine in Michigan.

U.S. reported consumption of salt in 1999 was 48.9 million tonnes. Mild winters have reduced the amount of salt used for deicing highways. The winter of 2001 in the Northeast U.S. was very mild into December. The chemical industry consumes about 50 percent of total salt sales. Salt for highway deicing took about 21 percent of the salt used. U.S. imports of salt in 1999 were 8.8 million tonnes. The major suppliers were Canada, China and Mexico.

World Production of All Salt In Thousands of Metric Tons

Year	Australia	Canada	China	France	Germany	India	Italy	Mexico	Poland	Spain	United Kingdom	United States	World Total
1993	7,737	10,900	29,500	6,980	12,688	9,503	3,730	7,490	3,817	3,410	6,790	39,300	187,000
1994	7,685	11,700	29,746	7,536	13,099	9,503	3,953	7,458	4,074	4,932	7,000	40,100	192,000
1995	8,148	10,957	29,780	7,539	15,224	12,544	3,552	7,670	4,214	4,776	6,650	42,200	199,000
1996	7,905	12,248	29,035	7,860	15,907	14,466	3,541	8,508	4,163	4,000	6,610	42,300	204,000
1997	8,801	13,264	30,830	7,085	15,787	14,251	3,510	7,933	3,859	4,000	6,600	41,500	207,000
1998	8,879	13,296	22,420	7,000	15,700	11,964	3,600	8,412	4,005	3,500	6,600	41,300	200,000
1999[1]	10,003	12,686	28,124	7,000	15,700	14,453	3,600	8,236	4,212	3,200	5,800	45,000	211,000
2000[2]	8,798	11,935	31,280	7,000	15,700	14,453	3,600	8,884	4,200	3,200	5,800	45,600	214,000

[1] Preliminary. [2] Estimate. *Source: U.S. Geological Survey (USGS)*

Salient Statistics of the Salt Industry in the United States In Thousands of Metric Tons

Year	Net Import Reliance as a % of Apparent Consumption	Average Value FOB Mine Vacuum & Open Pan $ Per Ton	Production: Total	Production: Open & Vacuum Pan	Production: Solar	Production: Rock	Production: Brine	Sold or Used Producers: Open & Vacuum Pan	Sold or Used Producers: Rock Salt	Sold or Used Producers: Brine	Sold or Used Producers: Total Salt	Sold or Used Producers: Value[3] Million $	Imports for Consumption	Exports: Total	Exports: To Canada	Apparent Consumption
1993	12	111.97	39,200	3,864	2,960	14,253	18,100	3,850	13,401	18,100	38,200	904.0	5,868	688	499	43,400
1994	18	115.35	40,100	3,960	3,020	15,100	18,000	3,930	14,900	18,000	39,700	990.0	9,630	742	573	48,600
1995	14	118.63	42,100	3,950	3,540	14,000	20,600	3,920	13,000	20,500	40,800	1,000.0	7,090	670	558	47,200
1996	19	120.54	42,200	3,920	3,270	13,500	21,500	3,900	14,500	21,500	42,900	1,060.0	10,600	869	710	52,600
1997	17	119.61	41,400	3,980	3,170	12,900	21,400	3,990	12,200	21,400	40,600	993.0	9,160	748	624	49,000
1998	17	114.93	41,200	4,040	3,190	12,900	21,100	4,040	12,700	21,100	40,800	986.0	8,770	731	533	48,800
1999[1]	16	112.49	44,900	4,190	3,580	14,400	22,700	4,190	14,700	22,700	44,400	1,110.0	8,870	892	730	52,400
2000[2]	15	113.95	45,600	4,200	3,810	15,000	22,500	4,190	13,600	22,500	43,300	1,040.0	8,960	642	500	51,600

[1] Preliminary. [2] Estimate. [3] Values are f.o.b. mine or refinery & do not include cost of cooperage or containers. *Source: U.S. Geological Survey*

Salt Sold or Used by Producers in the U.S. by Classes & Consumers or Uses In Thousands of Metric Tons

Year	Chemical[2]	Tanning Leather	Textile & Dyeing	Meat Packers	Canning	Baking	Agricultural Distribution	Feed Dealers	Feed Manufacturers	Rubber	Oil	Paper & Pulp	Metal Processing	Water Treatment	Grocery Stores	Water Conditioning Distrib.	Ice Control and/or Stabilization
1993	19,273	67	313	418	322	152	808	1,120	476	37	1,220	110	216	419	823	527	13,600
1994	18,400	82	304	410	342	157	842	1,070	478	33	1,290	150	239	440	934	505	16,400
1995	21,100	74	290	410	332	155	726	1,040	407	67	2,420	152	236	413	847	563	12,900
1996	22,400	83	288	407	336	169	661	1,150	403	71	2,430	122	199	534	855	719	17,700
1997	22,400	78	273	416	334	167	307	1,110	683	68	2,440	107	177	471	800	624	15,000
1998	22,000	93	250	440	275	219	362	1,190	536	68	2,320	115	170	531	807	598	9,490
1999	22,400	103	235	405	225	234	254	1,210	533	72	2,430	112	153	899	831	600	15,300
2000[1]	22,400	82	209	402	220	234	262	1,240	540	71	2,510	106	112	589	823	568	19,700

[1] Preliminary. [2] Chloralkali producers and other chemical. *Source: U.S. Geological Survey (USGS)*

Sheep & Lambs

The mid-2001 U.S. total of all sheep and lambs of 8.3 million head compares with 8.5 million in mid-2000. The inventory has trended down since 1942 when it reached a peak of 56.2 million head. Of the 2001 total, the breeding sheep inventory declined to 4.9 million head vs. 5.0 million respectively. The 2001 lamb crop of 4.42 million head compares with 4.62 million in 2000. Texas is the largest sheep producing state. The nation's number of sheep operations (whole or partial) totaled 66,000 in 2000 vs. almost 67,000 in 1999. Commercial 2001 U.S. lamb production of 223 million pounds compares with 230 million in 2000. The U.S. is a net importer of lamb, almost all from Australia and New Zealand, totaling 87.1 million pounds through the first tent months of 2001 vs. 77.1 million in the like 2000 period. However, the U.S. imports live sheep from Canada. Per capita, retail weight disappearance of lamb in the U.S. totals about one pound.

Choice wholesale slaughter lamb prices in late 2001 averaged near $70/cwt. compare with $75/cwt. towards late 2000, basis San Angelo, Texas. Feeder lamb prices generally run higher.

Although demand for sheep meat is low in the U.S., foreign demand is higher; especially in those countries with large sheep herds utilized for wool production from which there is a derived demand for meat. Thus, the price of wool is a key factor in determining the availability of sheep meat. World sheep (and goat) numbers decreased during the second half of the 1990's owing largely to declines in Australia and New Zealand, which counteracted gains in China.

World Sheep and Goat Numbers in Specified Countries on January 1 In Thousands of Head

Year	Argentina	Australia	China	India	Kazak-hstan	New Zealand	Romania	Russia	South Africa	Spain	Turkey	United Kingdom	World Total
1991	27,552	173,982	210,021	160,207	35,700	57,852	14,062	58,200	37,585	24,037	45,000	30,147	962,853
1992	25,706	161,073	206,210	161,084	34,556	55,162	13,879	55,255	36,076	24,625	44,700	28,932	931,903
1993	24,500	140,542	207,329	162,155	34,420	52,568	12,079	51,368	35,770	24,615	44,600	29,493	900,400
1994	23,500	120,900	217,314	169,569	34,208	50,298	12,276	43,700	33,800	23,872	44,000	29,333	881,258
1995	21,626	121,100	240,528	171,626	25,132	50,135	12,119	34,500	33,385	23,058	43,000	29,484	874,912
1996	17,956	121,200	279,535	173,519	19,600	48,816	11,086	28,336	35,145	21,322	42,400	28,797	897,009
1997	17,295	120,228	236,961	175,976	13,742	47,394	10,317	23,519	35,830	23,981	41,100	28,256	842,179
1998	15,232	117,494	255,055	178,462	10,896	46,970	9,747	20,697	36,821	24,857	39,500	30,027	853,061
1999[1]	13,953	117,091	268,143	180,130	9,556	46,150	9,167	18,213	34,910	24,199	37,300	31,080	857,109
2000[2]	13,800	117,191	271,130	180,885	9,000	45,800	8,700	15,698	35,000	23,700	34,400	30,800	852,745

[1] Preliminary. [2] Forecast. *Source: Foreign Agricultural Service, U.S. Department of Agriculture (FAS-USDA)*

Salient Statistics of Sheep & Lambs in the United States (Average Live Weight) In Thousands of Head

	-- Inventory, Jan. 1 --				--- Marketings[3] ---		---------- Slaughter ----------					Production (Live Weight)	Farm Value --------- Jan. 1 ---------	
Year	Without New Crop Lambs	With New Crop Lambs	Lamb Crop	Total Supply	Sheep	Lambs	Farm	Com-mercial	Total[4]	Net Exports	Total Disap-pearance	Mil. Lbs.	All Million $	$ Per Head
1993	10,201	10,906	6,379	17,285	1,952	6,752	74	5,182	5,268	750	7,180	688.6	714.2	70.6
1994	9,836	9,714	5,897	15,611	1,536	6,384	76	4,938	5,008	760	6,742	630.0	681.4	69.9
1995	8,989	8,886	5,606	14,492	990	6,228	69	4,560	4,628	680	5,807	599.4	663.4	74.7
1996	8,465	8,461	5,282	13,743	1,024	6,023	65	4,184	4,249	264	5,488	565.7	732.2	86.5
1997	8,024	8,024	5,356	13,380	1,011	5,709	62	3,907	3,969	----	5,946	591.3	761.7	96.0
1998	7,825	7,825	5,007	12,832	977	5,510	73	3,804	3,877	----	----	555.7	797.8	102.0
1999	7,215	7,215	4,733	11,948	790	5,208	67	3,701	3,768	----	----	533.6	637.6	88.0
2000[1]	7,032	7,032	4,622	11,654	825	4,852	69	3,460	3,529	----	----	506.0	668.8	95.0
2001[2]	6,965	6,965	4,495	11,460				3,216					660.5	96.0

[1] Preliminary. [2] Estimate. [3] Excludes interfarm sales. [4] Includes all commercial and farm. Source: Economic Research Service, U.S. Department of Agriculture (ERS-USDA)

Sheep and Lambs[3] on Farms in the United States on January 1 In Thousands of Head

Year	California	Colorado	Idaho	Iowa	Minnesota	Montana	New Mexico	Ohio	South Dakota	Texas	Utah	Wyoming	Total
1994	1,120	647	266	267	231	534	340	198	550	1,895	442	813	9,742
1995	1,060	545	270	294	190	490	315	162	530	1,700	445	790	8,886
1996	1,000	535	273	345	185	465	265	153	500	1,650	395	680	8,461
1997	960	575	285	285	180	432	235	130	450	1,400	375	720	7,937
1998	800	575	285	265	165	415	290	135	420	1,530	420	710	7,825
1999	810	440	265	260	175	380	275	125	420	1,350	400	630	7,215
2000	800	440	275	265	165	370	290	134	420	1,200	400	570	7,032
2001[1]	840	420	275	270	170	360	255	142	420	1,150	390	530	6,965
2002[2]	800	370	260	250	160	335	230	140	400	1,130	365	480	6,685

[1] Preliminary. [2] Estimate. [3] Includes sheep & lambs on feed for market and stock sheep & lambs. Source: Economic Research Service, U.S. Department of Agriculture (ERS-USDA)

SHEEP & LAMBS

Average Wholesale Price of Slaughter Lambs (Choice) at San Angelo Texas In Dollars Per Cwt.

Year	Jan.	Feb.	Mar.	Apr.	May	June	July	Aug.	Sept.	Oct.	Nov.	Dec.	Average
1993	69.88	73.38	75.50	71.25	62.50	57.75	57.00	58.97	66.08	63.75	65.69	68.44	65.85
1994	56.67	62.31	61.19	51.25	60.94	66.92	75.33	79.50	76.08	69.96	73.60	67.50	66.77
1995	65.38	75.08	73.75	68.58	77.20	81.63	83.70	87.00	80.00	75.50	72.00	70.50	75.86
1996	74.44	85.63	84.07	83.10	86.17	97.50	92.67	83.75	84.40	82.58	80.00	88.88	85.27
1997	94.63	100.81	97.50	95.50	83.17	83.25	78.94	90.25	85.45	82.75	80.33	83.52	88.01
1998	74.38	74.31	71.50	63.00	73.00	91.21	82.21	82.05	69.50	67.20	63.33	71.44	73.59
1999	69.31	67.88	68.54	70.50	82.70	81.06	77.29	81.17	77.00	74.81	78.00	83.29	75.96
2000	73.71	76.83	78.17	78.25	89.65	78.30	84.17	82.20	82.00	77.50	76.70	75.33	79.40
2001[1]	81.25	87.00	82.63	83.30	86.07	75.21	69.82	54.47	56.50	57.67	59.00	71.60	72.04

[1] Preliminary. *Source: Economic Research Service, U.S. Department of Agriculture (ERS-USDA)*

Federally Inspected Slaughter of Sheep & Lambs in the United States In Thousands of Head

Year	Jan.	Feb.	Mar.	Apr.	May	June	July	Aug.	Sept.	Oct.	Nov.	Dec.	Total
1993	380	384	476	461	396	462	394	413	410	391	403	430	5,000
1994	383	409	515	402	418	377	302	382	384	381	393	411	4,756
1995	373	363	456	420	355	347	296	355	344	356	364	358	4,388
1996	352	353	403	374	313	271	313	315	313	365	324	336	4,032
1997	294	317	386	321	308	293	295	288	310	324	299	337	3,771
1998	301	300	377	367	270	283	269	263	295	312	290	344	3,671
1999	260	291	411	295	260	259	253	283	294	293	317	341	3,557
2000	271	284	334	330	248	247	229	269	257	266	286	287	3,308
2001[1]	258	236	316	275	227	221	229	258	230	274	273	266	3,065

[1] Preliminary. *Source: Economic Research Service, U.S. Department of Agriculture (ERS-USDA)*

Cold Storage Holdings of Lamb and Mutton in the U.S., on First of Month In Thousands of Pounds

Year	Jan.	Feb.	Mar.	Apr.	May	June	July	Aug.	Sept.	Oct.	Nov.	Dec.
1993	7,864	6,343	6,620	6,661	11,064	11,181	13,152	13,495	12,241	12,615	11,843	10,161
1994	8,372	9,198	9,507	11,194	11,505	11,368	12,124	12,026	11,016	9,261	8,946	8,796
1995	10,913	11,621	10,825	12,679	14,934	13,992	12,306	10,679	10,240	7,412	7,503	7,846
1996	7,606	9,794	13,017	12,247	13,649	12,187	13,726	13,164	14,645	11,249	10,494	9,788
1997	8,899	9,473	9,862	11,163	13,027	15,220	16,594	18,535	19,383	16,119	16,894	16,534
1998	13,741	13,920	15,284	16,226	16,306	16,666	16,040	16,188	14,530	12,253	12,558	11,914
1999	11,721	10,452	12,134	12,374	13,146	12,313	12,459	11,975	12,240	9,815	9,210	9,446
2000	8,740	10,394	10,335	11,437	13,345	13,137	13,984	13,557	14,042	12,867	12,195	12,486
2001[1]	13,455	13,836	13,141	13,729	13,551	14,586	15,443	15,744	15,266	13,979	13,198	11,296

[1] Preliminary. *Source: Economic Research Service, U.S. Department of Agriculture (ERS-USDA)*

Average Price Received by Farmers for Sheep in the United States In Dollars Per Cwt.

Year	Jan.	Feb.	Mar.	Apr.	May	June	July	Aug.	Sept.	Oct.	Nov.	Dec.	Average
1993	33.10	35.20	36.10	27.30	29.10	28.90	29.00	28.50	25.80	24.60	25.70	30.30	29.47
1994	35.10	37.00	34.30	29.60	29.30	33.60	30.10	29.40	27.90	27.30	30.50	34.70	31.57
1995	32.80	37.50	31.90	29.50	27.90	28.30	28.60	27.00	26.00	24.50	23.80	26.00	28.65
1996	34.40	33.80	34.00	27.30	25.30	26.60	30.50	29.10	30.20	28.80	29.80	34.20	30.33
1997	41.80	41.30	42.50	37.50	34.00	36.60	39.40	38.40	33.90	35.80	38.90	37.70	38.15
1998	42.00	39.60	41.00	34.40	30.30	30.20	29.40	28.30	26.80	26.10	26.40	30.10	32.05
1999	32.40	30.20	32.70	31.80	31.50	28.90	32.00	29.80	29.20	26.40	30.20	33.40	30.71
2000	36.80	39.50	38.80	35.00	30.50	30.00	34.20	30.70	30.30	29.50	33.60	36.20	33.76
2001[1]	43.30	43.60	43.60	34.90	34.10	29.50	32.40	31.30	28.90	26.20	26.60	33.50	33.99

[1] Preliminary. *Source: Economic Research Service, U.S. Department of Agriculture (ERS-USDA)*

Average Price Received by Farmers for Lambs in the United States In Dollars Per Cwt.

Year	Jan.	Feb.	Mar.	Apr.	May	June	July	Aug.	Sept.	Oct.	Nov.	Dec.	Average
1993	67.30	72.70	76.00	68.10	61.50	55.70	53.90	59.20	64.50	64.50	65.80	66.00	64.60
1994	60.60	59.40	58.60	54.50	54.50	63.00	72.80	75.50	71.20	68.00	70.60	69.10	64.82
1995	67.50	70.40	74.80	74.60	80.40	85.70	85.70	85.60	82.70	77.60	77.10	76.50	78.22
1996	76.10	84.30	86.60	85.90	90.30	100.70	98.30	89.10	88.50	87.00	84.60	88.20	88.30
1997	94.60	99.80	99.70	96.40	90.80	86.50	81.10	92.70	90.20	87.20	83.10	83.90	90.50
1998	78.40	75.00	70.10	66.00	63.00	88.90	81.30	80.10	71.80	67.60	62.60	64.70	72.46
1999	68.20	67.20	67.40	67.40	82.80	81.30	77.00	80.30	75.30	72.60	76.30	77.60	74.45
2000	70.90	72.00	80.20	82.60	96.40	89.70	87.00	83.60	80.80	76.80	71.50	71.80	80.28
2001[1]	74.10	80.10	84.40	85.20	79.00	71.60	65.00	55.40	53.40	52.90	54.10	61.70	68.08

[1] Preliminary. *Source: Economic Research Service, U.S. Department of Agriculture (ERS-USDA)*

Silk

Silk is the cloth and thread made from silkworms. While there are different varieties of silk, the fiber used in commercial silk production is produced primarily by the mulberry silkworm. The silkworm, which is a caterpillar, has been domesticated for thousands of years. The basic process of silk production is for silkworm eggs to be put on mulberry leave. These hatch into caterpillars which feed on the leaves. As the caterpillar grows, it sheds its skin. The silkworm then makes or spins a cocoon and in about three weeks emerges as a moth. It is the silk threads that are released by the silkworm that form the cocoon. In a matter of a few days, one silkworm can spin a cocoon of unbroken thread as much as 600 meters in length. The process of collecting the silk fiber is called reeling. Reeling is the bringing together of two or more cocoons to form them into one continuous strand of silk.

The Food and Agricultural Organization of the United nations reported that world production of silk has seen little trend. Between 1988 and 1991, world production averaged 83,600 metric tonnes. In the mid 1990's it averaged over 100,000 tonnes. In 1997 world production was 83,000 tonnes. The world's largest producer of silk by far is China. Between 1989 and 1991, China increased its silk production by 20 percent. This allowed world production to increase by 16 percent. Between 1991 and 1994, production increased by 40 percent in China. After that it has declined. China is the largest producer as well as exporter of silk. In terms of production, China has a market share of just over 60 percent. In terms of imports, China's share of the market is about 38 percent. The next largest producer of silk is India. India's share of world production is about 19 percent. Other important producers of silk are North Korea, Japan, Brazil, Uzbekistan, Vietnam and Iran.

China's yearly exports of silk average about 15,000 metric tonnes. China has made an effort to reduce its surplus production capacity. China has a large amount of excess capacity in terms of the number of spindles devoted to silk. Uzbekistan, on the other hand, has been trying to increase silk production. Among the major importers of silk are France, Italy, Japan, India, Hong Kong and South Korea. Italy and Japan together import about 20 percent of the world's silk.

Futures Markets

Raw silk is traded on the Kansai Agricultural Commodities Exchange (KANEX). Dried cocoons are traded on the Chuba Commodity Exchange (CCE). Raw silk and dried cocoons are traded on the Yokohama Commodity Exchange.

World Production of Raw Silk In Metric Tons

Year	Brazil	China	India	Iran	Japan	North Korea	South Korea	Kyrgyzstan[3]	Thailand	Turkmenistan[3]	Uzbekistan[3]	Viet Nam	World Total
1990	1,693	55,003	11,000	537	6,000	4,200	971	----	1,250	----	4,094	500	85,987
1991	2,077	60,002	14,000	537	5,527	4,400	837	----	1,300	----	4,100	500	93,880
1992	2,296	70,302	15,000	537	5,085	4,500	870	1,200	1,300	600	2,200	500	105,220
1993	2,450	76,801	14,168	480	4,254	4,600	683	1,000	1,500	500	2,000	550	109,790
1994	2,450	84,001	14,500	600	2,400	4,700	700	1,000	1,600	500	2,000	600	115,796
1995	2,450	80,001	15,000	600	2,400	4,700	700	1,000	1,600	500	2,000	650	112,350
1996	2,000	51,000	16,000	1,000	3,000	5,000	----	1,000	1,000	5,000	2,000	1,000	88,000
1997	2,000	51,000	16,000	1,000	2,000	4,000	----	1,000	1,000	5,000	2,000	1,000	85,000
1998[1]	2,000	52,000	16,000	1,000	1,000	4,000	----	1,000	1,000	5,000	2,000	1,000	86,000
1999[2]	2,000	54,000	16,000	1,000	1,000	4,000	----	1,000	1,000	5,000	2,000	1,000	88,000

[1] Preliminary. [2] Estimate. [3] Formerly part of the U.S.S.R.; data not reported separately until 1992. *Source: Food and Agricultural Organization of the United Nations (FAO-UN)*

World Trade of Silk by Selected Countries In Metric Tons

	Imports							Exports					
Year	France	Hong Kong	India	Italy	Japan	South Korea	World Total	Brazil	China	Hong Kong	Japan	North Korea	World Total
1989	1,012	6,362	1,400	7,740	8,512	3,763	35,968	534	19,314	6,748	417	1,100	39,064
1990	796	3,928	1,647	4,775	7,111	3,204	27,322	1,064	13,066	4,102	380	1,200	27,977
1991	579	4,347	2,100	5,297	6,933	3,519	29,623	2,052	15,178	4,186	405	900	29,188
1992	693	4,400	2,843	4,337	5,137	3,627	28,239	1,552	13,474	4,358	701	800	26,433
1993	1,001	5,475	4,977	5,634	5,982	4,494	36,086	1,495	15,652	7,204	904	1,200	35,634
1994	1,047	6,165	5,750	9,235	5,772	4,128	44,136	1,739	21,004	6,149	1,265	1,400	41,998
1995	663	4,775	4,276	5,612	4,331	3,513	37,854	966	16,788	5,176	925	1,000	40,633
1996	675	3,978	2,980	4,400	6,098	3,737	37,615	1,071	15,791	4,165	946	1,000	38,587
1997	582	4,320	4,204	5,482	4,229	2,796	48,930	905	14,382	4,501	936	1,000	37,574
1998[1]	592	2,030	2,204	4,088	3,357	1,510	31,441	780	12,250	2,105	612	1,000	31,185

[1] Preliminary. *Source: Food and Agricultural Organization of the United Nations (FAO-UN)*

Silver

Silver prices in year 2001 moved lower until the events of September 11. Ahead of that day, silver at the COMEX Division of the New York Mercantile Exchange was trading for about $4.20 per ounce. Following September 11, silver prices edged higher though it took a number of sessions before prices reached nearly $4.80 before pulling back. In late 2001, silver was trading for close to $4.00 per ounce. Prices then started to move higher as lease rates, the cost to borrow and lend metal, increased. Silver prices moved from almost $4.00 back to about $4.70. In early 2002, lease rates declined and silver prices eased back.

The U.S. Geological Survey reported that world mine production of silver in 2000 was 17,900 metric tonnes, an increase of 1 percent from 1999 when production was estimated to be 17,700 tonnes. The U.S. is a major producer of silver with 2000 mine production of 2,060 tonnes, up 6 percent from the year before. The largest producer of silver in 2000 was Mexico with mine output of 2,500 tonnes, an increase of 7 percent from 1999. Silver production by Peru in 2000 was estimated at 2,000 tonnes, down 10 percent from the previous year. Australia's production at 1,850 tonnes was up 8 percent from the prior year. Canada's silver output in 2000 was 1,300 tonnes, up 4 percent from 1999.

World reserves of silver are estimated at 280,000 tonnes. More than two-thirds of the world's silver resources are located with copper, lead and zinc deposits. Much of this metal is located at great depths. The remaining silver is located in vein deposits with gold which is the most valuable metallic component. The most recent discoveries have been primarily gold and silver deposits but future silver reserves are expected to be found with base metals with silver as a byproduct.

Silver is basically an industrial metal. About 25-28 percent of silver demand is derived from photographic applications. In conventional photography, silver halide film is used. The new digital technologies convert images into electronic form and do not use silver. Silver halide pictures can be scanned into electronic form which uses silver to take and print the picture but also eliminates the need for silver in further processing. Silver finds use in many other products including jewelry and coins. There are a number of substitutes for silver. Aluminum and rhodium can be substituted for silver in mirrors. Tantalum can be used for silver in surgical equipment while stainless steel can be used in tableware. As an industrial metal, silver's use will follow the course of the economy. About two-thirds of the silver used is in photographic and industrial applications. The U.S. economy is expected to rebound in 2002 and that should increase the use of silver.

In the U.S., the largest silver-producing state is Nevada. About one-half of the domestic silver mined is found with precious metal ores. The other half is recovered as a byproduct of processing copper, lead, and zinc ores. There were 22 principal refiners of commercial-grade silver in 2000. There were about 30 fabricators of silver and they accounted for 90 percent of the silver used in arts and industry. On the industrial side, silver is used in electrical products, catalysts, brazing alloys, dental products and bearings. U.S. primary refinery production of silver in 2000 was 2,200 tonnes, while secondary refinery production was 1,600 tonnes.

U.S. mine production of silver in August 2001 was estimated at 132,000 kilograms. In the January-August 2001 period, production totaled 958,000 kilograms. For all of 2000, silver production was 2.02 million kilograms. Production by Nevada in August 2001 was 49,300 kilograms and in January-August 2001 it was 321,000 kilograms. Silver production in other states, including Alaska, Colorado, California and Missouri in August 2001 was 82,700 kilograms.

U.S. imports for consumption of silver bullion in July 2001 were 264,000 kilograms. The major suppliers were Canada and Mexico. For all of 2000, silver bullion imports were 3.81 million kilograms. Imports of silver waste and scrap in July 2001 were 201,000 kilograms.

Futures Markets

Silver futures are traded on the New York Mercantile Exchange, COMEX Division (COMEX), the Chicago Board of Trade (CBOT), the Mid America Commodity Exchange (MidAm), and the Tokyo Commodity Exchange (TOCOM). Options are traded on the Amsterdam Exchanges (AEX) and the COMEX.

World Mine Production of Silver In Thousands of Kilograms In Metric Tons

Year	Australia	Bolivia	Canada[3]	Chile	China	Kazak-hstan[4]	Rep. of Korea	Mexico	Peru	Poland	Sweden	United States	World Total[2]
1991	1,180	376	1,339	678	150	2,200	265	2,295	1,927	899	239	1,860	15,600
1992	1,218	282	1,220	1,029	800	500	333	2,098	1,614	798	210	1,800	14,900
1993	1,092	333	896	970	840	500	215	2,136	1,671	767	255	1,640	14,100
1994	1,045	352	768	983	810	506	257	2,215	1,768	1,064	276	1,490	14,000
1995	939	425	1,285	1,041	910	489	299	2,324	1,929	1,001	268	1,560	14,900
1996	1,013	384	1,309	1,047	1,140	468	254	2,528	1,970	935	272	1,570	15,100
1997	1,106	387	1,224	1,091	1,300	690	268	2,679	2,090	1,038	304	2,180	16,500
1998	1,474	404	1,196	1,340	1,300	726	339	2,686	2,025	1,108	299	2,060	17,200
1999[1]	1,720	422	1,174	1,380	1,320	904	489	2,467	2,231	1,100	300	1,950	17,600
2000[2]	2,060	434	1,161	1,242	1,600	927	591	2,621	2,438	1,100	300	1,860	18,300

[1] Preliminary. [2] Estimate. [3] Shipments. [4] Formerly part of the U.S.S.R.; data not reported separately until 1992.

Source: U.S. Geological Survey (USGS)

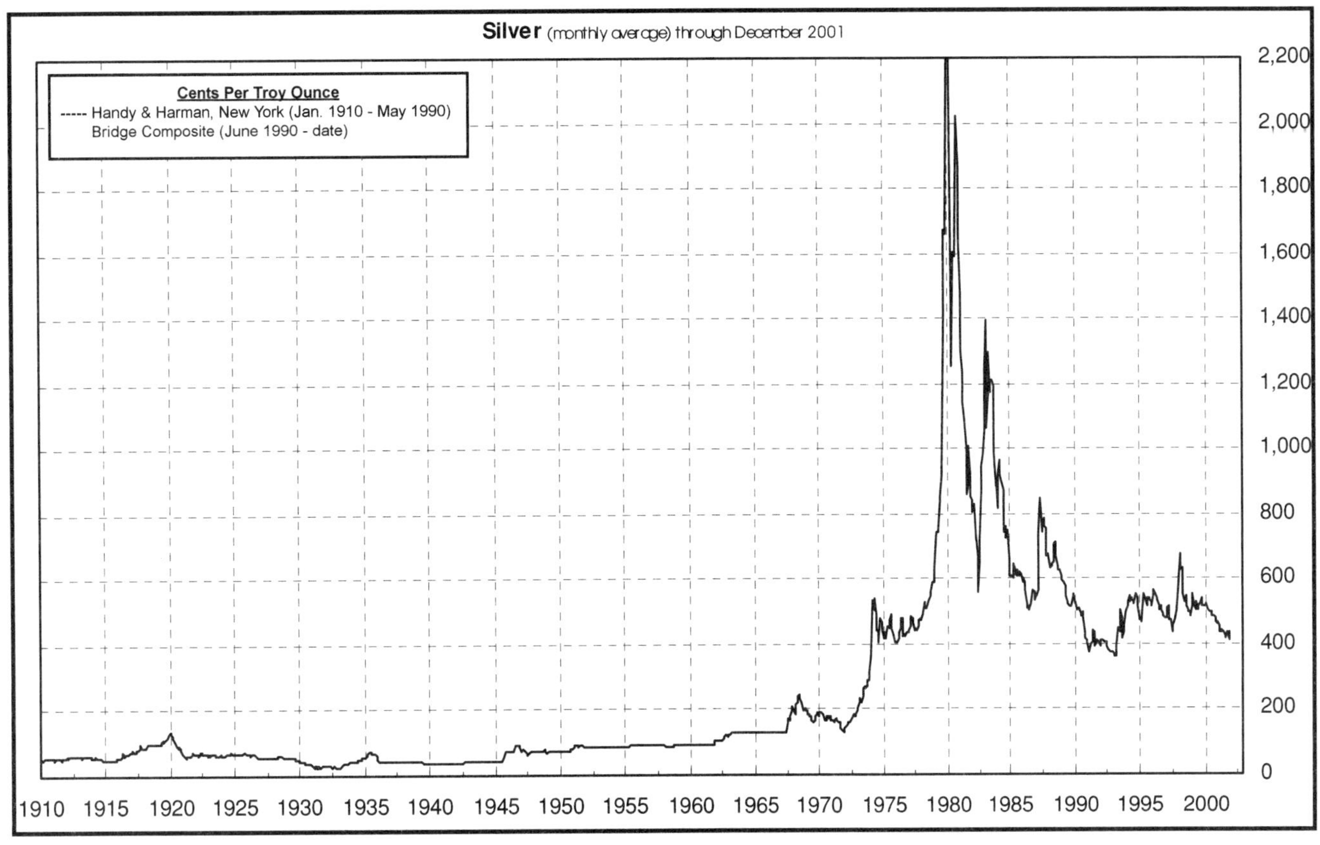

Average Price of Silver in New York (Handy & Harman) In Cents Per Troy Ounce (.999 Fine)

Year	Jan.	Feb.	Mar.	Apr.	May	June	July	Aug.	Sept.	Oct.	Nov.	Dec.	Average
1992	412.08	413.71	410.36	403.00	406.83	405.64	394.89	379.67	376.33	373.66	376.32	370.98	393.62
1993	367.93	364.39	364.80	396.36	445.02	437.50	503.74	480.61	417.19	433.45	450.25	496.83	429.84
1994	513.14	527.24	545.11	530.87	543.64	539.34	528.65	519.54	552.88	544.10	519.60	476.88	528.42
1995	476.36	469.53	464.83	552.42	555.25	535.27	517.58	539.59	540.78	534.48	529.30	514.75	519.18
1996	547.03	562.75	551.38	540.14	536.02	513.58	502.95	510.50	501.57	492.76	481.69	480.14	518.34
1997	483.70	508.76	519.88	476.41	475.80	474.60	435.96	451.36	472.69	501.15	507.30	571.53	489.07
1998	584.58	672.61	617.18	628.86	558.65	526.05	546.82	516.45	502.67	500.18	498.39	476.85	552.68
1999	511.61	554.55	519.85	509.21	529.83	507.73	522.81	529.36	527.86	541.67	519.20	521.95	524.75
2000	523.47	529.65	510.15	510.37	504.30	505.20	501.82	492.76	494.50	488.14	471.93	466.40	499.89
2001	470.19	457.34	439.93	439.25	443.59	436.79	425.45	420.72	441.09	441.87	412.35	437.98	438.88

Source: American Metal Market (AMM)

Average Price of Silver in London (Spot Fix) In Pence Per Troy Ounce (.999 Fine)

Year	Jan.	Feb.	Mar.	Apr.	May	June	July	Aug.	Sept.	Oct.	Nov.	Dec.	Average
1991	209.50	190.10	216.00	227.61	234.43	266.86	263.97	235.06	234.22	238.90	229.09	228.03	231.15
1992	227.68	233.21	238.36	230.72	225.02	219.32	206.74	197.03	203.89	226.06	246.94	240.01	224.58
1993	240.39	254.41	249.55	256.16	287.61	289.42	335.27	324.64	276.85	285.48	306.07	332.78	286.55
1994	344.48	354.77	364.74	358.95	360.86	353.28	341.86	336.67	353.15	339.73	326.64	306.49	345.14
1995	302.80	300.36	290.35	341.95	248.74	336.31	323.80	343.72	348.99	340.29	339.90	336.05	329.44
1996	359.20	367.64	362.03	392.85	354.25	334.68	325.81	330.93	322.98	310.78	290.51	289.77	336.79
1997	287.63	311.95	323.99	293.08	291.43	289.16	272.73	280.36	295.67	308.69	300.76	348.90	300.36
1998	359.62	416.55	375.76	378.77	339.42	319.05	331.87	317.74	297.40	295.41	298.72	291.77	335.17
1999	312.69	340.46	320.27	315.12	326.80	315.51	328.86	327.98	322.20	326.42	317.53	319.87	322.75
2000	316.08	327.90	320.87	319.61	330.53	331.24	329.35	327.80	340.75	332.24	327.71	317.47	326.94

Source: American Metal Market (AMM)

SILVER

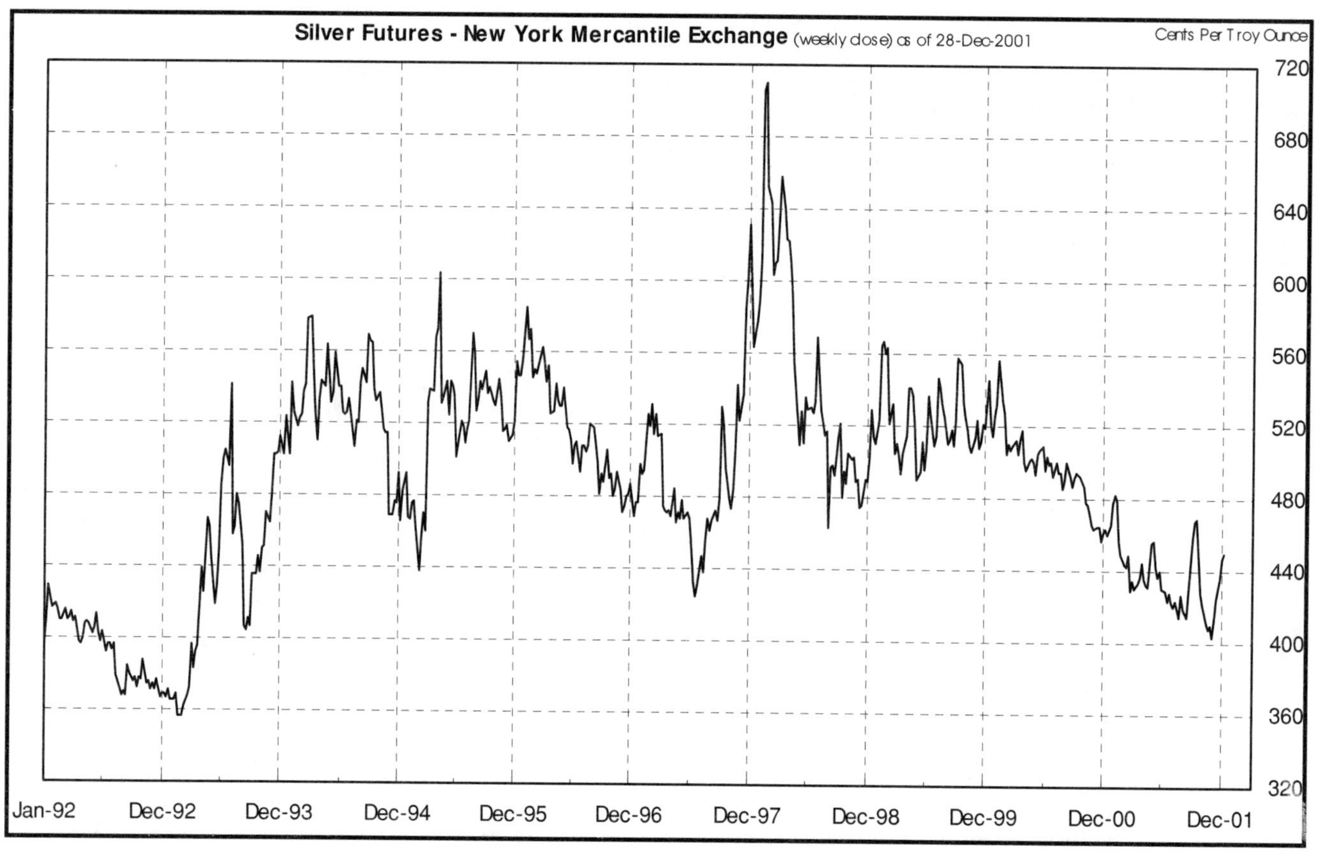

Average Open Interest of Silver Futures in New York (COMEX) In Contracts

Year	Jan.	Feb.	Mar.	Apr.	May	June	July	Aug.	Sept.	Oct.	Nov.	Dec.
1992	97,179	93,352	88,445	96,427	87,355	84,002	80,879	81,695	74,265	72,090	77,633	72,296
1993	80,155	86,241	87,127	100,985	105,931	102,539	107,537	109,427	93,891	93,316	101,576	110,029
1994	112,584	116,652	112,745	119,314	121,296	126,255	122,138	118,081	113,261	117,224	126,666	134,099
1995	132,158	139,806	132,317	129,063	112,723	108,941	101,842	111,251	95,433	101,763	105,453	95,551
1996	99,316	107,667	92,186	101,011	99,529	110,247	105,627	103,618	93,448	95,809	93,238	83,879
1997	91,385	94,539	90,531	97,434	87,510	90,145	96,777	89,250	79,344	100,464	96,695	93,761
1998	95,717	108,284	91,730	83,045	79,451	91,563	78,353	82,530	74,848	74,451	76,440	78,716
1999	77,946	97,593	82,435	82,824	78,745	78,943	78,151	86,601	77,490	86,577	80,564	70,275
2000	76,187	81,398	75,765	76,213	75,001	76,466	75,199	91,083	73,441	78,222	83,142	73,644
2001	69,408	72,798	74,337	71,589	67,328	67,429	75,019	75,830	65,533	66,530	74,228	66,903

Source: New York Mercantile Exchange (NYMEX), COMEX Division

Volume of Trading of Silver Futures in New York (COMEX) In Contracts

Year	Jan.	Feb.	Mar.	Apr.	May	June	July	Aug.	Sept.	Oct.	Nov.	Dec.	Total
1992	408,179	320,226	229,010	322,364	184,825	295,358	197,946	266,347	173,165	125,537	355,728	127,654	3,016,339
1993	167,201	315,916	242,974	476,554	433,460	523,961	503,935	531,772	428,366	338,189	520,591	373,005	4,855,924
1994	489,055	555,136	484,134	585,058	516,396	729,414	339,298	535,722	377,540	455,049	589,220	348,323	5,994,345
1995	390,453	501,454	541,807	592,620	500,522	476,481	280,651	655,854	344,182	272,362	447,095	179,755	5,183,236
1996	415,801	583,767	368,175	547,629	334,973	549,631	296,905	460,686	316,366	321,781	415,441	259,653	4,870,808
1997	401,995	530,514	360,871	493,999	280,536	472,306	340,245	425,471	335,400	430,397	488,024	333,762	4,893,520
1998	352,688	550,800	368,127	360,130	310,130	393,971	278,774	367,257	283,475	280,066	319,216	229,982	4,094,616
1999	315,165	550,271	355,559	424,822	274,002	373,662	288,480	422,653	328,907	318,256	344,289	161,434	4,157,500
2000	258,053	425,910	231,336	318,752	216,938	407,455	175,235	370,739	146,007	149,252	303,673	113,667	3,117,017
2001	175,026	302,035	155,658	252,486	204,552	281,846	112,956	267,711	160,329	210,266	266,077	180,256	2,569,198

Source: New York Mercantile Exchange (NYMEX), COMEX division

Mine Production of Recoverable Silver in the United States In Metric Tons

Year	Arizona	Idaho	Montana	Nevada	Total	Year	Arizona	Idaho	Montana	Nevada	Total
1989	171	439	194	625	2,007	1995	220	182	76	766	1,640
1990	173	442	220	646	2,125	1996	189	234	11	596	1,570
1991	148	337	[illegible]	578	1,848	1997	100	311	W	707	2,180
1992	153	255	195	586	1,740	1998	211	447	W	670	2,060
1993	157	190	125	713	1,610	1999	183	416	W	597	1,950
1994	183	158	71	602	1,390	2000[1]	132	416	W	633	1,860

[1] Preliminary. W = Withheld proprietary data. *Source: U.S. Geological Survey (USGS)*

Consumption of Silver in the United States, by End Use In Millions of Troy Ounces

Year	Brazing Alloy & Solders	Catalysts	Batteries	Mirrors	Electrical Contacts-Conductors	Photo-graphic Materials	Silver-plate	Jewerly	Sterling Ware	Total Net Industrial Con-sumption	Coinage	Total Con-sumption
1991	5.6	3.3	3.1	1.1	18.3	60.0	2.8	2.0	3.5	118.7	9.1	127.8
1992	7.1	3.8	3.1	1.2	18.3	64.4	2.9	3.0	3.9	118.9	8.1	127.0
1993	7.2	4.0	3.3	1.3	18.8	65.0	3.0	3.3	4.0	121.1	8.9	130.0
1994	7.5	4.2	3.6	1.5	19.5	71.0	3.1	3.7	4.2	130.1	8.1	138.2
1995	7.7	4.9	4.1	1.7	20.9	72.9	3.5	4.1	4.4	136.2	7.5	143.7
1996	8.2	5.5	4.5	2.1	22.3	78.3	3.9	4.4	4.8	146.7	5.0	151.7
1997	8.9	5.7	4.8	2.4	26.5	84.6	4.1	4.9	5.1	160.5	5.3	165.8
1998	9.3	5.9	4.9	2.6	28.4	91.0	4.5	5.5	5.7	172.3	5.6	177.9
1999	9.1	5.9	5.0	2.6	29.2	96.0	4.4	5.7	5.8	178.5	10.0	188.5
2000[1]	8.6	6.3	5.2	2.6	32.7	104.0	4.5	6.1	5.6	191.1	10.0	201.1

[1] Preliminary. *Source: The Silver Institute*

Commodity Exchange, Inc. (COMEX) Warehouse of Stocks of Silver In Thousands of Troy Ounces

Year	Jan. 1	Feb. 1	Mar. 1	Apr. 1	May 1	June 1	July 1	Aug. 1	Sept. 1	Oct. 1	Nov. 1	Dec. 1
1992	271,692	278,990	270,449	262,239	267,003	267,818	271,259	273,743	278,575	278,526	280,712	275,156
1993	272,824	273,629	271,856	265,580	270,800	273,947	277,228	278,745	276,819	275,370	277,666	263,138
1994	251,685	250,730	239,374	240,187	233,950	236,459	246,291	249,417	255,198	259,634	265,710	258,618
1995	260,708	264,045	235,114	211,028	189,668	184,570	181,269	175,764	156,544	156,529	156,110	156,932
1996	159,695	143,426	151,336	139,059	141,789	150,141	168,079	155,441	151,283	141,673	129,911	148,451
1997	204,051	195,450	193,381	191,676	189,498	201,682	184,691	169,079	164,296	138,775	133,470	128,252
1998	110,437	103,778	89,458	86,926	89,715	89,628	85,911	79,136	78,681	73,142	74,260	76,818
1999	76,301	75,017	78,135	79,664	79,415	76,976	73,973	77,592	80,126	79,388	78,738	78,416
2000	75,984	73,326	95,594	104,053	102,589	99,053	102,713	101,786	97,133	99,552	95,387	95,717
2001	93,069	99,876	98,659	96,690	95,745	95,876	NA	NA	NA	NA	NA	104,831

Source: New York Mercantile Exchange (NYMEX), COMEX Division

Production[2] of Refined Silver in the United States, from All Sources In Metric Tons

Year	Jan.	Feb.	Mar.	Apr.	May	June	July	Aug.	Sept.	Oct.	Nov.	Dec.	Total
1992	414	388	396	375	408	295	366	350	323	393	331	364	4,403
1993	359	406	374	357	315	266	293	275	292	293	261	303	3,794
1994	278	327	319	307	209	371	239	288	273	254	297	281	3,443
1995	279	273	340	281	381	355	331	404	364	340	384	351	4,083
1996	373	299	332	321	327	316	354	314	333	344	304	403	4,020
1997	343	262	296	331	250	326	292	344	331	281	340	382	3,778
1998	338	486	426	372	377	374	394	324	463	443	469	447	4,860
1999	424	420	441	356	368	394	404	316	354	371	364	396	4,608
2000	436	1,177	551	399	431	390	361	402	400	469	386	401	5,803
2001[1]	405	343	405	360	360	331	395	380	337				4,422

[1] Preliminary. [2] Through 1991; output of commercial bars .999 fine, including U.S. Mint purchases of crude. Production is from both foreign and domestic silver. Beginning 1992; U.S. mine production of recoverable silver plus imports of refined silver. *Source: U.S. Geological Survey (USGS)*

U.S. Exports of Refined Silver to Selected Countries In Thousands of Troy Ounces

Year	Canada	France	Germany	Hong Kong	Japan	Singapore	South Korea	Switzerland	United Arab Emirates	United Kingdom	Uruguay	Other Countries	World Total
1990	2,586	64	749	----	16,568	1,005	298	74	----	2,060	152	108	23,664
1991	736	22	350	755	6,519	1,593	2,823	8	3,462	8,628	259	73	25,318
1992	2,177	44	140	497	4,554	2,126	[2]	70	6,922	10,856	671	47	29,274
1993	4,910	[2]	34	1,002	3,414	2,500	1,492	38	4,403	3,673	530	44	22,673
1994	3,138	[2]	8	456	10,385	16	2,701	14	4,823	4,212	1,489	14	27,889
1995	1,665	431	[2]	[2]	5,819	2,209	2,932	1,177	10,288	63,980	939	5	90,462
1996	489	[2]	2	646	4,662	3,601	383	2,413	15,850	35,366	624	40	93,346
1997	903	[2]	2	797	6,044	[2]	547	5,305	16,751	62,694	402	17	96,038
1998	485	2,206	347	----	579	208	----	20	3,569	60,444	621	9	72,479
1999[1]	11	2	1	----	585	37	----	----	4,249	7,719	----	20	15,455

[1] Preliminary. [2] Included in other countries, if any. *Source: American Bureau of Metal Statistics, Inc. (ABMS)*

U.S. Imports of Silver From Selected Countries In Thousands of Troy Ounces

Year	Canada	Mexico	Other Countries	Total	Canada	Chile	Mexico	Peru	Uruguay	Other Countries	Total
1990	12	189	2	203	33,518	1,671	40,204	8,141	2,265	942	86,741
1991	42	277	29	348	25,389	6,640	34,448	13,748	[2]	973	81,198
1992	646	126	42	814	24,937	2,002	40,230	16,841	400	1,162	85,572
1993	299	836	12	1,147	28,622	1,058	27,241	12,709	[2]	559	70,189
1994	369	3,805	97	4,271	28,678	1,923	22,135	12,663	[2]	742	66,141
1995	338	6,655	243	7,236	27,649	2,003	31,957	13,728	[2]	9,197	84,534
1996	256	4,662	----	4,918	35,365	1,874	30,285	12,153	[2]	3,122	82,799
1997	7	4,437	85	4,529	29,385	608	28,774	8,873	[2]	376	68,016
1998	24	5,851	419	6,294	34,722	813	41,152	9,388	[2]	3,931	90,006
1999[1]	11	335	1	347	42,952	1,048	33,050	5,433	[2]	2,562	85,045

[1] Preliminary. [2] Included in other countries, if any. *Source: American Bureau of Metal Statistics, Inc. (ABMS)*

World Silver Consumption[1] In Millions of Troy Ounces

	Industrial Uses										Coinage							
Year	Canada	France	Germany	India	Italy	Japan	Mexico	United Kingdom	United States	World Total	Austria	Canada	France	Germany	Mexico	United States	World Total	Grand Total
1990	4.6	24.1	51.7	46.8	51.4	106.9	12.9	24.6	121.6	684.6	.5	1.9	2.1	2.6	1.2	9.4	32.1	716.7
1991	3.8	26.0	52.2	44.8	56.5	108.8	13.5	25.0	119.8	677.8	.6	.9	2.3	5.7	1.6	10.8	29.2	707.0
1992	1.5	28.8	49.3	58.1	60.1	104.9	14.2	26.3	127.1	681.1	.5	.8	2.1	5.6	8.7	8.5	33.5	714.6
1993	1.6	28.1	45.7	108.8	56.3	105.5	14.9	27.7	131.6	739.1	.5	1.2	2.1	2.8	17.1	9.2	41.5	780.6
1994	1.6	27.2	45.7	93.9	51.6	108.4	14.6	30.4	140.4	722.4	.5	1.5	1.0	7.1	13.0	9.5	43.8	766.2
1995	2.0	30.0	43.6	101.3	49.5	112.7	16.9	31.6	148.7	752.7	.5	.7	1.2	2.4	.6	9.0	24.7	777.4
1996	2.0	26.9	41.0	122.2	51.7	112.1	20.3	33.8	155.0	785.8	.5	.7	.3	4.6	.5	7.1	23.3	809.1
1997	2.2	28.3	42.3	122.9	56.1	119.9	23.3	34.9	166.3	828.2	.4	.6	.3	3.7	.4	6.5	28.5	856.7
1998	2.3	28.3	38.4	104.3	56.0	112.8	22.0	38.6	181.8	809.9	.3	1.1	.3	8.4	.2	7.0	26.1	836.0
1999[2]	2.1	26.2	35.1	109.0	62.0	125.2	23.0	39.3	193.9	850.4	.3	1.4	.3	5.4	.4	11.2	27.0	877.4

[1] Non-communist areas only. [2] Preliminary. *Source: The Silver Institute*

Soybean Meal

Soybean meal prices, basis Chicago futures, traversed a narrow $30/ton range during 2001 with seasonal firmness in the first half of the year followed by slippage during the second half. On balance the bias was bearish with the year's closing values about $30/ton under a year earlier.

Global supply/demand for soybean meal during the past decade shows steady growth and the trend is likely to persist owing largely to the expansion in world poultry numbers. Soybean meal, a high protein feed used in formulating livestock and poultry rations is obtained from the processing (crush) of soybeans and is the world's major protein meal with about two-thirds of total meal production--(124 million metric tons in 2001/02 out of a total of 183 million). Cottonseed and rapeseed meal account for a combined total of about 17%. The U.S. is the largest producer followed by Brazil and Argentina whose combined total lags U.S. production.

World soybean meal production in the late 1990's averaged less than 100 million metric tons. In 2001/02 a record large 124 million metric tons were produced, of which the U.S. produced a record 36.2 million tons vs. 35.7 million in 2000/01. Brazil's production reached a high record 18.2 million tons vs. 17.8 million in 2000/01 while Argentina's production at 15.6 million tons compares with 14 million tons, respectively. Part of the growth in meal production has been indirectly derived from the strong worldwide demand for vegetable oils, but the primary reason is that more countries have increasing livestock numbers and a burgeoning need for high protein feed; a fact underscored by the sharp expansion in the world's soybean meal trade with much of the recent gains emanating from developing nations in Latin America and Asia.

World soybean meal consumption in 2001/02 of a record large 123.86 million tons compares with 123 million in 2000/01 and less than 100 million as recently as 1997/98. The U.S. is the largest single consumer with about 28 million tons annually in recent years, but collectively the European Union and especially Asia have closed the gap with 29 million and 35 million tons, respectively. In 2001/02 Asia's use is forecast as particularly strong reflecting the growth in the region's poultry production. China's 2001/02 consumption of a record 17.4 million tons compares with an annual average of about 10.5 million tons in the late 1990's. Despite China's surging demand, imports have dropped, totaling only 300,000 tons in 2001/02 vs. a record large 4.2 million in 1997/98: early in the 1990's, China was a net exporter of soybean meal. France in 2001/02 was the largest single importer with 4.25 million tons, about 10% of the world total. Exports are dominated by Argentina and Brazil with a combined 26 million tons in 2001/02 out of a 43.1 million ton total. World carryover at the end of the 2001/02 season is forecast at 3.9 million tons, marginally higher than both initial estimates and the year earlier total (3.86 million tons); as usual, Brazil account for at least a quarter of the carryover.

U.S. soybean meal production (October-September) in 2001/02 of a record 40 million short tons compares with 39.4 million in 2000/01. Total 2001/02 supplies of 40.4 million tons compares with 39.7 million in 2000/01, including a small carry-in at the start of each crop year of about 300,000 tons. Total supplies in the early 1990's averaged near 30 million tons, but domestic usage has since climbed steadily and forecast at a record high 32.4 million tons in 2001/02 vs. 31.7 million in 2000/01 owing to increases in poultry production. Indeed, poultry demand now controls the U.S. soybean crush, and not the soybean oil factor. Cattle accounts for little soybean meal use, hogs somewhat more.

U.S. soybean meal exports in 2001/02 were forecast at 7.8 million short tons vs. 7.6 million in 2000/01 and a record large 9.3 million in 1997/98; the decline from the latter season reflecting smaller demand from China as well as the European Union and increased foreign competition from Brazil and Argentina.

U.S. soybean meal wholesale prices, basis 44%-- hi-protein, Decatur, Illinois, in 2000/01 averaged $173.62 per short ton vs. $167.62 in 1999/00 and the 1994-1999 average of $192 per ton. Rotterdam and Brazilian prices tend to average higher than prices. During 2001/02, domestic meal prices may be pressured somewhat as processors may crush more aggressively for oil which in turn increases meal output.

Futures Markets

Soybean meal futures and options are traded on the Chicago Board of Trade. A smaller futures contract is traded on the Mid-America Commodity Exchange.

World Supply and Distribution of Soybean Meal In Thousands of Metric Tons

Year Beginning Oct. 1	Production: Brazil	Production: China	Production: European Union	Production: United States	Production: Total	Exports: Brazil	Exports: United States	Exports: Total	Imports: France	Imports: Total	Consumption: European Union	Consumption: United States	Consumption: Total	Ending Stocks: Brazil	Ending Stocks: United States	Ending Stocks: Total
1992-3	13,161	3,634	10,991	27,546	77,489	9,301	5,673	29,032	3,500	28,046	22,249	21,981	76,101	526	185	3,329
1993-4	14,726	6,160	9,855	27,682	81,315	10,519	4,867	30,106	3,798	29,563	22,862	22,927	81,061	434	136	3,040
1994-5	16,977	6,958	11,825	30,182	89,302	11,471	6,092	32,389	3,792	31,588	25,068	24,081	87,812	640	203	3,729
1995-6	15,841	6,051	11,387	29,508	87,895	10,900	5,446	32,220	3,343	32,823	23,462	24,140	88,754	381	193	3,473
1996-7	14,863	5,963	11,987	31,035	89,607	9,800	6,344	32,593	3,266	34,389	22,334	24,785	91,785	344	191	3,091
1997-8	15,730	6,717	12,866	34,633	103,681	10,850	8,464	41,495	3,647	37,602	24,740	26,213	99,924	332	198	2,955
1998-9	16,600	10,023	12,912	34,285	107,743	10,150	6,461	38,871	4,106	39,476	27,655	27,812	107,363	457	300	3,940
1999-00	16,750	11,980	11,470	34,100	107,830	9,930	6,650	39,660	4,150	39,840	25,870	27,530	109,070	900	270	3,870
2000-1[1]	17,790	14,950	13,780	35,730	117,820	1,050	6,930	41,140	4,350	41,320	28,050	28,770	117,980	990	350	3,880
2001-2[2]	18,250	17,170	14,490	36,460	124,560	10,850	7,170	43,340	4,250	43,510	29,100	29,350	124,530	990	250	3,990

[1] Preliminary. [2] Forecast. *Source: Foreign Agricultural Service, U.S. Department of Agriculture (FAS-USDA)*

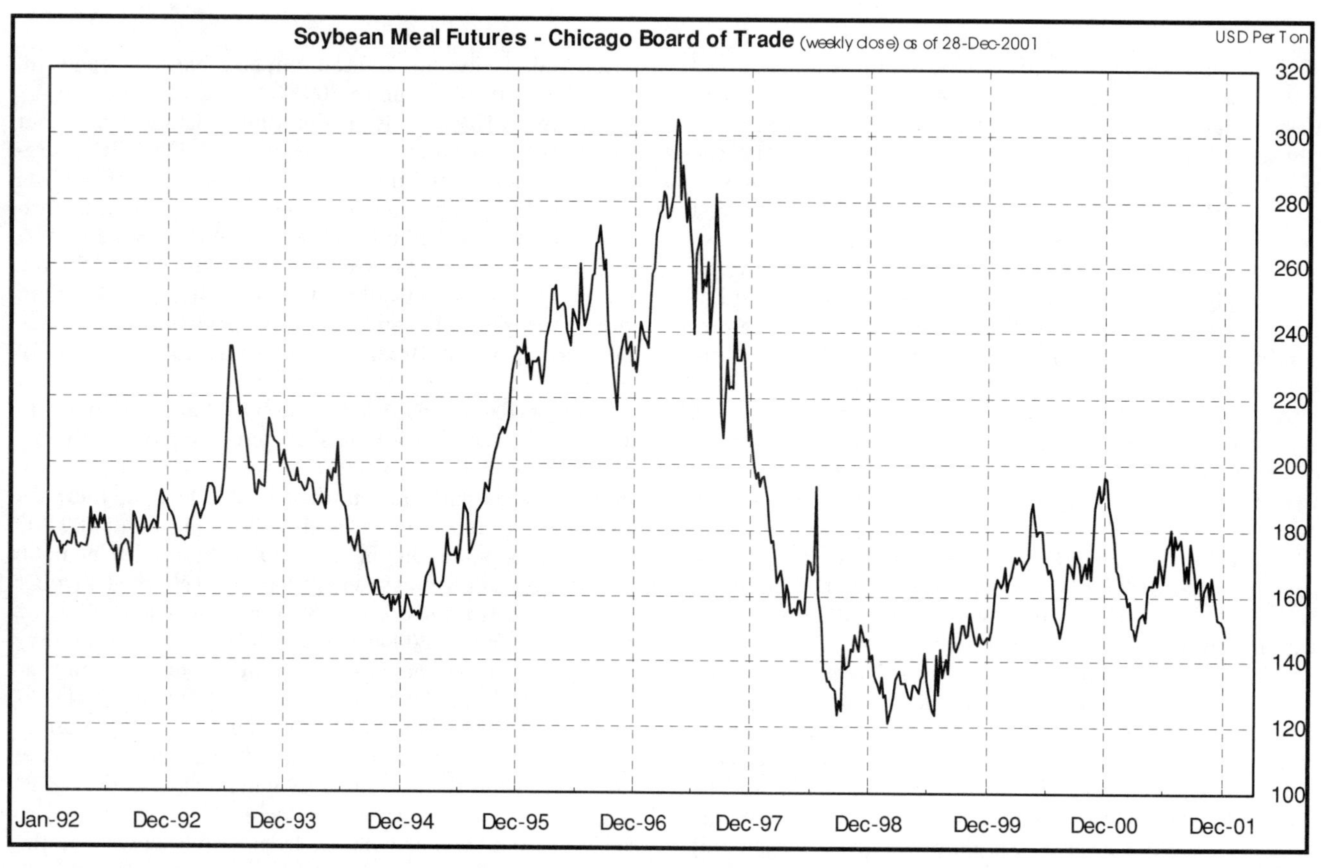

Average Open Interest of Soybean Meal Futures in Chicago In Contracts

Year	Jan.	Feb.	Mar.	Apr.	May	June	July	Aug.	Sept.	Oct.	Nov.	Dec.
1992	67,575	56,453	55,370	59,528	57,204	60,519	66,315	66,861	66,648	72,403	73,255	72,881
1993	63,178	70,384	64,550	66,121	78,386	74,191	91,435	73,770	75,267	77,065	83,802	85,039
1994	87,612	91,142	82,193	89,453	85,553	81,721	84,461	82,691	85,508	94,483	101,030	98,717
1995	97,661	101,253	101,846	99,898	90,237	86,090	83,712	74,233	79,450	85,290	103,824	110,193
1996	95,903	90,010	87,468	101,204	91,453	88,641	77,961	80,727	93,373	88,969	90,007	84,399
1997	86,204	97,618	107,763	111,413	113,848	110,780	114,372	108,923	111,447	118,409	125,201	116,760
1998	114,243	122,979	131,390	137,251	136,212	136,216	126,108	139,239	140,904	141,426	134,095	122,788
1999	123,041	130,473	121,435	112,155	104,176	108,134	116,464	121,202	120,462	112,426	117,523	104,246
2000	115,285	124,822	120,157	123,957	123,691	112,425	105,230	94,469	105,240	103,263	120,164	127,529
2001	111,880	108,047	107,253	116,888	119,644	135,046	134,982	129,536	123,644	121,845	145,996	147,576

Source: Chicago Board of Trade (CBT)

Volume of Trading of Soybean Meal Futures in Chicago In Contracts

Year	Jan.	Feb.	Mar.	Apr.	May	June	July	Aug.	Sept.	Oct.	Nov.	Dec.	Total[1]
1992	368,714	290,492	312,556	312,187	388,097	380,975	425,995	333,639	327,556	320,176	327,854	357,156	4,145.4
1993	295,555	273,673	346,607	323,253	356,757	518,212	575,510	460,550	402,399	315,643	469,343	380,593	4,718.1
1994	405,590	339,834	330,694	380,736	467,223	456,279	384,508	354,372	366,263	317,438	370,377	420,500	4,593.8
1995	283,623	307,477	404,387	410,860	532,694	479,589	610,833	491,775	481,949	449,009	523,440	625,606	5,601.2
1996	496,414	442,937	435,764	655,984	439,212	442,370	507,240	490,349	425,850	581,126	491,917	452,139	5,861.3
1997	479,001	481,841	509,515	576,564	581,886	569,760	579,748	452,188	531,299	589,542	561,133	512,471	6,424.9
1998	458,519	454,310	449,806	592,614	499,468	749,765	675,104	536,650	504,088	553,224	521,231	559,067	6,553.8
1999	420,240	509,348	476,104	477,102	390,527	646,806	710,110	597,026	568,859	511,503	572,194	447,078	6,326.9
2000	455,335	537,527	556,010	467,698	566,607	606,190	488,172	469,017	484,617	483,174	690,313	513,328	6,318.0
2001	530,193	431,822	470,608	485,106	584,352	625,089	709,973	630,909	491,398	652,931	659,328	472,063	6,743.8

[1] In thousands of contracts. *Source: Chicago Board of Trade (CBT)*

Supply and Distribution of Soybean Meal in the United States — In Thousands of Short Tons

Year Beginning Oct. 1	Supply: For Stocks Oct. 1	Supply: Production	Supply: Total Supply	Distribution: Domestic	Distribution: Exports	Distribution: Total	$ Per Ton Decatur 48% Protein Solvent	$ Per Metric Ton: Decatur 44% Protein Solvent	$ Per Metric Ton: Brazil FOB 45-46% Protein	$ Per Metric Ton: Rotterdam CIF
1992-3	230	30,364	30,687	24,251	6,232	30,483	193.75	201	185	207
1993-4	204	30,514	30,788	25,282	5,356	30,638	192.86	199	182	202
1994-5	150	33,269	33,483	26,542	6,717	33,260	162.55	167	172	184
1995-6	223	32,527	32,826	26,611	6,002	32,613	236.00	248	256	256
1996-7	212	34,211	34,525	27,321	6,994	34,316	270.90	286	289	278
1997-8	210	38,176	38,442	28,894	9,330	38,224	185.28	193	201	197
1998-9	218	37,797	38,114	30,662	7,122	37,784	138.55	145	150	150
1999-00[1]	330	37,591	37,970	30,346	7,331	37,677	167.70	176	182	180
2000-1[2]	293	39,389	39,733	31,713	7,636	39,350	173.60	192	205	209
2001-2[3]	386	39,839	40,275	32,350	7,650	40,000	150-170	192	205	209

[1] Preliminary. [2] Estimate. [3] Forecast. *Source: Economic Research Service, U.S. Department of Agriculture (ERS-USDA)*

U.S. Exports of Soybean Cake & Meal by Country of Destination — In Thousands of Metric Tons

Year	Algeria	Australia	Canada	Dominican Republic	Italy	Japan	Mexico	Netherlands	Philippines	Russia[2]	Spain	Venezuela	Total
1990	373.5	28.2	555.5	130.5	146.4	20.8	253.0	229.7	200.7	1,568.4	19.6	332.2	4,826
1991	323.5	99.4	651.2	142.6	33.5	24.1	303.6	339.8	150.4	2,271.0	5.5	405.9	5,536
1992	237.8	75.9	582.5	146.7	93.4	167.2	454.4	420.0	434.8	765.1	92.3	473.8	6,236
1993	266.1	90.6	646.7	200.8	91.5	208.7	187.8	580.8	295.7	697.1	203.8	425.0	5,536
1994	248.3	247.0	706.3	209.2	27.1	76.9	367.5	465.6	257.9	159.5	92.6	258.9	4,825
1995	216.7	190.2	798.7	219.2	70.2	246.7	340.0	751.6	593.4	11.1	127.7	181.4	5,890
1996	203.4	156.2	687.3	260.7	85.9	225.5	292.2	453.5	423.2	5.1	51.8	274.9	5,860
1997	250.8	134.1	651.6	261.1	284.1	263.0	142.1	451.2	483.1	8.3	329.1	336.7	6,994
1998	263.2	135.5	774.7	221.2	217.6	265.7	127.8	274.6	758.7	----	296.2	446.2	8,035
1999[1]	213.2	166.8	790.8	308.9	51.5	208.9	304.3	197.6	860.5	----	60.1	357.8	6,634

[1] Preliminary. [2] Formerly part of the U.S.S.R.; data not reported separately until 1992. *Source: The Oil World*

Production of Soybean Cake & Meal[2] in the United States — In Thousands of Short Tons

Year	Oct.	Nov.	Dec.	Jan.	Feb.	Mar.	Apr.	May	June	July	Aug.	Sept.	Total	Yield in lbs.
1991-2	----	7,920.4	----	2,665.5	2,393.8	2,544.4	2,411.3	2,262.5	2,372.4	2,434.2	2,429.0	2,397.3	29,831	47.51
1992-3	2,698.1	2,697.3	2,763.4	2,781.2	2,430.4	2,691.3	2,519.1	2,536.3	2,373.0	2,324.1	2,188.3	2,361.8	30,364	47.54
1993-4	2,707.1	2,714.8	2,696.7	2,632.3	2,458.1	2,696.3	2,510.0	2,446.4	2,330.7	2,398.0	2,406.6	2,517.1	30,514	47.62
1994-5	2,812.5	2,903.5	3,027.8	3,007.5	2,755.0	3,048.5	2,829.8	2,697.9	2,492.1	2,565.4	2,589.8	2,535.8	33,269	47.33
1995-6	2,893.2	2,948.9	2,972.3	2,945.2	2,652.1	2,757.5	2,683.1	2,534.6	2,566.2	2,656.3	2,513.4	2,404.1	32,527	47.69
1996-7	2,992.8	3,151.8	3,263.8	3,251.7	2,966.8	3,089.1	2,709.1	2,618.1	2,573.2	2,517.4	2,465.2	2,611.0	34,211	47.36
1997-8	3,344.0	3,390.6	3,624.2	3,592.1	3,279.2	3,484.0	3,172.5	2,956.7	2,795.2	2,941.5	2,665.6	2,930.7	37,176	47.41
1998-9	3,365.1	3,368.4	3,422.4	3,214.4	3,027.7	3,302.7	3,044.2	3,024.4	2,844.0	3,011.9	3,003.5	3,167.8	37,797	47.25
1999-00	3,573.4	3,400.4	3,413.5	3,332.8	2,998.2	3,123.6	2,906.1	2,882.5	2,845.4	3,118.8	2,906.8	3,089.7	37,591	47.76
2000-1[1]	3,573.9	3,432.8	3,399.4	3,524.2	3,085.2	3,412.0	3,151.5	3,180.4	3,091.1	3,256.2	3,203.1	3,079.2	39,389	48.01

[1] Preliminary. [2] At oil mills; including millfeed and lecithin. *Sources: Economic Research Service, U.S. Department of Agriculture (ERS-USDA)*

Stocks (at Oil Mills)[2] of Soybean Cake & Meal in the U.S., on First of Month — In Thousands of Short Tons

Year	Oct.	Nov.	Dec.	Jan.	Feb.	Mar.	Apr.	May	June	July	Aug.	Sept.
1991-2	ÑÑ	285.0	ÑÑ	281.0	258.3	291.3	315.6	310.4	310.2	274.7	260.5	209.9
1992-3	230.0	307.9	411.3	360.8	440.0	420.5	336.9	268.5	328.4	257.3	386.1	353.8
1993-4	204.4	375.1	282.3	290.1	230.0	283.1	277.3	333.0	325.2	254.3	267.5	144.9
1994-5	149.6	240.9	231.6	241.1	197.7	227.1	173.1	382.7	337.6	222.6	252.0	203.8
1995-6	223.4	196.9	241.3	394.8	302.2	229.9	369.3	382.1	306.8	406.2	298.8	218.3
1996-7	212.4	200.2	291.8	254.4	263.0	198.5	322.6	280.1	256.5	317.3	303.2	257.4
1997-8	206.6	218.2	412.2	262.0	269.3	280.7	238.0	210.4	290.2	193.1	205.3	187.2
1998-9	218.1	271.9	352.3	313.9	380.5	436.4	341.0	316.0	447.7	284.2	394.8	279.4
1999-00	330.2	467.6	460.2	436.5	489.8	482.5	350.2	441.2	325.0	260.2	305.8	225.9
2000-1[1]	292.9	317.4	343.8	423.7	334.0	325.8	309.2	313.4	287.0	341.4	338.1	274.0

[1] Preliminary. [2] Including millfeed and lecithin. *Source: Economic Research Service, U.S. Department of Agriculture (ERS-USDA)*

SOYBEAN MEAL

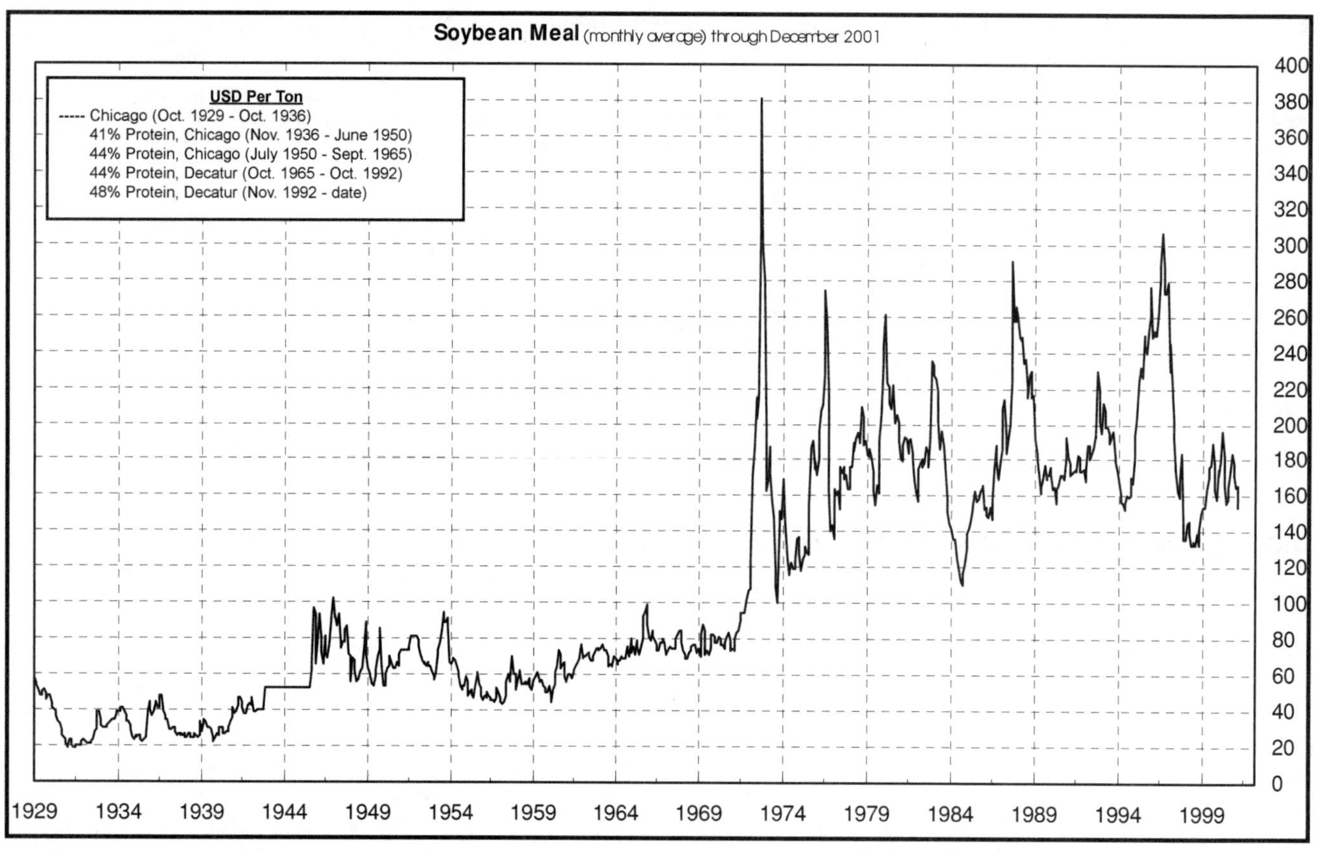

Average Price of Soybean Meal (44% Solvent) in Decatur Illinois In Dollars Per Short Ton -- Bulk

Year	Oct.	Nov.	Dec.	Jan.	Feb.	Mar.	Apr.	May	June	July	Aug.	Sept.	Average
1991-2	183.0	178.0	170.7	172.7	174.3	174.2	174.8	182.8	181.7	173.9	174.4	175.1	176.3
1992-3	168.6	170.9	176.4	175.6	167.5	172.4	175.6	181.7	181.3	217.6	206.9	186.5	181.8
1993-4	180.6	195.7	192.5	185.9	184.4	182.0	176.4	191.1	183.0	168.1	165.6	162.5	180.7
1994-5	156.4	150.9	145.4	145.1	149.4	145.7	151.0	148.1	149.1	160.1	157.5	171.8	152.5
1995-6	183.4	194.1	213.6	220.5	216.7	215.7	237.9	232.3	227.9	242.3	251.1	265.5	225.1
1996-7	238.0	242.7	240.9	240.7	253.6	270.4	277.7	296.0	275.9	261.5	261.6	265.7	260.4
1997-8	216.0	231.6	214.9	193.1	182.1	165.3	152.8	150.3	157.8	173.3	135.7	126.9	175.0
1998-9	129.4	139.3	139.6	131.0	124.4	127.2	128.6	127.0	131.7	125.7	135.9	144.1	132.0
1999-00	147.2	148.1	145.4	155.0	163.6	166.6	168.1	180.1	170.2	156.8	151.4	166.9	160.0
2000-1	166.0	173.7	187.9	183.2	166.1	156.3	158.5	165.1	172.6	184.3	178.5	171.5	172.0

Source: Economic Research Service, U.S. Department of Agriculture (ERS-USDA)

Average Price of Soybean Meal (48% Solvent) in Decatur Illinois In Dollars Per Short Ton -- Bulk

Year	Oct.	Nov.	Dec.	Jan.	Feb.	Mar.	Apr.	May	June	July	Aug.	Sept.	Average
1992-3	180.60	181.90	187.60	188.75	179.90	183.60	187.40	193.25	193.10	229.90	219.10	199.90	193.75
1993-4	194.50	209.40	206.00	198.30	198.40	195.40	188.90	193.75	195.50	181.10	178.60	174.50	192.86
1994-5	168.50	161.00	156.90	156.40	151.30	156.90	161.90	159.10	160.40	170.45	166.70	180.99	162.55
1995-6	193.90	204.10	223.60	232.00	228.30	226.57	249.30	244.30	238.80	252.50	261.20	276.40	235.90
1996-7	248.50	251.50	250.60	249.20	262.40	280.50	288.60	306.40	287.90	273.60	273.30	278.30	270.90
1997-8	229.30	245.30	222.50	202.85	192.75	174.20	162.50	160.00	168.55	183.40	146.25	135.80	185.28
1998-9	135.70	144.45	146.40	138.80	132.30	133.00	134.50	133.20	139.10	132.70	141.70	150.65	138.54
1999-00	153.57	154.70	154.00	163.41	170.85	175.50	177.53	189.34	177.45	163.38	157.48	174.60	167.65
2000-1	171.52	179.95	195.65	183.17	166.08	156.32	158.48	165.14	172.60	184.43	178.46	171.67	173.62
2001-2	165.45	166.10	154.18										161.91

Source: Economic Research Service, U.S. Department of Agriculture (ERS-USDA)

Soybean Oil

Soybean oil prices, basis nearest Chicago futures, rallied to a two-year high in mid-2001, largely on prospects of increased global demand, notably from China owing to their accession in the World trade Organization (WTO), but prices eased later in the year. The world's supply/demand for soybean oil shows protracted year-to-year gains to record highs. World production in 2001/02 of 28.4 million metric tons compares with the previous year's 26.9 million. The U.S., the world's largest bean oil producer, generally accounts for about a third of total production, producing nearly twice that of Brazil, the second largest producer. Of the important edible vegetable oils, soybean oil is the world's largest--about 31% in 2001/02-- followed by palm oil and rapeseed oil. World usage of soybean oil in 2001/02 of 28.4 million tons compares with 26.5 million in 2000/01. World carryover stocks at the end of 2001/02 were estimated at 2.40 million tons vs. 2.49 million a year earlier. The U.S. is the world's largest consumer with almost a third of the total followed by China with about half the U.S. total: 7.6 million tons and 3.9 million tons in 2001/02, respectively.

Global soybean oil exports in 2001/02 of a record 8.6 million tons compare with the previous year's 7.9 billion. Argentina is the largest exporter with 3.5 million tons in 2001/02. Importing nations are numerous: collectively, Asia is the largest importer followed by the Middle East.

The U.S. soybean oil crop year begins October 1. Production in 2001/02 of a record 18.8 billion pounds compares with 18.4 billion in 2000/01. In the mid-1990's, production averaged about 15 billion pounds. The oil content of U.S. soybeans correlates directly with temperatures and sunshine during the soybean pod-filling stages. Carry-in stocks on October 1, 2001 were estimated at 2.9 billion pounds vs. 2 billion a year earlier. The U.S. supply for 2001/02 of 21.7 billion pounds compares with 20.5 billion in 2000/01. Disappearance in 2001/02 of 19.2 billion pounds compares with 17.6 billion in 2000/01. Bean oil stocks were forecast to decline during 2001/02 to about 2.7 billion pounds as of September 30, 2002.

Domestic soybean oil use in 2001/02 is forecast at a record high 16.7 billion pounds vs. 16.2 billion in 2000/01 as domestic prices prove competitive to other fats and oils. U.S. exports have shown an irregular trend in recent years: estimated at 2.5 billion pounds in 2001/02 vs. 1.4 billion 2000/01 and the record high 3.1 billion in 1997/98.

Crude soybean oil prices (basis Decatur) in 2000/01 averaged 14.5 cents vs. 15.6 cents in 1999/00.

Futures Markets

Soybean oil futures and options are traded on the Chicago Board of Trade. A smaller contract trades on the MidAmerica Commodity Exchange (MidAm).

World Supply and Demand of Soybean Oil In Thousands of Metric Tons

Year	Production				Exports			Imports		Consumption					Stocks[3]	
Beginning		European	United			United					European		United		United	
Oct. 1	Brazil	Union	States	Total	Brazil	States	Total	India	Total	Brazil	Union	India	States	Total	States	Total
1992-3	3,154	2,545	6,250	17,446	771	663	4,268	42	3,799	2,342	2,002	562	5,903	17,141	705	1,826
1993-4	3,522	2,232	6,328	18,228	1,556	695	5,064	41	4,726	2,399	1,831	711	5,869	18,341	500	1,375
1994-5	4,061	2,672	7,082	20,161	1,643	1,217	6,287	60	5,986	2,500	1,927	555	5,857	19,209	516	2,026
1995-6	3,749	2,567	6,913	19,860	1,320	450	5,285	60	5,273	2,630	1,960	772	6,108	19,604	914	2,270
1996-7	3,521	2,685	7,145	20,318	1,075	922	6,004	49	5,904	2,676	1,871	706	6,471	20,544	690	1,944
1997-8	4,096	2,914	8,229	23,562	1,418	1,397	8,062	236	6,814	2,827	1,799	1,095	6,922	22,308	627	1,950
1998-9	4,040	2,926	8,202	24,735	1,463	1,076	8,191	833	7,981	2,816	1,834	1,805	7,101	24,525	689	1,950
1999-00	4,030	2,600	8,090	24,790	1,200	620	7,280	790	7,120	3,000	1,500	1,580	7,280	24,390	910	2,410
2000-1[1]	4,320	3,120	8,360	26,940	1,530	640	7,870	1,400	7,650	3,100	2,000	2,220	7,360	26,610	1,310	2,540
2001-2[2]	4,450	3,280	8,470	28,420	1,500	1,130	8,620	1,300	8,550	3,160	2,110	2,160	7,580	28,510	1,110	2,380

[1] Preliminary. [2] Forecast. [3] End of season. *Source: Foreign Agricultural Service, U.S. Department of Agriculture (FAS-USDA)*

Supply and Distribution of Soybean Oil in the United States In Millions of Pounds

						Domestic Disappearance								
						Food					Non-Food			
Year								Cooking						Total
Beginning	Pro-		Stocks		Total	Short-	Mar-	& Salad	Other	Total	Paint &	Resins &	Total	Disap-
Oct. 1	duction	Imports	Oct. 1	Exports	Domestic	ening	garine	Oils	Edible	Food	Varnish	Plastics	Non-Food	pearance
1992-3	13,778	10	2,239	1,419	13,054	4,465	1,970	4,717	254	11,505	38	95	296	14,473
1993-4	13,951	68	1,555	1,529	12,942	4,773	1,840	4,999	221	11,832	46	115	304	14,471
1994-5	15,613	17	1,103	2,680	12,916	4,714	1,693	5,546	222	12,175	49	124	287	15,597
1995-6	15,240	95	1,137	992	13,465	4,702	1,699	5,317	159	11,877	48	119	297	14,457
1996-7	15,752	53	2,015	2,033	14,267	4,578	1,667	6,119	68	12,432	51	132	333	16,300
1997-8	18,143	60	1,520	3,079	15,262	4,688	1,623	6,188	78	12,576	49	128	490	18,341
1998-9	18,078	83	1,382	2,372	15,651	4,842	1,589	6,191	120	12,743	37	117	576	18,024
1999-00	17,825	83	1,520	1,376	16,057	5,541	1,642	7,129	128	14,440	65	96	586	17,433
2000-1[1]	18,433	73	1,995	1,402	16,222	6,209	1,340	6,653	128	14,915	60	86	535	18,100
2001-2[2]	18,730		2,873	2,450	16,550						59	71	502	18,100

[1] Preliminary . [2] Forecast. *Source: Economic Research Service, U.S. Department of Agriculture (ERS-USDA)*

SOYBEAN OIL

Stocks of Crude Soybean Oil in the United States, at End of Month In Millions of Pounds

Crop Year	Oct.	Nov.	Dec.	Jan.	Feb.	Mar.	Apr.	May	June	July	Aug.	Sept.
1996-7	1,796.5	1,711.6	1,805.1	1,928.5	1,982.6	1,938.2	1,929.9	1,919.4	1,917.8	1,760.3	1,492.8	1,321.1
1997-8	1,307.0	1,303.6	1,439.8	1,518.8	1,459.1	1,498.6	1,533.3	1,577.6	1,451.7	1,535.9	1,240.1	1,167.4
1998-9	1,195.0	1,142.0	1,041.1	1,066.2	1,209.5	1,318.6	1,462.0	1,499.5	1,411.8	1,441.8	1,417.8	1,316.1
1999-00	1,378.3	1,422.9	1,516.5	1,742.4	1,829.7	1,847.2	1,847.5	1,760.3	1,802.9	1,903.7	1,831.3	1,773.4
2000-1	1,873.6	1,961.8	2,035.0	2,140.0	2,262.4	2,304.1	2,321.7	2,455.2	2,587.4	2,718.3	2,698.2	2,692.4
2001-2[1]	2,553.4	2,606.0	2,655.3									

[1] Preliminary. *Source: Bureau of the Census, U.S. Department of Commerce*

Stocks of Refined Soybean Oil in the United States, at End of Month In Millions of Pounds

Crop Year	Oct.	Nov.	Dec.	Jan.	Feb.	Mar.	Apr.	May	June	July	Aug.	Sept.
1996-7	196.4	186.8	222.0	243.8	220.6	233.1	233.9	223.9	220.1	217.8	207.1	199.0
1997-8	218.6	221.9	239.8	269.1	252.1	264.0	324.3	279.4	260.9	243.2	213.0	215.0
1998-9	221.7	264.4	246.5	246.7	296.1	289.0	254.2	267.8	235.6	229.4	213.0	203.4
1999-00	238.1	240.7	250.0	271.3	270.1	245.6	251.8	231.6	225.5	216.7	186.3	222.0
2000-1	187.2	205.7	263.1	239.3	211.5	199.9	184.1	200.9	189.3	177.2	171.7	184.8
2001-2[1]	171.4	181.4	208.4									

[1] Preliminary. *Source: Bureau of the Census, U.S. Department of Commerce*

U.S. Exports of Soybean Oil[1], by Country of Destination In Metric Tons

Year Beginning Oct. 1	Canada	Ecuador	Ethiopia	Haiti	India	Mexico	Morocco	Pakistan	Panama	Peru	Turkey	Vene-zuela	Total
1992-3	28,554	1,227	8,272	6,935	50,626	44,194	57,996	0	689	36,400	58,436	0	662,798
1993-4	4,401	0	24,011	1,747	47,705	18,499	31,563	72,204	248	24,081	34,920	26	694,544
1994-5	26,178	12,698	8,392	49,793	28,948	58,624	29,053	25,500	13,342	8,691	5,750	2,017	1,217,079
1995-6	43,912	1,155	4,426	15,041	20,841	46,644	0	0	9,512	35,999	1,960	1,877	449,876
1996-7	58,756	6,587	19,492	36,436	26,675	81,902	46,682	0	3,623	37,726	6,952	517	922,336
1997-8	26,711	10,897	4,175	14,191	38,610	102,950	30,493	0	13,591	49,426	2,452	654	1,396,755
1998-9	11,316	4,858	2,933	44,957	71,685	99,112	43,346	0	1,369	62,085	8,497	1,464	1,075,699
1999-00	22,715	0	13,627	25,214	23,413	118,079	14,091	0	299	66,686	15,680	414	623,651
2000-1[2]	54,933	9,849	5,224	5,937	54,062	75,447	0	62,999	4,558	60,606	0	577	637,891

[1] Crude & Refined oil combined as such. [2] Preliminary. *Source: Economic Research Service, U.S. Department of Agriculture (ERS-USDA)*

Production of Crude Soybean Oil in the United States In Millions of Pounds

Year	Oct.	Nov.	Dec.	Jan.	Feb.	Mar.	Apr.	May	June	July	Aug.	Sept.	Total
1992-3	1,238	1,200	1,239	1,247	1,102	1,216	1,148	1,152	1,083	1,070	1,006	1,078	13,778
1993-4	1,241	1,228	1,218	1,192	1,122	1,231	1,155	1,123	1,070	1,099	1,104	1,168	13,951
1994-5	1,328	1,342	1,403	1,400	1,289	1,419	1,333	1,275	1,183	1,205	1,228	1,208	15,613
1995-6	1,354	1,360	1,382	1,360	1,236	1,292	1,259	1,197	1,221	1,263	1,171	1,139	15,234
1996-7	1,401	1,430	1,473	1,474	1,348	1,413	1,254	1,216	1,196	1,176	1,141	1,231	15,752
1997-8	1,591	1,580	1,689	1,684	1,558	1,655	1,526	1,418	1,337	1,410	1,286	1,410	18,143
1998-9	1,598	1,598	1,611	1,528	1,439	1,587	1,453	1,450	1,383	1,451	1,452	1,528	18,078
1999-00	1,687	1,597	1,599	1,580	1,417	1,482	1,368	1,396	1,360	1,486	1,388	1,466	17,825
2000-1[1]	1,673	1,591	1,579	1,643	1,436	1,603	1,485	1,489	1,449	1,526	1,507	1,453	18,433

[1] Preliminary. *Source: Economic Research Service, U.S. Department of Agriculture (ERS-USDA)*

Production of Refined Soybean Oil in the United States In Millions of Pounds

Year	Oct.	Nov.	Dec.	Jan.	Feb.	Mar.	Apr.	May	June	July	Aug.	Sept.	Total
1993-4	1,094.3	1,053.5	1,030.8	960.1	945.5	1,056.6	1,018.5	1,012.0	1,017.3	968.0	1,107.2	1,044.6	12,308
1994-5	1,123.0	1,079.2	1,060.6	1,002.5	968.2	1,063.6	1,010.4	1,077.0	993.5	940.9	1,076.8	1,039.8	12,435
1995-6	1,119.2	1,088.8	1,018.5	979.9	934.3	1,042.6	997.3	1,009.3	962.8	971.9	1,115.8	1,058.7	12,299
1996-7	1,111.7	1,064.1	1,025.7	969.8	931.5	1,057.1	1,023.7	1,026.2	984.8	1,019.1	1,094.3	1,072.5	12,381
1997-8	1,173.9	1,156.3	1,110.1	1,092.6	1,047.4	1,148.2	1,094.8	1,140.7	1,053.1	1,083.9	1,173.4	1,114.5	13,389
1998-9	1,200.6	1,108.8	1,042.2	1,016.7	976.7	1,138.2	1,073.2	1,087.7	1,060.7	1,058.6	1,122.6	1,116.2	13,002
1999-00	1,201.1	1,195.2	1,150.4	1,056.9	1,045.1	1,173.7	1,109.6	1,141.4	1,063.8	1,080.2	1,176.0	1,177.7	13,571
2000-1	1,260.3	1,159.7	1,093.4	1,107.5	1,166.8	1,211.3	1,170.0	1,234.1	1,204.6	1,222.8	1,317.4	1,201.2	14,349
2001-2[1]	1,383.2	1,363.5	1,287.7										16,137

[1] Preliminary. *Source: Bureau of the Census, U.S. Department of Commerce*

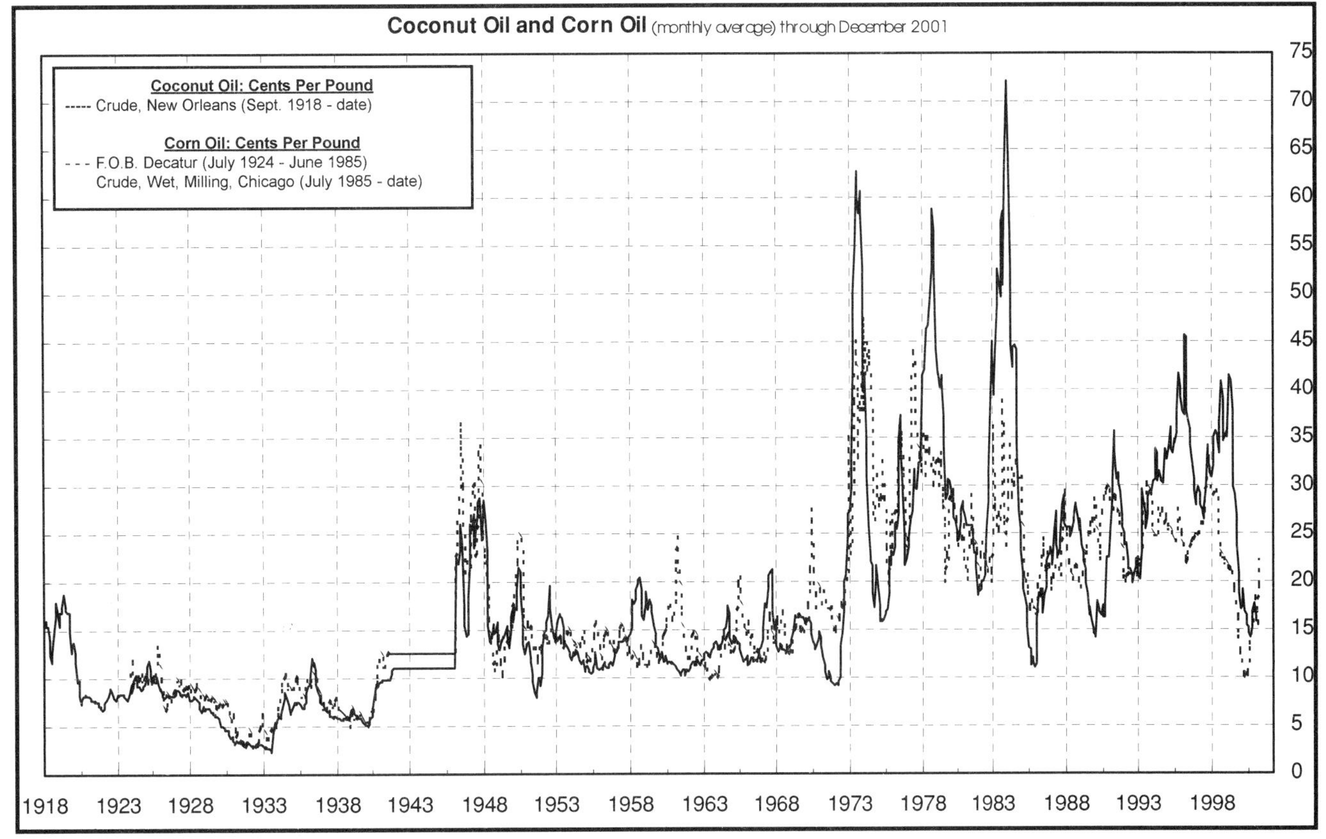

Consumption of Soybean Oil in End Products in the United States In Millions of Pounds

Year	Jan.	Feb.	Mar.	Apr.	May	June	July	Aug.	Sept.	Oct.	Nov.	Dec.	Total
1992	880.4	867.0	1,010.1	947.9	956.7	962.1	935.5	932.4	1,019.8	1,061.7	951.8	946.1	11,472
1993	934.5	942.2	1,092.6	1,044.6	981.2	1,036.0	1,019.3	1,097.3	1,103.3	1,123.6	1,092.1	1,029.2	12,496
1994	924.5	939.1	1,084.7	1,040.6	1,001.4	1,023.8	974.9	1,119.2	1,075.4	1,123.3	1,103.4	1,063.8	12,474
1995	991.1	950.0	1,093.8	1,006.2	1,077.3	1,020.8	948.7	1,046.1	1,042.3	1,092.0	1,067.7	1,002.6	12,339
1996	964.9	927.4	1,026.4	999.8	1,020.6	946.2	959.9	1,123.3	1,042.8	1,137.1	1,080.9	1,093.1	12,322
1997	1,086.0	979.7	1,104.9	1,060.4	1,034.1	995.2	991.4	1,126.1	1,067.8	1,128.5	1,100.0	1,087.8	12,762
1998	1,045.8	1,020.2	1,129.7	1,066.5	1,101.6	1,070.1	1,062.2	1,123.4	1,122.0	1,231.5	1,150.2	1,057.0	13,180
1999	1,031.5	979.0	1,156.1	1,087.7	1,091.9	1,079.5	1,082.9	1,185.0	1,185.7	1,183.0	1,199.3	1,135.6	13,397
2000	1,096.6	1,050.5	1,217.9	1,158.9	1,183.6	1,102.9	1,121.1	1,226.4	1,163.6	1,306.1	1,139.7	1,079.6	13,847
2001[1]	1,065.9	1,151.7	1,308.8	1,202.4	1,224.2	1,261.6	1,307.6	1,557.5	1,411.0	1,687.3	1,624.0	1,509.4	16,311

[1] Preliminary. *Source: Bureau of the Census, U.S. Department of Commerce*

U.S. Exports of Soybean Oil (Crude and Refined) In Millions of Pounds

Year	Jan.	Feb.	Mar.	Apr.	May	June	July	Aug.	Sept.	Oct.	Nov.	Dec.	Total
1992	140.0	171.9	134.6	155.4	69.1	129.1	163.7	205.2	142.5	169.5	113.2	91.6	1,686
1993	146.8	188.0	143.3	61.1	154.8	75.4	59.9	116.0	99.7	190.4	88.6	200.2	1,524
1994	120.4	144.6	94.4	46.1	111.6	36.1	57.7	184.6	254.0	154.8	303.2	305.9	1,813
1995	217.4	367.6	564.2	236.2	90.8	160.4	91.0	109.4	79.4	69.3	205.4	95.9	2,287
1996	189.1	97.0	68.0	75.3	63.9	16.1	27.1	28.0	56.7	121.0	303.8	213.3	1,259
1997	190.7	239.2	301.1	84.9	28.9	44.9	144.1	212.9	152.1	217.2	424.0	199.7	2,240
1998	449.4	387.6	268.6	191.1	148.1	204.7	161.8	316.0	108.9	189.6	343.5	376.7	3,146
1999	246.1	231.1	130.8	230.8	91.3	135.0	111.7	91.2	196.2	209.1	114.9	157.6	1,946
2000	98.4	152.1	161.3	91.6	48.2	111.0	104.6	56.8	68.0	44.9	115.1	256.2	1,308
2001[1]	130.4	191.6	142.4	105.8	51.0	109.9	89.4	96.3	68.8				1,314

[1] Preliminary. *Source: Economic Research Service, U.S. Department of Agriculture (ERS-USDA)*

SOYBEAN OIL

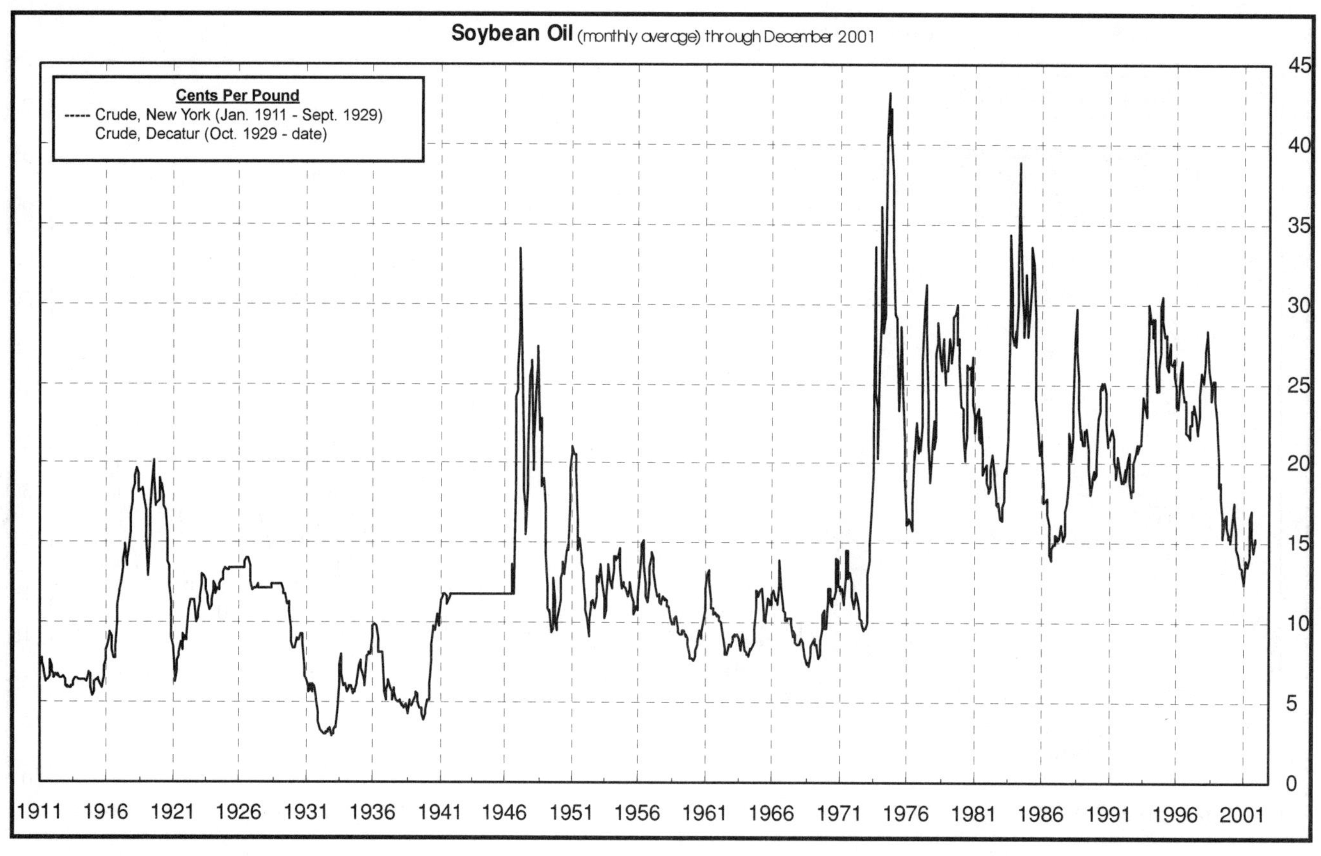

Stocks of Soybean Oil (Crude & Refined) at Factories and Warehouses in the U.S. In Millions of Pounds

Year	Oct. 1	Nov. 1	Dec. 1	Jan. 1	Feb. 1	Mar. 1	Apr. 1	May 1	June 1	July 1	Aug. 1	Sept. 1
1991-2	ÑÑ-	1,786.3	ÑÑ-	2,217.0	2,159.0	2,402.0	2,400.0	2,423.0	2,433.0	2,426.5	2,421.0	2,363.0
1992-3	2,239.4	2,076.4	2,110.8	2,280.1	2,410.1	2,336.8	2,246.1	2,297.9	2,240.8	2,174.0	2,060.7	1,719.8
1993-4	1,554.8	1,452.7	1,399.6	1,406.9	1,414.6	1,400.9	1,402.2	1,553.3	1,566.8	1,553.8	1,570.9	1,339.4
1994-5	1,103.1	1,055.5	1,026.9	1,055.2	1,116.8	1,128.8	1,059.5	1,089.6	1,130.4	1,111.6	1,142.0	1,100.0
1995-6	1,136.7	1,195.9	1,132.0	1,408.9	1,512.6	1,521.5	1,653.5	1,747.4	1,758.9	1,888.5	2,156.5	2,091.4
1996-7	2,015.4	1,992.9	1,898.4	2,027.1	2,172.3	2,203.2	2,171.3	2,163.8	2,143.2	2,137.9	1,978.1	1,699.9
1997-8	1,520.2	1,525.6	1,525.5	1,679.6	1,787.9	1,711.2	1,762.6	1,857.6	1,857.0	1,712.6	1,779.1	1,453.2
1998-9	1,382.4	1,416.8	1,406.5	1,312.9	1,505.6	1,607.6	1,716.2	1,640.5	1,767.3	1,647.4	1,671.2	1,630.8
1999-00	1,519.6	1,616.4	1,663.6	1,791.1	2,013.7	2,099.8	2,092.7	2,099.2	1,991.9	2,028.3	2,120.4	2,018.1
2000-1[1]	1,995.3	2,060.8	2,167.5	2,298.0	2,379.7	2,474.0	2,504.0	2,505.8	2,656.1	2,776.7	2,895.5	2,869.9

[1] Preliminary. *Source: Economic Research Service, U.S. Department of Agriculture (ERS-USDA)*

Average Price of Crude Domestic Soybean Oil (in Tank Cars) F.O.B. Decatur In Cents Per Pound

Year	Oct.	Nov.	Dec.	Jan.	Feb.	Mar.	Apr.	May	June	July	Aug.	Sept.	Average
1992-3	18.36	20.10	20.52	21.23	20.72	21.00	21.24	21.15	21.30	24.13	23.47	23.61	21.40
1993-4	22.98	25.37	28.09	29.91	28.84	29.03	27.94	29.10	27.60	24.53	24.51	26.11	27.00
1994-5	27.06	29.84	30.61	29.01	28.15	28.33	27.16	26.00	26.78	27.60	26.56	26.26	27.51
1995-6	26.56	25.41	24.76	23.69	23.65	23.60	25.82	26.50	24.95	24.10	23.99	23.92	24.70
1996-7	21.95	21.80	21.60	22.45	22.41	23.29	23.17	23.68	22.97	21.89	22.06	22.88	22.50
1997-8	24.31	25.73	25.08	25.09	26.51	27.09	28.10	28.28	25.83	24.88	23.99	25.13	25.84
1998-9	25.20	25.20	24.00	22.90	20.00	19.50	18.80	17.85	16.50	15.30	16.50	16.80	19.88
1999-00	16.08	15.63	15.30	15.63	15.09	16.21	17.52	16.75	15.65	14.70	14.34	14.24	15.60
2000-1	13.50	13.37	13.12	12.53	12.38	13.90	13.53	13.53	14.21	16.49	17.08	15.46	14.09
2001-2[1]	14.38	15.23	15.10										14.90

[1] Preliminary. *Source: Economic Research Service, U.S. Department of Agriculture (ERS-USDA)*

Average Open Interest of Soybean Oil Futures in Chicago In Contracts

Year	Jan.	Feb.	Mar.	Apr.	May	June	July	Aug.	Sept.	Oct.	Nov.	Dec.
1992	68,619	73,919	75,508	68,749	65,084	71,507	64,450	72,569	70,228	65,243	76,168	76,908
1993	73,683	68,887	66,803	68,598	65,814	73,892	83,730	72,746	64,927	62,348	80,136	94,990
1994	97,198	99,640	100,334	98,659	97,595	83,165	93,994	88,196	81,735	86,901	108,327	114,928
1995	101,171	103,856	97,715	87,300	76,175	75,171	81,650	77,064	70,410	71,652	85,241	84,138
1996	87,214	85,611	87,859	95,954	95,422	86,366	81,440	80,090	83,211	98,514	97,496	86,119
1997	89,112	89,348	102,388	101,191	101,544	104,433	105,346	95,282	94,521	107,471	119,877	106,406
1998	105,798	121,657	142,100	160,004	159,248	139,934	117,487	112,177	115,879	115,260	110,386	104,738
1999	115,407	131,875	136,967	133,404	131,993	147,749	157,999	147,280	146,239	155,768	163,439	144,798
2000	131,948	135,196	143,699	155,114	134,093	140,582	134,392	135,506	136,590	135,584	142,712	134,873
2001	134,677	133,497	123,770	128,360	142,877	151,713	162,395	166,318	159,467	164,521	167,803	154,589

Source: Chicago Board of Trade (CBT)

Volume of Trading of Soybean Oil Futures in Chicago In Contracts

Year	Jan.	Feb.	Mar.	Apr.	May	June	July	Aug.	Sept.	Oct.	Nov.	Dec.	Total[1]
1992	344,204	293,729	399,754	255,848	381,807	352,349	413,086	298,001	425,859	346,755	365,760	405,526	4,282.7
1993	341,366	267,022	378,389	306,092	261,620	434,704	513,329	444,559	449,338	302,084	465,173	448,553	4,612.2
1994	442,026	401,580	366,007	391,175	442,419	378,177	397,483	357,896	415,407	476,936	516,724	477,358	5,063.2
1995	424,387	363,695	464,413	355,884	457,682	418,182	377,355	330,507	303,893	317,201	431,711	366,426	4,611.3
1996	354,602	355,220	375,237	443,408	376,716	423,089	512,563	449,014	425,850	414,018	396,233	454,327	4,980.3
1997	473,290	381,921	503,998	445,848	389,741	439,626	442,846	375,122	417,970	413,722	489,541	511,369	5,285.0
1998	443,562	556,982	497,887	673,091	624,518	648,098	629,642	491,155	558,032	383,844	450,073	540,379	6,498.3
1999	367,303	555,097	520,622	463,236	350,850	489,184	516,205	552,198	523,376	395,243	497,090	433,491	5,663.9
2000	424,232	451,677	483,212	438,526	451,162	533,376	422,418	456,195	436,841	378,419	507,044	386,801	5,369.9
2001	327,570	458,445	416,718	443,454	403,110	541,194	751,299	612,349	447,390	550,995	579,460	502,341	6,034.3

[1] In thousands of contracts. *Source: Chicago Board of Trade (CBT)*

Soybeans

The soybean market, basis Chicago futures, has been in a broad trading range since 1999, with support and resistance levels between $4/bu and $5.50, basis nearest futures; in calendar 2001, the range was even tighter, about $4.25 to $5.25. Prices began the year on the defensive, trending lower into early spring before finding initial support near $4.25. then recovered into mid-summer, reaching about $5.25 before the rally failed. By yearend, prices were near their lows of the year and about $.50 per bushel below closing 2000 levels.

World soybean production during 2001/02 reach another new high, 182.8 million metric tons vs. 174.3 million in 2000/01 and the late 1990's average of less than 160 million tons. Soybeans now account for nearly 60% of the world's total oilseed production. The U.S. produces nearly 60% of the world's soybeans and Brazil, the second largest producer, about a fifth. Soybean production is expanding in a number of countries, but the U.S. ranking is well entrenched. A key question focuses on China and Argentina, the latter having reached the third largest producer level during the past few years, which until 1996/97 was held by China. In 2001/02 China's near record large crop of 15.3 million tons compares with the Argentine's record large 28.8 million and a late 1990's average of about 17 million tons. The odds would seem to favor a stronger growth in China than seen in recent years owing to their expanding poultry flocks and the derived need for high protein soybean meal. However, as China's economy becomes more market sensitive growers apparently have switch to higher price crops with more soybean acreage moved into corn and cotton production; it is possible that China's soybean acreage has peaked at around 9 million hectare, suggesting that further production gains will be dependent on higher average yields, which have yet to be realized, estimated at 1.70 tons per hectare in 2001/02 vs. 1.66 tons in 2000/01. Brazil's soybean crop is sown about the time the U.S. crop has been harvested and was forecast at a record large 41.5 million tons in 2001/02 vs. 39 million in 2000/01. Brazil's bean acreage of 15.5 million hectare compares with 14 million in 2000/01. Argentina's acreage increased to 11.1 million hectare from 10.3 million; average yield in both countries is about the same at 2.60 tons per hectare. However, unlike Brazil, Argentine soybean farmers have significantly lower production costs and a better transportation structure. Brazil's crop year encompasses February to January; Argentina's is April to March.

World soybean trade in 2001/02 of a record large 59 million tons compares with the previous high of almost 58 million in 2000/01, with soybeans accounting for about 80% of total world oilseed trade. The U.S. is the largest soybean exporter, with almost 46% (27.2 million tons) of 20001/02 world exports, but a somewhat lower percentage than seen in recent years. Brazil's exports of 17.5 million tons in 2001/02 compare with 15.5 million in 2000/01 and less than 10 million in the late 1990's. Argentina's exports are forecast at 9 million tons in 2001/02 vs. 7.5 million in 2000/01 and compare with the 1996-99 average of about 3 million. Clearly, the percentage gain in South American soybean exports since the late 1990's greatly exceeds the U.S.. Importing nations are more numerous; collectively Asia is the largest importer with almost 28 million tons in 2001/02 with China and Japan accounting for about 19 million tons. The European Union, formerly the largest importing bloc is forecast to import 19.6 million tons in 2001/02, marginally higher than a year earlier. Within the EU, Germany's imports of 4.6 million and the Netherlands 5.7 million are both about unchanged from 2000/01. The ending 2001/02 world bean carryover was expected at 29.1 million tons vs. with the year earlier 28.6 million; the U.S., Brazil and Argentina account about 22.4 million tons of the total vs. 21.2 million a year earlier.

U.S. farmers harvested a record large 74.1 million acres of soybeans in 2001 vs. 72.4 million in 2000. The average yield of a record 39.4 bushels per acre compares with 38.1 bushels in 2000. Iowa and Illinois are the largest producing states followed by Minnesota and Indiana.

The U.S. soybean crop year begins September 1. Carryover stocks on August 31, 2001 totaled 248 million bushels, down 42 million from a year earlier. Total 2001/2 supplies of almost 3.2 billion bushels compare with 3 billion in 2000/01. Total disappearance in 2001/02 was forecast at a record large 2.8 billion bushels, of which almost 1.7 billion will be crushed, 1.0 billion exported and about 175 million allocated to seed and residual. Carryover as of August 31, 2002 is forecast at 248 million bushels, unchanged from the 2001/02 carry-in.

U.S. soybean exports have seen a strong shift in regional demand during the past two years. The traditional European market has come to represent a smaller share of U.S. exports, while Asia and Mexico have increased their importance to U.S. exporters. Asia's share is expected to increase owing to the area's improved economies and the shift away from importing meal and choosing instead to process beans. Historically, When a more positive soybean usage outlook takes hold its apt to show in early calendar year prices. Demand bull years in soybeans generally show counter-seasonal strength in January and February, however, if total usage holds neutral and/or weakens then prices, manifested chiefly in futures, tend to witness what is referred to as the "February break." If the latter develops its not unusual for prices to penetrate the harvest lows of the previous October-December quarter.

The USDA's average price received by farmers in 2000/01 was $4.45 per bushel vs. $4.63 in 1999/00. Early 2001/02 crop farm prices were averaging about 30 cents under a year earlier. The highest farm price during the past decade was $7.35 in 1996/97 and the low was in 2000/01.

Futures Markets

Soybean futures are traded on the Bolsa de Mercadorias & Futuros (BM&F), the Mercado a Termino de Buenos Aires (MAT), the Dalian Commodity Exchange in China, the Tokyo Grain Exchange (TGE), the Chicago Board of Trade (CBOT), and the Mid-America Commodity Exchange (MidAm). Options are traded on the MAT, the TGE, the CBOT and the MidAm.

World Production of Soybeans In Thousands of Metric Tons

Crop Year[4]	Argentina	Bolivia	Brazil	Canada	China	India	Indonesia	Mexico	Paraguay	Thailand	United States	Ex-USSR	World Total
1992-3	11,350	513	22,500	1,455	10,300	3,106	1,700	572	1,750	480	59,612	581	117,380
1993-4	12,400	735	24,700	1,851	15,310	4,000	1,565	497	1,800	480	50,885	557	117,767
1994-5	12,500	810	25,900	2,251	16,000	3,236	1,680	523	2,200	450	68,444	451	137,696
1995-6	12,430	900	24,150	2,293	13,500	4,476	1,517	190	2,400	368	59,174	320	124,915
1996-7	11,200	1,040	27,300	2,165	13,220	4,100	1,460	61	2,771	360	64,780	299	132,217
1997-8	19,500	1,071	32,500	2,738	14,728	5,350	1,306	189	2,988	338	73,176	298	158,066
1998-9	20,000	960	31,300	2,737	15,152	6,000	1,300	143	3,050	335	74,598	333	159,807
1999-00[1]	21,200	1,200	34,200	2,776	14,290	5,200	1,300	123	2,900	330	72,220	379	159,880
2000-1[2]	27,200	950	38,800	2,703	15,400	5,250	1,150	115	3,400	330	75,060	420	174,280
2001-2[3]	28,750		42,500		15,300	5,600			3,400		78,670		182,830

[1] Preliminary. [2] Estimate. [3] Forecast. [4] Spilt year includes Northern Hemisphere crops harvested in the late months of the first year shown combined with Southern Hemisphere crops harvested in the early months of the following year. *Sources: Oil World; Foreign Agricultural Service, U.S. Department of Agriculture (FAS-USDA)*

World Crushings and Ending Stocks of Soybeans In Thousands of Metric Tons

	Crushings										Ending Stocks		
Year	Argentina	Brazil	China	Germany	India	Japan	Mexico	Netherlands	United States	World Total	Brazil	United States	World Total
1992-3	8,667	16,765	4,486	3,107	2,810	3,785	2,670	3,721	34,808	97,943	832	7,955	11,388
1993-4	8,718	18,736	7,605	2,781	3,600	3,700	2,640	3,582	34,716	102,071	651	5,691	9,045
1994-5	9,280	21,599	8,590	3,286	2,750	3,760	2,330	3,991	38,242	112,509	710	9,112	12,876
1995-6	9,927	20,154	7,470	3,242	4,046	3,700	2,436	3,940	37,273	110,733	825	4,993	8,506
1996-7	10,423	18,910	7,500	3,686	3,650	3,810	2,690	3,980	39,080	112,785	475	3,588	7,802
1997-8	16,782	21,900	8,450	3,950	4,770	3,720	3,600	4,205	43,464	130,080	6,800	5,440	25,070
1998-9	16,800	21,600	12,607	4,071	5,400	3,700	3,950	4,263	43,262	135,626	6,800	9,480	26,640
1999-00[1]	17,080	21,200	15,070	3,497	4,400	3,750	4,100	4,260	42,940	136,250	7,650	7,900	27,010
2000-1[2]	17,500	22,500	18,900	3,812	4,530	3,750	4,450	4,335	44,650	148,240	7,100	6,740	28,600
2001-2[3]	19,500	23,000	21,700		4,800	3,880	4,600		45,590	156,730	7,000	7,770	28,700

[1] Preliminary. [2] Estimate. [3] Forecast. *Sources: Oil World; Foreign Agricultural Service, U.S. Department of Agriculture (FAS-USDA)*

World Imports and Exports of Soybeans In Thousands of Metric Tons

	Imports							Exports					
Year	China	Germany	Japan	Mexico	Netherlands	Taiwan	World Total	Argentina	Brazil	Canada	Paraguay	United States	World Total
1992-3	150	3,308	4,866	2,136	4,257	2,506	29,939	2,274	4,184	211	1,250	20,972	29,804
1993-4	125	2,785	4,855	2,200	4,137	2,500	29,077	2,957	5,395	489	1,200	16,006	27,982
1994-5	155	3,363	4,837	1,867	4,624	2,598	32,686	2,614	3,492	542	1,450	22,867	32,251
1995-6	795	3,249	4,776	2,401	4,300	2,646	32,904	2,014	3,633	599	1,600	23,108	31,969
1996-7	2,274	3,681	5,043	2,720	4,450	2,632	37,387	750	8,328	478	2,150	24,110	37,044
1997-8	2,940	4,000	4,873	3,479	4,875	2,387	39,442	3,231	9,336	769	2,390	23,760	41,046
1998-9	3,850	4,095	4,807	3,764	5,007	2,150	40,585	3,200	8,973	876	2,300	21,898	38,731
1999-00[1]	10,100	3,440	4,900	3,950	5,260	2,300	47,720	4,130	11,160	900	2,120	26,490	46,670
2000-1[2]	13,240	4,570	4,840	4,400	5,650	2,400	55,590	7,450	15,500	900	2,520	27,170	55,220
2001-2[3]	14,000	4,610	5,000	4,530	5,720	2,300	59,380	8,750	18,000		2,520	27,490	59,260

[1] Preliminary. [2] Estimate. [3] Forecast. *Sources: Oil World; Foreign Agricultural Service, U.S. Department of Agriculture (FAS-USDA)*

Supply and Distribution of Soybeans in the United States In Millions of Bushels

Crop Year	Supply					Distribution			
	Stocks, Sept. 1								
Beginning Sept. 1	Farms	Mills, Elevators[3]	Total	Production	Total Supply	Crushings	Exports	Seed, Feed & Residual	Total Distribution
1992-3	105.0	173.4	278.4	2,190.4	2,470.8	1,279.0	771.0	128.0	2,178.0
1993-4	125.0	167.3	292.3	1,869.7	2,168.4	1,276.0	588.0	95.0	1,959.0
1994-5	59.1	150.0	209.1	2,514.9	2,729.5	1,405.0	840.0	149.0	2,394.0
1995-6	105.1	229.7	334.8	2,174.3	2,513.5	1,370.0	849.0	111.0	2,330.0
1996-7	59.5	123.9	183.5	2,380.3	2,572.6	1,436.0	886.0	118.0	2,440.0
1997-8	43.6	88.2	131.8	2,688.8	2,825.6	1,597.0	874.0	155.0	2,626.0
1998-9	84.3	115.5	199.8	2,741.0	2,945.0	1,590.0	805.0	202.0	2,597.0
1999-00	145.0	203.5	348.0	2,653.8	3,006.0	1,578.0	973.0	165.0	2,716.0
2000-1[1]	112.5	177.7	290.2	2,757.8	3,052.0	1,641.0	998.0	165.0	2,804.0
2001-2[2]	83.5	164.2	247.7	2,907.0	3,175.0	1,665.0	980.0	173.0	2,820.0

[1] Preliminary. [2] Estimate. [3] Also warehouses. *Source: Economic Research Service, U.S. Department of Agriculture (ERS-USDA)*

SOYBEANS

Salient Statistics & Official Crop Production Reports of Soybeans in the U.S. In Millions of Bushels

Year	Acreage Planted	Acreage Harvested	Yield Per Acre (Bu.)	Farm Price ($ / Bu.)	Farm Value (Million Dollars)	Yield of Oil	Yield of Meal	Aug. 1	Sept. 1	Oct. 1	Nov. 1	Dec. 1	Final
	---- 1,000 Acres ----							---- Crop Production Reports In Thousands of Bushels ----					
1992-3	59,180	58,233	37.6	5.56	12,168	10.84	47.54	2,079,487	----	----	----	----	2,190,354
1993-4	60,135	57,347	32.6	6.40	11,950	10.87	47.62	1,902,023	1,909,188	1,890,808	1,833,788	----	1,870,958
1994-5	61,670	60,859	41.4	5.48	13,756	11.08	47.33	2,282,367	2,316,077	2,458,087	2,522,527	----	2,516,694
1995-6	62,575	61,624	35.3	6.72	14,737	11.15	47.69	2,245,901	2,284,551	2,190,661	2,182,991	----	2,176,814
1996-7	64,205	63,409	37.6	7.35	17,495	10.91	47.37	2,299,675	2,269,505	2,346,220	2,402,610	----	2,380,274
1997-8	70,005	69,110	38.9	6.47	17,396	11.26	47.40	2,744,451	2,745,891	2,721,843	2,736,115	----	2,688,750
1998-9	72,025	70,441	38.9	4.93	13,513	11.30	47.25	2,824,744	2,908,604	2,768,919	2,762,609	----	2,741,014
1999-00	73,730	72,446	36.6	4.63	12,287	11.34	47.76	2,869,519	2,778,392	2,696,272	2,672,972	----	2,642,908
2000-1[1]	74,266	72,408	38.1	4.55	12,548	11.24	48.01	2,988,669	2,899,571	2,822,821	2,777,036	----	2,769,665
2001-2[2]	75,216	74,137	39.2	4.30	12,500			2,867,474	2,833,511	2,907,042	2,922,914	----	2,890,572

[1] Preliminary. [2] Forecast. *Source: National Agricultural Statistics Service, U.S. Department of Agriculture (NASS-USDA)*

Stocks of Soybeans in the United States In Thousands of Bushels

Year	On Farms Mar. 1	On Farms Jun. 1	On Farms Sept. 1	On Farms Dec. 1	Off Farms[1] Mar. 1	Off Farms[1] Jun. 1	Off Farms[1] Sept. 1	Off Farms[1] Dec. 1	Total Stocks Mar. 1	Total Stocks Jun. 1	Total Stocks Sept. 1	Total Stocks Dec. 1
1992	505,000	279,000	105,000	876,100	672,343	416,671	173,437	959,885	1,177,343	695,671	278,437	1,835,985
1993	576,900	319,800	124,970	697,400	638,667	363,613	167,314	876,220	1,215,567	683,413	292,284	1,573,620
1994	425,700	195,000	59,080	985,800	595,917	360,260	150,037	1,116,156	1,021,617	555,260	209,117	2,101,956
1995	635,300	348,800	105,130	861,500	734,898	443,072	229,684	971,929	1,370,198	791,872	334,814	1,833,429
1996	512,000	234,100	59,523	935,100	678,356	388,701	123,935	889,984	1,190,356	622,801	183,458	1,825,084
1997	514,000	216,000	43,600	1,048,000	541,912	283,890	88,233	951,417	1,055,912	499,890	131,833	1,999,417
1998	637,000	318,000	84,300	1,187,000	565,922	275,654	115,499	999,440	1,202,922	593,654	199,799	2,186,440
1999	815,000	458,000	145,000	1,150,000	642,338	390,573	203,482	1,032,666	1,457,338	848,573	348,482	2,182,666
2000	730,000	370,000	112,500	1,217,000	665,986	404,425	177,662	1,022,791	1,395,986	774,425	290,162	2,239,791
2001	780,000	365,000	83,500	1,240,000	623,908	343,180	164,247	1,035,713	1,403,908	708,180	247,747	2,275,713

[1] Includes stocks at mills, elevators, warehouses, terminals and processors. NA = Not avaliable. *Source: National Agricultural Statistics Service, U.S. Department of Agriculture (NASS-USDA)*

Commercial Stocks of Soybeans in the United States, on First of Month In Millions of Bushels

Year	Jan.	Feb.	Mar.	Apr.	May	June	July	Aug.	Sept.	Oct.	Nov.	Dec.
1992	76.0	75.9	67.1	67.8	58.5	57.2	51.7	32.1	18.6	59.0	75.1	79.9
1993	71.5	63.5	54.5	48.5	44.0	32.1	26.6	24.4	15.8	9.6	52.3	60.2
1994	62.6	65.3	54.4	46.3	40.7	34.7	29.9	24.3	19.8	11.5	68.1	83.4
1995	80.7	72.5	67.8	63.5	51.8	50.8	44.3	35.7	33.6	23.0	60.8	61.7
1996	57.2	57.2	59.2	54.7	56.2	44.9	36.9	32.7	12.0	5.3	55.2	50.6
1997	32.6	28.8	22.9	26.0	29.2	24.7	14.3	12.8	6.3	4.5	50.2	49.4
1998	35.3	31.2	22.9	18.4	14.5	14.2	10.2	9.7	8.7	18.6	43.5	40.6
1999	39.1	31.5	29.0	28.7	25.0	18.9	16.1	17.3	14.1	19.5	46.9	42.3
2000	34.1	28.3	30.0	23.9	23.8	20.6	17.0	12.3	8.6	15.5	38.2	37.9
2001	34.5	28.8	25.2	22.5	16.3	15.0	12.9	13.4	11.9	9.6	34.7	38.2

Source: Livestock Division, U.S. Department of Agriculture (LD-USDA)

Stocks of Soybeans at Mills in the United States, on First of Month In Millions of Bushels

Year	Jan.	Feb.	Mar.	Apr.	May	June	July	Aug.	Sept.	Oct.	Nov.	Dec.
1991-2	-----	-----	67.0	-----	126.9	121.4	109.6	94.7	79.8	73.5	65.7	56.2
1992-3	43.8	46.3	132.3	137.4	119.1	111.2	97.2	90.1	83.6	67.7	67.1	55.3
1993-4	42.0	28.0	108.6	114.9	120.9	126.1	118.5	119.7	98.7	97.8	90.0	63.5
1994-5	47.9	46.8	114.1	124.3	108.0	114.7	114.3	112.6	94.1	81.2	69.1	55.1
1995-6	52.8	54.2	125.6	129.1	120.0	123.3	121.9	110.6	104.2	92.5	70.4	57.4
1996-7	40.7	23.4	101.1	117.4	106.0	112.6	122.2	104.9	89.2	78.2	64.0	43.6
1997-8	28.3	37.0	126.4	124.3	110.3	98.7	93.4	72.0	56.9	41.0	42.5	44.1
1998-9	32.8	66.5	175.0	154.3	131.0	109.6	102.5	93.7	80.5	56.9	55.5	48.1
1999-00	41.7	70.8	162.9	144.7	144.2	140.3	137.8	129.6	98.7	78.7	78.4	52.1
2000-1[1]	52.1	56.8	179.4	166.8	137.8	142.9	126.6	120.2	94.5	85.7	78.9	68.6

[1] Preliminary. *Source: Economic Research Service, U.S. Department of Agriculture (ERS-USDA)*

Production of Soybeans for Beans in the United States, by State In Millions of Bushels

Year	Arkansas	Illinois	Indiana	Iowa	Kentucky	Michigan	Minnesota	Mississippi	Missouri	Nebraska	Ohio	Tennessee	Total
1992	104.3	405.5	194.4	359.5	42.2	47.5	172.8	59.5	161.5	103.3	147.2	33.3	2,190.4
1993	92.3	387.0	223.1	257.3	38.0	54.7	115.0	42.9	118.8	90.0	156.2	32.2	1,871.0
1994	115.6	429.1	215.3	442.9	42.4	57.0	224.0	57.0	173.3	134.4	173.6	38.3	2,516.7
1995	88.4	378.3	196.7	407.4	41.4	59.6	234.9	37.8	132.8	101.0	153.1	34.6	2,176.8
1996	112.0	398.9	203.7	415.8	44.8	46.7	224.2	54.3	149.9	135.5	157.2	38.5	2,380.3
1997	109.8	427.9	230.6	478.4	42.1	71.6	255.5	64.2	174.6	143.8	191.0	40.8	2,688.8
1998	85.0	464.2	231.0	496.8	36.0	73.7	285.6	48.0	170.0	165.0	193.2	35.1	2,741.0
1999	92.4	443.1	216.5	478.4	24.4	77.6	289.8	44.7	147.1	180.6	162.0	22.8	2,653.8
2000	80.3	459.8	252.1	464.6	45.2	73.1	293.2	34.8	175.0	173.9	186.5	28.8	2,757.8
2001[1]	97.4	481.8	283.2	481.8	50.8	65.7	252.0	43.2	181.3	212.3	197.0	36.8	2,922.9

[1] Preliminary. *Source: Agricultural Statistics Board, U.S. Department of Agriculture (ASB-USDA)*

United States Exports of Soybeans In Millions of Bushels

Year	Sept.	Oct.	Nov.	Dec.	Jan.	Feb.	Mar.	Apr.	May	June	July	Aug.	Total
1991-2	26.8	-----	235.6	-----	73.8	90.6	63.3	56.6	28.3	27.3	42.6	39.2	683.9
1992-3	50.1	98.0	84.2	73.6	89.1	104.7	79.7	48.7	34.6	39.4	42.7	24.6	769.5
1993-4	30.1	73.6	72.4	73.9	71.0	67.8	53.6	34.8	27.5	26.7	17.1	40.7	589.1
1994-5	42.3	99.9	78.5	104.2	89.3	91.4	83.1	80.7	45.2	35.5	41.2	46.7	838.1
1995-6	70.7	77.4	65.5	89.6	106.2	82.9	93.5	52.9	42.1	51.8	46.0	52.6	851.2
1996-7	41.6	95.8	152.4	121.6	106.5	105.7	68.2	58.8	43.0	32.4	23.2	36.5	885.9
1997-8	42.6	174.3	150.4	121.2	91.1	94.8	56.9	36.7	27.3	24.7	27.9	26.6	874.3
1998-9	27.9	135.6	106.3	90.4	84.3	66.8	72.4	52.5	37.8	36.4	36.7	57.5	804.7
1999-00	69.4	122.8	104.5	109.1	104.0	103.1	109.7	50.6	45.6	46.0	50.3	58.4	973.4
2000-1[1]	53.5	139.2	122.9	105.6	105.6	127.3	134.5	54.1	39.8	39.5	33.1	43.4	998.4

[1] Preliminary. *Source: Economic Research Service, U.S. Department of Agriculture (ERS-USDA)*

Spread Between Value of Products and Soybean Price in the United States In Cents Per Bushel

Year	Sept.	Oct.	Nov.	Dec.	Jan.	Feb.	Mar.	Apr.	May	June	July	Aug.	Average
1991-2	118	120	94	82	74	74	75	78	87	104	80	83	89
1992-3	98	93	87	93	94	77	77	79	82	84	120	97	90
1993-4	95	108	105	92	93	99	88	85	89	88	94	118	96
1994-5	117	134	114	107	104	103	85	72	58	74	62	65	91
1995-6	68	82	58	64	53	48	53	67	44	50	52	47	57
1996-7	84	92	105	92	74	74	62	54	82	67	94	123	83
1997-8	177	96	108	87	57	51	35	33	33	29	53	43	67
1998-9	53	53	38	40	33	30	35	37	34	36	47	45	40
1999-00	48	61	64	58	75	61	70	70	80	81	69	62	66
2000-1	81	81	82	89	85	60	65	73	68	81	111	92	80

Source: Economic Research Service, U.S. Department of Agriculture (ERS-USDA)

Soybean Crushed (Factory Consumption) in the United States In Milions of Bushels

Year	Sept.	Oct.	Nov.	Dec.	Jan.	Feb.	Mar.	Apr.	May	June	July	Aug.	Total
1991-2	98.9	-----	333.3	-----	112.0	100.8	107.2	101.6	95.2	100.0	102.3	102.3	1,254
1992-3	101.2	113.9	113.1	116.2	116.8	102.2	113.0	105.9	106.5	99.9	98.0	92.2	1,279
1993-4	98.4	113.7	114.4	114.1	110.7	103.3	113.3	105.6	103.0	97.2	101.0	101.0	1,276
1994-5	105.9	119.3	122.5	128.5	127.3	116.5	128.1	119.4	114.2	105.6	108.4	109.5	1,405
1995-6	107.4	120.6	123.4	125.1	122.8	111.2	115.5	112.1	106.3	107.5	111.9	105.7	1,370
1996-7	100.9	127.0	133.1	138.1	137.3	125.1	130.1	114.8	110.7	108.9	106.1	103.8	1,436
1997-8	110.8	142.2	142.8	153.1	151.8	138.3	147.0	134.0	123.9	117.5	123.8	111.9	1,597
1998-9	123.9	142.4	143.0	144.6	136.4	127.6	140.0	128.4	128.0	121.2	127.3	126.9	1,590
1999-00	133.8	150.2	142.8	143.0	139.2	125.4	130.4	121.5	121.0	117.9	130.2	122.2	1,578
2000-1[1]	128.9	149.1	143.1	142.3	146.7	128.9	141.8	131.0	132.7	128.0	135.5	133.5	1,641

One Bushel = 60 Pounds. [1] Preliminary. *Source: Economic Research Service, U.S. Department of Agriculture (ERS-USDA)*

Average Open Interest of Soybean Futures in Chicago In Contracts

Year	Jan.	Feb.	Mar.	Apr.	May	June	July	Aug.	Sept.	Oct.	Nov.	Dec.
1992	114,871	118,317	132,639	121,171	121,398	137,896	116,208	106,830	104,115	125,734	118,877	114,261
1993	121,726	126,682	126,681	138,155	137,821	142,721	199,681	183,422	163,647	159,641	161,170	168,694
1994	177,648	167,217	156,059	147,569	145,798	150,203	132,010	121,126	126,947	147,198	137,187	136,351
1995	138,345	138,794	137,843	138,624	133,533	143,119	143,671	135,584	144,409	167,200	174,775	194,021
1996	198,731	199,150	192,927	207,284	191,989	179,548	180,817	182,324	196,361	178,872	155,937	152,966
1997	157,728	176,242	189,352	188,617	186,792	159,720	141,658	133,732	150,606	172,098	148,760	150,201
1998	135,340	142,778	147,900	152,732	143,994	149,563	133,532	140,236	158,627	163,759	143,814	146,463
1999	152,757	166,003	162,690	166,565	164,777	163,663	157,433	134,105	146,087	174,583	164,306	153,693
2000	149,468	172,494	174,465	195,189	193,500	167,678	140,894	126,952	149,074	183,734	168,023	177,324
2001	160,730	164,017	148,190	156,781	137,227	153,190	181,194	165,630	167,677	195,366	175,522	173,116

Source: Chicago Board of Trade (CBT)

Volume of Trading of Soybean Futures in Chicago In Thousands of Contracts

Year	Jan.	Feb.	Mar.	Apr.	May	June	July	Aug.	Sept.	Oct.	Nov.	Dec.	Total
1992	804.4	738.4	688.0	558.8	873.8	1,054.6	933.2	630.8	572.2	867.4	613.2	665.4	9,000
1993	683.4	624.6	675.8	761.2	778.0	1,287.0	1,643.2	1,180.0	925.0	962.2	1,188.0	941.4	11,649
1994	1,134.6	898.5	922.0	919.3	1,158.4	1,197.0	892.4	688.4	622.6	857.0	825.8	633.2	10,749
1995	614.0	572.0	799.6	698.3	949.4	1,050.8	1,196.7	817.0	800.2	1,127.8	840.4	1,145.4	10,612
1996	1,302.6	1,122.9	1,009.4	1,683.2	1,149.3	989.5	1,295.9	989.8	1,050.2	1,002.7	1,695.6	940.1	14,231
1997	1,119.8	1,254.2	1,405.9	1,585.5	1,391.1	1,355.6	1,217.4	835.0	852.3	1,505.8	1,010.7	1,006.6	14,540
1998	875.7	971.2	935.9	1,116.2	973.6	1,378.8	1,286.3	884.5	864.4	1,264.6	867.0	1,012.9	12,431
1999	871.1	1,025.3	1,440.1	963.5	823.6	1,149.5	1,502.5	1,669.8	903.0	1,158.6	839.4	872.3	12,482
2000	1,071.9	1,099.3	1,191.6	1,079.1	1,321.6	1,302.0	883.4	801.4	860.9	1,188.8	932.5	895.3	12,628
2001	935.0	947.4	843.1	916.3	909.5	1,155.6	1,508.1	1,122.0	648.7	1,356.1	964.7	844.1	12,151

Source: Chicago Board of Trade

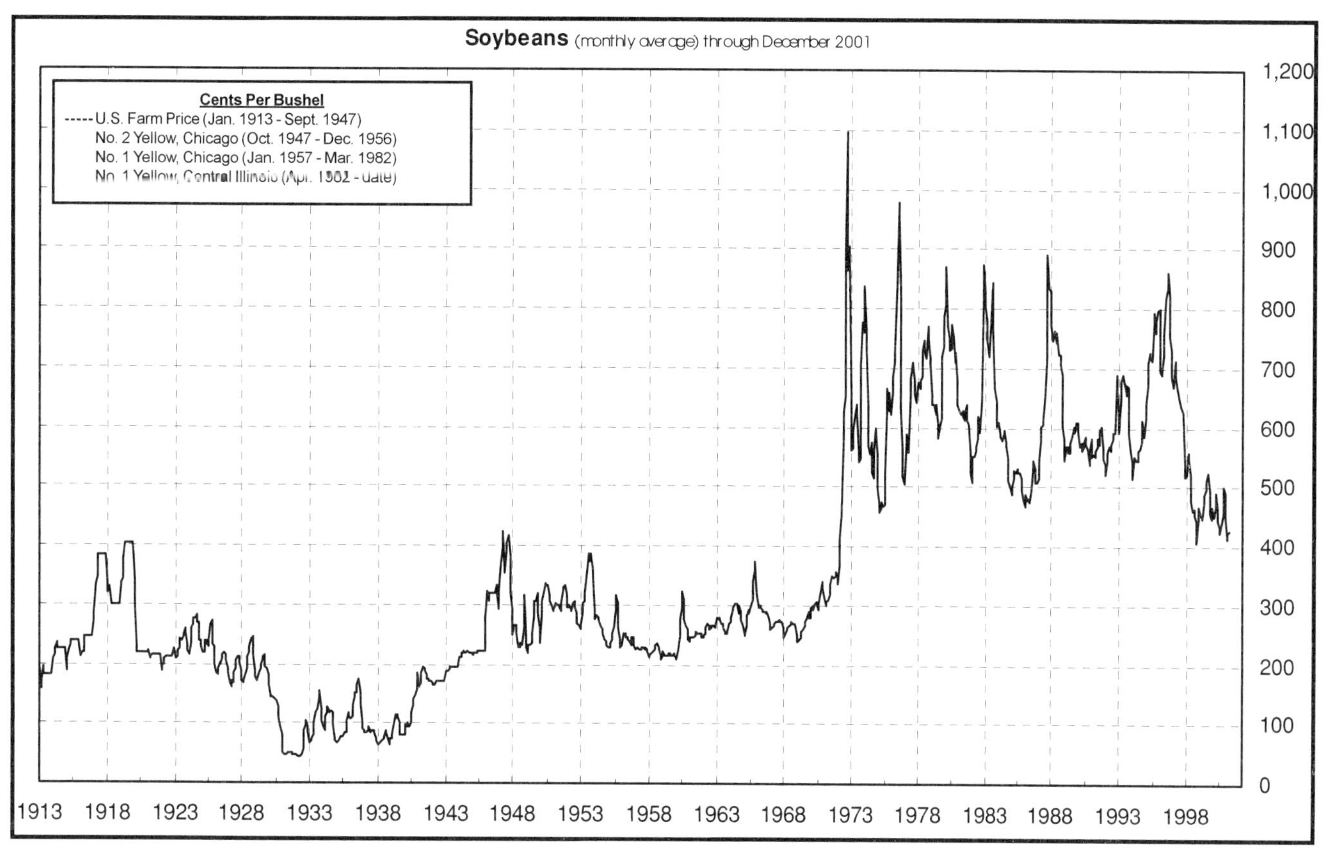

Average Cash Price of No. 1 Yellow Soybeans at Illinois Processor In Cents Per Bushel

Year	Sept.	Oct.	Nov.	Dec.	Jan.	Feb.	Mar.	Apr.	May	June	July	Aug.	Average
1991-2	598	568	571	568	577	581	593	585	609	619	580	564	584
1992-3	554	535	560	572	582	575	587	597	607	606	689	679	595
1993-4	643	606	664	694	701	686	692	670	689	685	603	576	659
1994-5	557	531	566	567	558	560	574	578	580	577	623	602	573
1995-6	632	656	686	717	737	730	726	791	808	778	795	816	739
1996-7	820	711	704	708	737	769	833	854	878	837	769	741	780
1997-8	703	684	727	699	679	680	662	649	649	640	642	556	664
1998-9	533	536	572	558	532	490	475	480	468	462	425	465	500
1999-00	485	470	464	460	473	500	513	529	542	510	474	463	490
2000-1[1]	484	468	483	506	477	457	451	441	457	474	517	510	477

[1] Preliminary. *Source: Economic Research Service, U.S. Department of Agriculture (ERS-USDA)*

Average Price Received by Farmers for Soybeans in the United States In Cents Per Bushel

Year	Sept.	Oct.	Nov.	Dec.	Jan.	Feb.	Mar.	Apr.	May	June	July	Aug.	Average
1992-3	536	526	536	546	558	556	565	573	581	590	656	656	556
1993-4	621	601	632	664	672	671	673	657	677	672	592	558	640
1994-5	547	530	536	541	547	540	551	555	556	568	590	583	548
1995-6	598	615	640	676	677	701	700	743	769	741	762	782	672
1996-7	779	694	690	691	713	738	797	823	840	816	752	725	735
1997-8	672	650	685	671	669	657	640	626	626	616	614	543	647
1998-9	525	518	540	537	532	480	461	463	451	444	420	439	493
1999-00	457	448	445	443	462	479	491	500	519	493	453	445	463
2000-1	459	445	455	478	468	446	439	422	433	446	479	485	455
2001-2[1]	453	409	416	413									423

[1] Preliminary. *Source: Economic Research Service, U.S. Department of Agriculture (ERS-USDA)*

Stock Index Futures, U.S.

The U.S. equity markets, using the Dow-Jones 30 industrial average as a benchmark, came under moderate bearish pressure in the first quarter of 2001, but then rallied into late May, reaching what proved to be the year's high of about 11,350. Bearish pressure once again then took hold which perhaps could have been checked were it not for the September 11, 2001 terrorist attack that set the stage for a collapse that carried the Dow to slightly above 8000, the year's low. After the initial shock to the domestic equities markets dissipated, a recovery once again took hold that erased much of the year's weakness and enabling almost all the indices to post only moderate percentile losses for the year. Still, by all market evaluations, technical and psychological, 2001 was the consecutive second year of disappointment and seemed to reinforce the likelihood that the pronounced bull market(s) of the late 1990's had not only run its course, but more importantly the damage ran so deep as to prevent any sustained recovery from taking hold for some time to come. Moreover, this negative scenario took on greater weight in late 2001 following the collapse and bankruptcy of a major oil trading company, the impact of which cut deeply into the confidence of equities traders and investors, a market intangible that is needed to both launch and sustain a viable bull market.

The bellwether price weighted Dow-Jones 30 industrial index, which includes some Nasdaq stocks lost 7.10% following a 6% loss in 2000. The market capitalization weighted S & P 500 index fell 13% vs. a loss of 10% in 2000; the Russell 2000, however, scored a 1.03% gain vs. a 4% decline in 2000 and the value line index lost about 6.1% vs. a 9% loss in 2000. Even the Dow-Jones Utility index, which rose by 45% in 2000, could not escape the downward pressure in 2001 and fell nearly 29%. Trading volume continued at a record pace: on the New York Stock Exchange about 308 billion shares vs. 263 billion in 2000 while the Nasdaq's volume topped 462 billion shares vs. 434 billion in 2000. As has been the case since the mid-1990's market volatility was the rule rather than the exception, partially reflecting burgeoning computer driven day trading that tends to feed upon itself. The markets' weakness in 2001, especially late in the year, also reflected a return to properly (if not honestly) evaluating corporate earnings as the traditional price determinant, which was not the case seen in much of the 1990' when time tested traditional analytical parameters were relegated to the backburner.

The U.S. economy officially slipped into a recession in early 2001 despite a series of Federal Reserve interest rates cuts implemented to hold the economy's weakness in check. Although there were late 2001 statistical signs that the economy was on the mend there was little consensus as to its staying power.—As for the 2002 outlook, conviction may prove to be lacking as to the market(s) direction, which if nothing else suggests another year of price volatility.

Futures Markets

The Chicago Mercantile Exchange (CME) IOM division trades index futures and options on the S & P 500, the S & P MidCap 400, the NASDAQ 100 and the Russell 2000. The Chicago Board of Trade (CBOT) lists futures and options on the Dow-Jones 30 industrial stock average. New York Stock Exchange Composite index futures and options are traded on the NYFE Division of the New York Board of Trade (NYBOT).

Dow Jones Industrial Average (30 Stocks)

Year	Jan.	Feb.	Mar.	Apr.	May	June	July	Aug.	Sept.	Oct.	Nov.	Dec.	Average
1992	3,227.1	3,257.3	3,247.4	3,294.1	3,376.8	3,337.8	3,329.4	3,307.4	3,293.9	3,198.7	3,238.5	3,303.1	3,284.3
1993	3,277.7	3,367.3	3,440.7	3,423.6	3,478.2	3,513.8	3,529.4	3,597.0	3,592.3	3,625.8	3,674.7	3,744.1	3,522.1
1994	3,868.4	3,905.6	3,817.0	3,661.5	3,708.0	3,737.6	3,718.3	3,797.5	3,880.6	3,868.1	3,792.5	3,770.3	3,793.8
1995	3,872.5	3,953.7	4,062.8	4,230.7	4,391.6	4,510.8	4,684.8	4,639.3	4,746.8	4,760.5	4,935.8	5,136.1	4,493.8
1996	5,179.4	5,518.7	5,612.2	5,579.9	5,616.7	5,671.5	5,496.3	5,685.5	5,804.0	5,995.1	6,318.4	6,435.9	5,742.8
1997	6,707.0	6,917.5	6,901.1	6,657.5	7,242.4	7,599.6	7,990.7	7,948.4	7,866.6	7,875.8	7,677.4	7,909.8	7,441.1
1998	7,808.4	8,323.6	8,709.5	9,037.4	9,080.1	8,873.0	9,097.1	8,478.5	7,909.8	8,164.3	9,005.8	9,018.7	8,625.5
1999	9,345.9	9,323.0	9,753.6	10,443.5	10,853.9	10,704.0	11,052.2	10,935.5	10,714.0	10,396.9	10,809.8	11,246.4	10,464.9
2000	11,281.3	10,541.9	10,483.4	10,944.4	10,580.3	10,582.9	10,663.0	11,014.5	10,967.9	10,441.0	10,666.1	10,652.4	10,734.9
2001	10,682.7	10,774.6	10,081.3	10,234.5	11,005.0	10,767.2	10,444.5	10,314.7	9,042.6	9,220.8	9,721.8	9,979.9	10,189.1

Average. *Source: New York Stock Exchange (NYSE)*

Dow Jones Transportation Average (20 Stocks)

Year	Jan.	Feb.	Mar.	Apr.	May	June	July	Aug.	Sept.	Oct.	Nov.	Dec.	Average
1992	1,378.7	1,412.2	1,409.0	1,356.9	1,380.4	1,333.3	1,303.1	1,254.6	1,275.2	1,286.1	1,375.9	1,430.2	1,349.6
1993	1,488.1	1,533.2	1,541.6	1,619.7	1,583.4	1,533.9	1,553.7	1,631.6	1,623.9	1,660.5	1,732.6	1,763.2	1,605.5
1994	1,812.1	1,810.4	1,719.9	1,614.7	1,602.2	1,619.2	1,596.2	1,602.8	1,553.7	1,485.8	1,473.7	1,415.3	1,608.8
1995	1,515.8	1,547.2	1,584.6	1,648.9	1,646.2	1,699.3	1,852.1	1,883.9	1,961.4	1,922.9	2,008.3	2,029.5	1,775.0
1996	1,932.7	2,030.0	2,136.0	2,180.0	2,229.1	2,213.4	2,053.1	2,060.4	2,050.8	2,100.1	2,224.3	2,273.9	2,123.7
1997	2,295.0	2,341.4	2,427.8	2,464.0	2,635.1	2,711.4	2,858.0	2,925.8	3,086.0	3,239.9	3,155.7	3,233.5	2,781.1
1998	3,275.8	3,456.8	3,521.5	3,586.5	3,401.9	3,373.2	3,459.3	3,021.1	2,763.0	2,647.8	2,953.4	3,027.6	3,207.3
1999	3,172.0	3,188.3	3,296.4	3,477.7	3,628.2	3,396.1	3,423.7	3,207.0	3,006.2	2,928.7	2,988.7	2,902.1	3,217.9
2000	2,812.2	2,483.4	2,534.5	2,823.9	2,813.2	2,717.2	2,822.3	2,835.6	2,641.5	2,491.0	2,792.3	2,822.9	2,715.8
2001	3,029.9	3,010.2	2,792.5	2,776.6	2,908.2	2,770.4	2,887.3	2,852.1	2,344.8	2,217.3	2,404.6	2,603.0	2,716.4

Average. *Source: New York Stock Exchange (NYSE)*

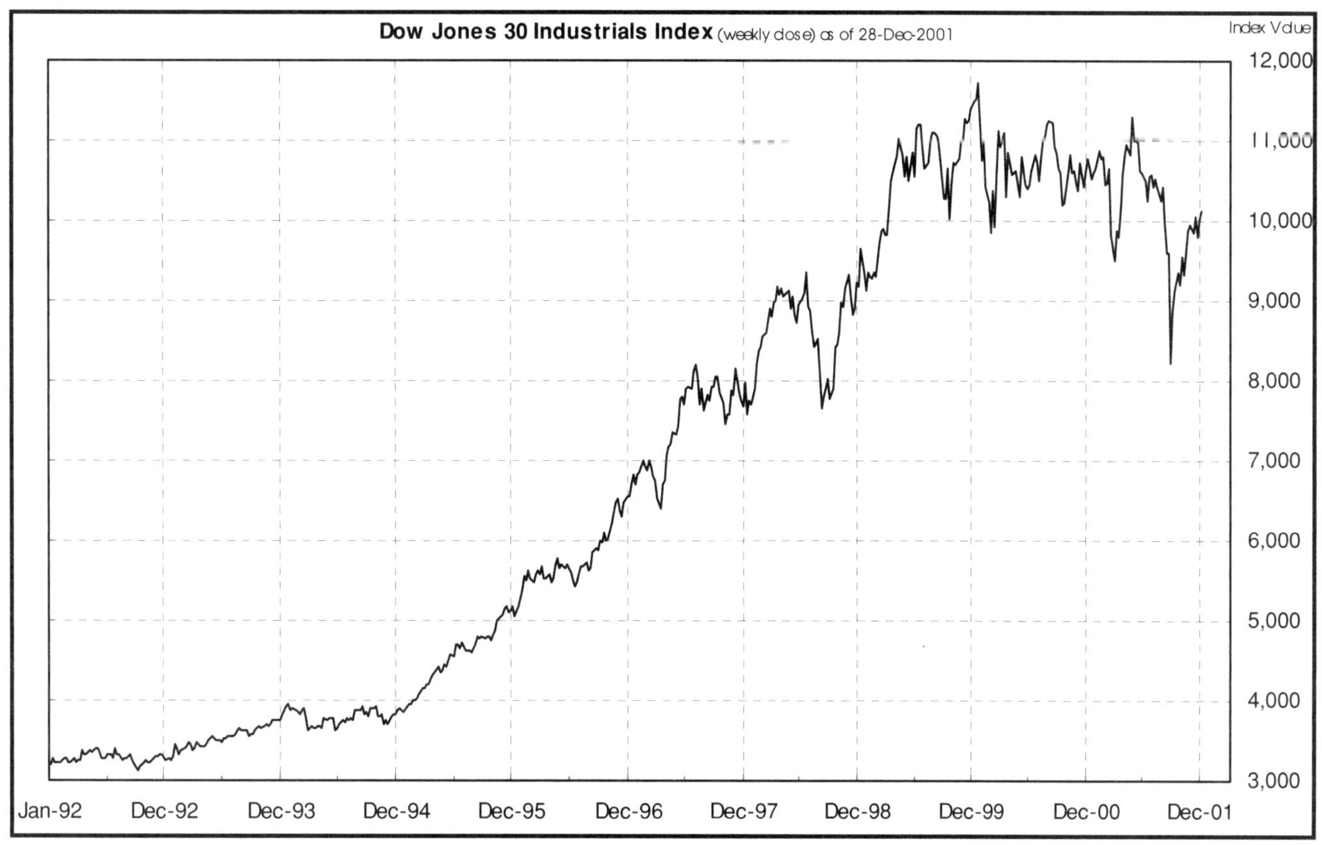

Dow Jones Public Utilities Average (15 Stocks)

Year	Jan.	Feb.	Mar.	Apr.	May	June	July	Aug.	Sept.	Oct.	Nov.	Dec.	Average
1992	215.7	206.8	204.4	206.1	213.2	212.5	219.1	220.2	220.0	217.2	217.7	220.2	214.4
1993	222.0	234.2	240.0	242.1	237.8	241.5	246.5	252.0	253.0	243.1	227.1	227.1	238.9
1994	222.3	215.6	207.0	196.5	185.5	182.9	181.8	188.9	179.6	179.9	177.7	181.0	191.6
1995	186.9	194.0	187.9	192.7	197.6	204.5	202.5	202.8	207.2	216.4	215.3	221.4	202.4
1996	228.4	228.6	216.3	209.5	211.2	210.0	212.8	214.8	217.2	222.3	234.0	232.1	219.8
1997	235.8	230.5	223.7	213.8	222.1	223.5	232.0	231.9	238.9	242.9	249.2	263.9	234.0
1998	265.6	267.9	279.0	285.4	281.2	291.1	289.3	279.4	289.1	307.0	308.1	309.0	287.7
1999	307.4	293.9	299.4	299.9	320.5	327.8	319.9	317.3	306.8	298.8	294.9	277.4	305.3
2000	300.6	302.3	285.4	307.0	325.2	322.2	325.0	355.6	384.2	386.9	392.5	394.9	340.2
2001	360.9	385.1	375.7	387.0	388.9	367.2	356.8	345.4	321.3	308.8	291.4	284.0	347.7

Average. *Source: New York Stock Exchange (NYSE)*

Standard & Poor's 500 Composite Price Index

Year	Jan.	Feb.	Mar.	Apr.	May	June	July	Aug.	Sept.	Oct.	Nov.	Dec.	Average
1992	416.1	412.6	407.4	407.4	414.8	408.3	415.1	417.9	418.5	412.5	422.8	435.6	415.7
1993	435.2	441.7	450.2	443.1	445.3	448.1	447.3	454.1	459.2	463.9	462.9	466.0	451.4
1994	473.0	471.6	463.8	447.2	451.0	454.8	451.4	464.2	467.0	463.8	461.0	455.2	460.3
1995	465.3	481.9	493.2	507.9	523.8	539.4	557.4	559.1	578.8	582.9	595.5	614.6	541.6
1996	614.4	649.5	647.1	547.2	661.2	668.5	644.1	662.7	674.9	701.5	735.7	743.3	662.5
1997	766.1	798.4	792.2	763.9	833.1	876.3	925.3	927.7	937.0	951.2	938.9	962.4	872.7
1998	963.4	1,023.7	1,076.8	1,112.2	1,108.4	1,108.4	1,156.6	1,074.6	1,020.7	1,032.5	1,144.5	1,190.0	1,084.3
1999	1,248.7	1,246.6	1,281.7	1,334.8	1,332.1	1,322.6	1,381.0	1,327.5	1,318.2	1,300.0	1,391.0	1,428.7	1,326.1
2000	1,425.6	1,388.9	1,442.2	1,461.4	1,418.5	1,462.0	1,473.0	1,485.5	1,468.0	1,390.1	1,375.0	1,330.9	1,426.8
2001	1,335.6	1,305.8	1,185.9	1,189.8	1,270.4	1,238.8	1,204.5	1,178.5	1,047.6	1,076.6	1,129.7	1,144.9	1,192.3

Average. *Source: Index and Option Market (IOM), division of the Chicago Mercantile Exchange (CME)*

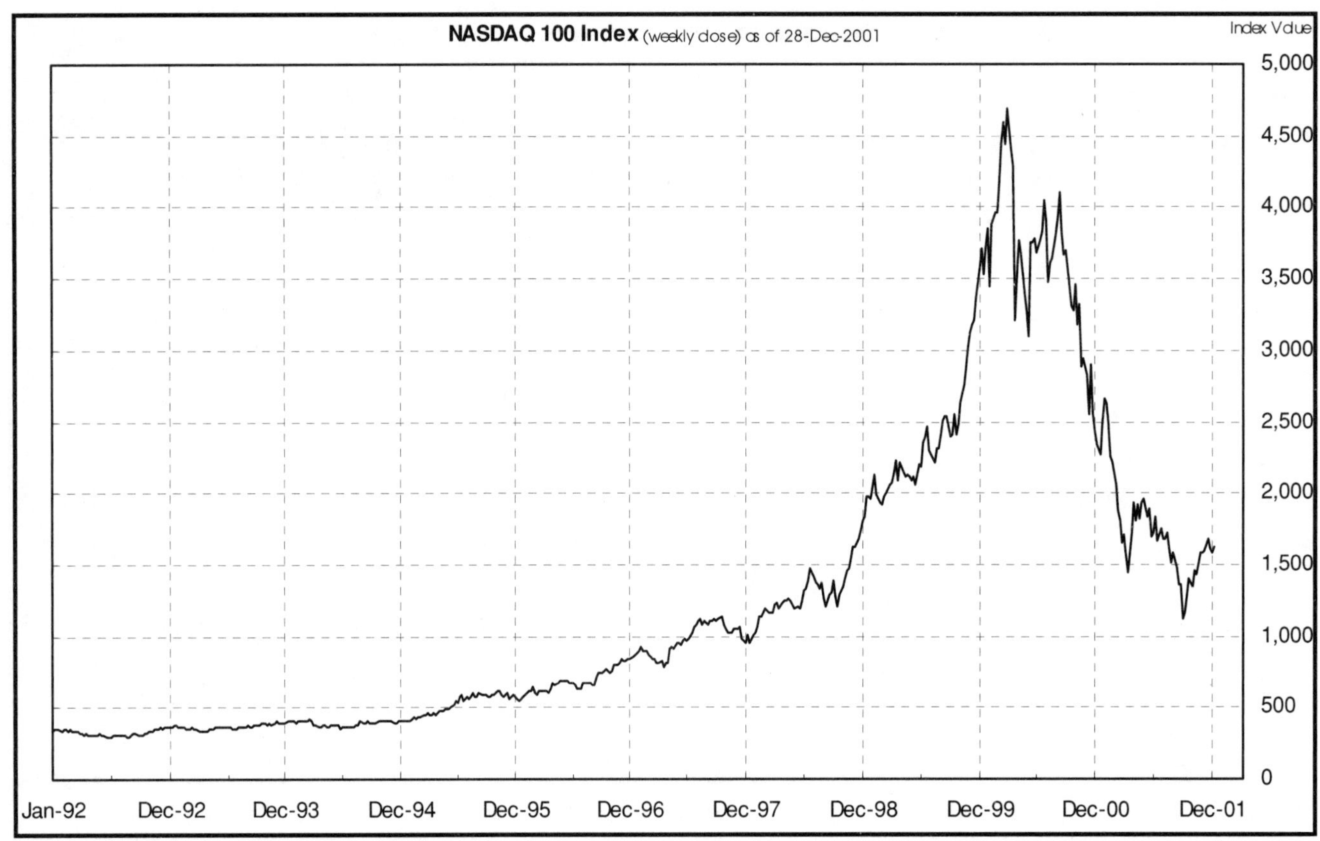

NASDAQ 100 Index (weekly close) as of 28-Dec-2001
Index Value
5,000
4,500
4,000
3,500
3,000
2,500
2,000
1,500
1,000
500
0
Jan-92
Dec-92
Dec-93
Dec-94
Dec-95
Dec-96
Dec-97
Dec-98
Dec-99
Dec-00
Dec-01

NYSE Composite Index (weekly close) as of 28-Dec-2001
Index Value
700
650
600
550
500
450
400
350
300
250
200
Jan-92
Dec-92
Dec-93
Dec-94
Dec-95
Dec-96
Dec-97
Dec-98
Dec-99
Dec-00
Dec-01

S&P 500 Index (weekly close) as of 28-Dec-2001
Index Value
1,600
1,500
1,400
1,300
1,200
1,100
1,000
900
800
700
600
500
400
300
Jan-92
Dec-92
Dec-93
Dec-94
Dec-95
Dec-96
Dec-97
Dec-98
Dec-99
Dec-00
Dec-01

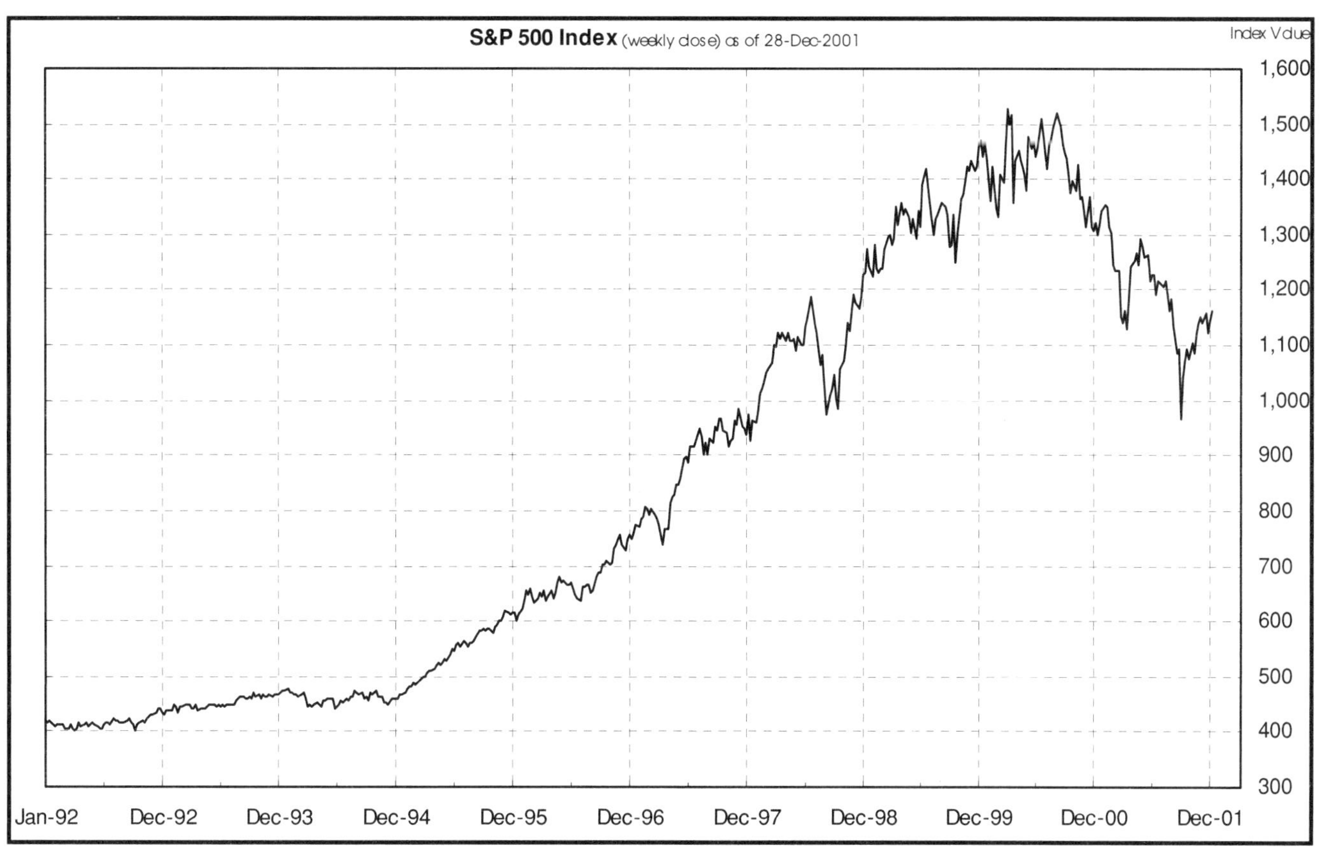

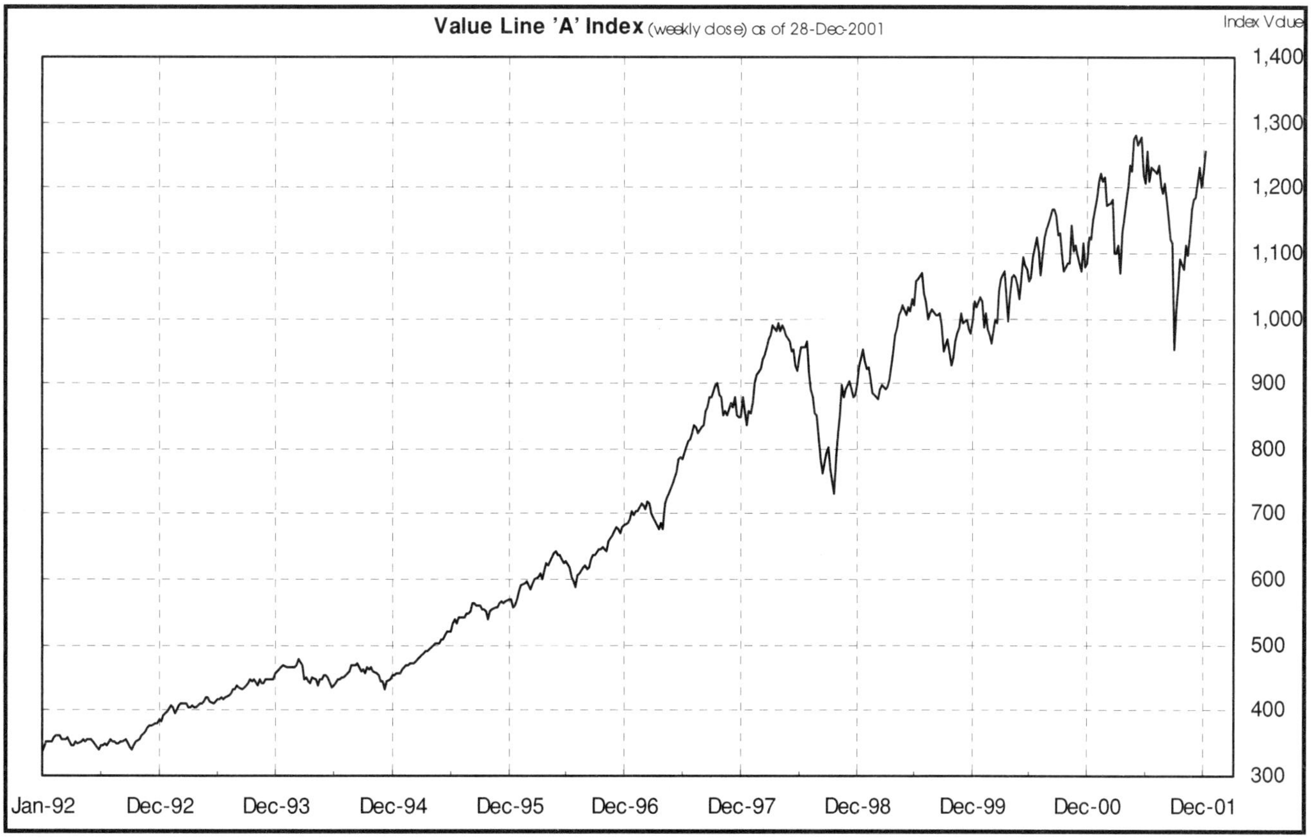

Value Line 'A' Index (weekly close) as of 28-Dec-2001
Index Value
1,400
1,300
1,200
1,100
1,000
900
800
700
600
500
400
300
Jan-92
Dec-92
Dec-93
Dec-94
Dec-95
Dec-96
Dec-97
Dec-98
Dec-99
Dec-00
Dec-01

STOCK INDEX FUTURES, U.S.

Composite Index of Leading Indicators (1992 = 100)

Year	Jan.	Feb.	Mar.	Apr.	May	June	July	Aug.	Sept.	Oct.	Nov.	Dec.	Average
1993	100.7	100.7	100.1	100.4	100.2	100.3	100.1	100.3	100.4	100.5	100.8	101.2	100.5
1994	101.2	101.0	101.5	101.4	101.4	101.4	101.2	101.5	101.4	101.5	101.6	101.6	101.4
1995	101.5	101.1	100.7	100.6	100.4	100.5	100.7	101.0	101.1	100.9	100.9	101.2	100.9
1996	100.5	101.4	101.6	101.8	102.1	102.3	102.3	102.4	102.5	102.5	102.5	102.6	102.0
1997	102.8	103.3	103.4	103.3	103.6	103.6	103.9	104.0	104.3	104.4	104.7	104.6	103.8
1998	104.8	105.2	105.4	105.4	105.4	105.2	105.6	105.6	105.6	105.7	106.2	106.4	105.5
1999	104.5	104.7	104.8	104.7	105.0	105.3	105.6	105.5	105.4	105.5	105.7	110.3	105.6
2000	110.7	110.3	110.5	110.5	110.5	110.4	109.8	109.9	109.9	109.5	109.2	108.8	110.0
2001[1]	108.9	109.0	108.7	1086	109.3	109.5	109.8	109.7	109.1	109.2	110.1	111.4	109.4

[1] Preliminary. *Source:* The Conference Board

Civilian Unemployment Rate

Year	Jan.	Feb.	Mar.	Apr.	May	June	July	Aug.	Sept.	Oct.	Nov.	Dec.	Average
1993	7.3	7.1	7.0	7.1	7.1	7.0	6.9	6.8	6.7	6.8	6.6	6.5	6.9
1994	6.7	6.6	6.5	6.4	6.0	6.1	6.1	6.1	5.9	5.8	5.6	5.4	6.1
1995	5.6	5.5	5.4	5.7	5.6	5.6	5.7	5.7	5.7	5.5	5.6	5.6	5.6
1996	5.7	5.5	5.5	5.5	5.5	5.3	5.4	5.2	5.2	5.2	5.3	5.3	5.4
1997	5.4	5.3	5.2	4.9	4.8	5.0	4.9	4.9	4.9	4.8	4.6	4.7	5.0
1998	4.6	4.6	4.7	4.3	4.4	4.5	4.5	4.5	4.5	4.5	4.4	4.3	4.5
1999	4.3	4.4	4.2	4.3	4.2	4.3	4.3	4.2	4.2	4.1	4.1	4.1	4.2
2000	4.0	4.1	4.1	3.9	4.1	4.0	4.0	4.1	3.9	3.9	4.0	4.0	4.0
2001[1]	4.2	4.2	4.3	4.5	4.4	4.5	4.5	4.9	4.9	5.4	5.7	5.8	4.8

[1] Preliminary. *Source: Bureau of Economic Analysis, U.S. Department of Commerce (BEA)*

Capacity Utilization Rates (Total Industry) In Percent

Year	Jan.	Feb.	Mar.	Apr.	May	June	July	Aug.	Sept.	Oct.	Nov.	Dec.	Average
1993	81.4	81.7	81.6	81.7	81.2	81.2	81.3	81.0	81.7	81.8	82.1	82.5	81.6
1994	82.6	82.8	83.2	83.3	83.7	83.9	84.1	83.9	83.8	84.1	84.4	84.9	83.9
1995	84.9	84.5	84.3	83.9	83.7	83.6	83.4	83.8	83.9	83.3	83.2	83.0	83.4
1996	82.4	83.2	82.6	83.1	83.2	83.5	83.2	83.2	83.1	83.0	82.5	82.5	82.4
1997	82.4	82.6	82.5	82.6	82.4	82.3	82.6	82.8	82.7	83.4	83.4	83.4	82.9
1998	83.0	82.6	82.6	82.6	82.6	81.5	81.1	82.0	81.3	81.5	80.9	80.6	81.8
1999	80.4	80.4	80.5	80.4	80.5	80.5	80.7	80.7	80.6	81.0	81.5	81.7	81.4
2000	81.9	82.0	82.2	82.5	82.7	82.7	82.3	82.6	82.4	81.2	80.7	80.2	81.8
2001[1]	79.3	78.9	78.5	77.8	77.5	76.7	76.7	76.4	75.5	74.9	74.5	74.4	76.8

[1] Preliminary. *Source: Bureau of Economic Analysis, U.S. Department of Commerce (BEA)*

Manufacturers New Orders, Durable Goods In Billions of Constant Dollars

Year	Jan.	Feb.	Mar.	Apr.	May	June	July	Aug.	Sept.	Oct.	Nov.	Dec.	Average
1993	129.56	133.47	128.50	130.20	126.93	131.29	128.27	128.99	130.31	133.01	135.60	136.82	131.08
1994	142.23	138.88	140.91	141.21	142.61	146.15	142.60	145.92	146.93	145.72	149.89	152.88	144.66
1995	153.42	151.82	151.72	146.32	149.74	148.21	147.45	152.12	156.78	154.37	154.09	158.89	154.10
1996	158.86	155.10	157.67	156.01	162.59	162.67	168.25	162.76	170.45	170.59	169.34	166.02	163.48
1997	171.73	174.80	170.02	173.13	177.05	176.93	175.82	181.08	181.15	181.33	189.71	181.44	177.03
1998	184.33	183.87	184.17	187.35	181.58	182.22	186.22	190.39	193.18	189.33	190.21	197.11	194.42
1999	211.18	203.31	209.39	204.68	206.78	207.27	216.02	218.02	214.83	212.77	215.34	229.47	209.76
2000	225.14	221.12	230.44	217.17	232.76	254.20	220.74	227.27	232.41	217.30	221.14	220.90	223.95
2001[1]	197.36	205.41	209.56	197.75	203.22	198.14	196.22	195.21	177.33	200.03			198.02

[1] Preliminary. *Source: Bureau of Economic Analysis, U.S. Department of Commerce (BEA)*

Change in Manufacturing and Trade Inventories In Billions of Dollars

Year	Jan.	Feb.	Mar.	Apr.	May	June	July	Aug.	Sept.	Oct.	Nov.	Dec.	Average
1993	34.9	31.8	66.7	43.7	12.9	25.6	7.3	39.0	34.8	27.2	63.2	1.6	32.4
1994	15.3	45.1	-8.1	42.1	114.2	56.3	60.8	98.6	60.3	71.8	65.3	64.5	57.2
1995	127.4	78.5	100.6	97.6	54.4	48.1	42.9	50.6	51.4	61.8	24.1	-39.7	58.5
1996	66.2	14.2	-27.7	61.5	-8.4	80.3	123.6	-272.1	90.6	143.4	86.1	72.0	19.9
1997	107.0	103.4	76.3	56.2	25.2	76.8	20.9	19.1	91.5	55.2	43.1	28.2	47.1
1998	27.8	86.1	85.7	38.5	5.5	11.4	-91.6	47.9	67.6	36.3	51.0		34.0
1999	10.4	36.8	66.7	31.2	44.4	61.6	67.2	42.5	58.0	50.4	121.1	70.9	50.6
2000	69.5	59.5	17.5	38.8	82.8	129.5	8.7	87.4	10.1	77.7	26.4	5.8	42.4
2001[1]	26.7	-40.5	-58.0	-22.0	-22.2	-85.5	-72.2	-31.0	-81.5	-197.8			-58.4

[1] Preliminary. *Source: Bureau of Economic Analysis, U.S. Department of Commerce (BEA)*

Comparison of International Stock Price Indexes (1990 = 100)

Year	Jan.	Feb.	Mar.	Apr.	May	June	July	Aug.	Sept.	Oct.	Nov.	Dec.	Average
United States													
1996	191.2	192.5	194.0	196.6	201.1	201.6	192.4	196.0	206.6	212.0	227.6	222.7	202.9
1997	236.3	237.7	227.6	240.9	255.0	266.1	286.8	270.4	284.7	274.9	287.2	291.7	263.3
1998	294.7	315.4	331.2	334.2	327.9	340.8	336.9	287.7	305.7	330.2	349.8	369.5	327.0
1999	384.6	372.2	386.7	401.3	391.3	412.6	399.4	396.9	385.6	409.7	417.5	441.6	400.0
2000	419.2	410.7	450.5	436.6	427.0	437.2	430.1	456.2	431.8	429.7	395.3	396.9	426.8
2001[1]	410.6	372.7	348.8	375.6	377.5	368.0	364.1	340.7	312.9	318.6	342.5		357.5
Canada													
1996	145.2	144.2	145.3	150.4	153.4	147.4	144.1	150.3	154.7	163.7	175.9	173.2	154.0
1997	178.6	180.0	171.0	174.7	186.6	188.2	201.0	193.3	205.8	200.0	190.4	195.8	188.8
1998	195.8	207.3	220.9	224.0	221.9	215.3	202.6	161.7	164.0	181.5	185.4	189.6	197.5
1999	196.7	184.5	192.9	205.0	200.0	204.9	207.0	203.8	203.4	212.1	219.9	245.9	206.3
2000	247.9	266.8	276.6	273.2	270.4	298.0	304.2	328.8	303.3	281.8	257.8	261.1	280.8
2001[1]	272.5	236.1	222.4	232.3	238.6	226.1	224.8	216.3	199.9	201.3	217.1		226.1
France													
1996	111.2	109.5	112.5	118.1	116.1	116.9	109.8	108.4	117.4	117.8	127.4	127.4	116.0
1997	138.5	143.5	146.2	145.2	142.2	157.3	169.2	152.4	165.5	150.7	157.3	165.0	152.8
1998	174.5	188.3	213.3	213.5	222.4	231.3	229.8	200.9	176.0	193.8	211.5	216.9	206.0
1999	233.9	225.2	231.0	242.4	239.4	249.6	241.1	252.5	252.6	269.0	293.9	327.8	254.9
2000	311.4	340.6	345.9	353.2	353.6	354.7	360.0	364.5	344.8	352.0	326.2	326.1	344.4
20011	330.0	295.3	285.0	310.3	300.1	287.5	279.8	258.0	224.4	238.9	246.3		277.8
Germany[2]													
1996	123.7	123.2	123.3	123.0	124.4	126.3	122.1	125.6	130.4	130.6	139.0	139.7	153.2
1997	147.0	157.8	167.8	167.1	172.2	183.8	209.6	184.1	195.3	177.8	186.0	196.3	221.4
1998	204.9	217.5	234.9	302.0	329.3	348.7	347.3	285.8	264.6	276.2	297.0	295.8	299.1
1999	305.1	290.4	288.8	318.9	299.8	318.0	301.6	311.6	304.5	326.7	348.6	411.4	318.8
2000	404.2	452.0	449.3	438.4	420.4	407.9	425.1	426.7	401.9	418.5	376.8	380.4	416.8
2001[1]	401.8	367.1	344.7	370.4	362.0	358.2	346.5	306.8	254.7	269.6	295.0		334.3
Italy													
1996	96.5	94.5	90.4	102.4	104.1	102.4	93.4	93.2	99.0	94.0	102.4	103.7	98.0
1997	119.8	115.4	115.3	119.5	117.9	130.0	144.5	136.6	155.0	144.6	149.4	164.0	134.3
1998	184.0	194.3	239.3	220.9	236.1	222.1	240.5	208.1	184.6	194.1	223.7	231.5	214.9
1999	231.7	234.1	245.4	245.9	237.1	237.5	221.5	230.4	231.0	226.5	241.3	282.8	238.8
2000	276.8	330.7	308.7	303.1	307.1	309.0	308.5	320.5	307.2	318.8	316.3	298.3	308.8
2001[1]	303.3	276.4	267.4	278.1	266.1	254.1	249.1	237.9	197.7	208.7	220.9		250.9
Japan													
1996	72.2	69.8	74.3	76.5	76.2	78.2	71.8	70.0	74.8	71.0	72.9	67.2	72.9
1997	63.6	64.4	62.5	66.4	69.6	71.5	70.5	63.2	62.1	57.1	57.7	52.9	63.5
1998	57.7	58.4	57.3	54.3	54.4	54.9	56.8	48.9	46.5	47.1	51.6	48.0	53.0
1999	50.3	49.8	54.9	57.9	55.9	60.8	62.0	60.5	61.1	62.2	64.4	65.7	58.8
2000	67.8	69.2	70.6	62.4	56.7	60.4	54.6	58.5	54.6	50.4	50.8	47.8	58.7
2001[1]	48.0	44.7	45.1	48.3	46.0	45.0	41.1	37.2	33.9	36.0	37.1		42.0
United Kingdom													
1996	170.2	170.0	170.3	176.9	174.2	171.5	169.6	177.0	179.7	180.8	183.4	186.0	175.8
1997	192.8	194.7	194.0	197.3	203.3	201.8	212.0	210.3	226.8	211.9	211.4	222.7	206.6
1998	234.3	247.9	257.0	257.6	258.9	253.4	252.6	225.5	216.6	231.4	242.7	247.0	243.7
1999	249.0	261.0	267.4	279.8	266.9	272.2	270.2	271.5	261.1	268.3	285.2	299.5	271.0
2000	274.9	276.2	287.3	277.3	278.7	279.9	282.9	296.3	279.8	284.4	272.1	275.6	280.5
2001[1]	279.9	264.9	250.5	265.0	259.7	252.0	246.1	239.3	216.2	222.9	232.2		248.1

[1] Preliminary. [2] Federal Republic of Germany. Not Seasonally Adjusted. *Source: Economic and Statistics Administration, U.S. Department of Commerce (ESA)*

Corporate Profits After Tax -- Quarterly In Billions of Dollars

Year	First Quarter	Second Quarter	Third Quarter	Fourth Quarter	Average	Year	First Quarter	Second Quarter	Third Quarter	Fourth Quarter	Average
1990	221.7	232.2	233.9	237.1	231.2	1996	493.5	501.0	500.9	515.4	502.7
1991	281.1	277.9	280.9	290.3	282.6	1997	530.7	549.4	573.8	566.9	555.2
1992	314.2	320.9	281.9	316.8	308.4	1998	491.8	485.0	480.1	472.2	482.3
1993	325.6	340.8	343.5	370.1	345.0	1999	509.2	511.2	515.1	557.7	523.3
1994	349.4	379.8	401.0	416.6	386.7	2000	567.8	581.6	583.4	563.0	573.9
1995	440.1	456.6	464.8	468.5	457.5	2001[1]	518.9	510.3	475.6		501.6

[1] Preliminary. *Source: Bureau of Economic Analysis, U.S. Department of Commerce (BEA)*

STOCK INDEX FUTURES, U.S.

Productivity: Index of Output per Hour, All Persons, Nonfarm Business -- Quarterly (1992 = 100)

Year	First Quarter	Second Quarter	Third Quarter	Fourth Quarter	Average	Year	First Quarter	Second Quarter	Third Quarter	Fourth Quarter	Average
1990	96.4	96.7	96.4	95.5	96.3	1996	101.5	101.7	102.0	102.4	103.7
1991	96.1	96.8	97.4	97.6	97.0	1997	103.4	104.0	105.6	105.9	107.2
1992	99.3	99.9	99.7	101.1	100.0	1998	106.6	106.6	107.3	111.5	110.2
1993	100.1	99.7	100.1	100.8	100.2	1999	112.2	112.4	113.6	115.8	113.2
1994	100.2	100.5	101.0	101.2	100.7	2000	116.2	118.0	116.7	117.8	117.2
1995	100.5	100.9	101.3	101.1	100.7	2001[1]	117.8	118.4	118.9		118.4

[1] Preliminary. *Source: Bureau of Economic Analysis, U.S. Department of Commerce (BEA)*

Consumer Confidence, The Conference Board (1985 = 100)

Year	Jan.	Feb.	Mar.	Apr.	May	June	July	Aug.	Sept.	Oct.	Nov.	Dec.	Average
1993	76.7	68.5	63.2	67.6	61.9	58.6	59.2	59.3	63.8	60.5	71.9	79.8	65.9
1994	82.6	79.9	86.7	92.1	88.9	92.5	91.3	90.4	89.5	89.1	100.4	103.4	90.6
1995	101.4	99.4	100.2	104.6	102.0	94.6	101.4	102.4	97.3	96.3	101.6	99.2	100.0
1996	88.4	98.0	98.4	104.8	103.5	100.1	107.0	112.0	111.8	107.3	109.5	114.2	104.6
1997	118.7	118.9	118.5	118.5	127.9	129.9	126.3	127.6	130.2	123.4	128.1	136.2	125.4
1998	128.3	137.4	133.8	137.2	136.3	138.2	137.2	133.1	126.4	119.3	126.4	126.7	131.7
1999	128.9	133.1	134.0	135.5	137.7	139.0	136.2	136.0	134.2	130.5	137.0	141.7	135.3
2000	144.7	140.8	137.1	137.7	144.7	139.2	143.0	140.8	142.5	135.8	132.6	128.6	139.0
2001[1]	115.7	109.3	116.9	109.9	116.1	118.9	116.3	114.0	97.0	85.3	84.9		107.7

[1] Preliminary. *Source: The Conference Board (TCB) Copyrighted.*

Average Open Interest of NYSE Composite Stock Index Futures in New York In Contracts

Year	Jan.	Feb.	Mar.	Apr.	May	June	July	Aug.	Sept.	Oct.	Nov.	Dec.
1993	5,033	5,083	4,113	3,613	4,222	4,340	3,714	4,178	3,997	4,315	4,721	4,539
1994	4,653	4,471	4,823	3,720	3,839	3,969	3,903	3,982	4,142	4,494	4,244	4,617
1995	3,695	4,159	4,113	3,476	3,396	3,254	3,205	3,029	2,966	2,683	3,125	3,403
1996	3,644	4,139	3,245	2,822	2,839	2,547	2,492	2,526	2,759	2,798	2,649	3,050
1997	3,126	3,232	3,194	2,801	3,154	2,744	2,316	2,823	2,780	2,384	3,005	4,354
1998	4,803	5,216	5,252	4,754	4,888	5,990	10,154	12,249	10,574	8,554	7,977	9,806
1999	8,299	8,661	5,457	4,050	4,169	3,849	3,419	3,882	3,730	3,958	4,447	4,260
2000	3,653	3,715	3,747	3,285	2,533	2,597	2,452	2,793	2,463	1,690	1,943	2,406
2001	2,387	2,648	3,510	3,694	2,929	2,408	5,271	5,802	5,451	6,448	6,884	6,617

Source: New York Futures Exchange (NYFE)

Average Open Interest of Value Line Stock Index Futures in Kansas City In Contracts

Year	Jan.	Feb.	Mar.	Apr.	May	June	July	Aug.	Sept.	Oct.	Nov.	Dec.
1993	330	393	382	375	497	449	387	455	413	359	519	534
1994	432	501	530	566	648	593	575	583	573	1,111	1,041	845
1995	678	792	951	1,108	1,132	972	839	1,042	966	980	1,193	1,138
1996	1,238	1,580	1,949	1,804	1,669	1,576	1,611	1,813	1,818	1,466	1,641	1,958
1997	1,459	1,354	1,338	1,448	1,326	1,686	2,160	2,523	1,980	1,477	1,213	1,675
1998	1,739	1,442	1,433	1,498	1,549	1,390	697	839	667	696	914	780
1999	746	738	699	725	900	967	515	503	381	314	300	283
2000	273	284	246	135	155	148	155	216	179	182	181	185
2001	233	333	377	233	275	285	283	268	222	125	249	368

Source: Kansas City Board of Trade (KCBT)

Average Open Interest of S & P 500 Stock Index Futures in Chicago In Contracts

Year	Jan.	Feb.	Mar.	Apr.	May	June	July	Aug.	Sept.	Oct.	Nov.	Dec.
1993	329,228	347,382	357,878	348,554	365,792	380,106	364,378	382,622	416,780	390,218	402,748	392,350
1994	376,450	391,648	420,130	401,636	438,218	599,134	434,056	455,742	475,868	461,188	487,162	502,740
1995	427,004	442,628	445,584	420,104	443,296	453,364	420,024	422,608	417,812	402,794	441,780	447,528
1996	406,400	428,058	419,688	368,620	399,070	407,914	369,248	382,266	413,944	374,726	416,102	448,382
1997	393,086	396,528	417,542	377,100	392,034	417,006	372,274	392,812	423,449	391,922	402,044	417,717
1998	394,410	408,851	417,721	365,746	371,732	412,739	370,410	385,820	434,838	405,395	421,928	435,907
1999	399,093	406,516	410,164	381,402	391,035	400,503	372,455	385,809	408,176	394,316	408,751	416,425
2000	369,295	374,365	400,089	379,651	383,677	409,448	380,118	391,867	416,600	413,912	447,245	498,049
2001	488,284	495,621	517,666	498,594	490,148	505,063	485,839	501,281	556,737	529,730	550,201	551,175

Source: Index and Option Market (IOM), division of the Chicago Mercantile Exchange (CME)

Average Open Interest of S & P 400 Midcap Stock Index Futures in Chicago In Contracts

Year	Jan.	Feb.	Mar.	Apr.	May	June	July	Aug.	Sept.	Oct.	Nov.	Dec.
1993	7,197	9,048	9,095	8,759	8,640	9,336	8,731	10,183	10,728	12,955	13,343	13,261
1994	13,183	11,999	12,748	10,801	10,829	11,902	11,970	12,369	15,002	13,702	13,896	14,494
1995	13,787	13,355	11,130	9,275	9,329	9,929	11,198	11,708	13,107	11,702	12,041	12,803
1996	11,088	10,474	11,375	8,700	9,254	10,403	9,763	10,867	11,168	9,641	10,596	11,107
1997	11,215	11,825	11,258	9,721	10,807	10,877	11,292	12,346	13,505	11,595	11,874	13,329
1998	12,688	13,319	14,363	14,130	13,352	13,940	12,964	13,589	14,893	16,645	16,768	17,569
1999	16,191	16,309	14,573	12,154	12,705	14,422	14,263	13,496	13,182	12,699	13,933	14,902
2000	12,810	13,119	13,965	12,495	13,355	14,040	12,957	13,162	15,026	16,143	16,510	17,479
2001	15,246	15,461	17,235	16,953	15,623	16,606	16,334	16,132	16,718	15,109	15,307	15,337

Source: Index and Option Market (IOM), division of the Chicago Mercantile Exchange (CME)

Average Open Interest of NASDAQ 100 Index Futures in Chicago In Contracts

Year	Jan.	Feb.	Mar.	Apr.	May	June	July	Aug.	Sept.	Oct.	Nov.	Dec.
1996	-----	-----	-----	1,364	3,336	6,182	5,977	4,737	7,957	10,999	10,465	8,897
1997	6,610	7,064	8,073	7,627	7,587	8,270	6,346	8,255	8,444	6,235	8,831	8,210
1998	6,918	8,184	9,314	7,652	8,833	11,128	9,991	9,507	9,233	8,187	9,176	10,838
1999	10,669	14,766	19,786	21,286	23,028	26,938	21,646	22,765	21,808	19,946	23,429	27,876
2000	27,242	34,555	37,795	36,512	37,578	35,314	29,974	32,922	34,754	35,559	44,022	48,757
2001	46,582	49,495	59,916	56,328	49,337	54,394	50,854	55,234	61,665	51,977	61,196	67,769

Source: Index and Option Market (IOM), division of the Chicago Mercantile Exchange (CME)

Average Open Interest of Dow Jones Industrials Index Futures in Chicago In Contracts

Year	Jan.	Feb.	Mar.	Apr.	May	June	July	Aug.	Sept.	Oct.	Nov.	Dec.
1997	-----	-----	-----	-----	-----	-----	-----	-----	-----	5,249	11,542	15,952
1998	14,853	15,558	14,421	13,846	14,464	16,226	15,707	17,586	18,569	17,416	17,795	17,597
1999	16,794	19,401	19,807	20,492	25,890	22,198	21,556	25,333	23,977	24,847	22,342	17,299
2000	13,713	16,331	20,443	18,157	19,253	17,394	14,367	15,748	14,840	15,087	19,113	20,966
2001	21,830	23,423	28,340	32,497	33,767	29,357	26,792	33,015	35,451	31,997	30,598	27,018

Source: Chicago Board of Trade (CBT)

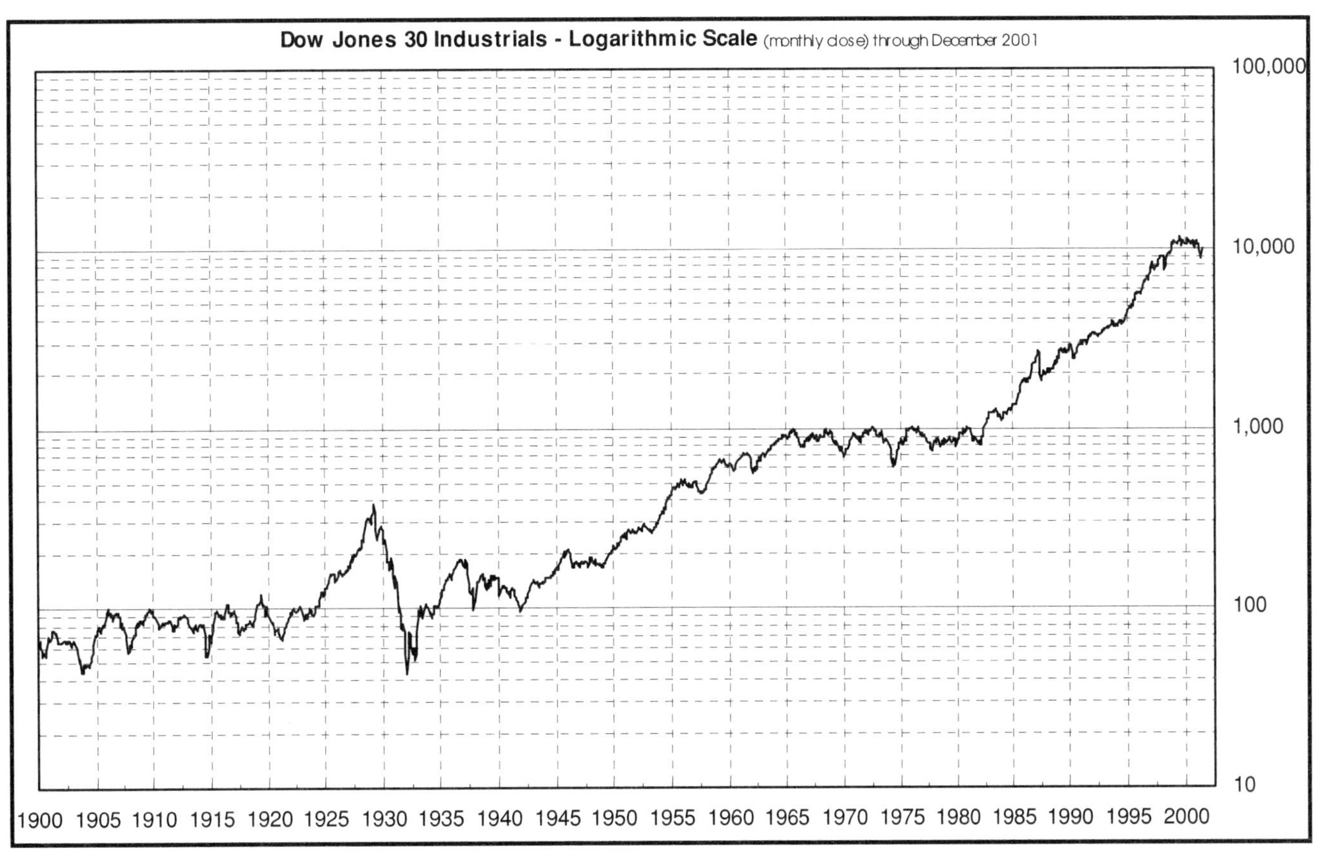

Stock Index Futures, Worldwide

The world's equity markets plunged to three year lows during 2001, reflecting a year that was marked by terrorism, military actions and uncertainty as to whether a global recession had taken hold and/or been avoided. The Dow-Jones World Stock Index, excluding the U.S., fell 21%, its second straight annual decline and the worst one-year performance seen in the ten years it has been compiled. Europe was probably the more disappointing of the world's equities areas, as it was believed the Continent could withstand the uncertainties that fell on the U.S. markets, but reality proved otherwise as it showed the mutual interdependence between the U.S. and Europe. Benchmark indexes in Paris, Milan, and Frankfurt all dropped at least 20% in 2001, but there were also some winners: Istanbul's market gained 46% despite a shaky economy. And in Japan, whose Nikkei index fell about 23%, the decline seemed to reflect a view that it could have been worse. Among the few markets that finished with gains in 2001 based on the performance of the local stock index, and not in U.S. dollar terms, were China with a near 93% gain, Iran up 24% and Russia up 56%: relative to the dollar, however, the gains are much less impressive, if not in negative territory by perhaps 20%.

In Europe, 2001 was one of the worst ever for equity markets. The Dow-Jones Stoxx index of 600 major European companies fell 17% vs. the previous record decline of almost 18% in 1990. Despite a late yearend rally, the technology sector dropped 42.5%, easily making it the worst performing sector. Britain's, FTSE's 100-share index fell 16%, its biggest decline since the index was created in 1983. with most of the blame for the slide focusing on technology and telecom stocks. In France, the blue-chip CAC-40 index fell 20%, which followed a 7% decline in 2000. Germany's DAX's of 30 blue chip stocks fell 19.8% vs. a 16.5% drop in 2000. Germany's Neuer Markt (Nemax-50 index), the apparent toast of Europe during the technology boom of the late 1990's proved a bust in 2001, slumping to about 641 by September' 01 vs. its record high of 9694 in March, 2000. Among other major European markets: the Swiss index fell 21%, Norway's oil-sensitive index plunged 51%, making it Europe's biggest loser, Italy's Milan index fell 26%, but in Vienna, the benchmark ATX index was up 6%, largely due to the relatively low U.S. exposure of Austrian companies. In Asia, Hong Kong's Hang Seng Index was one of the worst performers with a 24% slide and Singapore's Straits Times Index fell almost 16%. There were winners, however, South Korea's Composite index gained 37% and Malaysia's index eked out a 2.4% gain while Thailand's index gained almost 13%. Australia and New Zealand's stock indices both managed to finish 2001 higher, up 6.5% and 8%, respectively. In the Americas initial expectations for solid economic growth in Brazil failed to materialize and their stock index fell almost 25% in dollar term: but Mexico's index gained about 19%. Canada's economic growth sagged in 2001 and the Toronto 300 composite index fell about 19%.

Aside from the percentile swings, of continuing importance was the growth in Internet trading which caused a number of exchanges to consider merging to hold down costs. Although the merger impetus subsided somewhat in 2001, the Lisbon bourse agreed to merge with Euronext, which is a combination of French, Dutch and Belgium exchanges. The odds are that the coming years will see further consolidation and/or electronic link-ups.

As usual, the world economic setting was sharply divided in 2001, but early in the year very few people thought that the world equity markets would do so poorly, especially in view of easier monetary policies, fiscal stimulus packages and corporate downsizing in a number of countries. However, for most of the year, nothing really sparked a global interest in equities. Moreover, uncertainties were plentiful as 2002 came into view, specifically focusing on terrorism fears and the elusive U.S. led economic recovery, which seemed to be always a calendar quarter away. In Japan, for example, the country's economy had a record-breaking year, but it was all negative: unemployment reached an unheard of 5.4%, and bankruptcies were at a record high. In 2001, the benchmark Nikkei 225 index and the broader Topix index each fell more than 20%, the seventh losing year since 1990. By yearend 2001, there was deep-rooted uncertainty as to how Japan could fix its ailing economy.

The U.S. economy's near decade long expansionary phase ended officially in the first quarter of 2001 and a recession was declared. A sharply easier monetary policy was implemented during the year as well as a federal tax relief policy, but neither approach appeared capable of doing little more than holding the economy's slide in check. The bearish pressure on the U.S. equity markets reflected latent concern that had taken root before the September 11, terrorist attack. All the key equity indices finished lower in 2001 with the technology biased NASDAQ composite losing 21%. Although hopes for more fiscal stimulus in 2002 helped stocks recover in late 2001, price-earning ratios were still viewed as historically high which could still leave the U.S. equities market vulnerable to further corrections in 2002. However, European stocks have generally much lower price/earning ratios suggesting that if the world equities markets recover in 2002, it might be the key European equity markets that set the pace. Moreover, the U.S. markets have been shaken by a possible loss of confidence in corporate financial reporting which could prove to last longer than expected, effectively restraining investor interest and/or participation in U.S. equities. Price volatility, however, is still likely owing to the broad computer driven approaches to market action and short-term price swings.

Futures Markets

Futures and option trading on stock indices have expanded rapidly in recent years, taking their place alongside debt instruments futures and options as the most successful exchange traded contracts. Nearly every global futures exchange lists a variety of stock index contracts, primarily on those indices based on their domestic stock markets. The lists of stock indices traded worldwide has grown too large for this space, but a listing is available in the worldwide futures exchange volume tables in the front section of this Yearbook.

FT-SE 100 Stock Index (weekly close) as of 28-Dec-2001
Index Value
7,000
6,500
6,000
5,500
5,000
4,500
4,000
3,500
3,000
2,500
2,000
Jan-92
Dec-92
Dec-93
Dec-94
Dec-95
Dec-96
Dec-97
Dec-98
Dec-99
Dec-00
Dec-01

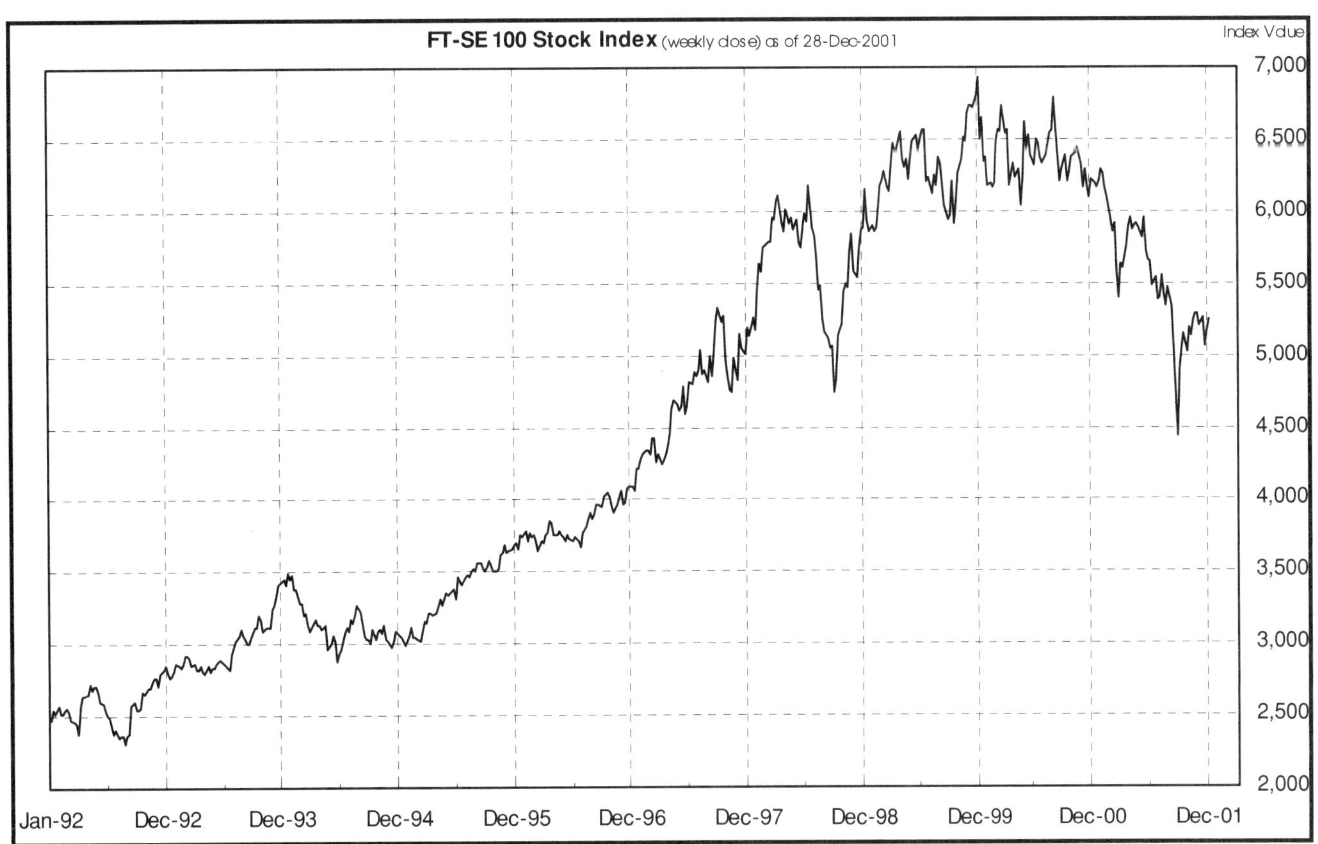

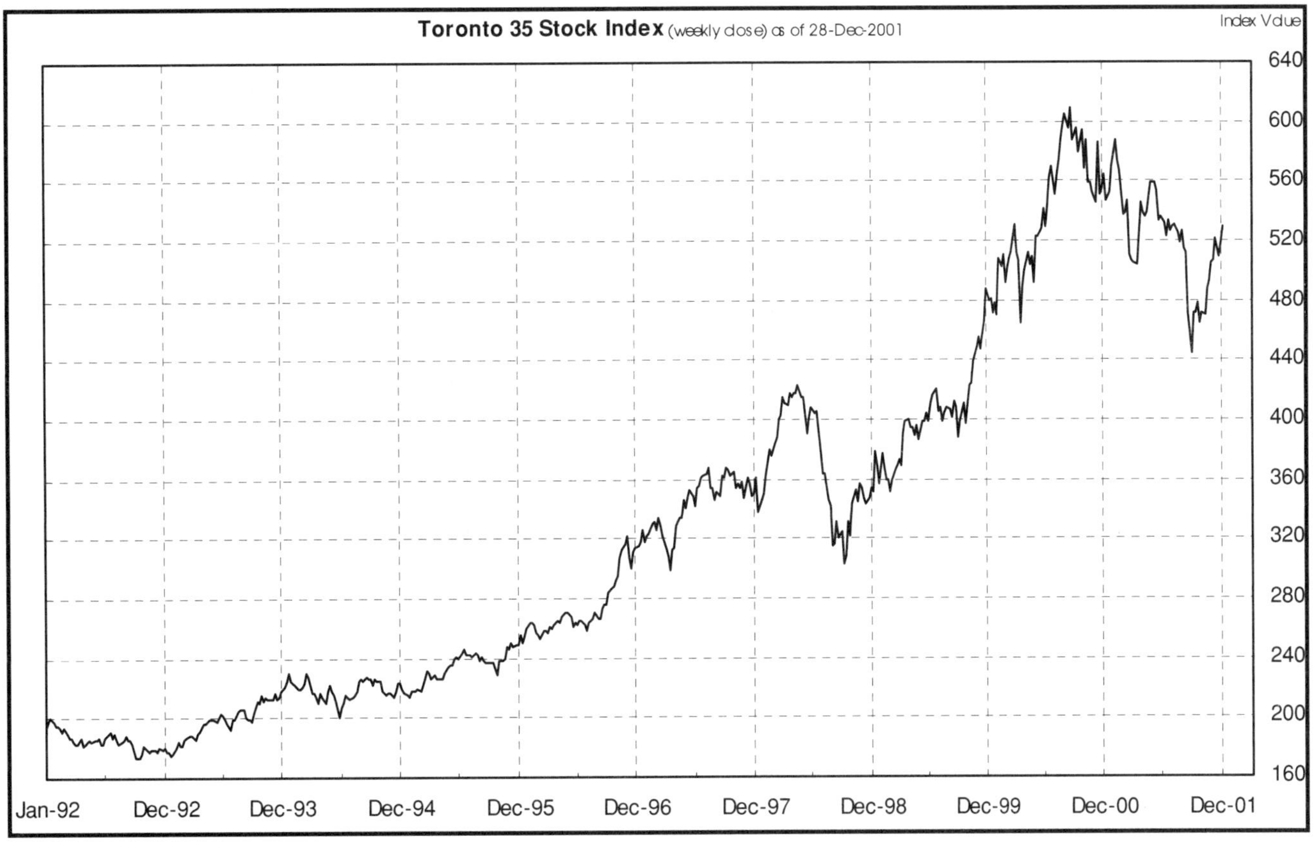

Toronto 35 Stock Index (weekly close) as of 28-Dec-2001
Index Value
640
600
560
520
480
440
400
360
320
280
240
200
160
Jan-92
Dec-92
Dec-93
Dec-94
Dec-95
Dec-96
Dec-97
Dec-98
Dec-99
Dec-00
Dec-01

STOCK INDEX FUTURES, WORLDWIDE

CAC-40 Stock Index (weekly close) as of 28-Dec-2001
Index Value
7,200
6,800
6,400
6,000
5,600
5,200
4,800
4,400
4,000
3,600
3,200
2,800
2,400
2,000
1,600
1,200
Jan-92
Dec-92
Dec-93
Dec-94
Dec-95
Dec-96
Dec-97
Dec-98
Dec-99
Dec-00
Dec-01

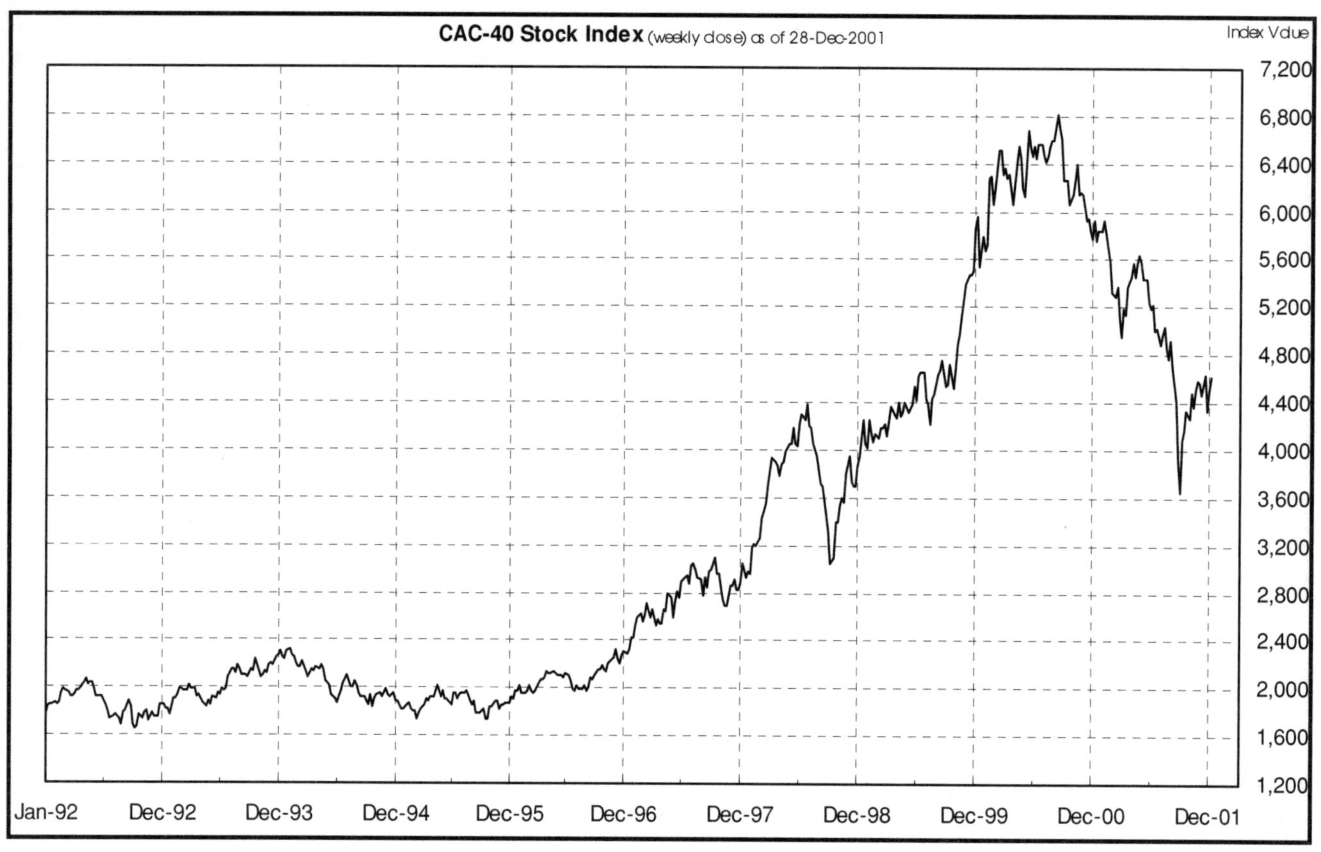

Deutscher Aktienindex (DAX) (weekly close) as of 28-Dec-2001
Index Value
8,500
8,000
7,500
7,000
6,500
6,000
5,500
5,000
4,500
4,000
3,500
3,000
2,500
2,000
1,500
1,000
Jan-92
Dec-92
Dec-93
Dec-94
Dec-95
Dec-96
Dec-97
Dec-98
Dec-99
Dec-00
Dec-01

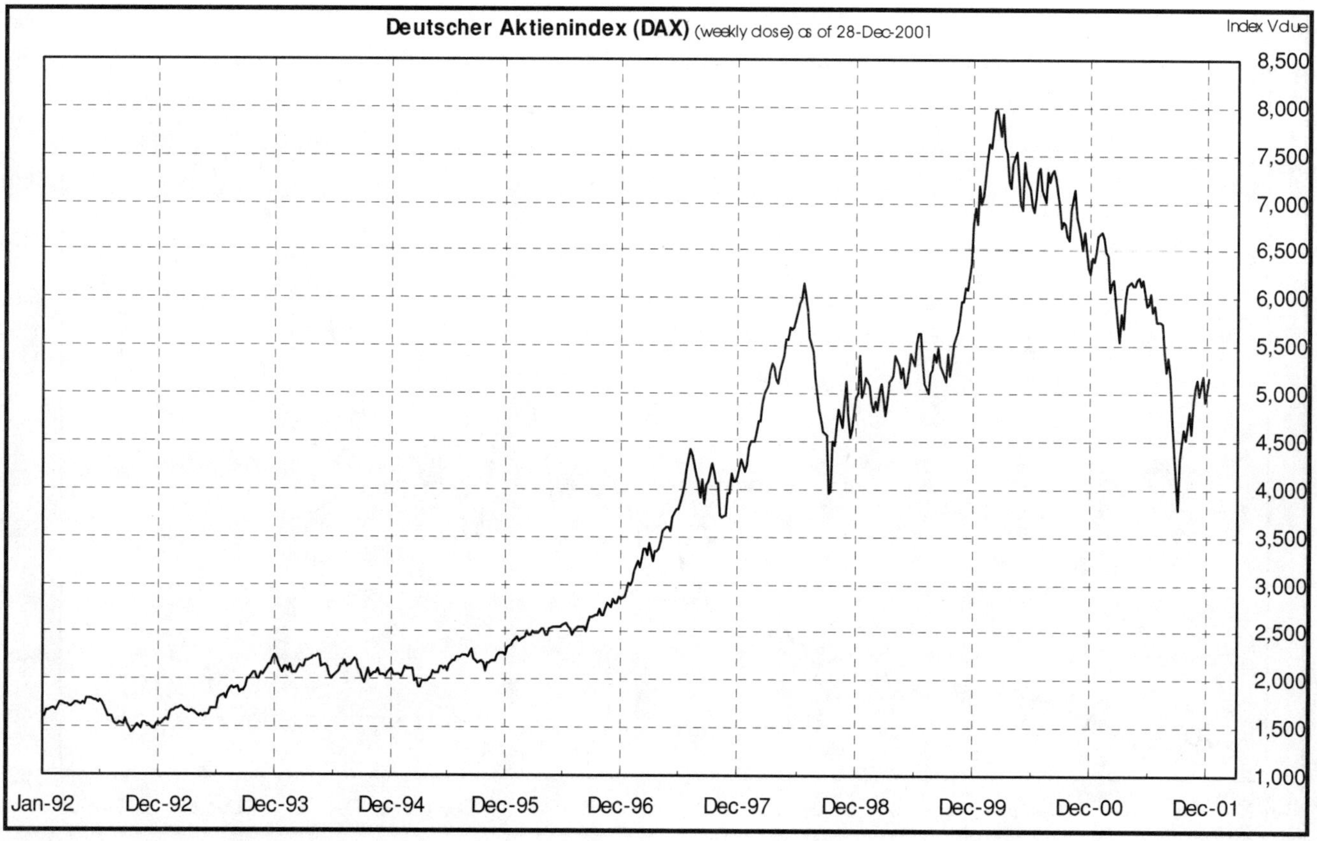

Hang Seng Stock Index (weekly close) as of 28-Dec-2001
Index Value
19,000
18,000
17,000
16,000
15,000
14,000
13,000
12,000
11,000
10,000
9,000
8,000
7,000
6,000
5,000
4,000
Jan-92
Dec-92
Dec-93
Dec-94
Dec-95
Dec-96
Dec-97
Dec-98
Dec-99
Dec-00
Dec-01

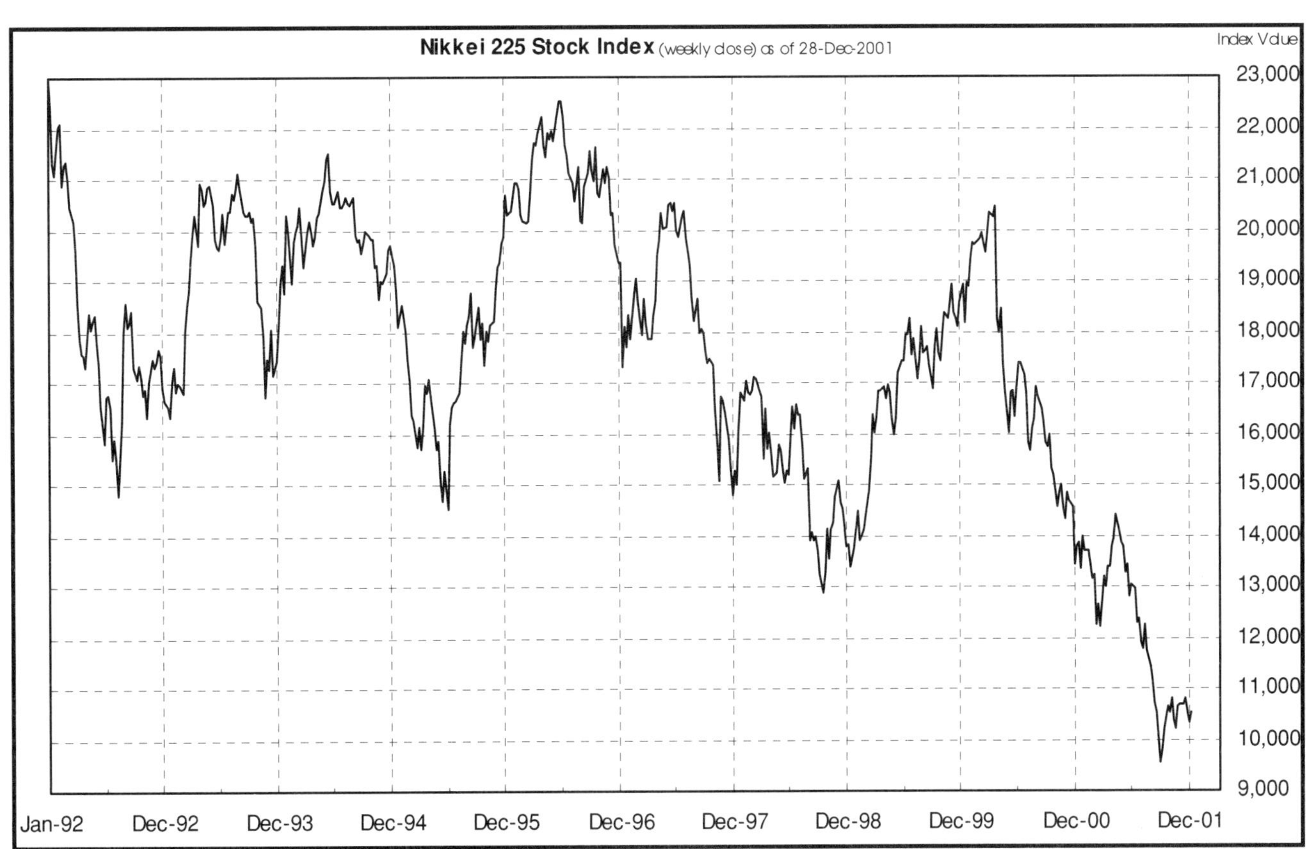

Nikkei 225 Stock Index (weekly close) as of 28-Dec-2001
Index Value
23,000
22,000
21,000
20,000
19,000
18,000
17,000
16,000
15,000
14,000
13,000
12,000
11,000
10,000
9,000
Jan-92
Dec-92
Dec-93
Dec-94
Dec-95
Dec-96
Dec-97
Dec-98
Dec-99
Dec-00
Dec-01

Sugar

Sugar prices moved lower in the third quarter of 2001 as a large sugarcane crop in Brazil came to the market. Futures prices for sugar on the New York Board of Trade moved down to almost six cents in October 2001. At that point prices began to move reaching over eight cents by early 2002. Driving prices higher were a smaller sugarbeet crop in Europe and consistent buying interest by Middle Eastern countries in the physical market. Despite the events of September 11, there continued to be interest in buying physical sugar. As prices edged higher in late 2001, the buying interest continued. many countries that import sugar are price sensitive in that as prices move higher they tend to back away from the market waiting for prices to move lower again. Among the countries buying physical sugar in late 2001 were Iran and Syria. Russia, a major buyer of sugar, bought some by what the market was missing was buying by countries that import large amounts of sugar. China, a large importer, was notably absent in late 2001.

The 2001/02 season was characterized by world production of sugar being somewhat less than world consumption. In late 2001, the U.S.D.A. estimated world production of sugar at 126.8 million metric tonnes, down 2 percent from the 129.7 million tonnes produced in 2000/01. The U.S.D.A.'s production estimate was up slightly from an estimate made earlier in the year. The U.S.D.A. forecast as increase in Brazilian sugar production while the European Union (EU) was expected to have a smaller crop. Global consumption of sugar was estimated at 130.7 million tonnes which was up 1.5 percent from the previous year.

As the new 2002/02 season approaches, the first crops to be harvested will be in the Southern Hemisphere. The major sugar producers there are Brazil, Australia and South Africa. By far the largest producer of sugar is Brazil which starts to harvest its sugarcane in May. The U.S.D.A. estimated the 2001/02 (May-April) Brazilian sugarcane crop at 272 million tonnes., up 6 percent from the previous season. In Brazil the sugarcane is processed into either sugar for the domestic and export market or alcohol for the fuel market. More sugarcane is used to produce alcohol than for sugar, but the proportion has been shifting toward sugar. In part this appears due to a decline in the value of the local currency which acts to encourage exports of sugar and other commodities. The U.S.D.A. estimated that Brazilian sugar production in 2001/02 would be 18.5 million tonnes, up from 17.1 million tonnes in 2000/01. The 2002/03 sugarcane crop is expected to be larger than in 2001/02 and the government has mandated a higher level of alcohol to be blended with gasoline.

The European Union is the larger producer of refined sugar. The U.S.D.A. estimated that EU sugar production in 2001/02 would be 16.2 million tonnes, a decline of 12.5 percent from 2000/01 when production was 18.5 million tonnes. The decline was attributed to late plantings and a poor growing season. Due to the smaller crop, EU exports of sugar in 2001/02 were projected to reach a record low of 3.7 million tonnes, down 44 percent from the previous year.

India is a major sugar producer as well as a major holder of sugar stocks. The U.S.D.A. forecast Indian sugar production in 2001/02 at 18.3 million tonnes. This would represent a decline of 10 percent from the previous crop in 2000/01 of 20.4 million tonnes. In addition to very high production, India also holds a large portion of the world's stocks. At the end of 2001, India's sugar stocks were estimated to be 12.4 million tonnes. At the end of 2002, stocks are estimated to be 11.7 million tonnes. India has also emerged as an exporter of sugar and looks like it will export about a million tonnes of sugar in 2002.

The U.S.D.A. in the January 2002 supply/demand report for the U.S. estimated 2001/02 (October-September) season production of 7.92 million short tons, down 9 percent from the 2000/01 crop of 8.67 million tons. Beet sugar production was estimated at 3.9 million tons, down 15 percent from the previous season. The cane sugar crop was 4.02 million tons, down 1 percent from the previous year. U.S. sugar imports in 2001/02 were forecast to be 1.63 million tons, up 4 percent from the previous season. Imports under the Tariff Rate Quota were 1.341 million tons, up 6 percent from 2000/01. Countries with quota allocations include Brazil and the Dominican Republic. Ending stocks of sugar were forecast to be 1.22 million tons, down 44 percent from 2000/01.

Futures Markets

Sugar futures are traded on the Bolsa de Mercadorias & Futures (BM&F), Chubu Commodity Exchange (C-COM), Kansai Commodities Exchange (KANEX), the Tokyo Grain Exchange (TGE), the London International Financial Futures and Options Exchange (LIFFE), and the CSCE Division of the New York Board of Trade (NYBOT). Options are traded on the KANEX, the TGE, the LIFFE and the NYBOT.

World Production, Supply & Stocks/Consumption Ratio of Sugar In 1000's of Metric Tons (Raw Value)

Marketing Year	Beginning Stocks	Production	Imports	Total Supply	Exports	Domestic Consumption	Ending Stocks	Stocks/ Consumption Percentage
1992-3	23,509	112,099	28,937	164,545	28,937	114,037	21,571	18.9
1993-4	21,570	109,731	29,565	160,866	29,565	112,054	19,247	17.2
1994-5	19,288	115,920	31,317	167,553	30,289	113,716	22,520	19.8
1995-6	22,756	122,212	32,457	179,250	34,282	116,574	26,569	22.8
1996-7	26,569	122,496	32,803	184,990	35,925	119,667	26,276	22.0
1997-8	26,276	124,997	32,494	186,659	35,386	122,918	25,463	20.7
1998-9	25,463	130,228	34,697	191,887	36,196	123,738	30,454	24.6
1999-00	30,454	135,641	35,110	205,652	39,557	126,859	34,789	27.4
2000-1[1]	34,789	129,653	35,528	200,967	36,525	128,787	34,658	26.9
2001-2[2]	34,658	126,795	33,645	195,989	34,536	130,718	29,844	22.8

[1] Preliminary. [2] Forecast. *Source: Foreign Agricultural Service, U.S. Department of Agriculture (FAS-USDA)*

World Production of Sugar (Centrifugal Sugar-Raw Value) In Thousands of Metric Tons

Year	Aus-tralia	Brazil	China	Cuba	France	Ger-many	India	Indo-nesia	Mexico	Thailand	United States	Ukraine	World Total
1992-3	4,367	9,800	8,300	4,280	4,723	4,401	12,447	2,300	4,330	3,750	7,111	3,965	112,099
1993-4	4,412	9,930	6,505	4,000	4,725	4,736	11,704	2,480	3,780	3,975	6,945	4,188	109,731
1994-5	5,196	12,500	6,299	3,300	4,363	3,991	16,410	2,450	4,556	5,448	7,191	3,600	115,920
1995-6	5,049	13,700	6,686	4,400	4,564	4,159	18,225	2,090	4,660	6,223	6,686	3,800	122,212
1996-7	5,659	14,650	7,789	4,200	4,594	4,558	14,616	2,094	4,835	6,013	6,536	2,935	122,496
1997-8	5,567	15,700	8,631	3,200	----	----	14,592	2,190	5,490	4,245	7,276	2,032	124,997
1998-9	4,997	18,300	8,969	3,760	----	----	17,436	1,492	4,985	5,386	7,597	2,000	130,228
1999-00	5,448	20,100	7,525	4,060	----	----	20,219	1,690	4,977	5,721	8,203	1,720	135,641
2000-1[1]	4,162	17,100	6,899	3,500	----	----	20,370	1,800	5,223	5,107	7,869	1,700	129,653
2001-2[2]	4,662	18,500	7,623	3,200	----	----	18,350	1,700	5,092	5,225	7,298	1,900	126,795

[1] Preliminary. [2] Forecast. *Source: Foreign Agricultural Service, U.S. Department of Agriculture (FAS-USDA)*

World Stocks of Centrifugal Sugar at Beginning of Marketing Year In Thousands of Metric Tons (Raw Value)

Year	Aus-tralia	Brazil	China	Cuba	France	Ger-many	India	Iran	Mexico	Philip-pines	United Kingdom	United States	World Total
1992-3	163	950	2,002	500	589	340	5,245	300	910	515	281	1,340	23,509
1993-4	125	880	1,508	130	701	358	3,502	400	1,040	679	416	1,546	21,570
1994-5	125	455	1,168	170	784	511	2,776	400	575	412	450	1,213	19,288
1995-6	152	710	3,215	647	437	271	5,990	270	601	100	453	1,126	22,756
1996-7	101	510	2,684	567	684	331	8,455	300	714	511	457	1,354	26,569
1997-8	228	860	2,784	484	----	----	6,979	330	634	345	----	1,350	26,276
1998-9	253	560	2,515	568	----	----	5,850	350	670	183	----	1,523	25,463
1999-00	183	1,010	2,548	468	----	----	7,374	350	665	454	----	1,487	30,454
2000-1[1]	518	710	1,851	518	----	----	10,710	398	630	330	----	2,013	34,789
2001-2[2]	573	860	850	318	----	----	12,400	368	790	322	----	1,990	34,658

[1] Preliminary. [2] Forecast. *Source: Foreign Agricultural Service, U.S. Department of Agriculture (FAS-USDA)*

Centrifugal Sugar (Raw Value) Imported into Selected Countries In Thousands of Metric Tons

Year	Algeria	Canada	China	France	Iran	Rep. of Korea	Malaysia	Morocco	Nigeria	Russia	United Kingdom	United States	World Total
1992-3	980	1,095	506	487	780	1,233	900	408	430	3,500	1,352	1,827	28,937
1993-4	990	1,219	1,469	156	950	1,258	958	417	510	3,150	1,363	1,604	29,565
1994-5	990	1,020	4,110	361	800	1,345	1,030	455	490	2,700	1,261	1,664	31,317
1995-6	1,000	1,174	1,775	523	940	1,411	1,120	477	542	3,200	1,361	2,536	32,457
1996-7	920	1,057	1,014	553	1,200	1,497	1,166	513	555	3,600	1,260	2,517	32,803
1997-8	925	1,061	420	----	1,110	1,424	1,065	586	660	4,210	----	1,962	32,494
1998-9	925	1,141	543	----	1,075	1,403	1,188	470	700	5,400	----	1,655	34,697
1999-00	930	1,142	687	----	1,315	1,514	1,158	590	825	5,170	----	1,484	35,110
2000-1[1]	955	1,170	1,000	----	1,200	1,520	1,257	497	714	5,200	----	1,405	35,528
2001-2[2]	950	1,110	1,432	----	1,200	1,545	1,400	455	760	4,350	----	1,480	33,645

[1] Preliminary. [2] Forecast. *Source: Foreign Agricultural Service, U.S. Department of Agriculture (FAS-USDA)*

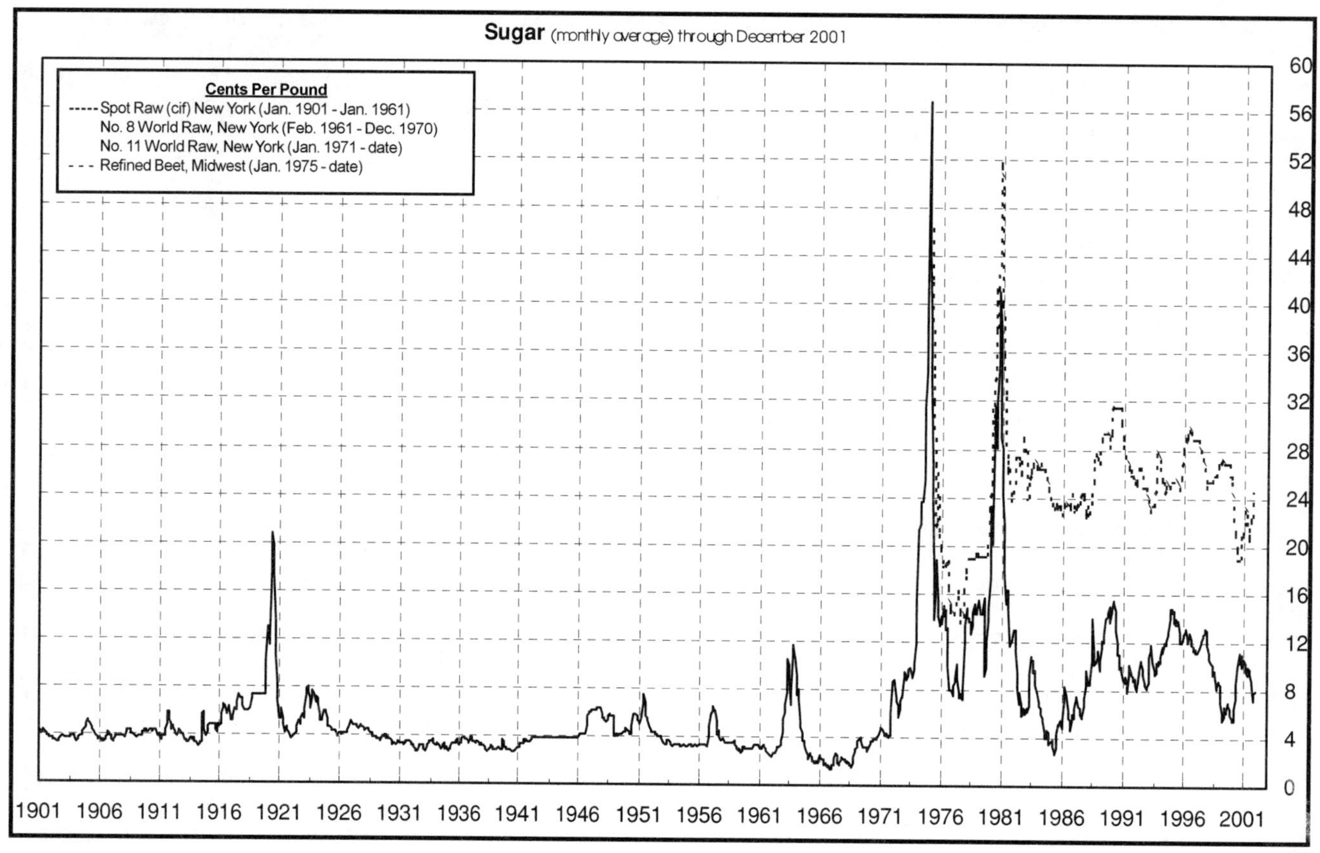

Centrifugal Sugar (Raw Value) Exported From Selected Countries In Thousands of Metric Tons

Year	Australia	Brazil	Cuba	Dominican Republic	France	Germany	Mauritius	Mexico	South Africa	Swaziland	Thailand	United Kingdom	Total
1992-3	3,476	2,425	3,800	327	2,822	1,607	621	0	123	409	2,332	300	28,937
1993-4	3,663	2,861	3,300	346	2,636	1,785	590	0	27	395	2,718	410	29,565
1994-5	4,321	4,300	2,600	295	3,004	1,417	508	235	369	296	3,809	263	30,289
1995-6	4,242	5,800	3,830	325	2,735	1,180	560	587	399	307	4,537	327	34,282
1996-7	4,564	5,800	3,598	364	2,730	1,430	602	750	1,056	293	4,194	388	35,925
1997-8	4,554	7,200	2,426	270	----	----	613	1,224	1,160	272	2,839	----	35,386
1998-9	4,076	8,750	3,200	191	----	----	626	590	1,355	271	3,352	----	36,196
1999-00	4,123	11,300	3,300	185	----	----	346	530	1,410	304	4,147	----	39,557
2000-1[1]	3,118	7,700	2,980	185	----	----	554	520	1,580	251	3,600	----	36,525
2001-2[2]	3,650	9,500	2,700	185	----	----	635	530	1,500	267	3,550	----	34,536

[1] Preliminary. [2] Estimate. [3] Forecast. *Source: Foreign Agricultural Service, U.S. Department of Agriculture (FAS-USDA)*

Average Wholesale Price of Refined Beet Sugar[1]--Midwest Market In Cents Per Pound

Year	Jan.	Feb.	Mar.	Apr.	May	June	July	Aug.	Sept.	Oct.	Nov.	Dec.	Average
1992	25.40	26.50	26.50	26.50	26.40	26.00	25.00	25.00	25.00	24.90	24.13	23.90	25.44
1993	23.25	23.00	23.00	23.50	23.50	23.50	25.50	27.75	27.50	27.50	27.25	26.50	25.15
1994	25.75	25.50	25.50	24.50	24.75	25.25	25.00	25.00	24.70	25.00	25.38	26.50	25.15
1995	25.50	25.50	25.50	25.50	25.13	25.10	24.75	24.75	25.50	25.75	28.13	28.85	25.83
1996	28.69	29.00	29.50	29.50	29.70	29.50	29.50	29.00	29.00	29.00	29.00	29.00	29.20
1997	29.00	29.00	28.13	28.00	28.00	27.50	27.00	26.65	26.38	24.90	25.00	25.50	27.09
1998	25.50	25.50	25.50	25.50	26.00	26.00	26.00	26.00	26.50	26.90	27.00	27.00	26.12
1999	27.20	27.13	27.00	27.00	27.00	27.00	27.00	27.00	27.00	26.00	26.00	25.20	26.71
2000	23.38	22.25	21.50	21.00	19.75	19.00	19.00	19.00	20.70	21.25	21.00	21.80	20.80
2001[2]	23.13	22.75	22.00	20.50	21.38	21.90	22.50	22.50	24.63				22.37

[1] These are f.o.b. basis prices in bulk, not delivered prices. [2] Preliminary. *Source: Economic Research Service, U.S. Department of Agriculture (ERS)*

Average Price of World Raw Sugar[1] In Cents Per Pound

Year	Jan.	Feb.	Mar.	Apr.	May	June	July	Aug.	Sept.	Oct.	Nov.	Dec.	Average
1992	8.43	8.06	8.22	9.53	9.62	10.52	10.30	9.78	9.28	8.66	8.54	8.15	9.09
1993	8.27	8.61	10.75	11.30	11.87	10.35	9.60	9.30	9.52	10.27	10.10	10.47	10.03
1994	10.29	10.80	11.71	11.10	11.79	12.04	11.73	12.05	12.62	12.75	13.88	14.76	12.13
1995	14.87	14.43	14.58	13.63	13.49	13.99	13.46	13.75	12.72	11.94	11.96	12.40	13.44
1996	12.57	12.97	13.07	12.43	11.94	12.54	12.83	12.33	11.87	11.65	11.29	11.38	12.24
1997	11.13	11.06	11.17	11.50	11.54	12.02	12.13	12.54	12.65	12.86	13.19	12.90	12.06
1998	11.71	11.06	10.66	10.27	10.17	9.33	9.70	9.50	8.21	8.24	8.73	8.59	9.68
1999	8.40	7.05	6.11	5.44	5.83	6.67	6.11	6.39	6.98	6.90	6.54	6.00	6.54
2000	5.64	5.51	5.54	6.48	7.33	8.72	10.18	11.14	10.35	10.96	10.02	10.23	8.51
2001[2]	10.63	10.26	9.64	9.27	9.96	9.80	9.48	8.77	8.60				9.60

[1] Contract No. 11, f.o.b. stowed Caribbean port, including Brazil, bulk spot price. [2] Preliminary. *Source: Economic Research Service, U.S. Department of Agriculture (ERS-USDA)*

Average Price of Raw Sugar in New York (C.I.F., Duty/Free Paid, Contract #12/#14) In Cents Per Pound

Year	Jan.	Feb.	Mar.	Apr.	May	June	July	Aug.	Sept.	Oct.	Nov.	Dec.	Average
1992	21.38	21.56	21.36	21.38	21.04	20.92	21.10	21.34	21.55	21.61	21.39	21.11	21.31
1993	20.76	21.16	21.56	21.76	21.36	21.42	21.89	21.85	21.97	21.80	21.87	22.00	21.62
1994	22.00	21.95	21.95	22.08	22.18	22.44	22.72	21.84	21.78	21.58	21.57	22.35	22.04
1995	22.65	22.69	22.46	22.76	23.10	23.09	24.47	23.18	23.21	22.67	22.60	22.63	22.96
1996	22.39	22.68	22.57	22.71	22.62	22.48	21.80	22.51	22.38	22.37	22.12	22.14	22.40
1997	21.88	22.07	21.81	21.79	21.70	21.62	22.04	22.21	22.30	22.27	21.90	21.93	21.96
1998	21.85	21.79	21.74	22.14	22.31	22.42	22.66	22.19	21.92	21.67	21.83	22.19	22.06
1999	22.41	22.38	22.55	22.57	22.65	22.61	22.61	21.24	20.10	19.50	17.45	17.87	21.16
2000	17.70	17.24	18.46	19.43	19.12	19.31	17.64	18.12	18.97	21.15	21.39	20.56	19.09
2001[1]	20.81	21.18	21.40	21.51	21.19	21.04	20.64	21.10	20.87				21.08

[1] Preliminary. *Source: Economic Research Service, U.S. Department of Agriculture (ERS-USDA)*

Supply and Utilization of Sugar (Cane and Beet) in the United States In 1,000's of Short Tons (Raw Value)

	Supply								Utilization						
	Production			Offshore Receipts									Domestic Disappearance		
Year	Cane	Beet	Total	Foreign	Territories	Total	Beginning Stocks	Total Supply	Total Use	Exports	Net Changes in Invisible Stocks	Refining Loss Adjustment	In Polyhydric Alcohol[4]	Total	Per Capita
1993-4	3,565	4,090	7,655	1,772	0	1,772	1,704	11,131	9,794	454	7	0	15	9,175	64.9
1994-5	3,434	4,493	7,927	1,853	0	1,853	1,337	11,117	9,876	502	37	0	10	9,239	64.3
1995-6	3,454	3,916	7,370	2,777	0	2,777	1,241	11,388	9,896	385	-43	0	13	9,441	65.1
1996-7	3,191	4,013	7,205	2,774	0	2,774	1,492	11,471	9,983	211	30	0	21	9,564	65.7
1997-8	3,631	4,389	8,020	2,163	0	2,163	1,488	11,671	9,992	179	-2	0	20	9,672	65.5
1998-9	3,951	4,423	8,374	1,824	0	1,824	1,679	11,877	10,238	230	-58	0	25	9,872	66.5
1999-00[1]	4,065	4,976	9,041	1,636	0	1,636	1,639	12,316	10,098	124	-137	0	32	9,993	66.1
2000-1[2]	4,072	4,600	8,672	1,610	0	1,610	2,219	12,500	10,435	125	50	0	35	10,125	66.4
2001-2[3]	4,195	4,150	8,345	1,631	0	1,631	2,126	12,102	10,605	125	90	0	35	10,270	67.2

[1] Preliminary. [2] Estimate. [3] Forecast. [4] Includes feed use. Source: Economic Research Service, U.S. Department of Agriculture (ERS-USDA)

Sugar Cane for Sugar & Seed and Production of Cane Sugar and Molasses in the United States

			Production					Farm Value		Sugar Production				
										Raw Value			Molasses Made	
Year	Acreage Harvested 1,000 Acres	Yield of Cane Per Harvested Acre Net Tons	for Sugar (1,000 Tons)	for Seed (1,000 Tons)	Total (1,000 Tons)	Sugar Yield Per Acre Short Tons	Farm Price $ Per Ton	of Cane Used for Sugar (1,000 Dollars)	of Cane Used for Sugar & Seed (1,000 Dollars)	Total 1,000 Tons	Per Ton of Cane in Lbs.	Refined Basis 1,000 Tons	Edible (1,000 Gallons)	Total[3] (1,000 Gallons)
1993	923.9	32.8	29,652	1,449	31,101	3.82	28.5	846,132	886,285	3,482	235	3,255	1,480	198,167
1994	936.8	33.0	29,405	1,524	30,929	3.96	29.2	857,438	900,827	3,595	----	3,308	----	193,628
1995	932.3	33.0	29,155	1,641	30,796	3.90	29.5	859,604	906,956	3,489	----	----	----	195,429
1996	888.9	33.1	27,687	1,777	29,464	----	28.3	784,113	833,297	----	----	----	----	----
1997	914.0	34.7	30,003	1,706	31,709	----	28.1	842,840	890,257	----	----	----	----	----
1998	947.1	36.6	32,743	1,964	34,707	----	27.3	893,049	944,562	----	----	----	----	----
1999	993.3	35.5	33,577	1,722	35,299	----	25.6	859,175	901,900	----	----	----	----	----
2000[1]	1,025.7	35.2	34,294	1,823	36,117	----	----	----	----	----	----	----	----	----
2001[2]	1,029.2	34.9	34,008	1,861	35,869	----	----	----	----	----	----	----	----	----

[1] Preliminary. [2] Estimate. [3] Excludes edible molasses. *Source: Economic Research Service, U.S. Department of Agriculture (ERS-USDA)*

U.S. Sugar Beets, Beet Sugar, Pulp & Molasses Produced from Beets and Raw Sugar Spot Prices

Year of Harvest	Acreage: Planted (1,000 Acres)	Acreage: Harvested (1,000 Acres)	Yield Per Harvested Acre Ton	Production 1,000 Tons	Sugar Yield Per Acre Sh. Tons	Price[3] Dollars	Farm Value $1,000	Sugar Production: Equivalent Raw Value[4] (1,000 Short Tons)	Sugar Production: Refined Basis (1,000 Short Tons)	Raw Sugar Prices: World[5] Refined #5 (Cents Per Pound)	Raw Sugar Prices: CSCE #11 World (Cents Per Pound)	Raw Sugar Prices: CSCE N.Y. Duty Paid (Cents Per Pound)	Wholesale List Price HFCS (42%) Midwest
1992	1,437	1,412	20.6	29,143	3.10	41.10	1,206,480	4,386	4,099	12.39	9.09	21.31	20.70
1993	1,438	1,409	18.6	26,249	2.87	39.00	1,023,687	4,047	3,792	12.79	10.03	21.62	18.83
1994	1,476	1,443	22.1	31,853	3.17	38.80	1,234,470	4,578	4,090	15.66	12.13	22.04	20.17
1995	1,445	1,420	19.8	28,065	2.78	38.10	1,070,663	3,944	----	17.99	13.44	22.96	15.63
1996	1,368	1,323	20.2	26,680	3.06	45.40	1,211,001	3,900	----	16.64	12.24	22.40	14.46
1997	1,459	1,428	20.9	29,886	3.00	38.80	1,160,029	----	----	14.33	12.06	21.96	10.70
1998	1,498	1,451	22.4	32,499	----	36.40	1,181,494	----	----	11.59	9.68	22.06	10.58
1999	1,561	1,527	21.9	33,420	----	37.20	1,242,895	----	----	9.10	6.54	21.16	11.71
2000[1]	1,565	1,374	23.6	32,436	----	----	----	----	----	9.97	8.51	19.09	11.32
2001[2]	1,368	1,331	21.1	28,081	----	----	----	----	----				

[1] Preliminary. [2] Estimate. [3] Includes support payments, but excludes Government sugar beet payments. [4] Refined sugar multiplied by factor of 1.07. [5] F.O.B. Europe. *Source: Economic Research Service, U.S. Department of Agriculture (ERS-USDA)*

Sugar Deliveries and Stocks in the United States In Thousands of Short Tons (Raw Value)

Year	Quota Allocation	Actual Imports	Deliveries by Primary Distributors: Cane Sugar Refineries	Beet Sugar Factories	Importers of Direct Consumption Sugar	Mainland Cane Sugar Mills[3]	Total Deliveries	Total Domestic Consumption	Stocks, Jan. 1: Cane Sugar Refineries[4]	Beet Sugar Factories	CCC	Refiners' Raw	Mainland Cane Mills	Total
1992	3,958.4	3,926.6	4,808	3,966	52	11	8,936	9,638	194	1,336	0	619	890	3,039
1993	[5]	[5]	4,781	4,087	52	15	9,064	9,577	183	1,640	0	507	895	3,225
1994	[5]	[5]	4,929	4,170	78	12	9,321	9,177	218	1,696	0	438	1,160	3,512
1995	2,413.2	2,308.0	4,808	4,486	44	15	9,451	9,337	192	1,600	6	448	906	3,139
1996	2,339.1	----	5,539	3,923	33	14	9,619	9,496	195	1,383	0	334	996	2,908
1997	----	----	5,553	3,997	27	----	9,755	9,578	196	1,520	0	323	1,156	3,195
1998	1,289.7	1,254.2	5,347	4,313	24	----	9,851	9,684	212	1,535	0	322	1,308	3,377
1999	----	----	5,419	4,536	41	----	10,167	9,996	255	1,499	0	332	1,335	3,422
2000[1]	----	----	5,508	4,433	36	----	10,091	9,977	208	1,554	0	356	1,737	3,855
2001[2]	----	----	----	----	----	----	----	----	251	1,500	794	274	1,519	4,351

[1] Preliminary. [2] Estimate. [3] Sugar for direct consumption only. [4] Refined. [5] Combined with 1992. *Source: Economic Research Service, U.S. Department of Agriculture (ERS-USDA)*

Sugar, Refined--Deliveries to End User in the United States In Thousands of Short Tons

Year	Bakery & Cereal Products	Beverages	Confectionery[2]	Hotels, Restaurant & Institutions	Ice Cream & Dairy Products	Canned, Bottled & Frozen Foods	All Other Food Uses	Retail Grocers[3]	Wholesale Grocers[4]	Non-food Uses	Non-industrial Uses	Industrial Uses	Total Deliveries
1991	1,632	204	1,277	100	439	331	623	1,182	2,079	88	3,469	4,594	8,063
1992	1,719	164	1,246	101	429	315	649	1,230	2,104	69	3,668	4,591	8,259
1993	1,785	158	1,292	108	424	336	725	1,235	2,075	85	3,589	4,805	8,394
1994	1,952	156	1,313	93	453	322	704	1,269	2,039	77	3,598	4,977	8,575
1995	1,905	169	1,372	103	452	279	863	1,236	2,173	64	3,701	5,103	8,804
1996	1,993	196	1,335	80	445	318	849	1,263	2,241	66	3,759	5,202	8,962
1997	2,161	158	1,350	78	436	308	793	1,281	2,283	66	3,828	5,272	9,100
1998	2,301	165	1,336	79	438	331	907	1,230	2,223	76	3,761	5,556	9,317
1999	2,312	179	1,361	72	499	346	862	1,263	2,257	71	3,804	5,630	9,434
2000[1]	2,264	168	1,328	71	499	330	817	1,242	2,241	85	3,893	5,491	9,383

[1] Preliminary. [2] And related products. [3] Chain stores, supermarkets. [4] Jobbers, sugar dealers. *Source: Economic Research Service, U.S. Department of Agriculture (ERS-USDA)*

Deliveries[1] of All Sugar by Primary Distributors in the U.S., by Quarters In Thousands of Short Tons

Year	First Quarter	Second Quarter	Third Quarter	Fourth Quarter	Total	Year	First Quarter	Second Quarter	Third Quarter	Fourth Quarter	Total
1990	1,837	1,911	2,154	2,149	8,051	1996	2,191	2,355	2,519	2,445	9,496
1991	1,878	1,955	2,173	2,057	8,063	1997	2,143	2,401	2,591	2,443	9,578
1992	1,985	2,178	2,390	2,273	8,826	1998	2,233	2,428	2,565	2,458	9,684
1993	2,039	2,172	2,432	2,277	8,920	1999	2,208	2,553	2,655	2,580	9,996
1994	2,121	2,265	2,532	2,260	9,177	2000	2,318	2,484	2,611	2,564	9,977
1995	2,105	2,311	2,542	2,379	9,337	2001[2]	2,370	2,485			9,710

Raw Value. [1] Includes for domestic consumption and for export. [2] Preliminary. *Source: Economic Research Service, U.S. Department of Agriculture (ERS-USDA)*

Average Open Interest of World Sugar No. 11 Futures in New York In Contracts

Year	Jan.	Feb.	Mar.	Apr.	May	June	July	Aug.	Sept.	Oct.	Nov.	Dec.
1992	96,255	105,166	93,774	109,137	95,101	106,310	96,038	87,089	77,740	69,023	74,292	93,039
1993	91,426	105,147	123,023	115,400	112,085	101,843	94,296	94,932	91,312	92,832	96,246	99,592
1994	108,936	123,148	137,582	115,060	117,030	126,843	106,749	118,057	141,361	140,011	171,843	191,801
1995	186,893	167,451	149,027	152,600	127,978	121,877	114,027	119,787	114,069	119,561	140,008	157,779
1996	156,047	159,563	150,093	142,773	137,897	148,447	144,527	153,845	153,202	144,830	150,866	150,573
1997	155,156	147,198	143,623	166,143	150,480	175,139	165,884	197,331	187,477	158,065	200,486	201,922
1998	206,100	212,072	183,472	182,770	171,555	186,978	149,536	152,754	155,076	138,762	139,896	148,983
1999	165,717	176,465	168,624	188,324	196,864	177,266	142,416	151,621	189,606	161,760	167,549	175,125
2000	191,464	199,031	193,554	187,810	201,756	200,973	172,361	171,808	160,809	154,101	148,035	145,760
2001	157,478	158,192	158,448	167,555	131,640	126,426	112,483	128,181	139,915	146,058	163,358	170,710

Source: New York Board of Trade (NYBOT)

Volume of Trading of World Sugar No. 11 Futures in New York In Contracts

Year	Jan.	Feb.	Mar.	Apr.	May	June	July	Aug.	Sept.	Oct.	Nov.	Dec.	Total
1992	376,704	395,793	255,501	583,535	246,360	454,854	264,528	275,677	334,962	163,263	168,470	147,844	3,667,481
1993	330,474	481,506	507,370	518,292	415,283	390,261	255,581	307,181	368,194	222,082	272,579	217,142	4,285,945
1994	289,593	486,222	360,787	472,388	407,343	443,002	252,012	349,079	471,899	316,330	484,943	387,620	4,719,218
1995	591,861	489,274	472,519	478,757	352,000	485,131	298,756	402,358	360,086	246,584	278,906	254,850	4,711,082
1996	550,780	544,514	341,940	526,255	384,302	496,745	279,707	290,732	562,082	264,290	203,921	306,584	4,751,852
1997	436,935	493,199	268,343	618,176	308,563	575,264	400,150	427,082	580,551	440,208	323,286	413,214	5,284,971
1998	601,378	688,036	431,818	551,628	364,203	686,997	294,354	370,179	527,270	303,951	358,096	346,201	5,524,111
1999	683,891	543,477	452,485	688,181	361,895	762,271	346,534	408,289	657,572	344,434	405,495	256,775	5,911,299
2000	422,527	609,793	501,115	617,633	523,939	717,700	376,769	420,611	622,350	507,562	371,824	242,027	5,933,850
2001	410,492	545,538	380,640	567,921	426,987	515,561	356,483	419,123	447,349	348,896	413,965	317,374	5,150,329

Source: New York Board of Trade (NYBOT)

Sulfur

Elemental sulfur is used in the synthesis of sulfur compounds. With its derivative product, sulfuric acid, sulfur is an important industrial raw material. More sulfuric acid is produced in the U.S. than any other chemical. The U.S. Geological Survey reported that in 2000, elemental sulfur and byproduct sulfuric acid were produced at 128 operations in 30 states and the U.S. Virgin Islands. Elemental sulfur production was 9.4 million metric tonnes in 2000. One mine used the Frasch method to mine sulfur and that mine closed during the year. Texas and Louisiana account for about 50 percent of the domestic production of elemental sulfur.

World production of all forms of sulfur in 2000 was estimated at 57.4 million tonnes, about 1 percent more than in 1999. The U.S. was the largest producer with output of 10.4 million tonnes, down 8 percent from the previous year. Canada produced 10.3 million tonnes, up 2 percent from 1999. Other large sulfur producers include Russia, China, Japan and Saudi Arabia. World resources of sulfur are estimated at 1.4 billion tonnes.

U.S. production of sulfur from petroleum in July 2001 was 545,000 tonnes. In the January-July 2001 period, sulfur production from petroleum totaled 3.68 million tonnes. For all of 2000 it was 6.35 million tonnes. Production of sulfur from natural gas in July 200 was 142,000 tonnes. In the first seven months of 2001 production was 1.03 million tonnes while for all of 2000 it was 2.91 million tonnes.

U.S. consumption of sulfur in June 2001 was 718,000 tonnes. In the January-June 2001 period, consumption totaled 4.63 million tonnes. For all of 2000, consumption was 11.1 million tonnes. U.S. imports of sulfur in the first half of 2001 were 995,000 tonnes. In 2000 they were 2.33 million tonnes.

World Production of Sulfur (All Forms) In Thousands of Metric Tons

Year	Canada	China	France	Germany	Iraq	Japan	Mexico	Poland	Russia	Saudi Arabia	Spain	United States	World Total
1993	8,430	6,360	1,260	1,260	450	2,922	906	2,120	3,720	2,400	768	11,100	51,600
1994	8,850	7,020	1,180	1,005	475	2,900	1,177	2,325	3,650	1,630	694	11,500	53,400
1995	8,953	7,030	1,170	1,110	475	3,110	1,241	2,591	3,840	2,400	786	11,800	54,000
1996	9,490	7,260	1,090	1,110	475	3,150	1,280	1,982	3,800	2,300	943	11,800	55,200
1997	9,480	7,640	1,060	1,160	450	3,380	1,340	1,985	3,750	2,400	967	12,000	57,100
1998	9,694	6,150	1,110	1,180	450	3,430	1,387	1,675	4,650	2,300	993	11,600	57,100
1999[1]	10,116	5,690	1,100	1,190	----	3,460	1,310	1,509	5,270	2,400	955	11,300	57,700
2000[2]	9,900	5,220	1,110	1,240	----	3,500	1,310	1,700	5,900	2,400	685	10,300	57,200

[1] Preliminary. [2] Estimate. *Source: U.S. Geological Survey (USGS)*

Salient Statistics of Sulfur in the United States In Thousands of Metric Tons (Sulfur Content)

	Production of											Sales Value of Shipments F.O.B. Mine/Plant		
	Elemental Sulfur											$ Per Metric Ton		
	Native - Sulfur[3] -	Recovered												
Year	Frasch	Petroleum & Coke	Natural Gas	Total	product Sulfuric Acid	Other Sulfuric Compounds	Production (All Forms)	Imports Sulfuric Acid[4]	Exports Sulfuric Acid[4]	Producer Stocks Dec. 31[5]	Apparent Consumption (All Forms)	Frasch	Recovered	Average
1993	1,900	4,820	2,905	7,725	1,430	3	11,100	2,440	145	1,382	12,600	51.60	25.06	31.86
1994	2,960	4,930	2,240	7,160	1,380	0	11,500	2,130	140	1,160	13,100	W	W	30.08
1995	3,150	5,040	2,210	7,250	1,400	0	11,800	1,920	170	583	14,300	W	W	44.46
1996	2,900	5,370	2,100	7,480	1,430	0	11,800	2,070	117	646	13,600	W	W	34.11
1997	2,820	5,230	2,420	7,650	1,550	0	12,000	2,010	118	761	13,900	W	W	36.06
1998	1,800	6,060	2,160	8,220	1,610	0	11,600	2,040	155	283	14,100	W	W	29.14
1999[1]	1,780	6,210	2,010	8,220	1,320	0	11,300	1,370	155	451	13,400	W	W	37.81
2000[2]	900	6,360	2,020	8,380	1,030	0	10,300	1,420	191	208	12,500	W	W	24.73

[1] Preliminary. [2] Estimate. [3] Or sulfur ore; Withheld included in natural gas. [4] Basis 100% H2SO4, sulfur equivalent. [5] Frasch & recovered.
[6] Data 1996 to date includes Frasch. W = Withheld proprietary data. *Source: U.S. Geological Survey (USGS)*

Sulfur Consumption & Foreign Trade of the United States In Thousands of Metric Tons (Sulfur Content)

	Consumption			Sulfuric Acid Sold or Used, by End Use[2]						Foreign Trade					
										Exports			Imports		
Year	Native Sulfur Frasch	Recovered Sulfur	Total Elemental Form	Total Sulfuric Acid	Pulpmills & Paper Product	Inorganic Chemicals[3]	Synthetic Rubber & Plastic	Phosphatic Fertilizers	Petroleum Refining[4]	Frasch	Recovered	Value 1,000 $	Frasch	Recovered	Value 1,000 $
1993	1,331	9,046	10,377	11,886	304	549	259	7,906	388	246	656	39,726	100	2,070	49,800
1994	W	11,100	11,100	11,300	295	448	256	8,040	236	----	899	48,400	----	1,650	62,000
1995	W	12,300	12,300	11,500	319	170	245	8,200	479	----	906	66,200	----	2,510	143,000
1996	W	11,500	11,500	10,900	343	152	270	7,380	525	----	855	51,700	----	1,960	70,200
1997	W	11,800	11,800	10,700	334	232	85	7,000	610	----	703	36,000	----	2,060	64,900
1998	W	11,900	11,900	10,600	134	174	69	7,590	632	----	889	35,400	----	2,270	58,400
1999	W	11,700	11,700	10,400	138	174	68	7,770	508	----	685	35,800	----	2,580	51,600
2000[1]	W	11,100	11,100	9,620	136	152	68	7,110	497	----	762	53,700	----	2,330	39,400

[1] Preliminary. [2] Sulfur equivalent. [3] Including inorganic pigments, paints & allied products, and other inorganic chemicals & products.
[4] Including other petroleum and coal products. W = Withheld proprietary data. NA = Not available. *Source: U.S. Geological Survey (USGS)*

Sunflowerseed, Meal and Oil

Sunflower seed ranks fifth among the world's major oilseeds. However, unlike soybeans for which most of the crop is crushed for meal, sunflower seed has nearly equal amounts of meal and oil produced. The U.S. produces only about 6% of global sunflower seed production, but has a larger role in world trade.

World sunflower seed production in 2001/02 dropped to an eight year low, 21.2 million metric tons, lower than initial forecasts and compares with 22.7 million tons in 2000/01. More significant during the past two seasons is the decline from the record large 1999/00 crop of 27.2 million tons owing larger to smaller subsequent crops in Argentina and Eastern Europe. Still, Argentina is the largest single producer with 3.4 million tons in 2001/02 vs. the late 1990's annual average of almost 6 million tons. The Russian Federation (FSU-12) remains the largest producing area--5.3 million tons in 2001/02 vs. 7.8 million in 2000/01. The world sunflower seed crush for 2001/02 is forecast at 19.1 million tons vs. 20.6 million in 2000/01. Sunflower seed is the third largest oilseed in foreign trade, in 2001/02 only 2.0 million tons vs. 3.47 million in 2000/01, and a fraction of soybeans. World stocks have generally averaged about one million tons, but at yearend 2001/02 are estimated at 640,000 tons. Sunflower meal production in 2001/02 of 8.66 million tons compares with 9.37 million in 2000/01; sunflower oil production of 7.7 million tons compares with 8.3 million, respectively.

The acreage planted to sunflower seed production in the U.S. tends to show an irregular year-to-year pattern as does average yield at times. The acreage planted for the 2001/02 of 2.5 million acres compares with a near record large 3.6 million in 1999/00. . Production (September/August) in 2001/02 of 1.59 million metric tons compares with 1.61 million in 2000/01. The Dakotas are the largest producing states with about two-thirds of total U.S. production. Following the crush more meal is generally produced than oil. However, domestic usage of meal is generally about three times larger than oil, but oil exports greatly exceed that of meal. Moreover, meal carryover supplies are small, averaging about 5000 tons, about a tenth that of oil.

The 2000/01 U.S. sunflower oil price averaged 16.2 cents per pound vs. 16.6 cents in 1999/00 and a late 1990's average over 20 cents, basis average crude Minneapolis. Sunflower meal prices in 2000/01 averaged $88.50 per short ton vs. $75 in 1999/00 and a mid-1990 average of more than $100. For 2001/02, higher oil prices are forecast, but lower meal prices. Abroad, the expected 2001/02 average sunflower seed oil price of $283/metric tons compares with $219/ton in 2000/01, basis Rotterdam; for protein meal the Rotterdam average of $119 per metric ton compares with $118, respectively.

World Production of Sunflowerseed In Thousands of Metric Tons

Crop Year	Argentina	Bulgaria	China	France	Hungary	India	Romania	South Africa	Spain	Turkey	United States	Ex-USSR	World Total
1991-2	3,800	434	1,420	2,570	797	1,194	612	174	900	650	1,639	5,621	21,658
1992-3	3,100	578	1,472	2,110	756	1,185	618	364	1,343	980	1,163	5,645	21,135
1993-4	3,850	440	1,282	1,640	700	1,400	696	390	1,215	700	1,167	5,251	20,600
1994-5	5,900	595	1,370	2,050	665	1,204	767	450	979	600	2,193	4,356	23,342
1995-6	5,600	650	1,270	1,900	730	1,400	933	755	575	750	1,819	7,368	25,720
1996-7	5,400	490	1,325	2,000	800	1,315	1,180	450	1,138	545	1,614	5,268	23,800
1997-8	5,500	500	1,176	1,940	545	1,150	858	562	1,373	650	1,668	5,368	23,206
1998-9	7,100	500	930	1,680	706	1,200	970	1,109	1,097	650	2,392	5,548	26,128
1999-00[1]	6,100	570	1,300	1,910	795	1,300	1,100	531	579	800	1,969	7,262	26,404
2000-1[2]	4,400	400	1,300	1,850	450	1,200	700	630	1,200	575	1,684	7,814	24,167

[1] Preliminary. [2] Forecast. *Source: Economic Research Service, U.S. Department of Agriculture (ERS-USDA)*

World Imports and Exports of Sunflowerseed In Thousands of Metric Tons

Crop Year	Imports: France	Germany	Netherlands	Spain	Turkey	World Total	Exports: Argentina	France	Hungary	Ex-USSR	United States	Uraguay	World Total
1991-2	7	320	434	134	104	2,481	300	1,075	75	360	144	----	2,214
1992-3	36	278	428	92	50	1,984	200	663	80	366	118	----	1,837
1993-4	194	331	427	170	100	2,615	580	516	250	755	99	----	2,545
1994-5	109	279	543	472	550	3,287	884	628	260	708	287	----	3,173
1995-6	300	366	617	681	500	3,972	550	480	249	1,750	224	----	3,647
1996-7	395	484	658	531	360	4,215	100	825	220	2,481	149	----	4,167
1997-8	220	345	563	524	583	4,063	453	911	155	1,825	189	----	3,930
1998-9	406	474	524	764	595	4,365	910	499	145	1,863	260	----	4,272
1999-00[1]	140	370	550	749	520	3,554	550	475	253	1,523	199	----	3,726
2000-1[2]	240	385	465	400	565	3,480	350	500	125	1,917	204	----	3,512

[1] Preliminary. [2] Forecast. *Source: Economic Research Service, U.S. Department of Agriculture (ERS-USDA)*

SUNFLOWERSEED, MEAL AND OIL

Sunflowerseed Statistics in the United States In Thousands of Metric Tons

Crop Year Beginning Sept. 1	Harvested Acres 1,000	Harvested Yield Per Cwt.	Farm Price $ Per Metric Ton	Value of Production Million $	Supply: Stocks, Sept. 1	Supply: Production	Supply: Imports	Supply: Total	Disappearance: Crush	Disappearance: Exports	Disappearance: Non-oil Use & Seed	Disappearance: Total
1992-3	2,043	12.55	215	249.8	262	1,163	47	1,472	923	118	362	1,403
1993-4	2,486	10.35	284	331.8	69	1,167	24	1,260	661	99	429	1,189
1994-5	3,430	14.10	236	517.4	71	2,193	42	2,306	1,313	287	603	2,203
1995-6	3,368	11.90	254	461.1	103	1,819	21	1,943	915	224	599	1,738
1996-7	2,479	14.36	258	416.4	205	1,614	18	1,837	844	149	648	1,641
1997-8	2,792	13.17	256	426.5	196	1,668	29	1,893	1,061	189	551	1,801
1998-9	3,492	15.10	225	559.0	92	2,392	34	2,518	1,178	260	849	2,287
1999-00	3,441	12.62	166	326.9	231	1,969	41	2,241	1,139	199	672	2,010
2000-1[1]	2,647	13.39	150	241.0	231	1,608	66	1,905	923	202	623	1,748
2001-2[2]	2,660	13.18	149-179	261.2	157	1,590	61	1,808	907	172	627	1,706

[1] Preliminary. [2] Forecast. *Source: Economic Research Service, U.S. Department of Agriculture (ERS-USDA)*

World Production of Sunflowerseed Oil and Meal In Thousands of Metric Tons

Year	Oil: Argentina	Oil: France	Oil: Spain	Oil: Turkey	Oil: Ex-USSR	Oil: World Total	Meal: Argentina	Meal: France	Meal: Spain	Meal: Turkey	Meal: United States	Meal: Ex-USSR	Meal: World Total
1991-2	1,400	605	380	299	1,883	7,836	1,470	785	425	271	498	1,821	8,828
1992-3	1,112	548	430	420	1,747	7,336	1,197	722	470	380	440	1,817	8,551
1993-4	1,280	478	440	319	1,542	7,083	1,393	642	550	289	327	1,521	8,340
1994-5	1,980	590	455	445	1,287	8,247	2,129	703	485	408	653	1,221	9,527
1995-6	2,000	593	470	482	1,920	9,018	2,100	720	485	430	458	1,805	10,198
1996-7	2,070	588	540	410	1,161	8,588	2,174	742	570	370	440	1,166	10,070
1997-8	1,990	566	525	506	1,292	8,258	2,092	707	550	463	494	1,232	9,545
1998-9	2,450	577	588	512	1,364	9,186	2,573	720	615	460	617	1,351	10,499
1999-00[1]	2,220	585	504	535	1,944	9,325	2,332	740	525	492	549	1,973	10,720
2000-1[2]	1,610	635	588	462	2,170	8,714	1,690	800	615	423	463	2,204	10,027

[1] Preliminary. [2] Forecast. *Source: Economic Research Service, U.S. Department of Agriculture (ERS-USDA)*

Sunflower Oil Statistics in the United States In Thousands of Metric Tons

Crop Year Beginning Oct. 1	Supply: Stocks, Oct. 1	Supply: Production	Supply: Total[3]	Disappearance: Exports	Disappearance: Domestic	Disappearance: Total	Minneapolis, Crude $ Per Metric Ton
1992-3	45	331	376	266	85	351	558
1993-4	25	263	291	204	58	262	683
1994-5	29	528	558	444	77	521	622
1995-6	37	390	428	285	76	361	560
1996-7	67	381	458	322	94	416	497
1997-8	42	435	480	370	83	453	608
1998-9	27	534	563	363	145	508	446
1999-00	55	474	531	286	174	460	364
2000-1[1]	71	398	472	251	160	411	356
2001-2[2]	62	408	472	272	168	440	353-419

[1] Preliminary. [2] Forecast. [3] Includes imports. *Source: Economic Research Service, U.S. Department of Agriculture (ERS-USDA)*

Sunflower Meal Statistics in the United States In Thousands of Metric Tons

Crop Year Beginning Oct. 1	Supply: Stocks, Oct. 1	Supply: Production	Supply: Total[3]	Disappearance: Exports	Disappearance: Domestic	Disappearance: Total	28% Protein $ Per Metric Ton
1992-3	6	440	451	48	401	449	98
1993-4	2	327	333	37	291	328	104
1994-5	5	653	658	89	564	653	72
1995-6	5	458	463	25	433	458	136
1996-7	5	440	445	21	419	440	122
1997-8	5	494	499	13	481	494	90
1998-9	5	617	622	41	576	617	72
1999-00	5	549	554	21	528	549	83
2000-1[1]	5	458	463	8	455	458	100
2001-2[2]	5	463	467	5	458	463	74-97

[1] Preliminary. [2] Forecast. [3] Includes imports. *Source: Economic Research Service, U.S. Department of Agriculture (ERS-USDA)*

Tall Oil

Tall oil is a product of the paper and pulping industry. Crude tall oil is the major byproduct of the kraft or sulfate processing of pinewood. Crude tall oil starts as tall oil soap which is separated from recovered black liquor in the kraft pulping process. The tall oil soap is acidified to yield crude tall oil. The resulting tall oil is then fractionated to produce fatty acids, rosin, and pitch. Crude tall oil contains 40-50 percent fatty acids such as oleic and linoleic acids; 5-10 percent sterols, alcohols, and other neutral components. The demand is for the tall oil rosin and fatty acids which are used to produce adhesives, coatings, and ink resins. The products find use in lubricants, soaps, linoleum, flotation and waterproofing agents, paints, varnishes, and drying oils.

Since tall oil and its production are derived from the paper and pulping industry, the amount of tall oil produced is related in part to the pulp industry and in part to the U.S. economy.

U.S. production of crude tall oil in January 2001 was reported by the U.S,. Department of Commerce to be 94.7 million pounds, down 7 percent from the year before. In recent years, U.S. production of crude tall oil has averaged 1.33 billion pounds. U.S. consumption of tall oil in inedible products in 2000 was 1.15 billion pounds. In recent years annual consumption has averaged 1.19 billion pounds. U.S. stocks of crude tall oil in February 2001 were 113.2 million pounds, down 14 percent from a year earlier. Refined tall oil stocks in February 2001 were 10.6 million pounds, up 8 percent from a year earlier.

Consumption of Tall Oil in Inedible Products in the United States In Millions of Pounds

Year	Jan.	Feb.	Mar.	Apr.	May	June	July	Aug.	Sept.	Oct.	Nov.	Dec.	Total
1994	117.4	98.8	124.0	118.4	115.0	118.8	106.8	114.9	119.8	113.7	101.9	113.0	1,363
1995	99.8	93.6	96.9	95.8	87.3	96.5	93.1	102.3	89.4	91.6	100.5	88.9	1,136
1996	93.1	103.4	89.2	104.1	100.5	96.6	85.4	100.7	94.9	111.5	101.4	98.8	1,180
1997	111.5	89.0	91.0	99.5	97.0	105.8	103.7	94.4	84.7	87.2	87.3	88.4	1,139
1998	86.7	114.4	113.2	120.0	108.0	101.8	117.2	114.8	120.3	111.6	119.0	121.0	1,348
1999	99.4	115.1	111.0	114.0	99.9	109.2	119.1	113.0	103.9	108.4	106.4	102.2	1,302
2000	91.7	88.1	106.4	97.5	90.9	98.8	91.8	106.6	94.9	93.7	89.4	96.2	1,146
2001[1]	97.7	96.4	104.4	101.6	105.1	100.7	99.9	98.3	102.4	81.4	87.7	74.4	1,150

[1] Preliminary. *Source: Bureau of the Census, U.S. Department of Commerce*

Production of Crude Tall Oil in the United States In Millions of Pounds

Year	Oct.	Nov.	Dec.	Jan.	Feb.	Mar.	Apr.	May	June	July	Aug.	Sept.	Total
1994-5	111.1	114.5	115.1	108.3	108.1	123.0	111.1	116.5	118.2	116.4	119.2	102.9	1,261.6
1995-6	109.8	105.2	105.2	115.5	123.3	126.9	108.9	120.3	120.3	120.5	124.9	112.9	1,281.0
1996-7	119.2	113.9	114.5	119.9	125.1	125.1	118.5	116.6	116.4	135.0	132.9	130.8	1,337.2
1997-8	122.7	115.4	135.4	137.7	126.6	127.5	132.3	131.2	131.1	132.0	120.2	121.1	1,540.6
1998-9	118.4	113.4	119.3	118.0	115.2	134.6	121.0	103.8	100.7	103.2	103.5	113.6	1,364.8
1999-00	93.8	101.6	107.8	101.3	104.6	115.2	95.4	91.8	99.5	94.5	97.0	86.5	1,202.6
2000-1	92.3	91.6	81.4	94.9	83.7	103.7	99.7	99.9	95.1	94.1	105.4	93.0	1,134.8
2001-2[1]	99.1	100.7	86.5										1,145.0

[1] Preliminary. *Source: Bureau of the Census, U.S. Department of Commerce*

Stocks of Crude Tall Oil in the United States, on First of Month In Millions of Pounds

Year	Oct.	Nov.	Dec.	Jan.	Feb.	Mar.	Apr.	May	June	July	Aug.	Sept.
1994-5	86.3	82.7	94.1	104.1	107.6	117.2	123.4	132.1	118.1	132.3	134.7	135.0
1995-6	120.9	117.5	112.9	100.7	105.7	120.3	146.0	131.8	127.0	130.5	138.7	147.3
1996-7	172.3	192.1	167.4	182.4	173.0	196.0	200.8	220.6	187.3	237.5	248.5	242.2
1997-8	208.6	187.9	209.7	202.1	202.8	219.4	256.8	254.1	239.1	259.1	278.4	245.2
1998-9	268.7	219.8	200.3	197.5	164.8	156.9	163.3	177.5	183.0	180.7	183.6	152.7
1999-00	146.8	130.9	135.3	121.5	131.8	153.5	136.6	138.5	154.6	130.5	136.7	117.1
2000-1	110.5	102.4	105.4	117.0	118.9	118.2	134.4	139.6	171.7	132.0	160.5	145.4
2001-2[1]	132.7	125.6	142.1	127.9								

[1] Preliminary. *Source: Bureau of the Census, U.S. Department of Commerce*

Stocks of Refined Tall Oil in the United States, on First of Month In Millions of Pounds

Year	Oct.	Nov.	Dec.	Jan.	Feb.	Mar.	Apr.	May	June	July	Aug.	Sept.
1994-5	12.0	14.4	16.3	13.5	15.4	14.1	11.7	10.8	10.2	10.0	9.9	8.9
1995-6	10.1	11.6	7.9	6.0	7.9	9.7	8.5	10.4	8.5	6.0	6.1	7.2
1996-7	8.3	7.0	7.5	8.9	6.5	26.5	17.4	31.7	20.9	32.0	13.2	16.6
1997-8	32.3	25.6	34.9	21.4	30.4	17.0	14.2	13.0	13.1	15.1	14.7	15.3
1998-9	15.1	14.9	17.0	12.5	14.8	9.9	7.2	7.6	7.2	7.3	6.3	7.0
1999-00	7.5	7.0	8.5	9.1	9.8	11.0	9.8	13.7	10.4	7.8	11.9	8.2
2000-1	9.6	9.0	9.9	10.2	10.7	12.5	11.8	13.9	12.6	19.5	13.4	21.6
2001-2[1]	22.4	17.2	17.1	19.9								

[1] Preliminary. *Source: Bureau of the Census, U.S. Department of Commerce*

Tallow and Greases

Production of tallow and greases is directly related to the number of cattle produced. Those countries that are the leading cattle producers are also the largest producers of tallow. World production of tallow and greases (edible and inedible) has averaged just over 8 million metric tonnes since 1991. Prices are responsive to changes in production. In 1996 world tallow production declined by 2 percent from the previous year. Average prices in 1996 were 3 percent higher for edible, loose, tallow in Chicago. In 1999, world production of tallow increased by almost 3 percent. In 1999, the average price of edible, loose, tallow in Chicago was down 21 percent from the previous year.

The U.S.D.A. estimated that global production of tallow and greases (edible and inedible) in 2000 was 8.3 million tonnes, down about 3 percent from the previous season. The largest producer of tallow and greases was the U.S. with 43 percent of the world total. The next largest producer was Australia with some 6 percent of the global output. Brazil's share of world output was also 6 percent. Other large producers of tallow and greases include Russia, Canada, and Argentina.

The U.S.D.A. estimated that U.S. stocks of edible tallow on January 1, 2000 were 33 million pounds, down 15 percent from the previous year. U.S. production of edible tallow in 2000 was 1.84 billion pounds, rendered basis. This was some 6 percent higher than the previous year. The total supply of tallow in 2000 was 1.88 billion pounds, up some 6 percent from the previous year. The overall trend has been for the production of edible tallow to increase.

In terms of use, domestic disappearance of tallow in 2000 was 1.59 billion pounds, an increase of 12 percent from 1999. Tallow finds widespread use in the baking and cooking industries. The months with the highest rates of edible tallow use are May through August. Per capita use of tallow shows some variation from year to year. Per capita use of edible tallow in 2000 was estimated to be 5.8 pounds. This was up 12 percent from the previous year. Between 1992 and 1998, per capita use of edible tallow was less than five pounds. In 1985 and 1986, per capita use was over six pounds. While per capita use of tallow in 2000 was 5.8 pounds, per capita use of lard was 2.3 pounds. Per capita use of butter was 4.7 pounds while per capita use of margarine was 8.5 pounds.

U.S. exports of tallow in 2000 were 248 million pounds, down 22 percent from the previous year. The total disappearance of edible tallow in 2000, domestic use and exports, was 1.84 billion pounds, up 6 percent from the previous year.

World Production of Tallow and Greases (Edible and Inedible) In Thousands of Metric Tons

Year	Argentina	Australia	Brazil	Canada	France	Germany	Rep. of Korea	Netherlands	New Zealand	Russia	United Kingdom	United States	World Total
1991	285	530	340	193	185	270	85	150	132	386	230	3,180	6,968
1992	268	472	336	212	275	197	121	150	134	352	225	3,309	7,077
1993	260	526	429	209	240	178	115	163	145	706	212	3,650	8,492
1994	250	446	435	213	206	167	120	159	135	437	215	3,851	8,258
1995	248	423	46	217	220	166	118	158	147	377	230	3,756	8,312
1996	240	397	467	242	220	168	198	161	155	400	165	3,581	8,184
1997	265	456	460	250	220	167	209	200	161	340	160	3,467	8,342
1998	220	560	467	265	220	166	235	190	150	340	170	3,694	8,374
1999[1]	235	565	480	285	220	165	230	168	135	330	180	3,855	8,584
2000[2]	230	540	505	290	220	165	230	192	142	310	195	3,562	8,312

[1] Preliminary. [2] Forecast. *Source: Foreign Agricultural Service, U.S. Department of Agriculture (FAS-USDA)*

Salient Statistics of Tallow and Greases (Inedible) in the United States In Millions of Pounds

	Supply				Consumption			Wholesale Prices, Cents/Lb.	
Year	Production	Stocks, Jan. 1	Total	Exports	Soap	Feed	Total	Edible, (Loose) Chicago	Inedible, No. 1 Chicago
1992	5,768	349	6,117	2,276	334	1,954	3,050	15.5	14.4
1993	6,621	309	6,930	2,117	300	1,995	3,018	16.2	14.9
1994	6,364	320	6,684	3,039	301	2,183	3,246	18.4	17.4
1995	6,481	350	6,831	2,486	264	2,071	2,334	21.4	19.2
1996	6,242	373	6,615	1,807	245	2,389	2,634	22.0	20.1
1997	6,249	266	6,515	775	245	2,401	2,646	23.5	20.8
1998	6,644	339	6,983	1,041	228	2,533	2,761	19.1	17.5
1999	7,079	437	7,516	877	229	2,847	3,076	15.1	13.0
2000[1]	7,035	405	7,440	791	146	2,727	2,849	11.6	10.0
2001[2]	6,822	347	7,170	618	107	2,830	2,839	13.7	12.0

[1] Preliminary. [2] Estimate. *Sources: Economic Research Service, U.S. Department of Agriculture (ERS-USDA); Bureau of the Census, U.S. Department of Commerce*

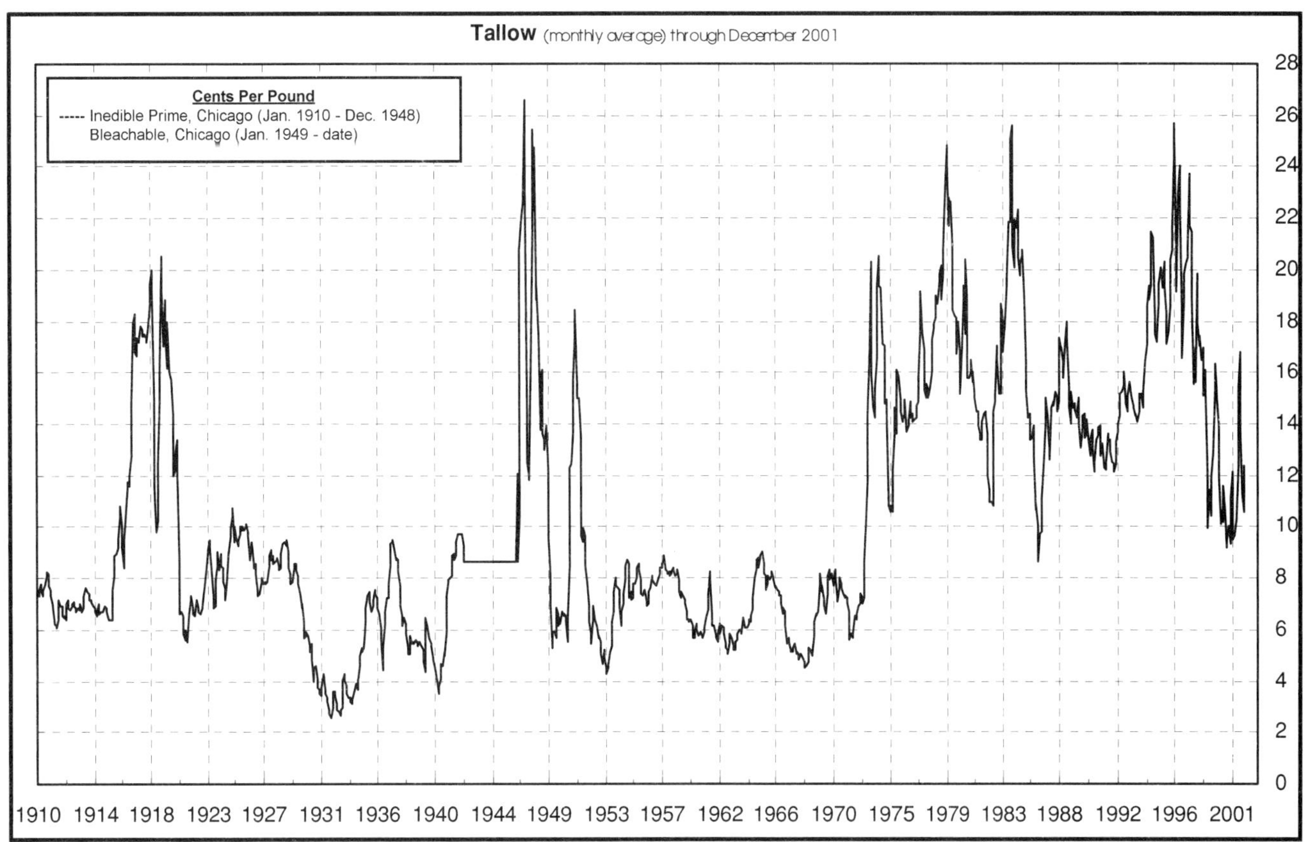

Supply and Disappearance of Edible Tallow in the United States In Millions of Pounds, Rendered Basis

	Supply			Disappearance					
Year	Stocks Jan. 1	Production	Total	Domestic	Exports	Total	Diret Use	Baking or Frying Fats	Per Capita (Lbs.)
1991	37	1,251	1,299	975	285	1,261	367	460	3.9
1992	39	1,527	1,571	1,205	333	1,538	610	427	4.7
1993	33	1,425	1,470	1,127	310	1,437	412	404	4.4
1994	33	1,510	1,606	1,275	295	1,570	639	405	4.9
1995	36	1,536	1,590	1,268	279	1,548	533	374	4.9
1996	43	1,520	1,568	1,317	218	1,535	602	320	5.0
1997	33	1,416	1,455	1,223	185	1,408	585	312	4.6
1998	47	1,537	1,586	1,301	246	1,547	868	259	4.8
1999[1]	39	1,729	1,775	1,425	317	1,742	998	262	5.2
2000[2]	33	1,840	1,881	1,593	248	1,841	1,137	284	5.8

[1] Preliminary. [2] Forecast. *Sources: Economic Research Service, U.S. Department of Agriculture (ERS-USDA); Bureau of the Census, U.S. Department of Commerce*

Wholesale Price of Tallow, Inedible, No. 1 Packers (Prime), Delivered, Chicago In Cents Per Pound

Year	Jan.	Feb.	Mar.	Apr.	May	June	July	Aug.	Sept.	Oct.	Nov.	Dec.	Average
1992	12.25	12.63	12.68	13.25	13.75	13.98	14.75	15.42	15.25	15.94	16.75	16.13	14.40
1993	15.36	14.70	15.24	16.15	15.41	14.51	14.36	14.53	14.66	14.62	14.69	14.63	14.91
1994	15.00	15.00	15.22	15.19	15.25	15.63	16.67	18.64	19.50	19.78	20.38	22.48	17.40
1995	21.75	18.86	18.00	17.75	17.50	17.89	19.61	19.81	19.53	19.46	19.75	20.08	19.17
1996	19.45	17.00	17.03	17.54	19.37	19.50	20.98	22.40	25.98	21.05	19.65	21.63	20.13
1997	23.40	22.88	19.35	17.39	18.09	19.64	19.65	20.10	20.88	22.13	22.88	22.60	20.75
1998	18.20	16.88	17.58	17.70	20.35	19.63	17.31	17.57	16.69	16.98	16.90	16.70	17.71
1999	16.30	12.53	11.18	11.38	10.40	11.49	11.50	11.69	14.38	16.37	14.95	13.88	13.00
2000	11.89	10.14	10.67	10.21	11.60	10.74	9.19	9.48	10.07	10.05	9.35	11.23	10.39
2001[1]	12.17	9.46	9.62	10.26	10.19	12.35	15.44	16.83	13.75	11.24	10.60	12.34	12.02

[1] Preliminary. *Sources: Economic Research Service, U.S. Department of Agriculture (ERS-USDA)*

Tea

Tea is produced in a number of countries around the world. It is usually grown on plantations. The tea plant is an evergreen shrub which can grow 15-30 feet tall in its natural state, though on a plantation it is kept to a height of about five feet. It thrives in tropical climates with plenty of rain. It does well at higher altitudes though it can be grown at sea level. Most commercial production of tea takes place near the equator.

Tea is usually classified in three classes. The first is black tea or fermented tea, the second is green tea or unfermented tea, and the third is oolong tea or semifermented. All of these teas are differentiated in processing, the tea leaves used are all the same. Black tea is made by taking tea leaves and fermenting them under damp clothes, then drying the leaves until they are black. The fermentation reduces the astringency and changes flavor. Green tea is steamed in a boiler with fermentation before drying the leaves. Oolong teas are partially fermented. After drying, teas are graded with orange pekoe being the highest quality.

World production of tea has been increasing about 1 percent per year in the last decade. Global production, as estimated by the Food and Agricultural Organization of the United Nations is about 2.7 million metric tonnes. The world's largest producer of tea is India with about 29 percent of the world total. India produces mostly black tea and has been putting more effort into producing higher quality teas. In June 2001, India approved futures trading in tea. Trading was expected to begin 6-8 months after the Forward Markets Commission, the commodity market regulator, gave approval for individual commodity exchanges to conduct trading. It was expected that this would lead to price stability with producers able to hedge and manage price risk.

The tea season in India starts in April and ends in January. India's production has exceeded the government target. Due to large stocks and low prices, some harvesting of tea leaves ended early in 2001. Tea production in India in 2000 was estimated to be about 846,000 metric tonnes. Production in 2001 was projected to be about 835,000 tonnes. The Indian Tea Board reported that tea exports in the January-October 2001 period were 150,000 tonnes, a decline of 11 percent from the 169,000 tonnes exported in the same period in 2000. Exports in October were reported to be 17,000 tonnes, down 19 percent from the October 2000 exports of 21,000 tonnes. Tea exports were reported to have declined due to reduced buying interest by Russia which is a major market for Indian tea. In the January-October 2001 period, tea production by India was 728,000 tonnes, up less than one percent from the same period in 2000. In October 2001, tea production was 94,000 tonnes, a decline of 7 percent from October 2000.

Another large tea producer was Sri Lanka. The Sri Lanka Tea Board reported that tea production in 2000 was 306,000 tonnes, up 8 percent from 1999. Year 2000 was the first time Sri Lanka surpassed 300,000 tonnes. Production in 2001 was expected to decline 7 percent.

World Tea Production, in Major Producing Countries In Thousands of Metric Tons

Year	Argentina	Bangladesh	China	India	Indonesia	Iran	Japan	Kenya	Malawi	Sri Lanka	Turkey	Ex-USSR[2]	World Total
1990	50.0	45.9	540.0	720.3	145.2	44.0	89.9	197.0	39.1	234.1	126.7	123.2	2,528
1991	40.0	45.2	542.0	741.7	133.4	45.0	87.9	203.6	40.5	241.6	135.3	110.0	2,541
1992	43.0	46.0	580.0	704.0	163.0	55.0	92.0	188.0	28.0	179.0	144.0	57.0	2,439
1993	55.0	55.0	621.0	758.0	165.0	57.0	92.0	211.0	39.0	232.0	117.0	81.0	2,643
1994	50.0	51.0	613.0	744.0	136.0	56.0	86.0	209.0	35.0	242.0	134.0	66.0	2,615
1995	47.0	52.0	609.0	753.0	154.0	54.0	85.0	245.0	34.0	246.0	103.0	44.0	2,613
1996	47.0	48.0	617.0	780.0	166.0	62.0	89.0	257.0	37.0	258.0	115.0	42.0	2,710
1997	54.0	53.0	637.0	811.0	149.0	69.0	91.0	221.0	44.0	277.0	140.0	39.0	2,791
1998	57.0	51.0	688.0	870.0	152.0	60.0	91.0	294.0	46.0	280.0	120.0	52.0	3,025
1999[1]	49.0	51.0	723.0	749.0	152.0	60.0	91.0	220.0	43.0	280.0	120.0	65.0	2,872

[1] Preliminary. [2] Mostly Georgia and Azerbaijan. *Sources: Foreign Agricultural Service, U.S. Department of Agriculture (FAS-USDA); Food and Agriculture Organization of the United Nations (FAO-UN)*

World Tea Exports from Producing Countries In Metric Tons

Year	Argentina	Bangladesh	Brazil	China	India	Indonesia	Kenya	Malawi	P. New Guinea	Sri Lanka	Vietnam	Zimbabwe	World Total
1989	43,335	23,426	9,400	204,584	211,622	114,709	163,188	39,891	5,439	203,763	15,016	12,768	1,121,251
1990	45,966	26,970	7,976	195,471	209,085	110,964	169,586	43,039	5,375	215,251	24,698	11,507	1,141,026
1991	36,029	26,860	7,347	190,188	215,144	110,207	175,625	41,185	3,747	212,017	7,953	11,304	1,206,282
1992	36,530	24,990	8,211	180,834	166,359	121,243	172,053	37,056	5,638	181,259	12,967	6,088	1,130,355
1993	44,258	29,620	8,335	206,659	153,159	123,925	199,379	35,264	6,441	134,742	21,200	8,065	1,193,144
1994	43,355	29,040	8,377	184,071	150,874	84,916	176,962	38,670	3,400	115,097	23,500	9,688	1,078,460
1995	41,175	26,445	7,252	169,788	158,333	79,227	258,564	32,600	4,200	178,005	18,800	9,156	1,179,705
1996	35,042	20,981	3,891	173,145	138,360	101,532	260,819	36,700	9,300	218,714	20,800	11,540	1,234,708
1997[1]	56,806	21,740	3,404	205,381	203,000	66,843	199,224	49,200	6,500	267,726	32,901	13,057	1,351,562
1998[2]	58,987	25,049	3,208	219,325	225,000	67,219	263,685	41,000	6,600	267,726	33,000	11,076	1,441,467

[1] Preliminary. [2] Estimate. *Source: Food and Agriculture Organization of the United Nations (FAO-UN)*

Tin

Tin is used in the manufacture of coatings for steel containers used to preserve food and beverages. Tin finds use in solder alloys, electroplating, ceramics, and in plastic. Research by the tin industry has focused on the use of tin in more products because of its non-toxic properties compared to other metals. Tin is relatively non-toxic compared with other metals and therefore the use of tin as a replacement for these metals is desirable. Some replacements would be for lead-free solders, tin shotgun pellets to replace lead, and the use of inorganic tin compounds to replace antimony in flame-retardant chemicals. The U.S. Geological Survey has estimated that the major uses for tin were: cans and containers, 30 percent; electrical, 20 percent; construction, 10 percent; transportation, 10 percent; other, 30 percent. In 1999 there was no domestic tin mine production in the United States. Outside of imports, tin is only produced by recycling old and new scrap.

U.S. production of secondary tin, including tin recovered from alloys and tinplate, in September 2001 was 900 metric tonnes, unchanged from the previous month. In the January-September 2001 period, secondary production of tin was 8,100 tonnes while for all of 2000 it was 10,800 tonnes.

U.S. consumption of primary tin in September 2001 was 3,300 tonnes, up less than 1 percent from August. In the January-September 2001 period, consumption of primary tin was 29,500 tonnes. For all of 2000, consumption was 42,000 tonnes. Consumption of secondary tin in September 2001 was 853 tonnes compared to 883 tonnes in August. For the January-September 2001 period, consumption of secondary tin was 7,800 tonnes while for all of 2000 it was 10,700 tonnes.

U.S. production of tin plate in July 2001 was 80,300 tonnes, gross weight, with a tin content of 514 tonnes. There were 6.4 kilograms of tin per tonne of plate. In June 2001, production was 80,600 tonnes with a tin content of 66.6 tonnes and 8.3 kilograms of tin per tonnes of plate. For all of 2000, tinplate production was 1.72 million tonnes with a tin content of 8,990 tonnes. There were 5.2 kilograms of tin per tonnes of plate in 2000. Shipments of tinplate in August 2001 were 185,000 tonnes, up 11 percent from July. For all of 2000, shipments were 2.26 million tonnes.

U.S. imports of tin metal in August 2001 were 2,910 tonnes, down 20 percent from July. In the January-August 2001 period, imports of tin metal were 27,600 tonnes. for all of 2000, imports of tin were 44,900 tonnes. In 2000, the major supplier of tin metal to the U.S. was Peru with 12,800 tonnes followed by China with 10,200 tonnes. Other large suppliers included Bolivia, Indonesia, Brazil and Chile. U.S. imports of other tin products in August 2001 were 1,240 tonnes, up almost 2 percent from July. In the January-August 2001 period, imports of other tin products totaled 15,700 tonnes. For all of 2000, imports were 16,800 tonnes. Imports of tin alloys in 2000 totaled 4,370 tonnes. Imports of tin waste and scrap were 2,340 tonnes while bars and rods were 993 tonnes. U.S. exports of tin metal in August 2001 were 292 tonnes. In the January-August period, tin metal exports were 3,210 tonnes while for all of 2000 they were 6,640 tonnes.

U.S. reported consumption of finished tin products in September 2001 was 3,260 tonnes while in August it was3,260 tonnes. In the January-September 2001 period, consumption was 29,200 tonnes while for all of 2000 it was 41,900 tonnes. In 2000, consumption of tin solder was 16,900 tonnes., consumption of tinplate was 9,020 tonnes and tin chemical use was 8,180 tonnes. Consumption of tin in bronze and brass products was 2,800 tonnes. U.S. stocks of tin at the end of September 2001 were 8,910 tonnes. Stocks of tin at the end of year 2000 were 10,400 tonnes.

World mine production of tin in 2000 was estimated at 200,000 tonnes, an increase of 1 percent from 1999. The largest producer of tin is China with 2000 production of 64,000 tonnes, an increase of 3 percent from 1999. The next largest producer was Indonesia with 2000 production of 50,000 tonnes, an increase of 4 percent from 1999. The third largest producer was Peru with 32,000 tonnes, an increase of 7 percent from 1999. Tin production by Brazil was estimated at 13,000 tonnes, the same as the previous year. Bolivia produced 12,000 tonnes. Other large producers of tin include Australia, Malaysia, Russia and Thailand.

World reserves of tin are estimated to be 9.6 million tonnes. The largest reserves are in China which had an estimated 3.5 million tonnes. Tin reserves in Brazil are estimated to be 2.2 million tonnes. Reserves in Malaysia are estimated to be 1.2 million tonnes. Other large reserves are located in Indonesia and Bolivia.

Futures Markets

Tin futures and options are traded on the London Metals Exchange (LME).

World Mine Production of Tin In Metric Tons (Contained Tin)

Year	Australia	Bolivia	Brazil	China	Indo-nesia	Malaysia	Nigeria	Peru	Portugal	Russia[3]	Thailand	United Kingdom	World Total
1991	5,708	16,830	29,253	42,100	30,061	20,710	217	6,558	8,333	13,500	14,937	2,326	201,000
1992	6,609	16,516	27,000	43,800	29,400	14,339	415	10,044	6,560	15,160	11,484	2,044	191,000
1993	8,057	18,634	26,500	49,100	29,000	10,384	200	14,310	5,334	13,100	6,363	2,232	190,000
1994	7,495	16,169	16,619	54,100	30,610	6,458	278	20,275	4,332	10,460	3,926	1,922	178,000
1995	8,656	14,419	17,317	61,900	46,058	6,402	357	22,331	4,627	9,000	2,201	1,973	201,000
1996	8,828	14,802	19,617	69,600	52,304	5,174	139	27,004	4,637	8,000	1,300	2,103	220,000
1997	10,169	12,898	19,065	67,500	55,175	5,065	150	27,952	2,667	7,500	746	2,396	217,000
1998	10,204	11,308	14,607	70,100	53,959	5,754	200	25,747	3,100	4,500	1,656	376	207,000
1999[1]	10,038	12,417	13,200	80,100	47,754	7,340	200	30,403	2,200	4,500	2,712	----	216,000
2000[2]	9,146	12,464	13,000	97,000	48,000	6,307	300	37,410	1,200	5,000	1,930	----	238,000

[1] Preliminary. [2] Estimate. [3] Formerly part of the U.S.S.R.; data reported separately until 1992. *Source: U.S. Geological Survey (USGS)*

TIN

World Smelter Production of Primary Tin In Metric Tons

Year	Australia	Bolivia	Brazil	China	Indo-nesia	Japan	Malaysia	Mexico	Russia[2]	South Africa	Spain	Thailand	World Total
1991	340	14,663	25,776	36,400	30,415	716	42,722	2,262	13,000	1,042	600	11,255	205,000
1992	240	14,393	27,000	39,600	31,915	821	45,598	2,590	15,200	592	600	10,679	194,000
1993	222	14,541	26,900	52,100	30,415	804	40,079	1,640	13,400	452	500	8,099	215,000
1994	315	15,285	20,400	67,800	31,100	706	37,990	768	11,500	43	500	7,759	216,000
1995	570	17,709	16,787	67,700	38,628	630	39,433	770	9,500	----	500	8,243	223,000
1996	460	16,733	18,361	71,500	39,000	524	38,051	1,234	9,000	----	150	10,981	211,000
1997	605	16,853	17,525	67,700	52,658	507	34,822	1,188	6,700	----	150	11,986	222,000
1998	655	11,102	17,500	79,300	53,401	500	27,201	1,078	3,000	----	100	15,353	226,000
1999	585	11,166	13,200	90,800	49,105	568	28,913	1,258	3,400	----	50	17,306	236,000
2000[1]	775	9,353	13,000	111,000	50,000	593	27,200	1,300	4,700	----	----	17,076	258,000

[1] Preliminary. [2] Formerly part of the U.S.S.R.; data not separately until 1992. *Source: U.S. Geological Survey (USGS)*

United States Foreign Trade of Tin In Metric Tons

		Imports for Consumption											
		Concentrates[2] (Ore)			Unwrought Tin Metal								
Year	Exports (Metal)	Total All Ore	Bolivia	Peru	Total All Metal	Bolivia	Brazil	China	Indo-nesia	Malaysia	Singa-pore	Thailand	United Kingdom
1991	970	1	1	-----	29,102	8,912	4,489	5,281	4,425	1,751	100	-----	344
1992	1,890	-----	-----	-----	27,314	4,623	8,167	5,389	3,854	2,799	320	427	-----
1993	2,600	-----	-----	-----	33,682	8,027	11,366	4,202	5,678	846	220	-----	6
1994	2,560	-----	-----	-----	32,400	7,260	9,990	3,230	6,620	1,390	142	-----	666
1995	2,790	-----	-----	-----	33,200	6,630	8,070	5,610	7,230	3,810	40	-----	97
1996	3,670	-----	-----	-----	30,200	6,290	9,460	2,760	7,550	965	120	-----	243
1997	4,660	57	-----	-----	40,600	6,680	8,610	4,710	7,610	1,640	120	600	20
1998	5,020	-----	-----	-----	44,000	5,160	4,710	9,870	7,880	1,870	822	540	790
1999	6,770	-----	-----	-----	47,500	3,850	4,700	13,900	7,930	944	60	20	60
2000[1]	6,640	-----	-----	-----	44,900	6,330	5,860	10,200	5,320	214	20	----	514

[1] Preliminary. [2] Tin content. *Source: U.S. Geological Survey (USGS)*

Consumption (Total) of Tin (Pig) in the United States In Metric Tons

Year	Jan.	Feb.	Mar.	Apr.	May	June	July	Aug.	Sept.	Oct.	Nov.	Dec.	Total
1992	3,800	3,800	3,800	3,800	3,700	3,800	3,800	3,500	3,600	3,600	3,400	3,300	45,090
1993	3,400	3,500	3,600	3,600	3,500	3,600	3,500	3,600	3,500	3,500	3,500	3,400	47,107
1994	3,500	3,700	3,700	3,600	3,600	3,700	3,500	3,400	2,500	3,600	3,600	3,400	42,700
1995	3,500	3,600	3,680	3,726	3,877	3,833	3,544	3,895	3,825	3,823	3,735	3,770	44,808
1996	3,862	3,938	3,940	3,878	3,894	3,976	3,926	3,996	3,687	3,779	3,908	3,730	48,800
1997	4,953	4,025	4,023	4,067	3,999	4,079	3,936	3,912	4,050	4,098	3,964	4,250	44,350
1998	4,410	4,493	4,445	4,508	4,388	4,483	4,273	4,300	4,404	4,402	4,348	4,268	52,720
1999	4,660	4,667	4,790	4,790	4,760	4,700	4,254	4,396	4,340	4,316	4,275	4,227	55,100
2000	4,362	4,466	4,430	4,377	4,466	4,470	4,398	4,476	4,397	4,460	4,244	4,157	47,040
2001[1]	4,252	4,185	4,095	4,141	4,148	4,128	4,055	4,163	4,153	4,198	4,244	4,148	52,694

[1] Preliminary. *Source: U.S. Geological Survey (USGS)*

Tin Stocks (Pig-Industrial) in the United States, on First of Month In Metric Tons

Year	Jan.	Feb.	Mar.	Apr.	May	June	July	Aug.	Sept.	Oct.	Nov.	Dec.
1992	3,024	3,022	3,369	2,844	2,877	2,901	2,651	3,111	3,321	3,454	3,654	3,178
1993	3,221	3,572	4,450	4,483	3,898	3,609	4,648	4,652	4,561	3,709	3,262	3,535
1994	3,651	4,635	3,775	3,967	3,471	3,470	3,825	3,027	2,891	2,980	2,844	2,908
1995	2,741	3,931	3,850	2,780	3,000	3,080	3,210	3,910	3,800	3,880	4,380	4,290
1996	4,580	6,000	5,200	4,390	4,880	5,590	5,760	5,640	4,790	4,580	4,810	6,810
1997	4,670	5,100	5,610	5,600	5,070	5,270	5,180	5,650	5,590	5,420	5,290	5,590
1998	6,100	5,570	5,390	5,840	6,170	5,940	5,830	5,580	6,660	6,270	5,880	5,710
1999	5,620	8,120	7,770	7,760	7,760	7,510	7,750	7,560	7,870	7,790	8,390	8,800
2000	8,300	8,330	7,960	7,580	7,810	7,930	8,090	8,240	7,820	8,210	7,200	7,970
2001[1]	8,140	8,330	8,360	8,460	8,270	8,640	8,760	8,760	8,920	9,030	7,630	7,970

[1] Preliminary. *Source: U.S. Geological Survey (USGS)*

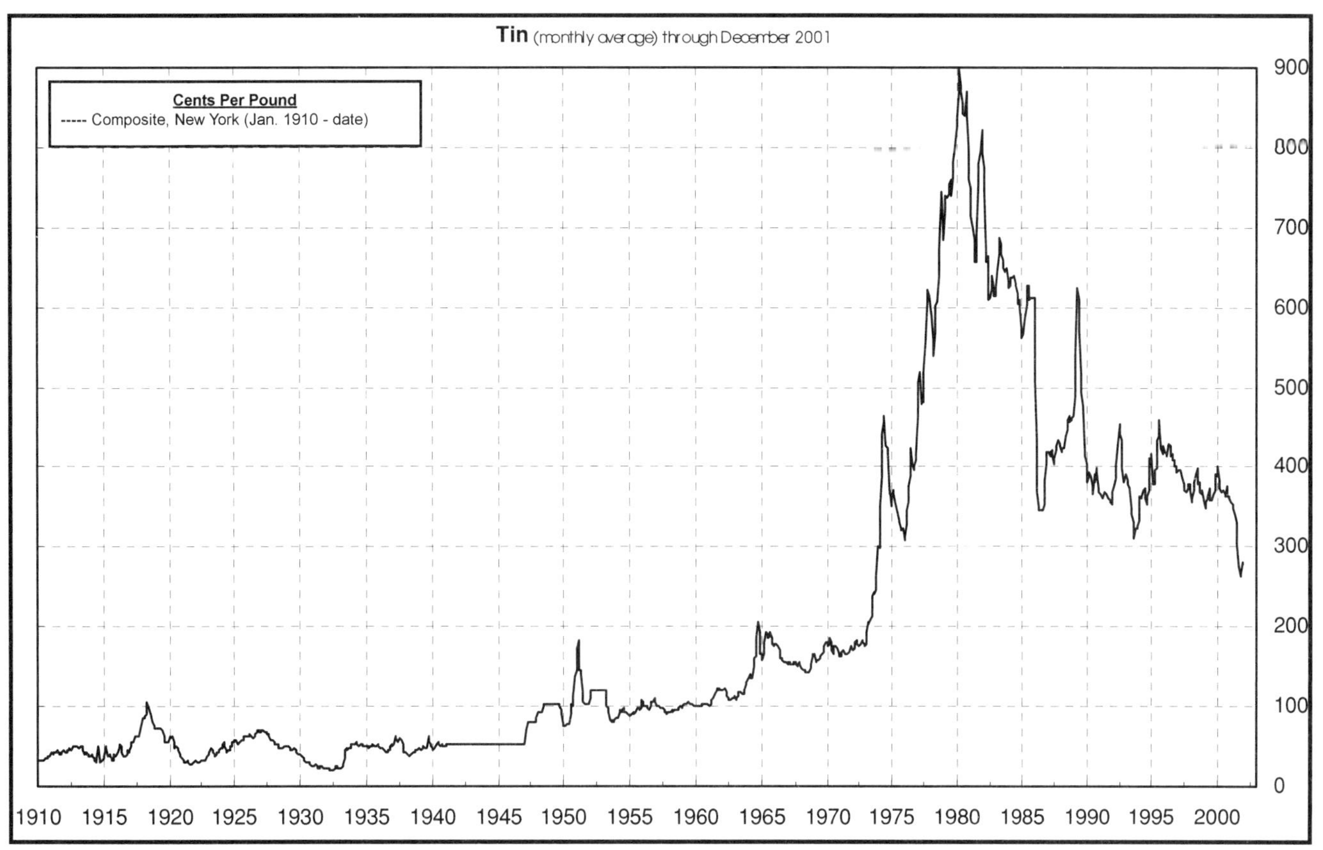

Average Price of Ex-Dock Tin in New York[1] In Cents Per Pound

Year	Jan.	Feb.	Mar.	Apr.	May	June	July	Aug.	Sept.	Oct.	Nov.	Dec.	Average
1992	261.30	267.79	267.52	277.20	290.05	313.07	331.10	322.19	315.66	291.60	268.54	271.76	289.82
1993	280.40	280.91	277.43	275.67	269.62	255.35	252.31	230.17	213.22	220.02	224.88	236.90	251.41
1994	249.55	267.55	261.20	258.49	264.18	264.45	254.83	249.18	255.10	262.46	293.72	284.99	263.81
1995	374.77	260.25	266.45	288.00	283.62	314.33	316.06	331.64	304.12	297.77	304.47	300.28	303.48
1996	299.55	297.45	296.68	308.49	306.71	296.20	298.47	291.30	292.13	285.11	285.87	280.61	294.88
1997	281.91	281.34	281.51	274.36	274.23	267.31	261.03	259.85	262.56	266.77	268.33	262.61	270.15
1998	249.39	252.65	262.36	271.65	279.50	284.27	268.87	270.98	260.79	259.17	261.82	251.75	264.43
1999	244.46	251.04	255.13	256.97	269.42	253.64	251.09	251.32	256.38	260.70	278.24	274.51	258.73
2000	283.63	271.70	263.42	259.59	259.70	260.16	257.77	255.92	262.54	254.56	253.64	252.19	261.24
2001	249.32	246.91	243.14	238.33	238.53	231.14	210.17	188.42	179.53	181.38	194.77	195.90	216.46

Source: American Metal Market (AMM)

Average Price of Tin (Straights) in New York In Cents Per Pound

Year	Jan.	Feb.	Mar.	Apr.	May	June	July	Aug.	Sept.	Oct.	Nov.	Dec.	Average
1992	367.89	375.70	375.25	386.88	402.70	431.63	453.05	441.89	434.02	398.27	380.41	380.89	402.38
1993	390.01	384.48	378.36	374.06	369.82	347.55	339.79	330.63	310.94	322.67	322.26	326.72	349.77
1994	334.38	362.81	361.86	363.65	371.63	372.59	360.45	353.85	362.48	371.82	411.63	401.31	369.04
1995	415.05	379.08	378.61	395.99	399.17	433.75	438.04	458.66	423.71	417.23	425.41	419.75	415.37
1996	418.68	415.65	414.71	429.34	427.24	413.65	416.63	409.12	407.79	400.25	400.65	394.46	412.35
1997	396.18	395.50	395.64	386.52	386.58	377.83	369.97	369.01	372.45	377.39	378.00	371.35	381.37
1998	356.97	359.76	370.96	381.99	392.16	397.36	377.72	380.02	368.89	366.87	370.49	357.69	373.41
1999	348.77	356.50	361.11	363.01	372.62	359.05	359.96	357.35	366.06	370.68	392.04	288.77	357.99
2000	400.90	384.13	372.50	368.42	370.13	370.81	366.49	364.65	375.25	363.54	362.94	360.68	371.70
2001	356.37	352.87	348.19	341.59	340.61	329.68	302.57	276.55	263.17	264.88	281.23	279.46	311.43

Source: Wall Street Journal (WSJ)

Tin Plate Production & Tin Recovered in the United States In Metric Tons

	------ Tin Content of Tinplate Produced ------												
		-------- Tinplate (All Forms) --------			---- Tin Recovered from Scrap by Form of Recovery ----								
Year	Tinplate Waste ---- Gross Weight ----		Tin Content (Tonne)	Tin Per Tonne of Plate (Kilograms)	Tin Metal	Bronze & Brass	Solder	Type Metal	Babbitt	Anti-monial Lead	Chemical Com-pounds	Misc.[2]	Grand Total
1987	141,842	2,302,173	10,357	4.5	1,353	10,245	3,765	66	77	623	W	30	16,159
1988	149,054	2,375,809	11,582	4.9	578	9,939	3,619	70	112	902	W	29	15,249
1989	153,542	2,263,769	11,764	5.2	569	10,305	3,225	46	116	952	W	W	15,213
1990	156,419	2,467,205	11,750	4.8	186	13,312	2,876	46	28	739	W	4	17,187
1991	166,647	2,468,769	11,482	4.7	234	11,719	W	44	24	928	W	2,705	12,949
1992	195,760	1,620,007	9,821	6.1	137	12,761	W	47	78	704	W	181	13,727
1993	196,874	1,625,132	9,945	6.0	112	10,670	W	43	51	796	W	W	11,672
1994	188,921	1,528,303	9,396	6.1	NA	NA	NA	NA	NA	NA	NA	NA	NA
1995	205,000	1,660,000	9,600	5.8	W	11,200	W	39	W	335	W	W	11,600
1996	181,100	1,551,000	9,617	6.2	W	11,400	W	37	34	171	W	W	11,600
1997	157,000	2,010,000	9,300	4.6	W	12,200	W	W	W	149	W	W	12,300
1998	W	1,700,000	8,900	5.2	NA	NA	NA	NA	NA	NA	NA	NA	NA
1999	W	1,750,000	9,080	5.2	----	----	----	----	----	----	----	----	----
2000[1]	W	1,720,000	8,990	5.2	----	----	----	----	----	----	----	----	----

[1] Preliminary. [2] Includes foil, terne metal, cable lead, and items indicated by symbol W. W = Withheld Proprietary data.
Source: U.S. Geological Survey (USGS)

Consumption of Primary and Secondary Tin in the United States In Metric Tons

Year	Net Import Reliance as a % of Apparent Consumption	Industry Stocks Jan. 1[2]	Net Receipts: Primary	Net Receipts: Secondary	Net Receipts: Scrap	Net Receipts: Total	Available Supply	Stocks Dec. 31 (Total Available Less Total Processed)	Total Processed	Consumed in Manu-facturing Products
1987	74	9,876	38,401	11,707	6,635	56,743	66,619	21,887	44,731	44,219
1988	78	10,217	39,421	12,472	6,707	58,600	68,817	23,586	46,232	45,602
1989	77	9,242	37,760	10,901	8,168	56,829	66,071	19,184	46,887	46,463
1990	71	13,551	38,473	9,501	6,534	54,508	68,059	22,578	45,481	45,165
1991	74	12,502	36,126	1,622	8,370	46,118	58,620	13,540	45,080	44,805
1992	80	12,038	34,327	2,279	8,412	45,018	57,056	11,669	45,387	45,120
1993	84	8,556	37,700	3,280	8,768	49,700	58,300	11,566	46,700	46,600
1994	83	9,540	35,400	4,210	4,940	44,500	54,100	11,600	42,500	42,200
1995	84	8,480	39,400	5,020	6,240	50,600	59,100	13,000	46,100	46,000
1996	83	9,300	39,200	2,750	6,140	48,100	57,300	12,500	44,900	44,700
1997	85	9,180	39,000	2,360	6,010	47,300	56,500	11,900	44,600	44,400
1998	85	9,280	39,900	2,490	6,240	48,600	57,900	12,000	45,800	45,700
1999	85	9,290	40,500	2,790	6,360	49,700	58,900	11,900	47,000	46,900
2000[1]	86	8,910	41,400	2,990	6,080	50,400	59,300	12,300	47,100	47,000

[1] Preliminary. [2] Includes tin in transit in the U.S. *Source: U.S. Geological Survey (USGS)*

Consumption of Tin in the United States, by Finished Products In Metric Tons (Contained Tin)

Year	Tinplate[2]	Solder	Babbitt	Bronze & Brass	Tinning	Chem-icals[3]	Tin Powder	Bar Tin & Anodes	White Metal	Other	Total	Total: Primary	Total: Secondary
1987	10,357	15,240	1,060	3,559	1,398	W	W	703	1,175	10,704	44,219	35,620	8,599
1988	11,582	15,288	926	3,934	1,406	W	W	557	1,131	10,777	45,601	37,529	8,072
1989	11,764	16,370	794	3,693	1,505	W	711	619	1,074	9,926	46,456	36,603	9,853
1990	11,750	16,443	763	3,166	1,707	6,275	563	603	1,045	2,850	45,165	36,770	8,395
1991	11,482	16,296	941	2,896	1,465	6,564	539	436	868	3,318	44,805	35,138	9,667
1992	9,821	18,461	916	2,916	1,275	6,301	573	919	974	2,964	45,090	34,983	10,137
1993	9,650	19,000	823	3,093	1,249	6,446	608	946	789	3,927	46,600	34,600	11,900
1994	9,480	15,100	831	3,080	1,230	5,740	625	1,190	992	3,990	42,200	33,700	8,530
1995	9,670	17,700	871	2,830	1,110	7,060	W	1,200	965	4,550	46,000	35,200	10,800
1996	9,340	15,600	851	2,760	2,050	7,520	573	1,150	1,340	3,230	44,700	36,500	8,180
1997	9,350	15,900	909	3,160	1,210	8,170	W	684	754	3,980	44,400	36,200	8,250
1998	8,900	16,900	1,020	3,610	1,100	8,180	W	704	778	4,260	45,700	37,100	8,620
1999	9,150	18,700	1,610	3,410	905	8,220	W	721	943	3,220	46,900	38,000	8,890
2000[1]	8,800	18,800	1,660	3,360	1,200	8,040	W	714	1,260	3,140	47,000	38,100	8,940

[1] Preliminary. [2] Includes small quantity of secondary pig tin and tin acquired in chemicals. [3] Including tin oxide. W = Withheld proprietary data.
Source: U.S. Geological Survey (USGS)

Titanium

Titanium is a metal known for its corrosion resistance and strength. It has a density half that of steel. Titanium occurs in a number of materials but primarily in ilmenite, leucoxene and rutile. With its properties of high strength and light weight, titanium is ideal as a construction material for airframes and engines. Pure titanium metal is called "sponge" because of its porous cellular form. Titanium sponge is processed to form an ingot, which is then processed by mills to make plate sheet tubing. Due to its weight-to-strength properties, titanium is finding use in products like golf clubs and bicycles. Titanium is used in the automotive industry as well as in pollution control devices and in chemical processing. About 95 percent of titanium is consumed in the form of titanium dioxide, a white pigment used in paints, paper and plastics. The largest producers of titanium are Australia and South Africa with over half of the world's mine production. Other producers include Norway, India and the Ukraine.

U.S. production of titanium in the second quarter of 2001 was withheld from publication. Production of titanium ingot in the second quarter of 2001 was 12,800 kilograms while in the first quarter it was 12,400 kilograms. For all of 2000, ingot production was 39,600 kilograms. Titanium mill products production in second quarter 2001 was 7,190 tonnes. In the first quarter of 2001, production was 7,230 tonnes. For 2000 mill product production was 25,900 tonnes.

U.S. consumption of titanium sponge in the second quarter of 2001 was 6,000 tonnes while in the first half of 2001 it was 12,300 tonnes. For all of 2000, titanium sponge consumption was 18,200 tonnes. Consumption of titanium scrap in the second quarter 2001 was 5,230 tonnes and in the first half of 2001 it was 9,570 tonnes. For all of 2000 it was 18,500 tonnes. Consumption of titanium ingot in second quarter 2001 was 8,820 tonnes while in the first six months of 2001 it was 17,800 tonnes. For all of 2000, ingot consumption was 27,400 tonnes. Total titanium product consumption in the first half of 2001 was 39,670 tonnes.

U.S. imports of titanium sponge in the January-May 2001 period were 5,070 tonnes while for all of 2000 they were 7,240 tonnes. In the first five months of 2001, imports of waste and scrap were 4,880 tonnes and for all of 2000 imports were 7,550 tonnes. Total titanium product imports in January-May 2001 were 12,400 tonnes while for all of 2000 they were 19,500 tonnes. Government stocks of titanium sponge at the end of the second quarter 2001 were 22,400 tonnes. Industry stocks of titanium sponge at the end of the quarter were 5,280 tonnes.

Average Prices of Titanium in the United States

Year	Ilmenite F.O.B. Australian Ports	Slag, 85% TiO2 F.O.B. Richards Bay, South Africa	Rutile Large Lots Bulk, F.O.B. U.S. East Coast	Rutile Bagged F.O.B. Australian Ports	Average Price of Grade A Titanium Sponge, F.O.B. Shipping Point	Titanium Metal Sponge	Titanium Dioxide Pigments, F.O.B. U.S. Plants	
	Dollars Per Metric Ton				Dollars Per Pound			
1991	68-76	295-325	606-650	515-545	5.25	4.75	.99	.99
1992	58-62	310	510-520	380-414	3.96	3.50-4.00	.99	.92-.95
1993	61-64	330	NA	370-400	3.75	3.50-4.00	.99	.92-.95
1994	74-80	334	410-430	450-480	3.96	3.75-4.25	.94-.96	.92-.94
1995	81-85	349	550-650	650-800	4.06	4.25-4.50	.92-.96	.99-1.03
1996	82-92	353	525-600	700-800	----	4.25-4.50	1.06-1.08	1.08-1.10
1997	68-81	391	500-550	650-710	----	4.25-4.50	1.01-1.03	1.04-1.06
1998	72-77	386	470-530	570-620	----	4.25-4.50	.96-.98	.97-.99
1999[1]	90-103	406	435-510	500-530	----	3.70-4.80	.92-.94	.99-1.02
2000[2]	83-105	407	470-500	480-570	----	3.70-4.80	.92-.94	.99-1.02

[1] Preliminary. [2] Estimate. NA = Not available. *Source: U.S. Geological Survey (USGS)*

Salient Statistics of Titanium in the United States In Metric Tons

Year	Titanium Dioxide Pigment: Production	Titanium Dioxide Pigment: Imports[3]	Titanium Dioxide Pigment: Apparent Consumption	Ilmenite: Imports[3]	Ilmenite: Consumption	Titanium Slag: Imports[3]	Titanium Slag: Consumption	Rutile[4]: Imports[3]	Rutile[4]: Consumption	Exports of Titaniu Products: Ores & Concentrates	Exports: Scrap	Exports: Dioxide & Pigments	Exports: Ingots, Billets, Etc.
1991	991,976	166,094	935,829	213,886	738,089	408,302	341,379	240,120	368,643	26,912	4,568	211,854	1,700
1992	1,137,038	169,260	999,930	294,585	684,882	537,118	539,323	317,399	460,969	34,665	2,770	270,422	1,455
1993	1,161,561	171,939	1,028,311	301,000	693,940	476,000	545,809	371,481	464,825	15,202	3,893	261,000	1,511
1994	1,250,000	176,000	1,090,000	808,000	W	472,000	583,000	332,000	510,000	19,000	4,120	313,000	1,559
1995	1,250,000	183,000	1,130,000	861,000	1,410,000	388,000	582,000	318,000	480,000	32,300	3,420	306,000	2,560
1996	1,230,000	167,000	1,070,000	939,000	1,400,000	421,000	----	324,000	398,000	15,500	3,410	292,000	3,130
1997	1,340,000	194,000	1,130,000	952,000	1,520,000	----	----	336,000	489,000	23,800	5,500	362,000	3,860
1998	1,330,000	200,000	1,140,000	1,010,000	1,300,000	----	----	387,000	421,000	59,700	7,010	356,000	3,780
1999[1]	1,350,000	225,000	1,160,000	1,070,000	1,280,000	----	----	344,000	494,000	9,380	8,130	344,000	3,390
2000[2]	1,400,000	218,000	1,150,000	918,000	1,250,000	----	----	438,000	537,000	18,900	5,060	423,000	2,980

[1] Preliminary. [2] Estimate. [3] For consumption. [4] Natural and synthetic. [5] 1994 to date includes Slag. W = Withheld proprietary data.
Source: U.S. Geological Survey (USGS)

TITANIUM

World Production of Titanium Illmenite Concentrates In Thousands of Metric Tons

Year	Australia[2]	Brazil	China	India	Malaysia	Norway	Sierra Leone	Sri Lanka	Thailand	Ukraine[3]	World Total	-- Titaniferous Slag[4] -- Canada	South Africa
1987	1,509	169.3	140.0	140.0	509.2	852.3	5.6	128.5	27.10	455	3,937	925	650
1988	1,622	142.2	150.0	229.7	486.3	898.0	42.1	74.3	18.30	460	4,033	1,025	400
1989	1,714	144.2	150.0	240.7	533.7	929.8	62.3	101.4	16.99	460	4,353	1,040	725
1990	1,621	114.1	150.0	280.0	530.2	814.5	54.6	66.4	10.67	430	4,072	1,046	840
1991	1,381	69.1	150.0	311.5	336.3	625.0	60.4	60.9	17.08	400	3,360	701	808
1992	1,806	76.6	150.0	300.0	337.7	708.0	60.3	33.3	2.97	450	3,920	753	884
1993	1,804	90.6	155.0	320.0	279.0	713.0	62.9	76.9	20.82	450	3,990	653	892
1994	1,817	97.4	155.0	300.0	116.7	826.4	47.4	60.4	1.68	530	3,970	764	744
1995	2,011	102.1	160.0	290.0	151.7	833.2	----	49.7	.03	359	4,010	815	990
1996	2,061	98.0	165.0	330.0	244.6	746.6	----	62.8	----	250	4,010	825	1,000
1997	2,265	97.2	170.0	332.0	167.5	750.0	----	18.0	----	500	4,470	850	1,100
1998	2,409	103.0	175.0	378.0	124.7	590.0	----	34.1	----	507	4,530	950	1,100
1999	2,022	96.0	180.0	378.0	127.7	600.0	----	----	----	537	4,160	950	1,100
2000[1]	2,183	96.0	185.0	380.0	110.0	610.0	----	----	----	577	4,770	950	1,120

[1] Preliminary. [2] Includes leucoxene. [3] Formerly part of the U.S.S.R.; data not reported separately until 1992. [4] Approximately 10% of total production is ilmenite. Beginning in 1988, 25% of Norway's ilmenite production was used to produce slag containing 75% TiO2. NA = Not available.
Source: U.S. Geological Survey (USGS)

World Production of Titanium Rutile Concentrates In Metric Tons

Year	Australia	Brazil	India	Sierre Leone	South Africa	Sri Lanka	Thailand	Ukraine[2]	World Total
1987	246,263	324	7,000	113,300	55,000	7,200	92	10,000	439,179
1988	230,637	1,514	5,000	126,358	55,000	5,255	128	10,000	433,892
1989	243,000	2,613	9,931	128,198	60,000	5,589	150	10,000	459,331
1990	245,000	1,814	11,000	144,284	64,056	5,460	NA	9,500	481,114
1991	201,000	1,094	13,635	154,800	77,000	3,085	76	9,000	460,000
1992	183,000	1,798	10,000	148,990	84,000	2,741	281	60,000	491,000
1993	186,000	1,744	13,900	152,000	85,000	2,643	87	60,000	501,000
1994	233,000	1,911	14,000	137,000	78,000	2,410	49	80,000	545,000
1995	195,000	1,985	14,000	----	90,000	2,697	----	112,000	416,000
1996	180,000	2,018	15,000	----	115,000	3,532	----	50,000	366,000
1997	214,000	1,742	14,000	----	123,000	2,970	----	50,000	406,000
1998	241,000	1,800	16,000	----	130,000	1,930	----	50,000	441,000
1999	190,000	4,300	16,000	----	100,000	----	----	49,000	359,000
2000[1]	237,000	4,000	17,000	----	100,000	----	----	58,600	417,000

[1] Preliminary. [2] Formerly part of the U.S.S.R.; data not reported separately until 1992. NA = Not available.
Source: U.S. Geological Survey (USGS)

World Production of Titanium Sponge Metal & U.S. Consumption of Titanium Concentrates

	Production of Titanium (In Metric Tons)						-- U.S. Consumption of Titanium Concentrates, by Products (In Metric Tons) --						
	Sponge Metal[2]						Ilmenite (TiO_2 Content)				Rutile (TiO_2 Content)		
Year	China	Japan	Russia[3]	United Kingdom	United States	Total	Pigments	Misc.	Total	Welding Rod Coatings	Pigments	Misc.	Total
1987	1,814	10,074	44,453	1,361	17,849	75,298	420,099	1,648	421,747	3,781	246,448	51,309	301,538
1988	2,000	16,500	46,000	1,500	24,000	88,000	429,736	590	430,326	3,737	262,998	64,641	331,376
1989	2,000	21,000	46,000	1,500	25,225	95,725	419,329	414	419,743	3,603	271,208	71,178	345,989
1990	2,000	25,630	47,000	1,500	24,679	101,000	445,502	726	446,228	4,047	271,637	71,373	347,057
1991	2,000	18,945	20,000	2,000	13,366	56,000	476,145	495	476,640	6,931	286,741	42,200	335,872
1992	2,000	14,554	20,000	2,000	W	38,554	425,876	647	426,523	W	405,875	32,553	438,428
1993	2,000	14,400	20,000	1,000	27,938	37,000	434,097	451	434,548	W	405,784	30,223	436,007
1994	2,000	14,400	12,000	----	29,510	33,000	W	637	W	W	460,000	18,500	478,500
1995	2,000	16,000	12,000	----	W	35,000	1,010,000	[4]	1,010,000	W	417,000	22,300	439,300
1996	2,000	21,100	18,000	----	W	51,000	1,010,000	[4]	1,010,000	W	341,000	24,200	365,000
1997	2,000	24,100	20,000	----	W	58,000	1,410,000	[4]	1,410,000	W	406,000	27,600	434,000
1998	----	----	----	----	----	----	1,290,000	14,000	1,300,000	W	384,000	37,300	421,000
1999	----	----	----	----	----	----	1,270,000	13,400	1,280,000	W	469,000	25,800	494,000
2000[1]	----	----	----	----	----	----	1,240,000	139,000	1,250,000	W	513,000	24,100	537,000

[1] Preliminary. [2] Unconsolidated metal in various forms. [3] Formerly part of the U.S.S.R.; data not reported separately until 1993. [4] Included in Pigments. NA = Not available. W = Withheld proprietary data. *Source: U.S. Geological Survey (USGS)*

Tobacco

The U.S. Department of Agriculture reported that the U.S. tobacco crop as of September 1, 2001 was forecast to be 1.20 billion pounds. The total crop was some 3 percent less than a year ago when tobacco leaf production was 1.05 billion pounds. Production of tobacco leaf did not change much because the tobacco quota did not decline very much in 2001. The production quota for flue-cured tobacco and burley declined about 1 percent. About 94 percent of U.S. tobacco output is used in cigarette production. Cigar leaf is about 1 percent of the total. The supply of U.S. grown tobacco in 2001 was expected to decline due to the decline in production as well as lower stocks.

Burley tobacco production as of September 1 was estimated at 372 million pounds, an increase of 3 percent from the previous season. Burley tobacco marketings this season could reach 360 million pounds which includes carryover tobacco. Total supplies of burley tobacco could be 1.27 billion pounds, down 6 percent from 2000. The major burley tobacco producing state is Kentucky with 2001 harvested acreage of type 31 105,000, a decline of 13 percent from 2000. The Kentucky yield was estimated at 2,2000 pounds per acre, up almost 9 percent from the previous year. The next largest burley tobacco producing state was Tennessee with 34,000 acres, down 8 percent from a year ago. The yield in 2001 was 2,000 pounds per acre. Other type 31 burley tobacco producing states include Virginia, North Carolina, Ohio, Indiana Missouri and West Virginia.

For flue-cured tobacco, marketings are expected to be 560 million pounds and stocks on July 1, 2001 were 948.3 million pounds. Supplies of flue-cured tobacco leaf were expected to decline some 19 percent compared to the previous year. Supplies of flue-cured tobacco in 2001 were expected to be lower than at any time since the late 1930's. As of September 1, 2001, the flue-cured tobacco crop was expected to be 582.2 million pounds while some 66 million pounds of the 2000 crop were carried into the season. The disappearance of flue-cured tobacco in the 2000 marketing year (July 2000-June 2001) increased about 3 percent from the previous year. Stocks of tobacco on July 1, 2000 were 1.189 million pounds. Use or disappearance of tobacco was 717 million pounds and stocks declined 13 percent.

Production of Maryland type 32 leaf grown in Maryland has declined due to the state sponsored buyout of tobacco. Production of tobacco in 2000 was 13.4 million pounds but in 2001 production was expected to be 69 percent less at 4.1 million pounds. Tobacco growers accounting for 82 percent of production are participating in the buyout. Beginning stocks of Maryland leaf tobacco on January 1, 2001 were 13.4 million pounds. With the crop of 13.4 million pounds, the supply was 26.8 million pounds. Use of Maryland leaf tobacco in the 2000/01 marketing year was expected to be close to 18 million pounds. Maryland leaf tobacco grown in Pennsylvania declined from 5.1 million pounds to 1.7 million pounds. There was no buyout in Pennsylvania. There has been increased acreage planted to low-nicotine leaf tobacco.

Fire-cured tobacco is used to make chewing tobacco, snuff and plug. Production of fire-cured tobacco leaf in 2000 was 51.6 million pounds, an increase of 36 percent from the previous season. For 2001, production is estimated at 39.5 million pounds. Production of Kentucky-Tennessee fire-cured tobacco as of September 1, 2001 was estimated at 37.2 million pounds, down 24 percent from a year ago. Production of Virginia fire-cured tobacco in 2001 was estimated at 2.3 million pounds, down 8 percent from 2000. About half of the fire-cured tobacco is exported. Total disappearance in the 2000 marketing year was expected to be 40 million pounds.

Cigarette output in 2000 was 594.7 billion pieces, less than in 1999 but higher than expected. Domestic taxable removals were 423.3 billion pieces compared to 429.8 billion in 1999. Exports were 148.3 billion pieces, some 3,1 billion less than in 1999. State cigarette tax increases were fewer in 2000. The only states to increase cigarette taxes were New York and Louisiana. In 2001, Maine increased its cigarette tax from 74 cents per pack to $1.00. Rhode Island increased its tax from 71 cents to $1.00. As of June 2001, 20 states had tax rates of at least 50 cents per pack and five states were at $1.00 or higher. Virginia is lowest at 2.5 cents per pack followed by Kentucky at 3 cents per pack. In April 2001, wholesale cigarette prices increased from $2.114 per pack to $2.254. The Federal excise tax increased five cents per pack on January 1, 2002 to 39 cents per pack.

World Production of Leaf Tobacco In Metric Tons

Year	Brazil	Canada	China	Greece	India	Indo-nesia	Italy	Japan	Pakistan	Turkey	United States	Zim-babwe	World Total
1991	422,000	78,704	3,030,700	165,650	555,900	164,850	193,296	69,897	80,806	239,405	754,949	178,107	7,262,539
1992	577,000	71,775	3,499,000	196,500	584,400	145,420	150,784	79,366	107,980	331,786	780,944	211,394	8,160,788
1993	608,000	86,094	3,451,000	148,000	580,600	152,800	135,698	67,430	105,966	338,068	731,914	235,286	8,261,069
1994	442,000	71,500	2,238,000	135,400	528,000	160,000	131,010	79,503	100,351	187,733	717,990	177,816	6,391,977
1995	398,000	79,287	2,317,700	131,875	587,100	171,400	124,492	78,212	80,917	204,900	575,380	209,042	6,376,704
1996	439,000	65,320	3,076,000	131,000	562,750	177,000	130,590	66,031	80,760	229,400	688,258	207,767	6,962,473
1997	576,600	71,110	4,251,000	132,450	623,700	184,300	140,634	68,504	86,279	310,850	810,154	192,144	8,822,851
1998	447,000	69,300	2,365,000	132,200	633,200	148,980	132,030	63,959	92,728	260,750	802,014	223,977	6,788,827
1999[1]	595,000	64,864	2,480,000	132,300	648,600	156,882	132,300	64,727	103,430	260,000	699,176	198,872	6,907,667
2000[2]	589,000	64,864	2,406,000	132,200	661,600	185,121	132,200	65,500	101,600	238,600	560,868	207,533	6,672,712

[1] Preliminary. [2] Estimate. *Source: Foreign Agricultural Service, U.S. Department of Agriculture (FAS-USDA)*

TOBACCO

Production and Consumption of Tobacco Products in the United States

Year	Cigarettes	Cigars[3]	Plug	Twist	Looseleaf	Total	Smoking Tobacco	Snuff[4]	Consumption[5] of Per Capita[6]: Cigarettes	Cigars[3]	Cigarettes	Cigars[3]	Smoking Tobacco	Chewing Tobacco	Total Products
	- Billions -	- Millions -	Chewing Tobacco: In Millions of Pounds						Number		In Pounds				
1992	718.5	1,741	5.9	1.2	61.6	68.7	14.9	57.5	2,647	24.5	4.62	.40	.18	.75	5.30
1993	661.0	1,795	5.3	1.1	58.0	64.4	13.7	59.1	2,543	23.4	4.70	.38	.17	.70	5.39
1994	725.5	1,942	4.6	1.1	56.8	62.5	13.4	15.1	2,524	25.3	4.23	.41	.16	.67	4.90
1995	746.5	2,058	4.1	1.1	57.7	62.9	12.2	60.2	2,505	27.5	4.22	.45	.13	.67	4.67
1996	754.5	2,413	3.9	1.1	56.0	61.1	12.0	61.5	2,482	32.7	4.20	.53	.12	.64	4.70
1997	719.6	2,324	3.5	1.0	53.7	58.1	11.4	64.3	2,423	36.9	4.10	.61	.12	.64	4.55
1998	679.7	2,751	3.1	1.0	49.2	53.3	12.5	65.5	2,320	38.0	3.70	.62	.12	.64	4.49
1999	606.6	2,938	2.8	0.9	47.2	50.9	14.7	67.0	2,136	39.5	3.60	.65	.14	.52	4.32
2000[1]	594.7	2,825	2.6	0.8	46.0	49.4	13.6	69.5	2,092	39.3	3.50	.64	.15	.49	4.22
2001[2]	580.0	2,800	2.3	0.8	44.1	47.2	12.0	70.1	2,051	38.6	3.40	.63	.16	.47	4.14

[1] Preliminary. [2] Estimate. [3] Large cigars and cigarillos. [4] Includes loose-leaf. [5] Consumption of tax-paid tobacco products. Unstemmed processing weight. [6] 18 years and older. *Source: Economic Research Service, U.S. Department of Agriculture (ERS)*

Production of Tobacco in the United States, by States In Thousands of Pounds

Year	Florida	Georgia	Indiana	Kentucky	Maryland	North Carolina	Ohio	Pennsvania	South Carolina	Tennessee	Virginia	Wisconsin	Total
1992	19,575	100,980	18,900	524,378	11,931	609,873	21,840	20,840	112,320	146,556	111,459	13,100	1,721,671
1993	18,673	96,320	17,415	455,080	12,255	608,415	18,900	18,260	110,760	139,423	99,544	6,643	1,613,319
1994	16,575	80,660	15,265	453,687	12,750	599,853	18,360	18,360	108,100	132,289	106,092	5,866	1,582,896
1995	17,676	84,000	13,601	328,581	11,475	484,599	15,015	15,685	105,000	92,907	81,269	6,220	1,268,538
1996	20,100	113,620	14,972	395,542	10,000	585,542	12,640	16,817	117,810	109,888	103,543	5,162	1,518,704
1997	19,053	89,225	18,690	497,928	12,000	731,199	22,230	17,020	126,360	114,292	117,576	5,690	1,787,399
1998	17,102	90,200	17,000	443,628	9,100	551,730	17,934	15,720	92,250	111,100	95,898	4,230	1,479,867
1999	15,312	64,020	11,700	408,492	9,100	448,980	17,052	11,170	78,000	122,601	88,855	2,818	1,292,692
2000	11,475	68,820	7,980	283,065	8,265	406,500	13,200	10,170	81,260	95,958	5,613	2,254	1,052,998
2001[1]	11,700	64,800	6,665	283,780	2,380	432,075	11,816	5,794	78,400	88,230	63,140	3,216	1,062,751

[1] Preliminary. *Source: Agricultural Statistics Board, U.S. Department of Agriculture (ASB-USDA)*

Salient Statistics of Tobacco in the United States

Year	Acres Harvested 1,000 Acres	Yield Per Acre Pounds	Production Million Pounds	Farm Price Cents/Lb.	Farm Value Million $	Tobacco (July - June) Exports[2]	Tobacco (July - June) Imports[3]	U.S. Exports of Cigarettes	Cigars & Cheroots	All Tobacco	Smoking Tobacco	Stocks of Tobacco[5] Various Types: All Tobacco	Fire Cured[6]	Cigar Filler[7]	Maryland
						- Million Pounds -		Millions		In Millions of Pounds					
1992	784.4	2,195	1,722	177.7	3,059	528.8	881.0	205,600	76	574	59.1	2,280	61.6	26.7	9.4
1993	746.4	2,161	1,613	175.3	2,830	529.7	706.1	195,476	67	458	62.5	2,412	64.0	26.7	7.5
1994	671.1	2,359	1,583	177.4	2,779	442.1	537.5	220,200	74	434	77.0	2,588	69.7	24.1	8.4
1995	663.1	1,913	1,269	182.0	2,305	432.6	623.3	231,100	94	462	91.8	2,541	80.5	20.5	11.7
1996	733.1	2,072	1,519	188.2	2,854	533.1	717.2	243,900	67	486	110.4	2,225	80.2	17.9	15.0
1997	836.2	2,137	1,787	180.2	3,217	450.1	565.8	217,000	86	487	118.2	2,031	83.3	13.2	18.7
1998	717.7	2,061	1,480	182.8	2,701	461.9	529.6	201,300	93	466	142.5	2,250	84.8	13.0	20.6
1999	647.2	1,997	1,293	182.8	2,356	390.3	480.3	151,400	84	418	151.1	2,301	86.7	11.4	16.0
2000	472.4	2,229	1,053	187.2	1,783	350.4	457.3	148,300	113	402	136.1	2,388	87.8	9.5	13.4
2001[1]	451.2	2,355	1,063			333.3	511.3	150,000	120	403	149.9	1,894	87.7	10.0	11.0

[1] Preliminary. [2] Domestic. [3] For consumption. [4] In bulk. [5] Flue-cured and cigar wrapper, year beginning July 1; for all other types, October 1. [6] Kentucky-Tennessee types 22-23. [7] Types 41-46. *Source: Economic Research Service, U.S. Department of Agriculture (ERS-USDA)*

Tobacco Production in the United States, by Types In Thousands of Pounds (Farm-Sale Weight)

Year	11-14	21	22	23	31	32	35-36	37	41	41-61	51	54	55	61
1992	906,025	2,567	23,736	10,486	719,552	18,771	10,332	124	14,000	30,098	1,484	8,460	4,640	1,514
1993	886,908	1,872	26,985	12,060	633,838	18,335	11,123	104	12,180	22,094	1,694	4,690	1,953	1,577
1994	869,920	2,403	31,723	14,205	612,398	19,770	11,797	124	11,340	20,680	1,808	4,180	1,686	1,666
1995	746,616	1,540	26,609	11,041	436,343	17,935	8,488	79	9,225	19,887	2,441	4,513	1,707	2,001
1996	908,345	1,738	29,461	13,029	520,483	16,545	8,550	112	10,272	20,441	2,901	3,610	1,552	2,106
1997	1,047,438	1,968	27,952	12,342	648,633	18,240	8,196	119	10,780	22,511	3,637	4,194	1,496	2,404
1998	812,797	2,340	25,922	11,573	582,336	15,370	9,663	122	9,450	19,744	3,633	3,270	960	2,431
1999	656,752	2,672	24,773	10,630	555,185	14,350	11,640	155	5,920	16,535	4,169	2,252	566	3,628
2000	598,915	2,548	34,167	14,920	362,788	13,395	15,896	165	5,040	10,204	1,070	1,825	429	1,840
2001[1]	618,950	2,340	26,320	11,830	373,056	4,054	12,860	150	4,120	13,191	3,855	2,640	476	2,000

[1] Preliminary. *Source: Agricultural Statistics Board, U.S. Department of Agriculture (ASB-USDA)*

U.S. Exports of Unmanufactured Tobacco   In Millions of Pounds (Declared Weight)

Year	Australia	Belgium-Luxem.	Denmark	France	Germany	Italy	Japan	Netherlands	Sweden	Switzerland	Thailand	United Kingdom	Total
1991	7.7	11.0	14.8	6.5	82.8	19.9	83.1	42.8	8.3	14.8	19.5	18.9	499.3
1992	6.9	21.4	15.6	4.2	93.3	19.0	131.0	49.9	8.8	7.5	16.9	24.3	574.4
1993	5.7	12.8	15.5	4.3	52.1	7.3	124.7	38.1	8.1	6.1	17.8	20.8	458.0
1994	6.4	12.3	14.9	3.1	54.1	11.3	126.2	30.9	7.3	6.0	19.0	14.7	433.9
1995	4.8	17.9	14.6	3.9	70.7	14.8	106.9	39.2	3.0	14.4	19.0	14.2	461.8
1996	5.6	39.7	15.1	3.2	60.1	17.3	88.7	40.4	3.7	14.9	15.9	34.4	485.5
1997	4.2	38.9	15.5	7.0	72.2	18.3	80.5	30.2	5.2	11.4	21.6	18.2	488.3
1998	5.0	25.2	14.9	6.6	84.6	14.0	85.3	44.0	2.6	10.3	14.2	15.6	467.2
1999	3.2	18.3	15.7	5.6	71.9	15.1	60.3	64.5	3.9	16.1	6.8	9.0	417.5
2000[1]	3.6	23.2	5.4	5.5	86.1	15.8	63.6	19.7	3.5	9.5	7.3	7.3	402.4

[1] Preliminary.   *Source: Economic Research Service, U.S. Department of Agriculture (ERS-USDA)*

U.S. Salient Statistics for Flue-Cured Tobacco (Types 11-14) in the United States   In Millions of Pounds

Crop Year	Acres Harvested 1,000	Yield Per Acre Pounds	Mar-ketings	Stocks July 1	Total Supply	Exports	Domestic Disap-pearance	Total Disap-pearance	Farm Price Cents/Lb.	Placed Under Gov't Loan Million Lb.	Price Support Level Cents/Lb.	Loan Stocks Nov. 30	Loan Stocks Uncom-mitted
1992-3	401.5	2,257	901	1,224	2,125	420	509	929	172.6	81.8	156.0	223.6	129.0
1993-4	400.1	2,217	892	1,196	2,087	359	433	792	168.1	204.9	157.7	330.5	317.5
1994-5	359.5	2,420	807	1,295	2,102	346	569	915	169.8	97.7	158.3	298.5	396.5
1995-6	386.2	1,933	854	1,187	2,041	345	531	875	179.0	12.0	159.7	157.6	62.3
1996-7	422.2	2,151	897	1,166	2,064	391	556	947	183.4	1.8	160.1	181.0	.0
1997-8	458.3	2,285	1,014	1,117	2,130	336	541	877	172.0	195.5	162.1	145.3	.0
1998-9	368.8	2,204	815	1,253	2,068	342	492	834	175.5	82.4	162.8	311.5	182.7
1999-00	303.8	2,162	654	1,234	1,888	262	437	699	173.7	136.4	163.2	318.3	144.9
2000-1[1]	250.0	2,396	564	1,190	1,754	238	479	717	179.3	27.4	164.0	256.9	135.9
2001-2[2]	247.5	2,501	560	948	1,420	250	434	684	185.8		166.0	93.2	65.0

[1] Preliminary.   [2] Estimate.   *Source: Economic Research Service, U.S. Department of Agriculture (ERS-USDA)*

Salient Statistics for Burley Tobacco (Type 31) in the United States   In Millions of Pounds

Crop Year	Acres Harvested 1,000	Yield Per Acre Pounds	Mar-ketings	Stocks Oct. 1	Total Supply	Exports	Domestic Disap-pearance	Total Disap-pearance	Farm Price Cents/Lb.	Gross Sales[3]	Price Support Level Cents/Lb.	Loan Stocks Nov. 30	Loan Stocks Uncom-mitted
1992-3	332.7	2,163	700	807	1,507	183	385	568	181.5	502.4	164.9	131.2	71.7
1993-4	299.7	2,115	627	939	1,566	152	399	552	181.6	492.4	168.3	178.8	141.9
1994-5	266.3	2,300	568	1,014	1,582	155	468	623	184.1	455.7	171.4	345.2	380.8
1995-6	234.2	1,863	483	959	1,441	165	386	551	185.4	341.6	172.5	212.5	50.8
1996-7	268.3	1,940	527	890	1,417	209	457	666	192.2	422.6	173.7	216.8	27.1
1997-8	335.3	1,934	628	751	1,379	168	379	548	188.5	337.9	176.0	105.6	38.5
1998-9	315.4	1,960	589	832	1,422	169	352	521	190.3	431.6	177.8	183.8	142.2
1999-00	300.6	1,829	551	901	1,453	139	273	413	182.9	356.6	178.9	226.6	186.7
2000-1[1]	185.4	1,957	311	811	1,122	142	289	431	195.7	169.7	180.5	420.7	336.5
2001-2[2]	167.0	2,122	354	690	1,044	135	279	414			182.6	119.3	

[1] Preliminary.   [2] Estimate.   [3] Before Christmas holidays.   *Source: Economic Research Service, U.S. Department of Agriculture (ERS-USDA)*

Exports of Tobacco from the United States (Quantity and Value)   In Metric Tons

	Unmanufactured							
Year	Flue-Cured	Value 1,000 USD	Burley	Value 1,000 USD	Total	Value 1,000 USD	Manufactured	Value 1,000 USD
1991	115,481	776,654	61,852	441,223	226,463	1,427,630	NA	4,574,086
1992	146,100	983,478	64,481	483,743	260,526	1,650,559	58,115	4,509,395
1993	111,636	752,646	51,892	389,964	207,747	1,306,067	49,669	4,253,286
1994	107,411	749,305	49,859	380,993	196,792	1,302,744	63,837	5,367,220
1995	123,040	866,208	47,129	365,206	209,481	1,399,863	77,135	5,221,487
1996	112,797	786,473	52,202	380,012	222,316	1,390,311	83,383	5,238,340
1997	116,457	832,381	56,803	454,849	221,510	1,553,314	85,734	4,956,392
1998	110,435	776,640	50,167	409,773	211,930	1,458,877	----	4,517,500
1999[1]	86,838	611,054	49,398	404,564	191,975	1,311,643	----	3,232,862
2000[2]	65,062	482,255	35,248	293,566	148,476	991,484	----	3,296,719

[1] Preliminary.   [2] Forecast.   NA = Not available.   *Source: Foreign Agricultural Service, U.S. Department of Agriculture (FAS-USDA)*

Tung Oil

Tung oil is a yellow drying oil produced from the seed of the tung tree. The seed or nuts of the tung tree are harvested and pressed yielding tung oil. Tung oil finds the most use as an industrial lubricant and drying agent. It finds use in paints and varnishes as well as in soaps, inks, and electrical insulators. Tung oil is poisonous, containing glycerol esters of unsaturated fats. It is the most powerful drying agent known. It finds use as a substitute for linseed oil in paints, varnishes, and linoleum. It is also used as a waterproofing agent. As such, it finds use in many industrialized countries.

The major producers of tung oil are China, Paraguay, and Argentina. Smaller producers include Madagascar, Malawi and Brazil. China produces tung oil from trees grown in the southern part of the country. China produces about 75 percent of the world's tung oil while Paraguay produces about 18 percent of the world supply. Total production is about 45,000 tonnes.

China is the largest exporter of tung oil. Exports vary from year to year but average about 20,000 tonnes which is about 75 percent of the world export total. Paraguay exports about 2,500 tonnes of tung oil. The major importers of tung oil are Taiwan, South Korea and the United States. Other importers include Japan, Germany and Hong Kong.

The Bureau of the Census data on tung oil use show that U.S. consumption of tung oil has been declining. In 1996, consumption of tung oil in inedible products was 21.6 million pounds. In 2000, consumption was 11.9 million pounds, a decline of 45 percent.

World Tung Oil Trade In Metric Tons

	Imports								Exports				
Year	Germany	Hong Kong	Japan	Nether-lands	South Korea	Taiwan	United States	World Total	Argen-tina	China	Hong Kong	Para-guay	World Total
1993	777	5,222	6,549	1,427	3,490	3,595	4,270	30,834	2,497	16,990	6,004	2,295	30,074
1994	912	7,843	8,628	1,663	4,594	7,454	5,401	43,082	2,415	30,582	6,476	4,603	45,182
1995	825	3,671	8,429	2,174	7,200	5,777	4,427	38,234	4,319	25,620	3,838	4,587	39,816
1996	863	1,247	3,619	1,253	7,317	4,244	3,944	27,250	2,427	18,205	1,266	3,156	27,068
1997	733	1,404	6,807	1,076	6,700	5,931	6,264	34,877	3,976	25,260	991	4,260	37,010
1998[1]	601	1,101	3,813	944	6,000	5,730	3,880	28,406	2,205	21,265	552	2,161	28,407
1999[2]	499	500	2,455	1,100	6,000	6,699	5,822	29,057	1,425	20,800	471	2,500	27,868

[1] Preliminary. [2] Estimate. *Source: The Oil World*

Consumption of Tung Oil in Inedible Products in the United States In Thousands of Pounds

Year	Jan.	Feb.	Mar.	Apr.	May	June	July	Aug.	Sept.	Oct.	Nov.	Dec.	Total
1995	427	503	976	1,389	1,437	1,387	1,886	2,830	2,549	2,645	2,455	2,126	20,610
1996	1,724	1,427	1,730	1,750	1,498	1,813	2,214	2,024	1,431	2,045	1,908	2,081	21,645
1997	934	1,922	2,720	2,170	1,335	2,034	2,618	1,262	1,267	1,099	857	1,157	19,375
1998	935	1,146	1,342	1,103	1,536	1,255	1,248	1,172	1,214	1,216	1,037	1,112	14,316
1999	862	797	967	1,071	2,137	1,140	1,519	1,043	1,012	933	962	937	13,380
2000	1,065	1,083	1,064	1,193	1,159	1,176	1,107	1,224	733	711	700	648	11,863
2001[1]	1,044	842	533	366	281	431	253	430	399	411	243		5,709

[1] Preliminary. *Source: Bureau of the Census, U.S. Department of Commerce*

Stocks of Tung Oil at Factories & Warehouses in the U.S., on First of Month In Thousands of Pounds

Year	Jan.	Feb.	Mar.	Apr.	May	June	July	Aug.	Sept.	Oct.	Nov.	Dec.
1995	1,764	1,490	1,055	3,193	2,554	2,551	2,369	2,116	2,038	2,361	2,210	2,048
1996	2,013	1,635	2,232	3,018	2,386	2,532	2,641	2,381	2,670	2,525	2,459	2,834
1997	2,373	2,754	3,417	2,808	2,134	2,230	2,230	1,561	2,525	2,535	2,311	2,326
1998	2,484	3,116	4,548	3,949	3,357	3,300	2,435	2,409	3,578	2,523	2,501	2,272
1999	2,010	3,427	5,427	3,740	3,078	2,788	2,710	2,346	2,047	1,959	1,359	1,002
2000	691	910	611	2,555	2,254	1,982	1,658	1,381	1,262	1,217	1,011	827
2001[1]	685	2,438	2,181	2,131	1,881	1,727	1,578	1,168	1,046	714	NA	NA

[1] Preliminary. *Source: Bureau of the Census, U.S. Department of Commerce*

Average Price of Tung Oil (Imported, Drums) F.O.B. in New York In Cents Per Pound

Year	Jan.	Feb.	Mar.	Apr.	May	June	July	Aug.	Sept.	Oct.	Nov.	Dec.	Average
1995	60.00	60.00	60.00	60.00	60.00	60.00	60.00	60.00	60.00	60.00	60.00	60.00	60.00
1996	60.00	60.00	64.00	64.00	64.00	64.00	64.00	64.00	64.00	64.00	64.00	64.00	63.33
1997	74.00	92.00	92.00	103.00	103.00	103.00	103.00	108.00	110.00	110.00	110.00	110.00	101.50
1998	110.00	110.00	110.00	110.00	100.00	100.00	100.00	100.00	100.00	100.00	100.00	100.00	103.33
1999	100.00	100.00	100.00	100.00	100.00	74.00	74.00	74.00	74.00	74.00	74.00	74.00	84.83
2000	59.00	59.00	59.00	59.00	59.00	59.00	59.00	59.00	59.00	59.00	59.00	59.00	59.00
2001[1]	60.50	62.00	62.00	62.00	62.00	62.00	62.00	62.00	62.00	62.00			61.85

[1] Preliminary. *Source: Economic Research Service, U.S. Department of Agriculture (ERS-USDA)*

Tungsten

Tungsten has a wide range of industrial uses. Tungsten has a high melting point, high density, good corrosion resistance, excellent wear-resistance, and excellent cutting properties. Most tungsten is used to produce tungsten carbide which is used in the production of cemented carbides. Cemented carbides are also called hardmetals and are used in mining, metal working, and construction. Tungsten is used to make dies, bearings, superalloys for turbine blades as well as armor-piercing metal projectiles. Tungsten metal wire, electrodes, and contacts are used in electrical, heating, welding and lighting applications.

The U.S. Geological Survey indicated that 2000 world mine production of tungsten was 31,500 metric tonnes, up 5 percent from the previous year. The largest tungsten producer in the world is China with 2000 output estimated at 24 million tonnes, the same as in 1999. The next largest producer was Russia with 3,700 tonnes, up 6 percent from the previous year. Other tungsten producers include Austria, Portugal, North Korea and Bolivia. Most of the world's reserves of tungsten are in China.

U.S. reported consumption of ferrotungsten in August 2001 was 43 tonnes. In the January-August 2001 period, consumption was 337 tonnes while for 2000 it was 476 tonnes. Consumption of tungsten metal powder in August 2000 was 92 tonnes while for the first eight months of 2001 it was 1,050 tonnes. For 2000, consumption was 1,770 tonnes. Tungsten carbide powder consumption in August 2001 was 482 tonnes. In the January-August 2001 period it was 3,930 tonnes while for 2000 it was 5,850 tonnes. Tungsten scrap consumption in January-August 2001 was 250 tonnes and in 2000 it was 387 tonnes.

World Concentrate Production of Tungsten In Metric Tons (Contained Tungsten[3])

Year	Australia	Austria	Bolivia	Brazil	Burma	China	Kazakhstan	Mongolia	Peru	Portugal	Rep. of Korea	Russia	World Total
1994	11	----	462	196	544	27,000	122	----	259	59	----	4,000	34,000
1995	----	738	655	98	531	27,400	249	34	728	875	----	5,400	38,500
1996	----	1,413	582	99	334	26,500	----	17	332	776	----	3,000	34,700
1997	----	1,400	513	40	272	25,000	----	26	280	1,036	----	3,000	33,200
1998	----	1,423	497	----	178	30,000	----	35	76	831	----	3,000	37,400
1999[1]	----	1,610	334	13	87	29,000	----	16	----	434	----	3,500	36,100
2000[2]	----	1,600	381	14	82	30,000	----	15	----	750	----	3,500	37,400

[1] Preliminary. [2] Estimate. [3] Conversion Factors: WO3 to W, multiply by 0.7931; 60% WO3 to W, multiply by 0.4758.
Source: U.S. Geological Survey (USGS)

Salient Statistics of Tungsten in the United States In Metric Tons (Contained Tungsten)

			Consumption of Tungsten Products by End Uses										Stocks at End of Year	
			Steel										Concentrates	
Year	Net Import Reliance as a % of Apparent Consumption	Total Consumption	Tool	Stainless & Heat Assisting	Alloy Steel[3]	Superalloys	Cutting & Wear Resistant Materials	Products Made from Metal Powder	Miscellaneous	Chemical and Ceramic	Exports	Imports for Consumption	Consumers	Producers
1994	95	3,630	529	20	19	300	5,920	1,200	W	108	44	2,960	756	44
1995	90	5,890	265	W	18	215	6,590	1,200	3,600	W	5	4,660	627	44
1996	89	5,260	434	107	177	371	5,960	687	0	97	18	4,190	569	44
1997	84	6,590	361	151	277	366	6,280	828	151	123	12	4,850	658	44
1998	78	3,210	[4]	532	219	333	6,640	1,270	532	97	10	4,750	514	W
1999[1]	81	2,100	W	486	189	306	5,910	1,860	----	93	26	2,870	W	W
2000[2]	68	W	W	408	W	403	5,960	W	----	89	70	2,370	W	W

[1] Preliminary. [2] Estimate. [3] Other than tool. [4] Included with stainless & heat assisting. W = Withheld proprietary data; included with Miscellaneous. *Source: U.S. Geological Survey*

Average Price of Tungsten at European Market (London) In Dollars Per Metric Ton

Year	Jan.	Feb.	Mar.	Apr.	May	June	July	Aug.	Sept.	Oct.	Nov.	Dec.	Average
1996	56.00	54.00	56.00	57.00	57.00	57.00	53.50	50.00	50.00	47.50	45.00	48.00	52.58
1997	48.00	49.00	50.00	50.00	50.00	50.00	50.00	43.00	43.00	43.00	46.00	46.00	47.33
1998	46.00	46.00	46.00	46.00	46.00	46.00	45.00	43.00	43.00	43.00	43.00	43.00	40.00
1999	37.38	38.50	38.50	38.50	38.50	38.50	38.50	40.36	43.00	43.00	43.00	43.00	40.25
2000	43.00	43.00	43.50	44.00	44.00	44.00	42.75	41.43	44.00	45.63	51.06	52.50	44.93

65% WO3 Basis, C.I.F., combined wolframite and scheelite quotations; data thru 1970 are for 60% WO3. *Source: U.S. Geological Survey (USGS)*

Average Price of Tungsten at U.S. Ports (Including Duty) In Dollars Per Short Ton

Year	Jan.	Feb.	Mar.	Apr.	May	June	July	Aug.	Sept.	Oct.	Nov.	Dec.	Average
1996	60.00	60.00	60.00	60.00	60.00	60.00	60.00	60.00	60.00	60.00	60.00	60.00	60.00
1997	60.00	60.00	60.00	60.00	60.00	60.00	60.00	60.00	60.00	55.00	50.00	50.00	57.92
1998	64.00	64.00	64.00	64.00	64.00	62.44	57.00	57.00	57.00	57.00	54.43	49.88	57.19
1999	49.50	49.50	49.50	49.50	48.57	48.75	49.16	50.88	51.50	54.44	54.75	54.75	52.00
2000	53.75	53.75	53.75	53.29	50.50	50.50	51.88	53.50	69.00	74.00	76.00	78.92	64.67

U.S. Spot Quotations, 65% WO3, Basis C.I.F. *Source: U.S. Geological Survey (USGS)*

Turkeys

U.S federally inspected turkey production increased more than 10% since the early 1990's, reaching a record high 5.5 billion pounds in 2001 vs. 5.4 billion in 2000. A further rise to 5.6 billion pounds is forecast in 2002. On the demand side, to help iron out the traditional late yearend holiday seasonality for whole birds, the industry in recent years shifted a larger proportion of retail sales to prepackaged turkey parts. The additional processing required to cut up and package turkey cuts, such as breast and legs, increased the supply of edible trimmings which processors sell in several forms, including mechanically deboned turkey (MDT). A strong market for the latter is exports; also, as a relatively low-cost meat protein MDT can be readily incorporated into sausage and other meat products.

Despite the record high output and effort to broaden domestic demand, U.S. per capita ready-to-cook retail weight turkey consumption has so far failed to match the record high 18.5 pounds in 1996. Usage in 2001 of 17.7 pounds compares with 17.8 pounds in 2000 and a forecast 17.9 pounds in 2002. The October-December period still accounts for more than a third of total domestic use followed by a sharp drop in the January-March period. November is the highest slaughter month with about 25 million birds. Prices follow a similar pattern, peaking generally in the fourth quarter and trending lower during the first quarter, basis 8-16 pound hens in New York. Heavier turkeys, 14-22 pounds, are classified as toms. However, with the industry's new marketing approach and changes in consumer food tastes, shifts in the traditional seasonalities may be taking root and many grocery chains are now more inclined to use turkeys as a loss leader in an effort to broaden same store purchases of other holiday related foodstuffs.

An estimated 270.4 million turkeys were raised in the U.S. in 2001 vs. 270 million in 2000. Six states account for about two-thirds of the turkeys produced with North Carolina and Minnesota the largest producers, 43 million and 44 million in 2001, respectively, vs. 41 million and 43.5 million in 2000.

U.S. turkey exports of 458 million pounds in 2000 compare with 379 million in 1999. Exports for 2001 are forecast to match the previous year. Mexico remains the largest importer with at least half the total followed by China/ Hong Kong and Russia. However, for Russia the exports are generally lower priced turkey parts.

Wholesale Eastern turkey prices in 2001 averaged 66.60 cents per pound vs. 70.50 cents in 2000 and forecasts of 64-69 cents in 2002.

Production and Consumption of Turkey Meat, by Selected Countries   In Thousands of Metric Tons (RTC)

	Production							Consumption						
Year	Canada	France	Germany	Italy	United Kingdom	United States	World Total	Canada	France	Germany	Italy	United Kingdom	United States	World Total
1992	132	558	159	269	226	2,167	3,916	129	354	272	268	210	2,072	3,761
1993	128	532	169	266	267	2,176	3,935	126	331	280	256	264	2,075	3,801
1994	133	568	180	269	266	2,239	4,055	128	330	295	245	271	2,110	3,894
1995	141	650	206	294	289	2,299	4,292	126	353	327	262	287	2,133	4,121
1996	146	671	217	315	293	2,450	4,372	123	352	361	277	298	2,225	4,185
1997	142	708	243	338	293	2,455	4,503	126	332	386	295	277	2,141	4,155
1998	139	725	256	361	268	2,366	4,452	130	360	396	302	276	2,214	4,285
1999	139	682	271	343	264	2,372	4,415	126	369	410	310	255	2,223	4,274
2000[1]	140	720	272	330	265	2,420	4,518	122	376	412	303	250	2,218	4,230
2001[2]	140	735	272	350	268	2,508	4,667	123	394	412	317	250	2,283	4,370

[1] Preliminary. [2] Forecast. *Source: Foreign Agricultural Service, U.S. Department of Agriculture (FAS-USDA)*

Salient Statistics of Turkeys in the United States

						Ready-to-Cook Basis					Production Costs		Wholesale Ready-to-Cook	
	Poults Placed[3]	Number Raised[4]	Liveweight Produced	Liveweight Price	Value of Production	Production	Beginning Stocks	Exports	Consumption Total	Consumption Per Capita	Feed	Total	Production Costs	3-Region Weighted Average Price[5]
Year	In Thousands	In Thousands	Mil. Lbs.	Cents/Lb.	Million $	In Millions of Pounds	In Millions of Pounds	In Millions of Pounds	In Millions of Pounds	Lbs.	Liveweight Basis	Liveweight Basis		
1991	308,083	284,910	6,114.6	38.5	2,353.0	4,603	306	122	4,523	17.9	22.72	36.42	61.83	60.79
1992	307,823	289,880	6,355.3	37.7	2,396.4	4,777	264	202	4,568	17.9	23.06	36.76	62.25	60.48
1993	308,871	287,650	6,432.6	39.0	2,509.1	4,798	272	244	4,577	17.7	22.20	35.86	61.12	62.83
1994	317,468	286,585	6,540.3	40.4	2,643.1	4,937	249	280	4,652	17.8	24.00	37.70	63.40	65.90
1995	320,882	292,356	6,761.3	41.0	2,769.4	5,069	254	348	4,705	17.9	21.90	35.60	60.80	66.20
1996	325,375	302,713	7,222.8	43.3	3,124.5	5,466	271	438	4,907	18.5	31.60	45.30	72.90	66.80
1997	305,612	301,251	7,225.1	39.9	2,884.4	5,478	328	606	4,720	17.6	28.20	41.90	68.70	63.80
1998	297,798	285,204	7,050.9	38.0	2,679.3	5,281	415	446	4,880	18.1	22.96	36.66	62.12	62.15
1999[1]	297,387	270,494	6,886.4	40.8	2,809.9	5,297	304	378	4,868	18.0	19.00	32.70	57.17	67.81
2000[2]	298,094	269,969	6,988.4	40.7	2,843.2	5,402	250	445	4,882	17.0	19.98	33.68	58.40	68.06

[1] Preliminary. [2] Estimate. [3] Poults placed for slaughter by hatcheries. [4] Turkeys place August 1-July 31. [5] Regions include central, eastern and western. Central region receives twice the weight of the other regions in calculating the average. *Source: Economic Research Service, U.S. Department of Agriculture (ERS-USDA)*

Turkey-Feed Price Ratio in the United States In Pounds[1]

Year	Jan.	Feb.	Mar.	Apr.	May	June	July	Aug.	Sept.	Oct.	Nov.	Dec.	Average
1992[3]	6.0	5.8	6.0	6.0	6.0	6.1	6.5	6.8	6.7	7.1	7.2	7.1	6.4
1993	6.3	6.4	6.6	6.5	6.6	6.7	6.4	6.4	6.9	7.2	6.7	6.0	6.5
1994	5.4	5.4	5.5	5.8	5.9	6.1	6.9	7.4	7.4	7.9	7.9	7.3	6.6
1995	6.8	6.4	6.5	6.4	6.3	6.3	6.0	6.3	6.4	6.4	6.5	5.7	6.3
1996	5.3	5.2	5.1	4.8	4.6	4.9	4.9	4.8	5.3	6.2	6.4	6.1	5.3
1997	5.4	5.1	5.0	5.1	5.3	5.6	6.0	5.9	6.1	6.2	6.2	5.8	5.7
1998	5.4	5.2	5.4	5.7	5.8	6.1	6.5	7.6	8.1	8.3	8.2	7.5	6.7
1999	6.5	7.1	7.5	7.8	8.2	8.7	9.7	9.5	9.6	10.0	9.9	9.2	8.6
2000	7.6	7.2	7.6	7.9	7.8	8.5	9.5	10.0	10.1	10.0	9.8	8.1	8.7
2001[2]	7.3	7.5	7.7	8.1	8.1	8.3	7.9	7.8	8.3	9.6	9.6	8.1	8.2

[1] Pounds of feed equal in value to one pound of turkey, liveweight. [2] Preliminary. [3] New data series due to NASS switching to basing ration costs on raw ingredient prices (corn and soybeans) rather than commercial feed prices. *Source: Economic Research Service, U.S. Department of Agriculture (ERS-USDA)*

Average Price Received by Farmers for Turkeys in the United States (Liveweight) In Cents Per Pound

Year	Jan.	Feb.	Mar.	Apr.	May	June	July	Aug.	Sept.	Oct.	Nov.	Dec.	Average
1992	36.3	35.5	37.0	37.0	37.7	37.7	37.9	37.8	37.5	38.5	39.4	39.3	37.6
1993	35.6	35.7	37.6	37.6	37.7	37.6	38.7	39.6	41.1	43.2	42.7	40.8	39.0
1994	37.0	37.3	38.4	39.2	39.9	40.3	40.6	42.1	43.1	44.5	44.3	42.2	40.7
1995	39.3	37.2	38.3	38.3	38.4	39.3	39.6	41.9	43.6	45.2	47.3	44.0	41.0
1996	40.9	42.4	41.8	42.2	43.2	44.4	45.0	44.3	44.2	45.1	45.5	43.2	43.5
1997	38.6	36.4	37.8	39.7	41.3	41.6	41.1	41.0	41.1	41.0	41.9	38.7	40.0
1998	35.5	34.0	34.6	35.7	35.5	35.9	37.5	38.6	40.2	42.7	43.8	40.3	37.9
1999	34.8	35.7	37.0	38.7	39.4	41.3	42.0	43.0	44.3	45.3	45.3	42.2	40.8
2000	36.4	35.7	38.2	40.0	40.8	41.8	42.2	43.2	44.8	46.1	47.1	40.5	41.4
2001[1]	36.6	36.3	37.1	37.8	38.3	38.5	38.6	38.8	40.4	44.0	44.3	38.5	39.1

[1] Preliminary. *Source: Economic Research Service, U.S. Department of Agriculture (ERS-USDA)*

Average Wholesale Price of Turkeys[1] (Hens, 8-16 Lbs.) in New York In Cents Per Pound

Year	Jan.	Feb.	Mar.	Apr.	May	June	July	Aug.	Sept.	Oct.	Nov.	Dec.	Average
1992	58.74	55.00	58.77	60.00	60.03	59.46	57.02	57.80	61.02	63.92	65.57	65.14	60.21
1993	58.05	56.83	58.41	58.98	58.81	58.35	59.76	63.43	66.73	71.28	71.76	68.20	62.55
1994	60.09	59.32	60.98	61.58	63.14	64.61	65.26	66.39	68.98	73.13	74.01	70.35	65.65
1995	60.71	58.54	60.04	60.05	60.57	62.76	64.78	68.52	72.92	76.73	80.31	70.35	66.36
1996	64.60	64.65	65.07	64.82	65.39	65.85	65.66	64.94	64.16	69.09	73.58	70.05	66.49
1997	59.71	57.84	59.30	62.93	66.64	68.60	68.59	68.20	67.89	67.33	70.07	62.18	64.94
1998	55.65	54.04	55.49	55.49	58.68	58.14	58.68	63.17	65.65	71.52	72.95	69.00	61.54
1999	57.67	58.84	61.69	63.02	65.55	68.89	71.62	73.57	76.28	79.30	78.99	72.39	68.98
2000	61.58	61.84	65.35	67.38	69.18	70.36	71.55	73.61	76.53	78.74	79.58	70.31	70.50
2001[2]	61.50	61.18	62.38	63.45	65.65	66.00	66.10	66.38	68.81	72.86	73.48	67.71	66.29

[1] Ready-to-cook. [2] Preliminary. *Source: Economic Research Service, U.S. Department of Agriculture (ERS-USDA)*

Certified Federally Inspected Turkey Slaughter in the U.S. (RTC Weights) In Millions of Pounds

Year	Jan.	Feb.	Mar.	Apr.	May	June	July	Aug.	Sept.	Oct.	Nov.	Dec.	Total
1992	362.9	331.7	361.3	385.2	374.2	435.0	451.8	411.9	431.3	467.6	423.0	393.1	4,829
1993	354.1	322.7	382.9	391.9	378.7	446.7	419.3	426.9	436.0	451.4	461.8	375.3	4,848
1994	347.8	342.0	400.9	380.6	415.6	457.9	405.6	483.6	447.7	459.1	453.9	397.5	4,992
1995	386.3	368.9	433.1	369.6	441.4	478.4	409.1	447.3	419.5	480.2	463.0	394.4	5,091
1996	412.4	426.5	422.3	430.9	483.0	454.7	484.8	476.6	440.9	518.1	465.9	406.1	5,422
1997	439.7	389.5	399.6	448.8	465.8	481.4	488.8	453.0	457.6	510.0	450.6	457.9	5,443
1998	430.5	407.7	437.8	444.0	419.1	454.2	456.0	409.9	425.3	470.5	459.5	428.2	5,243
1999	408.9	361.0	428.8	435.8	438.6	452.4	434.7	464.3	451.3	468.7	487.6	425.4	5,257
2000	396.9	412.4	466.2	413.5	489.2	479.4	422.8	481.6	423.0	494.7	478.2	396.5	5,354
2001[1]	454.7	404.4	456.7	416.8	483.3	460.2	465.9	488.5	409.2	536.2	477.7	413.2	5,467

[1] Preliminary. *Source: Economic Research Service, U.S. Department of Agriculture (ERS-USDA)*

TURKEYS

Per Capita Consumption of Turkeys in the United States In Pounds

Year	First Quarter	Second Quarter	Third Quarter	Fourth Quarter	Total	Year	First Quarter	Second Quarter	Third Quarter	Fourth Quarter	Total
1991	3.7	4.0	4.1	6.4	18.0	1997	3.5	4.0	4.2	6.0	17.6
1992	3.4	3.8	4.2	6.5	18.0	1998	3.9	3.9	4.2	6.0	18.1
1993	3.5	3.7	3.9	6.5	17.7	1999	3.8	3.8	4.4	5.8	18.0
1994	3.6	3.9	4.4	6.2	17.8	2000	3.7	4.2	4.4	5.5	17.8
1995	3.6	3.9	4.2	6.2	17.9	2001[1]	3.9	3.9	4.4	5.6	17.8
1996	3.7	3.9	4.6	6.2	18.5	2002[2]	4.0	3.9	4.2	5.7	17.9

[1] Preliminary. [2] Estimate. *Source: Economic Research Service, U.S. Department of Agriculture (ERS-USDA)*

Storage Stocks of Turkeys (Frozen) in the United States on First of Month In Millions of Pounds

Year	Jan.	Feb.	Mar.	Apr.	May	June	July	Aug.	Sept.	Oct.	Nov.	Dec.
1992	264.1	325.5	354.1	392.3	430.2	486.8	580.1	662.1	684.2	734.4	714.7	320.5
1993	271.7	314.7	359.8	359.2	424.4	474.0	556.1	624.2	678.6	713.8	683.6	290.6
1994	249.1	279.8	304.8	346.5	399.1	461.4	539.2	588.1	623.4	648.6	636.2	280.7
1995	254.4	312.9	359.5	432.1	466.2	536.3	598.8	651.1	678.2	686.0	644.2	270.1
1996	271.3	339.2	423.1	445.4	514.5	587.4	679.7	718.2	723.2	721.0	658.3	347.8
1997	328.0	401.0	446.4	496.5	543.3	611.8	667.9	714.3	742.0	770.7	736.6	438.6
1998	415.1	497.6	512.7	527.0	579.7	614.1	656.5	701.8	706.8	699.5	658.7	310.4
1999	304.3	363.8	375.6	374.9	455.4	494.3	556.1	599.0	580.3	596.4	494.5	252.3
2000	254.3	319.4	353.9	391.4	416.9	480.3	506.8	524.0	524.9	528.1	473.9	261.1
2001[1]	241.3	289.1	333.5	355.4	392.6	454.6	506.7	534.2	545.3	542.0	497.6	259.7

[1] Preliminary. *Source: Economic Research Service, U.S. Department of Agriculture (ERS-USDA)*

Average Retail[2] Price of Turkeys (Whole frozen) in the United States In Cents Per Pound

Year	Jan.	Feb.	Mar.	Apr.	May	June	July	Aug.	Sept.	Oct.	Nov.	Dec.	Average
1992	67.9	65.8	68.1	68.7	69.2	69.0	65.7	68.1	69.6	72.3	74.0	74.9	69.5
1993	67.9	67.2	67.9	68.8	68.4	68.2	67.1	72.1	74.9	78.4	80.1	75.0	71.3
1994	70.3	69.4	70.6	70.9	72.0	72.6	72.8	74.8	77.3	79.9	83.3	77.3	74.3
1995	69.5	67.1	68.5	68.6	70.1	72.5	74.2	77.8	81.6	84.9	86.5	77.5	74.9
1996	103.5	104.7	106.9	101.4	104.3	104.1	104.4	108.6	106.5	107.4	98.1	102.0	104.3
1997	106.3	106.7	104.7	103.2	104.5	107.8	107.4	109.2	108.9	106.2	97.6	98.2	105.1
1998	103.4	100.1	99.6	97.2	95.7	99.1	100.8	102.4	105.2	102.5	93.4	95.4	99.6
1999	96.9	100.1	98.4	93.6	97.5	100.5	103.1	101.5	101.8	102.5	96.4	97.6	99.2
2000	101.3	102.5	101.5	99.7	102.9	106.5	109.5	104.5	104.4	106.7	98.1	99.4	103.1
2001[1]	108.8	112.5	112.7	109.7	109.4	110.9	111.0	113.5	116.2	114.6	98.0	99.5	109.7

[1] Preliminary. [2] Data prior to 1996 are prices to selected retailers. *Source: Economic Research Service, U.S. Department of Agriculture (ERS-USDA)*

Average Retail-to-Consumer Price Spread of Turkeys (Whole) in the United States In Cents Per Pound

Year	Jan.	Feb.	Mar.	Apr.	May	June	July	Aug.	Sept.	Oct.	Nov.	Dec.	Average
1992	28.2	29.2	27.0	29.4	29.6	29.5	33.3	32.5	31.4	27.2	15.4	18.1	27.6
1993	30.0	31.7	32.6	31.9	32.3	34.5	35.8	29.7	27.7	25.0	13.6	20.4	28.8
1994	27.5	29.7	28.1	25.1	27.1	28.8	28.7	27.6	27.1	25.5	13.9	20.3	25.8
1995	28.5	32.0	33.7	32.1	32.7	32.8	30.8	28.2	27.0	20.1	10.6	21.2	27.5
1996	30.4	30.7	33.6	28.0	29.3	28.0	27.9	32.1	30.3	28.9	18.0	26.6	28.7
1997	38.3	40.7	37.5	32.0	29.6	32.0	32.0	34.5	34.3	31.9	20.0	26.9	32.5
1998	38.8	37.2	35.2	31.2	29.4	30.7	29.6	29.0	29.3	21.3	10.3	19.0	28.4
1999	29.9	32.7	28.6	21.3	22.5	22.6	23.2	29.1	18.5	17.6	12.0	19.6	23.1
2000	32.1	33.9	29.1	25.9	27.6	29.5	30.9	23.7	21.1	21.7	13.4	23.1	26.0
2001[1]	39.5	43.3	42.5	39.1	37.7	38.7	38.6	40.5	41.0	35.6	18.7	27.0	36.9

[1] Preliminary. *Source: Economic Research Service, U.S. Department of Agriculture (ERS-USDA)*

Uranium

In the wake of the events of September 2001, there was renewed interest in the role of nuclear power to produce energy such as electricity. The argument was that increased use of nuclear power would reduce the amount of petroleum that needed to be imported to produce electricity. One argument against the increased use of nuclear power was the long-term issue of how to safely dispose of nuclear waste. There is still no workable or agreed upon solution as to what to do with the nuclear waste material that has built up over many years.

Despite the important issue of waste disposal, the amount of electricity that is generated using nuclear power has been increasing. The U.S. Energy Information Administration reported that in August 2001, U.S. nuclear-powered generation of electricity totaled 68.3 billion kilowatthours, up less than 1 percent from a year ago. In the January-August 2001 period, nuclear electricity generation totaled 514.8 billion kilowatthours. In the same period in 2000, nuclear electricity generation was 509.6 billion kilowatthours. In the same period in 1999, electricity generation was 482.5 billion kilowatthours. For all of year 2000, electricity generation was 753.9 billion kilowatthours. In 1990, electricity generated by nuclear power plants was 577 billion kilowatthours. In 1980 the total was 251 billion kilowatthours while in 1973 it was 83.5 billion kilowatthours. In August 2001, nuclear's share of total electricity generated in the U.S. was 18.3 percent. In August 2000 it was 18.5 percent. In 1999 nuclear's share was 19.1 percent while in 1980 it was 11 percent. In 1973 it was only 4.5 percent.

World production of uranium oxide concentrate has been trending lower. In 1990 world production was estimated at 64,642 short tons while by 1999 that total had fallen to under 40,000 tons. Among the major producers of uranium oxide are the former countries that were in the Soviet Union, Canada, Australia, Niger, Namibia and the U.S. and South Africa. U.S. mine production of uranium concentrate in 2000 was estimated to be 3.123 million pounds. This was down 31 percent from 1999 when production was estimated to be 4.55 million pounds. In 1991 production was 5.18 million pounds. Much of the uranium concentrate produced is down by in-situ leaching. In 2000 there were a total of 10 mines and other sources producing uranium. There was one underground mine and four in-situ leaching sites. Other sources include production from mine workings.

In 2000, total exploration and development expenditures were $6.694 million, a decline of 25 percent from 1999. Surface drilling (exploration and development) expenditures in 2000 were $5.635 million. The number of holes drilled in 2000 was withheld to avoid disclosure. In 1999, there were 265 holes drilled in surface drilling exploration. That represented a decline of 81 percent from the previous year. The total acreage held for land exploration in 2000 was 685,000 acres, down 15 percent from 1999. Commercial inventories of uranium concentrate at the end of 2000 were 112.3 million pounds.

World Production of Uranium Oxide (U_3O_8) Concentrate In Short Tons (Uranium Content)

Year	Australia	Canada	China	Czech Rep. & Slovakia	France	Gabon	Germany	Namibia	Niger	South Africa	United States	Ex-USSR	World Total
1991	4,909	10,609	1,039	2,340	3,204	882	1,569	3,185	3,853	2,248	3,975	13,650	53,458
1992	3,032	12,087	1,039	2,040	2,755	702	325	2,199	3,855	2,449	2,822	11,205	46,124
1993	2,949	11,990	1,300	911	2,220	769	195	2,168	3,786	2,261	2,587	10,491	43,027
1994	3,050	11,950	----	----	1,700	750	----	2,500	3,800	2,250	1,950	----	41,750
1995	4,900	13,600	----	----	1,250	800	----	2,600	3,750	1,850	3,050	----	43,050
1996	6,450	15,250	----	----	1,200	750	----	3,150	4,300	2,200	3,150	----	46,650
1997	7,150	15,650	----	----	940	600	----	3,770	4,500	1,065	2,900	----	46,550
1998	6,350	14,200	----	----	660	950	----	3,590	4,850	1,250	2,435	----	44,110
1999[1]	7,875	10,680	----	----	450	380	----	3,495	3,790	1,195	2,325	----	39,640
2000[2]	9,830	----	655	795	525	----	5	2,430	3,270	1,305	1,890	655	29,600

[1] Preliminary. [2] Estimate. *Source: American Bureau of Metal Statistics, Inc. (ABMS)*

Commercial and U.S. Government Stocks of Uranium, End of Year In Millions of Pounds U_3O_8 Equivalent

	Utility		Domestic Supplier			DOE Owned & USEC Held	
Year	Natural Uranium	Enriched Uranium[1]	Natural Uranium	Enriched Uranium[1]	Total Commercial Stocks	Natural Uranium	Enriched Uranium[1]
1993	57.9	23.3	19.1	5.4	105.7	52.4	26.9
1994	42.4	23.0	17.4	4.1	86.9	57.2	28.0
1995	41.2	17.5	13.2	.5	72.5	82.0	28.8
1996	42.2	23.9	13.0	1.0	80.0	83.2	25.3
1997	47.1	18.8	10.3	30.1	106.2	53.2	0
1998	42.1	23.7	35.0	35.7	136.5	24.5	0
1999	44.8	13.5	29.5	39.4	127.1	53.1	0
2000	37.0	18.9	12.6	43.8	112.3	53.1	0

[1] Includes amount reported as UF_6 at enrichment suppliers. DOE = Department of Energy USEC = U.S. Energy Commission

Source: Energy Information Administration, U.S. Department of Energy (EIA-DOE)

Reported Average Price Settlements for Purchases by U.S. Utilities and Domestic Suppliers In $/Pound

Year of Delivery	Contract Price	Market Price[1]	Price & Cost Floor	Total	Contract & Market	Year of Delivery	Contract Price	Market Price[1]	Price & Cost Floor	Total	Contract & Market
	Averages of Reported Prices						Averages of Reported Prices				
1991	13.94	9.04	21.84	12.62	13.66	1996	13.40	13.66	16.13	14.91	13.72
1992	13.16	8.65	18.35	13.89	13.45	1997	13.33	11.20	14.52	12.11	13.13
1993	14.96	9.57	14.87	11.03	13.14	1998	12.53	9.33	13.50	10.31	12.37
1994	10.68	9.76	20.03	10.57	10.63	1999	12.72	9.52	14.75	11.16	12.57
1995	10.58	10.19	17.86	12.05	10.79	2000	12.31	9.11		11.04	

[1] No floor. Note: Price excludes uranium delivered *under litigation settlements. Price is given in year-of-delivery dollars.*
Source: Energy Information Administration, U.S. Department of Energy (EIA-DOE)

Uranium Industry Statistics in the United States In Millions of Pounds U_3O_8

Year	Production: Mine	Production: Concentrate	Concentrate Shipments	Employment: Exploration	Employment: Mining	Employment: Milling	Employment: Processing	Employment: Total	Deliveries to U.S. Utilities[1]	Average Price Delivered Uranium $/Lb. U_3O_8	Imports	Avg. Price Delivered Uranium Imports $/Lb. U_3O_8	Exports
1991	5.2	7.952	8.437	52	411	191	361	1,016	26.8	13.66	23.1	15.55	3.5
1992	1.0	5.645	6.853	51	219	129	283	682	23.4	13.45	45.4	11.34	2.8
1993	2.0	3.063	3.374	36	133	65	145	871	15.5	13.14	41.9	10.53	3.0
1994	2.5	3.352	6.319	41	157	105	149	980	38.3	10.40	36.6	8.95	17.7
1995	3.5	6.000	5.500	27	226	121	161	1,107	43.4	11.25	41.3	10.20	9.8
1996	4.7	6.300	6.000	27	333	155	175	1,118	47.3	14.12	45.4	13.15	11.5
1997	4.7	5.600	5.800	30	413	175	175	1,097	42.0	12.88	43.0	11.81	17.0
1998	4.8	4.700	4.900	30	518	160	203	1,120	42.7	12.14	43.7	11.19	15.1
1999	4.5	4.600	5.500	7	310	201	132	848	47.9	11.63	47.6	10.55	8.5
2000	3.1	4.000	3.200	1	157	106	137	627	51.8	11.04	44.9	9.84	13.6

[1] From suppliers under domestic purchases. *Source: Energy Information Administration, U.S. Department of Energy (EIA-DOE)*

Month-End Uranium (U_3O_8) Transaction Values[1] In Dollars Per Pound

Year	Jan.	Feb.	Mar.	Apr.	May	June	July	Aug.	Sept.	Oct.	Nov.	Dec.	Average
1991	9.40	9.45	9.35	9.30	9.30	9.20	9.15	8.95	8.70	8.35	7.45	7.50	8.84
1992	7.55	7.80	7.95	7.90	7.85	7.80	7.75	7.85	7.95	8.40	8.55	8.75	8.01
1993[2]	8.80	8.60	8.80	9.20	8.70	8.90	8.20	8.80	9.05	8.45	8.60	8.71	8.74
1994	8.58	8.45	8.25	8.25	8.23	8.25	8.23	8.15	8.13	8.10	8.13	8.25	8.25
1995	8.30	8.45	8.65	8.78	9.18	9.48	9.50	9.83	9.83	9.83	9.95	10.05	9.32
1996	10.20	10.48	10.93	11.70	13.03	13.25	14.93	15.18	15.40	15.53	15.48	15.38	13.45
1997	15.33	15.08	14.85	14.75	14.43	10.95	10.68	10.45	10.55	10.48	10.43	10.53	12.37
1998	10.63	10.63	10.60	10.05	10.00	9.80	9.80	9.73	9.55	9.35	9.25	9.05	9.87
1999	9.03	9.08	9.20	9.20	9.53	9.48	9.48	9.40	9.35	9.23	9.18	9.13	9.27
2000	9.03	8.70	8.55	8.50	8.40	8.18	8.13	7.98	7.88	7.40	7.15	6.80	8.06

[1] Transaction value is a weighed average price of recent natural uranium sales transactions, based on prices paid on transactions closed within the previous three-month period for which delivery is scheduled within one year of the transaction date; at least 10 transactions involving a sum total of at least 2 million pounds of U_3O_8 equivalent. [2] Beginning December 1993; data represents average of Unrestricted and Restricted.
Source: American Metal Market (AMM)

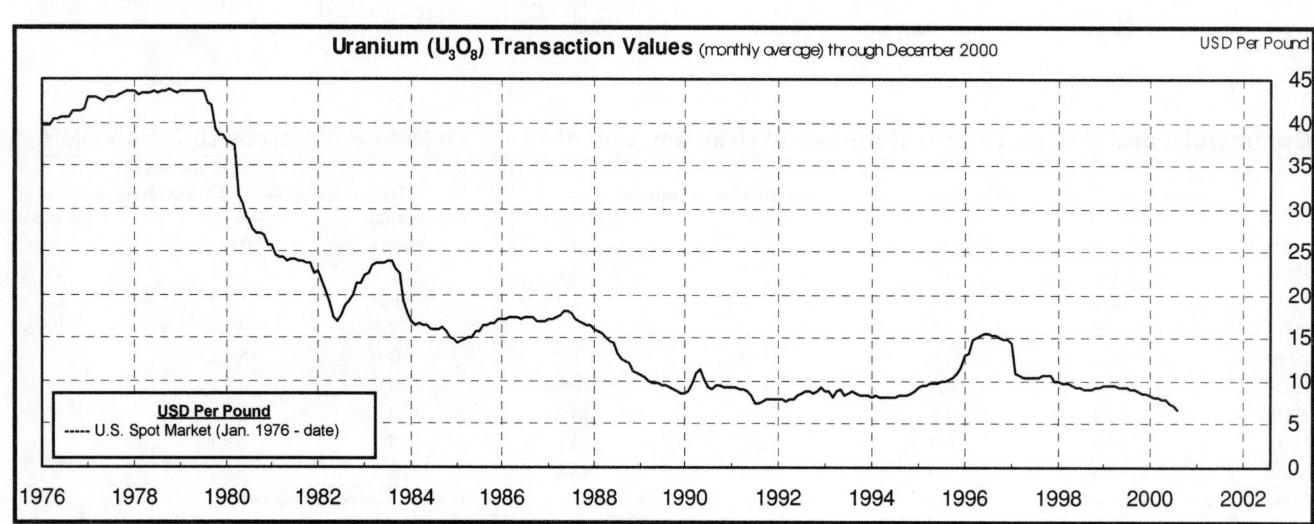

Vanadium

Vanadium is used in the production of carbon and alloy plates and steel, pipe steels and structural bars. Vanadium finds use as an oxidation catalyst and is used in tool production to provide strength and toughness. Ferrochromium is an iron alloy used in steel. Vanadium pentoxide is used in dyeing and painting applications. Vanadium is important in the production of aerospace titanium alloys and as a catalyst in the production of nucleic anhydride and sulfuric acid. There are some substitutes for vanadium in steels. Steels that contain other alloying elements can be substituted for steels containing vanadium. Among the metals that can to some degree be interchanged with vanadium are manganese, molybdenum, columbium, tungsten and titanium. In chemical processes, platinum and nickel are substitutes to some extent. There is no substitute for aerospace titanium alloys.

The U.S. Geological Survey reported that world mine production of vanadium in 2000 was estimated at 42,000 metric tonnes, down 2 percent from 1999. The largest producers of vanadium are South Africa and China. In 2000, South Africa produced 16,000 tonnes of vanadium, the same as in 1999. Production by China in 2000 was also 16,000 tonnes, the same as in 1999. Production by Russia in 2000 was 9,000 tonnes, unchanged from 1999.

U.S. consumption of ferrovanadium in July 2001 was 252,000 kilograms. In August 2001 consumption was 253,000 kilograms, contained vanadium. For all of 2000, consumption of ferrovanadium was 3.46 million kilograms. Consumption of other vanadium-containing products like vanadium metal, vanadium pentoxide and vanadium alloys in August 2001 was 37,900 kilograms, down 5 percent from the previous month. For all of 2000, consumption of these products was 403,000 kilograms. U.S. stocks of ferrovanadium in August 2001 were 186,000 kilograms. At the end of 2000, stocks were 228,000 kilograms. Stocks of vanadium-aluminum alloy in August 2001 were 7,990 kilograms. Stocks of other vanadium materials in August 2001 were 5,990 kilograms while at the end of 2000 they were 7,350 kilograms.

U.S. consumption of vanadium in steel in August 2001 was 249,000 kilograms. In the January-August 2001 period, vanadium consumption in steel was 2.07 million kilograms. carbon steel used 780,000 kilograms while high-strength low-alloy steel used 585,000 kilograms and full alloy steel took 510,000 kilograms. For all of 2000, steel production consumed 3.44 million kilograms of vanadium. In 2000 vanadium consumption in superalloy production was 16,800 kilograms.

World Production of Vanadium In Metric Tons (Contained Vanadium)

	From Ores, Concentrates and Slag						From Petroleum Residues, Ash, Spent Catalysts			
			Republic of South Africa							
Year	China[3]	Russia[4]	Content of Pentoxide & Vanadate Products	Content of Vanadiferous Slag Products	Total	Total[5]	Japan[4]	United States[7]	Total	World Total
1991	4,500	8,500	6,500	8,460	14,962	31,700	404	2,250	2,650	34,300
1992	4,700	11,000	6,300	7,730	14,285	31,600	245	1,347	1,590	33,200
1993	5,000	12,800	6,650	8,400	15,051	33,900	252	2,867	3,120	37,000
1994	5,400	11,900	6,050	9,600	16,350	34,700	252	2,740	2,990	37,700
1995	13,700	11,000	6,500	9,000	16,297	42,100	245	1,990	2,240	44,400
1996	14,000	11,000	----	----	14,770	40,900	245	3,730	3,980	45,800
1997	15,000	9,000	----	----	15,590	40,700	245	----	----	----
1998	15,500	9,000	----	----	18,868	44,500	245	----	----	----
1999[1]	16,000	9,000	----	----	17,612	43,600	245	----	----	----
2000[2]	16,000	9,000	----	----	17,000	43,000	245	----	----	----

[1] Preliminary. [2] Estimate. [3] In vanadiferous slag product. [4] Formerly part of the U.S.S.R.: data not reported separately until 1992. [5] Excludes U.S. production. [6] In vanadium pentoxide product. [7] In vanadium pentoxide and ferrovanadium products. Source: U.S. Geological Survey(USGS)

Salient Statistics of Vanadium in the United States In Metric Tons (Contained Vanadium)

		Vanadium Consumption by Uses in the U.S.									Exports			Imports			
Year	Consumer & Producer Stocks, Dec. 31	Tool Steel	Cast Irons	High Strength, Low Alloy	Stainless & Heat Resisting	Superalloys	Carbon	Full Alloy	Total	Average \$ Per Lb. V_2O_5	Vanadium Pentoxide, Anhydride	Oxides & Hydroxides	Ferrovanadium	Ores, Slag, Residues	Vanadium Pentoxide, Anhydride	Oxides & Hydroxides	Ferrovanadium
1991	935	242	15	919	37	14	919	739	3,293	2.85	700	1,110	94	882	133	110	420
1992	1,084	453	17	989	28	13	1,262	828	4,079	2.28	26	1,113	213	838	206	103	592
1993	900	373	21	981	33	13	1,413	789	3,973	1.45	126	895	219	1,454	70	19	1,630
1994	1,110	424	31	979	26	16	1,680	777	4,290	1.55	335	1,050	374	1,900	294	3	1,910
1995	1,100	443	40	1,070	32	20	1,870	833	4,640	4.63	229	1,010	340	2,530	547	36	1,950
1996	1,070	433	W	890	22	16	1,820	1,030	4,200	3.11	241	2,670	479	2,270	485	11	1,880
1997	1,000	481	W	944	20	24	1,800	908	4,730	7.40-11.00	614	385	446	2,950	711	126	1,840
1998	336	269	W	950	42	20	1,650	891	4,380	5.25-15.50	681	232	579	2,400	847	33	1,620
1999[1]	348	344	W	865	W	14	1,050	861	3,620	4.35-6.25	747	70	213	1,650	208	----	1,930
2000[2]	282	225	W	931	W	17	1,190	685	3,520	3.85-6.60	653	100	172	1,890	902	14	2,510

[1] Preliminary. [2] Estimate. W = Withheld proprietary data. *Source: U.S. Geological Survey (USGS)*

Vegetables

The U.S.D.A. reported that the area for harvest of 13 selected fresh market vegetables during the 2001 fall quarter was forecast at 177,400 acres, up 4 percent from the year before. Acreage increased for snap beans, broccoli, cabbage, carrots, celery, sweet corn, head lettuce, bell peppers and tomatoes while cucumbers registered the only decline. Acreage for cauliflower, eggplant and escarole/endive was unchanged.

During the summer quarter of 2001, acreage harvested to the major fresh market vegetables and melons was 454,800 acres, up 2 percent from 2000 but down 6 percent from 1999. Acreage harvested in the spring 2001 quarter was 319,600 acres, up 2 percent from 2000 but down 5 percent from 1999. Winter acreage in 2001 was 193,000, down 2 percent from 2000 but up 2 percent from 1999.

Acreage for fresh tomatoes for fall 2001 harvest was forecast at 24,600 acres, up 3 percent from 2000 but 15 percent less than in 1999. The California crop experienced a lot of variation in weather though the crop appeared to be making normal progress. Bell pepper acreage for fall harvest was forecast at 8,400 which was up 2 percent from 2000 and 5 percent more than 1999. The Florida crop experienced tropical storm Danielle with heavy winds and rains but only minimal damage was expected. Fall harvest acreage for head lettuce was forecast at 35,400 which was up 3 percent from 2000 and 2 percent more than in 1999. Arizona saw above average temperatures but no damage to the crop was seen due to use of irrigation. In California there were uncertainties about water which shifted some acreage from summer to the fall. The weather was initially unfavorable but improved during the season.

Index of Prices Received by Growers for Commercial Vegetables[1] in the United States

Year	Jan.	Feb.	Mar.	Apr.	May	June	July	Aug.	Sept.	Oct.	Nov.	Dec.	Average
1996	94	111	147	122	103	116	99	116	102	109	112	96	111
1997	111	105	118	113	106	112	112	122	119	145	122	136	118
1998	122	116	125	156	129	110	121	114	114	133	113	117	123
1999	105	112	121	131	118	110	104	106	105	98	98	115	110
2000	98	86	108	136	131	118	119	128	143	125	141	139	123
2001[2]	122	147	138	142	146	119	119	142	132	102			131

Not seasonally adjusted. 1990-92=100. [1] Includes fresh and processing vegetables. [2] Preliminary. *Source: National Agricultural Statistics Service, U.S. Department of Agriculture (NASS-USDA)*

Index of Prices Received by Growers for Fresh Vegetables (0113-02) in the United States

Year	Jan.	Feb.	Mar.	Apr.	May	June	July	Aug.	Sept.	Oct.	Nov.	Dec.	Average
1996	133.9	119.4	202.5	155.6	108.2	96.6	108.8	97.2	91.3	106.0	131.5	99.3	120.9
1997	105.2	126.2	150.4	109.6	103.2	112.2	115.7	125.2	121.8	143.1	124.7	118.5	121.3
1998	133.1	136.6	148.2	162.9	123.2	106.5	153.7	114.9	135.0	161.9	131.2	148.1	137.9
1999	131.9	93.1	117.4	144.4	111.3	125.8	103.4	113.7	117.5	101.6	100.9	151.6	117.7
2000	111.3	100.5	122.3	126.8	152.0	128.1	127.2	136.7	155.9	165.0	173.9	120.3	135.0
2001[1]	147.0	168.6	178.7	145.6	144.9	129.4	109.7	127.2	132.3	112.3	105.9	121.0	135.2

Not seasonally adjusted. 1990-92=100. [1] Preliminary. *Source: National Agricultural Statistics Service, U.S. Department of Agriculture (NASS)*

Producer Price Index of Canned[1] Processed Vegetables (0244) in the United States 1982 = 100

Year	Jan.	Feb.	Mar.	Apr.	May	June	July	Aug.	Sept.	Oct.	Nov.	Dec.	Average
1996	120.4	119.8	120.4	120.4	120.8	121.0	122.6	122.1	121.9	121.8	121.9	121.8	121.2
1997	121.5	121.1	120.5	120.1	119.8	119.9	119.1	119.3	119.3	120.2	120.3	120.7	120.1
1998	121.2	121.9	121.8	121.8	121.9	121.9	122.0	122.0	120.0	119.6	120.0	120.0	121.2
1999	120.6	120.6	120.9	120.9	121.0	121.0	120.8	120.9	120.7	120.7	121.3	121.3	120.9
2000	121.3	120.8	121.2	120.9	121.2	121.5	121.1	120.9	121.1	121.6	121.7	121.3	121.2
2001[2]	121.4	121.4	121.3	121.3	121.4	121.9	124.1	124.9	125.4	126.1	128.2	127.8	123.8

Not seasonally adjusted. [1] Includes canned vegetables and juices, including hominy and mushrooms. [2] Preliminary. *Source: Bureau of Labor Statistics, U.S. Department of Labor (BLS)*

Producer Price Index of Frozen Processed Vegetables (0245) in the United States 1982 = 100

Year	Jan.	Feb.	Mar.	Apr.	May	June	July	Aug.	Sept.	Oct.	Nov.	Dec.	
1996	125.1	124.8	124.6	124.9	125.0	125.4	125.5	125.8	126.0	125.7	125.8	126.0	125.4
1997	125.9	125.7	125.6	125.6	125.7	125.7	126.9	125.6	125.7	126.6	125.5	125.3	125.8
1998	125.2	126.0	124.8	125.7	125.0	124.6	125.5	125.6	125.3	125.6	125.5	125.2	125.3
1999	125.8	126.6	125.6	126.7	125.9	126.0	126.8	126.1	126.0	126.4	125.5	125.3	126.1
2000	125.4	126.2	125.7	126.3	126.3	124.9	125.9	126.4	126.2	126.9	126.1	126.2	126.0
2001[1]	127.6	128.5	127.7	128.7	128.4	127.7	128.7	128.6	128.1	129.5			128.4

Not seasonally adjusted. [1] Preliminary. *Source: Bureau of Labor Statistics, U.S. Department of Labor (BLS)*

Per Capita Use of Selected Commercially Produced Fresh and Processing Vegetables in the U.S.

Crop	1991	1992	1993	1994	1995	1996	1997	1998	1999	2000[9]	2001[10]
Asparagus, all	1.0	1.0	1.0	.9	1.0	.9	1.0	1.1	1.2	1.3	1.3
Fresh	.6	.6	.6	.6	.6	.6	.7	.8	.9	1.0	1.0
Canning	.3	.3	.3	.2	.3	.2	.2	.2	.2	.2	.2
Freezing	.1	.1	.1	.1	.1	.1	.1	.1	.1	.1	.1
Snap Beans, all	7.0	7.2	7.3	7.4	7.0	7.3	6.9	7.5	7.8	7.9	7.8
Fresh	1.1	1.5	1.5	1.6	1.7	1.5	1.4	1.7	2.0	2.1	2.0
Canning	4.1	4.0	4.0	3.8	3.6	3.9	3.7	3.8	3.8	3.9	3.8
Freezing	1.8	1.7	1.8	2.0	1.7	1.9	1.8	2.0	2.0	1.9	2.0
Broccoli, all[1]	5.4	5.8	5.7	6.8	7.0	7.2	7.4	7.3	8.9	8.1	7.9
Fresh	3.1	3.4	3.4	4.5	4.4	4.6	5.1	5.2	6.7	5.6	5.7
Freezing	2.3	2.4	2.3	2.3	2.6	2.6	2.3	2.1	2.2	2.5	2.2
Carrots, all[2]	11.2	12.3	14.8	17.1	15.6	17.2	18.5	17.3	15.6	15.6	15.5
Fresh	7.7	8.3	10.9	12.8	11.3	12.6	14.4	13.0	11.6	11.3	11.4
Canning	1.1	1.7	1.1	1.5	1.7	1.7	1.5	1.5	1.5	1.6	1.5
Freezing	2.4	2.3	2.8	2.8	2.6	2.9	2.6	2.8	2.5	2.7	2.6
Cauliflower, All[1]	2.6	2.5	2.8	2.6	2.3	2.2	2.2	2.3	2.4	2.5	2.5
Fresh	2.0	1.8	2.1	2.0	1.7	1.7	1.8	1.5	1.9	2.0	1.9
Freezing	.6	.7	.7	.6	.6	.5	.4	.8	.5	.5	.6
Celery, fresh	6.8	7.4	7.3	7.3	7.0	7.1	6.7	6.6	6.8	6.3	6.4
Sweet Corn, all[3]	26.4	27.8	28.0	27.6	28.9	29.5	27.9	28.9	28.9	27.9	27.4
Fresh	5.9	6.9	7.0	8.2	7.9	8.5	8.4	9.5	9.3	9.2	9.3
Canning	11.1	11.9	11.2	10.2	10.5	10.5	9.3	9.4	9.3	9.5	8.7
Freezing	9.4	9.0	9.8	9.2	10.5	10.5	10.2	10.0	10.3	9.2	9.4
Cucumbers, all	9.7	9.6	9.7	10.2	10.8	10.1	11.8	10.7	11.2	11.7	11.6
Fresh	4.6	5.0	5.3	5.4	5.7	6.0	6.5	6.6	6.9	6.7	6.7
Pickles	5.1	4.6	4.4	4.8	5.1	4.1	5.3	4.1	4.3	5.0	4.9
Melons, all	23.4	25.4	24.7	25.7	26.4	29.3	28.8	27.8	30.1	27.4	26.7
Watermelon	12.8	14.8	14.3	15.2	15.4	16.8	15.8	14.6	15.8	14.0	13.2
Cantaloupe	8.7	8.5	8.7	8.5	9.1	10.4	10.7	10.9	11.8	10.9	11.0
Honeydew	1.9	2.1	1.7	2.0	1.9	2.1	2.3	2.3	2.5	2.5	2.5
Lettuce, Head	26.1	25.9	24.6	25.3	22.5	21.9	24.3	22.0	24.4	24.9	24.8
Onions, all	17.3	17.6	19.3	18.1	19.3	19.6	20.0	19.7	21.2	20.6	20.3
Fresh	15.7	16.2	17.3	17.1	18.0	18.7	19.1	18.6	18.8	18.8	19.0
Green peas, all[4]	4.2	4.1	3.5	3.7	3.7	3.4	3.6	3.4	3.5	3.8	3.5
Canning	1.9	2.1	1.6	1.5	1.6	1.5	1.5	1.5	1.4	1.6	1.4
Freezing	2.3	2.0	1.9	2.2	2.1	1.9	2.1	1.9	2.1	2.2	2.1
Tomatoes, all	92.8	89.2	92.8	93.5	92.7	91.9	91.0	93.5	91.0	89.5	90.3
Fresh	15.4	15.5	16.4	16.4	17.1	17.7	17.1	17.9	18.2	17.8	17.6
Canning	77.4	73.7	76.4	77.1	75.6	74.2	73.9	75.6	72.8	71.7	72.7
Subtotal, all[8]	268.2	276.4	284.0	288.9	284.7	290.5	293.7	293.3	298.4	304.3	300.7
Fresh	134.3	145.5	150.2	157.2	153.2	160.6	166.1	163.2	170.6	176.1	173.5
Canning	110.8	108.8	109.6	108.6	107.2	105.5	104.3	106.4	102.3	103.7	103.5
Freezing	21.5	20.7	22.2	22.1	23.0	23.5	22.4	22.6	23.1	22.7	22.4
Potatoes, all	134.5	130.6	137.7	138.3	138.8	147.2	144.0	140.8	139.8	147.9	144.4
Fresh	50.4	48.6	50.5	50.2	49.9	50.7	49.4	47.9	49.2	51.1	49.3
Processing	84.1	82.0	87.2	88.1	88.9	96.5	94.6	92.9	90.6	96.8	95.1
Sweetpotatoes, all	4.0	4.3	3.9	4.7	4.5	4.6	4.5	4.1	4.1	4.4	4.4
Total, all items	422.1	423.2	437.2	444.6	440.3	454.6	454.3	451.0	455.5	469.9	462.3

[1] All production for processing broccoli and cauliflower is for freezing. [2] Industry allocation suggests that 27 percent of processing carrot production is for canning and 73 percent is for freezing. [3] On-cob basis. [4] In-shell basis. [5] Includes artichokes, brussels sprouts, eggplant, endive/escarole, garlic, radishes, and spinach. [6] Includes beets, chile peppers (1980-94, all uses), and spinach. [7] Includes green lima beans, spinach, and miscellaneous freezing vegetables. [8] Fresh, canning, and freezing data do not add to the total because onions for dehydrating are included in the total. [9] Preliminary. [10] Forecast. Source: Economic Research Service, U.S. Department of Agriculture (ERS-USDA)

VEGETABLES

Average Price Received by Growers for Broccoli in the United States In Dollars Per Cwt.

Year	Jan.	Feb.	Mar.	Apr.	May	June	July	Aug.	Sept.	Oct.	Nov.	Dec.	Season Average
1994	23.50	21.40	19.50	21.80	27.10	21.10	21.60	18.50	38.60	37.00	57.70	46.00	27.50
1995	24.70	34.30	54.40	34.00	26.50	27.30	19.50	31.30	27.70	23.60	20.80	26.90	29.30
1996	34.60	22.00	30.90	25.20	28.20	30.60	24.10	24.10	23.90	24.30	31.10	28.60	27.10
1997	36.80	27.80	25.90	24.20	23.10	30.30	27.50	23.30	31.20	40.70	27.00	30.20	29.10
1998	34.90	27.10	31.70	40.50	27.10	29.60	23.30	27.60	29.20	32.80	25.80	31.20	30.20
1999	27.70	20.10	23.20	20.20	18.60	23.10	18.70	27.40	29.30	23.00	22.10	35.00	24.10
2000	22.60	20.10	27.50	23.20	44.30	30.00	31.50	25.20	27.70	34.10	48.10	43.00	31.20
2001[1]	22.80	32.30	24.20	26.90	25.50	27.00	23.60	27.10	22.90	25.00			

[1] Preliminary. *Source: National Agricultural Statistics Service, U.S. Department of Agriculture (NASS-USDA)*

Average Price Received by Growers for Carrots in the United States In Dollars Per Cwt.

Year	Jan.	Feb.	Mar.	Apr.	May	June	July	Aug.	Sept.	Oct.	Nov.	Dec.	Season Average
1994	10.70	10.50	11.50	10.30	12.10	12.10	13.50	16.10	15.30	15.30	15.10	15.70	12.90
1995	19.20	16.90	18.70	19.40	19.20	15.20	15.00	16.10	16.10	15.30	15.50	13.00	16.70
1996	12.60	13.80	15.90	15.70	12.00	11.00	10.50	14.50	12.60	12.00	16.00	17.20	13.40
1997	15.00	14.70	13.40	12.60	12.60	12.60	12.60	13.10	12.70	12.10	12.50	16.80	12.90
1998	14.00	13.00	13.00	12.60	12.00	11.90	10.60	10.80	10.60	10.90	11.60	11.00	12.00
1999	16.70	20.20	22.00	26.90	25.30	21.90	15.80	12.60	10.10	10.50	11.20	11.60	16.80
2000	9.62	11.60	11.80	12.30	13.80	14.70	15.60	14.50	14.00	14.20	14.30	15.50	13.50
2001[1]	15.90	16.70	17.30	17.30	17.30	18.60	20.70	19.60	15.40	17.00			

[1] Preliminary. *Source: National Agricultural Statistics Service, U.S. Department of Agriculture (NASS-USDA)*

Average Price Received by Growers for Cauliflower in the United States In Dollars Per Cwt.

Year	Jan.	Feb.	Mar.	Apr.	May	June	July	Aug.	Sept.	Oct.	Nov.	Dec.	Season Average
1994	24.80	24.90	23.10	20.80	32.20	29.10	31.40	24.30	34.00	31.30	42.50	29.80	28.80
1995	31.40	31.50	53.90	68.40	47.70	37.60	26.70	34.20	25.40	21.10	22.60	33.20	34.70
1996	35.20	36.10	52.80	37.00	37.70	35.70	24.30	27.20	23.80	29.20	30.00	31.10	33.00
1997	30.40	34.70	32.90	27.90	20.70	31.20	38.90	23.40	34.60	47.10	27.60	36.20	32.30
1998	39.10	43.20	49.10	44.70	35.50	26.40	23.20	26.10	32.30	25.90	33.20	37.50	34.50
1999	29.40	31.10	42.80	46.40	23.40	25.50	19.60	25.40	21.70	22.30	35.10	55.50	30.00
2000	23.10	30.30	32.00	34.80	46.00	31.20	37.50	25.20	25.40	21.60	70.00	50.00	35.00
2001[1]	26.00	37.50	23.20	47.10	26.30	37.40	24.80	24.70	23.50	23.90			

[1] Preliminary. *Source: National Agricultural Statistics Service, U.S. Department of Agriculture (NASS-USDA)*

Average Price Received by Growers for Celery in the United States In Dollars Per Cwt.

Year	Jan.	Feb.	Mar.	Apr.	May	June	July	Aug.	Sept.	Oct.	Nov.	Dec.	Season Average
1994	11.40	8.85	7.78	8.34	13.50	8.92	12.40	14.90	12.60	12.00	13.90	25.50	12.50
1995	24.30	26.00	20.60	33.30	24.50	14.40	11.50	10.50	16.50	13.20	12.90	11.40	16.30
1996	7.90	8.50	12.20	11.60	8.90	11.50	11.50	10.30	11.60	9.79	12.40	13.40	10.50
1997	16.20	16.20	12.30	10.50	15.40	9.89	19.30	17.00	14.30	13.40	18.40	19.10	14.70
1998	11.20	11.40	16.40	13.80	15.40	12.40	10.60	10.30	10.50	10.40	11.90	14.00	12.30
1999	9.51	8.47	8.35	10.20	12.80	18.30	14.00	10.30	10.60	9.14	12.80	17.20	12.00
2000	19.20	16.00	12.90	21.20	25.60	29.10	18.10	20.00	15.10	12.80	19.50	20.00	18.40
2001[1]	14.60	15.00	15.80	19.10	24.00	33.70	13.50	10.30	10.20	8.76			

[1] Preliminary. *Source: National Agricultural Statistics Service, U.S. Department of Agriculture (NASS-USDA)*

Average Price Received by Growers for Sweet Corn in the United States In Dollars Per Cwt.

Year	Jan.	Feb.	Mar.	Apr.	May	June	July	Aug.	Sept.	Oct.	Nov.	Dec.	Season Average
1994	26.80	17.60	26.40	17.90	20.40	20.20	19.10	11.90	15.30	19.70	19.90	26.00	17.20
1995	25.00	44.70	27.80	16.60	24.50	18.80	18.60	17.10	18.50	20.70	24.00	23.30	18.30
1996	29.90	30.20	28.90	21.90	17.50	14.00	18.90	17.40	16.70	17.90	19.40	17.70	16.90
1997	29.00	25.80	33.90	26.10	21.20	17.10	18.60	18.00	16.60	15.20	18.90	19.90	17.70
1998	18.70	31.60	24.20	20.10	17.10	14.00	16.40	16.40	18.10	25.30	24.80	14.30	17.20
1999	19.60	23.30	21.80	18.90	18.50	15.00	17.30	16.60	17.30	16.50	28.40	40.70	17.20
2000	31.50	25.10	19.30	18.60	14.50	17.80	22.10	20.70	20.10	24.10	17.90	33.40	18.30
2001[1]	36.70	35.10	25.70	15.50	25.50	15.20	18.60	18.60	19.10	19.50			

[1] Preliminary. *Source: National Agricultural Statistics Service, U.S. Department of Agriculture (NASS-USDA)*

Average Price Received by Growers for Head Lettuce in the United States In Dollars Per Cwt.

Year	Jan.	Feb.	Mar.	Apr.	May	June	July	Aug.	Sept.	Oct.	Nov.	Dec.	Season Average
1992	7.23	6.75	11.90	9.91	11.20	9.84	13.00	19.90	21.00	13.60	9.63	16.30	12.50
1993	10.80	10.70	11.30	37.80	12.60	11.50	18.80	14.90	16.80	12.20	10.50	8.28	16.00
1994	7.91	11.80	9.71	11.70	11.40	13.80	10.60	10.90	17.30	22.10	22.40	37.20	13.30
1995	13.40	9.32	27.00	48.20	47.00	15.60	12.60	15.20	25.60	13.30	11.50	16.10	23.50
1996	11.30	14.90	16.50	13.20	13.30	15.20	12.70	23.50	13.70	15.40	17.70	8.87	14.70
1997	14.90	9.58	13.50	15.70	10.40	14.90	17.10	22.80	22.30	34.80	22.20	25.10	17.50
1998	19.00	10.90	12.50	27.20	14.30	11.80	15.50	16.40	14.00	21.00	10.80	12.50	16.10
1999	10.30	15.50	16.30	20.20	14.00	11.40	12.70	12.00	13.10	13.10	10.50	16.20	13.30
2000	14.60	9.29	14.10	22.80	23.60	13.50	15.00	19.20	29.40	16.20	18.70	18.70	17.50
2001[1]	13.70	23.20	15.00	21.60	18.50	12.00	16.40	26.90	26.20	11.90			

[1] Preliminary. *Source: National Agricultural Statistics Service, U.S. Department of Agriculture (NASS-USDA)*

Average Price Received by Growers for Tomatoes in the United States In Dollars Per Cwt.

Year	Jan.	Feb.	Mar.	Apr.	May	June	July	Aug.	Sept.	Oct.	Nov.	Dec.	Season Average
1992	40.50	76.00	80.70	32.40	16.70	21.90	28.30	23.50	29.30	60.10	39.10	34.30	35.80
1993	38.30	21.90	21.20	45.20	58.10	22.90	23.30	32.70	29.80	19.40	31.60	57.60	31.70
1994	41.50	19.30	24.50	16.50	20.60	31.30	26.90	30.60	22.70	28.50	31.20	37.40	27.40
1995	41.10	29.80	37.10	20.50	14.70	35.70	24.40	19.60	19.50	22.50	33.10	25.00	25.50
1996	18.40	40.00	81.70	50.50	24.40	24.20	26.00	22.10	23.40	28.30	29.70	30.40	28.10
1997	32.10	45.90	57.40	24.90	32.20	30.30	29.20	27.60	25.90	26.50	43.60	40.80	31.70
1998	26.40	44.00	34.00	37.20	36.50	29.00	40.90	25.10	28.40	43.00	42.10	42.20	35.20
1999	33.50	23.40	22.30	23.70	21.00	29.10	23.20	24.70	26.50	21.30	26.00	28.90	25.90
2000	21.40	21.10	33.00	34.80	23.00	22.60	24.70	34.00	29.60	42.10	47.50	45.90	31.40
2001[1]	43.80	28.70	56.50	22.90	37.50	27.00	24.90	28.20	20.80	25.10			

[1] Preliminary. *Source: National Agricultural Statistics Service, U.S. Department of Agriculture (NASS-USDA)*

Frozen Vegetables: January 1 and July 1 Cold Storage Holdings in the U.S. In Thousands of Pounds

	1997	1998		1999		2000		2001		2002[1]
Crop	July 1	Jan. 1	July 1	Jan. 1	July 1	Jan. 1	July 1	Jan. 1	July 1	Jan. 1
Asparagus	12,276	6,908	11,766	6,162	15,712	12,076	15,494	11,359	14,705	10,647
Lima Beans	28,015	72,221	37,659	75,469	38,390	71,993	29,220	46,930	23,911	64,324
Snap Beans	95,868	230,661	91,266	213,400	82,525	186,390	64,964	175,959	58,310	160,978
Broccoli	108,411	112,311	108,673	113,752	189,160	157,375	135,209	107,960	124,988	107,199
Brussels sprouts	7,975	19,926	7,485	18,745	15,145	25,649	14,913	19,632	12,244	17,622
Carrots	162,153	300,870	163,176	256,623	162,569	307,197	180,217	295,376	161,150	276,379
Cauliflower	32,785	58,512	38,028	5,298	32,894	57,812	37,597	44,974	26,866	38,086
Corn, Sweet[2]	203,740	532,645	228,765	673,315	255,389	585,866	226,980	570,912	172,149	617,277
Mixed vegetables	50,755	45,744	79,375	53,020	46,699	51,537	47,855	46,312	47,647	51,703
Okra	18,711	52,230	63,950	46,567	51,951	39,837	53,942	47,217	72,863	39,484
Onions	37,817	42,218	33,598	40,348	49,002	58,262	65,818	54,905	46,076	37,037
Black-eyed peas	2,952	9,344	6,654	8,039	5,598	6,517	3,517	4,438	3,257	4,482
Green peas	137,615	219,533	230,233	277,858	226,888	276,154	254,497	295,784	240,139	224,027
Peas and carrots	6,840	5,760	7,154	10,285	10,062	11,314	7,512	7,770	8,571	8,975
Spinach	104,073	67,092	10,369	69,232	142,617	73,349	99,820	50,765	97,278	63,163
Squash	48,184	75,397	64,966	70,272	49,942	58,254	41,097	42,572	31,839	43,078
Southern greens	16,681	20,771	37,660	32,765	39,455	26,944	36,237	38,934	28,131	35,913
Other vegetables	253,158	285,670	251,391	301,595	243,759	272,866	280,841	340,043	248,289	352,858
Total	1,317,049	2,303,007	1,539,168	2,317,745	1,657,757	2,279,392	1,595,730	2,201,842	1,388,413	2,153,232
Potatoes	1,271,316	1,163,547	1,316,450	1,151,294	1,234,126	1,165,389	1,186,310	1,189,663	1,355,134	1,256,149
Grand total	2,588,365	3,466,554	2,855,618	3,469,039	2,891,883	3,444,781	2,782,040	3,391,505	2,743,547	3,409,381

[1] Preliminary. [2] Cut-basis with cob corn converted to cut-basis using a factor of 0.4706. *Source: National Agricultural Statistics Service, U.S. Department of Agriculture (NASS-USDA)*

Wheat

Since 1998 U.S. wheat prices, basis Chicago nearest futures, had basically traded within a tight $.75 per bushel range, pivoting around $2.75/bu. For much of 2001 this range persisted, but with signs of an upward bias slowly taking hold. Towards yearend, prices broke through seemingly strong resistance near $2.80 and showed signs of testing $3/bu, a three year high. Although the latter resistance level held, the price action was seen as positive for carrying into 2002.

World wheat production in 2001/02 of 577 million metric tons compares with 582 million in 2000/01 and the record high 1997/98 crop of 609 million tons. Production in the late 1990's averaged about 590 million tons. Global usage in 2001/02, however, may reach a record high 596 million tons vs. 589 million in 2000/01. Ending 2001/02 world carryover of 140 million tons compares with nearly 161 million a year earlier; the total was moderately above initial estimates. The 2001/02 world stocks-to-usage ratio of about 24% compares with 27% a year earlier.

China remains the world's largest wheat producer, notwithstanding a sizable and steady drop in output during the past few years. China's 2001/02 crop of 94 million tons compares with nearly 100 million in 2000/01 and as much as 123 million in 1997/98. China has been allocating less acreage to wheat, 25.2 million hectare harvested in 2001/02 vs. 26.7 million in 2000/01 and almost 29 million in 1999/00. Average yield, however, has been erratic: 3.73 tons/hectare in 2001/02 vs. 3.74 in 2000/01 and 3.95 tons in 1999/00. China's domestic wheat use has held relatively stable, estimated at 113 million tons in 2001/02 vs. 114 million in 2000/01. Despite the supply/demand imbalance, China's recent import needs have been minimal at best, about 1 millions tons in 2001/02 vs. as much as 12.5 million in the mid-1990's. China's carryover stocks have dropped sharply during the past few years although the marketplace still tends to view the government's official totals as suspect: the ending 2001/02 carryover of 32 million tons compares with 50 million a year earlier and 71 million at yearend 1997/98.

The persistent decline during the 1990's in the former USSR's wheat production may have finally run its course: 2001/02 production estimates in the key republics were: Russia, 44.5 million tons vs. 34.5 million in 2000/01 and as little as 30 million in the mid-1990's; Kazakstan at 13 million tons vs. 9 million and the Ukraine at 21 million vs. 10 million, respectively. However, throughout the region any major improvements in average yield remains elusive. In Kazakhstan, once a major producing region of the Soviet Union, the two main barriers still holding production in check are a lack of investment in new equipment and the inadequate use of fertilizer. The Russian Federation, was once the world's largest importer; Russia's 2001/02 imports of 1 million tons compare with 1.5 million in 2000/01 and as much as 14 million tons a decade ago. The decline in domestic consumption among the Russian republics shows signs of slowing with Russia's use estimated at 37.5 million tons in 2001/02 vs. 35.1 million in 2000/01 and more than 50 million on average early in the 1990's. The Ukraine's 2000/01 use of 13.9 million tons compares with 11.4 million in 2000/01 and the early 1990's average of more than 20 million. Collectively, the European Union is a major producer of wheat, 92 million tons in 2001/02 vs. 105 million in 2000/01, with France generally accounting for about a third of EU production.

The 2001/02 world wheat trade is forecast at a record large 107.2 million tons vs. 102.8 million in 2000/01. Four countries generally account for about two-thirds of total exports: Argentina, Australia, Canada and the U.S. with the EU supplying much of the balance. The U.S., the largest exporter, is forecast to ship 28.5 million tons in 2001/021 vs. 27.9 million in 2000/01. Canadian 2001/02 exports were forecast at 15.5 million tons vs. 17.3 million in 2000/01; and EU exports of 11.5 million compare with 15 million in 2000/01. Australian exports of 17.5 million tons in 2001/02 compare with 16.8 million in 2000/01. Importing nations are scattered, among those taking up to 6 million tons in 2001/02 are Brazil, Egypt, and Iran.

The U.S. 2000/01 wheat crop (June/May) of 1.96 billion bushels compares with 2.23 billion in 200/01; the decline reflecting an average yield of 40.2 bushels per acre vs. 42 bushels and a sharp drop in harvested acreage to 48.6 million acres from 53.1 million, respectively. Winter wheat accounts for more than half of U.S. production with Kansas the largest producing state. North Dakota is the largest spring wheat and durum producing state. The 2001/02 durum wheat crop of 84 million bushels compares with 110 million in 2000/01; spring wheat production was put at 400 million bushels vs. 471 million, respectively.

The U.S. imports some wheat, mostly from Canada. Carryin stocks as of June 1, 2001 of 876 million bushels compare with 950 million a year earlier. The U.S. wheat supply for 2001/02 of 2.92 billion bushels compares with 3.28 billion in 2000/01. Total usage in 2001/02 of 2.27 billion bushels compares with 2.39 billion in 2000/01. Exports generally account for almost half the total disappearance. Food use takes at least three-quarters of domestic usage; feed about 20% and seed the balance. If the 2001/02 supply/demand estimates are realized, ending stocks on May 31, 2002 would fall to 652 million bushels, lowering the stock to use ratio to 29% vs. 37% a year earlier. This ratio is often used to forecast prices; the smaller it is the greater the likelihood for higher prices as the crop year progresses.

The 2001/02 average price received by farmers was forecast to range from $2.70-$3.00 a bushel vs. $2.62 in 2000/01.

Futures Markets

Wheat futures and options are traded on the Mercado a Termino de Buenos Aires (MAT), Sydney Futures Exchange (SFE), London International Financial Futures and Options Exchange (LIFFE), Marche a Terme International de France (MATIF), Budapest Commodity Exchange (BCE), the Chicago Board of Trade (CBOT), the Kansas City Board of Trade(KCBT), the Minneapolis Grain Exchange (MGE), the Mid America Commodity Exchange (MidAm)and the Winnipeg Commodity Exchange (WCE).

World Production of Wheat   In Thousands of Metric Tons

Year	Argentina	Australia	Canada	China	France	Germany	India	Pakistan	Russia	Turkey	United Kingdom	United States	World Total
1992-3	9,800	16,184	29,871	101,590	32,777	15,542	55,690	15,684	46,170	15,500	14,000	67,135	562,407
1993-4	9,700	16,479	27,232	106,000	29,253	15,767	57,210	16,157	43,500	16,500	12,890	65,220	558,740
1994-5	11,300	8,903	23,122	99,300	30,549	16,481	59,840	15,212	32,100	14,700	13,314	63,167	523,966
1995-6	8,600	16,504	25,037	102,215	30,862	17,763	65,470	17,002	30,100	15,500	14,310	59,404	538,410
1996-7	15,900	22,925	29,801	110,570	35,940	18,922	62,097	16,907	34,900	16,000	16,102	61,980	581,912
1997-8	14,800	19,224	24,280	123,289	33,764	19,827	69,350	16,650	44,200	16,000	15,018	67,534	609,185
1998-9	12,400	21,465	24,076	109,726	39,793	20,188	66,350	18,694	27,000	18,000	15,470	69,327	588,735
1999-00[1]	15,700	24,757	26,900	113,880	37,000	19,620	70,780	17,854	31,000	16,500	14,870	62,569	585,932
2000-1[2]	16,500	23,766	26,804	99,640	37,530	21,620	75,754	21,079	34,450	17,500	16,700	60,758	582,220
2001-2[3]	16,500	22,000	21,300	94,000	32,000	22,800	68,500	19,000	47,000	15,000	12,000	53,278	578,451

[1] Preliminary. [2] Estimate. [3] Forecast. *Source: Foreign Agricultural Service, U.S. Department of Agriculture (FAS-USDA)*

World Supply and Demand of Wheat   In Millions of Metric Tons/Hectares

Crop Year	Area Harvested	Yield	Production	World Trade	Utilization Total	Ending Stocks	Stocks as a % of Utilization
1992-3	222.9	2.52	562.1	113.1	549.6	170.0	30.9
1993-4	221.9	2.52	558.6	101.6	556.2	172.5	31.0
1994-5	214.5	2.44	524.0	101.5	546.9	149.5	27.3
1995-6	218.7	2.46	538.4	99.1	548.3	139.6	25.5
1996-7	230.0	2.53	581.9	100.1	576.0	145.6	25.3
1997-8	228.0	2.67	609.2	104.0	583.4	171.3	29.4
1998-9	224.8	2.62	588.7	101.9	584.0	176.1	30.2
1999-00[1]	216.6	2.70	585.9	112.3	591.4	170.6	28.8
2000-1[2]	219.0	2.66	582.2	103.3	589.0	163.9	27.8
2001-2[3]	214.6	2.70	578.5	107.4	588.9	153.4	26.1

[1] Preliminary. [2] Estimate. [3] Forecast. *Source: Foreign Agricultural Service, U.S. Department of Agriculture (FAS-USDA)*

Salient Statistics of Wheat in the United States

Crop Year	Planting Intentions	Acreage Harvested: Winter	Acreage Harvested: Spring	Acreage Harvested: All	Average - All Yield Per Acre in Bushels	Value of Production $1,000	Foreign Trade[5]: Domestic Exports[2]	Foreign Trade[5]: Imports[3]	Per Capita[4] Consumption: Flour	Per Capita[4] Consumption: Cereal
	1,000 Acres						In Millions of Bushels		In Pounds	
1992-3	72,219	42,123	20,638	62,761	39.3	8,009,711	1,353.6	69.4	139.0	4.7
1993-4	72,168	43,811	18,901	62,712	38.2	7,647,527	1,227.8	108.9	143.0	5.0
1994-5	70,349	41,335	20,415	61,770	37.6	7,968,237	1,188.3	91.9	144.0	5.2
1995-6	69,132	40,972	19,973	60,945	35.8	9,787,213	1,241.1	67.9	142.0	5.4
1996-7	75,105	39,574	23,245	62,819	36.3	9,782,238	1,001.5	92.3	149.0	5.4
1997-8	70,412	41,340	21,500	62,840	39.5	8,286,741	1,040.4	94.9	150.0	5.4
1998-9	65,821	40,126	18,876	59,002	43.2	6,780,623	1,042.2	103.0	146.0	5.4
1999-00	62,714	35,486	18,337	53,823	42.7	5,593,989	1,089.5	94.5	147.0	5.3
2000-1	62,629	35,072	18,061	53,133	42.0	5,970,197	1,061.5	89.8	----	----
2001-2[1]	59,617	31,295	17,358	48,653	40.2	5,481,000	1,000.0	95.0	----	----

[1] Preliminary. [2] Includes flour milled from imported wheat. [3] Total wheat, flour & other products. [4] Civilian only. [5] Year beginning June.
Source: Economic Research Service, U.S. Department of Agriculture (ERS-USDA)

Supply and Distribution of Wheat in the United States   In Millions of Bushels

Crop Year Beginning June 1	Supply: Stocks, June 1: On Farms	Supply: Stocks, June 1: Mills, Elevators[3]	Supply: Totl Stocks	Supply: Production	Supply: Imports[4]	Supply: Total Supply	Domestic Disappearance: Food	Domestic Disappearance: Seed	Domestic Disappearance: Feed & Residual[5]	Domestic Disappearance: Total	Exports[4]	Total Disappearance
1992-3	144.6	327.2	475.0	2,466.8	70.0	3,011.8	834.8	99.1	193.6	1,127.5	1,353.6	2,481.2
1993-4	183.8	345.3	530.7	2,396.4	108.8	3,035.9	871.7	96.3	271.7	1,239.7	1,227.8	2,467.4
1994-5	175.3	393.2	568.5	2,321.0	91.9	2,981.4	853.0	89.0	344.5	1,286.6	1,188.3	2,474.8
1995-6	163.4	343.2	506.6	2,182.7	67.9	2,757.2	882.9	103.5	153.7	1,140.1	1,241.1	2,381.2
1996-7	74.6	301.4	376.0	2,277.4	92.3	2,745.7	890.7	102.3	307.6	1,300.7	1,001.4	2,302.1
1997-8	154.6	289.0	443.6	2,481.5	94.9	3,020.0	914.1	92.5	250.5	1,257.1	1,040.4	2,297.5
1998-9	224.2	498.3	722.5	2,547.3	103.0	3,372.8	909.7	80.5	394.4	1,384.7	1,042.2	2,426.9
1999-00	277.7	668.2	945.9	2,299.0	94.5	3,339.4	928.9	91.8	279.4	1,300.1	1,089.5	2,389.7
2000-1[1]	226.8	723.0	949.7	2,232.5	89.8	3,272.0	956.4	79.8	298.2	1,334.4	1,061.5	2,395.9
2001-2[2]	197.3	678.9	876.2	1,957.6	95.0	2,928.8	950.0	83.0	225.0	1,258.0	1,000.0	2,258.0

[1] Preliminary. [2] Estimate. [3] Also warehouses and all off-farm storage not otherwise designated, including flour mills. [4] Imports & exports are for wheat, including flour & other products in terms of wheat. [5] Mostly feed use. *Source: Economic Research Service, U.S. Department of Agriculture*

Stocks, Production and Exports of Wheat in the United States, by Class In Millions of Bushels

Year Beginning June 1	Hard Spring Stocks June 1	Hard Spring Production	Hard Spring Exports[3]	Durum[2] Stocks June 1	Durum[2] Production	Durum[2] Exports[3]	Hard Winter Stocks June 1	Hard Winter Production	Hard Winter Exports[3]	Soft Red Winter Stocks June 1	Soft Red Winter Production	Soft Red Winter Exports[3]	White Stocks June 1	White Production	White Exports[3]
1992-3	131	707	438	55	100	47	194	967	464	41	427	210	54	266	195
1993-4	171	512	266	49	71	54	204	1,066	486	43	401	173	64	347	249
1994-5	201	515	292	28	97	40	227	971	422	45	434	212	67	304	222
1995-6	193	475	230	26	102	39	194	825	384	37	456	250	57	325	238
1996-7	106	631	300	25	116	38	154	759	286	35	420	140	55	352	237
1997-8	166	491	240	31	88	57	143	1,098	358	45	472	180	59	332	205
1998-9	220	486	247	26	138	40	307	1,180	453	80	443	105	90	301	198
1999-00	233	448	230	55	99	44	435	1,051	486	136	454	170	87	247	160
2000-1	218	502	230	50	110	50	458	846	403	133	471	176	91	303	203
2001-2[1]	210	476	220	45	84	50	411	767	365	135	400	210	75	232	155

[1] Preliminary. [2] Includes Red Durum. [3] Includes four made from U.S. wheat & shipments to territories. *Source: Economic Research Service, U.S. Department of Agriculture (ERS-USDA)*

Seeded Acreage, Yield and Production of all Wheat in the United States

Year	Seeded Acreage -- 1,000 Acres: Winter	Other Spring	Durum	All	Yield Per Harvested Acre (Bushels): Winter	Other Spring	Durum	All	Production (1,000,000 Bushels): Winter	Other Spring	Durum	All
1992	50,922	18,750	2,547	72,219	38.2	41.8	39.7	39.3	1,609.3	757.6	99.9	2,466.8
1993	51,587	18,340	2,241	72,168	40.2	33.7	33.6	38.2	1,760.1	565.8	70.5	2,396.4
1994	49,197	18,329	2,823	70,349	40.2	31.8	35.6	37.6	1,661.9	562.3	96.7	2,321.0
1995	48,686	17,010	3,436	69,132	37.7	32.2	30.5	35.8	1,544.7	535.7	102.3	2,182.6
1996	51,445	20,030	3,630	75,105	37.1	35.1	32.6	36.3	1,469.6	691.7	116.1	2,277.4
1997	47,985	19,117	3,310	70,412	44.6	29.9	27.6	39.5	1,845.5	548.2	87.8	2,481.5
1998	46,449	15,567	3,805	65,821	46.9	34.9	37.0	43.2	1,880.7	528.5	138.1	2,547.3
1999	43,331	15,348	4,035	62,714	47.8	34.1	27.8	42.7	1,696.6	503.1	99.3	2,299.0
2000	43,393	15,299	3,937	62,629	44.7	38.4	30.7	42.0	1,566.0	556.6	109.8	2,232.5
2001[1]	41,078	15,629	2,910	59,617	43.5	35.2	30.0	40.2	1,361.5	512.6	83.6	1,957.6

[1] Preliminary. *Source: Economic Research Service, U.S. Department of Agriculture (ERS-USDA)*

Production of Winter Wheat in the United States, by State In Thousands of Bushels

Year	Colorado	Idaho	Illinois	Kansas	Missouri	Montana	Nebraska	Ohio	Oklahoma	Oregon	Texas	Washington	Total
1992	70,500	55,250	62,100	363,800	64,800	65,250	55,500	59,095	168,150	42,900	129,200	102,000	1,609,284
1993	94,350	67,150	68,200	388,500	53,200	102,900	73,500	52,520	156,600	61,060	118,400	162,500	1,760,143
1994	76,500	56,880	50,400	433,200	50,400	64,750	71,400	68,440	143,100	55,680	75,400	124,200	1,661,943
1995	102,600	58,520	68,110	286,000	47,970	54,800	86,100	73,810	109,200	57,750	75,600	133,300	1,544,653
1996	70,400	68,800	41,800	255,200	48,750	61,380	73,500	51,870	93,100	58,680	75,400	164,500	1,469,618
1997	86,400	68,800	66,490	501,400	58,320	55,100	70,300	68,670	169,600	53,790	118,900	141,900	1,845,528
1998	99,450	63,140	57,600	494,900	57,500	48,750	82,800	74,240	198,900	52,930	136,500	136,500	1,880,733
1999	103,200	53,960	60,600	432,400	44,160	36,860	81,600	72,100	150,500	29,610	122,400	96,860	1,696,580
2000	68,150	65,700	52,440	347,800	49,400	44,550	59,400	79,920	142,800	45,260	66,000	131,400	1,562,733
2001[1]	69,700	54,670	43,310	344,400	41,040	19,000	66,300	60,300	125,400	32,900	102,000	106,750	1,385,048

[1] Preliminary. *Source: Crop Reporting Board, U.S. Department of Agriculture (CRB-USDA)*

Official Winter Wheat Crop Production Reports in the United States In Thousands of Bushels

Crop Year	May 1	June 1	July 1	August 1	September 1	Current December	Final
1992-3	1,618,017	1,618,017	1,573,901	1,600,931	-----	-----	1,609,284
1993-4	1,807,657	1,824,062	1,821,345	1,788,005	1,788,005	-----	1,760,143
1994-5	1,657,938	1,674,563	1,658,426	1,670,436	1,670,436	-----	1,661,043
1995-6	1,638,211	1,608,396	1,529,950	1,552,230	1,552,230	-----	1,544,653
1996-7	1,363,851	1,369,861	1,484,836	1,494,716	-----	-----	1,477,058
1997-8	1,561,470	1,603,580	1,780,554	1,855,474	-----	-----	1,845,528
1998-9	1,706,784	1,743,294	1,898,719	1,914,359	-----	-----	1,880,733
1999-00	1,614,799	1,611,559	1,673,222	1,688,582	-----	-----	1,696,580
2000-1	1,648,805	1,621,966	1,588,376	1,594,321	-----	-----	1,562,733
2001-2[1]	1,341,381	1,321,126	1,366,192	1,385,048	-----	-----	1,361,479

[1] Preliminary. *Source: Crop Reporting Board, U.S. Department of Agriculture (CRB-USDA)*

Production of All Spring Wheat in the United States, by State In Thousands of Bushels

Year	Durum Wheat: Arizona	California	Mon-tana	North Dakota	South Dakota	Total Durum	Other Spring Wheat: Idaho	Minne-sota	Mon-tana	North Dakota	Oregon	South Dakota	Wash-ington	Total Other
1992	0,740	5,115	1,851	81,700	000	00,006	44,840	137,500	79,050	382,200	4,900	85,000	17,640	757,608
1993	4,500	3,800	3,534	57,970	432	70,476	43,200	69,750	99,900	274,350	3,900	54,540	15,080	565,821
1994	8,554	5,605	5,340	76,375	598	96,747	43,400	70,000	100,500	278,775	2,900	51,480	9,800	562,291
1995	8,514	6,800	7,950	77,760	896	102,280	44,800	70,400	133,000	221,400	5,928	33,600	20,470	535,658
1996	14,760	13,800	7,000	79,380	720	116,090	50,400	105,000	106,600	313,500	6,405	83,250	18,170	691,680
1997	8,010	13,680	7,540	57,860	513	87,783	45,030	75,200	118,900	210,000	6,600	63,000	23,220	548,155
1998	15,120	15,750	12,040	94,400	624	138,119	39,270	78,720	108,000	211,200	4,560	59,200	20,925	528,469
1999	7,275	8,925	9,450	72,000	1,512	99,322	50,560	78,000	108,000	168,000	5,049	59,850	27,280	503,108
2000	8,075	9,700	13,160	78,300	468	109,805	42,750	95,550	77,500	230,400	5,750	60,040	33,480	550,902
2001[1]	7,917	8,262	13,250	56,250	----	86,459	34,000	81,400	74,750	231,000	4,020	64,350	25,200	519,570

[1] Preliminary. *Source: Crop Reporting Board, U.S. Department of Agriculture (CRB-USDA)*

Grindings of Wheat by Mills in the United States In Millions of Bushels (60 Pounds Each)

Year	July	Aug.	Sept.	Oct.	Nov.	Dec.	Jan.	Feb.	Mar.	Apr.	May	June	Total
1992-3	70.0	77.3	71.9	77.9	71.9	65.5	68.1	70.0	76.2	72.0	69.6	67.9	858.2
1993-4	69.2	75.2	74.1	75.8	77.0	76.3	70.0	68.3	81.1	73.0	73.0	70.6	883.8
1994-5	68.9	78.7	76.3	77.9	75.9	71.1	69.0	65.2	76.9	66.6	74.7	71.9	873.1
1995-6	69.8	77.8	74.2	78.4	74.8	70.0	70.1	72.4	72.1	69.4	72.6	67.7	869.1
1996-7	73.6	77.4	75.1	82.7	73.7	71.3	69.6	66.9	70.3	73.2	72.5	72.2	878.6
1997-8	76.4	75.8	78.4	82.7	75.3	74.8	-----	215.5	-----	-----	216.6	-----	895.5
1998-9	-----	224.7	-----	-----	238.6	-----	-----	213.5	-----	-----	228.0	-----	904.9
1999-00	-----	234.0	-----	-----	242.2	-----	-----	225.6	-----	-----	226.8	-----	928.7
2000-1	-----	244.7	-----	-----	247.7	-----	-----	228.1	-----	-----	225.1	-----	945.6
2001-2[1]	-----	234.6	-----	-----		-----	-----		-----	-----		-----	938.4

[1] Preliminary. *Source: Bureau of the Census, U.S. Department of Commerce*

Wheat Stocks in the United States In Millions of Bushels

Year	On Farms: Mar. 1	June 1	Sept. 1	Dec. 1	Off Farms: Mar. 1	June 1	Sept. 1	Dec. 1	Total Stocks: Mar. 1	June 1	Sept. 1	Dec. 1
1992	275.6	144.6	979.4	672.0	611.7	327.2	1,128.2	918.5	887.2	471.9	2,107.6	1,590.5
1993	378.0	183.8	987.0	653.1	670.3	346.8	1,145.6	932.6	1,048.3	530.7	2,132.6	1,585.7
1994	363.2	175.3	859.8	575.6	664.8	393.2	1,209.7	920.6	1,028.0	568.5	2,069.5	1,491.1
1995	335.3	163.4	743.6	477.0	633.8	343.2	1,137.5	861.3	969.1	506.6	1,881.1	1,338.3
1996	220.6	74.6	824.5	584.2	602.9	301.4	899.7	634.7	823.5	376.0	1,724.2	1,218.8
1997	320.8	154.6	794.4	604.0	501.1	289.0	1,282.0	1,015.2	821.8	443.6	2,076.3	1,619.2
1998	399.9	224.2	885.7	680.2	766.6	498.3	1,499.6	1,215.5	1,166.6	722.5	2,385.3	1,895.7
1999	471.2	277.7	888.1	647.4	979.2	668.2	1,557.0	1,236.3	1,450.4	945.9	2,445.0	1,883.7
2000	424.7	226.8	808.4	623.4	991.8	723.0	1,544.3	1,182.7	1,416.5	949.7	2,352.7	1,806.1
2001[1]	384.8	197.3	696.9	517.9	953.6	678.9	1,459.0	1,105.5	1,338.4	876.2	2,155.8	1,623.4

[1] Preliminary. *Source: National Agricultural Statistics Service, U.S. Department of Agriculture (NASS-USDA)*

Wheat Supply and Distribution in Canada, Australia and Argentina In Millions of Metric Tons

Crop Year	Canada (Year Beginning Aug. 1): Supply: Stocks Aug. 1	New Crop	Total Supply	Disappearance: Domestic	Exports[3]	Australia (Year Beginning Oct. 1): Supply: Stocks Oct. 1	New Crop	Total Supply	Disappearance: Domestic	Exports[3]	Argentina (Year Beginning Dec. 1): Supply: Stocks Dec. 1	New Crop	Total Supply	Disappearance: Domestic	Exports[3]
1992-3	10.1	29.9	40.0	8.1	19.7	2.9	16.2	19.1	4.2	9.9	.3	9.8	10.1	4.3	5.9
1993-4	12.2	27.2	39.4	9.3	19.1	5.0	16.5	21.5	4.1	13.7	0	9.7	9.7	4.3	5.0
1994-5	11.1	23.1	34.2	7.8	20.9	3.7	8.9	12.7	3.9	6.4	.4	11.3	11.7	4.3	7.3
1995-6	5.7	25.0	30.7	7.8	16.3	2.4	16.5	18.9	3.7	13.3	.2	8.6	8.8	4.2	4.5
1996-7	6.7	29.8	36.5	8.2	19.5	1.5	22.9	24.4	3.3	19.2	.2	15.9	16.1	5.1	10.2
1997-8	9.0	24.3	33.3	7.3	20.1	2.4	19.2	21.6	5.0	15.3	.8	14.8	15.6	4.5	10.7
1998-9	6.0	24.1	30.1	8.1	14.7	1.3	21.5	22.8	4.5	16.5	.4	12.4	12.8	4.1	8.4
1999-00	7.4	26.9	34.3	7.6	19.2	1.9	24.8	26.7	5.2	17.8	.3	15.7	16.0	4.1	11.6
2000-1[1]	7.7	26.8	34.5	8.2	17.3	3.6	23.8	27.4	6.9	15.9	.3	16.5	16.8	4.5	11.7
2001-2[2]	9.2	21.3	30.5	8.2	16.0	4.6	22.0	26.6	5.5	17.5	.6	16.5	17.1	4.2	12.5

[1] Preliminary. [2] Forecast. [3] Including flour. *Source: Foreign Agricultural Service, U.S. Department of Agriculture (FAS-USDA)*

Quarterly Supply and Disappearance of Wheat in the United States In Millions of Bushels

Crop Year Beginning June 1	Supply: Beginning Stocks	Supply: Production	Supply: Imports[3]	Supply: Total Supply	Disappearance: Domestic Use: Food	Disappearance: Domestic Use: Seed	Disappearance: Domestic Use: Feed & Residual[7]	Disappearance: Domestic Use: Total	Disappearance: Exports[3]	Disappearance: Total Disappearance	Ending Stocks: Gov't Owned[4]	Ending Stocks: Privately Owned[5]	Ending Stocks: Total Stocks
1991-2	868.1	1,980.1	40.7	2,889.0	789.5	97.2	244.5	1,131.2	1,282.3	2,413.5	152.0	323.0	475.0
June-Aug.	868.1	1,980.1	7.8	2,856.1	189.4	1.2	359.1	549.7	251.7	801.4	162.8	1,891.9	2,054.7
Sept.-Nov.	2,054.7	-----	7.3	2,062.0	213.0	62.2	-26.9	248.3	365.9	614.2	160.7	1,287.1	1,447.8
Dec.-Feb.	1,447.8	-----	10.7	1,458.5	192.9	2.4	-.5	194.8	371.7	566.5	156.9	735.1	892.0
Mar.-May	892.0	-----	14.9	906.9	194.2	31.9	-87.3	138.8	293.0	431.8	152.0	323.0	475.0
1992-3	475.0	2,466.8	70.0	3,011.8	834.3	99.1	194.2	1,127.6	1,353.6	2,481.2	150.0	380.7	530.7
June-Aug.	475.0	2,466.8	20.1	2,962.0	212.1	1.4	345.3	558.8	282.6	841.4	151.6	1,969.0	2,120.6
Sept.-Nov.	2,120.6	-----	16.4	2,137.0	218.8	63.4	-81.9	200.3	345.0	545.3	151.1	1,440.6	1,591.7
Dec.-Feb.	1,591.7	-----	17.4	1,609.1	196.7	2.6	5.2	204.5	356.3	560.8	150.4	897.9	1,048.3
Mar.-May	1,048.3	-----	16.1	1,064.4	206.7	31.7	-74.4	164.0	369.7	533.7	150.0	380.7	530.7
1993-4	530.7	2,396.4	108.8	3,035.9	871.7	96.3	271.7	1,239.7	1,227.8	2,467.4	150.3	418.2	568.5
June-Aug.	530.7	2,396.4	14.6	2,941.7	211.3	1.3	295.8	508.4	300.7	809.1	149.9	1,982.7	2,132.6
Sept.-Nov.	2,132.6	-----	30.1	2,162.7	225.3	60.9	-38.5	247.7	329.2	577.0	150.3	1,435.4	1,585.7
Dec.-Feb.	1,585.7	-----	26.9	1,612.6	211.0	2.3	39.0	252.3	332.3	584.6	150.4	877.6	1,028.0
Mar.-May	1,028.0	-----	37.2	1,065.2	224.1	31.8	-24.7	231.2	265.5	496.7	150.3	418.2	568.5
1994-5	568.5	2,321.0	92.0	2,981.4	852.5	89.2	344.9	1,286.6	1,188.3	2,474.9	142.1	364.5	506.6
June-Aug.	568.5	2,321.0	30.7	2,920.2	213.2	1.6	376.3	591.1	259.6	850.7	146.4	1,923.1	2,069.5
Sept.-Nov.	2,069.5	-----	21.4	2,090.9	229.3	61.1	-28.8	261.6	338.2	599.8	142.8	1,348.3	1,491.1
Dec.-Feb.	1,491.1	-----	17.7	1,508.8	201.5	2.2	25.6	229.3	310.4	539.7	142.3	826.8	969.1
Mar.-May	969.1	-----	22.2	991.2	208.5	24.3	-28.2	204.6	280.1	484.7	142.1	364.5	506.6
1995-6	506.6	2,182.6	67.9	2,757.1	882.9	104.1	153.0	1,139.9	1,241.1	2,381.1	118.2	257.8	376.0
June-Aug.	506.6	2,182.6	22.7	2,711.9	215.3	8.0	305.0	528.3	302.5	830.8	141.5	1,739.6	1,881.1
Sept.-Nov.	1,881.1	-----	16.3	1,897.4	232.2	64.9	-98.7	198.3	360.8	559.1	141.2	1,197.1	1,338.3
Dec.-Feb.	1,338.3	-----	11.8	1,350.0	215.8	3.0	13.3	232.1	294.5	526.6	137.5	686.0	823.5
Mar.-May	823.5	-----	17.2	840.7	219.6	28.2	-66.5	181.3	283.4	464.6	118.2	257.8	376.0
1996-7	376.0	2,277.4	92.3	2,745.7	890.7	102.3	307.6	1,300.6	1,001.5	2,302.1	93.0	350.6	443.6
June-Aug.	376.0	2,277.4	14.9	2,668.3	223.7	8.7	377.5	610.0	334.1	944.1	109.5	1,614.7	1,724.2
Sept.-Nov.	1,724.2	-----	20.7	1,744.9	233.8	59.9	-76.0	217.8	308.3	526.1	96.1	1,122.7	1,218.8
Dec.-Feb.	1,218.8	-----	27.1	1,245.9	212.7	1.8	30.3	244.7	179.3	424.1	95.3	726.5	821.8
Mar.-May	821.8	-----	29.7	851.6	220.5	31.8	-24.2	228.1	179.8	407.9	93.0	350.6	443.6
1997-8	443.6	2,481.5	94.9	3,020.0	914.1	92.5	250.5	1,257.1	1,040.4	2,297.5	94.2	628.3	722.5
June-Aug.	443.6	2,481.5	22.7	2,947.8	227.9	3.1	352.2	583.2	288.2	871.4	93.2	1,983.1	2,076.3
Sept.-Nov.	2,076.3	-----	22.8	2,099.1	238.7	58.6	-113.4	183.9	296.0	479.9	93.1	1,526.1	1,619.2
Dec.-Feb.	1,619.2	-----	23.8	1,643.0	219.2	2.1	.3	221.6	254.9	476.4	93.0	1,073.6	1,166.6
Mar.-May	1,166.6	-----	25.7	1,192.2	228.3	28.7	11.4	268.4	201.3	469.8	94.2	628.3	722.5
1998-9	722.5	2,547.3	103.0	3,372.8	909.7	80.5	542.1	1,532.4	1,042.2	2,574.6	127.9	818.0	945.9
June-Aug.	722.5	2,547.3	24.4	3,294.2	225.7	1.0	424.9	651.6	257.3	908.9	99.8	2,285.5	2,385.3
Sept.-Nov.	2,385.3	-----	23.9	2,409.2	240.7	54.9	73.8	369.5	291.8	661.2	126.6	1,769.1	1,895.7
Dec.-Feb.	1,895.7	-----	27.7	1,923.4	213.2	1.4	11.6	226.2	246.8	473.0	124.2	1,326.2	1,450.4
Mar.-May	1,450.4	-----	27.0	1,477.4	230.1	23.2	31.8	285.1	246.3	531.5	127.9	818.0	945.9
1999-00	945.9	2,299.0	94.5	3,339.4	924.7	91.6	283.8	1,300.1	1,089.5	2,389.6	103.9	845.8	949.7
June-Aug.	945.9	2,299.0	30.6	3,275.5	230.5	6.4	270.0	506.9	323.6	830.5	132.2	2,312.8	2,445.0
Sept.-Nov.	2,445.0	-----	19.5	2,464.5	241.1	54.6	-8.0	287.7	291.3	579.0	115.0	1,770.6	1,885.6
Dec.-Feb.	1,885.6	-----	19.4	1,905.1	220.9	2.3	30.7	253.9	235.9	489.8	108.7	1,306.6	1,415.3
Mar.-May	1,415.3	-----	25.0	1,440.3	232.2	28.4	-8.8	251.8	238.8	490.6	103.9	845.8	949.7
2000-1[1]	949.7	2,232.0	90.0	3,272.0	956.0	80.0	298.0	1,334.0	1,061.0	2,395.0	105.0	729.2	876.0
June-Aug.	949.7	2,232.0	20.0	3,203.0	239.0	1.0	324.0	564.0	286.0	850.0	108.9	2,243.8	2,353.0
Sept.-Nov.	2,353.0	-----	25.0	2,378.0	253.0	50.0	-24.0	279.0	293.0	572.0	102.9	1,698.9	1,806.0
Dec.-Feb.	1,805.0	-----	21.0	1,828.0	231.0	3.0	5.0	239.0	250.0	489.0			1,338.0
Mar.-May	1,340.0	-----	23.0	1,631.0	234.0	25.0	-7.0	252.0	233.0	485.0			876.0
2001-2[2]	876.0	1,958.0	95.0	2,929.0	950.0	83.0	225.0	1,258.0	1,000.0	2,258.0			671.0
June-Aug.	876.0	1,958.0	26.0	2,860.0	236.0	3.0	245.0	484.0	219.0	703.0			2,156.0
Sept.-Nov.	2,156.0	----	27.0	2,183.0	250.0	51.0	-26.0	275.0	285.0	560.0			1,623.0

[1] Preliminary. [2] Forecast. [3] Imports & exports include flour and other products expressed in wheat equivalent. [4] Uncommitted, Government only. [5] Includes total loans. [6] Less than 50,000 bushels. [7] Includes alcoholic beverages. *Source: Economic Research Service, U.S. Department of Agriculture (ERS-USDA)*

Wheat Government Loan Program Data in the United States Loan Rates (Cents Per Bushel)

Crop Year Beginning June 1	National Average	Target Rate	Corn Belt (Soft Red Winter)	Central & Southern Plains (Hard Winter)	Northern Plains (Spring & Durum)	Pacific Northwest (White)	Placed Under Loan	% of Production	Acquired by CCC Under Program	Total Stocks	Total CCC Stocks	CCC Loans	Farmer-Owned Reserve	"Free"
	Farm Loan Prices						In Millions of Bushels			Stocks Ending May 31		Outstanding		
1993-4	245	400	251	243	245	269	258	14.7	0.3	569	150	0	6	413
1994-5	258	400	253	257	258	271	231	10.0	0	507	142	0	0	365
1995-6	258	400	254	258	258	276	114	5.2	0	376	118	13	0	245
1996-7	258	NA	253	257	258	271	194	8.1	0	444	93	72	0	279
1997-8	258	NA	253	257	258	271	248		0	723	94	134	0	494
1998-9	258	NA	253	257	258	271			0	946	128	140	0	678
1999-00[1]	258	NA	253	257	258	271			0	950	104	62	0	784
2000-1[2]	258	NA	253	257	258	271			0	876	97	70	0	664

[1] Preliminary. [2] Estimate. [3] The national average loan rate at the farm as a percentage of the parity-priced wheat at the beginning of the marketing year. [4] Beginning with the 1996-7 marketing year, target prices are no longer applicable. NA = Not avaliable. *Source: Agricultural Marketing Service, U.S. Department of Agriculture (AMS-USDA)*

Exports of Wheat (Only)[2] from the United States In Thousands of Bushels

Year	June	July	Aug.	Sept.	Oct.	Nov.	Dec.	Jan.	Feb.	Mar.	Apr.	May	Total
1993-4	85,874	103,836	100,516	104,732	100,618	112,667	121,900	109,389	87,250	96,873	71,575	82,838	1,178,068
1994-5	73,364	66,314	103,941	117,555	101,450	107,549	104,139	93,735	97,478	98,876	85,251	75,006	1,124,658
1995-6	78,355	88,649	119,797	131,424	117,679	105,535	99,175	96,085	91,876	108,800	90,373	78,303	1,206,051
1996-7	73,715	108,437	145,840	125,910	98,302	75,245	50,979	63,431	59,039	55,936	69,821	47,640	974,295
1997-8	65,654	92,465	123,141	119,029	89,331	79,528	80,906	97,090	68,972	63,914	64,623	68,359	1,013,012
1998-9	67,372	86,605	96,664	90,507	109,168	81,913	96,486	73,017	63,794	65,522	86,066	85,057	1,002,171
1999-00	90,594	110,814	107,168	91,438	96,154	89,211	84,460	71,763	64,198	68,836	73,815	87,789	1,036,240
2000-1	88,581	82,739	104,944	113,785	82,716	86,034	94,705	60,743	85,797	71,502	83,157	68,908	1,023,611
2001-2[1]	59,190	64,911	89,582	86,941	94,598								948,533

[1] Preliminary. [2] Grains. *Source: Economic Research Service, U.S. Department of Agriculture (ERS-USDA)*

United States Wheat and Wheat Flour Imports and Exports In Thousands of Bushels

Crop Year Beginning June 1	Imports: Wheat: Suitable for Milling	Wheat: Unfit for Human Consumption	Grain	Flour & Products[2]	Total	Exports: P.L. 480	Foreign Donations Sec. 416	Aid[3]	Total Concessional	CCC Export Credit	Export Exhance-ment Programs	Total U.S. Wheat Exports
			Wheat Equivalent			In Thousands of Metric Tons						
1992-3	56,859	----	56,859	13,142	70,001	2,043	891	NA	4,001	8,538	21,806	36,081
1993-4	91,287	----	91,288	17,529	108,817	2,801	0	NA	3,527	5,874	18,157	31,145
1994-5	70,561	----	70,562	21,386	91,946	1,491	0	NA	1,948	4,202	18,073	32,088
1995-6	47,753	----	47,753	20,180	67,933	1,530	0	NA	1,530	5,662	570	33,708
1996-7	71,727	----	71,727	20,605	92,333	1,009	0	NA	1,155	4,844	0	24,526
1997-8	73,245	----	73,245	21,556	94,923	1,453	0	NA	1,727	5,460	0	25,791
1998-9	79,766	----	79,766	23,238	103,004	556	4,682	NA	5,334	3,621	0	28,806
1999-00[1]	72,408	----	72,408	22,099	94,506	869	2,343	NA	3,333	3,488	0	27,779

[1] Preliminary. [2] Includes macaroni, semolina & similar products. [3] Shipment mostly under the Commodity Import Program, financed with foreign aid funds. NA = Not available. *Source: Economic Research Service, U.S. Department of Agriculture (ERS-USDA)*

Comparative Average Cash Wheat Prices In Dollars Per Bushel

Crop Year Beginning June 1	Received by U.S. Farmers	No. 2 Soft Red Winter, Chicago	No. 1 Hard Red Ordinary Protein, Kansas City	No. 2 Soft Red Winter, St. Louis	Minneapolis: No. 1 Dark Northern Spring 14%	Minneapolis: No. 1 Hard Amber Durum	No. 1 Soft White, Portland, Oregon	No. 2 Western White Pacific Northwest	No. 2 Soft White, Toledo	Export Prices[2] (U.S. $ Per Metric Ton): Australian Standard Wheat	Canada Vancouver No. 1 CWRS 13 1/2%	Argentina F.O.B. B.A.	U.S. Gulf No. 2 Hard Winter	Rotterdam C.I.F. U.S. No. 2 Hard Winter
1994-5	3.45	3.52	3.97	3.62	4.26	5.98	4.16	3.75	3.37	162	199	131	150	210
1995-6	4.55	4.83	5.49	4.82	5.72	7.03	5.27	4.74	4.41	198	204	178	177	221
1996-7	4.30	3.92	4.88	4.10	4.97	5.59	4.54	4.26	3.71	229	230	218	207	235
1997-8	3.38	3.29	3.71	3.43	4.31	5.97	3.81	3.41	3.12	169	173	141	143	191
1998-9	2.65	2.46	3.08	2.40	3.83	4.06	3.02	2.64	2.27	148	158	116	119	180
1999-00	2.48	2.19	2.87	2.39	3.65	4.22	3.02	2.72	1.94	138	150	113	108	163
2000-1	2.62	2.34	3.30	2.39	3.62	4.59	2.99	2.72	2.22	152	149	124	127	164
2001-2[1]	2.80		3.25	2.75	3.65	4.98	3.60	3.24	2.64				125	

[1] Preliminary. [2] Calendar year. NA = Not available. *Source: Economic Research Service, U.S. Department of Agriculture (ERS-USDA)*

Average Price of No. 2 Soft Red Winter (30 Days) Wheat in Chicago In Dollars Per Bushel

Year	June	July	Aug.	Sept.	Oct.	Nov.	Dec.	Jan.	Feb.	Mar.	Apr.	May	Average
1992-3	3.60	3.39	3.09	3.24	3.39	3.60	3.59	3.77	3.67	3.58	3.72	3.19	3.49
1993-4	2.82	3.03	3.12	2.99	3.02	3.29	3.53	3.67	3.48	3.28	3.19	3.15	3.22
1994-5	3.21	3.14	3.37	3.75	3.83	3.63	3.76	3.68	3.55	3.39	3.40	3.56	3.52
1995-6	3.91	4.41	4.28	4.53	4.72	4.85	5.04	4.92	5.10	4.99	5.65	5.57	4.83
1996-7	4.94	4.64	4.49	4.33	3.96	3.57	3.54	3.47	3.29	3.49	3.77	3.57	3.92
1997-8	3.38	3.30	3.52	3.49	3.51	3.44	3.31	3.27	3.26	3.25	2.91	2.87	3.29
1998-9	2.72	2.51	2.39	2.32	2.56	2.58	2.49	2.46	2.28	2.63	2.31	2.24	2.46
1999-00	2.20	1.94	2.09	2.12	1.98	1.96	2.12	2.34	2.38	2.34	2.30	2.45	2.19
2000-1	2.41	2.14	2.08	2.13	2.36	2.42	2.47	2.57	2.49	2.56	2.52	2.51	2.39
2001-2[1]	2.40	2.56	2.57	2.57	2.68	2.75	2.83						2.62

[1] Preliminary. *Source: Economic Research Service, U.S. Department of Agriculture (ERS-USDA)*

Average Price[1] Received by Farmers for Wheat in the United States In Dollars Per Bushel

Year	June	July	Aug.	Sept.	Oct.	Nov.	Dec.	Jan.	Feb.	Mar.	Apr.	May	Average
1992-3	3.43	3.15	3.01	3.20	3.21	3.29	3.31	3.37	3.33	3.30	3.26	3.11	3.24
1993-4	2.84	2.85	2.96	3.10	3.25	3.47	3.63	3.58	3.60	3.70	3.56	3.43	3.26
1994-5	3.21	3.04	3.25	3.57	3.76	3.75	3.74	3.69	3.61	3.52	3.48	3.66	3.45
1995-6	3.84	4.10	4.26	4.53	4.72	4.81	4.88	4.83	4.98	5.07	5.32	5.73	4.55
1996-7	5.25	4.73	4.58	4.37	4.18	4.14	4.06	4.03	3.88	3.93	4.11	4.09	4.28
1997-8	3.52	3.23	3.56	3.67	3.55	3.50	3.45	3.33	3.27	3.32	3.15	3.06	3.38
1998-9	2.77	2.56	2.39	2.41	2.79	2.97	2.87	2.80	2.74	2.65	2.62	2.53	2.68
1999-00	2.50	2.22	2.53	2.58	2.57	2.66	2.52	2.51	2.54	2.59	2.57	2.59	2.53
2000-1	2.50	2.32	2.41	2.44	2.68	2.83	2.87	2.85	2.83	2.87	2.86	2.98	2.70
2001-2[2]	2.74	2.70	2.73	2.85	2.86	2.88	2.89						2.81

[1] Includes an allowance for unredeemed loans and purchases. [2] Preliminary. *Source: Economic Research Service, U.S. Department of Agriculture*

Average Price of No. 1 Hard Red Winter (Ordinary Protein) Wheat in Kansas City   In Dollars Per Bushel

Year	June	July	Aug.	Sept.	Oct.	Nov.	Dec.	Jan.	Feb.	Mar.	Apr.	May	Average
1992-3	3.91	3.52	3.27	3.56	3.60	3.78	3.81	3.97	3.75	3.74	3.59	3.51	3.67
1993-4	3.33	3.38	3.34	3.37	3.52	3.39	4.15	4.00	3.80	3.64	3.63	3.65	3.60
1994-5	3.60	3.48	3.70	4.05	4.31	4.24	4.27	4.00	3.98	3.87	3.80	4.22	3.97
1995-6	4.72	4.98	4.76	5.00	5.28	5.34	5.51	5.40	5.67	5.63	6.60	7.02	5.49
1996-7	6.12	5.34	5.01	4.70	4.76	4.78	4.70	4.61	4.52	4.58	4.78	4.61	4.88
1997-8	4.08	3.57	3.84	3.86	3.88	3.87	3.72	3.61	3.64	3.61	3.39	3.41	3.71
1998-9	3.16	3.02	2.74	2.81	3.30	3.42	3.31	3.27	3.05	3.02	2.94	2.89	3.08
1999-00	2.93	2.68	2.85	2.92	2.80	2.89	2.81	2.90	2.94	2.91	2.84	2.95	2.87
2000-1	3.07	2.97	2.89	3.13	3.41	3.45	3.47	3.54	3.35	3.45	3.41	3.49	3.30
2001-2[1]	3.32	3.20	3.15	3.18	3.28	3.37	3.26						3.25

[1] Preliminary. *Source: Economic Research Service, U.S. Department of Agriculture (ERS-USDA)*

Average Price of No. 1 Dark Northern Spring (14% Protein) Wheat in Minneapolis   In Dollars Per Bushel

Year	June	July	Aug.	Sept.	Oct.	Nov.	Dec.	Jan.	Feb.	Mar.	Apr.	May	Average
1992-3	4.42	4.04	3.65	3.79	3.85	3.94	3.88	4.05	3.87	3.87	3.80	3.71	3.91
1993-4	3.96	4.80	4.88	4.90	5.17	5.50	5.45	5.32	5.29	4.94	4.99	5.05	5.02
1994-5	4.20	4.14	4.00	4.27	4.40	4.41	4.37	4.21	4.09	4.11	4.30	4.61	4.26
1995-6	4.89	5.52	5.06	5.27	5.52	5.63	5.80	5.62	5.82	5.81	6.53	7.14	5.72
1996-7	6.73	6.04	5.29	4.63	4.69	4.64	4.51	4.62	4.45	4.62	4.78	4.58	4.97
1997-8	4.44	4.36	4.49	4.36	4.35	4.42	4.27	4.12	4.15	4.26	4.29	4.24	4.31
1998-9	4.01	3.89	3.58	3.53	4.03	4.15	3.97	3.92	3.78	3.79	3.65	3.61	3.83
1999-00	3.73	3.68	3.58	3.55	3.70	3.78	3.64	3.37	3.59	3.65	3.69	3.80	3.65
2000-1	3.78	3.50	3.29	3.17	3.69	3.77	3.52	3.79	3.68	3.63	3.73	3.88	3.62
2001-2[1]	3.81	3.72	3.54	3.52	3.71	3.69	3.59						3.65

[1] Preliminary. *Source: Economic Research Service, U.S. Department of Agriculture (ERS-USDA)*

Average Farm Prices of Winter Wheat in the United States   In Dollars Per Bushel

Year	June	July	Aug.	Sept.	Oct.	Nov.	Dec.	Jan.	Feb.	Mar.	Apr.	May	Average
1994-5	3.09	2.99	3.23	3.57	3.79	3.76	3.75	3.67	3.61	3.47	3.45	3.65	3.50
1995-6	3.77	4.05	4.22	4.47	4.70	4.78	4.88	4.80	5.01	5.06	5.39	5.81	4.75
1996-7	5.14	4.67	4.52	4.28	4.07	4.05	4.04	4.02	3.90	3.98	4.14	4.14	4.25
1997-8	3.42	3.16	3.39	3.47	3.42	3.31	3.25	3.16	3.16	3.15	2.94	2.90	3.23
1998-9	2.68	2.47	2.25	2.29	2.66	2.76	2.68	2.70	2.55	2.53	2.48	2.34	2.53
1999-00	2.32	2.12	2.35	2.46	2.47	2.42	2.27	2.32	2.37	2.37	2.32	2.44	2.35
2000-1	2.43	2.23	2.31	2.37	2.63	2.70	2.76	2.77	2.74	2.85	2.77	2.94	2.63
2001-2[1]	2.68	2.67	2.71	2.81	2.81	2.81	2.84						2.76

[1] Preliminary. *Source: National Agricultural Statistics Service, U.S. Department of Agriculture (NASS-USDA)*

Average Farm Prices of Durum Wheat in the United States   In Dollars Per Bushel

Year	June	July	Aug.	Sept.	Oct.	Nov.	Dec.	Jan.	Feb.	Mar.	Apr.	May	Average
1994-5	4.59	4.32	4.30	4.51	4.89	4.88	4.67	4.61	4.68	4.61	4.48	4.82	4.61
1995-6	5.20	5.29	5.33	5.87	5.80	5.78	5.75	5.66	5.72	5.73	5.63	5.62	5.62
1996-7	5.58	5.13	5.03	4.69	4.78	4.56	4.59	4.47	4.31	4.32	4.40	4.50	4.70
1997-8	4.21	4.61	5.23	5.35	5.09	5.25	5.17	5.02	4.71	4.68	4.45	4.29	4.84
1998-9	3.98	3.39	3.23	3.03	3.04	3.08	3.05	3.20	2.84	2.82	2.80	2.84	3.11
1999-00	2.93	2.89	2.76	2.29	2.30	2.64	2.96	2.90	2.88	2.63	2.89	3.02	2.76
2000-1	2.71	2.90	2.33	2.32	2.42	2.97	3.03	2.94	2.60	2.40	2.52	2.53	2.64
2001-2[1]	3.37	2.74	2.38	3.02	2.89	3.08	3.13						2.94

[1] Preliminary. *Source: National Agricultural Statistics Service, U.S. Department of Agriculture (NASS-USDA)*

Average Farm Prices of Other Spring Wheat in the United States   In Dollars Per Bushel

Year	June	July	Aug.	Sept.	Oct.	Nov.	Dec.	Jan.	Feb.	Mar.	Apr.	May	Average
1994-5	3.51	3.28	3.19	3.38	3.52	3.51	3.56	3.50	3.40	3.38	3.34	3.53	3.43
1995-6	3.78	4.26	4.19	4.27	4.45	4.61	4.72	4.66	4.81	4.88	5.21	5.67	4.63
1996-7	5.48	5.30	4.63	4.41	4.23	4.11	4.01	3.95	3.80	3.83	4.04	3.94	4.31
1997-8	3.74	3.66	3.75	3.64	3.49	3.55	3.51	3.45	3.34	3.42	3.41	3.31	3.52
1998-9	3.22	3.08	2.69	2.62	3.04	3.23	3.19	3.12	3.09	3.00	2.95	2.92	3.01
1999-00	3.01	2.93	2.86	2.86	2.79	2.94	2.87	2.82	2.82	2.85	2.89	2.92	2.88
2000-1	2.90	2.74	2.59	2.59	2.80	2.97	2.98	2.96	2.99	2.99	3.05	3.13	2.89
2001-2[1]	3.03	2.78	2.84	2.87	2.97	2.91	2.91						2.90

[1] Preliminary. *Source: National Agricultural Statistics Service, U.S. Department of Agriculture (NASS-USDA)*

WHEAT

Average Open Interest of Wheat Futures in Chicago In Contracts

Year	Jan.	Feb.	Mar.	Apr.	May	June	July	Aug.	Sept.	Oct.	Nov.	Dec.
1992	61,484	70,152	58,957	53,706	50,978	50,340	60,116	62,071	50,093	54,564	57,693	49,263
1993	50,329	47,858	44,885	48,354	51,353	55,829	58,705	64,335	58,603	61,496	62,877	50,523
1994	53,912	48,013	45,110	47,430	44,552	54,622	57,151	65,388	73,200	78,419	70,815	67,150
1995	66,715	67,768	55,973	55,612	67,875	90,208	101,351	90,800	91,505	103,987	102,475	99,422
1996	102,718	104,807	91,378	98,260	93,378	81,211	69,222	66,128	65,561	65,639	60,810	58,533
1997	63,388	71,304	76,747	85,516	84,721	83,675	92,815	105,320	104,587	108,480	101,089	90,386
1998	96,870	99,103	97,585	114,193	115,199	116,008	121,794	127,240	125,747	131,322	130,186	116,249
1999	119,096	131,961	118,503	117,905	111,541	117,075	120,365	129,748	128,403	135,884	140,798	124,063
2000	127,419	135,316	123,980	128,462	130,938	133,527	139,194	144,953	141,803	150,592	153,287	134,997
2001	145,802	146,927	137,377	138,876	134,051	151,951	142,399	143,574	136,514	126,772	113,456	104,975

Source: Chicago Board of Trade (CBT)

Volume of Trading of Wheat Futures in Chicago In Contracts

Year	Jan.	Feb.	Mar.	Apr.	May	June	July	Aug.	Sept.	Oct.	Nov.	Dec.	Total
1992	366,736	460,354	318,810	236,063	290,148	303,044	304,217	283,379	250,003	220,502	257,017	188,541	3,498,814
1993	246,125	237,936	277,632	217,898	173,607	268,206	366,414	266,893	202,308	256,329	310,464	195,817	3,019,629
1994	288,321	211,703	187,617	244,544	300,324	370,135	272,492	330,758	343,548	398,041	354,975	318,173	3,620,631
1995	353,603	302,950	316,330	279,099	345,455	598,762	507,876	527,716	436,145	472,794	454,352	359,985	4,955,067
1996	628,340	510,138	455,981	660,722	531,979	512,883	452,690	345,626	305,448	362,047	359,005	261,108	5,385,967
1997	312,680	373,411	368,547	567,099	422,935	469,158	470,992	493,225	401,277	405,978	432,621	340,722	5,058,645
1998	363,511	473,114	452,186	514,557	432,167	601,149	401,508	490,242	475,766	543,680	539,488	394,201	5,681,569
1999	426,524	597,448	710,375	559,211	444,696	674,580	523,516	665,897	536,014	437,689	613,633	380,442	6,570,025
2000	467,050	691,068	522,394	490,694	627,722	759,371	461,068	572,879	388,237	466,328	596,581	364,139	6,407,531
2001	551,756	595,312	536,141	579,992	537,836	720,350	695,339	600,341	385,930	629,479	614,734	354,331	6,801,541

Source: Chicago Board of Trade (CBT)

Commercial Stocks of Domestic Wheat[1] in the United States, on First of Month — In Millions of Bushels

Year	July	Aug.	Sept.	Oct.	Nov.	Dec.	Jan.	Feb.	Mar.	Apr.	May	June
1992-3	269.6	290.5	202.5	228.2	231.9	202.7	185.5	169.5	153.3	132.6	112.9	87.0
1993-4	102.9	145.1	171.8	194.9	199.3	174.9	169.5	168.3	162.2	143.8	127.3	111.3
1994-5	145.7	203.9	243.0	269.7	268.6	238.0	199.5	181.0	162.5	150.2	108.7	91.8
1995-6	92.3	161.7	201.1	234.3	228.3	200.2	178.7	170.8	156.6	137.7	107.6	87.2
1996-7	86.3	112.9	128.0	145.3	117.2	94.9	89.0	80.4	77.0	75.6	68.1	64.6
1997-8	80.1	186.3	235.2	268.1	258.1	231.4	196.8	178.1	170.6	158.0	146.4	145.7
1998-9	209.8	265.0	314.9	325.6	307.3	291.3	272.9	265.7	256.8	251.5	236.7	218.3
1999-00	248.6	294.9	335.8	354.0	334.6	301.5	277.4	273.7	267.8	266.3	247.6	240.3
2000-1	285.5	310.3	335.3	335.5	306.2	286.6	263.7	251.7	243.2	243.7	224.5	221.0
2001-2	271.0	296.6	318.7	321.9	291.9	251.8	224.5	251.7	243.2			

[1] Domestic wheat in storage in public and private elevators in 39 markets and wheat afloat in vessels or barges at lake and seaboard ports, the first Saturday of the month. *Source: Livestock Division, U.S. Department of Agriculture (LD-USDA)*

Stocks of Wheat Flour Held by Mills in the United States — In Thousands of Sacks -- 100 Pounds

Year	Jan. 1	April 1	July 1	Oct. 1	Year	Jan. 1	April 1	July 1	Oct. 1
1990	5,207	5,072	5,818	7,980	1996	6,869	6,927	6,400	6,350
1991	8,051	5,474	8,115	6,336	1997	6,671	6,040	5,820	6,330
1992	5,660	5,210	5,841	5,864	1998	6,343	6,245	6,210	7,345
1993	5,487	4,863	6,197	5,882	1999	7,544	5,920	5,697	4,265
1994	5,611	5,904	5,834	6,020	2000	5,099	5,217	5,062	5,244
1995	7,060	6,496	6,312	6,582	2001[1]	5,241	5,250	4,892	4,756

[1] Preliminary. *Source: Bureau of the Census, U.S. Department of Commerce*

Average Producer Price Index of Wheat Flour (Spring) — June 1983 = 100

Year	Jan.	Feb.	Mar.	Apr.	May	June	July	Aug.	Sept.	Oct.	Nov.	Dec.	Average
1992	109.7	116.4	111.5	110.3	109.2	111.0	104.9	99.6	104.1	104.4	104.7	103.5	107.4
1993	107.5	108.1	107.2	108.4	105.2	104.7	103.7	107.2	102.1	107.3	108.4	112.5	106.9
1994	111.8	110.5	108.9	107.9	109.4	106.4	100.8	101.2	109.1	112.0	110.9	111.4	108.4
1995	110.7	108.5	107.9	109.8	113.5	118.6	127.4	126.7	129.5	132.6	132.3	133.5	120.9
1996	130.4	138.0	136.6	137.6	160.1	146.8	138.0	127.0	121.5	125.7	121.7	121.4	133.7
1997	119.4	119.3	116.6	121.8	120.8	117.4	112.1	113.5	115.1	112.6	111.5	111.1	115.9
1998	106.8	108.1	111.5	110.1	109.9	106.4	105.5	101.8	100.9	106.6	107.8	104.8	106.7
1999	104.8	102.7	105.0	100.5	102.2	102.7	100.7	103.5	101.4	99.8	101.4	96.8	101.8
2000	99.9	99.9	100.2	99.4	100.1	101.7	100.2	100.4	101.2	105.2	103.6	104.4	101.4
2001[2]	104.7	105.1	106.2	105.7	106.9	108.2	107.9	106.8	107.0	108.4	108.6	107.1	106.9

[1] Standard patent. [2] Preliminary. *Source: Bureau of Labor Statistics, U.S. Department of Commerce (BLS) (0212-0301)*

World Wheat Flour Production (Monthly Average) — In Thousands of Metric Tons

Year	Australia	France	Germany	Hungary	India	Japan	Kazakhstan	Rep. of Korea	Mexico	Poland	Russia	Turkey	United Kingdom
1992	113.9	465.2	327.0	106.9	400.0	389.0	161.0	129.4	223.3	167.1	----	112.2	320.0
1993	116.3	480.6	336.4	75.0	399.4	399.3	155.3	129.5	214.0	113.4	449.5	122.1	331.0
1994	116.9	470.8	378.8	62.9	400.0	387.2	157.0	132.6	219.8	150.5	348.0	104.9	353.0
1995	112.6	473.1	382.3	84.0	400.0	389.3	131.0	139.9	210.7	156.9	274.6	119.7	358.0
1996	123.8	450.0	394.2	75.1	400.0	389.6	132.7	141.2	215.9	164.1	309.7	132.1	371.0
1997	129.7	----	404.8	77.7	412.5	388.1	127.3	145.9	216.0	175.3	361.9	159.1	369.0
1998	146.8	----	407.5	70.1	430.6	382.0	128.8	143.5	213.2	172.1	347.8	152.6	377.0
1999	----	----	423.6	69.1	182.2	386.7	105.2	152.8	204.8	125.0	360.0	156.6	----
2000[1]	----	----	405.5	73.9	202.5	386.0	79.5	155.9	206.0	125.4	405.0	162.0	381.0
2001[2]	----	----	395.1	76.7	200.8	381.2	73.7	154.7	212.8	125.3	402.5	143.3	373.7

[1] Preliminary. [2] Estimate. NA = Not available. *Source: United Nations (UN)*

Production of Wheat Flour in the United States In Millions of Sacks (100 Pounds Each)

Year	July	Aug.	Sept.	Oct.	Nov.	Dec.	Jan.	Feb.	Mar.	Apr.	May	June	Total
1993-4	30.7	33.3	32.9	33.5	34.0	33.8	30.9	30.2	35.9	32.3	32.2	31.1	390.8
1994-5	30.5	34.9	34.2	35.0	33.7	31.7	30.9	29.4	34.5	29.9	33.5	32.3	390.4
1995-6	31.0	34.5	33.0	35.1	33.4	31.2	31.6	32.3	32.2	31.2	33.2	30.6	389.3
1996-7	33.9	35.6	34.6	37.5	33.1	32.0	31.3	30.0	31.8	33.1	32.6	32.5	397.9
1997-8	34.0	34.3	35.1	37.2	33.8	33.5	-----	96.0	-----	-----	96.2	-----	400.1
1998-9	-----	100.2	-----	-----	106.5	-----	-----	96.1	-----	-----	103.5	-----	406.3
1999-00	-----	104.2	-----	-----	108.2	-----	-----	101.1	-----	-----	101.6	-----	415.2
2000-1	-----	108.8	-----	-----	109.7	-----	-----	101.0	-----	-----	98.7	-----	418.2
2001-2[1]	-----	103.9	-----	-----		-----	-----		-----	-----		-----	415.5

[1] Preliminary. *Source: Bureau of the Census, U.S. Department of Commerce*

United States Wheat Flour Exports (Grain Equivalent[2]) In Thousands of Bushels

Year	June	July	Aug.	Sept.	Oct.	Nov.	Dec.	Jan.	Feb.	Mar.	Apr.	May	Total
1993-4	4,408	3,793	1,811	3,642	3,840	3,416	3,170	5,838	4,390	6,099	4,198	3,368	47,973
1994-5	2,922	6,824	5,636	3,407	3,105	4,721	4,734	2,805	7,085	7,617	6,945	6,005	61,807
1995-6	2,822	5,018	7,520	2,249	2,080	1,221	3,458	808	2,537	1,230	2,415	1,831	33,189
1996-7	2,006	2,008	1,669	3,133	2,496	2,748	2,240	1,347	1,920	2,521	1,259	2,125	25,472
1997-8	1,803	2,900	1,621	3,101	2,524	1,634	3,118	1,426	2,725	1,309	1,269	963	25,393
1998-9	1,971	1,740	2,027	2,914	3,812	2,354	6,838	2,551	3,341	4,126	3,105	1,948	36,728
1999-00	4,160	3,638	2,586	6,503	4,576	2,332	3,023	2,924	6,108	2,615	3,193	1,286	42,944
2000-1	3,620	3,805	1,623	3,174	4,165	2,332	2,741	2,236	2,365	2,200	3,868	2,163	34,292
2001-2[1]	1,412	661	1,990	1,005	3,226								19,906

[1] Preliminary. [2] Includes meal, groats and durum. *Source: Economic Research Service, U.S. Department of Agriculture (ERS-USDA)*

Supply and Distribution of Wheat Flour in the United States

Year	Wheat Ground	Millfeed Production	Flour Production[2]	Flour & Product Imports	Total Supply	Exports: Flour	Exports: Products	Domestic Disappear-ance	Total Population July 1	Per Capita Disappear-ance
	- 1,000 Bu. -	- 1,000 Tons -	In 1,000 Cwt.						- Millions -	- Pounds -
1992	833,339	6,707	370,829	4,749	375,578	20,194	787	354,680	255.4	138.9
1993	871,408	6,963	387,419	5,786	393,205	22,731	687	369,976	258.1	143.4
1994	884,707	7,186	392,519	8,425	400,944	23,801	811	376,594	260.6	144.5
1995	869,296	7,144	388,689	8,918	397,607	23,615	857	373,135	263.0	141.9
1996	878,070	7,042	397,776	8,574	406,350	10,651	881	394,818	265.5	148.7
1997	885,843	6,886	404,143	8,684	412,827	11,038	1,167	400,622	268.0	149.5
1998	902,532	7,301	403,880	9,745	413,625	12,551	1,215	399,859	270.5	145.9
1999	917,797	7,040	411,968	9,305	416,354	17,568	1,610	393,377	272.9	144.0
2000[1]	935,747	7,248	415,093	9,663	424,756	16,053	1,685	407,018	275.4	147.8

[1] Preliminary. [2] Commercial production of wheat flour, whole wheat, industrial and durum flour and farina reported by Bureau of Census.
Source: Economic Research Service, U.S. Department of Agriculture (ERS-USDA)

Wheat and Flour -- Price Relationships at Milling Centers in the United States In Dollars

	At Kansas City					At Minneapolis				
		Wholesale Price of					Wholesale Price of			
Crop Year (June-May)	Cost of Wheat to Produce 100 lb. Flour[1]	Bakery Flour 100 lb. Flour[2]	By-Products Obtained 100 lb. Flour[3]	Total Products: Actual	Total Products: Over Cost of Wheat	Cost of Wheat to Produce 100 lb. Flour[1]	Bakery Flour 100 lb. Flour[2]	By-Products Obtained 100 lb. Flour[3]	Total Products: Actual	Total Products: Over Cost of Wheat
1992-3	8.53	9.65	1.28	10.93	2.40	8.91	10.12	1.15	11.27	2.37
1993-4	10.03	10.34	1.46	11.79	1.77	11.45	12.50	1.28	13.77	2.33
1994-5	9.25	10.50	1.21	11.71	2.46	9.71	11.01	1.04	12.05	2.34
1995-6	12.97	13.35	1.93	15.28	2.31	13.04	13.03	1.68	14.71	1.67
1996-7	11.22	11.89	1.92	13.81	2.60	11.32	11.68	1.87	13.54	2.22
1997-8	9.03	9.99	1.43	11.41	2.38	9.83	10.62	1.34	11.96	2.12
1998-9	7.91	9.06	1.08	10.15	2.23	8.76	9.80	1.02	10.82	2.06
1999-00	7.74	8.86	.98	9.84	2.10	8.29	9.30	.95	10.24	1.95
2000-1	7.90	9.21	1.11	10.32	2.42	8.14	9.15	1.00	10.15	2.01
June-Aug.	7.58	9.13	.79	9.93	2.35	8.03	9.10	.84	9.94	1.90
Sept.-Nov.	7.99	9.35	1.04	10.39	2.40	8.03	9.14	.95	10.09	2.07
Dec.-Feb.	8.13	9.15	1.49	10.64	2.51	8.35	9.20	1.21	10.41	2.06

[1] Based on 73% extraction rate, cost of 2.28 bushels: At Kansas City, No. 1 hard winter 13% protein; and at Minneapolis, No. 1 dark northern spring, 14% protein. [2] quoted as mid-month bakers' standard patent at Kansas City and spring standard patent at Minneapolis, bulk basis. [3] Assumed 50-50 millfeed distribution between bran and shorts or middlings, bulk basis. *Source: Agricultural Marketing Service, U.S. Department of Agriculture (AMS-USDA)*

Wool

U.S. wool production, along with rest of the world, has been in a protracted slide for years and the downtrend is likely to persist owing to the well-entrenched contraction in world sheep numbers. The U.S. sheep inventory since the mid-1980's has fallen from about 35 million head to less than 14 million by 2000. Globally, the world sheep inventory now totals about 850 million head vs. more than 1 billion head a decade or so ago. Notwithstanding the reduction in new supply, worldwide demand for wool has also fallen owing to changing consumer attitudes, which favor casual dress codes that use more cotton and manmade fibers than wool. In the U.S. most of the wool usage is allocated to apparel and a much smaller percentage to carpet production.

China now has at least one-quarter of the world's sheep inventory, believed to be more than 200 million head, well over the early 1990's total. In contrast, New Zealand's sheep herd is the lowest since the 1960's; and in Australia, the inventory has fallen by at least a third from the more than 175 million head in the early 1990's. Percentage wise, the largest decline has been in Russia with the sheep inventory down nearly 75% since the early 1990's.

U.S. shorn wool production (tops and noils) is insignificant; about 46.5 million pounds in 2000 vs. 46.6 million in 1999. In the early 1980's annual production averaged about 105 million pounds. The totals gleaned from 6.14 million sheep in 2000 vs. 6.16 million in 1999. The major wool producing state is Texas with at least a fifth of the total followed by California. The value of the calendar year 2000 U.S. wool crop was $15.4 million vs. $17.9 million in 1999 with an average price per pound of 33 cents vs. 38 cents, respectively.

In line with the world's declining wool production and use, foreign trade has also fallen. Australia remains the largest exporter followed by New Zealand, the two nations accounting for the bulk of world exports. Importing nations are numerous; but China leads followed by Japan, the U.K., Italy and France. Australian wool accounts for most of U.S. imports. The U.S. also imports a relatively small quantity of wool tops. However, the U.S. also exports small amounts of raw wool and a moderately larger amount of wool tops. Global wool prices are a function of origin and grade; South African wool tends to be much higher than Australian prices while the latter is generally moderately higher than New Zealand's and U.S. prices.

Futures Markets

Wool futures are traded on the Sydney Futures Exchange (SFE). Wool yarn futures are traded on the Chubu Commodity Exchange (CCE), the Osaka Mercantile Exchange (OME) and the Tokyo Commodity Exchange (TOCOM).

World Production of Wool In Metric Tons--Degreased

Year	Argentina	Australia	China	Kazak-hstan	New Zealand	Pakistan	Romania	Russia	South Africa	United Kingdom	United States	Uruguay	Total
1991	75,400	699,000	123,000	62,640	227,000	28,900	19,196	122,700	51,000	51,055	20,830	56,500	1,953,339
1992	74,200	574,000	121,500	63,000	221,000	29,600	16,800	107,400	48,500	50,876	19,980	50,700	1,780,613
1993	58,000	557,000	122,000	56,800	193,000	30,300	15,600	95,000	45,000	48,329	18,520	49,410	1,688,806
1994	48,000	570,000	130,000	55,000	214,000	31,000	17,000	73,000	40,000	47,000	16,000	50,000	1,693,000
1995	44,000	475,000	141,000	35,000	214,000	32,000	16,000	56,000	35,000	48,000	15,000	46,000	1,512,000
1996	39,000	457,000	152,000	25,000	199,000	32,000	16,000	46,000	37,000	46,000	13,000	43,000	1,459,000
1997	36,000	472,000	130,000	21,000	228,000	34,000	13,000	36,000	34,000	46,000	13,000	46,000	1,440,000
1998[1]	36,000	452,000	141,000	15,000	219,000	34,000	12,000	29,000	32,000	48,000	12,000	42,000	1,404,000
1999[2]	36,000	460,000	143,000	15,000	191,000	34,000	13,000	29,000	34,000	48,000	12,000	42,000	1,394,000

[1] Preliminary. [2] Estimate. *Source: Food and Agriculture Organization of the United Nations (FAO-UN)*

Production of Wool Goods[1] in the United States In Millions of Yards

Year	First Quarter	Second Quarter	Third Quarter	Fourth Quarter	Total	Year	First Quarter	Second Quarter	Third Quarter	Fourth Quarter	Total
1992	45.7	47.2	43.9	39.5	176.3	1997	42.7	49.7	42.3	40.5	175.2
1993	48.4	48.9	43.9	42.8	184.0	1998	38.8	37.5	29.6	26.3	132.2
1994	49.1	51.1	39.4	39.0	178.6	1999	25.0	20.9	17.4	14.6	77.9
1995	46.8	45.9	35.2	34.3	162.2	2000	17.9	18.0	13.4	17.4	66.7
1996	44.8	43.6	30.8	32.8	152.0	2001[2]	20.9	12.6	11.2		59.6

[1] Woolen and worsted woven goods, except woven felts. [2] Preliminary. *Source: Bureau of the Census, U.S. Department of Commerce*

Consumption of Apparel Wool in the United States In Millions of Pounds--Clean Basis

Year	First Quarter	Second Quarter	Third Quarter	Fourth Quarter	Total	Year	First Quarter	Second Quarter	Third Quarter	Fourth Quarter	Total
1992	36.4	35.1	33.6	31.1	136.1	1997	33.1	33.8	30.6	32.8	130.4
1993	35.5	35.9	35.5	34.4	141.4	1998	29.3	29.6	21.9	17.5	98.4
1994	36.3	35.6	32.7	34.0	138.6	1999	17.3	16.8	15.8	13.6	63.5
1995	36.3	35.5	29.4	28.1	129.3	2000	17.1	15.7	14.1	13.9	60.8
1996	39.1	36.2	27.4	26.8	129.5	2001[2]	16.6	13.0	11.2		54.4

[1] Woolen and worsted woven goods, except woven felts. [2] Preliminary. *Source: Bureau of the Census, U.S. Department of Commerce*

WOOL

Salient Statistics of Wool in the United States

								Raw Wool (Clean Content)							
Year	Sheep & Lambs Shorn[4]	Weight Per Fleece	Shorn Wool Production	Price Per Lb.	Value of Production	Support	Payment Rate	Total Wool Production	Domestic Production	Exports Domestic Wool	Dutiable Imports for Consumption[3] 48's & Finer	Total New Supply[2]	Duty Free Imports (Not Finer than 46's)	Mill Consumption -- Apparel	Mill Consumption -- Carpet
	-1,000's-	-In Lbs.-	1,000 Lbs.	Lb.	1,000 $	--Cents Per Lb.--		In Thousands of Pounds							
1992	10,521	7.88	82,943	74.0	60,162	197	123.0	82,943	43,794	3,413	65,457	129,640	23,802	136,143	14,695
1993	9,976	7.77	77,535	51.0	39,077	204	153.0	77,535	40,938	2,529	76,001	138,286	21,876	141,380	15,431
1994	8,877	7.73	68,577	78.0	52,377	209	131.0	68,577	36,209	2,863	64,889	122,880	24,645	138,563	14,739
1995	8,138	7.80	63,513	104.0	64,277	212	108.0	63,513	33,535	6,042	63,781	116,313	25,039	129,299	12,667
1996	7,279	7.79	56,669	70.0	39,659	----	----	56,159	29,921	5,715	54,063	99,575	20,971	129,525	12,311
1997	7,032	7.70	53,889	84.0	45,172	----	----	53,578	28,630	4,732	51,484	100,344	24,295	130,386	13,576
1998	6,428	7.70	49,255	60.0	29,415	----	----	49,239	30,321	1,700	45,760	102,528	23,121	98,373	16,331
1999	6,150	7.60	46,549	38.0	17,852	----	----		24,800	3,700	21,221		20,081	63,535	13,950
2000[1]	6,100	7.60	46,400	42.0		----	----		24,500	6,600	23,884		20,043	60,294	14,514

[1] Preliminary. [2] Production minus exports plus imports; stocks not taken into consideration. [3] Apparel wool includes all dutiable wool; carpet wool includes all duty-free wool. [4] Includes sheep shorn at commercial feeding yards. *Source: Economic Research Service, U.S. Department of Agriculture (ERS-USDA)*

Shorn Wool Prices

		Australian Offering Price, Clean[2]						Graded Territory Shorn Wool, Clean Basis[4]				
Year	U.S. Farm Price Shorn Wool Greasy Basis[1]	Grade 70's Type 61	Grade 64's Type 63	Grade 64/70's Type 62	Grade 60/62's Type 64A	Grade 58's-56's 433-34	Market Indicator[3]	64's Staple 2 3/4" & up	60's Staple 3" & up	58's Staple 3 1/4" & up	56's Staple 3 1/4" & up	54's Staple 3 1/2" & up
	-Cents/Lb.-	In Dollars Per Pound					-Cents/Kg.-	In Dollars Per Pound				
1992	74.0	2.58	2.32	2.17	2.10	1.94	557	2.04	1.61	1.47	1.35	1.23
1993	51.0	2.08	1.70	1.84	1.49	1.44	488	1.37	1.13	1.05	.99	.94
1994	78.0	3.72	2.43	3.01	1.96	1.86	547	2.12	1.50	1.26	1.27	1.21
1995	104.0	3.22	2.81	3.01	2.49	2.33	888	2.49	1.93	1.77	1.63	1.53
1996	70.0	2.81	2.34	2.54	1.96	1.84	619	1.93	1.54	1.43	1.31	1.22
1997	84.0	3.56	2.57	2.90	2.06	1.95	615	2.38	1.78	1.64	1.43	1.14
1998	60.0	2.70	1.94	2.02	1.74	1.60	663	1.62	1.31	1.21	1.06	.94
1999	38.0	2.63	1.58	1.76	1.46	1.33	527	1.10	.85	.74	.66	.59
2000	42.0	2.80	1.60	1.79	1.47	1.30	NA	1.08	.75	.65	.57	.53

[1] Annual weighted average. [2] F.O.B. Australian Wool Corporation South Carolina warehouse in bond. [3] Index of prices of all wool sold in Australia for the crop year July-June. [4] Wool principally produced in Texas and the Rocky Mountain States. *Source: Economic Research Service, U.S. Department of Agriculture (ERS-USDA)*

Average Wool Prices[1] --Australian-- 64's, Type 62, Duty Paid--U.S. Mills In Cents Per Pound

Year	Jan.	Feb.	Mar.	Apr.	May	June	July	Aug.	Sept.	Oct.	Nov.	Dec.	Average
1992	259	270	277	264	268	246	NA	224	210	192	195	193	236
1993	186	176	170	158	179	169	167	154	153	171	175	176	170
1994	204	216	205	223	249	258	243	248	259	256	273	297	244
1995	281	297	302	302	307	308	292	284	266	236	242	237	280
1996	240	237	238	234	242	245	236	234	228	220	225	232	234
1997	234	261	254	261	279	287	NA	270	262	250	245	240	258
1998	218	225	247	205	214	179	NA	144	144	140	156	147	184
1999	158	150	157	156	150	149	152	148	139	139	143	137	148
2000	154	146	144	156	156	154	155	151	149	146	140	148	150
2001	160	168	164	158	164	166	167	172	169	159	166		165

[1] Raw, clean basis. NA = Not available. *Source: Economic Research Service, U.S. Department of Agriculture (ERS-USDA)*

Average Wool Prices --Domestic[1]-- Graded Territory, 64's, Staple 2 3/4 & Up--U.S. Mills In Cents Per Pound

Year	Jan.	Feb.	Mar.	Apr.	May	June	July	Aug.	Sept.	Oct.	Nov.	Dec.	Average
1992	163	203	195	196	199	218	210	188	210	193	168	168	193
1993	158	148	132	127	135	140	138	140	130	129	133	133	137
1994	140	150	170	201	226	230	230	235	250	238	238	252	213
1995	245	252	265	288	295	285	261	250	235	185	208	192	247
1996	188	192	197	197	195	192	192	192	192	192	190	190	192
1997	190	190	208	228	248	255	255	255	255	255	260	260	238
1998	236	195	195	188	177	170	170	150	115	115	115	115	162
1999	115	115	115	110	117	122	116	110	105	100	110	95	111
2000	95	95	101	110	125	125	125	120	107	105	105	97	109
2001	95	100	108	129	137	125	127	122	126	130	122		120

[1] Raw, shorn, clean basis. *Source: Economic Research Service, U.S. Department of Agriculture (ERS-USDA)*

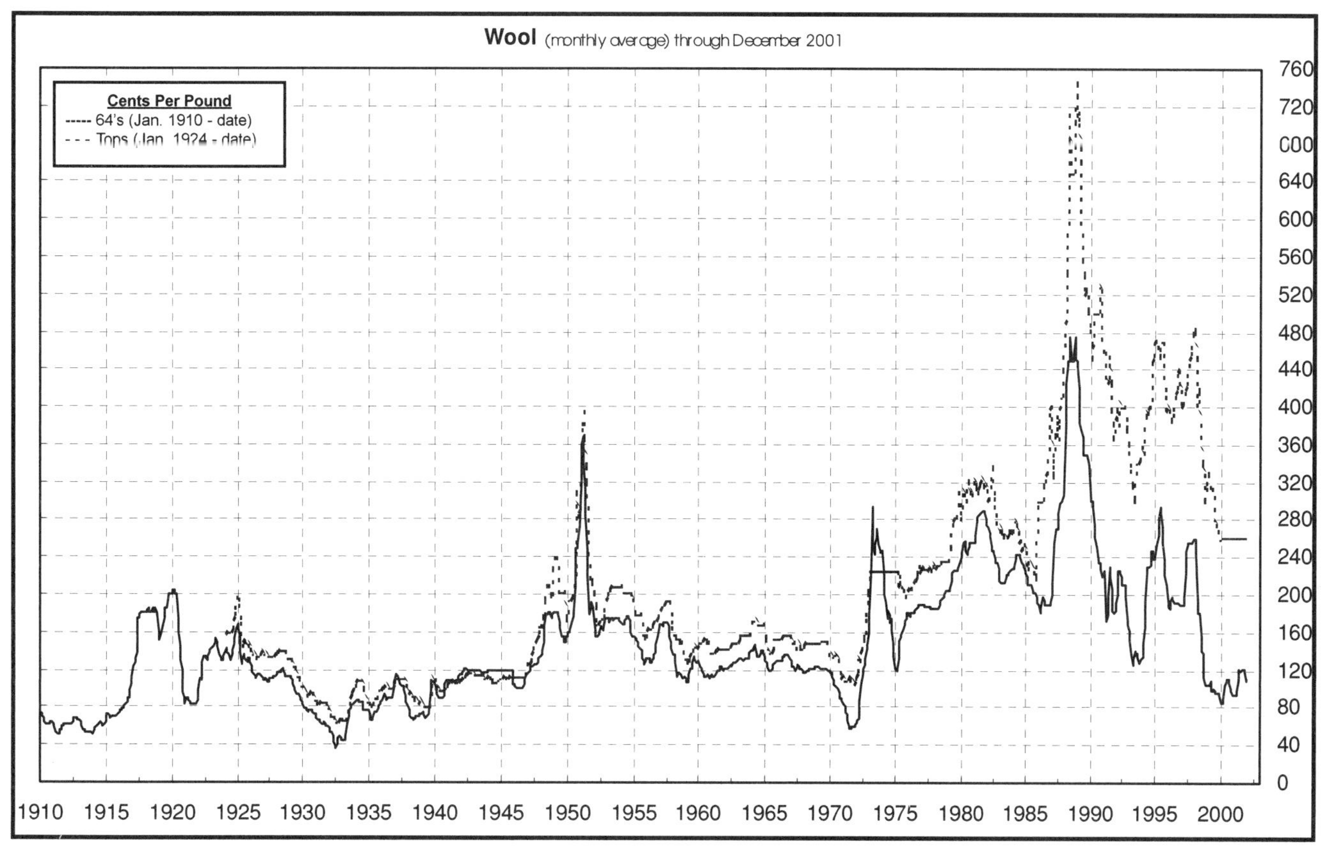

Wool: Mill Consumption, by Grades in the U.S., Scoured Basis In Millions of Pounds

	Apparel Class[1]							
	Woolen System			Worsted System				
Year	60's & Finer	Coarser Than 60's	Total	60's & Finer	Coarser Than 60's	Total	All Total	Carpet Wool[2]
1991	31,961	26,599	58,560	56,521	22,106	78,627	137,187	14,352
1992	33,878	25,600	59,478	58,495	18,170	76,665	136,143	14,695
1993	40,895	26,624	67,519	58,834	15,027	73,861	141,380	15,431
1994	35,960	26,038	61,998	59,599	16,966	76,565	138,563	14,739
1995	30,211	27,089	57,300	54,980	17,019	71,999	129,299	12,667
1996	42,141	27,575	69,716	46,057	13,752	59,809	129,525	12,311
1997	49,038	21,303	70,341	48,153	11,892	60,045	130,386	13,576
1998	31,258	15,079	46,337	42,243	9,793	52,036	98,373	16,331
1999[3]	18,379	10,772	29,151	27,429	6,955	34,384	63,535	13,950
2000[4]	18,503	13,432	31,935	NA	NA	30,106	62,041	15,205

[1] Domestic & duty-paid foreign. [2] Duty-free foreign. [3] Preliminary. [4] Estimate. *Source: Economic Research Service, U.S. Department of Agriculture (ERS-USDA)*

United States Imports[1] of Unmanufactured Wool (Clean Yield) In Millions of Pounds

Year	Jan.	Feb.	Mar.	Apr.	May	June	July	Aug.	Sept.	Oct.	Nov.	Dec.	Total
1992	10.2	8.1	7.3	10.6	8.8	6.2	6.9	5.0	3.9	5.5	9.1	7.8	89.4
1993	7.8	8.7	8.5	9.3	11.0	9.6	9.7	8.7	5.7	7.7	7.2	8.4	102.2
1994	10.0	7.7	7.7	12.7	7.5	7.7	6.9	6.5	4.1	5.7	8.1	7.0	91.7
1995	10.4	7.7	10.8	6.0	11.5	5.2	7.3	7.3	4.9	7.9	7.7	4.1	90.6
1996	9.6	9.1	8.8	5.6	7.0	5.9	5.3	6.6	3.1	4.6	4.6	5.1	75.3
1997	5.1	5.8	5.8	6.6	5.8	4.2	4.9	4.2	4.8	8.5	7.3	8.6	71.5
1998	8.8	5.4	5.4	7.2	5.9	5.5	5.7	4.4	3.3	7.3	4.9	4.3	68.0
1999	6.2	3.6	3.9	7.9	3.5	3.0	3.7	3.1	2.6	3.8	2.8	2.5	46.3
2000	4.9	3.8	3.8	4.6	5.1	2.7	3.2	3.7	4.3	3.2	3.5	2.4	45.0
2001[2]	4.9	4.3	4.3	1.5	2.9	2.8	4.0	1.9	2.0				38.2

[1] For consumption. [2] Preliminary. *Source: Economic Research Service, U.S. Department of Agriculture (ERS-USDA)*

Zinc

Zinc is utilized as a protective coating for other metals, such as iron and steel, in a process known as galvanizing. Zinc also finds use as an alloy with copper to make brass and as an alloying compound with aluminum and magnesium. There are a number of substitutes for zinc in chemical, electronic, and pigment uses. Aluminum, steel, and plastic substitute for galvanized sheet. Aluminum alloys can replace brass.

The U.S. Geological Survey reported that world mine production of zinc in 2000 was 8 million metric tonnes, about the same as in 1999. The largest zinc producer was China with output in 2000 of 1.4 million tonnes, up 2 percent from 1999. The next largest producer was Australia with 1.25 million tonnes, up 8 percent from the previous year. Canada produced 900,000 tonnes, down 11 percent from 1999. U.S. zinc production in 2000 was 860,000 tonnes, up 7 percent from the previous year. The reopening of a zinc mine in Tennessee along with increased production at a mine in Alaska resulted in the higher U.S. output. The U.S. is the world's largest exporter of zinc concentrates and is also the largest importer of zinc metal. Other large producers of zinc include Peru and Mexico.

The world reserves of zinc are estimated to be 190 million tonnes. The largest reserves of zinc are estimated to be in Australia with 34 million tonnes followed by China with 33 million tonnes. U.S. reserves are estimated to be 25 million tonnes. Other large reserves are in Canada, Peru and Mexico.

U.S. mine production of zinc (recoverable zinc) in August 2001 was 70,300 tonnes, up 3 percent from the previous month. In the January-August 2001 period, mine production was 544,000 tonnes. For all of 2000, mine production was 837,000 tonnes (recoverable zinc). Smelter production of zinc (refined) in August 2001 was 19,800 tonnes, up 5 percent from the previous month. In the January-August 2001 period, smelter production of zinc was 215,000 tonnes while for all of 2000 it was 363,000 tonnes. U.S. production of zinc oxide in August 2001 was 1,360 tonnes, compared to 605 tonnes the previous month. In the January-August 2001 period, zinc oxide production was 52,900 tonnes while for all of 2000 it was 107,000 tonnes.

U.S. shipments of refined zinc in August 2001 were 20,600 tonnes compared to 29,200 tonnes the year before. In the January-August period, shipments totaled 217,000 tonnes while for all of 2000 they were 365,000 tonnes. Stocks of refined zinc in August 2001 were 6,580 tonnes while in August 2000 they were 7,860 tonnes. Shipments of zinc oxide in August 2001 were 70 tonnes, well below the year ago total of 8,490 tonnes. For all of 2000, shipments were 107,000 tonnes while in the January-August 2001 period they were 54,200 tonnes. Stocks of zinc oxide in August 2001 were 2,140 tonnes while in August 2000 they were 3,390 tonnes.

U.S. apparent consumption of refined zinc in August 2001 was 76,600 tonnes, down 27 percent from the previous month. In the January-August 2001 period, consumption was 778,000 tonnes. For all of 2000, zinc consumption was 1.32 million tonnes. In the January-August 2001 period, sheet and strip galvanizing took 319,000 tonnes of refined zinc. Other galvanizing uses took 113,000 tonnes. Refined zinc used in brass and bronze was 108,000 tonnes. Use of refined zinc in zinc-base alloy was 138,000 tonnes. refined zinc for other uses like chemical, alloys and castings consumed 101,000 tonnes. U.S. consumption of zinc ore (zinc content) in August 2001 was 19 tonnes. In the January-August 2001 period, zinc ore consumption was 152 tonnes while for all of 2000 it was 225 tonnes. Consumption of zinc-base scrap (zinc content) in August 2001 was 18,600 tonnes while for the January-August 2001 period it was 149,000 tonnes. For all of 2000, zinc-base scrap consumption was 223,000 tonnes. Copper-base scrap (zinc content) consumption in January-August 2001 was 141,000 tonnes and for all of 2000 it was 211,000 tonnes. In August 2001, producer stocks of refined zinc were 6,580 tonnes.

Futures Markets

Zinc futures and options are traded on the London Metals Exchange (LME).

Salient Statistics of Zinc in the United States In Metric Tons

	Slab Zinc ----- Production -----			---- Imports for Consumption ----		----- Exports -----		--------- Consumption ---------			Net Import Reliance as a % of Con-	High-Grade, Price
Year	Primary	Secondary	Mine Production (Recovered)	Slab Zinc	Ore (Zinc Content)	Slab Zinc	Ore (Zinc Content)	Slab Zinc	Consumed as Ore	All Classes[3]	sumption	-Cents/Lb.-
1991	253,276	124,078	517,804	549,137	45,419	1,253	381,416	931,000	2,098	1,160,000	24	52.77
1992	272,000	128,000	523,430	644,482	44,523	565	307,114	1,050,000	2,400	1,290,000	33	58.38
1993	240,000	141,000	488,374	723,563	33,093	1,410	311,278	1,120,000	2,200	1,340,000	36	46.15
1994	216,600	139,000	570,000	793,000	27,374	6,310	389,000	1,180,000	2,400	1,400,000	35	49.26
1995	232,000	131,000	603,000	856,000	10,300	3,080	424,000	1,230,000	2,400	1,460,000	35	55.83
1996	226,000	140,000	586,000	827,000	15,100	1,970	425,000	1,210,000	1,400	1,450,000	33	51.11
1997	226,000	141,000	592,000	876,000	49,600	3,630	461,000	1,260,000	----	1,490,000	35	64.56
1998	234,000	134,000	709,000	879,000	46,300	2,330	552,000	1,290,000	----	1,580,000	35	51.43
1999[1]	241,000	131,000	771,000	966,000	74,600	1,880	531,000	1,340,000	----	1,610,000	30	53.48
2000[2]	228,000	143,000	786,000	915,000	52,800	2,770	523,000	1,330,000	----	1,610,000	60	55.61

[1] Preliminary. [2] Estimate. [3] Based on apparent consumption of slab zinc plus zinc content of ores and concentrates and secondary materials used to make zinc dust and chemicals. *Source: U.S. Geological Survey (USGS)*

World Smelter Production of Zinc[3] In Thousands of Metric Tons

Year	Australia	Belgium	Canada	France	Germany	Italy	Japan	Kazak-hstan[4]	Mexico	Poland	Spain	United States	World Total
1991	326.5	384.2	660.6	299.6	345.7	263.8	778.7	800.0	189.1	126.0	262.2	376.0	7,310
1992	333.0	310.6	671.7	318.7	383.1	252.6	780.6	260.0	151.6	134.6	351.0	300.0	7,260
1993	321.0	299.6	650.0	310.0	380.9	182.0	744.6	263.0	209.9	149.1	341.6	382.0	7,360
1994	328.0	306.2	691.0	306.0	359.9	203.6	713.0	172.4	209.2	154.4	294.7	356.0	7,330
1995	325.0	301.1	720.3	300.0	322.5	180.4	711.1	169.2	222.7	162.7	358.0	363.0	7,370
1996	331.0	234.4	715.6	324.3	327.0	269.0	642.3	190.0	221.7	163.1	360.8	366.0	7,610
1997	317.0	244.0	703.8	346.0	251.7	227.7	650.2	189.0	231.4	171.0	364.2	367.0	7,920
1998	322.0	205.0	745.1	321.0	334.0	231.6	652.7	240.7	230.3	175.0	360.0	368.0	8,160
1999[1]	348.0	232.4	776.9	330.0	330.0	152.8	683.6	249.3	218.9	178.0	375.0	371.0	8,570
2000[2]	500.0	251.7	787.5	348.0	325.0	168.0	700.5	260.0	230.0	175.0	385.0	371.0	9,050

[1] Preliminary. [2] Estimate. [3] Secondary metal included. [4] Formerly part of the U.S.S.R.; data not reported separately until 1992.
Source: U.S. Geological Survey (USGS)

Consumption (Reported) of Slab Zinc in the United States, by Industries and Grades In Metric Tons

		By Industries					By Grades			
Year	Total	Gal-vanizers	Brass Products	Zinc-Base Alloy[3]	Zinc Oxide	Other	Special High Grade	High Grade	Remelt and Other	Prime Western
1991	764,038	364,629	97,952	169,883	64,035	67,539	421,316	91,468	57,786	189,930
1992	814,228	396,480	112,990	165,598	71,224	67,936	414,661	119,660	56,185	223,723
1993	1,035,000	532,400	139,500	222,000	63,448	141,100	403,696	116,500	71,202	182,309
1994	859,000	395,000	107,000	196,000	68,300	92,400	486,000	112,000	68,400	192,000
1995	1,240,000	390,000	91,500	194,000	70,900	90,800	135,000	98,200	54,400	251,000
1996	788,000	398,000	87,400	142,000	[4]	161,000	385,000	111,000	54,000	238,000
1997	672,000	347,000	76,800	107,000	[4]	141,000	319,000	88,700	57,200	207,000
1998	647,000	320,000	60,300	122,000	[4]	145,000	331,000	72,800	51,700	192,000
1999[1]	614,000	308,000	78,200	105,000	[4]	124,000	317,000	58,400	55,400	184,000
2000[2]	640,000	293,000	82,800	123,000	[4]	NA	332,000	60,600	41,500	206,000

[1] Preliminary. [2] Estimated. [3] Die casters. [4] Included in other. *Source: U.S. Geological Survey (USGS)*

United States Foreign Trade of Zinc In Metric Tons

	Imports for Consumption							Zinc Ore & Manufactures Exported						
								Blocks, Pigs, Anodes, etc.		Wrought & Alloys				
Year	Ores[1]	Blocks, Pigs, Slabs	Sheets, Plates, Other	Waste & Scrap	Dross, Ashes, Fume	Dust, Powder & Flakes	Total Value $1,000	Un-wrought	Un-wrought Alloys	Sheets, Plates & Strips	Angles, Bars, Rods, etc.	Waste & Scrap	Dust (Blue Powder)	Zinc Ore & Con-centrates
1991	45,419	549,137	539	31,596	6,483	15,424	687,879	1,253	4,224	10,385	6,151	96,314	5,737	381,416
1992	44,523	644,482	171	31,176	11,813	17,051	910,289	5,886	----	----	----	82,088	5,889	307,114
1993	33,093	723,563	135	38,079	11,862	16,218	799,999	8,765	----	----	----	46,385	6,727	311,278
1994	27,374	793,482	475	51,676	12,152	11,954	878,100	13,220	----	----	----	58,297	6,603	389,488
1995	10,300	856,000	332	42,300	10,900	11,700	1,018,620	----	----	----	----	55,900	8,840	424,000
1996	15,100	827,000	16,900	31,900	14,500	10,300	1,001,800	----	----	----	----	45,500	11,100	425,000
1997	49,600	876,000	19,200	29,600	----	11,700	1,340,390	----	----	----	----	46,100	9,980	461,000
1998	46,300	879,000	16,900	29,200	----	17,600	1,098,690	----	----	----	----	35,000	5,530	552,000
1999[2]	74,600	966,000	22,600	26,600	----	21,300	1,133,890	----	----	----	----	28,200	5,050	531,000
2000[3]	52,800	915,000	9,380	36,500	----	23,000	1,272,750	----	----	----	----	36,100	4,830	523,000

[1] Zinc content. [2] Preliminary. [3] Estimate. NA = Not available. *Source: U.S. Geological Survey (USGS)*

Mine Production of Recoverable Zinc in the United States In Thousands of Metric Tons

Year	Jan.	Feb.	Mar.	Apr.	May	June	July	Aug.	Sept.	Oct.	Nov.	Dec.	Total
1992	41.5	48.8	47.7	40.3	40.7	40.4	46.2	49.1	47.6	36.2	40.4	42.2	520.1
1993	48.0	42.5	46.4	39.5	43.0	40.7	33.5	32.1	35.9	41.8	41.4	43.4	488.3
1994	43.2	40.2	48.4	44.0	47.9	47.1	52.5	47.1	50.1	41.6	46.0	48.0	557.0
1995	49.8	48.1	52.8	45.6	54.5	50.0	50.2	55.0	48.1	52.0	47.8	48.1	601.0
1996	52.4	48.9	49.7	45.5	50.7	49.9	53.7	48.1	46.8	43.4	43.1	42.6	600.0
1997	46.2	45.7	45.8	47.9	49.7	45.3	45.9	49.8	53.0	47.6	44.2	48.4	574.0
1998	50.1	48.3	56.5	56.2	56.7	55.0	59.5	57.2	60.1	55.7	62.0	61.9	722.0
1999	61.4	57.6	63.0	67.0	61.7	62.8	68.2	72.1	60.8	67.8	61.2	65.9	808.0
2000	64.4	56.6	68.5	64.5	70.2	65.3	68.1	71.4	59.6	62.3	63.5	67.2	814.0
2001[1]	68.4	60.5	62.2	65.2	66.9	66.1	66.7	67.6	60.9	65.0			779.4

[1] Preliminary. *Source: U.S. Geological Survey (USGS)*

ZINC

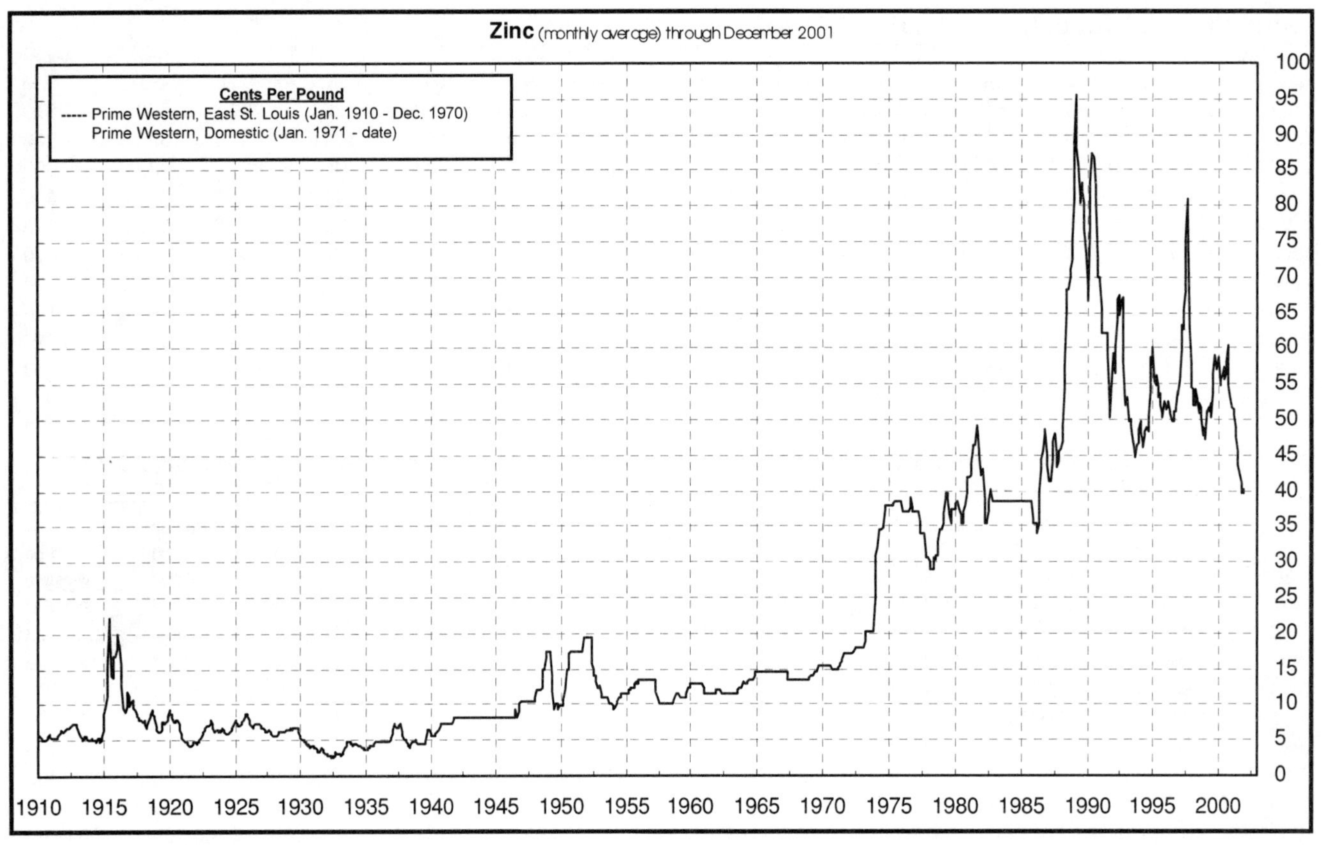

Consumption of Slab Zinc by Fabricators in the United States In Thousands of Metric Tons

Year	Jan.	Feb.	Mar.	Apr.	May	June	July	Aug.	Sept.	Oct.	Nov.	Dec.	Average
1992	93.8	77.2	85.0	89.9	76.0	76.9	47.2	53.8	52.2	53.5	50.3	47.6	814.2
1993	50.9	49.2	55.8	59.2	60.8	55.7	44.6	49.1	47.0	52.7	50.9	51.0	774.0
1994	50.8	53.7	55.7	58.5	58.7	52.7	48.0	53.2	53.6	53.9	52.5	45.0	623.0
1995	51.3	57.8	56.3	57.9	53.4	58.0	44.0	44.0	58.8	57.0	56.0	54.5	838.0
1996	56.3	55.6	59.3	55.7	56.3	55.9	48.9	48.1	54.4	56.4	54.2	53.1	788.0
1997	47.2	43.1	48.6	50.1	48.1	45.3	45.1	45.5	50.9	49.6	44.3	46.2	588.0
1998	46.3	45.2	47.4	44.8	45.4	49.0	46.0	45.0	45.9	45.9	40.5	43.9	647.0
1999	40.5	45.4	43.8	40.3	42.5	47.1	37.8	40.1	42.0	42.8	41.1	39.7	614.0
2000	41.8	44.6	47.7	45.6	44.4	49.1	42.0	43.3	42.6	47.5	43.8	40.2	640.0
2001[1]	45.4	43.5	44.1	42.7	43.6	38.2	30.6	39.2	37.7	35.7			480.8

[1] Preliminary. *Source: U.S. Geological Survey (USGS)*

Average Price of Zinc, Prime Western Slab (Delivered U.S. Basis) In Cents Per Pound

Year	Jan.	Feb.	Mar.	Apr.	May	June	July	Aug.	Sept.	Oct.	Nov.	Dec.	Total
1992	57.62	56.40	60.19	64.12	66.83	67.29	64.57	66.47	67.12	57.84	52.16	52.71	61.11
1993	52.70	53.18	49.72	50.07	49.27	46.75	46.90	45.08	44.54	46.21	46.54	48.69	48.30
1994	49.64	48.29	46.70	46.16	47.66	48.42	48.81	48.26	50.55	53.81	58.64	57.41	50.36
1995	60.11	55.44	54.84	56.08	54.61	53.08	53.75	52.00	50.77	50.42	52.52	51.60	53.77
1996	51.38	51.86	52.66	51.03	50.76	49.75	49.86	50.86	51.22	51.76	53.81	53.39	51.53
1997	55.64	59.82	63.28	62.62	65.65	67.78	75.29	80.89	78.96	62.55	57.83	54.45	65.40
1998	55.43	51.86	51.98	54.31	52.77	50.78	52.23	51.64	50.29	47.63	48.74	48.44	51.23
1999	47.29	51.11	51.68	51.07	52.20	50.35	53.73	56.28	59.12	57.07	56.91	58.75	53.84
2000	58.44	54.67	55.60	56.14	57.44	55.67	56.52	58.04	60.53	54.67	53.07	53.00	56.15
2001	51.82	51.29	50.55	48.95	47.54	45.56	43.62	42.53	41.14	39.53	39.99	39.25	45.15

Source: American Metal Market (AMM)